OXFORD PAPERBACK REFERENCE

The Concise Oxford Dictionary of WORLD RELIGIONS

Professor John Bowker, Fellow of Gresham College, London, and Adjunct Professor at North Carolina State University (formerly Professor of Religion at the University of Lancaster, Fellow of Trinity College, Cambridge, and Adjunct Professor at the University of Pennsylvania), is a highly regarded authority on religious studies and a well-known broadcaster on BBC Radio and the World Service. His many books on the subject include *Is God a Virus?*, *Genes, Culture and Religion*, *Problems of Suffering in Religions of the World*, *What Muslims Believe*, *The Meanings of Death* (Harper Collins Religious Book Award, 1993), *World Religions*, and *The Complete Bible Handbook* (Benjamin Franklin Award, 1999).

The Concise Oxford Dictionary of

WORLD RELIGIONS

Edited by
JOHN BOWKER

OXFORD UNIVERSITY PRESS

OXFORD
UNIVERSITY PRESS
Great Clarendon Street, Oxford OX2 6DP

*Oxford University Press is a department of the University of Oxford.
It furthers the University's objective of excellence in research, scholarship,
and education by publishing worldwide in
Oxford New York
Athens Auckland Bangkok Bogotá Buenos Aires
Calcutta Cape Town Chennai Dar es Salaam
Delhi Florence Hong Kong Istanbul Karachi
Kuala Lumpur Madrid Melbourne Mexico City Mumbai
Nairobi Paris São Paolo Singapore
Taipei Tokyo Toronto Warsaw*

*with associated companies in
Berlin Ibadan*

*Oxford is a registered trade mark of Oxford University Press
in the UK and in certain other countries*

*Published in the United States
by Oxford University Press Inc., New York*

First published 1997 as The Oxford Dictionary of World Religions

This abridged and updated edition published as an Oxford University Press paperback 2000

*British Library Cataloguing in Publication Data
Data available*

*Library of Congress Cataloging in Publication Data
Data available*

ISBN 0-19-280094-9

4

Typeset by Interactive Sciences Ltd, Gloucester

Printed in Great Britain by
Printed in Great Britain by
Clays Ltd, St Ives plc

For Margaret

'Kind is my Love today, tomorrow kind,
Still constant in a wondrous excellence'

PREFACE

WHEN Mr Brooke, in *Middlemarch*, stated that if he went into Parliament, he would emulate Wilberforce and work at philanthropy, 'Mr Casaubon bowed, and observed that it was a wide field.' Religion is even wider; and while this Dictionary would not be able to keep pace with Mr Brooke's 'impetuous reason', it has been written for those who wish to pause and to understand religion and religions better. Vague impressions of religion can do great harm, not least by giving offence to the adherents of religions by seeming to be casual about the things that matter to them. Even the choice of an illustration for the dust jacket of this book shows how difficult these things can be. The photograph of a Thai Buddhist meditating was chosen because it suggests a general religious atmosphere of prayer. Prayer and meditation, however, are not the same thing, and this image ignores the fact that many Buddhists regard their following of the Buddha's teaching as a non-theistic philosophy and not as a religion. It seems perhaps a trivial detail, but detail, in the case of religion, matters.

The details, however, are daunting. Each religion has a long history of its own, with its attendant people and texts and ideas. The Dictionary was planned, therefore, to help those who have an interest in religions, but who find the subject vast. At the time we began, the first-year course at Lancaster University on the Introduction to Religions had more than a hundred students on it. They, and others who come to religions for the first time, find themselves, not simply in Baudelaire's 'forest of symbols', but in a forest also of concepts, texts and practices, languages and histories, teachers and preachers, guides, gurus and gods. The purpose of the Dictionary is to provide initial bearings on new and unfamiliar ground, not just for students, but for the general reader as well. Some entries are brief, because such items as Congé d'élire or Dalmatic do not, in this context, need more than a short definition. But in most articles an attempt has been made to offer something more than a definition, so that the reader can gain some sense of what the item is and why it has been included, even though a full treatment is obviously impossible.

The Dictionary has been far too long in the making. It was delayed by the sheer volume of the work; even the headword lists took far longer than I had expected. It was delayed further by my return to Cambridge and by my illness. But all clouds have linings, and during this period, I have written almost exactly half the book. I have also supplied most of the brief suggestions for further reading. In a book covering so much ground in so many entries, it was clearly impossible to provide full bibliographies. The books listed are, therefore, *only suggestions*: they are limited to one or at the most two, offering a possible 'next step' for those who require further information. Some were suggested by contributors, but most come from myself, and thus represent a highly personal reading list, the illustration no doubt of a misspent life. There will surely be other and more recent books, which a library catalogue will disclose. As it is, I broke my own rule, and I have listed more than two books on a number of major topics where the pressure on space made it impossible to do more than point at a large horizon.

Pressure on space: given that there are multi-volume encyclopedias on each of the religions, and one-volume dictionaries on many, it was rash to attempt a one-volume work on the major world religions. But neither general readers nor students have a reference library beside them all the time. We therefore decided to give the maximum space to text, rather than to illustrations. Religions are expressed as much in pictures and signs as they are in words, and although entries on art and music have been included, it was out of the question to do justice to these areas in a single-volume work. There remains yet to be written a companion dictionary of religious art and music. In the meantime I have edited for Dorling Kindersley *World Religions*, which is based on illustration, and gives a glimpse of that other side of religion.

Pressure on space has also meant that a careful system of cross-reference has been used, so that information is not too often repeated. If major concepts (for example, karma) were to be explained each time they appear, we would be back with the many volumes. For the same reason, I have also compiled an Index of major themes. This has reduced the number of times an article ends with 'See also . . .' In the case of such things as cosmology or mysticism, the book would otherwise have been greatly lengthened, since each 'See also' list would have had to be repeated at the end of several entries. The making of the Index was an immense task in its own right. It was made possible, first through the generosity of Gresham College, London (who paid for both the hardware and software involved), and secondly through the skills of Dr Martin Richards, of the Computer Laboratory of Cambridge University. My gratitude to them is great indeed.

My thanks go also to many others: to the contributors, and especially for their patience in accepting the delay in publication; to Lamea Abbas Amara Krishan Bhugtiar, David Bowker, Gene d'Aquili, Sean Hughes, and Professor C. F. D. Moule who offered advice or corrections on particular entries; to Lavinia Cohn-Sherbok for undertaking a whole area of the Dictionary when another, at a late stage, withdrew; to Dr Christopher Hancock, Dr Newman Brooks, and Dr Margaret Bowker who rescued the book, when, at the very end, promised articles failed to turn up; to Professor Roger Corless who gave me the will to go on when it seemed impossible; to Trinity College for lending me books; to the late Peter Nailor, and to Gresham College, for support and friendship; and to Dr Stephen Wroe and Mrs Sarah Brunning who, among many others, have cared for me through my illness and enabled me to take up this work again. In the early years, Dr J. F. Coakley, in addition to being a contributor, undertook the immense work which was necessary to get the whole project under way. His admirable efficiency and care laid the foundations on which the rest could be built. My thanks go also to the Press (not least, again, for their patience), to the skill of those in India who typed in a difficult manuscript, to proof-readers, and to the development editor, Pam Coote, and the copy-editor, Jane Robson. Above all, my thanks go to Alysoun Owen, and her production and design colleagues John Mackrell and Nick Clarke: this book was extremely complicated to design and set, with many substantial changes at very late stages: her dedication to getting things right has been extraordinary.

Finally, words cannot possibly express adequately my thanks to my wife Margaret. Quite apart from the entries she has written, she has sustained me at every point. It is certain that without her, the Dictionary would have been abandoned long ago. She is, in a real way, the joint-author of it.

John Bowker

Cambridge, 1996

EDITORS

JOHN BOWKER, Gresham Professor, Gresham College, London and Adjunct Professor at the University of Pennsylvania and North Carolina State University; formerly Professor of Religion, University of Lancaster and Fellow of Trinity College, University of Cambridge, UK
General editor and contributor

ADRIAN ABBOTTS, Head of Religious Studies, Sir Jonathan North Community College, Leicester, UK
Consultant editor and contributor for Tibetan religion

DR PETER B. CLARKE, Professor of the History and Sociology of Religion and Director, Centre for New Religions, King's College, University of London, UK
Consultant editor and contributor for new religious movements

LAVINIA COHN-SHERBOK, Honorary Research Fellow, University of Kent, Canterbury, UK
Consultant editor and contributor for Judaism

PROFESSOR JOHN R. HINNELLS, Professor of Comparative Religion, University of London and Head of the Department of the Study of Religions, School of Oriental and African Studies, UK
Consultant editor and contributor for Zoroastrianism/Parsis

JOSEPH KITAGAWA, lately of the Divinity School, University of Chicago, USA
Consultant editor for Far Eastern religions

DR ELEANOR NESBITT, Lecturer in Education, Warwick Religions and Education Research Unit, University of Warwick, UK
Consultant editor and contributor for Sikhism

DR HAROLD TURNER formerly Founder-Director of Interact Centre, Selly Oak Colleges, Birmingham, UK
Consultant editor and contributor for new religious movements

DR MARTIN WILTSHIRE, Department of Religion and Philosophy, Edith Cowan University, Western Australia
Consultant editor and contributor for Buddhism

CONTRIBUTORS

Dr Gina Alexander
Jungian analyst
British Association of Psychotherapists
UK
Jung

Claire Baillargeon
Santa Barbara
California, USA
Hinduism

Revd P. M. Ballaman
Anglican deacon
UK
Modern Christian thought

Dr Jerome H. Bauer
Department of Asian and Middle Eastern Studies
University of Pennsylvania
USA
Indian civilization; South Asian religion and philosophy; Hinduism

Revd Dr Jeremy Begbie
Vice Principal
Ridley Hall
Cambridge, UK
Calvin and Calvinism; modern systematic theology

David Bowker
Teacher of religious studies
UK
Religions; religious studies

Dr Margaret Bowker
Emeritus Reader
University of Lancaster
UK
Church history; Christianity

Andrew Braddock
Ridley Hall
Cambridge, UK
Church history

Dr Peter Newman Brooks
Fellow
Robinson College
Cambridge, UK
Reformation

Dr Raymond Brown
Sometime Principal
Spurgeon's College
London, UK
Christianity

Mr Robert F. Campany
Associate Professor
Department of Religious Studies
Indiana University, USA
Chinese religion

Professor D. R. Catchpole
St Luke's Foundation
Professor of Theological Studies
University of Exeter, UK
New Testament

Professor Henry Chadwick
Emeritus Professor
University of Cambridge and Former Master of Peterhouse
Cambridge, UK
Anglican-Roman Catholic International Commission

The Late Professor K. S. Chen
Former Chairman of the Department of Oriental Languages
University of California
Los Angeles, USA
Chinese Buddhism

Professor Julia Ching
University of Toronto
Canada
Chinese religion

Professor J. P. Clayton
Professor of Religious Studies
University of Lancaster
UK
Religious studies

Dr J. F. Coakley
Senior Lecturer in Near Eastern Languages
Harvard University, USA
Christianity

Professor R. J. Corless
Associate Professor of Religion
Duke University, USA
Buddhism (general) and Far Eastern Buddhism

The Revd Canon
C. F. Coussmaker
Anglican chaplain in Moscow
Russia
Orthodox Christianity

Dr Kenneth Cragg
Former Anglican bishop in Jerusalem and
Warden of the Central College,
Canterbury, UK
currently Visiting Professor
Union Theological Seminary
New York, USA
Islam

David Craig
Head of Religious Broadcasting
BBC World Service
UK
World religions

Dr Brian Davies, OP
Regent
Blackfriars, Oxford, and
University Research Lecturer
University of Oxford, UK
Christianity

Dr Wade Dazey
Associate Professor
Department of Philosophy
and Religious Studies
University of Wisconsin-
Whitewater, USA
General Hinduism and Advaita Vedanta

Professor J. C. Dobbins
Associate Professor of
Religion and East Asian
Studies
Oberlin College
Ohio, USA
Japanese Buddhism

Professor Richard
H. Drummond
Florence Livergood Warren
Professor of Comparative
Religions
University of Dubuque
Seminary
USA
Christian mission

Professor Gary L. Ebersole
Associate Professor
History of Religions
University of Chicago
USA
Japanese religion

Professor L. W. Fagg
Research Professor
Department of Physics
Catholic University of
America
Washington DC, USA
Time

Dr Gavin Flood
Lecturer in Religious Studies
Department of Theology
and Religious Studies
University of Wales
Lampeter, UK
Hinduism

Dr Richard Gardner
Sophia University
Faculty of Comparative Culture
Ichigaya Campus
Tokyo, Japan
Japanese religion

Ed Gilday
Formerly Research Student
Centre for Far Eastern Studies
University of Chicago
USA

Dr David Gosling
Cambridge Teape Fellow
Clare Hall
University of Cambridge
UK
South-East Asian Buddhism

Mary Griffith
Santa Barbara
California, USA
Hinduism

Mr John S. Guest
Trustee Emeritus
Robert College of Istanbul
Turkey
Yezidi religion

Revd Dr C. D. Hancock
Holy Trinity Church
Cambridge, UK
Anglicanism

Dr F. E. Hardy
Reader in Indian Religions
King's College
University of London
UK
Indian religions

Dr Ian Harris
Reader in Religious Studies
University College of
St Martin
Lancaster, UK
Buddhism

Dr Paul Heelas
Reader in Religion and
Modernity
Department of Religious
Studies
University of Lancaster
UK
Study of religion

Professor Y. T. Hosoi
Associate Professor
Oregon State University
Corvallis
Oregon, USA
Japanese religion

The late Trevor Huddleston
Former Archbishop of the
Indian Ocean and President
Anti-Apartheid Movement
Africa

Zahid Hussein
Former research student
University of Lancaster
UK
Islam

Professor Paul Ingram
Professor of Religion
Pacific Lutheran University
Tacoma
Washington, USA
Japanese Buddhism

Dr Penelope Johnstone
Tutor in Arabic
Oriental Institute
University of Oxford, UK
Islam

Dr H. A. Kanitkar
Lector
Department of Anthropology and Sociology
School of Oriental and African Studies
University of London, UK
Hinduism

Mr V. P. Hemant Kanitkar
Former schoolmaster and author of books on Hinduism
UK
Hinduism

Professor T. Kasulis
Professor of Comparative Studies in the Humanities
Ohio State University
Columbus, USA
Japanese Buddhism

Dr Ruth Katz
Former Associate Professor of Religion
Florida State University
USA
Hinduism

Dr Damien Keown
Lecturer in Indian Religion
Department of Historical and Cultural Studies
Goldsmith's College
University of London
UK
Buddhism

Professor H. J. Kim
Professor Emeritus
Department of Religious Studies
University of Oregon, USA
Korean Buddhism

Professor H. Kiyota
Chairman
Buddhist Studies Program
Department of South Asian Studies
University of Wisconsin-Madison
USA
Buddhism

Dr Linda L. Lam-Easton
Associate Professor
Department of Religious Studies
California State University
Northridge, USA
Chinese religions; history of religions

Dr Gerald J. Larson
Professor of Religious Studies
University of California
Santa Barbara, USA
Hindu and Buddhist traditions; history of religions

Professor Andrew Louth
Professor of Cultural History
Goldsmith's College
University of London
UK
Christianity

Professor Theodore M. Ludwig
Professor of Theology
Valparaiso University
Indiana, USA
Japanese religion

Dr Nancy McCagney
Assistant Professor of Philosophy
Department of Philosophy
University of Delaware
USA
Indian Mahayana Buddhism

Mark MacWilliams
Assistant Professor
Religious Studies
Bucknell University
USA
Japanese religion

Professor M. M. J. Marasinghe
Professor of Buddhist Philosophy
University of Kelaniya
Sri Lanka
Buddhism

Dr F. Matchett
Honorary Research Fellow in Indian Religions
Department of Religious Studies
University of Lancaster
UK
Hinduism

Professor Jeffrey J. Meyer
Professor and Chair of Religious Studies Department
UNC Charlotte
North Carolina, USA
Chinese religion

Dr Alan John Milbank
University Lecturer and Fellow of Peterhouse
University of Cambridge
UK
Christianity

Professor Alan L. Miller
Professor of Religion
Miami University
Oxford
Ohio, USA
Japanese folk religion

Revd Gareth Moore, OP
Prior
Couvent de l'Épiphanie
Rixensart, Belgium
Christian ethics

Dr P. E. Nosco
Formerly, Institute of Asian Studies
St John's University
New York, USA
Shinto

The late Maurice Oldfield
Cumbria
UK
Jainism

Emily Groszos Ooms
Elementary school teacher
The Willows Community School
Los Angeles, USA
Japanese religion

Jeanne Openshaw
Research Fellow
Lucy Cavendish College
University of Cambridge
UK
Bauls

Professor Roger O'Toole
Professor of Sociology
University of Toronto
Canada
Sociology of religion

Dr Lloyd Pflueger
Assistant Professor of Philosophy and Religion
Truman State University
Kirksville, USA
South Asian philosophy and religion

Dr Richard B. Pilgrim
Associate Professor
Department of Religion
Syracuse University
New York, USA
Japanese religion

Professor Don A. Pittman
Associate Professor of the History of Religions
Tainan Theological College and Seminary
Tainan, Taiwan
Chinese religion

Dr Y. Raef
Professor of Arabic and Islamic Studies
American University in Cairo
Egypt
Islam; Islamic thought

Revd Chris Russell
UK
Charismatic movement

Lamie Abbes Samora
Mandeans

Dr P. J. Sherry
Reader
Religious Studies Department
University of Lancaster
UK
Christianity; philosophy of religion

Dr Peter Smith
Visiting Professor in History and Social Sciences
International Students Degree Program
Mahidol University
Thailand
Babi; Baha'i

Mr P. J. Stewart
Lecturer in Ecology
University of Oxford
UK
Contemporary Islam

Dr Laurence G. Thompson
Professor Emeritus of East Asian Languages and Cultures
University of Southern California
Ventura, USA
Confucian classics; Chinese religion

Very Revd Simon Tugwell, OP
President of the Dominican Historical Institute
Rome, Italy
Dominicans

Professor Taitetsu Unno
Jill Ker Conway Professor of Religion
Smith College
Northampton, Massachusetts
USA
East Asian Buddhism

Professor Manabu Waida
Professor of the History of Religions
University of Alberta
Edmonton, Canada
Japanese religion

Dr Michael Walsh
Librarian
Heythrop College
University of London
UK
Christianity

Professor L. H. Yearley
Walter Y. Evans-Wentz Professor
Stanford University, USA
Chinese religion

Professor D. C. Yu
Formerly, Department of Religion
Maryville College
Tennessee, USA
Chinese religion

NOTE TO READER

ENTRIES are arranged in letter-by-letter alphabetical order up to the first punctuation in the headword. For example, the entry on **Jerusalem** comes before **Jerusalem, Synod of**, which in turn precedes **Jerusalem Conference**. Some longer entries have been divided into sections each of which deals with an individual religion. These sections are either arranged in the logical order for the specific entry and discussion, or grouped as Semitic religions (Judaism, Christianity, Islam), Asiatic religions (Hinduism, Jainism, Buddhism, Sikhism, Chinese, Japanese); other religions (e.g. Zoroastrianism) usually appear at the end. The religions of the former group are referred to by the abbreviation W. (western), and the latter by E. (eastern), although all religions are now found in eastern and western parts of the world.

Cross-references are indicated by an asterisk or the use in brackets of 'see' followed by the entry headword, or part of the headword, to which the reader is being referred. Sometimes the flagged word in the text will differ from the exact form of the headword, but it is always clear where the reader is being directed. For example, *Ecumenical Movement is asterisked, but the actual form of the entry is Ecumenism. 'See also' followed by a headword in small capitals is also used at the end of an entry to cross-refer the reader to subjects of related interest. The reader is also cross-referred to the Topic Index at the back of the book. So, under the entry **Meditation** there are in-text cross-references *inter alia* to *contemplation and *Jesuits and at the end of the entry: See also MENPEKI; ZAZEN; Index, Meditation.

A cross-reference item is normally marked with an asterisk only at its first appearance in any entry and is included only where reference is likely to increase understanding of the entry being read. Frequently recurring terms (such as God and the names of the major religions, all of which have their own entries) are not cross-referenced. Signpost entries (i.e. entries which simply direct the reader to a main entry where the discussion of them appears) include short descriptions to enable readers to decide whether they wish to pursue the cross-reference. Thus: **Hsing** (human nature): see HSÜN TZU and **Vaudois** (adherents of Christian reform movement): see WALDENSES.

Use of italics The titles of books and texts are in italics except for some foundational texts, such as the Adi Granth, Bible (and its individual books) and Qur'an. These are in normal text (roman) type. Foreign and transliterated terms are usually in italics, unless they are asterisked as cross-references and thus have their own entry, in which case they are in roman type throughout the entry. The text includes a large number of transliterated terms which may be unfamiliar to the reader; for ease of reading we have tried to keep the use of italics to a minimum.

Foreign words Foreign scripts have been transliterated. However, there are often different systems of transliteration for each language, and preferred transliterations are often changing. Most obviously, Chinese transliteration has changed from the Wade–Giles system to Pinyin. Most older books will have followed the Wade–Giles system, and for that reason it is usually used in the Dictionary, since it is the form readers will most frequently meet. But an index has been provided at the back of the book that lists all Chinese headwords with their Pinyin alternatives. With other languages, we have tried to provide the form that a general reader is most likely to encounter today. This leads to a necessary inconsistency in the case of diacriticals. In the case of some languages (e.g. Greek, Hebrew) diacriticals are now almost always left out in books for the general reader, whereas in the case of others (e.g. Sanskrit, Pali) they are increasingly being added. Plurals are given in English form.

Some words have alternative transliterations which conform to general patterns. For example, words starting with **c** may also commonly begin **ch** as for cela or chela; caitya or chaitya. Likewise, **sh** may also appear as ṣ or ś; ḥ as ch. Other common variants are b/v; f/ph; g/gh; k/q; v/w. The form used sometimes varies across entries, and for major items the alternative spellings are given. This has, clearly, not been possible in every instance, and readers who fail to find an entry are advised, in the above instances, to look for the alternative spelling.

In the case of the Arabic definite article al- ('the'), the letter 'l' is assimilated to the letters known as *alhuruf ashshamsiya* (i.e. the Sun letters), t, th, d, dh, r, z, s, sh, ṣ, ḍ, ṭ, ẓ, l, n. Thus al-shams, the sun becomes ash-shams. Since these forms are less commonly followed in English books, the form al- has been retained in the dictionary, including the alphabetical order—thus al-Razi not ar-Razi, al-Shaf'i not ash-Shaf'i. Note also that such entries appear under 'A', not under the first capital letter: R, Sh, etc.

Abbreviations In order to make the text as readable as possible abbreviations have been kept to a minimum (but see also Index under Acronyms and Abbreviations). The following have been used:

Languages

Arab.	Arabic	Ital.	Italian
Aram.	Aramaic	Jap.	Japanese
Chin.	Chinese	Lat.	Latin
Eng.	English	Pers.	Persian
Fr.	French	Skt.	Sanskrit
Germ.	German	Syr.	Syriac
Gk.	Greek	Tib.	Tibetan
Heb.	Hebrew	Yid.	Yiddish

Others

AH	After the Hijra, *Anno Hegirae* (see entry HIJRA)
b. [in names]	ben, ibn (son of)
B.	*Babli* (Babylonian Talmud)
BCE	before the common era
CE	in the common era
P. or *J.*	Palestinian or Jerusalem Talmud
R.	Rabbi
$\sqrt{}$	from the root of

RELIGION

The Meaning of Religion

A strange thing about religion is that we all know what it is until someone asks us to tell them. As *Augustine said of *time: 'What, then, is time? If no one asks me I know; but if I have to say what it is to one who asks, I know not.' That has not stopped people trying to define religion, but their definitions are clearly different:

Religion is the sigh of the oppressed creature, the heart of a heartless world, just as it is the spirit of a spiritless situation. It is the opiate of the people (Karl *Marx)

Religion is a daughter of Hope and Fear, explaining to Ignorance the nature of the Unknowable (Ambrose Bierce)

A religion is a unified system of beliefs and practices relative to *sacred things, that is to say, things set apart and forbidden—beliefs and practices which unite into one single moral community called a *Church, all those who adhere to them (Émile *Durkheim)

It seems best to fall back at once on this essential source, and simply to claim, as a minimum definition of religion, the belief in Spiritual Beings (Edward *Tylor)

*Psychoanalytic investigation of the unconscious mental life reveals that religious beliefs correspond closely with the phantasies of infantile life, mainly unconscious ones, concerning the sexual life of one's parents and the conflicts this gives rise to (Sigmund *Freud)

Religion is what the individual does with his own solitariness (A. N. *Whitehead)

A brief, handy definition of religion is considerably more difficult than a definition of evolution, so, for limited purposes only, let me define religion as a set of *symbolic forms and acts which relate man to the ultimate conditions of his existence (R. N. Bellah)

Viewed systemically, religion can be differentiated from other culturally constituted institutions by virtue only of its reference to superhuman beings. All institutions consist of *belief systems*, i.e., an enduring organisation of cognitions about one or more aspects of the universe; *action systems*, an enduring organisation of behaviour patterns designed to attain ends for the satisfaction of needs; and *value systems*, an enduring organisation of principles by which behaviour can be judged on some scale of merit. Religion differs from other institutions in that its three component systems have reference to superhuman beings (Melford Spiro)

Without further ado, then, a *religion* is: (1) a system of symbols which acts to (2) establish powerful, pervasive and long-lasting moods and motivations in men by (3) formulating conceptions of a general order of existence and (4) clothing these conceptions with such an aura of factuality that (5) the moods and motivations seem uniquely realistic (Clifford *Geertz)

Religion is the human attitude towards a sacred order that includes within it all being—human or otherwise—i.e., belief in a cosmos, the meaning of which both includes and transcends man (Peter Berger)

Pure religion and undefiled before God and the Father is this: to visit the fatherless and widows in their affliction, and to keep oneself unspotted from the world (Letter of *James).

These and the many other definitions of religion (J. H. Leuba began his book *A Psychological Study of Religion* . . . (1912), with nearly fifty of them, sorted into three different types) tell us much about religion, but because of their diversity, none of them on its own can tell us what religion is. Some emphasize the personal, others the social; some the beliefs, others the uses; some the structures, others the functions; some the private, others the public; some the mundane, others the transcendent; some the truth, others the illusion. We might, perhaps, attempt to put them all together, but that would produce a juggernaut (*jagganatha) even more unwieldy than the lumbering giant of Orissa.

Would the origins of the word itself take us any further? The Latin *religio* refers to the fear of *God or the gods, and (much later) to the ceremonies and rites addressed to the gods. But it does so through its reference also to the scrupulous and often over-anxious way in which *rituals are conducted. The Latin poet Lucretius addressed strong words against religion:

> Tantum religio potuit suadere malorum . . .
> Religio peperit scelerosa atque impia facta.
> (*De rerum natura*, 1.101, 183)

(How many evils has religion caused! . . . Religion has brought forth criminal and impious deeds.)

But Lucretius had in mind the sacrifice of Iphigenia at Aulis as a demonstration of the disastrous consequences of an over-scrupulous insistence on the exact detail of ritual. So the Latin word supports the modern sense of 'doing something religiously', i.e. with an obsessive attention to detail (when it was reported in 1995 that Honda UK was supplying air conditioning kits containing the highly pollutant R12 refrigerant, despite the Montreal Protocol which looked for its elimination, Honda UK issued a statement saying: 'The Montreal Protocol is being religiously adhered to by Honda UK. . . . The only R12 kits being sold are from existing stocks held', *Daily Telegraph*, 12 Aug. 1995, p. C3). But this sense of the word is far too restricted. When people do things religiously, they not only do them scrupulously: they do them devotedly, generously, *ecstatically, *prayerfully, *sacrificially, superstitiously, *puritanically, ritualistically, and in many other ways as well.

So does the underlying etymology of the word help us further? A problem is that the etymology of *religio* is not certain. Cicero took it from *relegere*, to gather things together, or to pass over the same ground repeatedly. But most have taken it from *religare*, to bind things together. And if that is so, it certainly draws attention to one of the most obvious and important features of religion: it binds people together in common practices and beliefs: it draws them together in a common enterprise of life—so much so that Durkheim regarded religion as being the social in symbolic form (hence his definition above): religion is the social fact (and the experience of it by individuals as being real and greater than themselves) being made objective outside the lives of individuals. As a result, the social has a legitimate and emotional demand on them:

> Society is a reality *sui generis*; it has its own peculiar characteristics, which are not found elsewhere and which are not met with again in the same form in all the rest of the universe. The representations which express it have a wholly different content from purely individual ones and we may rest assured in advance that the first add something to the second. . . . Religion ceases to be an inexplicable hallucination and takes a foothold in reality. In fact we can say that the believer is not deceived when he believes in the existence of a moral power upon which he depends and from which he receives all that is best in himself: this power exists, it is society. . . . It is society which classifies beings into superiors and inferiors, into commanding masters and obeying servants; it is society which confers upon the former the singular property which makes the command efficacious and which makes *power.* So everything tends to prove that the first powers of which the human mind had any idea were those which societies have established in organising themselves; it is in their image that the powers of the physical world have been conceived. (*The Elementary Forms of the Religious Life* (1912), tr. J. W. Swain (New York: Collier, 1961), 28, 257, 409)

Durkheim may have concentrated too much on the entirely speculative origin of religion. He hoped that by examining the acorn he would be able to understand the oak. He may also, as *Weber thought, have paid too little attention to the creation of religious meaning, innovation, and change. But his grasp of the importance of the social in understanding religion was a breakthrough. Religions are organized systems which hold people together.

Religions as Systems: Natural Selection and Survival

The question then becomes obvious: why

are these systems necessary? The basic answer to that lies in the most fundamental condition of human life and survival, as we now understand it. Natural selection through the sifting process of evolution sets an impartial rule against the experiments of life. Those which are best adapted to the environmental conditions survive long enough to replicate more of their genes into another generation; those which are ill adapted may not survive at all. It is from this perspective that bodies have been regarded (admittedly in too casual and inaccurate a way) as gene-survival machines: a chicken is an egg's way of making another egg (Samuel Butler). So the skin is the first defensive boundary of the gene-replication process. But humans have then built a second defensive system outside the boundary of the body, in their shared cultural achievements; so that *culture is the second defensive skin in which the gene-replication process sits.

Religions are the earliest cultural systems of which we have evidence for the protection of gene-replication and the nurture of children. Obviously, our early ancestors knew nothing of how gene-replication works. But that is irrelevant to the evolutionary point. It is not understanding, but successful practice which is measured by survival. That is why religions have always been preoccupied with *sex and *food, creating food laws and systematic agriculture, and taking control of sexual behaviour, *marriage, and the status of *women. Sometimes the close relation between sexual and religious emotion has been promoted, on occasion exploited. This necessary connection between religion, sex, and food is the reason also why the family is the basic unit of religious organization, even in religions where *celibacy is seen as a higher vocation. On this basis, sociobiology (the study of the interaction of genes and culture which claims that culture can be best understood as a consequence of choices which have proved beneficial in protecting gene-replication) has claimed that religions have had value, not because their beliefs might happen to have been true (though sociobiologists generally assume that they are not), but because they have served the purposes of survival and selection.

There is much about sociobiology that is clearly wrong (for a critical survey, see J. W. Bowker, *Is God a Virus? Genes, Culture and Religion* (London: SPCK, 1995), but it is at least correct in observing that religions are highly organized protective systems. And they have worked. For millennia religions have been the social context in which individuals have lived their lives successfully, success being measured in terms of survival and replication. Even now, more than three-quarters of the population of the world regard themselves as being attached to some religion, however much or little they do about it.

Gene-Protein Process and Preparation for Religion

But still the question has to be asked, why *religious* systems? After all, animals, birds, and fish live in many different kinds of social organization without saying their prayers (so far as we know, though some religions have thought otherwise). But that is simply to say that the emergence of the human brain carries with it immensely greater possibilities, not least in the development of consciousness and language. It is here that we can locate the emergence and development of religion. These possibilities are latent in the brain, in the sense that they are a consequence of the particular structures and substances which the gene-protein process builds in the brain—and builds, therefore, not in a random way, but with great stability and consistency from generation to generation. This means that although there are differences in human populations which are derived from the gene-protein process (for example, skin pigmentation, colour of eyes, average height), there is much more that is held in common. That is why *biogenetic structuralism can claim that humans are prepared from the gene-protein process for many of their characteristic behaviours: they are prepared, for example, for sexual development and behaviours, for sleeping and waking, for eating and drinking, for linguistic competence. The gene-protein process does not *determine* what individuals will do with their preparedness, but it does give stable opportunities to create in culture both the expression and the control of what that process has prepared in the human brain. Biogenetic structuralism makes the point that humans are also prepared, in this gene-protein sense, for those characteristic behaviours which have been called religious. This at once explains why there is much that is universal and common in religious behaviour, but why, nevertheless, there are many different religions and why there are radical differences among them: that happens because what people in societies and cultures do with their preparedness is not determined. But the basic universality, at the level of brain/body competence and opportunity, means that whereas the sign held up in the crowd used to read, 'Prepare to meet thy God', it should now be amended to read, 'Prepared to meet thy God'. It means also that religion, or what is sometimes called 'religiosity', is inevitable in the human case unless there are major alterations in the human DNA.

Somatic Exploration and Discovery

So the basic argument of sociobiology is correct, that religions are early and, for millennia, successful protective systems tied to the potentialities of the brain and body, and to the necessity for survival. The point then becomes obvious, that once successful protective systems are established, people are given the confidence and security to do many other things as well. They are set free to explore their own nature and society, as well as the world around them. These explorations of human possibility, and of the environments in which it is set, opened the way to the specifically religious. Where human possibility is concerned, the exploration is primarily of the human body. It is therefore known, from Greek *soma* = 'body', as 'somatic exploration'. What is this body capable of experiencing? What is it capable of being and of becoming? In some religions, the emphasis has been on exploration inwards: they have sought and found truth within the body, in terms of *enlightenment, peace, emptiness (see e.g. *śunyata), the *Buddha-nature, and are therefore known as 'inversive systems'. The exploration of what *Thoreau called 'the private sea', the streams and oceans of our inner nature, has led to such religions as *Jainism and *Buddhism. In other religions, the emphasis has been on exploring the meaning and value of what has been discovered outside the body, and of the relationships into which people enter. It was this which culminated in communion, or even union, with God. This exploration of the value in relationship has produced religions like *Judaism, *Christianity, and *Islam. These systems, in which value and meaning are found in relationship, are known as 'extraversive systems'. In both cases, it is a matter of emphasis: an inversive system is never unattentive to that which concerns extraversive systems, and vice versa. In both cases, also, the realities of evil and wickedness are recognized and mapped as well.

The consequences of somatic exploration are vast. They are indeed the subject matter of this book. The system, or more often subsystem, of a religion provides the context within which sanctions and rewards, approval and disapproval, inspiration and ideation are held in common. As a result, the context becomes one of security, a security within which people are set free from a great deal of anxiety and uncertainty. As they internalize the constraints of the system, they are able, if they wish, to move on into further exploration and discovery of their own (on the importance of 'constraint', see further p. xxii). What might give rise to these discoveries, or what, in other words, might exist waiting to be discovered, is described in faltering languages, and it is approached through imperfect practices. However, both words and practices are winnowed, corrected, and reinforced through time. No language, whether verbal or non-verbal, can encompass God or the Buddha, *heaven or enlightenment, but language opens up the way to these and other possibilities. The languages are corrected and reinforced precisely because that to which they point interacts so consistently with those who seek, that frequently, though not invariably, they find a truth or a reality far beyond their languages and independent of them. To find God or the Buddha is more like being found by them.

As the consequences of somatic exploration in the past are realized in the present, so the characteristic practices of religions become apparent, in *worship, *meditation, *prayer, *yoga, *zazen, and much else. All of these are appropriations of past and tested achievements and experience, realized and extended in the present. The consequent power and peace are, for many, so real and unequivocal that all else in human life fades in comparison. The Buddha-nature is intelligible to anyone as a proposition; but the Buddha-nature as the universe and one's own appearance within it is true in a transforming sense only to those who have realized it by the ways so carefully preserved and transmitted. God may be the subject of philosophical debate; but God as source and goal of life is known only to those who receive him as gift, demand, and invitation—so much so that Rudolph *Otto could offer the distinct experience of the *Holy, of *mysterium tremendum et fascinans* (the wholly other who both terrifies and yet attracts, who 'appears and overthrows, but who is also the mystery of the self-evident, nearer to me than my *I*', Martin *Buber) as a *Kantian a priori category of human judgement (see esp. *The Idea of the Holy*, chs. xiv and xvii):

> We conclude, then, that not only the rational but also the non-rational elements of the complex category of 'holiness' are *a priori* elements and each in the same degree. Religion is not in vassalage either to morality or to teleology, '*ethos*' or '*telos*', and does not draw its life from postulates; and its non-rational content has, no less than its rational, its own independent roots in the hidden depths of the spirit itself. (p. 140)

Paradoxically, therefore, somatic explorations require human initiatives, but all of them, whether inversive or extraversive, have ended up with the realization that human initiatives cannot achieve the furthest goals without profound help which is not of their own making: guides, *gurus, and *grace take us further than even the furthest exploration can imagine.

Even so, somatic exploration *has* made supreme discoveries about human possibility. It has led people into assurance, union, trance, and ecstasy, and it has enabled them to understand and reverence the cosmos as the bearer of meaning and value. So religions open people up to possibility in this life, and now beyond *death as well. Initially, the latter point did not obtain: the belief that there will be a worthwhile life after death is late in religious history. This means that the great religious traditions of both East and West did not *in origin* have any strong belief that the purpose of life and religion is to obtain rewards or avoid punishments after death. It follows that the enduring religious traditions of the world were not, as so many assume, established on the basis of an offer of 'pie-in-the-sky'. They were established on the basis of this-life experience and exploration, not on the promise of a reward after death (for the detail of this, see J. W. Bowker, *The Meanings of Death* (Cambridge: Cambridge University Press, 1991)).

Yet eventually the belief that there will be enduring consequence through and beyond death became firmly established. This was mainly a matter of inference from the nature and quality of what had been discovered in the process of somatic exploration. Since those discoveries were so many and so diverse, it is not surprising that the subsequent beliefs differ greatly in their descriptions of what may be the case through and after death. This is reinforced by the fact that the different somatic explorations, which have led to different religions, have produced radically different accounts of human nature, that is, different religious anthropologies. Here already we can begin to see that the different religions really are different: religious differences *do* make a difference. But all of them protect and transmit important discoveries about the possibilities of human life.

The consequences of somatic exploration are not simply a matter of practice: there is also somatic exegesis, the interpretation of what has been discovered which produces elaborate belief systems and world pictures, as also it produces texts to sustain them. Somatic exegesis points to worlds vivid with gods and spirits, full of power and presence. To enquire further (for example, into their *ontology or existence) leads into those human reflections, so important in the history of religions, of *philosophy and *theology.

The importance of all this begins to explain why religions are protective systems: they protect much that is indispensable for human life and flourishing of a kind, and in ways, which necessarily evoke a distinctive word ('religion'). Religions in fact have even more to protect and transmit than all that has so far been described, but that alone, ranging from sex to salvation, is far too important to be left to chance. It is information which has to be organized if it is going to be saved and shared. Religions are systems for the monitoring, coding, protecting, and transmitting of information which has proved to be of the highest possible value, from person to person and (even more important) from generation to generation.

The Organization of Religions

The ways in which religions do this are again extremely varied. So far as organization is concerned, religions may be large-scale and coherently organized and hierarchical: an example is *Roman Catholicism, which has a strong centre of authority and control, the *Vatican, and a clear hierarchy of *Pope, *cardinals, *bishops, *priests, male *religious orders, female religious orders, *laity, running in parallel with a spiritual hierarchy of *apostles, *saints, *martyrs, *confessors, *doctors. But equally, they may be large-scale and *loosely* organized, with virtually no overall structure at all: an example is *Hinduism; but among Hindus there are extremely strong subsystems, based, for example, on gurus or *temples or holy places. Or again, they may be small-scale and local, extending perhaps only to the borders of a village. Between the extremes, there are many variations on the theme of protecting information and transmitting information, of allowing or denying access to the religious system (a powerful means for controlling aberrant beliefs or practices, see e.g. *excommunication, *heresy), and of sharing or restricting knowledge with the wider outside world. For that last reason, religions vary between mystery religions and *missionary religions: the former set and maintain conditions before access is allowed; the latter feel impelled to share what has been entrusted to them. Organization also evokes many different kinds of religious specialist—*priests, *witches, *shamans, *gurus, *imams, *rabbis, *monks, *nuns, *bhikṣus—an almost endless list.

The organization of religions is so important for some that the preservation and efficiency of the system become for them an end in itself. The risk involved in this is that they may become curators of a museum, or persecutors of those who do not conform. The system as an end is reinforced by the fact that religion is extremely big business. The numbers alone of those who secure all or part of their livelihood from religion make religion one of the largest global industries. When the Pope made his six-day visit to Britain, a company, Papal Visits Ltd., was set up to raise the costs estimated at £1 million per day. When it appointed Mark McCormack of the International Management Group, better known for managing the investments of sporting millionaires, he commented in an interview: 'They said that when the Pope had visited the Church in Ireland a couple of years ago, it cost the Church several million pounds and that everyone and his brother had made money except the Church.' On this occasion, it was estimated that the Church would make money and that McCormack would make, from his 20 per cent share of the profits, £1 million. With money inevitably goes power. It is an observation at least as old as Polybius (*c.*125 BCE) that 'since the masses of the people are inconstant, full of unruly desires, passionate and reckless of consequence, they must be filled with fears to keep them in order; the ancients did well therefore to invent the gods and the belief in punishment after death'. The financial exploitation of this is a familiar theme in religious history. Money is the root of much religion. A history of religion might well be written as a history of authority, control, and power, since the sanctions and rewards of religious systems are pervasive, and often subtle, in the extreme.

Life as Project: Ethics and the Nature of Time

It is easy, therefore, for religious organizations to become an end in themselves. But the creative health of religions lies in the recognition that the system is not an end, but a means to ends which transcend the organization—indeed, a means to *the* End (*eschatology), the final destiny of all that is. All human life is lived as project. That is so because humans are conscious that there is a future, but they know extremely little about it. Life as project (towards acknowledged but largely unknown futures) means that evaluation is built into the formation of human actions: is this wise or is it foolish? is it rash or is it prudential? is it harmful or is it beneficial? is it good or is it bad? This is clearly the foundation of *ethics and of evaluating behaviours and people as moral or immoral, and religions have done much to create stable ethical evaluations which obtain throughout a particular system and culture.

It is a reason also why acceptance and rejection, approval and disapproval, are so central to religious life: the terms on which these obtain are fundamental, for good and for ill, in the forming of human lives, groups, and societies. They include the ways in which self-approval and self-acceptance become possible. Religions, each in different ways, map the conditions and terms of approval and disapproval, and of acceptance and rejection. This may, of course, create major difficulties, social as well as psychological, for those who cannot accept or meet the terms. But on the other hand, it has had the huge advantage of making life as project less unpredictable.

Religions have done even more to make the future less unknown: they have produced, despite Augustine's perplexity, descriptions of the nature of time which allow the process of time to tell a significant story: the experience of moving from past to present to future is no longer 'one damn thing after another', but a vehicle of destiny in which people and societies are characterized in particular ways. The ways vary greatly, because the understandings of time vary greatly. Thus in the broadest division (for examples, see *time*), time in some religions is regarded as cyclical (but with lives being lived linearly, with as many as 84 million *rebirths or reappearances), while in others time is linear, moving from creation to end (but with lives lived cyclically, going round repeated years of commemorative *festivals). In many religions, both the past and the future can be visited: the past in order that it may continue to live in the present, and so that wrongdoing may be repaired and forgiven (*retrogressive rituals, which 'visit' past events and enable people to relive or deal with them, are common), the future so that it is not wholly unknown. Religions have produced a multitude of different ways in which the future can be foretold, and they have also portrayed what the ultimate future will be like—and by what ways that future state can be reached. They have even attempted to create proleptic societies which anticipate the final state.

In these ways, religions make life as project a little easier. They protect and transmit the means to attain the most important goals imaginable. Some of these goals are proximate: they are goals which can be attained within this life (a wiser, more fruitful, more charitable, more successful, way of living) or within the process of rebirth. But others are ultimate, and have to do with the final condition of this or any other human person, and of the cosmos itself. These ultimate goals may be at the extremes of joy or pain, of reward or punishment; which means that death, for most religions, is the threshold of judgement, or the place of judgement itself. The picture is complicated by the fact that for religions with a belief in rebirth or reappearance, such as Hinduism, Jainism, Buddhism, the possibility of punishment after death, in the equivalent of *hell, is only a proximate goal: it is not an ultimate destiny; and even in religions like Christianity or Islam, where the judgement after death is ultimate, it has always been a matter of debate whether punishment is eternal (*universalism). But even with the many qualifications which the immense diversity of religions always makes necessary, the general point remains that religious systems protect and transmit the means through which the proximate and ultimate goals of life, as they are designated within the systems themselves, can be attained. Furthermore, they give accounts of the state of the dead of such a kind that the living can either remain in some form of communication or communion with them, or can have assurance about them and can continue to care for them. Religions extend the family beyond the grave (or funeral pyre: see *ancestors).

Text, Tradition, and Story

How is all this information to be secured and conveyed? The family is of paramount importance, but so too is the social gathering, in forms which emerge eventually in *ekklesia* and its equivalent in other religions. The Greek word *ekklesia,* which means a summoning out of individuals into a group, refers often to political organizations; but it came to be the word used for the Christian Church—as in the English 'ecclesiastical' or *ecclesiology. But there is an ecclesial necessity in all religions, whether in village assembly, *synagogue, *mosque, *gurdwara, or *temple. Religion binds people together in a common enterprise; and it is in the forms and modes of religious assembly that much of the transmission of religious information takes place. Much is transmitted orally, and much, again, is entirely non-verbal: that is why so much of religion is expressed in gestures, symbols, *art, and silences; even that most fundamental of human necessities, *breathing, becomes a vehicle of religious exploration and discovery.

But the precious nature of religious information, whether verbal or non-verbal, means that writing became of paramount importance: in the beginning was the Word, or Sound, *Logos, or *Śabda. The Word extends its powers when it is written down, and Sound becomes more repeatedly accessible when it is translated into text. Text always runs in parallel to oral transmission, and by no means all religions became text-based. But text as authority and *revelation builds into religious life one of its most powerful constraints. The *Bible says . . . ; but so also does *Tanach (Jewish *Scripture), the *Qur'an, *Śruti, the *Angas, the *Guru Granth Sahib, the Book of *Mormon. The fact that they do not all say the same thing, and may indeed contradict each other, reinforces the radical divide between religions; but it also means, more simply, that revelation is always contingent—that is, no matter how strong the claims may be that a particular text or collection of texts comes from heaven or from God, it is always related to the particular historical circumstances in which it first appeared. And that means, in turn, that it is related to the transmission of a particular system.

The importance of texts extends beyond revelation. The work of *exegesis is continuous in all religions, which means, in other words, that the working out of the meaning of any particular tradition is a continuing task. Again, much of this is practical, a working out in life of what the tradition requires, enables, and expects. But much is committed to writing, so that the *scribe (especially before the invention of printing), although sometimes feared, is almost invariably honoured as a midwife of meaning. Text as the protector of information immediately creates the problems of exegesis and *hermeneutics (whose meaning is the true meaning of the text? and who decides which it is?), but it also creates opportunity: it becomes a transforming constraint on individual lives, and it releases the possibility of a brilliant kaleidoscope of different kinds of writing, in philosophy, poetry, story and drama, all of which owe much to the religious contexts in which they came into being.

In these ways religions have protected and transmitted the information which has been tested and winnowed through time, and they have thus created worlds of confidence: they have created worlds in which people can recognize who they are, why they are, where they are, and where they are going. They can know how they should live and behave. Religions establish codes of recognition, so that in potentially hostile environments, people can recognize whether those approaching them are friends or foes, whether their intentions are hostile or friendly. Religions create extended families—extending them, in some cases, far beyond even the kinship group and tribe, to make into one community 'all the nations of the earth' (see, for example, 'UMMA). Religions are usually tribal, but the tribe may be extremely large and metaphorical. The codes of recognition and of expected behaviour, even beyond the scope of ethics, bring order into society, often organizing hierarchies. Even more importantly, from a religious point of view, they give to all members, including the poorest and least privileged, the opportunity of religious success, however that is described. The codes of recognition and behaviour need to be secure and well established for that to be possible. In all these many ways, religions make life a little more predictable. They enable people to recognize the many different kinds of limitation which lie before the project of their lives, and how to accept or deal with them.

So important is the role of religions in creating meaning that the great pioneer of the modern study of religion, Max Weber, regarded it as their primary function. In his view, religions create theodicies. '*Theodicy' usually has a more restricted meaning, that of justifying claims made about the love and power of God in the face of suffering and evil. In Weber's usage, theodicies are explanations which will account for the inequalities and injustices of life: you live long, I die young; you are rich, I am poor; you are male, I am female; you are well, I am sick. Religions pour meaning and explanation into the gaps of inequality, and organize societies so as to be a living expression of a particular theodicy.

But although Weber extended the sense of the word, he did not really extend it enough. The meanings and values which religions create and sustain extend far beyond the range of even his understanding of theodicy, important though that is. Religions create entire worlds of order and entertainment, in which the place of each part can be recognized and identified. The biography of any individual is set within a far larger narrative, the components of which are constantly translated into that biography, thereby completely transforming its nature and outcomes. Much of this translation into life will be entirely unconscious, but much also will be a deliberate appropriation of the ways in which a religion makes the story, or components of the story, available—for example, in scripture-reading, preaching, *liturgy, or *pilgrimage. 'Religion as story' (to quote the title of the book edited by J. Wiggins, University Press of America, 1985) may be applied literally through story-telling, with the story-teller highly valued in all religions (see e.g., K. Narayan, *Storytellers, Saints and Scoundrels: Folk Narrative in Hindu Religious Teaching* (Delhi: Motilal Banarsidass, 1992)), but it may also lead to imaginations of time and space on such a large scale that they provide the conceptual context of life in a particular religion. Thus, for example, religions create cosmogonies and *cosmologies. Often these have been evaluated as quasi-scientific accounts, and have then been measured for worth against current cosmological theories in the natural sciences. In fact, a religion may have many cosmogonies, often contradictory of each other, each of which serves a different purpose. There are at least five creation stories in Jewish Scripture, and many more than that among Hindus. The point is that religions devise and elaborate cosmogonies and cosmologies, not in order to anticipate the brief episode of twentieth-century science, but in order to display the universe as an arena of opportunity, the opportunity to live in the ways and for the purposes which a religion suggests or demands. By providing maps of time and space, religions enable people to deal with (or to accept) the many limitations which stand across the project of their lives.

The cosmos as the bearer of meaning demands particular ways of acting and living. Religions, therefore, regard people as being both responsible and accountable: their lives move to some reckoning, whether it is spoken of as *Judgement or as *Karma (or in other ways), and whether the dialectic is described as *sin and *salvation, or as ignorance (*avidya) and enlightenment; and all religions have an imagination of hell. Religions may stress the inadequacy of human actions without help (grace and *redemption, or their equivalents, in other religions, of rescue and repair). But the belief that humans should do nothing and leave it all to God, guru, or grace, the extreme versions of which end up in *antinomianism, is rare.

Religious Creativity: Myth, Ritual, and Symbols

So religions (as Weber insisted) pour into the gaps not only meaning but also actions; and that is why religions are a constant force for change, despite the fact that they are also, as systems, necessarily conservative. But as in biology, so here: constraints are the condition of freedom, and once the constraints of a religion are internalized, people are set free to act and think in creative ways (on the meaning and importance of constraint in biology and religion, see J. W. Bowker, *A Year to Live*, Introduction (London: SPCK, 1991); *Is God a Virus . . . ?*, 96 ff.)

The supreme intellectual instruments of this religious creativity are *myth, *ritual, and *symbol. The word 'myth' has been debased in recent years so that it is now, in popular usage, another word for something false or invented. Yet myth is in fact one of the greatest of human achievements. Myths are narrations, usually stories, which point to truths of a kind that cannot be told in other ways—for example, in the categories of natural science. That is why myth was seized upon in the nineteenth century by those like Wagner who accepted that science has a true story to tell, but a limited one: it cannot, for example, tell us anything about the experienced truths of human love and suffering. Myth places individual biographies and local events into a much larger context and story, thereby giving them meaning and significance. Myth may provide explanations of ritual, but rituals may also be independent of myth. Rituals are actions repeated in regular and predictable ways which create order in the otherwise random process of time. They may therefore be entirely secular (as, for example, on New Year's Eve or at the opening of an Olympic Games), but they are extensive in religions. Some are *rites of passage (marking the movement of individuals or groups through significant moments of life and death), others mediate protection into dangerous worlds; some initiate, others terminate membership of a religious group; some seek to effect change, others to express meaning. Ritual is the enacted language through which human hopes and fears are articulated and dealt with, and life is constantly renewed. So much is expressed through ritual that it is impossible to summarize all that it means and does.

So too with symbols: language is important (to say the least) in expressing religious beliefs and ideas, but symbols are at least as much so. Symbols are compressed expressions of religious beliefs and ideas in visible form, some of which are enacted, but many of which are transcribed. Symbols rarely attempt to portray what they purport to be about, because they are economies of statement, feeling, and belief, usually achieved and established in religions and simply appropriated by particular individuals. Rather than reproducing something, they act as entrances to religious worlds and imaginations, much as the Looking Glass admitted Alice to wonder and delight—and to terror. Symbols are possessed of power and may encompass a universe in a space not much larger than a small room—or God in a *host the size of a coin.

From all this flows religious art and architecture, and much more besides. Religions are the resource and inspiration of virtually all the most enduring and timelessly moving of human creations—not just in art and architecture, but in agriculture, *music, *dance, *drama, poetry, and in the explorations of the cosmos which issued eventually as the natural sciences (it is only in very recent centuries that science has become decoupled from religion as a way of exploration). In practice and presentation, religions in human experience have been fun and they have been entertainment. Long before Hollywood began to dream in dollars, religions were mounting spectacles, heightened, often, by terror, and enhanced by high degrees of audience participation.

Boundaries and Border Incidents: Religions and Conflict

The protection and transmission of all of this requires organized systems, which religions necessarily are, and systems require boundaries. The boundaries may be literal, being established in relation to particular geographies, or they may be metaphorical. In either case, boundaries will be required; and where there are boundaries, there will be border incidents. Whenever boundaries come under threat, religions are likely to become either offensive or defensive. The threat may be one of literal invasion and displacement, or it may be metaphorical, as, for example, when it seems that *secular values and interests are displacing those of the inherited religion. In either case, at least some religious people will seek to hold, or even to extend, their ground. For this reason, religious wars are common, either between subsystems within the same religion, or between religions, or between religions and the non-religious world. The seriousness of the issues affords a powerful reinforcement of *fundamentalism, that is, the determination to identify and maintain certain fundamental and non-negotiable markers of true or legitimate religious identity. Maintaining that identity and defending boundaries against invasion or erosion leads repeatedly to religious wars, or wars in which religions are involved. All religions defend the legitimacy of war in some circumstances (see Just War), even those religions which insist on non-violence or on **ahimsa*. The cir-

*cumstances are restricted, and careful rules of limitation are usually specified. But war, particularly in defence, is recognized.

That is one reason why virtually all the long-running and apparently insoluble problems in the world, in Northern Ireland, Bosnia, Cyprus, the Middle East, Kashmir, *Khalistan, Sri Lanka, India and Pakistan, East Timor, the Philippines, have deep religious roots. If you wish to see where future conflicts will occur, draw on a map of the world the lines where religions, or subsystems of religions, meet. It is true that religions are capable of coexisting with each other, and often have done so for long periods of time: that has been the case, for example, until very recently, with Jewish communities in Muslim lands. But they do so only so long as the continuity of each of the religions in question does not seem to be threatened.

The reason why religions are so intransigent is because they protect and transmit all that information which is of such high and tested value, at least to those who see things that way. People would rather die than abandon such inherited treasure, especially when they have often tested it and proved it to be of worth in their own case. This is the paradox of religious urgency: religions are such bad news (when they are) only because they are such good news: they protect so much that is so important and so well tested through time that people would die rather than lose it. There is no doubt that one can point to many kinds of damage which religions have done, in terms, for example, of spiritual terrorization or of the subordination of women, in most aspects of their lives, to the decisions and determinations of men. But religions also remain now as they have been in the past, the major resource for the transformation of life and the transfiguration of art. There will always, therefore, be many who will resist a threat to their religion and the ruin of all that goes with it.

The Future of Religion

War and fundamentalism, however, are not the only responses to novelty. Religions are open to change, and have indeed changed much through the centuries. Change is invariably resisted by some, as being the kind of threat summarized in the previous paragraphs. Sometimes it is so strongly resisted that new *sects, new *cults, even *new religions split off and begin a history of their own. But because religions protect and transmit information of such high value and proven worth in the transformation of life, the appropriation of that information into life often demands transformation and change in the institution. The procedures of change are different in each religion, but the fact of change is a part of religious history, even though change has often, perhaps usually, been resisted. Religions are the custodians of collective memory: they carry the constraints from the past which control human life into distinct, but within the boundaries shareable, outcomes, so that a Buddhist, for example, is recognizable in any country or any generation, even though no Buddhist is identical with any other. But collective memory may demand change in order that the values and goals of a system can be appropriated and lived in new circumstances. The importance of collective memory is that it enables religions to maintain identity while at the same time being open to change.

What of the future of religion? Human religiosity will not diminish except by way of atrophy (by non-use, if that happens), because the preparation for it is so deeply embedded in the brain—and, many would say, because it then develops and flourishes in relation to what is truly discovered, however approximately and corrigibly this is described. Thus the extraordinary discoveries of somatic exploration and exegesis will not become unattainable, even if, for the sake of argument, the neurophysiology of the underlying brain events is better understood. But the forms of expression will certainly change. Partly that is a matter of language, and partly one of organization. All our languages about anything, even about something as relatively obvious as the universe, are approximate, provisional, corrigible, and frequently wrong, at least from the point of view of later generations; and yet, as in the case of the natural sciences, they can be extremely reliable. If that is true of the universe, it will certainly be true also of God, *Brahman, and the Buddha-nature: what we say will always be approximate and incomplete, but it will continue to achieve great reliability. It is the corrigibility and approximate nature of all languages which opens up the necessity of faith. But faith, as trust in the tradition and the teacher, then sets out on journeys which for many (not inevitably, and certainly not for all) reveal the truth of that for which it yearns. 'Eternity in time', to quote the phrase of Henry *Vaughan, is no longer a paradox but a persuasion. Meditation enters into meaning far beyond common senses, and rests in that supreme condition which leaves behind it even such treasures as beauty, excitement, and delight. Prayer is presence, before One who elicits praise, thanksgiving, and joy, as well as *penitence and sorrow. Because prayer is the greatest of the human languages of love, it connects others to God as well.

The truth of all this is so well known and practised that it will endure, even in the midst of great changes. So far as organization is concerned, we are on the edge of unimaginable transformations in the methods and speed of communication. The *ecclesia* of the internet does not require physical presence. And yet humanity does. The ecclesial necessity which helped to bring religions into being may yet serve purposes of humanity which could scarcely be envisaged until the last decade.

What, finally, of the definition of religion? Has it come any closer into our sights? Clearly not. We have simply shown that *Wittgenstein was right when he observed of games that it is easier to recognize a game than to define it—or at least, than it is to define the word 'game' in such a way that all the characteristics of all games are embraced within it (see e.g. *Philosophical Investigations,* nos. 66 f., on 'family resemblances'). We can recognize a religion when we see one because we know what the many characteristics of religion are; but we would not expect to find any religion which exhibited all the characteristics without exception. That process of discerning the characteristics is the first level of *phenomenology, and it is the reason why Ninian Smart (*The World's Religions* . . . (Cambridge: Cambridge University Press, 1989), 12–21) has proposed that we can gain a more balanced and comprehensive view of 'the luxurious vegetation of the world's religions' by observing what is the case in seven different dimensions: the practical and ritual; the experiential and emotional; the narrative or mythical; the doctrinal and philosophical; the ethical and legal; the social and institutional; and the material (art, architecture, and sacred places). It will still remain the case that the second level of phenomenology remains to be done, the testing and examination of what has brought the brilliant and majestic creation of religion into being in the first place, and has sustained it to the present. Religion is a risk of intolerance, cruelty, bigotry, social oppression, and self-opinionated nastiness. Within that 'luxurious vegetation' are ruthless predators of power and ambition. But religion also remains, as that first definition of Marx recognized, the heart and soul of what might otherwise be (and in the twentieth century all too often has been) a heartless world.

John Bowker

A

A (1) Symbol of emptiness (*śūnyatā) and of the undifferentiated source of appearance in *Zen Buddhism. In Japanese esoteric Buddhism (*mikkyō), *aji*, the first sound in the Sanskrit alphabet, contains the epitome of all truth, and as such is a key element in meditation. *Aji-kan* is meditation on the letter A.

A (2) (Gk., alpha). First letter of the Greek alphabet, combined with the last, *Ω* (omega), to refer to God as the beginning and the end, the all-encompassing.

A (3) Letter of negation in several languages, as in, e.g., *atheism, *adharma.

Aaron (*c.*13th cent. BCE). Elder brother of *Moses. He was perceived in biblical literature as the archetypal *priest and the founder of the hereditary priesthood (see AARONIDES).

In the Qur'ān, he appears as Hārūn, a *prophet and helper to his brother Mūsā (Moses).

Aaron ben Elijah (?1328–69). *Karaite Jewish philosopher and exegete. His greatest work was the trilogy *Ez Hayyim* (Tree of Life), *Gan Eden* (Garden of *Eden), and *Keter Torah* (Crown of the Law).

Aaron ben Jacob ha-Kohen of Lunel (13th/14th cent. CE). French Jewish *Talmudist. His most famous work, *Orhot Ḥayyim* (Ways of Life), was a compilation of Jewish law which was widely quoted.

Aaronides. Descendants of *Aaron and members of the Israelite *priesthood. According to Numbers 18. 1–7, there is a clear distinction between members of the house of *Levi and the direct descendants of Aaron who 'shall attend to your priesthood for all that concerns the altar and that which is within the veil' (v. 7).

Aaron of Baghdad (mid-9th cent. CE). A Babylonian Jewish scholar who lived in Italy and is regarded as a link between the Babylonian *academies and W. Jewish culture. He is described by *Eleazar ben Judah of Worms in the 13th cent. as *av kol ha-sodot* ('the father of all secrets').

Ab-. For words beginning Ab-, check also alternative spelling, AV-, e.g. 'Abodah is under 'Avodah.

Abaddon (Heb.). Place of destruction, mentioned in the *Wisdom literature (e.g. Job 31. 12, Psalm 88. 12). In the *Talmud, it is a name given to *Gehenna.

'Abādites (Muslim sect): see 'IBĀDIYA.

Abangan (Javanese, 'brown coloured'). Javanese who are culturally (rather than observantly) Muslim. They have come under increasing pressure from observant Muslims (*santri*) to conform, but remain resistant to the eradication of indigenous customs.

Abarbanel (Jewish statesman): see ABRABANEL.

Abba (1) (Aram., 'Father'). An address to God used by *Jesus. The Aramaic word is found in Mark 14. 36, Romans 8. 15, and Galatians 4. 6; it is a term both of a child's respectful relation to its father and of a confidential relation to an esteemed person, not 'Daddy'.

Abba (2) (late 3rd/early 4th cent. CE). Jewish Babylonian *amora, who later settled in *Israel. He was seen as a link between the two centres.

Abba bar Kahana (late 3rd cent. CE). Jewish Palestinian *amora. He was regarded as one of the greatest exponents of *aggadah of his era.

Abbahu (3rd/4th cent. CE). Jewish Palestinian *amora. He held a prominent position in the Jewish community of Caesarea and was well-known for his generosity, wealth, and excellent relationship with the Roman authorities. He issued proclamations and introduced customs such as the order of *blessing the *shofar on *Rosh ha-Shanah.

'Abbās (uncle of *Muḥammad and source of the *'Abbāsid dynasty): see AL-'ABBĀS.

Abba Saul (mid-2nd cent. CE). Jewish Palestinian *tanna. He passed on traditions concerning the human embryo and the structure and furnishing of the *Temple.

'Abbās Effendi (one-time head of Bahā'ī faith): see SHOGHI EFFENDI.

'Abbāsids (Arab., *al-dawlah al-'abbāsiya*, from *Banū al-'Abbās*). Muslim dynasty in power 749–1258 CE (AH 132–656). Their name is derived from their ancestor *al-'Abbās, the uncle of *Muḥammad. After the death of *'Alī b. Abī Tālib, the rule passed to the *Umayyads with their capital in *Damascus (660–750 CE (AH 41–132).) Social, economic, political, and religious factors combined led to an uprising with strong Persian and *Shī'ite elements, and the

Umayyads were ousted, nearly all of them killed, and al-Saffāḥ ('the spiller', i.e., of Umayyad blood) took over power as the first of the 'Abbāsid rulers. The next caliph, al-Manṣūr, founded the city of Baghdād. One of the most famous of the 'Abbāsid caliphs was Hārūn al-Rashīd (764–809 (AH 147–194); his splendid court is reflected in *The Thousand and One Nights*). His son al-Ma'mūn (813–33 (AH 198–218)) founded the *Bayt al-ḥikma* (house of wisdom) for the translation from Gk. of classical texts of philosophy, science, and medicine. Under the 'Abbāsids, the *Mu'tazilite school of theology enjoyed a brief period of supremacy, but the more orthodox schools eventually regained their dominant place. Although the 'Abbāsids were the nominal rulers throughout the Muslim empire, various dynasties gained effective control of parts of this vast region. The Buwayhids, from Persia, actually entered Baghdād and controlled affairs from 945 (AH 334) for just over a century. The *Fāṭimids in Egypt, a *Shī'a dynasty, took power in 909 (AH 297) but were finally ousted by the Ayyūbids under *Ṣalāḥ al-Dīn (Saladin) in 1171 (AH 567). One survivor of the massacre of the Umayyads, 'Abd al-Raḥmān, made his way to Spain (al-Andalus) and founded an independent dynasty with its capital at Cordoba.

In 1258 (AH 656) the Mongols captured and sacked Baghdād, rolled up the body of the last caliph in a carpet and rode their horses over it. Thus the 'Abbāsid caliphate came to an end, although another branch reigned in Cairo 1261–1517 (AH 659–923), when they were supplanted by the *Ottomans.

Abbaye (late 3rd/4th cent. CE). Jewish Babylonian *amora. As head of the *academy at *Pumbedita, he debated legal points with the most prominent scholars of his time. Abbaye was the first to make explicit the distinction between the literal and the figurative meaning of a text.

Abbé (French). Title for a clergyman.

Abbess. Feminine form of *abbot, dating back to 6th cent. An abbess is elected by a community of *nuns as its superior.

Abbey. Building or buildings used (or once used) by a religious order of *monks or *nuns.

Abbot (Aram., Syr., *abba*, 'father'). The head of a Christian monastic community, especially in the *Benedictine or *Cistercian traditions. The term is used in translation for the head of communities in other religions: e.g. *roshi, the Tibetan *mkhan-po* (also, following the pronunciation, *khenpo*).

'Abd (Arab., 'servant' (pl. *'ibād*) or 'slave' (pl. *'abīd*). In the religious sense, a 'servant' or 'worshipper' of *Allāh. In the secular sense, the *Qur'ān speaks of *slaves, of 'a slave possessed (by a master)' (*'abd mamlūk*, 16. 75). The Qur'ān accepts slavery as a fact, but encourages kind treatment of slaves, and to free them is an act of piety (2. 177). Women slaves could be taken as concubines, but could also become legal wives.

Abdal (Arab., 'substitutes'). A numerical set of seventy *Sūfī holy people, constant in number until the end of the world, when their number diminishes and the world ends. The central figure (known only to God) is the *qutb, or axis, of the world; around him are four pegs (*awstād*), so that together the abdal form a tent of protection for the world.

'Abd al-Bahā (one-time head of Bahāī faith): see 'ABDU'L-BAHĀ.

'Abd al-Jabbār (*c*.935–*c*.1025 (AH 322–415)). A leading Muslim *Mu'tazilite theologian. He wrote many books, of which the best-known is *al-Mughnī fī abwāb al-tawhīd wa'l-'adl*.

'Abd al-Karīm al-Jīlī (*c*.1365/6–*c*.1412 (AH 767–815)). A Muslim mystic who was a follower of *Ibn al-'Arabī's system and wrote the *Sūfī treatise **Al-Insān al-Kāmil* (The Perfect Man), dealing with cosmic, metaphysical, and ontological problems.

Jīlī elaborated the doctrine of *Muḥammad as the *Logos, the Perfect Man *(al-Insān-al-Kāmil). This absolutely Perfect Man is the Prophet Muḥammad, and in every age the Perfect Men are an outward manifestation of the essence of Muḥammad. Muḥammad should be loved and adored as the most perfect manifestation of the Lord.

'Abd Allāh ibn Maimūn al-Qaddāḥ (*c*.10th cent./AH 3rd cent.). A revered figure among *Shī'a Muslims, who did much to establish and organize *Ismā'īliya; but the details of his own life remain obscure.

'Abd Allah ibn Yāsīn (Muslim revivalist): see ALMORAVIDS.

'Abd al-Muṭṭalib ibn Hāshim (of the tribe of Quraysh). Grandfather of *Muḥammad. When Muḥammad's father died, he became guardian of the child, but himself died when Muḥammad was aged 8, and the guardianship passed to his uncle *Abū Ṭālib the father of *'Alī.

'Abd al-Qādir al-Jīlī (more often Jīlānī, 1077–1166 (AH 470–561)). Preacher, *Ḥanbalite theologian, and supposed founder of the

*Qādirīya *Sūfī order. His fame as an orator attracted students from all over the Muslim world. It is said that his sermons converted many Jews and Christians to Islam, and many Muslims to the spiritual life. Financial support from his many followers enabled him to establish a *ribāt* (Sūfī centre), where the poor and needy were cared for. He served as *muftī, teacher of Quranic exegesis, *ḥadīth, and *fiqh.

'Abd al-Qādir's sober Sufism gained wide acceptance amongst the orthodox circles, and therein lies the reason for the great spread of the Qādirīya order throughout the Muslim world. He was given the title Ghawth-al-A'ẓam (the greatest of all helpers) and his tomb in Baghdād still attracts many devotees.

'Abd al-Rāziq, 'Alī (1888–1966). Egyptian writer and scholar whose *Islām wa Usūl al-Hukm* (Islam and the Principles of Government) caused a sensation in 1825. Responding to the demise of the *Ottoman Caliphate the previous year, he claimed that Islam had never been essentially political, that the Caliphate was dispensable, and that Islam was a purely spiritual loyalty.

'Abduh, Muḥammad (1849–1905 (AH 1266–1322)). Egyptian Muslim theologian, known as *al-ustad al-iman* (master and guide). He was the founder of the Egyptian Muslim modernist school. He was from a peasant family in lower Egypt, and studied at *al-Azhar University, and in Paris, where he met *al-Afghānī and became his closest disciple (founding with him the *Salafiyya). 'Abduh emphasized the important function of reason in Islam, that although faith and reason operate in different spheres, they must not conflict but must positively co-operate in human advancement. By restating Islam in such a way, 'Abduh attempted to open the door, by way of *ijtihād, to new influences and the acquisition of modern knowledge.

'Abduh's major work, *Risālat-al-Tawhid* (1897), and the journal *al-Manār* (1897), were widely read and supported by many Muslims, but also provoked bitter hostility from orthodox circles. In 1899, 'Abduh obtained the highest religious position in Egypt, that of state *muftī, which he held till his death. 'Abduh used this powerful position to push through many reforms.

He regarded his commentary (*tafsīr) on the *Qur'ān as his most important work, but it was unfinished at his death, and was completed (and revised) later, by Muḥammad Rashīd Riḍā.

'Abdu'l-Bahā (1844–1921, lit. Servant of Bahā). Title of 'Abbās Effendi, eldest son and appointed successor of *Bahā'u'llāh as head (1892–1921) of the *Bahā'ī faith. Successfully rebutting a challenge to his leadership from his half-brother, Mīrzā Muḥammad 'Alī, he superintended the expansion of the Bahā'ī religion to North America and Europe, delineated its further expansion, and guided the Iranian Bahā'ī community through the turbulent years of the constitutional movement. He died in Haifa on 28 November 1921, having appointed his eldest grandson, *Shoghi Effendi Rabbānī to be his successor.

Abel. A herdsman, in Jewish *scripture, the younger son of the first human beings, *Adam and *Eve. According to Genesis 4. 1–9 he was murdered by his elder brother, the farmer, *Cain.

Abelard, Peter (1079–1142). Christian philosopher and theologian. Born at Pallet, near Nantes, he was one of the most brilliant and controversial theologians of his day. His academic career was cut short after his love-affair with Héloïse in Paris, where he was a popular lecturer. He challenged current philosophical orthodoxy, preparing the way for *nominalism, and was condemned for his teaching on the *Trinity. His doctrine of the *atonement, emphasizing the love of Christ, manifest in his life and passion, which calls forth a human response of love, has had a continuing influence: His works include *Christian Theology*, *Ethics*, and his letters to Héloïse.

Abercius, St (d. *c*.200 CE). Christian *bishop of Hieropolis in Phrygia Salutaris. He is known from an important inscription apparently set up by him over his future tomb.

Abgar V, 4 BCE–50 CE, King of Edessa. According to a popular tradition as early as *Eusebius (and also in the *Doctrine of *Addai*) he wrote a letter to *Jesus asking him to visit and heal him.

Abhabba-ṭṭhāna (Pāli, 'condition of being incapable'). A characteristic of the *Arhat in Buddhism, who is regarded as incapable of certain kinds of moral transgression.

Ābhāsa-caitanya (Skt., 'reflection' + 'consciousness'). The way in which, in Hinduism, absolute consciousness (*cit) is reflected in human awareness. The world-entangled self (*jīva) takes this reflection to be the reality and thus fails to break through to the true realization of *Brahman, and of the true self (*ātman) as Brahman.

Abhava (Skt.). In Hinduism, the non-reality or non-existence of manifest appearances, hence (by the realization that this is so) release (*mokṣa) from entanglement in them. In Buddhism, abhava reinforces *Nāgārjuna's argument for *śūnyatā.

Abhayākaragupta (11th/12th cent.). Buddhist monk and scholar, especially of *Tantric Buddhism. He was born a *brahman, but became Buddhist in response to a vision. He wrote many works on monastic discipline, issues in *abhidhamma, and tantra. The tr. of his works into Tibetan began under his own supervision, thus extending his influence.

Abhaya-mudra (Skt., 'fearlessness' + *mudra). The gesture of being without fear (only acquired in full in the condition of *mokṣa).

Abhaya-vacana (Skt., 'fearlessness' + 'words'). The capacity in Hinduism to speak without mortal or bodily fear, when one has achieved spiritual insight.

Abheda-bodha-vākya (Skt., 'identity' + 'alertness' + 'utterance'). A formula in Hinduism to invoke the absolute truth.

Abhibhāvayatana (Skt.; Pāli *abhibhāyatana*). Eight fields of mastery or control of the perception of manifest appearances, an early practice in Buddhism.

Abhibhāyatana (control of perceptions): see ABHIBHĀVAYATANA.

Abhicāra (magic form of ritual): see CHINNAMASTA.

Abhidhamma (Pali; Skt., *abhidharma*, 'special teaching'), *Buddhist reflection, often analytic, on the meaning of the Buddha's teaching. The *Abhidhamma Piṭaka thus forms one of the 'three baskets' (*Tripiṭaka) of Buddhist text collections.

Abhidhamma Piṭaka (Pāli; Skt., Abhidharma Piṭaka). The third and final section of the Buddhist *canon (*tripiṭaka). Each school of early Buddhism had its own particular version of the Abhidhamma Pitaka, though the only complete versions now extant are those of the *Sarvāstivādins (in Chinese and Tibetan) and the *Theravādins (in Pāli).

Abhidharma-kośa Śāstra. A systematic *Sarvāstivāda Buddhist treatise composed by (or attributed to) *Vasubandhu in the period before he embraced *Mahāyāna Buddhism. The work comprises two parts: verse (*Abh.k. kārikā*) and prose commentary (*Abh.k. bhāṣya*). As an encyclopaedia of Abhidharma, the work became absolutely central to the tradition of study within Buddhism in subsequent cents.

Abhijñā (supernatural powers): see ABHIÑÑĀ.

Abhimāna (Skt., 'self-esteem'). The self in Hinduism that has made a declaration of independence, i.e. of self-sufficiency, and is therefore far removed from the true realization of the unity of all appearance in relation to *Brahman.

Abhinavagupta (960–1050 CE). A Hindu theologian of *Kashmir *Śaivism who wrote extensively on poetics, aesthetics, and religious doctrine and practice. In his work *Tantrism finds its philosophical articulation. His comprehensive *Light on Tantra* (*Tantrāloka*, Ital. tr. R. Gnoli *Lucce delle sacre scritture*, 1960) is a synthesis of the traditions, teaching, and practice of Kashmir Śaivism. His ideas are summarized in his *Essence of Supreme Meaning* (*Paramārthasāra*, Fr. tr. L. Silburn, 1957). He also contributed to aesthetics (*rāsa), writing a commentary (*locana*) on the great aesthetician Ānandavardhana's *Dhvanyāloka* and Bharata's *Nātya Śāstra* (Eng. tr. R. Gnoli, *The Aesthetic Experience According to Abhinavagupta*, 1956). Abhinavagupta was probably the first Indian philosopher to link aesthetic and religious experience, maintaining that the aesthetic emotions (rāsa) originate in the aesthetic emotion of tranquility (*śāntarasa*) which is also an experience of the absolute. Applying the categories of aesthetic to religious experience was developed much later by the Gosvamins, *brahmans who are descendants of Nityāndanda.

Abhiniveṣa (love of the world): see ASMITA.

Abhiññā (Pāli), **Abhijñā** (Skt., 'higher knowledge'). In Buddhism, any of six supernormal powers: (i) psycho-kinesis, (ii) clairaudience, (iii) telepathy, (iv) knowledge of the rebirth of others and of the karmic factors, (v) knowledge of one's own former rebirths, (vi) knowledge of the extinction of the *āsavas.

Abhirati. The *paradise of the *Buddha *Akṣobhya, the 'Realm of Joy'. It is the Eastern paradise (see SUKHĀVATI), but in the sense that Buddhist heavens or hells have only the degree of reality that humans confer upon them. They seem real to those who are still in ignorance.

Abhisamayālankāra (The Treatise on the Exposition of the Perfection of Wisdom). An important commentary work of the Buddhist Mahāyāna tradition attributed to *Maitreya and probably composed in the 4th cent. CE.

Abhiṣek(a) (Skt., *abhi* + *ṣich*, 'sprinkle water'). In Hinduism, a general word for anointing or sprinkling, especially in order to consecrate: Abhiṣeka in later Hinduism is transferred to a religious context and is sometimes a synonym for *dīkṣa or sometimes follows from dīkṣa.

In Buddhism, abhiṣeka is the means by which the guru transmits the power and authority to a pupil to engage in specific forms of meditation. It is important especially in Tibet (Tib., *dbang.bskur*, 'empowerment'), where it is an *initiation ritual in Tibetan Buddhism preceding *Tantric practice.

Abhiṣeka-bhūmi (highest stage of perfection): see BHUMI.

Abhuta-dharma (miracle): see ABUDATSUMA.

Abi (Jap.; Skt. *avīci*). The lowest part of Buddhist *hell, a place of such pain that no one cries out, and anguished silence prevails. However, as with all Buddhist hells, it is not a place of everlasting torment, since there is nothing permanent in the Buddhist perspective.

Abidatsuma-kusha-ron. Jap. for *Abhidharma-kośa-bhāṣya*, the survey of *Theravāda teaching by *Vasubandhu.

Abidatsumazō. Jap. for *Abhidhammapiṭaka, one of the three (*sanzō*) or five (*gozō*) divisions of Buddhist texts or 'scriptures'.

Abimelech (date uncertain, 19th–16th cents. BCE). King of Gerar, whom both *Abraham and *Isaac tried to deceive by presenting their wives as their sisters (Genesis 20, 26. 1–11). He also appears in connection with both *patriarchs in disputes over wells (Genesis 21. 25, 26. 15–21). Because of the similarities between the stories, most scholars regard them as different versions of the same incidents. According to the *aggadah, Abmilech is described as a *'righteous gentile' (*Mid. Ps.* 34).

Abimelech (12th cent. BCE). In the Jewish scriptures, the son of *Gideon by his Shechemite concubine (Judges 8. 31). He slaughtered sixty-nine of the seventy sons of Gideon and became ruler of the city of Shechem (Judges 9. 1–5). Subsequently he destroyed the city, but was mortally wounded during the siege of Thebez (Judges 9. 39–54). Although Abimelech is not counted as one of the judges, his story may reflect the changing attitude of Israelites towards the institution of monarchy at that time.

Abjad. Muslim method of calculating from the numerical value of letters—alif = 1, ba' = 2, etc. The letters are moved on squares, or the numbers are substituted for letters, to gain secret meanings, predictions, and the like. In that respect it resembles Jewish *gematria.

Ablutions. Ritual cleansings to remove impurity and to mark transitions from profane to sacred states, etc. They are often, therefore, associated with *rites of passage. In Judaism, ablution is ritual washing intended to restore or maintain a state of ritual *purity is rooted in *Torah. A complete list of when it is required was compiled by Samson b. Zadok (13th cent. CE): see Joseph *Caro's *Shulḥan Arukh*. OH 4. 18.

In Christianity, in addition to the general sense in which *baptism might be regarded as 'an ablution', the word has a technical sense. The ablutions are the washing of the fingers and of the *communion vessels after the communion.

In Islam, ritual purity (*ṭahāra) is required before carrying out religious duties, especially *ṣalāt (worship). Ablution is of two kinds: *ghusl and wuḍū' (regulations being given in the *Qur'ān, 5. 7), with a third kind substituting for the others where necessary:

1. Ghusl, major ablution: complete washing of the body in pure water, after declaring the *niyya (intention) to do so. It is obligatory after sexual relations whereby a state of *janāba* (major ritual impurity) is incurred. It is recommended before the prayer of Friday and the two main feasts (*'id al-aḍḥā and *'īd al-fiṭr), and before touching the Qur'ān. For the dead, ghusl must be carried out before burial.

2. Wuḍū', minor ablution, is required to remove *ḥadath, minor ritual impurity which is incurred in everyday life. Wuḍū' should usually be carried out before each of the five times of daily prayer.

3. Where water is not available, clean sand may be used, rubbed upon the body; this method, *tayammum*, can be substituted for wuḍū' and, occasionally, for ghusl.

For ablution among Hindus, see TARPAṆA, ŚODHANA. Since Sikhs concentrate on inner cleanliness ('True ablution consists in the constant adoration of God', Ādi Granth 358), ritual ablutions are much diminished.

Aboab, Isaac (end of 14th cent. CE). A Jewish *rabbinic writer. He was a member of a prominent *Sephardic family which produced several outstanding scholars. Isaac was the author of *Menorat ha-Ma'or* (Candlestick of Light), which was widely popular.

Abodah (Jewish ritual): see AVODAH.

Abomination of Desolation. Tr. of the Gk. *bdelugma erēmōseōs* from 1 Maccabees 1. 54 and the Heb. *shiqquz shomen* from Daniel 12. 11. It refers to something *idolatrous which was set up on the *altar of the *Jerusalem *Temple in obedience to the command of Antiochus IV (Epiphanes)—possibly an image of Antiochus. It is then picked up in the New Testament (Matthew 24. 15, Mark 13. 14), where again the exact reference is uncertain.

Abō Rasetsu. A guardian of *hell in Japanese Buddhism.

Abortion. The artificial termination of an established pregnancy. In all religions, there is a general tendency to disapprove, but the fact and severity of disapproval varies with circumstances. Thus it may depend on the stage which the pregnancy has reached; on the welfare of the pregnant woman; on the status, value, or (in more recent times) rights of the unborn human life; the assumed gender of that life; the interests of others (e.g. the father); the requirements of whatever is authoritatively determinative of decisions in this area (e.g. scripture). Some religions are thus more definite, in so far as they have normative scriptures in which prescriptions can be found (or from which they can be derived).

Abot(h) (Jewish treatise): see AVOT.

Abrabanel (Abravanel). Isaac ben Judah (1437–1508), Jewish statesman, commentator, and philosopher. He succeeded his father as treasurer to the Portuguese king Alfonso V, but was compelled to flee to Spain when he was suspected of participating in rebellion against his successor. Although in the service of Ferdinand and Isabella of Spain, he failed to prevent the expulsion of the Jews in 1492, and went into exile, eventually settling in Venice where he died. By the age of 20 he had written *Ateret Zekenim* (The Crown of Elders) examining divine providence. In *Rosh Amanah* (The Principles of Faith) he defended *Maimonides, although he also maintained that the isolation of some dogmas as seemingly more important than others is wrong, since the whole of *Torah is a seamless robe. He wrote commentaries on many biblical books.

Abrabanel, Judah (also known as Leo Hebraeus, *c.*1460–*c.*1523). Jewish Portuguese philosopher, poet, and physician. He served as personal physician to the Spanish viceroy in Naples and was the author of *Telunah 'al ha-Zeman* (Complaint against Time) and four poems about his father *Isaac. His most famous work was a philosophical dialogue on the theme of love (*Dialoghi di amore*).

Abraham (originally named Abram). *Patriarch of the Israelite people whose story is told in *Genesis.

In the *aggadah, Abraham is seen as an ideal figure who kept the *oral law even before it had been revealed. As the first to recognize God, he is the father of all *proselytes.

In Christianity, Abraham is an exemplar of the efficacy of faith without law (Romans 4, Galatians 3. 6–9) and of faith as such (Hebrews 11. 8 ff.). In James 2. 20–4, his faith (in his willingness to sacrifice *Isaac) is an illustration of *justification by works. He was believed to have been one of the just liberated by *Christ on his descent into *hell. See also ABRAHAM'S BOSOM.

In Islam, his name (in the Qur'ān) is Ibrāhīm. He is seen as a *prophet and the one who together with his son Ismā'īl (Ishmael) restored the original monotheistic worship at the *Ka'ba in *Mecca. (Qur'ān 2.125). Ibrāhīm is considered as the original Muslim, who submitted to *Allāh as a *ḥanīf (monotheist) and muslim (3. 67). Islam is itself referred to as the 'religion of Ibrāhīm' (*millat Ibrāhīm*, 2. 130).

Abraham, Apocalypse of. A literary work of the 2nd cent. CE. It tells the story of *Abraham's visit to the seven heavens.

Abraham, Testament of. A book of unknown date containing the apocryphal story of the death of *Abraham.

Abraham bar Hiyya (d. *c.*1136). Jewish Spanish philosopher and translator. He produced several works of philosophy, the best known of which are *Hegyon ha-Nefesh ha-Azuvah* (Meditation of the Sad Soul), the encyclopaedic *Yesodei ha-Tevunah u-Migdal ha-Emunah* (Foundation of Understanding and Tower of Faith), a book of astronomy *Hokhmat ha-Hizzayon* (Wisdom of the Revelation), and one on *astrology, *Megillat ha-Megalleh* (Scroll of the Revealer).

Abraham ben David of Posquières (*c.*1125–98 CE, also known as Rabad). Jewish French *Talmudist. His criticism of *Maimonides' *Mishneh Torah* (especially for not giving sources or explanations, and for the very tendency to codify) established his reputation, and his most famous work, the *Ba'alei ha Nefesh* (Masters of the Soul) discussed the laws related to *women.

Abraham ben Moses ben Maimon (1186–1237 CE). Leader of Egyptian Jewry, philosopher, and son of *Maimonides. He introduced various new ritual practices, influenced by the Muslim *Sūfīs, and therefore aroused strong opposition. He defended his father's works in various publications and produced an encyclopaedic work on Judaism entitled *Kifayat al-Abidin* (Comprehensive Guide for the Servants of God).

Abrahamites. A Christian Judaizing sect flourishing in Bohemia between 1747 and 1781. They rejected the doctrine of the *Trinity, kept Saturday as the *Sabbath, did not eat pork, and even occasionally practised *circumcision.

Abraham's bosom (Heb., *be-heiko shel Avraham*). An expression indicating the location of righteous souls. It led to the famous 'malapropism' of the Hostess in Shakespeare's *Henry V*: 'Nay, sure he's [Falstaff] not in hell; he's in Arthur's bosom, if ever a man went to Arthur's bosom.'

Abram (Jewish Patriarch): see ABRAHAM.

Abravanel (Jewish statesman): see ABRABANEL.

Abrogation (Muslim): see NASKH.

Absalom. Son of *David. After the rape of his sister Tamar by their half-brother Amnon, Absalom murdered Amnon and fled the court. Having raised rebellion against his father David, he was killed in the subsequent battle, evoking David's lament (2 Samuel 13–18).

Absolute Dependence, Feeling of: see SCHLEIERMACHER, F.

Absolute unitary being: see BIOGENETIC STRUCTURALISM.

Absolution. The statement and the enactment of the forgiveness of *sins, and of release from them. It is a sacrament in the *Roman Catholic and *Orthodox (Gk., *metanoia, exomologesis*) Churches, with absolution being pronounced by a *priest or *bishop. In *Russian Orthodoxy, the form of absolution is in the form of a prayer (precatory), 'May our Lord and God *Jesus Christ forgive you', followed by the statement (indicative), 'I, n., through the power given to me by him, forgive you and absolve you. . . .' In the Catholic tradition, the indicative form became standard from the time of the Council of *Trent onward. When the rite of penance was revised after *Vatican II, a precatory form was added.

Abstinence. The practice of not eating certain foods: see also ASCETICISM; CELIBACY. As a Christian technical term it is distinguished from fasting (eating little or nothing).

Abu (1). A mountain in Rājasthān, sometimes called the 'Olympus of India'.

Abu (2) (Arab.). In Muslim names, 'father of'.

Abubacer (Muslim philosopher): see IBN TUFAYL.

Abu Bakr (d. 634 (AH 13)). The first adult male convert to Islam, a close friend of the Prophet *Muḥammad, and first Caliph (*Khalīfa) of the Islamic *'umma. His faithfulness to Muḥammad at *Mecca earned him the title of *al-Siddīq* ('the truthful one').

Upon Muḥammad's death in 632 (AH 11), the forceful *Umār persuaded the Madinans to accept Abu Bakr as the Prophet's successor.

Abu Bakr accelerated Arab integration under Islam: captured tribal leaders were treated with respect, and consequently became active supporters of Islam (i.e. a united, God-fearing community). Thus Abu Bakr gave to Islam, the religion, the means of political expression, and therein lies his greatness. On his death he was buried beside Muḥammad.

Abudatsuma (Jap., for Skt., *abhuta-dharma*). An unusual or praeternatural event, a miracle performed by a deity in Hinduism, or by a *Buddha in Buddhism.

Abū Dāwūd al-Sijistānī (817–89). Muslim compiler of one of the six *ṣaḥīḥ, or canonical, collections of aḥādīth (see ḤADĪTH).

Abū Dharr al-Ghifāri (d. 652/3 CE (AH 31/2)). Close companion of the Prophet Muḥammad. The Prophet named him 'the shining truth' because of his unswerving belief in the oneness of *Allāh.

Traditions state that his character bore great similarity to that of 'Isa/*Jesus. Abu Dharr held a 'communistic' interpretation of Islam, and was ultimately banished to the desert village of al-Rabadha. Thus ended a phase in the struggle between the idealists and the pragmatists in early Islam.

Abū Ḥanīfa (d. 767 (AH 150)). Muslim theologian and jurist, and founder of the *Ḥanafites (Kufan) law school (*sharī'a). Abū Ḥanīfa's use of *qiyās (analogy), *istiḥsān (juristic preference), ra'y (personal judgement) to resolve new legal problems arising in the expanding Muslim world, characterized his law school, in contrast to the other *schools of law. Furthermore, he stressed the idea of an international Muslim community, unified by the *Qur'ān and *Sunna, avoiding extremes. In his personal life, he suffered punishment and imprisonment at the hands of the Umayyads and *'Abbāsids because of his independent viewpoint and his refusal to accept the official post of qādī in Kūfa. He died in prison in Baghdād. His school of law is extensively followed and applied in the Muslim world.

Abū Huraira (d. 676–8 (AH 57 or 58). Companion of the Prophet *Muḥammad, and prolific transmitter of *Ḥadīth: nearly 3,500 ḥadīth have come down from him.

Abulafia, Abraham ben Samuel (1240–*c*.1291). A wandering Spanish *kabbalist. He wrote a number of *mystical essays, and in 1280 went to Rome to persuade the pope to relieve the sufferings of the Jews. He was condemned to death, but was reprieved after the pope's death. He attracted a considerable following and announced that the *messianic era would begin (according to Jewish calculation) in 5050 (i.e. 1290). Arousing the opposition of

Solomon ben Abraham *Adret, he responded with various polemical works.

Abulafia, Me'ir (1170?–1244, also known as Ramah). Spanish *Talmudic Scholar. He is best known for his controversy with *Maimonides on the doctrine of the *resurrection, but, despite this dispute, he had great respect for the philosopher, as is shown by the elegy he composed for him after his death.

Abu Madyan, Shu'aib b. al-Ḥusain (1126–98 (AH 520–94)). *Sūfī poet, teacher, and adept. Born in Spain, he settled in Biijayah (Bougie) in Algeria, where disciples gathered to him. He was recognized as the *qutb al-Ghawth (the axis on whom the mystical support of the world turns), and he remains the spiritual guardian of Algeria.

Abuna (Ethiopic and Arab., 'our father'). The *patriarch of the *Ethiopian church.

Abu Sufyān b. Harb b. Umayyā (d. 653 (AH 32)). A notable Quraysh aristocrat, a wealthy merchant and financier, with hardly any equals in *Mecca for intelligence and business acumen. Like most of the Meccan merchants, he was originally hostile to Muḥammad and Islam, but he became a Muslim at the fall of Mecca, and then supported Islam with vigour and enterprise. The Prophet made him governor of Najrān, and later, during the Islamic conquests, he saw active service against the Byzantines as a military general. He fought in the historic battle of Yarmuk (636 CE), and died in Palestine.

Abū Ṭālib (d. 619 CE). An uncle of the Prophet *Muḥammad. He was the chief of the Hāshim clan of the Quraysh tribe. Though Abū Ṭālib remained loyal and protected his kinsman Muḥammad from his enemies, he never converted to Islam. It was his son *'Alī, raised by the Prophet, who brought fame to his name.

Abu 'Ubaida b. al-Djarrah (d. 639 (AH 18)). One of the earliest converts to Islam, he distinguished himself by his piety, intelligence, bravery, and devotion to the Prophet *Muḥammad. The Prophet nicknamed him 'al-Amin' (The Trustworthy), and promised him paradise. He conquered *Damascus, Hims, Antioch, and Aleppo, and successfully administered those territories. He died of the plague which claimed the lives of many Muslim warriors.

Abū Yūsuf, Ya'kūb (Muslim writer on law): see ḤANAFITES.

Academies. An established gathering of Jewish scholars. The *Talmudic terms are yeshivot ('sitting'), also *bet ha-midrash (Heb., 'House of Study'), *bet din gadol (Heb., 'the great house of law'), and *metivta rabba* (Aram., 'the great session'). After the destruction of the Temple in 70 CE, several academies were founded, the most famous being that of *Johanan b. Zakkai at *Jabneh. Later academies were established in Babylonia at *Sura and *Pumbedita which survived until approximately the middle of the 11th cent. CE. The Academy on High (*yeshivah shel ma'lah*) is a rabbinic belief in an assembly in heaven of scholars and others who acquired merit on earth, by studying and keeping Torah. To be 'summoned by the Academy on High' is a euphemism for death. Academies may also refer to institutions in other religions, e.g. *sojae* (private academies) and shrine schools in Korea.

Acamana (Skt., 'cleansing of mouth'). Washing out the mouth, in Hinduism, in order to purify what enters and what leaves it.

Ācāra. Hindu term for custom and for law and behaviour according to custom—as in *Manusmṛti, where, e.g., rules of behaviour for different *castes are laid down. The opposite are *viruddha-ācār* (conduct contrary to custom) and *bhrashṭācār* (fallen out of customary use). See also ĀCĀRYA.

Ācāra-aṅga (one of the twelve Aṅgas): see AṄGA.

Ācariya-muṭṭhi (Pāli, 'teacher's fist'). A teacher's reluctance to impart the whole of his knowledge and skill to his pupils. Buddhism stresses that its founder is definitely not this kind of a teacher.

Ācārya (Skt., 'one who knows or teaches the *ācāra, the rules of right conduct'). 1. The title ācārya is primarily applied to a Hindu teacher who invests the student with the sacrificial thread (*vajñopavīta*) and instructs him in the *vedas and the religious law (*dharma). By extension it is applied to a spiritual preceptor, or to anyone learned in the Hindu tradition. This title is frequently affixed directly to the proper name, e.g. *Śaṅkarācārya.

2. In particular, a group of Tamil *Vaiṣṇava teachers regarding the *Āḻvārs as incarnations of *Viṣṇu's instruments/weapons. The first was *Nāthamuni (9th cent. CE).

3. In Buddhism Pāli, *ācāriya*), teacher of the *dhamma, in contrast to *upāydhyāya*, who taught discipline and the rules.

4. Among Jains, the ācārya holds a vital place in teaching and in the transmission of lineage (for an example, see BHIKṢU, ĀCĀRYA).

Accidie (Gk., *akēdia*, 'negligence', 'indifference'). In ascetical terminology, one of the principal temptations, or *deadly sins. Accidie is a listlessness tempting one to give up prayer and the spiritual life. In the later English tradition it is translated as sloth, which is an oversimplification.

Acculturation (acquiring cultural characteristics): see CULTURAL RELATIVITY.

Acedia (lack of commitment): see ACCIDIE.

Acinteyyāni (Pāli, *acinteyya*, 'that which cannot or should not be thought'). Certain notions or thought-topics considered by *Theravāda Buddhism to lie beyond the scope of imagination or speculation. Prolonged reflection on them is discouraged because it leads to no satisfactory answers, only to frustration and anguish. They are the notions of what it is like to be a Buddha; what a higher state of consciousness is like (see SAMĀDHI); what are the particular fruits of *karma; who created the world. See also AVYĀKATĀNI.

Acintya-śaktī (Skt., *acintya*, 'unthinkable, incomprehensible, the Absolute'). The literally incomprehensible force associated with a *mantra, which cannot be contained by reason or by bodily power.

Acit (Skt., opposite of *cit, 'consciousness'). That which is inert, the material universe. In *Rāmānuja's system, acit forms the body of God.

Acoemetae (Gk., *akoimētai*, 'sleepless ones'). *Orthodox ascetics in general, and in particular monks following the rule of *Basil. The term may be applied more generally to Eastern Christian *ascetics.

Acolyte, In the W. Church, one of the minor *orders, first heard of in 251 in Rome. His function is to assist the priest and deacon at the *mass, but later, acolytes and *subdeacons take over most functions in the liturgy of the other minor orders.

Acquisition, doctrine of (Muslim): see QADAR.

Action Française, a political group, with a journal (from 1908 a daily newspaper) of the same name, having strong *Roman Catholic connections. It was founded in 1898, after the *Dreyfus affair. It sought the restoration of French national unity and pride, under a restored monarchy.

Acts of the Apostles, The. Fifth book of the New Testament. It recounts the history of the earliest church. It is almost the only source for Christian history in the period 30–64 CE. Acts is generally accepted as the work of the same author as the third gospel. Dates from as early as 64 CE (before Paul's death) up to the 2nd cent. have been suggested.

Acupuncture. One of the nine branches of Chinese traditional medicine. Since the body acts as a channel, especially for *ch'i, the points of insertion of the needles of acupuncture do not have to be proximate to the place of pain and disorder: they stimulate and promote the body's own ability to treat itself; thus the carefully mapped points of insertion (the numbers vary from 350 to 450) are related to the body's internal system of communication and control.

'Ād (pre-Islamic people): see HŪD.

Adalbert of Prague, St (*c*.956–97). Christian *bishop and martyr. His name was Voytech, but he adopted the name of Adalbert, the bishop of Magdeburg. Although young, he was made bishop of Prague in 982, but the political conflict and opposition made him withdraw to Rome in 990. Pope John XV sent him back to his diocese, where he founded the *abbey of Brevnor, but continuing opposition forced him once more to return to Rome. This time he was sent to the unconverted Pomeranians, by whom he and his fellow-missionaries were killed. His influence remained extensive. He was canonized in 999. Feast day, 23 April.

Adam (Heb., 'man'), In W. tradition, the first human being. According to the first creation account in Genesis, Adam was created in the image of God (1. 27) on the final day of creation. In Genesis 2, he is said to have been made from the dust of the earth (Heb., *adamah*, 'earth') and to have become a living *soul after God had breathed into him (2. 7) As a result of disobedience God punished them by evicting them from the Garden of *Eden and condemning the man to toil for his living (Genesis 2. 5–3. 24). Despite the punishment, Judaism does not understand the *fall of Adam as having created a radical fault, as does Christianity, requiring the second Adam (i.e., *Christ) to deal with the fault and its effects. The 'fall' is a fall upwards, into new opportunities of action and knowledge.

In Islam, Adam is not only the first human being but the first *prophet, entrusted by *Allāh with a message for humankind. Allāh is said to have made a *covenant with Adam and with his descendants (7. 172), and he is thus in a special sense the father of all humankind.

Adam, Books of. Apocryphal books. They include the *Book of the Life of *Adam and *Eve* (probably composed in Palestine between 100 BCE and 200 CE), the *Cave of Treasures* (a Syriac work), the Ethiopic *Book of Adam and Eve*, and various Armenian compositions dealing with the Adam and Eve legend.

Adam Kadmon (Heb., primordial Man). A *kabbalistic notion, summarizing, in mystical terms, the divine symbolism of the human body. Isaac *Luria described Adam Kadmon as the most perfect manifestation of God that the human mind can contemplate, and his followers contrasted Adam Kadmon with *Satan, 'adam beliyya'al' (the evil man). Later still Adam Kadmon was identified with the *messiah, and *Shabbetai Zevi was regarded as an incarnation of Adam Kadmon by his disciples.

Adam's Bridge or **Rāma's Bridge.** The chain of small islands linking S. India to N. Śri Lankā, which could be crossed on foot until the 15th cent., when storms widened the gaps. According to **Rāmāyaṇa*, *Hanumān built the link to enable *Rāma to cross and rescue *Sītā. According to Muslim tradition, *Adam crossed here after his expulsion from the Garden of *Eden.

Adam's Peak. Śrī Pada. Sacred mountain in Śri Lankā, at the top of which (a place of *pilgrimage) a hollow shape is identified by adherents of the relevant religions as the *footprint of *Adam, the *Buddha, *Śiva, or the *apostle *Thomas.

Adar: see CALENDAR (JEWISH).

Adat. Traditional, often unwritten, law, the customary part of legal regulation in Muslim countries, which often comes from pre-Islamic times, and has therefore to be integrated (so far as it can be) with *sharī'a.

Addai. Traditional founder of the important church of Edessa in N. Mesopotamia. According to the Syriac *Doctrine of Addai* he was one of *Jesus' seventy disciples (Luke 10. 1) and was sent by St *Thomas to heal the local King *Abgar.

Ādhān. The call to worship (*ṣalāt) given by the mu'adhīn (Muezzin) traditionally from the manāra (minaret), before each of the five daily times of ṣalāt.

The words incorporate the *Shahāda (profession of faith):

(i) *Allāhu Akbar* (God is most great)
(ii) *Ashhadu anna lā ilāha illā Allāh* (I bear witness there is no god but God)
(iii) *Ashhadu anna Muḥammadan rasūl Allāh* (I bear witness Muḥammad is the messenger of God)
(iv) *Ḥaiya 'alā al-ṣalāt* (Come to prayer)
(v) *Ḥaiya 'alā al-falāḥ* (Come to wellbeing)
(vi) *Al-ṣalāt khayrun min al-nawm* (Prayer is better than sleep)
(vii) *Allāhu Akbar* (God is most great)
(viii) *Lā ilāha illā Allāh* (There is no god but God).

Ādhāra (Skt., 'container'). The Hindu understanding of the way in which *ātman is contained in the five *kośas or sheaths.

Adharma (Skt.). In Hinduism, the opposite of *dharma, synonym of *pāpa: evil, sin, what is not right or natural, or according to *śāstras.

Adharma is personified in Hindu mythology as the son of *Brahmā and brother of *Dharma, born from Brahmā's back.

Adhvaryu (performer): see SACRIFICE (HINDU).

Adhvenak (image): see FRAVASI.

Adhyāropa (Skt., 'false covering'). The way in which in Hinduism, illusory or false understandings impose themselves on what is truly the case, which ultimately must be *Brahmān. The classic example is that given by *Śaṅkara of a rope on a path which is believed to be a snake, an error which arises from *avidyā (ignorance). It follows that release from ignorance requires instructed attention to what is real, and to the ways leading to that knowledge.

Adhyāsa (Skt.). In philosophical Hinduism, superimposing reality on what is not real. It is false attribution, as when a rope is mistaken for a snake.

Adhyātma (Skt., 'that which pertains to the *ātman'). 1. In Hinduism the inner self or soul of the individual; but because of the relation of ātman to *Brahmān, it is also the supreme self, or (theistically conceived) the deity.

2. In Jainism, the inner self, which *Banārsīdās discovered could be cultivated to the realization of supreme truth. It is the name of a movement devoted to that end.

Adhyātma Rāmāyaṇa. A version of **Rāmāyaṇa* composed by different authors, based on the original Skt. work of Vālmikī. Its tendency is to move the epic in an *Advaitin and spiritualized direction.

Ādhyātma-Yoga. A yogic discipline in Hinduism which elucidates the difference between *ātman and its *kośas (containers), thus leading to the state of *ādhyātma-prasāda*, which is equivalent to the liberated self (*jīvanmukti).

Ādi (Skt., 'original'). The first, primordial or archetypical, found in many compound words.

Adiaphora (Gk., 'things indifferent'). The view that certain items in a controversy are not sufficiently central to warrant continuing division or dispute. Adiaphorism is thus of importance in *ecumenical discussions or arguments, and particularly in the attempts to hold together many varied views in *Anglicanism.

Ādibrahmacariyaka-sīla (Pāli, 'conduct regarding the fundamentals of the holy life'). Collectively, the three precepts of the Eightfold Path (see AṢṬANGIKA-MARGA) relating to ethical behaviour: right speech, right action, and right livelihood.

Ādi Brāhma Samāj. The 'original' *Brahmo Samāj (according to its adherents) when the movement split.

Ādi Buddha (Skt.; Tib., *dang.po'i.sangs.rgyas*). Primordial Buddha, the highest being in Tibetan Buddhist cosmology. Although teachings regarding the Ādi Buddha existed in India at least as early as the 7th cent. CE, they did not enter Tibet until the arrival of *Atiśa in 1042, after which the Ādi Buddha, known in India as Vajradhāra, became identified as Dorje Chang (Tib., *rDor.rje.ch'ang.*, 'Holder of the Thunderbolt') by all schools except the *Nyingma, who know him as Kuntu Zangpo (Tib. *kun.tu. bzang-.po.*, 'Goodness in all Ways'; Skt.: *Samantabhadra).

The Tibetan traditions have avoided the attribution to him of theistic qualities by stressing his nature as *śūnyatā, and by seeing his purpose as essentially that of a device within the confines of tantric practice. His *bīja *mantra is OM.AH.HUM., which represents the *body, speech, and mind of all buddhas.

Ādi Granth (Pañjābī, 'first volume', the second being *Dasam Granth, i.e. 'tenth book'). Sikh scriptures. The Ādi Granth is usually called the Gurū Granth Sāhib in recognition that it is the embodiment of the *Gurū. Sikhs also call it *Gurbāṇī (the Gurū's utterance). They believe that before his death Gurū *Gobind *Siṅgh declared the Ādi Granth his successor. The *Ardās concludes with the injunction 'Gurū mānio granth' ('acknowledge the Granth as Gurū'). Any room in which the Ādi Granth is appropriately installed is a *gurdwārā. The scriptures are treated with the same detailed devotion as would be shown to a human Gurū—e.g. a *chaurī is waved over it and the volume is ceremonially laid to rest at night.

The Ādi Granth consists of 1,430 pages, each copy having standard page length and numbering.

The contents are metrical and, excepting the opening *Japjī, are intended for singing.

Despite the diversity of authorship and language, the message of the Ādi Granth is unanimous: salvation depends not upon *caste, ritual, or asceticism, but upon constant meditation on God's name (*nām) and immersement in his being:

Ādinātha (Skt. 'first lord'). Title given to first Jain *tīrthaṅkara of this present time span (*avasarpiṇī*), *Ṛṣabha. The Ādinātha temple on Mount *Abu in S. Rajasthan provides an outstandingly beautiful example of Jain architecture and is a major centre of Jain pilgrimage today. As a title of *Śiva, see SIDDHA.

Ādi-purāṇa. 1. An occasional title of *Brahma purāṇa*.

2. A Jain work in Skt. on the 'origin' and past history of the world. It was written by *Jinasena in S. India, and completed by his disciple Guṇabhadra who also continued the narrative in the *Uttara-*purāṇa*, which his own disciple Lokasena finished in *c.*892 CE. These two parts, also called together *Mahā-purāṇa*, contain the Jain world history, from its beginnings up to the time of the *Mahāvīra, the last *tīrthaṅkara (and historical founder of Jainism). Within the framework of the (mythical) adventures of the sixty-three *śalākā-puruṣas* (lit. 'staff-men', denoting here 'heroic men'), a vast store of Indian and specifically Jain story material has been arranged.

Jinasena's intention was to provide, in an increasingly 'Hindu-conscious' southern Indian environment, a Jain answer to the Hindu *purāṇas.

Aditi (Skt., 'boundlessness'). Unlimited space and consciousness, hence infinity, eternity. Manifested as a goddess (frequently mentioned in the **Ṛg Veda*), she is the inexhaustible source, the mother of the *Ādityas under whose constraint the universe is alone possible.

Ādityas. In Hinduism, the ruling principles which constrain the universe into its outcomes. In personified form, they are the sons of *Aditi. They are associated closely with the sun as the source of life, and became eventually twelve in number to correspond to the twelve solar months. The original eight are identified with the Vasus, the eight spheres of existence. When the number was extended to twelve, and they were identified with the twelve ruling principles, they were usually (but with occasional variants) listed as Aṁsā (the share of the gods), Aryaman (generous nobility), Bhaga (due inheritance), Dakṣa (ritual skill), *Mitra (constancy in friendship), Pūṣan (prosperity), Śakra (courage), Savitṛ (power of words), Tvaṣṭṛ (skill in craft and technique), *Varuṇa (fate), *Viṣṇu (cosmic law), Vivasvat (social law). In later times, the name Āditya came to be applied to any god (so fundamental are the twelve principles to the sustenance of the cosmos). In Buddhism, Āditya is a name given to the Buddha.

Ādityavarṇa. A Hindu spiritual practice and experience based on the intense light of the sun. Cf. NŪR in Islam.

Adloyada (Heb.). *Purim carnival. The expression derives from the Hebrew *'ad de-lo-yada'* (until one no longer knows). According to the *rabbis, participants should celebrate on Purim until they no longer know the difference between 'Blessed be Mordecai' and 'Cursed be Haman'. The celebration involves processions of carnival floats through major *Israeli towns.

Adonai (Heb., 'my Lord'). Jewish title of God. It is commonly used to replace the *tetragrammaton (JHWH) when reading the text of the Hebrew scriptures, and its vowels, inserted into JHWH, thus produce the form Jehovah.

Adon 'Olam (Heb., 'Lord of the World'). A Jewish hymn praising God's greatness. A version appears in George Borrow's *Lavengro*.

Adoptianism. A Christian *heresy in 8th-cent. Spain: the *Logos, as true Son of God, must be distinguished from *Christ, who is Son in a different sense, as a consequence of the Word 'adopting' humanity.

More generally, the term, usually spelt adoptionism, refers to the view that *Jesus was a man whom God adopted as his son.

Adoptionism: see ADOPTIANISM.

Adret, Solomon ben Abraham (Shelomoh b. Avraham, *c*.1235–*c*.1310, commonly known as Rashba). Spanish Jewish scholar. He was considered the outstanding student of *Naḥmanides, and for forty years held the position of *Rabbi of Barcelona. He was the author of many *responsa which were gathered together for future guidance. He also refuted the attempt of Raimundo Martini in *Pugio Fidei* to argue from the Talmud against the Jews; and he argued against *ibn Ḥazm, contesting the divine origin of the *Qur'ān.

Adrian IV (*c*.1100–59). The first and so far only Englishman to be *pope. He was born Nicholas Breakspear, and after education partly in France, he became a monk near Avignon. In 1137, he was elected *abbot. In 1150–3 he was *papal legate in Scandinavia, where his skill in reordering the church led him to be called 'The Apostle of the North'. He was elected pope in 1154. In the conflicts of the time, he sought an alliance with the German king, Frederick I Barbarossa, crowning him in front of his army as Holy Roman Emperor in 1155, in a ceremony designed to emphasize Frederick's subservient position.

Adṛṣṭa (Skt., 'unseen'). Unseen force; in Indian philosophy related to and sometimes synonymous with *karma. It designates an imperceptible constraint on any given event, accounting for such forces as gravity and magnetic attraction as well as the unseen causes of one's present life-situation, i.e. actions performed in previous lives.

Adultery. The way in which religions have played so vital a role in the protection of what would now be recognized as gene-replication and the nurture of children has contributed to a strong condemnation of adultery in all religions—though what counts as adultery is diversely defined: thus, according to Jewish law, sexual relationship between a married man and an unmarried woman, although sinful, is not considered adulterous; In Islam (see ZINĀ'), there is no distinction between men and women (Qur'ān 24. 3), but there has been considerable dispute about the permissibility of extra-marital sex between Muslim men and their unmarried slave women. At issue in the religious evaluation of marriage and adultery has been the stability of families within the continuing structure of society (hence the importance of known parentage and descent), along with the predictability and reliability of humans in relations of commitment to each other.

Advaita (Skt., 'not-dual'). The state in which there is only, without differentiation, whatever there is, in which all appearances of distinction (e.g. between subject and object, perceiver and perceived) are known to be a consequence and product of inadequate understanding, or ignorance (*avidyā, *adhyāsa). This state can only be ascribed to God or to *Brahman as Absolute. This perception of non-duality underlies *Advaita Vedānta.

Advaita Vedānta. One of the three major philosophical/theological systems in Hindu *Vedānta, whose leading protagonist was *Śaṅkara. *Brahman is the Absolute and underlying ground of all appearance: for those with (trained) eyes to see, Brahman can be perceived as the real and the unchanging lying within or behind the manifold appearances which the senses encounter. There cannot, therefore, be any truth in the human propensity to differentiate objects, or parts of objects, as though they have the reality of their superficial appearance. There is only Brahman, which is necessarily undifferentiated. It follows that there cannot even be a difference, or duality, between the human subject, or self, and Brahman, for

Brahman must be that very self (since Brahman is the reality underlying all appearance). The goal of human life and wisdom must, therefore, be the realization that the self (*ātman) *is* Brahman—hence the famous formula (*mahāvākya), *tat tvam asi*, thou art that. See also AJĀTIVĀDA; ŚRĪ HARṢA; Index, Advaita.

Advaya (Skt., non-duality). The essential nature of things when truly understood, according to Buddhist thought.

The term is more commonly encountered in the literature of the *Mahāyāna. In the *Prajñāpāramitā* (see PERFECTION OF WISDOM) corpus it is often found as a synonym of suchness (*tathatā) since, from the ultimate point of view, reality cannot be determined on the basis of dichotomies, such as subjectivity and objectivity, which operate according to worldly convention.

Advent (Lat., *adventus*, 'coming', i.e. of Christ). The season of the church year preceding *Christmas. Originally a season of fasting, in the *Orthodox Church it begins in November. In the W. Church, fasting is no longer obligatory, and the season is shorter, beginning on the Sunday closest to 30 Nov. Concerned with the *Four Last Things, Advent prepares for the *parousia, as well as for Christmas.

Adventists. Members of Christian sects who believe that the Second Coming of *Jesus Christ is literal and imminent. Seventh Day Adventists, derived from William Miller (1781–1849) who predicted the end of the world in 1843–4, believe that the Advent is delayed because of the failure to keep the *Sabbath. Sabbath-keeping was confirmed in the visions of Ellen G. White (d. 1915), who was a prolific writer of Adventist literature. *Dietary laws from the Old Testament are also observed, and the further belief, that the Advent will occur when the *gospel has been proclaimed throughout the world, leads to vigorous proselytization.

Advocatus Dei: see DEVIL'S ADVOCATE.

Advocatus diaboli: see DEVIL'S ADVOCATE.

Advowson. The right, in the Christian Church, to present to a *bishop a nominee for appointment to a *parish or other benefice. This right may be in the hands of the bishop, in which case it is usually described as 'collating'. In the 20th cent. in England the right of advowson or patronage has been increasingly concentrated in the hands of ecclesiastical authorities.

Ādya-śrādha. A Hindu anticipatory funeral rite, performed during their lifetime by those who have no son to perform the appropriate rites for them after death, or by those who for some other reason believe that the rites will not be performed after death.

Aelia Capitolina. The post-135 CE Roman name for *Jerusalem when, after the *Bar Kokhba revolt, the Emperor Hadrian tried to deprive the city of its Jewish character.

Aelred, St (1109–67). *Cistercian monk of Rievaulx; author, as novice-master, of *Speculum Caritatis* (The Mirror of Love), emphasizing God's love as restoring fallen humans into their true image. He was *abbot of Revesby in 1143 and of Rievaulx in 1147. He wrote a major work on Christian friendship, based on Cicero's *De Amicitia*, but showing how friendship is transformed and spiritualized in relation to Christ (hence the title, *De Spirituali Amicitia*). He has, consequently, been adopted as the equivalent of a *patron saint by some gay (*homosexual) Christians.

Aeon: (Gk., *aion*, 'age, time'). A period of time, usually lengthy. As 'time without end', it became synonymous with eternity. For the Hindu *manvantara*, see MANU.

Aetiology (account of causes or origins): see MYTH.

Aetos (Gk.). In Greek Orthodoxy, the inset in the choir floor which marked the position of the emperor's throne. From this it became a decorated mat on which *bishops stand at their consecration in order to recite the *Creed and their profession of faith.

Affective prayer. A way of prayer which makes use of the emotions or feelings or the will, as opposed to prayer of the intellect.

Affirmative way. The approach to God which affirms that something can be discerned of his being and nature through reason and from the created order. It is therefore in contrast to the *via negativa. A classic expression occurs in Christianity in the five arguments advanced by St *Thomas Aquinas (*Quinque Viae) from which he concluded that 'the existence of God can be demonstrated from those of his effects which are known to us' (*Summ. Theol.* 1, qu. 2, art. 2): it can be known *that* God is, but not, without revelation, *what* God is. The affirmative way is even stronger in some other religions, especially in Islam, where creation offers demonstrations of God subsumed under the same word (*ayā) as that which is used for the verses of the *Qur'ān; and in Hinduism, where the cosmic appearance may be the body of God (see e.g. *Rāmānuja), and where in any case the true reality underlies all appearance. The affirmative way is the foundation of kataphatic theology in contrast to *apophatic, though the two are necessarily linked, since even the ultimate kataphatic claim of *Jesus, that 'he who has seen me has seen the Father' (John 14. 9) does not produce God as an object among objects.

Affliction, cults of. Cults and their associated ritual activities which deal with the occurrence of affliction, especially disease. The cause may be thought to be human or supernatural. The rituals often take the form of contest against the cause of the affliction and thus merge into possession and *exorcism.

Afghānī: see AL-AFGHĀNĪ, JAMĀL AL-DĪN.

Afikomen (Heb.). The middle of three pieces of *mazzah which is broken and set aside during the *Passover *Seder and is left to be eaten at the end. In *Ashkenazi households, it has become the custom for the children to hide the afikomen from the leader and only return it after a ransom has been paid.

African-American religion. The religious beliefs of so large and diverse a population cannot be unified into a single, artificial scheme. The African dispersion has now mingled with many other sources, and black Americans look to more roots than those of their African origin (thus *black Muslims may absorb Islam *ab origine*, not simply via Africa, and black Catholics advert to St Martin de Porres, a 17th-cent. Peruvian of Afro-Hispanic descent); and in any case, the nature of the religious beliefs in any particular area depends on a creative interaction with existing beliefs and customs. In relation to Christianity, they have been marked by a strong independence (for the first African-American Church, see AFRICAN METHODIST EPISCOPAL CHURCH), ranging from the 'storefront churches' to the African Orthodox Church (founded by Marcus *Garvey and an Episcopalian priest, G. A. McGuire), in which the *Madonna and *Christ are visualized as black. At one stage (*c.* 1960) the National Baptist Convention numbered more than 6 million members. In relation to Islam, see NATION OF ISLAM, BLACK MUSLIMS.

Despite the extreme vitality and diversity of African-American religion, H. A. Baer and M. Singer (*African-American Religion in the 20th Century*, 1992) have suggested that African-American religion falls into four broad types: (i) messianic-nationalist (cf. MESSIAH); (ii) *thaumaturgic; (iii) conversionist; (iv) mainstream. In addition, it is clear that all types are united by a profound involvement in the religious possibilities of music and dance. R. F. Thompson (*Flash of the Spirit*, 1983) has singled out as recurrently characteristic the dominance of a percussive style, propensity for multiple metre, overlapping call and response, inner pulse control, suspended accentuation patterning, and songs and dances with social allusion.

African Apostles. Two distinct independent Christian movements in central Africa, both beginning in Zimbabwe in 1932, the Masowe Apostles and the Maranke Apostles. The former derive from John Masowe (?1910–73). His followers became called VaPostori (Shona, 'the Apostles'), but their anti-government and anti-church attitudes led to harassment which drove them to seek freedom by settling as the Apostolic Sabbath Church of God in the Korsten slum of Port Elizabeth, South Africa, in 1947. Here their manual skills led to the popular name of the Basketmakers' Church. Deported in 1962, they moved north *en route* to Ethiopia and Jerusalem, but most settled in Zambia near Lusaka, where they established a range of small industries; others established the church in some nine adjacent countries, and Masowe died in Tanzania.

The Maranke Apostles were founded by Johane Maranke (1912–63), brought up in the American *Methodist mission, who had a *pentecostal experience and also visions of going to heaven, which were later recorded in 'The New Revelation of the Apostles' as an addition to the Bible.

African Greek Orthodox Church. A complex development from E. *Orthodoxy around an *Anglican Ugandan, Reuben Mukasa (1899–1982), nicknamed Spartas. After hearing of Marcus *Garvey's independent African Orthodox Church in America, he founded his own counterpart in Uganda in 1929. Upon finding the Garvey Church to be heterodox, Spartas separated and affiliated in 1933 with the Greek Orthodox Patriarchate in Alexandria.

African Instituted Churches. Indigenous churches in Africa, characterized by their independence from the history (and originally missionary) churches. Hence they were first known as African Independent Churches. The initials AIC became common, so that the new and current name (adopted by the churches in question to emphasize that they are founded and led by Africans, and are not to be defined by their relationship to the historic and missionary churches) allows the same initials to be used. For examples, see AFRICAN APOSTLES; AFRICAN ISRAEL CHURCH NINEVEH; AIYETORO; ALADURA; BAYUDAYA; BRAID(E); BWITI; DÉÏMA; EAST AFRICAN REVIVAL; ETHIOPIANISM; FEDEN; GODIANISM; GOD'S KINGDOM SOCIETY; HARRIS MOVEMENT; JAMAA; KIMBANGU; KITAWALA; LUMPA CHURCH; MAI CHAZA'S CHURCH; MARIO LEGIO; MUSAMA DISCO CRISTO; NAZARITE CHURCH; PROVIDENCE INDUSTRIAL MISSION; ZION CHRISTIAN CHURCH; ZIONIST CHURCHES.

African Israel Church Nineveh. An early independent church in Kenya, mainly among the Luhya and the Luo. It was founded by the highly charismatic David Zayako Kivuli (1896–1974) who was baptized in 1925 in the Pentecostal Assemblies of East Africa (a Canadian mission), had a mystic experience in 1932, became a teacher and evangelist, and led a small peaceful secession in 1942. By 1960 it was spreading to Uganda and Tanzania, and in 1975, when it joined the *World Council of Churches, it claimed 76,000 members.

African Methodist Episcopal Church. The first church in the USA to be made up entirely of African-Americans. It came into being in 1787 when those with black skin refused to be segregated in the seating in St George's church in 4th St, Philadelphia. There was some scuffling, and Richard Allen (elected the first *bishop of the ensuing church) led the founding members of the church out of the building.

African Orthodox Church: see AFRICAN-AMERICAN RELIGION.

African religion. No single religion corresponds to the term 'African religion', nor could it. The geography of Africa ranges from rain forests to uninhabitable deserts; its peoples are organized in many different social ways, from itinerants to villages to tribes to urbanized communities; and the vast continent has been invaded by other religions which frequently dominate particular areas, especially Christianity and Islam, but also to a lesser degree Hinduism. These in turn have often been appropriated and given a new and distinctive African style and content (see e.g. AFRICAN INSTITUTED CHURCHES).

Nevertheless, although there is no such 'thing' as 'African religion', attempts have been made to draw out some of the recurrent and characteristic emphases to be found in Africa.

1. There is strong reverence for a supreme God.

2. The power of God to inspire particular individuals or functionaries is emphasized.

3. Religion is important in maintaining both social and cosmic order.

4. The importance of *ancestors is noted. 'Ancestor worship' is too strong and too misleading a term; in fact it is commonly believed that each individual is made up of several different 'souls', including the continuing effects of the ancestors as guardians; the ancestors are not saved out of the world, but rather continue to be related to the ongoing family, and remain a part of it—until they are removed by the extending gap of succeeding generations.

5. *Rites of passage maintain stability and order.

6. *Magic and witchcraft are emphasized.

7. The oral tradition is powerful; myth is rich and eloquent.

8. There is emphasis on the sacred and often sacrosanct nature of the environment, almost any aspect of which may carry religious meaning.

Afro-Brazilian cults. New (syncretist) religions based on survivals of African religions among the black slave population, originally in the north-east but now over most coastal areas and in southern cities. Some exhibit traditional Yoruba religion little changed from W. Africa. Candomblés are the forms developed in Bahia early in the 19th cent. (also called Xango, i.e. *Shango). These vary according to whether the African origins are Congolese-Angolan, Yoruba, or Islamic Negro (Hausa, etc.), and to the presence of Amerindian or Catholic elements. 'Macumba', more in Rio de Janeiro and São Paulo, emphasizes possession by ancestral spirits rather than deities, and tends to pass over into *magic and to forms known as Quimbanda. Batuque in Belem is more Brazilianized, with songs in Portuguese and members from all races, although lower class.

Afscheiding (Dutch Reformed separation): see DUTCH REFORMED CHURCH.

Afterlife. The condition awaiting humans and the cosmos after *death or at the end of time. Beliefs vary greatly between religions, though in origin the major continuing religious traditions, both East and West, had no belief that there would be a worthwhile existence after death. They could not deny that in some sense there is a trace of the dead, in memory and dreams, or in the resemblance of offspring to ancestors; but whatever state the dead may be in, it is a condition of extreme weakness, in which all connection with God and with the living is cut off, and certainly to be avoided or postponed as long as possible: it is, in Sophocles' words, *ton apotropon Haidan*, Hades to be shunned. The most militant reaction to this occurred in China, in the quest for immortality; and gradually both traditions came to realize that there may be about us that which does endure through the process of time and therefore perhaps through the event of death.

The Jewish tradition has come to believe that the life of human beings continues through death, and that there will be a consummation of the purposes of God in the *messianic age. Today, *Orthodox Jews still maintain a belief in bodily resurrection, but most Reform Jews are only concerned with spiritual survival. The

Jewish equivalent of *hell is derived from the mundane 'valley of Hinnom', *Gehinnom, Gk., Gehenna.

Christian beliefs were formed in the context of acute Jewish debates, in the period of the second *Temple, about the likelihood and nature of the afterlife, and are controlled by the astonished and grateful acceptance of the resurrection of *Jesus Christ. Jesus himself had affirmed belief in life after death, arguing against the Sadducees, but not going into detail. Early Christianity put together the two Jewish forms of speculation, thereby talking of the resurrection of the body, but also of the continuing life of the soul in the interval before the resurrection body is restored to it—a 'gap' which eventually allowed the doctrine of *purgatory.

The afterlife in Islam is known as *al-akhira*. The Muslim understanding of the afterlife is based on vivid and literal pictures in the *Qur'ān.

The early understandings in India of human nature and its destiny much resemble in attitude those of the Jewish Bible. The *Vedic imagination could conceive only of this life as a place of guaranteed worth. Neither *samsāra nor *ātman as immortal soul are present in the *Vedas. The advance to ātman was made in the *Brāhmaṇas and *Āraṇyakas via *prāṇa, breath—the recognition that prāṇa is the support of life. Prāṇa is like the *logos in the W., since it not only supports life, but is the creator of sound (*vāc, see e.g. *Jaiminīya Upaniṣad Brāhmaṇa* 8. 2. 6), and becomes equated with Brahman as creator. Thus the life-principle in humans (and other manifestations) is eventually believed to be not other than the undying Brahman—so that ātman is Brahman. Rebirth carries the soul through many appearances, so that rebirth has become an evil to be brought to an end. The many hells belong firmly within the process of rebirth, not to any eternal destiny—an understanding which is true of Eastern religions in general.

For Jains, the afterlife is mapped onto a cosmography in which the Middle World includes the part inhabited by humans. Below are a series of hells of increasing unpleasantness; above are a series of heavens of increasing brightness, including the abode of the gods. But those heavens are not the desirable state: this is the Isatpragbhara, the slightly curved (shaped somewhat like curved space in a parabola), where the *jīvas which have ceased to be encumbered by bodies abide.

Buddhists pressed further in resisting the Hindu move toward an eternal ātman. While there is continuity of consequence through samsāra, there is no eternal and undying subject of this process (*anātman). The process may move through heavens and hells, but these are no 'abiding city'. The afterlife may involve being reborn as an animal or attaining the condition of *arhat: between the two, many *Theravādin Buddhists aim for a better outcome in the next birth without aiming too far. In Mahāyāna, the realization of the ultimate goal was brought closer within reach, particularly through devotion to *bodhisattvas, whose role it is to save all sentient beings. While sharing Hindus' presuppositions about rebirth, Sikh teaching emphasizes the possibility of attaining *mukti during one's present life.

Agadut Israel (Jewish movement): see ḤAFETS ḤAYYIM.

Aga Khan (Pers., Āghā Khān). Title conferred on the *Ismā'īlī *imām (spiritual leader), Ḥasan 'Alī Shāh (d. 1881) and to his successors as leaders of the Nizārī Ismā'īlīs. They claim descent from *'Alī and *Fāṭima (the daughter of *Muḥammad).

Āgama (Skt.). In Hinduism, a general term for scripture, but more specifically, a body of medieval *Vaiṣṇava (specifically *Pāñcarātra), *Śaiva, and *Śakta literature in Sanskrit and Tamil, called respectively the Pāñcarātra Saṃhitās, the Śaiva Āgamas, and the Śakta Tantras. There is also a collection of Jain Āgamas.

In Buddhism, āgama is the *Mahāyāna name for the collections of writings known in Pāli as *nikāya. Thus Dirghāgama is equivalent to Digha Nikāya, *et al.* In Jap., āgama is *agon*, as in *agon-gyō*, the four Chinese collections of *sūtras. In Jainism, it is the term, along with *siddhānta* (established teachings); for the 'canonical' texts: see AṄGA.

Āgāmi-karma: see KARMA.

Agape (Gk.). 1. 'Love' (avoiding the sexual associations of *erōs*), the word used in the New Testament for the love of God or Christ, or of Christians, of a new and different quality.

2. The 'love feast' celebrated by early Christians (1 Corinthians 11. 17–34).

Agastya or **Agasti**. A great *Vedic sage said to have been born of Mitra and *Varuṇa in a large earthenware pot (*kumbha*), hence known as Kumbhayonī. He is the legendary pioneer of the *Āryan occupation of peninsular India.

Age of Aquarius (time of spiritual advance): see NEW AGE.

Aggadah/Haggadah (Heb., 'narrative'). Rabbinic teaching which is not *halakhah and which includes stories, legends, history, ethical maxims, and witticisms. The *rabbis themselves maintained that aggadah was not authoritative and insisted that 'no halakhah may be derived from the aggadot' (*TJ Pe'ah* 2. 6, 17a); but its status in relation to insight and piety is high.

Aggadat Bereshit. An *aggadic *midrash ('commentary') on the book of *Genesis. It probably should be dated in the 10th cent. CE.

Aggadic. Pertaining to *aggadah.

Aggiornamento (Ital., 'updating'). The renewal of the *Roman Catholic Church which Pope *John XXIII hoped would come from the Second *Vatican Council and would lead to the reunion of all Christians; especially the renewal of the religious life of Catholics, and the bringing up to date of the Church's teaching, discipline, and organization.

Aggregates, Five (composition of human beings): see SKANDHA.

Āghā Khān (spiritual leader): see AGA KHAN.

Aghlabids. Muslim dynasty in N. Africa and Sicily, 800–909 (AH 184–296), after when they were overthrown by the *Fāṭimids.

Aghorī (Skt., 'non-terrific'). A *Tantric *Śaiva sect existing to the present day, renowned for *antinomian practices which include consuming ordure and corpse-flesh. They venerate a tradition of *gurus and worship *Śiva as Aghora, or the goddess as *Śītalā, Parnagīrī, or *Kālī. Like their predecessors, the *kāpālikas, they carry a skull which they use as a bowl, dwell in cremation grounds, and cover themselves in the ashes of corpses. Some take an intoxicating drink of *bhanga. Aghorī gurus were not cremated but buried in an upright meditation posture.

Agnes, St. Christian virgin and martyr. There is no certain information about her death or its date, but she has been venerated in Rome since the 4th cent. She is represented with a lamb (Lat., *agnus*). Feast day, 21 Jan.

Agni (Skt., 'fire'; cf. Lat., *ignis*). The god of fire in Hinduism, of great importance, especially in the *Vedic period. As *sacrifice is at the centre of Vedic religion, Agni is at the centre of sacrifice. As messenger of the gods, Agni is mediator between humankind and the heavenly realm. All offerings must pass through the sacred fire to reach their divine destinations. Agni is the witness of all sacred transactions, the benefactor and protector of people and their homes, and guardian (*loka-pāla*) of the south-east quadrant of the universe. His three principal forms include not only fire on earth, but also lightning in the atmosphere and the sun in the sky. In a sense Agni personifies all the gods, the power of the divine, immanent in all things. He is understood as the source of knowledge (the *Veda), both god of priests and priest of the gods, and potent enemy of darkness. Ever youthful, he bestows life and immortality.

Agnihotra. Hindu daily ritual of offering milk, oil, and gruel, in the morning and the evening, to *Agni, in the domestic (*gārhapatya*) and sacrificial (*āhavanīya*) fires.

Agnihotri (1859–1928). Hindu founder of the Dev Samaj. Originally called Shiv Narayan, he was born into a *brahman family and became a teacher in Lahore. He joined the *Brahmo Samāj, and was a fiery opponent of *Ārya Samāj. He broke away from Keshub Chandra Sen in 1887, but his Dev Samaj only took on distinctive ideas when he adapted Herbert Spencer to ideas of *Brahman/*ātman, thus viewing ātman as an 'inanimate' life-force, evolving to altruism.

Agnosticism (Gk., *a* + *gnōstos*, 'not know'). A position distinguished from *theism and *atheism equally, by its view that neither in principle nor in fact is it possible to know God's nature or even whether he exists. In its broadest sense, agnosticism is compatible with deep religious commitment, as in the case of *Nicholas of Cusa or of Henry Mansel (1820–71); in its narrower and more specific sense, however, it normally implies a certain detachment in matters religious. The term itself was coined by T. H. Huxley (1825–95), who defined its basic principles as repudiation of all metaphysical speculation and of most Christian doctrine as unproven or unprovable, and the application of scientific method to the study of all matters of fact and experience.

Agnus Dei (Lat., 'Lamb of God'). The hymn derived from John 1. 29 sung or said during or after the breaking of the bread at *communion in W. churches.

Agon[-gyō]: see ĀGAMA (Buddhist).

Agonshu. Japanese *new religion. It was founded by Kiriyama Seiyu (Tsutsumi Masao, b. 1921), being given its present name in 1978. It is based on the *Agama (Jap., *agon*) sutras and on belief in enlightenment in this life. It has developed fire rituals and a *hoshi matsuri* (Star Festival) at its base in *Kyoto that attract huge crowds. It numbers about 300,000 members.

Agra. City on the Yamuna river in India, capital city for some of the *Mughal rulers. It is particularly famous for the *Taj Mahal, and for the fort containing the Pearl Mosque (Moti Masjid) of Shah Jehan.

Agrapha (Gk., 'unwritten [sayings]'). Words of Jesus recorded outside the four *gospels.

Agudat Israel (Yisra'el). 'Union of Israel', abbreviated as Agudah, a world movement of *Orthodox Jews. It was founded in 1912, from a number of Orthodox communities as a counterweight to the programmes of the *Zionist Congresses. Although it is not a party with a programme, it has developed *da'at Torah*, the understanding of Torah on particular matters —i.e. the application by scholars of Torah to all aspects of life. See also ḤAFETS ḤAYYIM.

Agunah (Heb., 'tied woman'). A married woman who cannot remarry, either because her husband has not given her a divorce, or because there is no proof of his death. The term is also applied to a widow who cannot obtain release from a *levirate *marriage. There has been much *halakhic discussion on the problem of the agunah, but no satisfactory solution has been found.

AH (Muslim dating): see HIJRA.

Ahad ha-'Am ('One of the People'). Asher Hirsh Ginsberg. (1856–1927), essayist and Jewish *Zionist leader. His article *Lo Zeh ha-Derekh* (The Wrong Way), published in 1889, argued that educational work should take place before an immediate indiscriminate settlement in the land of *Israel. He became spiritual leader of the secret order of Benei Moshe ('sons of Moses') and the editor of the monthly literary periodical, *Ha-Shilo'ah* (The Coming One) which contributed to the development of modern Hebrew literature. Although he had a role in the obtaining of the *Balfour Declaration, he favoured group action rather than negotiation. His thought has been influential in Zionist thinking, both in Israel and in the *diaspora.

Aḥai of Shabḥa (Jewish writer on law): see CODIFICATIONS OF LAW.

Ahalyā (also called Maitreyi). The wife of the *ṛṣi Gautamā. She committed adultery with *Indra, the King of the Heavenly region. When Gautamā discovered her infidelity, he cursed her and, in some versions, made her invisible; in others he turned her into stone as a punishment.

Aham Brahman asmi (i.e. aham brahmāsmi). 'I am Brahman' (*Bṛhadāraṇaya Upaniṣad* 1. 4. 10). Hindu formula through which the identity of the self (*ātman) with *Brahman is proclaimed. It is one of the *mahāvākyas, great precepts.

Ahaṃkāra (Skt., 'I maker'). In Indian (especially *Sāṃkhya) philosophy, the principle of the ego. In general ahaṃkāra is the ego or ego principle responsible for one's individuality, one's self-awareness. In Sāṃkhya, ahaṃkāra is understood as the second evolution of unmanifest *prakṛti and the immediate product of the *buddhi (or *mahat) principle. The products of ahaṃkāra predominant in *tamas (also called *bhutādi*) are the five subtle elements (*tanmātras*), the building blocks of the objective world.

Āhāra ('food' or 'nutrition'). In the Pāli *Nikāyas, āhāra sums up the whole teaching of the *Buddha in relation to the living being, including the 'Doctrine of Dependent Origination', *paticca-samuppāda. The basic perception is that 'all beings live on food' (*sabbe sattā āhāraṭṭhitika*, *Digha Nikāya* iii. 211). This statement covers the whole nature of a living organism, which depends not only on material food but also psychic food, for its sustenance.

Aharonim (Heb., 'later ones'). Later (from Middle Ages onward) rabbinic authorities—contrasted with earlier authorities, the *Rishonim.

Āhavanīya (sacrifice): see AGNIHOTRA.

Ahikar, Book of. An *Aramaic folk-work, known during the period of the Assyrian Empire. It consists of the life of Ahikar (also mentioned in the *apocryphal book of *Tobit) and his sayings to Nadan his adopted son.

Ahiṁsā (Skt., 'not-harming'). Avoiding injury to any sentient creature through act or thought, a principle of basic importance for Indian religions, but especially for Jains and Buddhists, whose emphasis on ahiṁsā reinforced their rejection of sacrifice (since sacrifice necessarily involves violence against animals). It is the first of the five precepts of Buddhist life (*śīla). For Jains, it is the first of the *Five Great Vows. Good conduct (*cañta*) is ahiṁsā put into practice. It was a Jain, Śrīmad *Rājacandra, who greatly influenced *Gāndhī, through whose teaching, practice, and example nonviolence became a powerful instrument of dissent and political action in the 20th cent. See Index, Ahiṁsa.

Ahl al-Hadith (People of the Tradition). A relatively small but vigorous Islamic reform movement. It first appeared in India at the end of the 19th cent., and its characteristics are similar to the *Wahhābī movement of Arabia. Their creed is 'whatever the Prophet *Muḥammad taught in the *Qur'ān and the authentic traditions, that alone is the basis of our religion'. On matters of Islamic law, the ahl-al-Hadith far exceed Wahhābī puritanism. They cast aside the four orthodox schools of law, and instead contend that every believer is free to follow his own interpretation of the Qur'ān and the traditions, provided that he has sufficient learning to enable him to give a valid interpretation.

Ahl al-Kitāb. 'People of the Book', i.e. possessing a *scripture; the name given by the Qur'ān to the Jewish (Banū Isrā'īl) and Christian (*Naṣārā) communities, possessors respectively of the *Tawrāt (Torah) and Zabūr (Psalms) and of the *Injīl (Gospel), and later extended by Muslim law to the Sabeans and the *Zoroastrians. To these people was given the status of *dhimma, 'protection'. Although the Qur'ān allows them to keep their own religion, and affords them protection, they are expected to pay a special tribute, the *jizya (9. 29). Because of this special status, it is a vital issue in community relations whether the category can be extended to include others, e.g., Hindus.

Ahl al-Mantalka (Arab., 'people of the girdle'). *Copts and Syrian Jacobites, so called as a mark of humility (cf. HABIT, RELIGIOUS), but also as a sign of humiliation, from the Muslim insistence that Christians in Egypt should wear a girdle, in order to be identified.

Ahl al-Suffa. A group of poor Muslims, who were given permission by the Prophet *Muḥammad to live in a corner of the *Madīna mosque. Later generation of Muslims, especially the *Sūfīs, venerated the pious and ascetic character of the ahl al-Suffa as a model for themselves.

Ahl al-Sunna wa'l-jamā'a (non-Shi'ite Muslims): see SUNNA.

Ahl-i-Haqq ('People of the Truth'). A secret religious sect found in W. Persia and Kurdistan, dating back to the 11th cent. It incorporates *Zoroastrian, *Manichaean, Jewish, Christian, and *Sūfī ideas into a popular *messianic cult.

Aḥmad al-Badawī, Sidi (*c.* 1199/1200–1276 (AH 596–675)). *Sūfī adept, immensely revered in Egypt. Boisterous in youth, he underwent some kind of inner conversion in *c.*627 and withdrew from human contact, including marriage, to seek God alone. He made pilgrimage to the tombs of many of the great Sūfīs, e.g. *al-Jīli and *al-Ḥallāj. Settling finally at Tanditā in Egypt, he developed even more ascetic ways. After his death, 'Abd al-'Āl became his *khalīfa, and organized his followers under strict rule.

Aḥmad al-Tijānī (1737–1815). Founder of the African *Sūfī order, the *Tijāniya. He was born in Algeria, and early in life joined several Sūfī orders before withdrawing for five years to a remote community. In 1781, he saw *Muḥammad in a vision, and received from him the command to establish his own order. He attracted little support until he received royal support in Morocco. After his death, the order spread rapidly in N. and W. Africa, becoming increasingly aggressive against French colonialists and non-Muslims. This use of the *jihād, combined with the personal cult of al-Tijānī, makes the order suspect to other Muslims.

Aḥmadīy(y)a. The movement founded by Mirzā Ghulām Aḥmad Qādiyānī (*c.*1835–1908), hence the later name Qādī. In *Barāhīn-i-Aḥmadiyya* (1880), Aḥmad claimed to be *al-Mahdī, and in due course also the *Messiah, the *avatāra of *Kṛṣṇa, and the reappearance of *Muḥammad. The Aḥmadīya believe, with other Muslims, that 'Isa/*Jesus did not die on the cross, but they do not believe that he was received into heaven. Rather, they hold that he visited India to preach, and died there, aged about 120. His tomb is at Srinagar. While sharing many Muslim beliefs, they are nevertheless regarded by Muslims as heretical and to be treated as such. The Lahore group (Aḥmadīya Anjuman-i-Ishā'at-i-Islam) has spread widely and established the Woking mosque as its UK centre.

Ahmad Khan, Sir Sayyid (1817–98). Often known simply as Sir Sayyid, founder of Islamic Indian modernism and an educational reformer. Sir Sayyid's greatness lies in restoring Muslim confidence and bringing them into the modern age through a practical programme of social and educational reform. He recognized the weakness of Indian Muslims and the futility of armed insurrection against strong British rule (e.g. the failure of the Indian Mutiny, 1857). The only course of action for him was to recognize British rule and raise the standard of the Muslims by working from within. His establishment of a Muslim college at Aligarh (1875) modelled on the lines of Cambridge and Oxford, provoked violent reaction from *al-Afghānī, the *Shīa, and the orthodox *'ulamā. His two major works *Essays on the life of Mohammed* (1870) and a Quranic commentary (1880–95) were attempts to demythologize the *Qur'ān, and to offer psychological and naturalistic interpretations of Islam. He also, unusually, wrote a *Bible commentary, *Tabyīn al-kalām*.

Aḥmad Sirhindī (b. 1563 (AH 971)). A leading figure in the *Naqshbandi *Sūfī order, who did much to restore Sunni orthodoxy to *Mughal India. He became a Naqshbandi adherent of Khwāja Bāqī Bi'llah in 1600 and succeeded him as *shaykh in 1603. His claim to strong spiritual authority led to a period in prison, but his followers recognized him as 'the Renewer'. In his teachings (mainly collected in his letters), he abandoned the pervasive Sūfī doctrine, derived from *ibn 'Arabī, of *waḥdat al-*

wujūd, the oneness of being: this claims that everything which exists can only do so because it is created by God, and might therefore be regarded as an aspect of Divine Reality—'Wherever you turn, there is the face of God' (Qur'ān 2. 115). The obvious risk here is that of *pantheism, so close to the surrounding Hinduism which Sirhindī contested strongly. Instead, he emphasized *waḥdat al-shuhūd*, the unity of witnessing consciousness, a single awareness.

Ahriman (source of evil): see ANGRA MAINYU.

Ahura Mazda. The Wise Lord (or possibly more correctly 'The Lord Wisdom'), God in *Zoroastrianism. Zoroaster was convinced he had seen Ahura personally and had been called by him. This injected into the foundations of Zoroastrianism a concept of a personal God. In the *Gāthās, Ahura is referred to as the creator of all things, of the heavens, of humanity, both materially and spiritually. In the developed Zoroastrian tradition, the emphasis is on Ahura Mazda's goodness and knowledge, but not on his *omnipotence, for he is restricted by the activities of the wholly independent evil *Angra Mainyu. The first creations of Ahura were the *Amesa Spentas, the heavenly forces. Beneath them in the heavenly hierarchy are the *yazatas*, or worshipful beings. In modern Zoroastrian exegesis, the Amesa Spentas are often compared to the archangels and *angels of Judaism and Christianity. Ahura Mazda is the Good Creator (*Bundahisn) who will ultimately triumph over evil (*Frasokereti). In that battle he has his helpers (*hamkars*) chief among whom are humans.

Ai. 1. Love in *Mo Tzu's system, usually in the form chien ai, universal love. Universal love is in a different category from *jen, being more related to utilitarian considerations: altruism has benefits running in both directions.

2. In Japanese Buddhism, ai (lust as well as love) is fundamental desire which may go in either of two opposite directions. It may become self-interested and self-satisfying, or, it may be self-denying and disinterested in the pursuit of the good of another, and is thus supremely the love of a *buddha or *bodhisattva, a transfigured love.

AIC: see AFRICAN INSTITUTED CHURCHES.

Aidan, St (d. 651). Christian *apostle to Northumbria. He was a monk of Iona brought to *Lindisfarne as bishop by King Oswald to evangelize his territory. His gentle commitment and personal asceticism made his many missionary journeys successful. He educated a small group of boys to be church leaders, among them St Chad. Feast day, 31 Aug.

Ailred (Cistercian monk): see AELRED.

Ainu. A Japanese people and religion. They were early inhabitants of Japan, driven northward from *c.*7th cent. CE. They are now mainly assimilated into mainstream Japanese culture, though some of their beliefs and practices can be traced in later religion—e.g. their animistic belief that spirits or spiritual powers (*kamuy*) are causative in natural events.

'Ā'isha bint Abī Bakr (d. 678 CE (AH 59)). Daughter of *Abu Bakr, born in *Mecca about 614 CE, and wife of *Muḥammad. She was married to him not long after the death of his first wife *Khadīja, and he admitted freely that she was his favourite wife of all those he subsequently married.

At Muḥammad's death in 632, 'Ā'isha was only about 18 years old, and played no part in political life until towards the end of the reign of *'Uthmān, the third Caliph, when she joined the growing opposition party. In 656, 'Uthmān was assassinated; 'Ā'isha, together with Ṭalḥa and al-Zubayr, took control of Baṣra, and in Dec. 656 fought against *'Alī b. Abī Ṭālib, the successor of 'Uthmān. This event was known as the Battle of the Camel, because the camel-litter carrying 'Ā'isha was in the thick of the fighting. Ṭalḥa and al-Zubayr were killed, but 'Ā'isha survived, and from then on kept to her house in *Madīna, where she died in 678. She was said to be both pious and learned, and is quoted as the source for many (1,210) *ḥadīth, especially those concerning Muḥammad's personal life.

Aitareya Upaniṣad. A short work of three chapters: the first deals with creation of all things from the One (*ātman), bringing out the correspondences between macro- and microcosm; the second with the three births, conception, natural birth, and extension through one's son; and the third with the nature of ātman.

For trs., see UPANIṢAD.

Aiyetoro (Yoruba, 'happy city'). A utopian Christian community, the Holy Apostles, in Nigeria, founded by a group of persecuted members of the *aladura-type Cherubim and Seraphim society. In 1947 they migrated to a mudbank in the coastal lagoons 160 miles east of Lagos, built a model town on piles, and set up a radical form of economic communism under a priest-chief. Several branch communities developed, but by the 1970s internal dissension and litigation had appeared and the original impetus had faded.

Aizen-myō-ō (Jap.; Skt., Rāgarāja or Vajrarājapriya). In Japanese esoteric Buddhism, a protective deity who destroys all evils and passions.

Aja Ekapād (Skt., 'the one-footed goat'). A *Vedic god. The exact nature of Aja Ekapād is obscure. He is mentioned only six times in *Ṛg *Veda*, usually in connection with Ahi Budhnya, an atmospheric deity. Later traditions connect Aja Ekapād with *Agni or the sun. He has been interpreted as Agni in the form of lightning.

Ajaṇṭā. An impressive series of about twenty-eight (numbers vary because of interconnections) humanly constructed caves in W. India, cut into a cliff overlooking the Waghora River, Maharashtra. Started in the 2nd cent. BCE and continued until the 6th cent. CE Ajaṇṭā is a series of monastic residences (*vihāras) with four associated *caitya halls. The wall-paintings, from all periods of construction, reached a peak of achievement during the Gupta era (320–650 CE). This Gupta style celebrates a fusion of the sacred and the aristocratic, and, through the visits of Chinese pilgrims, exercised a powerful influence on the painting of the T'ang (618–906 CE).

Ajapa-mantra (Skt.). Hindu *Haṭha-Yoga belief that every breathing creature must repeat a *mantra with every *breath in and out: *seham*, He am I, *hamsa*, I am He. This may therefore be an involuntary affirmation.

Ajari. Jap. tr. of *ācārya, hence title of a Buddhist monk in general, or teacher in particular, especially among *Tendai or *Shingon Buddhists.

Ajātivāda (Skt., 'the doctrine of non-origination'). According to the teaching of the early *Advaita Vedānta philosopher *Gauḍapāda, the entire phenomenal world characterized by the objects of sense experience is unreal, a mere appearance like the visions experienced in a dream, and the Self is not separate from the objects of experience. There is only one changeless Reality (Consciousness, *vijñāna, or *Brahman, or *ātman), and all causality is mere appearance.

Aji-kan (meditation on A): see A (1).

Ajita Kesakambala. One of the notorious six heretical teachers criticized by the Buddha for propounding false doctrines. The epithet 'kesakambala' derives from the hair garment worn by Ajita which the Buddhists described as foul-smelling and repellent. In spite of his austere garb Ajita was a materialist who denied the doctrine of the retribution of actions (*karma) and the purpose of the religious life.

Ajīva (Skt. 'not jīva', i.e. 'not living'). In Jainism the insentient constitution of the physical universe which forms one of the two major divisions of all existing things, the other being *jīva (the sentient soul).

Ājīvaka (Skt., 'one who practises a way' (?)). A heterodox sect founded by Makkhali Gosala, a contemporary and opponent of the *Buddha. According to Buddhist sources, Makkhali was a determinist who compared the course of a man's life to a ball of string which, when thrown down, rolls along unwinding in a pre-ordained course until it reaches its end.

Ajñāna (Skt.). In Hinduism, the opposite of *jñāna, but particularly ignorance of the identity of *ātman and *Brahman, and thus in consequence equivalent to *avidyā.

Ājur Veda (sacrificial prayer): see YAJUR VEDA.

Akāl (timeless): see AKĀL PURUKH; AKĀL TAKHT; AKĀLĪ.

Akalanka (8th cent. CE). A *Digambara Jain philosopher and logician. According to biographies written centuries after his death, he regarded Buddhists as his greatest intellectual opponents, and he organized his arguments to eradicate their viewpoint. The relativism of his outlook required a careful defence of Jain epistemology. His main achievement was to realize that the traditional division of inference (*svārthānumāna* and *parārthānumāna*) can be extended, so that something akin to the abductive inference of Peirce is anticipated.

Akālī (Pañjābī, 'deathless'). Designation by Gurū *Gobind Siṅgh of those devotees of Akāl (i.e. God), the Timeless one, who were prepared to die for the Sikh cause. Their fearlessness won the title *'Nihaṅg', although the two terms have since gained widely differing connotations. The Akālī Dal (political party) first met in 1926 and, despite division, has continued to dominate the *Shiromaṇī Gurdwārā Parbandhak Committee and to campaign actively—e.g. for a Pañjābī-speaking state (achieved in 1966) and for greater Sikh autonomy.

Akāl Purukh. 'Being beyond time', Sikh designation of God. 'Akāl Purukh' is the theological affirmation of God's absolute transcendence. *Vāhigurū is the designation more common in devotion, but Akāl Purukh is the foundation on which Sikh faith and confidence rest.

Akāl Takht (Pañjābī, 'immortal throne'). The foremost *takht among Sikh shrines, located in *Amritsar. The Akāl Takht was founded by Gurū *Hargobind for the organization of the *panth's secular and military affairs. In June 1984, during fighting between the Indian army and supporters of Jarnail Siṅgh *Bhindrānwāle, the Akāl Takht was severely damaged, but it has since been rebuilt.

Ākāśa (Skt., 'open space, vacuity, ether'). 1. One of the five gross elements (*mahābhūtas) of Hindu philosophy (albeit the finest), the ether which pervades the universe and is the vehicle of life and sound. See also BHŪTA.

2. In *Matsya* **Purāṇa*, Ākāśa is a god of house-building.

3. In Buddhism, space, either as limited by the boundaries of bodies, or unlimited space.

4. For Jains, see ASTIKAYA.

Akathistos (Gk., 'not sitting', because it is sung standing). A *Greek hymn in twenty-four stanzas in honour of the Virgin *Mary. It is sung in *Orthodox churches on the fifth Saturday in *Lent.

Akbar the Great (Jalāl ud-Dīn Muḥammad, 1542–1605). One of the ablest rulers of *Mughal India, who built a durable base for stable Muslim rule. Akbar ruled for forty-eight years and created a strong central government to administer the vast Mughal empire; he extended it from Afghanistan to the Godavari river in S. India.

During the latter part of his reign, Akbar, while maintaining that he remained Muslim, promulgated Dīn-i-Ilāhī (Divine Faith, also called Tawḥīd-i Ilāhī) as a new religion for his empire. It was a syncretization of various creeds and an attempt to create a pure theism. Although he was illiterate himself, he founded an 'Ibādat-khāna (house of worship) where leaders of different religions could discuss their faiths. However, Akbar's Dīn-i-Ilāhī met with very little success (it was strongly opposed by *Aḥmad Sirhindī), and it died with him.

Akdamut Millin (Heb., 'Introduction'). Introductory words of an *Aramaic poem written by R. Meir b. Isaac Nehorai. It consists of ninety lines, praising God, the Creator and Lawgiver.

'Akeda/'Aqeda (Heb., 'Binding' (of *Isaac)). The story of *Abraham's intended *sacrifice of Isaac, told in Genesis 22. In Jewish thought, this incident is regarded as the supreme example of obedience to God's will. Traditionally the *Temple was believed to have been built over the site where the 'akeda took place.

À Kempis (Christian writer): see THOMAS À KEMPIS.

Akhaṇḍ Kīrtanī Jathā (Pañjābī, 'continuous hymn-singing group'). A non-political organization emphasizing strict allegiance to Sikh discipline. The Jathā draws inspiration from the devout and learned fighter for Indian independence, Bhāī Randhīr Singh (1878–1961). From the Akhaṇḍ Kīrtanī Jathā have come many members of the more political and militant Babbar Khālsā, campaigning for an independent state, *Khālistān.

Akhaṇḍ pāṭh (Hindī, Pañjābī). 'Uninterrupted reading' of the *Ādi Granth. Akhaṇḍ *pāṭh is a relatively recent Sikh practice. Anyone wishing to mark a happy or sorrowful family occasion may arrange for akhaṇḍ pāṭh, providing food for all who read or attend during the forty-eight hours.

Akhārā ('wrestling arena', i.e. a monastery): see NIRMALĀ.

Akhlāq (ethics): see ETHICS (Islam).

Akhun(d): Persian for *Mulla.

Aki Matsuri (harvest festival): see NIINAME-SAI.

Aki no Higan (festival): see FESTIVALS AND FASTS (Japanese).

Aki no Shanichi (protective festival): see FESTIVALS AND FASTS (Japanese).

Akiva/Aqiba (*c*.50–135 CE). Jewish scholar and *martyr. Akiva was one of the leading scholars of his age and is credited with systematizing the *midrash. He set up his own school at Bene Barak, and his pupils included R. *Meir and R. *Simeon bar Yoḥai. He recognized Simeon bar Kokhba as the *messiah in his revolt against the Romans in 132 CE, applying to him the verse (Numbers 24. 17) Ultimately he died as a martyr, being flayed alive by the Romans.

Akṣara (Skt., 'unchangeable'). That which cannot perish, the immutable, a name for *Brahman.

Akṣara-puruṣa (Skt., 'unchangeable' + *puruṣa). The uninvolved Self which keeps aloof and detached from the changes which occur in *prakṛti, and simply observes its processes.

Akṣobhya (Skt., 'imperturbable'). In Buddhism, one of the five Jinas or *Dhyāni-Buddhas who inhabits the pure land of the East (*Abhirati). Akṣobhya is mentioned briefly in the earliest *Mahāyāna sources but comes to prominence in later *Tantric Buddhism. His paradise in the East is described, in a manner similar to the *pure land of Amitābha/*Amida in the West, as a utopia without evil, ugliness, or suffering, wherein the virtuous are reborn.

In Tantric Buddhism he is the father of the spiritual lineage which has Vajrapāni for *bodhisattva and Kanakamuni as the earthly Buddha. His consort is the earth goddess Locanā, and he is usually depicted in iconography in the gesture (*mudra) of touching the earth to call witness to his enlightenment. He is symbolically associated with the colour blue and with the aggregate (*skandha) of consciousness.

Aku-byōdō (Jap., 'bad-sameness'). A subtle error in Zen Buddhism whereby the sameness of all things when they are experienced in enlightenment (*byōdō), is confused with a belief that all things are the same—thereby overlooking their provisional distinctions.

Akum (non-Jewish star worshipper): see GENTILE.

Akuśala (Skt., opposite of *kusala. Unskilful action. Actions are called 'unskilful' because of their undesirable effects, since they contain the seed of unhappy destiny or rebirth. These actions are rooted in greed (*lobha), hatred (*dosa), or delusion (*moha), the three unfavourable roots (akuṣala-mūla). See also KARMA/KAMMA.

Akusō (Jap., 'evil monk'). Common term from the Heian period in Japan for monks who had abandoned their monastic orders (and rules) and had become warriors. They constituted the *sōhei*, soldier-monks who were only overcome in the 16th cent.

Akuśu-kū (Jap., 'wrong understanding' + 'emptiness'). A wrong understanding, in Zen Buddhism, of the true nature of ku (Skt., *śūnyatā). In this error, ku is understood as equalling 'nothing', the negation of existence. But Ku/śūnyatā is the repository and source of all appearance, so that appearance is neither more nor less than it.

al-ʿAbbās b. ʿAbd al-Muṭṭalib (d. 652–3 (AH 32)). An uncle of the Prophet *Muḥammad. The *ʿAbbāsid dynasty took its name from him, being descended from his son.

Aladura (Yoruba, 'praying people'). The general name for a wide range of prophet-healing independent churches that have developed in W. Nigeria since about 1918, spread as far as the Cameroon and Sierra Leone, and established branches in Britain.

al-Afghānī, Jamāl al-Dīn (1838–97 (AH 1254–1314)). A Muslim modernist and reformer, and strong anti-colonialist. He was born in Iran, but his formative years were spent in Afghanistan. From 1871, he taught in Cairo, but subsequently travelled widely, following political opportunity. Freedom and liberation from foreign rule were to be followed by the establishment of a pan-Islamic state, the union of the Muslim people under one *khalīfa.

Al-Afghānī argued that Islam was not incompatible with Western reason or science (he contested, in particular, E. Renan's lecture 'Islam and Science'), but as a Muslim rationalist, he repudiated blind faith and conjecture, and instead believed that true happiness sprang from wisdom and clear-sightedness.

al-Aḥsāʾī (Muslim founder of the Shaykhīs): see SHAYKH AHMAD IBN ZAYN AL-DĪN.

al-Akhira (the hereafter): see AFTERLIFE.

al-ʿAqīqah (sacrifice at time of a birth): see SACRIFICE (Islam).

al-Aqṣā Mosque: see JERUSALEM.

al-Arbaʿayn (commemoration of departed): see FUNERALS RITES (Islam).

al-ʿArsh (the throne of God): see KURSĪ.

al-Ashʿarī, Abū 'l-Ḥasan ʿAlī ibn Ismāʿīl (873–935 (AH 260–324)). Foremost Muslim theologian, who is often regarded as the founder of *kalām. In early life, he was a *Muʿtazilite, but he became doubtful about the power of human reason to solve theological problems when he raised the issue of the condemnation of those whom God might have brought to death earlier (thus avoiding the deeds for which they were condemned). He moved more toward the *Ḥanbalites and contested the arguments of the Muʿtazilites, while using some of their methods. He insisted that the *Qur'ān is uncreated (against the view that anything which appears in or through material form must be created). In affirming attributes of God (e.g. the hand of God), al-Ashʿarī held that they are truly posited (they are not metaphors), but that it is impossible to say in exactly what way they pertain to God—thus producing the famous formula, *bilā kaif(a)*, 'without knowing how'. He also dealt with the problem of how humans can be accountable for their actions if God determines all things, by developing the doctrine of acquisition (*kasb*, see QADAR): God creates all possibilities, but humans acquire a particular act in the action itself. Among many works, he wrote *al-Ibānah ʿan Uṣūl al-Diyānah* (Discourse on the Foundations of Religion) and *Maqālāt al-Islāmiyyīn* (The Treatises of the Islamic Schools).

al-Asmāʾ al-Ḥusnā (names of Allāh in Islam): see NINETY-NINE BEAUTIFUL NAMES OF GOD.

Alawi (a Shīʿa Muslim movement): see NUṢAIRĪ.

ʿAlawiyya. Sūfī movement derived from the *Shādhiliyya.

Ālaya-vijñāna ('receptacle-consciousness'). In Yogācāra (Buddhist Idealism, also known as *Vijñānavāda) the continuum of subjective consciousness underlying cognition and personal experience through time (given that there is no 'self' supplying this continuity). The concept was introduced by *Asaṅga in the 4th cent. CE as an elaboration of the *Abhidharmic notion of a stream of consciousness (*bhavaṅga-sota*) which constitutes personal continuity over a series of lives. See also ANĀTMAN; ARAYA-SHIKI.

al-Azhar (Arab., 'the most resplendent'). One of the principal *mosques in Cairo, also a centre of learning and later a university. It was founded in 969 CE by the *Fāṭimid rulers of Egypt. Since they were Isma'īlī, al-Azhar was (for two centuries) a centre for Isma'īlī teaching, until the Ayyubids under Ṣalāḥ al-Dīn (*Saladin) deposed the Fāṭimid dynasty in the late 12th cent. In the 1950s, and especially in the reform of 1961, further expansion added facilities for a much wider range of studies (including sciences, languages, and business studies) and in the 1970s a section for women was opened. Al-Azhar remains to this day one of the leading and most influential universities in the Islamic world.

Alb. A Christian eucharistic *vestment, derived from the Graeco-Roman *tunica talaris*. It is a long white (Lat., *albus*) garment usually with tight-fitting sleeves and held in at the waist by a cord ('girdle').

al-Baiḍāwī. 'Abdallah b. 'Umar al-Baiḍāwī, of Persian origin, author of one of the best known works of *tafsīr (*Qur'ān commentary). Al-Baiḍāwī belonged to the *Shāfi'ī school of law, and wrote on law, grammar, and scholastic theology. He became chief *qāḍi (judge) in Shirāz, and died in 1286 CE.

Alban, St. The first Christian *martyr in Britain. The date of his death is either *c*.209 or *c*.305. He was converted to Christianity by a fugitive priest he sheltered, in whose cloak he was arrested. He was subsequently put to death. His shrine is in St Albans Abbey. Feast day, 20 June.

al-Bannā (founder of Sūfī movement): see ḤASAN AL-BANNĀ'.

al-Baṣrī (Sūfī): see ḤASAN AL-BAṢRĪ.

Albertus Magnus, St (*c*.1205–80). Christian philosopher and theologian. He was born in Bavaria, studied at Padua and Bologna, and became a *Dominican in 1222/3. He held one of the Dominican chairs of theology at the University of Paris, where Thomas *Aquinas was one of his pupils, and later (1260–2) he became bishop of Ratisbon. Allowed to resign, he resumed teaching at Cologne. He preached a *crusade in Germany, 1263–4. As well as Magnus, he was called Doctor Universalis. He was canonized and proclaimed a Doctor of the Church in 1931. He wrote commentaries on the Sentences of *Peter Lombard and on Pseudo-*Dionysius, and a *Summa de Creaturis*. He left incomplete a *Summa Theologica*.

Albigenses. A branch of the *Cathars of S. France. Christian *dualist heretics, Pope Innocent III failed to convert them; a savage *Crusade, led by Simon de Montfort, went on until 1218; and in 1233, the *Dominican *Inquisition undertook to eliminate them. Their main centre was Albi (hence the name); they may have had remote ancestry in the teaching of *Maṇi.

al-Bīrūnī, Abū Rayḥān (973–1049 (AH 362–442)). Muslim scholar of wide-ranging interests, not least in other religions. His study culminated in *Kitāb al-Hind* (The Book of India). On this basis, he developed work of his own on a wide scale, particularly, but by no means exclusively, in astronomy.

al-Bisṭāmī, Abū Yazīd/Bāyazīd (d. 875 (AH 261)). A Persian *Sūfī, who was given to a life of asceticism and solitude. His only desire in life was to attain a direct experience of divine reality. He wrote no work, but his ecstatic utterances have been preserved in writing by such contemporaries as *Dhu'l-nūn and *al-Junaid. His particular method of attainment was one of subtraction, or stripping away, of the attributes of personality until not even personality is left—as when a snake finally sloughs its skin; Al-Bistāmī is much quoted by the Sūfīs, and had a far-reaching influence on Sufism in the direction of a pantheistic doctrine.

Albo, Joseph (15th cent. CE). Spanish Jewish preacher and philosopher. Albo was the author of *Sefer ha-'Ikkarim* (Book of Principles), a reasoned presentation of the articles of the Jewish *faith, explained in the light of contemporary ideas. He was familiar with Islamic philosophy and Christian *scholasticism and was greatly influenced by the teaching of Hasdai *Crescas. He formulated three principles of Judaism—the existence of God, divine *revelation, and reward and punishment (though he added eight further derivative principles). Subordinate to the principles are six dogmas, namely the creation of the world *ex nihilo*, the status of *Moses as supreme *prophet, the validity of Mosaic law, the possibility of attaining human perfection, the *resurrection of the dead and the coming of the *messiah. The work achieved great popularity and went through many edns.

al-Bukhārī, Muḥammad b. Ismā'īl (810–70 (AH 194–256)). Compiler of one of the main collections of *ḥadīth, known as *Ṣaḥīḥ* ('sound', 'genuine'). He travelled extensively in search of ḥadīth, which he subjected to careful scrutiny—much needed, since spurious ḥadīth were circulating. The *Ṣaḥīḥ* contains over 7,000 narratives, though because some are repeated, the total is under 3,000. Together with the *Ṣaḥīḥ* of *Muslim (d. 875 (AH 261)), al-Bukhārī's collection is accepted as the main definitive compilation of reliable ḥadīth, and as such, comes second only to the *Qur'ān as a source of principles for legislation and religious practice.

Alchemy (Arab., perhaps from Gk. via Syriac, *al-kīmiyā*). The endeavour (minimally) to find the key to the transformation of chemical substances, especially of base metals into precious ones; and beyond that, to find 'the elixir of immortality'. The word and practice of 'alchemy' thus underlie modern chemistry. In its earlier forms it pervades all religions, though moving increasingly to interior and spiritual transformations. Thus in Taoism, there were two different levels: practitioners of Wai-tan (external alchemy) sought a potion for immortality, based on a belief that a person's vital energy (*yüan-ch'i) was a particular balance of *yin-yang, which, if it is disturbed, produces illness and death; gold and cinnabar have the power to restore the balance. The practitioners of Nei-tan (internal alchemy) aimed to develop an immortal soul from *ching, *ch'i, and *shen, by meditative exercises, especially breathing and control of bodily functions.

European alchemy seems to have begun in Hellenistic Egypt around the 1st cent. CE, and possibly even earlier. It enjoyed flourishing periods in 2nd- and 3rd-cent. Greece, and in various parts of the Arab world in the 7th and 8th cents., thus taking its name from the Arab. *al-kīmiyā*, the Syriac *kīmīyā*, and the Gk. *chēmeia*. In the 10th cent., alchemy re-entered Europe via Islamic Spain, where it also received influence from the *Kabbalah. At its peak in Renaissance Europe, in addition to having produced a well-developed medical system under such as Paracelsus, alchemy came for some to rival the Church as the epitome of *Hermetic philosophy.

Alcohol (Arab.). Intoxicants which in some religions are prohibited. In Islam, they are *harām* (see KHAMR), and in Buddhism, abstention from alcohol is one of the five basic principles of moral conduct (pañca-*śīla). Among Hindus, *surāpāna*, drinking intoxicants, is the second of the five great sins (*mahāpātaka), although there is much commentarial discussion on what counts as an intoxicant. Drinking alcohol is forbidden for initiated *khālsā Sikhs, as is the taking of drugs—though *Nihaṅg Siṅghs take an infusion of cannabis ritually to aid meditation. In Judaism and Christianity, wine is extolled as part of the bounty of God, but again, in moderation.

Al-Dajjāl (Arab.). The perjurer or false accuser, a figure in Islamic *eschatology, the '*anti-Christ' whose wiles and deceptions 'cover' (a root meaning) and resist the truth. He is not mentioned in the *Qur'ān. By some he is identified with *al Shaytan al-Rajīm, 'the accursed Satan', whom pilgrims on the *ḥajj repudiate by hurling stones against his 'pillar' outside *Mecca.

Aleinu le-Shabbe'ah (Heb, 'It is our duty to praise'). Prayer now recited at the end of the prayerbook services. In the *Ashkenazi *liturgy, it is customary to prostrate oneself during the recital of the Aleinu on *Rosh ha-Shanah and *Yom Kippur. It begins, 'It is our duty to praise the Lord of all things, to ascribe greatness to the Creator, that he has not made us like the nations of other lands, nor placed us like the other families of earth'.

Alexandria. City in Egypt, notable in Christian tradition (stemming, traditionally, from St *Mark) for its catechetical school in the 2nd and 3rd cents. and in the 4th and 5th cents. especially for the 'Alexandrian theology' represented by *Origen, *Athanasius, and *Cyril.

al-Fārābī, Abu Nasr Muḥammad Ibn Tarkhān (*c*.870–950 (AH 257–339)). A philosopher-mystic of Turkish origin who lived during the height of *'Abbāsid rule in Baghdād. His philosophy contained elements of Aristotelanism, Platonism, and *Sufism. Al-Fārābī wrote on many diverse subjects. Among Muslim philosophers he is considered the Second Teacher (*al mu'allim ath-thāni*) after Aristotle. Al-Fārābī's chief work, *Attainment of Happiness*, defends the basis of *revelation (i.e. *prophecy) against the strong attacks of such free-thinkers as Al-Rawandī.

He reconciled the various modes of human reflection and enquiry by dividing the intellect (the extension of Being into the human) into three: the active intellect, the potential intellect and the acquired intellect. In this way he could affirm the equal validity of many human arts and skills. His *Kitāb al-Musiqa* (The Book of Music) laid the foundations for an Islamic theory of music, drawing attention to relations between mathematics and music; and his *Risalah fi ara' ahl alMadina al-fadilah* (Treatise on the . . . Virtuous City) was widely influential in the development of political science.

Alfasi, Isaac ben Jacob (known as Rif, 1013–1103). N. African codifier of Jewish law. His *Sefer ha-Halakhot* (Book of the Commandments) was the best known code before the *Mishneh Torah* (Second Law Code) of *Maimonides. It was much admired. Joseph *Caro regarded Alfasi, Maimonides, and *Asher b.

Jehiel as the three pillars of learning on which Judaism rested, and he used their work as a foundation for his own **Shulḥān Arukh* (Arranged Table).

al-Ghaz(z)ālī, Abū Ḥāmid Muḥammad (d. 1111 (AH 505)). The 'Proof of Islam' (*hujjat al-Islam*), often considered the greatest religious authority after the Prophet *Muḥammad. As a result of the esteem accorded to him by his contemporaries, al-Ghaz(z)ālī deeply influenced the direction of Islamic thought, in particular Islamic jurisprudence (*sharī'a), dialectical theology (*kalām), philosophy, and mysticism (*taṣawwuf).

He was born at Ṭūs and was educated there and at Nishapur. He rose to be a distinguished professor at the Baghdād Nizamiya, a formidable scholar in Islamic law and theology. However, in 1095, he underwent a crisis brought on by a search for inner conviction, and by an awareness that although he was lecturing *about* God, he did not know God. He therefore abandoned his high position for the life of a *Sūfī, seeking to know the reality of which, hitherto, he had only spoken. After ten years, he returned to Nishapur and wrote his *magnum opus*, *'Ihyā 'ulūm al-dīn* (The Revival of the Religious Sciences) and other key works, such as *Mishkāt al-anwār* (Niche of the Lamp), *al-Qistās al-mustaqīm* (The Just Balance), *Kīmiya' al-Sa'āda* (The Alchemy of Happiness), and *Tahāfut al-Falāsifah* (The Incoherence of the Philosophers) in which the inadequacy of reason outside its appropriate spheres points to the necessity for revelation and mystical knowledge. It was his achievement that he successfully harmonized Sufism into the field of orthodoxy and gave it acceptance as an inner dimension of Islam. At the same time, his emphasis on the limits of reason in relation to faith led eventually to a withdrawal of Islam from the leadership it had given to the world in science and philosophy.

al-Hakim (Druze holy figure): see DRUZES.

al-Halal wa'l-Harām. The permitted and the forbidden in Islam. This constitutes the fundamental division between what *Allāh permits and what he forbids. The creation principle (*asl*) is that everything which God has created is for human use (Qur'ān 2. 29; 31. 20; 45. 13), but that for specific reasons in each case, some things are prohibited.

More particularly, the word halal is used as a short-hand for the permitted way of slaughtering animals—by severing blood-vessels, while naming the name of Allāh over the animal. This is usually done by cutting through the throat of the animal until the jugular veins are severed. The meat is then halal, permitted. Cf. SHEḤITAH.

al-Hallāj, Abu 'l-Mughīth al-Ḥusain b. Mansur (d. 922 (AH 309)). One of the most controversial figures in Islam: he was acclaimed as a saint by the masses and condemned as a heretic by the jurists. It is said that he was called Hallāj al-asrar (Carder of Consciences) because he could read the secret thoughts of others. He embraced the doctrine of *fanā' (extinction of personal consciousness) and other notions such as *hulul* (union and identity with God). Al-Hallāj aimed to bridge the abyss between humans and God: 'I am He whom I love and He whom I love is I. We are two spirits dwelling in one body. When you see me, you see Him.' However, to the jurists of his time, he appeared blasphemously to contradict the Islamic notion of *tanzīh (transcendence of God), and even to threaten the social order.

He paid the supreme penalty for his choice. After many years of extensive teaching and travelling throughout Central Asia and India, he was arrested, imprisoned and finally brutally executed in Baghdād. His only work to have survived is *Kitāb al-Tawāsīn* (902 CE). This contains the famous phrase *'ana' l-Haqq* (I am the Truth). It is important to read it in its proper context: 'If you do not recognize God, at least recognize his signs. I am that sign, I am the Creative Truth (*'ana' l-Haqq*) because through the Truth I am a truth eternally.' (*Kitāb al-Tawāsīn*, pp. 51–2). Cf. also AL-INSĀN AL-KĀMIL.

al-Ḥaqq (the True, i.e., God): see HAQQ.

al-Hasan b. 'Ali (d. 669–70 (AH 49)). Second *Shī'a *Imam, son of *'Alī and *Fāṭima, and claimant to the Caliphate until he renounced the office in favour of *Mu'āwiyyah. Mu'awiyyah rewarded him with a generous settlement and a subsidy of a million dirhams. The Shī'a contend that Hasan was a *martyr by being poisoned to death by Mu'āwiyyah. However, this is unlikely since Mu'āwiyyah had already neutralized him and Mu'āwiyyah was not a man to commit an unnecessary crime when his design had already succeeded. It is more likely that he died of consumption.

al-Ḥasan b. al-Sabbah (d. 1124 (AH 518)). Founder of the *Nizārīs (popularly known as *Assassins). Very little is known of his early life. His followers captured the strong mountain fortress of Alamūt in 1091 (AH 483) and established it as a power centre of the Assassin movement. He did not introduce assassination as a religious duty, for it had already been practised by other sects; nor is it clear that he even advocated this. But from him derived a movement which gained considerable strength, and which terrorized parts of the Muslim world, until Alamūt was captured and destroyed by the *Mughals in the 13th cent.

'Al Het (Heb., 'for the sin'). First words of a Jewish prayer of confession recited on *Yom Kippur. 'Al het consists of an alphabetical list of sins expressed in the first person plural. Each section concludes with the words, 'and for all these God of forgiveness, forgive us, pardon us, grant us *atonement'.

al-Ḥusain b. 'Ali (626–80 (AH 4–61)). Third *Shī'a *Imām, known from his death as Sayyid al-Shuhadā', 'the Chief of Martyrs'. He was the son of *'Alī and *Fāṭima, and, acc. to numerous *ḥadīth, was much loved by *Muḥammad. During his youth, Ḥusain distinguished himself for his devotion and service to his father. He remained in the background during *Mu'āwiyya's reign, but refused to acknowledge Yazīd as heir-apparent. Upon Yazīd's accession (680), he escaped from *Madīna with his family and relatives to Mecca, and then headed for Kūfa to muster support for his cause. However, Ḥusain and his party were intercepted by Umayyad troops near Karbalā. They were surrounded, and cut off from access to water for ten days. On 10 Muḥarram, Ḥusain's weary supporters (92 males) gave battle against 4,000 soldiers. During the fierce engagement, Ḥusain's party was annihilated.

The Karbalā tragedy became the focus of the Shī'a faith: Ḥusain, impelled by a desire to fulfil the demands of true Islam, had stood up against the evil Umayyads; his sacrifice was to redeem Islam, and to teach people the need of revolt against an unjust (*zalim*) government.

'Alī b. Abī Ṭālib (d. 661 (AH 40)). Cousin and son-in-law of the Prophet *Muḥammad, and the fourth Caliph (*Khalīfa) in Islam. 'Alī was one of the ten to whom paradise was promised by Muḥammad. He distinguished himself in all the early battles as a courageous warrior and was consequently nicknamed Haidar (lion) and Murtada (he in whom God is well pleased). During the rule of the first three Caliphs, 'Alī served as an adviser. After 'Uthmān's murder, 'Alī was proclaimed *khalīfa* (Caliph) by the Medinans. However, 'Alī's reign was an unhappy and frustrating one, marked by the first civil war in Islamic history, the beginnings of the overt *Sunni/*Shī'a split in Islam which persists to the present (Shī'a being the party of 'Alī).

Inconclusive military conflict at Siffīn (657 (AH 37)) led to the famous incident where the Syrians hoisted copies of the Qur'ān on spears, and invited the combatants to resolve the problem by recourse to the Holy Book. 'Alī was forced to accept arbitration by most of his army, and was thus politically outmanœuvred by Mu'āwiyya's stratagem. 'Alī's support diminished, a section of his army rebelled (those averse to arbitration) and these were crushed at Nahrawan (658 (AH 38)). The remnants of this defeated group later became known as the *Kharijites. During 'Alī's preparations for further battle, he was assassinated by a Kharijite in the mosque of Kūfa (661 (AH 40)).

Since the period of 'Alī's caliphate is a controversial time in Islamic history, it is open to various interpretations. Both Sunni and Shī'a sources agree that 'Alī was a powerful orator, a leading authority on the Qur'ān and the *Sunna of the Prophet Muḥammad, and that his piety was beyond question. 'Alī's sermons, lectures, and discourses have been preserved in *Nahj-ul-Balagha* (collected in the 11th cent.). However, while Muḥammad, *Abu Bakr, and *'Umar had displayed great pragmatism in the handling of worldly affairs, 'Alī lacked political insight: on the assumption of authority, he reversed all of 'Uthmān's policies, appointed new governors, initiated a programme of tribal reorganization, and moved the capital to Kūfa. 'Alī's opponents constituted the Quraysh élite, particularly the Umayyah clan who had proved their administrative skills in the rapidly expanding empire. The Arab-Islam polity could only function with the co-operation of the Quraysh. The Mu'awiyya/'Alī struggle had deeper implications for the Islamic community than merely the avenging of 'Uthmān's murder, or the dominion of Syria or Iraq; it opened up the two different directions of the Muslim community. 'Alī's programme was utopian, looking for the pure Islamic state, whereas that of Mu'awiyya was more of a secular nature.

In Shi'ite understanding, 'Alī is *walī Allah*, 'the friend of God', closest to him in sanctity. As such he is distinguished from Muḥammad, who is (merely!), *nabī, prophet. The family descent via 'Alī designates the legitimate *Imām, which can never, for a Shi'ite, be a matter of election—the most fundamental division from the Sunnis.

Ali Hujwīrī (Sūfī): see SŪFĪS.

al-Ikhwān al-Muslimūn. 'The Muslim Brotherhood', a religio-political movement founded in Egypt by *Ḥasan al-Bannā' (1904–49) in 1928. Its adherents urge a return to the fundamentals of Islam. The Ikhwan's main objectives were to free Egypt from British domination and then to establish an Islamic state in accordance with the *Qur'ān. A parallel women's movement, 'The Muslim Sisters', seeks to restore the Islamic status of women. All attempts by the authorities to liquidate the Ikhwan have met with failure, for as soon as one group is eradicated, another springs up and takes its place. Moreover, persecution has increased their prestige and popularity amongst Egyptians, for they are honoured as martyrs in the defence of Islam and enjoy grassroot support.

al-Insān al-Kāmil (The Perfect Man). An expression perhaps first compounded by *Ibn 'Arabī in *Fuṣūṣ al-Ḥikam* (*Bezels of Wisdom*): 'Everything the world contains is subject to man. This is known to him who knows, that is to say, to the Perfect Man, and is not known by him who does not know, that is to say, to man the animal. He (The Perfect Man) is the mirror by which God is revealed to himself.' Ibn 'Arabī identified the Perfect Man with the Prophet *Muḥammad the archetype of the universe and humanity; the first symbol of the Lord was Nūr Muḥammad (Light of Muḥammad), and it is in him and through him that prophets and saints find their perfection. *'Abd al-Karīm al-Jīlī elaborated this notion further: 'The Perfect Man is the pole (*qutb) around which the spheres of existence turn, from the first to the last.' For al-Jīlī, he (the Perfect Man) is unique for all time but appears in different guises and names: there is no reincarnation but merely the irradiation of the reality of Muḥammad on each occasion upon the most perfect of men, who thus become Muḥammad's representatives on the plane of manifestation. In another development (cf. AL-HALLĀJ), the Creator (al-*Ḥaqq) and the Perfect Man (al-Ḥalq) are seen as complementary constituents of total or absolute Being: 'Man unites in himself both the form of God and the form of the universe . . . God is necessary to us in order that we may exist, but we are necessary to him in order that he may be manifested to himself' (Ibn 'Arabī). Such a way of union was of profound importance in *Sūfīsm.

'Aliyah (Heb., 'ascent'). 1. Emigrating from the *diaspora to the land of *Israel to become a permanent resident.

2. The calling up of a member of the congregation in a *synagogue to recite a *blessing or to read from the *Torah scroll (in full, 'aliyah la-Torah).

3. Making *pilgrimage to *Jerusalem.

al-Jamāl wa'l-Jalāl (mercy and majesty): see NINETY-NINE BEAUTIFUL NAMES OF GOD.

al-Jīli (Jilāni) (Sūfī philosopher): see 'ABD AL-KARĪM AL-JĪLĪ; 'ABD AL-QĀDIR AL-JĪLĪ.

al-Junaid, Abū 'l-Qāsim (d. 910 (AH 298)). *Sūfī teacher, who influenced *al-Hallāj, and who laid the foundations of much of the development of Sufism. From his instructors he received his strong insistence that religious law and orthodox behaviour and belief control Sūfī experience. He thus distanced himself from the extreme statements of such men as al-Hallāj, and has therefore been known as the advocate of 'sober Sufism'. Little of his own writing has survived, apart from fragments collected in a work given the general title of an Epistle, *Rasa'il*.

al-Khamriyya (The Wine Ode): See OMAR KHAYYAM.

al-Kharkī (Sūfī master): see MA'RŪF AL-KARKHĪ.

al-Kursi (the footstool/throne of God): see KURSĪ; THRONE OF GOD.

Allāh. Arab. for God: if from earlier Semitic languages (e.g. Aram., *alāhā*), perhaps *the* God (Arab. *al* = 'the'). Before the birth of *Muḥammad, Allah was known as a supreme, but not the sole, God. Muḥammad became aware, early in his life, of conflict between religions and of contest, therefore, between 'gods'. From his experience in the cave on Mount *Ḥirā' (with possible influence from *ḥanīfs), Muḥammad saw that if God is God, it is God that God must be: there cannot be division of God into separate or competing beings. From this absolute realization of *tawḥīd (oneness of God), the whole of Islam is derived—as indeed is the whole of the created order. Hence the fundamental mark of *islām* (allegiance to God) is the *shahāda, *lā ilāha illā Allāh* . . . This involves Islam in necessary conflict with polytheism, idolatry, and what was taken to be the Christian understanding of the *Trinity.

In the *Qur'ān, Allah is described by many epithets, contributing eventually to the *ninety-nine beautiful names of God. Controlling all are the two descriptions (occurring in the *basmala) *rahmān* (merciful) and *rahīm* (compassionate). In later Islam, fierce arguments developed: about the status of the attributes of God (too much status would confer ontological, or truly existent, reality on them, thus converting them into something like independent parts of God); about anthropomorphic statements (e.g. the Qur'ān says that God sits on a *throne: to take this literally would limit God in space. This particular issue was resolved agnostically by saying that he does so, *bilā kaifa wa lā *tashbīh*, without knowing how and without comparison, sc. with our way of sitting; and also by *tanzīh); and about the power of God to determine all things. This last issue is focused on the term *qadar. The Qur'ān emphasizes the absolute power of God to determine all things, which suggests strong *predestination (as held e.g. by the Jabriya); in that case, how can humans be held accountable for their deeds and be judged accordingly (the question raised e.g. by the Mu'tazilites)? The eventual solution (at least for the Ash'arites (acquisition) was formulated in the doctrine of *iktisāb*, see AL-ASH'ARI).

Theological and rational reflection on God is complemented, in Islam, by the direct and immediate relation of the believer with God, above all in *salāt: to everyone, God is closer than the vein in the neck (50. 16). This close and direct relation to God led into the cultivation of the experiential awareness of God, which culminated in *Sūfism.

For the controlling and all-important Sūra of Unity (112), which, if a Muslim says it with conviction, leads to the shedding of sins as a tree sheds its leaves in autumn, see TAWḤĪD.

Allāhābād (Hindu place of pilgrimage): see PRAYĀGA.

Allāhu Akbar. 'God is great' (literally, 'greater'), fundamental and repeated proclamation by Muslims of the absolute supremacy of God.

al-Lāt. Meccan goddess, apparently recognized in the verse of the *Qur'ān insinuated by Shaitān/*Satan, but repudiated by *Muḥammad. See SATANIC VERSES.

al-Lawḥ (tablet): see UMM AL-KITĀB.

Allegory A narrative expressing abstract ideas as concrete symbols; a description of a topic or subject under the guise of another which is suggestive of it, an extended comparative metaphor. There is often little distinction between an allegory, a *parable, a simile, or a metaphor. In Judaism, the *Song of Songs has been interpreted allegorically, as a description of the relationship between God and his people. Allegory is also to be found in *Talmudic and *kabbalistic literature. It was especially prominent in *Philo, who regarded allegory as 'the rules of a wise architect'. Yet he also insisted that the literal sense and practice must be maintained (see e.g. *De Abrahamo*, 89–93). In Christianity, allegorical exegesis is that which treats a text as if it were an allegory, and was thus important for Christians as a way of relating Jewish scripture (from their point of view, the Old Testament) to Christianity.

Alleluia, Lat. and Gk. form of the acclamation *hallelujah, used in many places in Christian worship. In Catholic but not Orthodox practice, it is omitted from the liturgy at certain penitential times of the year.

Allen, Richard (first bishop of the African Methodist Episcopal Church): see AFRICAN METHODIST EPISCOPAL CHURCH.

All Saints' Day. The feast which celebrates *all* the Christian *saints, whether known by name or not. The date in the W. is 1 Nov., and in the E. the first Sunday after *Pentecost. The W. 'All Souls' Day' is a commemoration of the faithful departed on the following day (or on 3 Nov. if 2 Nov. is a Sunday).

Almagest (Lat. form of Arab., *al-majisti*, which in turn is the Arab. form of Gk. *megalē syntaxis*). Ptolemy's work on astronomy, which became the basis of the extensive Muslim work in that field.

al-Mahdī (Arab., 'the guided one'). In *Sunni Islam, one who receives guidance from God (God is al-Hādī, the Guide, Qur'ān 22. 54; 25. 31). The term may apply to figures in the past (e.g. the first four caliphs; see KHALĪFA; cf. AR-RĀSHIDŪN), or to those who revive Islam, but more often it refers to a future, *eschatological figure, who will come to herald in the end of all things.

In Shī'a Islam, even stronger beliefs surrounding al-Mahdī as the hidden Imām, who will emerge at the end of time, developed among the Twelvers (*Ithna 'Ashariy(y)a). The twelfth Imām, 'Ali ibn Muḥammad Simmarī, was born in Samarra' in 869 (AH 255). On the death of his father in AH 260, he became Imām but was kept in seclusion (the first so-called occultation, *ghaiba, *ghaibat-i-sughra*), being seen (if at all) on rare occasions only by senior figures. He answered questions through a succession of deputies (*wakīl*). Shortly before the death of the fourth *wakīl* in 939 (AH 329), it was announced that there would be no further Imām, that the major occultation would occur (*ghaibat-i-kubra*), and that the Imām would remain hidden until God gave him permission to manifest himself. Meanwhile, the hidden Imām gives guidance, hears prayers, and intercedes. al-Mahdī is also known as Imām-i-'Aṣr (the Imām of the Period), al-Muntazar (the Awaited), and Ṣāḥib al-Zamān (the Lord of the Age). See also MUḤAMMAD AḤMAD (the Mahdi of the Sudan).

al-Majlisī, Muḥammad Bāqir ibn Muḥammad al-Tāqī (1628–99 (AH 1038–1111)). Leading *Shi'ite theologian ('alim, see *'ulamā), whose opinions became a formative influence on the development of Twelver Shi'ite (*Ithna 'Ashariyya) practice and organization. He was strongly opposed to the rationalizing of religion through philosophy, to the *Sūfīs and to the Sunnis, whom he saw as intransigent competitors, and whom he succeeded in persuading the Shah to have banned from Isfahan. His major work was *Biḥār al-anwār* (The Ocean of Lights), a many-volumed work assembling *ḥadīth. His opposition to the Sunnis may have induced the Afghan invasion of 1722, but this in turn opened the way to the reconquest by the Qajars: they established a dynasty in 1794 (AH 1209) which endorsed the programme of al-Majlisī, making Teheran the capital. They in turn were overthrown by Reza Khan, whose short-lived Pahlavi dynasty could not possibly capture the Shi'ite devotion of the old order, still less displace the authority of the Hidden Imām exercised through the *mullas as al-Majlisī had established it.

Almanac. Especially in China, an annually published lunar calendar containing weather and harvest prognostications, lucky and unlucky days, festival dates and birthdays of the gods, moral maxims, and, most thumbed, a variety of fortune-telling systems. In the West, almanacs were originally connected with *astrology, suggesting a rational order in the cosmos.

al-Masīḥ (name for Jesus in Islam): see MESSIAH (ISLAM).

al-Māturīdī, Abū Mansūr Muḥammad (d. 944 (AH 333)). Contemporary of *al-Ash'arī, and founder (like him) of an important school of orthodox, conservative theology, which admitted a place for human reason, but not a paramount one. The differences between Ash'arites and Maturidites were reckoned as thirteen, of which the most substantial was the former's emphasis on the absolute power of the will of *Allāh, and the latter's emphasis that humans have freedom and responsibility.

Almemar. Platform in *synagogue where the reading stand is placed. In *Ashkenazi circles, it is usually described as the *bimah, and among the *Sephardim as the *tebah*.

Almohads (Arab., *al-muwwaḥḥidūn*, 'those who espouse Oneness'). Spanish name of a Muslim dynasty in N. Africa and Spain, 1130–1269 (AH 524–667). Their name summarizes their character as protestants against the lax style of prevailing Islam, especially under the *Almoravids. They derived their inspiration from *ibn Tumart, but it was his successor, 'Abd al-Mu'min, who extended territorial control. In 1170 (AH 566) Muslim Spain fell to them. The 'Almohad arch' is sometimes interpreted as a physical manifestation of sūra 94 in the *Qur'ān, The Grand Mosque in Seville, the Giralda, is now a cathedral, but still illustrates the vision. After their defeat at Las Navas de Tolosa in 1212 (AH 609), their eclipse was only a matter of time.

Almoravids (Arab., *al-murābiṭūn*, 'those who espouse defence'). Spanish name of a Muslim dynasty in N. Africa and Spain, 1056–1147 (AH 448–541). Initially it was a rigorist revival movement in Sudan under 'Abd Allāh ibn Yāsīn. Invited into Spain, the Almoravids defeated Alfonso VI at Sagrajas in 1086 (AH 479)—thereby initiating among Christians a determination to create a more united front against Islam. From their initial austerity and zeal, the Almoravids declined into a more lax and ostentatious lifestyle, until supplanted by the *Almohads.

Almsgiving. A work of merit, and sometimes of obligation, in most religions. In part, it establishes reciprocity, as in the N. American Kwakiutl potlatch ceremony, where 'a whole people was caught up in an exchange system that conferred greatest prestige on the individual who gave away the greatest amount of the most valuable goods'. In terms of reciprocity, the formality of exchange issued in systems of merit, whereby especially benefits could be transferred to the dead (see e.g. DĀNA; INDULGENCE). In Buddhism, this was elaborated into a social structure of mutual support between laity and *saṅgha. But equally, almsgiving is evoked by a religious sense of charity, where there is no calculation of consequence beyond the good of the recipient. This is prominent in Judaism and in Christianity. In Islam, *zakāt is an obligation, and one of the *Five Pillars.

al-Muḥāsibī ('he who examines his conscience'), Abū 'Abd Allāh Ḥārith (*c*.781–857 (AH 165–243)). *Shāfi'ite theologian who turned to ascetic renunciation and moral purification, and is regarded as the first *Sunni mystic (*Sūfī) to organize a theologically systematic approach to God. He was a prolific writer, with about 200 works ascribed to him. His *Kitāb al-ri'āya li-ḥuqūq Allah* (The Book of Observance of that which is Owed to God) is a book of spiritual advice, which includes the importance of self-examination (Arab., *muḥāsaba*), hence his name.

al-Nasā'ī, Abu 'Abd al-Raḥmān Aḥmad (d. 915 (AH 303)). Muslim collector of *Ḥadīth: his collection became one of the six Ṣaḥīḥ (Sound) collections, and was admired particularly by the *Shāfi'ites.

al-Naẓẓām, Ibrahīm b. Saiyār (d. *c*.840 (AH 225)). Leading *Mu'tazilite theologian and accomplished poet. But he was strongly rejected, even by other Mu'tazilites, for his dogmatic style.

al-Niffarī, Muḥammad (d. *c*.965 (AH 354)). *Sūfī who developed the notion of *waqfa*, a condition in which the mystic hears God directly—and perhaps is moved to write automatically at God's will. He claimed also that the vision of God is possible in this world.

Alobha (Pāli). Being without greed, one of the three root or conditioning attitudes which produce good *karma in Buddhism.

A-lo-pen (7th cent. CE). Chinese name of a Persian Christian (Nestorian) monk who was a missionary in China. According to a stele discovered by Jesuits in 1625, the emperor Tai-tsung (627–50) gave permission to A-lo-pen and sixty-seven others to work as missionaries in Sian-fu. These missions established an extensive church which was ended by Ming persecutions.

Alphonsus Liguori (moral theologian): see LIGUORI.

al-Qadam al-Sharīf (the noble footprint, i.e. example, of Muḥammad): see FOOTPRINT OF MUḤAMMAD.

al-Qamar (the crescent moon): see CRESCENT MOON.

al-Quds (the Holy [Place]): see JERUSALEM (ISLAM).

al-Rāshidūn (first four 'rightly guided' caliphs in Islam): see KHALĪFA.

al-Rāzī, Abū Bakr Muḥammad ibn Zakariyyā (850–925 (AH 236–313)). Muslim philosopher, physician, and pre-eminent medical writer; in Europe he became known as Rhazes (Rasis in Chaucer). He wrote a large number of books, including *Kitāb al-Mansūrī* (tr. into Lat. as *Liber Almansoris*), *Kitāb al-Mulūkī* (*Liber Regius*) and a vast encyclopaedia, completed after his death by his pupils, *Hāwī* (*Continens*, first tr. in 1279 and later one of the first books to be printed, five times between 1488 and 1542). He ended his days blind, and refused treatment, saying that he had been in the world so long that he had seen enough of it.

al-Rāzī, Fakhr al-Dīn (1149–1209 (AH 543–606)). Prominent Muslim theologian and philosopher, who contested *Mu'tazilites until compelled into exile, eventually settling in Herāt. There he founded a *madrasa and was accorded the title of *Shaykh al-Islām. He attracted many pupils, but because of his determination to show how theology and philosophy can be reconciled, he was accused by some of betraying Islam. His death may have been caused by poison.

al-Sādiq, Ja'far (sixth Shī'a Imām): see ISMĀ'ĪLIYYA.

al-Sanūsī, Sīdī Muḥammad (1791–1859 (AH 1206–76)). Founder of the Sanūsiya order (the Senusis). After a period in *Mecca, he returned to N. Africa, and at Jaghbūb, made freed slaves welcome. He was initiated into *Qadiriya mysticism, and attempted to harmonize orthodox practice with mystical attainment, with special emphasis on *dhikr.

al-Shāfi'i, Abū 'Abd Allāh Muḥammad (d. 820 (AH 204)). Founder of the *Shāfi'ite school of Muslim law (*sharī'a). He was taught by *Mālik b. Anas (amongst many others), but differed from him in paying particular attention to the methods of applying Qur'ān and *sunna, and for that reason is regarded as the founder of uṣūl al-*fiqh (the principles of fiqh). Thus he attempted to establish rules governing the exercise of *qiyās (analogy); but having done so, he was prepared to use it to establish a middle way between conservative traditionalism and innovation.

al-Shaikh al-Akbar: see IBN (AL)-'ARABĪ.

al-Shaybānī, Muḥammad b. al-Ḥasan: see HANAFITES.

al-Shaytan: see SATAN (ISLAM).

al-Shibli, Abū Bakr Dulaf b. Jahdar (*c*.861–945 (AH 247–334)). *Sūfī mystic of Baghdād. He was originally a high government official but turned to the mystic life at the age of 40. Although he belonged to *al-Junaid's sober school of Sufism, he distinguished himself as an extreme and eccentric Sūfī, whose excessive behaviours and practices (e.g. rubbing salt in his eyes to prevent sleep) led to his committal to a lunatic asylum, where he would offer discourses on the Sūfī way to distinguished visitors. His tomb in Baghdād is still venerated.

al-Sirhindī: see SŪFĪS.

al-Tabarī, abū Ja'far Muḥammad ibn Jarīr (*c*.839–923 (AH 224–310)). Prominent Muslim scholar, best known for his history of the world, *Ta'rīkh al-Rusul wa'l-Mulūk* (Chronicle of Apostles and Kings). He also composed a vast commentary (*tafsīr) on the *Qur'ān, in which he gathered together earlier exegesis on an equally large scale. It became a standard work of reference for later exegetes, and is used to the present day. He also founded a school of *sharī'a, known as Jariyya, but it was so close to the *Shāfi'ites that it did not persist.

Altar (Lat., *altare*, 'to raise up'). A structure, often raised, either natural or humanly made, usually with a flat surface, on which offerings are made to God or gods. In Hinduism, the *vedi* (altar) is the centre of the world, *axis mundi*, because the divine comes into the world at that point. The word *bēma* (Gk., 'altar') may refer to the whole sanctuary, *hiera/hagia trapeza* ('sacred/holy table') being reserved for the altar.

Altar of Earth. A structure built to the north of the old Inner City of Beijing (Peking) in 1530 CE, as a counterpart in symmetrical relationship to the *Altar of Heaven in the south. The original name of the complex was *fang tse* (literally, 'square watery place') altar, indicating that Sovereign Earth, worshipped there by late Ming and Ch'ing emperors on the summer solstice, was conceived as the chthonic spirit which ruled over the entire sublunary world, and thus the counterpart of Heaven.

Altar of Heaven. An architectural complex located south of the old Inner City of Beijing (Peking), just to the east of the north–south axial way. Venerated Chinese writings such as the *Classic of History* and the *Book of Rites* mention the Shang and early Chou emperors worshipping at 'suburban altars', and each of the succeeding dynasties built an Altar of Heaven south of their capital city for this purpose. Although Beijing's Altar of Heaven is the most recent example, a roofless, three-tiered circular platform constructed of concentric circles of paving stones. See also ALTAR OF EARTH.

Altered States of Consciousness. Neurophysiological states in which ordinary consciousness is suspended or replaced by other states. In this broad sense, sleep itself is an altered state of consciousness, but the phrase is used more often of induced states, ranging from those induced by drugs to those induced by meditation practices. Controversy has arisen over whether the states so induced are identical, or whether there is a difference in those which occur in religious contexts. However, the debate has made it clear that the phrase itself may be a category mistake, by giving the impression that there are discrete brain states which can be subsumed under this single heading.

Alternative Service Book 1980. *Church of England service-book. It is an 'alternative' to the *Book of Common Prayer to which it corresponds in content.

al-Tirmidhī, Abu 'Īsā Muḥammad (d. *c*.889 (AH 275)). Author of one of the six authoritative collections of *ḥadīth, which is known sometimes as **Ṣaḥīḥ*, but more often as *Jāmi'*. He was attentive to the reliability of the *isnād, as well as the content, and, as a result, his collection is shorter (and less repetitious) than those of *al-Bukhārī and *Muslim.

al-Ṭūsī, Muḥammad ibn Ḥasan (995–1067 (AH 385–460)). Leading *Shi'ite scholar. Born in Ṭūs (hence the name), he played an important part in stabilizing the religion in practice after the occultation (see *hidden Imām) of the twelfth *Imām. He collected Shi'ite traditions in *al-Istibṣār* (The Examination) and in *Tahdhīb al-Aḥkām* (The Correcting of Judgements), which form part of the 'Four Books' of authoritative traditions. Even more influential was his *Kitāb al-Nihāya* (The Book of Method), which lays out the basis of Shi'ite legal procedure, and which became the foundation of a legal school which endured for centuries after his death. After riots, during which his library was burnt, he moved to al-Najaf where he died.

al-Ṭūsī, Nasīr al-Dīn (1201–74 (AH 598–673)). Shi'ite scholar and theologian. Born in Ṭūs (hence the name), he worked under an *Ismā'īlī ruler in Alamūt (the centre for the *Assassins), and wrote Ismā'īlī works of accepted and great authority, but his own personal allegianace is uncertain. He compiled the astronomical tables known as *Zīj al-Khānī*, and introduced into astronomy 'the Ṭūsī couple'. Writing on virtually all subjects, his most enduring works were *al-Akhlāq al-Nāsiriyya* (1235, The Nasiriyyan Ethics) and *Tajrīd al-I'tiqādāt* (The Definition of the Articles of Faith).

al-Tustarī (Muslim theologian and mystic): see SAHL AL-TUSTARĪ.

Alumbrados (Span., also known from Lat., as *Illuminati). Movements for reform, based on personal holiness and enlightenment, in 16th/17th cent. Spain. At least three different groups have been identified, attracting both educated and uneducated adherents. Because of their supposed connection with *Lutheranism, they were fiercely persecuted by the *Inquisition; yet prominent figures (e.g. *Ignatius Loyola, *John of the Cross, *Teresa of Avila) were all accused of illuminism, illustrating how close were the goals of holiness for these diverse figures.

A-luo-ben (Persian Christian monk): see A-LO-PEN.

Āḻvārs (Tamil, 'saintly masters'). A group of (allegedly) twelve Hindu poets of the 6th to 9th cent. CE from South India. They wrote in the vernacular *Tamil on *Viṣṇu/*Kṛṣṇa religion, and their works were collected in the **Nāl-āyira-divya-prabandham*. Like their *Śaivite contemporaries (the *Nāyaṉmār), they promulgated a new, *bhakti-oriented form of religion in the South which soon gained enormous popularity. No external historical document about them is known. The traditional number is twelve, but because not all poems are 'signed' (in the concluding stanza), this cannot be verified from the *Divya-Prabandham* itself. Many of the traditional names by which they are referred to are honorific titles and differ from the names actually mentioned. The most important Āḻvārs are: *Nammāḻvār ('Our Saintly Master', real name: Caṭakōpaṉ); Tirumaṅkai-Āḻvār ('the Saintly Master from the region of Tirumaṅkai [near modern Sirkazhi]', real names: Parakālaṉ,

Kalikaṉṟi); Periyâḻvār ('the Great Saintly Master', real name: Viṭṭucittaṉ); Āṇṭāḷ ('the Lady', real name: Kōtai); and Kulacēkaraṉ ('Peak of his Lineage', his real name). Thus there is one woman among them (Āṇṭāḷ, allegedly the adopted daughter of Periyâḻvār).

Alwah (works of prophet-founder of Bahā'ī Faith): see BAHĀ'U'LLĀH.

al-Zamakhsharī, Abu'l-Qāsim Maḥmūd ibn ʿUmar (1075–1144 (AH 467–538)). Muslim grammarian and *Qur'ān commentator. He was born in the Khwārizm province of N. Persia, where, apart from a period of study in *Mecca, he spent most of his life. His commentary on the Qur'ān, *al-Kashshāf 'an Ḥaqā'iq Ghawāmid al-Tanzīl* (The Unveiler of the Truths of the Sciences of Revelation), takes each verse, phrase by phrase, and gives an interpretation which goes back to the theological rationality of the *Mu'tazilites. At the same time, al-Zamakhsharī's linguistic interests allowed him to make many points about the rhetorical and literary beauty of the Qur'ān, and this endeared the commentary to subsequent generations.

Ama, et fac quod vis (love and do what you will): see ETHICS (Christianity).

Amal (ritual power): see MAGI.

Amarakośa (Skt., 'deathless vocabulary'). Dictionary of classical Sanskrit, compiled by Amara-simha, a Buddhist of *c.*7th cent. CE.

Amarāvatī (Skt., 'abode of the deathless'). 1. The 'deathless' are the gods, hence A. is the abode of the gods, i.e., heaven. 'To enter Amarāvatī' = 'to die'.

2. A Buddhist ceremonial and pilgrimage centre situated along the Kistna river, Andhra Pradesh. The site dates from the Śuṅga period (185–75 BCE). However, the central building, the Great *Stūpa, is the most important structure dating from the late Āndhra (25 BCE–320 CE).

Amarāvikkhepikas (Pāli, 'eel-wrigglers'). A name in the Buddhist *Nikāyas for a school of sceptical philosophers who were contemporaries of the *Buddha. They are supposed to have refrained from giving any categorical answers on questions relating to ethics and speculative knowledge. They adopted the stance that things are intrinsically unknowable, and that, as a consequence, the only remaining worthwhile goal is the pursuit of subjective states of tranquillity.

Amar Dās, Gurū (1479–1574 CE). Third Sikh *Guru. Gurū Amar Dās, the son of Tej Bhān, was born into a Bhallā *Khatrī family to Lachhmī in Bāsarke village, *Amritsar District, *Pañjāb. In 1552 Amar Dās was installed as Gurū by *Aṅgad.

As Gurū, Amar Dās was responsible for establishing practices distinctively Sikh yet reminiscent of Hindu custom: (i) he instructed Sikhs to gather to worship the one God on the first days of the Hindu months, *Vaiśākhi (April–May), Māgha (Jan.–Feb.) and on *Dīvālī; (ii) he had a deep well dug at Goindvāl as a Sikh *tīrath; (iii) he provided distinctive rituals for birth and *death, replacing the Sanskrit *śaloks with *hymns of the Gurūs; (iv) also ascribed to Gurū Amar Dās is the *Mohan Pothī*, a two-volume collection of hymns (composed by himself, his two predecessors, and six bhagats, *Kabīr, *Nāmdev, Trilochan, Seiṇ, *Ravidās, and Jaidev), which served as a nucleus for Gurū *Arjan Dev's compilation of the Ādi Granth; (v) Gurū Amar Dās emphasized the importance of the *Gurū-kā-laṅgar in the motto '*pahale paṅgat picche saṅgat*', i.e. 'First sit in a laṅgar row, then sit in the congregation.' This denial of *caste distinction antagonized the *brahmans.

Aged 95, Amar Dās died at Goindvāl.

Amaterasu-ō-Mikami (Jap., 'heavenly-shining-deity'). The central deity (*kami) of the classical Shinto tradition. This female deity, usually associated with the sun, plays a central part in the most important myth cycles of Shinto, and subsequently in the ritual traditions of Shinto—especially as connected to the imperial household and the sense of a national religion. The mythologies tell us that she was born of the original parent deities, *Izanagi and Izanami, and became the ruling deity in the 'high heavenly plain' (*takama-no-hara*) where the myriad heavenly deities dwell. Subsequently, she sent her grandson, Ninigi, to subjugate and rule the land of Japan. Out of this process the earthly kami were subjugated to the heavenly kami, and the imperial line came into being.

As the ancestral deity of the imperial family, Amaterasu was enshrined in the central shrines of Shinto at *Ise. There, through the centuries, emperors and peasants alike have worshipped her, sought her help in times of trouble, and appealed to her life-giving power of renewal—especially on behalf of the whole nation.

Amba. Title of the Christian *Coptic *patriarch.

Ambā, Ambikā. One of the names of the Hindu Goddess. Literally it means 'mother', like the related *ammā/ammaṉ. A particular goddess-figure is denoted by it only in the context of regional cults centred on temples.

Ambapālī. A beautiful courtesan of Vesali and devotee of the *Buddha. She eventually renounced the world, gained insight into impermanence through contemplating the ageing of her own body, and attained *arhatship.

Ambedkar, Bhīmrāo Rām (1891–1956). Indian lawyer and politician, also known as Babasaheb. Born the fourteenth child of untouchable (Mahar) parents in Indore State he succeeded, against all the odds, in graduating from Elphinstone College in 1912. His career developed on two fronts: he was called to the bar in 1923, and became Principal of the Government Law College, Bombay. Politically, he became active fighting for the rights of untouchables. In 1924 he founded an organization for the 'moral and material progress of untouchables' and employed the technique of *satyāgraha (passive resistance) in a successful attempt to allow untouchable access to Hindu temples and tanks. Shortly before his death he initiated the Bharatiya Buddha Mahasabha as an organization to promote the spread of Buddhism in India. Deprived of his strong leadership many untouchable converts to Buddhism have since reverted to Hinduism.

Ambrose, St (*c*.339–97). *Bishop of Milan. He was trained in rhetoric and law, and assumed the *see in *c*.374, after having been civil governor. He was famous as a preacher and champion of orthodoxy (e.g. against the *Arians). He was a strong advocate of *monasticism, writing on asceticism, and also interpreting Eastern theology for the West. He is one of the four original *Doctors of the W. Church. Feast day, usually 7 Dec.

AMDG (Lat., Ad Maiorem Dei Gloriam, 'to the greater glory of God'). The motto of the *Jesuits, but it appears more widely as well.

Amen (Heb., 'So be it'). An individual or congregational endorsement of a *prayer or *blessing. In Islam, the form is *āmīn*, spoken as a form of inclusion and assent to the words of prayer.

Ame no Koyane. One of four *kamis of the Kasuga shrine in *Nara. Ame no Koyane cooperated with *Amaterasu and *Hachiman to establish and then endorse the Japanese imperial system.

American Jewish Committee. Oldest Jewish defence organization, founded in 1906. It was formed in response to the extensive Russian *pogroms of the time, and it lobbied for a liberal US immigration policy. From this committee grew the American Jewish Relief Committee and other philanthropic organizations, and it has sponsored numerous publications including *The American Jewish Yearbook*.

Amesa Spentas. The 'Bounteous' (or Holy) Immortals in Zoroastrianism. *Zoroaster mentions a number of heavenly forces, the creations of, and therefore subservient to, *Ahura Mazda, but powers through which Ahura and his worshippers are linked. In the later tradition they form a coherent system of seven beings, although there is some difference about which figures are included in the seven, notably whether Ahura is himself one of the seven or not (in which case the ancient figure of Sraosa becomes one instead). Each of the seven protects one of the seven creations which is represented in major rituals by its symbol. The Amesa Spentas are, therefore, part of theology and liturgy. Apart from Ahura Mazda, and his unique Holy Spirit (Spenta Mainyu) each of these forces represents both an aspect of Ahura and a feature of the good Zoroastrian. The six other than Ahura are: (i) Vohu Manah, the Good Mind; (ii) Asa, righteousness or truth; (iii) Armaiti, spoken of as feminine, represents devotion; she is the personification of faithful obedience, harmony, and worship, and is said to have appeared visibly to Zoroaster; (iv) Khsathra, the personification of Ahura's might, majesty, dominion, and power; (v) and (vi), Haurvatat and Ameretat, two feminine beings, always mentioned together in the texts, representing wholeness, totality, or fullness (often translated as integrity). Haurvatat is the personification of what salvation means to the individual. Ameretat, literally deathlessness, is the other aspect of salvation—immortality.

ʿAm ha-Arez (Heb., 'people of the land'). In biblical Hebrew, the term refers to the general population, particularly that of Palestine, which harassed the returning Jewish *exiles. In the era of the second *Temple, the ʿam ha-arez were contrasted with the observant *pharisees, and in rabbinic times the term was pejorative to indicate those who were not scholarly and well-versed in *Torah.

Amice. A Christian *eucharistic vestment. It is an ornamented linen neckcloth worn above the *alb so as to form a kind of collar.

Amida or **Amita.** In Far Eastern Buddhism the name of the principal *Buddha of the *Pure Land lineages, the Jap. pronunciation of the Chinese transliteration (O-mi-t'o) of the Skt. (Amita, 'Immeasurable One'). The titles Amitābha (Skt., 'He of Immeasurable Light') and *Amitāyus (Skt., 'He of Immeasurable Life') are, contrary to the Tibetan tradition, regarded by the Japanese as synonyms for Amida. The invocation (*nembutsu) to Amida is *namu Amida butsu*, 'veneration to the Buddha Amida', the 'Original Vow'. In Chinese, it is *namo o-mi-to-fo*, 'veneration to Amitābha'.

For the basic text, *Amida-kyō*, see SUKHĀVATĪVYŪHA. See also AMITĀYUS.

ʼAmidah (Heb., 'standing'). A Jewish prayer consisting of eighteen *benedictions which is a core part of the structure of each of the three daily services. It is also known as the Shemoneh-Esreh ('eighteen') or, in *Talmudic sources, as *ha-tefillah* ('the prayer'). It is said standing (facing in the direction of Jerusalem), and is recited in different forms on weekdays, *Sabbaths, and *festivals.

Āmīn (so be it): see AMEN.

Amish. A group of strict *Mennonites now settled mainly in the eastern USA, particularly in Ohio, Pennsylvania, and Indiana. The sect originated at the end of the 17th cent. with Jacob Ammann (*c.*1644–*c.*1725), a Swiss minister who insisted on strict discipline, including avoidance of those under the ban of excommunication, even within the family. Members of the sect began to emigrate to N. America soon after 1700. They now number about 130,000.

The 'Old Order' Amish separate themselves from the society around them by retaining the dress and customs of that early period. There is no missionary activity, and marriage is always within the Amish community; the growth or maintenance of their numbers is due to the large size of families. Some other Amish groups, in various ways more liberal, have separated from the Old Order Amish.

Amitābha (Pure Land Buddha): see AMIDA.

Amitābha-Sūtra. One of the three basic *sutras of the *Pure Land School (with **Amitāyurdhyāna-Sūtra* and **Sukhāvatīvyūha*). It survives in Chinese translations, and describes the fundamental practice of reciting Amitābha's name (*Amida).

Amitāyurdhyāna-Sūtra ('Sūtra on Contemplation on *Amitāyus'). One of the three basic *sūtras of the *Pure Land School (with **Amitābha-Sūtra* and **Sukhāvatīvyūha*). It describes the pure land and the moral life which prepares for it.

Amitāyus (Skt.; Tib., *tshe.dpag.med*, 'Limitless Life'). In Tibetan Buddhism an aspect of *Amida/Amitābha (Skt.; Tib., *'d.dpag.med*, 'Limitless Light') concerned with long life. Amitāyus is generally portrayed surrounded by his 108 *emanations, each of which have separate names which, recited together, form the *mantra of the practice devoted to him. In Japanese Buddhism, Amitāyus is simply an epithet, rather than an aspect of Amitābha.

Ammā (Skt., Marathi, etc.), **Amman̠** (Tamil, etc.). Literally 'mother' (compare AMBĀ, AMBIKĀ). It is frequently used with reference to Hindu goddesses, and appears in compound names of regional and local *grāmadevatās, etc., e.g. *Māriyamnam, *Yellammā.

Ammann, Jacob: see AMISH.

Amoghasiddhi (Skt., 'the unerring achiever of the goal'). One of the five transcendent *Buddhas in *Mahāyāna and *Zen Buddhism. His *mudra is that of fearlessness, and his emblem is *vajra, the absolute and indestructible, as a diamond.

Amoghavajra (Chin., *Pu-k'ung Chin-kang*; Jap., *Fukū (kongō)*). An influential teacher of esoteric Buddhism in 8th cent. China, 6th patriarch of Chen-yen (*Shingon). He studied under Vajrabodhi, and the two together went to China in 720 and established esoteric Buddhism there. He spent about five years in India from 740, collecting Skt. texts, and on his return, he engaged in a major work of translation, numbering in the end more than 100 works. He based his own teaching especially on *Vajraśekhara-Sūtra*, a wisdom text. He was given the title Kuang-chih San-tsang (Kōchi Sanzō) in 765.

Amoraim (Aramaic, 'spokesmen'). Jewish scholars who interpreted the *Mishnah in Palestine and Babylonia between 200 CE and 500 CE. Those scholars ordained by the *nasi and the *Sanhedrin in Palestine were given the title *'Rabbi' whereas the Babylonian scholars were known as 'Rav'.

Amos (8th cent. BCE). A *prophet of the northern kingdom. The biblical book of his prophecy is considered to be the earliest of the prophetic books.

ʼAmr b. ʻUbaid (co-founder of Islamic theological school): see MUʻTAZILITES.

ʼAmr ibn al-ʼAṣ (d. 663 (AH 42)). Muslim statesman. A Qurayshite, ʼAmr was a late convert to Islam, but the Prophet *Muḥammad recognized his talents and immediately sent him as an envoy to Oman where he met with great success. His real fame rests as the conqueror of Egypt during *ʻUmar's caliphate. He held Egypt by his political skills and even seems to have gained the support of the *Coptic Church. At the battle of Siffin, ʼAmr commanded *Muʻawiyyah's cavalry against *ʼAlī, and devised the plan of arbitration by *Qur'ān. Muʻawiyyah rewarded ʼAmr's faithful service by appointing him governor of Egypt, where he remained until his death.

Amrit (Pañjābī, 'undying'; Skt., 'ambrosia'). The nectar of immortality. For Sikhs, amrit has several related meanings. 'Taking amrit' (amrit *chhakaṇā*) means receiving initiation (*amritsanskar*) at the *khaṇḍe-dī-pāhul ceremony with sweetened baptismal water. In popular usage, amrit is often holy water believed to have healing properties, especially water which has been close to the *Ādi Granth during a *pāṭh (reading). Used metaphorically in the Ādi Granth, amrit suggests both immortality and sweetness particularly as a result of meditation upon God's name (*nām simaran), e.g. 'Ambrosial (amrit) is the True Name' (Ādi Granth 33). The 'amrit velā' is the hour before dawn especially precious for prayer. See AMRITDHĀRĪ; AMRITSAR.

Amritdhārī (*Pañjābī, 'one who has received amrit'). An initiated Sikh.

Amritsanskar (Sikh initiation): see AMRIT.

Amritsar (*Pañjābī, 'pool of nectar'). Sikhs' spiritual capital. Amritsar, *Pañjāb, is 400 km. NNW of Delhi and 30 km. from Pakistan. It is especially holy to Sikhs on account of the *Harimandir (Golden Temple). Amritsar, first known as Gurū kā Chak, Rāmdāspur, and Chak Rām Dās, was founded 1577 CE by Gurū *Rām Dās, who built a brick temple there. The city took its name from the pool. In 1984, the Indian army stormed the Harimandir to dislodge Sikh militants.

In 1919, many Sikhs who, disregarding the Rowlatt Acts, had gathered on *Vaisākhī in Jalliānwālā Bāgh, were killed by British soldiers under the command of Brigadier General Dyer. This event, of great significance for the Independence movement in India, and for establishing 'minimum force' as a rule in crowd control, is known as the Amritsar massacre.

Amṛta (Skt., 'not-death'). The nectar of immortality, as in *Amrit; but in Hinduism (especially *Vedas), it is *soma.

Aṁśa (share of the gods): see ĀDITYAS.

Aṃśāvatāra (partial incarnation of Hindu deity): see AVATĀRA.

Amulets: see CHARMS.

Anabaptists ('re-baptizers'). Various *radical or left-wing *Reformation groups who reinstated the *baptism of believers on profession of personal faith. Two Zürich Reformers, Conrad Grebel and Felix Manz, formed the first congregation at Zollikon in 1525 (later called 'the Swiss Brethren'). Others were established in Moravia, led by Jacob Hutter (so Hutterites), in S. Germany, led by Balthasar Hubmaier and Hans Denck, and in NW Germany and the Low Countries, inspired by Melchior Hoffmann, a leader who combined unorthodox *christology and *millenarianism with deep piety. Forced by persecution to leave their homes, many Anabaptists came to regard baptism as initiation into Christian suffering, with Christ as the proto-martyr of their faith. Some Anabaptist exiles, influenced by the fanatical views of Jan Matthys and Jan Bockelson (John of Leyden), introduced polygamy in the city of Münster (1533–5) which was eventually besieged. The episode was not only a stigma on Anabaptism, but led inevitably to increased persecution with the loss of many thousands of lives. The Münster débâcle also issued in a fresh definition of Anabaptist thought by writers such as Dirk Philips, and especially Menno Simons, whose spirituality, pacifism, and social ideals continue to be treasured by the *Mennonites.

Anāgāmin (Skt., Pāli, 'not-returner'). Theravādin Buddhist who is free of the five fetters (*saṃyojana) and is on the third stage of the path towards attainment (*ārya-mārga).

Anāgārika (Pāli, 'without home'). Groups in India, before and during the time of the *Buddha, who had left home for a more ascetic life.

Anagogical Interpretation (Gk., *anago*, 'I lead up'). Interpretations of scripture (*hermeneutics) which point to the meaning of a text in relation to its eternal or heavenly meaning: it is the spiritual sense of scripture which anticipates what the Church is or will be in heaven. See ALLEGORY.

Anahana (Jap., from Skt., *ānāpāna). Awareness of *breathing in *Zen Buddhism, as a natural rhythm.

Anāhata-śabda (Skt., 'not-struck sound'). Awareness of pure sound beneath audible sounds (as of *Brahman underlying appearances).

Analects. Accepted English rendering of *Lun Yü*, the *Dialogues* or *Conversations* of *Confucius and his personal disciples. It is one of the *Confucian Classics, considered by scholars to be the most nearly contemporary, verbatim transcription of some of the Master's sayings. The *Analects* is not only the cornerstone of the Confucian School, but has been one of the most influential books in all human history, studied and revered as much in other E. Asian civilizations as in China itself.

Analogy. A proportional similarity. Most theological discussion of analogy has been concerned with analogical predication, a mode of predication in which terms familiar in one context are used in an extended sense elsewhere. Thus it is claimed that terms like 'love', 'wisdom', and 'living', which are learnt in everyday contexts, are applied to God by analogy because of some relationship (e.g. likeness, exemplarity, participation, and causation) between God's perfections and these human attributes.

According to Thomas *Aquinas, such a mode of predication is midway between univocity and equivocation (*Summa Theologiae*, 1a, xiii. 5). Terms like 'family resemblance', 'open texture', and 'systematic equivocation', used in 20th-cent. analytic philosophy, may be regarded as akin to analogy. See also TANZĪH; NYĀYA (for *upamana*).

Anamchara (soul-friend): see CELTIC CHURCH.

Anamnesis (Gk., 'remembrance'). A prayer in the Christian *eucharist which follows the words of institution, commemorating the *passion, *resurrection, and *ascension of *Christ.

Ananaikyo. A New Sect Shinto organization (see SECT SHINTO) founded in 1949 by Nakano Yonosuke. It is deliberately eclectic: the name means 'the teaching' (*kyo*) of 'the three' (*ana*) and 'the five' (*nai*), referring to the religious traditions from which it draws inspiration. It practises *kami possession and ecstasy, through a technique known as *chinkon kishin*, 'stilling the self to become one with the kami'. The principal kami worshipped is Kuni Tokotachi no Mikoto.

Anan ben David (8th cent. BCE). Jewish Babylonian sage, regarded as the founder of *Karaism. According to Karaite legend, when the *exilarchate of Babylon was bestowed on Anan's younger brother, Anan consequently founded an alternative sect. His immediate followers, the Ananites, rejected the *Talmudic tradition and relied on the *Bible alone as the source of divine law. Anan's own book, *Sefer ha-Mitzvot* (Book of Precepts), became an important text in the later Karaite movement.

Ānanda (Skt.). 1. A chief disciple and first cousin of the *Buddha. Though not an intellectual, Ānanda could explain the 60,000 words of the Buddha and was known as the Dhammabhaṇḍāgārika, 'treasurer of the Teachings'.

2. Initially a qualitative attribute of *Brahmā, it became, especially in *Vedānta, the consciousness that is free from all entanglements in *samādhi. It is usually found in association with *sat and *cit, hence in the fused form, Satchidānanda, Being, Consciousness, Bliss. A *saṁnyāsin in the Śankara tradition is given the word ānanda as part of his name—e.g. Vivekānanda.

Ananda Marga (Skt., 'path of bliss'). Movement founded in India in 1955 by Shree Shree Anandamurti, known to his followers as Baba and regarded by them as a *thaumaturge or miracle-worker. Imprisoned in India in 1971 on a charge of murder and later released when Indira Gandhi fell from power, Anandamurti's career, as well as that of his movement, evoked controversy.

Though it has been suggested that this 'revolutionist' movement has several million adherents, the actual membership is undoubtedly very much smaller.

Ānandamayī Mā (1896–1982). Hindu responsive teacher and spiritual attainer, who reached the goal without studying the scriptures, and without a *guru. She was married at 12, but gave priority to spiritual development. She passed through the attainments of *yoga within six years, and she became known as 'the mother filled with bliss', instead of her original name, Nirmala Sundari Devi.

Anandamurti (founder): see ANANDA MARGA.

Anand Karaj (Sikh marriage): see MARRIAGE (SIKH).

Anand Marg: see ANANDA MARGA.

Anaṇḍpur (Sāhib) (*Pañjābī, '(respected) city of bliss'), Sikh holy place, in NE *Pañjāb. Gurū *Tegh Bahādur founded Anaṇḍpur in 1664, and it was here that in 1675 his son *Gobind received his severed head. This was cremated where *Gurdwārā Śīś Gañj now stands. For *Holā Mahallā, thousands flock to Anaṇḍpur and witness the *Nihaṅgs' swordplay in what is now an impressive Sikh centre. In 1972, the *Akālī Dal met at Anaṇḍpur and drew up the Anaṇḍpur Sāhib Resolution, which summarized Sikh aspirations for the designation of an enlarged Pañjāb as a Sikh homeland.

Anand Sāhib (Pañjābī, 'bliss'). Composition by Guru *Amar Dās, included as part of the *Ādi Granth. It can be found on pp. 917–22.

Ananites (movement): see ANAN BEN DAVID.

Ananta. *Śeṣa, 'the infinite one', the constantly coiling cosmic snake on which *Viṣṇu reclines.

Ānāpāna (Skt.). Control of *breathing in Hindu *yoga. Ānāpānasati (Pāli) is a corresponding Buddhist technique (in sixteen stages or ways), counting breaths in and out, which calms the mind and is a preparation for attainment of the *dhyānas. Cf. also Anahana in *Zen Buddhism.

Ānāpānasati: see ĀNĀPĀNA.

Anaphora (Gk., 'offering'). The central part of the Christian *eucharist, known in the West as the *canon), and in the East as the Eucharistic Prayer. The W. Syrian Annaphuras are variant liturgies which are claimed to go back to early days.

ʿAnas b. Mālik (d. 709/11 (AH 91/3)). A prolific transmitter of *ḥadīth who served the Prophet *Muḥammad as his servant from an early age, and grew up in his house.

Anat Anath. A Goddess worshipped widely in the ancient Near East, the consort of *Baʿal.

Anathema. A sentence of separation from a Christian congregation. The word is the equivalent of Heb. *ḥerem.

Anātman (Skt., 'not-self'; Pāli *anatta*). Fundamental perception in Buddhism that since there is no subsistent reality to be found in or underlying appearances, there cannot be a subsistent self or soul in the human appearance—in contrast to Hinduism, where the understanding of *ātman and *jīva is equally fundamental to its understanding of the human predicament and how to escape it. If all is subject to *dukkha (transience and the grief that arises from trying to find the non-transient within it), then human appearance is no exception. The human is constituted by five aggregates (*skandha) which flow together and give rise to the impression of identity and persistence through time. Thus even if there is 'no soul', there is at least that which has the nature of having that nature. There were major disputes about the best candidates for constituting this impression (see especially PUDGALA; ĀLAYA-VIJÑĀNA), but agreement was in general reached that there is no soul which, so to speak, sits inside the human body, like the driver of a bus, and gets out at the end of the journey. There is only the aggregation of components, which is caused by the previous moment and causes the next. Thus while there is momentarily some one person who is rightly identified as the Dalai Lama, there is no one person who the Dalai Lama always is (cf. **Milindapañha*). In *Mahāyāna Buddhism, this term was extended to apply to all appearance which arises from *Śūnyatā and is therefore devoid of substance, empty of self.

Anatta: see ANĀTMAN.

Anbhav Prakash. Experience of *enlightenment among Sikhs. It is the perception of reality which means that a person has become centred on God (*gurmukh).

Ancestors. The maintaining of ancestors in memory is a fundamental part of religious life and practice. Even during the millennia in which belief in personal life after death was extremely rare, this remembering—and often veneration—of ancestors was extensive. Yet the term 'ancestor-worship' is usually misleading (see AFRICAN RELIGION): it is not so much that ancestors were worshipped as that they continued in relation to the living family, both sustaining it (provided they were in fact appropriately remembered) and being sustained by it. If they were forgotten or neglected, they might well turn into restless or hungry or avenging figures. Rituals therefore developed to ensure proper respect to these continuing members of the family, as well as to provide means of consulting them.

Anchorite, Anchoress (Gk., *anachōreō*, 'withdraw'). One who withdraws from the world in order to offer prayer and mortification, frequently understood in sacrificial terms. Anchorites are precursors of the development of *monasticism, and are related to the hermits who are attached to monastic orders (e.g. among *Camaldolese or *Carthusians). The term became more strictly applied to those who live in a cell (restricted dwelling-place). In the later M. Ages, such cells were sometimes attached to parish churches. *Julian of Norwich is (thought to be) a notable example.

Andrew, St. One of the twelve *apostles of *Jesus. He was the brother of *Peter, and is mentioned by name in several stories in the gospels (e.g. John 6. 8). According to the *Acts of Andrew*, a 3rd-cent. work now partly lost, he was crucified in Patras in Greece. The tradition that his cross was X-shaped goes back no further than the 10th cent. He is *patron saint of Russia and of Scotland. Feast day, 30 Nov.

Andrewes, Lancelot (1555–1626). *Anglican *bishop. In 1601 he became Dean of Westminster, was consecrated bishop in 1605, becoming bishop of Winchester in 1619. He was famous as a preacher, and it is on his sermons and his *Preces Privatae* (Private Prayers) that his importance rests. T. S.*Eliot regarded his sermons as ranking 'with the finest English prose of their time, of any time' (*For Lancelot Andrewes*): 'He takes a word and derives a world from it.'

Anekāntavāda (Skt., *anekānta* = 'non-one-sidedness' or 'manysidedness'). In Jain philosophy, the doctrine of the manysidedness of reality. The doctrine claims that seven assertions, apparently contradictory, but perfectly true, can be made about anything: (i) *syādasti*, maybe it truly is (for example, a cold room); (ii) *syānnāsti*, maybe it truly is not (if you enter it from a colder one); (iii) *syādastināsti*, maybe it truly is and is not (two different people's opposite statements could be true); (iv) *syādavaktarya*, maybe it is exhaustively indescribable (if two opposite statements are relatively true); (v) *syādastyavaktarya*, maybe it is and is indescribable; (vi) *syānnāst yavaktavya*, maybe it is not and is undescribable; (vii) *syādastināstyavaktavya*, maybe it is and is not and is indescribable.

Aṅga (Skt., 'limb, part'). 1. The eight steps of *Rāja-Yoga in Hinduism.

2. A Jain term to denote the twelve 'limbs' of revered and basic texts. Among Jains, 'scripture' is a fluid, even a contested, concept (see DIGAMBARA). The Śvetāmbara have a *'canon', defined by 19th-cent, European scholars as the '45 text canon', but while this defines the core texts, more texts are revered, and groups among the Śvetāmbara do not identify identical texts. Nevertheless, the basic texts for both Digambara and Śvetāmbara are the Twelve Aṅgas, but Śvetāmbara believe (xii) below to be lost: (i) *Ācāra-aṅga* ('Behaviour', rules for ascetics); (ii) *Sūtrakṛta-aṅga* ('On Heretical Views', attitudes to rituals, and to other views); (iii) *Sthāna-aṅga* ('Possibilities', options especially, in relation to *jīva, and numerical descriptions; (iv) *Samavāya-aṅga* ('Combinations', similarities, as in (iii), also describing the aṅgas); (v) Digambara, *Vyākhyā-prajñapti-aṅga*; Śvetāmbara, *Bhagavatī-aṅga* ('Explanations Expounded', 60,000 questions, and answers, to, and from, the *tīrthaṅkaras); (vi) *Jñātradharma-katha-aṅga* ('Accounts of *Jñāna and *Dharma'); (vii) *Upāsakādhayna-aṅga* ('Ten Chapters on Lay Responsibilities', the vows and rules of conduct for lay people, especially for the eleven stages of a householder's life); (viii) *Antakṛddaśā-aṅga* ('Ten Chapters on End-Achievers', the extreme methods of ten ascetics who freed themselves from *karma); (ix) *Anuttaraupapādikadaśa-aṅga* ('Ten Chapters on Arisers in Heaven', on ten ascetics who are reborn in the five heavens, *anuttaravimāna)*; (x) *Praśnavyākaraṇa-aṅga* ('Questions and Expositions', instructions on how to reply to questions); (xi) *Vipākasūtra-aṅga* ('Text on Ripening', an exploration of Karma); (xii) *Dṛṣṭipravāda-aṅga* ('Disputation about Views, parts only, divided into five parts, *Parikarma* (on the geography of earth and sky), *Sūtra* (on false views), *Prathamānuyoga* (on sixty-three illustrious figures), fourteen *Pūrvaguta* (in fourteen sections), and five *Cūlikā* (on magical skills).

Associated with the twelve aṅgas, are for Śvetāmbara, twelve dependent texts (*upaṅgas*). Also revered are six Cedasūtras, four Mūlas ('Root') sūtras (the foundation of an ascetic life), ten Prakīrṇakas and two Cūikāsūtras. The Śvetāmbara 'canon' is said to have been fixed at the Assembly at Valabhī (453 or 466 CE), but there is no list of what was actually agreed.

3. In Buddhism, the nine (or twelve) 'branches' within the *canon of literary types: *sutta* (*sūtra), *geyya* (recitation), *veyyākaraṇa* (prophecies), *gāthā* (verse), *udāna* (solemn pronouncement), *ittivuttaka* (discourses beginning, 'This has been said by the master'), *jātaka, *abhutadhamma* (stories of accomplishments), *vedalla* (analysis and explication). In N. (Skt.) Buddhism the three additional aṅgas are *nidāna* (linking introduction), *avadāna (biographies), and *upadeśa* (explanations).

Aṅgad, Gurū. (1504–52). Second Sikh Gurū. Lehṇā (Lahaṇā) as he was originally called, a Trehaṇ *Khatrī, lived at Khaḍūr, *Pañjāb. His devotion to *Durgā turned to loyal service of Gurū *Nānak at *Kartārpur. Impressed by his selfless obedience, Nānak renamed him Aṅgad (Pañjābī *aṅg*, 'part of one's body'), and proclaimed him his successor rather than the disappointed *Srī Chand.

Angel (Gk., *angelos*, 'messenger'). An intermediary between heaven and earth. In the early religious imagination of the Jews, the connection between heaven and earth was thought to be literal, as in the attempt to build a tower of Babel (Genesis 11. 1–9). For that reason, *Jacob had a vision of angels ascending and descending a ladder between *heaven and earth (Genesis 28. 12). It was only later (perhaps under Persian influence) that they developed their own means of propulsion with wings. There are various references to angels (Heb., *malakhim*, 'messengers') in the *Bible. Later reflection named many (e.g. *Gabriel, *Michael, *Metatron, *Raphael, *Raziel, *Uriel): they carry prayers to God, they teach *Torah to each embryo in the womb, and they accompany Jewish fathers as they walk home on the evening of *Sabbath.

Jewish angelology was taken over by early Christianity. Catholic teaching includes few pronouncements on angels, but enjoins a cult similar to that of the *saints. In Christianity, the notion of fallen angels is developed further. These refuse to return or acknowledge the sovereignty and love of God: they are not destroyed but have a limited scope of subversive activity.

In Islam, angels (Arab., *malā'ika*, pl., of *malak*) are 'messengers with wings' (Qur'ān 35. 1, the *sūra of angels). They were created before humans, and protested to Allāh at his plan to create human beings (2. 30–3), though they agreed to bow down to *Adam (2. 34), except for Iblīs (see DEVIL).

The angel of revelation is Jibrīl (*Gabriel), who 'brings down (the revelation) to your heart, by Allah's permission' (2. 97), and he is mentioned together with Mikā'īl (2. 98). The angel of death (32. 11) is not named, but tradition calls him 'Izrā'il, while the angel who will announce the Day of Judgement is Isrāfīl. Two angels, *Munkar and Nakīr, question people, on their first night in the grave, about Muḥammad: if they answer that he is *rasūl

*Allāh, the messenger of God, they are left in peace until *Yaum al-Qiyama, the day of Resurrection. For others, there ensues the 'punishment in the tomb'.

Angel of Death. God's messenger who brings *death to human beings. There is no constant figure of the angel of death in the *Bible, but in the *Talmud, *Satan and the evil *inclination are both identified with him. For Islam, see ANGEL.

Angelus. A Catholic thrice-daily devotion (early morning, noon, and evening), consisting of three *Ave Marias with *versicles and a *collect.

Angelus Silesius (1624–77). Joannes Scheffler, Christian mystical writer and controversialist. A *Lutheran who, in 1653, became RC, he was ordained priest in 1661. Remembered for his mystical poems, the collection *Heilige Seelenlust* (1657) interprets the mystical life in the imagery of the *Song of Songs; and *Der Cherubinische Wandersmann* (1675) is deeply influenced by the tradition of German mysticism inspired by *Eckhart.

Angkor. Capital in central Cambodia of the Khmers, a people of N. Indo-Chinese origin, established by Yaśovarman II (889–910 CE). A successor in the dynasty, Sūryavarman II (1112–52), raised Angkor Wāt (*wāt*, 'city temple') on the site as a fortress-temple dedicated to Devarāja and to himself as an *avatāra of *Viṣṇu.

Close by is Angkor Thom which was established as a new capital by Jayavarman VII (1181–*c.*1210), with the Bayon as its ceremonial centre.

Anglican Chant. The music of the Psalms and canticles as sung in many Anglican churches, developed out of the *plainchant psalm-tones about the end of the 17th cent. See also liturgical use of PSALMS.

Anglicanism, from the Latin *Anglicana ecclesia* (lit., English Church), as found in clause 1 of *Magna Carta*, 1215, used to differentiate the 'English Church' from the Church elsewhere in Europe even if under the jurisdiction of the king of England: it was subsequently, in the Act of Supremacy in 1534, described as the *Church of England, which Henry VIII also described as *Anglicana Ecclesia* to distinguish it as the Church over which he alone had the power of authority and reform. 'Anglicanism' is now used to describe the diverse character, practice, and faith of 37 autonomous Churches of the international Anglican Communion and its *c.*70 million members world-wide. It is held together by the *Lambeth Conferences, Primates' meetings, and the Anglican Consultative Council. Structurally, therefore, it resembles the diffused but collegial responsibilities of the *Orthodox Church much more than it does the centralizing control of the *Vatican in *Roman Catholicism. In different parts of the Anglican Communion it may carry a different name, as e.g. ECUSA (the *Episcopal Church in the USA), the Church of Ireland, the Scottish Episcopal Church, Nippon Sei Ko Kai (the Holy Catholic Church of Japan). In addition to the Provinces of Canterbury and York, the main Churches and Provinces are in Aotearoa, New Zealand and Polynesia; Australia; Brazil; Burundi; Canada; Central Africa; Indian Ocean; Ireland; Japan; Jerusalem and the Middle East; Kenya; Korea; Melanesia; Mexico; Myanmar; Nigeria; Papua New Guinea; Philippines; Rwanda; Scotland; SE Asia; S. Africa; S. Cone of America; Sudan; Tanzania; Uganda; USA; Wales; W. Africa; W. Indies; Zaire.

Anglicanism is an episcopal (with *bishops) Church, in continuity with Catholicism, but also accepting much from the *Reformation. It is thus described as 'both Catholic and reformed'. The *via media* 'Reformed Catholicism' of the 17th cent. 'Caroline Divines' is deemed more in keeping with the spirit of Anglicanism today than the strong Protestantism of Bishop Jewel's earlier *Apology of the Church of England* (1562); and *via media* has often been used as a description of Anglicanism. This 'comprehensiveness' is the experience of shared and tolerating faith which characterizes such Anglicans as Richard *Hooker, William *Temple and Desmond *Tutu.

There is nevertheless a common focus in that Anglican theology is based on an appeal to scripture, tradition, and reason, expanded in the dictum of Lancelot *Andrewes: 'One *canon, ... two *testaments, three *creeds, four general *councils, five centuries and the series of *fathers in that period ... determine the boundary of our faith.' Comprehensiveness involves a necessary agreement on certain 'Fundamentals' (as the 1968 Lambeth report stressed) and a containing of both Protestant and Catholic elements in a national Church. It may thus still be 'the privilege of a particular vocation', as the 1948 Lambeth Conference held, for the Anglican Communion to contain in microcosm the diversity elsewhere divided into disparate denominations.

Anglicanism's pioneering role in *ecumenicism had an early start (e.g., individual explorations of reunion with the Orthodox), but takes its rise in modern times from the Chicago-Lambeth Quadrilateral (usually referred to simply as the Lambeth Quadrilateral) of 1888, prompted by W. R. Huntingdon's *The Church Idea* (1870). It identifies four elements 'on which approach may be, by God's blessing, made toward Home Reunion', namely, the holy scriptures as containing all things necessary for salvation, the Creeds as the sufficient statement of Christian faith, the sacraments of *baptism and *Holy Communion, and 'the Historic Episcopate, locally adapted in the methods of its administration to the varying needs of the nations called of God into the Unity of His Church.' There have been some practical results, as in the former Churches of N. and S. India: Methodists and Anglicans are close to recovering the unity from which they began; in 1993, conversations between British and Irish Anglican Churches and Nordic and Baltic Lutheran Churches produced the Porvoo *Common Statement* (the Porvoo Declaration, 1993), which called for a relationship of communion, with structures for collegial consultation and interchangeable ministries; this was approved by participating Churches in 1995. Otherwise, there have been continuing agreed statements and conversations, as with Lutherans, Reformed Churches, Orthodoxy and Roman Catholics (see ARCIC).

Underlying all of the foregoing has been a long and deep commitment to a practical spirituality.

It is a tradition in which a creationist poet like Thomas *Traherne, an apologist like C. S. *Lewis, or a writer like T. S. *Eliot can equally explore God's truth in Christ in relation to the glory and misery and mystery of life; it is a tradition which turned *Wilberforce to the abolition of slavery and Archbishop Trevor Huddleston to the abolition of apartheid. It is the theological and spiritual context in which an incarnational sacramentalism prevails.

Anglican/Roman Catholic International Commission: see ARCIC.

Anglo-Catholics. *Anglicans who embrace *Catholic doctrines, especially of the *church and *sacraments, stressing continuity from the early Church.

Angra Mainyu (Pahlavi Ahriman). The 'Destructive Spirit' or 'devil' in *Zoroastrianism. He is thought to have existed 'from the beginning', independent of *Ahura Mazda (i.e. he is coeval). Angra Mainyu is the source of all that is evil, of pollution (e.g. the smoke afflicting the good flame of the fire), of that which destroys (e.g. decay and rust), of misery, suffering, and death. By instinct his will is to destroy. To aid him in his conflict with the Good Creation he (mis-)created the demon forces, the *daevas, such as Wrath, Greed, Procrastination. In the material world, his work is carried out by the creatures who embody his destructive aims, the *khrafstras*. Azi Dahaka is the personification of the Lie, often depicted in mythology as a terrible dragon with three heads, six eyes, and three jaws, whose body is full of *khrafstras*. In modern Zoroastrian thought, Angra Mainyu is commonly demythologized and interpreted as an evil tendency within human nature.

Anguttara-Nikāya (Pāli, 'graduated collection'). The fourth part of the Sūtra-*piṭaka of the Buddhist Pāli canon.

Angya (Jap., 'wander on foot'). Pilgrimage of *unsui (Zen monk who has completed the first phase of his training), preferably through dangerous territory, as a test of his detachment.

Anicca (Pāli, 'impermanent', 'not enduring'), **Anitya** (Skt.), One of the *Three Marks of Existence in Buddhism. The teaching of the impermanence or transitoriness of all things is central to the whole of Buddhist philosophy and practice. It involves the affirmation, as a truth statement, that all phenomena, both mental and physical, are without exception impermanent.

There are various ways in which the truth of the universality of impermanence is spoken of. Figuratively, the action of time is compared to the wheel of a moving chariot (which only touches the ground at one point at a time), an ever-flowing mountain stream, a bubble, a mirage, the sound of a bell. Analytically, 'impermanence', is to be observed in the fact that all things exist in dependence on something else, arise out of and become something else: no thing exists in isolation, no thing possesses stability. It is precisely in this respect that *nirvāna is to be understood as the direct antithesis of anicca, that is, as comprising duration, stability, and permanence, and why it is regarded as worthy of our aspiration, unlike the things of this world. The teaching on anicca links up with the Buddhist doctrine of 'dependent origination' (*paticca-samuppāda) which states that 'all things have a beginning' and that 'all things with a beginning must have an end'; the doctrine of anicca draws attention to the fact of their demise. The paramount importance of anicca in Buddhist teaching is spotlighted in the Buddha's last words, 'decay is inherent in all things'.

In consequence of all this, Buddhism teaches the practice of *aniccānupassanā* ('contemplation of impermanence'; cf. VIPASSANĀ) as the way of realizing the truth of impermanence. The actual process of contemplation involves 'watching' the rise or appearance of a given datum, verifying its 'dependent' or 'caused' origin; then, by the same token, 'watching' its subsidence or disappearance and verifying its transient characteristic.

Acceding intellectually to the truth of impermanence is termed in Buddhism the acquisition of 'right view' (*sammā-diṭṭhi*; see AṢṬANGIKA-MĀRGA) and is synonymous with entry on to the path to enlightenment.

Ani Ma'amin (Heb., 'I believe'). A short Jewish creed of unknown authorship. It is based on *Maimonides' principles of the Jewish faith (*articles of faith), and dates back at least to the 15th cent. More particularly, it is the title of Elie Wiesel's cantata, for which see the HOLOCAUST.

Animals. The resemblances between many animals and humans, not least in their dependence on food and air, has given to animals a special status in all religions. Thus it has been widely believed that suprahuman realities, not least divine and diabolic, can take on the form of animals. They can also epitomize, in the form of *totems, the networks of relationship which constitute a human society. Bearing, as they do, the obvious signs of vitality, animals have been a major part of *sacrifice, becoming instrumental in expressing the many needs which humans have felt in their relation to God and to each other. Some religions (e.g. Islam) have retained animal sacrifice (*'Id al-Aḍḥā), but others have reacted strongly against the efficacy of such acts (e.g. Buddhism and Jainism). However, even in religions where the sacrifice of animals has taken, or does take, place, animals may be given a high and revered status. Judaism and Islam emphasize that they come from the hand of the Creator, and while they are to some extent given to humans for their use and food (e.g. Qur'ān 16. 5–8), this is within limits, and must always be in the context of kindness. Among Hindus, there is a controlling sense that that which alone is truly real (whether conceived of as *Brahman or as God) underlies and guarantees the subsistence of all appearance: 'This form is the source and indestructible seed of innumerable incarnations within the cosmos, and from it the appearances of all different living beings are created, heavenly beings, animals, humans, and all other kinds. . . . Thus you should regard deer, camels, monkeys, donkeys, rats, reptiles, birds and flies as though they are your own children' (*Śrimad-Bhagavatam*). This underlying attitude is epitomized in the sacred cow (*go). Not surprisingly, animals can be the focus of worship and in particular can be the forms of incarnation (*avatāra). The principle of *ahiṁsā, emphasized and reinforced among Jains and Buddhists, led to a strong preference for vegetarianism (for this issue in general, see FOOD). An attempt to mobilize the resources of religion for greater care of the environment and of animals within it was made in the Assisi meetings and declarations in 1986.

Anima naturaliter Christiana ('naturally Christian soul'): see TERTULLIAN.

Animism. The belief that perhaps all appearances, but certainly living appearances, are animated by spirits (are made vital by an *anima*, Lat., 'spirit'). *Tylor introduced the term as part of his explanation of the origin of religions, and for decades his view dominated the *anthropology of religion. Now, at most, animism would be, either a recognition of soul-beliefs in particular societies, or a casual synonym for pre-literate societies and their religions.

Ānimitta (Skt., 'signless'). In *Mahāyāna Buddhism a synonym for both emptiness (*śūnyatā) and the desireless (*apraṇihita*). In the Pāli **Tripiṭaka* the signless comprises one of the three entrances to liberation (*vimokṣa-mukha*).

Aniruddha (manifest power of Viṣṇu): see VIṢṆU.

Anitya (Skt., 'not-permanent'). In Hinduism, the characteristic of *māyā, understood not in its derived sense of 'illusion', but as transitory nature of all appearance. In Buddhism (Pāli *anicca), the concept became even more fundamental.

Anjin, Anshin (Jap.). Peace in mind-consciousness (*kokoro), attained in *Zen Buddhism especially through the unsuccessful search for the mind: if the mind cannot be found, 'it' cannot give rise to disturbance. Also known as *dai-anjin*, great peace.

Annaphura (W. Syrian liturgies): see ANAPHORA.

Annapurna (Skt., 'one who gives nourishment'). Household Goddess for Hindus, who guarantees to her worshippers that food will not fail.

Aññatitthiya Paribbājakas (Pāli), **Anyatirthika Parivrājakas** (Skt.). Wanderers of other views. In Buddhist scriptures, the name for groups of non-Buddhist *ascetics that were contemporaries of the *Buddha. Because they were seen as rivals and competitors to Buddhism, they are generally represented unfavourably, though there is some evidence to suggest that the Buddha himself may have regarded them more highly than his own followers.

Anne, St. Mother of the Virgin *Mary, of whom nothing certain is known: she does not appear in the Bible, but only in legends beginning with the *Protogospel of *James*. Her cult, by then widely popular, was attacked by the Reformers. Feast day, in the W. (with St Joachim her husband), 26 July; in the E., 25 July.

Annihilationism (doctrine of no afterlife): see UCCHEDAVĀDA.

Annunciation. The announcement to the Virgin *Mary by the angel *Gabriel that she would conceive a son *Jesus (Luke 1. 26–38). The Christian festival, also called 'Lady Day', is celebrated on 25 Mar., exactly nine months before *Christmas, even though the date falls in *Lent.

Anointing

Judaism Pouring oil on a person symbolizes their elevation of status, especially in relation to God. In *Israel, it was performed at the inauguration of kings, the consecration of *priests, and the cleansing of lepers. The Hebrew term *mashiaḥ* ('anointed one') came to mean king or *high priest, and was then transliterated into English as *messiah.

Christianity In the New Testament anointing is found as a *charismatic means of healing: see UNCTION. From early times anointing has also been used in the rites of *baptism, *confirmation, and *ordination, as well as in the consecration of churches, altars, bells, etc. See also CHRISM.

Anonymous Christians (view that all in the exercise of humanity are related to Christ): see RAHNER, K.

Ansar (early supporters of Muḥammad in Madīna): see HELPERS.

Anselm (*c.*1033–1109). Monk and *archbishop of *Canterbury. Born in Aosta, the son of a Lombard landowner, he left Italy and became a monk of Bec, Normandy, in 1060. In 1063 he succeeded Lanfranc as prior, and in 1078 became abbot. In 1093 he succeeded Lanfranc as archbishop of Canterbury, inheriting a conflict with the king. He was in exile 1098–1100 and on his return was involved in the Investiture controversy (see GREGORY VII), spending a further period in exile 1103–7. A prolific theologian, his two most famous works were the *Proslogion* (1078–9) and **Cur Deus Homo* (1097–8). Two famous phrases express his conjunction of faith and reason: *fides quaerens intellectum* ('faith seeking understanding', his first proposed title for the *Proslogion*) and *credo ut intelligam* ('I believe in order that I may understand'.

An Shih-kao (2nd cent. CE). Buddhist monk, converted when crown prince in Parthia, who went to China and undertook and organized the first translations of Buddhist texts into Chinese. Since they were mainly concerned with *dhyāna, he became the founder of the *Dhyāna School of Buddhism.

Antakṛt-daśa-aṅga: see AṄGA.

Āṇṭāḷ (S. Indian bhakti poetess): see ĀḶVĀR.

Antarā-bhava (Skt., 'intermediate state'). The period, according to Hindus, which intervenes between death and rebirth. The term was taken into Buddhism, although there is no soul (*ātman) being reborn. In Japanese, the intermediate state is *chūu* or *chūin*.

Anthem (from Gk., *antifōnon*, 'that which is sung by alternate voices'). A musical setting of words usually from the *Bible, sung by a choir in church.

Anthony: see ANTONY.

Anthony, Susan (advocate of women's suffrage): see FRIENDS, THE SOCIETY OF.

Anthropology of religion. In the co-ordinating of anthropology as a discipline in the later 19th cent., the study was concerned with what were thought to be 'primitive' religions, i.e. those which were believed to be closer to an original state, cruder and simpler than developed, historical religions. Few anthropologists today think that the religions of non-westernized small-scale societies are different in kind from religions of the *great traditions. Instead, they tend to be impressed by the fact that similar beliefs, *rituals, *myths, etc., can be found in both contexts. Religion is seen as a major part of the ways in which individuals and societies organize and sustain their lives. Anthropologists tend to focus on such issues as kinship organization, myth, ritual and *symbols, *magic and *witchcraft. During the first half-century, anthropologists of religion developed both structuralism and functionalism. But structure/function has ceased to dominate analysis, and in recent years there has been a return to the social and individual construction of meaning and significant space.

Anthropomorphism (Gk., 'of human form'). The attribution of human qualities to the divine, as also to other items in the environment, hence the conceiving of God or the gods, or of natural features, in human form. The status of such language and descriptions has been a matter of fierce debate in those religions which rely on revelations which describe God in terms of human qualities—e.g. sitting on a throne (in Islam, see TANZĪH). In general the limitations of *analogical language and of *symbols led in the direction of the *via negativa. That is true even of Hinduism, but in that case the prevailing sense of God underlying all appearance makes the occurrence of anthropomorphism deceptive: there is a real presence through the image, and thus through sound and language (see e.g. ŚABDA; MANTRA; MAṆḌALA).

Anthroposophical Society, The. Organization founded by the Austro-Hungarian Rudolf Steiner (1861–1925) in 1912, which has for its principal aim the development of new perspectives for the study of humanity. Matter, in Steiner's view, is a necessary evil, for without descending into matter, spirit cannot rise up and acquire an individuated form. Humans are the high point of this process of the evolution of spirit.

Antichrist. An eschatological figure first mentioned in the epistles of John in the New Testament. He is described as a pseudo-*messiah who stands against Jesus at the end of days. Similar ideas can be found in Jewish *eschatology where the powers of evil are finally overcome in the ultimate great battle. In later Christian tradition Antichrist has been identified with *Satan; with the emperor Nero *redivivus*; with other particular enemies of the faith; and sometimes by Protestants with the pope.

In Islam, al-Dajjāl is an anti-religious figure who is often identified with Shaitān/Satan. In particular, he is the opponent and tempter of ʿĪsā/*Jesus, who will fight a final battle with him when ʿĪsā returns at the end of days.

Anticlericalism. Hostility (expressed usually by laypeople) against the privileges enjoyed by the Christian clergy, and a criticism of their failure to maintain the undertakings of their calling, to look after those committed to their care and to preach and teach the Christian gospel. In the American Constitution (and subsequent amendments), Church and State were rigorously separated, with anticlericalism playing a part. The attacks made by Pope *John Paul II on the *Enlightenment as the source of 'the culture of death' (which now, in his view, is dominant), combined with issues of celibacy and child abuse among the clergy, have led to a resurgence of anticlericalism, as clergy become identified with an authoritarian Church not open to criticism.

Anti-cult movement. Collectively, those groups and organizations that began to emerge in the 1970s in the United States, Europe, Australia, and elsewhere, in response to what were considered to be the harmful effects of *new religions on recruits.

These bodies, which include the Spiritual Counterfeits Project (SCP) in the USA, FAIR (Family Action Information and Rescue) in Britain, and ADFI (Association pour la defénse de la famille et de l'individu) in France, disseminate literature on new religions, carry out research, and seek to counsel and advise those distressed by the fact that a friend or relative has become a member of a new religion.

Antidoron (Gk., 'instead of the gift'). In the Byzantine *liturgy the part of the *eucharistic loaf which is not consecrated, but is blessed and distributed to the congregation at the end of the service. Non-Orthodox thus receive it 'instead of' communion, and it is considered a symbol of *ecumenical fellowship. A similar custom ('pain bénit') survives in the Roman Catholic Church in France.

Antinomianism (Gk., *anti*, 'against', + *nomos*, law) A tendency in all religions, for some among those who believe to regard themselves as so possessed of grace/salvation/enlightenment, etc., that existing laws are no longer applicable. It may also apply to an attitude which regards the keeping of rules and laws as an impediment on the way to freedom/release/salvation, etc., because it produces a legalistic understanding of actions and rewards. See Index, Antinomianism.

Antioch (modern Antakya in SE Turkey). City associated in Christian tradition with a tendency in theology opposed to that of *Alexandria. Its exponents include John *Chrysostom, *Theodore of Mopsuestia, *Nestorius, and *Theodoret. 'Antiochene' exegesis of scripture looked for historical rather than for hidden meanings, and was critical in holding some parts of the Bible more valuable than others. Antioch is now the *see of five *patriarchs, the *Greek Orthodox, Syrian Orthodox, *Melkite, *Maronite, and Syrian Catholic.

Antiphon (Gk., *antiphōnon*, 'responsive'). 1. In the W. Church, sentences, usually from the *Bible, recited before and after the *Psalms and *canticles in the divine *office, by alternative choirs or voices. They vary with the season or feast.

2. In the Orthodox liturgy, in addition to responsories, it may be any of the three anthems at the beginning of the *eucharist; or any 'alternate utterance' in which psalms or other words are sung alternately.

Antipope. A person in Christianity who claims (or exercises) the office of *pope illegitimately. The RC Church lists thirty-seven, from Hippolytus (d. *c*.235) to Felix V, who abdicated in 1449. The major and serious conflict over the papacy took place in the W. schism, 1378–1417. After the election of Urban VI in 1378, some cardinals, claiming that he was mentally unstable, elected Clement VII, who returned to Avignon as the centre of papal authority. Attempts to heal the schism included the election of a third pope, Alexander V, at Pisa. The attempt to locate continuing authority in these circumstances led directly into the conciliar controversy, raising the possibility that a general council, or the college of *cardinals (with or without such additional figures as certain university professors), had the ultimate authority—a position condemned by Pius II in the Bull *Exsecrabilis*, and also by the First *Vatican Council. The schism was ended by the elevation of Oddo at the Council of Constance (1414–18) to become Martin V.

Anti-semitism. Hostility against the Jewish people. The term was first used by Wilhelm Marr in Germany) in 1879, but prejudice against the Jews appeared in ancient times. With the triumph of Christianity, Jews were increasingly persecuted, marginalized, and deprived of civil rights. In 1215, the 4th Lateran Council decreed special clothing for Jews, thereby increasing their isolation. They were accused of desecrating the Christian *host, of poisoning wells, and of killing Christian children.

Although Jews fared somewhat better in Islamic lands, they did not achieve full civil rights in Christian Europe until the 19th cent. Anti-Semitic feelings did not disappear then, however, as is illustrated by the *Dreyfus case in France in 1894, the pronouncements of Richard Wagner in Germany, the circulation of such spurious works as *The Protocols of the Elders of Zion*, and the huge numbers of Jews who emigrated to the United States to escape the *pogroms of E. Europe, culminating in the *Holocaust. The foundation of the state of Israel was believed by Zionists to be the only solution to anti-Semitism, but as a result of the Arab–Israeli conflict, Muslim anti-Semitism is today even more virulent than its Christian counterpart.

Antony, St (also called 'the Great' or 'of Egypt', *c*.250–356). Christian hermit whose life and actions lie at the foundation of *monasticism. He withdrew into the desert in *c*.285, in order to develop holiness of life away from the distractions of the world. Athanasius wrote the *Vita Antonii*, from which details of his life are derived. He is regarded as 'the father' of Christian monasticism.

Antony of Padua, St (?1195–1231). Christian *Franciscan, *patron saint of the poor. His zeal, especially against the Cathars, earned him the title of *malleus haereticorum*, 'hammer of heretics'. As his cult developed, he became associated with the power to restore or locate lost property—perhaps because of an incident in which a novice was forced, by an apparition, to return a psalter which he had taken. He was canonized in 1232 and made a Doctor of the Church in 1946. Feast day, 13 June.

Antyeṣṭi, Antyeshti ('cremation'). The sixteenth sacrament in Hinduism, dealing with funeral rites. There is no other *saṃskāra for the body after the last rites. In modern times, when cremation can be by gas or electricity, only a token ceremony is performed and *mantras are recited, but generally no oblations can be offered.

On the third day, the near relatives go back to the funeral ground and collect the few remaining bones and either bury them in the ground nearby or throw them in the river. The *Vedas do not mention any rites, yet in practice on the twelfth day, relations and friends are invited for the feast of the wake. The annual *śrāddha (ancestor veneration) is performed by the surviving relatives.

Aṇu (Skt., 'tiny, minute'). In *Vaiśeṣika, a point in space without dimension which evolves from the subtle elements (*tanmātras*). Aṇus are eternal, invisible, and intangible, and are in a constant state of disintegration and reintegration. The material universe is evolved through the coming together of aṇus. There are four basic *paramāṇus* which are the essential components of earth, water, fire, and air. These correspond to the *mahābhūtas of other Indian philosophical systems. In *Kashmir Śaivism, aṇu is the soul or basic particle of *Śiva. For the application among Terapanth Jains, see BHIKṢU, ĀCĀRYA.

Anubhava (Skt., 'experience'). In *Vedānta, 'experience' or 'intuition' as the basis of an individual's knowledge of *Brahman, the Absolute. For *Śaṅkara brahman-anubhava, the 'intuition of Brahman', is the ultimate experience—impersonal, transcendental, and abstract. In *Advaita Vedānta, enlightenment is not a matter of speculation or emotion, but a direct and immediate anubhava.

Anubhāvi-guru (Skt.). The *guru who is witness of the highest truth, because he has direct experience of it.

Anubhūti (direct experience of Brahman): see REVELATION.

Anu Gītā. The miniature Gītā, a summary and recapitulation of the *Bhagavad-gītā*, given to *Arjuna by *Kṛṣṇa at the end of the Great War, because, as Arjuna says, 'the instruction already given has gone out of his degenerate mind'. It is selective (e.g. it does not recapitulate the devotional parts of the *Gītā*), and inclines to an emphasis on *jñāna-yoga.

Anugraha (uncompelled action, grace): see RĀMĀNUJA.

Anumāna (inference): see RĀMĀNUJA; NYĀYA.

Anupassanā (Pāli), **Anupaśyanā** (Skt., *anupaśyati*, 'look at'). Contemplation, observation; the mode of meditation in Buddhism through which insight (*vipassanā) takes place. Anupassanā works on the basis of looking at the object of thought not in terms of the quality or attribute which it seems to the natural, unenlightened mind to possess but in terms of its contrary or opposite, that is, its *true* characteristic.

Anupodisesa-nibbāna (nirvāna with no conditions remaining): see NIRUPADHIŚEṢA-NIRVĀṆA.

Anurādhapura. Capital of Sri Lanka until 10th cent. CE. The Mahāvihāra monasteries were established here, along with many temples and *stūpas. Of particular importance are the two great dagobas, Ruwanweli and Thūparāma. A branch or cutting of the *Bo tree (under which the *Buddha became enlightened) was planted in the 3rd cent. BCE, which survives to the present as (reputedly) the oldest tree in the world.

Anuruddha. 1. A close companion of the *Buddha, who was present at his death. To him is attributed the recitation and thus preservation of *Anguttara-Nikāya.

2. Theravādin Buddhist scholar of uncertain date (but within centuries either side of 10th cent. CE), author of *Abhidhammattha-sangaha* which summarizes Theravādin teaching.

Anusaya (Skt., *anuśaya*). In Buddhism a latent tendency or disposition towards vice. According to Buddhist psychology these dispositions are carried over to the next life and exist even in the newly born infant.

Anusim (Heb., 'forced ones'). People compelled unwillingly to convert from Judaism to another faith. Instances of forced conversion have occurred throughout Christian history and include the baptism of the Jewish community of Clermont-Ferrand in 576 CE, compulsory conversions in the Rhineland in the 10th cent. and the Conversos or *Marranos of Christian Spain.

Anussati (Pāli, 'recollection'). Contemplative practices in Buddhism which break attachment to the three destructive roots (*akuśala). Initially six, they are now reckoned as ten.

Anussava (Pāli), **Anuśrava** (Skt., 'that which has been heard or reported'). Tradition: according to early Buddhism, that which is passed on by word of mouth from one person to another and from one generation to another. In the *Nikāyas it is chiefly used with reference to the *brahmans who appealed to tradition as sacrosanct, believing their own *Vedas to be divine revelation and the exclusive source of all knowledge and truth. However, Buddhism maintained that the claim for any doctrine or teaching to represent knowledge or truth cannot rest exclusively on the fact that it is part of or belongs to tradition. In order for a body of teaching to be regarded as valid knowledge three criteria need to be met: the teacher or transmitter of the doctrine must be observed as someone who is free of attachment (*rāga), hate (*dosa), and delusion (*moha); the meaning of the teaching should be tested by the pupil independently of the teacher; and the teaching has to be tested in practice.

Anuttaravimāna. The five heavens of the Jains. The detail of how ten great ascetics attained these heavens is found in *Anuttoropapādaka-daśa-anga* (see AÑGA).

Anuttarayogatantra (division of tantric texts): see TRIPIṬAKA.

Anuttoropapādaka-daśa-aṅga: see AṄGA.

Anuvrata. The 'lesser vows' which Jain laypeople take, as a kind of parallel to the great vows of the ascetics. They are applied to the practice of daily life. The *gunavratas* are three supplementary vows, restricting unnecessary travel (in the light of (i) above, and counteracting self-indulgence and extravagance). The *śikṣavratas* are three vows of instruction, relating to specific religious duties.

Aṇuvrata Movement, (Skt., *aṇu*, 'lesser', + *vrata*, 'vows'). Indian moral revival movement based on the *anuvrata vows of Jains. Founded in 1948 by Acharya Tul(a)si, head of the Jain Śvetāmbara Terāpantha sect, the movement aims to purge corruption and uplift the moral tone of the life. To further these goals, an international branch of the movement was established in Jaipur in 1984. See further BHIKṢU, ĀCĀRYA.

Anuvyañjana. In Buddhism, one of the secondary or minor physical attributes of a 'Great Man' (*mahāpurusa*), and especially of the *Buddha. There are said to be eighty such features. Several versions of the full list occur in textual sources although the specific attributes and the order of the items vary: see LAKṢAṆA.

Apacāyana (respect to elders): see DASAKUSALAKAMMA.

Apadāna (part of Pāli canon): see KHUDDAKANIKĀYA.

Āpaddharma (Skt., *āpad*, 'misfortune', + *dharma*, 'law'). In Hinduism, a practice only permissible in time of calamity, distress, or misfortune; the *dharma of emergencies.

Apara-vidya (Skt., 'not-direct knowledge'). Knowledge by hearsay or report in Hinduism, as opposed to para-vidya, direct knowledge by way of experience, hence also known as Brahma-vidya.

Aparigraha (Skt.). 1. The state in Hinduism of detachment from all possessions and desires, one of the five virtues required on the first step of *Rāja-Yoga, according to *Patañjali's account. The others are *satya* (truthfulness), *ahiṁsā (non-injury of others), *asteya* (not stealing), and *brahmacarya (continent and holy life). They constitute the Mahāvrata, the Great Vow which remains in force for all the other steps.

2. Jain vow of detachment: see FIVE GREAT VOWS.

Apartheid (policy of separate development): see DUTCH REFORMED CHURCH.

Apasmāra (Skt., 'epilepsy'). The demonic dwarf who in Hindu mythology personifies ignorance and forgetfulness.

Apāya (Skt.). The four lower modes of rebirth possible for humans. They are animals, *narakas (beings in torment), *pretas (hungry ghosts), and *asuras (roughly, demons, but only in the sense that they are complementary to *devas, and may thus be reckoned as among the good, or higher, modes of existence, *gati).

Aphrahat, Aphraates (early 4th cent.). 'The Persian sage', earliest of *Syriac church *fathers. He was a *bishop in Persia during the persecutions of Shapur II (310–79). His twenty-three *Demonstrations*, dated between 337 and 345, give a survey of the Christian faith.

Apikoros (probably from Gk., 'Epicurean'). A person who abandons the *rabbinic *tradition. Today it is used to describe anyone with heretical or heterodox views.

Apocalypse, Apocalyptic (Gk., 'revelation'). Jewish and Christian literature of revelations, making known the features of a heavenly or future time or world, or, in general, things hidden from present knowledge; hence 'apocalyptic books' or literature.

In Christianity, the controlling example is the Book of Revelation, although apocalyptic words are attributed to *Jesus: thus Mark 13 is often referred to as 'The Markan Apocalypse'. Because apocalyptic is often concerned with catastrophic events, e.g. the end of the world, it lends itself to such titles as *Apocalypse Now*, a film exploring the Vietnam War on the basis of Joseph Conrad's *Heart of Darkness*.

Apocalypse of Ezra: see ESDRAS, BOOKS OF, 3 and 4.

Apocatastasis (Gk., *apokath'istēmi*, 'to restore'). The restoration of the created order to a condition, either of its intended perfection, or to its source (e.g. God as creator). It is thus associated with the end of the present cosmos. However, it has also been adopted by those who hold that creation is eternal (see COSMOLOGY): in that case, apocatastasis refers to the phase in which the absolute condition of perfection is attained. In Hinduism, something akin to apocatastasis occurs in the *mahāpralaya. In Buddhism, the equivalent is the point at which the condition of nirvāna is universally realized.

Apocrypha (Gk., 'hidden things'). Jewish books associated with the *Bible, but not included in the Jewish *canon. These are works regarded by the sages as *Sefarim hizonim* (extraneous books). They include (i) *Esdras; (ii) *Tobit; (iii) *Judith; (iv) additions to *Esther; (v) *Wisdom of Solomon; (vi) Ecclesiasticus; (vii) *Baruch; (viii) *Song of the Three Children; (ix) *Susanna; (x) *Bel and the Dragon; (xi) The Prayer of *Manasseh; (xii) 1 *Maccabees; (xiii) 2 Maccabees. In addition, there are many other books, known as *Pseudepigrapha (frequently *apocalyptic in character), which were written in the same period.

Apocryphal. Of the same form as a book of scripture but excluded from the *canon as doubtful or spurious. Among Jewish writings the word is best applied not to the *Apocrypha proper but to the wider class of *Pseudepigrapha, and thus to the 'Apocryphal Old Testament'. The 'Apocryphal New Testament' includes gospels, acts of apostles, epistles, and apocalypses.

Apollinarius or **Apollinaris** (*c*.310–*c*.390). Christian *heretic. Although as *bishop of Laodicea he was an orthodox opponent of *Arianism, his *christological teaching was condemned, finally in 381 at the Council of *Constantinople. He left the church *c*.375. Apollinarianism is the view which defends the divine nature in *Christ by refusing to allow that there could be moral development during his lifetime. There can be a human body and soul, but the *Logos replaces the human spirit and is thus not subject to change. Such a view, according to opponents, means that Christ was not fully human.

Apollonian and Dionysiac religion. Contrasted forms of religion, the former being reflective and rational, the latter ecstatic and fervent. The distinction in its modern form derives from the work of *Nietzsche.

Apologetics (Lat., *apologia*, 'defence'). The defence, or commendation, of a religion.

Among Christians, the name 'Apologists' is given to the earliest group of Christian writers who (*c.*120–220) composed defences of Christianity addressed to educated outsiders. They include Athenagoras, *Justin Martyr, *Minucius Felix, *Tatian, and *Tertullian. A notable later example is *Augustine's **City of God*. *Calvin's *Institutes of the Christian Religion* is addressed to Francis I (the French King) to persuade him of his error in pursuing a policy of persecution.

Apologists: see APOLOGETICS.

Apophatic theology. Another name for 'theology by way of negation', according to which God is known by negating concepts that might be applied to him, stressing the inadequacy of human language and concepts to say anything of God. It is characteristic of mystical theology and Eastern *Orthodoxy, and shows parallels with Indian *Advaita Vedānta: see e.g. NETI, NETI.

Apostasy, (Gk., 'stand away from'). The act or state of rejecting one religious faith for another. Apostasy has been regarded with horror by Jews, although a distinction was always made between apostates who converted for gain and the *anusim or *Marranos who were forced to convert and tried to maintain their Judaism secretly. According to the *halakhah, an apostate remains a Jew: he can contract a valid Jewish marriage, and the child of an apostate mother is considered a Jew. However, as the law stands at present, an apostate Jew is not entitled to immigrate to *Israel under the *law of Return.

In Christianity, the debate mainly took the form of the ability of one elected to salvation to fall from *grace (see e.g. ARMINIUS). In Islam, the issue is extremely prominent, involving the argument whether it requires the death penalty: see MURTADD.

Apostle (Gk., *apostolos*, 'one sent out'). 1. An important early Christian title, used in two senses: (i) an authoritative missionary; and (ii) one of *Jesus' chosen twelve disciples. For (ii) see Index, Apostles.

2. The name given to the *Epistle in the *Orthodox liturgy.

3. An official of the *Catholic Apostolic Church.

Apostle of the North: see ADRIAN IV.

Apostles' Creed. A statement of faith used in W. Christian Churches.

There is no basis to the tradition that it was composed by the *apostles; rather, it evolved from the baptismal *creed used at Rome in the 2nd cent. In the 20th cent. has been treated as a basis for *ecumenical agreement.

Apostles of the Southern Slavs (Christian missionary brothers): see CYRIL AND METHODIUS.

Apostle to the apostles: see MARY MAGDALENE.

Apostolicae Curae. Bull issued by *Leo XIII in 1896, declaring that *Anglican *ordinations 'are absolutely null and utterly void', because of double defect of form and intention.

Apostolic Council. The meeting in Jerusalem described by *Paul in Galatians 2. 1–10 between himself, *James, *Peter, and *John. It approved Paul's missionary preaching to gentiles independent of the Jewish law. The account in Acts 15. 1–21 attributes to the council a set of minimal stipulations (to abstain from anything polluted by idols, from fornication, from meat of strangled animals, and from blood. The event is usually dated to 48, less often to 51 CE.

Apostolic Delegate. A papal appointment to represent the pope in those countries which do not have diplomatic relations with the *Holy see (cf. NUNCIO). Permanent apostolic delegations were established in the USA in 1893, and in Great Britain in 1938.

Apostolic Fathers. The Christian fathers of the period immediately after the New Testament. They are *Clement of Rome, *Ignatius, *Hermas, *Polycarp, and *Papias, and the authors of *The Epistle of *Barnabas*, *The Epistle to *Diognetus*, 2 **Clement*, and the **Didache*.

Apostolic Succession. A belief in Christianity that the authority of the ordained ministry, in word and *sacrament, is protected by the continuous transmission of that authority through successive ordinations by those who were themselves validly ordained.

Apotheosis (Gk., *apo*, 'from', + *theoun*, 'to deify'). The elevation of a human being to the rank and status of a god. See also EUHEMERISM.

Apotropaic (Gk. 'turn away from'). Name given to *rituals designed to turn away some threatened or threatening evil.

Appar (Late 6th or 7th cent. CE). A *Tamil poet, one of the sixty-three *Nāyaṇmārs. A devotee of *Śiva, his 312 surviving hymns remain in use. He is a model of the self-effacing servant of the Lord.

Apratiṣṭhita-nirvāna (Skt., 'not-fixed nirvāna'). The state, in *Mahāyāna Buddhism of one who has attained *nirvāna, but suspends final attainment in order to help those who are still on the path to liberation—i.e. a *bodhisattva.

Apsarā (Skt., 'move in water'). The dancers in *Indra's *svarga (heaven) in Hinduism. They are frequently depicted in Hindu relief art. In Buddhism, they are depicted as richly adorned attendants on *Sakka (i.e. Indra).

Apsarasa: see GANDHARVA.

Apse (Gk., *apsis*). The rounded end of a church, especially in Greek Orthodoxy: it is derived from the Constaninian basilicas which incorporated the pagan *apsis* where judges and legal advisers sat.

'Aqeda(h) (Abraham's intended sacrifice of Isaac): see 'AKEDA.

Aqib[v]a (Jewish scholar and martyr): see AKIVA.

'Aqīda (articles of faith): see CREED (ISLAM).

Aqṣā Mosque: see JERUSALEM.

Aquarius, Age of (time of spiritual advance): see NEW AGE.

Aquila (2nd cent. CE). Translator of the Hebrew *Bible into Greek. It survives only in fragments. Rabbinic sources confuse Aquila and Onkelos, the author of the *Targum on the Pentateuch.

Aquinas, Thomas, St (*c*.1225–74). *Dominican philosopher and theologian, recognized as one of the greatest thinkers of the Catholic Church. He was *canonized in 1323 and declared a *Doctor of the Church in 1567. Feast day, 28 Jan. Aquinas's major works include commentaries on Aristotle and the Bible, general treatises (*Summae*) on Christian doctrine, and discussions of particular topics such as Truth and Evil. Central to his outlook is the notion of God as Creator *ex nihilo* (out of nothing). On Aquinas's account, God is the cause of there being anything apart from himself. In the light of this view, Aquinas further argued that God is not one of a class of spiritual beings; he is *sui generis*, not an individual, omniscient, omnipotent, changeless (meaning 'timeless'), perfect, incomprehensible, and the cause of all that comes to pass, including the choices of his creatures. Aquinas rejected determinism and believed in free will, but he also insisted that the free actions of creatures are directly caused by God as Creator of everything.

In the areas of ethics and psychology Aquinas resembles Aristotle. He rejected a sharp mind–body dualism, and he held that criteria of human goodness are discovered by a study of human nature which is essentially bodily and social. But according to Aquinas, human beings can be transformed by *grace to a level not anticipated by philosophy. He also held that by faith one can have access to truths about God not themselves demonstrable philosophically. These truths include doctrines like the *Trinity and the *Incarnation, which Aquinas believed to be revealed by God. See also THOMISM; QUINQUE VIAE.

'Arabi (Sūfī mystic): see IBN (AL-)'ARABĪ.

Arabic. The language of the *Qur'ān, and thus the most sacred language for all Muslims, since it is the language of the final and uncorrupted language of revelation. For that reason, the Qur'ān cannot be translated: it can only be interpreted or paraphrased in other languages. Arabic is the language of the obligatory prayers (*ṣalāt).

Ārādhana (Skt.). Adoration of God in Hinduism, and aspiration to attain union with him, especially by repetition of his name.

Ārādhya: see LIṄGĀYAT.

'Arafā(t). Muslim place of *pilgrimage, a plain about 19 km. from *Mecca. According to tradition, after *Adam and *Eve were expelled from *paradise, they separated, but met again at this place, and recognized (Arab., *'arifa*, 'know') each other. Pilgrims on the *ḥajj assemble here toward the end of the obligatory duties for at least a short time. The massive assembly is said to resemble, in anticipation, the Day of Judgement.

Ar(a)ha(n)t (in Buddhism, one worthy of reverence, having reached the stage before nirvana): see ARHAT.

Arai Hakuseki (1657–1725). Confucian statesman and scholar during Japan's Tokugawa (1600–1868) period. He exerted considerable influence on government policy and administration, and in his later years he devoted himself to scholarship, especially in the fields of ancient Japanese history, Shintō theology, and historical linguistics.

Arakan. Jap. for *arhat.

Arama, Isaac b. Moses (*c*.1420–94). Jewish communal leader in Spain. He was the author of *Akedat Yizhak* (Binding of *Isaac; see 'AKEDA), a philosophical and *allegorical commentary on the *Pentateuch. In his philosophy, he was critical of *Maimonides' rationalism and was influential on such thinkers as Isaac *Abrabanel.

Aramaic. A Semitic language written generally in *Hebrew script. Ancient (from 700 BCE) inscriptions have been found as far afield as Afghanistan, Turkmenistan, and the Caucasus. In the later period of the second *Temple, the *Pentateuch was translated into Aramaic (these translations are known as *targumim* (*targums)).

Āraṇyaka (Skt., 'that which pertains to the forest'). In Hinduism, the genre of texts within the *Vedic corpus developed as an adjunct to the *Brāhmaṇas. They are explanatory and speculative in nature, intending to give the secret aspects of rituals obtainable only by the advanced student instructed in the seclusion of the forest. They are generally listed as being four in number: the *Aitareya*, *Kausītaki*, *Taittirīya*, and *Jaiminīya Āraṇyakas*.

Ārati, Aratrika (Skt.). Evening *pūjā (worship) in Hinduism, with incense, flowers, and chant, and with lights swung in front of the image.

Araya-shiki (Jap., for Skt., *ālaya-vijñāna, 'storehouse-consciousness'). The eighth and foundational level of consciousness in the Buddhist Hossō (see DŌSHŌ) school. It stores impressions received from other forms of consciousness and retains them as a potential for further actions and thoughts.

Arba'ah minim (four plants used in Jewish rite of Sukkot): see FOUR SPECIES.

Arbada (mountain in India): see ABU.

Arba kosot (Heb., 'four cups'). Four cups of wine traditionally drunk at the *Passover *seder. The tradition is based on a *midrashic interpretation of Exodus 6. 6–7, where four different terms for deliverance are used.

Arba Kushiyot: see FOUR QUESTIONS.

Arcāvatāra: see AVATĀRA.

Archangels (in the hierarchy of angels): see ANGELS.

Archbishop. Title of certain Christian *bishops, approximately equivalent to *metropolitan.

Archdeacon. In *Anglican churches, a priest having administrative charge over part of a diocese. He exercises a general supervision of the parish clergy and deals with matters of church buildings and other property. He is styled 'Venerable'.

Arches, Court of. The *consistory court of the province of *Canterbury, so-called because formerly it met in the E. London church of St Mary-le-Bow (Lat., *S. Maria de Arcubus*).

Archetypes: see MYTH.

Archimandrite (Gk., *archi*, 'ruler of', + *mandra*, 'fold'). Title given in the early church (later also Archimandret, Slavonic) to a monastic superior. In the *Orthodox Church it has become a title of honour; for the Copts, an archimandrite is second only to a *patriarch.

Archimedean point: see CULTURAL RELATIVITY AND RELIGION.

Architecture: see ART.

Archpriest. A title of certain clerics in the *Roman Catholic and *Orthodox Churches. From the 5th cent. on, the archpriest was the senior *presbyter of a city, who might take the *bishop's place at liturgical functions.

ARCIC (*Anglican/*Roman Catholic International Commission). Created by Pope Paul VI and Archbishop Michael Ramsey of Canterbury in consequence of the Second *Vatican Council's positive decree on *ecumenism (1965). From 1971 to 1981 ARCIC produced four agreed statements on *eucharist, ministry, and *ordination, and (in two stages) authority. Principles governing the conversations were (*a*) avoidance of polemical language inherited from late medieval and 16th-cent. formulas designed to exclude; (*b*) avoidance of statements on essential doctrines which could be interpreted in incompatible senses by the two parties.

Although Anglican official endorsement of the agreed statements came reasonably rapidly the Roman Congregation for the Doctrine of the Faith under Cardinal Ratzinger accompanied the publication of the four reports (*Final Report*, 1982) with predominantly negative 'Observations'. The official Vatican verdict (December 1991) was in tone less negative than the 1982 Observations.

After 1982 ARCIC was continued with largely new members and was increased in size, from 18 to 24. The large agenda assigned to it began with the most intricate of all articles of faith, *Justification. An agreed statement, *Salvation and the Church*, appeared (1987), followed by *Church as Communion* (1991), and, after further changes in membership, by a statement on moral issues, *Life in Christ: Morals, Communion and the Church* (1994), recognizing differences on divorce and contraception but denying that the issues are church-dividing.

Ardās (Pañjābī, 'petition' from Persian 'arżdāsht). The Sikh Prayer. The Ardās marks the conclusion of Sikh congregational worship in the *gurdwārā and is to be repeated daily after the *Rahirās and *Kīrtan *Sohilā.

The Ardās is not in the Ādi Granth, and only the opening passage (concluding with veneration of Gurū *Tegh Bahādur) is attributable to Gurū *Gobind Siṅgh. The prayer evolved in the 18th cent., providing insight into contemporary ideals although lines have been added since. It is printed as part of *Nitnem. See NIRAṄKĀRĪ; RAVIDĀSĪ.

Ardhanārī (Skt., 'half-female'). The androgynous form of a Hindu deity, especially of *Śiva as Ardanārīśvara, 'Hermaphrodite Lord'. In painting or sculpture, the ardhanārī is represented with the left side of the body as female and the right side as male. On the one hand, this symbol of the union of male and female polarities within the Supreme Being is an image of erotic desire (*kāma) and divine creativity. On the other hand, ardhanārī symbolizes the perfect balance of male and female, of all dualities and limitations within the transcendent, impersonal *Brahman. In *Tantric belief the balance of male and female elements within the individual, achieved by various techniques (sexual and non-sexual), results in *enlightenment and bliss. Although the most common ardhanārī is that of Śiva, *Viṣṇu, *Kṛṣṇa, and other deities are also portrayed in this form.

Ardhanārīśvara: see ARDHANĀRĪ.

Arendt, Hannah (1906–75). Philosopher and political scientist, ending her career as Professor in the Graduate Faculty of the New School for Social Research in New York. She was deeply concerned with the way in which the atomization, alienation, and anomie of mass society left it open to totalitarian take-over. In her view, freedom and thought depend on the separation of political life (the public realm) from social and economic life (the private realm)—as in the Greek polis or in the system envisaged in the American revolution. The modern world has seen the advent of the opposite, with public and private realms coerced together into the social and economic sphere, depriving thought of its necessary privacy and converting politics into economic administration. This allows totalitarian *ideology to take over, and opens the way to 'the banality of *evil'. All this keeps pace with *antisemitism, since the stateless Jew cannot rely on any vague notion of human rights: rights are subordinated to ends.

Arghya (Skt.). Sacrificial offering during Hindu *pūjā (worship).

Arhat (*arhati*, 'be worthy of'; Pāli *arahat*). In Buddhism, one who is worthy of reverence because he has attained the penultimate state of perfection (Chin., *alohan*, **lohan*; Jap., *arakan*; Korean, *arahan*, *nahan*). The term was originally applied to all ascetics, but it came to be applied to those who are no longer bound to *punabbhava ('again-becoming') and have become completely detached from the Triple World of sense, form, and formlessness. Since, in *Theravāda, there can be only one *Buddha in each world cycle, the condition of arhat is the highest to which one can aspire in this cycle (since the Buddha has already appeared).

They possess four faculties of discernment and exegesis not possessed by ordinary mortals, and five kinds of transcendent knowledge, so that they are characterized by supreme wisdom, and are known as *prajñāvimukta*. They can hear and understand all sounds in the universe, know the thoughts of others, and remember previous existences. At death, they attain *nirvāna completely.

*Mahāyāna Buddhism, in contrast, regards the notion, especially the limited goal, of arhat as selfish. The development of the *bodhisattva, who might attain the goal but returns to help others, is held to be the logical application of the example of the Buddha and of his teaching.

Among Jains, the arhat is one who is worthy of absolute reverence. In effect, these are the *tīrthaṅkaras.

Ari (acronym): see LURIA, ISAAC BEN SOLOMON.

Arianism. The Christian *heresy according to which the Son of God was a creature and not truly God. In the Arian system the Son could be called 'God', but only as a courtesy title; he was created (not begotten) by the Father, and he achieved his divine status by his perfect obedience to him. As a creature, it must be said of Christ *ēn pote hote ouk ēn* (a famous slogan), 'there was once when he was not'. The chief proponent of the doctrine was the Alexandrian priest *Arius (*c*.250–*c*.336).

Aridity. A state of emptiness or listlessness in which it is difficult to pray. Its cause may be physical illness or sinfulness. But much W. (as opposed to E.) Christian spirituality teaches that such aridity may mark the beginning of the *dark night of the soul (cf. JOHN OF THE CROSS).

Aristeas, Letter of. An anonymous Jewish composition written probably in the late 2nd cent. BCE. It is supposedly composed by Aristeas, a Greek at the court of Ptolemy II Philadelphus (285–246 BCE) and describes the translation of the Hebrew scriptures into Greek. It seems to be designed to enhance the status of a Gk. translation.

Aristotle (384–322 BCE). Greek philosopher whose influence on W. theology and philosophy has been prodigious—though it was not so much by a strict exegesis of his ideas as by an eclectic adaptation combined particularly with *Neoplatonism. But the influence and adaptation are not surprising. In his own thought, a theology or science of God is the primary form of knowledge, partly because God is the source (*arche*) of all things, and partly because God alone possesses knowledge in the highest degree. The human desire to know is thus the highest truth of our being, and is potentially a sharing in God's knowledge of himself. This aspiration may in the past have been handed down in *myth, but through *nous* (intellect or intelligence which is the essence of God's nature) humans attain to God. The insistence on the rationality of God and of the human possibility of entering into union with God through *nous* laid foundations for a theological and rational spirituality which flourished especially in Islam—albeit by then in a form which was Platonic. The real influence of Aristotle on W. Christian theology came in the 13th cent., mediated by Jews and Muslims, becoming a source of controversy (Aristotelianism was condemned in Paris in 1277), but providing nevertheless the philosophical basis for *scholasticism, especially in St Thomas *Aquinas.

Arius (*c*.250–*c*.336). Christian theologian who gave his name to the *Arian heresy, eventually condemned at the Council of *Nicaea in 325. The Arian controversy was renewed in later centuries and has been a recurrent interpretation of the person of Jesus by those who fear that otherwise they will compromise the transcendence and unity of God.

Ariyaratne, A. Y. (founder): see SARVODAYA.

Ariya-satta/sacca (foundation of the Buddha's teaching): see FOUR NOBLE TRUTHS.

Arjan Dev, Gurū (1563–1606). Fifth Sikh *Gurū, poet and first Sikh *martyr. Arjan Mal, the youngest son of Gurū *Rām Dās and Bībī Bhānī, was born in *Goindvāl, *Pañjāb. He married Gaṅgā who bore one son, *Hargobind. In preference to his elder brother, *Prithī Chand, Arjan was invested as Gurū in 1581 by *Bhāī *Buḍhā at the request of Gurū Rām Dās. Prithī Chand's jealousy proved a continuing source of harassment to Arjan.

Gurū Arjan Dev completed the excavation of sacred pools at Rāmdāspur, later renamed *Amritsar, extended the town and superintended the construction of the *Harimandir. He also built *Kartārpur and Srī Hargobindpur on the Beās River, both in Pañjāb.

In 1594 he returned to Amritsar and, finding that Prithī Chand was composing hymns to further his ambition, Arjan decided to make an authentic collection of hymns. This volume, the *Ādi Granth, was completed in 1604 and installed at Amritsar but is now at Kartārpur in the possession of the *Sodhī family.

Jealousy and conflict led to Arjan Dev, now known as the 'True Emperor', being charged with sedition as well as with creating communal dissension. He was subjected to prolonged torture. According to Sikh tradition he had to sit in a red hot cauldron and was bathed in boiling water. Before his death he appointed Hargobind to succeed him.

Gurū Arjan Dev's 2,216 hymns are the largest contribution to the Ādi Granth. In the spirit of his predecessors his verses proclaim the saving power of God's name (*nām), the blindness of sinful man, the greatness of God, and the need for constant devotion to God. Of his compositions, the greatest is the *Sukhmanī.

Arjuna. In the **Mahābhārata*, the third, or middle, *Pāṇḍava, a fabulous warrior best known for his skill as an archer, in many ways the hero *par excellence* of the epic. Son of *Kuntī by the god *Indra, Arjuna wields the bow Gāṇḍīva, carries the monkey *Hanumat on his battle standard, and rides a chariot drawn by white horses.

Arjuna's close friendship with *Kṛṣṇa is central to the *Mahābhārata*'s structure. Among Arjuna's wives is Subhadrā, Kṛṣṇa's sister: the son of Arjuna and Subhadrā is Abhimanyu, who dies in the Kurukṣetra war. During the Kurukṣetra war, Kṛṣṇa serves as Arjuna's charioteer and adviser, often inciting him and the other Pāṇḍavas to tricky means to their end of victory. Perhaps the most famous incident in the *Mahābhārata* is Arjuna's failure of nerve before the war, in which he will have to kill his Kaurava relatives, resulting in Kṛṣṇa's expounding of the **Bhagavad-gītā* to encourage him to fight. In truth, the *Mahābhārata* tells us, Arjuna and Kṛṣṇa are incarnations of *Nara and Nārāyana; it is as though Arjuna's friendship with (devotion to) Kṛṣṇa brings him beyond the human state to semi-divinity.

Ark. 1. The vessel in which *Noah supposedly saved his family and a breeding pair of each animal and bird species from the destruction of the great flood (Genesis 6. 1–9. 18).

2. The 'ark of the *covenant' (*aron ha-berith*) was a container, made by God's command during the Wilderness wandering of Israel, to contain the tablets of the covenant.

3. The niche in the *synagogue in which the *Torah Scrolls (*Scrolls of the Law) are kept. It is located on the wall which faces towards the Temple Mount in Jerusalem and is considered the holiest part of the building. A *ner tamid* ('eternal light') is kept burning in front of the

Ark. In *Ashkenazi circles, the Ark is called the *aron* or *aron kodesh* ('holy Ark'), and among the *Sephardim, it is known as the *heikhal* ('sanctuary').

Arkān ud-Dīn (fundamentals of Muslim life): see FIVE PILLARS OF ISLAM.

Armageddon. In Christian *eschatology, the scene of the last battle between good and evil. The name appears only in Revelation 16. 16, where it is said to be 'Hebrew'; it is usually taken to be from Har Megiddo, mountain of Megidda.

Armaiti (one of the Holy Immortals): see AMESA SPENTAS.

Armenian Church. One of the *Oriental churches, sometimes incorrectly called 'Armenian Orthodox'. Armenia was the first country to adopt Christianity as a state religion, after the conversion of King Tiridates III by St Gregory 'the Illuminator' *c.*294 (hence the name 'Armenian Gregorian Church' which is sometimes used). A major factor in the preservation of Armenian national consciousness has been membership of the Church, and non-ethnic Armenians cannot be admitted to membership, though this does not prevent children becoming members by baptism if one parent is Armenian.

The Armenian Church was much influenced by contact with the *Crusaders, of which one result was a temporary (12th–13th cents.) union of much of the Church with Rome. Another was the adoption of the *mitre as the liturgical headgear of its *bishops. The present *Uniat church, the Armenian Catholic Church of *c.*100,000 members, goes back only to 1740.

Under the Ottoman Turks the Armenians suffered notorious persecutions, culminating in massacres as late as 1920 which left practically no Armenians in Turkish territory. Of the 3½ million Armenians, most live now in the ex-Soviet Republic of Armenia, where conflict with Azerbaijan over the disputed territory of Nagorno-Karabakh is exacerbated by memories of persecution. There is a large *diaspora, including ½-million in the USA.

The Armenian Church has two classes of *priests: the *vardapets* or doctors, who are unmarried, and the *parish priests who, unless monks (*monasticism) must be married before *ordination as *deacons. Bishops are usually chosen from among the *vardapets*. The Armenian *liturgy is celebrated in the ancient Armenian language, having been translated (with the Bible) in the early 5th cent. by St *Mesrob, who himself invented the Armenian alphabet. For the *eucharist the Armenians use unleavened bread, and do not mix water with the wine. They follow the Julian *calendar. Following the ancient Eastern practice, the birth of Christ is not celebrated as a separate feast at *Christmas, but at *Epiphany. An organ or harmonium is often used to accompany the choir, in contrast to the *Orthodox churches, where such instruments are forbidden.

Armenian Massacres: see ARMENIAN CHURCH.

Arminius, Jacobus (1560–1609). Dutch theologian who gave his name to the system of theology known as Arminianism. He became professor at Leiden, where there were arguments over *predestination, leading to severe divisions. Arminius held that God willed that all people should be saved, and that it is only because God foresaw the belief or unbelief of individuals that he can be said to have predestined some to salvation, others to damnation. After his death, his followers issued the Remonstrance of 1610, from which the major differences from strict Calvinism can be discerned: (i) Christ died for all; (ii) God's saving grace can be resisted; (iii) Christians can fall from grace; (iv) the Holy Spirit is necessary to help the achievement of what is good; (v) salvation is for those who believe in Christ and who persist in holiness, obedience, and faith. Arminius and Arminianism had a wide (though always contested) influence, including such figures as Grotius and John *Wesley.

Armour of Faith (Zoroastrian): see NAUJOTE.

Armstrong, Herbert W. (b. 1892). Leader of the 'Worldwide Church of God'. Armstrong began as a preacher on radio in the USA in the 1930s, and became widely known through the radio programme 'The World Tomorrow', after 1955 continued by his son Garner Ted.

Armstrong's doctrines owe much to British Israelism. Their major theme is the reference of biblical prophecy to Britain and America and to current events (e.g. war in the Middle East as a 'sign of the times' and precursor of *Armageddon). Worship is on the Sabbath (Saturday), and Jewish festivals are observed rather than Christmas and Easter; the *Ten Commandments figure prominently; several *tithes are required of church members. Medicine is deprecated in favour of spiritual healing. Since the 1970s the organization has suffered from scandals over the style of life of some of its leaders.

Arnauld, Antoine (known sometimes as 'the Great', 1612–94). Christian philosopher and controversialist. He studied and taught at the Sorbonne until he was expelled (1656) for his *Jansenist views. In 1643 he had published a book on frequent communion (of that title) stressing the need for thorough preparation and appropriate disposition, and in 1644 an anonymous apology for Jansen. His major writings were *The Art of Thinking* (with Pierre Nicole, 1662), also known as the *Port Royal Logic*, and *Concerning True and False Ideas* (1683). He developed (while criticizing) Cartesian logic and views, pointing out, for example, the circularity in one of *Descartes arguments: the idea of God depends on the clarity and distinctness of our perception of him, while the truth of our clear and distinct perceptions depends on God's existence. In theology, he, more than anyone else, was responsible for diffusing Jansenist ideas.

Aron: see ARK (2).

ar-Rāshidūn (the (first) four caliphs): see KHALĪFA.

Art. Although religions are usually studied through their words and texts, religious people live at least as much (probably more) through their non-verbal modes of expression—through *ritual at least as much as through *myth, through rhythm as much as through song. Beyond ritual, religious art extends the human ability to communicate through complex sign-systems, locking on, especially, to the imagination of worlds and states which cannot be directly seen. Religious art is profoundly connected to the human ability to recognize and take delight in truth, beauty, and goodness. What *counts* as beautiful or good may differ from one religion to another (or from one age to another in any religion), but not the human ability to recognize those absolutes within the change and contingency of human circumstance. Thus religious art is extensively concerned with celebration, worship, thanksgiving, and praise. Art and prayer are connected in that, according to one artist (R. Raistick), an artist must spend 'hour after hour looking at the one subject', just as those who pray spend hour after hour looking at the One Subject. Above all, the demands of religious art have offered the supreme challenge and opportunity to the human ability to create—to be the creator of artefacts, to be an artist. Not surprisingly, religions have been the resource and inspiration of almost all the most enduring art and architecture throughout the whole of human history, at least until very recently; and religions (i.e. religious people or institutions) have been evocative of art through patronage on a massive scale.

Yet at the same time, each religion develops its own distinctive art, *dance, architecture, and *music. That is because such art cannot be detached from the entire network of 'information' which constitutes the characteristic nature, form, and content of each religion (obviously, the sub-systems of any religion may themselves be competitive in such a way that the very status of art may itself be contested). Thus Judaism produces synagogues, Christianity produces churches, Islam mosques, Hinduism temples, Buddhism *stūpas, etc. Partly this is a function of available materials and current technology. But also (and much more), these characteristic 'shapes' are controlled into their outcome by the ideology (represented through signs, *symbols, and *icons) of the religion in question. These sign-systems provide the controlling metaphors for religious art; but then, conversely, religious art mediates those basic, controlling metaphors back into the lives of believers, transforming them into outcomes that could not otherwise occur.

Religious art does this at many different levels and in equally many different ways. At its most basic (and often most banal), religious art can be propaganda; not far beyond that, it can be exploitation (the attempt to elicit religious emotions at an immature level, what Rose Macaulay summarized as 'bleeding hearts in convent parlours'). It can be coercive (Doré's engravings of heaven are perfunctory, of hell terrifying), it can be repetitive and dull, it can simply be illustration. But moving again beyond that, religious art can both be, and be the instrument of, a reawakening of forgotten or abandoned truths about ourselves and our possibilities: it can open eyes to a new seeing of an otherwise prosaic world. At this level, the controlling metaphors become, not restriction, but opportunity, not least because they evoke contrasted meanings. Finally, the manifestations of religious art can be epiphany: they can *be* what they purport to be about, the incursion of whatever it is that is true into the midst of time and space. Art is then holy rather than religious. See also Index, Art; Aesthetics.

Judaism Jewish art is a dialectic between strong prohibitions against making images or likenesses of living creatures (Exodus 20. 4, Deuteronomy 4. 16–8, 5. 8) and the celebration of craftsmanship in the building of the Temple and its appurtenances. In general, Jewish art has focused on the synagogue and its contents, and on Torah manuscripts and Torah ornaments (e.g. the *keter* or crown, the *rimmonim*, the finials on the rollers holding the scroll). Jewish symbols reconnect with the lost temple, most recurrently through the *menorah. Among other books beautifully produced, the Passover Haggadah has been the most frequent.

Synagogue architecture has seen many different styles of hall or building appropriated through the ages. Apart from the necessity to separate women from men (in Orthodox synagogues), the main requirement is to give prominence (and protection) to the Torah Scroll, and to provide a pulpit for the reading of scripture.

Christianity Beginning from simple emblems of identity and allegiance (e.g. the sign of a fish, since the Gk. for 'fish' is *ichthus*, the letters of which stand for Jesus Christ, God and Saviour) Christian art and architecture developed into the most diverse forms of expression. The representation of biblical scenes, and of the Last Judgement, were visual aids in the instruction of largely illiterate or uneducated populations. But the power inherent in such representations led directly to the development of *icons—and to the eventual controversy about the extent to which, if at all, they were/are idolatrous. Mosaics (those of Ravenna being especially fine early examples) and wall-paintings were reinforced in churches by stained glass. But church buildings themselves summarized Christian truths and affirmations in their layout: thus the secular basilica, or assembly hall, was adapted to draw attention to the celebration of the *eucharist, and to the role of the *bishop in presiding; or again, Gothic cathedrals extended the shape to make it cruciform, and to enhance the vast and mysterious unknowability of God who can only be approached in penitence and praise. Redevelopment of Christian art simply cannot be summarized: resting frequently on a strong doctrine of creation (as also on developing systems of patronage and commissioning), it is, at its best, a deliberate extension of the work of the Holy Spirit in bringing order and beauty out of chaos and ugliness. At its worst, it is the illustration of a text, sometimes allied to the spiritual terrorization which can on occasion characterize Christian missionary zeal.

Islam Muslim art is controlled by the prohibition on rivalling God as creator, and thus on portraying the human figure. The work of the artist or architect in Islam is limited, therefore, to the work of giving praise to *Allāh, or to expressing allegiance (*islam). Supremely this is seen in *mosque architecture, which may be extremely simple—nothing more than a hut—or classically elegant and cool. It needs little more, internally, than the niche indicating the direction of prayer towards *Mecca (*mihrab*; see MOSQUE) and the pulpit for the delivering of the sermon (*khuṭba), and externally the minaret from which the faithful are summoned to prayer. But it calls also for the reminder of the primacy of the *Qur'ān over life through the carving of texts from the Qur'ān. This, as also the writing of copies of the Qur'ān, led to the most distinctive of Islamic art forms, *calligraphy.

Hinduism Of all religions, Hinduism is most vivid in its *iconography, because of its belief that the underlying source of all appearance (*Brahman) is present in all appearance. Thus the work of the sculptor, etc., is to make manifest what is already there in the material, not simply to illustrate a story about the gods. They can thus produce the state of *rasananda* (see RASA), blissful union with the god, often regarded as the equivalent of *samādhi. But the same is possible in all the arts (e.g. *dance, *music, drama) because there is nothing in the cosmos which is not sustained in being by Brahman. The recognition of this is equally obvious in the attention paid to the sacred orientation of space. The order made apparent in astronomy, geometry, mathematics (hence the early Hindu commitment to these arts which the West would regard as sciences) led to a mapping of that cosmic order on to space in miniature (e.g. through the *maṇḍala) or in the planning of towns, but above all in the architecture of temples and shrines.

The temple is the major source and expression of Hindu art. Its shape, laid down in the *śāstras, was originally a square, designed to concentrate force. Above the shrine is a tower (the *śikara*, a symbolic mountain), channelling the deity into the shrine and the worshipper, and radiating power upward as well. From the temple derive carving (to entice the deities or spirits), dance, the creation of manuscripts, and the decoration of textiles. The temple then reaches out into everyday life through the corresponding decoration of house and body. Thus the creation of the classical music, the *rāga, is understood as the 'building of a temple': 'In the improvised pieces, you start like building a temple: you lay the foundations, then gradually you build up the building, then you do the decorative things, like the painting and carving. Finally you bring out the deity, into that temple.'

Jainism Jain art is devoted mainly to the decoration of temples (*sāmavasarāna*, regarded as assemby halls of the *jinas, not as places where God or gods are worshipped) and to reverence for the jinas. While Jain art shares much of the styles and techniques of Indian art in general, it is different in important respects. Above all (since a controlling metaphor of paramount importance for Jains is *ahiṁsā), the atmosphere of Jain art is one of great peacefulness. For the same reason, materials are avoided which might involve the taking of life, e.g. clay and ivory. The main figures represented are those of the jinas, but the *śāsanadevatās are also common. Also distinctive are *ayagapata*, small carvings, incorporating elaborate symbolism, which express devotion. They may be related to *yantras and *maṇḍalas.

Sikhism See ICONOGRAPHY.

Buddhism Buddhist art, with the possible exception of *Zen art (see below), did not arise from such deep theoretical considerations as did the Hindu. It arose from grateful recognition of the work of the *Buddha in teaching the way to the cessation of *dukkha. The Buddha is therefore represented increasingly with the marks indicating his status or his achievement of *nirvāna. The elaboration of saviour-figures in Mahāyāna and Tibetan Buddhism led to an immense proliferation of sculpture and wall-painting, with extremely careful codes of iconographic symbols. The devotion of thanksgiving to the Buddha (and eventually to buddhas and *bodhisattvas) led to the building of *caityas and stūpas; and the formal organization of Buddhism into communities of monks (*bhikṣu) required the building of accommodation in monasteries (*vihāra). The development of these into large temple and monastic complexes is particularly impressive in Japan.

Ch'an/Zen art occupies a special place in Buddhism. Ch'an/Zen is a way of seeing through the superficial claims of appearance in reality, enticement, endurance, etc., to the true buddha-nature of all appearance. Zen realization, is both attained and expressed through the arts. Architecture of monasteries is thus related to environment, especially by the development of *gardens leading into the natural landscape. Rock gardens, with carefully swept sand, challenge the perception of the ordinary; the tea-garden surrounded the tea-ceremony (see CHADŌ).

In addition to architecture, *calligraphy is central in Ch'an/Zen art. Calligraphy precedes Ch'an in China, but it was raised to new heights by Ch'an practitioners, especially in the Sung period. In Japan, it was known originally as *shojutsu*, but later as *shodō*. The importance for Zen lies in the complete connection between the artist and the art: nothing serves so well to overcome the opposition between worker and work: the medium is the messenger; the connection from heart-mind, through brush and ink, to paper realizes the unity of the one buddha-nature.

Artha (Skt., 'goal', 'advantage', 'wealth'). 1. In Hinduism, a goal of life. There are four traditional arthas; *dharma (duty, law), artha (advantage, utility, goal-oriented activity), *kāma (erotic or aesthetic expression), and *mokṣa (release, liberation). Artha is success in one's worldly pursuits. See also ARTHAŚĀSTRA.

2. In *Sāṁkhya and *Yoga philosophy, the object of the senses.

Arthaśāstra (Skt., *artha*, 'advantage' + *śāstra*, 'teaching'). A Sanskrit text concerned with *artha, worldly advantage, especially the advantage of the prince (*rājanya*) and universal monarch (*cakravartin).

One of the most influential works of political philosophy, it is attributed to Kāuṭilya (or Caṇakya) a minister of Candragupta Māurya.

Kāuṭilya presupposes the traditional S. Asian concept of *matsyanyāya*, or 'law of the fishes', according to which large fish prey upon smaller fish.The role of the king, established through a pact made with the people, is to mitigate this law by providing protection for all *bhūtas, all human and non-human beings. Kāuṭilya maintains that warfare or *daṇḍanīti* is necessary to uphold the sanctity of the pact, the basis of social and cosmic peace. For Kāuṭilya, peace is not the absence of war, but the order maintained through war.

Arthur's Bosom (location of righteous souls): see ABRAHAM'S BOSOM.

Ārtī. Hindu offering of light during *pūjā (worship). It evoked from Gurū *Nānak the hymn *Sohilā, which remythologizes the ceremony.

Articles of faith (*ikkarim*, Heb., 'roots'). Formulations of Jewish belief. These are not as important as are *creeds in Christianity, since every person born of a Jewish mother is automatically a Jew irrespective of religious conviction. The *Shema', recited twice daily, is the fundamental Jewish article of faith. *Philo spoke of eight basic principles, Hananel b. Hushi'el isolated four articles, and *Maimonides set down thirteen *principles. These became the basis of later formulations, including *ani ma'amin of the Prayer Book, the 'ikkarim' of David Kokhavi, Hasdai *Crescas' *'Or Adonai* (Light of the Lord), and Joseph *Albo's *Sefer ha-Ikkarim* (Book of Roots). In the 12th cent., the *Karaite Judah Hadassi produced ten articles of faith, and in the 19th cent., Moses *Mendelssohn, the pioneer of modernism within Judaism, identified three essential principles.

Articles, Thirty-Nine: see THIRTY-NINE ARTICLES.

Aruṇācala (Skt., 'red mountain'). A holy mountain in Tamil Nadu, S. India, at whose foot lies the Arunācalasvara temple dedicated to *Śiva.

Arūpadhatu: see LOKA.

Arūpaloka: see LOKA (Buddhist).

Āryadeva or **Deva** (*c*.3rd cent. BCE; Tib., 'Phags-pa-lha). The foremost disciple of *Nāgārjuna and a leading exponent of the Buddhist *Mādhyamaka school of philosophy. His most celebrated work is the *Four Hundred Verses* (*Catuḥśataka*) which is in sixteen chapters: the first eight chapters expound the Mādhyamaka philosophy while the remaining eight are a refutation of rival Buddhist and non-Buddhist schools. It became a basic work for *San-lun.

Aryaman (generous nobility): see ĀDITYAS.

Ārya-mārga (Pāli, *ariya-magga*). Sacred path to the full and final attainment in Buddhism. It has four stages, divided according to whether the *arya-pudgala* (person on the path) is still on the way or has gained the fruit (*phala*): (i) is the stream-enterer (*srotāpanna); (ii) is the once-returner (*sakrdāgāmin); (iii) is the not-returner (*anāgāmin); (iv) is the attainer (*arhat).

Āryans. A group of Indo-European speaking people who spread through Iran and N. India in the early 2nd millenium BCE. This is the so-called Aryan invasion.

Arya-pudgala: see ĀRYA-MĀRGA.

Ārya Samāj. A Hindu reform movement founded by a *brahman, *Dayānanda Sarasvatī, in 1875. The followers of Dayānanda are against idol-worship and meaningless rituals in modern Hinduism, and aim to return to the *Vedas in their beliefs and ritual. Dayānanda's interpretation of the Vedas is to be found in his book *Vedabhāshya*. Followers of Ārya Samāj do not tolerate *caste divisions in Hindu society, and they introduced the novel idea of converting people of other faiths to Hinduism. The followers of Ārya Samāj do invaluable work to remove social and religious injustices. It is now a worldwide organization.

Ārya-satya (foundation of Buddha's teaching): see FOUR NOBLE TRUTHS.

Asa (one of the Holy Immortals): see AMESA SPENTAS.

Asahara Shoko (Japanese cult leader): see AUM SHINRIKYO.

Āsā kī Vār, Āsā dī Vār. *Hymn by *Gurū *Nānak, including some *śaloks by Gurū *Aṅgad repeated daily in Sikh morning *worship after *Japjī.

Asamprajñāta (Skt., 'non-differentiated', 'non-discerned') or **nirbīja** (Skt., 'without seed'). A stage of *samādhi in *rāja *yoga following from *samprajñāta ('differentiated') or *sabīja* ('with seed') samādhi. The **Yoga Sūtra* (1. 51) says that this state of consciousness is achieved upon the cessation (*nirodha) of all contents of consciousness (*citta), and that in it karmic impressions (*saṃskāras) are terminated.

Asaṃskṛta (Skt., 'not-conditioned'; Pāli *asankhata*). The state in Buddhism of anything that is beyond conditioned existence—the opposite, therefore, of saṃskṛta, the state in which all things are transient, coming into being, changing, and passing away.

Āsana (Skt. 'sitting', 'posture'). A posture assumed for the practice of *yoga; the third 'limb' of *Patañjali's 'eight-limbed' (*aṣṭāṅga) or *rāja yoga. Āsana keeps the body still, regulates physical processes, and so allows the yogin to concentrate his mind. In *Haṭha-yoga, āsana takes on central importance, and Haṭha-yoga and *Tantric texts describe and give lists of different āsanas. Perhaps the most famous is the 'lotus posture' (*padmāsana) in which the yogin sits with the right foot placed on the left thigh and the left foot on the right thigh, soles facing upwards, with the hands placed between the thighs palms facing up. The eyes are directed to the tip of the nose and tongue placed at the root of the front teeth.

Asaṅga (Skt., 'not-bound'). 1. In Hinduism, the state of the true self (*ātman) which knows itself to be what it is—not bound to, or identified with, the mind or body.

2. 4th cent. CE. Founder of the Buddhist Yogācāra/*Vijñānavāda school of idealism and elder brother of *Vasubandhu, from whose biography the details of Asaṅga's life are known. Numerous works are attributed to Asaṅga including the monumental *Yogācārabhumiśāstra*, *Mahāyānasutrālaṃkāra*, and *Mahāyānasaṃgraha*.

Asankhata: see ASAṂSKṚTA.

Asaññasatta (Pāli, 'unconscious being'). In Buddhism, a class of celestial beings who through the practice of meditation have reached a lofty state of existence in which mental activity is suspended for great lengths of time.

Asat (Skt., 'not-being'). Linguistically the opposite of *sat (being), but not in the sense of annihilation or nihilism. Asat is the unimaginable, that which is in the absence of objects. It is thus the Absolute without qualities in *Advaita Vedānta.

Asava (in Buddhism, the destructive poison of desire): see DAŚABALA.

Āsava or **Āśrava** (Pāli/Skt., 'outflow', as from a sore). In Buddhism, a group of basic defects or defilements which are the cause of repeated rebirth. There is an original list of three which is often supplemented by a fourth. Among Jains, āśrava is the incursion of consequence from *karma, which has to be recognized by appropriate attention before it can be eliminated.

ASB (Church of England service book): see ALTERNATIVE SERVICE BOOK.

Ascama (rabbinic approval of halakhic decision): see HASKAMAH.

Ascension. The withdrawal of *Christ into heaven witnessed by the *apostles forty days after his *resurrection (Acts 1. 9).

'Ascension' may also refer to the ascent of the Prophet *Muḥammad to heaven: see MI'RĀJ.

'Ascension' is then applied to many descriptions of other-world journeys, especially among *shamans.

Ascetical theology (Gk., *askēsis*, 'exercise', 'training'). The theological discipline concerned with the ways of reaching Christian perfection, and especially with the human activities involved: ways of overcoming temptation, cultivating the virtues, fasting, and prayer. It overlaps with, and is with difficulty precisely distinguished from, moral theology and *mystical theology.

Asceticism (Gk., *askesis*, 'exercise', as of an athlete). The practice of self-denial or self-control as a means of religious attainment through discipline. Asceticism occurs in all religions, since in all religions there are more important things in life than living, and to attain particular goals, or to serve others, the giving up of some things on one's own behalf may be the only way forward. Nevertheless, asceticism is somewhat suspect in Judaism (but see BAḤYA BEN JOSEPH) and in Islam, because it seems to imply a denial of the goodness of God's creation. Even so, *ṣawm (fasting during the month of Ramadhan) is one of the *Five Pillars of Islam; see also ZUHD.

In Hinduism, the most basic structure of ordinary life, the four stages of life (*āśrama) are marked by discipline, culminating in complete renunciation; the practice of asceticism is marked *pravrajya (going forth from home). The efficacy of self-mortification (*tapas) is so great that even the gods engage in it. This is even more marked in Jainism, where the ideal is the one who dies his death before it actually occurs (see SALLEKHANĀ). The practice of control becomes literally manifest in the many techniques of *yoga.

All of these were practised by Gautama in the early stages of the quest for enlightenment which culminated in his becoming the *Buddha.

Renouncing these practices as counterproductive, the Buddha came to be critical of contemporary ascetic movements, and in several discourses he describes and criticizes their many and varied practices. Although the Buddha prohibited extreme practices, he allowed twelve optional practices (*dhutanga) of a moderately ascetic kind but resisted the attempt to make five of them compulsory for monks; thirteen are listed in *Visuddhimagga* 11.

Among Jains, the commitment to asceticism is the central dynamic of the whole system. Those far enough advanced in the emancipation of *jīva from *karma (see GUNASTHĀNA) undergo initiation (*dīkṣa) and take the *Five Great Vows (*mahāvrata*); but the laity are closely integrated, by being on the same path, and by the formality of *dāna, gifts in support of the ascetics. The two immediate aims of the Jain ascetic counterbalance each other, *saṃyama being restraint, and *tapas being the generation of 'heat' (i.e. spiritual power).

Among Sikhs, asceticism is viewed with caution: the *Gurus advocated for all Sikhs full involvement in family life coupled with self-discipline. For the *amritdhārī this frequently means a vegetarian diet and avoidance of *alcohol. Austerities and penances are considered painful, irrelevant and not conducive to spiritual development. (see GRAHASTI; NIRMALĀ; SRĪ CHAND; TOBACCO.)

The origins of Christian asceticism are to be found in the strongly *eschatological consciousness of early Christians who looked forward to an imminent end of the world in which good would triumph over evil in a holy war. They were to prepare themselves by watchfulness, prayer, fasting, and, for many, sexual continence (cf. 1 Samuel 21. 5), anticipating martyrdom as the test of their faithfulness and a sign of the imminence of the final struggle. With the triumph of Christianity in the 4th cent. this attitude of eschatological awareness was inherited by the *monastic movement, and Christian asceticism became archetypically monastic. A systematic understanding of the demands of such asceticism on human nature was developed, notably by *Evagrius, and later by *Cassian and Dorotheus. The Renaissance brought a reaction against Christian asceticism, intensified by the Reformation with its tendency to suggest the worthlessness of human effort. See Index, Asceticism.

Aseity (Lat., *a se*, 'in himself', that which God is): see NOMINALISM.

Asenath. Daughter of the Egyptian high priest of On and wife of *Joseph. Her two sons, Manasseh and *Ephraim, were the *patriarchs of their eponymous tribes.

Ash or **ashes.** In Western religions, ashes generally represent human frailty and mortality. Thus in Christianity, ashes are smeared on the forehead during the *Ash Wednesday ritual. The words of committal in the Anglican **Book of Common Prayer* are, 'We commit this body to the ground, earth to earth, ashes to ashes, dust to dust.' But in Indian religions, and especially among Hindus, ash represents the pure substance left when the impure accidents of life have been removed. Ash is therefore smeared on the body as a mark of commitment to the process of liberating the true self from all that encumbers it. *Saivites are distinguished by three horizontal ash marks across the forehead.

Ashamnu (Heb., 'we have sinned'). Opening words of the Jewish penitential *prayers.

Ash'arī (Muslim theologian): see AL-ASH'ARI.

Asher. One of the twelve tribes of Israel.

Asherah. A Canaanite goddess and a wooden cult figure. Asherah was the mother Goddess and apparently the consort to *El, the father and creator of the gods.

Asher b. Jehiel/Yeḥi'el (also known as 'Asheri' and 'Rosh' *c.*1250–1327). Jewish *Talmudic authority. After the imprisonment of his teacher, *Meir of Rothenburg, he became the leader of the German Jewish community, but later fled from Germany and became *rabbi of Toledo. He encouraged the Spanish leaders to support Solomon *Adret's ban on the study of philosophy for those under the age of 25, and his *responsa were hugely influential throughout Europe.

Asher Hirsh Ginsberg (Jewish Zionist leader): see AHAD HA-'AM.

Asheri: see ASHER B. JEHIEL.

Ashes: see ASH.

Ashkenazim. German Jewry and its descendants in other countries. Originally the Ashkenaz referred to a small group of Jews settled on the banks of the Rhine. Gradually the term included all Jews from northern France, through Germany to Poland and Russia, and now includes their descendants in Israel, Australia, and the USA. The Ashkenazim are specifically contrasted with the *Sephardim, the Jews whose cultural origin was in Spain. Ashkenazi and Sephardi customs and rituals remain distinctive from one another.

Ashkenazi, Zevi Hirsch b. Jacob (also known as the Ḥakham Zevi, 1660–1718). Jewish *halakhist. Despite his *Ashkenazi origin, he adopted *Sephardi customs and was appointed *Ḥakham of the community of Sarajevo. His chief work was a collection of responsa, *Ḥakham Zevi* (Rabbi Zevi) which dealt with such matters as the relationship between the Ashkenazim and Sephardim, and also with more specific questions—as, e.g., whether a *golem can be counted to make up the requisite number for prayer.

Ashoka (Indian ruler): see AŚOKA.

Ashram: see ĀŚRAMA.

Ashrei (Heb., 'happy are they'). First word of a reading from the book of Psalms used in the Jewish *liturgy.

Ashtoreth or **Astarte.** Pagan Goddess. Frequently designated in the Bible as the feminine version of *Ba'alim and generally used to mean pagan worship.

'Ashūrā' (Arab., from Heb., *'āsōr*, 'tenth [of the month]'). The Jewish *Day of Atonement, observed as a day of fasting by the early Muslim community in *Madīna. It became a voluntary fast day on 10 *Muḥarram, often observed by the pious. For *Shī'a Muslims, this is the anniversary of the death of *al-Husain at the hands of the Caliph Yazīd, and it is observed often with displays of self-inflicted wounds indicating willingness for martyrdom, and by martyrdom plays (*ta'ziya).

Ash Wednesday. So-called because of the practice of marking with *ash the foreheads of clergy and people at the beginning of *Lent.

Asmi-māna (Pāli, 'pride of "I am" '). In Buddhism, self-pride, egoism, conceit; considered to be a major obstacle to moral and spiritual development at any stage along the path to *nirvāna. One of the ten fetters (*saññojana*) and an important factor in Buddhist teaching on no-self (*anatta), it is combated specifically by meditation on impermanence (*anicca).

Asmita (Skt., 'I am-ness'). The error in Hinduism of supposing that the immediately experienced self is the true self: it is one of four kinds of error or ignorance (*avidyā), to be overcome in *yoga. The others are *rāga (attachment), *dvesa* (aversion, which indicates that one is still involved, albeit by a feeling of revulsion), and *abhiniveṣa* (love of material and physical life).

Asmodeus or **Ashmedai.** An evil spirit. He first appears in Tobit and subsequently in the *Testament of Solomon*. In folklore he often appears as the butt of jokes and is frequently seen as a kindly spirit and the friend of human beings.

Aśoka (3rd cent. BCE). Indian ruler of the Mauryan dynasty who converted to Buddhism and did much to promote the faith, while at the same time allowing freedom of worship to all creeds. He proclaimed his ethical principles throughout his empire by means of *Edicts inscribed upon rocks, pillars, and walls of caves. From the Edicts it may be seen that the content of Aśoka's *Dharma is essentially that of a lay Buddhist: it consists of 'Few sins and many good deeds, of kindness, liberality, truthfulness and purity' (Pillar Edict 2). But no reference is made to the technical aspects of Buddhist doctrine as expounded in the *Four Noble Truths.

Asparśa (Skt. 'non-touching). In Hinduism, keeping apart from the worldly and carnal influences of the world.

Āśrama, Āśram. 1. A centre (usually Hindu) for religious study and meditation.

2. The four stages of life for a Hindu following the *Vedic way: *brahmacarya (receiving instruction), *gṛhastha (householder), *vānaprastha (forest dweller), *saṁnyāsa (renouncer).

Āśrava (defilement): see ĀSAVA.

Āśraya (Skt., 'basis'). In Buddhist Sanskrit sources, a term used mainly in a philosophical sense to refer to the receptacle-consciousness (*alaya-vijñāna) as the basis or support of the other six consciousnesses (*vijñāna) or sense-modalities. Less commonly the term is used of the body itself as the substrate or support for conscious experience.

Assassins (Fr., from Arab., *ḥashīshī*, 'one who consumes hashish'). An *Ismā'īlī (Nizārī) sect at the time of the *crusades, founded by *al-Ḥasan b. al-Sabbah, who resorted to assassination supposedly under the influence of the drug (though the name *ḥashīshī* is not often used outside Syrian texts). Taking advantage of the confused conditions, the sect gained considerable strength, but was driven out of its mountain strongholds in the 13th cent. CE. The ruler of the Syrian assassins was known as *shaikh al-jabal*, 'the Old Man of the Mountain'.

Assemblies of God. Christian denomination. It was organized in 1914 in Hot Springs, Arkansas, USA, from previously independent *Pentecostal churches. It became the largest white Pentecostal body in the USA, with 1.4 million adherents in 10,000 autonomous congregations throughout the country.

Assimilation. The process of so integrating with another culture that distinctive Jewish identity is lost. From biblical times, there has been a fear of Jews being assimilated into the pagan cultures of the surrounding nations, and early Christianity is seen by some Jewish communities as a process of assimilation of the early Jewish Christians into a *gentile mode of life. Since the second half of the 18th cent., assimilation has been a serious threat to the continued existence of Judaism and the Jewish people. Thus the modern community is increasingly polarized between the almost completely assimilated and those who are affirming their Jewish character more strongly than ever.

Association For Research and Enlightenment. A movement founded in Virginia Beach, Virginia, USA, in 1931 by the so-called 'sleeping prophet', Edgar *Cayce, and continued under Hugh Lynn Cayce, son of the founder. It is characterized by religious tolerance, holistic health practices, metaphysical teachings, and effective marketing techniques. The ARE, with its occult practices, shares with many other New Age groups a belief in reincarnation, parapsychology, astrology, Atlantis, and novel interpretations of Christianity, such as the belief that *Jesus travelled to India, Tibet, and Egypt for training.

Assumption of the Virgin Mary. The Christian belief that *Mary was taken body and soul into heaven at the end of her life. The doctrine first emerged in various New Testament *apocrypha of the 4th cent., and on the strength of a passage in pseudo-*Dionysius became accepted in orthodox circles by the 7th cent. Finally in 1950 Pope *Pius XII, in the decree *Munificentissimus Deus*, defined it as a divinely revealed dogma. In Orthodox Churches, the belief is generally held but with less precise definition. Feast day in the W., 15 Aug.

Assyrian Church. A name used since the 19th cent. for the *Church of the East. It became popular especially in *Anglican circles as a way of avoiding the name *Nestorian, which was disliked by the Syrians themselves and appeared to prejudge their orthodoxy.

Aṣṭamangala (Skt.). In Hinduism, eight objects to make auspicious an important occasion, e.g. the coronation of a king. They are variously listed, but a typical list includes: a lion, bull, elephant, banner, trumpet, water-jar, fan, lamp. For a lesser occasion the list might include: a king, *brahman, cow, sun, water, fire, gold, ghee.

In Buddhism, the practice was adapted to express veneration of the *Buddha as universal sovereign. The eight symbols are often placed before images of the Buddha. They are: parasol (power and protection); two fish (kingship); conch shell (conqueror); lotus blossom (purity); water-jar (nectar of *amṛta); banner (victory of the spirit); knot (endless eternity); wheel of teaching (*dharma-cakra).

Aṣṭāṅga-yoga (Skt., 'eight-limbed yoga'). A name in Hinduism for *Rāja-yoga, which has eight steps (aṅga): for details, see RĀJA-YOGA.

Aṣṭangika-mārga (Skt.; Pāli, *aṭṭangika-magga*). The eightfold path which leads, in Buddhism, to release from *dukkha (transience and the suffering involved in it). It is the last of the *Four Noble Truths, and one of the thirty-seven 'limbs' of enlightenment (*bodhipākṣika-dharma). Each of the eight is described as *samyak* (Skt.), *samma* (Pāli), often translated 'right'; but the meaning intended is not 'correct' as opposed to 'incorrect', but rather 'complete' or 'perfected'. They are: (i) perfected view (*samyak-dristhi/sammā-ditthi*), which understands the Four Noble Truths and their dependence on no persistent substantiality (*anātman); (ii) perfected resolution (*s.-kalpa/s.-sankappa*) in the direction of non-attachment, *ahiṁsā, etc.; (iii) perfected speech (*s.-vāc/s.-vāchā*), free from malice, gossip, lies, etc.; (iv) perfected conduct or action (*s.-karmānta/s.-kammanta*) in accordance with *śīla; (v) perfected livelihood (*s.-ājīva*), avoiding work which might harm others; (vi) perfected effort (*s.-vyāyāma/s.-vayāma*) in setting forward that which produces good *karma/kamma; (vii) perfected mindfulness (*s.-smriti/s.-sati*), as summarized in *satipaṭṭhāna; (viii) perfected concentration (*s.-samādhi/s.-samādhi*), especially in *jhāna.

In *Mahāyāna Buddhism they become: (i) insight into *dharmakāya* (*trikāya); (ii) cessation of mental superimpositions; (iii) silence in absorption of *dharma; (iv) withdrawal from all actions with karmic consequence; (v) living in a way that dharma neither arises nor ceases; (vi) abandoning all intentionality; (vii) giving up reflection on unprofitable questions; (viii) no reliance on ideas or concepts at all.

Aṣṭapadī (Pañjābī, 'eight stanzas'). A poem of eight or occasionally more verses. In the *Ādi Granth, within each *rāg the *Gurūs' aṣṭapadīs are grouped between the last *chaupad and the first *chhant.

Aṣṭasāhasrikā-Prajñāpāramitā-Sūtra. Early (*c*.100 BCE) *perfection of wisdom *sūtra, 'The Sūtra of Perfect Wisdom in 8,000 Lines'. It elevates the *bodhisattvas as the practitioners of the six perfections (*pāramitā), and therefore points the way to the practice of *jhāna (meditation).

Aṣṭāvakra. The teacher of *Patañjali.

Aṣṭa-vimokṣa (Skt.). Eight liberations, a meditation exercise in Buddhism which leads to detachment from dependence on forms of appearance.

Asterisk (Gk., 'a star'). A metal (usually gold or silver) instrument used in Greek Orthodoxy to cover the *paten so that the covering veils do not touch the consecrated bread during the *eucharist.

Asteya (Indian vow against stealing): see APARIGRAHA (I).

Asthangika-mārga (Buddhist eightfold path): see AṢṬANGIKA-MARGA.

Āstika (Skt.). Hindu name for the six philosophical systems (*darśana) which adhere correctly to the *Vedas, acknowledging their authority. The opposite are the *nāstika systems.

Astikaya ('it exists' + 'a body'). The five elements of Jain ontology. According to Jains, there are five elements which pervade the universe (*loka) and which keep it in being: (i) *jīva, 'life-permeation'; (ii) *dharma, 'movement'; (iii) *pudgala*, 'atomic individuals'; (iv) *ākāśa*, 'space'; all of these making up the fifth category of non-jīva, *ajīva.

Astrology. The belief that the stars and planets have effects on human life and affairs. It is entangled in astronomy, and while the two, in some religions, reinforce each other, they may also be in serious conflict.

In Hinduism, decision-making on all serious matters (e.g. the date and time of a wedding) and on many everyday matters is referred to astrology (*jyotiṣa).

In general, Buddhism adopted the Hindu scheme of astronomy but rejected the latter's preoccupation with astrology. The position and movement of the celestial bodies were of interest to Buddhists for pragmatic purposes only.

Astrology and divination are stigmatized as practices unworthy of a monk, and the *Buddha is singled out for praise as one not devoting himself to such 'low arts' (*tiracchāna-vijjā*). However, the practice of divination by monks was never eradicated. In practically all Buddhist cultures monks officiate as advisers to the laity and employ techniques of divination.

Sikhs return to a more basic condemnation of astrology. Although some Sikhs may consult horoscopes, astrology is condemned by the *Rahit-Maryādā in accordance with the *Gurūs' teaching. See CALENDAR; SANGRĀND.

In both Judaism and Christianity, astrology is officially condemned (e.g. *Catechism of the Catholic Church* (1994), 2116), because it detracts from the sovereignty of God, as though stars and planets can be lesser creators in God's world; but unofficially, at the level of folk-religion, the consulting of horoscopes is simply one example of how tenacious these beliefs are.

In Islam, the contest between astronomy and astrology (*'ilm al-nujūm*) became explicit in *al-Ghaz(z)ālī: he commended astronomy as a part of the study of the signs of God in God's creation (*aya), but strongly condemned astrology as spurious. Even so, the same term was still being applied to both, *'ilm ahḳam al-nujūm*, and the practice of astrology did not abate, at least at the popular level. See Index, Astrology.

Aśubha (Skt., 'not-beautiful'). The contemplation in Buddhism of disgusting objects, sometimes equated with reflection on the unpleasing features of the body, especially of corpses in different stages of decay. It is thus a dramatic instance of *memento mori*.

Asura (Skt.), power-seeking and power-hungry being, not unlike a Titan, often, but somewhat misleadingly translated as 'demon'; or, *anārya* (non-*Āryan) people of ancient India. The derivation of asura is uncertain.

Asuras are not necessarily evil, nor are devas necessarily good. They are consubstantial, distinguished only by their mutual opposition, which is not conceived as an absolute ethical *dualism.

Aśvaghoṣa (2nd cent. CE). A court poet of the Kusāna king Kaniṣka and author of literary works in Sanskrit on Buddhist themes. He is known to be the author of three such works: *The Acts of the Buddha* (*Buddhacarita*), *Nanda the Fair* (*Saundarananda*), and *The Story of Sariputra* (*Sāriputraprakaraṇa*). His most famous work is the first of these, a biography of the *Buddha in epic *mahākāvya* style.

Aśvamedha. A Hindu, *Vedic, ritual of horse-sacrifice. It was performed by kings as a symbolic representation of their supreme power and authority, as well as, sometimes, for such boons as the birth of a son to ensure succession. For one year the chosen horse might wander as he pleased, unmolested and protected by an armed guard. Should he trespass into another kingdom, its ruler would have to give battle or submit. At the end of the year the horse was brought back to the capital with due ceremony, and sacrificed along with other animals. The fertility element of the ceremony is evident from the way in which, symbolically, the senior queen would lie beside the dead horse. Jaya Siṇha II of Jaipur was the last prince to perform this sacrifice, in the 18th cent.

Aśvin(s) (Skt., *aśva*, 'horse'). Two Hindu, *Vedic, deities, who appear at dawn, drawn in a golden carriage by horses or birds. They are associated with light and the sun, and are particularly auspicious and helpful.

Atami (religious centre): see SEKAI KYŪSEIKYŌ.

Āṭānatiyā (part of Buddhist Pāli canon): see DIGHA-NIKĀYA.

Atas. Fire, in *Zoroastrianism one of the seven Good Creations of *Ahura Mazda, the one most commonly bound up with worship. There are many levels to the symbolism. The ritual fire is the focal point of Zoroastrian ceremonies, interpreted by some as radiating the power of God, and by others as the best symbol of 'He who is himself pure undefiled light'. All Zoroastrians believe that when they stand in purity and in devotion before the sacred fire, they stand in the presence of God. The common label 'fire-worshipper' is offensive to them, because they rightly believe it fails to do justice to the richness of the symbolism and the religion.

When the *Parsis first settled in India, they maintained only one permanently burning ritual fire for many centuries. In Muslim Iran, many temples were desecrated and destroyed, and mosques were built on the ruins to highlight the Muslim triumph. The home, therefore, continued to be the main setting for much Zoroastrian devotional life.

There are three categories of fire, and two types of fire temple. The different grades of fire are distinguished by the manner of their consecration. The highest, the *Bahram* fire, involves the bringing together and consecrating of sixteen different types of fire (e.g. fire which has cooked dead matter and has thus been involved in the greatest pollution, goldsmith's fire, a shepherd's fire, and one caused by lightning). The rites are so complex they last a year. Temples housing such fires are sometimes referred to as 'Cathedral Fire Temples' because of their status. There are four such temples in Iran, and eight in India (four in Bombay and the oldest of all, which has burnt for over 1,000 years, at Udwada). They are treated as royalty, with a crowning dome, and the wood is laid on them in the shape of a throne.

The second grade of fire, the *Adaran* fire, is the one which burns in most temples, and its consecration is much less complicated, combining only four types of fire (that of priests, warriors, farmers, and artisans). Like the Atas Bahram it can be tended only by a ritually pure priest. The third grade of fire, the *dadgah*, may be tended by a lay person in the home, but is also used in the 'inner' or 'higher' ceremonies in the temple where it is tended by the priest. In both Iran and India, temples are commonly referred to as *Dar-i-Mihrs* (Gateway or Court of Mithra), or in India by the Gujarati as *Agiary*, or 'House of fire'.

Atatürk (Turkish Leader known as 'father of the Turks'): see OTTOMAN EMPIRE.

Athanasian Creed. A statement of faith formerly widely used in W. churches. It begins: 'Whosoever will be saved, before all things it is necessary that he hold the Catholic faith. Which faith except everyone do keep whole and undefiled, he shall perish everlastingly.'

The opening words thus furnish the alternative title 'Quicunque Vult'. It was composed in the 4th or 5th cent. (certainly after the time of *Athanasius) in Latin.

Athanasius, St (*c*.296–373). Bishop of *Alexandria and important church *father. He opposed any compromise with *Arianism at the council of *Nicaea (325), and so was repeatedly deposed and exiled from his *see while that party was in the ascendant. He was finally restored in 366. Athanasius's most important work (written before *c*.318) was *On the *Incarnation*. Athanasius's (probably genuine) *Life of *Antony* stimulated the monastic movement in Egypt and made it known in the West.

Atharvan. The priest who in Indian religion was the first to generate fire, to institute its worship, and to offer *soma (*Ṛg Veda* 1. 83. 5). For those reasons he was called 'the father of fire'. His descendants, the Atharvānas, have inherited his responsibilities in relation to domestic rituals. See also ATHARVA VEDA.

Atharva Veda (Skt.). The *Vedic collection of hymns used by the *Atharvan priests in the domestic rituals. Because of its lack of connection to the larger, more public Vedic sacrifices, the *Atharva Veda* early on was relegated to a secondary position and denied the title *Veda accorded the *trayī vidyā* (threefold knowledge), i.e. the *Ṛg*, **Sāma*, and **Yajur Veda*. The Atharvan school responded by claiming the office of the domestic priest (*purohita) and officiating priest (*brahman), by adding a final section of hymns (book 20) devoted specifically to one of the major sacrifices, the *soma sacrifice, and by expounding a tradition of the fourfold Veda. The Atharva Veda consists of sundry hymns not easily divided into these categories. Charms, curses, hymns intended for healing, recovering, or inflicting injury are mixed with hymns of praise and speculation.

Athavale, Pandurang Vaijnath Shastri (1920–), known as Dadaji, founder of the Hindu movement, Swadhyaya. Born in Maharashtra, he reacted against formal and institutional religion, regarding these as leading to intolerance and divisiveness. He urged people instead to make a total offering of their time and creative energy to God, taking as their focus the recognition of God in others. Swadhyaya draws people together so that this endeavour is reinforced in cooperation. In 1997, he received the Templeton Prize for Progress in Religion.

Atheism. Disbelief in the existence of God; to be distinguished from *agnosticism, which professes uncertainty on the question. Modern atheists make a variety of claims to defend their position: that there is little or no real evidence for the existence of God, that *theism is refuted by the existence of *evil in the world, that it is meaningless because unverifiable, that it is inauthentic because it attacks human autonomy, and that it is unscientific.

In Indian religion and philosophy, atheism is addressed to different understandings of what God is and does (according to those who believe), and is often more subtle. Thus Jains and Buddhists allow that within the domains of appearance, that which might be labelled 'God' is no less (but no more) real than other transient appearances, and is of effect; but in practice, 'God' must be left behind for true progress to be made. Among Hindus, several systems interpreted the tradition without involving God, e.g. Carvaka; Saṁkhya was initially atheistic, though God was later able to be accommodated in the system; and Pūrva and Uttara Mīmāṃsā debated the worth of arguments pointing to God.

Athos, Mount. Peninsula in NE Greece (*c*.48 × 10 km. in area), named for the mountain at its end. Known as the 'Holy Mountain' (Hagion Oros), it is the principal centre of *Orthodox monasticism. It is an autonomous monastic district, in effect a theocratic republic from 1927. Its importance dates from the foundation of the monastery of the *Lavra in 962. Most communities are *coenobitic, with the 'idiorrhythmic' houses, in which each monk arranges his own work and meals, gradually disappearing.

Of the twenty monasteries, seventeen are Greek; there is one Russian, one Serbian, and one Bulgarian. A rule forbids women, or even female animals, to set foot on the peninsula.

Atiśa (also Atīśa and Dīpaṅkaraśrījñāna; *c*.982–1054). Indian teacher who strongly influenced the development of Buddhism during its 'second diffusion' in Tibet. As one of the most revered teachers in India, Atiśa left to enter Tibet in 1042 at the invitation of King Byang.chub.' od, and stayed until his death.

On arrival in Tibet, Atiśa found that Buddhism was only beginning to reassert itself there following the earlier persecution by King Langdarma, and that the monks lacked guidance on interpretation of the 'old' *tantras such as Atiśa found at Samye, and the 'new' tantras being freshly introduced by the great traveller-translators such as Rinchen Zangpo. Atiśa's main task was to correct their superficial interpretations. Atiśa accomplished this essentially by emphasizing monastic discipline, the grounding of *Tantrism in the philosophy and ethics of the *sūtras, and the need for a pupil to devote himself to a single teacher.

Atiśa is credited with the introduction into Tibet of the worship of *Tārā, and of the popular system of meditation and philosophy known as Lojong (*blo.sbyong*, 'mind training'), which involves such meditations as the consideration of all beings as having been one's mother in a previous existence. Of more than 200 works ascribed to Atiśa, his most famous is *Bodhipathapradīpa* (A Lamp for the Path to Enlightenment), elucidating the correct development of the *bodhisattva.

Atiyoga (exceptional or perfect yoga): see DZOGCHEN.

Atlanteans. A philosophical society founded in 1957 from the teachings of a 'spirit guide' named Helio-Arcanophus. These teachings place emphasis upon the importance of the individual and the need to find a meaning to life which can help sweep aside frustration and allow one to develop spiritually.

Ātmabodha. A short treatise on 'knowledge of the Self', attributed to *Śaṅkara. In sixty-eight verses (*ślokas*) it covers the most important points of *Advaita-Vedānta.

Ātman (Skt.). For Hindus and Sikhs, the real or true Self, which underlies and is present in human appearance. In the Vedas, that sense had not developed. In the **Ṛg Veda* it means breath, or the whole body, as opposed to parts of it. It may even simply be a reflexive pronoun (cf. *nafs in Arabic). It was only in the period of the *Āraṇyakas and *Upaniṣads that attempts were made to define and describe the nature of this 'self' more precisely. *Brihādaranyaka Upaniṣad* 1. 3. 22 states that the vital force, ātman (now much more than breath) is present and operative in every form of life, not just in humans. Ātman is therefore necessarily identical with *Brahman.

In Buddhism, this idea of ātman was profoundly contradicted: see ANĀTMAN (= *anatta*). For Sikhs, the immortal ātman is the means of relation to God—indeed, the union (for those who attain it) is so close that it comes close at times to identity: 'God abides in the ātman, and the ātman abides in God' (*Ādi Granth 1153).

Atonement

Judaism (Heb., *kapparah*). Reconciliation with God. According to Jewish belief, human sin damages the relationship with God and only the process of atonement can restore it. According to biblical teaching, *sacrifice was the outward form of atonement (Leviticus 5), provided human beings also purified themselves spiritually (e.g. Isaiah 1. 11–17). After the destruction of the *Temple in 70 CE, (the only means of atonement were *prayer, repentance, fasting, *charity, and full restitution. See also DAY OF ATONEMENT.

Christianity In Christian theology, atonement is the reconciliation ('at-one-ment') of men and women to God through the death of Christ. The word was introduced by W. *Tyndale (in 1526) to translate *reconciliatio*.

Although there have been no official Church definitions of the doctrine of the atonement, there have been many accounts of how the life, death, resurrection, and ascension of Jesus effect for others the forgiveness and reconciliation with God which he clearly mediated to many during his lifetime and ministry: in other words, these accounts attempt to answer the questions of what the death of Jesus adds to his life, or of how the 'atonements' effected in his life are still achieved after his death. In general, these accounts claim that the death of Jesus universalizes what would otherwise have been a local and restricted transaction. There are five major accounts falling into two groups, objective and subjective theories. Objective theories claim that something factual has been done for us which has dealt with the reality of sin, and which we could not have done for ourselves. The penal (or juridical) theory claims that Christ has borne the penalty instead of us, so that God can now forgive freely: sin, being an infinite offence against God, required a correspondingly infinite satisfaction which only God could make (see ANSELM). Literally interpreted, this may lead to claims that Christ is a substitute for each individual who deserves the penalty, hence substitutionary theories of atonement. Equally objective are sacrificial theories, which claim that Christ is the sinless offering who makes a universal expiation of the stain of sin—or, with less biblical and religious warrant, that he propitiates the deserved wrath of God; in neither of these cases is Christ a substitute: the New Testament seems to think more in terms of Christ as the representative of human beings. Again objectively, the atonement has been understood as a victory (perhaps by way of being a ransom or a 'bait') against evil and sin personified in the Devil: this is often called the classic or dramatic theory, also the *Christus Victor theory (the title, in English, of G. Aulén's influential article, subsequently book, *Den kristna forsonnigstanken*, 1930/1). Subjective theories, also known as moral or exemplary theories, claim that the extent of God's love revealed in Christ and especially in his acceptance of a brutal and unjust death, move us to repentance. This theory is especially associated with *Abelard. All these theories have an individualistic emphasis, as has the missionary appeal based on them. The advent of the *sociology of religion has led in the 20th cent. to an increasing stress on the corporate nature of atonement, on the death and resurrection of Christ, recapitulated in *baptism and the *eucharist, constituting people as his body. This social understanding of atonement has been expressed especially through *Liberation Theology.

Attangika-magga (Buddhist eightfold path): see AṢṬANGIKA-MĀRGA.

'Aṭṭār, Farīd al-Dīn (d. *c.*1229 (AH 627)). Persian mystic (*Sūfī) and poet. He is particularly remembered for *Mantiq al-Ṭā'ir* (The Language of the Birds). 'Aṭṭār composed an allegory of the spiritual journey, with all the birds following the Hudhud (Hoopoe) bird. In the end they come to an indivisible union with the King. But he wrote many other, often epic, poems, e.g. *Muṣībatnāmah* (Book of Affliction), *Ilāhīnāmah* (Divine Book).

Aṭṭha-loka-dhamma (Pāli, 'eight worldly concerns'). Buddhism teaches that there are eight matters which are common human preoccupations. They are 'gain and loss, fame and obscurity, praise and blame, happiness (*sukha*) and suffering (*dukkha)'. Looking at the world in these terms, however, is regarded as inherently unsatisfying, and perfect happiness (*paramasukha*) is not possible until they are abandoned.

Auden, Wystan Hugh (1907–73). A poet increasingly involved in the exploration and expression of Christian themes. After the death of his mother (a committed Anglo-Catholic) in 1941, he became increasingly concerned with religion. This is particularly evident in a Christmas oratorio (written for Benjamin Britten), *For the Time Being* (1944) and a reflection on Good Friday, *Horae Canonicae* (1955). Acknowledgement of guilt becomes the ground of freedom: to live in the tangle of human history makes one, inevitably, an accomplice, but to acknowledge complicity is the beginning of *grace.

Augsburg Confession. A summary of the Christian faith drawn up during the *Reformation for the Diet of Augsburg, and presented to the emperor Charles V. It was written by *Luther, *Melanchthon, and two others. A final authorized text was issued, to create the document which remains of foundational importance in Lutheranism. The first twenty-one articles deal with similarities and dissimilarities between Lutherans and Roman Catholics, the last seven with abuses in the existing church.

Augustine of Canterbury, St (d. 604 or 605). Missionary to England and first *archbishop of *Canterbury. He was sent by Pope *Gregory in 596 to re-establish the church in England. A few months after his landing in 597, Christianity was formally adopted by King Ethelbert of Kent. About 603 he attempted but failed to reach an agreement with the Celtic Church on matters of discipline and practice. At Canterbury, he helped to establish the monastery of Sts Peter and Paul, where the first ten archbishops were buried.

Augustine of Hippo, St (354–430). Christian *father and *doctor of the Church. He was a native of Tagaste in N. Africa. His mother *Monica was a Christian, but as a young man he gradually abandoned what Christian belief he had. For nine years he was associated with the *Manichaeans, but had left this religion also by the time he came to Rome as a teacher of rhetoric. Becoming a professor of rhetoric at Milan, he became a Neoplatonist and, under the influence of *Ambrose, was converted to Christianity in 386, after responding to a command, 'Tolle, lege', and opening the New Testament at Romans 13. 13 f. He returned to N. Africa, was ordained priest in 391 and became *bishop of Hippo (modern Bōne in Algeria) *c.*396. His own life and conversion were the subject of his deeply moving *Confessions*.

Augustine's influence on Christian thought and theology, especially down to the 13th cent., has been immense. His own theology was formulated in controversy with three opponents in particular. First, against Manichaeism, he defended the essential goodness of all that God, as sole creator, has created. Thus evil could only be *privatio boni*, the absence of the good which ought to be. Second, the *Donatist controversy caused him to formulate systematic doctrines of the church and *sacraments. Augustine's last battle was with the *Pelagians, clarifying his teaching on the *fall, *original sin, and *predestination. He held that man's original endowment from God was lost by the fall of *Adam, so that now all suffer from an inherited defect and liability from Adam's sin; and from this the whole human race is justly *massa damnata*, to be saved only by the grace of God. Since God knows what he intends to do, Augustine is inevitably predestinarian to some extent, and this influenced especially *Calvin and other Reformers. Apart from his polemical works, the *Confessions* and *The *City of God* are most important.

Augustinians. Augustinian or Austin Friars, a Christian religious order drawn together from disparate orders of hermits in 1256. It was based on the Rule of St *Augustine, with a constitution drawn from the *Dominicans. The Rule (*Regula Sancti Augustini*) appears to have been drawn up by one of Augustine's followers, perhaps during his lifetime. Among those adopting the Rule were *Canons Regular, Premonstratensians, and *Dominicans. The Rule was also adopted by Orders for women (e.g. the Augustinians of the Assumption of Mary, known as Assumptionists, Bridgettines, Salesian Sisters, and Ursulines).

Aulén, G.: see ATONEMENT; CHRISTUS VICTOR.

AUṂ: see OṂ.

Aumbry. A recess in the wall of a church or sacristy in which sacred items (and sometimes the *reserved Sacrament) are kept.

Aum Shinrikyo, Supreme Truth Movement. A Japanese syncretistic movement, with a strong eschatological emphasis. Under its leader, Asahara Shoko, to whom dedication as to a guru was required, it became notorious in 1995 because of its claimed association with two attacks using poison gas on a random population. The second of these, on the Tokyo subway, killed or injured hundreds of people. The members of the movement believed that the end of the world cycle was due in 1997; in preparation for the end, new recruits were required to demonstrate their loyalty by arduous programmes of self-denial—including near-starvation. Its main headquarters were near Mount Fuji (*Fujisan), an association which has linked the movement (inappropriately) with the older Shinrikyo. Shinrikyo was founded by Sano Tsunihiko (1834–1906), who had belonged to Ontakekyo, one of the mountain worship cults. Shinrikyo, while being eclectic, is nevertheless conservative: it worships *Amaterasu and the **kojiki* deities, it emphasizes loyalty to emperor and family, and it requires participation in rituals as well as the practice of kado (flower meditation: see IKEBANA) and *chadō (tea ceremony). Shinrikyo has given rise to at least four break-away groups, but none of a radical, 'end of world' kind.

Auraṇgzéb (1618–1707) 6th Mughal emperor in India, son of Shāh Jahān and Mumtāj Mahal.

When Shāh Jahān became ill in 1657, Auraṇgzéb attacked and captured Agrā, imprisoned his aged father and declared himself Emperor, assuming the title 'Alamgīr Gazī'. He struggled unsuccessfully to conquer the Marāṭhās for twenty-five years and died, supposedly of a broken heart, at Ahamadnagar in 1707.

Among historians, he is a particularly controversial figure. One view praises him for maintaining the Islamic character of the Mughal Empire, while the other holds him responsible for the downfall of the Mughals because of his religious fanaticism. It is clear that he identified the interests of the Muslim *Sunnī orthodoxy with those of the Mughal Empire. Overcome by religious zeal, he failed to note the practical requirements of administering a multi-religious community, especially of a Muslim minority ruling over a Hindu majority.

He enlarged the Empire to its greatest extent, but it was so weakened internally that it fell apart soon after his death. Auraṇgzéb bequeathed an empty treasury and a divided India to his successor.

Aureole (symbol or mark of holiness): see HALO.

Aurobindo, Śri (1872–1950). Born Aurobindo Ghose in Calcutta, he became a widely known Hindu teacher. Committed to prison for a year for his work against British rule, he there had his first spiritual experiences. On his release, he turned to the practice of *yoga, but he came to regard the classical ways of yoga as too one-sided: they aim to raise the yogi towards a goal, whereas in his view, the true technique should be to integrate the goal into life. Hence his system became known as Pūrna-Yoga, or Integral Yoga.

Threatened with further arrest, he took refuge in 1910, in the French enclave of Pondicherry, and remained there until his death. He met there Mira Richard (Alfassa) who became his constant support and companion. She established the Aurobindo-ashram (*āśrama) and, after his death, a town, Auroville, to embody his teaching. She is known as 'the Mother'.

The chief works (among many) of Śri Aurobindo are *The Life Divine*, a commentary on the **Bhagavad-gītā*, and *The Synthesis of Yoga*.

Aurva. In Hindu mythology, the son of *Cyavana and the grandson of *Bhṛgu. The Aurva-fire, sometimes called *vāḍavāgni* (Skt., 'mare-fire') because it has a mare's head, awaits the time when it is unleashed to destroy the universe.

Auschwitz. The largest Nazi concentration camp. Established in 1940 on the outskirts of Oseiecim, Poland. It has become a symbol of the horrors of the *Holocaust—as also of the extreme issues of *theodicy, of 'Theology after Auschwitz' (see HOLOCAUST).

Authorized Version. An English translation of the *Bible published in 1611. It was ordered by King James I (hence the American name 'King James Version') and was the work of *c.*50 scholars. The words 'Appointed to be read in Churches' appear on the title-page, but it has never otherwise been 'authorized'.

Autocephalous (Gk., *autos*, 'self' + *kephalē*, 'head'). Term describing an *Orthodox church whose hierarchy is independent of any other. Thus 'the Orthodox Church' comprises a variable number of autocephalous 'Orthodox churches', whose *patriarchs are ranked only in honour (1. Constantinople, 2. Alexandria, 3. Antioch, 4. Jerusalem, 5. Moscow, etc.). Some autocephalous churches are very small, e.g. Sinai (one monastery) and Czechoslovakia (autocephalous since 1951).

Auto-da-fé (Portuguese, 'act of faith'). The elaborate public ceremony of the *Inquisition, especially in Spain, at which, after a showy procession, mass, and sermon, the sentences were read. Heretics were dressed in a yellow gown and mitre. Those sentenced to death were handed over to the secular power.

Autonomy of the liminal (independence in ritual of the transitional stage): see RITES OF PASSAGE.

Auto Sacramental (Spanish religious plays): see THEATRE AND DRAMA.

Av, Ninth of (Heb., *Tishah be-Av*). A day of *mourning in the Jewish calendar for the destruction of the Jerusalem *Temple. According to the *Talmud, five disasters occurred on 9 Av: (i) the Israelites could not enter the *Promised Land; (ii) and (iii) the first and second Temples were destroyed; (iv) the last Jewish stronghold in the *Bar Kokhba war was destroyed; (v) Emperor Hadrian established a heathen temple in Jerusalem.

Avadāna literature. One of the twelve types of literary composition traditionally found in Buddhist Sanskrit literature. The Avadānas are essentially popular moral tales which seek to inspire the believer to exertion in the faith and the performance of good deeds. The most important examples of this type of literature include the **Avadāna-Śataka*, the *Aśoka-Avadāna*, *Divya-Avadāna*, and the later *Avadāna-Kalpalatā*.

Avadāna-Śataka (Skt. 'the 100 Avadānas'). An ancient collection of tales or moral stories from the *Theravāda Buddhist tradition, dating to 1st or 2nd cents. BCE.

Avadhūt-Gītā ('Song of an Illumined One'). A Hindu work of 193 verses composed by Mahātmā Dattatraya. The *Avadhūt-Gītā* is a compressed summary of the way in which the *Upaniṣads were moving in the direction of *Advaita Vedānta.

Avalokiteśvara (Skt., 'the lord who looks in every direction', or 'of what is seen'). One of the most important *bodhisattvas in *Mahāyāna Buddhism. He embodies compassion (*karuṇā), and is thus called Mahākarunā (the other necessary constituent of a *buddha being wisdom, *prajña, which is embodied in Mañjuśri). Avalokiteśvara is the manifestation as bodhisattva of the power of the equally compassionate buddha, Amitābha (*Amida). He is the supremely compassionate helper, and is often depicted with a thousand arms and a thousand eyes for that purpose. He is also eleven-headed, because when he looked at suffering humanity, his head split open from pain. From a single tear shed by Avalokiteśvara, *Tārā was born who ferries the faithful across on their way to *nirvāna, or to the Western Paradise (see SUKHĀVATĪ). He responds instantly to all who 'with all their mind call on his name'.

In China, Avalokiteśvara is known as Kuan-yin, 'he who hears the sound of the world'. In addition to the characteristics and representations of Avalokiteśvara, Kuan-yin frequently has a child on one arm, and appears (under Taoist influence of complementary properties) increasingly with feminine characteristics. She becomes the all-compassionate mother-goddess, perhaps the most popular deity in China, represented in a flowing white robe, holding a *lotus.

In Japan, 'he' (see below) is known as Kannon (Kanzeon, Kwannon), the Bodhisattva of Compassion, one of the most popular deities in Mahāyāna Buddhism. According to the **Lotus Sūtra*, Kannon perceives the sufferings of all sentient beings and devises ways to assist them, to answer their prayers, and to lead them to salvation. This compassion of the Bodhisattva is reflected in his fuller name Kanzeon, meaning 'He Who Regards the Cries of the World'. In Japan, as in China, Kannon was frequently portrayed in feminine form, possibly stemming from the *Lotus Sūtra*'s statement that the Bodhisattva will take on the guise of a woman or any other figure in order to lead sentient beings to salvation, and perhaps suggesting feminine representation to be more expressive of compassion.

In Tibet, he is known as sPyan-ras-gzigs, or in the West as Chenrezi. The king Songsten-Gampo who brought Buddhism into Tibet (see TIBETAN RELIGION) is regarded as an incarnation of Avalokiteśvara, as are the successive *Dalai Lamas.

Avanti: see SACRED CITIES, SEVEN.

Avasthā (Skt. 'condition', 'state'). In Hinduism a state of consciousness or condition in a world (*loka, *bhuvana*). A common classification of different states of consciousness (*avasthā*) is found in the *Upaniṣads, notably **Māndūkya*.

Avatamsaka literature. An important and extensive literary compilation in *Mahāyāna Buddhism centring on the *Avatamsaka-sūtra*, also known as *Buddhāvatamsaka-sūtra* (Sutra of the Garland of Buddhas; Chin., *Hua-yen ching*; Jap., *Kegon-kyo*). Most of the Skt. original of the work, reputedly extending to 100,000 verses, has been lost, but several translations exist in Tibetan and Chinese. Several chapters became revered as important sūtras in their own right, such as 'The Ten Stages of a Bodhisattva's Career' (*Daśabhūmika-sūtra*) and the 'Entry into the Absolute' (*Gaṇḍavyūha-sūtra*), these being the only parts, in consequence, which survive in Sanskrit.

Throughout the text the Buddha is portrayed as the focal point of all the spiritual energies of the universe which coalesce into a magnificent cosmic unity. The *Avatamsaka-sūtra* rapidly became popular in China with the Hua-Yen school, in Korea, and especially in Japan with the development of the Kegon school. Doctrinally it embraces Yogācāra/*Vijñāvāda idealism, *Mādhyamaka, and *Tantric elements, which it weaves together into a rich metaphysical tapestry. Underlying the apparent diversity in the world is a complex mesh of interdependence and interpenetration of phenomena illuminated and energized by the compassion of the cosmic Buddha (*Vairocana). No part of the whole exists in isolation and there is complementarity and mutual identification between all entities in a grand harmonious unity. Elements which appear to be separate are in fact subtly linked like jewels which reflect their brilliance upon one another.

Avatāra (Skt., 'descent'). The earthly manifestations (or 'incarnations') of a Hindu deity. More specifically, it is an earthly manifestation of Viṣṇu due to his free choice (i.e. not due to the laws of *karma or a curse) and taking the form of a full human life (including conception, birth, and natural death), for the sake of a specific cosmic purpose. This allowed for the inclusion of other popular heroes and figures of worship under the general umbrella of Viṣṇu religion. Already at a relatively early stage, the *Vedic figure of Trivikrama was included, now under the name of *Vāmana, 'the Dwarf'. By widening the definition of the term, cult-figures like the *Varāha (Boar), *Kūrma (Tortoise), *Matsya (Fish), and Nṛsiṃha/*Narasiṃha (Man-Lion), could be included. Somewhat later also *Rāma, *Balarāma or Baladeva (Kṛṣṇa's half-brother), and *Paraśurāma (Rāma with the Axe) entered the group. Even the *Buddha was appropriated by certain traditions. A future manifestation is connected with *Kalkin.

Many other figures were regionally, or at times envisaged as avatāra of Viṣṇu, e.g. Nayagrīva, *Dattātreya, the Haṃsa (Goose), etc. But by the close of the first millennium CE a set of ten had acquired the widest currency (Baladeva, the Buddha, and Paraśurāma being somewhat less rigidly included in such lists of ten). Another extension of the concept that proved particularly useful was the idea of an *arcâvatāra*, viz., the descent and permanent residence of a deity (particularly Viṣṇu) in the sculpture of a temple image (*arcā*).

Finally, various religious movements have tended to regard their founder or their sages as avatāras of their own specific deity. The concept of an *aṃśâvatāra*, 'partial incarnation', remained unproductive outside the circles of the scholastics; in some areas *aṃśa* is actually used as a synonym of avatāra.

The belief put forward in **Bhāgavata-purāṇa*, that humans can become avatāras by a divine infilling, has allowed the title to be extended to religious leaders, such as *Gāndhī and Satya *Sai Baba, or to non-Hindus, such as *Jesus or *Muḥammad.

Avelei ha-Rahamim (Heb., 'Merciful Father'). Memorial *prayer for Jewish martyrs which is found in a *Prayer Book* of 1290.

Avelei Zion (Heb., 'Mourners of Zion'). Groups of Jews dedicated to mourning the destruction of the *Temple in Jerusalem. With the conquest of Palestine by the Seljuk Turks in 1071, they disappeared from Jerusalem.

Ave Maria. Christian, mainly Catholic, salutation and invocation addressed to *Mary.

Averroes (Spanish Muslim theologian): see IBN RUSHD.

Averroism. The views associated with Averroes (*Ibn Rushd), which became influential in Jewish and Christian philosophy from 1230 onward. Since these attributed views included the absolute separation of God from his creation, the eternity of matter and its potentiality, and the notion of 'double truth', one (literal in relation to revelation) for the uneducated and the other allegorical, much of the Christian response became hostile: Averroism was condemned in 1270 and 1277, and was strongly criticized by *Aquinas. Nevertheless, Averroist philosophers continued to defend this outlook, the most prominent being Siger of Brabant (*c*.1235–1284).

Avesta. The holy book of *Zoroastrianism (the word probably means 'The Injunction [of Zoroaster]'). Only approximately one-quarter of the original is extant. That which has survived is basically the liturgical material which continued in use in regular worship. The content of the 'canon' includes material from many ages. There are some pre-Zoroastrian 'hymns' (some of the *Yásts*, such as *Yt.* 10 to Mithra) and 'Litanies' (*Nyayes*). The anti-demonic law, the *Vendidad*, contains much ancient material, although its present structure was probably Parthian. The liturgy of the *Yasna* is especially ancient, probably much of the substance deriving from Indo-Iranian times. Embedded in the

Yasna are the seventeen hymns of Zoroaster, the *Gāthās*. They are in two blocks (*Ys.* 28–34 and 43–53) either side of the *Yasna Haptanhait* liturgy, which, if not by Zoroaster, is certainly early. The *Gāthās* are embedded in the *Yasna* the 'act of [daily] worship', because that is the liturgical context within which the prophetic hymns have been preserved. Their fragmentary nature, combined with the allusive poetic imagery and metrical form, make them extremely difficult to translate. They are intensely personal in style, passionate outpourings of an individual spirit, following visions of God. For Zoroastrians, they are the most powerful holy *manthras*.

In modern religious practice, Zoroastrians use a *Khorda Avesta*, a collection of essential prayers for daily use by lay people.

Avicebron (Jewish poet): see GABIROL, SOLOMON.

Avicenna (Muslim philosopher): see IBN SĪNĀ.

Avidyā (Skt.) or **avijja** (Pāli), Literally 'non-knowledge' or ignorance. A term in Indian religions which, in its broadest connotation, means that which keeps a person bound on the wheel of transmigration (*saṃsāra) due to his/her action (*karma) and so is a condition of suffering (*duḥkha).

1. Avidyā in Hinduism.

In the *Vedas avidyā means ignorance of ritual and moral obligations and so implies absence of knowledge rather than an ontological condition of bondage. In the *Upaniṣads it comes to mean spiritual delusion and the non-knowledge of *Brahman. In *Sāṃkhya-*yoga ignorance, which is the cause of bondage and suffering, is regarded as the non-discrimination of the individual self (*puruṣa) from matter (*prakṛti) in which it appears to be entangled. For *Advaita Vedānta bondage is similarly due to beginningless ignorance which, in contrast to Sāṃkhya, is the creation of distinctions where none exist; in reality there being only Brahman. For *Rāmānuja's Viśiṣṭādvaita, ignorance is the absence of knowing that the self (*jīva) is distinct from, yet also merged into, Brahman, while for the *Dvaita school of *Madhva, avidyā is ignorance of the self's eternal distinction from God.

2. In Buddhism, avijja/avidyā is ignorance of the true nature of reality, the non-emancipated state of mind; it is specifically expressed in Buddhist writings as lack of experiential knowledge of the *Four Noble Truths. Avijja refers to moral and spiritual ignorance, not ignorance of a factual and scientific kind, and is only finally extinguished with the attainment of nirvāna.

Avinu Malkenu (Heb., 'Our Father, our King'). A Hebrew liturgy recited on the Ten Days of *Penitence, and in some communities on other fast days.

Av kol ha-sodot (the father of all secrets): see AARON OF BAGHDAD.

Avodah (Heb., 'Service'). Description of the complicated sacrificial ritual practised in the Jerusalem *Temple on the *Day of Atonement, and now recited as the central part of the *Musaf service on that day.

Avodah Zarah (Heb., 'idolatrous worship'). Tractate of the *Mishnah, *tosefta, and *Talmud, assigned to the order of 'Nezikim' (torts). It includes both *halakhic and *aggadic material, and deals with the laws concerning *idolatry and relations with idol-worshippers.

Avot (Heb., 'Fathers'). A treatise of the *Mishnah placed at the end of the order of 'Nezikim'. Often known as *Pirkei Avot* (the Chapters of the Fathers), it presents a series of sayings of the sages going back from the *tannaim in an unbroken chain to *Moses' revelation on Mount *Sinai.

Avvakum (1620–82). Archpriest of the Russian Church, leader, and eventually *martyr, of the Raskolniki, or *'Old Believers'. As *archpriest of Our Lady of Kazan in Moscow, he opposed the liturgical reforms of *Patriarch *Nikon, while establishing the ascetical and highly moral group of 'The Old Believers'. For his opposition, he was exiled to Siberia in 1653. He returned on the death of Nikon (1664), but was again exiled, imprisoned, and punished for refusing the continuing reforms. Finally he and his companions were condemned to death at the stake. He wrote a fine autobiography.

Avyākata (Pāli; Skt., *avyākṛtavastūni*, 'that which cannot be expressed'). The four issues or questions on which the *Buddha was pressed, but concerning which he remained silent. The silence was not because the questions are unanswerable, but because any answer would lead to a false sense of apprehension within the limits of his hearers' understanding. See *Brahmajāla Sutta* 28; but it does not follow from that that he was agnostic. The true answers require insight which is itself a consequence of enlightenment or of considerable progress toward it.

Avyākṛta(vastūni) (inexpressible issues): see AVYĀKATA.

Avyakta. The unmanifest in Hinduism, either the power of God, or of *prakṛti, before it becomes manifest in created appearance or *Brahman.

Awakening of Faith (Mahāyāna Buddhist text): see MAHĀYĀNAŚRADDHOTPĀDA-ŚASTRA.

Awliya' (pl., friends of God): see WALĪ.

Axial age. Period around the 6th cent. BCE, when religions were instrumental in effecting great changes in history and civilization. The term was used by Karl Jaspers to draw attention to the rise to prominence of great religious leaders and innovations which established the basis of the great civilizations until the disturbance of those patterns by the European enlightenment and expansion of trade and empire. He drew attention to *Zoroaster, the *Upaniṣads, the *Buddha, *Mahāvīra, *Confucius, the emergence of *Taoism.

Axis mundi. The central pivot of the earth or of the entire cosmos. For examples, see BODHIMAṆḌA; TEMPLE (JAIN); MERU. The idea is applied in the *Sūfī *qutb. See Index, Axis mundi.

Ayā (pl. *āyāt*; Arab., 'sign' or 'mark'). In the *Qur'ān, a mark of Allāh's existence and power (2. 248; 3. 41; 26. 197), and especially 'a *miracle'. The greatest sign and miracle of Allāh is the Qur'ān, and sections of the Qur'ān, shorter than *suras, are referred to as *āyāt*. From this usage, the word has come to mean the verses of the Qur'ān. See also ʿILM.

Ayam Ātman Brahman (Skt., 'This Self is Brahman': *Bṛhadāraṇyaka Upaniṣad* 4. 4. 5) one of the *Mahāvākyas in Hinduism, the realization that *ātman is *Brahman.

Aya Sofya (mosque, formerly basilica): see HAGIA SOFIA.

Ayatollah (Arab., 'sign of God'). Title of high-ranking Shi'ite Muslim authorities, especially in Iran. It is a recent (20th cent.) title for exceptional jurists (*mujtāhid*), whose authority rests on that of the infallible *Imām—though in 1979, the Ayatollah Khomeini (see KHUMAYNI) adopted the title of Imām for himself. An Ayatollah's decisions (*fatwā) have authority only for those who examine and agree with them–in theory; in practice, Ayatollahs gain personal followings, among whom their decisions are accepted as binding. The extension of these personal followings to even wider communities is again a recent innovation.

Ayatollah Khomeini (figure head of Islamic Revolution in Iran): see KHUMAYNI, RUḤ ALLAH.

Ayn al-Quzat (Persian Sūfī of 12th cent.): see SHARĪʿATĪ, ʿALĪ.

Ayodhyā ('Invincible'). One of the Hindu seven *sacred cities (equally sacred to Jains and Buddhists) in Uttar Pradesh.

Āyur veda (Skt., 'Knowledge of Life'). The ancient and traditional Hindu school or system of healing, regarded as a supplement to the *Atharva Veda*. The major early works are the *Caraka-saṃhitā* and the *Suśruta-saṃhitā*, 1st–4th cents. CE. The maintenance of relationship and balance is the principle of cure and care in ayurvedic medicine, which continues to be widely practised. For a spiritual equivalent, cf., BHŪTAŚUDDHI.

Azalī Bābīs. Followers of Mīrzā Yaḥyā Nūrī, called Ṣubḥ-i Azal (Morn of Eternity) (1830/1–1912), the appointed successor of the Bāb (see BĀBĪS). After the Bāb's execution (1850), Babism ceased to be a united movement. Ṣubḥ-i Azal was involved with the militant faction which unsuccessfully plotted the assassination of the Shah (1852). In the consequent purge he went into hiding, later joining his older half-brother *Bahā'u'llāh in Baghdād. Increasingly overshadowed by Bahā'u'llāh, he maintained the leadership of a small radical faction of *Bābīs. He was exiled to Ottoman Cyprus in 1868 and died in Famagusta on 29 Apr. 1912. Some of his younger disciples became free-thinkers and were prominently involved in the political opposition to the Qajar regime which culminated in the Iranian constitutional movement of the early 1900s.

Azazel. Place to which the *scapegoat was consigned on the *Day of Atonement. There is a dispute as to the exact meaning of Azazel; some rabbis identified it as a cliff or a place of rocks, while others saw it as a supernatural power, perhaps made up of two fallen *angels, Uza and Azael. 'Go to Azazel!' is the equivalent in modern Hebrew of 'Go to hell!'

Azhar (Cairo mosque): see AL-AZHAR.

Azharot (Heb., 'exhortations'). Jewish didactic poems used in liturgy. Azharot as compositions summarize and celebrate *halakot, and were recited initially at *Shavu'ot, itself the thanksgiving for the giving of *Torah.

Azi Dahaka (the Lie): see ANGRA MAINYU.

Azymites. A name given to the *Roman Catholic Church by the *Orthodox at the time of the *schism of 1054. It refers to the Latin use of unleavened bread (Gk., *ta azyma*) in the *eucharist, which was a special object of attack from the Eastern side, since it was held to invalidate the eucharist.

B

Baʿal (Phoen., Ugaritic, etc., 'Lord'). The weather god of the western Semites. Many of Baʿal's attributes were ascribed to the Israelite God, and certain aspects of Baʿal liturgy were taken over and adapted to the praise of the God of Israel.

Baʿal ha-Tanya (founder of Jewish movement): see SHNE'UR ZALMAN OF LYADY.

Baʿal ha-Turim (Jewish halakhic authority): see JACOB BEN ASHER.

Baʿal Shem (Heb., 'master of the divine name'). Title given in *ḥasidic and *'kabbalistic literature to those who possess secret knowledge of God's name. See also ISRAEL BEN ELIEZER, who, as a founder of ḥasidism, assumed the title Baʿal Shem Tov.

Baʿal Shem Tov (founder of E. European Jewish Ḥasidism): see ISRAEL BEN ELIEZER.

Baʿal teshuvah (Heb., 'master of repentance'; also *chozer bi-teshuvah*). One who returns to the observance of religion, and also (more recently) a Jew who is newly observant. The Baʿal Teshuvah movement was a reaction in Israel to the miraculous outcome of the Six Day War, and elsewhere to what seemed to be the excesses of personal freedom in society.

Bāb: see BĀBĪS.

Bābā (Pañjābī term of endearment for old man). Sikh title given to Gurū *Nānak and other saintly men regardless of age.

Babasaheb (Indian lawyer and politician): see AMBEDKAR, B. R.

Babbar Khālsā (Sikh organization): see AKHAṆḌ KĪRTANĪ JATHĀ.

Babel, Tower of. The enterprise which, acc. to the Bible, was the cause of the multiplicity of languages in the world: see Genesis 11. 1–9.

Bābīs. Followers of Sayyid ʿAlī Muḥammad Shīrāzī (1819–50), a merchant from southern Iran who ultimately claimed to be the bearer of a new religion in succession to Islam. His initial claim, made in the spring of 1844 after a series of revelatory visions, was that he was the *Bāb* ('gate') to the *Hidden Imám of Twelver Shiʿism (see ITHNĀ ʿASHARĪYA). Later he claimed to be the Imām himself, returned as *al-Mahdī at the end of the age. Finally he claimed to be the *Nuqta* ('point') of a new revelation from God. Teaching a complex combination of esoteric and messianic ideas, the Bāb initially attracted many *Shaikhīs to his cause, but the movement soon gained a wider following, becoming well established in many parts of Iran. Orthodox religious leaders sought to stem its growth, and in response to persecution the Bābīs steadily became more militant. After armed struggles followed (1850–1), and on government orders, the Bāb was executed (8/9 July 1850), and the movement was suppressed. The movement then fragmented. Ultimately most of the remaining Bābīs gave their allegiance either to Ṣubḥ-i Azal (*Azalī Bābīs), or to *Bahā'u'llāh (see also BAHĀ'Ī FAITH).

Babu (Skt., 'Lord'). Honorific title of respect in India, especially for a holy person.

Babylonian captivity. Period (586–538 BCE) during which many Israelites were held in exile in Babylon. The phrase was applied by Petrarch to the Church during the period when the papacy was at Avignon (1309–77): see ANTIPOPE.

Babylonian Talmud (Jewish authoritative development of Mishnah): see TALMUD.

Bach, J. S. (German composer): see MUSIC.

Bacharach, Jair (1638–1702). German *Talmudist. Under his leadership thirteen scholars met to study and prepare themselves for *redemption. Serving as the *rabbi of Koblenz and Worms, he collected the writings of *Shabbeti Tzevi and was the author of collections of *responsa, mainly of a conservative trend.

Bacon, Roger (*c*.1214–92). *Franciscan philosopher. Born in England, he was one of the first to show interest in *Aristotle's scientific works, then becoming known in the West. He devoted himself to languages, mathematics, and experimental science, and became a Franciscan. Later, in Paris, he wrote his encyclopaedic work, the *Opus Maius*, for Pope Clement IV, after whose death in 1268 he came under suspicion of novelty and dangerous doctrine.

Badā' (Arab., 'appearance'). The occurrence of new circumstances which bring about the alteration of an earlier determination on the part of God. The issue related to this term is extremely controversial in Islam, because it implies that God can 'change his mind'—i.e. it threatens the attribution of immutability, omnipotence, and *qadr (see ALLĀH).

Badā' rests particularly on the Quranic claim that God will change his determination to punish sinners, provided that they repent. It is reinforced by mansukh (*naskh, abrogation of one part of the Qur'ān by another).

Bādarāyaṇa ('descendant of Badara'). The ancient Indian sage, living around the 1st cent. BCE (though some suggest much later, e.g. 3rd/4th cent. CE), who propounded the basic teachings of *Vedānta which are expressed in the *_Brahmasūtra_ and later developed by *Śaṅkara, *Rāmānuja, and their successors. Although Śaṅkara attributed the authorship of the _Brahmasūtra_ to Bādarāyaṇa, others have attributed the work to the legendary compiler of the *_Mahābhārata_ epic, Vedavyāsa. It is unlikely that Bādarāyaṇa and Vedavyāsa are two names for the same person, but the later tendency to identify these two may be seen as a way of reconciling divergent views. The teachings, as given in the _Brahmasūtra_ passages mentioning Bādarāyaṇa by name, can be summarized as follows: (i) the aim of human life is liberation (*mokṣa); (ii) liberation is effected by the direct knowledge of *Brahman; and (iii) direct knowledge of Brahman is independent of, and not subordinate to, ritual acts.

Badr. Small town SW of *Madīna, the site of the first victory of the Muslim community after the *Hijra. This success, against numerical odds, was claimed by the Muslims as a sign of *Allāh's favour.

Baeck, Leo (1873–1956). German *rabbi and leader of *progressive Judaism. He was a rabbi in Berlin from 1912 (serving as an army chaplain during the First World War). From 1933 he defended the rights of Jews in Nazi Germany and, refusing all invitations to leave, he was deported in 1943 to Theresienstadt concentration camp. After the war he moved to London, and then to the USA, to continue teaching. His best known work was _Wesen des Judentums_ (The Essence of Judaism, 1905) in which, reacting against *Harnack's _Essence of Christianity_, he argued that Judaism was essentially a dialectic between 'mystery' and 'command' within a system of ethical monotheism.

Bahā'ī Faith. A religion founded by *Bahā'u'llāh in the 1860s. After his death in 1892, it was led successively by his eldest son, *'Abdu'l-Bahā (from 1892 to 1921), his great-grandson, *Shoghi Effendi (from 1922 to 1957), and then (in 1963, after a brief 'interregnum') by an elected body, the *Universal House of Justice.

Claiming to be the promised one of all religions, and preaching a message of global socio-religious reform, Bahā'u'llāh initially drew his followers from amongst the *Bābīs, most of whom became Bahā'īs. Significant expansion in the non-Muslim Third World began in the 1950s and 1960s, Bahā'īs from these areas now constituting the majority of the world's five million Bahā'īs.

Bahā'ī is monotheistic, but as God is regarded as in essence completely transcendent and unknowable, religious doctrine centres on the belief in a series of 'Manifestations of God' (_mazāhir-i ilāhī_). These individuals reflect and manifest the attributes of God and progressively reveal the divine purpose for humankind. The Manifestations include *Abraham, *Moses, *Zoroaster, Gautama *Buddha, *Jesus, *Muḥammad, the *Bāb, and for the present age, Bahā'u'llāh. At a societal level, the present age is regarded as unique. The unity of all the peoples and religions of the earth is the destined hallmark of the age.

Religious life centres on various individual acts of devotion (daily obligatory prayer and moral self-accounting, an annual nineteen-day fast), and a communal 'Feast' held once every nineteen days at the beginning of each month in the Bahā'ī calendar. Bahā'ī communities come together to commemorate various Holy Days, including the Bahā'ī New Year at the vernal equinox (usually 21 Mar.), and the Riḍvān festival (21 Apr.–2 May) marking the anniversary of Bahā'u'llāh's first declaration of his mission (1863). With no priesthood, administration rests with locally and nationally elected councils ('Spiritual Assemblies'), supreme authority resting with the *Universal House of Justice.

Bahā'u'llāh (1817–92) (Arab., 'the Glory/Splendour of God'), Religious title adopted by Mīrzā Ḥusayn 'ali Nūrī, the prophet-founder of the *Bahā'ī Faith. Born into a wealthy land-owning family in N. Iran, he chose to follow a life of religious involvement rather than that of a courtier. In 1844 he became a *Bābī. Imprisoned in the Black Pit of Tehran in 1852, he experienced a number of revelatory visions, and after his exile to Ottoman Iraq withdrew to the mountains of Kurdistan where he lived as a pious ascetic. Returning to Baghdād in 1856, he soon became the leading figure in a revival of Babism. Although he demanded that his followers should abandon militancy, the Iranian government was alarmed, and sought his removal from Iraq. Accordingly in 1863 he was summoned to Istanbul, and thence dispatched to Edirne (Adrianople) (1863–8) and then to the prison-city of Akka (Acre) in Ottoman Syria (1868–92). Immediately before his departure from Baghdād he apparently made the first declaration of his claim to be a new messenger from God, the promised one foretold by the Bāb. In Edirne this claim was made openly (1866), that he was 'he whom God shall manifest'; and the Bābī community soon became divided between the followers of Bahā'u'llāh (Bahā'īs) and those of his half-brother Ṣubḥ-i Azal (*Azalīs). Turning over much of the task of organizing the movement to his eldest son and eventual successor, 'Abbās Effendi (*'Abdu'l-Bahā), Bahā'u'llāh devoted his final years to his writings. These were now all regarded as revelations from God, and besides thousands of letters to his followers, included a number of lengthy books and 'Tablets' (*alwāḥ*). In his *Most Holy Book* (*c.*1873), he formulated the basis for a distinctive Bahā'ī Holy Law, and in a number of final works he delineated his principles for social reconstruction in a new world order (*Tablets of Bahā'u'llāh*). He died in the vicinity of Akka on 29 May 1892. His remains were buried at the Bahjī, which is now a shrine for pilgrims, and the direction of prayer for believers (*qibla).

Bahir, Sefer ha (Book of Light). An early Jewish *kabbalistic work. It was ascribed to R. Nehunya, and it is an anthology of statements attributed to various *tannaim and *amoraim; probably it has been handed down in a mutilated form. It is the earliest work which deals with the *sefirot (divine attributes) which are given symbolic names.

Baḥīrā. A Syrian monk who in Islamic tradition is said to have recognized the signs of prophethood on the young *Muḥammad, when the latter was on a trading journey to Syria.

Bahiraṇga-sādhana (Skt.). The development in Hinduism of an increasing detachment from the external world. The first three stages (*yama, *niyama, and *āsana) of *Patañjali's yoga are means to this end.

Bahubali (first person to achieve liberation in this world cycle): see PILGRIMAGE (JAIN); DIGAMBARA.

Bahya ben Asher (13th cent. CE). Jewish commentator and *kabbalist. Serving as *Dayyan in Saragossa, he produced a commentary on the *Pentateuch (*Be'ur'al ha-Torah*, 1291) which interpreted the text literally, homiletically, rationally and kabbalistically. It was very popular. He is important in the history of Kabbalah in that he preserves and quotes the mystical teaching of *Naḥmanides' contemporaries. He adopted a four-level interpretation of scripture: (i) *peshat*, plain or literal; (ii) *midrash, homiletical; (iii) *sekhal*, reasoned and argued; (iv) *sōdh*, derived from mystical union with God. This approach is summarized under the mnemonic, pardes.

Baḥya ben Joseph ibn Paquda (Pakuda) (late 11th cent. CE). Jewish philosopher, known only through his major work *Kitab al-Hidaya ila Fara'd al-Qulub* (tr. into Heb. as *Ḥovot ha-Levavot*, Duties of the Hearts). It discusses the ritual and ethical obligations of the *Torah, and attempts to lead the reader through various mystical stages towards union with God.

Bāhya-pūjā (Skt.). The external forms of devotion in Hinduism, especially to *avatāras; but equally constituting the *karma-kāṇḍa (ritual requirements) of the *Vedas.

Baidawi (Islamic scholar): see AL-BAIḌĀWĪ.

Baigan, Ishida (founder of Japanese religious movement): see SHINGAKU.

Baimasi (Buddhist monastery): see PAI-MA-SSU.

Bairāgī. An order of Hindu *yogis, derived from Bhatrahāri, a ruler who was persuaded by *Gorakhnāth to give up his throne and become a disciple. The term is more often encountered in the Sikh reinterpretation, in which the bairags are those who devote themselves to God while remaining with their families.

Baisākhī, V(a)isākhī. Hindu spring festival. The first day of the Hindu solar month Vaiśākha (Apr.–May), it is New Year's Day by the solar calendar of S. India and a spring harvest festival in N. India, celebrated with *melās, dances, and folksongs. Celebrated on or near 13 Apr., Baisākhī is of special importance to Sikhs. *Gurū *Amar Dās enjoined Sikhs to assemble in the presence of the Gurū. After abolishing the *masand order *Gobind *Siṅgh bade Sikhs to contribute directly to the treasury of the Gurū on Baisākhī. In 1699 he instituted the *khālsā on Baisākhī. Sikhs everywhere commemorate this event with *akhaṇḍ pāṭh and *kīrtan. The previous year's *Niśān *Sāhib is replaced and the flagpole cleaned. Often new initiates receive *amrit, and *gurdwārā presidents and management committees are elected. The *Harimandir Sāhib, Amritsar, is illuminated. See GURPURB; SAṄGRĀND.

Baker, Augustine (1575–1641). Influential Benedictine (see BENEDICT) writer, especially on spirituality and *asceticism, in particular through his *Holy Wisdom* (*Sancta Sophia*, 1657).

Bala (Skt., Pāli). The five powers developed in Buddhism by the strengthening of the five roots (*indriya), which lead to enlightenment.

Balaam. A biblical character. He was instructed by Balak, king of Moab, to curse Israel, but after a vision of an *angel he blessed the Israelites instead: see Numbers 22. 1–24. 25.

Bālak Siṅgh (1797–1862). Spiritual preceptor of *Rām Siṅgh, who founded the *Nāmdhārī Sikh movement. He exhorted his followers to live simply and practise no religious ritual apart from repetition of God's name (*Nām, hence the name of the movement). Devotees regard Bālak Siṅgh as a reincarnation of Gurū *Gobind Siṅgh.

Balarāma. In Hindu mythology, *Kṛṣṇa's elder brother, son of *Vāsudeva and *Devakī. He is also called Saṃkarṣaṇa (Skt., 'extraction, ploughing'). He is often said to be a manifestation of the cosmic serpent *Śeṣa. He is also said to be a manifestation of *Viṣṇu, and his name sometimes appears in the eighth place in the standard *avatāra list.

Bālā Sandhū. *Bhāī Bālā, Hindu companion of Gurū *Nānak. In popular iconography he is shown fanning his master while *Mardānā plays the *rabāb*.

Baldachino. In Christian churches, originally in *Coptic-rite churches, a domed canopy supported on four columns and covering the main *altar.

Balfour Declaration. British declaration of sympathy with *Zionism. It was made in a letter of 2 Nov. 1917, from the British Foreign Secretary (i.e. Balfour) to Lord Rothschild. The declaration was endorsed in 1920 by the allies at the San Remo Conference. It was, however, in apparent conflict with the McMahon correspondence, which made commitments to the Arabs.

Bali. An offering, in Hinduism and Buddhism, of grain or rice to gods and spirits, in particular, part of the daily offering of the *gṛhastha (householder) which ensures that at death he will attain *Brahman.

Bali. In Hindu mythology, one of the leaders of the *daityas (demons) and grandson of Prahlāda. According to one legend he was offered the choice of entering heaven with one hundred fools, or hell with one wise person. He chose the latter, because a hundred fools will turn heaven into hell, but one wise person will turn hell into heaven.

Bālmīkī. Pañjābī community venerating *Vālmīki. This movement, of Hindu/Sikh origin, gives enhanced identity to devotees of chūhṛā (sweeper) status in the *caste hierarchy. Bālmīkī leaders in Britain prefer the spelling 'Vālmīkī'. See also Mazhabī, Raṅghṛetā, Ravidāsī.

Balokole (Christian renewal movement): see EAST AFRICAN REVIVAL.

Balthasar, Hans Urs von (1905–88). *Roman Catholic theologian. In 1969, he was appointed to the International Theological Commission, and in 1988 was nominated to be a *cardinal but died before this could be put into effect. As a philosophical theologian, von Balthasar emphasized the necessary openness of human nature to exploration and creativity. In his *Herrlichkeit: Eine theologische Asthetik* (Eng. tr., *The Glory of the Lord: A Theological Aesthetics*, 1982, 1984, 1986), he insisted on the importance of the form which is more than the sum of its parts: to perceive the beauty of an object or of a harmony is to grasp the wholeness of it which is never exhausted. Thus God reveals himself, not simply in truth and goodness, but as beauty. Here is the perfected form of love, which is so urgent in its self-giving that it draws the one who contemplates it into a corresponding act of unreserved giving. On this basis, von Balthasar completed his massive trilogy with his *Theodramatik* (1973, 1976, 1978) and *Theologik* (1985, 1985, 1987): because God has dramatically expressed his love and displayed his glory in his Son, so we can know that he has spoken a definitive word of truth.

Baluan Native Christian Church (Papua New Guinean Church): see PALIAU MALOAT.

Bāmiyān. Buddhist holy place with carved and decorated caves, in Afghanistan. The caves served as *caityas for the Buddhist monks who lived nearby.

Banāras (sacred city of India): see KAŚI.

Banārsīdās (1586–1643). Jain layperson and reformer, who maintained that spiritual development and experience are not a specialist preserve. He made a record of progress in *Ardhkathanak*, his *Half a Story*, so-called because it is an autobiography of his first fifty-five years, half the ideal life-span. It is a remarkable and vivid record, ranking with the spiritual autobiographies of *Augustine and *al-Ghaz(z)ali.

Bancroft, Richard (1544–1610). *Archbishop of *Canterbury. His aversion to *Puritanism is expressed in his writings. An uncompromising man of considerable academic ability, he was committed to the importance of clerical learning.

Bandā Siṅgh Bahādur (1670–1716 CE). Sikh military leader. Bandā Siṅgh, originally Lachman Dās, became a *bairāgī (Hindu renunciant) in early youth, adopting the name Mādho Dās. He settled as a hermit at *Nander where he later became Gurū *Gobind Siṅgh's ardent follower, renamed Bandā (slave). The gurū authorized him to punish the persecutors of the Sikhs. After eight years of fighting against the Mughals he was besieged at Gurdās-Naṅgal and cruelly executed in Delhi.

Bāṇī ('speech'). Common abbreviation among Sikhs for *gurbāṇī, the writings contained in the *Ādi Granth. See also BHAGAT BĀṆĪ.

Banka (Jap., 'evening portion'). The recitation in Zen monasteries of the evening *sūtra (also 'bansan'). Banka-zoji, which follows, is the careful cleaning of the monastery.

Bankei Eitaku (Yōtaku), also **Kokushi** (1622–93). Japanese *Zen teacher of the *Rinzai school. When young, he wandered through Japan, attending various Zen teachers, and then retired into seclusion to practise *zazen. Neglecting his health, he had an enlightenment experience at a moment of critical illness. He received further instruction from Dōsha Chōgen, who bestowed on him the seal of recognition (*inka-shōmei), but Bankei seized it and tore it up—he had no need of written authority. In 1672, he was appointed abbot of Myōshin-ji (monastery) in *Kyōto, and at this point the extreme simplicity of his teaching led to a Rinzai revival, in which ritual preoccupations were transcended. Although he prohibited the recording of his teaching, some instructions and dialogues have survived.

Banno, Bhāī (16th–17th cents. CE). Disciple of Sikh Gurū *Arjan Dev; early version of *Ādi Granth. According to tradition, Arjan Dev either entrusted his compilation to Banno for binding in Lahore or reluctantly lent it on condition he did not keep it for more than one night in his village, Māṅgaṭ. By travelling extremely slowly Banno contrived to copy the entire Ādi Granth before returning it. Unlike the *Kartārpur version, the Banno version, also known as the Māṅgaṭ version or bitter version (*khārī bīṛ*), contains a *hymn by *Mīrābāī, a hymn of Sūr Dās of which only the first line appears in the Kartārpur version and a hymn by Arjan Dev in Rāmakalī *Rāg of which the Kartārpur version has only a couplet. The reasons for these discrepancies are uncertain.

Banū Isrā'īl (children of Israel): see AHL AL-KITĀB.

Baoli (place of ritual bathing): see PILGRIMAGE.

Bapak (father): see SUBUD INTERNATIONAL BROTHERHOOD.

Baptism. The rite of admission into the Christian church, practised by all denominations. Its origin is probably to be sought in (i) the Jewish practice of baptizing proselytes; and (ii) the baptism administered by *John the Baptist 'for the forgiveness of sins' (Mark 1. 4).

The doctrine which attended baptism in the early church was variable. Baptism might be, for example, the washing away of sins (Acts 2. 38), a dying with Christ (Romans, 6. 4), a rebirth (John 3. 5), or the occasion of the gift of the Holy Spirit (1 Corinthians 12. 13).

The theology of baptism gained precision in the 3rd and 4th cents., notably in the West in the writings of *Augustine. The Catholic view which emerged was of a rite which works *ex opere operato, which confers a 'character' on the recipient (who thus can never be rebaptized, even after *apostasy).

The 16th-cent. Reformers modified that theology: *Luther, reconciling the necessity of baptism with his doctrine of justification by faith alone, regarded baptism as a promise of divine grace after which a person's sins are no longer imputed to him or her. *Zwingli, on the other hand, saw baptism only as a sign of admission to the Christian community. *Calvin taught that baptism can only be of effect for the elect, who have faith (without which the rite is vacuous). The radical *Anabaptists understood baptism exclusively as a response of faith on the part of the individual to the gospel, and thus rejected infant baptism.

In the most usual form of early Christian baptism, the candidate stood in water, and water was poured over the upper part of the body. This is technically called 'immersion', but the word is now more often used to refer to the method (used e.g. by Baptists and Orthodox) of dipping the whole body under water.

Baptism, forced. see ANUSIM.

Baptist Churches. Christian denomination. Baptists form one of the largest *Protestant bodies with a worldwide membership of over 40 million, plus a greater number of adherents. Its beginnings can be traced among the *Anabaptists, and to the ministry of the English *Puritan John Smyth (*c*.1554–1612), and his fellow separatist exiles, who made believers' *baptism the basis of their gathered church fellowship in Amsterdam. In England a Baptist 'General Union', formed in 1813, was gradually transformed into the Baptist Union of Great Britain and Ireland (1873).

Concerned, since the publication of Helwys's *Mystery of Iniquity* (1612), about religious liberty, some early 17th-cent. Baptists sought freedom in America. Roger Williams began Baptist work at Rhode Island in 1639 which, after early difficulties, spread rapidly throughout the USA, largely inspired by the mid-18th-cent. *Great Awakening in New England. The majority of their present congregations belong to either the 'American Baptist Churches in the USA' with 1.6 million members in 1983, the *Southern Baptist Convention with 13.9 million, and two (largely black) National Conventions with a combined membership of 10.3 million. Additional smaller bodies provide a total Baptist membership in the USA of 26.7 million.

Baqā' (Sūfī state of attainment): see FANĀ'.

Baraita (Aram., for Heb., *hizonah*, 'outside'). Every Jewish tradition of the *tannaim which is found outside Judah ha-Nasi's *Mishnah. The beraitot (pl.) were used to supplement mishnaic teaching or to solve a new problem which had arisen.

Baraka. *'blessing' (Arab., cf. Heb., *bārakh*). In Islam, a quality or force emanating originally from *Allāh but capable of transmission to objects or to human beings. The word appears in the *Qur'ān in the plural, *barakāt*, 'blessings' (7. 94; 11. 50, 76), and the term *mubārak*, 'blessed', is used, for example, of the Book (6. 92, 155), the *Kaʿba (3. 90), an olive tree (24. 33). *Muḥammad, *prophets, and holy persons in general are especially credited with baraka, and in popular Islam baraka can be acquired by touching a shrine or the tomb of a *walī (holy person), and above all from the *Black Stone in the Kaʿba. A baraka from God initiates a *Sūfī order: see SILSILAH. Great Sūfī *shaykhs also become possessed of baraka which is transmitted to others and may remain associated with their tombs, thereby evoking *pilgrimage.

Baramon-sōjō (Indian Buddhist monk): see BODHISENA.

Barbarossa (German King): see ADRIAN IV.

Barclay, Robert (exponent of Quaker beliefs): see FRIENDS, THE SOCIETY OF.

Bardaisan or **Bardesanes of Edessa** (154–222). Christian speculative thinker, by the 4th cent. classed as a *heretic. His Syriac *Book of the Laws of Countries* is a more or less orthodox treatment of fate.

Bardo (Skt., *antarabhāva*, 'intermediate state'). In *Tibetan Buddhism, the state after death and before rebirth. A distinction is made, however, in the *Nyingma, *Kagyü, and *Sakya traditions (which follow the **Tibetan Book of the Dead*) between six bardos, three of life and three of death. The subject experiencing these bardos is not an unchanging soul (which concept does not exist in Buddhism) but the constantly changing continuum of consciousness which, according to spiritual advancement, becomes either sharpened or bewildered after disjunction from the body.

Bardo Todrol (Tibetan afterdeath state): see TIBETAN BOOK OF THE DEAD.

Barelvi. Indian and Pakistani school of Muslim thought with over 200 million followers. The Dar-al-uloom was founded in 1904 by the Qadiri *Sūfī master, Imām Ahmad Reza (d. 1921) at Barelvi in N. India. Imām Ahmad Reza perceived the moral and intellectual decline of Indian Muslims at the beginning of the 20th cent. His solution was to strengthen the ordinary person's Islam by having the *Hanafi *shariʿa propagated through well-respected channels such as Sūfī *shaykhs and *ʿulamā.

Barelvi is a stronghold of *Sunni orthodoxy against the *Wahhābī and *Ahmadīyya movements. See also DEOBAND.

Baresnum (purification): see PURITY.

Bar-Ilan (Orthodox Jewish University): see BERLIN, N. Z. J.

Bar Kokhba, Simeon (d. 135 CE). Leader of Jewish revolt against Rome. His name ('Son of a Star') seems to have been understood as a fulfilment of the verse in Numbers 24. 17. He was accepted as *messiah by R. *Akiva, the leading authority of his day, and the revolt seems to have lasted for three years, 132–5 CE. He was eventually killed by the Roman army after a siege at Bethar which traditionally was taken on the 9 *Av.

Barlaam and Joasaph, Sts. Heroes of a medieval Christian romance. In it, an 'Indian' king Abenner tries to keep his son Joasaph from becoming a Christian as a seer had prophesied at his birth. The boy is brought up in a palace alone in strict ignorance of any of the ills of life and of Christianity. He is eventually allowed to go for a drive, sees men who are maimed, blind, and old, and becomes troubled. A Christian ascetic Barlaam, disguised, then preaches to him a series of parables and converts him. The story continues with a contest between Christianity and paganism and with Abenner's own conversion. The dependence of the tale on the legendary life of the *Buddha is obvious.

Barmecides (Muslim government adviser): see WAZĪR.

Barmen Declaration. Document issued in May 1934 by the Confessing Synod of Barmen. It was drafted by K. *Barth, and consists of a preamble and six theses. Each thesis quotes, then expounds, a New Testament text, then rejects an opposing thesis. 'Barmen' marked the beginning of organized opposition by the *Confessing Church to the Nazi government.

Bar mitzvah (Heb., 'Son of the Commandment'). The ceremony and status of boys (aged 13) attaining religious adulthood in Judaism. Girls are considered to have reached religious maturity at the age of 12, but except in *Progressive Judaism, this tends to be a fairly muted occasion. See BAT MITZVAH.

Barnabas, St. A Jew of Cyprus who became a member of the earliest Christian church at Jerusalem and was the companion of *Paul on his first missionary journey (Acts 4. 36, 9. 27, 13. 2, etc.). Feast day, 11 June.

The *Letter of Barnabas* is an anonymous treatise seeking to attack Judaism by claiming the *Old Testament for Christians alone.

Barth, Karl (1886–1968). Christian theologian, of dominating importance in 20th cent. Beginning his career at the end of the long 19th-cent. ascendancy of liberal and reductionist theology in Germany (e.g. *Feuerbach, *Schleiermacher, and *Strauss), epitomized for Barth in the figure of *Harnack, Barth entered his first and massive protest against this in his *Der Römerbrief* (1919). This introduced what came to be known as 'dialectical theology', or 'the theology of crisis' (Gk., *krisis*, 'judgement'). God cannot be found by humans as the conclusion of an argument, or as the experience at the end of a religious or mystical quest. God, rather, speaks his Word through the words of 'the strange new world of the Bible'. Although he published many works, his major commitment was to the many-volumed *Church Dogmatics*. The first volume appeared in 1932; 13 volumes later, it was unfinished at his death. He increasingly stressed the human vocation to co-operate with the initiatives of God in creation, and saw a place for human wisdom and knowledge as a prolegomenon to the acknowledgement of the sovereignty of God.

Bartholomew, St. One of the twelve *apostles (Mark 3. 18). Feast day in W., 24 Aug.; in E., 11 June.

Baruch. Scribe and companion of the *prophet *Jeremiah. In *apocryphal literature, several books are attributed to him, and further fragments of such books have been found among the *Dead Sea Scrolls.

The Book of Baruch (*1 Baruch*) is one of the additions to the book of Jeremiah in the *Septuagint.

2 Baruch (Syriac *Apocalypse of Baruch*) describes the Babylonian capture of Jerusalem, written to encourage Jews after the destruction of the second *Temple.

3 Baruch (Greek *Apocalypse of Baruch*) describes Baruch's vision of the seven heavens.

The *Rest of the Words of Baruch* (*4 Baruch* or *Paralipomena Jeremiae*) is a legendary account of Jeremiah's return from exile and his death.

Barukh Shem (Heb., 'Blessed be his name'). The beginning of an ancient Jewish doxology probably based on Nehemiah 9. 5, 'Bless the Lord your God from everlasting to everlasting. Blessed be your glorious name which is exalted above . . .'. It is regularly used after the first verse of the *Shemaʿ, and in the *Orthodox tradition, it is pronounced in a whisper.

Barzakh (Arab., 'an obstacle', 'separation', 'hindrance', or 'barrier'. The word is found three times in the Qur'ān (23. 100, 25. 53, 55. 20), and is understood differently by commentators, with moral, physical, and metaphysical interpretations.

Basava or Basavaṇṇa (*c*.1106–67/8). A Hindu religious reformer, associated with the founding of the *Liṅgāyata, also known as Vīraśaivism. He was a devotee of *Śiva from an early age, but he soon found *caste and ritual impeding progress. He became a devotee of the Lord of the Meeting Rivers, Kūḍalasaṅgamadēva, to whom reference is made in almost all his poems. After study of the *Vedas under a *guru, he began to worship with his own chosen *liṅga, *iṣṭaliṅga*, later to become characteristic of the Liṅgāyats. His egalitarian community of followers grew rapidly, evoking the opposition of traditionalists. Basava espoused non-violence, but when he could not control his followers, he returned to Kappaḍisaṅgama, where he died. His most practical and characteristic teaching aimed to re-establish the body as the true temple, a theme which he often expressed in poems of the vacana style—*vacana* ('that which is said') being a religious lyric in Kannada free verse.

Base Communities: see LIBERATION THEOLOGY.

Bashō (Matsuo Bashō, Japanese poet): see HAIKU.

Basil, St, 'the Great' (*c*.330–79). One of the three *Cappadocian fathers, and the first of the three Holy Hierarchs of the E. Church. Besides his eloquence and personal holiness, Basil was known for his talent for administration. His two monastic rules (see below) determined the structure of E. Christian monasticism ever since. He built hospitals and hostels alongside church buildings in Caesarea, and organized relief for the poor. His writings, in addition to letters, are a treatise *On the Holy Spirit*, three anti-Arian books *Against Eunomius*, and homilies. Feast day in W., 2 Jan.; in the E., 1 Jan.

The *Rule of Basil* has two forms, each set out as a series of questions and answers about the monastic life. Stopping well short of the extreme deprivations of the desert hermits, it prescribed liturgical prayer at fixed hours, manual work, poverty and chastity, community life, care for the poor, and the education of children. The present form of the rule is a revision by *Theodore of Studios (d. 826).

The Liturgy of Basil is used in the E. Church in place of that of *Chrysostom on a few fixed days (e.g. the Sundays in *Lent) each year.

Basilica. A Christian church building, derived in form from Roman empire buildings. In R. Catholicism, it is a title given to four ('major') churches in Rome, and to several ('minor') churches in Rome and elsewhere.

Basilica of Notre Dame de Paix. A vast church built at Yamoussoukro in the Ivory Coast, at the instigation of President Felix Houphouet-Boigny. It is 17 metres taller than St Peter's in Rome, and its dome is about three times the size of St Paul's in London.

Basilides (2nd cent. CE). An Alexandrian Christian theologian who inclined to *gnosticism. According to *Hippolytus he taught that under the supreme God were various good world-rulers, including the God of the Jews. *Jesus was endowed with a heavenly light to summon the elect, who will ascend to the highest heaven.

Basketmakers Church: see AFRICAN APOSTLES.

Basle, Council of (1431–49). The council which inherited the problems of the council of *Constance, convened by Martin V and dissolved by his successor, Eugenius IV, later in the year. It refused to be dissolved and reaffirmed the decrees of Constance on the superiority of a general *council over the *pope. The continuing council of Basle deposed the pope and elected the *anti-pope, Felix V, in 1439. After his abdication, the council submitted to the pope in 1449.

Basmala (Arab.). The saying of *Bismi'llah*, 'in the Name of *Allāh', invoking a blessing upon every action and undertaking of a Muslim. The full form is *bismillāhi (ar-)raḥmāni (ar-)raḥīm*, 'in the Name of Allah the merciful the compassionate'. Cf. also ḤAMDALA, the saying of *al-ḥamdu li 'illāh*, 'praise belongs to Allāh', which precedes the writing of any formal document.

Baso Dōitsu (leader of Ch'an/Zen school): see MA-TSU TAO-I.

Bassevi, Joseph (prominent Jew allied to ruler in Prague): see COURT JEWS.

Bassui Zenji (Tokushō) (1327–87). Jap. Zen teacher of the *Rinzai school. When he was 7, his father died, and this prompted him into *dai-gidan, probing questions based on doubt which form one of the three foundation pillars of *zazen, especially after *Hakuin. This led to a number of enlightenment experiences, and to monastic ordination. He eventually consented to become abbot of a monastery, and died sitting in the lotus position (see PADMĀSANA), saying, 'Do not be deceived: Look closely: what is this?' His letters and some of his *dharma instruction have been preserved: see P. Kapleau, *The Three Pillars of Zen* (1980).

Bast (Arab., 'expand', cf. Qur'ān 2. 245). In *Sūfī Islam, a technical term describing a state of exalted joy.

Bāṭinīy(y)a (Arab., *batana*, 'conceal'). Name for several Muslim sects, characterized by their seeking the inner, or secret, or esoteric meaning of the *Qur'ān. Bāṭinī is any doctrine which is esoteric or secret.

Bat Kol or **Qol** (Heb., 'daughter of a voice). A divine voice which reveals God's will. After the cessation of *prophecy, it became for Jews the only direct means of communication between God and human beings and occurred at the death of martyrs and occasionally in dreams.

Bat mitzvah (Heb., 'daughter of the commandment'). The status for a girl of attaining religious adulthood (cf. BAR MITZVAH for a boy). No ceremonies are laid down in the law, but a liturgy is contained in the Reform *New Union Prayer Book* (1975); the ceremonies are more elaborate in *Progressive Judaism.

Batuque: see AFRO-BRAZILIAN CULTS.

Baugs (places for worship): see PARSIS.

Bāul (Bengali, 'mad'). In India a kind of minstrel, mystic, and/or adept in esoteric practice, as well as a category of 'folk-song' composed and sung by such people. Those called 'Bāul' belong to the Bengali-speaking region of S. Asia: W. Bengal (India) and Bangladesh.

'Bāuls' are to be found among both Hindus and Muslims, and some Bāul lineages recruit from both these communities.

One meaning of the word 'bāul' is 'mad', and Bāuls are associated with madness in part through their liminal status. Their challenge to and partial transcendence of conventional structures and boundaries has caused them to be both extolled and vilified.

Most of their practices are esoteric (often classified as Tāntric) and are centred on the human body, almost invariably in conjunction with a partner of the opposite sex.

Baur, Ferdinand Christian (1792–1860). German Protestant theologian, who was Professor of Theology at Tübingen from 1826 to his death, and founded the *'Tübingen school'. Influenced by F. D. E. *Schleiermacher and by G. W. F. *Hegel's understanding of history, he saw conflict and synthesis as the key to understanding early Christianity. So, e.g. in his controversial work on Paul (1845; Eng. tr. 1873–5), he held that only the letters reflecting his lifelong opposition to the older disciples (viz., Galatians, 1–2 Corinthians, Romans) were authentic. He applied similar historical criticism to the development of Christian doctrines, especially the *atonement, *Trinity, and *incarnation.

Baxter, Richard (1615–91). *Puritan writer and theologian. Shropshire born and largely self-educated, Baxter was influenced by two *Nonconformist preachers, Joseph Symons and Walter Craddock. Ordained *deacon in 1638 by the bishop of Worcester, he served as curate at Kidderminster. At the Restoration he refused the bishopric of Hereford, taking his place with other ejected Nonconformists. His total literary output of 141 books and pamphlets includes such outstanding works as *The Saints' Everlasting Rest* (1650) and *Gildas Salvianus: The Reformed Pastor* (1656). His lengthy autobiography, *Reliquiae Baxterianae*, was edited by Matthew Sylvester and published posthumously in 1696. Some of his hymns are still in use (e.g. 'Ye holy *angels bright').

Bay ʿat (pact among Sūfīs): see INITIATION.

Bayram. In Turkey denotes *ʿīd, feast.

Bayudaya (Luganda, 'the Jews'). An African community in E. Uganda, officially known as 'The Propagation of Judaism in Uganda—Moses Synagogue'. The founder, Semei Kakungulu (?1850s–1928), was an outstanding Ganda political and military leader who became a *Protestant in the 1880s, but when disappointed in not being made Kabaka ('king'), he turned to religion and joined the semi-Christian, anti-medicine Bamalaki movement which had Judaic features. After deep study he took the *Old Testament literally and left in 1919 to form his own Bayudaya movement which insisted on *circumcision, the biblical festivals, and ritual slaughter.

BCP: see BOOK OF COMMON PRAYER.

Bdud-joms Rin-po-che or **Dudjom Rinpoche** (1904–87). Head of the *Nyingma order of Tibetan Buddhism. When 3 years old, he was recognized as the reappearance of the 'treasure-finder', Bdud-joms gling-pa (1835–1903). As a refugee in 1959, he settled first in Darjeeling and in Nepal, but then increasingly in the USA, and Europe, where he established Nyingma centres. He was thus a major figure in securing the Tibetan *diaspora.

Beard: see HAIR.

Beas (river providing name of religious movement): see RĀDHĀSOĀMĪ SATSAṄG.

Beatification. In the *Roman Catholic Church, the penultimate stage in the process which leads to the *canonization of a *saint. A person who has been beatified receives the title of 'Blessed'.

Beatific vision. The vision of God granted to the redeemed in *heaven. The term is used mainly in Catholic theology where it was the subject of much debate in the later Middle Ages. In Islam, the vision of God is the culminating experience of the rewarded in heaven, though the impossibility of seeing God directly is usually defended by affirming that a general manifestation of God is interpreted in the forms of habitual devotion.

Beatitudes. Promises of blessing, and specifically the sequence of eight or nine sentences beginning 'Blessed are the poor in spirit' in *Jesus' *Sermon on the Mount (Matthew 5. 3–11). The version in Luke's 'sermon on the plain' (6. 20–2) is shorter with more marked contrast of present and future.

Beautiful Names of God (in Islam): see NINETY-NINE BEAUTIFUL NAMES OF GOD.

Becket, Thomas à, St (*c.*1117–70). *Archbishop of *Canterbury and *martyr. A friend of Henry II, who appointed him chancellor in 1154 and, despite his protestations, archbishop of Canterbury in 1162, Thomas almost immediately came into conflict with the king over Henry's claim to judge 'criminous clerks', and, receiving little or no support from the other English *bishops, he had to flee abroad in 1164. An apparent reconciliation was achieved in 1170, but in a fit of temper Henry expressed the wish to be rid of the archbishop (according to tradition, 'Will no one revenge me of the injuries I have sustained from one turbulent priest?'), and four of his knights took him at his word: they murdered Thomas in Canterbury Cathedral on 29 Dec. He was canonized three years after his death (feast day, 29 Dec.), and his tomb rapidly became a centre of pilgrimage.

Bede, St, 'the Venerable' (*c.*673–735). English scholar. He spent his life as a monk at Jarrow in Northumbria. His most important work is the *Ecclesiastical History of the English People*, a main source for early English history, and also for an understanding of spiritual life at the time. In 1899 he was made a *Doctor of the Church. Feast day, 27 May.

Bedikat ḥamez (search for leaven): see LEAVEN.

Bedwardites. Followers of Alexander Bedward (1859–1930), a prophet-healer at August Town, Kingston, Jamaica. He was successor to an American Negro, Woods, founder of the Jamaica *Baptist Free Church in 1891, who had appointed his convert Bedward as *bishop with the title 'Shepherd'. Shepherd Bedward emphasized prayer, fasting, baptism by the *Holy Spirit, prophecy, and healing through water from the Mona River.

Beelzebub. A name equivalent to *Satan found in the gospels (Mark 3. 22–6 and par.). The Gk. text is *Beelzeboul*, which may correspond to Heb. *Baal-zebel*, 'lord of filth'. The English form -bub is due to the influence of Baal-zebub ('lord of flies') in 2 Kings 1. 2.

Beghards (lay Christian movements): see RHENO-FLEMISH SPIRITUALITY.

Beguines (lay Christian movements): see RHENO-FLEMISH SPIRITUALITY.

Behemoth. A monster described in the book of Job. In Job 40. 15–24.

Behrends, L. (prominent Jewish administrator/banker): see COURT JEWS.

Beijing. Capital of China for most of the last seven centuries under Yüan, Ming, Ch'ing dynasties, and currently under the People's Republic. Built according to ancient cosmic principles, it was oriented to the four directions, bisected by a North-South axial way, and modelled on the capital city of the God (*Shang Ti) in the Heavens. Religiously, the most important monuments of the capital were the *Altar of Heaven to the south of the city, the *Altar of Earth to the north, the Imperial Ancestral Temple and the Altar to Land and Grain, and the *T'ai Ho Tien* or Imperial Hall of Audience, where the emperor sat on his 'dragon throne'.

Being-itself: see TILLICH, PAUL.

Beit (house of, as in Beit-Hillel): see BET.

Bektāshīy(y)a. Turkish Derwish order, originating in about the 12th cent. CE, of a particularly eclectic kind. The traditional founder was Hajji Bektash Vali, but very little is known of him. They are *Shi'ite in so far as they acknowledge the Twelve Imāms, but different from other Muslims in disregarding such obligations as *ṣalāt, and in allowing *women to take part in rituals without the veil.

Bel and the Dragon. Two stories which appear together in the *Apocrypha, and at the end of *Daniel in *Roman Catholic Bibles. They are directed against idolatry.

Belial (Heb., 'worthlessness'). A description of people acting in a worthless manner and, in post-biblical literature, the name of the Prince of Evil.

Bellarmine, Robert, St (1542–1621). Italian *Jesuit *cardinal and controversialist. He was born in Montepulciano, Tuscany, and entered the Society of Jesus at Rome in 1560. He was ordained priest in 1570 in Louvain—where he was the first Jesuit to hold a chair—but shortly afterwards returned to the Roman College, now the Gregorian University, to teach controversial theology to priests destined for England and Germany. His lectures provided the basis for his famous work, *De Controversiis* or *Controversies*, published at Ingolstadt between 1586 and 1593. He was made a cardinal in 1599, and briefly (1602–5) served as *archbishop of Capua. In 1616 he was obliged to censure Galileo, although he had considerable sympathy for his views. In later life Bellarmine produced a number of popular devotional works. He was declared a *Doctor of the Church in 1931.

Benamozegh, Elijah ben Abraham (1822–1900). Italian *rabbi and philosopher. Serving as rabbi in Leghorn, he produced numerous books and articles which attempted to reconcile traditional Judaism, including *Kabbalah, with the secular philosophy of his day.

Benares: see KĀŚI.

Ben Asher, Aaron ben Moses (called Abu Sa'id; early 10th cent. CE). Jewish biblical scholar. A contemporary of Saadiah *Gaon, he was well known as a masorete (see MASORAH). Although a *Karaite, his vocalization of the scriptures carried enormous prestige. His *Sefer Dikdukei ha-Te'amim* (Book of the Decreed Grammar) laid the basics of Hebrew grammar.

Ben Asher, Jacob (author of Jewish law text): see CODIFICATIONS OF LAW.

Bene Berith (Jewish charitable organization): see B'NAI B'RITH.

Benedicite (Lat., 'bless ye'). The song of praise beginning 'O all ye works of the Lord, bless ye the Lord'. It forms part of the *Song of the Three Children.

Benedict, St (*c*.480–*c*.550). Christian monastic leader. Little is known of his life. He withdrew from the world to live in a cave at Subiaco in *c*.500, where a community grew up around him. He moved with a small number of monks *c*.525 to Monte Cassino, where he remained and composed his Rule—although he does not seem to have intended to found an order. Feast day in W., 11 July; in E., 14 Mar.

The *Rule of St Benedict* is a fundamental rule of W. Christian monasticism. The opening chapters seem to have been based on the anonymous *Rule of the Master* emanating from a smaller monastery in SE Italy; *Basil, *Pachomius, and *Augustine were also influential. It consists of seventy-three terse chapters, dealing with both spiritual matters and questions of organization, liturgy, and discipline. Stability and obedience are paramount.

Benedict XV (1854–1922). *Pope from 3 Sept. 1914. His pontificate was dominated by the First World War: the first of Benedict's twelve *encyclicals dealt with peace, and he was deeply distressed by the failure of his 1917 peace initiative. He speeded the publication of the first code of *canon law, and worked for an understanding between the *Holy See and the kingdom of Italy.

Benedictines: see BENEDICT, ST; Index, Benedictine.

Benediction (with the Blessed Sacrament). Catholic eucharistic devotion. As a separate evening service, benediction is first found in the 15th cent. In the modern service in its most solemn form, the consecrated host is exposed to view in a *monstrance; hymns are sung; the sacrament is censed twice; and the priest blesses the congregation with it. See also REAL PRESENCE; EXPOSITION.

Benedictions. Formulas of blessing. Among Jews, according to the *Talmud, the formulation of benedictions goes back to the time of *Ezra. According to R. *Meir, every Jew has a duty to pronounce one hundred benedictions every day (*B. Men.* 43b). Special benedictions are grouped in three categories: (i) *birkhot ha-nehenim*, blessings for enjoyment (e.g. before and after meals, over fragrant odours); (ii) *birkhot ha-mitzvot*, blessings on performance of commandments; (iii) *birkhot hoda'ah*, blessings of gratitude (e.g. on witnessing natural phenomena, such as thunderstorms, rainbows, earthquakes, or on ritual occasions). Everything in life, whether it gives rise to sorrow or to joy, has its ultimate source in God.

Benedictus. Title of two Christian liturgical hymns. 1. The song of Zechariah (Luke 1. 68–79). 2. The 'Benedictus qui Venit', forming the end of the *Sanctus at the *eucharist ('Blessed is he who comes in the name of the Lord').

Bene Israel (Heb. 'Sons of Israel'). Early Jews (of the biblical period), but more particularly a Jewish community in India. Indian Jews claim their community dates back to the days of the *Maccabees and survived in complete isolation. By 1969, 12,000 had emigrated to *Israel, although the religious establishment initially raised questions of personal status and legitimacy: in 1964, the Chief Rabbinate declared them 'full Jews in every respect'.

Ben'en; also **Enni Ben'en** (also known as Shoichi Kokushi; 1202–80). Japanese *Zen master of the *Rinzai Yogi school. In 1242, he became abbot of the Tōfuku-ji (monastery) in Kyōto. Enni was thus a man of wide education, but while he was prepared to take part in Tendai and Shingon rituals, he believed that Zen was the true way to the goal. In *Jisshūyōdōki* (Essentials of the Way of the Ten Schools), he claimed that Zen was not simply 'a school among schools', but that it was the 'bowl which carries the Buddha mind' through history.

Ben Gurion, David (1886–1973). First prime minister of *Israel. His own faith he summarized as, 'We have preserved the Book, and the Book has preserved us.'

Ben ha-matserim (between the disasters commemorated by Jews on 17 Tammuz and 9 Av): see THREE WEEKS.

Benjamin. Youngest son of the patriarch *Jacob, full brother to *Joseph and forefather of the tribe of Benjamin.

Bensh (Yid., 'Bless'). Jewish expression used for making a *blessing. A bensh can refer to grace after meals, blessing a child, or other *benedictions.

Ben Sira, Wisdom of (also called *Ecclesiasticus*, the Church (book), and *Sirach*, the Gk. for Sira). Book of the *Apocrypha. It was probably composed in the 2nd cent. BCE. It directs humanity to the ways of wisdom, virtue, and moderation, and emphasizes the importance of well-ordered family life.

Ben sorer u-moreh (Jewish Commandment): see REBELLIOUS SON.

Beraitot (paragraphs): see TOSEFTA; BARAITA.

Berakhot (Heb., 'benedictions'). The first tractate of the *Talmud. The tractate discusses prayers and *blessings, including the laws involved in the recital of the *Shema', the *'Amidah and the various *benedictions.

Berdyaev, Nicolas (1874–1948). Russian philosopher. Originally a sceptic with Marxist sympathies, he embraced *Orthodoxy after the revolution of 1905, and from 1922 lived as an *émigré* in Paris. His religious philosophy was deeply influenced by *Dostoevsky and also *Boehme. There is thus a *gnostic tinge to his philosophy, which attracted the suspicion of the Orthodox hierarchy.

Bereshit (Heb., 'in the beginning'): see GENESIS.

Berit (Heb., 'covenant'): see COVENANT.

Berkowits, E. (Jewish writer): see HOLOCAUST (3).

Berlin, Naphtali Zevi Judah (known as ha-Neziv, 1817–93). Jewish *Talmudic scholar. From 1854, he was head of the *yeshivah at Volozhin which became the spiritual centre of Russian Jewry. Ultimately he was exiled by the

Russian authorities and the yeshivah was closed.

His son, Meir Berlin (Bar-Ilan), 1880–1949, was prominent in religious Zionism, and became a leader in the *Mizraḥi movement, first in Berlin, then (1915–26) in the USA. From 1926 he settled in Palestine, where he was involved in initiating the Talmud Encyclopedia. The Orthodox university, Bar-Ilan, was established in 1955 to honour his memory.

Bernadette, St (1844–79). Bernadette Soubirous was born into a humble family at *Lourdes, where, at the Massabielle Rock, she received eighteen apparitions of the Virgin *Mary between 11 Feb. and 16 July 1858. She was beatified in 1925 and canonized in 1933. The importance of Lourdes as a place of pilgrimage, and its association with healing, has made her among the most popular modern *saints.

Bernard of Clairvaux, St (1090–1153). Christian monastic reformer and mystical writer. He joined the *Cistercian monastery at Citeaux in *c.*1111, and established at Clairvaux in 1115 a daughter house in which he insisted on rigorous observance and discipline. He combined an emphasis on the love and mercy of God with vehement controversy on this earth. He was officially charged with preaching the Second *Crusade. He was canonized in 1174 and proclaimed *Doctor of the Church in 1830. Feast day, 20 Aug.

Bernard's understanding of spiritual life is *affective, dominated by the way in which the human freedom to consent is met by God's *grace so that the consequence of love flows forth.

Bertinoro, Obadiah ben Abraham Yare (*c.*1450–*c.*1516). Italian Jewish commentator on the *Mishnah. His commentary on the Mishnah became the standard work, comparable to *Rashi's commentary on the *Talmud and drawing heavily on it. His acronym is Ra'av (Rabbenu Ovadyah mi-Bartenura).

Beruryah (2nd cent. CE). Jewish woman scholar of the *Talmud. The wife of R. *Meir, she was the only woman in Talmudic literature whose *halakhic opinions were respected. In the so-called Beruryah Incident, R. Meir tested her integrity by sending to her a student to seduce her into adultery: after submitting, she committed suicide.

Besant, A.: see THEOSOPHICAL SOCIETY.

Beshara. *Sūfī-inspired movement, started in London *c.*1970. The name of the founder, a Turk, is unknown, and while members stress that there is no leader as such, Beshara teaching is grounded in the writings of the mystics *Ibn Arabi (1165–1240) and *Jalāl al-Dīn Rūmī (1207–73).

Besht (founder of E. European Ḥasidism): see ISRAEL BEN ELIEZER (i.e. Ba'al Shem Tov).

Bet Din (Heb., 'house of judgement'). Jewish court of *law. Traditionally the establishment of the bet din as an institution is ascribed to *Ezra. In *Israel, the bet din is the rabbinic court which has jurisdiction in such areas as personal status, while the bet mishpat (also 'house of judgement') deals with secular cases.

Bet (ha-)Midrash (Heb., 'house of study'). Houses of study in Judaism go back at least to the second century BCE, when Simeon Ben Sira asked people to 'dwell in my bet midrash' (*Ecclesiasticus* 51. 47). They were the community centre where Jewish culture and learning were preserved and disseminated.

Bethel. Town approximately 10 miles north of Jerusalem. According to Genesis, *Abraham built an altar between Bethel and Ai (12. 6–8), and *Jacob had a vision of *angels ascending and descending on a ladder stretching between heaven and earth (28. 10–22). The name Bethel means literally 'house of God' and the place was said to have been so called by Jacob.

Bet Hillel. One school of Jewish interpretation of the oral *law. It is frequently contrasted with the other school, Bet Shammai. The schools existed in the 1st and 2nd cents. CE, and *tannaitic literature records many of the controversies. In general, Bet Hillel was considered to be the more lenient of the two.

Bethlehem. Town located 5 miles south of Jerusalem. On the basis of Micah 5. 2, *Jesus' birth in the city is understood by Christians as the fulfilment of prophecy (Matthew 2. 1–12; Luke 2. 1–20).

Bet mishpat: see BET DIN.

Betrothal (in Judaism): see SHIDDUKHIN.

Bet Shammai: see BET HILLEL.

Betsugedatsukai. Jap. ('individually liberating precepts') for *prātimokṣa, the precepts for Buddhist monks.

Beza, Theodore (1519–1605). French-born successor to *Calvin in Geneva as the leader of Reformed Protestantism (see REFORMATION). Educated for a legal career, he renounced *Roman Catholicism after a severe illness in 1548. Academically, he devoted himself to biblical study, especially to study of the Greek text. During the wars of religion (1560–98) he provided a theological argument and basis for resistance to usurped political authority. His strong defence of biblical literalism, double predestination and firm church discipline laid deep foundations for Calvinism and initiated what has been called 'Reformed Scholasticism'. However, the precise connection of Beza with this has been much disputed.

Bezalel. Head builder of the *tabernacle (Exodus 31. 1–11; 36–9).

Bhadrakalpika-sūtra (Skt., 'Sūtra of the Fortunate Age'). *Sūtra of *Mahāyāna Buddhism of a type which became extremely popular: it focuses on the legends of the thousand *buddhas of the fortunate age, of which the Buddha *Śākyamuni is the fifth.

Bhaga (due inheritance, social order): see ĀDITYAS.

Bhagat (Pañjābī form of Skt., *bhāgavata). Among Sikhs, those whose compositions are included in the *Ādi Granth, but who are either non-Sikhs or Sikhs who are not *Gurūs.

Bhagavā, Bhagavant, (Pāli, Skt.). 'Lord', 'Master', 'Exalted One', 'Blessed One'; reverential title used of the *Buddha by his disciples and others.

Bhagavad-gītā (Skt., 'the song of the *Bhagavā'). A fundamental text for Hindus—for many, the most sublime. It forms part of book vi of the **Mahābhārata*, and in eighteen sections of 700 verses, it explores the situation which has brought the warrior Arjuna to a crisis of conscience: he is opposed in battle by members of his own family; should he attack and perhaps kill them? Offered the assistance of *Kṛṣṇa Devakīputra, he accepts and receives instruction on appropriate conduct and attitudes. The main part of the *Gītā* records this instruction. Kṛṣṇa points Arjuna to the three paths (*marga), of knowledge (*jñāna-marga), of action with detachment (*karma-marga), and of devotion to God (*bhakti-mārga). Since these are ways of being united to the ultimately true and real, they are also known as karma-yoga, jñāna-yoga, and bhakti-yoga, the latter amounting to *rāja-yoga.

The *Gītā* appears to have been addressed (the date is uncertain, but *c*.200 BCE is likely) to a situation in which major unease about the excessive and costly rituals of *Brahmanical religion had led to a reaction so severe that it had isolated both Buddhism and Jainism as separate religions. The *Gītā* appears to make a deliberate attempt to show the worth of the major ways of the continuing tradition (though obviously it corrects any non-theistic system if taken in isolation). It therefore reads as a deliberate attempt to reconcile and hold the line against further schism. It achieves a profound reconciliation; not surprisingly, therefore, it is the most revered and influential text among Hindus.

Bhagavān (Skt., 1st person nom. of *bhagavat*, 'having shares', from √*bhaj*, 'distribute, partake'). Hindu epithet for God as constantly concerned for human well-being, and as 'one who receives his share' (sc., of offerings and honour). Although the term can be used as a title of respect for honoured individuals, especially teachers (it is used of the *Buddha, see BHAGAVĀ, or more recently in the form 'Bhagwan' in *Rajneeshism), it is most commonly used of God as Lord. A Bhāgavata is one who is devoted to Bhagvān, in a disposition of *bhakti. Major texts of this devotion are **Bhagavad-gītā* and **Bhāgavata-purāṇa*.

Initially, Bhāgavatas were not organized as a movement or sect. Subsequently many bhakti movements of Bhāgavatas came into being.

Bhāgavata. One devoted to *Bhagavān.

Bhāgavata-purāṇa. A Hindu mythological work in Skt., one of the eighteen *mahapurāṇas. The title must be derived from *Bhagavān, which means here *Kṛṣṇa/*Viṣṇu, the central deity of the text. It is usually included in the list of the eighteen mahā-purāṇas (Major Purāṇas), but among these it is the most idiosyncratic and unusual work. Innumerable versions of it were produced in almost all vernaculars of India, and many religious movements (among them the schools of *Caitanya and Vallabhā) made it their scriptural authority. It is a complex work, fusing many different traditions, hence its wide popularity. Its basic structure and content derive from the **Viṣṇu Purāṇa* (with traces of influence also from the **Mārkaṇḍeya-purāṇa*). But unlike that source, and the earlier purāṇas generally, it uses highly sophisticated lyrical metres and descriptions (often presented as songs). Also, the form of devotion it advocates—an intense emotionalism that aims at *ecstasy—is quite different from earlier *bhakti texts (such as the **Bhagavad-gītā* or the *Viṣṇu Purāṇa*). Its influence is still felt today, not only in India, but—because of its use by the Kṛṣṇa Consciousness movement—throughout the world.

Bhāgo, Mātā or Māī (Pañjābī, 'mother'; b. 17th cent. CE). Sikh heroine. Māī Bhāgo rallied the 'forty immortals' at *Muktsār, vowing that she would, if necessary, die for Gurū *Gobind Siṅgh. Wearing men's clothing, she fought bravely, killing several men of the local Mughal governor, Wazir Khān, and was blessed by the

Gurū. Apparently she subsequently lost her reason and died at *Nander.

Bhagwan (founder of Indian-based movement): see RAJNEESH.

Bhāī (Pañjābī, 'brother'). Title for Sikh men which indicates particular esteem. The equivalent for women is *bībī.

Bhāī Kanayhā (model of selfless Sikh): see SEVĀ.

Bhairava (Skt.). 1. A ferocious form of *Śiva, akin to *Kālī, revered in *Tantrism especially by the Kāpālikas and in *Kashmir Śaivism. By meditating on this terrible form of the deity, the adept (*sādhaka) eventually sees through the ferocity and apprehends the transcendent beyond form. He is accompanied by his *śakti *Bhairavī who is likewise terrible.

2. The name/title of one who seeks to enter a Tantric sect.

Bhairavī (Skt.). A ferocious form of the Goddess (*Devī) in Hinduism especially in *Tantrism, the *śakti of *Bhairava. Like *Kālī, Bhairavī is described as having a terrible appearance, garlanded with severed heads. She is the active principle of the cosmos dancing on the passive principle of *Śiva, often represented as a corpse. Like Kālī, Bhairavī represents the terrible aspects of existence which have to be embraced in order to achieve liberation (*mokṣa).

Bhaiṣajyaguru (more fully: Bhaiṣajyaguru vaiḍūryaprabha tathāgata, 'Radiant lapis-lazuli Master of Healing Buddha'; Tib. sman.bla; Chin., Yao Shih Fo; Jap., Yakushi Nyōrai; Korean, Yaksa). The *Buddha of healing, frequently called 'Medicine Buddha', popular in the *Mahāyāna Buddhism of Tibet, China, and Japan, whose dispensation also includes longevity, protection from disasters, and the transmutation of negative states of mind (all illnesses in Buddhism, by virtue of their *karmic origin, being considered to some extent psychosomatic).

The earliest evidence of the Healing Buddha is the Chinese translation from the Skt. of *Bhaiṣajyagurusūtra* (early 4th cent. CE), and as this has close similarities with the **Lotus Sūtra* (*c*.2nd cent. CE) in which the *bodhisattva King of Healing (Bhaiṣajyarāja) is prominent, it is likely that Bhaiṣajyaguru was a development bestowing increased importance to Bhaiṣajyarāja. He presides over the *Pure Land of the East (cf. *Sukhāvatī, the Western Paradise).

Bhājā (Buddhist monastic establishment): see VIHĀRA.

Bhajana (chant): see MANDIR(A): WORSHIP.

Bhakti (Skt., either from √*bhaj*, 'to share, be loyal', or √bhañj, 'to separate'). Devotion in love and adoration, especially to one's chosen manifestation of the divine (*iṣṭadeva); but it may be guru-bhakti (surrender to a guru) or vaidhi-bhakti (willing acceptance of a guru's instructions). In its theistic form, it perhaps appears in the **Ṛg Veda* (5. 85. 7 f.; 7. 87. 7), in hymns imploring *Varuṇa to forgive the offences of his devotees. But it became a major way of Indian religious life (owing much to the religion of *Tamil Nadu), in which the grace (*prasāda) of God modifies the strict causality of *karma. Bhakti-marga (the way of bhakti) has produced some of the world's most moving theistic poetry, as well as the formalization of the stages through which union with God can be attained, in Bhakti-yoga. The **Bhagavad-gītā* is the foremost exposition and expression of bhakti addressed to *Kṛṣṇa. See also VAIṢṆAVA; ŚAIVA; ŚRI-VAIṢṆAVISM; Index, Bhakti.

Bhaktivedanta Swami Prabhupada (founder of ISKCON): see PRABHUPADA.

Bhandarkar, Ramkrishna Gopal (1837–1925). Eminent Indian academician, who was Professor of Sanskrit at Deccan College, Puné, 1884–93, and Vice-Chancellor of Bombay University 1893–5. His writings are numerous, and he is especially noteworthy for his search for Skt. manuscripts in Western India and Rajasthan, and the editing of Bhavabhūti's *Mālatī Mādhuva*.

Bhanga or **bhang.** A narcotic (*cannabis sativa*) used in India to assist divination and produce ecstatic states. According to **Atharva Veda* 9. 6. 15, it is one of the five kingdoms of plants ruled by *Soma.

Bharata. The tribe which took part in the war described in the *Mahābhārata, and the name of several notable *Āryans; hence also the name (Bharat) of modern India.

Bharata natya. S. Indian *dance, performed originally by *Deva-Dāsīs. Although it fell into disuse, it has been reconstructed by following the dance poses as they are sculpted in Indian temples.

Bharatya Janata Party. Indian political party committed to the preservation of Hindu identity. Committed to the Constitution, it has nevertheless run the risk of being taken over on the streets by far more extreme groups, e.g. Rashtriya Svayamsevak Sangh (RSS), founded as a self-defence militia in pre-Independence days; and Viśva Hindu Paraśad (VHP), which has tried to give 'Hinduism' a more systematic ideology.

These and other groups were involved in the destruction of the *Ayodhyā mosque.

Bhārhut. In Madhya Pradesh, this is the earliest surviving Buddhist *stūpa. Based on a Mauryan relic mound, the stūpa was decorated in the Śuṅga period, about 100 BCE.

Bhāsa (early: *c.* 4th cent. CE?). Hindu dramatist. His works were lost until 1912, when thirteen plays attributed to him were published, including the admired *Svapna-vāsavadatta*.

Bhāṣya. Hindu commentary on sacred texts, especially *sūtras. Because sūtras are compressed and aphoristic, bhāṣyas are a vital key to understanding them.

Bhāṭṛā, N. Indian pedlar community claiming *brahman descent. They trace their origin to Mādho Mal of Śri Lankā, whose descendant, Chaṅgā Bhāṭṛā, reputedly became a disciple of Gurū *Nānak. Many Bhāṭṛās are Sikhs. There is no intermarriage between Bhāṭṛā Sikhs and Sikhs of other *castes, and in some cities they have formed separate *gurdwārās.

Bhāṭṭa (Skt.). A follower of *Kumārila Bhaṭṭa; also in Hinduism, an honorific title given to learned *brahmans.

Bhattaraka (Skt., 'learned man'). Head of a group of naked monks in *Digambara Jainism. Buildings (*maṭha*) to accommodate these ascetics began to be built from about the 5th cent. BCE, and the bhattarakas became in effect the presidents of them.

Bhāva (Skt.). 1. In *Sāṃkhya, a set of psychological predispositions either eight or fifty in number. The more concise numbering renders them as virtue (*dharma), vice (adharma), knowledge (*jñāna), ignorance (ajńāna), nonattachment (*virāga*), attachment (*rāga), power (*aiśvarya*), and impotence (*anaiśvarya*).

These dispositions are an inherent part of human nature. They create the environment in which karma is accumulated or overcome.

2. The emotional dispositions in Hinduism of the bhakta (one engaged in *bhakti) to the chosen deity (*iṣṭadeva): (i) *śanta*, peace; (ii) *dāsya*, servant to master; (iii) *sākhya*, friend to friend; (iv) *vātsalya*, parent to child; (v) *madhura*, wife to husband, lover to beloved.

3. In Buddhism, 'being', every kind of manifestation in the three domains of appearance (triloka: see LOKA). It is also the tenth link in chain of conditioned-arising (*paticca-samuppāda).

4. For Jains, bhāva, with *dravya, enters deeply into the dynamic of lay and ascetic life. In the quest to disentangle *jīva from *karma, bhāva represents the spiritual elements whose priority must be secured over against the physical constituents of material appearance (dravya).

Bhavacakra (Skt., the 'wheel of existence'). Buddhist, and especially Tibetan, painting which portrays the relentless process of recurrent birth, death, and rebirth, *saṃsāra, as a wheel. Pictures on the wheel convey the conditions of saṃsāra together with the moral and mental factors which cause the individual to remain within saṃsāra. The wheel is shown clasped by the hands and feet and being devoured by a demon monster, *Māra, symbolizing the all-pervasive nature of death and impermanence.

According to the **Divyāvadāna*, the Buddha himself instituted the drawing of the bhavacakra as a pedagogic device for the instruction of the non-literate in Buddhist truths. The earliest known example of the bhavacakra is a fresco (*c.*6th cent. CE) of *Ajaṇṭā.

Bhāvanā (Pāli, Skt., 'to make become', 'to nurture', 'to develop', √*bhu* = 'to be'). In early Buddhism, *meditation in the broadest sense: methods of mental training and discipline leading to mind-control and spiritual insight.

Bhavanga-sota (stream of consciousness): see Ālaya-vijñāna.

Bhavānī. A name of the Hindu Goddess. Theoretically it can be derived from Bhava, a synonym of *Śiva. This would then denote the goddess as Śiva's consort, similar to *Pārvatī, *Durgā, or Gaurī. However, in the context of regional cults connected with temples, Bhavānī may figure independently from Śiva.

Bhāvaviveka (also 'Bhāvya' and 'Bhāviveka'; *c.*500–70 CE). Major Indian philosopher of the *Madhyamaka school of Buddhism.

A major mark of Bhāvaviveka's thought is the division of reality into ultimate truth (*paramārthasatya*) and conventional truth (*saṃvṛtisatya*), by which self-existence (*svabhāva) is asserted as a conventional truth but not as an ultimate one.

Bhāvaviveka's principal works are the *Prajñāpradīpa* (Light of Wisdom), which is a commentary on *Nāgārjuna's *Mulamadhyamakākarikās*, and the *Madhyamakahṛdayakārikās* (Verses on the Essence of the Middle Way), with his own commentary the *Tarkajvāla* (Blaze of Reasoning), which assesses the *brahmanical systems.

Bhave, Vinoba: see VINOBA BHAVE.

Bhāvya: see BHĀVAVIVEKA.

Bhīkanji: see BHIKṢU, ĀCĀRYA.

Bhikkhu, bhikkhunī: see BHIKṢU/BHIKṢUṆĪ.

Bhikṣu/bhikṣuṇī (Skt.; Pāli, *bhikkhu*, *bhikkhunī*; Chin., *pi-ch'iu*; Jap., *biku*; Korean *pigu*). Male/female members of the Buddhist *saṅgha, usually translated as 'monks', 'nuns'.

The life of the saṅga is laid down in the rules of the *Vināya-piṭaka, underlying the basic principles of poverty, chastity, and peacefulness. The bhikṣu relies on begging for his food, and his clothing, made of three parts (*tricīvara*), is preferably ragged. Initially, all bhikṣus spent their lives wandering, but were then allowed to spend the rainy season in a monastery (*vihāra), which has now become the norm for the saṅgha. It is required (or at least desirable) that a layman should spend a period during the rainy season living as a bhikṣu.

The *Buddha initially resisted the formation of an order of bhikṣuṇīs, fearing for distraction and moral disorder. But this was introduced by Mahāprajāpati Gautami, the Buddha's stepmother. There is no difference in principle between Theravada and Mahāyāna monastic observances, but the Mahāyāna list of precepts is longer. Mahāyāna bhikṣus observe 250 precepts while bhikṣuṇīs observe 348. Theravādin nuns adopt the habit and tonsure but observe only the ten precepts (Pāli, *dassasīla*) of the novice (Pāli, *sāmaṇari*) and are called *dasasīlavanti*, 'those of the ten precepts'.

Bhikṣu, Ācārya (also Bhīkanji, 1726–1803). Founder of the Jain reforming sect, the Terapanth. He founded the Terapanth in 1759 on the basis of extreme discipline and rigour. He followed the life of a wandering beggar, and by the time he died, he had initiated forty-nine monks and fifty-six nuns.

The name 'Terapanth' is variously explained: *tera* means (in Rajasthani) both 'thirteen' and 'your'. Thus the 'Thirteen Path' may be the reliance on the thirteen basic elements of ascetic practice which Bhiksu was restoring (the *Five Great Vows, the Five Attentive Actions, *samiti*, and the Three Protections, *gupti*); or it may be the number of early followers (thirteen monks and thirteen laymen); or it may be the devotion to '*you*, Lord *Mahāvīra'. He elevated the role of the ācārya, to become the sole authority over adherents, and to appoint his own successor. The eighth ācārya, Tulsi, who succeeded in 1936, took this out into the world (especially of politics and economics), arguing that the accelerating power of humans to destroy must be counteracted by an accelerating power to reform spiritually. He therefore founded the *Anuvrata Movement, from *aṇu ('atom', with deliberate reference to 'atom bomb') and *vrata, 'vow': 'A small, or atomic, vow alone has the power to ward off and counter the threat of an atom bomb.'

Bhīma or **Bhīmasena.** In the **Mahābhārata*, the second oldest *Pāṇḍava, of the strong and wild warrior type, whose weapon, when not simply a tree trunk, is the mace.

Bhindrānawāle, *Sant Jarnail Siṅgh (1947–84). Controversial Sikh leader. Jarnail Siṅgh was the leader of a religious institution, Damdamā Sāhib Taxāl, which was reputedly founded by the 18th-cent. Sikh hero, Bābā Dīp Siṅgh. He opposed the Sant *Nirañkārīs, and inspired militant support for *Khālistān. He was killed in the *Akāl Takht by the Indian army during Operation Blue Star.

Bhīṣma. In the **Mahābhārata*, the 'Grandfather' of the *Pāṇḍavas and *Kauravas. Really the sky god *Dyaus (one of the eight Vasus: see ĀDITYAS) incarnate, Bhīṣma is born as the son of King Śaṃtanu and the river Ganges (*Gaṅga). While waiting to die, he rests on a bed of arrows, and exhorts Yudhiṣṭhira with the legal and spiritual instruction which constitutes books xii and xiii of the *Mahābhārata*, the **Śānti-* and *Anuśāsanaparvans*.

Bhog (Pañjābī, 'enjoyment, climax'). Among Sikhs, the ceremonial conclusion of a complete reading of the *Ādi Granth.

Bhoga (Skt.). In Hinduism, food offered to a form of God; also sensory pleasure.

Bhṛgu. In Hindu mythology, a divine seer, son of *Brahmā (or of *Varuṇa, or of *Indra, or of *Prajāpati), and eponymous ancestor of the Bhṛgu or Bhārgava clan.

Bhubaneswar (formerly Bhuveneśvara, 'Lord of the world', an epithet of Śiva). City in Orissa with many temples dedicated to Śiva, especially Lingavaj temple.

Bhūmi (Skt., 'ground', 'level', 'stage'). In *Mahāyāna Buddhism, a stage in a systematized scheme of progress to spiritual maturity and perfection in enlightenment (*nirvāna). Most schools of Buddhism recognize a scheme of states or stages which are passed through, beginning with conversion and the taking up of the religious life and ending in enlightenment. *Theravāda lists the four stages of the *arya-mārga, and the theory of the bhūmis may be thought of as an outgrowth of this or as an extension of the scheme of progress in the Eightfold Path (*aṣtangika-mārga) through morality, meditation, and wisdom. The most popular sequence involves a list of ten bhūmis although some texts refer only to seven.

In the 10th stage, the Cloud of the Dharma (*dharmamegha*), the bodhisattva reaches full perfection and is consecrated as a fully enlightened Buddha. He sits, surrounded by bodhisattvas, on a lotus in the Tuṣita heaven. This stage is also known as abhiṣeka-bhūmi.

Bhumi ('earth'): see LOKA.

Bhūta (Skt., √*bhu*, 'being'). 1. In S. Asian philosophy, an element, especially a *mahābhūta (gross element) but also a tanmātra (subtle element: see AHAṂKARA). Hindu systems of philosophy list five gross elements: ether (*ākāśa), air, fire, water, and earth.

2. Spirits; in the *Brāhmaṇas, human and non-human beings; in later texts, malignant spirits or goblins.

Bhūtaśuddhi (Skt., 'purification of the elements'). The ritual purification of the body in *Tantrism, so as to render the body sacred in order to worship a deity. The body corresponds to the cosmos, so bhūtaśuddhi recapitulates at a personal level the process of cosmic dissolution (*pralaya). Bhūtaśuddhi is a preliminary rite in all forms of Tantric pūjā.

Bhūtatathatā (Skt., 'suchness of existents'). In Buddhism, the true nature, as opposed to the appearance, of the manifest world. It is 'that which really is', in contrast to all that is transient, and thus in *Mahāyāna, it is the *buddha-nature.

Bhuvaneśvara ('Lord of the world', title of Śiva): see BHUBANESWAR.

Bībī. Honorific title for Sikh women, e.g. Bībī Nānakī, Gurū *Nānak's elder sister.

Bible. The collection of sacred writings of Jews, or that of Christians. The word derives from Gk. *biblia*, 'books', which came to be used as a singular noun as the books of the Bible were thought of as a unity. See also CANON and articles on individual books. The Hebrew Bible is divided into three sections, *Torah (law), Nevi'im (*prophets) and Ketuvim (*writings). From the initial letters, the acronym Ta Na Kh is formed, which thus becomes a common name for the Bible i.e. Tanach, Tanak, etc. Torah includes *Genesis, *Exodus, *Leviticus, *Numbers, and *Deuteronomy (collectively known as the *Pentateuch). Nevi'im includes *Joshua, *Judges, *1 and 2 Samuel, *1 and 2 Kings, *Isaiah, *Jeremiah, and the twelve prophets. The Ketuvim are *Psalms, * Proverbs, *Job, the five *scrolls (the *Song of Songs, *Ruth, *Lamentations, *Ecclesiastes, *Esther), *Daniel, *Ezra, *Nehemiah, and *1 and 2 Chronicles. This division into three parts goes back at least to the 2nd cent. BCE. Other books which are not regarded as canonical are to be found in the *Apocrypha and *pseudepigrapha. Much was translated into Greek (*Septuagint) and Aramaic (*Targum) before Christian times.

The earliest Hebrew term for the Bible was *ha-seferim* (the books), the Greek translation of which is *ta biblia*. The notion of a canon of scripture is distinctively Jewish, and the Jews saw themselves as separate from other people in their devotion to the Bible (cf. the aphorism of BEN GURION).

The Christian Bible consists of two parts, the Old and the New Testaments. The Christian Old Testament corresponds to the Hebrew Bible. *Roman Catholic and *Orthodox Bibles also include other books and parts of books which belonged to the *Septuagint version of the Jewish scriptures. Until recently Roman Catholics usually cited the names of books in the *Vulgate form. Protestant Bibles restrict the Old Testament to the Hebrew canon, segregating these other writings as the Apocrypha, or omitting them.

The New Testament was formed as the second part of the Christian Bible when at an early date churches began to regard certain of their own writings in Greek, especially if of apostolic origin, as of equal authority and inspiration to those inherited from Judaism. It attained its present form in the 4th cent., comprising four *Gospels, Acts, thirteen epistles of Paul, seven catholic epistles, and Revelation. By the 5th cent. there were translations of the New Testament into Syriac, Armenian, Coptic, Latin (see VULGATE), and Ethiopic. See also CANON.

Christian understandings of the provenance of the Bible are unlike that of Muslims of the *Qur'ān. While recognizing the initiative of God (especially through (the agency of) the Holy Spirit) in bringing these words into being, they have largely abandoned theories of 'divine dictation', as though the human author/poet/prophet, etc., simply 'took down' the words dictated. The process is seen as one in which the work is concursive, with God not by-passing, or overruling, the human competence and social circumstances of the writer. For this reason, Muslims, who acknowledge Jews and Christians as 'people of the Book' (*ahl al-kitāb), regard the Bible as defective and compromised when compared with the Qur'ān.

For a list of books, see Index, Biblical books.

Bible Belt. The southern states of the United States of America, where the mainstream of Christianity is characteristically *fundamentalist, stressing the literalism and inerrancy of the Bible. See also BRANCH DAVIDIANS.

Biblical theology. A movement in Christian theology, especially in the 1930s–1950s, which sought to expound a common, 'biblical' (usually, 'Hebraic') viewpoint and language in the Old and New Testaments.

Bidʿa (Arab., 'innovation'). Belief or practice for which there is no precedent in the *sunna of Prophet *Muḥammad. Generally speaking, bidʿa as 'innovation' has a bad sense, since it implies unconsidered disruption of what God has revealed and intended in *Qur'ān. However, jurists such as Imām *al-Shāfiʿi recognized that allowances must be made for changes in environments and other conditions, and in the development of knowledge. He therefore taught that there were good and even necessary innovations as long as they did not contradict Qur'ān, *sunna, and *ijmāʿ.

Big Wild Goose Pagoda: see SIAN.

Bihbahānī, Vahid (Aqa Muḥammad Baqir ibn Muḥammad Akmal, 1706–92 (AH 1118–1207)). Shiʿite scholar and definer of the Uṣūlī system of jurisprudence. In contrast to the traditionalist Akhbārīs (who required precedent for all decisions), he recognized the legitimacy of *ijtihād and of the work of the mujtāhidūn, who apply principles to current issues and arrive at novel and unprecedented decisions. Aggressive in the extreme, he declared the Akhbārīs to be *kāfirs (expelling them to a marginal existence in such places as S. Iraq), and he employed a religious police (*mirghadabs*, 'executors of wrath') to enforce his views— a kind of precursor of the Revolutionary Guards. He also greatly strengthened the authority of the *ʿulamā, allowing the *Mullas to follow his example and to declare themselves Mujtāhids and representatives of the Hidden *Imām on earth. This theory of ijtihād, which led to the authoritarian development of Shiʿite Islam, is set forth in *Risalat al-ijtihad wa'l-akhbar.*

Bīja (Skt., 'seed, potency'). In both Hinduism and Buddhism, the latent power underlying every manifest appearance. In particular, bīja is the power concentrated in a symbolic sound, which a *guru has learnt in experience, and which he passes on to a pupil in a bīja *mantra (seed syllable). An aspect of the absolute reality is thus concentrated in the mantra.

Biku. Jap. for *bhikṣu.

Bilā kaif(a): see ALLĀH; AL-ASHʿARĪ.

Bilāl b. Rabāḥ. (d. *c.*641 AH 20). One of the first Muslims, best known as the first *muezzin of *Muḥammad. Of African origin, he was a slave in *Mecca and possibly the first adult convert after *Abu Bakr. He suffered persecution for his faith, was freed by Abu Bakr, and became a personal servant to Muḥammad.

Bimah (Heb., 'elevated place'). *Synagogue platform on which the *Torah reading stand is placed. Alternative names for the bimah are *almemar or *tevah*.

Bimbisāra, Seniya. King of Magadha at the time of the *Buddha. He had ruled for fifteen years when Gautāma, at the age of 30, passed through his capital on his quest for enlightenment. Thereafter the two had a long and cordial relationship, and after hearing the Buddha preach, Bimbisāra gained the stage of *srotāpanna (stream-enterer). He became a patron of the Buddhist *saṅgha and donated a park for the use of monks.

Binding of Isaac: see ʿAKEDA.

Bindu (Skt., 'drop' or 'particle'). A complex term of varied though related meanings in Hinduism and especially in *Tantrism.

1. In a general sense it is the expression of the highest consciousness (*samvid*) as *Śakti which is subtle, eternal, and pervades the whole universe, yet is also the centre of creation.

2. More specifically in *Śāivism and *Śaktism, bindu is a technical term for the material cause of pure creation (see KASHMIR ŚAIVISM). It is contrasted with *māyā, the material cause of impure creation, though both must be regarded as two aspects of one reality which interpenetrate each other.

3. Bindu is equated with the *anusvāra*, the nasalized vowel in Sanskrit (ṃ) represented in devanāgarī as a dot with the letter. It has great symbolic significance in *mantra as the absolute contracted to a point, the pure potential out of which the universe emanates and to which it returns.

4. Cosmic evolution (the macrocosm) is located within the body (the microcosm) in Tantrism. Thus bindu is located between the eyebrows as a drop which is the object of meditation. It is sometimes identified with *Kuṇḍalinī, within which *laya yoga* is called bindu *sādhana.

5. In its grossest sense, bindu is a synonym for semen, cosmic potential reduced to an individual level.

6. Bindu is depicted as the point in the centre of the *Śrī yantra.

Biogenetic structuralism and religion. Biogenetic structuralism is an account of the way in which the gene-protein process in the formation of the human body, and especially of the brain, prepares human beings for characteristic behaviours and for a range of different competence. It thus prepares us for linguistic, sexual, musical, etc., competence, without dictating what we do with each competence. The claim is that we are prepared also for religious competence, and that religious beliefs and behaviours are consequently an inevitable part of human life. Biogenetic structuralism proposes two operators arising from different parts of the brain: the causal operator, which operates in the same way as a mathematical operator: it organizes a given 'strip of reality' into what is subjectively perceived as causal sequences taken back to the initial source of that strip. If the initiating source is not given by sense data, the causal operator generates a source automatically. When these are personalized, they produce the religious consequence of gods, powers, spirits, devils, demons, etc. When the strip of reality is the entire universe, the initial source produced by the causal operator is *Brahman, the unproduced Producer of all that is *Aristotle's unmoved Mover, and the like. The second operator is distinct from that concerned with control. It produces those states commonly described as *mystical. In the human autonomic system are two subsystems, the sympathetic (concerned with short-term energy expending, e.g. 'fight or flee', hence called ergotropic) and parasympathetic (concerned with energy-conserving in body-function maintenance, hence called trophotropic). Rhythmicity in the environment, whether visual, auditory, tactile, or propriocentive, drives the sympathetic-ergotropic system to maximal capacity with intermittent spillover and simultaneous activation of the parasympathetic-trophotropic system, thus creating unusual subjective states. Other effects (e.g. the use of *incense), by stimulating the pleasure system, reinforce the attainment of ecstatic unitary states. Of these, the sense of absolute unitary being (often summarized as AUB) is described in virtually all religions: the difference between one's self and any other is obliterated, there is no sense of the passing of time, and all that remains is a perfect, timeless, undifferentiated consciousness. The state may in fact (and in time) be extremely brief, but qualitatively it leads to self-transcendence of such a kind that the contingencies of life (including death) seem comparatively unimportant.

Birkat ha-mazon: see GRACE.

Birkat ha-minim (Heb., '*benediction concerning heretics'). The twelfth benediction of the Jewish *Amidah. It invokes God's wrath on the 'kingdom of arrogance'. It originates from the time of the second *Temple and has been used against collaborators, *Sadducees, and Judaeo-Christian sects.

Birkat ha-Torah (Heb., '*Blessing of the *Law'). The blessing required by Jewish law before reading or studying the *Torah.

Birth and population control. In general, religions give to birth the highest possible value. In W. religions, it tends to be seen as a matter of responsibility, aligned with the will of God: it is indeed a matter of pro-creation. In E. religions, birth continues the sequences of reincarnation or of reappearance (*punabbhāva). Although, to varying degrees and in different ways, each religion allows contraception, the emphasis is on the marvel and opportunity of birth.

In Judaism, some (not all) methods of contraception are allowed in some circumstances. The most general circumstances are those which involve threat to the woman or a potential foetus. *B.Ket.* 39a requires contraception for those under 12 (at that time able to be married), pregnant mothers, and nursing mothers. The methods of contraception tend to favour those used by women (i.e. not the condom), since women may not be under the obligation of the command. *Progressive Judaism extends the notion of welfare to include the existing family, allowing family planning.

Christianity has followed the same instinct to forbid contraception, though (generally) without the same attention to detail. Churches apart from the *Roman Catholic Church have come to emphasize the whole marriage act, including the sustenance of the family, as a matter of love-endowed responsibility. The RC Church was moving in the same direction until 1968, when Pope Paul VI issued the *encyclical, **Humanae Vitae*, which reaffirmed the condemnation of artificial measures to prevent conception (against the majority advice of the commission set up in 1963 to assess the issue).

In Islam, 'the preservation of the human species is unquestionably the primary objective of marriage' (al-Qaradāwi), but contraception is allowed for valid reasons: danger to the mother or a potential foetus, the burden of a further child on the existing family, protecting a suckling infant.

Biruni (Muslim scholar): see AL-BĪRŪNĪ.

Birushan(a) (Jap.) (transcendent Buddha): see VAIROCANA.

Bishop (Anglo-Saxon via Lat. from Gk., *episkopos*). In Christian Churches, recognizing a threefold ministry (*deacons, *priests, bishops), the bishop is the highest order. In New Testament times, the offices of *episkopos* (literally, 'overseer') and *presbyteros* ('elder') are not distinguished (e.g. Titus 1. 5, 7).

Among the insignia traditional to the bishop are the throne in his *cathedral, *mitre, pastoral staff, pectoral cross, and ring. The most usual style of bishops is 'Right Reverend', or for *archbishops 'Most Reverend'.

For individual bishops, see Index, Bishops.

Bismillah ('in the Name of Allāh'): see BASMALA; SŪRA.

Bistāmī (Persian Sūfī): see AL-BISTĀMĪ.

Bitter herbs (eoder at Jewish Passover): see MAROR.

Bittul ha-tamid (Heb., 'abolition of the daily offering'). Interruption of *synagogue *liturgy to draw attention to a wrong. It was a custom mainly practised by *Ashkenazi Jews in the Middle Ages.

Bittul ha-yesh (the presence of God alone in creation): see ḤABAD.

BJP (Indian Political Party): see BHARATYA JANATA PARTY.

Black American religion: see AFRICAN-AMERICAN RELIGION.

Blackfriars. A specifically English medieval nickname given to the *Dominicans because of the black cape they wear.

Black Jews. Members of cults that emerged in Harlem, New York City, shortly after the First World War. Prophet F. S. Cherry, one of the first leaders of the Black Jews, maintained that his followers were the true Israelites of the Bible, and that *Jesus was black. Another important early Black Jewish figure was Arnold Ford from Barbados. Though grouped into a number of different sects, all Black Jews claim that they are descendants of Ethiopian Hebrews (cf. FALASHAS) who were deprived of their religion, sacred language (Hebrew), and names, during the era of slavery.

Black Mass. Usually a blasphemous caricature of the *mass, with an inversion of symbols and a worship of *Satan, not God. But the term is also used colloquially for the requiem mass for the dead when black vestments are used.

Black Muslims. Members of an African American nationalist religious movement. It was founded in Detroit in the 1930s by Wallace D. Fard (sometimes Ford, later known as Wali Farad). He was known as Prophet Fard, the Great *Mahdi, and the Saviour. The movement was called originally The Lost-Found Nation of Islam, subsequently The World Community of Islam in the West. Fard hailed black (as they were then called) people as the founders of civilization, and predicted the destruction of Caucasians and Christianity and the establishment of a Black Nation after the final judgement of the white race.

*Elijah Muhammad took over the movement on Fard's disappearance in 1934, assuming the titles 'Minister of Islam' and 'Prophet'. *Malcolm X became Elijah Muhammad's chief aide in 1963 before breaking away to found the Muslim Mosque, Inc., and the Organization of Afro-American Unity. He was assassinated in Feb. 1965.

When Elijah Muhammad died in 1975, his son, Warith Deen (Wallace D.) succeeded and endeavoured to bring the movement closer to mainstream Islam throughout the world. A splinter group, led by Louis Farrakhan (see ELIJAH MUHAMMAD), took the name Nation(s) of Islam. This continued the emphasis on separation from white people, and included a theme of *anti-semitism.

Black Pagoda (Konārak temple): see SŪRYA.

Black shamanism (contest against malevolent spirits): see SHAMANS.

Black Stone (*al-ḥajar al-aswad*). A stone said to be of meteoric origin, variously thought to be of lava or basalt, and reddish-black in colour, some 12 inches in diameter, embedded in the eastern corner of the *Kaʿba in *Mecca. As the Kaʿba is the focus of Muslim devotion, being the 'house of *Allāh', so is the Black Stone the holiest object.

Blake, William (1757–1827). Poet, artist, and visionary. Trained as an engraver, he soon combined his talent for illustration with his poetic gifts and, with *Songs of Innocence* (1789), began a series of works, engraved and combining text and coloured illustration. His vision combined a positive acceptance of, and delight in, the world of the senses, both the immediately pleasing and that which is darker and more threatening: it was expressed through verbal and visual imagery that became increasingly complex and allegorical. The key to all this Blake found in various occult traditions—hermetic, *Neoplatonic, *gnostic, and especially the theosophy of *Swedenborg.

Blasphemy (Gk., 'speaking evil'). Impious or profane talk, especially against God; and in many W. legal systems, the offence of reviling God or *Jesus Christ or an established church. The appearance of Salman Rushdie's *The *Satanic Verses*, raised the issue whether blasphemy should be extended to become a more general offence (in the UK), or whether it is an offence in the domain of inciting unrest.

In Judaism, 'blasphemy' is speaking scornfully of God (Heb., *gidduf*, *ḥeruf*) and is described euphemistically as *birkat ha-Shem* ('blessing the

Name', i.e. God). According to Leviticus 24. 10–23, the penalty for cursing God is death.

The nearest equivalent in Islam is *sabb*, offering an insult to God.

Blavatsky, H. P.: see THEOSOPHICAL SOCIETY.

Blessing. A two-way movement of (from humans to God) thanksgiving and praise, and of (from God to humans) power and goodness/good fortune. Blessings (in both senses) are prominent in Judaism, where it is said that there is a blessing for every occasion. See also BENEDICTIONS.

In Christianity, blessings occur especially in worship and in the *liturgy—e.g. at the end of the *eucharist and other services, where the congregation is blessed.

In Islam, *baraka was associated originally with fecundity and having many descendants. From this it came to mean success or prosperity in more general terms. The source is always God.

Blondel, Maurice (1861–1949). French *Roman Catholic philosopher. His *Letter on Apologetics* (1896; Eng. tr. 1964) and *History and Dogma* (1904; Eng. tr. 1964) concern issues raised by the *Modernist crisis, though their importance transcends this context.

Blood. Commonly held in religions to be the sign and condition of life, and therefore a fundamental constituent of *sacrifices. Because of its importance in relation to God's gift of life, the Jewish *Bible contains an absolute prohibition against swallowing the blood of an animal (see Leviticus 3. 17; Deuteronomy 12. 15–16). The justification for this is the belief that the blood contained life (Leviticus 17. 11). The prohibition leads directly to laws of *kashrut* (see DIETARY LAWS) and *sheḥitah (the method for slaughtering animals). Eating meat was itself a concession on the part of God after the *Flood.

In Christianity, the shedding of the blood of *Christ came to be understood as the continuation and culmination of the *Temple sacrifices, achieving completely that which they had partially anticipated. From this developed devotion to the Precious Blood (from the *Vulgate tr. of 1 Peter 1. 19), decreed as a feast day for the whole Church by Pius IX in 1859, though transferred to a votive mass after *Vatican II.

Bloodguilt. In Judaism the liability for punishment of those who have shed blood. The blood-avenger is known as *goel ha-dam* (see e.g. Judges 8. 18–21, 2 Samuel 3. 27, 13. 28 ff.). If someone has killed accidentally, he must flee to a *city of refuge.

Blood-libel. The accusation that *Jews murder non-Jews to obtain *blood for *Passover rituals. This accusation was repeated in many places in the Middle Ages and was the cause of anti-Jewish riots and massacres. It was a regular motif in *anti-Semitic propaganda until the Second World War.

Blood of the martyrs, seed of the Church (Christian evaluation of martyrdom): see PERSECUTION; TERTULLIAN.

Blue Cliff Record (Chinese Ch'an verses): see HSÜEH-TOU CH'UNG-HSIEN.

B'nai B'rith (Heb., 'Sons of the *Covenant'). Oldest and largest Jewish *charitable organization. It was founded in 1843 in New York, and has a total membership of approximately half a million people throughout the world.

Bo, as in Bo Tree: see BO TREE.

Boanerges. The surname given by *Jesus (Mark 3. 17) to *James and *John.

Bodai. Jap. version of Skt., *bodhi, via Chinese. It is thus the state of *kokoro, the completely enlightened mind and complete *Buddha realization. Bodaishin is the 'enlightenment mind', the determination to find complete enlightenment.

Bodaidaruma. Jap. for *bodhidharma.

Bodhgāya. On the Nairañjana River, Bihar, the legendary site of the *Bo Tree under which the *Buddha gained final enlightenment. A major place of pilgrimage, tradition ascribes the foundation of a temple on this spot to *Aśoka. See also DHARMAPĀLA.

As Gayā, it is sacred to Hindus as one of the seven *sacred cities. Its temple is dedicated to the lotus feet of *Viṣṇu.

Bodhi (Skt., Pāli, 'awakened'). In Hinduism, perfect knowledge, personified as Bodha, a son of Buddhi (intellect).

In Buddhism, it is the experience of enlightenment, which, unlike *nirvāna, can be given an approximate description: it is the attainment of perfect clarity of mind in which things are seen as they really are—as in the experience of Gautāma under the tree (hence called Bodhi or *Bo tree) through which he became the Buddha. Cf. BODAI.

In later Buddhism, the bodhis are the four stages of the *ārya-mārga.

In *Mahāyāna, bodhi is wisdom based on insight into the undifferentiated sameness of all appearance.

Bodhicaryāvatāra (Entering upon the Practice of Awakening). A practical work by Śantideva on the Buddhist six perfections (*pāramitā), which include, as the fifth, *jhāna (meditation). Of Śantideva, nothing certain is known, apart from the fact that he was the supposed author of an analytic work, *Śikshāsamuccaya*. *Bodhicaryāvatāra* is a much revered and used work.

Bodhicitta (Skt., 'thought of enlightenment'). An important concept in *Mahāyāna Buddhism, having both a personal and a cosmic aspect. In the personal sense it denotes the spontaneous generation of the resolve to strive for enlightenment. The cosmic aspect of the doctrine locates the seed or first stirrings of this impulse in a transpersonal matrix or resource along absolutistic lines. Here it is reality itself, under its various denominations such as the 'Body of Truth' (*dharmakāya), the 'Womb of *Tathāgatas' (*tathāgatagarbha), or 'True Suchness' (*bhūtatathatā), which engenders the possibility of enlightenment.

In *Tantric Buddhist symbology bodhicitta is identified with the seed or semen which is produced through the union of male and female, representing the fusion of wisdom (*prajña) with compassion (*karuṇā) in the bliss of perfect enlightenment.

Bodhidharma (Chin., *P'u-t'i-ta-mo* or *Tamo*; Jap., *Bodaidaruma* or *Daruma*, *c.*5th cent. CE). The 28th successor (*hassu) in line from Śākyamuni Buddha, and the first Chinese patriarch of Ch'an/Zen Buddhism. According to the traditional accounts, he engaged in motionless *zazen for nine years (hence the name of this period, *menpeki-kunen, nine years facing the wall). Hui-k'o joined him as a pupil, and became the second patriarch. The forms of meditation taught by Bodhidharma were based on the *Mahāyāna sūtras, with especial emphasis on **Laṅkāvatāra-sūtra*. It produced *Dhyāna Buddhism, with dhyāna (meditation) understood in a broad sense: it was this which fused with Taoism to produce the distinctive form of Ch'an.

Tradition also attributes six treatises to Bodhidharma, of which one, *The Two Ways of Entrance*, is translated by D. T. Suzuki, *Essays in Zen Buddhism*, iii (1970). But this, and the whole tradition about Bodhidharma is extremely uncertain.

Bodhidharma is usually portrayed with an appearance of fierce concentration, and Daruma-dolls are given in Japan to those who have attained a goal through perseverance.

Bodhimaṇḍa. The site of the *Buddha's enlightenment under the *Bo Tree. In iconography the Buddha is depicted as seated on the bodhimaṇḍa with his right hand touching the earth to call it to bear witness to his enlightenment.

Bodhipakkhiya-dhamma: see BODHIPĀKṢIKA-DHARMA.

Bodhipākṣika-dharma (Pāli, *bodhipakkhiya-dhamma*, 'things pertaining to enlightenment'). In Buddhism, the thirty-seven necessities for the attainment of enlightenment. They are divided into seven groups: (i) the four foundations of right attention (*satipaṭṭhāna); (ii) the four perfect efforts (*sammā-padhāna); (iii) the four components of concentrated power (*iddhi-pāda); (iv) the five roots (*indriya); (v) the five powers (*bala); (vi) the seven contributions to enlightenment (*bojjhanga); (vii) the Eightfold Path (*aṣṭangika-mārga).

Bodhiruci (translator of Buddhist scriptures): see PURE LAND SCHOOLS.

Bodhisattva (Skt.; Pāli, *bodhisatta*, 'Enlightenment-Being'; Chin., P'u-sa; Jap., Bosatsu; Korean, Posal; Tib., byang.chub sems.dpa, 'Hero of the Thought of Enlightenment'). In *Theravāda Buddhism a title exclusively identifying historical *Buddhas (i.e. *Śākyamuni) in their previous lives, before their Buddhahood was attained; and in *Mahāyāna Buddhism to describe any being who, out of compassion, has taken the *bodhisattva vow to become a Buddha for the sake of all sentient beings. Strictly, an ordinary person who has 'engendered *bodhicitta' (generated a desire for enlightenment in order to save all beings from suffering) and taken the bodhisattva vow is a bodhisattva, but there are also 'celestial bodhisattvas', such as *Mañjuśrī and *Avalokiteśvara, who are almost Buddhas in their attainments.

A bodhisattva's progress is determined by his practice of the six (sometimes given as ten) perfections (*pāramitās) which are: generosity and morality; patience and energy; meditation and wisdom.

This contrast between the bodhisattva and the arhat or pratyekabuddha ideals is the principal distinction between the Mahāyāna and Theravāda schools, since the overwhelming message of the Mahāyāna is that the *nirvāna with which the arhats and pratyekabuddhas content themselves is not the highest goal. Some bodhisattvas, such as *Avalokiteśvara, who in some Tibetan schools is considered to have already attained Buddhahood, even enter the hell-realms in order to alleviate pain there. The Mahāyāna notion of the bodhisattva as a being who views his own comfort (and sometimes his vows) as concerns subordinate to the needs of others, thus increased the social dimension of Buddhism and emphasized the value of lay life alongside monkhood. In *Vimalakīrtinirdeśa-sūtra* (*c.*2nd–3rd cents. CE), for example, it is the lay bodhisattva Vimalakīrti who is the hero, and *Mañjuśrī is the only other bodhisattva deemed wise enough to converse with him. For examples, see Index, Buddhas, Bodhisattvas.

Bodhisattva-śīla (Skt.). Rules of discipline for the forming of a *bodhisattva, which are obligatory in *Mahāyāna Buddhism for both monks and laypeople. They are laid down in the **Brahmajala-sūtra*. They are not rigid, in the sense that they can be broken if the welfare of another is at stake.

Bodhisattva vow (Skt., *praṇidhāna*). The vow in *Mahāyāna Buddhism to follow the six *pāramitās (perfections) and attain Buddhahood, the taking of which is deemed as the first entering of the Mahāyāna path. The core of the bodhisattva vow is: 'I vow to attain enlightenment for the sake of all sentient beings'. For the 'four great vows' in Zen, see HONGAN SHIGUSEIGAN.

Bodhisattva-yāna. The 'Vehicle of the *Bodhisattvas', an alternative designation for the *Mahāyāna or 'Great Vehicle', is the way, means or method by which bodhisattvas pursue their religious career.

Bodhisena (704–60). Indian Buddhist monk, commonly referred to as Baramon-sōjō (Jap., 'the *brahman abbot'). Bodhisena, Emperor *Shōmu (who conceived the idea), Rōben (the first chief abbot), and *Gyōgi, a charismatic monk, are known as the four founders of Tōdai-ji. Tōdai-ji was the central monastery (Sōkokubun-ji), unifying all the provincial monasteries and nunneries built by imperial edict. The casting of the Great Buddha (*daibutsu) demonstrated the majestic power of the emperor and the unity of the nation.

Bodhi Tree (tree under which Buddha gained enlightenment): see BO TREE.

Bodhyanga (in Buddhism, the seven contributions to enlightenment): see BOJJHANGA.

Body as temple (teaching of Basava): see BASAVA.

Body/bodies in Hinduism: see ŚARĪRA.

Body, speech, and mind: A frequent division, especially in *Tibetan Buddhism, of the sentient being into his three functional aspects which *tantric practice or *sādhana practice aims to transmute into the body, speech, and mind of a *Buddha.

Boehme, Jakob (1575–1624). German *Lutheran theosophical writer. Son of a farmer, from 1599 to 1613 he lived as a cobbler in Görlitz in Silesia. He claimed to be a mystic, writing under direct divine inspiration. From the publication of his first work, *Aurora* (1612), he provoked official opposition. Most of his works were published posthumously, including the famous *Signatura Rerum* and *Magnum Mysterium*. Boehme is obscure and difficult, using much abstruse terminology. Boehme was enormously influential, especially on German idealism, and also in England.

Boethius (*c*.480–*c*.524). Roman philosopher and statesman. His most famous work, *On the Consolation of Philosophy*, is not specifically Christian, but was popular among Christians for its description of the soul attaining knowledge of the vision of God through philosophy.

Boethusians. A Jewish sect of the 1st cent. BCE/CE. They may be the Herodians referred to in the New Testament.

Boff, C. and L.: see LIBERATION THEOLOGY.

Bogomils. A *dualist Christian sect which flourished in Bulgaria from the 10th to as late as the 17th cent., and more widely in the Byzantine Empire in the 11th–12th cents. The name comes from their founder, a priest who took the name Bogomil (= Gk., *Theophilos*). They espoused the dualist and neo-*gnostic doctrines of the Paulicians (e.g. belief in the devil as the creator of humanity and the world, *docetic ideas of Christ, rejection of the Old Testament). They were also strongly ascetic, rejecting sex, marriage, and possessions, and not eating meat, believing that the soul must be freed from evil and thus the body. Bogomil influence can be discerned in the later *Catharism of W. Europe.

Bohemian Brethren (Christian movement): see MORAVIAN BRETHREN.

Bojjhanga (Pāli; Skt., *bodhyanga*). The seven contributions, in Buddhism, to enlightenment. See also BODHIPĀKṢIKA-DHARMA.

Bōkatsu (Jap., 'stick' + 'shout'). Zen Buddhist training technique, using blows from a stick (*kyosaku) or a shout (*ho), not as a punishment, but—at the exactly right moment—to help the breakthrough to enlightenment.

Bokuseki (Jap., 'marks of ink'). Zen Buddhist *calligraphy. The purpose is not aesthetic, but to express Zen experience. The words executed are usually those of the Zen masters (*hōgo), but the text may be simply one letter or one word. Outstanding practitioners were *Muso Soseki, *Ikkyu Sōjun, *Hakuin Zenji, and more recently *Yamamoto Gempō.

Bokushū Chinsonshuku (Ch'an teacher): see MU-CHOU CH'EN-TSUN-SU.

Bollandists. A small group of Belgian *Jesuit scholars of hagiology. It was begun by John van

Bolland (1596–1665) to publish the *Acta Sanctorum*, a massive critical collection of the lives of Christian *saints.

Bön (Tib., 'invocation'). The non-Buddhist religion of Tibet which was indigenous and unorganized before the first diffusion of Buddhism there (7th cent.), but which became organized at the time of the second diffusion (11th cent.). In spite of claims of uninterrupted continuity, however, any connection between ancient and modern Bön is extremely tenuous.

The nature of original Bön—beyond probable *animism and *shamanism and definite non-literacy—is hard to determine, since all early descriptions of it are Buddhist and intended to discredit. Contrary to the popular misconception that Buddhism was significantly influenced by Bön when it entered Tibet, it is clear that what is known of Bön today is almost completely influenced by *Mahāyāna Buddhism, which was itself transplanted from India into Tibet virtually unchanged.

Bon (rituals, festival of the dead): see ULLAMBANA; FESTIVALS.

Bonaventura (1221–74). Govanni di Fidanza, Christian mystic and saint. Born near Viterbo in Italy, he believed that he had been rescued from illness by the intercession of St *Francis. He entered the order of the Friars Minor, and became minister-general in 1256. His *Itinerarium Mentis in Deum* describes the way that leads to God by the path of his illumination. *Leo XIII called Bonaventura 'the prince of mystics'; E. *Gilson called him 'a St Francis of Assisi gone philosopher and lecturing at the university of Paris'.

Bonfire of vanities (burning of frivolous or lewd items): see SAVŌNAROLA, GIROLAMO.

Bonhoeffer, Dietrich (1906–45). German pastor and Christian (*Lutheran) theologian. Bonhoeffer took a leading part in drafting the *Barmen Declaration. He attempted to found a seminary for pastors of the *Confessing Church, but this was soon closed down. He continued to oppose Hitler, and was arrested in Apr. 1943. His *Letters and Papers from Prison* are a moving testament. He was executed on 9 Apr. 1945, commemorated in the nearby church by a tablet which states, 'Dietrich Bonhoeffer, a witness of Jesus Christ among his brethren.'

His theological work was, obviously, unfinished. He accepted with *Barth that religion as a human enterprise was an inevitable failure; but in contrast, indeed, he envisaged a 'religionless Christianity', commensurate with 'a world come of age'.

Boniface, St (680–754). Christian 'apostle to Germany'. He was a native of Devon who, after earlier missionary visits, received the support of the pope for his work in Germany in 722. The challenge involved in felling the Oak of Thor at Geismar led to a breakthrough in recognition, and not much later he laid the foundations of church organization in Germany. After becoming archbishop of Mainz, he returned to missionary work in Frisia where he was martyred. Feast day, 5 June.

Boniface VIII (*c*.1235–1303). *Pope from 24 Dec. 1294. He was born Benedict Gaetani, and after studying law, served in a variety of posts in the Roman *curia. As a *cardinal he was instrumental in 1294 in persuading Celestine V to resign the papacy, and was elected in Celestine's place. His pontificate was dominated by the struggle with Philip the Fair of France, which led to the bull *Unam Sanctam* proclaiming that there is no salvation or remission of sins outside communion with the bishop of Rome (see EXTRA ECCLESIAM NULLA SALUS). Boniface was on the point of excommunicating Philip in Sept. 1303 when his palace at Anagni was attacked by the Colonnas and French-led mercenaries. The pope was briefly held captive, and died a month later as a consequence of his treatment.

Bonpu-no-jōshiki (Jap., 'every person's awareness'). According to Zen Buddhism, ordinary, everyday consciousness, which is fraught with delusion (*mayoi)—as opposed to the enlightened mind.

Book of Changes: see I-CHING.

Book of Common Prayer (often *BCP*). The major prayer book of the *Anglican Church, and official service book of the *Church of England. Its centrality and continuing use is advocated by the Prayer Book Society.

Book of Heavenly Commandments (Chin., *T'ien-t'iao shu*). A key religious document in the *T'aip'ing rebellion. The text lays down rules to govern the lives of members of the T'aip'ing ('Great Peace') community, including 'ten commandments' which approximate to those of Exodus 20.

Book of Jashar. A lost Israelite book of poetry.

Book of life (Heb., *Sefer ha-Ḥayyim*). A book in *heaven in which Jews believe the names of the righteous are inscribed. In Psalm 69. 28, the poet declares that his enemies should be 'blotted out of the book of the living; let them not be enrolled with the righteous'. According to *Ashkenazi belief, God's judgement is sealed during *Sukkot, when a slip of paper recording each person's fate falls from heaven—hence the

Yiddish greeting, 'A gute kvitl', 'A good slip/seal!'

Book of the Covenant. The laws found in Exodus 20. 22–23. 33.

Book of the Dead: see TIBETAN BOOK OF THE DEAD.

Book of the Yellow Emperor (Chin., *Huang-ti nei-ching*, 'The Inner Classic of the Yellow Emperor'). Compiled sometime during the Han era (206 BCE–220 CE), this work, consisting of two parts (the *Su-wen* or 'Candid Questions' and the *Ling-shu* or 'Spiritual Pivot'), expounds a comprehensive theory of medicine based on systems of 'correspondence', 'correlation', or 'resonance' among various parts and aspects of the human person, and between those and other parts and aspects of the larger world.

Booth, William (1829–1912). Founder and first General of the *Salvation Army. His White-chapel 'Christian Mission' changed its name in 1878 to the 'Salvation Army'. A strong advocate of rousing music (and of denying to the *devil all the best tunes), he also introduced 'the standard of the London cab-horse', pointing out that many had to live on less money than was expended on maintaining cab-horses: the standard of the London taxi produces a similar result.

Borobudur. The largest of Buddhist monuments, situated in mid-Java, probably built in the 9th cent. CE. The whole structure is believed to represent the Buddhist cosmology as a *maṇḍala, successive levels corresponding to stages on the path. The meaning of the name Borobudur is unclear.

Bosatsu (abbr. of Jap., *bodaisatta*). Jap. equivalent of Skt., *bodhisattva; also a title of respect given by emperors to outstanding monks, the first instance being *Gyōgi.

Bossey. An *ecumenical institute near Geneva in Switzerland, run by the World Council of Churches.

Bo Tree, Bodhi Tree (Skt., *bodhi*, 'enlightenment'). The tree (*ficus religiosa*) under which the *Buddha is believed to have gained enlightenment. Situated in Bodhgaya, Bihar, the present tree is not particularly large and is unlikely to be the original.

It became customary to plant a Bodhi Tree (a cutting when possible), usually surrounded by a low railing, in the courtyard of a *vihāra to signify the presence of the *Dharma, and this practice continues to the present day.

Boxer Rebellion. A major anti-foreign uprising in north China in 1899–1900 by a Chinese secret society known to Westerners as the 'Boxers'. The I-ho ch'uan, or 'Righteous and Harmonious Fists', was a secret religious society associated with the *Eight-Trigram Society. It was noted for its practice of the old-style Chinese callisthenics, the movements of which suggested to Westerners the name 'Boxers'. With court patronage, they destroyed churches and foreign residences, murdered missionaries and Chinese Christians, and attacked foreign legations. In Aug. 1900, a large allied Western force defeated the Boxers. The Boxer Rebellion thus ended with an even further debilitated Ch'ing dynasty and, consequently, new popular support for the radicals' call for a republican revolution and a new China.

Brahmā (to be distinguished from *Brahman or its alternative Brahma). In Hinduism, a post-*Vedic deity. Brahmā is the god of creation and first in the Hindu triad of Brahmā, *Viṣṇu and *Śiva. He is represented as red in colour, with four heads and four arms, the hands holding, respectively, a goblet, a bow, a sceptre, and the *Vedas. Today Brahmā is seldom worshipped, and his shrines are few; only two major temples in India are dedicated to him: one at Pushkar, near Ajmere, the other at Khedbrahmā. Nevertheless, Brahmā does figure in both Buddhism and Jainism.

Brahmacarin. In Hinduism, following a pathway of discipline to attain an end, e.g. in *Yoga or *Tantra. It became equated with *celibacy, brahmacārin, and is the first of the four *āśramas, or stages of life, of a Hindu. See also BRAHMACARYA.

Brahmacarya (Skt., 'behaviour or conduct (*caryā*) appropriate to Brahman'), 1. In Hinduism, the mode of life of an unmarried student of the *Vedas, characterized especially by sexual continence and service to the teacher (*guru).

Frequently the term brahmacarya is encountered in modern Hindu literature as a synonym for celibacy and self-control.

2. In Buddhism, a life lived in accordance with Buddhist rules of conduct (*śīla), especially by *bhikṣus.

3. Among Jains, it is one of the *Five Great Vows.

Brahmachari, Dhirendra (1925–94). Hindu *guru and teacher of *yoga, who exercised much influence on Indira Gandhi—he was known by those who mistrusted him as India's Rasputin. When her son, Sanjay, was killed in an air-crash, she seemed to relate to Brahmachari almost as a surrogate son. He taught her yoga and persuaded her that yoga classes should be introduced into Indian schools.

Brahmajala-sūtra (Sūtra of the Net of Brahman). A *Mahāyāna Buddhist *sūtra, containing basic instruction on the rules of moral life (*śīla). It contains fifty-eight rules, of which the first ten are esp. important: see BODHISATTVA-ŚĪLA.

Brahmajijñāsā (Skt., literally, 'the desire to know *Brahman' or 'the enquiry into Brahman'). The subject-matter of the **Brahmasūtra* is pronounced in its famous first verse: *athāto brahmajijñāsā*, 'Then therefore the enquiry into Brahman.' In his commentary on this verse, *Śaṅkara explains that the knowledge of Brahman is the highest aim of humans, yet the desire for knowing Brahman depends on certain antecedent conditions already having been fulfilled (hence the use of the word 'then' in the verse).

Brahma Kumari. A Hindu-oriented movement composed in the main of unmarried women and founded in Hyderabad in 1937 by the one-time Sind diamond merchant, Dadi LeKray. Women are clearly the spiritual and moral leaders in this *millennial movement, in which the traditional role of wives and husbands has been reversed.

Through the practice of celibacy and *yoga, souls can attain unity with the founder, Shiv Baba as he came to be known, and a right of entry to the golden age. In the late 1960s the movement, with headquarters in Mount Abu, India, began to acquire a following in the West.

Brahmaloka (Skt., 'domain of Brahmā'). Hindu *heaven in the company of Brahmā and the gods.

Brahman or **Brahma** (Skt., literally, 'growth' or 'expansion'). The one supreme, all-pervading Spirit; the impersonal Absolute, beyond attributes, which is the origin and support of the visible universe. This neuter noun, Brahman (or Brahma) should be distinguished from the masculine form, *Brahmā, the personal Creator-god in the Hindu triad of *Brahmā, *Viṣṇu and *Śiva.

The etymology of Brahman is obscure, but is traditionally derived from the verb root *bṛh* or *bṛṁh*, 'to grow great', 'to increase'. In the earliest use of the word in the *Vedas, and especially in **Atharva Veda*, the meaning of Brahman is the mysterious force behind a magical formula. It then means the sacred utterance through which the *devas become great, and thus also ritual power and those in charge of it (i.e. *brahmans). In the *Śatapata Brāhmaṇa*, and then in the Upaniṣads, the word Brahman comes to mean the source of power, and thus the impersonal, supreme, eternal principle behind the origin of the universe and the gods. It is this later meaning that is developed in the systematic philosophy of *Vedānta which teaches that Brahman, the impersonal Absolute, is the essence, the Self (*ātman), of all beings. Ātman and Brahman are one, and the knowledge of Brahman (*brahmavidyā*; see APARAVIDYA) is the supreme goal of human life as it confers liberation (*mokṣa) from the ongoing cycle of suffering and rebirth (see e.g. ŚAṄKARA). See Index, Brahman.

Brahman (often Anglicized as brahmin; Skt., *brāhmaṇa*). A member of the highest of the four *varna, or categories, of *Vedic society, hence *Brahmanism.

The brahmans were traditionally the custodians, interpreters, and teachers of religious knowledge, and, as priests, acted as intermediaries between humans, the world, and God. They alone knew and could perform the rituals of correct worship, making them acceptable to God.

Brāhmaṇa (Skt., 'that pertaining to *brahman*'). In Hinduism, the explanatory portion of the *Veda developed as a commentary on the *mantra portions of the text. Commonly they are dated between 1,000 BCE and 650 BCE. The most important are the following: the *Aitareya* and *Kausītaki* (*Śāṅkhāyana*) Brāhmaṇas of the **Ṛg Veda*; the *Jaiminīya* and *Pañcaviṃsa* (*Tāṇḍyamahā*) Brāhmaṇas of the **Sāma Veda*; the *Taittirīya* Brāhmaṇa of the Black and the *Śatapatha* Brāhmaṇa of the White **Yajur Veda*; the *Gopatha* Brāhmaṇa of the **Atharva Veda*. To the Brāhmaṇas were then added the *Āraṇyakas.

Brahmānanda. In Hinduism. 1. The absolute, undifferentiated bliss of *Brahman.

2. Disciple of Sri *Ramakrishna. Born Rakhal Chandra Ghosh, he became head of the order when Ramakrishna died. He was a close friend of Svārni *Vivekānanda who also became a disciple.

Brahmanical religion: see BRAHMANISM.

Brahmanirvana (Skt.). Final union with *Brahman in which all traces of dual relationship have been eradicated.

Brahmanism. Religion of early India which came to prominence in the *Vedic period, and is effectively to be identified with Vedic religion and its continuity. It emphasized sacrifice and ritual under the control of the *brahmans as those who have access to the rituals and control of them.

Brahman satyam, jagat mithya (Skt.). A sentence which summarizes for Hindus the entire teaching of *Advaita Vedānta: Brahman is the real reality (cf. SAT), the world is deceptive (because its apparent reality is superimposed on Brahman.

Brahmārandhra (Skt.). The place in the crown of the head through which, according to Hindus, the self escapes at death.

Brahma-samādhi (Skt.). An absorption state (*samādhi) of *brahman-consciousness attained through the repetition of a *mantra (*japa).

Brahmasūtra. An ancient Indian work which systematizes the teachings of the *Upaniṣads concerning *Brahman, Ultimate Reality, in 555 elliptic verses or *sūtras. It is attributed to *Bādarāyaṇa, a sage of the 1st cent. BCE, but may have been compiled in its final form several centuries later. Other names for the *Brahmasūtra* are encountered in Indian literature: the *Vedāntasūtra* or *Uttaramīmāṁsāsūtra*, because it outlines the philosophy of Vedānta; the *Bādarāvaṇasūtra*, named after its supposed author; the *Vyāsasūtra*, so-named by another tradition which credits its authorship to the sage Vyāsa; and the *Śārīrakasūtra*, because it is an investigation of 'that which is embodied', i.e. the individual self according to Śaṅkara, or Brahman according to Rāmānuja. See also BRAHMAJIJÑĀSĀ.

Brahma-vidya (knowledge by hearsay in Hinduism): see APARA-VIDYA.

Brahma-vihāra (Skt., Pāli, 'dwellings of Brahmā'). Meditational states and attitudes in Hinduism, taken up and reapplied in Buddhism as central meditation practice.

Brahmin: see BRAHMAN.

Brahmo Samāj. 19th-cent. Hindu reform movement. It had its antecedent in the Brahmo Sabha (1828) of Rām Mohan Roy (1772–1833), who was impressed by Western achievements, but who believed that Indian spirituality was greater. The Brahmo tradition of reinterpreting early Hinduism in the light of new knowledge led to the organizing of Brahmo Samāj in 1843 by Debendranath *Tagore (father of the poet). The presence of Keshub Chandra *Sen in the movement led to Tagore continuing with the Adi Samāj, while Sen led the Brahmo Samāj to further division and a cult-like focus on himself—though he also engaged in much social reform. The movement continued into the 20th cent., but rapidly declined in influence and membership.

Braid(e) Movement. The first modern prophet and revival movement in Nigeria, and one of the first in Africa. It arose in Nov. 1915 at Opobo, within the semi-independent *Anglican community among the Ijaw people in the E. Niger delta, through the healing and prayer ministry of a lay leader in the Bakana parish, Garrick Braid (*c*.1880–1918). The independent 'Christ Army' churches that appeared continued after his death, and many churches in E. Nigeria now claim him as founder.

Brain-washing. Coercive methods of conversion or changes in behaviour. Based on (i) Pavlov's discovery that fear among his laboratory dogs (induced by floods) led to the erasing of certain learned behaviours and to relatively greater ease in implanting new ones; and (ii) the use of deprivation techniques in breaking down political and other prisoners, it was argued that religious threats of hell-fire (e.g.), followed by promises of salvation (accompanied by rhythmic and emotional music), produced conversion by comparable mechanisms.

Branch Davidians. Cult derived from Seventh Day *Adventists, whose centre, at Waco in Texas, was destroyed after an FBI siege intended to arrest its leader, David Koresh. The name of the cult goes back to the promises of Isaiah 11. 1, 'A branch will spring from the stock of Jesse [the father of David], a new shoot will grow from his roots: on him will rest the spirit of the Lord, the spirit of wisdom and insight . . .'.

Braslav Ḥasidim (Jewish group): see NAḤMAN.

Brautmystik (bridal or nuptial mysticism): see RHENO-FLEMISH SPIRITUALITY.

Breastplate. Metal pendant hung in front of the covered *Torah scrolls among the Jewish *Ashkenazim.

Breath. As a necessary and manifest condition of life, breath and breathing have a literal and metaphorical importance in religions. Basic words which come to identify a real and continuing self originate as 'breath' (see e.g. *ruaḥ* in Hebrew, RŪḤ (NAFS), ĀTMAN); and 'breath' becomes the vehicle of divine communication and presence—hence Ruaḥ ha-Qodesh, i.e. the *Holy Spirit, and the invocation, 'Breathe on me, Breath of God, Fill me with life anew . . .'. The understanding and control of breath is an important part of *yoga, especially within *Haṭha-yoga, and as prāṇayama, the fourth in the eight stages (mentioned by *Patañjali, 1. 34, 2. 29 and 49, but later much elaborated). In W. religions, breathing is used for the control of the mind and for bringing a person without reserve or distraction into the presence of God. In Christianity, see JESUS PRAYER; HESYCHASM; in Islam, see DHIKR, in which a common technique is that of saying *la ilaha* ('there is no God') while breathing in, and *illa Allah* ('except God') while breathing out. See also Index, Breathing.

Breeches Bible (Calvinist Bible): see GENEVA.

Brethren, Plymouth. A movement within Christianity, so-called from the location of its first tract depot in England, although it had been founded previously in Ireland (1828). An early leader was J. N. Darby (1800–82). It sought to establish life and the Church on Biblical, especially New Testament, principles, and laid emphasis on the *millennium and on separation from evil. There have been a number of divisions, notably between the Open and the Exclusive Brethren.

Brethren of Purity (secret movement founded in Iraq): see IKHWĀN AL-ṢAFĀ'.

Brethren of the Common Life (Christian community): see GROOTE, G.

Breviary. The book containing the divine *office of the *Roman Catholic Church.

Bṛhadāraṇyaka Upaniṣad (Skt., 'of the Great Forest'). The longest and perhaps oldest of the principal Upaniṣads. Composed in prose style between *c*.8th and 6th cents. BCE, it consists of six chapters attached to the final book of the **Śatapatha Brāhmaṇa*. The central religious and philosophical themes adumbrated in this Upaniṣad have been variously interpreted in important commentaries by *Śaṅkara, *Rāmānuja, and other pivotal religious thinkers of Hinduism.

Bṛhaspati (Skt., *bṛh*, 'prayer', + *pati*, 'Lord'). 1. A *Vedic god who embodies, not a natural phenomenon, but reason and moral judgement.

2. A Hindu teacher of materialism: see CĀRVĀKA.

Bricolage (Fr., 'doing odd jobs'). A characteristic (according to C. *Lévi-Strauss) of the early human mind, in contrast to modern scientific thinking. But bricolage is entirely rational (i.e. not pre-rational). A *bricoleur* is one who improvises and uses any means or materials which happen to be lying around in order to tackle a task. In the making of *myth, bricolage is the use of whatever happens to be 'lying around', so that myth is both rational and also improvisatory.

Bridegroom of the Law. In Judaism, the reader who is called up to read the last portion of the *Pentateuch (Deuteronomy 33. 27–34. 12) in the morning service on the Jewish festival of *Simḥat Torah ('the Rejoicing in the Law'). It is common for the 'bridegrooms' to give a party for the congregation after the service.

Bridget of Sweden, St (d. 1373). Founder of the Brigittines. She experienced visions (whose content she dictated to the abbot of a nearby monastery), one of which commanded her to found the Order of the Most Holy Saviour, later known as Brigittines. The Order followed the *Augustinian rule, and was organized in parallel communities of women and men. It flourished until the *Reformation, but was banished from Sweden in 1595. It was reintroduced to Sweden in 1923. Bridget was canonized in 1391.

Bridgid, St. Regarded by many as the second *patron saint of Ireland, but there is no unequivocal evidence that she existed. Her festival is at the start of spring ploughing and sowing (1 Feb.), and is marked by young men (known as Biddies) visiting houses in disguises to ward off evil.

Brigittines: see BRIDGET OF SWEDEN.

British Israelites: see TEN LOST TRIBES.

Broad Churchmen. Christians who seek to avoid narrow theological definitions and interpret the creeds and other formulae in a 'broad', liberal sense.

Bronze vessels. Containers of food and drink for ritual use, produced from the Shang to the Chou *dynasties in China. The bronzes are perhaps most famous for the so-called *t'ao-t'ieh* ('ogre masks'), which show, in split representation, an animal with a single head and two bodies extending out more or less flatly toward the two adjoining sides of the vessel. For the most part, scholars have seen in these motifs symbols of life renewal, fecundity, sacred sovereignty, and cosmic order; but equally, these zoomorphic forms may represent animal helpers or 'familiars' connected with *shamanistic activities which were of great importance in ancient China for communicating between *Heaven and Earth.

Brothers and Sisters of the Common Life (Christian community): see GROOTE, G.

Brunner, Heinrich Emil (1889–1966). Christian (Swiss Reformed) theologian, for most of his working life Professor of Theology at Zurich. He maintained a distinct position from Karl *Barth, but endeavoured to retain a dialectical theology, with the utter distinctiveness of God nevertheless already 'prepared for', by way of recognition, in his creation. Thus in *The Mediator* (1927, 1934) he claimed that the command to love God wholly and solely is unrealistic apart from Christ's own fulfilment of it which opens the way to our own.

Bsam. yas (first monastery in Tibet): see SAMYÉ; TUCCI, G.

Bstan-'dzin-rgya-mtsho (current Dalai Lama): see DALAI LAMA.

Buber, Martin (1878–1965). Jewish philosopher and *Zionist leader. As a Zionist, influenced by *Aḥad ha-'Am, Buber emphasized the importance of education. As a 'Hebrew humanist', he emphasized the rights of the Arabs, stating 'the Jewish people proclaims its desire to live in peace and brotherhood with the Arab people and to develop the common homeland'. His *Ich und Du* (I and Thou) was published in 1923 (Eng. edn. 1937) and contains his famous philosophy of dialogue. He distinguished between 'I–It' relationships, which are impersonal interactions designed to achieve a particular end, and 'I-thou' relationships which are mutual, direct, and open. This leads to the characterization of God as the 'eternal thou'—the one who is only known through direct personal relationship.

Bucer, Martin (1491–1551). Christian Reformer and theologian. A *Dominican friar, he was attracted in 1518 to *Luther's teaching. Released from his monastic vows in 1521, he led the *Reformation in Strasbourg and was noted for his tolerance and diplomacy in theological debates. His *De Regno Christi* offers a stimulating interpretation of ideal Christian society.

Buchman, Frank (1878–1961). Founder of *Moral Re-Armament. A *Lutheran pastor in Pennsylvania, Buchman embarked for Europe in 1908 after a disagreement. There he began a campaign along evangelical lines. In Oxford in 1921 he founded the 'First-Century Christian Fellowship' or Oxford Group Movement, the chief activity of which was house parties including group confessions, prayers and listening for God's guidance, having as their aim the 'changing' of lives. The Oxford Group became Moral Re-Armament in 1938.

Buddha (Pāli, Skt.; Chin., *fo*; Jap., *butsu*; Korean, *pul*). 1. An enlightened person, literally, 'one who has awakened' to the truth. Traditional Buddhism teaches that there are two sorts, samyaksaṃbuddha (see SAMMASAMBUDDHA) and *pratyekabuddha; and that *Gotama is one in a series of the former kind. *Mahāyāna Buddhism extends the notion of a buddha into a universal principle: all beings possess a 'buddha-nature' and are therefore prospective buddhas.

2. Title applied to Gotama (Skt., Gautama), the historical founder of Buddhism (hence, the Buddha Gotama or Gotama Buddha).

Gotama Buddha is also known, especially in Mahāyāna, as Buddha *Sākyamuni (i.e. the Wise One, or Sage, of the Śakya clan). There are uncertainties about his dates. According to the Long Chronology, he lived just over 200 years before *Aśoka, giving approximate dates of 566–486 BCE. According to the Short Chronology, he lived 100 years before Aśoka, i.e. *c.*448–368. He was born Siddhārtha Gotama or Gautama, in *Kapilavastu, in modern-day Nepal. After his enlightenment, he became known as the Buddha, the Enlightened One. Although many stories of his life are told, and immense bodies of teaching are attributed to him, it is not possible to reconstruct his biography or his own teaching with any historical certainty—nor, from a Buddhist point of view, is it in the least desirable. The Buddha is a physician who diagnoses illness and suggests treatment; but the worth or the value lies, not in the biography of the physician, but on whether the patient is cured.

Buddhist biographies are late (see e.g. **Buddhacarita*, **Lalitavistara*). They, and texts in the *Pāli canon, suggest that Gotama was brought up in a royal household (perhaps son of the rāja of Kapilavastu), and that he married (perhaps more than one wife). His wife Yaśodharā bore a son, Rāhula. Although his father tried to protect Gotama from disturbing experiences, he ordered a carriage and saw, on separate occasions, a sick man, an old man, and a dead man. Disturbed by the thought that these conditions awaited him, he wondered how to escape them. On a fourth trip, he saw an emaciated religious *ascetic. Gotama abandoned his wife and son, and embarked on extreme asceticism. He discovered that such practices attain their goal—but no more than their goal; and these goals do not lead to escape from suffering and death.

In disillusionment at the limited attainments of asceticism, Gotama reverted to 'the middle way' (a characteristic name for 'Buddhism') and sat beneath a tree (*Bo Tree), concentrating on 'seeing things as they really are'. He passed through the four stages or layers of progressive insight (*jhānas), and reached enlightenment.

His initial response was to remain where he was, but eventually he was prevailed upon (by the god *Brahmā) to share the truth, on the grounds that humans are like lotuses in a pool: all are rooted in mud; most are swamped below the surface; but a few are struggling to the light and some have already blossomed. The Buddha agreed to teach according to the capacity of his audiences (*upāya-kauśalya).

The rest of his life (when he had in fact attained *nirvāna, but the residual appearances of *karma kept him in apparent form on this earth) was spent wandering, with an increasing band of disciples, in the area of the larger Ganges basin. According to *Majihima Nikāya*, his last words before death were, 'Decay is inherent in all compounded things, so continue in watchfulness' (or '. . . work out your own salvation with diligence'). See Index, Buddha's life; Buddhas, Bodhisattvas.

Buddhabhadra (359–429). Buddhist *Sarvāstivāda monk, who was born in Kashmir, and entered the *saṅgha at 17. He met Chih-yen, who advised him to go to China. There he translated basic works (e.g. **Mahāparinirvāna-sūtra* and *Vināya-piṭaka), but came into conflict with *Kumārajīva monks, and took refuge, away from the capital, in *Lu-shan. There he became an interpreter of the teaching of *Hui-yuan.

Buddhacarita. 'The Acts of the Buddha', a biography of the Buddha in the style of Sanskrit epic poetry (*mahākāvya*) written by *Aśvaghoṣa about the 2nd cent. CE.

Buddhadāsa (Skt; Thai, Putatāt). Thailand's most influential Buddhist scholar and reformist monk. Born in 1905, Buddhadāsa (i.e. 'servant of the Buddha') was ordained at the age of 20, but soon afterwards became disenchanted with conventional monastic life. He decided to embark on a career of *vipassanā (insight meditation), and established a centre for this purpose at Suan Mokkhabalārāma (The Grove of the Power of Liberation) near Chaiya in S. Thailand in 1932. He remained there, paying occasional visits to Bangkok and abroad. He gave a lecture at the Sixth Great Buddhist Council held in Rangoon, 1954–6.

Following King Mongkut's disregard for the literal understanding of Buddhist cosmology, Buddhadāsa *demythologizes many traditional beliefs. Thus gods and demons become states of mind, rebirth a moment-to-moment experience, and the doctrine of *anatman (no-self) a statement of the need to move away from an existence characterized by 'ego' or 'self-ness' to *nirvāna (Pāli), here and now.

Buddha-dharma. Teaching of the *Buddha and thus an appropriate name for 'Buddhism'. In *Zen, buddha-dharma is *buppō*. In SE Asia, 'Buddhism' is also known as buddha-sāsana, the practice of Buddhist morality and meditation.

Buddha-family: see BUDDHAKULA.

Buddha-fields: see BUDDHA-KṢETRA.

Buddhaghosa (Pāli, Skt., 'Buddha-voice'). Theravādin Buddhist, who was born in a *brahman family at the end of the 4th cent., traditionally at *Bodhgāya. He wrote commentaries on many works in the Pāli canon, but is best remembered for *Visuddhimagga*, *The Way of Purity*, a work of great importance in understanding post-canonical Buddhism.

Buddha-kāya. The 'bodies' (i.e. forms of manifestation) of the buddha-nature, more usually known as *Trikāya.

Buddha-kṣetra (Skt., 'Buddha-field'). The sphere of influence and activity of a *Buddha. The most famous of the pure buddha-fields or *Pure Lands is the paradise of the Buddha Amitābha (*Amida) in the west, described in the *Sukhāvatívyūha Sūtras*, into which all may be reborn by calling upon the name of Amitābha. The existence of these pure buddha-fields became immensely important in the development of popular devotional Buddhism especially in China and Japan.

Buddhakula (Skt., 'buddha-family'). The five basic qualities found in the Mahāyāna buddhas. The five qualities are different aspects of *prajña (wisdom).

Buddha-nature: see BUDDHATĀ; TATHĀGATA-GARBHA; and Index *ad loc.*

Buddhapālita. A teacher and commentator of the *Prāsaṅgika branch of the *Mādhyamaka school who lived most probably in the 5th cent. CE. He is the author of the *Mūla-mādhyamaka-vṛtti*, a commentary on the *Mādhyamaka-kārikā* of *Nāgārjuna, the 2nd-cent. CE. founder of the school.

Buddha-sāsana. Buddha-discipline, a term embracing the practice and teaching of the Buddha, and thus is a name for 'Buddhism': see also BUDDHA-DHARMA.

Buddhas of the three times. The *buddhas of the three periods, past (Kaśyapa, but often in iconography *Dīpaṃkara), present (Śākyamuni, i.e. Gotama), and future (*Maitreya).

Buddha's tooth (Buddhist relic): see PILGRIMAGE (BUDDHISM).

Buddhatā (Skt., 'buddha-nature'). In Mahāyāna Buddhism, the real and undifferentiated nature of all appearance. Since this nature constitutes all beings, they all have equal opportunity to realize this fact and to attain enlightenment. In Zen Buddhism, the equivalent (Jap.) term is *bussho, or *hossho*, and the awakening to the truth of that nature and one's identity with it is *mujōdō-no-taigen. See also HUA-YEN; TATHĀGATA-GARBHA; Index, Buddha-nature.

Buddhavacana: see BUDDHIST SCRIPTURES.

Buddhavaṃsa (stories of previous Buddhas): see KHUDDAKA-NIKĀYA.

Buddhāvatamsaka-sūtra (Mahāyāna sūtra): see AVATAMSAKA LITERATURE.

Buddhi (Skt., 'intellect'). In Skt. (Hindu) literature, the higher mental faculty, the instrument of knowledge, discernment, and decision. Buddhi is understood in slightly different ways in the different philosophical systems.

Buddhism. This began historically (although, of course, in its own account it has always been the truth, with a long pre-history) in the 6th and 5th cents. BCE, in India, with the enlightenment of Gotama, who became thereby *muni of the Śakya clan (i.e. Śākyamuni) and (in his own self-description) *Tathāgata. As presented now in the texts, he taught in the context of the basic components of Hindu *cosmology and psychology (long cycles of time, and equally long periods through which a self or soul, *ātman, is reborn as it moves, controlled by *karma as cause, toward freedom or salvation, *mokṣa), but modified them drastically: he saw all appearance as characterized by *dukkha (transience, *anicca, accompanied by the suffering which arises if one seeks something permanent or eternal in its midst). It follows that there cannot be a soul, but only the sequence of one moment giving rise to the next, constituting appearances with characteristic possibilities (human, e.g., as opposed to animal, through the *skandhas, aggregations). The no-soul doctrine is referred to as *anātman.

The teaching of the Buddha is summarized in the *Four Noble Truths (the truth of dukkha and how to escape it), the Eightfold Path (*aṣṭangika-marga) (the route to escape or enlightenment), and *paticca-samuppāda (the analysis of the twelve-step chain of cause which gives rise to entanglement in *saṃsāra, the continuing process of reappearance (*punabhāva).

Buddhist commitment can be summarized in the *Three Jewels or Refuges: I take refuge in the Buddha; I take refuge in the Dhamma (Pāli for Skt., dharma); I take refuge in the *Saṅgha. The saṅgha is the communal organization of the *bhikṣus (bhikkhus), or monks.

The Buddha's teaching was gathered, over a long period, into canonical collections, especially the *Tripiṭaka and the *Sūtras, though the status, particularly of the latter, may be disputed (see BUDDHIST SCRIPTURES). From about the end of the 4th cent. BCE, different interpretations of the teaching were leading to different schools, and especially to the major difference between Theravāda ('teaching of the elders'), with its eighteen schools, and Mahāyāna ('great vehicle', hence their derogatory reference to Theravāda as Hīnayāna, 'minor vehicle'), with its innumerable styles and divisions; for these, see BUDDHIST SCHOOLS. The spread of Buddhism was greatly accelerated during the reign of *Aśoka (3rd cent. BCE).

Under this endorsement, popular Buddhism flourished, especially in *pilgrimages, in the development of *stūpas and the rituals and beliefs associated with them, and in the proliferation of art and image-making. But philosophy (*abhidhamma) also began its quest for more exact analysis of Buddhist concepts: three major schools emerged in the 3rd cent. BCE): Puggalavāda (Skt., Pudgalavāda), Sarvastivāda (Pāli, Sabbatthivāda), and Vibhajjavāda (Skt., Vibhajyavāda). Later, and even more important, came the development of 'the Great Vehicle', Mahāyāna, between the 2nd cent. BCE and 1st CE. It was not a single school or movement, but a drawing out of elements of practice and belief which had been in Buddhism from the outset, but without formal elaboration. Nevertheless, as the implications of these elements *were* elaborated, a new style of Buddhism began to emerge. In particular, the emphasis was no longer on making one's own way as near to enlightenment as possible (*arhat), but on attaining what the Buddha promised and then turning back from selfish attainment in order to help others (*bodhisattva). This led to entirely new cosmologies, as the whole spectrum of buddhas and bodhisattvas was mapped into its place. But even more disjunctively, new philosophical realizations were achieved of what the true buddha-nature must be, and how there cannot be other than that nature which is empty of self and of all differentiation (*buddhatā; *bussho; *śūnyatā). A key figure here was *Nāgārjuna and the *Mādhyamaka school.

The reasons for the decline and virtual disappearance of Buddhism in India remain a matter of academic dispute. Long before the decline, Buddhism had begun to expand, in three different geographical directions, which produced very different versions of Buddhism (for which see following articles and TIBETAN RELIGION): north into Tibet; east into China, Korea, and Japan; and south-east into Śri Lankā, Burma, and Thailand. For the development of Buddhism through schools/sects, see BUDDHIST SCHOOLS.

Buddhism in China. Buddhism was introduced into China about the beginning of the Christian era by Buddhist monks who travelled the overland route across Central Asia. During the first two centuries it maintained a precarious existence in its new surroundings, but with the downfall of the Han dynasty in the 3rd cent., a period of disunity and social turmoil ensued which affected the fortunes of the religion. The message of Buddhism, that existence is suffering (*dukkha), that life is transitory (*anicca), that there is an iron law of rewards and retribution (*karma), and that all beings can achieve salvation, proved to be an attractive magnet drawing the Chinese to the religion.

To refute the charge of unfiliality, the Chinese Buddhists observed memorial services for the departed ancestors, just as the Chinese did. Indian deities (such as the future Buddha *Maitreya) took on a Chinese appearance as the fat jovial *Laughing Buddha with children climbing all over him, while the *bodhisattva *Avalokiteśvara became the female Kuan-yin, the giver of children, in which form she was worshipped by countless numbers of Chinese women anxious to have children.

The accommodation to the Chinese scene may also be seen in the two most popular Chinese schools of Buddhism which flourished during the T'ang dynasty, the *Pure Land and *Ch'an. Major efforts at translation led to the monumental Chinese Buddhist canon, the latest modern edition of which was printed in Japan during 1922–35, consisting of 55 volumes, each one approximately 1,000 pages in length.

Buddhist art also played a prominent role in the dissemination of the religion among the Chinese. Images of Buddhist deities were carved out of the rocks in such centres as *Yün-kang and *Lungmen which may still be seen today as mute testimony to the emotional fervour of the faithful devotees.

By the end of the 8th cent., however, the fortunes of Buddhism in China began to decline. The persecution of 845 in China accelerated the process. Though the religious community in later centuries continued to ordain monks and carry on religious activities, it became clear that the religion was no longer a creative spiritual and intellectual force in Chinese society. Chen-yen, a form of Mantrayāna (stressing the effectiveness of the *mantra) died out in China under persecution, but was of importance in Korea and Japan. On the many other schools in China, see BUDDHIST SCHOOLS.

Buddhism in Japan. The dominant religious tradition of Japan, Buddhism first entered Japan *c.*5th or 6th cent. CE, from the Chinese mainland (traditionally in 538 from Korea). Initially, a few powerful clans opposed the new religion, but by the end of 6th cent. the emperor himself embraced Buddhism, and it received the devotion and patronage of the highest levels of Japanese society. Shōtoku Taishi or Prince Shōtoku (574–622) was instrumental in consolidating Buddhism in Japan (see NARA BUDDHISM).

Japan's schools of Buddhism are generally categorized according to the historical period in which they emerged: Nara period (710–84), Heian period (794–1185), and Kamakura period (1185–1333). During these periods the Japanese assimilated the content of Buddhism, while also adapting it to their own religious sensibilities. *Nara Buddhism consisted of six schools which were virtual transplants from China: Hossō, Kusha, Sanron, Jōjitsu, Kegon (Chin., *Hua-yen), and Ritsu. These were not separate sectarian organizations but mostly philosophies of Buddhism studied side by side in the major temples of the ancient capital of Nara.

Heian Buddhism was comprised of two schools: *Tendai (Chin., *T'ien-t'ai) founded by *Saichō (767–822) and *Shingon founded by *Kūkai (774–835).

Japanese Buddhism reached its height in the Kamakura period with the *Pure Land schools of *Hōnen (1133–1212), *Shinran (1173–1262), and *Ippen (1239–89); the *Zen schools of *Eisai (1141–1215), known as Rinzai (Chin., Linchi), and *Dōgen (1200–53), known as Sōtō (Chin., *Ts'ao-tung); and the Nichiren school of *Nichiren (1222–82). Each of these was strongly sectarian in outlook, emphasizing one specific practice to the exclusion of others. Amalgamation with Shinto, pursuit of worldly benefits, rigorous observance of vows, celibacy, study and meditation, clerical rights all became less important, and simple practices aimed at personal salvation emerged as the central concern. These new forms of Buddhism appealed to ordinary believers who could not meet up to the requirements of the earlier schools. Hence, Kamakura Buddhism became the religion of the masses, and it eventually overshadowed the Nara and Heian schools. To this day the Kamakura schools claim the vast majority of Japan's population as adherents.

Buddhism in Korea. Chinese Buddhism was officially introduced to Korea during the Three Kingdoms period (*c.*350–668) when the country was divided into Koguryŏ, Paekche, and Silla. The teachings were transmitted first to Koguryŏ, then to Paekche, both in the 4th cent. CE, and finally spread to Silla in the 6th cent. The new religion allied itself with the court, embraced indigenous *shamanism and folk religion, gradually penetrating to the populace. Buddhism in Silla contributed to the formation of the *Hwarang Do, a unique institution which trained young aristocrats in civil and military virtues, through devotion to Mirŭk (*Maitreya Bodhisattva) and observance of Buddhist precepts.

During the unified Silla period (668–935) Buddhism took root and flowered in Korean soil. Many monks went to China and even to India in pursuit of Buddhist truth. The five major schools were formed: Yŏlban (Nirvāna), Kyeyul (Vinaya), Pŏpsŏng (Dharma-nature), Hwaŏm (Hua-yen), and Pŏpsang (Consciousness-only). In addition, the nine lineages (Nine Mountains) of *Sŏn (Ch'an/Zen) were transmitted from China. However, Hwaŏm Buddhism played the crucial role: *Wŏnhyo (618–86) and *Ŭisang (625–702) contributed to making Silla Buddhism syncretic and nationalistic, traits which have since been the hallmarks of Korean Buddhism. Faith in Kwanŭm (Kuan-yin) was also widely held among the people.

The Koryŏ dynasty (935–1392) marks the zenith of Korean Buddhism. Buddhism absorbed religious *Taoism and Buddhist *esotericism; the halls of the seven stars (of the Dipper) and the halls of mountain gods were built along with the Buddha halls. *Maṇḍalas of buddhas, bodhisattvas, and gods were painted. Two new sects were established in this period: the Ch'ŏnt'ae (*T'ien-t'ai) sect, by *Ŭich'ŏn (1055–1101), and the Chogye sect, by *Chinul (1158–1210), through a unification of the nine existing Sŏn lineages. The publication of the *Korean Tripiṭaka in the 13th cent. was a brilliant achievement of Koryŏ Buddhism. For all of this, Buddhism was plagued by increasing internal corruption and external discontent.

The rulers of the Yi dynasty (1392–1910), adopting *Neo-Confucianism as the state orthodoxy, advanced a series of anti-Buddhist policies which dealt a crippling blow to Buddhism. King T'aejong (r. 1401–18) reduced the eleven existing sects to seven, and King Sejong (r. 1419–50) reduced those seven sects to just two: the doctrinal school (*kyojong*) and the meditational school (*sŏnjong*). The number of monasteries was drastically diminished.

During the period of Japanese rule (1910–45), Korean Buddhism, under the influence of its Japanese counterpart, made some reforms but also suffered serious set-backs. The two surviving Buddhist groups were forced in 1911 to merge with the Chogye sect. In 1919 countless Buddhists together with other religionists and patriots participated in the March First Movement against Japanese colonial rule.

Since Korea's independence in 1945, Buddhism has coped with the challenges of the modern world. Shedding its seclusion in deep mountains, it is nowadays active in the cities. The Chogye sect remains influential. Young people are involved in Buddhist studies, meditation, the monastic way of life, and social services. The activities of nuns are noteworthy. *Won Buddhism is the most popular lay Buddhist movement today.

Buddhism in South-East Asia. SE Asian Buddhism is mostly *Theravāda and historically related to the *Sthaviras (i.e. elders) who emerged in the 3rd cent. BCE, in what is now Śri Lankā. During the following centuries monks carried the teaching of the *Tripiṭaka to Thailand, Burma, Laos, and Cambodia, where it flourished, though not without substantial accommodation to popular Hinduism and animism.

A major reason for the rapid spread of Buddhism in SE Asia was its acceptance by monarchs. Thai Buddhism, for example, owes much to King Mongkut (1804–68). He founded a new branch of the saṅgha known as the Dhammayutika Nikāya ('those who adhere to the Dhamma'). The older group subsequently became known as the Mahānikāya ('the great branch').

The Dhammayutika monks became popular among the educated élite, and a parallel group came into being in Cambodia. The former remained subject to a single patriarch, whereas the latter had one for each branch. Mongkut's insistence on the *Vinaya, the first of the Tripiṭaka (Skt.), as the cornerstone for reform, influenced Thai, Cambodian, and to a lesser extent Laotian monks by making them more careful to observe its detailed rules.

Nuns are rare in SE Asia, though provision exists for women to ordain to the level of *anāgārika, which is intermediate between the five precepts for a lay Buddhist, and the ten undertaken by the novice. They wear white robes. In Thailand they are known as *mae chii*, and their role is gaining in importance.

In Laos and Cambodia the political events of the 1970s have severely curtailed the activities of Buddhist monks. In Burma, *pongyis* ('great glory') played a prominent role in the movement for independence from Britain, and supported U Nu in his 1960 election campaign. But more recently, since the advent of Ne Win, saṅgha and State have parted company.

Thailand's continuous tradition of monarchy and saṅgha unchecked by colonial powers produced some important manifestations of Buddhism. Mongkut's rejection of supernaturalism has encouraged educated members of the saṅgha to present Buddhism in modern scientific dress. *Buddhadāsa (Skt.; Putatāt, Thai) has reformulated cardinal doctrines.

Other leading monks share the progressive outlook of Buddhadāsa, but are famous primarily as meditation teachers (Achan Mun) or practitioners of development (Phra Maha Narong Cittasobhano).

Vietnamese Buddhism differs from that of other mainland SE Asian Buddhist countries in that it was both Theravādin and Mahāyānist from an early stage, and has been heavily influenced by Confucianism and Taoism. The comparatively high proportion of Theravādins in the south is the legacy of the Cambodian presence between the 15th and 19th cents. Vietnamese monks have been heavily involved in politics, and in 1963 Thich Quang Duc, a 73-year-old monk, performed self-immolation as a protest against the Diem regime. The United Vietnamese Buddhist Church, which came into being during the religious and political ferment of the 1960s, united Theravādins and Mahāyānists in a single ecclesiastical structure. Thich Nhat Hanh is representative of the moderate political wing of the Church.

*Cao Dai and *Hoa Hao are even more syncretistic than their parent Vietnamese Buddhism. The former, founded in 1926 by Ngo Van Chieu (1878–1932), tries to draw together Confucianism, Taoism, Buddhism, and Christianity into a single religion of the Way (Tao). Hoa Hao, founded by Huynh Phu So in 1939, is more distinctively Buddhist and reformed in its opposition to religious rituals.

Thus SE Asia Buddhism is a highly complex system of interlocking historical, geographic, political, and cultural traditions. Although common features exist, such as the role of the monarchy and accommodation between Buddhism and pre-Buddhistic animism and Hinduism, there is an enormous diversity which characterizes not only the differences between countries in the region but also significant distinctions which exist between the Theravāda Buddhism of SE Asia and its historical parents in Śri Lankā and India.

Buddhism in Tibet: see TIBETAN RELIGION.

Buddhist Councils: see COUNCILS, BUDDHIST.

Buddhist lineages: see BUDDHIST SCHOOLS.

Buddhist schools (sometimes referred to as 'sects'). These are felt by Buddhists to be primarily a matter of lineage more than credal confession. A Buddhist is a *Bauddha* (Skt., 'Follower of *Buddha') and takes refuge in the *Three Jewels, thus becoming a part of the *saṅgha with a particular interpretation of the *dharma, and will often refer to a particular person as 'my teacher'. This teacher will have been certified by another teacher in a lineage which, if complete, can be traced back to the Buddha. Controversies then arise over the authenticity of a lineage and/or the correctness or completeness of its understanding of the dharma. Since divisions over the interpretation of dharma have often impressed scholars as philosophical, they have been called schools rather than sects, or the neutral term 'tradition' may be used. Within Tibetan Buddhism the theoretical divisions called *siddhānta* (Skt., 'finality', 'explanation') have been translated as 'system' although they come closest to being philosophical schools. No one term in Buddhism corresponds to any of these divisions, and for convenience the word 'lineage' will be used here.

There are two major lineage groups: *Theravāda and *Mahāyāna. *Vajrayāna is sometimes counted as a third grouping and sometimes as a subset of Mahāyāna. Theravāda is most simply viewed as a single major lineage. Mahāyāna is a family of lineages that may be grouped into two main cultural types: Tibeto-Mongol and Sino-Japanese. Tibeto-Mongol Buddhism sees itself as the inheritor of later Indian Mahāyānist scholar-monks and places much emphasis on philosophical precision. Sino-Japanese Buddhism (which includes Korean and Vietnamese forms) developed lineages independently of Indian Mahāyāna.

Early Buddhism is said to have divided into eighteen lineages on the basis of scholarly disputes about the nature of all three of the Three Jewels. None of the earliest lineages can be clearly identified in later Buddhism, but Theravāda may be seen as the oldest surviving lineage. It has become the dominant form of Buddhism in SE Asia. Theravāda has been repeatedly split over questions of monastic discipline (see VINAYA) and ordination practice, and the relative importance of doctrine and meditation.

Tibetan Buddhism has four main lineages divided into two major groups: Nyingmapa (Tib., 'Ancient Ones'), a single lineage attributed to the Indian missionary *Padmasambhava (9th cent. CE), which arranges the dharma into nine vehicles (Skt., *Yāna); and Sarmapa (Tib., 'New Ones'), a group containing the three lineages of the Later Transmission: Kagyupa founded by Marpa (1012–*c*.1098), Sakyapa founded by Konchog Gyalpo (1034–1102), and the Gelugpa reform of Tsongkhapa (1357–1419). The Nyingma and Sarma groups differ over their understanding of *śunyatā and the interpretation of Tantra. The sub-divisions of the Kagyu are the most complicated. There are two main divisions, Shangpa and Dragpo. The Dragpo has four divisions, of which the Karma Kagyu is the best known. Another division, Phagtru, itself has eight divisions, of which the Drikung and Drukpa are best known. Drukpa has further sub-divided into three. Tsongkhapa's lineage, Gelugpa, attempts a synthesis of what it considers the best features of all Sarma groups. The *Dalai Lamas belong to the Gelugpa. The Tibetan lineages spread into Mongolia and mixed with the indigenous *shamanism but without producing distinctly new lineages.

Chinese Buddhist lineages may be divided into three main types: modifications of Indian lineages, native scholastic lineages, and native popular lineages. All these lineages interact with each other in complex ways and this classification, although designed to be helpful, is in no way absolute. The major lineages based on Indian forms are one Hīnayāna, Chü-shê or Ābhidharmika; and two Mahāyāna, San-lun or *Mādhyamaka, and Fa-hsiang or Yogācāra/Vijñānavāda. These, and many smaller lineages, provided the theoretical basis for the development of the two great comprehensive Chinese systems of *T'ien-t'ai, based on the **Lotus Sūtra* and founded by Hui-ssŭ (515–76); and Hua-yen, based on the **Avatamsaka Sūtra* and founded by Tu-shun (557–640). Lineages with a wider appeal among layfolk are *Zen (Chin., Ch'an), attributed to the Indian missionary *Bodhidharma (*c.*5th cent.) and *Pure Land (Chin., Ching-t'u), perhaps founded by Hui-yüan (334–416). During the Sung and Ming Dynasties Zen and Pure Land were synthesized to form the basis of modern Chinese Buddhism.

Korean Buddhist lineages were at first extensions of the Chinese, with the Hua-yen (Hwaŏm) being the most important and forming the doctrinal basis for all later Korean Buddhism. A distinctively Korean lineage, Popsong (Dharma Nature) was founded by *Wŏnhyo (617–86) who attempted a comprehensive system based on the Awakening of Faith (*Mahāyānaśraddhotpāda-śastra*) and the teaching of One Mind. Zen *Sŏn was introduced by Pŏmnang in *c.*630 and sparked a major controversy between itself and scholastic Buddhism (collectively known as Kyo) which still affects Korean Buddhism. Sŏn itself divided into nine lineages, called 'mountains', which disputed with each other. The highly respected Master *Chinul (1158–1210) attempted to resolve the controversies by teaching the identity of the enlightenment achieved through Sŏn practice and Kyo study, i.e. the identity of the 'tongueless' and the 'tongued' dharma transmissions. The government forcibly united the lineages at various times, and in 1935 all lineages were unified as the Chogye.

Japan received many of the Chinese lineages through Korea in the 6th cent. CE, with some importance again being given to Hua-yen (Kegon). *Kūkai (774–835) combined two streams of Chinese Chen-yen (Vajrayāna) to form *Shingon, an original synthesis which became considerably more popular than its parents, and with his ability to align Buddhism with native folk religion he became a cultural hero. Zen and Pure Land have remained distinct lineages in Japan, with three forms of Zen modified from Chinese forms (*Sōtō, *Rinzai, and *Ōbaku) and two main forms of Pure Land (*Jōdo and *Jōdoshin) developed indigenously by *Hōnen (1133–1212) and *Shinran (1173–1263) respectively. *Nichiren (1222–82) founded a vigorously exclusivist lineage of which a later subbranch, *Nichiren Shōshū, is socially (as *Sōka Gakkai) and politically (as the Kōmei Party) highly visible in present-day Japan. As Korea has tried to reduce the number of lineages, so Japan has allowed them to proliferate. Nearly 170 lineages, divided amongst 14 major groupings, are currently listed by the Japanese Agency for Cultural Affairs.

Vietnam received lineages from the rest of SE Asia around 1st cent. CE and from China between the 6th and 17th centuries. The SE Asian lineages have formed a Hīnayāna base for Vietnamese Buddhist practice supporting a superstructure of Chinese Mahāyāna, chiefly Zen (Vietnamese *Thiền*). The *Tha'o-Đu'ò'ng* lineage, a form of the Chinese Sung Dynasty synthesis imported in the 11th cent., had great influence on the character of Vietnamese Buddhism as a harmony of Zen (emphasizing wisdom) and Pure Land (emphasizing compassion). An indigenous form of Lin-chi (Vietnamese, *Lâm-Tế*) was founded by Liễu-Quán (d. 1743) and became the dominant lineage. All lineages were merged into the Unified Buddhist Church of Vietnam (Vietnamese, *Việt-Nam Phật-Giáo Thống-Nhất Giáo-Hội*) in 1963.

Buddhist Scriptures. These are extensive and variously classified. The fundamental division is into the word of the *Buddha (Skt., *buddhavacana*) and the authorized commentaries. The written scriptural tradition is secondary to the oral transmission and there is no single body of texts that might be called a 'Buddhist Bible'. For the basic canon, see TRIPIṬAKA.

Buḍhā, Bhāī (16th cent. CE). Respected contemporary of the first six Sikh *Gurūs. In 1604 he became the first *granthī, upon the installation of Arjan Dev's compilation of the *Ādi Granth in the *Harimandir whose construction he had supervised. Following the Gurū's execution and during the imprisonment of Gurū Hargobind, whose adviser he was, Bhāī Buḍhā and Bhāī *Gurdās administered the Sikh community.

Budo (martial ways): see MARTIAL ARTS IN JAPAN.

Buffalo (icon, myth, and sacrifice): see MAHIṢA.

Bugaku (Jap., 'dance music' or 'dance entertainment'). Ceremonial *dance and *music used in Shinto, Buddhist, and Imperial Court festivals and rituals of Japan since the early days of Japanese history. The music, when performed alone, is called *gagaku* ('refined/ceremonial music').

Bugei (martial arts): see MARTIAL ARTS IN JAPAN.

Buji-zen. In Zen Buddhism an unwarranted self-confidence whereby an individual believes that since he is the universal buddha-nature (*buddhatā) as a matter of fact, there is no need to engage in discipline or meditation to realize it.

Bujutsu (martial skills): see MARTIAL ARTS IN JAPAN.

Bukan (Buddhist teacher): see HAN-SHAN.

Bukhārī (compiler of Muslim ḥadīth): see AL-BUKHĀRĪ.

Bukkyo or **Buppo:** Jap. for *buddha-dharma.

Bulgakov, Sergei or **Sergius** (1871–1944). Russian philosopher and Orthodox theologian. He was ordained in 1918, but was then expelled from Russia in 1923, ostensibly for unorthodoxy, but more probably for political reasons. He sought to interpret all doctrine in the light of the divine Sophia, or Wisdom. Of his many works, *The Orthodox Church* (1935) and *The Wisdom of God* (1937) summarize his main ideas.

Bull (Lat. *bulla*, 'seal'). A papal document or mandate, so-called because sealed officially. For examples, see Index, Bulls, encyclicals, etc.

Bullinger, Heinrich (1504–57). Swiss Reformer. Biblical and patristic study, the reading of *Luther's and *Melanchthon's writings, and *Zwingli's preaching, led Bullinger to support the *Reformation movement. He succeeded Zwingli as Chief Minister in Zürich, devoting his energies to educational reform, participation in the eucharistic debate amongst Protestants, and voluminous literary activities including influential correspondence with the English Reformers.

Bultmann, Rudolf (1884–1976). Christian interpreter of the New Testament and its environment, associated especially with the programme of *demythologization. He pioneered the study of *form-criticism, developing scepticism about the possibility of recovering much, if any, historical detail about Jesus, beyond his summons to decision. His commentary on John argued for dependence on *gnostic ideas, and in an essay on NT and mythology (circulated from 1941, but published in H. W. Bartsch, *Kerygm and Myth*, Eng. tr. 1953) he claimed that the pre-scientific world view of the Gospels and NT needed to be demythologized (decoded, so that its essential message could be extracted from the accidents of its environment).

Bundahisn. 'Creation' in *Zoroastrianism, and a text with this title which assumed its final form 9th/10th cents. CE in the Pahlavi language. It starts with the 'event' of creation (a Zoroastrian counterpart to Genesis); much of the central section is dedicated to priestly schematic classifications of types of creation (types of mountains, rivers, birds, animals, etc.) and concludes with an account of the end of history (*Frasokereti).

The Zoroastrian cosmology, as expounded in the *Bundahisn* and other Pahlavi works, encapsulates Zoroastrian belief about God (*Ahura Mazda), the world, human nature, and destiny.

Zoroastrian ethics are founded on this understanding of cosmogony. By nature men and women are perfect, free of all suffering, and sinless. As evil is in essence destructive, it is humanity's duty to expand the Good Creation both through expanding the world (e.g. in farming), and by having children. It is a religious obligation to enjoy the Good Creation, and to refrain from despoiling or abusing it.

Bungan. A revitalization movement among the Kenyah and Kayan peoples of Indonesian Borneo and Sarawak. Though declining by the 1970s, Bungan has still not died out entirely.

Bunyan, John (1628–88). *Puritan preacher and writer. He served in the Parliamentary army for a period during the Civil War and was a vigorous preacher. He was partially 'silenced' during the Restoration period, spending most of twelve years in prison. Calvinist in ethos, he was a prolific writer, his main works, *Grace Abounding to the Chief of Sinners* (a spiritual autobiography, 1666), *Pilgrim's Progress* (part i, 1678; part ii, 1684), and *The Holy War* (1682) have become spiritual classics.

Buppō (Jap., 'Buddhist instruction'). Buddhist teaching, i.e. Buddhism. Hence buppō-sha, one who studies and practises Buddhism, a Buddhist.

Buraku, or **burakumin.** Category of people in Japan outside the social orders. They were involved in contaminating work (especially involving dead bodies), who thereby transmitted impurity. They were known as *eta* ('great filth') and later (during the Tokugawa period, 1600–1868) as *hinin* ('non-persons').

Burāq. The winged beast which the Prophet *Muḥammad is said to have ridden during the miraculous Night Journey and the Ascension (*mi'rāj). The name burāq is connected with the Arab. root *baraqa* ('to lighten', 'to flash') and suggests that the beast received its name 'the lightning flash' on account of its speed.

Burdah (Arab.). 1. A mantle, but especially one of the Prophet *Muḥammad's mantles, given away as a gift. The *Ottomans claimed to possess a cloak of the Prophet, and this *khirqa-i-sharif* formed part of their claim to be authentic caliphs (*khalīfa).

2. The name of a famous, often-recited, poem, al-Burdah, praising the Prophet, by al-Buṣīrī (1213–96 CE (AH 610–95)).

Burials: see FUNERAL RITES.

Burning bush. The plant from which occurred God's revelation to *Moses in Exodus 3. 1–4. 17. During the Middle Ages, the burning bush became a Christian symbol for *Mary, as e.g. in Chaucer, Prologue to the Prioress' Tale.

Burning of books. A recurrent political and religious activity, indicating the power of words and ideas to call in question the validity and authority of existing systems. Familiar examples are 'the burning of the books' under Ch'in Shih Huang Ti (Qin Shihuangdi) (213 BCE), Ch'eng Yi (*Ch'eng Hao), the burning of the library of *Alexandria, the burning of the works of *Maimonides, the burning of books under the Nazis.

Burnt offerings: see SACRIFICE.

Bushidō or **Warrior Code** (Jap., 'Way of the Warrior'). The code of honour, valour, and duty governing the behaviour of the *samurai (warrior class) in Japan.

The central virtue of bushidō is loyalty. The noblest way to die was in battle, but bushidō included more than training in martial arts. Other values in bushidō, like austerity, self-control, and contempt for possessions or personal gain, all served to reinforce the core virtue of loyalty. See further MARTIAL ARTS.

Busshi (Jap., 'son of the Buddha'). A disciple of the *Buddha (i.e. a 'Buddhist'). More generally, busshi embraces all living beings, since the Buddha regards them as his family and children. Thus busshi also includes all *bodhisattvas.

Bussho. Jap., for *buddhatā, the buddha-nature in *Zen Buddhism. See Index, Buddha-nature.

Busshō-dento Kokushi. Posthumous name of *Dōgen.

Busso (Jap., 'patriarchs'). The *Buddha and the patriarchs (*soshigata), from whom *Zen Buddhism is derived. Busso may also refer to the Buddha Śākyamuni.

Bu-ston (1290–1364). Tibetan teacher, translator, and historian of Buddhism belonging to the Bkah-brgyud-pa ('ka-ju-pa') sect. By the age of 30 he had studied under all the great teachers of his day and began to compose treatises in his own name and to translate and edit the canon. By the age of 32, he completed his *History of Buddhism in Tibet* to which he appended a theoretical classification of the canon based on a distinction between the direct teachings of the *Buddha or *Bkah-ḥgyur* ('Kan-jur'), and the treatises of commentary thereon or *Bstan-ḥgyur* ('Ten-jur'). This became the accepted form of classification for the Tibetan canon.

Butler, Joseph (1692–1752). Anglican *bishop and philosopher. From 1718 to 1726 he was preacher at the Rolls Chapel, where his sermons won him fame. He then became a parish priest in Co. Durham, where he wrote his *Analogy of Religion* (1736). He was consecrated bishop of Bristol in 1738 and became bishop of Durham in 1750. His own mistrust of the irrational and of appeal to the praeternatural in religion is contained in his remark, 'The pretending to extraordinary revelations and gifts of the Holy Ghost is a horrid thing, a very horrid thing.'

Butler, Josephine Elizabeth (1828–1907). Christian social reformer. She was initially committed to the improvement of educational opportunities and facilities for women, but she became equally concerned with the desperate plight of women made destitute in various ways. She is recognized in the *Anglican calendar of Lesser Commemorations on 30 Dec., as 'Social Reformer, Wife, and Mother'.

Butsu, or **Butsuda.** Jap. for *Buddha.

Butsudan. Japanese shrine or altar in Buddhist temples (or, in smaller versions, in homes).

Butsuden (Jap., 'Buddha-hall'). The building in which the images of *buddhas and *bodhisattvas are placed.

Butsudō (Jap., 'buddha-way'). The teaching of the Buddha (cf. BUKKYO, BUPPO). In *Zen, it may refer to the attainment of that enlightenment.

Butsumyō-e (Jap., 'a buddha's name'). The former annual ceremony in Japan of reciting the names of buddhas in the past, present, and future to expiate sins.

Butterfly dreaming: see CHUANG-TZU.

Bwiti. A range of *syncretist movements among the Fang and other tribes in Gabon and neighbouring territories. It began in the late 19th cent. as a creative synthesis of elements from traditional and Christian sources.

Byakuren-sha. Jap., for *Pai-lien-tsung, the White Lotus School.

Byams pa (earthly buddha): see MAITREYA.

Byōdō (Jap., 'sameness'). The undifferentiated nature of all manifest appearance, in *Zen Buddhism, since it arises from *śūnyatā and is the same buddha-nature (*buddhatā). Byōdō-kan is the experience of all things in this way.

Byrd, William (1543–1623). Composer especially of liturgical music, who remained a Roman Catholic although writing often for the Church of England.

Byzantine. That which pertains to the Church and the *patriarchate of *Constantinople; though the term in practice is often used to refer to the whole Eastern *Orthodox Church.

C

Cabasilas (Greek Orthodox theologian): see CAVASILAS.

Cabbala(h) (teachings of the Jewish mystics): see KABBALAH.

Cab-horse, standard of: see BOOTH, W.

Cabrini, Frances-Xavier, St (1850–1917). Founder of the Missionary Sisters of the Sacred Heart, and first saint of the USA. She was born in Italy and had hoped to become a missionary in China, but she was rejected on grounds of health. Sent to New York by Pope Leo XIII, she began work among Italian immigrants in 1889, producing a network of support in practical form. She was known as Mother Cabrini, and she became the *patron saint of immigrants and displaced persons. She was canonized in 1946. Feast day, 13 Nov.

Cain. Eldest son of *Adam and *Eve and brother of *Abel: see Genesis 4. 1–16.

Cairo (Arab., al-Qāhira, 'the victorious', but also from al-Qāhir, Mars, the city of Mars). Capital city of the *Fāṭimids, established by al-Mu'izz in 969 (AH 358). It was originally called al-Manṣūriyya until al-Mu'izz entered it, and only then was it called 'the victorious city of al-Mu'izz'. Under the Mamluke dynasty (1250–1517 (AH 648–922)), many of the great *mosques were built, including *al-Azhar.

Cairo Genizah (Heb., 'storing'). A storeroom attached to the Ezra *synagogue in Cairo which contained valuable Hebrew historical documents. It was rediscovered and explored by Solomon *Schechter in 1896.

Caitanya (Skt.). 1. In Hinduism, the spiritually awakened consciousness; hence among followers of *Ramakrishna it is the title of the initiated *bhakti-caitanya.

2. A devotee of *Kṛṣṇa, and source of the Caitanya or Gauḍīya Sampradaya (movement), who lived *c.*1485–1533, and was a major influence on the development of devotion to Kṛṣṇa (Kṛṣṇa-bhakti). In 1510, he was initiated as an *ascetic and took the name Śrī Kṛṣṇa Caitanya. He rapidly became renowned for his ecstatic devotion, expressed in dance and song, and was believed to be an *avatāra of the joint figure of Kṛṣṇa and *Rādhā. His ecstatic, even wild, forms of devotion were later thought (by his disciple, Rūpa Gosvāmī) to be a participation in the divine *līlā, or play, the source of creativity itself. The so-called 'Six Gosvāmīs' were disciples who gave some order and structure to the inspiration which Caitanya left, and which continue to the present, not least in the Hare Krishna (see INTERNATIONAL SOCIETY . . .) movement.

Caitya (Skt., 'a shrine', also **cetiya**). 1. In Indian religions, a shrine or monument, a place of worship, a burial mound.

2. In Buddhism, any object of veneration such as a burial mound, a sacred tree, a robe, etc., but more specifically a particular kind of Buddhist temple.

Caityagiri (Buddhist centre in India): see SĀÑCHĪ.

Caityavandana (interior devotion in Jainism): see PŪJĀ.

Cajetan, Tommaso De Vio (1464–1534). *Dominican scholar and exponent of *Aquinas. He entered the Dominican order in 1484 against his parents' wishes, and became a prolific author, with more than 100 works attributed to him. The best-known, *De Ente et Essentia*, attacked *Averroism. He strongly defended the monarchical authority of the *pope at the (Ps.-) Council of Pisa, and was accordingly made cardinal in 1517. In 1518, he held three disputations with *Luther, but failed to convince him. His commentary on the *Summa Theologica* of Aquinas led to a revival of Thomism.

Cakra (Skt., 'wheel'). A centre of psychic energy in the body conceived as a *lotus, especially in *Tantrism. Six main cakras connected by the *suṣumnā* *nāḍī (in Buddhism called *avadhūtī*) came to be recognized in Hinduism, the *mūlādhāra* ('root support') at the base of the spine, the *svādhiṣṭhāna* ('own place') in the genital region, the *maṇipūra* ('jewel city') at the navel, the *anāhata* ('unstruck') at the heart, the *viśuddha* ('pure') at the throat, and the *ājña* ('command') between the eyebrows. Just above here are two minor cakras: the *manas and *soma*. Above the top of the head is the thousand-petalled lotus (*sahasrāra padma*; or *ūṣṇīṣa kamala* for Buddhists), the abode of bliss which is not classified as an ordinary cakra. See also MAṆḌALA.

For its meaning in non-Tantric Buddhism, see DHAMMA-CAKRA.

Cakra pūjā (Skt.). 'Circle-worship', *Tantric worship by an equal number of male and female disciples of the same line of *gurus (guru *paramparā), who form a closed circle.

Cakravartin (Skt., 'wheel-turner'). A 'universal ruler'. In Hinduism, it refers to a ruler, in the ordinary sense, in this world, but an ideal ruler, one who creates a union between heaven and earth. In Buddhism (and in Jainism), it is extended to ethical sovereignty (e.g. in the *Edicts of Aśoka); and it became an epithet for a *buddha whose teaching is universally true throughout the cosmos.

Calcutta. Kālīghāt, the place in India where the major temple to *Kālī was built in the 16th cent. CE.

Calderón, P. (Christian dramatist): see THEATRE AND DRAMA.

Calendar

Judaism The Jewish calendar is fixed according to the number of years since the creation of the world (traditionally 3761 BCE. Thus the year 5000 began on 1 Sept. 1239 CE. When using the secular calendar, Jews use the terms BCE (before common era) and CE (common era) rather than BC and AD. The year follows a 354 day year of twelve lunar months. To harmonize this with the solar year of 365¼ days, an extra month, Adar II, is added into seven of every nineteen years. The months received Babylonian names during the *Exile: Tishri (Sept./Oct.), Heshvan (Oct./Nov.), Kislev (Nov./Dec.), Tevet (Dec./Jan.), Shevat (Jan./Feb.), Adar (Feb./Mar.), Adar II (see above), Nisan (Mar./Apr.), Iyyar (Apr./May), Sivan (May/June), Tammuz (June/July), Av (July/Aug.), Elul (Aug./Sept.). The year begins with 1 Tishri, Rosh ha-Shanah.

A day begins and ends at sunset. *Rosh ha-Shanah (the new year) is kept on 1 Tishri. It is followed by the days of repentance and Yom Kippur on 10 Tishri. The season of *Sukkot (tabernacles) begins on 15 Tishri and concludes with Shemini Azeret (the Closing Festival) and *Simḥat Torah (the rejoicing in the *law) on 22/23 Tishri. *Ḥanukkah (Lights) begins on 25 Kislev and ends on 2 Tevet. 10 Tevet is a fast day and 15 Shevat is the new year for trees. *Purim (Lots, the Feast of Esther) is celebrated on 14 Adar. It is preceded by the Fast of Esther (13 Adar) and succeeded by Shushan Purim (15 Adar). Pesaḥ (*Passover) begins on 15 Nisan and ends on 21/22 Nisan. 27 Nisan is Yom ha-Sho'ah (Day of the *Holocaust) and 5 Iyyar is Israel Independence Day. Lag ba-Omer (the thirty-third day of the counting of the *omer) is celebrated on 18 Iyyar and *Shavu'ot (Pentecost) takes place on 6/7 Sivan. There are fast days on 17 Tammuz and 9 Av, and 15 Av is a minor holiday.

Christianity The Julian calendar was reformed by Pope Gregory XIII in 1582 when it was realized that the Christian calendar was ten days in advance of the solar year. The reformed calendar is known as the Gregorian (or New) Style, the unreformed as the Julian (or Old) Style. The difference between the two calendars is now thirteen days, so that some Orthodox observe Christmas, 25 Dec. (Old Style), on 7 Jan. The Christian calendar follows each year the preparation for the coming of *Christ, his life, death, and *resurrection, and the being of God (see FESTIVALS AND FASTS). Thus, it begins with *Advent, which has four Sundays, and then either one or two Sundays after Christmas bridge the gap to the *Epiphany (6 Jan.). Thereafter 'Sundays after Epiphany' are reckoned until what used to be known as *Septuagisma, *Sexagesima, and *Quinquagesima (Sundays before Lent); Ash Wednesday introduces the forty days of *Lent, with its six Sundays; and five Sundays after Easter lead up to *Ascension day with its following Sunday and *Pentecost (Whitsunday). The remaining Sundays until Advent are numbered 'after Trinity' or 'after Pentecost'. The Sundays of the Orthodox year fall into three segments: *triodion* (the ten weeks before Easter), *pentecostarion* (the paschal season), and *octoechos* (the rest of the year). See also FESTIVALS AND FASTS.

The system of dating years AD (Lat., *Anno Domini*, 'in the year of the Lord') goes back to Dionysius Exiguus ('the Small'; *c*.500–50). The abbreviations CE (Common Era) and BCE to replace AD and BC began with Jewish historians in the 19th cent., in order to avoid a religious confession within the words abbreviated.

Islam The Muslim calendar is lunar, with twelve months of twenty-nine or thirty days. Because this is not adjusted to the solar calendar (contrast the Jewish system), the religious festivals and holidays advance around the seasons: thus the month of fasting, *Ramaḍān, moves around the entire solar year, occurring sometimes in summer and sometimes in winter (intercalation is forbidden in the *Qur'ān 9. 37). The months are: Muḥarram; Ṣafr, Rabī' al-Awwal, Rabī' al-Thānī, Jumādā al-Ūlā, Jumādā al-Thāniyya, Rajab, Sha'bān, Ramadhān, Shawwal, Dhū al-Qa'dah, Dhū al-Ḥijjah. The years are numbered from the *Hijra, the move of the Prophet *Muḥammad from *Mecca to *Madīna in 622 CE. 1 Muḥarram of that year was 16 July 622, which begins the first year of the Muslim era. The years are referred to as AH, i.e. 'after the Hijra'.

Hinduism The Hindu religious calendar is lunar, with the months divided into a bright (*śulapakṣa*) and a dark (*kṛṣṇapakṣa*) half, with fifteen *tithis* (days) in each. The correlation of human activity with the whole cosmic process (made evident in the movement of heavenly bodies) is of paramount importance. The religious calendar is then a proliferation of special observances, for some of which see FESTIVALS AND FASTS. There are six seasons (*ṛtu*): (i) Vasanta (spring); (ii) Grīṣma (hot season); (iii) Varṣa (rainy season); (iv) Śarad (autumn); (v) Hemanta (winter); (vi) Śiśira (cold). To each of these is allocated two months (Caitra, Vaiśākha; Jyaiṣtha, Aṣāḍha; Śrāvana, Bhādarapada; Aśvinā, Āśvayuja; Mārgaśīrṣa, Pauṣa; Māgha, Phālguna. Every two or three years a thirteenth month was added to adjust the lunar year to the solar year.

Buddhism The spread of Buddhism did not take with it a calendar which it then imposed on other countries; rather, it adapted to local calendars, and worked its own *festivals into the local scene. Buddhist calendars thus vary from culture to culture.

Sikhism The Sikhs' religious calendar is a modified form of the Bikramī calendar. The year is solar (23 minutes 44 seconds shorter than the Christian year) and the months are lunar. Lunar month dates, varying within fifteen days, are used for *gurpurbs. So in 1984 Gurū *Gobind Siṅgh's birthday fell on both 10 Jan. and 29 Dec. Solar months, based on the twelve zodiac signs, are also used, e.g. for *saṅgrānds, *Baisākhī, and Lohṛī. The anniversaries of the battle of Chamkaur, martyrdom of the younger *sāhibzāde, and battle of *Muktsar are solar dates. Because of the discrepancy between the Bikramī and Christian solar year these dates advance one day in sixty-seven years.

Chinese The Chinese have traditionally followed both a solar and a lunar calendar. These run concurrently and coincide every nineteen years. The solar calendar divides the year into twenty-four periods, named (mainly) according to the weather expected in that period in the N. China plain. The only festival fixed by the solar calendar is at the beginning of the fifth period, *Ch'ing Ming. The lunar calendar is used to record public and private events. The New Year begins with the second new moon after the winter solstice, between 21 Jan. and 20 Feb. The months have no names and are known by numbers; but they are associated with the five elements of the cosmos, wood, fire, earth, metal, and water; and also with animals; hence each year is known as 'the year of'. Thus 2000 is the year of the dragon; 2001 the snake; 2002 the horse; 2003 the sheep; 2004 the monkey; 2005 the chicken; 2006 the dog; 2007 the pig; 2008 the rat; 2009 the ox; 2010 the tiger. The traditional starting-point for chronological reckoning is the year in which the minister of the emperor, Huang-ti, worked out the sixty-year cycle, i.e. 2637 BCE.

Zoroastrian See FESTIVALS AND FASTS.

Caliph (successor, representative): see KHALĪFA.

Calligraphy. The skill and art of writing is admired in all religions and advanced to a great height in some. In Judaism, the work of a *scribe was related to the proper transmission of judgements in courts of law. In Christianity, the same work of carefully transmitting sacred texts led to the illumination of manuscripts. In Islam, the importance of calligraphy reflected the prominence of the absolute and uncorrupted nature of the Word of God expressed through the *Qur'ān. Not only in text, but also on buildings, the elaboration of the visible word became a major form of art. No less important was calligraphy in China, being an expression of underlying philosophies in which word and painting are necessarily at one. This was taken to a consummate level in *Zen calligraphy (see BOKUSEKI) where the very act of putting brush to paper is to participate in the single buddha-nature of all things.

Call to prayer (Muslim): see ĀDHĀN.

Calvary, Mount (Lat., *calvaria*, 'skull', translating Heb., *Golgotha*). The place of *Jesus' crucifixion, outside the walls of *Jerusalem (John 19. 20) and near the tomb. The traditional site is within the church of the Holy Sepulchre. A less likely site is 'Gordon's Calvary', by a cliff outside the N. wall of the city.

Calvin, John (1509–64). Christian *reformer and theologian. Under *Protestant influence in Paris, he experienced a decisive change in religious outlook. Under the threat of persecution, he was forced to leave Paris and spent about three unsettled years travelling between Europe's main cities. During this period he wrote his *Psychopannychia* (1534) and the 1st edn. (1536) of his finest work, the *Institutes of the Christian Religion*. Passing through *Geneva, a city which had already committed itself to reform, Calvin was persuaded to settle there by the reforming preacher, Guillaume Farel. Calvin was soon appointed a preacher and pastor, but the measures he and others proposed for church reform were such that Calvin and Farel were forced to flee. In exile in Strasbourg, Calvin ministered to a French refugee congregation and developed a close friendship with Martin *Bucer, whose influence is evident in the next edn. of the *Institutes*, translated into French in 1541. In Feb. 1541 Calvin was invited to return to Geneva where he remained until he died. The reform of the Genevan church was accomplished in large part through the *Ecclesiastical Ordinances* (1541). He died at the age of 55, one of the most influential figures of the Western world.

At the heart of the Christian life lies 'union with Christ', an utterly unmerited relationship effected through the Holy Spirit. Calvin maintained a lifelong commitment to the Bible's importance for reforming every aspect of Christian faith and life, and the primary purpose of the Bible was to focus attention on Jesus Christ. See CALVINISM.

Calvinism. The religious ideas of bodies and individuals who were profoundly influenced by the 16th-cent. church reformer John *Calvin, or by his writings. In Calvinism there is typically a strong stress on the sovereignty of God over every area of life, and on the supremacy of *scripture as the sole rule of faith and practice, an authority confirmed by the inward witness of the Holy Spirit. The doctrine of *predestination was never a leading axiom of Calvin's thought. But many of Calvin's early followers (e.g. Theodore *Beza) were quick to establish the divine 'decree' (to eternal life and death) as the principle from which all other ideas were derived, and on this basis elaborated logically rigorous theological systems. Calvinist theology reached powerful expression in the *Helvetic Confession (1566) and at the Synod of Dort (1618–19). The latter expounded the so-called 'five points' of Calvinism: total depravity, unconditional election, limited *atonement, irresistible *grace, and the final perseverance of the *saints.

Calvinistic Methodists. Those members of the Church in Wales who responded to the revivalistic preaching of Griffith Jones (1684–1761), Howel Harris (1714–73), and Daniel Rowland (1713–90). Now known as the Presbyterian Church of Wales, the denomination has a membership of about 80,000.

Camaldolese (etym. uncertain, perhaps from *campus Romualdi*, 'field of Romuald'). A Christian monastic order derived from the reforms of Romuald (*c.*920–1027), who did penance for his father in Ravenna, and came into contact with monastic life of various kinds. He founded a number of communities, including the hermitage of Camaldoli in the mountains near Arezzo, below which developed the monastery which became the centre of the Camaldolese Order. *The Life of the Five Brothers*, by St Bruno-Boniface, was written before Romuald died and contains the short rule of Romuald. The Congregation of Camaldoli is part of the Benedictine (see BENEDICT) confederation.

Cambridge Platonists. A group of Anglican philosophical theologians who flourished between 1633 and 1688. Prominent among them were Benjamin Whichcote (1609–83), John Smith (1618–52), Henry More (1614–87), and Ralph Cudworth (1617–88). They found in Platonism and the Greek Fathers a rational philosophical structure that enabled them to distance themselves from contemporary enthusiasm, whether *Puritan or *High Church, by submitting the claims of revelation to the bar of reason by which we participate directly in God's *Logos (word, reason).

Camisard revolt: see HUGUENOTS.

Campbell, Alexander (1788–1866). Founder of the 'Campbellites' or 'Disciples of Christ', and the *Churches of Christ. A voluminous writer, Campbell rejected all credal formulas, being persuaded that Christianity's only demands are personal confession of Christ in baptism.

Campbell, Joseph (writer on myth): see MYTH.

Campion, Edmund, St (*c.*1540–81). *Jesuit *priest and *martyr. He was ordained *deacon in the *Church of England in 1569, but then left for Dublin. He returned to England two years later and went on to *Douai, then to Rome, where he entered the Society of Jesus. He was ordained in Prague in 1578 and shortly afterwards left for England with Robert Parsons. He landed at Dover in June 1580. He escaped arrest for a year, though his writings, especially *Decem Rationes*, won him considerable fame. He was arrested at Lyford Grange in Berkshire, and was hanged, drawn, and quartered at Tyburn on 1 Dec. 1581. He was *canonized as one of the *Forty Martyrs of England and Wales in 1970. Feast day, 20 Oct.

Cāmuṇḍā. A form of the goddess *Durgā appearing from her forehead in her fierce aspect as the destroyer of the demons Caṇḍa and Muṇḍa.

Canaan. Land which later became Palestine, promised, according to Jewish belief, by God to the Israelites. Early Canaanite religion is revealed particularly in the *Ugaritic texts.

Caṇḍī (Skt., 'vicious, fierce, violent'). 1. One of the names of the Hindu Goddess (also Caṇḍikā). It does not denote a specific goddess and tends to be used with reference to the more violent manifestations of *Devī.

2. In Bengal, an originally autonomous folk Goddess (similar to *Manasā). From *c.*14th cent. onwards, this Goddess became increasingly drawn into the mythology of the *purāṇas and

thereby got fused with the Skt. Caṇḍī (see (1) above).

3. In N. India, an alternative title of the Devīmāhātmya in the *Mārkaṇḍeya Purāṇa.

Candīdās, Baru. Author of *Srikrsnakitana*, an early *Vaiṣṇava text. Nothing is known of the author, not even his dates.

Candlemas. A Christian festival kept forty days after *Christmas, i.e. on 2 Feb. in most churches. It is also known as the Purification of the Virgin Mary, the Presentation of Christ in the Temple, and in the East, *Hypapantē* ('meeting', *sc.* with *Simeon), all with reference to the story in Luke 2. 22–39.

Candles

Judaism Traditionally oil was considered a more appropriate fuel for liturgical lights, because candles tended to be made from ritually unclean animals. However, by the Middle Ages, possibly influenced by their use in the *Roman Catholic Church, candles were employed for *Sabbath lights, for the *Havdalah (dividing) ceremony, for searching for leaven at *Passover, for *Ḥanukkah (Lights), for the *ner tamid* (*eternal light) hanging before the *synagogue *ark, and for *Yahrzeit (commemoration of the dead).

Christianity In liturgical churches it is usual to have two or more candles ('altar lights') on the *altar, and they may also be carried in procession. Votive candles are also lit before statues or *icons in churches (Catholic and Orthodox respectively) as personal offerings.

Candrakírti (Tib., *Zla-ba-grags-pa*; Chin., *Yüeh-cheng*; Jap., *Gesshō*). A distinguished Buddhist teacher of the *Mādhyamaka school who flourished in the 7th cent. CE. Candrakīrti championed the *Prāsaṅgika form of the Mādhyamaka doctrine in his commentaries on the work of *Nāgārjuna, the founder of the school, and *Āryadeva, his disciple. According to this, the method of the Mādhyamaka is to reduce to absurdity the position of the opponent through a dialectical process which reveals the internal contradictions of his argument. The alternative interpretation of Mādhyamaka, that of the Svātantrika-Mādhyamaka sub-school led by *Bhāvaviveka, was that the Mādhyamaka should seek to establish a positive thesis of its own, and that a purely negative dialectic was inadequate.

The contribution of Candrakīrti to an understanding of the terse aphorisms of Nāgārjuna, most notably through his 'Clear Words' (*Prasannapadā*) commentary cannot be overestimated. Also of great importance is his own composition, *An Introduction to the Mādhyamaka System* (*Mādhyamaka-Āvatāra*).

Canisius, Peter, St (1521–97). *Jesuit theologian and controversialist. His interest in education led him to publish, in 1555, the first of three *catechisms, the second (and perhaps most influential) of which appeared in 1556. In 1925 he was both canonized and, on the strength of his catechetical writings, declared a *Doctor of the Church. Feast day, 21 Dec.

Canon. 1. Title of a member of the *chapter of a cathedral or *collegiate church.

2. (Gk., *Kanon*, 'rule'). The determination of books which have authority in a religion, either because they are believed to be inspired or revealed, or because they have been so designated. In both Judaism (see BIBLE) and Christianity, the decision about which books were to be included or excluded was a long process—not leading to unanimity in Christianity, where Roman Catholics, relying on the Latin translation of the Greek translation of the Hebrew, included additional books not recognized by Jews or other Christians (*Apocrypha). The earliest witness to the present canon of the New Testament is the *Festal Letter* of *Athanasius for 367 CE; and the canon of both Testaments was probably finally fixed in Rome in 382.

The term 'canon' is then frequently applied to collections of sacred or holy texts in other religions. For Hinduism, see ŚRUTI; SMṚTI; VEDA; VEDĀNTA; and further refs. *ad loc.* For Buddhism (Pāli canon, etc.), see BUDDHIST SCRIPTURES; TRIPIṬAKA. The term 'canon' has been applied to revered and authoritative Jain texts (e.g. 'the 45 text canon'), but the term is particularly awkward in this case: see DIGAMBARA; AṄGA. For Sikhs, see ĀDI GRANTH. For the Taoist canon, see TAO-TSANG. In Japan, the **Nihongi* and **Kojiki* were given a status which made them effectively 'canonical'. See also Index, Canonical Collections.

3. The central prayer of consecration in the Roman *mass, and in all *eucharistic liturgies in different forms. It assumed its present form under *Gregory the Great (590–604). Unlike the practice in Eastern churches (see ANAPHORA), the RC Church maintained a single invariable prayer until recent times. Applied to other liturgies, 'canon' is practically synonymous with the more usual term 'eucharistic prayer'.

4. A type of hymn sung at the E. (Byzantine) Orthodox morning *office.

Canonization. The action by which the Christian church declares a deceased person to be a *saint. (The word can also refer broadly to a church's official approval of a doctrine, writing, etc.) In the Roman Catholic Church since *c.*13th cent. it has been reserved to the pope.

According to present canon law the process begins with *beatification. This allows the pope to confer the title 'Blessed' and to permit the public veneration of the beatified person in a particular place or among a religious order. Thereafter, if further miracles are attested, the cause may be taken up again, and if it is favourably concluded, the servant of God is declared a saint. In the Orthodox Church canonizations are usually made by synods of bishops of an *autocephalous church, but sometimes a cult comes to be accepted without formal authority.

Canon law. The body of rules or laws developing gradually, imposed by church authority in matters of its own organization and discipline (extending also to matters of belief).

Canons Regular. Roman Catholic *priests following a quasi-monastic form of common life.

Canopy (for Jewish marriage ceremony): see HUPPAH.

Canossa (place): see GREGORY VII.

Canterbury. In Kent, SE England, chief see of the *Church of England. Its history goes back to 597 with the arrival of *Augustine in England. He had been ordered to organize the church into two provinces with *archbishops at London and York, but Canterbury displaced London from the first. The struggle for precedence with York was ended in Canterbury's favour in the middle of the 14th cent. The archbishop is styled *Primate of All England. He is, however, also head of the *Anglican Communion (of which the Church of England is a numerically small part), and some expect to see a non-English archbishop in the future.

Canticle. A song or prayer from the Bible (other than a *Psalm) used in Christian worship. The Canticle of the Sun is a hymn of praise to God revealed in nature, composed by St *Francis, probably in 1225.

Cantillation. The musical reading of the Jewish Bible, *Talmud, or other liturgical passages. There is no scholarly agreement over the cantillation of Jewish liturgy.

Cantonists. Jewish children conscripted into the Russian army between 1827 and 1856. The children were snatched from their homes to fulfil the government quota.

Cantor (Heb., *ḥazzan*). One trained to lead the Jewish *synagogue prayer service.

Cao Dai (Vietnamese, 'supreme palace' or 'altar', and now the name for the supreme God). Syncretist religious and nationalist movement arising in the Mekong delta of Vietnam from spirit seances giving a new 'third revelation' through a civil servant, Ngo Van Chieu, in 1919. The first and second revelations had produced *Confucianism, *Taoism, Spirit worship, *Buddhism, and *Christianity, but Cao Dai would now unite and complete them. In 1923, a businessman, Le Van Trung, began to develop Cao Dai as a strong organization on the *Roman Catholic model under a pope, although this later split into several sects.

Capital punishment. This was the penalty for serious offences in the ancient world, summarized in the biblical injunction, 'Life for life' (Exodus 21. 23; cf. Genesis 9. 6).

Christianity inherited the biblical injunctions, and lived in a world where executions were practised: hence the acceptance in Romans 13. 1–7 that such executions may be instruments of God's wrath. However, Christianity derived itself far more from the demand of *Jesus to forgive enemies and not to pursue vengeance. Christians have therefore been divided over the permissibility of capital punishment. Muslim attitudes are controlled by the verse in the *Qur'ān, 'Do not take the life which Allāh has made sacred except for justice' (6. 151). In practice, capital punishment is required for *murtadd (apostasy which has been followed by an attack on Islam), *zinā' (adultery), and unjust murder (see QIṢĀṢ).

Capital sins: see DEADLY SINS.

Cappadocian Fathers. Three 4th-cent. Christian theologians, *Basil of Caesarea, his brother *Gregory of Nyssa, and *Gregory of Nazianzus. They were all born in Cappadocia (now in modern Turkey). They were engaged in opposing *Arianism after the Council of *Nicaea, and were influential in its defeat at the Council of *Constantinople in 381. More than this, the Council also canonized their doctrine of the *Trinity which defended the deity of the Holy Spirit alongside the Father and Son as three persons in one substance.

Capsali, Moses ben Elijah (1420–96). Turkish *rabbi. He served as rabbi of Constantinople during the Muslim conquest of the city in 1453 and was much respected by Sultan Mehmet II.

Capuchins. Reformed branch of the Christian *Franciscan order. In 1525, Matteo da Bascio (1495–1552) sought to return to the greater simplicity of the early Franciscans. He wore the pointed cowl or hood (*capuce*, hence the name) of St Francis, and he and his companions devoted themselves to care of plague victims.

Cardinal. A member of the 'Sacred College' of priests selected by the pope to assist him in governing the *Roman Catholic Church. In 1994 there were 167 cardinals in all. On the death of a pope they meet in secret session to elect his successor; since 1971 those over the age of 80 may not vote.

Cardinal directions. The division of space, in Hindu cosmology, into the 4 directions, NSEW, of great importance in sacrifice, orientation of towns and buildings, etc. With the *triloka* (see LOKA), they make up 'all this', i.e. the totality of space.

Cardinal virtues (Lat., *cardo*, 'hinge'). Four particular virtues in Christianity, on which all others are said to depend: prudence, justice, fortitude, temperance. They were extended by the *Scholastics to seven, by adding the three 'theological virtues' of faith, hope, and charity.

Cargo cults. The popular name for *millennial movements in Melanesia. During the last 100 years, hundreds of these have come into being from Fiji to Irian Jaya, and also in other tribal cultures. Local myths of a golden age encourage *prophets to announce the imminent return of *culture heroes or ancestors bringing spiritual or material 'cargo' of the kind discovered through Western contacts. This will inaugurate a new era of human fulfilment and equality with whites. Some movements are religious in form, as with *Manseren cults, the *Vailala Madness, and *Jon Frum. Others also attempt realistic development, as with *Paliau and *Yali, and the Peli and Pitenamu Societies.

Cariyā-piṭaka (part of Buddhist Pāli canon): see KHUDDAKA NIKĀYA.

Carlstadt or **Karlstadt** (*c*.1480–1541). Radical German *Reformer, Andrew Bodenstein, who took his name from his birthplace in Bavaria. He became teacher at Wittenberg, was several times Dean, and came to support *Luther's teaching. Luther's initial conservatism and Carlstadt's radical views were soon in conflict, especially during Luther's refuge in the Wartburg, when Carlstadt married, abandoned *vestments, celebrated *Communion in both kinds, disparaged infant *baptism, destroyed pictures and statues, and removed music from the *liturgy. He was compelled to leave Wittenberg (1528–9) for Switzerland where he finally taught in Basle.

Carmelites. Christian (Roman Catholic) religious order, deriving from hermits on Mount Carmel in Palestine, *c*.1200. Migrating to Europe as the failure of the Crusades began to lead to a break-up of the Latin Kingdom (*c*.1240), they were organized along lines of solitude, abstinence, and prayer. They were joined by nuns in 1452 as the Carmelite Second Order. Increasing laxity prompted the radical reforms of *Teresa of Avila, earning the name Discalced (i.e. not wearing sandals). *John of the Cross extended the reform to male houses of the order. Not having a founding figure (as e.g. *Dominic, *Francis, or *Benedict), they take Elijah and Mary as their founders. See Index, Carmelites.

Carnatic music: see MUSIC.

Caro, Joseph ben Ephraim (1488–1575). *Rabbinic authority and author of the ***Shulḥān Arukh*. Having lived much of his life in Turkey, in 1534 he settled in Safed where he was regarded as the leading scholar. His *Beit Yosef* (House of Joseph, 1555), on which he worked for twenty years, was a commentary on the *Arba'ah Turim* (Four Rows) of *Jacob b. Asher; he investigated every law, discussed its development, and gave a final decisive ruling. His aim was to lay down the definitive *halakhah so that there would be 'one Law and one *Torah'. *Shulḥān Arukh* (Prepared Table, 1597) was a digest of the *Beit Yosef* designed for 'young students'. Caro also produced many *responsa and a commentary on *Maimonides' *Mishneh Torah* (Second Law), the *Kesef Mishneh* (Silver Repetition) (1574).

Caroline Divines (17th-cent. bishops in England): see ANGLICANISM.

Cartesian doubt: see DESCARTES, R.

Cartesian dualism: see DESCARTES, R.

Carthusians. Roman Catholic monastic order, so-called from their mother-house, La Grande Chartreuse (Lat., *Cartusia*, 'Charterhouse') near Grenoble, founded in 1084 by St Bruno of Cologne (1032–1101). Carthusian monasticism emphasizes *eremitic over *coenobitic elements. Their austere form of life has changed little since being first codified *c*.1127 in the *Customs* of Guigo I, fifth prior of La Grande Chartreuse. Thus the Order is traditionally characterized as 'never reformed because never deformed'.

Cārvāka. A school of Indian materialism, also known as Lokāyata dārśana (i.e. restricting truth to this world (*loka)). The traditional founder is said to have been Bṛhaspati, of uncertain date (*c*.6th cent. BCE?) to whom is attributed *Bārhaspati Sūtra*, a work which has long since disappeared, although it is quoted in later works. Carvakins see no permanence, but constant change, in all appearance, so that the self is nothing more than the sum of its parts. Since there cannot be a future personal immortality, the only wise course is to grasp life now—but with the moral control that a good action is more likely to produce happiness than the reverse.

Caryatantra (division of tantric texts): see TRIPIṬAKA.

Cassian, John (*c*.360–435). Christian monk. He came from the East to Marseilles, where *c*.415 he founded two monasteries and where he wrote his two main books. The *Institutes* sets out the ordinary rules for the monastic life. It was the basis of many W. rules, being drawn on e.g. by *Benedict. The *Conferences* record his conversations with monastic leaders of the East.

Cassiodorus (*c*.485–*c*.580). Roman author and Christian monk. He retired from public affairs in 540 to a monastery of his own foundation at Vivarium. He made it a kind of academy of secular and religious learning, which, by its example, did much to protect and continue classical learning and culture through the so-called 'Dark Ages'.

Cassock. Ankle-length garment worn by Christian clergy (and, in church, by vergers, choristers, etc.).

Caste (Portuguese, *casta*, 'breed kind'). Term which indicates the unique hierarchical structure of S. Asian society, which, although originating from Hindu belief, has permeated all religions and communities of the subcontinent, having as its bases and sanctions religious as well as secular tenets. In modern India, the more common word for caste is the indigenous term *jāti (Skt., *jāta*, 'race').

The castes (and sub-castes), numbering many thousands, fit into the divinely originated *varna framework, though their origin is later and usually based on secular criteria relating to occupation and area of origin.

Criteria of caste maintenance such as pollution, hereditary occupation, and commensality are necessarily gradually disappearing in public places in urban, industrialized India, but in the countryside (where *c*.80 per cent of the populace still lives), and in home life, such beliefs and the discriminatory practices related to them still prevail.

Caste has long been the target of reforming groups, both within Hinduism and from the outside. Gurū *Nānak and successive Sikh Gurūs declared caste irrelevant to salvation. However, intercaste marriage has always been rare among Sikhs, and at least at that level, caste is far from being eradicated among Sikhs: see BĀLMĪKĪ; BHĀṬṚĀ; JAṬ; KABĪR; KHATRĪ; MAZHABĪ; MISL; RĀMDĀSĪ; RĀMGAṚHĪĀ; RAVI DĀS; RAVIDĀSĪ. See also Index, Caste.

Casuistry. The art of applying principles of moral theology to particular instances (Lat., *casus*, 'case').

Catacombs (Gk., *kata kumbas*, 'by the hollows', an area south of Rome). In these long underground burial chambers (outside the city walls as burial was not permitted within) the bodies of the departed were placed in coffin-like recesses, in rows usually about four deep. Christian catacombs seem to be copied from Jewish ones. Six Jewish catacombs have been found in Rome. Catacombs are found outside many cities, but the most famous and extensive—several hundred miles of them—are at Rome. Services commemorating *martyrs buried there were held, and they became centres of *pilgrimage as the cult of martyrs developed.

Catechism (Gk., *katēcheō*, 'instruct'). An elementary manual of Christian doctrine. In the Middle Ages books were produced containing explanations of the *Lord's Prayer and *creed, lists of mortal sins, etc. It was the *Reformation, however, with its insistence on religious instruction, which brought forth the catechisms known today. Catechisms normally contain expositions of the creed, Lord's Prayer, and the Ten Commandments; RC ones add instructions on the *Hail Mary, *sacraments, virtues and vices, and extend into virtually every area of doctrine and behaviour.

Catechumen. One who is undergoing training and instruction (Gk., *katachesis*) prior to Christian *baptism. See also NEO-CATECHUMENATE.

Categorical imperative. In Kantian ethics, the universal moral law, by which all rational beings are by duty constrained to act. The term was introduced in the *Foundations of the Metaphysics of Morals* (1785).

Category mistakes: see MYTH.

Cathars (Lat., *Cathari*, from Gk., *katharoi*, 'pure ones'). Christian dualist *heresy in W. Europe, which, in the 13th–14th cents., was a serious threat to the Catholic Church especially in S. France (see ALBIGENSES) and N. Italy. The origins of the movement are obscure, and although its doctrines were influenced by the *Bogomils of Bulgaria, it remains a possibility that its dualism was an independent development or inheritance.

The inner circle of the Cathars were the 'perfects', who followed a life of rigorous asceticism and praying the *Lord's Prayer. Admission to this circle was by the rite of *consolamentum* after an arduous probation, but other adherents received it on their deathbed. Those thus 'consoled' saw themselves as the only true Christians and denied the title to Catholics.

Cathedral (Gk., *kathedra*, 'seat'). The Christian church building in which a *bishop has his official seat.

Catherine of Alexandria, St (*c.*4th cent.?). Christian *martyr. Despite her wide popularity in the Middle Ages, extremely little (some would say nothing) is known of her. She is said to have been martyred during the persecution under Maxentius, by being tied to a wheel (hence the Catherine wheel), tortured, and beheaded. Her feast day (25 Nov.) was suppressed in 1969.

Catherine of Genoa, St (1447–1510). Christian mystic. Born of a noble family, Caterinetta Fieschi married young. Ten years later she experienced a sudden conversion and gave herself to the selfless care of the sick in a hospital in Genoa, at the same time experiencing strange, almost pathological, religious experiences, and supposedly receiving the *stigmata. Her spiritual doctrine is contained in the *Dialogues on the Soul and the Body* and *Treatise on Purgatory*: *purgatory is the final cleansing of the soul from self-love, to be accepted, therefore, with joy.

Catherine of Siena, St (1347–80). Christian saint who saw a vision of Christ when she was 7, after which she took a vow of virginity. She became a member of the Third Order of *Dominicans when she was 16 (or perhaps 18), and committed herself to work among the poor and the sick. Her holiness became widely known and she attracted many followers. In 1376 she went to Avignon to persuade Pope Gregory XI to return to Rome, and in the Great Schism which followed his death, she urged support for Urban VI. She looked for a Church renewed in holiness ('The only desire of God is our sanctification'), united under the pope. Many of her letters survive, as does the *Dialogo* (tr. F. Noffke, 1980), a spiritual work in which she relates contemplation and action. She was canonized in 1461 and made a Doctor of the Church in 1970; feast day 29 Apr. (30 Apr. until 1969). Raymond of Capua's *Life* was translated by C. Kearns, 1980.

Catherine wheel: see CATHERINE OF ALEXANDRIA.

Catholic (Gk., *katholikos*, 'universal'). A term used variously with reference to Christian belief and institutions.

1. Most generally, of the *Church in the whole world, as distinct from local congregations.

2. Especially in historical writers, of the great body of Christians in communion with the major sees and not divided by *heresy or *schism.

3. Of churches, institutions, and doctrines which claim as their basis a continuous tradition of faith and practice from the *apostles—the claim is contrasted with *Protestant appeals to the *Bible alone. See also ANGLO-CATHOLICS.

4. As a synonym for *Roman Catholic; it then applies to all churches, including the *Uniat churches, in communion with the bishop of Rome. See also OLD CATHOLICS.

Catholic Action. The organization of non-clerical members of the *Roman Catholic Church for apostolic action. It was defined by Pius XI in 1922 as 'the participation of laymen in the hierarchical apostolate'.

Catholic Apostolic Church. A Christian denomination founded in 1832 by followers of Edward Irving, and so also called Irvingites. Irving was a Church of Scotland pastor (expelled in 1833) and exponent of *millennarianism and of the gift of tongues (*glossolalia). The new church sought to re-establish a biblical church order with 'apostles', 'prophets', and 'evangelists', as well as, later, a local ministry of 'angels' (bishops), priests, and deacons. The substantial church built in Gordon Square, London (1853) became the Anglican chaplaincy to Univ. of London. See also NEW APOSTOLIC CHURCH.

Catholic Israel (Jewish ecumenical concept): see KENESET YISRAEL.

Catholikos (Gk., *katholikos*). A title of the *patriarchs of the *Church of the East, the *Armenian Orthodox Church, and the *Georgian Church.

Caussade, J. P. de (1675–1751). French *Jesuit and ascetic writer. His principal work is *Abandonment to the Divine Providence*. His teaching can be crystallized in his phrase 'the sacrament of the present moment', through which our will is to be united to God's at every moment through abandonment to, and trust in, God.

Cavasilas, Nikolaos, St (*c.*1320–95). Greek theologian and mystical writer in the Orthodox Church. He wrote *An Exposition of the Divine Liturgy* and *Life in Christ*, both of which exerted an influence long after his death. In the former he makes the worship on earth an anticipation of the worship in heaven; the connection is real, since the participation in the *sacraments is not merely symbolic. In the latter, the incarnate life of Christ is continued into the lives of the faithful through the sacraments, leading into union with God. He was canonized in 1983; feast day, 20 June.

Cave of Machpelah (burial place, Jewish): see MACHPELAH, CAVE OF.

Caves of a thousand Buddhas: see TANHUANG.

Cayce, Edgar (1877–1945). The 'Sleeping Prophet', an American psychic healer and clairvoyant. For the last thirty or so years of his life, Cayce gave some 14,000 'readings' throughout the USA. He saw his gifts as spiritual in origin, and used them to aid those 'who seek to know better their relationship to their Maker'.

Cecilia, St (2nd–3rd cent.). A perhaps legendary virgin martyr of the Roman church. Her *Acts* date from the 5th cent., and she is unknown to earlier writers. Since the 16th cent. she has been best known as patron saint of music and musicians. Feast day, 22 Nov.

Celā or **ceṭa.** A student, especially in relation to a *guru, of whom complete trust and acceptance is required.

CELAM (Episcopal Conferences): see LIBERATION THEOLOGY.

Celestial Buddhas. Those Buddhas, or those manifestations of the one buddha-nature, who appear in the *trikāya forms of manifestation, in the *sambhoga-kāya. They are accompanied by *bodhisattvas. They are prolific in number. Major celestial Buddhas are Amitābha/ *Amida, *Akṣobhya, *Vairocana, *Ratnasaṃbhava, *Amoghasiddhi, and various Buddhas associated with *Vajrayāna. In *Tantric Buddhism, there are also terrifying or *wrathful Buddhas, e.g. *Heruka, Hevajra, and Śaṃvara.

Celestial Kings (Skt. *devarāja*; Chin., *t'ien-wang*; Jap., *shi-tenno*). The four world protectors in Buddhism. They dwell on Mount *Meru and guard the four quarters of the world. Images of the Celestial Kings are widespread in China and Japan, and few monasteries are without them.

Celestial Master (founder of Taoist school of Wu-tou-mi): see CHANG TAO-LING; WU-TOU-MI TAO.

Celestial Master School (Taoist): see WU-TOU-MI TAO.

Celibacy. A state of life without marriage, undertaken for religious or spiritual reasons. Celibacy was not practised among the Jews.

In Christianity, celibacy rests on the demand for the renunciation of family ties 'for the sake of the kingdom' (Mark 10. 29, Luke 18. 29). In the early church, it was an individual vocation. In the Eastern Orthodox church, the norm became one of unmarried bishops; other clergy could be married. In the West, celibacy was increasingly imposed, until from the time of Pope Gregory VII (d. 1095) it was assumed to be the rule. The Protestant *Reformation abolished mandatory celibacy.

In other religions, celibacy may also be a permanent vocation (e.g. for Buddhist monks, *bhikṣus, unless their ordination is temporary), or it may be a temporary stage (e.g. the fourth *āśrama for Hindus). It may be tolerated, as it is among Sikhs, though regarded as less than ideal.

Celsus (2nd cent.). Philosopher and opponent of Christianity. His *True Discourse* (*c.*178) is largely quoted in *Origen's reply *Against Celsus* (mid-3rd cent.).

Celtic Church. The Christian Church in parts of Britain before the arrival of St *Augustine from Rome in 596–7. Its early history is uncertain, but it was sufficiently organized to send delegates to the Synod of Arles (314). The Celtic Christians resisted the Roman Christianity of Augustine, and although agreement was reached, e.g. over the date of Easter at the Synod of Whitby (664), the conformity to Roman practice was not accepted everywhere. Celtic Christianity is marked by a kind of heroic devotion, with a simplicity of prayer and art. It was strongly *ascetical, and emphasized the importance of *anamchairdeas*, soul-friendship, and of the *anamchara*, soul-friend, for counsel in the spiritual life. Many prayers (e.g. *Loricae*, breastplate prayers, as of the one attributed to St *Patrick) have survived and are in increasingly common use today.

Cenobitic (monasticism in community): see COENOBITE.

Cerinthus. Early Christian *heretic. He seems to have been a *gnostic of *docetic tendencies.

Certain because it is impossible: see TERTULLIAN.

Ceṭa (student): see CELĀ.

Cetas (Skt.). In *Yoga, the power of consciousness. It is a general term, perhaps parallel to the *antaḥkarana* of *Sāṃkhya.

Cetasika (quality of mental experience): see CITTA.

Cetiya (earth-mound): see CAITYA.

Ch. May be spelt C; check at appropriate place (e.g. chela/cela; chaitya/caitya).

Chaddor (veil): see ḤIJĀB.

Chadō or **cha-no-yu** (Jap., 'tea-way'). Zen Buddhist way to overcome ordinary consciousness, in which entities are differentiated, in themselves, or in subject–object distinctions. The translation 'tea-ceremony' is thus misleading if it implies a ritual involving tea, although its actions and context are highly formalized. Like other forms of Zen practice in the aesthetic domain (e.g. flower-way—not flower-arranging, *kado*, *ikebana), it is a means of mind-realization of the single buddha-nature (*buddhatā) of all appearance. The preparation and drinking of tea (religiously) began in China, apparently for medicinal purposes (reviewed by Lu Yü in *Ch'a Ching*). Sen no Rikyū (1521–91) organized tea-drinking practices into a single system, and also instructed Hideyoshi, who became the great master of cha-no-yu.

Chai (Chin., 'fasting'). Formal fast in Taoism, especially before sacrifice. It developed into an occasion during which pupils confess their faults to their teacher or master. This may last for days. Generally, these rituals begin with the participants stepping into a designated space, dishevelled or smeared (e.g. with charcoal in *t'u-t'an chai*) to indicate penitence. They repeat the twelve vows of repentance, then confess their sins to the accompaniment of rhythmic dreams. This, combined with thrice-daily repetition and little food, produces physical and ecstatic states. Among the different Tao schools, chai ceremonies are especially important in *Ling-pao p'ai, *T'ai-ping tao, and *Wu-tou-mi tao; in these, the connection between sickness and sin is explicit, so that the repentance rituals are tied to healing expectations.

Chaitanya: see CAITANYA.

Chakugo (summary of kōan): see JAKUGO.

Chalcedon. City in Asia Minor near Constantinople and venue of the fourth ecumenical *council in 451. By drawing up a statement of faith, the so-called Chalcedonian definition, it attempted to end the controversy between *Alexandrian and *Antiochene *christologies. The strong *Monophysite party in the E. never accepted the definition, and until Islamic times repeated attempts were made by 'neo-Chalcedonians' to remove its offence without actually rescinding it. The *Oriental Orthodox churches still remain 'non-Chalcedonian'.

Chalice (Lat., *calix*, 'cup'). The vessel containing the wine at the *eucharist. Present Roman Catholic law requires a chalice to be made of strong (i.e. not breakable and not able to absorb liquid) materials, preferably those which are valued in the country of use.

'Cham (Tibetan ritual drama): see MUSIC.

Chamār. An untouchable *caste of leather-workers common in N. and Central India.

Champa (heavenly Buddha): see MAITREYA.

Ch'an. Chin. for Jap., *Zen.

Chānaṇī (Pañjābī, 'canopy'). Decorative awning. In some *gurdwārās a large square of cloth is suspended over the *Ādi Granth in lieu of a wooden canopy (*pālkī*).

Chancellor. An administrative officer in a Christian diocese.

Chandogya Upaniṣad. One of the earlier *Upaniṣads, attached to the Sāmaveda. It includes the dialogue between Uddālaka Āruni and his son Śvetaketu, in which the teaching on the way in which *Brahman, the Absolute, permeates the universe, culminates in the focal (*mahāvakya) sentence, *tat tvam asi*, That thou art.

Ch'ang (Chin., 'enduring'). The permanent and eternal in Taoism, as opposed to the transient and mutable, and as such, one of the symbols of Taoism.

Ch'ang-an. Chinese capital of the Former Han (202 BCE to 9 CE) and Sui-t'ang (590–906 CE) dynasties. The present city on the site is *Sian (Xian).

Chang Chüeh (d. 184 CE). Founder of the Taoist school of *T'ai-p'ing tao (the way of supreme peace). He attracted a huge following, and led the Yellow Turban rebellion, so-called from the yellow cloth (*huang-chin*) worn by his followers. The rebellion was suppressed and Chang Chüeh was killed.

Chang Hsien (Chin., 'Chang the Immortal'). The immortal (*hsien) figure who protects children and bestows male offspring.

Chang Hsiu. Founder of a Taoist movement much like the *wu-tou-mi tao of *Chang Lu—who murdered him in 190 CE. The emphasis was on healing accompanied by sacrifices to the Three Rulers (*san-kuan): Earth, Water, and Heaven.

Chang Kuo-lao (one of eight Immortals): see PA-HSIEN.

Chang Ling (founder of Taoist school of wu-tou-mi): see CHANG TAO-LING.

Chang Lu. One of the secondary founder members, in the 2nd/3rd cent. CE, of the Taoist movement, *wu-tou-mi tao. With the help of *Chang Hsiu (whom he then removed), he established a strictly governed religious state in N. Szechwan. He took further the organization of the 'Celestial Master's Way', introducing the *tao-shih (often translated as 'the Taoist priest'), with a local temple and a hierarchy leading up to the T'ien-shih. The 'five pecks of rice' was also extended into a more extensive system of fees, enabling the pervasive presence of the tao-shih in Chinese society—and the survival of religious Taoism in this form down to the present, at least in Taiwan.

Chang Po-tuan (practitioner and teacher): see NEI-TAN.

Chang San-feng. Taoist immortal and source of *Ch'üan-chen tao; he is also said to be the founder of a school of Chinese boxing.

Ch'ang-sha Ching-ts'en (d. 868). Chinese Ch'an Buddhist master. He had no set school or monastery, but wandered in China, allowing his teaching to arise from whatever he encountered.

Ch'ang-sheng Pu-ssu (Chin., 'long-lasting', 'immortal'). The goal of Taoism in many of its practices. Initially, Taoism was concerned with literal and physical immortality (see ALCHEMY), which involved the quest for substances and exercises which might produce this (e.g. *tao-yin* (see GYMNASTICS), *fang-chung shu). The attainer of immortality (*hsien) ascends to heaven (*fei-sheng) visibly, or else seems to die and is buried, but when the coffin is opened, it is found to be empty.

The more reflective Taoism of *Lao-tzu or of *Chuang-tzu regarded spiritual immortality as more important—and indeed as alone attainable.

Many symbols of immortality appear in Chinese art under Taoist influence. Particularly frequent are peaches (cultivated by *Hsi Wang mu), the herb or mushroom of immortality (*ling-chih*), a crane (often holding the *ling-chih*), pine trees, a gnarled stick of wood.

Chang Tao-ling or **Chang Ling** (2nd cent. CE). Founder of the Taoist school of *wu-tou-mi tao, which emphasized the connection between sin and suffering, and which introduced repentance and healing ceremonies (see CHAI), for which were required payment of five pecks of rice—hence the name for the school. The movement was further organized and developed by *Chang Hsiu and *Chang Lu. After his death, he has continued to be revered as the Celestial Master (religiously as Chang T'ien Shih) down to the present day.

Chang T'ien Shih (Celestial Master): see CHANG TAO-LING.

Ch'an-na. Chin. for *dhyāna.

Channing, William Ellery (1780–1842). American Christian pastor, originally a *Congregationalist: in the schism between conservatives and liberals, Channing espoused the liberals, rejecting the *Trinity and the radical consequence of *original sin. He is thus regarded as a leading *Unitarian thinker, but he said that he belonged only to 'the community of free minds'. He supported social reform, though not at first the abolition of slavery. Rebuked for this, he published *Slavery* (1835), which became a key text for the opponents of slavery.

Cha-no-yu (way of tea): see CHADŌ.

Chantry. Provision (Christian) made for the saying (or singing) of *mass for the souls of the dead, especially for the one making the endowment, but also for family and friends. The term thus applies to the endowment and the office, and also on occasion (if the bequest was large enough) to the chapel in which the masses were said.

Ch'an-tsung (Jap., *zenshu*, literally 'the Ch'an school'). By this term, the different routes or paths in Zen Buddhism are recognized. For details, see BUDDHIST SCHOOLS.

Chao-chou Ts'ung-shen or **Jōshū Jūshin** (778–897). Leading Ch'an/*Zen master in China. He had a profound experience of enlightenment when he was 18, which simply indicated to him that there was a way worth pursuing further (i.e. enlightenment is not an end, but a step on a path).

Chao-chou was especially important in showing how Ch'an and *Tao relate together, opening the way to creative coexistence. His enlightenment is known as *funi daidō*, 'the nonduality of the great Tao'—which is a near synonym for the buddha-nature empty of self and differentiation.

Chaos. The primordial condition from which (or onto which) order is imposed, according to many religions, so that the cosmos can appear.

Chapter. The members of a Christian religious community or of any similar body. From the 9th cent. cathedrals often had separate 'chapter houses'.

Charan pāhul (Pañjābī, 'foot-initiation'). Hindu initiation ritual continued by Sikh *Gurūs. Gurū *Gobind Siṅgh replaced charan pāhul with *khaṇḍe-dī-pāhul, initiation with the *khaṇḍā on *Baisākhī day 1699. See also AMRIT.

Chardin (French Jesuit theologian): see TEILHARD DE CHARDIN.

Chariot (of God, in Ezekiel's vision): see MERKABAH MYSTICISM.

Charismatic (movement). Christian belief that the *Holy Spirit imparts particular gifts and inspiration, which have visible and internally recognizable consequences. This movement of the Holy Spirit in the historic denominations was characterized by experience of *'baptism in the Holy Spirit' or 'second baptism' and by a new informality in *liturgical worship, anticipation of the Second Coming of Christ, and renewed emphasis on the present reality of the gifts of the Spirit, especially *healing, *prophecy, and speaking in tongues (*glossolalia).

Charismatic authority. Type of leadership, not confined to religions, exercised by gifted individuals. It was defined by *Weber as 'a certain quality of an individual personality, by virtue of which he is considered as extraordinary and treated as endowed with supernatural, superhuman, or at least exceptional powers or qualities'.

Charity (Lat., *caritas*; Gk., *charis*). An openness and generosity to others, especially in the support of those in need. (see also ALMSGIVING). In Judaism, the nearest Heb. word to express this concept is *ẓedekah*, linked to *ẓedek*, justice. In contrast to the wider *gemilut ḥasadim* ('acts of loving-kindness'), *ẓedekah* involves the obligation to give to the poor.

In Christianity, charity came in English to be associated with the deeply characteristic virtue of *agape, through the Authorized Version translation of 1 Corinthians 13: 'Though I speak with the tongues of men and of angels, and have not charity, I am become as sounding brass, or a tinkling cymbal .... And now abideth faith, hope, charity, these three; but the greatest of these is charity.'

In Islam, charity is formalized through *zakāt, but generosity (*sadaqāt*) to those in need is meritorious, as are other gifts to support religious purposes (see WAQF).

In Hinduism, the nearest equivalents to charity lie in the obligations of *dharma: acts of charity will lead to good *karma. In Buddhism, the alleviation of *dukkha (suffering) is equally indispensable for progress toward the ultimate goal. In *dāna, a mutual structure of support is established between laypeople and the *saṅgha (community of monks).

Charms and amulets. These are universal, in all religions, even those where they might be expected to compromise trust in God alone. In Judaism, an amulet might seem to come close to breaking the command against graven images. Yet so many charms were excavated from the rabbinic period that it almost seemed to some that they were observing an alternative Judaism. Amulets (Heb., *kemea*) continued as a part of Judaism, worn round the neck or attached to a wall. They may be to protect against devils, thieves, or enemies, to obtain love, wisdom, or an easy childbirth.

In Islam amulets (Arab., *ḥijab*, *ḥamā'il*; in W. Africa *gri gri*) are permitted in *ḥadīth, and are used everywhere in the Muslim world, cf. also HAND OF FĀṬIMA.

In other religions, amulets are equally common and less surprising. Thus in Hinduism, the way in which all appearance is permeated by the spiritual and the divine makes the amulet (Skt., *rakṣa*; from *rakṣ*, 'guard, protect') entirely natural.

Amulets are an equally indispensable part of Chinese folk religion. Frequently pasted over doorways, they may also be worn, or else burnt, with the ashes being used to make a medicinal paste or drink.

Charoset (Jewish food): see ḤAROSET.

Charvaka (school of Indian materialism): see CĀRVĀKA.

Chasidim (members of Jewish devotional movement): see ḤASIDIM.

Chasuble. The outermost vestment, usually richly decorated, worn by the celebrant at the Christian *eucharist.

Chaturvarga-chintāmaṇī: see HÉMĀDRĪ.

Chaupad (Pañjābī, 'Four stanzas'). A poem of four stanzas. In the *Ādi Granth, the Gurūs' chaupads, plus some *hymns of two, three, five, and six stanzas, are grouped first in each *rāg, followed by the *aṣṭapadīs.

Chaupaī (Pañjābī, 'verse of four lines'). Sikh hymn; specifically, the Bentī Chaupaī or hymn of supplication, a composition of Gurū *Gobind Siṅgh.

Chaur(ī). Indian symbol of authority, now typically Sikh. A chaurī is a ceremonial whisk made of the tail hair of a white horse or yak embedded in a wooden or silver handle.

Cheese Sunday. Amongst Greek Orthodox Christians, the last Sunday before *Lent on which cheese and eggs may be eaten. It is also known as Forgiveness Sunday.

Ch'eng (sincerity): see CHUNG YUNG.

Ch'eng-chu (Chinese philosopher): see CHU HSI.

Ch'eng Hao, also **Ming-tao** (1032–85). Brother of Ch'eng Yi (or I, also I-ch'uan, 1033–1107), with whom he formed the neo-Confucianism of the Sung dynasty. Both of them opposed the far-reaching reform programme of Wang An-shih (Wang Anshi) (1021–86): Ch'eng Hao was dismissed in 1080 and went into retirement in Lo-yang; Cheng Yi was not in an official post until 1086. In Ch'eng Hao's view, human nature does not change from one age to another, so that reform must be, not to innovate, but to recover 'the laws established by the wise kings of old'.

Ch'eng Yi, in contrast, believed that true insight can be achieved only by the minute analysis of all things, in order to discover their fundamental constitution and thus the part that each plays in the whole.

Ch'eng-huang. Chinese gods who protect a city, and who guide the souls (*hun, *p'o) of the dead out of torment.

Ch'eng I: see CH'ENG HAO.

Cheng-i tao (Chin., Tao of unity). The collective term for Taoist schools who use *fu-lu (talismans) or amulets (*charms).

Cheng-kuan (teacher in Hua-yen Buddhism): see HUA-YEN.

Ch'eng-shih (Chinese school): see SAUTRĀNTIKAS.

Cheng-yi (Taoist movement): see WU-TOU-MI TAO.

Ch'eng Yi: see CH'ENG HAO.

Chen jen (Chin., 'perfected' or 'true man'). A term used by both Buddhists and Taoists in China to denote a person who has achieved the highest religious ideal.

Chenrezi (bodhisattva): see AVALOKITEŚVARA.

Ch'en T'uan (10th cent. CE). Taoist scholar of both outer and inner *alchemy, who lived on Mount Hua-shan as a hermit. On the face of the rock he carved the diagram of the supreme emptying, (*wu-ch'i-tu*). He is also reputed to have originated the other diagram of great importance to neo-Confucians, the diagram of the immortal heaven (*hsien-t'ien-tu*).

Chen-yen (Chinese Esoteric Buddhism): see BUDDHISM IN CHINA; SHINGON.

Cherub (from Heb., *keruv*). A winged heavenly creature.

Cherubic hymn or **Cherubikon.** The hymn, probably of the 6th cent., sung at the *Great Entrance in the Orthodox liturgy.

Chhant (Pañjābī, 'poem, song'). In the *Ādi Granth, the chhants are *hymns between a *chaupad and an *aṣṭapadī in length, i.e. usually four stanzas of six lines. Within each *rāg the chhants follow the aṣṭapadīs and precede the *vārs.

Ch'i (Chin., 'air, breath, strength'). The vital energy (in Chinese religion, medicine and philosophy) which pervades and enables all things. 'Nourishing the life spirit' (*yang ch'i*) by a variety of exercises, including diet, *breath control, and sexual control, became pervasive. It is thus closely associated with *yüan-ch'i and *nei-ch'i*. It is gathered in the human body in the 'ocean of breath' (*ch'i-hai*) just below the navel, where it must be carefully fostered, especially through breathing practices, above all *hsing-ch'i*, which allows the breath/energy to permeate the whole body, by imagining the breath as a visible line or lines moving through the body; or *t'ai-hsi* which reverts one's breathing to that of an embryo or foetus in the womb, and which, by transferring ordinary breathing (outer ch'i or *wai-ch'i*) to dependent but directed breathing, is powerful in leading to cures and immortality (see ALCHEMY). Medically, ch'i was developed into the exercises of *ch'i-kung*, also known as outer exercises (*wai-kung*). See also FU-CH'I; LIEN-CH'I; T'IAO-CH'I; YEN CH'I.

Chiang-I (Taoist ritual dress): see HABIT, RELIGIOUS.

Chiang Kai-shek (1887–1975). Military and political leader of the Chinese Kuomintang party and the Nationalist government on mainland China and Taiwan. Chiang Kai-shek promoted in 1934 the New Life Movement, which emphasized cardinal virtues both of the Confucian tradition and of the Christian faith, to which he had converted. The success of Mao's Red Army forced Chiang in 1949 to flee for refuge to the island of Taiwan.

Chiao (teaching): see CHINESE RELIGION.

Chiao (Chin., 'sacrifice'). Originally a wine offering (or 'toast') at the coming of age of a son, or at a wedding. Later it became a more general ritual offering among Taoists for a wide range of purposes (e.g. to ward off illness, to protect from fire, to bring peace or to procure blessings).

Chicago-Lambeth Quadrilateral (basis for ecumenicism): see ANGLICANISM.

Chief Khālsā Dīwān. Religio-political Sikh association, Amritsar, established in 1902.

Chief Rabbi. Central religious authority among Jews for a region.

Ch'ieh-lan, abbreviation of *ch'ieh-lan shen*, spirits of the *ch'ieh-lan* (monastic premises; Sanskrit: *saṅghārāma*). As tutelary deities of Chinese Buddhist monasteries, these spirits received prayers at appointed times of the day, and sometimes had shrines or halls dedicated to them within the monastery grounds. Best known among them was Kuan Kung, the red-faced god of war.

Chien ai (universal love): see JEN.

Chien-chen (Chinese Buddhist master): see GANJIN.

Ch'ien tzu wen (Chin., 'Thousand-Character Text'). An important Chinese primer for children written by Chou Hsing-te in the 6th cent. CE.

Chigū (Jap., 'rare encounter'). An encounter with a *buddha or with the *Buddha's teaching.

Chih (Cardinal virtue in Confucianism): see WU-CH'ANG.

Ch'i-hai (ocean of breath): see CH'I.

Chih-i or **Chih-che** (538–97). The third patriarch, but in effect founder, of the *T'ien-t'ai Buddhist school in China (his Jap. name is Chigi Chisha). In 576 he withdrew to Mount T'ien-t'ai (hence the name of the school), where his fame attracted to him the title 'man of wisdom', *chih-che*. He completed the first organized system of Buddhist teaching in China, and developed the practice of *chih-kuan (Jap. *shikan*), as extensively practised still as his works on meditation are widely read: e.g. *Liu-miao famen* (The Six Marvellous Gates of Dharma), *T'ung-meng chih-kuan* (Chih-Kuan for Beginners).

Chih-kuan (Skt., śamatha-*vipaśyanā; Jap., *shikan*). Meditation methods in the *T'ien-t'ai Buddhist school. 'Chih' is the calming of the restless and distracted mind; 'Kuan' is the insight which then arises.

Chih-tun or **Chih Tao-lin** (314–66). Founder of the Prajña (wisdom) School of Chinese Buddhism. His particular importance was his adaptation of Chinese concepts in a Buddhist direction, thereby enabling the rapid assimilation of Buddhism into China.

Chijang. Korean for *Kṣitigarbha.

Chijō tengoku (heaven on earth): see SEKAI KYŪSEIKYŌ.

Chikamatsu Monzaemon (1653–1724). Playwright for the Kabuki theatre and puppet theatre (Jap., *ningyō jōruri* or *bunraku*), generally regarded as Japan's greatest dramatist. The plays are deeply imbued with the teachings of both Confucianism and Buddhism. Most of Chikamatsu's characters are also followers of *Pure Land Buddhism.

Ch'i-kung (breathing exercises): see CH'I.

Children of God or **The Family.** A *cult founded in California in 1968 by David Berg (1919–94), who assumed the name David, and became known to his followers as Mo. The movement established a number of communes in the USA before moving to London in 1971. According to The Family, humanity is now living in the last days and the signs of the Second Coming of *Jesus are evident: the destruction of the materialistic culture of capitalism will follow that of communism (predicted by Mo), to be replaced with a 'godly socialism', with an emphasis (borrowed from *Acts) on sharing. This extends to the sharing of sexual partners, which includes the use of sex to attract new members (known as 'flirty fishing'). Reports of this led to strong opposition to The Family, which was accused also of encouraging and practising the abuse of children. However, no successful prosecutions were sustained (although children were taken into care in several countries, including Australia and France).

Chiliasm (Gk., *chilioi*, 'a thousand'). Another name for *millennialism, the theory that Christ will reign for a thousand years before the final consummation of all things.

Chimere. A silk or satin gown without sleeves worn over the rochet by *Anglican *bishops.

Ch'in (musical instrument): see MUSIC.

China and Tibet (as 'patron and priest'): see 'PHAGS-PA.

Chinese religion. Religion in China is not a single system of belief and practice. It is a complex interaction of different religious and philosophical traditions, of which four main strands (themselves by no means uniform) are particularly important: popular or folk religion (vivid with festivals, spirit-worlds, procedures in crises, and care of the dead), *Confucianism, *Taoism, and Buddhism (see BUDDHISM IN CHINA). In addition, Islam and Christianity have substantial followings in different parts of China, but they are distinguished from the others by appearing to the Chinese to require separation from the other religions/philosophies. In contrast, the Chinese in general have no problem in being entirely eclectic, being, for example, a Confucian in public life, a Taoist in the quest for immortality, a Buddhist in relation to ancestors, and dependent on folk wisdom in crisis or illness, or when buying a house. Thus religion is defined more by cultural geography than it is by bounded systems of beliefs and practices (though schools or traditions of teaching were formally organized). From *c.*1100 to 206, the Six Ways (*yin-yang sched, *Confucianism, *Mo Tzu, *Fa-chia, *Logic, and *Taoism) developed which constitute some of the main themes of Chinese religious history.

There is no exact equivalent in Chinese for the word 'religion'. *Men* means 'door', i.e. door leading to enlightenment, immortality, etc.; *tao* means 'way', and both are used. But more usual now is *chiao*, 'teaching', 'guiding doctrine' (as in *fo-chiao*, the religion of the Buddha; *ju-chiao*, the way of Confucius; *tao-chiao*, religious Taoism), usually in combination with *tsung*, 'ancestral, traditional', 'devotion, faith': *tsung-chiao*, the nearest equivalent to 'religion'.

Traditionally, religious history in China has been divided into four stages named after the seasons of spring, summer, autumn, and winter.

Chinese Rites Controversy. A dispute (18th cent.) in the Roman Catholic Church about the propriety of adopting Chinese customs and terms into Christian liturgy and vocabulary. Cf. also MALABAR RITES.

Chinese Tripiṭaka (Chin., *San-ts'ang*, 'Triple Treasury', or *Ta Ts'ang-ching*, 'Great Treasury of Scriptures'). The collection of *Buddhist scriptures in Chinese. It contains versions of most of the texts found in the Tripiṭaka with the addition of *Mahāyāna *sūtras , commentaries, histories, biographies, encyclopaedias, and even some non-Buddhist writings. The number of texts is not fixed. Various editions have appeared since the 1st printed edn. in 10th cent. CE. The most commonly used is the *Taishō Shinshū Daizōkyō* (Tokyo, 1924–9 and reprs.) containing 2,184 texts in 55 vols. In 1982 the State Council of the Peoples' Republic of China established the Chinese Tripitaka Editorial Bureau, charged with producing a new version, which is projected to contain 4,100 texts in 220 vols.

Ching (Chin., 'semen'). One of the three life forces in Taoism, the others being *ch'i (breath) and *shen (conscious mind). Ching is both semen and the menstrual flow, not so much in their literal manifestation, as in the power inherent in them.

Ch'ing-ming (Chin., 'clear and bright'). The fifth of the twenty-four periods of the Chinese solar *calendar. It is also the name of the festival which is additionally called 'the sweeping of the tombs': families sweep and tidy the graves of ancestors, offering food to them—and afterwards consuming food with them near the site.

Ch'ing-t'an (Chin., 'pure conversation'). The cultivation in China among the educated or literati or erudite and philosophical conversation. Sometimes referred to as a 'neo-Taoist school', they were in fact a tradition, embracing more than neo-Taoists (e.g. Buddhists). Among many groups, the Seven Sages of the Bamboo Grove were especially famous.

Ching-te Ch'uan-teng-lu (The Passing on of the Lamp; Jap., *Keito-ku Dentō-roku*). An early work (1004) of Ch'an/*Zen Buddhism, describing the history, via biographies, of the transmission of enlightenment, up to *Fa-yen Wen-i, founder of the *Hōgen school.

Ching-t'u (Chin., Jap. *jōdo*). *Pure Land, or the untainted transcendent realm created by the *Buddha Amitābha (*Amida) to which his devotees aspire to be born in their next lifetime. Ching-t'u Tsung is thus the Pure Land School.

Chinju (Jap., *chin*, 'to pacify' + *ju*, 'a lord': to protect). A Japanese tutelary shrine, temple, or deity.

Chin-lien (Golden Lotus): see CH'ÜAN-CHEN TAO.

Chinnamasta ('the headless'). A Tantric Hindu form of *Durgā. She is the fifth *mahāvidya who represents the end of life, especially when a sacrificial victim is beheaded. The Buddhist Tantric equivalent is Vajrayoginī, who is also depicted iconographically without a head. She is of particular importance in *abhicāra* (magic ritual) directed to the injury of enemies, or to other maleficent ends.

Chin-tan (Chin., 'golden cinnabar'). The elixir of immortality in Taoist *alchemy.

Chinul (1158–1210). Reformer of Sŏn (Ch'an/*Zen) and revitalizer of *Buddhism in Korea during the Koryŏ period (935–1392). Chinul, known also as National Teacher, Puril Pojo ('Universal Illuminator of Buddha-sun'), integrated the nine lineages ('Nine Mountains') of Sŏn Buddhism into the Chogye order and synthesized Sŏn and Hwaŏm (Hua-yen) placing primacy upon the former.

Chinzei. A school of Jōdo (*Pure Land) founded by Benchō. Of its many subsequent subdivisions, Shirahata-ryū is the strongest continuing group, often regarded as the main-line continuity of Jōdo.

Chi-Rho. The Greek letters X and P, being the first two letters of the word *Christos*, 'Christ'. It was an ancient abbreviation of the name.

Chironomy (hand gestures in cantillation): see MUSIC.

Chisha: see CHIH-I.

Chishti, Mu'īn al-Dīn Muḥammad (1142–1236 (AH 537–633)). Indian Sūfī, who mediated an important order (*tarīqa) into India. The Sūfī movement derived from him, the Chishti(y)ya, continues to make music central: it developed the *qawwāli* (singers) whose songs of love and devotion to *Allāh are a feature of holidays and festivals. He died at Ajmer, and his tomb is a celebrated place of pilgrimage.

Chishtiy(y)a: see CHISHTI.

Chi-tsang (549–623). Buddhist teacher of the *San-lun school, who wrote many commentaries on *Sūtras and *Mahāyāna texts. Of immense importance in the development of San-lun (Chin. for Mādhyamaka), Chi-tsang's pupil, Ekwan, took the San-lun school to Japan, where it is known as *Sanron.

Chöd or **gcod** (Tib., *gcod*, 'cutting'). A *meditation prominent in *Tibetan Buddhism, which is traced to the great female *yoginī Machig Labdron (*ma.gcig lab.sgron) and her teacher Father Dampa Sangye (pha.dam.pa-sangs.rgyas; equated in one legend with *Bodhidharma). The meditation is normally performed in a charnel ground or known haunted place, where the *yogin, with the aid of *mantra, hand-drum and human thigh-bone trumpet, *visualizes the cutting up of his own body and the offering of it to demons as sacrificial food.

Chödrug: see NARO CHOS DRUG.

Ch'oe Che-u (founder of Tonghak): see KOREAN RELIGION.

Chogye (Buddhist sect): see BUDDHISM IN KOREA.

Chōhōji (Japanese temple): see ROKKAKUDŌ.

Choir. Singers assisting in worship. Known in Christianity from the 4th cent., they customarily sang the music which was too difficult for the congregation.

Choka (Jap., 'morning part'). The Zen Buddhist morning *sūtra recitation, part of the daily routine in a Zen monastery (*tera).

Cholent ('stew'). Traditionally a Jewish housewife would prepare cholent in advance and put it in the oven before the *Sabbath began. It cooked slowly overnight and thus provided something hot to eat on Sabbath morning without breaking the Sabbath law against kindling a light or cooking.

Ch'ŏndo-gyo or **Ch'ŏndo-kyo** (Sect of the Way of Heaven): see KOREAN RELIGION.

Chorepiscopus. In E. churches, a minister intermediate in rank between *priest and *bishop. In modern times it is practically an honorary title.

Chōrō (Jap., 'elder'). A title of respect for a senior monk, and in *Zen for the head of a temple.

Chorten (*mchod.rten*, 'receptacle of offerings'). The Tibetan development of the Indian Buddhist *stūpa. The chorten is similar in function to the stūpa as a receptacle for the remains of a holy person and as a shrine containing texts, images, etc., but differs in its architectural development.

Along with the two types of stūpa common in India—the basic form and the form with a raised walkway (which in Tibet is usually too narrow to be anything more than symbolic)—a chorten comprising an archway may be found at the entrance to a city, and the uniquely Tibetan Multiple Door (*sgo.mang*) chorten is especially prolific.

Chōsan (Jap., 'morning devotion'). The *zazen (meditation) with which each day begins in a Zen monastery (*tera).

Chos drug (Kagyu teaching): see NĀRO CHOS DRUG.

Chosen people. A designation for the Jewish people, though also used of groups or people in other religions who have a strong sense of election. Despite the Christian claim that the Jews had forfeited the right to be the true Israel, through centuries of persecution the idea of election persisted. The doctrine of chosenness has been caricatured by *anti-Semites, who argued that it was the basis of the world conspiracy for Jewish domination. In the 19th and 20th cents., many Jews have become uneasy with the concept, and the *Reconstructionists in particular have eliminated all references to it in their liturgy.

Chöten: see CHORTEN.

Chou. Chin. for *mantra.

Chou Tun-(y)i, also **Chou Lien-ch'i** (1017–73). *Neo-Confucian scholar, who reordered Confucian cosmogony. Creating a sequential process from *t'ai-chi, he accounted for the proliferation of appearance from one unproduced producer.

Chrism (Gk., *chrisma*, from *chriō*, 'anoint'). A mixture of olive oil and balsam used in Catholic and (with other ingredients, including wine, nuts, and gum) Orthodox churches. It is used in anointings at *baptism, *confirmation, and *ordination, and at other consecrations (but not in the anointing of the sick: see UNCTION).

Christ (*christos*, 'anointed one'). The Gk. translation of Heb., *māshiach*: Messiah. Applied to *Jesus it was originally a title (John 7. 41, Acts 3. 20), but the forms 'Christ Jesus', 'Jesus Christ', and 'Christ' very soon became used indifferently by Christians as proper names.

Christadelphians. Christian denomination founded by John Thomas (1805–71), a physician in Richmond, Virginia, who broke away from the Christian Church of Alexander *Campbell in 1844. The name Christadelphians ('Christ's brethren') reflects Thomas's claim to return to the beliefs and practice of the earliest disciples. Christadelphians take no part in politics, voting, or military service.

Christian Fellowship Church or **Etoism.** The main independent church in Melanesia, founded on New Georgia in the Solomon Islands in 1959 by Silas Eto (b. 1905). As a *catechist-teacher in the *Methodist mission, he developed deviationist practices from the 1930s, and, in disillusionment with staid mission forms, began his own true church. Despite incipient *messianism concerning Eto himself, relations with Methodists, now in the United Church, were being re-established in the 1970s.

Christianity. The origins of Christianity lie, historically, in the life and ministry of *Jesus, extended through his death, *resurrection, and *ascension.

Christianity exists in a vast diversity of different styles and forms of organization, but all are agreed that the figure of Jesus is the disclosure of God and the means of human reconciliation with him.

In the early years, 'Christianity' was one interpretation, among many at that time, of what God's covenant with Israel and his purpose in creation should be; but in this interpretation, it was believed that Jesus was the promised *messiah (Heb., *ha-Mashiach* = messiah = Gk., *ho Christos*, hence the name 'Christianity', which was first used, according to Acts 2. 26, in *c.*40 CE).

Characteristic Christian doctrines emerged from the demand of the New Testament evidence (and from the experience which brought it into being). Jesus mediated the consequence and effect of God, so that on the one hand it was evidently God who was acting and speaking in and through him, and yet on the other it was clear that Jesus addressed God (e.g. in prayer) as apart from himself, as Father (see ABBA): this produced a quest in the early centuries to find ways of speaking of these two natures in one person (*Christology). At the same time, God was clearly present to the life of Jesus (e.g. at his birth and his baptism, and in the directing of his mission), in the ways traditionally spoken of as the *Holy Spirit. This led to a further quest to find ways of speaking of the interior nature of God, as being in itself, not an abstract unity, but social and relational (i.e. as *Trinity).

It was also recognized that what Jesus had done during his life for some particular people, in reconciling them to God when they had become estranged from him and from each other, was, as a consequence of his death, resurrection, and ascension, extended to others, and indeed made universal, at least as an opportunity for those who respond in faith. This led to doctrines of *atonement.

This extension of the consequence of Christ was made immediately realistic, and thus realizable, through the enacted signs of *baptism and of the *last supper (*eucharist).

During the New Testament period, the nature of Christian community (the Church) changed dramatically: the original metaphor of the Church as the Body of Christ, with all parts being of equal importance under the headship of Christ, was changed into a metaphor derived from the Roman army, with a hierarchical organization and vertical levels of authority of *bishops, *priests, and *deacons: the clericalization of the Church and the subordination of the *laity have remained characteristic of most parts of Christianity down to the present. After the support of *Constantine and the recognition of Christianity as the religion of the Empire under Theodosius I (emperor, 379–95), Christianity became the major religion of the Roman world.

Faith and practice were constantly disputed and contested, leading to a series of *Councils in which attempts were made to achieve unity and conformity. Creeds developed from baptismal formulae (which served as 'passwords') to summaries of approved and legitimized faith. But major divisions emerged, some of which (e.g. Monophysites) persist as continuing Churches to the present. Especially serious was the schism between E. and W. Christianity. Despite attempts at repair, the *Orthodox (i.e. E.) Church (itself comprising several different traditions, disciplines, and practices) remains resistant to the claims of the bishop of Rome (the pope) to teaching and jurisdictional authority. W. Christianity was disrupted by the *Reformation, with the Reformed Churches dividing further, and repeatedly, on issues of doctrine and practice.

The early involvement of Christianity with the Roman Empire led to the development of a religious life which was deliberately separated from the world. It began with the *desert fathers and spread across the known world. It eventually found expression in the *monastic orders, notably that of St *Benedict, and it gained its evangelical outreach in the *religious orders of the 13th cent. onward.

Throughout its history, the Christian quest to share the good news (*gospel) of Christ has produced an emphasis on *mission, especially in the 19th cent., 'the century of mission', culminating in the Edinburgh Conference, 1910. As a result, Christianity is found in all parts of the world, and makes up more than a quarter of the world's population.

Liturgically, Christians follow the life, death, resurrection, and ascension of Jesus throughout each year, marking particular days as *festivals, and celebrating also those who have been exemplary in faith and practice (*saints). The practices of *prayer (in its many forms) and worship are fundamental in Christian life.

Vital also is the fact that Christian life should be the manifestation of a pervasive quality of love (*agape). From this has arisen the recent view that *orthopraxy is at least as important as orthodoxy (perhaps more so): see LIBERATION THEOLOGY. It is this stress on the transformation of human life into love which has led through the centuries to the founding of schools and hospitals, and to the care of the poor, and to the recognition of such people as *Francis of Assisi as exemplary.

Christian Science. The Church of Christ (Scientist) was founded by Mary Baker Eddy (1821–1910). She had been a semi-invalid who, in 1862, began to learn from Phineas Quimby the possibility of cures without medicine. In 1866 (the year in which Quimby died), she claimed a cure from a severe injury (after a fall on ice) without the intervention of medicine. She devoted herself to the recovery of the healing emphasis in early Christianity, and in 1875 she completed the 1st edn. of *Science and Health with Key to the Scriptures*. In 1879, the Church of Christ (Scientist) was incorporated with the purpose of 'commemorating the word and works of our Master'. She became chief pastor of the Mother Church, and wrote *The Manual of the Mother Church* to govern its affairs.

Christian Socialists and **Christian Socialism.** A group led by F. D. *Maurice, and including Charles Kingsley, which rejected *laissez-faire* economics and competition as conforming to the will of God, and envisaged instead a kind of 'organic' society, in which co-operative societies and education would reduce poverty and class hostility. The group published pamphlets and set up co-operatives (which failed), and it only lasted from 1848 to 1854.

Christians of St John (name given to the Mandeans): see MANDEANS.

Christmas. The Christian feast of Jesus' birth, celebrated on 25 Dec. Its observance is first attested in Rome in 336. Probably the date was chosen to oppose the feast of the 'birthday of the unconquered sun' on the winter solstice. In the E. the date 6 Jan. for the nativity generally gave way to 25 Dec. by the 5th cent., although at Jerusalem the older custom was kept until 549 and the *Armenian Church still observes it (see also EPIPHANY).

Christology (Gk., *christos*, *Christ, + *logos*, 'reflection'). The attempt in Christianity to account for the relation of *Jesus to God, especially in his own nature and person. From the outset, New Testament writers related Jesus so closely to God that he could be seen as the initiative of God in seeking and saving that which was lost, even to the extent of being the manifestation of God so far as that can be seen or conveyed in human form. This led inevitably to questions of how the being of God is related to the humanity of Jesus in such a way that both are truly contained and present in one person.

The answers given to those questions are necessarily speculative. They range across a spectrum (in the history of the Church) from a view that he was a remarkable teacher and healer who was promoted by the faith of the early Christians into God, to the view that the pre-existent Son is God as God always is, and that the eternal and unchanging nature of God was truly present to the humanity of Jesus, both as co-agent of his activity and subject of his experience, without the humanity being obliterated or the divine nature compromised. The former are known as *Euhemeristic or Adoptionist Christologies (see e.g. ARIUS). The latter culminated in the *Chalcedonian definition, which sees the person of Jesus as (in the words of *Aquinas) *instrumentum coniunctum divinitatis*, the conjoined instrument of the Godhead. See Index, Christology.

Christus Victor. Christ as victor: Christian belief that *Jesus as Christ overcame all powers of evil and the devil.

Chronicles, Book of (Heb., *divre ha-yamim*). Historical book (now generally divided into two books) in the Hebrew *Bible. The Gk. title is *Paraleipomena* ('things left over', *sc.* from Samuel and Kings), but the work is more of a *midrash on those books, having affinities with Ezra and Nehemiah.

Chronology: see CALENDAR.

Chrysostom, John, St (*c.*347–407). Bishop of Constantinople and *Doctor of the Church. He served as priest at Antioch from 386, where his great powers of oratory (the name Chrysostom means 'golden-mouthed', more often expressed as 'golden-tongued', whence 'silver-tongued Smith', of the 16th-cent. preacher Henry Smith) were directed against moral and paganizing lapses in the nominally Christian city. Feast day in the W., 13 Sept.; in the E., 13 Nov.

The Liturgy of St Chrysostom has been, since the 13th cent., the *eucharistic liturgy in general use in the Orthodox Church, except on the few days for which that of *Basil is prescribed.

Chthonian religion (Gk., *chthon*, 'earth'). Religions and religious practices which are concerned with the gods and goddesses or life forces of the earth—in contrast to Olympian religion, which has to do with the gods and goddesses on high.

Chu. Korean for *mantra.

Ch'üan-chen tao (Chin., 'way of realizing truth'). A major form of religious Taoism also known as Pure Yang (*chung-yang*) and Golden Lotus (*chin-lien*). The school was founded by Wang Ch'un-yang (1112–70 CE). The objective for every disciple is to realize Tao in experience, by understanding his own nature and mind in relation to Tao. To this end he drew on classic sources (e.g. *Prajñāpāramitā Sūtra*, outer *alchemy and inner *nei-tan), but also on sources outside the Taoist tradition, especially *Zen Buddhism, and to some extent *Confucianism. His system is thus eclectic. Of several movements derived from Ch'üan-chen tao, the most important (or at least enduring) has been Lung-men, the Dragon Gate school, with its monastery at *Pai-yün kuan.

Chuang-tzu, also **Chuang chou** (*tzu* means 'master', *c.*370–286 BCE). Considered by Taoists to be (with *Lao-tzu) one of the founders of philosophical Taoism.

He is traditionally the author of the work bearing his name, *Chuang-tzu* (or *Nan-hua chen-ching*). Of its thirty-three chapters, 1–7 (the 'inner books') are perhaps his own, the fifteen 'outer' and eleven 'mixed' chapters are thought to be by his pupils. As with Lao-tzu, the *Tao and its *te are open to realization by all people. It requires well-directed and unattached action (*wu-wei) and meditative concentration on the constantly changing nature of the world, which, when realized and discarded, leaves only the Tao.

Wisdom consists in recognizing distinction and perceiving the relation:

Chuang Chou dreamed that he was a butterfly, fluttering about, not knowing that it was Chuang Chou. He woke with a start, and was Chuang Chou again. But he did not know whether he was Chuang Chou who had dreamed that he was a butterfly, or a butterfly dreaming that he was Chuang Chou. Between Chuang Chou and the butterfly there must be some distinction: this is what is called, 'the transformation of things'.

Chu Hsi (1130–1200). Chinese philosopher, who developed the analysis of neo-Confucian concepts, accepting influence from both Buddhism and Taoism, in a form which persisted to the 20th cent. Since he attended closely to the work of his predecessor, Ch'eng Yi (see CH'ENG HAO), his school is often known as that—i.e Ch'eng-chu, though also as 'the school of principle', Li-hsüeh. In practical terms, he did much to establish the Four Classics as the basis of education. He wrote commentaries on the *Confucian Classics, insisting on a realism in the pursuit of *jen (true humanity) which he contrasted with Buddhism. He is therefore often held to be the beginning of positivistic or scientific method in Chinese thought.

Chu-hung (1535–1615). A Chinese monk who combined *Zen and *Pure Land Buddhism to produce a practical path for lay Buddhists. He developed a way in which nembutsu, meditation on a *kōan, and a disciplined life, all reinforce each other, without any necessity for entering the saṅgha.

Chūin or **chūu** (intermediate state): see ANTARĀ-BHAVA.

Chū Kokushi (Ch'an/Zen master): see NAN-YANG HUI-CHUNG.

Ch'un Ch'iu. The *Springs and Autumns*, one of the *Confucian Classics.

Chung-kuo-shih (Ch'an/Zen master): see NAN-YANG HUI-CHUNG.

Chung-li Chuan (one of eight Immortals): see PA-HSIEN.

Chung-yang (form of Taoism): see CH'ÜAN-CHEN TAO.

Chung Yüan. Chinese festival (predominantly Buddhist), held to assist the hungry ghosts. It is held on the fifteenth day of the seventh month, and from this day until the end of the month offerings are made, or gifts contributed, which will assist those who have died with none otherwise to remember them, those without graves, and those without descendants.

Chung Yung ('Central Norm', often referred to as 'The Doctrine of the Mean'). A work attributed to Tzu Ssu, *Confucius' grandson (5th cent. BCE), but more probably a compilation of two or more works, being extracted from **Li Chi*. It advocates the discernment of a basic norm of human action which, if then put into effect, will bring life into harmony with the process of the universe. This requires a life controlled by *ch'eng*, sincerity, genuineness, and integrity. In this way, the natural order embraces both cosmos and ethical life; and those who live accordingly experience a mystical union between heaven and earth.

Chün tzu (ideal person): see ETHICS (CONFUCIAN).

Chuppah (canopy used at Jewish weddings): see ḤUPPAH.

Church (from Gk., *kuriakon*, 'belonging to the Lord'). The institution of *Christianity. The word may refer to the whole number of organized Christians everywhere, to a particular denomination, to a local congregation, or to a building where Christians assemble. Reflection on the nature of the church, 'ecclesiology' (Gk., *ekklēsia*), is also a traditional part of Christian teaching.

In *Orthodox understanding, the Church must be constituted by the *apostolic succession, and be *episcopal in character. It must accept the first seven *Councils, and its doctrine is held within that parameter.

For *Catholics, the Church is characterized as 'one, holy, catholic and apostolic'. Thus conceived, it is a visible body; its membership, its orders of ministers, and its unity are all constituted by participation in visible *sacraments.

The *Reformation gave rise to two major doctrines of the Church: (i) that it is a visible body, and, in God's intention, one (though divided if corruption and error have demanded a reformation); and (ii) that the true church is an invisible body, since it is by the personal commitment of faith that a person is saved and made a member of it.

For individual Churches see Index, Churches.

Church Army. Anglican evangelizing organization of lay workers founded in 1882 by Wilson Carlile on the model of the *Salvation Army.

Church Commissioners. Body which manages the endowments of the *Church of England.

Churches of Christ. Christian denomination, also known as 'Disciples' and 'Campbellites' after its founder A. *Campbell. Organized in the USA, the earliest 'Disciples' came to adopt *baptism by immersion and the weekly observance of the Lord's Supper for baptized believers; each local church practised a *Congregational form of church government. The Churches of Christ participated in ecumenical discussion in the present century, and in 1981 the majority of the Churches of Christ in Great Britain became part of the *United Reformed Church.

Church Fathers. Christian writers of the first eight centuries CE. The study of these writers is known as Patristics or Patrology. See Index, Fathers.

Church Missionary Society (Anglican missionary society): see CMS.

Church of England. The Christian Church which is 'by law established' in England. The Church of England is a consequence of the Reformation, as this was mediated under the 16th-cent. Tudor sovereigns. As the expression of *Anglicanism, it is the continuity of Christianity from the earliest times (see e.g. CELTIC CHURCH), as that changes through time.

Church of the East. The *Syrian Church, more popularly known as *Nestorian, or *Assyrian, which descends from the ancient church in the Persian Empire. Its foundation is traditionally associated with Mari, a disciple of *Addai, or with St *Thomas himself. It adopted a strongly dyophysite (*Antiochene) christology which by the 7th cent. hardened into Nestorianism.

The church undertook very extensive missionary work, and even had outposts in China from 635 until 'foreign' religions were expelled in 845 (see HSI-AN FU). At present, the Nestorians form a very small community in Iraq (the patriarchate was restored to Baghdād in 1976 with the election of Mar Denḥa IV), together with other small populations in the Middle E., N. and S. America, and S. India (this being a dissident body from the Syro-Malabar Church).

Church-sect typology. The attempt to classify religious groups according to their typical relationships with society. First developed by *Troeltsch, the distinction has been influential in the *sociology of religion. A Church 'utilizes the State and the ruling classes, and weaves these elements into her own life; she then becomes an integral part of the existing social order'. Sects, on the other hand, are protest groups (on this view; for a fuller typology, see SECTS).

Churning of the ocean (*samudramathana*). A Hindu myth, which tells how a great flood covered the earth, as a result of which many precious objects were lost, especially *amṛta. In order to recover them, *Viṣṇu, in his incarnation (*avatāra) as a tortoise (*Kūrma) dived to the ocean floor so that Mount *Mandara could be set up on his back. The gods and demons then coiled the serpent Vāsuki round the mountain, and, by pulling on each end, churned up the ocean until the missing objects were recovered. However, a poison, Halāhala, was also churned up, which *Śiva drank, in order to protect humanity, with the consequence that his throat is dyed blue.

Cintāmani (Skt.). 1. In Hinduism, a magical jewel which has the power to grant every wish, hence an epithet for God.

2. In Buddhism, the same jewel, but now an attribute of *buddhas and *bodhisattvas, hence a symbol for the mind which has attained its (proper) desire.

Circumambulation. The movement around a holy object, or of a holy object. The completion of a circle of protection, or of community, creates an integrity which is otherwise hard to find in this world. The application of this in religions is diverse: examples include *Ḥajj (the Muslim circumambulation of the *Ka'ba); the *Prayer Wheel (in Tibet); the *stūpa and the *Bo tree in Buddhism (see RELICS (BUDDHIST)); the respect shown to the *Ādi Granth on entering a *gurdwārā; *Lāvān; the Hindu 'following the sun' round the sacred fire and, in the temple (and, in *pradakṣina*, to go around any sacred object, person, or place, including the whole of India; the seven circuits (*hakkafot) around a cemetery before a burial by *Sephardi and *Hasidic Jews.

Circumcision

Judaism (Heb., *berit milah* '*covenant of circumcision'). Following Genesis 17. 11–12, any child born of a Jewish mother is Jewish whether circumcised or not. None the less it is the duty of a Jewish father to have his son circumcised on the eighth day (*Shulḥān Arukh* YD 260. 1). The operation is done by a *mohel who must be an observant Jew (*Sh.Ar.* YD 264. 1).

Islam *Khitān* is male circumcision. It is obligatory, though the details, and the age at which it is done, vary. *Khafḍ* is female circumcision, which is not obligatory, but which is nevertheless regarded by many as according to *sunna—i.e. customary in the strong and religious sense.

Cistercians. *Roman Catholic monastic order, also called 'White Monks'. The mother-house, Cîteaux (Lat., *Cistercium*) in Burgundy, was founded in 1098. In contrast to the comparative luxury of the monasticism of *Cluny, then at its height, they were austere in diet, clothing, architecture, and liturgy.

In the 17th cent. a party of 'Strict Observance' emerged, advocating, among other rigours, total abstinence from meat. Its most important figure was A. de Rancé (d. 1700), abbot of La Trappe, whence is derived the name *Trappists, applied from the 19th cent. onward to Cistercians of the Strict Observance.

Cit (Skt., 'See'). In Hindu thought, pure consciousness as the essential and irreducible quality of the eternal self or *Brahman. In *Vedānta, cit is often grouped together with being (*sat) and bliss (*ānanda) as a description of Brahman.

Citta (Skt., 'that which has been seen', i.e. belonging to consciousness, cf. CIT). In Hinduism, the reflective and thus conscious mind; in Buddhism, an equivalent to *manas (reflective mind) and *vijñāna (continuing consciousness). It belongs to all beings above the level of plant life. The nature of citta received particular analysis and emphasis in *Vijñanavāda (also known as Yogacāra)—so much so that the school is also known as Cittamātra, Mind only. In *Abhidhamma, the analysis differentiates 121 types of citta, each of which may be combined with any one of fifty-two *cetasikas* (the accompanying qualities of experience), thus producing the extremely large variety of mental events.

Cittamātra (mind only): see VIJÑĀNAVĀDA; VIJÑAPTI-MĀTRA.

Citt'ekaggata or **cittassa ekaggata** (Pāli, 'one-pointedness of mind'). The mark of having reached full concentration (*samādhi) during Buddhist meditation.

***City of God, The*:** see DE CIVITATE DEI.

City of Refuge. A place to which, in Judaism, those who have accidentally killed may flee. According to Numbers 35. 13, there were six cities of refuge in biblical times.

Cīvara (part of Buddhist dress): see HABIT, RELIGIOUS.

Civil religion. The term used by R. N. Bellah to describe the complex of symbolic meanings shared by many Americans and uniting them in a moral community. Beyond the specific use of Bellah, 'civil religion' has come to refer more loosely to the evident necessity of all communities to find symbols and rituals which will take the place of the religious rituals and symbols which no longer command adherence: see further SECULARIZATION.

Classics, Confucian: see CONFUCIAN CLASSICS.

Clement of Alexandria, St (*c*.150–*c*.215). Christian *father (patristic theologian). He was head of the catechetical school of *Alexandria from 190. His chief works are the *Protrepticus*, or 'Exhortation to the Greeks', the *Paedagogus* on Christian life and manners, and the *Stromateis*, or 'Miscellanies'. He shared the emphasis of the *desert fathers on the unknowability of God (see APOPHATIC THEOLOGY). His name occurs in the early martyrologies, but it was excised by Pope Clement VIII on the grounds of his doubtful orthodoxy.

Clement of Rome, St. Traditional third *bishop of Rome, perhaps to be connected with the fellow worker of *Paul (Philippians 4. 3). A letter from the Roman church to that of Corinth is ascribed to him and is known as *1 Clement*.

A mass of other early Christian literature circulated under Clement's name. The most important are the *Clementine Homilies* and *Recognitions* (3rd–4th cents.).

Clergy (Gk. *kleros*, an object used in casting lots, as by Jewish priests, Deuteronomy 18. 1 ff.). Designated religious leaders, especially in

Christianity by means of *ordination. The term 'clergy' is sometimes used of functionaries in other religions (e.g. mullahs in Islam), but none have anything like the same order or succession or duties.

Cloud of Unknowing, The. English mystical treatise of the 14th cent. The author, whose anonymity has remained inviolate, stands in the line of *Dionysian influence. The author teaches that God cannot be known by human reason and that in *contemplation the soul is conscious of a 'cloud of unknowing' between itself and God which can only be penetrated by 'a sharp dart of love'.

Cluny. Benedictine (*Benedict) *abbey in Burgundy (France), founded in 909/10. It became a centre of renewal in the Church and in monastic practice. During the 12th cent., the influence of Cluny began to decline, although the abbey itself survived until 1790.

CMS or **Church Missionary Society.** Anglican society founded in 1799 'to proclaim the Gospel in all lands and to gather the people of all races into the fellowship of Christ's church'. Its theology has always been *evangelical.

Coal. A description among Coptic, Ethiopic, and E. Syrian Christians of the sacramental body of *Christ. The description is derived from Isaiah 6. 6 f.

Cobb, J. (exponent of process theology): see PROCESS THEOLOGY.

Codex Iuris Canonici (Lat., Code of *Canon Law). The collection of all laws obtaining in the Roman Catholic churches of the Latin Rite—the Eastern or Oriental Rite churches have their own Codex.

Codifications of Law. In Judaism, successive attempts to bring order to the proliferating interpretations and applications of the original *Torah. Among the earliest were *Mishnah and *Tosefta, leading to the Palestinian and Babylonian *Talmuds, though these are not in the form of codes. Pioneers of the latter were the *She'iltot* of the Babylonian Aḥai of Shabḥa, and *Halakhot Pesukot* of Yehudai Gaon. Prominent in the transition to codes was *Saʿadiah Gaon. But the most ambitious was *Mishneh Torah* of *Maimonides. This remains a point of reference, but other codes have appeared, often condensing and reorganizing—e.g. Jacob ben Asher's *Arba'ah Turim* (Four Rows; *Tur* for short), which was the basis for **Shulḥān Arukh* of Joseph *Caro. For Jewish Codes and Codes in other religions, see Index, Codes.

Coenobite (Gk., *koinos*, 'common', + *bios*, 'life'; hence coenobitic). A religious who lives in a community, as opposed to a hermit.

Cohen, Hermann (1842–1918). German Jewish philosopher. As a philosopher, he brought a new interpretation to the thought of Immanuel *Kant. He argued that as the *chosen people of God, Jews have a particular duty to bring about the unity of humanity and establish God's Kingdom on earth. This duty is linked specifically to Torah and the keeping of its commands. His major work, *Die Religion der Vernunft aus den Quellen des Judentums* was published a year after his death.

Colenso, John William (1814–83). *Anglican *bishop of Natal. He is remembered principally for the controversy caused by his papers on *The Pentateuch and the Book of Joshua Critically Examined* (1862–79). His studies looked especially at the implications of numbers taken literally, and challenged the historical accuracy of the books and their authorship by *Moses. He was censured by the English bishops and deposed by his *metropolitan. He contested the deposition, and a schism ensued in Natal which was eventually healed in 1911.

Coleridge, Samuel Taylor (1772–1834). Poet and thinker. Born at Ottery St Mary in Devon, he studied (somewhat chaotically) at Cambridge where he met William Wordsworth. With him he published *Lyrical Ballads* in 1798. Already he had, with Robert Southey, attempted to set up a communal society, Pantisocracy, putting into practice the ideals of the French Revolution. In 1798, he went to Germany to study *Kant, and came under the influence of Schiller and Goethe. On his return he lectured and wrote. In religion he represents the Romantic reaction against both rationalism and dogmatic religious systems, seeing the heart of religion in human religious need. He is sometimes called the 'father of the *Broad Church'.

Collating (appointing to a benefice): see ADVOWSON.

Collect. A short variable prayer used in W. Christian worship.

Collective representations. A theoretical term closely associated with *Durkheim, referring to forms of knowledge which exist over and above any particular member of society. Religious and moral systems, categories of space, time, and the person, even much scientific knowledge, have *sui generis* characteristics. As traditions, they transcend individuals: people come and go, traditions live on.

Collegiate church. A church which is governed by a *chapter of *canons, but is not, like a *cathedral, a bishop's see.

Colossians, Letter to the. An epistle of *Paul and book of the New Testament.

Colours, liturgical: see LITURGICAL COLOURS.

Columba, St (*c*.521–97). Christian abbot and missionary, trained in Irish monasteries, who, in *c*.563 established himself and twelve companions on the island of Iona. He remained there as a base for evangelizing the Scottish mainland and establishing monasteries on other nearby islands. Though not a bishop, he exercised ecclesiastical authority in the area, and consecrated the new king of the Scots in 574. He is also known for three Latin poems and for his skill as a scribe. Feast day, 9 June.

Columbus Convention: see REFORM JUDAISM.

Commandments: see MITZVAH; SIX HUNDRED AND THIRTEEN COMMANDMENTS; TEN COMMANDMENTS.

Common Life, Brothers and Sisters of (Christian devotional movement): see GROOTE, GEERT.

***Common Prayer, Book of*:** see *Book of Common Prayer*.

Communicatio idiomatum (Lat., 'interchange of properties'). A doctrine of *christology put forward by several *patristic writers. It emphasizes the separateness of the human and divine natures in Christ, but holds that what may only strictly be said of the one may also be said of the other, because of their union in the one person. It is most clearly stated in the *Tome* of Pope Leo (449).

Communion. The partaking of the consecrated elements at the Christian *eucharist. Along with *Lord's Supper it is also (as in the **Book of Common Prayer*) another name for the whole service of the eucharist.

Communion of Saints. A belief professed in the Christian *Apostles' creed. It points to the whole company of the faithful, living and dead, in union with Christ and with each other. The Latin *communio sanctorum* could also mean 'communion of holy things', i.e. a sharing especially in the *sacraments.

Companions (Arab. *Aṣḥāb* or *Ṣaḥāba*). The men closest to *Muḥammad during his time in *Mecca and *Madīna; foremost among these, the first four caliphs (*khalīfa): *Abu Bakr, *ʿUmar, *ʿUthmān, and *ʿAlī b. Abī Tālib. See also ṢAHĀBA.

Compassion (characteristic Buddhist virtue): see KARUṆĀ.

Compline. The traditional last of the day *hours in the W. Church, said before retiring at night. The corresponding office in the Orthodox Church is the *apodeipnon* (Gk., 'after supper').

Compostela: see PILGRIMAGE.

Concelebration. The celebration of the *eucharist by a number of priests saying the eucharistic prayer, or the words of *consecration, together.

Concept of positive freedom (space for human effort in a deterministic system): see SPINOZA.

Conciliar controversy (dispute about the relative authority of a council or a pope): see ANTIPOPE.

Concordat. An agreement between a religious group and the government of a country on matters of mutual concern. Thus the *Vatican entered into concordats with both Nazi Germany and Fascist Italy. An important model is the Pactum Callixtinum, or Concordat of Worms (1122) whereby the contest between the Popes and the Holy Roman Emperors over the right to appoint bishops was resolved in favour of the Popes.

Concrete logic or **science** (of Lévi-Strauss): see MYTH.

Concursive revelation (a co-operative (i.e. between God and humans) understanding of revelation): see REVELATION.

Confessing Church or **Bekennende Kirche.** The *Protestant church in Germany organized in opposition to the official Nazi church organizations and policies. (see KIRCHENKAMPF).

Confession

Christianity 1. An affirmation or profession of faith: (i) the testimony of a *martyr or *confessor (e.g. 1 Timothy 6. 13); (ii) a doctrinal statement in the Orthodox Church; (iii) Protestant professions of faith, especially of 16th/17th cents.

2. An acknowledgement of *sin. In Christianity, this may be made either in worship by a congregation ('general confession'), or privately to a priest ('auricular confession': Lat., *ad auriculam*, 'to the ear'), who mediates God's willingness to forgive, and pronounces God's *absolution.

The recognition and acknowledgement of fault occurs in all religions, and the term 'confession' is applied widely, although what is happening in the context of each religion may be very different.

Judaism Confession of sin in Judaism (Heb., *viddu'i*) is an essential prequisite of expiation. Prayers of confession are part of the *synagogue liturgy, particularly at *Rosh ha-Shanah and Yom Kippur, and well-known prayers include Ashamnu (We have incurred guilt) *'Al het (For the sin), and *Avinu malkenu (Our father, Our king).

Buddhism In Buddhism confession is not made to a divine power and there is no concept of absolution or the forgiveness of sins. The act of confession (*pāpa-desanā*) is the owning-up to one's failings or shortcomings in order to cultivate greater self-awareness and be freed from the burden of persecutory guilt. The occasion for confession in monastic Buddhism is a formal public event which takes place at the *Uposatha ceremony. There is no counterpart to this formal ceremony for lay Buddhists.

Jainism Confession (*alocana* and *pratikramaṇa*) occurs twice daily for monks; laypeople make confession to their *guru.

Confessor. 1. In the early church, a person who suffered for 'confessing' (i.e. maintaining) the faith but not to the point of *martyrdom. After the time of persecutions, the term was extended to apply to those whose lives were manifestly holy (as Edward the Confessor, declared to be so in 1161).

2. A Christian priest who hears (private) *confessions and administers the sacrament of *penance.

Confirmation. The Christian rite in which the *Holy Spirit is conveyed in a renewed or fuller way to those who have already undergone *baptism, derived from John 14. 15–21, and Acts 2. 37 f., which suggests a division between the two. In the Middle Ages it came to be counted as one of the seven *sacraments.

Confucian Classics. A canonical collection of works whose prestige in traditional China was comparable to that of Greek and Roman classics in the W., and whose authority was as unassailable as that of biblical scripture.

Three of them predate *Confucius: the *Shih* (Song Lyrics), the **Shu* (Historical Documents of Archaic Times), and the **I* or *Yi* (Change). The **Ch'un Ch'iu* (Springs and Autumns) is supposed to be from the brush of the Master himself. Texts on ritually correct behaviour are collectively called **Li Chi* (Ritual Scriptures). A canon of ritual music (*Yüeh Ching*) is said to have been lost before the 3rd cent. BCE, but its contents can be surmised from other, surviving texts. All these works were supposed to have been edited by Confucius, or have him as their figure of authority; hence the term, Confucian Classics.

The corpus of Confucian Classics varied over the course of time. The Five Scriptures taught in the state college of the Han dynasty (from 136 BCE–220 CE) were *Shih*, *Shu*, *Yi*, *Ch'un Ch'iu*, and *Li* (at first the **Yi Li*, or Ceremonials and Rituals, and later the **Li Chi*, or Records of Rituals). To these there were then added the *Lun Yü* or **Analects*, and the **Hsiao Ching*, or *Scripture of Filiality*, to make up Seven Scriptures. In the T'ang period (618–907) the Canon comprised Nine Scriptures, including *Shih*, *Shu*, *Yi*, the Three Ritual Collections (*Yi Li*, *Li Chi*, and *Chou Li* or *Chou Kuan*, an idealized description of governmental institutions in early Chou times, ?1111–256 BCE), and the Three Exegeses, meaning the *Ch'un Ch'iu* with its ancient exegeses (*chuan*) named for their putative authors: *Kung-yang Chuan*, *Ku-liang Chuan*, *Tso Chuan*. The final version of the Confucian Classics was the *Thirteen Scriptures with Notes and Commentaries*, which appeared at the very end of the 12th cent. In addition to all of the above enumerated texts, it included the book of the philosopher Meng (*Meng Tzu*, or **Mencius*) and the earliest dictionary, called *Er Ya*.

The neo-Confucian philosophers of the Sung dynasty (960–1279) identified a corpus within this corpus which they called the *Four Books, or Books of the Four Philosophers (*Ssu Shu*): the *Analects*, *Mencius*, *Ta Hsüeh* (**Great Learning*), and *Chung Yung* (*Doctrine of the Mean), the latter two being small texts extracted from *Li Chi*.

Confucianism (Chin. equivalent, *ju-chia*, *ju-chiao*, *kung chiao*: School of Scholars or of *Confucius). The school and teaching of Confucius, which formed the mainstream in Chinese philosophy during most of the past 2,000 years. While Confucius' teachings are best found in the *Analects*, Confucianism regards as its special texts the Confucian Classics, for which see above. Confucian philosophy became dominant in Han China (206 BCE–220CE) only after much uncertainty, and by losing some of its doctrinal purity and integrity. Confucianism became eclectic, accepting many elements from Legalism. In Chinese terms, Confucianism is a religion (*chiao*, literally, 'doctrine') as well as a philosophy (*chia*, literally, 'a school of transmission'). But it is different from those W. religions which emphasize revealed doctrines and belief in God. While Confucius appears to have believed in a supreme deity, he preferred to teach a doctrine of humanism open to the transcendent. (For developments, see NEO-CONFUCIANISM). See also Index, Confucians.

Confucius. The Lat. rendering of K'ung Futzu (Master K'ung), whose name was K'ung Ch'iu and also styled Chung-ni. Little can be established about his life, forebears, and family, although legends (including very early ones) are abundant. The best source is probably the *Analects (Lun-yu). He became a ssu-k'ou (police commissioner?) at about the age of 50, but only for about a year. It was the highest public position he ever occupied. In over ten years of travel (497–484 BCE), K'ung visited many other feudal states of his time, seeking a ruler who would use his services, but never finding one. According to the *Annals of Tso*, he himself died aged 73, in the sixteenth year of the reign of Duke Ai (479 BCE). His political ambitions remaining unfulfilled, K'ung was remembered especially as a teacher, and by many as *the* great moral teacher of E. Asia. Above all, he was interested in the difficult art of becoming a perfectly humane (*jen) person, and regarded those who made efforts in that direction as the real gentlemen, rather than those born of high rank. His teachings give primary emphasis to the ethical meaning of human relationships, grounding the moral in human nature and its openness to the transcendent. Although he was largely silent on God and the after-life, his silence did not bespeak disbelief. His philosophy was clearly grounded in religion—the inherited religion of the Lord-on-high or Heaven, the supreme and personal deity. He made it clear that it was Heaven which gave him his message and protected him.

Congé d'élire (Fr.). 'Permission to elect' a *bishop, granted in the *Church of England by the Crown to the dean and *chapter of the cathedral of the diocese.

Congregational churches. Those churches which assert the autonomy of the local congregation. Their historical roots are in Elizabethan Separatism, with its insistence that the 'gathered church' in any given locality consists of those who commit themselves to *Christ and to one another. Its members believe in a *covenant of loyalty and mutual edification, emphasizing the importance of discerning God's will whilst 'gathered' together in Church Meeting. In 1831–2 they gave wider geographical expression to their unity in the formation of the Congregational Union. Renamed the Congregational Church in England and Wales (1966), it joined with the Presbyterian Church of England in 1972 to form the *United Reformed Church. Those churches which maintained that this union threatened their congregational principles joined either the newly formed Congregational Federation or the Fellowship of Evangelical Congregational Churches.

Congregation for the Doctrine of the Faith: see INQUISITION.

Congregations, Roman. The departments of the Roman *curia responsible for the central administration of the Roman Catholic Church.

Congruism (between grace and will): see SUAREZ, F. DE.

Conscience: see ETHICS (CHRISTIANITY).

Consecration (*Lat., cum*, 'with', + *sacrum*, 'sacred': i.e. making connection with the sacred). In Christianity: (i) the act in the *eucharist through which the elements become Christ's body and blood; (ii) the *ordination of bishops; and (iii) the dedication of altars, churches, and eucharistic vessels.

In a more general sense, consecration is the act or ritual which invests objects, places, or people with religious significance, often by way of power and holiness.

Conservative Evangelicals. *Evangelical Christians whose view of the *Bible is 'conservative', i.e. who either reject critical study of the Bible or else hold that such study confirms its authority and historical accuracy. See also FUNDAMENTALISM.

Conservative Judaism. A progressive movement within mainstream Judaism. Conservative (originally 'Historical') Jews acknowledge that certain changes in the Jewish way of life are inevitable since the Enlightenment, but that the traditional forms of Judaism are valid; thus changes in religious practice should only be made with great reluctance. The movement arose in both Europe and the USA in the late 19th cent. Its Jewish Theological Seminary has become an institution of great academic eminence over the years. None the less, the Conservative movement's rulings on divorce, the ordination of women, the celebration of the second day of festivals, and *conversion have not been accepted by the Orthodox.

Consistory

Judaism Official organization of the French Jewish Community. Its constitution was drafted at the Assembly of Jewish Notables called by the Emperor Napoleon in 1806, whose purpose was to integrate Jews as 'useful citizens'.

Christianity Any of certain ecclesiastical courts (the consistory being the room in which Roman emperors administered justice). In the Roman Catholic Church, the consistory is the assembly of *cardinals convoked by the pope and conducted in his presence. It may be public (e.g. to appoint new cardinals) or private to consider Church business. In the Church of England the consistory court is the bishop's diocesan court.

Constance, Council of (1414–17). Convened at the insistence of the Emperor Sigismund to end the *Great Schism, to reform the *Church, and combat heresy. There were three rival *popes: the council asserted its superiority to the papal office, the three rivals all resigned or were deposed, and in 1417 Martin V was elected pope. Among measures to promote reform, the council enacted that there should be regular General Councils. In these ways the council was important in the history of conciliarism (see ANTIPOPE).

Constantine I or **the Great** (*c*.288–337). First Roman emperor to accept Christianity. On the eve of the battle of the Milvian Bridge, in 312, he saw in a dream, according to Eusebius, a cross bearing the inscription, 'In hoc signo vinces': 'In this sign you will conquer'. Following his victory, he gave favoured status to the Church, but whether this was formalized (in, e.g., the Edict of Milan, 313) is disputed.

Constantinople (modern Istanbul). The chief see of the E. Roman Empire from the 5th cent. By the Treaty of Lausanne (1923) the Turkish Republic is bound to protect the Greek Christians in Constantinople; but the patriarch must be a Turkish citizen.

Constantinople was the venue for three *ecumenical councils. Constantinople I (381) marked the end of the *Arian controversy. See also NICENE CREED.

Constantinople II (553) secured the condemnation of *Theodore of Mopsuestia, and certain writings of *Theodoret and Ibas of Edessa. The council also condemned *Origenism.

Constantinople III (680) was convoked to settle the *Monothelite controversy.

Constitution of Madina: see MADĪNA.

Consubstantial. Of one and the same substance, hence also being. In Christian use the word refers especially to the relationship among the persons of the *Trinity. The Lat. *consubstantialis* is the Western counterpart of Gk. **homoousios*, the test-word of anti-*Arian orthodoxy.

Consubstantiation. The doctrine according to which the substances *both* of the body and blood of Christ *and* of the bread and wine coexist in the *eucharistic elements after their consecration.

Contarini, Gasparo (1483–1542). Christian *cardinal, who led those proposing reform of the Church to Pope Paul III. By 1511, he had already come to the conclusion that humans are justified by faith, not works, and this conclusion enabled him to view *Protestant claims with sympathy. He was papal legate to the Regensburg Colloquy (1541), where Protestants and Roman Catholics sought terms on which to reunify the Church. Both sides rejected his proposal of double *justification. He died a year later as papal governor of Bologna.

Contemplation. In modern Western use, mental *prayer that is non-discursive and thus distinct from *meditation. At this stage, prayer usually begins to be less the fruit of human effort and more the result of direct divine *grace, a distinction suggested by the traditional contrast between 'acquired' and 'infused' contemplation.

Contraception: see BIRTH AND POPULATION CONTROL.

Conversion. Conversion is a process common to all religions in its preliminary sense of 'conversion of manners'—i.e. the turning of one's life more deliberately toward the goals of the religion in question. But conversion also has a stronger sense, namely, the transfer of a person (or group of people) from one religion to another, or from no religion to belief. Conversion in that stronger sense is an extremely complex phenomenon, having a different status and priority in different religions. Judaism, for example, became highly resistant to seeking converts, not least because Judaism is a particular vocation to one people, and gentiles are *already* members of the *Noachide covenant, and have no need to undertake the laws of *Torah in addition.

In some religions the imperative to convert others is non-negotiable. In Christianity it is tied to the view that there is no other way to salvation (John 14. 6). Such conversion involves *baptism. In a comparable way, Muslims are under obligation to make known the will and the way of *Allāh, revealed in the *Qur'ān; yet 'There is no compulsion in religion' (Qur'ān 2. 256/7), and Muslims recognize that the People of the Book (*Ahl al-Kitāb) should be treated with respect, and that they are not obliged to convert to Islam.

The psychology and neurophysiology of conversion are understood, as yet, only in very preliminary ways. At one extreme, the techniques associated with the term *brain-washing were explored in connection with religious conversion by W. Sargant, *Battle For the Mind* (1957). At the other extreme, conversion may be undramatic and a consequence of a long process of reflection. Between the two is the phenomenon of 'snapping', in which a convert to one religion or religious movement is precipitated into several others in rapid succession. See also (with examples in other religions) Index, Conversion.

Convocations. The two provincial assemblies (Canterbury and York) of the clergy of the *Church of England.

Coomaraswamy, Ananda (1877–1947). A philosopher of aesthetics, who worked from the basis of the history of art to develop a form of the 'perennial philosophy' (*philosophia perennis*). Treating art as an 'affective expression of metaphysical theses', he emphasized the inspirational. It is a form of knowledge with the power to effect transformation of being.

Cope. Christian *vestment.

COPEC (conference): see TEMPLE, WILLIAM.

Copper Scroll. A document found at *Qumran. It consists of an inventory of treasure, conjectured to be the treasure seized from the *Temple before the Jewish revolt of 67 CE.

Coptic Church (Arab., *qibṭ*, from Gk., *Aigyptios*, 'Egyptian'). The national Christian church of Egypt.

Its position under Islam has, however, always been difficult. There were occasional persecutions under the *khalīfas, besides the legal disabilities imposed on non-Muslims as *dhimmis. Many restrictions (e.g. on church building and publication) still exist.

The Coptic Church was a founder member of the World Council of Churches in 1948. Its vitality appears in its Sunday schools and in a recent repopulation of some of the ancient desert monasteries. The number of Copts in the 1976 census was given as 2.3 million, but Coptic leaders claim it is 5 million or more, and that the figures were falsified to serve the picture of Egypt as an Islamic state.

Coptic liturgies and ceremonial preserve some very archaic features. The traditional liturgical language is Coptic, although it gave way to Arabic as a spoken language as early as the 9th cent.

Corban (Heb., 'oblation'). An obligatory or free-will offering at the temple altar (Leviticus 1. 2, etc.).

Cordovero, Moses (1552–70). *Kabbalistic scholar. Cordovero was a disciple of Joseph *Caro and the teacher of Isaac *Luria. He attempted to construct a speculative kabbalistic system based on traditional medieval philosophy and the teachings of the **Zohar*. His two great systematic works were *Pardes Rimmonim* ('Orchard of Pomegranates') and *Ellimah Rabbati*; and he also wrote a long commentary on the *Zohar*, *Or Yaqar* (Precious Light). His *Tomer Devorah* (Palm Tree of Deborah) is a popular work showing how Kabbalah is, in practice, a way leading to God.

Corinthians, Letters to the. Two epistles of *Paul and books of the New Testament.

Corpus Christi (Lat., 'body of Christ'). The Christian feast commemorating the origin of the *eucharist. It is celebrated in the W. church on the Thursday after *Trinity Sunday.

Corpus Hermeticum: see HERMETICISM.

Correlation (the relating of questions and religious symbols): see TILLICH, P.

Cosmic embryo (source of creation): see HIRAṆYAGARBHA.

Cosmogony: see COSMOLOGY.

Cosmological arguments. A family of arguments for the existence of God, which start from the existence of the world or some very general feature of it, e.g. causality, change, or contingency, and argue thence to the existence of a First Cause or Necessary Being, which is identified with God. Such arguments were attacked by *Hume and *Kant in the 18th cent. and by subsequent thinkers; but they are still defended by many *neo-Thomists and some analytic philosophers. Their modern proponents see the arguments as an expression of the human mind's search for total intelligibility in the world, and contend that we should not set *a priori* limits to the search for ultimate explanations.

Cosmology (Gk., *kosmos* + *logos*). Reflection on, and account of the world/universe as a meaningful whole, as embodying or expressing an order or underlying structure that makes sense: cosmogony is concerned with the coming into being of the cosmos, and cosmography with the description of its extent.

It is rare for religions to give a single cosmology or cosmogony purporting to be a description of the origin of the universe, in the way in which a scientific cosmology might aim to give a critically realistic account of the origin and nature of the universe. Religious cosmologies give accounts of origin and nature, but principally in order to display the cosmos as an arena of opportunity; and for that reason, a religion may offer, or make use of, many cosmogonies without making much attempt to reconcile the contradictions between them. It is this aesthetic and spiritual relaxation which allows religions to address cosmological issues from the point of view of accountability and responsibility (as at the present time over issues of ecology), not as competitors with a scientific account: thus the Vancouver Assembly of the World Council of Churches (see ECUMENISM) decided 'to engage member churches in a conciliar process of mutual commitment (covenant) to justice, peace and the integrity of creation (subsequently known as JPIC)'; while this (especially the word 'covenant') depends on a particular understanding of creation, and thus of cosmogony, it has moved far beyond concerns about identifying the 'correct' account of the cosmos and its origins. See Index, Cosmology.

Judaism *Tanach (Jewish scripture) contains at least six different types of creation narrative, all of which are integrated to the overriding cult of *Yahweh. The controlling accounts are those in Genesis: God created everything that exists in six days and rested on the seventh (1–2. 4). A second, more anthropocentric account (Genesis 2. 4–24), although differing in detail, also emphasizes that God is the origin of everything. The world is created solely in obedience to the divine will.

Christianity Christians inherited the Jewish cosmology, but virtually from the outset (as early as *Paul's letters) they associated Christ with the activity of the Father in creation. Furthermore, creation now has its end and purpose in him. Not surprisingly, therefore, Christian interest in cosmology and creation has seen them as a matter, not of technique, but of relationship—i.e. the relation of dependence which the created order has on its creator, not just for its origin, but for its sustenance. Thus God is the cause, not simply of things coming to be, but also of their being. The prevailing cosmography for millennia was one of a 'three-decker' universe (heaven above, earth in the middle, and hell below), but its 'correction' by modern cosmologies has not affected the more fundamental point of the earlier (or of any) religious cosmology which mapped the universe as an arena of opportunity. For that reason, a three-decker universe may well persist indefinitely in liturgy.

Islam The Qur'ān strongly affirms God as creator and disposer of all that is. By a simple word, *kun* ('Be'), he commands and it is (2. 117, 6. 73). God is al-Khāliq (the Creator, from *khalaqa*, 'he created'), and has the power and authority to bring about all things as he disposes (*qadar, *Allāh). Everything that he has created is a sign (*ayā), not only *of* God for those who have eyes to see, but also *that* God has power to continue his creative act in relation to humans by bringing them from the grave for judgement (e.g. 50. 6–11). The creation of a first man and first woman, and of the earth and seven heavens in two days, and of the cosmos in six, is described in such a way that, given the nature of the Qur'ān, any apparent conflict with other accounts (e.g. in the natural sciences) would have to be resolved in favour of the Qur'ān.

Hinduism Vedic religion displays a clear sense of an ordered universe in which *ṛta prevails. There are many different accounts of how the universe came into being, some implying agency, others emanation from a pre-existing state in which there is neither beginning nor end. Thus *Śaṅkara understood the emanation as a progress from the subtle to the gross constituents of the world. But earlier than that, there had developed a sense of an unending process like a wave, with elements rising up into organized appearance, but then lapsing into a corresponding trough during 'the sleep of Brahmā', a period of dissolution (*pralaya). It was thus possible that the cosmos arose from infinite space and consciousness, a belief expressed through *Aditi. In truth, Indian religion accepted that the origin of the cosmos could not be known, but that the conditions of ordered life could be extremely well known. Cosmology lays out the terms for achieving that understanding—cosmology, again, as the arena of opportunity—while remaining agnostic about detail.

There was a greater confidence in cosmography. Vertically, the world was understood to be made up of seven continents (*dvipas*), ranged in circles with intervening oceans around the central point of Mount *Meru. Vertically, if one takes a cross-section of the Brahmāṇḍa, one finds a series of layers. At the top are the *lokas of the gods and high attainers; next are the planets, sky, and earth; then the underworlds, and finally the twenty-eight *narakas or hells. See also CARDINAL DIRECTIONS.

Jainism and **Buddhism** The Indian scepticism about the work of the gods or God in creating this cosmos was taken to a further extreme in both Jainism and Buddhism. The Jains inherited the *triloka* (see LOKA), and envisaged it as something like an hour-glass, squeezed in at the middle. Above (*Urdhvaloka*) are a series of heavens of increasing brightness, at the top of which is 'the slightly curved place' (*Iśatpraghhara*) where dwell the liberated and disembodied souls. In the middle is the *Madhyaloka*, which includes the continent inhabited by humans. Below is the *Adholoka*, a series of increasingly terrible hells—from which release is eventually certain, though the intervening time may be unimaginably long.

Buddhism inherited the same basic cosmography, but adapted it greatly. It envisages a series of levels, all of which are open to the process of reappearance: at the summit are the four realms of purely mental rebirth, (*arūpa-avacara*); below them are the realms of pure form (*rūpa-avacara*), where the gods dwell in sixteen heavens, five of which are known as 'pure abodes' (*suddhāvāsa*), the remaining eleven of which arise out of the *jhānas (meditational states). Lower still are the sense-desire heavens, including those of the Tāvatiṃsa gods (the thirty-three Vedic gods, the chief of whom, *Indra, known as Sakka, has become a protector of Buddhism) and of the Tusita gods (where *bodhisattvas spend their penultimate birth, and in which *Maitreya now dwells). The world is simply a process, passing through cycles (*kappa*) of immense length.

Costa, Uriel da: see DA COSTA, U.

Councils: Formal assemblies for religious purposes: see Index, Councils.

Buddhism According to tradition three important councils were held in the early centuries after the passing away of the *Buddha. There is considerable uncertainty surrounding the date, location, deliberations, and conclusions of these councils, and while the traditional account may be accepted as reliable in some respects it should not be regarded as historically accurate in all.

The First Council is reported to have been held at Rājagriha in the year of the Buddha's death (486 BCE) with the objective of establishing the canon or at least two or its three divisions or 'baskets' (*tripiṭaka).

The Second Council took place 100 or 110 years after the first and was held at *Vaiśālī. It arose out of a dispute concerning monastic practices, and in particular the handling of money by monks.

The Third Council at *Pāṭaliputra in 250 BCE is the most important of the three and resulted in the 'Great Schism' between the 'Elders' (*Sthaviras) and the 'Great Assembly' (*Mahāsāṃghikas), which was to have a profound effect upon the later tradition.

Christianity A council is a formal assembly of *bishops and representatives of churches for determining doctrine or discipline. Local councils, as of provinces or *patriarchates, are more usually called *synods. The meeting described in Acts 15 is traditionally the first council. General, or *ecumenical, councils are those made up of bishops and other representatives from the whole world; but the term refers specifically to those seven whose decisions have been taken to represent a true consensus and to be authoritative. These are, with dates: 1. *Nicaea I (325) 2. *Constantinople I (381) 3. *Ephesus (431) 4. *Chalcedon (451) 5. Constantinople II (553) 6. Constantinople III (680–1) 7. Nicaea II (787): see ICONOCLASM.

Counsels of perfection. Certain injunctions of *Jesus taken in Christian tradition (in contrast to 'commandments') as a standard of perfection for only a few disciples (cf. Matthew 19. 21). They are specifically: poverty, the renunciation of property; chastity, abstinence from sexual relations; and obedience, the submission of the will in all things to a superior. These three form the basis for the monastic life.

Counterculture. The mainly middle-class, Western youth culture of the 1960s which opposed the *rituals, forms, structures, ideologies, calculating rationality, and leadership of the wider society. It was from among these casualties of the counterculture that a number of new religions of total commitment, such as the Unification Church (see MOON, SUN MYUNG) and Hare Krishna (see INTERNATIONAL SOCIETY . . .), gained many of their first converts in the West.

Counter-Reformation. Movement of revival and reform in the *Roman Catholic Church during the 16th and early 17th cents. The term was used in the 19th cent. to describe that Church's response to the *Reformation and the rise of *Protestantism, but this is too limiting a concept. The early leaders of the Counter-Reformation (such as Cisneros in Spain, *Pole or Giberti in Italy), the revival of *religious orders such as the *Augustinians and the *Carmelites, or the foundation of new orders such as the *Jesuits, owed little or nothing to the reaction to Protestantism. However, the summoning of the *Council of *Trent was a consequence of the spread of *Lutheranism, and much of the debate at Trent, especially that on the *sacraments, took place in the light of positions adopted by the *Reformers. Even though the Counter-Reformation may not have owed its origin to *Luther's revolt, it had the effect of hardening the *schism between the two branches of W. Christianity, and it was responsible, at least in part, for the century of religious wars which ended in 1648.

Court Jews. Prominent Jews used by European rulers to administer estates and develop credit systems. The institution of the Court Jew emerged gradually in the 16th and 17th cents. Well-known examples include Joseph Bassevi of Prague, Samuel Oppenheimer of Vienna, and Leffmann Behrends of Hanover. Influential and *assimilated, they played a prominent part in the development of the banking system of Europe.

Covenant

Judaism In the Bible, covenants were established between individuals, between marriage partners and between God and *Israel. *Circumcision itself is frequently known as *berit* (covenant).

Christianity The term 'New Testament' (Lat., *testamentum* = 'covenant') underlines how early Christians saw themselves in a new covenant.

'Covenant theology', or 'federal theology' (Lat. *foedus*, 'covenant'), was a particular development of the New Testament doctrine in *Calvinism in the 16th–17th cents.

Islam The *Qur'ān speaks of a covenant made in pre-existence with all of humanity, (7. 171) with Adam (20. 115), with the *prophets (3. 81), with the Children of Israel (5. 13, 2. 83, 3. 187), and with the *Christians (5. 15). The actual terms of the covenants are not specified in detail, but imply the belief in, and worship and service of, the One God.

Covenant, Book of: see BOOK OF THE COVENANT.

Covenanters. Scottish *Presbyterians who expressed their convictions through the signing of covenants. In particular they signed the National Covenant of 1638 and the Solemn League and Covenant of 1643, defending the Reformed faith and in effect rejecting the imposition of *episcopacy.

Covenant Service. A *Methodist service of dedication, usually at the New Year.

Coverdale, Miles (1488–1568). Translator of the Bible. The English Bible of 1539, known as the 'Great Bible', was his work, based mainly on earlier translations rather than on the Heb. and Gk. The Psalms in the **Book of Common Prayer* derive from this version.

Cow, sacred: see GO.

Cranach, Lucas, 'the Elder' (1472–1553). German artist whose altar-pieces, drawings, woodcuts, and portraits of leading Reformers gained him wide recognition. Once attracted to the *Reformation cause, he became *Luther's protector and close friend.

Cranmer, Thomas (1489–1556). *Archbishop of *Canterbury, *Protestant reformer, scholar, and liturgist. Cranmer played a crucial part in the Henrician *Reformation in England and in shaping the English *catechism, *prayer books and Articles (see THIRTY-NINE ARTICLES). A fellowship at Jesus College, Cambridge, and ordination allowed him to study for his doctorate in Divinity (1526) and to evaluate the work of Biblical scholars, including *Fisher, *Luther, and both Catholic and other Reformers. Asked by Henry VIII to put his views on the King's proposed divorce into book-form, he was subsequently used by the king to argue for the divorce at Bologna, Rome, and eventually Ratisbon and Nuremberg. There he encountered German Lutherans, and also met and married Margaret, the niece of Andreas Osiander (a Reformation theologian) in 1532. This unusual and uncanonical step was thrown into high relief when he was summoned from these Lutheran circles to become archbishop of Canterbury in 1533.

His belief in the scriptural warrant for the authority of the prince and not the *pope as head of the Church guaranteed a measure of protection from Henry VIII and Edward VI, to whom he acted as spiritual guide and tutor. This in turn enabled Cranmer to advance some reformed views, especially on the desirability of vernacular scriptures, the abolition of superfluous *saints' days, and the translation of the *liturgy and catechism into English. The limits of his loyalty to the Crown were tested by the accession of Queen Mary in 1553, who required his allegiance to the crown to be transferred to the papacy. He wavered and recanted at first, but finally came to the view that loyalty to the monarch had to be subordinate to loyalty to the word of God. He was accordingly burnt as a heretic on 21 Mar. 1556.

Craving (Buddhist): see TAṆHĀ.

Creation: see COSMOLOGY.

Creationism. 1. The view that the universe and all things in it were created directly by God and are not the result of a long evolutionary process, in contrast to the theory of evolution associated with Charles Darwin. The immediate ancestry of creationism can be found in the inter-war attempts of fundamentalists to get state laws passed which would ban the teaching of evolution in public schools. These attempts received a set-back in the Scopes trial in Tennessee (1925): John Scopes was convicted for teaching Darwin's theory, but the conviction was later overturned. Creationism emerged more specifically in the 1960s when creationists demanded equal time for the teaching of creationism (hence the importance of insisting on the equal validity of both as theories). The Creation Research Society supports the publication of creation science papers, but these have not been recognized as serious science outside the movement.

2. The view that God creates a soul for each human being, in contrast to pre-existence (that souls pre-exist bodies and enter into them) and traducianism (that souls generate souls as and when bodies generate bodies).

Credence. A small table or shelf in the sanctuary of a church near the *altar, to hold the bread, wine, and water to be used at the *eucharist.

Credo quia absurdum est (Lat., 'I believe because it is absurd'). A saying frequently used to mock the 'credulity' or dogmatic irrationality of religious believers. The saying is sometimes attributed to *Tertullian, though his nearest statement has a different nuance: 'Et mortuus est Dei Filius; prorsus credibile, quia ineptum est' (in paraphrase, so paradoxical is it to say that the Son of God has died that it would have to be a matter of belief). Such a saying does not preclude the recognition of rational support or reasons making evident what has evoked the statement: cf. ANSELM. It appears also in the form, 'credo quia impossibile est'.

Credo ut intelligam (commitment to the coherence between rationality and belief): see ANSELM.

Creed. A concise statement of what is believed (Lat., *credo*, 'I believe'). For examples, see Index, Creeds.

Judaism See ARTICLES OF FAITH.

Christianity Creeds originated as confessions of faith by candidates for *baptism. The Council of *Nicaea (325) put in a credal form the profession of faith as a standard of orthodoxy, and the use of creeds for this purpose rapidly spread. The most important creeds, the *Nicene Creed, *Apostles' Creed, and *Athanasian Creed, are also used liturgically.

Islam The basic 'creed' is the *shahāda, but this affirmation of allegiance (*islām*) is not a credal profession, with articles of faith. The nearest equivalent to that is the *'aqīda*, several of which appeared in the early history of Islam.

Cremation. Method of disposing of dead bodies by burning. It is the natural method of disposal in those religions (e.g. Hinduism: see ANTYEṢṬI) which regard the body as a dispensable vehicle for an immortal soul (*soma sēma*, 'the body a tomb'), or, as in the case of Buddhism, where the process of reappearance alone continues. But in religions such as Judaism, Christianity, and Islam, where there is belief in resurrection of the body, burial has been preferred as, intuitively, suggesting an easier reconstitution of the parts.

Crescas, Hasdai (*c.* 1340–*c.*1412). Jewish Spanish philosopher and statesman. He wrote *Or Adonai* (The Light of the Lord) to refute the philosophical teachings of *Maimonides and Jewish Aristotelianism. This was initially intended to be the first part of a larger work *Ner Elohim* (Lamp of God), and the second part, the *Ner Mitzvah* (Lamp of Commandment), was intended to supersede Maimonides' *Mishneh Torah* (A Second Law). Although Crescas' ideas were rejected by Isaac *Abrabanel and Shem Tov ben Joseph, he was later influential on *Spinoza.

Crescent moon (Arab., *al-qamar*). Religious emblem of Islam, derived from the Quranic (e.g. 36. 39) recognition of the waxing and waning of the moon as a sign of God's unchanging purpose and control.

Crosby, Fanny. Mrs F. J. Van Alstyne (1823–1915), American hymn-writer. She was blind from the age of six weeks. Her more than 2,000 hymns include '*Jesus, keep me near the cross', 'To God be the glory, great things he hath done', and 'Safe in the arms of Jesus'.

Cross. Chief of Christian symbols, deriving from the *crucifixion of Christ. It is used in various forms (plain, *crucifix, *icon) in the furnishing of churches and *altars, and as an object of private devotion. The claimed wood of the 'true cross' (see INVENTION OF THE CROSS) was divided and redivided, and now most of the *relics are very small.

Crown of thorns. An instrument of Christ's passion (John 19. 2). He is frequently depicted wearing this in *passion art and music: 'O sacred head, sore wounded . . .'.

Crowther, Samuel Ajayi (*c.* 1806–91). Anglican *bishop and pioneering African Church leader. He was baptized in 1825 and became a leading worker for the *CMS. Under the 'three-self' policy of Henry *Venn, he became the first African bishop of W. Africa beyond colonial limits, in 1864.

Crozier. The ceremonial staff carried by Christian bishops (and sometimes by abbots and abbesses).

Crucifix. A representation of the *cross of Christ, usually with the figure of Christ. *Evangelicals sometimes have a horror of it as idolatrous or as suggesting a dead rather than a risen Christ; at best, therefore, for them the cross should be empty (i.e. not bearing a figure).

Crucifixion. The punishment of death suffered by *Jesus (and, traditionally, a few other Christian *martyrs). Realistic crucifixion scenes emerged in the West with devotion to the passion, which developed in the 12th–13th cents.

Crusades (Lat., *cruciata*, 'cross-marked', i.e. *cruce signati*, those wearing the insignia of scarlet crosses). Military expeditions in the name of Christianity, directed chiefly against Muslim territories to recapture the Holy Land, but sometimes also against other non-Christians, and occasionally against Christian *heretics. Of the crusades to reconquer the Holy Land, the traditional count lists eight.

Juridically, a crusader was one who had 'taken the cross', i.e. vowed to go on a crusade. Failure to fulfil the vow might entail *excommunication, but in return for it the Church granted *indulgences (crusade bulls by the mid-13th cent. promised full remission of temporal punishment incurred by *sin) and security of a crusader's property in his absence on the crusade. These privileges came to be offered by the *papacy to those engaging in almost any campaign which could be presented as a defence of the Church including, in the 13th and 14th cents., the defence of the Church's property in Italy.

Cry of dereliction (of Jesus on the cross): see SON OF MAN, THE.

Crypto-Jews. Jews who secretly practised their religion while officially converting to either Christianity or Islam. Well-known examples are the *Almohads of Spain and N. Africa of the 12th cent, the neofiti of S. Italy (late 13th–16th cent.), the Conversos or *Marranos of Spain (15th and 16th cents.) and the Jadid al-Islam of Meshed, Persia (19th cent.). See ANUSIM.

Crystal night (Nazi terror against Jews): see KRISTALLNACHT.

Cudworth, R.: see CAMBRIDGE PLATONISTS.

Cuius regio, eius religio ('whose region, his religion'). A summary of the Peace of Augsburg (1555) whereby rulers decided whether the religion of their own area should be Roman Catholic or Lutheran.

Cūlavaṃsa (The Short Chronicle). The history of Śri Lankā from 302 CE to the 19th cent. It is a continuation of the **Mahāvaṃsa*, written by at least three authors.

Cult. A term which refers to many non-traditional religious movements. Academics sometimes contrast cults with sects (see CHURCH-SECT TYPOLOGY) on the grounds that the former (e.g. *Cargo cults) are more alienated from traditional religions than the latter (e.g. *Jehovah's Witnesses); or that cults are more innovatory.

Cults of affliction: see AFFLICTION, CULTS OF.

Cultural relativity and religion. Compared with the social organization of any of the higher primates, human communities are clearly different to a marked degree in the ways in which they organize, protect, and transmit their beliefs, values, social orderings, technologies, expectations, or whatever it is that might belong to a definition of *culture. But 'culture' not only marks humans off from primates: it marks human communities off from each other. Given that the basic biology and its needs are virtually identical in all humans, what is the status of the differences in culture which can so readily be observed? At one extreme are anthropologists who regard cultural diversity as nothing much more than a change of clothes: the clothes worn are no doubt well-chosen (i.e. well-adapted for the ecological niche which a particular group inhabits), but they cover the same basic human body. At the other extreme are anthropologists (and philosophers) who regard cultural diversity as profound: there is no such thing as 'human nature' or 'the person'; there are only mental and linguistic constructions which create entirely different ways of understanding and interacting with the world. In the succinct statement of E. Sapir (which underlies the Sapir-Whorf hypothesis about the way in which different languages create different worlds). 'The worlds in which different societies live are different worlds, not merely the same world with different labels attached.'

It is the second of these views which leads to cultural relativity, since if each culture creates and then imposes its own view of what reality is, then there is no neutral ground (no 'Archimedean point'—as in Archimedes' observation, 'Give me a place on which to stand and I will move the earth') on which to stand in order to give a neutral account or evaluation of any society or culture.

Beyond the issue of the incommensurability of different cultures, cultural relativism has raised equal questions for morality and *ethics. For if judgements are relative to the context in which they are produced, there cannot be any universal agreement on the good or the beautiful—though oddly, there *is* more agreement on the true. The intermediate holds that cultures elaborate different worlds in which differences make such a difference that they cannot be understood except on their own terms of reference; but on the other hand, limits are set upon viable worlds by the conditions set in nature—both in the external environment, and also in the human body. Religions can then be understood as consequences of extremely long-running transmissions of somatic exploration and exegesis (i.e. long-running explorations and interpretations of the competence of the human body and its possible experiences).

Culture. A many-layered concept with at least three dimensions: the cultivation of human natural capacities, the intellectual and imaginative products of such cultivation, and the whole way of life of a group or a society. Religion is fundamental in all accounts of culture, leading, e.g., C. *Geertz to reformulate the concept of culture as a socially constructed and historically transmitted network of *symbol systems (*The Interpretation of Cultures*, 1974).

Cupitt, D. (reductionist theologian): see SECULARIZATION.

Curate. A Christian clergyman who has the charge ('cure') of a parish.

Cur Deus Homo? The title of Anselm's famous treatise on the *Atonement (1097–8), meaning: Why did God become man?

Curé d'Ars (French priest): see VIANNEY, J.-B. M.

Curia, Roman. The collective organization which conducts the day-to-day affairs of the Roman Catholic Church.

Cursing. The reverse side of *blessing, and therefore believed to bring actual power to bear. For that reason, casual cursing is as much disapproved of as is the taking of oaths which bring the name of God into disrepute, or, even more, which imply a claim to control the power of God.

Cusanus (Christian philosopher): see NICHOLAS OF CUSA.

Custom (Jewish): see MINHAG.

Cuthbert, St (d. 687). Bishop of *Lindisfarne from 685. After the synod of Whitby, he was instrumental in winning acceptance of Roman usages at Lindisfarne. The cult of Cuthbert was especially popular from this time in N. England. Feast day, 20 Mar.

Cuti-citta (Skt., 'death consciousness'). In the scholastic Buddhism of the Theravāda tradition, one of the fourteen functions of the life-continuum (*bhavaṅga* (see ĀLAYA-VIJÑĀNA)). According to the medieval commentators it is the final moment of consciousness in an individual's life and is followed immediately by the first moment of consciousness at conception (*patisandhi-citta*) in the new appearance.

Cyavana. In Hindu mythology, son of *Bhṛgu.

Cyprian, St (d. 258). *Bishop of Carthage and *martyr. He was elected bishop only two years after his conversion to Christianity *c.*246. During the persecution of Decius (249–51) he ruled his church from exile. After his return he pursued the policy of reconciling the 'lapsed' (i.e. those who had *apostatized during the persecution), not easily, but after appropriate penance and delay. The subsequent schism of *Novatian gave rise to the question whether *schismatics returning to the Church needed rebaptism. Cyprian's writings in Latin include a number of short theological works, among them *On the Unity of the Catholic Church* (251), and letters. Feast days variously 16 and 26 Sept., 2 Oct.

Cyril, St (d. 444). Patriarch of *Alexandria from 412, and church *father. His career after *c.*430 was dominated by the controversy over church authority (he drove out schismatic followers of *Novatian), *christology, and specifically by his opposition to *Nestorius. The *Neoplatonist philosopher, Hypatia, was murdered by the mob, *possibly* at Cyril's instigation. The episode evoked a novel by Charles Kingsley. In the E. he is 'the Seal of the Fathers', in the W. a doctor of the Church (since 1882).

Cyril and Methodius (d. 869, 885). Christian missionary brothers, known as 'the *apostles of the (southern) Slavs'. Their activity was mainly in Moravia, subsequently among Croats, Serbs, and Bulgars, and was constantly subject to rivalry and opposition.

D

Da'at Torah (Torah understanding): see AGUDAT ISRAEL.

Da Costa, Uriel (1585–1640). Rationalizing Jewish freethinker. He was born in Portugal of a *Marranos family. After beginning a career as a church lawyer, he abandoned Christianity when he read the Hebrew Bible. Da Costa insisted on *sola scriptura* ('by scripture alone'), and rejected later *halakhic accretions, as well as ritual. He cast doubt on the immortality of the *soul; his first publication (1624) was duly burnt, and he was excommunicated (*ḥerem). In 1633, he formally submitted, though remaining privately sceptical. Such views led to a second excommunication (1633). His decision to recant required public humiliation and punishment, the thought of which led him to suicide.

Dādā Gurūs. Affectionate name (roughly, 'Grandad') of four Jain teachers (*suri*) in the Śvetāmbara (see DIGAMBARA) Kharatara *Gaccha (sect). The Gaccha traces its origins back to a monk, Vardhamana (d. 1031), who broke free from temple-dwelling monks in order to re-establish purity of teaching. Among his disciples was Jineśvara, whose skill in debate led to the name Kharatara, 'keen-witted'. His most celebrated successor was Jinadatta (1075–1154), who undertook hazardous missionary journeys into Muslim territory to win converts. Jinadatta, with three later *suris* make up the four Dādā Gurūs: Maṇidhāri Jinacandra (1139–65), the 'jewel-wearer', from the jewel in his forehead with which he performed miracles; Jinakuśala (1279–1331), who won many converts; and Jinacandra (1537–1612), who won concessions for Jains and protection for Jain holy places from Muslim rulers, perhaps from *Akbar. Places associated with the Dādā Gurūs are still the object of veneration.

Dādū Dayāl (c.1543–1603). A saint of N. India in the *Sant tradition who composed poetry in Hindi. Dādū gathered a group of disciples about him who collected his poems together in a volume called *Dāduvāṇi*. These poems, some of which are intensely personal, speak of devotion (*bhakti) to a God beyond qualities (*nirguṇa) and the anguish of separation from God. His biography was written by Jan Gopal, *Dādū Janam Līla*, (*c.*1620).

Daena (conscience): see FRASOKERETI.

Daeva (Old Pers., *daiva*; Middle Pers., *dēv*: 'shining one'). One of a group of gods in Ancient Persia (cf. DEVA) who were denounced by *Zoroaster as demonic and as gods of war and strife.

Daf Yomi (Heb., 'daily page'). Prescribed daily passage of *Talmud study. Devised by R. Meir Shapira in 1928, a double page of Talmud is prescribed for study each day. The entire Babylonian Talmud can be completed in seven years.

Dāgaba (Pāli *dhātu*, 'element, essence' + *garbha*, 'chamber, cave'). A Buddhist mound where *relics are kept, hence occasionally a relic-container. A dāgaba usually has the same form as a *stūpa but not all stūpas are dāgabas, because not all stūpas contain relics.

Dahara-vidya (Skt., 'small space' + 'knowledge'). The realization in Hinduism of *ātman within the body, specifically in the 'domain of *Brahman', the interior of the heart.

Dai-anjin (great peace): see ANJIN.

Daiba (datta). Jap. for *Devadatta (the Buddha's cousin).

Daibosatsu (Jap., 'great bodhisattva'). The title of *Hachiman understood as the incarnation of a great *bodhisattva. Daibosatsu is, therefore, any bodhisattva (Jap., *bosatsu) who has reached the stage (*futai*) of not falling back into a lower state, and who is thus assured of becoming a *buddha. It is used as a title of respect for an outstanding monk.

Daibutsu (Jap., 'great Buddha'). Statues of *Buddhas or *Bodhisattvas exceeding a height of 4.8 metres and found throughout Asia.

Dai-funshi (Jap., 'great resolve'). One of the three pillars of *zazen, the determination to counterbalance, through development of the *bodhi-mind, *dai-gidan*, 'great doubt'. *Dai-gidan* is not mild scepticism, but rather the necessary concomitant of enlightenment certainty: the more one knows by experience the truth of Zen, the more insistent the continuing presence of pain, strife, and suffering in the world must be as a question. The question is not to be evaded, but wrestled with from the perspective of dai-funshi. The third pillar is *dai-shinkon*, 'great faith'.

Dai-gedatsu (Jap., 'great liberation'). In Zen Buddhism, the attainment of enlightenment, and thus of the realized buddha-nature. Hence, it is a synonym for *nirvāna.

Dai-gidan: see DAI-FUNSHI.

Daigon (Jap., 'great incarnation'). The appearing in, or as, the human form of a deity.

Daigo-tettei (profound enlightenment): see DAISHI.

Daigu Ryokan (Zen poet and monk): see RYŌKAN DAIGU.

Daiji (Jap., 'great compassion'). The great compassion which is the goal and practice of *bodhisattvas. It is often used as the title of particular bodhisattvas, e.g. daiji daihi no satta, 'of great compassion and mercy', is Jizō; daiji daihi no honji is Kannon.

Daiji (Jap., 'important matter'). The one thing necessary in Japanese Buddhism for the attainment of enlightenment, namely, the desire and intention to seek it.

Daijō. Jap. term for *Mahāyāna.

Daijō-kai (Jap.). 'Rules of the great vehicle', i.e. rules for monks and laypeople in *Mahāyāna Buddhism, as e.g. in *jujukai.

Daijô-sai. The first First Fruits Ceremony (*Niiname-sai) following the accession of a new emperor in Japan. The entire sequence of official preparations and performances, promulgated during the 10th cent., is contained in *Engi-shiki Procedures of the Engi Era [Books VI-X]*, tr. F. Bock (1970), 27–56.

Daikoku. A Japanese deity (said to have been introduced to Japan by *Saichō, 767–822), identified in the popular mind as one of the seven gods of luck (Shichi-fuku-shin). The name is a Sino-Jap. tr. of the Skt. *Mahākāla, an Indian deity whose character in Japan is manifested variously as a deity of war, of wealth and agriculture, and of the underworld.

Daikyō. The 'Great Doctrine' promulgated by the new imperial Japanese government in the late 19th cent., as part of its effort to create a state religion. The Great Doctrine stated three central moral-religious tenets: (i) reverence for the national gods, (ii) the importance of the Law of Heaven and the Way of Humanity, and (iii) loyalty to the throne and authorities.

Daimoku. (Jap., 'sacred title'). The practice of chanting the *mantra *namu myōhō renge kyō*, 'I take refuge in the Lotus of the Wonderful Law Sūtra' (*Lotus Sūtra) followed by *Nichiren Buddhists. The Japanese monk Nichiren (1222–82) believed all Buddhist teaching and practice is concentrated in this mantra, which he also calligraphically inscribed on a tablet called the *gohonzon*, 'object of worship'.

Dainichi (Jap.; Skt., *Mahāvairocana*). The cosmic *Buddha of *Shingon or esoteric Buddhism. All phenomena point to the reality of Dainichi, and at the same time they are all manifestations of that reality. More concretely, it is said that the six elements—earth, water, fire, wind, space, and consciousness—create all Buddhas, all sentient beings, and the material world, Dainichi revealing the six elements in perfect harmony. The basic practice of esoteric Buddhism is to integrate the microcosmic activities of the body, speech, and mind with the *samādhi of the macrocosmic Dainichi.

Dainichi Nōnin or **Jimbō Zenji** (12th/13th cent.). Zen Buddhist Japanese master of the *Rinzai school. Initially introduced to *Tendai teaching, he reached enlightenment without formal instruction from a master, and founded the Sambō-ji (monastery). He is also credited (e.g. by *Nichiren) with the founding of the Daruma-school. Daruma teaching pushed the doctrine of all appearance being empty of attributes, and all therefore equally bearing the buddha-nature, to a logical extreme. Although Daruma-shu was repudiated by Jap. Zen, Nōnin was himself acknowledged as a profound master.

Dainihon Kannonkai. Early form of *Sekai Kyūseikyō.

Daiō Kokushi (Zen master): see NAMPO JŌMYŌ.

Daiosho (Jap., 'great priest'). Honorific title of Zen masters, used particularly in the daily recitation in Zen monasteries of the lineage of tradition running back to the *Buddha Śākyamuni.

Daishi (Jap., 'great master'). Buddhist title of respect for a *buddha or high official. It is used especially of *Kūkai.

Daishi (Jap., 'great death'). In Zen Buddhism, the death of (or to) the differentiated self, which leads to profound enlightenment (*daigo-tettei*). This is called 'the death on the mat' (*zagu*), the consequence of undertaking the Zen way which the *zagu* epitomizes.

Dai-shinkon (great faith): see DAI-FUNSHI.

Daitoku-ji. The Monastery of Great Virtue, one of the largest Zen Buddhist monasteries in Kyōto. It was built in 1319 and formed part of the Gosan (literally, 'five mountains'), a confederation of five monasteries, based on the model established by the Sung emperor, Ning-tsung.

Daityas. Sons of the *Vedic Goddess, *Diti, and demons, or giants, in post-Vedic Hinduism.

Daiun Sōgaku Harada (1870–1961). Japanese Zen master. He entered a *Sōtō monastery at the age of 7, but also trained in a *Rinzai monastery, Shōgen-ji. He became abbot of Hosshin-ji. His teaching was continued by his *dharma successor, Hakuun Ryōko Yasutani, whose 'Introductory Lectures' appear in P. Kapleau, *The Three Pillars of Zen* (1980).

Daiva (Skt.; cf. Lat., *deus*). Sacred or divine power at work, hence divinity itself; usually the influence of powers outside the observable workings of nature. *Daivī-māyā* is thus the way in which *Brahman brings manifestation into its apparent forms. In Zoroastrianism, daivas were taken to be malevolent and were condemned as *demons.

Dajjāl (Muslim form): see ANTICHRIST.

Ḍākiṇī (Skt., 'female witch'; Tib., *mkha'.'gro-.ma*, 'Female one who moves through the sky'). A class of Goddesses in Tibetan Buddhism attendant upon *yogins. Historically, ḍākiṇīs were known in India as flesh-eating attendants of *Kālī, and as the sexual partners of yogins. Iconographically, ḍākiṇīs are usually consorts of other deities, but it is *only* iconographically that they correspond to the Hindu *śaktis: the ḍākiṇīs are associated with wisdom, not with power, for which reason they are referred to as *prajñas (wisdoms).

Dakṣa (ritual skill): see ADITI; ĀDITYAS.

Dakṣinā (Skt., *da*, 'give', or perhaps *dakṣ*, 'causing the incomplete to be completed'). The Indian gift offered to the priestly officiants by the initiator of a sacrifice. Dakṣinā was also personified as a Goddess who is (mother nature) the giver of life and is propitious. Dakṣinā is associated with the right hand, the propitious or clean side, and thus with masculinity.

Dakṣinācāra (Skt., 'night hand' + 'custom'). *Tantric Hinduism of the pure kind, hence 'right-handed Tantra', as opposed to *vāmācāra, or 'left-handed Tantra'—the left hand being the one with which impure acts are undertaken.

Dakṣināgni. The southern of the three fires in which Hindu offerings are made, in this case to the *pitṛs (the ancestors who dwell in the south).

Dalada Maligawa (shrine of tooth relic): see TOOTH RELIC TEMPLE.

Dalai Lama. The office of temporal and spiritual leadership of the Tibetan peoples, of which the present holder, Tenzin Gyatso (Bstan-'dzin-rgya-mtsho) is the fourteenth. The history of the office begins with Gendun Drub (Dge-'dun-grub-pa, 1391–1475), the third successor of *Tsong Khapa as head of the *Geluk school. Gendun Drub was the first member of the Geluk to adopt the *tulku system of reincarnating *lamas. His successor was Gendun Gyatso, whose own successor Sonam Gyatso (1543–88) accepted an invitation to renew the Tibetan–Mongolian priest–patron relationship. In a respectful exchange by Lake Kokonor in 1578, Altan Khan gave Sonam Gyatso the Mongolian title 'Ta le' (Ocean [of Wisdom]) Lama, which, retrospectively applied to his two predecessors, made Gendun Drub the first 'Ta le' Lama ('Dalai' being a W. transcription).

The current Dalai Lama, Tenzin Gyatso, has based himself in Dharamsala, India, from where he has become well-known internationally, and been styled a 'god-king' by the Western press. This potentially misleading term stems from the Tibetan consideration of eminent beings as emanations of *Buddhas or *bodhisattvas, and the Dalai Lama in particular as an emanation of *Avalokiteśvara, the bodhisattva of compassion. Among Tibetans, he is more commonly called 'Gyalwa Rinpoche' (Precious Eminence), or simply 'Kundun' (Presence). An active statesman, Tenzin Gyatso continues to negotiate improved conditions for his people and terms for his own return, and has overseen the transformation of the previous theocratic government into a democratically elected autonomous body (albeit in exile). In 1989 he received the Nobel Peace Prize for his adherence to the Buddhist principle of non-violence in the Tibetan struggle, although in the 1990s a wing of the Tibetan Youth Congress advocating armed resistance has become more vocal.

Dalit (the oppressed), name given, by themselves, to the *untouchables of Hindu society, about a quarter of the whole. Their organization into a politically coherent group owed much to S.R. *Ambedkar, and serious riots broke out in 1997 in Maharashtra state when a statue of Ambedkar was desecrated. In 1997, K.R. Narayanan became the first Dalit to be president of India.

Dalmatic. A Christian eucharistic *vestment. It is a decorated tunic reaching to the knees.

Damadamā Sāhib Taxāl (Sikh movement): see BHINDRĀNAWĀLE, J. S.

Damaru. The drum of the Hindu god, *Śiva. It accompanies him as Naṭarāja, the Lord of the *Dance. It is shaped like an hour-glass, with each half representing the *liṅga and the *yoni. From the symmetry between the two, the cosmos is created.

Damascus or **Dimashq.** Capital of Syria, claimed to be the oldest continuously inhabited city in the world. Saul was converted to Christianity on the way to Damascus (hence 'a Damascus road experience' for any life-changing event); and 'the street called Straight' (i.e. Via Recta, Acts 9. 11) still runs for about a mile E.–W., with Roman gates at each end. When the *Umayyads came to power in 661 (AH 41), Damascus became their capital. The greatest monument is the Umayyad mosque, now restored after fire in 1893.

Damascus Document. Manuscript of a Jewish sect which left *Judah to settle in 'Damascus'. It reflects opposition to the *Hasmonean *high priesthood.

Damayantī. The heroine of *Nalopākhyānam*, the 'Story of Nala' in **Mahābhārata*, which was told to console Yudhiṣṭhira after his gambling losses.

Damdamā or **Damdama Sāhib** (Pañjābī, 'resting place'). Village in S. Pañjāb where Guru *Gobind Siṅgh dictated the *Ādi Granth.

Damian, Peter (monk and cardinal): see PETER DAMIAN.

Dan. One of the twelve tribes of *Israel.

Dāna (Pāli, 'gift'). In Indian religions, a gift, especially for a religious purpose. In Buddhism, it is an act of generosity to any creature, but more usually a particular gift to a *bhikṣu or to the *saṅgha, bringing *merit to the giver (or transferring that merit to others). In origin, it may have deliberately replaced the Hindu *dakṣinā offered to *brahmans officiating at sacrifices. Dāna is one of the Six Perfections (*Pāramitā), one of the Ten Contemplations (*anussati), and one of the most important works of merit (*puṇya).

Dance. Like all pervasive religious behaviours, the dominant importance of dance in religious and especially *ritual behaviours can be traced back to its genetic role (see Introduction and BIOGENETIC STRUCTURALISM). Dance, by its rhythm and exclusion of other external stimuli, induces brain behaviours (often leading to trance or ecstasy) which underlie claims to *shamanistic or divine possession. At the least, they become evidence of connection with the divine (e.g. dervishes/*derwīsh, *ḥasidic dancers), or of a manifestation of the divine (e.g. in Hindu temple dance). Among Hindus, dance reiterates the cosmic process, epitomized in Śiva, who, as Naṭarāja, the Lord of the Dance, is the patron of dancers, creating, sustaining, destroying, and bringing to birth. Much Hindu dance draws on the *Nātya Śastra* (*c*.1st cent. BCE or CE), which lays out the rules for the dramatic manifestation of the divine. *Kathak* (teller of tales) is an example in N. India, which syncretizes elements from Islam. *Kathākali* (story-tale) occurs at Kerala in S. India, drawing on the epics. The vernacular *nāc* (for nāṭya) gave rise to the Eng. 'nautch dancers'. *Kṛṣṇa's dance among the gōpīs is reflected in dance in honour of Kṛṣṇa (e.g. *Caitanya), visible in the streets today in the Hare Krishna (*International Society . . .) movement. See also GHOST DANCE; DENGAKU.

Dance of Death or **Danse Macabre** or **Totentanz.** A defiant reaction, principally in medieval Europe, to the unpredictable but inevitable occurrence of death. It was evoked especially by the spread of bubonic plague in the 14th cent., when sufferers danced in graveyards. Of many illustrations, Holbein's woodcuts, 'Totentanz', are particularly well-known. This deliberate confronting of death has a remote parallel in the Buddhist contemplation of death and of the frailties in the body which lead to it: see e.g. DEVA-DŪTA; DHĀTU-VAVATTHĀNA; FOUR LAST THINGS.

Daṇḍa (Skt.). Staff or rod, symbolizing power. In the hand of *Kālī, it symbolizes the irreversible power of time. Daṇḍa is also the personified form of punishment, especially as penitential, thus ameliorating the punishments of a future birth. *Yama's staff is a form of Yama himself, creating fear of the next life and better behaviour in this. A daṇḍa is bestowed during the sacred thread ceremony (*upanayana), and it is carried by a student (*brahmacarya) as a symbol of his renunciation of worldly, distracting pleasures.

Daṇḍadhara. The title of the Hindu god *Yama as judge of the dead.

Daṇḍin. 1. *Saṁnyāsin who carries a staff, and thus one who is on the fourth stage of life (*āśrama).

2. Early (*c*.7th cent. CE) writer of Sanskrit prose whose style is held out as a perfect model.

Dan-Gyo (Zen work): see LIU-TSU-TA-SHIH FA-PAO-T'AN-CHING.

Daniel, Book of. A book numbered among the *Writings of the Hebrew Bible and among the prophets in the Christian Old Testament.

Daniélou, Alain, or **Shiva Sharan** (1907–94). Musician and scholar of Indian religions. While in Benares, he converted to Hinduism, taking the name Shiva Sharan. He translated texts (notably *Kāma Sūtra*; see KĀMAŚASTRA) and wrote many books, notably *Hindu Polytheism* (1964), *La Musique de l'Inde du Nord* (1985), *Le Mystère du culte du Linga* (1993), and *La Sculpture* *érotique hindou* (1973). For Daniélou, polytheism surpasses monotheism because 'divinity can only be reached through its manifestations'.

Dante Alighieri (1265–1321). Italian poet. Little is known of his early life, but as a child he met 'Beatrice' with whom he fell in love. She died in 1290, the wife of another, provoking a crisis for Dante resolved by his writing *Vita Nuova*. In that, he promised her a poem 'such as had been written for no lady before'. That poem was his *Divine Comedy*, written sometime between 1305 and 1314. It is set in a period over Easter 1300 during which Dante travels from a dark forest (in which he has lost his way) through *hell and *purgatory to *paradise.

Daoism: see TAOISM.

Darajah (rank or degree): see MARRIAGE (ISLAM).

Dār al-ḥarb (Arab., 'abode of war'). Territory outside Muslim jurisdiction; the opposite of *dār al-Islām. In theory, *jihād is commanded, since inhabitants of such territory are at war with the Muslim *'umma. Qur'ān 9. 5 commands the Muslims to fight and slay the polytheists. There has been, more recently, an increased emphasis on a *third* category, the 'domain of covenant' or 'of agreement', *dār al-ṣulḥ.

Dār al-Islām (Arab., 'abode of Islam'). Territories within the Muslim *'umma's supremacy and in which Islamic law prevails. (Not to be confused with DARUL ISLAM.)

Dār al-ṣulḥ (Arab., 'abode of the Truce'). Non-Islamic territories no longer hostile but having a treaty agreement with the adjoining Muslim state, to which they pay tribute.

Dārā Shikoh (1615–59). Muslim heir-apparent of Shāh Jahān, who sought common ground between Hinduism and Islam. He regarded the two religions as 'the confluence of two oceans' (Qur'ān 18. 65): his views issued in *Majma' al-Bahrayn* ('Mingling of the Two Oceans', 1655). He also believed that the *Upaniṣads were 'the book that is hidden' (56. 78). As a result he began to translate Upaniṣads into Persian, in a work issuing in *Sirr-i Akbar* ('The Great Secret', 1657)—a work which, when translated into French by Anquetil Duperron (1801–2), had a great influence on European (e.g. Schopenhauer) attitudes to the East.

Darazī. A founder of the *Druzes, when he recognized the *Khalīfa al-Ḥākim as the incarnation of the universal reason (or *Logos) which had first been bestowed on *Adam, and had then been transmitted through the prophets to *'Alī, and thence to the Fātimid caliphs (*khalīfa). He was probably assassinated, but for reasons which are uncertain.

Darbār Singh (Divine Court). A name of the Golden Temple of *Amritsar, *Harimandir Sāhib.

Dardura-siddhi (Skt., 'frog' + 'praeternatural power'). The power to raise one's body through yogic practices, i.e. levitation.

Dark Night of the Soul. A term of Western mystical theology. According to the classical exposition of *John of the Cross, the dark night is the stage in which the soul is purified in preparation for union with God. The 'Dark Night of the Soul' is more technical, and a great deal more profound, than the colloquial usage, which debases the phrase into a general malaise.

Darqawiy(y)a (Sūfī order): see SHĀDHILIYYA.

Darśana (Skt., 'viewing'). 1. In post-Vedic times, the term refers to the 'schools' or 'viewpoints' of Indian philosophy, both orthodox and heterodox. The orthodox (*āstika) Hindu darśanas include six different systems which share certain presuppositions, in particular the authority of the *Veda as an infallible source of knowledge. These six darśanas are traditionally listed in pairs in the following order: *Nyāya, founded by Gautama, and *Vaiśeṣika by *Kaṇāda; *Sāṃkhya, founded by *Kapila and *Yoga by *Patañjali; *Pūrva-mīmāṁsā founded by *Jaimini and *Vedānta by *Bādarāyaṇa.

In dynamic interaction with the orthodox systems are the three main heterodox (*nāstika) darśanas, *Cārvāka, *Jaina, and Buddhist, which modify and adapt traditional views and challenge the authority of the Veda as well as the *brahman priesthood.

2. Paying respect or homage to ('viewing' with respect) a holy image, person or place, and receiving merit or blessing in return. Among Sikhs, the 'viewing' is of the *Ādi Granth, and hearing its contents.

3. In Buddhism (Pāli, *dassana*), insight based on reason to defeat false views (*dṛṣṭi*; Pāli, *diṭṭhi*) and mental defects (*kleśa; Pāli, *kilesa*).

Darshan (Heb., 'expounder'). A professional expounder of Hebrew scripture.

Darul Islam (from Arab., *dār al-Islām). A revolutionary movement in Indonesia whose aim was to establish an Islamic state. Its leader was Sekarmadji Maridjan Kartosuwirjo (1905–62), who declared the Islamic State of Indonesia in 1949.

Daruma. Jap. for *Bodhidharma, hence the occurrence in several terms: Daruma-ki, his date of death (5th day of 10th month); Daruma-shu, his school of teaching, hence a name for

Zen; Daruma-sōjō, the authentic transmission of his teaching via dharma-successors (*hassu) and patriarchs in succession (*soshigata).

Daruma school (Zen school): see DAINICHI NŌNIN.

Darwin, C. (theory of): see CREATIONISM.

Darwīsh (member of Muslim religious fraternity): see DERWĪSH.

Daśabala (Skt.; Pāli, *dasabala*). The ten powers of a *Buddha which confer knowledge on him of: (i) what is possible and impossible; (ii) the consequence of actions (*vipāka); (iii) the abilities of other beings; (iv) the direction of their lives; (v) the constituents of manifest appearances; (vi) the paths leading to the different domains of existence; (vii) those leading to purity and impurity; (viii) the states of meditation (*samādhi) and absorptions (*dhyāna); (ix) deaths and reappearances; (x) the eradication of all defilements (the three destructive poisons, Skt., *āśrava* Pāli, *āsava*: of desire, *kāma, of becoming in manifest form, *bhāva, and of ignorance, *avidyā/avijja).

Daśabhūmika-sūtra: see AVATAMSAKA LITERATURE.

Daśahrā or **Dussehra.** Ten-day Hindu *festival, celebrated at the beginning of Āśvina (see CALENDAR) in recognition of conquests of evil, especially of *Durgā over Mahiṣa and of *Rāma over *Rāvaṇa.

Dasakusalakamma (Pāli, 'ten meritorious actions'). A common Buddhist list of activities which bring good kamma (*karma) into effect and acquire (and transfer) merit: (i) *dāna; (ii) *śīla; (iii) *bhāvanā; (iv) *apacāyana* (showing respect to elders); (v) *veyyāvacca* (attending to their needs); (vi) *pattidāna* (transferring merit); (vii) *pattānumodana* (delighting in the merit of others); (viii) *dhammasavaṇa* (attending to the *dharma/dhamma of the *Buddha); (ix) *dhammadesanā* (preaching the dhamma); (x) *diṭṭhijjukamma* (adhering to right beliefs).

Daśalakśanaparvan (Jain observance): see FESTIVALS AND FASTS.

Dasam Granth or **Dasven Pādśāh Kā Granth** (Pañjābī, 'tenth book, book of the tenth Gurū'). Compilation of compositions traditionally ascribed to Gurū *Gobind Siṅgh and venerated by Sikhs. Despite its one-time canonical status, much of the Dasam Granth is seldom read, although it is especially important to the *Nihaṅgs.

Daśanāmī (Skt., 'having ten names'). A Hindu order of wandering monks founded by the great philosopher *Śaṅkara and upholding his philosophy of *Advaita Vedānta. It is a loose federation of *Śaivite *saṁnyāsins ('renouncers'), consisting of ten monastic lineages, the members of each lineage bearing a distinctive title or 'name' (*nāman*), which is suffixed to their individual monastic names at the time of initiation.

Dassana (Buddhist insight based on reason): see DARŚANA.

Dassera (period of Hindu festivals): see FESTIVALS AND FASTS.

Dastur (Zoroastrian high priest): see MAGI.

Daswandh. The Sikh donation of a tenth of one's income for the purposes of the *Panth.

Datsuma. Jap. for *dharma.

Dattātreya. A Hindu sage or god-figure. In the **Mārkaṇḍeya Purāṇa*, Dattātreya appears as an *antinomian sage. In other *purāṇas he is listed among the *avatāras of *Viṣṇu. *Iconography depicts him with three heads, although often in between Brahmā and Śiva.

Daughters of Zion. Biblical phrase: 'Daughter of Zion' generally refers to *Jerusalem or the Jewish people, as, for example, in, 'Rejoice greatly, O daughter of Zion ... lo, your king comes to you' (Zech 9. 9).

David

Judaism Second king of *Israel. David was the youngest son of Jesse, grew up in *Bethlehem and was said to be descended from *Ruth. He defeated the Philistines, the Moabites, the Arameans, the Ammonites, and the Edomites, and he made his capital in *Jerusalem. With the support of the religious establishment, the belief was fostered that God had chosen David and his descendants to rule over the Israelites forever (2 Samuel 7. 16), and he is traditionally believed to have written many of the *Psalms. In the *aggadah David is generally exalted as the great poet and scholar king. The unique status of the Davidic line of kingship is particularly emphasized. See also MESSIAH.

Islam Dāwūd or Da'ūd, is one of the line of *prophets, and listed as such in the *Qur'ān (6. 84). He is given the *zabūr*, a book—representing the Psalms—which is mentioned elsewhere in the Qur'ān as one of the former scriptures.

David ben Samuel/ha-Levi, or **Taz** (1586–1667). Jewish *halakhic authority. At the end of his life, persuaded by his sons, he seems to have given his support to *Shabbetai Zevi. His most important work, *Turei Zahav* (The Rows of Gold), a commentary on the four parts of Joseph *Caro's **Shulḥān Arukh*, has greatly influenced later halakhic decisions.

David ben Solomon Ibn Abi Zimra or **Radbaz** (1479–1573). Jewish *Talmudist and *kabbalist. Between 1517 and 1553, he was head of the Egyptian Jewish community and made several significant reforms. He subsequently moved to Safed. His most important works were collections of *responsa.

Davven or **Davnen** (Yid., uncertain origin). 'To pray': widely used among *Ashkenazi Jews.

Da'wa (Arab., from *da'ā*, 'call', 'summon'). Invitation, call; prayer (see DU'Ā', from the same root). It is the 'summons' to the way of Allāh, to the true religion (Qur'ān 14. 46). It is used today to denote the effort to spread the teachings of Islam, and in this sense is roughly equivalent to the concept of 'mission' in Christianity.

Daxma. Often referred to as a 'Tower of Silence', the place where *Zoroastrians expose their dead to vultures. Because death and decay are seen as weapons of evil, a corpse is traditionally seen as the place where *Angra Mainyu and his forces are powerfully present. All dead matter is polluting, but especially the corpse of a righteous person, for that represents a great (albeit temporary) victory of evil. It cannot therefore be buried in the earth, cremated, or disposed of at sea, for each of these is the good creation of Ahura Mazda. Zoroastrian funerals have two main concerns: to care for the soul and to restrict the pollution. It is important that a priest is called quickly after death. Traditionally the priest is accompanied by the Zoroastrian holy animal, a dog, who both protects people from threatening forces and is especially sensitive to an alien presence, and who therefore ritually 'sees' the corpse (Sagdid rite). There is an annual *muktad* ceremony where the souls of all the deceased are remembered.

Day, Dorothy (1897–1980). US Christian activist on behalf of the poor and underprivileged. In 1933, she founded (with Peter Maurin) the journal and movement, the Catholic Worker. She organized hospitality houses to care for the homeless and hungry, identifying herself with them. Among many books, see *House of Hospitality* (1939), *Loaves and Fishes* (1963), and her autobiography, *The Long Loneliness* (1981).

Dayāl Bābā (founder of Sikh reform movement): see NIRAṄKĀRĪ.

Dayānand(a) Sarasvatī (1824–83). Mul Shankara, founder of the neo-orthodox Hindu movement, *Ārya Samāj. After a long period as a wandering yogi, he settled in 1860 in Mathura, studying with the *Vedic scholar, Virajananda. Under his influence, Dayānand rejected the accretions of post-Vedic Hinduism and started a public campaign for a return to Vedic values.

Day of Atonement (Heb., Yom Kippur). The most important day in the Jewish liturgical year. (Leviticus 16. 30). After the destruction of the temple, it was believed that the day itself rather than the temple ritual atoned for *Israel's sin. The Day of Atonement liturgy begins in the evening of 9 Tishri (see CALENDAR) with the *Kol Nidrei (all the vows) service in the *synagogue. Services continue through the next day until sunset, when it is customary to blow the *shofar to indicate the end of the fast.

Day of Judgement: see DAY OF THE LORD.

Day of Judgement (Islam): see YAUM AL-DĪN.

Day of the Lord. In Jewish understanding, day of God's judgement on the world. The Day of the Lord is mentioned by *Isaiah, *Joel, *Amos, *Obadiah, *Ezekiel, *Zechariah, and *Zephaniah.

Days of Awe. In Judaism, the twelve days which begin with *Rosh ha-Shanah and end with Yom Kippur (*Day of Atonement).

Dayyan (Aram., 'judge'). Members of Jewish religious courts.

Dayyeinu (Heb., 'it would have satisfied us'). Title of the chorus of a Jewish *Passover song. The song lists all the good things God did for the Israelites in the *Exodus story.

Dbang bskur (Tibetan, empowerment): see ABHIṢEKA.

Deacon (Gk., *diakonos*, 'servant'). Christian minister next below *priest.

Deaconess. A woman Christian having an office akin to that of *deacon.

Dead Ḥasidim (follower of Naḥman of Bratslav): see NAḤMAN OF BRATSLAV.

Deadly sins or **capital sins.** In Christianity the root sins, usually listed as seven: pride, envy, anger, sloth, avarice, gluttony, and lust. Cf. the three 'deadly' faults of Buddhism; the *five deadly sins; *gogyaku-zai; *five evil passions.

Dead Sea Scrolls. Collection of manuscripts found in caves near the Dead Sea. The scrolls, discovered between 1947 and 1956, date mainly between *c.*150 BCE and 68 CE. They seem to have belonged to a succession of communities based at *Qumran, the last of which was destroyed by the Romans in the first Jewish revolt. They include manuscripts which seem to relate to a community or communities based in Qumran: the *Manual of *Discipline*, the **Damascus Document*, the **Thanksgiving Psalms*, and the **War Scroll*.

The identification of those who produced the sectarian documents has been much disputed. Scholarly consensus favours a group closely related to the *Essenes. However, it is at least equally likely that Qumran, because of its remoteness, was a haven of refuge for conservative groups in more than one period, who disapproved of (or were persecuted by) those who were running the *Temple in Jerusalem.

Dead Sea sect: see DEAD SEA SCROLLS; QUMRAN COMMUNITY.

Dean. The title of various Christian officials, of which the most important are: (i) the head of the *chapter of a *cathedral; and (ii) the head of the chapter of a *collegiate church which is a 'peculiar' (independent of any episcopal authority), e.g. Westminster Abbey.

Death. The human and religious imagination of the nature and meaning of death has been prolific: virtually everything that can be imagined about death has been imagined. Yet almost universally the major religious traditions did not in origin have any belief that there will be some worthwhile continuing life after death. This is in strong contrast to the popular impression that religions came into being to offer 'pie in the sky'—i.e. some compensation for the miseries and inequalities of this life. This erroneous view was elevated to a formal theory by such anti-religious theorists as *Marx and *Freud.

In fact, the early human imagination of death was entirely realistic: since the breath returns to the air and the body to the dust, there is nothing that *can* survive. Thus in both E. and W., the emphasis originally was on the positive worth of *this* life, not on some imagined heaven or hell.

The development of beliefs that there may be life beyond death (see AFTERLIFE) came about historically in different ways and with different anthropologies (accounts of human nature) in different religious traditions. In the Judaeo-Christian tradition, the belief developed in the 3rd or 2nd cent. BCE that the 'friendship with God' (as *Abraham's relationship with God was described) might perhaps be continued by God through death. The imagination of how God might bring that about then varied.

In the E., the sense that death can be contested and, in favourable circumstances (especially with the help of sacrifices), be postponed, led to the belief in Hinduism that a self or soul is reborn many millions of times as it moves toward *mokṣa (release). In early Buddhism, it was accepted that there is continuing reappearance, but no self or soul being reborn. In China, the caution of *Confucius was widely prevalent: 'Confucius said, "If we are not yet able to serve humans, how can we serve spiritual beings?" Tzu-lu then said, "Then let me ask you about death." Confucius said, "If we do not yet know about life, how can we know about death?" ' But in the Immortality Cult, and even more in the development of *Taoism, the quest for immortality was undertaken in the schools of *alchemy, sometimes literally, more often in spiritual terms.

On the basis of these understandings of death, different religions have expressed different preferences in the treatment of dead bodies: see CREMATION; FUNERAL RITES. They have also been in agreement to a large extent that excessive grief or mourning is inappropriate. See also AFTERLIFE and Index: Death, beliefs; Death, funerals.

Death, anniversary of (Jewish commemoration): see YAHRZEIT; FUNERAL RITES.

Death, kiss of. According to traditional Jewish belief, the death reserved for the righteous was like a hair being removed from milk (*B.Ber.* 8a).

Death of God. *Nietzsche proclaimed that the death of God was 'a recent event' in 1887. Belief in God had become *unglaubwürdig* (incredible). In that view he was anticipated by many major figures in the 19th cent., not least by the Young Hegelians: *Feuerbach, *Strauss, and *Marx. The first two attempted to 'deconstruct' theological language and to show that it is really language about ourselves; the last claimed that religion and theology are distorted and socially inhibiting reflections of unjust social and economic relations. In both cases, belief in a transcendent God, independent of this or any other universe, seemed to have become incredible. In the 20th cent., 'Death of God' theology (the view that theology is at best anthropology) was accelerated into prominence by the further considerations that, in a Newtonian universe, the God of traditional theism cannot intervene or make any difference in a universe of this kind; and that even if he could, he evidently has not, to judge from the enormity of such evil episodes as the *Holocaust. 'Death of God' theology then became associated with religionless Christianity.

Deborah. Hebrew judge. Deborah led the Israelites against Jabin, king of *Canaan (Judges 4 and 5).

Decalogue: see TEN COMMANDMENTS.

De Chantal, Jane-Francis (Jeanne-François), St. (Founder of Visitandines): see DE SALES.

De Chardin, T. (French Jesuit theologian): see TEILHARD DE CHARDIN.

De Civitate Dei ('The City of God'), Christian work by St *Augustine, which has had a major influence on political and social theory: it explores the relations between heaven and earth, and between divine *providence and human history.

Decretal. A papal letter; strictly, one in response to a question. Decretals are an important source of Roman Catholic *canon law.

Deer Park (site of the Buddha's first sermon): see SĀRNĀTH.

De fide (Lat., 'of the faith'). In Roman Catholic parlance, a term used of a proposition that has been explicitly and formally declared and defined by the Church to be true.

De Foucauld, Charles Eugène (1858–1916). Christian hermit. Brought to Roman Catholicism by Abbé Huvelin, he sought a life of poverty and solitude, finally as a hermit in the Sahara amongst the Muslim Tuaregs. He won their respect by his sympathy with their language and way of life, but was assassinated by one in 1916. His missionary ideal of prayerful presence, by way of commitment to a local circumstance, inspired the Little Brothers and the Little Sisters who follow a rule he composed, though in his lifetime no one joined him. See also PETITS FRÈRES.

Deg teg (Pers., 'kettle', 'sword'). A summary of the Sikh obligation for the *Panth to provide food and protection for the hungry and the unprotected.

Deguchi Nao (1836–1918). Female *shaman and founder of the new Japanese religion, Ōmoto-kyō. Through spirit writing, originally scratching these communications with a nail, she began to attract a large following. She met Ueda Kisaburo in 1898, and in 1900 recognized him as the promised saviour. He married Sumi, Nao's daughter, and became known as Deguchi Onisaburo. Deguchi Nao is venerated as *Kaiso* (spiritual founder) and Onisaburo as *Kyōso* (doctrinal founder).

Déïma or **Dahima.** The largest (after the *Harris churches) of the new religions in the Ivory Coast, with some 50,000 members among the Godié, Dida, Bakwé, and Bété peoples. Guigba Dahonon (1892–1951), a childless Godié, widowed in 1922, had various mystical experiences before developing a new teaching and movement, the Église Déïmatiste (a neologism), in 1942.

Deipara (mother of God): see THEOTOKOS.

Deism. The name of a heterogeneous 'movement' (it was not organized, and so-called Deist writers do not follow a single programme) of the late 17th and 18th cents., concerned to defend the rationality of religion and belief in God in the face of scepticism, or the perceived implications of Newton's laws. There is much emphasis on natural religion. Important works of Deist writers are: J. *Locke, *Reasonableness of Christianity* (1695); J. Toland, *Christianity not Mysterious* (1696); M. Tindal, *Christianity as Old as the Creation* (1730), the so-called 'Deist Bible'.

Delusion. A fault as fundamental in E. religions (e.g. *moha in Buddhism) as sin is in W. religions. Delusion is to see and interpret manifest appearance, including one's own nature and being, in the wrong way, mainly by superimposing wrong perceptions or ideas upon it. It is thus ignorance (in Hinduism *avidyā, in Buddhism *avijja, in Jap. Zen *mayoi*). See Index, Delusions.

Demiurge (Gk., *dēmiourgos*, 'craftsman'). The divine being in *Plato's account (in *Timaeus*) of the formation of the visible world. In *gnostic thought, it was used disparagingly of the inferior deity who created the material universe, distinguished from the supreme God.

Demon (Gk., *daimōn*, 'a spirit'). Originally an unseen reality influencing a person's life, speech, or actions (e.g. the *daimōn* of Socrates), it became associated with malevolence or evil. Sometimes identical with the *devil, demons (in the plural) become more often servants or agents of the devil.

Demythologization. A programme associated particularly with Rudolf *Bultmann which endeavoured to penetrate and re-express the meanings of biblical myths. For Bultmann demythologization was the attempt to express the content of myth in the non-imaginative form of the analysis of existence. In his view, the account of existentialists, especially M. Heidegger, is 'no more than a secularised, philosophical version of the New Testament view of human life'. See also HERMENEUTICS.

Dengaku (Jap., 'field entertainments'). Ritual music and dance forms within the agricultural folk religion of medieval Japan (*c*.11th–17th cents.).

Dengyō Daishi (founder of Tendai): see SAICHŌ.

Denkō-Roku (Sōtō stories): see KEIZAN OSHŌ DENKŌ-ROKO.

Denne (also **Den'e**, **Den-i).** In *Zen Buddhism, the handing on of the robe as a symbol of the transmission of *buddha-dharma in the lineage of patriarchs (*soshigata) to a successor (*hassu).

De Nobili, Roberto (1577–1656). Christian *Jesuit missionary. Despite family opposition, he became a Jesuit in 1596/7 and was sent to India in 1605. In contrast to the established missions which sought a disjunctive conversion from all things Indian, de Nobili learnt the languages and adopted the style of a *saṁnyāsin. Other Christians objected on grounds of a betrayal of Christianity, and he was inhibited from activity. His appeal to Rome was eventually upheld, in *Romanae Sedis Antistes*. His pioneering attempt (like that of *Ricci in China) to distinguish the gospel from the external aspects of the Church was an important step on the path to the indigenization of Christianity.

Denomination. A religious group within a major religion, having the same faith and organization. See also SECTS.

Densetsu (Jap., 'explanations of tradition'). Narratives of Japanese tradition describing acts of prominent figures, especially holy men who have attained religious powers, and are not entirely legendary (i.e. they had historical existence). Most of them are Buddhist. Particularly well-known are *Kobo densetsu*, the tales of *Kūkai. Comparable as genres of religious stories are *engi* (which tell especially of miracles and portentous events associated with holy places) and *reigenki* (stories of Buddhas and *bodhisattvas, in particular, of their efficacious powers of intercession). See also SETSUWA; SHINWA.

Deoband. A seat of Muslim learning, situated in Saharanpur, India. It was founded by Mawlana Qasem Nanawtawi in 1867. During the 20th cent. it gained extensive influence throughout the Muslim world and ranks with *al-Azhar in importance. Its aim is to resuscitate classical Islam, and to rid the Muslims of theological corruption and ritual malpractices. It blocks any innovation, e.g. it is resolutely opposed to compulsory education for Muslim girls.

Deontological ethics (from Gk., *dei*, 'it is necessary'). *Ethics which are grounded in objective principles and demands, rather than in an evaluation of consequences.

Dependent origination (nexus of cause in Buddhist analysis which brings appearances into being): see PATICCA-SAMUPPĀDA.

Deprogramming. A technique devised in the early 1970s by the American Ted Patrick as an antidote to the alleged *brain-washing or 'programming' methods used in recruitment by some *new religions.

Derash (Heb., 'interpret'). A Jewish method of interpreting scripture. Derash is contrasted with *peshāt as the homilectical rather than the literal exposition of the text. It is one of the four traditional methods of interpretation: see BAHYA BEN ASHER.

Derekh erez (Heb., 'way of the world'). In Judaism, acceptable behaviour. According to R. Ishmael b. Nahman, derekh erez preceded the giving of the *Torah by twenty-six generations. Two minor tractates of the *Talmud, *D. E. Rabbah*, and *D. E. Zuta*, provide rules of conduct and guides to behaviour.

Derwīsh or **dervīsh** (Pers., 'beggar'). A member of a Muslim religious fraternity (although the word may mean simply a religious mendicant, in Arab. *faqīr). The fraternities perhaps began in the custom of groups gathering around a particular *Sūfī teacher. The particular ritual of a group is as important as *ṣalāt (prayer). The elimination of outward stimuli is achieved by many different techniques, of which the best-known is the whirling *dance—hence the 'whirling dervishes', more correctly known as *Mawlawīy(y)a, transliterated as Mevlevis.

De Sales, Francis, St (1567–1622). Christian *bishop and spiritual director and, with St Jane Frances de Chantal (1572–1641), the founder of the Salesian style of spirituality. Educated at Paris and Padua his life after ordination was active and much involved in the world and his diocese; whereas Jane de Chantal was more inclined to contemplation and the creation of holy space in her life. Together they founded the community of the Visitation of the Holy Mary. The purpose of Salesian spirituality is to establish devotion to God in the midst of everyday life.

A number of Salesian Orders were subsequently founded, e.g. the Salesians of St John Bosco, the Oblates of St Francis de Sales.

Descartes, René (1596–1650). Philosopher. Educated at the *Jesuit college of La Flèche, in 1613 he went to Paris. Having devoted himself to philosophy, he settled in Holland. In 1649, at Queen Christina's invitation, he went to Sweden, where he died. His philosophy—expounded principally in his *Meditations* (1641), *Principles* (1644), and *Discourse on Method* (1637)—is based on a method of radical doubt. But even doubt leaves an awareness of self—his famous *cogito ergo sum* ('I think, therefore I am')—which becomes the pivot of his philosophy. From this point Descartes established, by pursuing 'clear and distinct ideas', a radical distinction (Cartesian dualism) between mind and matter —'thinking' and 'extended' reality—the existence of God (principally by a form of the *ontological argument), and thence the reliability of the world perceived through the senses.

Descent (of Christ) into Hell. A subject of Christian affirmation in, e.g., the *Apostles' Creed. The belief that Christ descended into *hell between his death and resurrection is based, though quite uncertainly, on such passages as Matthew 27. 52 f. and 1 Peter 3. 18–20. Some have understood the descent as an expression of Christ's victory over the evil powers (the 'harrowing of hell'); others, as the occasion of Christ's preaching to the pre-Christian righteous waiting in *Sheol.

Desecration of host: see HOST, DESECRATION OF.

Desert Fathers. The earliest Christian monks of Egypt, *c.*3rd–5th cents. Their names and way of life were made famous in the Greek and Latin world through *Athanasius' *Life of *Antony*, the writings of *Jerome, the *Life of *Pachomius*, the anecdotal *Lausiac History* (*c.*419) of *Palladius, a similar *History of the Monks of Egypt*, and the *c.*6th-cent. collections known as the *Apothegmata Patrum* (Sayings of the Fathers). The emphasis in all these works is one of *asceticism, tempered by quiet devotion.

Determinism. The view that events and behaviours are determined before they occur, by the laws of the universe or by God. In religions, determinism takes different forms: in Christianity, see *Augustine and *Calvin; in Islam, *qadar and *kasb, *Allāh; in Hinduism *et al.*, *karma. See also PREDESTINATION.

Detraditionalization (the erosion of tradition in religion and society): see ENTTRADITIONALISIERUNG.

Detroit Conference (1975): see LIBERATION THEOLOGY.

Deus absconditus (Lat., 'hidden God'). The apparent absence of God from those who seek him, or from circumstances where the godly are in extreme trouble.

Deus ex machina (Lat., 'God out of the machine'). The device in classical theatre of bringing God on to the stage and into the action to resolve a problem in the plot; hence the introduction of an artificial solution to a problem.

Deus otiosus (Lat., 'inactive God'). God understood as removed or detached from activity in relation to humans or the created order.

Deus sive Natura (God or Nature): see SPINOZA.

Deuterocanonical books. Biblical books belonging to a second or secondary *canon, and specifically the books of the *Apocrypha, accepted by the RC Church as belonging to the canon of the (Hebrew) Old Testament.

Deutero-Isaiah (Isaiah 40–55): see ISAIAH.

Deuteronomic history. The name given by scholars to the theory of history in the biblical books Deuteronomy–2 Kings: obedience to the commands of God leads to success, and disobedience to disaster.

Deuteronomy. The fifth book of the *Pentateuch in the Hebrew Bible and Christian Old Testament. The English title ('second law') derives from the Septuagint Gk. version of 17. 18. The usual Hebrew title *Devarim* ('words') is the second word of the text.

Deva (Skt., perhaps connected with *dyaus*, 'bright sky'). 'Shining One'. In Hinduism, a deva is a celestial power (cf. *Chandogya Upaniṣad* 6.3), and particularly a manifestation (*not* a personification) of a natural power, generally beneficent, especially if propitiated through offerings (see SACRIFICE, HINDU). In that way, it became a term for all the Vedic gods, generally reckoned as thirty-three (*Ṛg Veda* 1. 139. 11, 1. 45. 2). The introduction of goddesses, *devīs, appears to have been secondary.

In Buddhism, devas are manifest forms of reappearance (*punabbhāva) in 'heaven', i.e. in one of the good domains of manifestation (*gati).

Deva (Buddhist Madhyāmaka philosopher): see ĀRYADEVA.

Deva-dāsī. 'Slaves of the *deva', women in Hindu temples devoted to the God or gods, especially *Śiva, the lord of the *dance, hence temple-dancers. But their dedication was also understood as a marriage to the God, the sexual realization of which was enacted by *brahmans and by other devotees, until eventually they were liable to become temple prostitutes.

Devadatta ('god-given'). In Hinduism, (i) the name of *Arjuna's conch shell; (ii) the white horse that Pārāśraya (*Kalki as universal ruler) will ride; (iii) a *prāṇa (cosmic energy) stream initiated by yawning to distribute power/ *breath to an exhausted body.

In Buddhism, the cousin of the *Buddha (known in Japanese as Daiba (datta)), who joined the *saṅgha after hearing a discourse of the Buddha, but who plotted to murder him.

Deva-dūta. The Buddhist 'messengers from the *deva', sickness, old age, and death.

Devagṛha (house of God): see MANDIR(A)

Devakī. In Hindu mythology, daughter of Devaka, and wife of *Vasudeva.

Devālaya (house of God): see MANDIR(A).

Devaloka. 'Domain of the devas', a rough equivalent to *heaven, in Indian religions.

Deva-mātṛ (mother of the gods): see ADITI.

Devapūjā (worship of deities): see PŪJĀ.

Devarāja (Skt., 'god' + 'ruler'). A cult developed at *Angkor, in which the king was recognized as divine, or perhaps as ruler of the gods.

Devarāja (four world protectors): see CELESTIAL KINGS.

Devatā(s) (Skt.). In Hinduism, a group of lesser gods and spirits, often related to village life. The many classes of devatās include tree spirits, water spirits, village gods, demons of disease, etc.

Devayāna. 'The path of the deva', the way, in Hinduism, followed by the truly faithful after death, leading to the realization of *Brahman. Less mythologically, it is the path of wisdom and spiritual knowledge.

Devekut (Heb., 'cleaving'). Communion with God, derived from Heb., *davak*, being devoted to God. It is a concept and an attainment of great importance in *Ḥasidism.

Devī. Hindu Goddess. The term can be applied to any of the many forms of the Goddess. Initially, they may simply have been the feminine counterpart of the *devas, but already by the *Vedic period they appear as manifestations of the power inherent in natural phenomena, as e.g. *Uṣas (dawn), Rātrī (night), *Gaṅgā (Ganges), and other sacred rivers. In the post-Vedic period, many of these features were assimilated in Mahādevī (Great Goddess), who is the source of energy in the cosmos (*śākti), the dynamic counterpart of *Śiva. For Śāktas, Mahādevī is more than a counterpart: she is the ultimate source, for whom the other gods are servants and agents.

The major forms of Devi are *Durgā, *Pārvatī, and *Kālī. See Index, Devi.

Devī-Bhāgavata-Purāṇa. Hindu mythological work in Skt., belonging to the genre of the *purāṇas, 'the purāṇa that imitates the **Bhāgavata Purāṇa* but is dedicated to the Goddess'. Its date of composition will not be much earlier than the 15th cent. CE. The Goddess is envisaged as Bhuvanêśvarī, 'Empress of the World', and as residing in the supreme heaven of Maṇidvīpa.

Devil. In Jewish scripture, the figure of *Satan is that of an adversary (1 Kings 11. 14), allowed by God to engage in his probing work (Job 1–2, Zecheriah 3. 1 f., 1 Chronicles 21.1; cf. 2 Samuel 24. 1). In later Judaism, although Jewish folklore includes stories about Ashmedai, the king of *demons and Lilith his queen, the figure of the devil is not significant.

In both Christianity and Islam, the devil and Satan are at times identified, and yet also appear as separate figures.

The devil is named in the *Qur'ān Iblīs, perhaps from Gk., *diabolos*, though Muslims derive the name from Arab., *balasa*, 'he despaired' (*sc.* of the mercy of God). But he is also al-Shaitān, Satan, and 'the enemy of God'.

Although Iblīs and (al-)Shaitān are identified, Shaitan also has a distinct existence, perhaps as the leader of the *jinn.

See also DEMON for near-equivalent figures in other religions.

Devil's advocate or **advocatus diaboli.** Person appointed by the Roman Catholic Congregation of Rites to contest the claims of those put forward for beatification or canonization (i.e. being recognized officially as saints). His more correct name is *promotor fidei* (promoter of the faith); the supporter of the proposal is known as *advocatus Dei* (advocate of God).

Devotio Moderna (Christian community): see GROOTE, G.

Dev Samaj (Hindu movement): see AGNIHOTRI.

Devshirme (young Christian conscripts to Islam): see JANISSARIES.

Dew, prayer for (Heb., *tefillat tal*). Supplication for moisture forming part of the Jewish *'Amidah during the dry season.

Dge-'dun-grub-pa: see DALAI LAMA.

Dge lugs (school of Tibetan Buddhism): see GELUK.

Ḍhamaru (drum, Hindu): see DAMARU.

Dhamma or **Dharma** (Pālī, Skt.). Check alternative spellings at appropriate place.

Dhammabhaṇḍāgārika (chief disciple of Buddha): see ĀNANDA (1).

Dhamma-cakka or **dharma-cakra** (Pālī, Skt.). 'The Wheel of the Doctrine'. The motif of the many-spoked wheel is the distinctive symbol of Buddhism. It originally signified the Buddha's act of proclaiming his doctrine (*dharma) to the world (see FIRST SERMON). The dhamma-cakka has come to signify Buddhist teaching and doctrine generally.

In earliest *iconography (*c.*2nd cent. BCE), the dhamma-cakka features as an aniconic symbol for the Buddha. When eight spokes are depicted, this signifies the Eightfold Path (*aṣṭangika-mārga) or the cardinal points of the compass.

Dhamma-cakkappavattana-sutta. 'The Setting in Motion of the Wheel of Dhamma', the title of what is regarded as the *Buddha's *First Sermon, preached in the Deer Park at Isipatana (*Sārnāth), near Benares. The sermon is recorded in **Saṃyutta-Nikāya* 5. 420.

Dhammapada (Teaching of the Verses). A collection of 423 key Buddhist texts (verses), of wide influence and importance throughout the Buddhist world. Spiritual teachers in India were expected to conclude a discourse with a key verse (*gatha*), and the *Buddha frequently followed that custom. The *Dhammapada* is a collection of such verses.

Dhanvantari. The physician of the gods in Hinduism, who emerged from the *Churning of the Ocean bearing the cup of *amṛta.

Dharam yudh ('war of righteousness'). Sikh recognition that in some circumstances war is necessary. Gurū *Nānak insisted that tyranny and injustice must be resisted, and Gurū *Amar Dās told members of the *Kṣatriyas that it was their *dharma to establish a protective fence of justice. However, it was not until the time of Gurū *Gobiṅd Singh (10th Gurū) that the rules of war were drawn up. He laid down five conditions of a justifiable war: (i) it must be action of the last resort; (ii) the motives must be pure; (iii) it must not be for the purpose of gaining territory; (iv) the soldiers must be committed Sikhs who therefore conduct themselves according to Sikh standards; (v) minimum force must be employed. See, in comparison, JUST WAR.

Dhāraṇā (Skt., 'support'). 1. One-pointed concentration (*ekāgrata) in *yoga; the fifth 'limb' of *Patañjali's 'eight-limbed' (aṣṭāṅga) or *rāja-yoga resulting from *prāṇāyāma.

2. A term denoting a level of sonic cosmogony in *Tantrism. For example, in *Kashmir Śaivism the Devanāgarī phonemes *ya*, *ra*, *la*, and *va*, which represent certain levels of the cosmic hierarchy, are dhāraṇās, the idea being that sound (*nāda, *śabda) is the support of manifestation.

Dhāraṇī. In Hinduism, the earth Goddess; and (as also in Mahāyāna and Tantric Buddhist sources), a magical formula often composed of random syllables, the recitation of which is thought to produce supernatural effects or bestow magic powers.

Dharma or **Dhamma** (Skt., Pālī): check alternative spellings at appropriate place in compound words.

Dharma (Skt., *dhar*, 'hold', 'uphold'). 1. In Hinduism, dharma is a fundamental concept, referring to the order and custom which make life and a universe possible, and thus to the behaviours appropriate to the maintenance of that order. Initially, dharma applied more to ritual and religious rules (especially sacrifices) than to ethics (e.g. *Ṛg Veda* 3. 17. 1), but by the time of the *Brāhmaṇas, the term includes also the rules which govern (and enable) society. These were gathered in the *Dharmasūtras and *Dharmaśāstras, of which the most important are the law-codes of Manu and Yajñavalkya. In the *Upaniṣads, dharma is related more to the ways appropriate for the attainment of *Brahman, than to ethics.

2. In Buddhism (Pālī, *dhamma*), the Hindu sense of cosmic law and order is retained, especially as it works out in *karma and reappearance according to the law of karma. But it was rapidly applied also to the teaching of the *Buddha (*pariyatti*) who is himself a manifestation of the truth that is dharma. Dharma is then understood as the practice (*paṭipatti*) of that truth, and as its realization in stages (*paṭivedha*) up to *nirvāna, of which in this way dharma becomes a synonym.

3. Among the Jains, dharma may simply be the teaching of the *Jinas, so that *adharma* is its opposite—error and immorality. However, both of these are also regarded as basic constituents of the universe: dharma is the all-pervasive medium of motion or activity, and adharma, also pervasive, offers the circumstance of rest. Both are understood as real substances, in the Jain sense that without the ontological truth of the Five Elements (*astikaya), there could be no distinctions in the universe, which is palpably false.

Dharmacakra (Skt.). The wheel of *dharma, the teachings of the *Buddha. See (Pali) DHAMMA-CAKKA.

Dharma character school (school of Chinese Buddhism): see FA-HSIANG.

Dharma Contest (mutual encouragement between master and pupil in Zen Buddhism): see HOSSEN.

Dharmadhātu (Skt., element of phenomena'; Tib., *chos.kyi.dbyings*, 'expanse of phenomena'). A term in Buddhist philosophy which began as a *Hīnayāna concept, indicating the true nature of phenomena as ultimately specific entities subject to dependent origination (Skt., *pratītyasamutpāda*; Pālī *paticcasammupāda), but which grew in importance in the

*Mahāyāna to describe the true nature of all phenomena collectively as indivisible and empty (*śūnyatā) of own-being (*svabhāvaśūnya*). In modern Western usage it generally, and perhaps inadequately, simply indicates 'the absolute'.

Dharmaguru (Orthodox Hindu): see NĀSIK.

Dharmakara (name of king who vowed to found a Buddha-land): see AMIDA.

Dharmakāya. (One of three aspects of the buddha-nature): see TRIKĀYA.

Dharmakīrti. A Yogācāra/Vijñānavāda Buddhist logician of the 7th cent. CE, and author of seven treatises originally intended as commentaries on the work of *Dignāga but eventually superseding the latter as the basic materials for the traditional study of Buddhist logic and epistemology.

Dharmapāla (Skt., 'guardian of the *dharma'). 1. *Vajrayāna Buddhist deities, called on by Vajrayāna to protect the dharma wherever it is under threat.

2. *Yogācāra Buddhist philosopher (*c.*7th cent. CE), who was abbot of the Mahābodhi monastery at *Bodhgayā. Almost all his commentary writing has been lost, apart from Chinese trs.

Dharmapala, Anagarika (1864–1933). Sinhalese Buddhist reformer who laid foundations for the revival of Buddhism. He was born Don David Hewavitarne, but he renounced his European name in 1881 and took the name 'Guardian of Truth'. In 1891, he founded the Maha Bodhi Society for the renaissance of Buddhism and for the rescue of Buddhist sites in India.

Dharmasagara (Jain controversialist): see GACCHA.

Dharmaśāstra (Skt., *dharma*, 'law' + *śāstra*, 'teaching'). Any of a class of Sanskrit texts concerned with rules of conduct and law. Dharmaśāstras tend to be longer and more systematically organized than *dharmasūtras, and treat some topics neglected in the dharmasūtras, such as *vratas (religious vows); *utsarga* and *pratiṣṭhā* (dedication of public utilities, shrines, and temples); *kāla* (auspicious times); and *tīrtha (pilgrimages to sacred places).

Of the more than 2,000 surviving dharmaśāstras, the most influential is certainly the *Manusmṛti* or Laws of Manu (see DHARMA). The *Yājñavalkyasmṛti* has had an indirect influence upon modern Indian law *via* the commentary of Vijñāneśvara.

Dharma-successor (one in succession of Buddhist teachers): see HASSU.

Dharmasūtra (Skt., *dharma*, 'law' + *sūtra*, 'aphorism'). Any of a class of Sanskrit prose texts concerned with law and rules of conduct (*dharma). Dharmasūtras differ from *dharmaśāstras in that the former consist of prose or mingled prose and verse, while the latter consist exclusively of verse. Dharmasūtras tend to be briefer than dharmaśāstras, consisting of terse *sūtras or aphorisms which are seldom arranged in any systematic fashion.

Major dharmasūtras include the *Gāutamadharmasūtra*, *Bāudhāyana-dharmasūtra*, *Āpastamba-dharmasūtra*, *Vasiṣṭha-dharmasūtra*, *Viṣṇusmṛti*, and *Vāikhānasa-smārtasūtra*.

Dharmsālā (Sikh community): see SIKHISM.

Dhātu (Skt., Pāli, 'region, element'). A word occurring frequently as a component in longer Buddhist terms, e.g. as one of the three worlds or domains, *kāmadhātu*, *rūpadhātu*, *arūpadhātu*—see LOKA. In its own right, it refers to elements of many different kinds, e.g. the physical elements (earth, water, wind, fire), the eighteen elements of sentience and consciousness (eye, ear, nose, tongue, mental awareness, etc.), the six states of appearance (solid, liquid, temperature, moving, spatial, conscious or not), the remains of a body after *cremation.

Dhātu-vavatthāna (Pāli). Buddhist analysis of the elements of the body, and thus one of the forty meditation exercises advocated by the *Visuddhimagga* (for which see BUDDHAGHOSA).

Dhikr (Arab., 'remembrance'). Basically a Quranic word, commanding 'remembrance of God', an act of devotion during and after the *ṣalāt (prayer). However, the *Sūfīs consider dhikr a spiritual food, and it is one of their main practices. Each Sūfī order has a dhikr of its own, constructed by its founder; the litanies and incantations are derived from the Qur'ān and taught by the *murshid* (Sūfī guide) to the initiate. It should be noted that the dhikr does not bring union with God: it is a device to purify the heart so that it may become a fit receptacle of the divine attributes.

Dhimma. Official protected status granted by the Muslim ruling power to the non-Muslims, known as Ahl al-Dhimma, an individual being termed a Dhimmī. These were in origin generally of the *Ahl al-Kitāb, People of the Book (scripture), i.e. Jews and Christians, a status extended to *Zoroastrians (Majūs) and others as time went on until it has come to refer to non-Muslims living in a Muslim state. Unlike pagans (*mushrikūn*), Dhimmīs are allowed to retain their religion and generally to practise it unhindered, though subject to certain conditions and to *jizya (poll tax).

This practice was continued and elaborated by the Ottoman 'millet' system.

Dhīr Mal (17th cent. CE). A claimant to being the Sikh Gurū. His followers were called Dhīrmalīās.

Dhītika (Buddhist sage): see NĀGASENA.

Dhoti. Loin-cloth, common in India, and compulsory in some temples, as a mark of *ascetic poverty before God.

Dhṛtarāṣṭra. In the **Mahābhārata*, the blind 'king', father of the *Kauravas (Dhārtarāṣṭras), who, despite the meaning of his name ('he whose kingdom is firm'), is too weak to stop his evil sons from playing their dice game against the *Pāṇḍavas and fighting the *Kurukṣetra war.

Dhṛtarāṣṭra's blindness has been interpreted as a metaphor for the blindness of fate.

Dhruva (Skt., 'fixed, constant'). In Hindu mythology, the son of Uttānapāda and grandson of *Manu. His constancy has made him the symbol of fidelity in Hindu marriage ceremonies.

Dhū'l-Ḥijja. The Islamic month of pilgrimage (*ḥajj). It is the last month of the Muslim calendar.

Dhū'l-Nūn (Arab., 'owner of the fish'). A Quranic name for the Prophet Yūnus (*Jonah), after whom sūra 10 is named.

Dhu'l-Nūn al-Misrī (d. 859 (AH 245)). An Egyptian mystic who travelled widely in search of truth and certainty. He became a leading authority on *ma'rifa* (knowledge of inner truth) and was considered to be the *qutb (spiritual head) of the *Sūfīs of his time. Dhu'l Nun classified knowledge into three categories; (i) the knowledge of religious commands and observances, which is for both the elect and the common people; (ii) the knowledge gained by proof and demonstration, which is for the elect; and (iii) *ma'rifa*, which is beyond the power of human learning and reason (which is why so many reject it). He equated it with the love of God.

Dhūtanga (Skt., Pāli, 'shaking off'). Twelve optional practices allowed by the *Buddha (see further ASCETICISM): (i) wearing patched robes; (ii) wearing a robe made of three pieces (*tricīvara*); (iii) eating only begged-for food; (iv) eating once a day; (v) refraining from excess at any meal; (vi) taking only a single portion of food; (vii) living in seclusion; (viii) living where bodies are cremated; (ix) living under a tree; (x) living in the open; (xi) living in whatever place one chances to arrive at; (xii) sitting and not lying down.

Dhyāna (Skt., 'meditation', 'absorption'). In Indian religions, a term denoting both the practice of *meditation and a higher state of consciousness (generally involving *enstasy), though the term takes on more precise meanings in different traditions; thus the Buddhist use of the term is distinct from the Hindu—see JHĀNA.

In *Tantrism dhyāna comes to mean *visualization of one's own deity (*iṣṭadevatā), *maṇḍala, centres (*cakra) of the subtle body (*liṅga/*sūkṣma śarīra), or *guru, accompanied by *mantra repetition (*japa) and symbolic hand gestures (*mudra). Dhyāna as visualization is thus the visual equivalent of auditory mantra and corporeal mudra and is an essential part of *sādhana.

Dhyāni-Buddhas (Meditation Buddhas). Term coined by B. H. Hodgson, early 19th-cent. British diplomat in Nepal, to describe the jinas ('eminent ones') who appear in a *tantric context in the *Maṇḍala of the Five Jinas. Although the term 'Dhyāni-Buddhas' does not seem to occur in any Buddhist literature (other than *Dharmakośasamgraha* written by Vajrācārya Amṛtānanda in 1826 at the request of Hodgson), it has nevertheless been widely adopted by W. commentators.

Diaconate. Pertaining to, or belonging to, the order of *deacon.

Dialogue. Religions historically have been traditional discriminators within humanity, sacralizing identity by force of doctrine and culture, and establishing (indeed, being) systems for the protection and transmission of highly valued, non-negotiable information.

But in recent decades 'dialogue' has come to be a word in frequent currency among theologians—not the Socratic-style dialogue which assumed and sought the single thread of reason and logic, but a much more perplexing engagement with the authority and interrelation of truth-systems claiming disparate, if not rival, sanction in and by the transcendent.

The Vatican Secretariat for Non-Christian Religions, the Unit on Witness and Dialogue of the World Council of Churches, and the Committee for Relations with People of Other Faiths of the British Council of Churches, have published studies in the theology of dialogue and guidelines for relations with other faiths and with the ethnic groups which hold them. Observers from other faiths, firmly excluded from the 1961 Assembly of the World Council of Churches, were officially invited and welcomed at its 1983 Assembly in Vancouver.

Diamond Cutter: see DIAMOND SŪTRA.

Diamond Maṇḍala: see TAIZO-KAI MANDARA; SHINGON.

Diamond Sūtra. A short Buddhist text from the corpus of the *'Perfection of Wisdom' (*prajñāpāramitā*) literature which compresses the essential teachings into a few short stanzas. Composed around 300 CE, it was translated into Tibetan and Chinese and has remained immensely popular as a summary of the doctrine of 'emptiness' (*śūnyatā) or 'voidness' which lies at the heart of the Perfection of Wisdom writings. The full title of the text is 'The Diamond-Cutter Perfection of Wisdom Sutra' (*Vajracchedika-prajñāpāramitā-sūtra*), and, as its name suggests, it is thought to have the power to cut through ignorance like a diamond for those who study and reflect upon its profound meaning.

Diaspora (Gk., 'dispersion'; Heb., *galut*, 'exile', is the nearest equivalent). Jewish communities outside the land of *Israel. Today, increased *assimilation, higher rates of intermarriage, low birth rates, and increased secularism are threatening the identity of Jews in the Diaspora, except among the ultra-*orthodox. The *Zionist dream and support for the state of Israel, however, has proved a unifying focus for the diaspora communities.

Diaspora is also widely used for members of other faiths living outside their spiritual homeland, e.g. Hindus, Sikhs, Zoroastrians.

Diatessaron (Gk., 'through four'). The gospel story compiled into one narrative from the four gospels by *Tatian *c.*150–60 CE.

Dibbuk or **dybbuk.** An evil spirit in Jewish folklore. The term appeared in literature in Germany and Poland in the 17th cent. The spirit was supposed to enter a person as a result of a secret sin. The dibbuk is connected with belief in *ibbur*, a limited transmigration of souls: the *ibbur* is the birth in a good person of a righteous soul, thus reinforcing that person's goodness. It was a natural extension to suppose that an evil spirit could take up residence in another.

Didache (Gk., 'teaching'). Christian instruction in prayer, ethics, church order, etc. It is distinguished from *kerygma, 'preaching'.

The *Didache of the Twelve Apostles* is a short early Christian manual of morals (chs. 1–6), church practice (7–15), and *eschatology (16).

Dies Irae (Lat., 'day of wrath'). Opening words of the *sequence in the Catholic *mass for the dead. Composed in the 13th cent., it first appeared in a printed missal in 1485. Until 1969 it was obligatory also on All Souls' Day (2 Nov.).

Dietary laws: In Judaism the term *kasher*, or *kosher*, refers to food that is ritually fit for consumption—hence *kashrut*, fitness. According to Genesis, God gave all fruits and vegetables for human food (1. 29). Dietary laws, therefore, are primarily concerned with animals, birds, and fish, and their products. Animals that have a cloven hoof and chew the cud, such as the ox, sheep, and goat are kosher (Deuteronomy 14. 6), but creatures that fulfil only one of those criteria, such as the pig or camel, are forbidden (14. 7–8). Creatures must be slaughtered (*sheḥitah) in the ritually correct manner, and this must be carried out by a trained and licenced slaughterer (*shohet*). After slaughter, the animal or bird must be hung so that as much blood as possible drains out. Leviticus specifically forbids the eating of blood (7. 26–7), so meat must be salted and washed before it is cooked. *Reform Jews generally ignore the dietary laws.

For other Religions, see FOOD AND RELIGION.

Digambara (Skt., 'clothed in air'). 1. A Hindu *sādhu who goes about naked, having left sexual identity and desire far behind; a title, therefore, of *Śiva in his naked *asceticism.

2. One of two major divisions among Jains, the other being Śvetāmbara. The major divisions between the two are not mainly doctrinal, and it was often Digambara Jains who took the lead on behalf of both in controverting Hindu and Buddhist opponents (e.g. Akalanka, 8th cent. CE). They can live harmoniously in close proximity, though serious disputes arise over the ownership of, and access to, holy places (e.g. Bahubali, in S. Maharashtra; over 130 places are currently in dispute).

The origins of the split are obscure. The division appears to have been formalized at the Assembly of Valabhi (453 or 466 CE), which only Ś. attended, making an attempt to agree on what would count as scripture—a concept rejected by the D. in any case.

There are five major issues between them: (i) Ś. monks and nuns wear clothes, D. monks do not; (ii) Ś. use a bowl for begging and for eating, D. do not; (iii) according to Ś., the *kevalin (fully omniscient being) requires food, according to D., not so; (iv) according to Ś., women can attain deliverance, according to D., they must first be reborn as men; (v) Ś. accept ancient writings as *āgama/siddhanta (scripture), D. believe that scripture has been lost in the age of decline.

On (v), both groups believe that, from the tīrthaṅkaras' preaching, the most fundamental texts, the Purvas, are now lost. But D. believe that what remains of the tīrthaṅkaras' preaching is a kind of resonating echo, transmitted orally by successions of disciples, whereas the Ś. have a '45-text canon' (though actually they give equal respect to texts outside that boundary). However, the D. have sacred texts of their own (e.g. *Satkhandāgama*, 'Āgama of Six Parts' and *Kasayapahuda*, 'Treatise on the Passions'), and both D. and Ś. revere some texts in common, e.g. *Tattvārtha Sūtra, by a disciple of the D. Kundakunda.

There remain some differences concerning Māhavīra: Ś. hold that he was born with a miraculous change of wombs, D. do not; Ś. that he was a pleasure-loving prince who experienced sudden conversion, D. that he was always full of insight, but that he respected his parents' wishes, until they died, not to renounce the world; Ś. that he was married, D. that he was not.

Diggers. A radical expression of the mid-17th-cent. Leveller movement, whose adherents described themselves as 'True Levellers'. Inspired by the leadership of Gerard Winstanley and William Everard, the Diggers formed communal settlements, dug and sowed common land in several English counties (1649–50), vigorously maintaining that the earth was a common treasury.

Dīgha Nikāya (Skt., *Dīrghāgama*). The '*Long Collection*', the first of the five nikāyas of the Sūtra/Sutta Piṭaka of the Pāli canon. The Pāli version has thirty-four suttas, the Chinese (Mahāyāna) thirty; twenty-seven are common to both. It is divided into three sections, or 'books' (*vagga*): (i) ethical rules, and refutation of false views; (ii) the Great (Mahā-) section, in which some discourses (e.g. that on the final passing away, **Mahā-parinibbāna-sutta*) have become important works in their own right; (iii) the Pāthika section, i.e. the section beginning with the *Pāthika*, of which two discourses, *Sīgalovāda* (code for lay Buddhists) and *Āṭānatiyā* (providing protection) often appear separately.

Dignāga or **Diṅnāga.** Buddhist logician who flourished towards the end of the 5th cent. CE. His greatest work is the *Pramāṇa-samuccaya* which combines many of his earlier insights into a complete system of epistemology.

Dīkṣa (Skt.). Initiation; in Indian religions, the means of access into a religious tradition, religious or social condition. Dīkṣa is given by the preceptor or *guru and often involves the giving of a new name to the initiate which symbolizes the end of one condition and birth or entrance into a new.

In Hinduism, in the *Vedas, dīkṣa was a necessary prerequisite for the *soma sacrifice undergone by the sacrificer (*yajamāna*) and his wife, involving asceticism (*tapas) and fasting. In the *Upaniṣads, initiation into an ascetic life involves undergoing hunger, thirst, and abstention from all pleasure (**Chandogya Upaniṣad* 3. 17. 2). The importance of dīkṣa carries on into classical and medieval Hinduism where sub-traditions within the central traditions of *Vaiṣṇavism, *Śaivism, and *Tantrism all required dīkṣa.

There are different kinds and various stages of dīkṣa particularly in *Tantrism where the utmost secrecy is maintained. In *Śaivism the 'collective' (*samaya*) and 'particular' (*viśeṣa*) initiations give access to the cult of *Śiva.

In Jainism, dīkṣa is the ceremony whereby a person passes from lay status to being an ascetic.

Dilthey, W.: see HERMENEUTICS.

Dimensions of religion: see Introduction.

Dīn (Arab.). Life-way or religion, most particularly Islam. The whole system is sometimes referred to as dīn wa-dawla, 'religion and state (combined)', there being no distinction within Islam between 'religion and politics'. The word as used in the *Qur'ān is probably derived from a Christian source which had already borrowed from the Iranian *dēn*, religion. Other Arabic meanings are: judgement or retribution (as in *yaum al-dīn, day of judgement); custom or usage.

Dina de malkutha dina (Aram., 'the law of the country is the law'). The Jewish *halakhic principle that the law of the land is binding. The rule, originally laid down by the *amora Samuel in the 3rd cent. CE, states that *diaspora Jews are bound to obey their country's code of law—even, on some occasions, if it conflicts with Jewish law.

Dīn-i Ilāhī (religion of unity based on the oneness of God): see AKBAR.

Din Torah (Heb., 'ruling of the law'). A Jewish legal judgement.

Dionysiac (religion): see APOLLONIAN AND DIONYSIAC RELIGION.

Dionysius the pseudo-Areopagite (*c*.500). The name given to the author of a corpus of theological writings; until the end of the 19th cent., their authorship was generally ascribed to the Dionysius whom Paul had converted (Acts 17. 34).

Four of his works (*The Celestial Hierarchy*, *The Ecclesiastical Hierarchy*, *The Divine Names*, and *The Mystical Theology*) and ten letters are extant. The central characteristic of these works is the synthesis of Christian and *Neoplatonic thought. The leading theme is that of the intimate union (*henōsis*) of God and the soul, and the progressive deification of the human (*theiōsis*), by a process of unknowing in an ascent to God through the three ways of the spiritual life: *purgative, *illuminative, and *unitive.

Dionysius exerted a profound influence on Christianity. See also NEOPLATONISM.

Dīpaṃkara (Skt., Pāli, Dīpankara). 'Kindler of lights', best-known and first of the twenty-four *Buddhas who preceded Buddha Śākyamuni. With him and *Maitreya, Dīpaṃkara is one of the Buddhas of the three ages, past, present, and future. See also FORMER BUDDHAS.

Dīpāvalī (Hindu festival): see DĪVĀLĪ.

Dipavaṃsa. 'Island Chronicle': account of the Buddhist history of Śri Lankā from its beginnings to the 4th cent. CE. The record is taken up in the **Cūlavaṃsa*, and is paralleled by the **Mahāvaṃsa*.

Diptychs (Gk., *diptychon*, 'two-leaved folder'). The lists of names, contained originally on two-winged tablets of ivory or bone or metal, of living and dead Christians for whom special prayer is made in the *liturgy of both E. and W. churches. In art, the term also applies to an altar-piece with two folding side-wings.

Dīrghāgama (Indian division of Sūtra Piṭaka): see TRIPIṬAKA.

Dīrghatamas (Skt., 'long darkness'). A Ṛg Vedic *ṛṣi. Dīrghatamas or Dirghatapas ('long austerity') is traditionally known as the author of *Ṛg Veda* 1. 140 and 1. 164, one of the most philosophical and obscure hymns.

Discalced (not wearing sandals): see CARMELITES.

Disciplina arcani (Lat., 'discipline of the secret'). The practice of concealing certain rites and doctrines from outsiders. It used to be adduced by Catholic writers to explain the scarcity of early Christian evidences on such subjects as the *Trinity, *mass, and number of *sacraments.

Discipline, Manual of. One of the *Dead Sea Scrolls. It contains a description of the customs of the Dead Sea sect including the annual renewal of the *covenant. This is followed by an explanation of the spiritual status of the sect. The document concludes with three hymns of praise. The *Manual* is thought to date from approximately 150 BCE.

Dispensation. A licence granted by ecclesiastical authority to do some act otherwise canonically illegal or to remit the penalty for breaking such a rule.

Dispensationalism. *Millennial scheme of biblical interpretation. It divides history into seven 'dispensations', in which God deals differently, and progressively, with humanity. Dispensationalism is earliest associated with the Plymouth Brother (*Brethren, Plymouth), J. N. Darby (1800–82).

Disruption, The. A split in the Church of Scotland in 1843 over the right of presbyteries to veto proposed appointments. 474 out of 1,203 ministers seceded and formed the *Free Church of Scotland.

Distensio (unfolding of the universe): see GILSON.

Distinctionists (alternative name of the followers of Vātsīputrīya): see VĀTSĪPUTRĪYA.

Diti. In Hindu mythology, daughter of Dakṣa and wife of *Kaśyapa. As her name suggests, Diti is the counterpart of *Aditi, who is her sister and rival wife.

Diṭṭhi (Pāli, 'seeing'; Skt., *dṛṣṭi*). Wrong seeing in Buddhism. A speculative view, especially the seven false views: (i) belief in a sub-stantial self; (ii) rejection of *karma; (iii) espousing eternalism or (iv) nihilism in relation to the destiny of a self; (v) endorsing false *śīlas; (vi) confusing good with bad karma; (vii) doubting the *dharma of the *Buddha.

Dīvālī or **Dīwālī** or **Dīpāvalī.** The most important Hindu *festival which, unlike other festivals (such as the New Year, Makar Sankrānta, or *Holī), lasts for four or five days (the variation depending on the lunar calculation). It falls in Oct.–Nov. each year. Dīvālī is a short form of Dīpāvalī—a line of lamps. Dīvālī is celebrated by all Hindus, but it is the most important festival for merchants, bankers, and businessmen, because the main religious event is the worship of *Lakṣmī, the Goddess of wealth in Hindu mythology.

The festival of Dīvālī is a joyous occasion during which there should be light in every heart as there is light everywhere else.

Sikhs share the Dīvālī celebrations. Like *Baisākhī and Māghī, Dīvālī was a festival ordained by Gurū *Amar Dās for Sikh congregations. According to tradition *Bhāī Buḍhā completed his reading of the *Ādi Granth on Dīvālī and Gurū *Hargobind was released from Gwālior gaol. See MANĪ SIṄGH.

Dīvān (Urdū, Pañjābī, 'court, congregation'). Sikh assembly for worship, which takes its name from the royal audience of the Mughal emperors. The *sangat gather for worship in the *gurdwārā. See also KĪRTAN.

Divination. The art or skill of divining (*sc.*, by use of 'divinity' or deity) that which is unknown—e.g. the future, the identity of culprits, lost items, the best partner for marriage, etc. Divination may be entirely divorced from the gods, and usually is undertaken by recognized and designated specialists who use mechanical means or manipulative techniques. J. Collins (*Primitive Religion*, 1978) attempted a classification of ten methods: (i) by dreams; (ii) by presentiments; (iii) by body actions; (iv) by ordeals; (v) by possession; (vi) by necromancy; (vii) by animals or parts of dead animals; (viii) by mechanical means, using objects; (ix) by patterns in nature; and (x) by observing other patterns, e.g. that death always comes in threes. Index, Divination.

Divine Comedy, The (*La Divina Commedia*). A long poetic work by *Dante, describing the three domains of the life to come, Inferno, *Purgatory, *Paradise. Begun *c.*1307, it was completed shortly before his death in 1321. The poet is guided by Virgil through the circles of *hell to the rim of purgatory, and in company with Beatrice is granted a glimpse of the *beatific vision.

Divine Light Mission. Religious movement founded by Sri Hans Ji Maharaj in 1960. He was acclaimed Gurū Maharaj Ji (often Maharaji) and Satguru. The movement was largely run by his mother, Mata Ji, until a schism, with Maharaji renaming his part of the movement Elan Vital. Central to the movement's teachings is a belief that *Buddha, *Kṛṣṇa, *Christ, *Muḥammad, and a number of lesser masters have taught what is termed the Knowledge, which consists essentially of techniques of *meditation. This Knowledge is transmitted from one master to another, each one being the only perfect or true teacher, *satguru*, during his lifetime. Followers or 'premies' believe that Guru Maharaj Ji is the present satguru.

Divine messengers (the reminders of human destiny in Buddhism: sickness, old age, and death): see DEVA-DŪTA.

Divine right of kings. A high view of monarchy resting on biblical texts which associate kings closely with God through their anointing. Because of this sacramental association, the early view held that the character of the king was irrelevant: the virtue lay in the office, not in the person. The execution of Charles I did not break the hold of this belief (indeed, it contributed to the view that Charles I was a *martyr, to be remembered as such in the **Book of Common Prayer*); it persisted as a motive for many of the non-Jurors. They refused to accept the accession of William and Mary, on the ground that this involved breaking their previous oath to James II and his successors. The divine right of kings meant that at most they could engage in passive obedience to the usurper. Nine *bishops (including the *archbishop of Canterbury, W. Sancroft) and about 400 priests were deprived of their posts. Sancroft perpetuated the succession of non-juring bishops by securing the *congé d'élire from James II in exile. Gradually the non-Jurors were absorbed into the Anglican Church, the last bishop, Robert Gordon, dying in 1779.

Divorce: see MARRIAGE.

Divya-Prabandham (Tamil hymns and poems): see NAL-ĀYIRA-DIVYA-PRABANDHAM.

Divya-siddhis. Praeternatural powers in Hinduism arising through meditation, which may nevertheless be highly dangerous—either physically to the meditator, or by way of distraction, as of a child by toys.

Divyāvadāna. One of the earliest Buddhist literary compositions in the *Avadāna style, being a collection of moral stories relating how good and evil deeds receive their appropriate retribution in the course of time.

Djinn (fiery spirits in Islam): see JINN.

Dmigs pa (component in Tibetan Buddhist meditation): see VISUALIZATION.

Dō (Jap., *michi* or 'way'; Chin., *tao*). Used in Japan to identify some particular practice or discipline as religious; as a spiritual path. The term was borrowed out of similar usage in China (*tao*) and came to be associated not only with all the religions of Japan (e.g. *Shinto as shin-dō or kami-no-michi, the 'way of the *kami'; Buddhism as *butsudō, or the 'way of *buddha'), but also the fine and the martial arts (e.g. *gadō/kadō*, or the 'way of flowers' (*ikebana); *chadō, of tea; and *kendō, of the sword). In general, an external skill is attained which helps the realization of an internal spiritual refinement. The room or hall where these are practised is known as dōjō.

Docetism (Gk., *dokeō*, 'I seem'). The doctrine that the humanity and sufferings of Christ were apparent rather than real. The view that Jesus miraculously escaped death on the cross (such as, on the usual or orthodox understanding of the Arabic, in the Qur'ān, 4. 157) may also be termed docetic.

Doctors of the Church. Title given by the Roman Catholic Church to certain *saints who were also outstanding theologians. The first to be named were *Gregory the Great, *Ambrose, *Augustine, and *Jerome, by Pope Boniface VIII in 1298.

The title *doctor* is also unofficially used with distinguishing adjectives for the various *scholastic teachers, e.g. *Doctor Angelicus* (Thomas *Aquinas), *Doctor universalis* (*Albertus Magnus), etc.

Doctrine of the Mean. Eng. rendering of **Chung Yung*, one of the group of *Four Books in the *Confucian Classics. Like the **Great Learning* (*Ta Hsüeh*) it was extracted from the *Records of Rites* (**Li Chi*) by the *neo-Confucians of the Sung dynasty (960–1279) because of its relevance to their pursuit of sainthood through self-cultivation. The text deals with the existential situation of humans as moral beings in a moral universe, and the burden on the noble individual (*chün tzu*) to act and live accordingly. This expressed exactly the religious philosophy of the neo-Confucians.

Doenmeh (Turk., 'apostates'). Followers of the Jewish false *messiah, *Shabbetai Zevi, who converted to Islam. Shabbetai Zevi himself converted to Islam in 1666, and a small group of his disciples felt it was their duty to follow his example. By the 1720s, there were three Doenmeh sects, the Izmirim, the Jakoblar, and the Karakashlar, probably numbering about 600 families. They were generally believed to be sexually promiscuous and orgiastic ceremonies were claimed to have taken place on the Spring *Festival, Hag ha-Keves (Festival of the Lamb); but such accusations are common against *new religious movements. Although compelled to move from Salonika in 1924, and despite widespread *assimilation, still exists.

Dōgen Kigen, Zenji (1200–53). Founder of the *Sōtō Zen school in Japan and a major figure in Japanese intellectual history. He entered the Mount Hiei *Tendai Shū monastery at the age of 13. Here he was assailed by 'the Great Doubt' (see *dai-funshi): if, as the *sūtras maintain, all beings are endowed with the buddha-nature, why is such strenuous effort and training necessary to attain enlightenment? He left and studied Zen under *Eisai (1141–1215), but went to Sung China in 1223 for further study. There he became a disciple of Jü-ching (Rujing) (1163–1268) of T'ien-t'ung-ssu, attaining enlightenment by realizing the truth of 'Mind and body dropped off; dropped off mind and body'. In 1227 he returned to Japan and embarked on a mission to spread Zen, but, frustrated in his plans because of oppositions from various quarters, he retreated to present-day Fukui Prefecture where he founded *Eihei-ji. He devoted his life to the training of his disciples and the writing of his major work, *The Treasury of the Eye of True Dharma* (*Shōbōgenzō*) in ninety-five chapters (of which **Genjō-Kōan* is an especially revered part). His sayings are collected in *Eihei Kōroku*, and his rules of discipline for the community are in *Eihei Shingi*. His introduction to *zazen is in *Fukan Zazengi*. He was given the posthumous name and title of Busshōdento Kokushi in 1854, and of Jōyō Daishi in 1879.

Dogen is recognized as a towering figure in the development of Zen. His name is linked especially to the practice of zazen—indeed, his way is known as exactly that, *shikan taza*, zazen alone.

Dogen did not deny the importance of religious ritual or devotion to *Buddhas and *bodhisattvas—indeed, he said the opposite: without a proper sense of gratitude and reverence, it is impossible to develop the buddha-mind. The truth is that in religion, ritual, and ethics, provided these are rooted in zazen, one is always in the midst of realizing the one buddha-nature (*bussho; *śūnyatā; *tathāgatagarbha). This is most profoundly worked out in Dogen, who made a simple but all-important shift from the formula he inherited, and thereby solved 'the Great Doubt'. Whereas it had been said that all things *have* the buddha-nature, he stated that all things *are* the buddha-nature. There is nothing to do but realize what you already are—and always have been. Dogen thus denied the reality of the experience of time, since there never can be a before or after in that which is without exception the same buddha-nature: being is time and time is being (*uji*). In all things and in all experiences, the buddha-nature can be realized, especially by not trying to realize it.

Dogma (Gk., 'opinion'). Originally a good or acceptable opinion of philosophers, it became also a decree of a public or political authority; in that latter sense it is found in both Septuagint and New Testament. In Christian history (attaining among *Roman Catholics a formal definition at the First *Vatican Council) it is a truth revealed by God and presented to the Church for belief, either through a *council or a *pope or the *episcopacy.

Dōjō (room for dō): see DŌ; ZENDŌ.

Dokusan (Jap.). The meeting of a Zen pupil with his instructor, in private (as opposed to the group training sessions). The content of dokusan is necessarily secret, for it is the relation of heart-mind to heart-mind in a creative unity which is idiosyncratic to a particular partnership.

Dōkyō (Japanese Zen monk): see ICHIEN.

Dōkyō Etan (teacher of Hakui): see HAKUIN.

Doleantie (Dutch Reformed separation): see DUTCH REFORMED CHURCH.

Dome of the Rock (Arab., Qubbat al-Ṣakhra). A Muslim building in Jerusalem which covers the rock from which *Muḥammad is believed to have ascended to heaven. From the Rock on which the earth is founded (*eben shetiyyah), Muḥammad was taken by *Jibrīl through the seven heavens to the furthest limit. The Rock split at that moment, because it longed to follow Muḥammad to heaven. His footprint can still be seen. The building is also known (piously, but unhistorically) as the Mosque of 'Umar.

Dominic, St (1170–1221). Founder of the *Dominicans. Born in Old Castile, he became a *canon regular in Osma. With his bishop, Diego d'Azevedo, he initiated a new style of evangelization in Languedoc, characterized by humility and rigorous poverty. From this evolved the Order of Preachers, which he established in 1215. He was canonized in 1234: feast day, 7 Aug.

Dominicans. The 'Order of Friars Preachers', founded by St *Dominic in 1215 and confirmed in 1216. From the first foundation in Toulouse it spread rapidly; today its members work in most regions of the world. The goal of the order is to proclaim the word of God by preaching and teaching. It espoused *mendicant poverty, simplified conventual life and study as its main observances. There are also monasteries of enclosed nuns under the jurisdiction of the order, and a large number of congregations of active sisters attached to the order, though juridically independent. There are also Dominican lay fraternities and secular institutes. See Index, Dominicans.

Dominus vobiscum (Lat., 'the Lord be with you'). A formal Christian greeting, used especially in the *liturgy.

Donation of Constantine. A spurious document designed to strengthen the authority of the church and of Rome, purporting to report how Constantine conferred on Pope Sylvester I (314–35) the primacy over other sees and secular rule in the W. Empire.

Donatism. A *schism in Christian N. Africa in the 4th cent. The Donatists refused to accept the *consecration of Caecilian as *bishop of Carthage in 311 because his consecrator had been a *traditor* (one who had given up copies of the Bible for confiscation) in the recent persecution of Diocletian. The local bishops consecrated a rival to Caecilian, and he was soon succeeded by Donatus, from whom the schism is named. Their opponents, especially *Augustine, held that the unworthiness of ministers did not invalidate the sacraments, since their minister was Christ.

Dönmeh (followers of Jewish false messiah): see DOENMEH.

Donne, John (1571/2–1631). Christian *Metaphysical poet and priest. Brought up a Roman Catholic, he became an Anglican in the 1590s, after studying at Oxford and possibly Cambridge. He was ordained in 1615, becoming Dean of St Paul's in 1621. He wrote both love poetry and religious verse: the ingenious love poet becomes an explorer of the paradoxes of God's mercy and grace.

Door gods. Three Chinese tutelary deities, derived, traditionally, from three officials of the emperor T'ang Tai Tsung (d. 649), of whom the best known was Wei Cheng. When the emperor was afflicted by bad dreams, the three officials stood outside his door to ward off visiting spirits. They were later replaced by painted representations, and can be found in this form on the doorposts of Taoist temples, and sometimes of homes.

Dorje (Tib., *rdo-rje*). 'Lord of stones'. It was originally the thunderbolt (*vajra*) weapon of the Hindu god *Indra, and thus the source of the name for *Vajrayāna Buddhism. The dorje became identified with the immoveable and indestructible, as a diamond, and from there it shifted to the clear, translucent essence of all reality, which is emptiness of all qualities, *śūnyatā. In Tib. Buddhism, the dorje is the masculine symbol of the skilful (*upāya) path to enlightenment, while the ritual bell (*drilbu*) is the feminine symbol of the path of wisdom (*prajña).

Dorje Chang (Adi Buddha): see ADI BUDDHA.

Dort, Synod of: see DUTCH REFORMED CHURCH.

Dosa or **dveṣa** (Pāli, Skt.). Ill-will, hate; with attachment (*rāga) and delusion (*moha) forming the three dispositions of mind which, according to Buddhism, produce bad *karma.

Dōshō (629–700). Japanese Buddhist monk who founded the Hossō school. Hossō is 'the dharma-characteristics' school: it maintained that all appearances are reducible to the consciousnesses, which in turn are necessarily of the same nature. It was one of the six schools of the Nara period (710–94).

Dositheus (1641–1707). Orthodox patriarch of Jerusalem from 1669. His best-known achievement was the Synod of *Jerusalem convened in 1672 to resist Protestant influence in the Greek Church. The decrees of the Synod are also known as the 'Confession of Dositheus', and form an important Orthodox dogmatic text.

Dōsojin (Sino-Jap., *dō*, 'way', + *so*, 'ancestor', + *jin*, 'deity'). A Japanese folk deity, especially associated with crossroads, mountain passes, and village entrances, attested from medieval times to the present, and having a complex syncretistic history. The name Dōsojin seems to come partly from this Shinto tradition (road or path deities) and partly from Chinese folk belief in ancestral influence upon the health and prosperity of subsequent generations. Stones carved with human couples and labelled 'Dōsojin' can still be found in Japan and are thought to be guardians of marital harmony and fecundity.

Dostoevsky, Fyodor Mikhailovich (1821–81). Russian novelist. In 1849, he was arrested for suspected revolutionary activity and condemned to death (or at least was taken to the scaffold and to the last moments before execution before the true sentence of four years in prison and four years as a private in the Siberian army was read out). He was released from the army in 1858. The immediate fruit of this experience was his remarkable *House of the Dead* (1861). Other novels followed which display a profound understanding of the depths of the human soul. *Notes from the Underground* (1864) sets rational egoism (which proffers reasons for treating others as instruments) against irrational selfishness which treats others as enemies. *Crime and Punishment* (1866), *The Idiot* (1868), and *The Devils* (also translated as *The Possessed*, 1871) led up to his great achievement, *The Brothers Karamazov* (completed in 1880). With the Slavophils, Dostoevsky venerated the *Orthodox Church, and was deeply impressed by *Staretz Amvrosy whom he visited at Optina. But his sense of goodness was neither facile nor naïve. He saw human freedom as something so awesome that most people are ready to relinquish it. This is epitomized in the Legend of the Grand Inquisitor. In his speech accepting the Nobel Prize for Literature, *Solzhenitsyn quoted Dostoevsky, 'Beauty will save the world.' But the Church, in contrast, has continued, as Dostoevsky feared to the last that it would, on its path of authority and control.

Douai. Town in N. France. In the 16th cent., when it formed part of the Spanish Netherlands, Douai was a gathering place for English *recusants. William Allen established a college there in 1568 to train clergy for the English *mission, and a translation of the Bible, still known as the Douai version (though much of the work was done at Rheims where the college was from 1578 to 1593, hence Douai-Rheims), was begun there.

Double predestination (of both condemnation and salvation): see PREDESTINATION.

Double truth (levels of truth appropriate for the capacity of different people): see IBN RUSHD.

Douglas, Mary (anthropologist): see SACRED AND PROFANE.

Doukhobors (Russ.). 'Spirit-fighters', a Russian sect of unknown origin, which seems to have appeared among peasants in the district of Kharkov, moving later to the Caucasus. They called themselves 'the People of God', and were called by their opponents 'doukhobors', i.e. spirit wrestlers. Its members believe in one God manifested in the human soul in memory (Father), reason (Son), and will (*Holy Spirit), have an adoptionist (*adoptionism) understanding of *Christ, believe in *transmigration of the human soul, and adopt an allegorical understanding of the *scriptures and Christian *dogmas. They found sympathy from *Tolstoy, who, with the *Quakers, arranged for most of them (*c.*8,000) to emigrate to Cyprus and Canada at the end of the 19th cent., where most survive—few only in Russia.

Do ut des (reciprocal understanding of sacrifice): see SACRIFICE.

Dov Baar of Lubavitch (son of founder of Ḥabad): see ḤABAD.

Dov Baer of Mezhirech (d. 1772). An early *ḥasidic leader. A *Talmudic and *kabbalistic scholar, Dov Baer was generally recognized as the successor of the Baal Shem Tov (*Israel ben Eliezer). He lived an *ascetic life and, by his saintliness, set a pattern for future *Zaddikim (Ḥasidic leaders). His doctrines have been preserved through collections of his sayings and through the works of his disciples. His activities were strongly condemned by the *Orthodox in Vilna, who pronounced a ban of excommunication (*ḥerem) on the movement, and this is said to have hastened Dov Baer's death.

He is also known as 'the Great Maggid' because of his powerful preaching and aphorisms. His teachings were collected after his death in *Maggid Devarav le-Ya'aqov* (1781).

Dove. A bird of the pigeon family. Much symbolism is focused on the dove which ancient natural history (wrongly) regarded as a gentle and humble bird, noted for its fidelity. As the bird that returned to the *ark with an olive-branch, it is a symbol of peace (cf. Genesis 8. 11); as the bird that descended on Christ at his baptism, it is a symbol of the Holy Spirit (cf. Mark 1. 10). The dove is also a symbol of the Church, the faithful human soul, or divine inspiration. The 'eucharistic dove' was a popular vessel in medieval Europe for the *reservation of the Blessed Sacrament.

Dowie, John Alexander (1847–1907). Founder of the 'Christian Catholic Apostolic Church in Zion'. An Australian *Congregational minister, he moved to the USA in 1888 after a personal healing experience. There he established divine healing homes, and then in 1896 his own healing and *adventist church in Chicago. A continuing community of several thousand includes some Navajo Indians, but the Church no longer rules Zion City as a theocracy.

Doxology. A short hymn ascribing glory (Gk., *doxa*) to God. In the *eucharist the doxology is the ending of the eucharistic prayer. See also GLORIA, for the lesser doxology.

Dōzoku-shin (Sino-Jap., *dozoku*, 'family', + *shin*, 'deity'). A class of native Japanese deities, belief in whom combines social, geographical, and consanguinary relationships. Dōzoku is the extended family in traditional Japan, always consisting of a *honge*, or main family, and a number of branch families reckoned through the male line of descent. Traditionally all members of the dōzoku live in the same village, so that family rituals can be carried out in a spirit of mutual co-operation. Thus dōzoku-shin may be said to combine *ancestor reverence with a sense of the sacredness of locality.

Dragon Gate Caves: see LONGMEN CAVES.

Dragon Gate school (Taoist movement): see CH'ÜAN-CHEN TAO.

Dragon kings (Taoist mythological figures): see LUNG-WANG.

Dragons (Chinese). These are imagined by the Chinese as supernatural expressions of natural forces, sky or water animals.

The Dragon Boat Festival (Tuan Yang Chien) takes place on the fifth day of the fifth lunar month, and commemorates the death by drowning of Chu Yüan (? 3rd/late 4th cent. BCE). He is said to have committed suicide as a protest against corruption in government, and against the incessant conflict of the warring states.

Drama (religious): see THEATRE AND DRAMA.

Draṣṭṛ. The one who looks on, the true self in Hinduism, which observes the phenomenal involvement in the world, without getting entangled in it.

Draupadī. Also called Kṛṣṇā, the heroine of the *Mahābhārata*, princess of Pāñcāla. Born from a sacrificial altar, she is said to be an incarnation of the Goddess *Śrī (Prosperity). Outside the *Mahābhārata*, Draupadī is known as a S. Indian village Goddess.

Dravya (Skt., 'substance'). In Indian religions and philosophies, a term for the basic constituents of reality. The concept gave rise to philosophical debate and was a central factor in doctrinal divergence. For Jains, dravya represents the materiality of the cosmos from which the *jīva seeks to be emancipated. It is basically opposed to *bhāva, but for laypeople dravya must be related to bhāva, especially in ritual, as the base from which the ascent to *mokṣa necessarily begins. Dravya is thus related to bhāva in ritual. Early Buddhism denied the idea of substance, all objects being a linguistic construction.

Dreaming or **dream-time.** The sense of identity, in Australian aboriginal culture, with the primordial guarantee of life and land by commanding figures (deities), together with the actions which sustain that identity and relatedness. Many different terms (e.g. *alcheringa*, *bugari*, *djugurba*) express this sense of reverent relatedness to the land and the conditions of its peace and prosperity. The 'dream-time' is the state in which those of the present-day live, in the company of the ancestors, in this ideal (but realizable) state.

Dreams. The interior consequences of continuing brain activity during periods of sleep; day-dreaming arises from the cessation (or suppression) of ordinary modes of consciousness or attentiveness, allowing other modes and contents of thought to take place. Both forms of dream have been important in religions, the former because it allows the possibility of insight, information and warning that would not otherwise be accessible, the latter because it exists on the edge of trance states and altered states of consciousness.

Dream yoga (one of the six teachings of Nāropa): see MILAM.

Dreidel (spinning top): see ḤANUKKAH.

Drepung monastery: see LHASA.

Dress: see HABIT, RELIGIOUS; and Index, Dress.

Dreyfus case. Alfred Dreyfus (1859–1935) was a Jewish officer in the French army accused of betraying French military secrets to the Germans in 1894 and condemned to life imprisonment. He remained on Devil's Island in solitary confinement until 1898, when it was discovered that much of the evidence against him had been forged. At a retrial, the military court refused to admit the error, and found Dreyfus guilty, but with extenuating circumstances. He was sentenced to a further ten years' imprisonment. Two weeks later he was pardoned and reinstated in the army. The affair prompted anti-Semitic riots on the one hand, and enormous liberal agitation on the other, including an open letter from the novelist Émile Zola. Dreyfus was completely exonerated, but the whole affair made a strong impact on the Jewish community and led Theodor *Herzl in particular to *Zionism. Among Roman Catholics, the affair (apart from evoking the latent anti-Semitism in pre-*Vatican II Catholicism) is usually held to have retarded the adaptation, which the Church eventually had to make, to being an independent institution within a secular society in France.

Dṛg-Dṛśya-Viveka. A Skt. Hindu work of forty-six ślokas, which initiate into the deepest understanding of *Vedānta. Attributed to (among others) *Śankara, the most probable author was Bhārati Tīrtha (14th cent. CE).

Drilbu (ritual bell): see DORJE.

Droṇa. In the **Mahābhārata*, a *brahman, the weapons-teacher of both the *Pāṇḍavas and the *Kauravas.

Dṛshti-pravāda-aṅga: see AṄGA.

Drugpa Künleg or **'Brug-pa Kun-legs** (1455–1570). Tibetan, best-known as one of the 'holy fools' of Tibet. He was trained in the Drugpa school of the *Kagyüpa, but he adopted the ascetic life of a wanderer, which was nevertheless demonstrated in consumption of beer and women—in a quasi-*Tantric style of non-attachment even in action. He is believed to be the reappearance in bodily form of Saraha and Śavaripa, two *mahāsiddhas.

Druzes (Arab., Durūz). Members of a religious group numbering about half a million, mainly in S. Lebanon, SW Syria, and Hawran district of Israel/N. Palestine. A closely knit community, mainly landowners and cultivators, the Druzes practise a secret religion which conceals doctrines and practices from the uninitiated, a fact which has prevented until modern times a clear understanding of its origins, doctrines, and practices.

The Druze religion was derived from *Ismāʿīlīya, and was established in the 11th cent. in Cairo, Egypt, around the cult of the Fāṭimid *Khalīfa al-Ḥākim (disappeared in 1021 (AH 411)). Al-Ḥākim was first recognized as incarnate reason by al-Darazī, from whom the name Druze derives. The two most sacred books of the Druzes are *Al-Naqd al-Khafi* (Copy of the Secret) by *Ḥamza b. ʿAlī, often regarded as founder of the faith; and *Al-Juz'al-Awwal* (Essence of the First) by al-Muqtāna Bahā'uddin (d. 1031 CE), its main propagator. The main dogmas of the Druze faith are: confession in the unity of God; belief in successive manifestations of the deity (or of the Universal Intelligence, al-ʿAql al-Kulli) in human form; acceptance of al-Ḥākim as the last and greatest of these divine incarnations; recognition of five ministers who manifest aspects of the Divine Essence, Ḥamza b. ʿAlī being the supreme saint (*wali-al-zaman*); belief in *metempsychosis and in predestination; and observance of the seven precepts of Ḥamza who, on behalf of al-Ḥākim, absolved his followers from the obligations of Islam. Ḥamza's seven precepts are: veracity in speech; protection and mutual aid to the Druze community; renunciation of all forms of former worship and false belief; repudiation of Iblīs (the devil) and all forces of evil; confession of the divine unity in humanity, concentrated in 'Our Lord', Ḥākim, who is not dead but hidden; acquiescence in all al-Ḥākim's acts no matter what they be; and absolute submission and resignation to his divine will.

Dry shit stick (person, acc. to Zen, attached to this world): see KAN-SHIKETSU.

Duʿā' (Arab., *daʿā*, 'call' or 'summon', whence *daʿwa). In Islam, supplication or personal invocation, 'calling upon' *Allāh; private request or prayer, as contrasted with *ṣalāt, the ritual worship.

Dualism (Lat., *dualis*). The conjunction of two (usually opposing) entities or principles. The term was used by T. Hyde in 1700 (*The Ancient Persian Religions*) to describe the conflict between good and *evil (Ormazd and Ahriman) in *Zoroastrianism; but it is used of many religious and philosophical dualities, e.g. mind and matter (as in Cartesian dualism), material and spiritual (as in *Manichaeism), *yin and *yang.

Dudjom Rinpoche (head of Tibetan Buddhist order): see BDUD-JOMS RIN-PO-CHE.

Dukhobors (Russian sect): see DOUKOBHORS.

Dukkha or **duḥkha** (Pāli, Skt.). The second of the *Three Marks of Existence in Buddhism and the subject of the *Four Noble Truths. There is no satisfactory equivalent to the word in English, and it has been variously translated as 'suffering', 'unsatisfactoriness', 'frustration', 'unhappiness', 'anguish', 'ill', 'dis-*ease*' (opposite: *sukha*, 'ease, well-being'): it is essentially transience and all that arises from the experience of transience.

Traditional Buddhism defines 'dukkha' in a number of different ways. 1. In the Four Noble Truths, dukkha is represented as 'birth, old age, sickness and death; grief, sorrow, physical and mental pain, and despair; involvement with what one dislikes and separation from what one likes; not getting what one wants; in summary, the five groups of grasping (*pañc'upādānakkhandhā*, cf. SKHANDHA) are a source of suffering'. 2. Threefold dukkha is ordinary mental and physical pain (*dukkha-dukkhatā*), that is, pure or intrinsic suffering; suffering as the result of change (*viparināma-dukkhatā*), owing to the impermanent and ephemeral nature of things; and suffering due to the formations (*saṅkhāra-dukkhatā*; *sankhara), that is, the sense of *saṃsāra or our own temporality and finiteness. 3. It is maintained that all sentient beings—whether gods, humans, *pretas, animals, or inhabitants of hell—are subject to dukkha. Gods suffer the least in the hierarchy of different beings, and the inhabitants of hell the most.

It is by comparison with *nirvāna that everything is apprehended as suffering. Therefore, the 'truth' of suffering is something which has to be discerned or discovered, like the truth of anicca. Hence it figures as a subject of contemplation (*dukkhānupassanā*, cf. VIPASSANĀ) in Buddhist meditational practice.

Duleep Singh (son of Rañjit Siṅgh): see RAÑJĪT SINGH.

Dumézil, Georges (1898–1986). French scholar of Indo-European thought and structure. Much influenced by *Durkheim and Mauss, he made wide-ranging comparative studies, seeking to demonstrate the underlying importance of tripartite structures and functions (for an example see PĀṆḌAVAS), and also of paired relations between heavenly beings and earthly counterparts. Although accused of imposing patterns and 'shaving the corners', his views were influential for a time in the study of religion.

Dunhuang (town in NW China): see TANHUANG.

Duns Scotus, Johannes (*c.*1265–1308). Medieval Christian philosopher. His principal work was his commentary on the *Sentences* of *Peter Lombard, which survives in three versions. In his metaphysics he developed the idea that the principle of individuation is not matter, but a kind of individual uniqueness (*haecceitas*), that by virtue of which any being is *this* being.

Duperron, A. (French translator): see DĀRĀ SHIKOH.

Duran, Simeon Ben Zemah, known as **Rashbaz** (1361–1444). *Rabbinic authority and philosopher. He emigrated from Majorca to Algeria in 1391 where he became *Chief Rabbi in 1408. He was regarded as a great legal authority and was well-known for his careful judgements. He respected, but did not always agree with, the philosophy of *Maimonides. His major philosophical work was *Magen Avot* (Shield of the Fathers), written as an introduction to **Avot*. He maintained that many so-called *dogmas were open to argument (and substantiation), but that Judaism must insist on three foundational beliefs which were not to be disputed: the existence of God; the divine origin of *Torah; and reward and punishment after death.

Durgā. The one who is difficult to approach, among Hindus the fearsomely protective aspect of *Śiva's consort (see Mahādevī in *Devī), a slayer of demons who threaten the *dharma of creation. Notable among these was the buffalo-demon *Mahiṣa, who could not be slain by man or beast. Durgā being both a woman and divine, slew the creature easily (hence her name, Mahiṣāsuramardiṇī), using weapons given her by the gods.

Durgā, the ten-armed, is shown carrying a variety of weapons, and accompanied by her vehicle, a lion or tiger, symbolic of her ferocity and aggression. She is supported by eight demonesses (*yoginī), whose task it is to finish the destruction. Durgā is considered as another aspect of *Kālī, and, like her, is a popular deity in Bengal, where Durga-pūja, celebrated Oct.–Nov., is a major festival. Unlike Kālī, Durgā is shown as beautiful, though warlike. See also ŚAKTI; DAŚAHRĀ.

Durkheim, Emile (1858–1917). Only rivalled by Max *Weber as the father of social science. He founded the Année Sociologique, a group which made major contributions to the study of religion, 'représentations collectives' (*collective representations), modes of thought, and forms of classification. Jewish by birth, Durkheim adopted a positivistic attitude towards religion. His classic *The Elementary Forms of the Religious Life* (1912; tr. 1915) utilized Australian aboriginal material to attempt to show that religious life originates as a response to experiences of society. It is now generally taken for granted that comprehensive understanding of religions involves a social perspective. See also SACRED AND PROFANE (including his definition of religion).

Durvāsas. In Hindu mythology, the son of Atri and Anasūyā. He is also regarded as a manifestation of *Śiva.

Duryodhana. In the **Mahābhārata*, the eldest of the *Kauravas. His magical ability to hide himself under the surface of a pool of water after most of his army has been destroyed suggests serpent affiliations, and has been identified by some as an Indo-European theme.

Dusserah. Alternative spelling of Dassera, nine-day Hindu celebrations: see FESTIVALS AND FASTS.

Dutch Reformed Church or **Hervomde Kerk.** Major Christian (Protestant) Church, originally in the Netherlands, but spreading to other parts of the world through missionary work. It was organized during the revolt of the Low Countries against Spain in the 16th cent. Many different threads of Reformed theology and church order were entangled together until the Synod of Dort (1618–19) led to the character of the Church as Calvinist in theology and Presbyterian in government. The synod produced the Canons of Dort, which became one of the doctrinal foundations of the Dutch Reformed Church. The synod was involved in political contest, and was directed against the *Arminians or Remonstrants (so-called because in 1610 the followers of Arminius issued a remonstrance against unconditioned *predestination). The Remonstrants were ejected, and in the 17th cent., during a period of Dutch power, the Dutch Reformed Church was of central importance. During the 19th cent., the prolonged struggle between conservative and modernizing tendencies led to several splits (e.g. the *Afscheiding* ('Separation') in 1834, the *Doleantie* in 1886, forming with the earlier separatists the Gereformeerde Kerk), but the Dutch Reformed Church remained the largest. Meanwhile it had spread with colonization to the E. and W. Indies, and through settlement to the USA. Its most prominent settlement was in S. Africa, from 1652. When the Cape Colony came under British control, the Dutch, the Boers, trekked north and formed their own states, Orange Free State and Transvaal—carrying with them strong biblical associations with the move into a Promised Land. Equally biblical in its claimed foundations was the view (originally formulated in the Netherlands to justify the apparent anomaly of divisions in that territory) of apartheid. Apartheid as a religious doctrine rests in a debate in one of the 19th-cent. separatist churches, the Nederduitse Gereformeerde Kerk: in 1829, its synod declared that people of different colours (i.e. races) should receive communion together, but in 1857 its synod ruled that because of the weakness of some, segregation should be allowed. In 1974, the NGK produced a report, *Human Relations and the South African Scene in the Light of Scripture*, which offered justification of apartheid, but in 1982, the World Alliance of Reformed Churches declared apartheid to be heretical. An amended position appeared in *Church and Society* (1986), but it did not eradicate apartheid. At this stage, two groups (Nederduitsche Hervomde Kerk and Afrikaanse Protestante Kerk) seceded and refused to attend the consultation in 1990 which led to the Rustenburg declaration. This made a confession of guilt for the damage done by apartheid and proposed forms of restitution.

Dūtī pūjā (Skt.). In *Tantrism, worship of a beautiful woman involving the use of the *pañca-makāra. This union is symbolic of the union of *Śiva and *Śakti, and the bliss of sexual intercourse is said to be akin to the bliss of the absolute state.

Dvaita (Skt., 'dual'). The Hindu philosophy and religious attitude which maintains that the subject–object, *I–Thou, relationship between a worshipper and God persists, even in the final union; and that such union cannot be regarded as absorption (in contrast to *Advaita). This position is particularly associated with *Madhva, and is then known as Dvaitavedānta.

Dvārakā: see SACRED CITIES, SEVEN.

Dvātriṃśadvara-lakṣana (Skt.). The thirty-two marks of a *cakravartin, especially of one who is a *buddha of universal teaching. The marks feature in representations of the Buddha. For a typical list, see *Dīgha Nikāya* 3. 142.

Dveṣa (aversion): see ASMITA.

Dvija (Skt.). The twice-born in Hinduism, the members of the three upper castes (*varna).

Dyāl Dās (Sikh reformer): see SIKHISM.

Dyāvā-pṛthivi (Mother Goddess of Hindus): see PṚTHIVI.

Dybbuk (evil spirit in Jewish folklore): see DIBBUK.

Dying and rising Gods. Deities found in the Mediterranean world which suggested a general 'myth and ritual' pattern, which in turn was then applied to many other figures, including *Jesus. The pattern was supposed to be one in which the king represented God in a New Year ritual, in which he was symbolically slain, thereafter rising from the dead: this was supposed to have secured fertility. Figures such as Adonis, Isis and Osiris, Marduk, Tammuz/Dumuzi were claimed for this pattern.

Dynasties, Chinese. Legendary dynasties are the Three Sovereigns, the Five Emperors. In Ancient China the dynasties are Hsia/Xia (uncertain dates); Shang (Yin) (*c.*1766–1123 BCE); Chou/Zhou (*c.* 1122–256 BCE). The dynasties in

Imperial China are as follows: Ch'in/Qin (221–207 BCE); Former Han (206/2 BCE–9 CE); Hsin (9–23); Latter Han (25–220); The Three Kingdoms (Wei, Shu, Wu: 220–80); Chin/Jin (divided, *c*.280–420); The Six Dynasties, with China divided (450–589); Sui (589–618); T'ang/Tang (618–907); The Five Dynasties (907–60); Sung (960–1279); Yuan (1260–1367); Ming (1368–1644); and Ch'ing (1644–1911). The Republic lasted 1912–49 and the People's Republic began in 1949.

Dynasties, Muslim. The dynasties frequently mentioned here are listed in chronological order, beginning with al-Rashidun/ar-Rashidun, the Four Orthodox Caliphs, 632–61 (AH 11–40): *Abu Bakr, 632–4 (AH 11–13), *ʿUmar, 634–44 (AH 13–23), *ʿUthmān, 644–56 (AH 23–35), ʿAlī, 656–61 (AH 35–40). Umayyad (*Damascus), 667–750 (AH 41–132); ʿAbbasid (Baghdād), 750–1258 (AH 132–656); Umayyad of Cordova, 756–1031 (AH 138–422); Fāṭimids (Mahdiya and Cairo), 909–1171 (AH 297–567); Mamluk(e)s: Bahri, 1250–1390 (AH 648–792) and Burji, 1382–1517 (AH 784–922); Seljuq (Persia and Iraq), 1037–1157 (AH 429–552). The Ottoman Empire lasted 1299–1923 (AH 699–1341). Shahs of Persia include: Safavid, 1502–1736 (AH 907–1148), Qajar, 1779–1909 (AH 1193–1327), and Pahlavi, 1925–79 (AH 1344–99). In India dynasties include the Ghaznavid, 976–1186 (AH 366–582), and Mughal (Mogul), 1526–1858 (AH 932–1276). For further detail, see Index, Dynasties.

Dyophysites (Gk., 'two natures'). Those Christians who maintain the *Chalcedon definition of two natures in the one person of Christ, in contrast to *monophysites.

Dyoya-dṛṣṭi (Skt.). The third eye, or divine-seeing eye, which is located for Hindus between the eyebrows.

Dysteleology. A lack of purposiveness or design in the universe. If teleology is regarded as evidence for God's existence, then it would seem that dysteleology is *prima facie* evidence against it. See also EVIL, PROBLEM OF.

Dzogchen (Tib., rDzogschen). 'Great perfection', in the *Nyingma school of Tibetan Buddhism (*Tibetan religion), the highest of the nine *yānas (ways) which lead to perfect completion; and as the highest of the ways, it is also used sometimes as a synonym for Nyingmapa teaching itself. It is known also as *ati-yoga* (Atiyoga, exceptional *yoga), beyond which nothing is required (or indeed possible) in order to reach the goal. Central to Dzogchen is the realization that nothing, either mental or physical, has reality underlying its appearance, and that the mind, which cannot be measured or weighed, and is neither square nor round, is the threshold of truth (once it is disentangled from ignorance and delusion) because it is realized as being purely what it is. Dzogchen leads to the direct awareness of 'mind' as it is: the buddha-nature without qualification or attribute.

E

E (Jap., 'gather, understand'). An assembly or gathering in Japan, especially for religious purposes.

E. The name of a putative source used in the composition of the Pentateuch. See further PENTATEUCH.

East African Revival or **Balokole** (Luganda, 'saved ones'). A widespread Christian renewal movement with several independent origins. In the 1930s it spread among Ugandan *Anglicans and then into Kenya and Tanzania, working alongside the churches and avoiding schism, although meeting at first with a mixed reception from church leaders. It is essentially a lay movement, African in style and control, that has transcended tribal, racial, and church divisions, and has produced its own theology, organization, and hymns; one revival chorus, 'Tukutendereza' ('We praise thee, Jesus'), is now widely known.

Easter. The Christian feast of the *resurrection of *Christ. According to *Bede, the name is connected with an Anglo-Saxon spring goddess 'Eostre'. The derivation is uncertain, but some Easter customs, e.g. the giving of eggs as gifts, are certainly pre-Christian.

The primitive Christian feast known in the 2nd–3rd cents. as the Pasch (Aramaic, *pasḥa*, '*Passover') formed the Christian counterpart to the Jewish festival.

Since the Council of *Nicaea (325) Easter has been fixed for the Sunday following the full moon after the vernal equinox. However, there is still a divergence between E. and W. Churches, mainly because almost all Orthodox Churches, even those who otherwise use the Gregorian *calendar, use the Julian date for the equinox. Thus the date of 'Orthodox Easter' sometimes coincides with the W. date, but it is usually one, four, or five weeks later.

Eastern Catholic Churches: see UNIAT(E) CHURCHES.

Eastern Orthodox (Church). Those Christians who belong to the Churches which accepted the *Chalcedon definition of two natures in the one person of *Christ, and did not depart in the *great schism between E. and W. They are consequently *dyophysite as opposed to *monophysite. The term thus covers much more than the Greek Orthodox Church (for which it is nevertheless sometimes used as a synonym), and slightly less than all E. Christians. See further ORTHODOX CHURCH.

Eastern Paradise (Buddhist world of attainment): see BHAIṢAJYAGURU.

Eastern Rite Catholics. Christians who are in union with Rome, but who have followed rites other than the Latin rite. They are known also as Oriental Rite Catholics. See UNIAT(E) CHURCHES.

East Syrian Churches. Collective name for *Nestorian and Chaldaean Churches.

Easy Path: see PURE LAND SCHOOLS.

EATWOT (Ecumenical Association of Third-World Theologians): see LIBERATION THEOLOGY.

Eben Shetiyyah. The rock on which, according to Jews and Muslims, the world is founded. It is to be seen in Qubbat al-Sakhrah, the *Dome of the Rock, in *Jerusalem. From this Rock, *Muḥammad ascended to heaven on his Night Journey (*miʿraj): the rock split at that moment because it wanted to follow Muḥammad to heaven; the split can still be seen in the rock.

Ebionites (Heb. *ebyōnīm*, 'poor men'). A sect of Jewish Christians of the early centuries CE. The sect emphasized the ordinary humanity of *Jesus as the human son of *Mary and Joseph, who was then given the *Holy Spirit at his *baptism; it also adhered to the Jewish *Torah.

Ebisu (Jap., of uncertain meaning, possibly 'foreigner'). A Japanese folk deity of good fortune especially associated with occupational success.

Ecclesiastes (Heb., *Qoheleth*). A book in the Hebrew scriptures. Written by ha-Qoheleth (often tr. as 'the preacher', but more accurately 'the convoker'), 'Son of David, king in Jerusalem', the book is traditionally ascribed to *Solomon and is one of a group, collectively described as the five *scrolls. The writer argues that everything is ordained by God and that ultimately the life of humanity is transient: 'vanity of vanities! All is vanity!' (1. 2). The impression of scepticism is enhanced in the English by the translation of *ḥebel* as 'vanity': it is a word for 'mist' or 'steam in a bathroom', hence transience.

Ecclesiasticus (book of the Apocrypha/Bible): see BEN SIRA, WISDOM OF.

Ecclesiology (Gk., *ekkesia*, 'assembly'). Originally the study of Christian church architecture, but now reflection on the nature of the *Church. Ecclesiology points at one extreme to the hierarchical and authoritarian system of Vatican Catholicism (modified in theory, but not yet in practice, by conciliarity: see ANTIPOPE), and at the other to the *koinōnia* (communion) of the New Testament which is translated into house churches, local gatherings networked into monitoring organizations.

Eck, John (1486–1543). German Roman Catholic theologian and opponent of *Luther. Eck was appointed Professor of Theology at Ingolstadt in 1510, a post he held throughout his life. After the *indulgence controversy, he opposed Luther's teaching, engaged in public debate with him and *Carlstadt at Leipzig in 1519, and exerted his influence to procure their condemnation in the papal *bull **Exsurge Domine* of 1520. He wrote against Luther, *Melanchthon and *Zwingli, and defended the papacy.

Eckankar (union with God; cf *Ik Onkar). A new religious movement (the Religion of Light and Sound) 'revived' by Paul Twitchell (1908–71) in San Francisco in 1965. Its teaching is *pantheistic. The movement has many centres in the USA and Europe, and reports a worldwide membership of 50,000 chelas or students.

Eckhart, Meister (*c.* 1260–1327). German Christian mystic. Accused of *heresy in 1326, he died during the proceedings. In the 14th cent., his insistence on the reality of God's gift to humanity of himself in his son, a gift which deifies the human, sounded *pantheistic; conversely, his development of *seelenfünklein*, the spark of the soul, achieving union with God, sounded as though the two are merged.

Despite his condemnation, his influence, largely mediated by *Tauler and *Henry Suso, was considerable.

Ecology: see ANIMALS.

Ecstasy (Gk., *ek-stasis*, 'standing out of'). The experience, common in all religions, of being carried beyond ordinary, everyday experience into moments of extreme and intense transcendence. The word is used of such a wide range of such experiences that no common core can be identified. Thus it is used of the out-of-the-body experiences of *shamans, the third (and next to highest stage) of the analysis of mystical union of *Teresa of Avila, trance states, *fanā' among *Sūfīs, the *rapture of spirit possession. The neurophysiology of these (usually) brief states is not yet understood (but see BIOGENETIC STRUCTURALISM), though it is well-known that the inhibition or exclusion of external stimuli (even by the insistent repetition of one stimulus, e.g. by drumming) can lead to dramatic brain consequences, some of which approximate to some of the conditions defined as ecstatic.

The converse is *enstasy.

Ecumenical Councils: see COUNCILS (CHRISTIAN).

Ecumenical patriarch. Title of the patriarch of *Constantinople. In spite of its literal meaning, 'universal patriarch', he has only a primacy of honour over the other *Orthodox patriarchs.

Ecumenism or **ecumenicism** (Gk., *oikumene*, 'the inhabited world'). The Christian quest for recovered unity among the many different Churches of Christendom. The Ecumenical *Councils are claimed to represent the mind of the whole Church and thus to have distinct authority. The beginning of the modern ecumenical movement is usually traced to the Edinburgh Conference of 1910, when many (but no Roman Catholic) missionary societies met, at the end of a century of immense but competitive expansion, to explore the nature of mission and the ways to overcome debilitating divisions. The World Council of Churches, a direct descendant, was formed in 1948. This preoccupation with internal Christian affairs began to seem to some parochial, who called for a 'wider ecumenism', one which would explore the relations between religions. Spiritual ecumenism seeks to gather and share the spirituality of separated parts of the Church, or of religions. See Index, Ecumenicism.

Eddy, Mary Baker (1821–1910). Founder of the *Christian Science Movement. In 1875, she published *Science and Health* . . ., and in 1879, she founded the Church of Christ, Scientist, in Boston. The movement eventually (1891) became the First Church of Christ, Scientist. She started the publication of *The Christian Science Monitor* in 1908.

Edels, Samuel Eliezer ben Judah Halevi (known as **Maharsha**, 1555–1631). Talmudic commentator. He lived successively in Posen, Lublin, and Ostrog, and was the founder of a large *yeshivah. The author of *Hiddushei Halakhot* (Tracts on the Commandments), he was held in high esteem. The *Hiddushei* is one of the classics of Jewish literature and is printed in most editions of the Talmud. A further work, *Hiddushei Aggadot*, gives rationalizing exegesis of *aggadot, often explaining otherwise improbable claims as *parables.

Eden (perhaps Heb., 'be fruitful', or Sumerian 'flat plain'). The dwelling place created by God for *Adam and *Eve. The *rabbis described the ultimate destiny of the righteous as *gan Eden* (garden of *Eden), Eden became, in the Jewish imagination, the epitome of perfection.

Edict of Nantes (decree of toleration): see HUGUENOTS.

Edicts of Aśoka. A collection of inscriptions by the Buddhist emperor of India *Aśoka (*c.*274–232 BCE). A total of thirty-two have been found to date inscribed upon rocks, pillars, and caves in various parts of India. The edicts proclaim Aśoka's policy of rule by *dharma (righteousness) and his belief in the virtues of kindness, toleration, and upright conduct as the means to the happiness and well-being of his subjects both here and in the afterlife.

Edinburgh Conference (1910): see MISSION; ECUMENISM.

Edwards, Jonathan (1703–58). American *Calvinistic theologian and philosopher. Following his conversion at Yale, he was ordained into the *Congregational ministry and became pastor at Northampton, Mass., in 1724. His outstanding preaching there led to the 'Great Awakening' in 1734–5, which spread more widely in 1740–1. His *Faithful Narrative of the Surprising Works of God* (1737), which carefully describes the revival at Northampton, was widely influential.

Eel-wrigglers (philosophers): see AMARĀVIKKHEPIKAS.

Eger, Akiba ben Moses, known also as **Akiva Gins** (1761–1837). German *rabbi. Despite the opposition of the *reform movement, he became unofficial *chief rabbi of Posen where he established a large *yeshivah. Various editions of his *responsa were published both in his lifetime and after his death.

Egeria or ***Etheria, Pilgrimage of.*** An account of the journey of an abbess or nun (probably Spanish) to Egypt, Palestine, Edessa, Asia Minor, and Constantinople at the end of the 4th cent.

'Ehad mi yode'a (Heb., 'Who knows one?'). A concluding *Passover song in the *Ashkenazi rite. The aim of the concluding songs 'is to keep children awake' (*B.Pes.* 108b). It is a progressive number song and probably originated in Germany in the 15th cent.

Ehō (contingent and secondary consequences): see SHŌBŌ (2).

Eight auspicious symbols (in Hinduism): see AṢṬAMANGALA.

Eighteen benedictions (part of Jewish prayer): see 'AMIDAH.

Eighteen Schools of Early Buddhism. According to Buddhist tradition, in the early centuries after the *Buddha's death the original unity of his followers quickly gave way to disagreement and schism, resulting in the formation of eighteen different schools. Eleven of these schools identified themselves with the conservative tradition of the 'Elders' (*Sthaviras), while the remaining seven constituted the innovative movement of the 'Great Assembly' (*Mahāsāṃghikas). Chief among these schools were the *Theravāda, *Sarvāstivāda, *Sautrāntika, and Vātsīputrīya. Of the eleven schools of the Elder tradition only the Theravāda has survived, while the seven schools of the Great Assembly coalesced in the emergence of the *Mahāyāna.

Eightfold path (Buddhist way): see AṢṬANGIKA-MĀRGA.

Eight immortals (Taoist figures): see PA HSIEN.

Eight liberations (Buddhist meditation exercise): see AṢṬA-VIMOKṢA.

Eight masteries (Buddhist control of perception): see ABHIBHĀVAYATANA.

Eight Trigram Society. A general designation for various religious sects which staged a rebellion in N. China in 1813. The sects, which were closely related to the *millennarian White Lotus tradition, were galvanized into revolt by their belief that the millennium had arrived. See further BOXER REBELLION.

Eight Ways (Buddhist control of perception): see ABHIBHĀVAYATANA.

Eight ways of commendation (of the Jain way): see PRABHAVANA.

Eihei-ji. The Zen monastery of Eternal Peace, founded by *Dōgen Zenji in N. Japan, in 1243. With *Sōji-ji, it is one of the two main monasteries of the *Sōtō school. For its uneasy history with its companion monastery, see SŌJI-JI. It is now a major meditation centre, with about 15,000 linked centres worldwide.

Einhorn, David (1809–79). *Reform Jewish theologian. Because he could not find rabbinical employment in Europe on account of his radical views, he emigrated to the United States in 1855 and became *rabbi of Congregation Adath Israel, New York, in 1866. He strongly believed in introducing vernacular prayers and rejected the divine origin of the *Talmud. In his view, 'the doctrinal and moral law of Scripture' is 'the imperishable spirit of Judaism'; other laws are marks of the *covenant, which can change with the times if necessary.

Ein-Sof (Heb., 'the Infinite'). *Kabbalistic designation of God in his transcendence. The term first appeared in the 13th century in the circle of *Isaac the Blind. It was used to distinguish between God-in-himself and his *sefirot (emanations) by which humanity can know him. For comparable reticence in other religions, see VIA NEGATIVA.

Eisai or **Yōsai** (1141–1215). A *Tendai monk who established the *Rinzai Zen Buddhist school in Japan. He began his career at Mount Hiei, studying Tendai esotericism, but went to China in 1168. He returned to Japan in 1191 and built the first Rinzai Zen temple, Shōfukuji. In spite of the strong opposition from Mount Hiei against the establishment of Zen, he was successful in founding Kenninji (monastery) in Kyôto and Jufukuji in Kamakura. His polemical work, *Kōzen gokoku ron* (Dissemination of Zen for the Defence of the Nation), argues for the need of an independent Zen school, although he himself taught a synthesis of Tendai, esotericism, and Zen. He is also famous for introducing the cultivation of tea (see CHADŌ) to Japan and writing the first book on the merits of tea drinking, *Kissa yōjōki*. He instructed *Dogen, and for that reason, although his own lineage died out, he is often regarded as the founding figure of Zen in Japan. He was given the posthumous title of Senkō Kokushi.

Eisegesis (reading meanings into a text): see EXEGESIS.

Eisendrath, M. N. (1902–73). US *Reform *rabbi. While he was president of the *Union of American Hebrew Congregations, he presided over the change in direction of the Reform movement to a new *rapprochement* with tradition. He was also greatly involved in civil rights, social action, and interfaith activities.

Eka (Skt.). One; the unity (*Ṛg Veda* 10. 129) which precedes the manifestations of creation.

Eka (Second patriarch of Ch'an/Zen in China): see HUI-K'O.

Ekādaśi (Skt.). The eleventh day after a full or new moon, when Hindus fast and meditate, especially through the chanting of the name of God.

Ekāgrata (Skt., 'one-pointedness'). Concentration on a single point in Hindu and Buddhist *yoga, especially *rāja yoga, which controls the fluctuations of the mind (*cittavṛtti*) generated by sense activity (*indriya) and karmic residues (*saṃskāras). Through concentration, all distractions are eliminated and the mind eventually achieves such one-pointedness that *samādhi is reached.

Eknāth or **Ekanātha** (*c*. 1535–99). *Marāṭhī Hindu scholar and poet.

His most important service to the Marāṭhī language is undoubtedly the editing of *Jnāneśverī*. He obtained the manuscripts written 300 years previously and restored the famous commentary to its original form. He died at Paiṭhaṇ on the banks of the Godāvarī River, where a temple is dedicated to him.

Eko (Jap.). The Buddhist transference of *merit to another, especially through a religious practice or gift (e.g. chanting a *sūtra). It may also be the transference of merit to a *buddha as a gift in order to attain the same state.

Ekoddiṣṭa. Post-Vedic funeral rites in Hinduism, performed after cremation of the body, to unite the deceased person with the ancestors (*pitṛ).

Ekottarāgama (Indian division in Sūtra Piṭaka): see TRIPIṬAKA.

Ekwan (Korean monk): see SANRON.

El (Heb., 'God'). The name of the supreme God of the Canaanite pantheon (known e.g. from the *Ugaritic texts), which became the name of the God of Israel.

Elan Vital (name of religious movement): see DIVINE LIGHT MISSION.

Elder

Judaism A group of respected citizens who form a consulting body. In the *Talmudic period, the term was used of scholars, particularly members of a *bet din, and the word means 'one who has acquired wisdom' (*B.Kid.* 32*b*).

Christianity In the New Testament period, elders (Gk., *presbyteroi*) were church officials with a collective authority and oversight (they are called *episkopoi*, cf. *bishops, in Acts 20. 28, Titus 1. 5–7) over local congregations. In *Reformed churches, there are both teaching and ruling elders.

Elders of Zion, Protocols of the Learned. An *anti-Semitic forgery. The book purports to be the report of a conference of world Jewry in which the leaders plot world domination.

Eleazar. The name of various prominent Jewish *tannaim and *amoraim. Eleazar ben Arakh (late 1st cent. CE) was the most outstanding pupil of R. *Johanan b. Zakkai who described him as 'a spring flowing with ever-increasing force'. Eleazar ben Azariah (1st–2nd cent. CE) was a *priestly descendant of *Ezra and became *nasi to replace Rabban *Gamaliel II. Eleazar ben Damma (early 2nd cent. CE) was the nephew of R. *Ishmael. Eleazar ben Judah of Bartota (early 2nd cent CE) was a student of R.

Joshua. He was famous for his generosity. Eleazar ben Matya (early 2nd cent. CE) was a pupil of Tarfon. He is said to have understood seventy languages (*TJ, Shek* 5. 1, 48a). Eleazar ben Parta (early 2nd cent. CE) was arrested by the Romans for publicly teaching Torah, but was miraculously delivered. Eleazar ben Shammua (*c*.150 CE) was a student of *Akiva and the teacher of *Judah ha-Nasi. Eleazar ben Simeon (late 2nd cent. CE) was thought to be the author of much of the **Zohar*. Eleazar ben Yose I (late 2nd cent. CE) is said to have exorcized the Roman emperor's daughter. Eleazar ben Zadok (late 1st cent. CE) practised *asceticism to try to prevent the destruction of the *temple in *Jerusalem. Eleazar Hisma (early 2nd cent. CE) transmitted *halakhot in the name of Joshua b. Hananiah, and Eleazar of Modin (late 1st cent. CE), said to be the uncle of Simeon *bar Kokhba, was much respected by R. *Gamaliel.

Eleazar ben Judah of Worms, known as **Eleazar Roke'aḥ,** (*c*.1165–*c*.1230). Medieval German Jewish scholar. Eleazar was a major scholar of the *Ḥasidei Ashkenaz movement. Based in Worms, he wrote many *piyyutim (liturgical poems) as well as works of theology, ethics, exegesis, and *halakhah. In *Roke'aḥ* (the opening chapters of which were often reprinted as separate works), he explored the mystical meaning of halakot and prayers. In *Sodei Razayya* (The Secret of Secrets), he attempted to summarize the teachings of Ḥasidei Ashkenazim.

Election: see CHOSEN PEOPLE.

Elements. 1. In Christianity, the materials of bread and wine used in the *eucharist.

2. In Hinduism, the components and forces which constitute the universe: see *BHŪTA.

3. In Buddhism, constituents of appearance, *dharma (2).

Elephanta (Gharapuri). An island off the coast of Bombay, containing a famous representation of the *trīmurti *Śiva in a cave temple. The date is uncertain, but *c*.5th–7th cent. CE.

Elephantiné. City situated on an island in the Nile river. Elephantiné was the site of the discovery of a collection of papyri written in *Aramaic dating back to the 5th cent. BCE. They include legal documents, fragments of the *Book of Ahikar* and letters. Two goddesses seem to have been worshipped there as well as the Hebrew God.

Elevation. The lifting up of the *elements of the *eucharist by the celebrant. The purpose is both to symbolize their offering to God and to focus the devotion of the congregation.

Eliade, Mircea (1907–86). Advocate of what is called 'history of religions', which in his case is better seen as an attempt to discern elemental, timeless, patterns of religious life. Religion is taken to be the manifestation of 'Being'. Symbolic forms, redolent of the sacred, are influenced by historical circumstances but are not themselves the product of history. The task is to use the comparative method to arrive at what is constant; to arrive at what goes beyond the contingencies of time.

Working with a model of the human as *homo religiosus*, of the human as motivated by an irreducible religious intentionality, Eliade drew most of his material from archaic cultures. Supposedly providing the most powerful evidence of the 'morphology of the sacred', these cultures are held to signal the contemporary need for greater *ontological rootage. See also SHAMANISM.

Eliezer ben Hyrcanus (end of 1st cent. CE). Jewish *tanna. Eliezer was described by *Johanan b. Zakkai as outweighing all the sages of *Israel (*Avot* 2. 8). Both literally and metaphorically, he regarded the transmission of the Jewish inheritance as imperative. After his discussion with the *Sanhedrin on ritual purity, his view was rejected and he was excommunicated (*ḥerem). Only after his death was he reinstated as one of the foremost halakhists of his time. *Pirkei de-Rabbi Eliezer* (Sayings of Rabbi Eliezer) are ascribed to him.

Elijah (9th cent. BCE). Israelite *prophet. After choosing *Elisha as his successor, he was taken up to *Heaven in a fiery chariot (2 Kings 2. 1–18). According to the book of Malachi, he will return to earth 'before the great and terrible *day of the Lord' (4. 5). In *aggadic literature, Elijah was recognized as the forerunner of the *messiah. Consequently, the *gospels record speculation that John the Baptist, who wore the same clothes as Elijah (Mark 1. 6; 2 Kings 1. 8) was a reincarnation of the prophet. Subsequently Elijah was believed to be a partner of the messiah who will overthrow the foundations of the heathen (*Gen.R* 71. 9) and bring about the *resurrection of the dead. He most frequently was said to appear on the eve of *Passover to help the poor prepare for the *seder. It is customary to place a cup for Elijah in the middle of the table, and the door is opened during the seder for the prophet to come in and herald the days of the messiah. At *circumcision ceremonies, an unoccupied chair is placed for Elijah.

Elijah ben Solomon Zalman (1720–97). The Vilna Gaon, known as Ha-Gra, a Lithuanian Jewish spiritual leader. He was famous for his great learning and produced more than seventy works and commentaries on the *Bible, the *Talmud, the *midrashim, the *Zohar, *Shulḥān Arukh*, on Hebrew grammar, and on scientific subjects. He was a brilliant *halakhist, and was also devoted to the study of *Kabbalah. Philosophy he regarded as 'accursed', and he opposed all changes in customs and liturgy. Ḥasidism was rejected because he believed its emphasis on the love of God undermined the value of the Torah.

Elijah Muhammad (1897–1975). Leader of the Nation of Islam, the American Black Muslim movement, called more fully 'The Lost-Found Nation of Islam', or, from 1976, 'The World Community of Islam in the West'. He was born in Georgia with the name Elijah Poole. Moving to Detroit, he became a follower of Wallace D. Fard (Wali Farad, known as Prophet Fard) who had founded the Temple of Islam to affirm 'the deceptive character of the white man and the glorious history of the black race'. He advocated self-help, especially through education, and he produced two manuals which guided the movement, *The Secret Ritual of the Nation of Islam* and *Teaching for the Lost Found Nation of Islam* ... He became the chief aide of Fard, who gave him his new name, and when Fard disappeared in 1934, Elijah Muhammad took control. The original goals of the Nation of Islam were continued in what was originally a splinter group, but which rapidly grew in size, led by Louis Farrakhan (b. 1933). A fiery and inspiring orator, Farrakhan has often been dismissed as a racist and anti-Semitic orator, but he speaks from great intelligence and culture. His political ambitions on behalf of the movement came to an end with the failure of Jesse Jackson (in the presidential nominations) in 1984, but the march of a million men in 1995 re-established Farrakhan and the nation of Islam as a political force.

Elimelech of Lyzhansk (1717–87). Jewish *Ḥasidic leader. Elimelech was the pupil of *Dov Baer, and after some wanderings, settled in Lyzhansk in Galacia. He formulated the doctrine of the *Zaddik and taught that he should lead his community in all spheres of life, not merely the religious. He believed that the Zaddik had a direct connection with the higher world, and that 'every utterance of the Zaddik creates an *angel and influences higher spheres'. His main work was a commentary on *Torah, *No'am Elimelekh* (1787), but it is in effect an exposition of Ḥasidic ideology, and has remained an important guide for subsequent generations.

Eliot, Thomas Stearns (1888–1965). Poet and critic. His religious background was Unitarian, which gave way to a despairing agnosticism which finds expression in his early poems and, especially, *The Waste Land* (1922). Many religious traditions appealed to him, including Hindu philosophy, *Neo-Thomism, and the classical Anglicanism of *Andrewes and the *Metaphysical poets (though an *anti-Semitic note is also evident), and in 1927 he was baptized and declared himself 'an *Anglo-Catholic in religion'. His later poems (especially *Four Quartets*, 1935–42) and his plays explore human doubt and scepticism within an intellectual framework, with deep traditional roots in the mystics, *Dante, and the Greek tragedians: what is believed is more readily lived than expressed in words.

Elisha (9th cent. BCE). Israelite *prophet. *Elijah chose Elisha to be his successor. In the *aggadah, it was taught that Elijah's promise to bestow a double portion on Elisha (ch. 2. 14) was fulfilled by Elisha's performing sixteen miracles to Elijah's eight.

Elisha ben Abuyah (early 2nd cent.). Jewish *tanna who subsequently renounced Judaism. Although he was the teacher of R. *Meir who quoted his sayings (e.g. *Avot* 4. 20), the reason for his *apostasy was not known. He is referred to in the Talmud (even by R. Meir when quoting him) as *aḥer*, 'another', in order to avoid mentioning his name.

Elixir. (Arab., *al-iksīr*). Substances believed, especially in China, to confer immortality or simply longevity and magical powers, and as such the object of much herbal lore, myth, and *alchemy. In China, the elixir is based on preparations to unite *yin and yang and synchronize the microcosm and macrocosm.

Eliyyahu ben Shelomoh Zalman (Vilna Gaon): see ELIJAH BEN SOLOMON ZALMAN.

Elkesaites. A Jewish Christian group which arose *c.*100 CE in the country east of the Jordan, having affinities with the *Ebionites (e.g. in their *asceticism and in their use of only the gospel of *Matthew) and deriving their name from Elkesai who received a revelation from an angel 96 miles tall.

Ellorā or **Elūrā**. A complex of cave and rock temples in Maharashtra, India. Sacred to Hindus, Jains, and Buddhists, its thirty-four temples, monasteries, and sanctuaries come from all three religions. They were constructed from the 5th to the 9th cents.

El male raḥamim (Heb., 'God full of compassion'). A Jewish prayer for the dead. It is normally recited at *funerals, for *Yahrzeit, and on visiting family graves.

Elmo, St. The customary name for St Peter González (*c.*1190–1246), the patron saint of seamen. His 'fire' (i.e. electrical discharge on masts of ships) was taken as a sign of his protection. Feast day, 14 Apr.

Elohim (Heb., God(s)). A name for the God of the Jews. Its plural form may once have been literal—'mighty ones'—but it became subsumed in the accumulating Jewish sense that if God is indeed *God*, then there can only be what God is: One, and not a plurality of gods.

Elūrā (sacred Indian cave temples): see ELLORĀ.

Ema (Jap.). Pictorial votive offerings. *Koema* (small ema) is a small flat wooden plaque, which may be rectangular, square, or pentagonal in shape, with a picture painted on its front surface. *Ōema* (large ema), which appeared after the 15th cent. is a work of art in many cases, painted by famous painters at the request of their rich patrons. Both *koema* and *ōema* are offered to the *kami of a shrine or to the deity of a temple for making wishes and for the fulfilment of the wishes.

The word *ema* (picture + horse) suggests its origin as a substitute for a live horse.

Emaki (Jap.). A picture scroll. A long scroll, viewed from right to left, contains a series of pictures, often with the text that illustrates a story.

Its motifs range from the secular to the religious. *Jigoku zōshi* (the Scroll of Hells), made in the 12th cent., is a religious emaki, in which the gruesome scenes of *hells based on Genshin's **Ōjōyōshū* (The Essentials for Salvation) are vividly illustrated. Temples and shrines supplied legends and miracle stories, and as a result of the spread of Buddhism in the Kamakura period, the lives of exemplary people were added to its themes.

Emanation(s). Expressions of power or wisdom from a higher being, making connection between an uninvolved or uncontaminated source, and imperfect (because contingent) appearance. Emanations are characteristically *gnostic, and appear strongly in the *Neoplatonic system of *Plotinus. They appear with idiosyncratic genius in the poetry of *Blake. Under Neoplatonic influence, they are paramount in the *sefirot of *kabbalistic Judaism. In Tibetan Buddhism (*Tibetan religion), an emanation expresses either the profound influence of, or complete projection from, a higher being. The *Dalai Lama is said to be an 'emanation' of the *bodhisattva *Avalokiteśvara.

Emancipation, Jewish. Liberation from legal restrictions and political and social disabilities. Jewish emancipation depended on the political and social conditions of a particular country. Despite political emancipation, manifestations of *anti-Semitism have continued to occur. Campaigns for emancipation (as opposed to simply waiting for it to happen) were often fuelled by a perception of the dangers of *assimilation.

Ember days (OE, *ymbren*). Four groups of three days (Wednesday, Friday, and Saturday) in the W. church year, fast days 'around' or 'about' four seasons, Advent (mid-Dec.), *Lent (*Ash Wednesday), *Pentecost, and Holy Cross Day (14 Sept.), kept as days of fasting and abstinence. They are now associated, as days of preparation, with *ordination.

Emden, Jacob, pen-name **Yavez** (1697–1776). Jewish *halakhist and *kabbalist. Emden was an indefatigable campaigner against the followers of *Shabbetai Zevi, and his most famous controversy was against Jonathan *Eybeschuetz, whom he accused of secret Shabbateanism. From this, Emden went on to criticize and question the antiquity of some passages of the **Zohar*.

Emei (mountain in China): see PILGRIMAGE.

Emerald Buddha. The Buddha image, now in the Grand Palace in Bangkok, which epitomizes the Buddha's protection of the king and people of Thailand.

Emerson, Ralph Waldo (1803–82). Author and essayist, a leading figure among the New England Transcendentalists (the Transcendental Club met at his house from 1836 to give expression to revolutionary and visionary ideals). He was born in Boston in a *Unitarian family, and after study at Harvard, he became pastor of the Unitarian Second Church of Boston. However, his questioning of the tenets of faith, and a dispute over the administration of the Lord's Supper, led to his resignation. The break confirmed him in his conviction that the quest for truth can never be compromised. He gave up preaching in 1838, and regarded himself as 'God's child, a disciple of Christ', without ecclesiastical affiliation.

Emic/etic (by analogy from phonemic/phonetic). The contrast in the study (mainly in anthropology) of peoples and their religion either according to the principles, methods, and interests of the observer (etic) or by an attempt to understand the viewpoint of the people themselves (emic). The emic/etic contrast raises acutely the issue of whose meaning is the meaning of the meaning (cf. HERMENEUTICS) since it is now recognized that the aim of a value-free account of religious beliefs and practices is unattainable.

Emigrants (Arab., *Muhājirūn*). Those who accompanied *Muḥammad on his emigration (*hijra) from *Mecca to *Madīna in 622 CE or followed shortly afterwards. The term became a title of respect, describing those who had left their homes and property.

Emin Foundation. A *new religious movement started in London in 1973 by Raymond Armin (b. Shertenlieb), known to the members as Leo. The founder, whose supposed healing abilities rest on the use of electric force within peoples' bodies, is said to have discovered the laws that govern everything.

Empō Dentō-roku. A work of the Japanese Zen monk, Shiban Mangen (*c*.1627–1710), which contains the biographies of more than a 1,000 Zen monks.

Emptiness (the condition of all appearance being essentially devoid of characteristics): see ŚŪNYATĀ.

Enchin (founder of Jimon-shū): see TENDAI (-SHŪ).

Encratites. Groups of early Christians whose ascetic practices (and related teaching) were condemned by mainstream writers such as *Irenaeus.

Encyclical (Gk., *en*, 'in', + *kyklos*, 'circle'). A pastoral letter intended for circulation among all the churches of an area. By Roman Catholics they are restricted to letters sent out by the pope.

Engaku-ji. Zen Buddhist monastery of Complete Enlightenment (*engaku* is the enlightenment attained by a *buddha), founded in 1282 by the Chinese Ch'an master, Wu-hsüeh Tsu-yüan (Jap. Bukkō Kokushi or Mogaku Sogen). It was part of the Kamakura complex (*gosan), of the *Rinzai school, and it remains active to the present day.

Engi (Japanese stories): see DENSETSU.

Engishiki (Procedures of the Engi Era). A Japanese corpus of regulations for governmental administration and ceremonies in fifty books. The compilation of these procedures was initiated in 905 CE.

The *Engishiki* can be divided into two parts in accordance with the two major divisions of the government: the *Jingi-kan* concerned with *kami (deities) affairs or Shinto religion for the well-being and prosperity of the national community, and the *Dajō-kan* dealing with all the 'secular' business of the government. All matters handled by the *Jingi-kan* are found in the first ten books of the *Engishiki*.

Engo Kokugon (Japanese name of Rinzai master): see YÜAN-WU K'O-CH'IN.

Enlightenment (attainment of insight, illumination, wisdom, truth, etc.): see Index, Enlightenment.

Enlightenment (Germ. *Aufklärung*). A period in European thought and art, *c*.1720–80. It is sometimes also called 'the Age of Reason'—misleadingly, since it implies that other 'ages' are, at least comparatively, irrational. It is thus sometimes a term of conflict, implying an emancipation from 'the dead hand of dogma'. See also DEISM; HASKALAH (Jewish Enlightenment).

Enni Ben'en (Zen master): see BEN'EN.

Ennichi (Jap., *en*, 'connection', + *nichi*, 'day'). An auspicious day; a holy day at Japanese shrines and temples.

Ennin (794–864). Third chief abbot (*zasu) of the Japanese *Tendai school, also known by his posthumous title, Jikaku Daishi. He became a disciple of *Saichō (767–822), the founder of Tendai, at the age of 15, and in 838 he went to China for further study of *T'ien-t'ai and Esoteric Buddhism (*Mikkyō). His foremost contribution to history is the establishment of Tendai esotericism (Taimitsu) in contrast to the Shingon esotericism (Tomitsu) of *Kūkai (774–835), Saichō's great rival. No less important is his introduction of the *Pure Land practice of *Wu-t'ai-shan which initiated the Tendai Pure Land tradition. The bestowal of posthumous titles begins with Ennin, who preceded both Saichō (Dengyō Daishi) and Kūkai (Kōbō Daishi) in receiving the honour.

En-no-gyōja (founder of mountain Buddhism): see SHUGENDŌ.

E'nō. Jap. for *Hui-neng.

Enoch. Descendant of *Adam (7th generation), in the Hebrew *Bible. According to Genesis 5. 24, he was one who 'walked with God and he was not; for God took him'. From this, he became central in *apocalyptic speculation. Many legends became attached to him and several pseudepigraphical books bear his name.

1 Enoch, or *Ethiopic Enoch*, contains a series of revelations to Enoch. The book is composite, and chs. 37–71, the 'Similitudes' or 'Parables', have attracted special attention because of their use of the term '*Son of Man'.

2 Enoch, *Slavonic Enoch*, or *The Book of the Secrets of Enoch*, recounts a tour by Enoch of the seven heavens.

3 Enoch is a Hebrew *Merkabah text to be dated perhaps to the 5th–6th cents. CE.

In Islam, the figure in the *Qur'ān (19. 57 f., 21. 85) of Idrīs is usually identified by Muslims with Enoch.

Enryaku-ji (centre of Tendai): see SAICHŌ; TENDAI SHŪ.

Ensō or **ichi-ensō** (Jap., 'circle'). The symbol especially in Zen Buddhism, of the absolute and uncontained reality, enlightenment. It occurs frequently in Zen painting, executed in a single, flowing stroke of the brush.

En Sof (the God beyond description in Judaism): see EIN-SOF.

Enstasy (Gk., *en-stasis*, 'standing into'). The experiences, or abolition of experience, arising as a consequence of those meditational, etc., techniques which withdraw the practitioner from the world, and even from awareness of the self. The word was coined in contrast to *ecstasy. Examples are *dhyāna, *jhāna.

Entelechy (Gk., *en* + *telos*, 'end', + *echein*, 'to have'). Aristotelian term pointing to the capacity of an entity to have complete reality and also the power to achieve through development completeness or perfection. The term was adopted by *Leibniz to describe his monads.

Enthusiasm. A religious attitude of extreme commitment, frequently leading to acts and utterances which (in the eyes of those outsiders who regard themselves as more sober) seem extraordinary. *Holy fools often exhibit those characteristics which evoke the word.

Entia non sunt multiplicanda . . . ('entities ought not to be multiplied . . .'): see WILLIAM OF OCKHAM.

Entrance, Little and Great. In Orthodox Christianity, the processions which (i) lead up to the reading of the *gospel, and (ii) bring up the *elements to be consecrated.

Enttraditionalisierung (Germ., 'detraditionalization'). The phenomenon of the erosion of tradition in society in general and in religion in particular. Tradition has been a strong source of constraint and order, since religions are systems which protect information (both verbal and non-verbal) which has been tested through millennia and has proved effective (i.e. effective in relation to goals, some of which are set by evolution and natural selection at one extreme, others of which are set by ultimate attainments, such as the *beatific vision or *nirvāna at the other). The endorsement of individual choice and responsibility in democratic societies (which have had dominant economic power, and have thus increasingly made choice realizable), followed far more recently by the revolution in communications, has threatened and eroded the security of traditional boundaries which hitherto have protected (and often coerced) the transmission of information from one generation to another.

Environment: see ANIMALS.

Ephesians, Letter to the. One of the epistles of *Paul and a book of the New Testament.

Ephesus. City in Asia Minor (near the W. coast of modern Turkey and now a ruin), and venue of the third *ecumenical council in 431.

A second synod was held in Ephesus in 449 to deal with *Eutyches. Presided over by the bishop of *Alexandria, it exonerated him; deposed instead the bishop of *Antioch; and refused to receive the *Tome* sent by Pope *Leo I. Its decisions were reversed by the Council of *Chalcedon in 451. The second synod is often known as the Latrocinium (Robber Synod).

Ephod (Heb.). A Jewish sacred garment. It was evidently part of the vestments of the *high priest. The ephod and Urim and Thummim were used as a means of seeking God's will. Consultation of the ephod, however, had certainly died out by the time of the second *Temple.

Ephraem of Syria (Syriac church father): see EPHREM, ST.

Ephraim. Younger son of *Joseph. According to the *midrash, the tribe of Ephraim left slavery in Egypt early, and many were killed by the *Philistines. In order to avoid their bones, God led the Israelites a circuitous route to the *Promised Land. It was these bones which came to life in *Ezekiel's vision of the valley of the dry bones (ch. 37) (*B.Sanh* 92b).

Ephrem, St (*c*.306–73). 'The Syrian', the most important of church *fathers in the *Syrian churches. He was born in Nisibis (Nusaybin in E. Turkey) where after his baptism he joined the ascetic and celibate circle in the church known as 'covenanters'. He attended the famous theological school in Nisibis, and was ordained *deacon (never *priest). After the Roman cession of Nisibis to Persia in 363 he moved to Edessa. His biblical commentaries (e.g. on the **Diatessaron*) and anti-heretical works (against *Bardaisan, Mani (see MANICHAEISM), *Arius) come from his last ten years. Ephrem is however best known in Syriac tradition for his large number of *hymns, which figure largely in liturgical books and which influenced later Syriac and even Greek hymnography. He was made a *Doctor of the Church in 1920.

Epiclesis (Gk., 'invocation, prayer'). A prayer in the Christian *eucharist which asks the Father to send the *Holy Spirit upon the bread and wine to make them the body and blood of Christ.

Epikoros (in Judaism, one with heterodox or heretical views): see APIKOROS.

Epiphanius, St (*c.*315–403). Church *father and bishop of Salamis in Cyprus. He was a strong supporter of *Nicaea, and opponent of *heresy. His most important writing was the *Refutation of all Heresies* (in Gk. the *Panarion*, 'medicine chest'), in which he attacked all heresies (or all that he knew) up to his own time.

Epiphany (Gk., *epiphaneia*, 'manifestation'). An appearance of a divine or superhuman being. In Christian use it refers specifically to a feast celebrated on 6 Jan. It originated in the E., where it celebrated the baptism of Jesus and, at least in a secondary way, his birth. Epiphany spread to the W. Church in the 4th cent., but here it became associated with the 'manifestation of Christ to the Gentiles' in the person of the *Magi of Matthew 2. 1–12.

Episcopacy. The system of church government by *bishops (*episcopoi*). *Anglican churches are, specifically, known as 'Episcopal' or 'Episcopalian', as in ECUSA, the Episcopal Church of the United States.

Episcopal Church in the USA or **Protestant Episcopal Church.** The *Anglican Church in the United States. Its organization dates from the consecration of Samuel Seabury as first bishop in 1784.

Episcopi vagantes (Lat., 'wandering bishops'). *Bishops who have been consecrated in an irregular manner or who, having been regularly consecrated, have ceased to be in communion with any major Church.

Epistemology (reflection on how knowledge arises): see ONTOLOGY.

Epistle. The usual word for a letter, especially of the New Testament, and in liturgical use.

Epoche (bracketing out): see PHENOMENOLOGY.

Equiprobabilism (ethical choice where more than one possibility obtains): see LIGUORI, ALPHONSUS.

Erasmus, Desiderius (*c.*1466–1536). Christian humanist. Taught by the Brethren of the Common Life (see GROOTE, G.) at Deventer, Erasmus became an Augustinian monk in 1486 and was ordained priest in 1492. Erasmus was Europe's most outstanding scholar in the early 16th cent. His merciless satire exposed ecclesiastical abuses, but he was not remotely tempted to join the *Reformers, fearing radicalism and the cost of change. His influential writings include *Adagia* (1500), a popular edn. of Gk. and Lat. proverbs, *The Christian Soldier's Dagger or Handbook* (1504), and *The Praise of Folly* (1509).

Erastianism. The view that the state has the right and responsibility to intervene in and control the affairs of the Christian Church as it appears in a particular State. The view was proposed by Thomas Erastus (Germ. Liebler, Lieber, or Lübler), 1524–83, against the *Calvinists.

Eremetical (Gk., *erēmos*, 'wilderness'). That which pertains to the life of those who go into solitary or isolated places to seek religious goals—hence hermits.

Erez Israel (Heb., 'Land of Israel'). The Jewish *Promised Land. Erez Israel was the Hebrew name given to the land governed by the British mandate, 1919–48.

Erhard Seminar Training: see EST.

Eriugena/Erigena, John Scotus (*c.*810–*c.*877). *Neoplatonic philosopher. He was an Irishman who became head of the palace school at Laon, but little else is known about his life. His importance lies mainly in his knowledge of Gk. and his work as translator and interpreter of *Dionysius the Areopagite, *Maximus the Confessor, and Gregory of Nyssa. His influence was muted by his condemnation in the 13th cent., and the inherent difficulty of his thought. His own treatise, *Periphyseon* (On the Division of Nature), represents the first important influence of Neoplatonism on the W. since Boethius.

Erlebnis (lived experience): see HERMENEUTICS.

Eruv or **erubh** (Heb., 'mixing'). A symbolic act, by which *Sabbath restrictions can be circumvented. Such acts include carrying burdens on the Sabbath by amalgamating holdings; walking further than the permitted Sabbath distance by amalgamating boundaries, and cooking for the Sabbath on a Friday festival by amalgamating meals. The tractate *Eruvin* follows naturally from *Shabbat* in the Order *Mo'ed* in *Mishnah *et seq.*

Ervad (Zoroastrian priest): see MAGI.

Esau. Elder son of the patriarch *Isaac, and twin brother of *Jacob. The relationship between the two brothers was the subject of much *aggadot, particularly since Esau/Edom was taken to represent Rome and all hostile governments.

Eschatology (Gk., *eschatos*, 'last'). That which is concerned with the last things, the final destiny both of individuals and of humanity in general, and of the cosmos. The word was first used in the 19th cent., in discussing the Bible, but it refers to a concern in those religions which have a sequential (from a beginning to an end) understanding of time, and by application to religions which envisage an end to this particular cosmic cycle.

Esdras, Books of. Various Jewish biblical books. 'Esdras' is the Gk. and Lat. form of Ezra. Confusion results from the differences between the books of this title in the *Septuagint, *Vulgate (and hence some Catholic Bibles) and *Apocrypha in English Bibles. These correspond as follows:

Septuagint	*Vulgate*	*English Bibles*
Esdras A	3 Esdras	1 Esdras
Esdras B	1 Esdras	*Ezra
	2 Esdras	*Nehemiah
—	4 Esdras	2 Esdras

2 Esdras, and specifically chs. 3–14, is also known as the '*Ezra Apocalypse*'. It describes seven visions: the first three concern the destruction of Jerusalem and the problem of evil; the sixth (ch. 13) is of the victorious *Messiah, described as 'son of man'. It is usually dated toward the end of the 1st cent. CE.

Eshet hayil (Heb., 'A woman of valour'). Title, from opening words, of a Jewish song, derived from Proverbs, praising virtuous women. In *Kabbalistic Judaism, *Eshet Ḥayil* is taken as applying to the *Shekhinah of God as his bride.

Eshin Sōzu (Japanese monk): see GENSHIN.

Esoteric Buddhism: see MIKKYŌ; SHINGON; and Index *ad loc.*

Essenes. Jewish sect, of a communal kind, active during the later part of the period of the second *Temple. The name was taken by *Philo (*Hypothetica* 11. 1–18, *Every Good Man is Free* 12. 75–13. 91) to mean 'holy ones', but others have suggested 'silent ones', 'healers', or 'pious ones'. In addition to Philo, the sect is known about from *Josephus (*War* 2. 119–61, *Antiquities* 18. 18–22, *Life* 2. 9–11), Pliny (*Natural History* 5. 73), and *Eusebius. Its beliefs and practices bear some resemblance to those described in the sectarian documents found at Qumran (see DEAD SEA SCROLLS), but it is too simple to identify the two: a more probable relationship is that they are variations on a theme, not least because of transient membership between the two.

est. An acronym for Erhard Seminar Training. Established by Werner Erhard in 1971, seminars provide 'a sixty-hour educational experience which creates an opportunity for people to realize their potential to transform the quality of their lives'. The Centres Network, as Erhard's organization is now called, aims to eradicate hunger (The World Hunger Project), transform what it is to work, and in general make a difference to social life.

Established Church. Any Church recognized by state law as the official religion of a country. An example is the *Church of England.

Esther. Heroine of the Jewish Book of Esther.

The Book of Esther is the only book in the *Bible which does not mention the name of God. The name 'Esther' is therefore read as the Hebrew verb, 'I will hide': God is constantly active even when he does not directly reveal his action.

Eta (category of excluded people): see BURAKU.

Eternalism. A belief refuted by Buddhism. In *Theravāda, it is the false belief that the self is independent of the body-mind continuum and therefore survives death unchanged (Pāli, *sassata-diṭṭhi*). In *Mahāyāna, it is the false belief in the inherent existence (Skt., *svabhāva, 'own-being' or 'essence') of anything whatsoever (Skt., *śāśvata-dṛṣṭi*). It is the opposite of *nihilism. See further SASSATAVĀDA.

Eternal light (Heb., *ner tamid*). The light kept burning before the *ark in the Jewish *synagogue. The *ner tamid* is a symbolic reminder of the golden seven-branched candlestick (*menorah) which burned continually in the *temple.

Eternity. Not a long time, since 'eternity' does not enter into the dimension of time. *Brahman and God have been thought of as 'being' of that eternal state, where there is no passing of *time, although the passing of time is simultaneously present to Brahman/God. Thus Boethius defined eternity as *interminabilis vitae tota simul et perfecta possessio* ('the total, simultaneous and absolute possession of unlimited life').

Etheria (early pilgrim to Jerusalem): see PILGRIMAGE, CHRISTIANITY.

Ethical monotheism. The worship of, and adherence to, one God which is based on practice, rather than arrived at as the conclusion of a philosophical argument. An example is the gradual insistence on *Yahweh to the exclusion of other gods in the biblical period of Judaism.

Ethics. The human concern for what is right and wrong, good and evil. Ethics arise from the human awareness of the future, combined with a lack of detailed knowledge about it. Lives and actions have to be projected into acknowledged but unknown futures, which at once makes evaluation inevitable: is a possible action right or wrong, wise or foolish, prudential or risky, good or evil? The attribution of value then extends to much else, and produces the characteristic recognition by humans of truth, beauty, and goodness, not as contingent or arbitrary, but as independent of the moment which gives rise to them—i.e. as absolutes. What *counts* as good or evil varies from age to age, culture to culture, though even then there is a considerable convergence which overrides what is known as *cultural relativity.

Religions are aware of these universals as a matter of experience. They know that thoughts and actions based on the absolutes of truth, beauty, and goodness are to be endorsed and encouraged, and perhaps are to be rewarded after death, even if not in this life. Religious ethics are concerned, far more than secular ethics are, with the causes and consequences of evil. Nevetheless, they affirm (and give good grounds for doing so) the sovereignty of good.

On the basis of the experience of the human universal to make moral judgements and recognitions, religions have believed, in general, that there is a naturally good way to live and behave. In the E., this tends to be summarized under *dharma, in the W. under *natural law. Roughly speaking, if there is a consistent way for things to behave appropriately in the natural order (e.g. for stones to fall when dropped, or for the movement of planets to be predictable—hence the interest in the connections between those regularities and humans in *astrology), it would be extremely odd if there were not a naturally good way for humans to live with each other. In the W., this led Aristotle to propose what has subsequently been elaborated as eudaïmonism—human flourishing. What has been a matter of contest, within religions as well as between them, is whether what counts as 'flourishing' has been fixed for all time (e.g. in the word of God in revelation, whether Vedic, Biblical or Quranic), or whether there is a constant exegesis of the eudaimonic—no doubt on the basis of previous experience and revelation (where applicable), but nevertheless prepared to move and change. Aristotle, after all, could not imagine a world without slaves and the subordination of wives to husbands—it was both natural and eudaimonic for those concerned; we do not agree, because the detail of the eudaimonic is not fixed for all time in all respects.

On the same basis of the human universal to make judgements of what is right and wrong, good and evil, religions have developed many different styles of moral living and accountability. But all religions believe that we have some competence to take charge of the lives we project into whatever futures there may be, and to allow moral considerations to act upon our decisions. This is what it means to be human. If there is a basic human right (concerning which, in such terms, religions say little), it is the right to be human in this way—to be sufficiently free to exercise responsibility and accountability in this way.

Judaism Jewish ethics are derived from *Torah as the God-given revelation of the way in which the broken human condition (described graphically in the opening chapters of *Genesis) can be repaired. Humans are not radically evil (the story of *Adam and Eve is not understood as Christians understand it): they are confronted by the two *inclinations. In this context, law merges with morality—and it was a dispute among the *rabbis whether an act to be moral had to go *beyond* what the law required (*lifnim mi-shurat ha-din*, 'beyond the boundary of the law'). It is perhaps simplest to say that law is the necessary, but not the sufficient, condition of the good life. In the vital *imitatio Dei* (*imitation of God), the details are all derived from Torah itself. Judaism, while based on law, is not legalistic. There are in fact only three moral absolutes, summarized in *kiddush ha-Shem; otherwise, much rabbinic discussion is devoted to ranking obligations in order of priority: saving life having precedent over keeping the *Sabbath is an example.

Christianity Christian ethics derive from the occasion when *Jesus was asked, as teachers, especially rabbis, often were at that time, to give his *kelal* of Torah (choice of verse which summarizes Torah). His choice, the love of God and the love of one's neighbour, was neither unique nor controversial. This context-independent command of love had to be made context-specific: it had to be related to the circumstances in which the early and subsequent Christians found themselves. This is exactly what one finds *Paul and others doing in the writings which became eventually the New Testament. For example, in 1 Corinthians, Paul states how they should deal with a case of incest, with dietary scruples, with marriage and virginity, with support of ministry, with the behaviour of women in services, until he bursts out, almost in exasperation, 'I will show you a more excellent way'; and he reverts to the controlling, but context-independent, command of love. Christian ethics have oscillated through history between these extremes: on the one side, Situation Ethics, associated with Joseph Fletcher, emphasized the importance of each situation determining what is the most loving thing to do (echoing *Augustine's, *Ama, et fac quod vis*, 'Love, and do what you will'); on the other, when the *pope defines a matter of morals (as also of faith), it is infallibly decided. Between the two, most Christians refer to the Bible (though with great division about whether or not the Bible, or at least the New Testament, should be treated as containing commands, applicable as non-negotiable law) and live their lives somewhere between the two extremes by the exercise of conscience. In the main forms of Christianity, conscience is the absolutely inviolable and sacrosanct centre of the person as human, as responsible for her or his decisions.

Islam Since God has given to humans his guidance for their behaviour in the Qur'ān, Muslim ethics (*akhlāq*) are necessarily grounded in the Qur'ān. But as with all revelations, not every conceivable circumstance is covered in the Qur'ān. A second major source of guidance, therefore, lies in *ḥadīth: Muḥammad and his Companions were the first living commentaries on Qur'ān, and although ḥadīth is not in the same category of authority as the Qur'ān, nevertheless the example of *insān al-kāmil* (the perfect man) is of constant importance. Life as God desires it was eventually formulated more systematically in the schools of *sharīʿa (law), which detail the things which are lawful and prohibited (*al-halal w'al haram) for a Muslim. However, by no means all things are specified, and the principle applies that whatever God has not forbidden is allowed (as a mark of his generosity), though always within the boundaries of 'what God wills' as revealed in more general terms in the Qur'ān. Lives are judged by God (*judgement) on the basis of good and evil done, controlled always by intention (*niyya).

Hinduism Hinduism is a coalition of widely differing styles in religious life and belief, but shared in common is the belief that humans are bearers of souls (*ātman) which are reborn many millions of times (*saṃsāra)—so long, in fact, as they are entangled in bodies which desire transient appearances more than the truth. In each life, *karma accumulates—for good and for ill—which is worked out in subsequent lives, until one orders one's life in the direction of release, which necessarily involves good actions. 'Hinduism' is a map of the many ways in which one may so live that the ātman attains its goal and obtains *mokṣa (release). In other words, Hinduism is a map of *dharma (appropriateness), and its own name for itself is *sanātana dharma*, everlasting dharma: in the Hindu way, it is dharma that has primacy as ethics, because it corresponds to *ṛta, the cosmic order in which natural law is grounded. Central to this in relation to ethical behaviour is *varṇāśramadharma, one's duty in relation to class/caste (*varna) and the four stages of life (*āśrama), which still obtains for many (though as always, not for all) Hindus.

Buddhism While the Buddha rejected the Hindu belief in an undying ātman passing from life to life, he nevertheless affirmed continuity of consequence flowing from one life to another, working out the consequences of karma and *taṇhā (thirst or clinging). His 'middle way' to enlightenment included the necessity for right conduct. This is summarized for laypeople in the Five Precepts (Pañca-*śīla), which are not so much commands as promises which a person makes to himself/herself each morning; and the Ten Precepts for the members of monastic communities. The Buddha's own lives are exemplary in defining what is good—the plural 'lives' being a reminder that the Buddha-to-be appeared in previous lives, stories concerning which are found in the *Jātaka collections. Of the Five Precepts, the first, *ahiṃsā (non-injury) has further implications, because no exception was made for the killing of animals for sacrifice. *Dāna (giving) developed as a substitute, leading to the characteristically dynamic relationship between laypeople and the *saṅgha (monastic community), and to generosity at the heart of ethical life. The aim is the development of mahā-*karuṇā, great and unlimited compassion.

Confucianism The teaching of Confucius and of the Confucian school is addressed to the good of society, not simply to individual behaviour, or the attainment of individual goals. It is often summarized in the phrases, 'The Three Bonds' (between parent and child, husband and wife, ruler and subject), and 'The Five Relationships' (including those between brothers and between friends). Confucius believed that, with the help of heaven (*t'ien) or a positive moral force (*te), people can produce the all-important characteristics of *jen and *li. The moral issue can then be put as a question: 'How would the wise person (*sheng-jen) or ideal person (*chün tzu*) respond with te, and in accord with jen and li, in this situation?' Although Confucian ethics may seem to stress the desirability of hierarchical or vertical relationships, in fact the key factor stressed by Confucius is *shu* (reciprocity), even if the principle of authority has also been upheld in these relationships. Confucianism was open to attack and criticism which also affected the development of the dominant school: see e.g. MO TZU, HSÜN TZU, and (at the root of Taoism) LAO TZU and CHUANG TZU.

Sikh 'Truthful living' is the aim of Sikh life which necessarily embraces ethics (Ādi Granth 62). It requires a positive action and effort (*kirat karna*) in a constant work of service (*seva) to others: 'Only by the self-forgetting service of others can God be reached' (AG 26). This is expressed particularly in *vand chakna*, sharing with others. Because all humans are subverted by *haumai, this effort is not easy to initiate or sustain, but Sikhs receive help from the grace of God, the teachings of the scriptures, and the example of the *Gurus.

Ethics of the Fathers: see AVOT.

Ethiopianism. A term used to identify one type of African independent church, which first emerged in the 1880s in Ghana, Nigeria (here called the 'African churches'), and in S. Africa, where the term was first used by Mokone's Ethiopian Church in 1892. It is based on references to Ethiopia in the Bible, especially in Psalm 68. 31, and on the ancient Christian kingdom of Ethiopia; together these provide a charter for dignity and independence.

Ethiopian Jews: see FALASHAS.

Ethiopian Orthodox Church. The *monophysite national church of Ethiopia. The Church entertains legends of its origin in the preaching of Matthew or the eunuch of Acts 8. 26–39, but the planting of Christianity in the country actually dates from the 4th-cent. work of Frumentius at the royal court. Frumentius was consecrated the first *Abuna (patriarch) by Athanasius of Alexandria (*c*.340), thus establishing the dependence of the Church on the Church of Egypt. It became isolated from the rest of Christendom by the Islamic conquests of the 7th and 8th cents.

The Ethiopian Orthodox Church is in communion with the other *Oriental Orthodox Churches. It is unique, however, in its observance of Jewish practices, e.g. the keeping of the *Sabbath, *circumcision, and the distinction of clean and unclean meats. The Church also claims a connection with biblical Israel through the Queen of Sheba. How these Jewish themes and legends in Ethiopian Christianity are to be explained is very obscure. See also FALASHAS.

Eto: see CHRISTIAN FELLOWSHIP CHURCH.

Etrog. Citron fruit used on the Jewish *festival of *Sukkot. The etrog is one of the *four species used as part of the liturgy.

Eucharist (Gk., *eucharistia*, 'thanksgiving'). The principal service of Christian worship, at least in non-*Protestant churches. It is also variously called (Holy) *Communion, the *Lord's Supper, and the *Mass. The earliest account of the eucharist is *Paul's reference to the 'Lord's supper' in 1 Corinthians 11. 23–5, which attributes its institution to the words and actions of *Jesus at the *Last Supper and identifies the bread and the 'cup' with his body and blood.

Euchologion (Gk.). The book containing the text and rubrics for the Orthodox liturgy of the *eucharist, fixed parts of the daily *office, and the other sacraments and minor rituals.

Eudaimonism (human flourishing): see ETHICS.

Euhemerism. From Euhemerus (*c*.320 BCE), who argued that the gods developed out of elaborated legends concerned originally with historical people. Applied to Jesus, the question becomes, not **cur Deus homo?*, but *cur homo Deus?* Why (or how) was the man Jesus promoted to become the Son of God? The historical evidence supporting this interpretation of Jesus is negligible, not least since the letters of Paul, among the earliest writings of the New Testament, associate Jesus closely with God, with extremely high titles and claims.

Eusebius (*c*.260–*c*.340). Bishop of Caesarea in Palestine and church historian. Eusebius's most important work was the *Ecclesiastical History*, containing an immense range of material, including many extracts from earlier writers, about the Church from the beginning to his own time. Among his other historical works are a *Chronicle*, containing tables synchronizing events in ancient history; a *Life of Constantine*, to whom he was theological advisor; and an account of the *Martyrs of Palestine* in the persecution of 303–10. His most important theological writings are the two apologetic works, *Preparation for the Gospel* (refuting Greek polytheism) and *Demonstration of the Gospel* (proving Christianity from the Old Testament).

Eutyches (*c*.378–454). Christian *heretic, who opposed *Nestorianism so strongly that he was accused in 448 of the opposite error of confounding the two natures in Christ, and of denying that Christ's manhood was consubstantial with ours. He was deposed, then reinstated at *Ephesus in 449, and finally condemned at *Chalcedon in 451.

Evagrius of Pontus (346–99). Christian spiritual writer. He was a noted preacher in *Constantinople, but left the temptations of the capital for Jerusalem and (in 382) the Nitrian desert of Egypt, to devote himself to prayer among the monks. He became a disciple of St *Macarius. His mystical works, largely in the form of aphorisms, were the main channel through which the ideas of *Origen passed to later writers. His *Centuries* is preserved in Syriac, where, however, it was heavily edited to alter the more Origenistic statements.

Evam mayā śrutam ekasmin samaye or **evam me sutam ekam samayam** (Skt., Pāli). 'Thus have I heard. At one time . . .', the form of words occurring at the beginning of Buddhist *sūtras to show that a discourse of the Buddha is being related.

Evangelical Alliance. An interdenominational body formed in 1846 as a response to *Tractarianism and as an expression of unity 'on the basis of great evangelical principles'. The Alliance's 20th-cent. work in England was given more vigorous expression after the Second World War by promoting evangelistic crusades, conferences for ministers, accommodation for overseas students, and active co-operation among interdenominational missionary societies. Prominent amongst its more recent achievements was the formation of TEAR Fund which raises money for relief work throughout the world.

Evangelical and Reformed Church. Formed in 1934 by a merger of two American churches of German background: the Reformed Church in the United States (called 'German Reformed Church' until 1869), and the Evangelical Synod of North America. The new denomination accepted *Reformed and *Lutheran standards of belief equally. In 1957 it merged with the *Congregational Christian churches to become the *United Church of Christ.

Evangelicals. *Protestant Christians who stress belief in personal conversion and salvation by faith in the atoning death of Christ, and in the Bible as the sole authority in matters of faith: stress is also laid on evangelism.

Evangelist. 1. In the New Testament (e.g. Ephesians 4. 11), an itinerant missionary.

2. Any of the authors of the four canonical *gospels: Sts *Matthew, *Mark, *Luke, and *John. This usage dates from the 3rd cent. The four evangelists are traditionally symbolized by a man, a lion, an ox, and an eagle, respectively, on the basis of Ezekiel 10. 14 and Revelation 4. 6–10. The four signs are known as (Gk.) tetramorphs.

Evans-Pritchard, Sir Edward (1902–73). British anthropologist who concentrated on religion and related cultural phenomena. Involved with fieldwork in the S. Sudan during the period 1926–39, Evans-Pritchard's main intention was to show the rationality and coherence of the cultural domain, in order to refute the Lévy-Bruhl thesis of primitive mentality. *Theories of Primitive Religion* (1965) is a sustained attack on scientific theories of religion, and *Nuer Religion* (1956) is one of the first detailed studies of a pre-literate religion in which the religious domain is treated non-reductionistically. His approach (known as *hermeneutic explanation) is in strong contrast to *nomothetic explanation (Gk., *nomos*, 'a law') which seeks to find covering laws or generalizations—e.g. Evans-Pritchard's near-contemporary, A. Radcliffe-Brown (1881–1955). Radcliffe-Brown sought to establish structural principles governing human relationships.

Evans-Wentz, Walter Yeeling (1878–1965). Pioneer in revealing and interpreting *Tibetan Buddhist philosophy to the West. In 1919 in Gangtok, Evans-Wentz met the Lama Kazi Dawa Samdup (former teacher of Alexandra David-Neel who wrote *Magic and Mystery in Tibet*, 1965) and together they began translating the *Tibetan Book of the Dead*, 1927, a totally unknown manuscript which Evans-Wentz had picked up in a Darjeeling bazaar. Other books haphazardly followed: *Tibet's Great Yogi*, *Milarepa*, (1928); *Tibetan Yoga and Secret Doctrines*, (1935); *Tibetan Book of the Great Liberation*, (1954) (pt. 2 of which he considered his most important work), and *Cuchama and Sacred Mountains*, (1981) (posthumously).

Eve (Heb., Ḥavvah). According to Jewish scripture, the first woman. According to the *aggadah, Eve was Adam's second wife after *Lilith had left him, and the serpent approached Eve rather than Adam because it knew women are more easily tempted (*ARN* 1. 4). Eve is buried beside Adam on Mount *Machpelah.

In Islam the wife of Adam is mentioned in the *Qur'ān, but not by name. Further details, including the name Eve (Arab., Hawwā'), are given in legends, probably from Rabbinic and Syriac sources. Ḥawwā' died two years after Adam and was buried beside him at *Mecca.

Evening Prayer or **Evensong.** The evening office of the *Anglican Church. 'Evening prayer' is also a title for Roman Catholic vespers. See also MORNING PRAYER.

Even Shetiyyah (rock on which, according to Jews and Muslims, world is founded): see EBEN SHETIYYAH.

Evil. The furthest reach of wrongdoing and wrong being. Although *Kant maintained that the only evil thing is an evil will, there is much in human experience which evokes the word which is not a product of the will. Indeed, Hannah *Arendt, observing the Eichmann trial, spoke of the banality of evil, lying as it does so far outside the compass of will, and being 'excused' by the appeal that, in a totalitarian regime, to obey orders and not to think is the only behaviour possible. Religions tend to see the occurrence of evil as the consequence of personal agency in the cosmic order (personified as *Satan, the Devil or Iblīs, *Māra, etc.), which if made absolute leads to *dualism, an eternal principle of evil; and in either case, religions offer resources both to recognize and combat evil.

See also THEODICY; EVIL, PROBLEM OF.

Evil, problem of. If God is both almighty and perfectly good, why is there *evil in the world? This challenge, made by Epicurus (341–270 BCE), has been repeated over the centuries, either as a response to the *Teleological Argument for God's existence or, more radically, to attack *theism. The book of *Job is one of the earliest treatments of the question. Attempts to show that evil in the world can be reconciled with God's power and goodness are known as theodicies (*theodicy).

According to the Free Will Defence: moral evil is regarded as the result of human freedom, a price worth paying either because freedom is an intrinsic good or because its good effects outweigh its bad ones.

Evil eye. The eye is widely believed to have the power to convey mischief or damage, and is then known as the evil eye. According to Jewish sages, Sarah cast the evil eye (Heb., *ayin ra'ah* or *ayin ha-ra*) on Hagar (*Gen.R.* 45. 5), as did Joseph's brothers on *Joseph (*Gen.R.* 84. 10). In Islam, the evil eye (Arab., *'ayn*) can take effect even without the intention of the person possessing it, causing harm or death to human beings or animals, damage to crops or goods, etc.

This whole concept is disapproved of by orthodox Islam since it seems to deny or bypass the absolute divine power and decree, but it is virtually impossible to eradicate, and survives today in folklore, on the fringes of religion and medicine.

Evil spirits. The sense of evil being a consequence of active agents is common in all religions. They may be synonymous with *demons (q.v. for examples), but evil spirits take on many other forms. In Zoroastrianism, as *daevas, they form a fundamental part of the dynamic of the whole system. Evil spirits are frequently the spirits of the dead who have not received appropriate care from the living, and who are therefore restless until they receive support: for examples, see KUEI, PRETA. Evil spirits may take possession of other lives, not least those of humans. They are then contested through *exorcism or other rituals. They may also be contested by exclusion from the existing human community, a strategy which resulted in the execution of *witches and others believed to have been possessed. See Index, Evil agents.

Exaltation of the Cross. The feast, also known as Holy Cross Day, kept in honour of the cross of Christ on 14 Sept.

Exarch. In some E. churches a *metropolitan whose office is of high status, though not as high as that of *patriarch.

Ex cathedra (Lat., 'from the seat/throne'). Authoritative statements in Roman Catholicism.

Such definitions are 'irreformable', because they do not rely on the consent of the Church. The phrase colloquially has therefore come to refer to statements made with the kind of authority that brooks no argument.

Exclusive Brethren (Christian sect): see PLYMOUTH BRETHREN.

Excommunication. A censure imposed by the *Christian Church which deprives a person of the right to administer or receive the *sacraments or to hold office in the church.

The term is then applied to the process of expelling members from the, or a, community in other religions—e.g. the expulsion of a member of the Buddhist *saṅgha (monastic community) if he has committed one of the four offences which are known as *pārājika* (involving defeat): sexual misconduct, theft, murder, boasting of supernatural powers. See also (in Judaism) ḤEREM.

Exegesis (Gk., 'bring out'). 1. The task of 'bringing out' the meaning of a text. Exegesis raises immediately the central question of *hermeneutics, whose meaning is the meaning of the meaning? The task of exegesis is to seek out legitimate meaning in the light of continuing and developing understanding. However, if the text does not exercise some control over proposed meanings, interpretation easily becomes eisegesis (reading meaning into a text).

2. A seminar-based organization devoted to 'the business of transformation'. Running from 1976 until 1984, Robert D'Aubigny's Exegesis Standard Seminar has attracted *c*.5,000 people. This *est-like manifestation of the human potential movement, the first of its kind to be developed in Britain, has also attracted considerable controversy. Psycho-spiritual growth combines with mysticism in action in the modern world—shades of *Gurdjieffian, 'the work', and an attempt to fulfil socially as well as individualistically envisaged human potential.

Exempla of the Rabbis. A medieval manuscript containing more than 300 Jewish stories, as edifying examples of admirable conduct.

Exilarch. Lay head of the Babylon Jewish community. The first clear evidence of the existence of the exilarch dates back to the 2nd cent. CE. The office of exilarch (Aramaic *resh galuta*) was hereditary; its holder was traditionally a member of the house of *David. He was recognized by the royal court as chief representative of the Jews. By the 13th cent., however, most of the powers of the exilarch had been transferred to the *academies.

Exile, Babylonian. Exile of the Jews in Babylon in the 6th cent. BCE. From this experience and history derives the phrase, 'a Babylonian exile', to describe other periods of exile from a home circumstance. See also DIASPORA and GALUT.

Existentialism. A disparate trend concentrated mainly in the second quarter of the 20th cent. but with roots in 19th-cent. European thought, especially in the writings of S. *Kierkegaard, F. *Dostoevsky, and F. *Nietzsche. Existentialism is more a pervasive 'mood' than a united movement or 'school' of thought. However, recurrent features are: (i) deep suspicion of the claims of permanent systems or traditional ideologies, whether religious, metaphysical, or political; (ii) contempt for most academic philosophy as superficial and irrelevant to basic human needs and central human concerns; (iii) concern for the human condition as determined by the ever-present threat of death and ultimate meaninglessness; (iv) conception of human nature as unfixed and unfinished; (v) life as a series of ambiguous possibilities; and, (vi) disengagement from public issues and focus on the solitary individual and the decisions s/he is required to make in 'the moment'.

Exodus. The Jewish liberation from *slavery in Egypt. The story of the Exodus is contained in a series of narratives in the book of Exodus. It became the epitome of God's power to rescue his people.

Exodus, Book of. The second book of the Hebrew Bible and Christian Old Testament. The English title follows that of the Septuagint Greek version, the usual short Hebrew title *Shemoth* ('names') being the second word of the text. Like the rest of the *Pentateuch the book is traditionally ascribed to Moses but is held by modern critics to be a composite work of the 9th to 5th cents. BCE. Miriam's song in 15. 21 may be among the oldest passages in the Bible.

Ex opere operato (Lat., 'from the act done'). The objective mode of operation of the *sacraments as understood in Catholic theology. The claim that a sacrament is effective *ex opere operato* means that so long as the conditions of its institution are properly observed and fulfilled, the defective qualities of the minister and recipient are no impediment, and *grace is conferred.

Exorcism (Gk., *exorkosis*, 'out-oath'). The removing of that which has taken possession of a person or object or building. This is usually taken to be an *evil spirit or *demon.

Ex oriente lux (Lat., 'out of the East, light'). The belief that greater wisdom and deeper spirituality can be found in E. religions than in the materialistic West. Given impetus by such people as *Schopenhauer and Sir Edwin Arnold (his *Light of Asia* appeared in 1879), it led to an extensive and serious academic endeavour to study the religions of the East, and to publish texts and translations.

Expiation. The removal of an offence by means of some act or offering by, or on behalf of, the offender. According to one understanding of *atonement in Christian theology, *Christ made expiation vicariously for the sins of human beings.

Exposition of the Blessed Sacrament. The displaying of the eucharistic *host for the purpose of devotion, e.g. by opening the doors of the *tabernacle where it is reserved, or in a *monstrance. See also BENEDICTION; CORPUS CHRISTI.

Exsurge Domine. A *bull issued in June 1520 by Pope *Leo X, threatening the excommunication of *Luther. The *Reformer appealed for a general *council to discuss the issues but, having no success, burnt the bull publicly in Wittenberg, Dec. 1520.

Extra ecclesiam nulla salus (est) (Lat., 'outside the church there is no salvation'). The view, expressed first by *Origen and *Cyprian, that formal membership of the Church is necessary for salvation. The *bull *Unam Sanctam* (1302) of Pope *Boniface VIII declared that 'there is one holy, catholic and apostolic Church, outside of which there is neither salvation nor remission of sins', and that 'it is altogether necessary to salvation for every human creature to be subject to the Roman pontiff'. The bull mentions specifically 'the Greeks' (i.e. the Greek Orthodox): *a fortiori*, those in other religions must be in equally great peril.

The apparent severity to non-Christians and non-Catholics is modified by *invincible ignorance.

This caution issued in the teaching of Vatican II (especially *Lumen Gentium*) that those who live by conscience outside the Church may be saved. See also Anonymous Christians in RAHNER, K.

Extreme unction (rite of anointing): see UNCTION.

Eybeschuetz, Jonathan Ben Nathan/ Nata also **Eybeschitz** (1690/5–1764). Jewish *talmudic and *kabbalistic scholar. When *rabbi of 'the three communities' (Altona, Hamburg, and Wandsbeck), he came into controversy with Jacob *Emden over his supposed leanings towards Shabbateanism (see SHABBETAI ZEVI). Eventually he was vindicated by the Council of the Four Lands in 1753. He was an outstanding preacher, and published several homiletic works, as well as thirty treatises on *halakhah. Scholars do not agree whether there is any substance in the Shabbatean charges. His book on the Kabbalah, *Shem 'Olam* (Everlasting Name) can be interpreted in different ways, and doubt has been cast on its authorship. Eybeschuetz published a refutation of the charges in *Luḥot Edut* (1755).

Eye: see EVIL EYE.

Ezekiel. Hebrew prophet of the 6th cent. BCE and name of a prophetical book of the Hebrew Bible and Christian Old Testament. Ezekiel is the last of the three 'major prophets', after *Isaiah and *Jeremiah. As well as fears about mystical speculation, the book caused embarrassment because of the contradiction between chs. 40–8 and the laws of the *Pentateuch, as well as the fierce diatribes against Jerusalem in ch. 16. The Talmud (*B.Ḥag* 13a) records that the book was almost suppressed.

Ezra. A *priest and *scribe after whom a book in the Hebrew *Bible is named. Ezra himself was described as both a priest and scribe, and he had a major role in the rebuilding of the *Jerusalem *Temple after the Babylonian *exile. Ezra was regarded as second in piety only to *Moses.

Ezra and Nehemiah, Books of. Two books belonging to the *Writings of the Hebrew Bible and to the historical books of the Christian Old Testament. In some Roman Catholic Bibles the titles are 1 and 2 *Esdras respectively. The books continue the history of *Chronicles down to the end of the 5th cent. BCE, and may be the work of the same compiler ('the Chronicler').

Ezrat Nashim (Heb., 'Court of Women'). A courtyard in the *Jerusalem *temple. *Women were not permitted to pass beyond the Ezrat Nashim, and later, the term was applied to the section of the *synagogue reserved for women.

F

Fa. Chin. for *dharma.

Face/body marks in Hinduism: see TILAKA.

Fa-chia (political philosophy) One of the Six Ways of Chinese Religion. The historian Ssu-ma Tan (d. 110 BCE) wrote of its followers: they advocated deterrent law and punishment, especially in Han Fei Tzu, and in his work of that name, often compared to Machiavelli's *The Prince*; in Fa-chia, the Tao is simply the working out of power politics: the past is not revered as a repository of wisdom, as it was for Confucius and Mo Tzu: what matters is how the ruler exercises 'the two handles' of reward and punishment'.

Fackenheim, E. (Jewish writer): see HOLOCAUST; SHO'AH.

Fa-hsiang. A school of Chinese Buddhism, also known as Dharma-character, which continued the teaching of *Vijñavāda (Yogācāra), based on the writings of *Asaṅga and *Vasubandhu. It was founded by *Hsüan-tsang (600–64), whose work and translation, *Ch'eng wei-shih lun* (*Vijñaptimātratā-siddhi*) expounds the school's teaching. Everything is a *projection of mind, and possesses no reality in itself. Consciousness is analysed into eight types, in order to account for the different forms of appearance. The school began to decline in the 9th cent., but continued as a philosophical influence for many centuries.

Fa-hsien (*c*.338–*c*.422). Chinese Buddhist monk, who left China in 399 on pilgrimage to India, via the Himālayas. He collected Buddhist texts, and on his return to China in 414 he translated **Mahāparinirvāna-sūtra* and the *Mahāsāṃghika version of the *Vināya-piṭaka. But he is chiefly remembered for his account of his travels, *Fu-kuo chi*, for which see Li Yung-hsi, *A Record of the Buddhist Countries* (1957).

Faith. The disposition of believers toward commitment and toward acceptance of religious claims. It has a distinct importance in Christianity because of *Paul's insistence on *justification by faith alone (Romans 4. 5, 9. 30; Galatians 3. 2), and his inclusion of faith in the three paramount virtues (along with hope and love, 1 Corinthians 13. 13). In this sense, faith can only be received from God as a gift of *grace, and becomes the means through which belief is formed (*fides qua creditur*, 'faith by which it is believed'). But faith also becomes 'the Faith', the gradual accumulation through time of that which is believed by Christians, faith as *assensus*, assent (*fides quae creditur*, 'faith which is believed').

For faith in Buddhism, see ŚRADDHĀ; in Islam, see ĪMĀN.

Fa-ju: see SOUTHERN AND NORTHERN SCHOOLS.

Fa-jung (Jap., Hōyū), 594–657, Ch'an Buddhist master, who founded the Gozu ('Oxhead') school, which is Ch'an/Zen related, but is not reckoned as belonging to the Five Houses/Seven Schools (*goke-shichishū) of the mainstream tradition. The Oxhead school appears to have been eclectic, drawing on what it regarded as wisdom in other traditions.

Fa-lang (507–81). *San-lun Buddhist teacher. He devoted himself to combining in practice *Vinaya rules and *dhyāna meditation. In 558 he established a school at (present-day) Nanking, and his teaching was continued by a pupil, *Chi-tsang.

Falashas. Jews of Ethiopian origin. The Falashas themselves claim to be descended from Menelik, the son of King *Solomon and the Queen of Sheba (1 Kings 10. 1–13). Most experts believe they belong to the Agau family of tribes to whom Judaism spread from S. Arabia. They call themselves 'Beta Esrael' (House of *Israel) and live in their own separate villages, the best known of which are near the town of Gondar. They keep the ritual *food law of the *Pentateuch; they *circumcise their sons on the eighth day; they observe the *Sabbath and *Day of Atonement, and they offer *sacrifice and eat unleavened bread (*mazzah) during the *Passover season. Their precise personal status as Jews is still in some dispute among the Israeli religious establishment. In 1985, many Ethiopians demonstrated in Jerusalem against the *Chief Rabbi, who had demanded symbolic conversion for those among them who wished to marry—because of doubts about their divorce procedures and personal status. The insistence on symbolic recircumcision was withdrawn, but not ritual immersion.

Falk, Jacob (1680–1756). Jewish *halakhic authority. As *rabbi of Lemberg, his *yeshivah became the largest in Poland. He was a determined opponent of *Shabbateanism, siding with Jacob *Emden against Jonathan *Eybeschuetz. He is best known as the author of *Penei Yehoshu'a* (The Face of Joshua) published in separate parts (1739, 1752, 1756, and 1780), which is a series of novellae on the *Talmud, and a defence of *Rashi, still respected and consulted.

Fall. The act of disobedience of *Adam and Eve which according to the Bible story in Genesis 2–3 was responsible for the human condition of pain, toil, and (already in ancient exegesis) mortality. The Jewish interpretation of the Genesis story does not see in it anything like the same radical, vitiating, fault: there is a sense in which 'the fall' is a fall upwards, into the opportunity of choice, action, and responsibility: see FELIX CULPA.

Falun Gong (Wheel of Dharma). A Chinese movement founded by Li Hongzhi in 1992. Drawing on ancient practices in the Chinese tradition, mainly Taoist and Buddhist, Falun Gong secured many adherents in the 1990s, perhaps as many as 2 million in China (including members of the Communist party) and more overseas. Its teaching, Falun Dafa, is advocated in Li Hongzhi's book, *Zhuan Falun*. It draws particularly on meditation and breathing (*ch'i) techniques to offer its adherents control over life and its vicissitudes, including illness and death. Following a demonstration of 10,000 members in Beijing in 1999, it was condemned and attacked by the Chinsese authorities, who identified it as the latest in the many Chinese religious *societies that have combined religious assurance with political dissent (see, e.g., *Boxer rebellion, *Eight Trigram Society, *Taiping rebellion). Falun Gong claimed not to be an organization, despite a closely connected membership, achieved not least through the internet.

Falsafa (Arab., *falṣafa*, from Gk. *philosophia*), the pursuit of philosophy in Islam. The Muslim delight in philosophy (at least in the early centuries) rests on a confidence that God is the creator of all things, and that *knowledge (*'ilm) leads to a deeper understanding of him and of his works. For examples, see Index, Philosophers; Philosophy; and Theologians/Philosophers; all under sub-heading Muslim.

Family: see CHILDREN OF GOD.

Fan (return to the source in Taoism): see FU.

Fanā'. 'Annihilation, dissolution', the *Sūfī state of attainment or perfection, achieved by the annihilation of all human attributes until God is all. It is 'to die before one dies'. It is the threshold of *baqā'*, perpetual being in relation to God, i.e. eternal life.

Fan Festival (Buddhist festival): see NARA BUDDHISM.

Fang-chang: see FANG-SHIH.

Fang-chung shu (Chin., 'arts of the inner chamber'). Taoist practices aiming at immortality (inner or outer, see ALCHEMY and NEI-TAN) through union with the powers of the opposite, i.e. through union of *yin and yang. This might be through union of *ch'i, breath, but the *ho-ch'i* practices (at new moon and full moon) were linked to sexual union—to which fang-chung shu refers as a general term.

Fang-shih (Fangshi) (Chin., 'master of techniques'). *Shamanistic controllers of *magic in China in the centuries BCE (though their techniques continued in popular religion long after). They were guides to the islands of the immortals (Fang-chang, *P'eng-lai, and Ying-chou), and custodians of the techniques which secure both life and immortality.

Fang Yen-kou. Chinese Buddhist ceremony for the 'release of the burning mouths'. The 'burning mouths' are a type of hungry ghost (*preta). The monks break open the gates of hell (*naraka), with incantation and the ringing of bells.

Fanon, F.: see LIBERATION THEOLOGY.

Faqih. One who possesses religious knowledge in Islam. The name refers more usually now to one well-versed in religious law (*fiqh, *sharī'a). See also FUQAHA.

Faqīr (Arab., 'poor man', pl., *fuqarā*). One who has physical or spiritual needs. It may refer to a beggar in a miserable state, but within a religious context it implies dependence on God.

Fārābī (Muslim philosopher): see AL-FĀRĀBĪ.

Fara'zis (from Arab., *fard). Adherents of a movement in India, founded in 1818, to bring the observance of Islam to all sectors of society. The movement continues to the present day, but without the same revolutionary impetus.

Farḍ (Arab., *faraḍa*, 'prescribe'). That which is absolutely obligatory in Islam, as, particularly, the *Five Pillars. This is held to be the same as *wājib* (duty), except by *Ḥanafites who confine *wājib* to obligations imposed by law.

Fard (Arab., 'alone'). One who, in Islam, is filled with the realization of truth and illumination on his own—i.e. without belonging to a community or *Sūfī order.

Farquhar, John Nicol (1861–1929). Christian student of Hinduism who argued for a 'fulfilment theory' of the relation of Hinduism to Christianity. In 1913 he published his most influential work, *The Crown of Hinduism*. He left India in 1923 due to ill health, and became the second Professor of Comparative Religion at Manchester University.

Farrakhan, L. (leader of the Nation of Islam): see ELIJAH MUHAMMAD.

Fa-shun (patriarch of Chinese Buddhist school): see TU-SHUN.

Fasts, fasting: see FESTIVALS AND FASTS; ASCETICISM; SAWM.

Fateh (Urdu, Pañjābī, 'victory'). 1. Son of Gurū *Gobind Siṅgh. See SĀHIBZĀDE.

2. See VĀHIGURŪ.

3. Exchange of Sikh greeting. To the cry, 'Jo bole so nihāl' (anyone will be blessed who says), comes the response, '*Sat śrī akāl'.

Father. The ancient Christian title of a *bishop, from which two different modern senses derive.

1. Since the 19th cent. in English-speaking countries, the title has been used by and of all *Roman Catholic priests, and it is also customary in *Orthodox and *Anglo-Catholic usage.

2. The 'Fathers of the Church' are those Christian writers (not necessarily bishops) characterized by antiquity, orthodoxy of doctrine, holiness of life, and the approval of the church.

See Index, Fathers.

Father of secrets (Babylonian Jewish scholar): see AARON OF BAGHDĀD.

Fathers (text in the Mishnah): see AVOT.

Fātiḥa, al-Sūra al-Fātiḥa, or **Fātiḥat al-Kitāb.** The 'opening *sūra' of the *Qur'ān, also sometimes called *Umm al-Kitāb ('mother of the book'), since it is said to contain the essentials of the entire Qur'ān.

Fatima. Shrine of the Virgin *Mary in central Portugal. It was the scene of six appearances of Mary to three shepherd children from 13 May to 13 Oct. 1917. At the last of these, the Virgin revealed that she was Our Lady of the *Rosary. In 1982 *John Paul II visited the shrine to give thanks for his surviving the attempt on his life. The reported 'secret' made known in the apparitions has not been disclosed publicly, despite many accounts of what it is.

Fāṭima. Daughter of *Muḥammad and *Khadīja who married Muḥammad's nephew *'Alī b. Abī Ṭālib. She bore him two sons, *al-Ḥusayn and *al-Ḥasan, and two daughters. Al-Ḥusayn, the younger son, was killed at the battle of *Karbalā' (680), and this defeat, the 'martyrdom' of al-Ḥusayn and his companions, marked the real beginning of the *Shī'a party and sect. Numerous legends have grown up around the person of Fāṭima, especially among the Shī'a; Muḥammad is said to have named her as one of the four best women of Paradise, the others being Maryam (*Mary), *Khadīja, and the wife of Pharaoh.

Fāṭimids. *Ismā'īlī dynasty, 909–1171 (AH 297–567), extending from Palestine to Tunisia, which founded *Cairo (al-Qāhirah) as its capital in 969 (AH 358). The Fāṭimid *Khalīfas were Ismā'īlī *Imāms, the means of God's presence in the world—though the claim of one of them, al-Hākim (d. 1021 (AH 411)) to *be* God was a claim too far. The dynasty was succeeded by the Ayyubids, founded by *Salāḥ ud-Dīn.

Fa-tsang or **Hsien-shou** (643–712). Third patriarch and major organizer of the *Hua-yen school of Chinese Buddhism. He arranged Buddhist teachings into 'five levels and ten qualities', with Hua-yen at the height, and he integrated different teaching by affirming the interdependence and interpenetration of all phenomena.

Fatwā (Arab.). In Islamic law, a legal opinion, given on request to an individual or to a magistrate or other public official, concerning a point of law wherein doubt arises, or where there is not an absolutely clear ruling in existence. One qualified to give such an opinion is a *muftī, who would pronounce according to a particular *madhhab* ('school of law'). A fatwā may be contested, but only on the basis of existing precedent and law; it cannot, therefore, be regarded as an 'infallible pronouncement', but it commands assent where it can be seen to be well-grounded. See also SHAIKH AL-ISLĀM.

Faust. Initially a reprobate man who made a pact with the *devil and met a commensurate end. However, he became (through the *Enlightenment and into the 19th cent.) a heroic figure who sets his face against the supposed limitations of humanity.

Fa-yen Wen-i (Fayan Wenyi, Jap., Hōgen Bun'eki; 885–958). Chinese Ch'an/Zen Buddhist teacher, successor (*hassu) of *Lo-han Kuei-ch'en, whose work was continued by *T'ien-t'ai Te-shao (Jap., Tendai Tokushō). Few of his works survive. His sayings are gathered in a late work, *Ch'ing-liang Wen-i-ch'an-shih yü-lu*. They are characterized by paradox, and by the technique of answering a question with the same words.

Fazl Allāh (founder of Shi'a movement): see ḤURŪFĪ.

Feast of Fools (New Year Christian medieval festival): see HOLY FOOLS.

Feasts: see FESTIVALS AND FASTS.

Feden Church (Akan, 'children of Eden'). Formerly Eden Revival Church. A Ghanaian independent church founded by Yaw Charles Yeboa-Korie (b. 1938), a *Presbyterian secondary school teacher whose ill-health vanished after prayer, fasting, visionary experiences, and Bible study. In 1962 he founded an ancillary healing society, the Garden of Eden, at Nsawam, but his leadership qualities and travels abroad led to expansion and to the founding of Eden Revival Church, which became a member of the Ghanaian Council of Churches in 1970, and through a dream revelation became the Feden Church in 1975.

Feeling (of absolute dependence, as foundation of religion): see SCHLEIERMACHER, F.

Feinstein, Mosheh (1895–1986). *Orthodox Jewish *rabbi. Feinstein was a leading *halakhic authority (*posek). Many of his *responsa covered questions raised by modern science and technology, and also by the *Holocaust and by air disasters, which magnified the problems of *agunah (a woman whose husband's fate is unknown). His responsa are published in *Iggerot Mosheh* (7 vols).

Fei-sheng (Chin.). Ascending to heaven in daylight, one of the marks in Taoism of attaining immortality (see CH'ANG-SHENG PU-SSU).

Felix culpa (Lat., 'happy fault'). The Christian sense that sin has at least this to be said for it, that it evoked so great a redeemer. For a more general sense of this theme in Judaism, see INCLINATION; TESHUVA (repentance).

Fellowship of Isis. A *neo-pagan movement dedicated to the worship of female deities such as Isis, Venus, or Maia.

Feminine symbols and religion. Although masculine images reflect the male control of religion for at least the last 2,000 years, the earlier pervasive and dominant importance of feminine imagery has not been entirely lost, persisting as it does in most religions (though less so in the later arrivals such as Islam). Early archaeological evidence is always open to speculation in the absence of text controls, but the abundance of images of the fruitful woman certainly suggests dominant cults of the Goddess rather than the God. But *Tanach (Jewish scripture) displays the passion and vigour with which the cult of *Yahweh, under the control increasingly of men, drove out the feminine in the cult, adapting myths to make woman the cause of fault, pain, and sorrow. The cult of the feminine persisted in Christianity in devotion to the Virgin *Mary (especially in syncretistic assimilation in such countries as Mexico), but even that image was reduced in male interpretations to one of submissive obedience.

In India, the same early reverence for the female as the source of life is evident from the archaeological remains, and here it would seem that the Goddess remained undiminished, with the cult of the Goddess still being of paramount importance, especially for *Śaktas (see e.g. DEVĪ, ŚAKTI, KĀLI, DURGĀ, RĀDHA, SARASVATĪ, LAKṢMĪ, GAṄGĀ, PĀRVATĪ, amongst many). Yet still the Goddess has often been brought into a relationship with the God, which means that most of her activities are expressed as extensions of his power, except, usually, when the power is negative.

The reassertion of the feminine imagination of the sacred is gaining ground, but usually against much male resistance in the historical religions (hence the importance of Wicca and *witchcraft). The loss in the intervening centuries has been a kind of intellectual genocide—the eradication of the vision of half the human race. See also Index, Names of Goddesses; Women.

Feminist theology. Theological reflection which acknowledges from the outset that the greater part of theology so far in human history has been male-dominated, has been an expression of patriarchy, and has been saturated with masculine imagery, relegating feminine imagery to the edges. In relation to the Judaeo-Christian tradition, G. Lerner calls this male domination 'the androcentric fallacy', which distorts the whole structure and life of the Church—though the same would be true, *mutatis mutandis*, of other theistic religions. The androcentric fallacy draws attention to the extreme distortions which result in life and imagination when only, or predominantly, masculine language and images are used. This cannot be corrected by using non-sexist language, or by adding 'sisters' to 'brothers' and 'mothers' to 'fathers'.

Feminist theology recognizes the cultural relativity of the biblical period, in which the *incarnation did not obliterate circumstances, but set humans to the task of changing the world in the direction of love: the maintenance of patriarchy in Church or in society is then seen as precisely that demonic condition which has resulted from the *Fall, and from which Jesus has died to set humans free.

Fénelon, François de Solignac de la Motte (1651–1715). Spiritual writer. In 1695 he became archbishop of Cambrai. Through his friendship with Mme Guyon and his defence of her doctrine of pure love, he became involved in the *Quietist controversy and was attacked by Bossuet, as a result of which he was banished from the court in 1697. His letters of spiritual direction have long been greatly valued.

Feng-kan (Ch'an teacher): see HAN-SHAN.

Feng-shui (Chin., 'wind-water'). Chinese art or skill of *geomancy. Taking account of the five elements and the two forces of *yin and yang, the practitioners use a circular wooden plate on which the outline neo-Confucian cosmography is inscribed. They then determine the best site for buildings, graves, temples, etc.

Fenollosa, Ernest Francisco (1853–1908). An American educator, poet, and pioneering scholar of E. Asian fine arts and culture.

His published works include *East and West* (1893), a collection of poetry, *The Masters of Ukiyoe* (1896), and his *magnum opus*, *Epochs of Chinese and Japanese Art* (published posthumously in 1912).

Fen-yang Shan-chao (early collector of kōans): see KŌAN.

Feria. In Christian liturgical usage, a weekday on which no feast or *festival (despite Lat., *feria*, 'feast') falls. The word 'weekday' is now more common than feria.

Festivals and fasts. Festivals are celebrations, usually having an ordered and ritualized (see RITUAL) character. Festivals arise from the fact that 'no man is an island', or more exactly, from the fact that no one can live in isolation on an island in the midst of life: we are selves in a field of selves, requiring each other for the very process of life. Festivals give communal expression to the meaning of that process, in a shared affirmation of value and commitment. So universal is the religious fact of celebration that *Durkheim was able to make it a quintessential feature of religion itself: individuals experience the social as a fact over and above their own individuality, and therefore recognize this factual reality outside themselves in symbolic forms and ritual actions.

In that context, festivals manifest the demands of social existence in many different ways. At the simplest level, they affirm the worth of individuals in a social context (e.g. birthday parties, anniversaries). They mark *rites of passage; they express the dependence of human life on food and water, which are themselves uncertain in the context of the passing of seasons or the unpredictability of hunting; they mark occasions in the history of the community; they celebrate the epiphanies of power or grace which have offered the transformation of life in the direction of hope, especially when these have come from God or from the source of life itself—e.g. *ti'en, Heaven, or the *Tao. Such festivals are marked by trust and thanksgiving; and the dramatic nature of the celebration ties drama and the theatre to ritual in ways which have not yet been separated in India or China.

But festival cannot be divorced from fast. Fasts express the public recognition of unworthiness—to receive benefits, for example, or to participate in the community itself; or again, fasting may express a human desire to move beyond a present circumstance into some better outcome: little of worth is achieved without cost. Fasting may be isolated and specific, or they may be prolonged over a regular period each year: *sawm, observed by Muslims during the daylight hours of the month of *Ramaḍān, is one of the *Five Pillars of Islam. Fasting may equally be a form of protest against perceived injustice or tyranny, as it may also be a form of preparation for some endeavour. The preparation of *Jesus for his ministry sent him for 'forty days and forty nights' into the wilderness—a preparation which was imitated by Christians during the seasons of (originally) *Advent and of *Lent.

The conservative importance of festivals is precisely what seems negative about them to reformers. There is, in this respect, a constant tension in religions, exemplified in the Jewish *prophets and their protest against relying on the proper observance of festivals and fasts as the definition of appropriate behaviour before God. Yet even religious reformers find that the human need for festival and fast has to be satisfied.

Judaism Among Jews, the festivals and fasts (following a lunar *calendar) are a mixture of agricultural and New Year observances, combined with those which commemorate the history of God's dealings with his people. The days of festival are known as (in the singular) *yom tov*, 'a good day'. Those commanded in the *Pentateuch include the three pilgrim festivals (*Passover, *Shavu'ot, and *Sukkot), the *New Year (*Rosh ha-Shanah), the *Day of Atonement (Yom Kippur), and the first day of the lunar month (Rosh Ḥodesh). Later festivals are the feast of *Esther (*Purim), the feast of Lights (*Ḥanukkah), and various memorial days. Fixed fast days were first mentioned by the *prophet *Zechariah (ch. 8. 19); 10 Tevet commemorates the beginning of the siege of Jerusalem; 17 *Tammuz, the breaking of the walls; 9 *Av, the destruction of the *Temple, and 3 Tishri, the assassination of *Gedaliah. The other two fasts of the Jewish calendar are 13 Adar, Fast of *Esther, and 14 Nisan, Fast of the Firstborn (commemorating the ten plagues in Egypt).

Christianity Christian festivals follow an annual cycle, beginning with the advent of Christ and his birth, and tracing his life on earth: they culminate in his *ascension and status in the Holy and Undivided *Trinity. But at the same time, they commemorate and celebrate faithful followers of Christ, the *saints, *martyrs and *Doctors of the Church. Fasting is designed to strengthen the spiritual life by overcoming more immediate attractions of 'the world, the flesh and the *devil' (**Book of Common Prayer*). The observance of regular fasting began with weekly fast days, Wednesday and Friday. To these were added the fast of Lent; in the E., three further forty-day fasts throughout the year; and in the W., *vigil fasts and *ember days. The only two fast days now are *Ash Wednesday and *Good Friday.

Christian feasts are of three main kinds: (i) *Sunday, (ii) movable feasts, and (iii) immovable feasts. The movable feasts (*Easter, and *Pentecost seven weeks later) vary in date because of their origin in the Jewish lunar *calendar. See also CALENDAR.

Islam Among Muslims (who follow a lunar calendar), the major festivals and fasts are linked to the command of the *Qur'ān or to the life of *Muḥammad. They are Ra's al-ʿĀm (New Year, 1 Muḥarram); ʿĀshūrā' (10 Muḥarram, for *Sunnis a day of blessing, but for Shiʿites the anniversary of the martyrdom of *al-Husain); Mawlid al-Nabī (12 Rabīʿ al-Awwal, Muḥammad's birthday); Laylat al-*Miʿrāj (27 Rajab, the Night Journey); Laylat al-Barāʿah (15 Shaʿbān, the night on which sins are forgiven and the destiny of the next year is fixed); Ramaḍān, a month of fasting during daylight hours which includes on the 10th the commemoration of the *Exodus, and on the 27th, *Laylat al-Qadr, the night of the descent of the Qur'ān; *ʿĪd al-Fiṭr (1 Shawwal, feast of fast-breaking); *ʿĪd al-Aḍḥā (10 Dhu -'l-Ḥijjah, feast of sacrifice, commemorating Ibrahīm's (Abraham's) willingness to sacrifice his son; 8–10 are the days of pilgrimage to *Mecca); ʿĪd al-Ghadīr (18 Dhu-'l-Ḥijjah, Shiʿites only, the designation by Muḥammad of *ʿAlī as his successor).

Hinduism It is said that Hindus have a festival (*vrata, celebration) for every day of the year. That is a serious underestimate. P. V. Kane, *History of Dharmasastra*, v/1, pp. 253–452, lists more than a thousand; and in addition, each temple will have its own local vrata (of which the pulling of the chariots (*ratha*) of *Jagannātha is simply one example). Major festivals which are likely to be observed by most Hindus are Kṛṣṇajayānti (*Janamaśtami, during Śrāvaṇa, Kṛṣṇa's birthday, celebrated at midnight after a day of fasting); Rakhi Bandhan (full moon of the same month, when friendships are renewed); Ganeṣa Catūrthī (during Bhadra, when the instruments of work are placed before *Ganeṣa to evoke his blessing); Dassera (the first half of the month Aśvina, a series of festivals, including Navarātri, the first nine days leading to Daśahrā— i.e. *Durgā *Pūjā; *Dīvālī or Dipavālī (second half of Aśvina, the festival of lights); Nāgapañcami (mainly in S. India, the reverence of the cobra as guardian); Śivarātri (during Magha, devotion to Śiva and anointing of the *liṅga; *Holī (during Phalguṇa, a carnival of reversals and riot).

Buddhism Among Buddhists, festivals depend on the country and style of Buddhism: since Buddhism absorbed rather than obliterated the customs of the countries into which it spread, the accumulation of festivals makes it impossible to list them. However, certain major days are held by *Theravādin or *Mahāyāna Buddhists. Among Theravādins, the full moon dominates. New Year is observed with ceremonies of cleansing. Full moon in the month Vesakha is the major celebration (Vesakha Pūjā) of the Buddha's birth, enlightenment, and parinibbana (*nirupadhiśesa-nirvana). On the next full moon (in Śri Lankā) is Poson, celebrating the arrival of Buddhism in Śri Lankā; on the next full moon is Āsālha Pūjā, celebrating the Buddha's renunciation and First Sermon, and marking the beginning of the three month rain-period (*Vassa) during which laymen may join the *saṅgha, and during which the *bhikṣus stay in their monasteries. Mahāyāna adds many local festivals, but most Mahāyāna developments recognize the anniversaries of the birth, enlightenment, and parinirvana of the Buddha as separate occasions.

Jainism Jains have a large calendar (when local celebrations are included) which is complicated by the fact that few festivals are celebrated on the same day by *Digambaras and Śvetāmbaras. An exception is Mahāvīra Jayanti, the birthday of *Mahāvīra, which is celebrated on the 13th of the bright half of Caitra. Otherwise, the same feast or fast is observed at different times (e.g. Jñanapañcami honours scripture among the Śvetāmbaras, Śrutapañcami among the Digambaras) or the same goal is reached by different occasions: thus Paryushan (*Paryūsana) among Śvetāmbaras is an eight-day period of penitence, *confession, and effort to accomplish what should have been done during the year; the near equivalent for Digambaras is Daśalakśanaparvan, which starts exactly as Paryushan ends. The ritual year ends with Divālī, but the lights are reinterpreted as a commemoration of the lights lit to acknowledge the death of Mahāvīra.

Sikhism Sikh festivals are tied particularly to the Gurūs and to the founding of the *khālsā. Thus *Gurpurbs commemorate the births, accessions, or deaths of the Gurūs; and even those which have been received from Hinduism have been adapted: thus the lights on Divālī celebrate the release of Guru Hargobind on this day in 1619, and Hola-Mohalla (Holi) was given a specifically Sikh character by Guru Gobind Siṅgh in 1680. Of particular importance is *Baisakhi, commemorating the founding of the khālsā in 1699.

Zoroastrianism For Zoroastrians there are six seasonal festivals (*gahambars*) which together with New Year (No Ruz) constitute an annual cycle of religious obligation for all Zoroastrians. Along with the *sudre/kusti* prayers (*Naujote), they are in fact the only compulsory practices of the religion. They exhibit the traditional spirit of joyful worship of *Ahura Mazda (misery is a sin in Zoroastrianism), focusing on hospitality, the sharing of food and drink in which everyone has the religious obligation to undertake charitable giving to others, even if that be simply their labours. The last five days of the year are dedicated to each of the traditional five divisions of the *Gāthās (*Avesta) and are therefore known as 'Gatha days'. Other religious days of the year observed are Pateti (Parsi name for No Roz), when the Patet or prayer of repentance is recited seeking forgiveness for the past. Khordadsal celebrates the birthday of *Zoroaster and Zarthoshtno Diso his death. The time of greatest merrymaking among diaspora Zoroastrians is probably Jamshedi No Roz which is generally celebrated on 21 Mar.

Japanese Since *Japanese religion is 'a brocade of religious traditions', the festivals (*matsuri) of all the religions involved will be a part of the Japanese scene. But there are also annual festivals which are more specifically Japanese, and which, in general (at least until recently) are observed by a large proportion of the population. Of the annual observances (*nenjū gyōgi*), the following are important: Shōgatsu (New Year, for about one week from 1 Jan., prepared for by cleaning homes and putting up a straw rope, *shimenawa, symbolizing the binding of the home to divine power); Koshōgatsu (lesser New Year, following the lunar calendar, 15 Jan.); Setsubun (the turning of the seasons, held on the last day of winter, with the driving out of evil spirits from the home ('Oni wa soto')); Hana matsuri (3 Mar., the doll festival, associating the girls of the family with illustrious figures); Haru no shanichi (the day for the veneration of the protective deity, or *kami; the full veneration, Aki no shanichi, is held at the autumn equinox); Haru no higan (festival of the spring equinox; but because *higan* means, for Buddhists, 'the further shore', people visit their homes and ancestral graves; Aki no higan is held at the autumn equinox); Hana matsuri (8 Apr., the festival of flowers, observed by ascending a hill and gathering wild flowers, which, when they are brought home, lead the mountain deities (*yama no kami*) to follow); Tango no sekku (5 May, festival for celebrating the growth and achievements of boys); Suijin matsuri (15 June and 1 Dec., festivals of the kami of water, to seek their protection against the vindictive *goryō*); Tanabata (star festival, when craftsmen seek improvement in their skills by writing poems and floating them away on bamboo leaves on streams); Bon (sometimes O-bon, 13–16 July, feast for the dead, when the spirits of ancestors are welcomed back into the home and visits are made to attend to graves); Tsukimi (viewing the moon, 15 Aug. according to the lunar calendar, with offerings of the first-fruits of rice).

See Index, Festivals.

Festival of Light. Interdenominational movement founded in 1971 to promote action based on informed Christian opinion concerning declining moral values, particularly in the field of family ethics. It was renamed CARE (Christian Action Research and Education) in 1983.

Fetish (Port., *feitiço*, 'made thing'). An object held in awe or reverence. The term has had a wide range of uses and meanings. In origin, it derives from the observations made by early traders and travellers in W. Africa of objects (often worn) held in high regard. From this it was concluded that a fetish was an idol. It was then recognized that these objects were not so much worshipped as used to exercise power, and the word began to be used of objects containing force. Beyond that, the word 'fetish' was taken up in psychoanalysis to refer to a sexual tendency to obtain erotic satisfaction from objects rather than people, even if only of objects associated with people. Colloquially, a fetish is an object of obsessive preoccupation, 'making a fetish of something'.

Feuerbach, Ludwig (1804–72). German philosopher and religious thinker whose theory of *projection greatly influenced, among others, Karl *Marx. In *The Essence of Christianity* (1841) and then again in *Principles of the Philosophy of the Future* (1843), Feuerbach argued that God is humanity's self-alienated essence projected onto a cosmic screen: in worshipping God, people are simply worshipping themselves. Theology is reduced without remainder to anthropology. Anything less leads necessarily to contradictions.

Fideism. The view that true knowledge of God can be attained only by faith on the basis of revelation. Reason is therefore subordinated to faith where otherwise problematic issues or questions arise.

Fides quaerens intellectum ('faith seeking understanding'): see ANSELM.

Fifth Monarchy Men. Members of a short-lived elitist *millennarian movement in England in the mid-17th cent. Its members, mainly artisans, journeymen, and apprentices, anticipated the establishment of the 'fifth monarchy' of Daniel 2. 44. Following Venner's rebellion (1661) the movement died out.

Filaret of Moscow (1782–1867). *Russian Orthodox renewer of the Church, and Metropolitan of Moscow. Through the Holy Synod from 1819, he worked for the independence of Church from State, but in 1842 he was excluded from the synod because of his support for translations of scripture into modern Russian. He devoted much time to the reform of clergy education, producing *The Longer Catechism* (1823, rev., 1839).

Filial piety (Confucian influenced virtue in E. Asian ethics): see HSIAO.

Filioque (Lat., 'and the Son'), the formula in the W. form of the *Nicene Creed which expressed the 'double procession' (i.e. from both Father and Son) of the *Holy Spirit. Since the time of *Photius, a strong opponent, the *filioque* has been a central point of controversy between E. and W. Churches. The Orthodox point to the original creed omitting it, and to the need for a single 'fount of divinity' (*pēgē theotētos*, viz. the Father) within the Godhead.

Final solution. Nazi plan for the extermination of the Jews. The expression 'final solution' was first used in 1941. After the Wannsee Conference of 1942, Adolph Eichmann was authorized to implement the total destruction of European Jewry in the occupied lands. See HOLOCAUST.

Finkelstein, Louis (b. 1895). US *Conservative *rabbi. As president (1940–51) of the *Jewish Theological Seminary and the Rabbinical Assembly, his was the most prominent voice in the Conservative movement of his time. He was also a prolific writer. Under his leadership, Conservative Judaism became the largest organized body of American Jews.

Fiqh (Arab., 'intelligence, knowledge'). Jurisprudence, the science of the religious law in Islam. Fiqh covers all regulations of religious, political, civil, and social life; family, private, public, and criminal law. One who pursues the study of fiqh is a *faqih.

Four main schools of law (*madhāhib*, sing. *madhhab*) have survived, based on the teachings of *Shāfi'ī (d. 820 (AH 205)), *Mālik b. Anas (d. 795 (AH 179)), Aḥmad b. *Hanbal (d. 855 (AH 241)), and *Abū Ḥanīfa (d. 767 (AH 150)). Mālik's *Muwaṭṭa'* (The Path) is one of the earliest of all books of fiqh, and remained influential.

Firdaws ('paradise'): see HEAVEN (ISLAM); PARADISE (ISLAM).

Firdawsi, Abu-l-Qasim Mansur (940–1020 (AH 328–411)). Iranian poet who preserved many Zoroastrian traditions. He placed little emphasis on religion beyond a vague monotheism compatible with Islam. He was called Firdawsi by the Sultan Maḥmūd of Ghaznah, who said that his compositions turned the court into the rooms of paradise (*firdaws*, see PARADISE (ISLAM)).

Fire (in Hinduism): see AGNI.

Fire 'worship' (Zoroastrian): see ATAS.

First Amendment. The first amendment to the US Constitution, which states that 'Congress shall make no law respecting an establishment of religion, or prohibiting the free exercise thereof.' The 'free exercise' provision has been interpreted very broadly by the courts, only excluding e.g. polygamy and *snake-handling.

Firstborn. Jewish law gives first-born males a special status. The detailed laws are in the tractate *Bekhorot* in the Mishnah *et al.*

First diffusion (period in history of Tibetan Buddhism): see TIBETAN RELIGION.

First fruits (Heb., *bikkurim*). The portion of harvest which, according to Jewish law, must be given to the *Temple. In Israel today first-fruit celebrations are still held on Shavu'ot and donations are made to the Jewish National Fund.

First Sermon. Of the *Buddha, preached at Benares. It expounded the *Four Noble Truths and the Eightfold Path (*aṣṭangika-mārga). It is known as 'the first turning of the *dharma-cakra (wheel of dharma)': see DHAMMA CAKKAPPAVATTANA SUTTA.

Fiscus Judaicus. A tax on Jews levied in the Roman Empire. The fiscus Judaicus was a poll tax levied from 71 CE until the early 3rd cent.

Fish. As a Christian symbol, its use goes back to 2nd-cent. writers. The symbol itself may be derived from the acrostic spelling of *ichthus

(Gk., 'fish') from the Gk. first letters of 'Jesus Christ, God and Saviour'.

Fisher, John, St (1469–1535). *Bishop of Rochester and *martyr. Though himself a severe critic of standards in the Church, he was a vigorous opponent of *Lutheranism. He was eventually imprisoned for refusing to take the oath attached to the Act of Succession on the grounds that it contained an admission of royal supremacy over the Church in England. He was made a *cardinal in 1535. He was executed on 17 June that year, and canonized 400 years later. Feast day, 22 June.

Fiṭra (Arab.). An important term in Islamic doctrine about humans and their moral constitution as creatures of God's creation. The pivotal passage is Qur'ān 30. 30. Most exegesis takes fiṭra to mean human nature as designed and intended for 'religion'—understood as Islam. But some take fiṭra to mean Islam itself.

Five animals (Taoist exercises): see WU-CH'IN-HSI.

Five auspicious moments (Jain): see TRIŚALĀ.

Five Classics (of Shinto): see HONJISUIJAKU.

Five deadly sins. Five offences in Buddhism which deliver the offender (via *karma) into *naraka (hell): patricide, matricide, killing an *arhat, injuring a *buddha, creating schism in the *saṅgha. See also (in Japan) GOGYAKU-ZAI.

Five degrees (of enlightenment): see GO-I.

Five elements (in Chinese and Taoist understanding of the cosmos): see WU-HSING.

Five elements (Jain): see ASTIKAYA.

Five evil passions. In Sikh teaching, passions which typify the *manmukh (wayward individual) whose *man is prey to *haumai (egoism). They result in suffering and rebirth. They are *kām* (lust), *krodh* (anger), *lobh* (covetousness), *moh* (attachment to worldly things), and *haṅkār* (pride).

Five faces (of Śiva): see PAÑCĀNANA.

Five fetters: see SAṂYOJANA.

Five great vows (*mahāvrata*). Vows undertaken by Jain ascetics, accepted as fundamental to *Mahāvīra's teaching by both *Digambaras and Śvetambāras. They are (i) *ahiṁsā, the avoidance of killing any life-form; (ii) *satya*, speaking and thinking the truth, and avoiding lies; (iii) *asteya*, not taking what is not given; (iv) *brahmacharya, renunciation of all sexual activity, including any kind of contact with women; (v) *aparigraha*, detachment from all objects of the senses, and from possessions. A later sixth vow forbids eating after dark. For the lay (and less demanding) equivalents, see ANUVRATA.

Five heavens (Jain): see ANUTTARAVIMĀNA.

Five hindrances (Buddhist): see NĪVARAṆAS.

Five holy beings (Jain chant): see NAMASKĀRA-MANTRA.

Five Homages (basic Jain mantra): see FIVE SUPREME BEINGS.

Five houses. Five schools of Ch'an Buddhism (Tsung-men shih-kuei lun) during the later T'ang period and under the 'five dynasties'—though the roots of each are usually older: (i) *Ts'ao-tung (Jap., *Sōtō); (ii) *Lin-chi (Jap., *Rinzai); (iii) Yün-men (Jap., *Ummon); (iv) *Kuei-yang (Jap., Igyō; (v) Fa-yen (Jap., *Hogen).

The term was first used by *Fa-yen Wen-i (885–958), who described (i)–(iv).

Five impediments (Buddhist): see JÑĀNA.

Five Ks, Pañj Kakke. Sikh symbols. *Khālsā Sikhs, male and female, are identifiable by five emblems which they wear. These are called the five Ks because their Pañjābī names all commence with 'kakkā' (k).

1. Keś, uncut hair.

2. Kaṅghā, a small comb, usually of wood or ivory. This keeps the hair neat and so symbolizes controlled spirituality. Often a miniature kirpān (see below) is embedded in the kaṅghā.

3. Kirpān, steel sword. The kirpān signifies courage in defence of right.

4. Kaṛā, steel bangle, worn on the right wrist.

5. Kachh, long shorts. These replaced the 'dhotī', customarily worn by men, enabling swift action in war.

See KHAṆḌE-DI-PĀHUL; SAHAJDHĀRĪ; TURBAN.

Five Mountains (Buddhist temples in Japan): see GOZAN.

Five Ms (actions ordinarily forbidden which induce power in Tantrism): see PAÑCA-MĀKĀRA.

Five Peaks (pilgrimage centres): see PILGRIMAGE.

Five pecks of rice (school of religious Taoism): see WU-TOU-MI TAO.

Five periods, seven stages (Taoist analysis of progress to the goal): see WU-SHIH CH'I-HOU.

Five Periods and Eight Schools. T'ien-t'ai classification, initiated by *Chih-i, of the *Buddha's teaching to reconcile the immense divergences that had grown up since his death.

Controlled by the acceptance that the Buddha adapted his teaching to the levels of his audiences (*upāya-kauśalya), the five periods are chronological in his life, producing (i) **Buddhāvatamsaka-sūtra* in the first three weeks; (ii) the *Āgamas in the next twelve years; (iii) the Vaipulya-sūtras, the first level of *Mahāyāna, stressing superiority of *bodhisattva over *arhat, in the next eight years; (iv) *Prajñāpāramitā-sūtra* (*Perfection of Wisdom), unfolding *śūnyatā, in the next twenty-two years; (v) the **Lotus Sūtra* and **Mahāparinirvāna-sūtra* in his last eight years. But since the Buddha's teaching is indivisible, it was always present in each of the five periods, so that the stress on one aspect more than another led to eight different schools. T'ien-t'ai and the *Lotus Sūtra* re-establish the primordial unity.

Five Pillars of Islam (more literally, Pillars of the Faith, Arab., *arkān ud-Din*). These are the fundamental constituents of Muslim life. They are (i) ash-*Shahada, the witness; (ii) *ṣalāt, formal prayer; (iii) *zakāt, tithe for the poor; (iv) *ḥajj, pilgrimage to *Mecca; (v) *sawm, fasting during *Ramaḍān.

Five powers (Buddhist): see BALA.

Five precepts (Buddhist): see ŚĪLA.

Five Ranks (school of Ch'an/Zen Buddhism): see TS'AO-TUNG.

Five roots (Buddhist): see INDRIYA; BALA; BODHIPĀKṢIKA-DHARMA.

Five Scrolls (books of Hebrew scriptures): see SCROLLS.

Five species. Varieties of cereals or grains which are indigenous to the land of Israel, and are therefore subject to biblical and rabbinic laws governing such produce.

Five Supreme Beings (*pañca paramesthin*, those at the highest stage), the five exemplary modes of being for Jains. Highest are the *tirthaṅkaras; next are the *siddhas, the liberated souls (*jīva); then the guides on earth (*acarya) who lead monks and nuns; then the teachers of monks and nuns (*upadhyāya*); then monks. They are approached in reverence and homage through *pañca namaskāra* (the five homages), a *mantra which offers homage to each of the five groups.

Five virtues (Hindu virtues): see APARIGRAHA.

Five virtues (in Confucianism): see WU-CH'ANG.

Five vows (Jain): see FIVE GREAT VOWS.

Five ways (arguments pointing to the existence of God): see QUINQUE VIAE.

Five ways of Ch'an/Zen. Early classification of five styles of meditation, made by Kuei-feng Tsung-mi (780–841), also known as Tsung-mi. The five styles are: (i) Bonpu, *zazen for restricted aims, e.g. improving health or mental relaxation; (ii) Gedō, meditation sharing Zen aims, but practised outside (e.g. by Hindus or Christians); (iii) Shōjō, aimed at emancipation from reappearance (*punabbhava), and from a *Mahāyāna point of view, selfish; (iv) Daijō, 'great vehicle' (i.e. Mahāyāna) attainment of enlightenment (*kensho, *satori) etc.; (v) Saijōjō, highest form of Zen, in which the realization of the buddha-nature in all appearance (*bussho) occurs.

Fletcher, J. (exponent of Situation Ethics): see ETHICS (CHRISTIANITY).

Flight of the alone to the Alone: see NEOPLATONISM.

Flirty fishing (conversion technique of The Family): see CHILDREN OF GOD.

Flood. Deluge described in Genesis 6. 1–9. 18. For the flood of Manu in India, see PRALAYA.

Florence, Council of (1438–45). Council which effected a brief reunion of the Catholic and Orthodox Churches. Long sessions at Ferrara, then at Florence, discussed the problems of the *filioque, unleavened bread (see AZYMITES) in the *eucharist, *purgatory, the *epiclesis, and the primacy of Rome. The union was doomed by the fall of Constantinople in 1453 and was formally repudiated in 1472. The Council of Florence also established short-lived unions with other Eastern churches. See also LAETENTUR COELI.

Florenz, Karl A. (1865–1939). German scholar in the early 20th cent. who translated the ancient *Shinto texts into German and wrote extensively on Shinto and *Japanese religion and literature.

Flower contemplation ('arrangement', Japanese religious practice): see IKEBANA.

Fo. Chin. for *buddha.

Folk religion. 1. Religion which occurs in small, local communities which does not adhere to the norms of large systems. Folk-urban typology was developed by Robert Redfield as a basis for the comparison of societies, and for the study of urbanization.

2. In a wider sense, folk religion is the appropriation of religious beliefs and practices at a popular level. This may occur as much in urban as in rural environments, and may also be the way in which individuals or groups belonging to mainstream religions practise

their religion: it may be at considerable variance from what is officially supposed to be the case, and is thus also referred to as non-official religion.

Food and religion. Religions, as systems of control and protection which were tested for efficacy (originally) in straightforward terms of natural (evolutionary) selection, have as profound a concern in relation to food as they do in relation to sex. Consequently, the ways in which food is related to religious ideas and practices are extremely complex and varied—as in the following examples.

1. The rejection of particular foods. Such *taboos frequently operate on a social level also, defining the boundaries around the particular religious group.

2. The association of abstinence with spiritual practices: *asecticism frequently extends to diet.

3. The structuring of food according to religious categories: these can be categories of people, as in the Hindu caste rules or monastic observance; or they can be categories of time, as in yearly patterns of FESTIVALS AND FASTS such as *Lent or *Ramaḍān.

4. The use of food in religious ceremonies: food is one of the commonest forms of religious offering.

5. A vital means through which *women have secured their own identity, and also degrees of control, in a male-dominated world.

Hinduism Hindu food rites are embedded within a larger hierarchy of caste and purity. Uncooked food (i.e. untransformed: raw, unmixed, dry, unpeeled), since it has not yet taken on the qualities of the preparer, is broadly acceptable from the hands of all, regardless of caste. *Pakka* food, i.e. cooked in clarified butter, one of the products of the cow and therefore relatively resistant to pollution, can be accepted from a relatively wide range of people. It is thus the food of feasts; in distinction to *kakka* (baked or cooked in water) which is only acceptable from someone of similar or higher caste. Vegetarianism in India both relates to concepts of purity and to the wider development of the ideal of *ahiṁsā. Among meats, beef is the lowest regarded, and is consumed only by *Untouchables and non-Hindus like Muslims, who often act as butchers.

Sikhism The diet of most Sikhs is *Pañjābī, i.e. spiced vegetables, pulses, and the staple wheat chapātīs, plus dairy produce. Beef is avoided because of Hindu influence. Gurū *Gobind Siṅgh forbade *amritdhārī Sikhs to eat *halal* (see AL-HALAL) meat. The *Gurū-kā-laṅgar is vegetarian. See also ALCOHOL; NĀMDHĀRĪ.

Buddhism The *Buddha's advice concerning dietary habits is addressed primarily to those who have embraced the monastic life rather than to lay society. An important principle underlying Buddhist monasticism is that monks should be dependent upon the laity for alms and should go out daily into the local community to beg for food.

The general principle is that monks should accept with gratitude whatever they are given and not be selective in preferring or rejecting particular dishes. In *Theravāda Buddhism there is no prohibition on eating meat, providing that the monk has not seen, heard, or suspected that the animal was slaughtered specifically on his behalf.

Under the influence of Mahāyāna Buddhism, which stressed the virtue of compassionate concern for all sentient beings, vegetarianism came to be regarded as the most appropriate diet. Beyond that, the Buddha had clear views on the importance of both psychic and material food (see ĀHĀRA), and urged moderation.

Judaism In Judaism the fundamental division is between food that is *kasher* (see DIETARY LAWS), fit, and that which is *terefah*, unfit. The categories are defined in *Torah, though they receive greater elaboration and definition in *Talmudic writings.

There are rules concerning slaughter (*sheḥitah). For meat to be *kasher* it must be slaughtered according to the prescribed ritual rules of sheḥitah. Performed by a ritual slaughterman (*shoḥet*) it involves complex regulations, part of which at least aim at the removal of blood from the carcass.

Islam Quranic food rules express a simplified form of Judaic rules. The Qur'ān defines which foods are lawful, *halal*, and which unlawful, *haram*. The unlawful include blood, pig meat, carrion, and the meat of sacrifices. The rules around Islamic slaughter (see AL-HALAL) broadly follow the Jewish form.

Christianity The central rite of Christianity is a food rite (*eucharist), although one whose meal-like aspects are varyingly stressed. Dominant Christianity contains no explicit food taboos, though monastic observance—in general the avoidance of meat, particularly red meat—and the patterning of fast and feast days, extended to the laity in Friday fasting, draws on a more pervasive structure of meanings.

Fools: see HOLY FOOLS.

Footprint of Ibrāhīm (Abraham). An impression of a footprint claimed to be that of *Abraham, which is preserved near the *Ka'ba in *Mecca.

Footprint of Muḥammad. An impression in rock, said to be the point from which he took off on his ascent to heaven: see DOME OF THE ROCK. The metaphorical idea of 'following in the footprints of the Prophet' (*al-qadam al-sharīf*, 'the noble footprint') is strong in Islam, underlying as it does the importance of Muḥammad as the first living commentator on *Qur'ān.

Footprint of the Buddha: see PILGRIMAGE (BUDDHIST).

Forgiveness: see ATONEMENT.

Form criticism. A method of analysing a text in terms of its pre-history in oral tradition. It was first applied (1901) by H.*Gunkel to the narratives of Genesis, and has been most significantly used since then in studying the *Gospels, as well as the *Psalms and *Pentateuch. The term (Germ., *Formgeschichte*) comes from the preoccupation of the pioneer critics with the forms of oral material.

Former Buddhas. Members of a lineage of Perfectly Awakened Ones (*sammāsanbuddhas) who are alleged by tradition to have preceded *Gotama, the historical *Buddha. Earliest Buddhist texts record the names of six: Vipassi (the earliest), Sikhi, Vessabhu, Kakusandha, Konāgamana, and finally Gotama's immediate predecessor, Kassapā.

In later texts the number of former buddhas becomes gradually multiplied: the **Buddhavaṃsa* lists twenty-four, the **Lalitavistara Sūtra* fifty-three, the *Larger *Sukhāvatīvyūha Sūtra* eighty-one, and the **Mahāvastu* five hundred. Eventually, in accordance with the expansive cosmology and mythology of the Mahāyāna, their number becomes incalculable. See also DĪPAṂKARA; MAITREYA.

Formgeschichte (form criticism): see FORM CRITICISM.

Forty hours devotion. A Christian (mainly Roman Catholic) adoration of the blessed sacrament in a *monstrance (i.e. exposed to view).

Forty Martyrs of England and Wales. Forty Roman Catholics from England and Wales put to death between 1535 and 1680. The group is representative of a larger number of martyrs. They were canonized by Pope Paul VI in 1970: feast day, 25 Oct.

Foucauld, C. de (founder of Little Brothers): see DE FOUCAULD, C.

Four Books **or** ***Ssu Shu.*** A group of texts within the *Confucian Classics, singled out for special attention by the literati (*ju) of the Confucian renaissance in the Sung period (960–1279). It included *Lun Yü* (**Analects*), *Meng Tzu* (**Mencius*), *Ta Hsüeh* (**Great Learning*), and *Chung Yung* (**Doctrine of the Mean*). These works, equipped with the commentaries of Chu Hsi (1130–1200), provided the classical authority for the neo-Confucian programme of self-cultivation for the attainment of sainthood.

Four Captives. A Spanish medieval story of four *rabbis captured by Muslim pirates. The story is preserved in Abraham *ibn Daud's *Sefer ha-Kabbalah*.

Four certainties (Hindu): see VAIŚARADYA.

Four Foundations (Buddhist): see SATIPAṬṬHĀNA.

Four goals of life (among Hindus): see PURUṢĀRTHA.

Four Horsemen of the Apocalypse. Biblical figures signalling the beginning of the *messianic age. They occur in Revelation 6.

Four Kings/Guardians (four world protectors in Buddhism): see CELESTIAL KINGS.

Four last things. The Christian awareness of the ultimate realities awaiting humanity and the cosmos. They are the second coming of Christ, the day of judgement, heaven, and hell, epitomized in death.

The mindfulness of death is a central part of Buddhist meditation. *Buddhaghosa's **Visuddhimagga* 8. 1–41 summarizes the method of realizing the imminence and inevitability of death, making it real and personal to *me*.

Four mountains. In China, sacred in association with *bodhisattvas: (i) Chiu-hua-shan/Ti-ts'ang (Skt., *Kṣitigarbha); (ii) P'u-t'o-shan/Kuan-yin (Skt., *Avalokiteśvara); (iii) O-mei-shan/P'u-hsien (Skt., *Samantabhadra); (iv) Wu-t'ai-shan/Wen-shu (Skt., *Mañjuśrī).

Four noble truths (Skt., *catvāri-ārya-satyāni*. Pāli, *cattari-ariya-saccāni*). The foundation of the *Buddha's insight and teaching: (i) the first truth is the recognition of the all-pervasive and universal nature of *dukkha; (ii) the second truth is the recognition of what gives rise to suffering, summarized in the thirst (*taṇhā, Skt., *tṛṣṇa) for satisfaction in things that necessarily pass away, or for permanence (e.g. a self or soul) in the midst of the transient; (iii) the third truth is that dukkha can nevertheless be brought to cessation, by the eradication of taṇhā, and that this cessation is *nirvāna; (iv) the fourth truth is the summary, in the Eightfold Path (*aṣṭangika-mārga), of the means to that eradication.

Four perfect efforts (Buddhist): see SAMMĀPADHĀNA; BODHIPĀKṢIKA-DHARMA.

Four questions (Heb., *arba kushiyot*). Questions asked at the *Passover *seder. Traditionally they are asked by the youngest competent person present. In response the leader of the seder explains the Passover tradition.

Four species (Heb., *arba'ah minim*). The four plants which form part of the *Sukkot rite. Traditionally the fruits are *etrog and the leafy trees are myrtle. During the ceremony, the branches are bound together and held in one hand while the etrog is held in the other.

Four stages of life (Hindu): see ĀŚRAMA.

Fourteen stages of Jain progress (Jain): see GUNASTHĀNA.

Fox, George (1624–91). Founder of the Society of *Friends (also known as *Quakers). Despite poor health he travelled widely throughout England, Ireland, the West Indies, N. America (where *Penn found him 'civil beyond all forms of breeding'), and Holland. His famous *Journal* was published three years after his death (ed. J. L. Nickalls, 1952; R. M. Jones, 1976).

Foxe, John (1516–87). Author of 'Foxe's book of *martyrs'. Foxe wrote the book, *Acts and Monuments of matters happening in the Church*, while in exile in Europe during the reign of Queen Mary. Its chief purpose was to draw attention to the sufferings and endurance of the Protestant martyrs of Mary's reign.

Fraction. The breaking of the bread which, in all liturgies of the *eucharist, precedes *communion. It recalls Jesus' action at the *Last Supper (Matthew 26. 26) and reflects 1 Corinthians 10. 16b f.

Francis, St, of Assisi (1181/2–1226). Christian ascetic and founder of the Franciscan order. Son of a wealthy textile merchant, Francesco Bernardone had dreams of chivalric heroism and a bent toward frivolity until, in his early twenties, he underwent a conversion. He began to devote himself to care of lepers, whom he had formerly found repellent, and soon renounced his patrimony in the public square, returning even his clothes to his father. Embracing poverty, which he spoke of as his bride, he acquired his food by begging, and applied himself to repairing ruined churches. In 1208 or 1209, after hearing at mass *Jesus' commission to the disciples (Matthew 10. 7–19), he set out to preach. Companions soon followed, forming with him a band that became the Franciscan Order. He drew up a simple Rule based on Gospel commands and sayings (the *Regula Primitiva*). In 1212, Clare followed him in establishing a group of women, the Second Order of St Francis, commonly known as *Poor Clares. In 1217, provinces were established, and in 1219 he went to Egypt, at the time of a *crusade, appearing before the Sultan to argue the case for Christ. In 1221, he established 'a third order', i.e. Tertiaries, for those living in the world, but aspiring to his ideals. He reasserted his ideals in his Rule of 1221 (*Regula Prima*), but was obliged to compromise in the definitive Rule (*Regula Bullata*) of 1223. Thereafter, increasingly ill, he withdrew somewhat from the affairs of the Order and spent periods in contemplative solitude, receiving the *stigmata in 1224. He dictated his *Testament* shortly before he died. He was canonized in 1228.

The appeal of Francis remains vast, sustained by a large body of hagiographical works, among which the Italian *Little Flowers of St Francis* (*c.*1375), a partial translation of a Latin work of *c.*1325 by Ugolino of Monte Giorgio, is especially popular, although unreliable for historical detail.

Franciscans. Christian religious orders derived from St *Francis and St Clare of Assisi. Basic to them is the initial determination of Francis that they should be brothers and sisters 'living according to the form of the Holy Gospel'.

Francis (François) de Sales (Christian bishop and spiritual director): see DE SALES.

Francis Xavier, St (1506–52). Spanish *Roman Catholic (*Jesuit) priest and missionary to Asia, canonized, 1622: feast day 3 Dec. Xavier was won over by his Basque fellow countryman, *Ignatius Loyola, to become one of the original band of the Society of Jesus (he was one of those who took vows with him at Montmartre in 1534). Xavier committed himself to obey the pope's command to serve in the already vast and growing overseas colonies of Portugal and sailed for India on 7 Apr. 1541, arriving in Goa a year later.

Xavier's commission from both the king of Portugal and the pope extended to the whole of Asia, and he spent some months of 1546 and 1547 in what is now Indonesia. His primary goal, however, was Japan, and with a Japanese convert and a small band of co-workers landed on Kagoshima on 15 Aug. 1549. Xavier remained in Japan only two years and three months, leaving about 2,000 Christians to the ministrations of fellow Jesuits, after which he returned to Goa and then came back to die on an island near the coast of China on 3 Dec. 1552. His body was taken to Goa, where it is still venerated.

Among Xavier's greatest contributions to the mission to Japan was his deep and growing respect for the Japanese as persons and as bearers of a high culture which could be the foundation of Christian life.

Francke, A. H. (Pietist devoted to the poor): see PIETISM.

Frank, Jacob (1726–91). Founder of a Jewish sect. Born in Poland, Frank declared himself to be *messiah and the successor of *Shabbetai Zevi. He was *excommunicated in 1756 after he had attracted many disciples and had been accused of encouraging sexual immorality. Jacob appealed to the bishop of Kamenetz-Podolsk who offered protection in exchange for the Frankists renouncing the *Talmud. The Frankists also declared their belief in the Trinity of the three 'equal faces'. Initially Frankists only married within the sect, but by the mid-19th cent., the number of mixed marriages increased and many of their descendants became prominent members of the Polish nobility.

Frankel, Zacharias (1801–75). Bohemian *rabbi. Frankel was the first rabbi to preach in German; he acted as *Chief Rabbi of Dresden and founded what he called 'the positivist-historical school' which influenced the *Conservative movement. His seminary set a standard of rabbinic training which was imitated by all similar academies.

Frankists: see FRANK, JACOB.

Frasokereti (Pahlavi, *Frasogird*). Literally, the 'making fresh' (or 'restored') in *Zoroastrian *eschatology. In Zoroastrian *cosmology (*Bundahisn*) the world and humanity are created perfect but are assaulted by evil. Zoroastrianism is, however, an optimistic religion and teaches that evil will ultimately be eradicated. Frasokereti is the process by which the good is triumphant. There are two aspects to Zoroastrian eschatology: individual and cosmic. At death, every individual faces judgement by the balances whereby good thoughts, words, and deeds are weighed against the evil. At death, the soul is led by its *daena* (conscience), either to a heavenly existence or to the abyss of *hell. However, this stay in hell (or heaven) is not eternal, for eternal punishment could not be corrective, as punishment should be. Zoroastrians, therefore, believe in a resurrection and a second judgement which forms part of the cosmic Frasokereti. This in turn is related to the teaching of the four ages.

The last of these is broken down into three periods, each of a thousand years, in which a saviour (*sōšyant*) is born. With evil expunged from the Good Creation all can finally dwell with God as the heaven and earth come together in what is the best of all possible worlds. Evil is defeated, and Ahura Mazda is now not only all-good, but also for the first time all-powerful.

Fravasi. The 'heavenly self' or 'eternal soul' in *Zoroastrianism. There are many Zoroastrian theological analyses of human nature. The most common is to divide a human being into five parts: the *tan* (body, i.e. the material or *getig* dimension); the vital spirit (*jan*); soul (*urvan*); 'image' (*adhvenak*); and fravasi. The *tan* is that which remains on earth after death, and the *urvan* is that which proceeds to the judgement to be confronted by its *daena* (conscience). The fravasi is thought of as the aspect of human nature which pre-exists birth. In some *Pahlavi literature there is a concept of human destiny. Each person has his/her *khwarr*, the destiny which Ahura has set before them, but all have the freedom to reject that destiny. The essence of a person is sometimes said to be his/her reason (*khrat*). Although there are these various parts of human nature, nevertheless the person is by nature a unity. *Angra Mainyu seeks to destroy that unity, that balance of the parts, and thus to destroy them, through greed, arrogance, despair, and the Lie.

Frazer, Sir James George (1854–1941). A British cultural anthropologist whose views were, for a period, influential in the study of religion. His major work, *The Golden Bough* (13 vols., 1890–1937), is vitiated by crude evolutionary assumptions. As E. Leach pointed out, he wrote little of originality, except perhaps as concerns the ethnographic 'facts'; facts which he often devised so as to suit his picture of the 'savage'.

Free churches. Churches free from state control; specifically, the Protestant churches of England and Wales other than the established church. The Free Church of Scotland separated from the Church of Scotland at the *Disruption (1843). A minority, the 'Wee Frees', did not take part in the subsequent union which formed the United Free Church of Scotland (1900) and has survived as an independent body with 21,000 members (1980), mostly in the N. and NW of Scotland.

Freud, Sigmund (1856–1938). A major founding figure of psychoanalysis, with strong views on the mainly negative role of religion in human life and society. He had a *nomothetic ambition to become the first to uncover laws as invariant as those of Newton, but in his case governing, not cosmic, but psychological behaviour.

Religion, for Freud, emerges as a collective expression of neurosis, and as an attempt on the part of individuals to escape from the realities of a hostile and indifferent universe.

Since individuals recapitulate the history of the human race, the phylogenetic and ontogenetic explanations are variations on the same theme, as can be seen in one of his major analyses of religion, *Totem und Tabu: Über einige Übereinstimmungen im Seelenleben der Wilden und der Neurotiker* (1913; Totem and Taboo: Resemblances Between the Psychic Drives of Savages and Neurotics, 1917): religious solidarity and restraints begin in a primeval rebellion of the sons against the father. In *Der Mann Moses* ... (1939; Moses and Monotheism, 1939), he drew on abandoned speculations of biblical historians to produce a theory of Mosaic religion. In *Die Zukunft einer Illusion* (1927; The Future of an Illusion, 1928), he made his most explicit attack on the error of humanity in relying on the collective neurosis of religion. Religion rests on an attitude of *als-ob*, 'as-if', in which people seek comfort in a universe which is indifferent to them. They seek it, therefore, in the only place it can be found, in the illusory world of make-believe, in a heaven and God which they project. In a long correspondence with Oskar Pfister (*S. Freud/O. Pfister: Briefe 1909–1939*, 1963), Freud constantly reviewed his estimate of religion, expressing occasional doubt about detail but not about the fundamentally illusory and neurotic nature of religion. This itself was deeply embedded in his own lifelong fear of death. His account of religion is generally contradicted by evidence, but his outlook and terminology have remained pervasive.

Friar (Lat., *frater*, 'brother'). As applied to Christian religious, a usage which passed into the Romance languages and English, a friar was one who belonged to a mendicant order, as distinguished from those who belonged to monastic orders and were not itinerant. The best-known orders of friars are the *Dominicans, *Franciscans, *Carmelites, and *Augustinians.

Friday prayer (of Muslims): see JUMʿA.

Friedlaender, David (1750–1834). A forerunner of *Reform Judaism. He argued that prayers for friends and country should be substituted for the *messianic hope, and that secular law should be studied rather than *Talmud. He also was tireless in his efforts for Jewish political and civil rights in Prussia.

Friends, The (Religious) Society of, often called **Quakers.** A religious group of Christian derivation, emerging in the 17th cent. under the leadership of George *Fox. His followers first called themselves 'children of the light', following Fox's emphasis on the inner light which takes precedence over external guidance. They came to be called 'Friends' from the statement of Jesus (John 15. 14), 'You are my friends if you do what I command you.' They were first called Quakers in 1650, when Fox commanded a magistrate to tremble at the name of the Lord—though the name occurs earlier, of those who experienced tremors in a religious ecstasy. The Friends oppose warfare (partly on grounds of the command of Christ, partly because warfare demonstrates a diseased humanity), and refuse to take *oaths (since walking in the light means telling the truth). They were committed to the abolition of slavery (John Woolman, 1720–72), women's suffrage (Lucretia Mott, 1793–1880; Susan Anthony, 1820–1906), prison reform (Elizabeth Fry, 1780–1845), and the care of the mentally ill.

The resistance of the Friends to 16th-cent. laws of religion led to considerable persecution. Many fled to the American colonies, where William Penn (1644–1718) founded Pennsylvania. Their spirit of personal truth was given classic expression in Robert Barclay's *Theologiae Verae Christianae Apologia* (1676: *Apology for the True Christian Divinity*, 1678). Despite Fox's *Rule for the Management of Meetings* (1688), which gave cohesion to the movement, there have been four subsequent divisions, especially that of the Hicksites, following Elias Hicks (1748–1830).

Friends of the Western Buddhist Order: see WESTERN BUDDHIST ORDER.

Fringes (to Jewish garments): see ZITZIT.

Frum (figure in cargo cult): see JON FRUM.

Fry, Elizabeth (prison reformer): see FRIENDS, THE SOCIETY OF.

Fu, also **fan** (Chin., 'return'). The movement of the *Tao in *Tao-te ching* (16), whereby all things return to their source. In meditation, this 'returning to the root' is the means to enlightenment.

Fu-ch'i (Chin., 'sustaining by breath'). Breathing (*ch'i) technique in Taoism, directing breath to all parts of the body. It precedes *t'ai-hsi*, embryonic breathing.

Fudō (Jap., 'immoveable'). One of the deities, in Japanese Buddhism and folk-religion, who protects Buddhism and its true adherents, or simply, those who appeal to him. These protective deities are known as *myōō*, and they usually take frightening forms.

Fugen (a bodhisattva): see SAMANTABHADRA.

Fugyō-ni-gyō (Jap., 'doing by not doing'). Zen action which arises from deep enlightenment, and which is not intended or premeditated, but simply arises as the absolutely appropriate action in relation to the contingent circumstance.

Fuhōzō (Jap.). The transmission of the *buddha-dharma in Zen Buddhism through the lineage of patriarchs (*soshigata), and also a person in that lineage (see HASSU).

Fujifuse (Jap., 'neither give nor accept'). A 'branch' (*ha*) of the *Nichiren school of Japanese Buddhism established by Nichiō (1565–1630) in 1595. This branch of Nichiren Buddhism teaches that both lay persons and monks and nuns should neither give nor receive alms from persons belonging to other schools and sectarian movements of Buddhism. Although originally suppressed by secular authorities, adherents of this sect continued practising their faith in secret, calling themselves *nai-shinja*, 'secret believers'. In 1874, the government finally granted the Fujifuse Branch legal recognition. Its headquarters temple is the Myōkakuji in Okayama Prefecture.

Fujikan. A meditation practice in Japanese Buddhism, in which Skt. letters, especially *A, are written on various parts of the body; their power is then absorbed into the body.

Fujisan. Mount Fuji (usually known in the W. as Fujiyama from a confusion arising from the Chinese character which can be pronounced 'yama' or 'san'), a cone-shaped dormant volcano, the highest mountain in Japan (3,776 metres), about 75 miles SW of Tokyo, greatly revered for its beauty and sacred character. Although adherents of all Japanese religions revere Mount Fuji, it was made particularly sacred by the Yamabushi, the mountain *ascetics.

Fujiyama: see FUJISAN.

Fukasetsu (Jap., 'the unsayable'). The Zen insistence that the experience of enlightenment (*kensho, *satori) cannot be described or communicated. Anyone who realizes his *bussho (buddha-nature) is like a dumb man after a beautiful dream. It follows also that words are always approximate and corrigible: they are the sign that points to the moon, but not the moon itself. Hence arises the famous formula of 'transmission outside the scriptures', i.e. through the direct interaction of *mondō or *hossen, attributed first to *Bodhidharma, but perhaps from *Nan-chuan Pu-yuan: *kyoge betsuden* (transmission outside the formal teaching), *furyu monji* (transmission outside the scriptures), and *jikishi ninshin* (direct pointing to the human being or heart) lead to the realization of one's buddha-nature (*kenshō jōbutsu*).

Fukasetsu has its parallel in Zen, *fukashigi*, 'the unthinkable', that which can be experienced (enlightenment) but cannot be conceptualized.

Fukashigi: see FUKASETSU.

Fuke (flute-playing school of Zen): see KAKUSHIN; KOMUSŌ; P'U-HUA.

Fukko Shintō (from Chin., *fu-ku*, 'restore the ancient way'; Jap., 'Restoration Shintō'). A *Shinto movement that arose in the 18th cent. and sought to reconstruct ancient Japanese native religious practices as they were imagined to exist prior to the introduction of foreign creeds like Buddhism and Confucianism. The major figures of this movement include Kada Azumamaro (1669–1736), *Kamo no Mabuchi (1697–1769), *Motoori Norinaga (1730–1801), and Hirata Atsutane (1776–1843), all of whom were also known as 'National Learning' (*kokugaku) scholars.

Fuko (Buddhist teacher): see AMOGHAVAJRA.

Fukyo (Jap.). Communal recitation of *sūtras in Zen monasteries.

Fu-lu (pai). *Apotropaic talismans in religious Taoism (especially *cheng-i tao, *t'ai-ping tao, and *wu-tou-mi tao).

Fumie. Japanese flat image of a Christian symbol, usually the crucifixion, designed to be stepped on. Suspected Christians were required to step on the representation to prove that they were not believers.

Functionalism (accounts of religion which focus on the functions which religion serves): see SOCIOLOGY OF RELIGION.

Fundamentalism. In general, a description of those who return to what they believe to be the fundamental truths and practices of a religion. It can thus be applied to this attitude in all religions (e.g. the resurgence of conservative Islam is sometimes called 'Islamic fundamentalism'). But this use is often resented by such people, because of its more usual identification with those, in Christianity, who defend the *Bible against charges that it contains any kind of error. More specifically, it denotes the view of *Protestant Christians opposed to the historical and theological implications of critical study of the Bible.

To avoid overtones of closed-mindedness, Christians in the Fundamentalist tradition often prefer to be called *Conservative Evangelicals.

The word (Arab. equivalents are *salafiyya and *uṣūliyya) is used of Muslims, when it refers to those who assert the literal truth of the *Qur'ān and the validity of its legal and ritual commandments for modern people. See Index, Fundamentalism.

Funeral rites. From extremely early times (and possibly even among the Neanderthals), archaeology reveals that humans have treated the bodies of the dead with care and respect.

However, despite much speculation, it is not possible to state what beliefs about the status of the dead accompanied these early practices. By the time texts mediate beliefs about the dead, it is clear that almost universally there was no belief that there would be a worthwhile life after death. The funeral rites of the major world religions now express and reflect the consequence of subsequent human experience and reflection in which a continuity of life beyond death is clearly more probable, and is certainly a matter of faith expressed through the rituals and liturgies.

On the importance of being buried/cremated in particular places see KAŚI; KARBALĀ'; MASHHAD. See also DEATH; CREMATION; RITES OF PASSAGE; Index, Death, Funerals.

Judaism In biblical times, the dead were buried preferably near their family graves—hence the expression, 'slept with his fathers'. Traditionally, men are buried wrapped in their *tallit, and coffins were not used until the Middle Ages. Different communities observe different burial practices, but normally the coffin is escorted to the grave and *Kaddish is recited. Burial in the land of Israel is a desideratum, but failing that, earth from Israel should be placed on the head or under the body. Among *Reform Jews, embalming and cremation are permitted.

Christian Christian respect for the body, and expectation of its resurrection, derive from the resurrection of *Christ. *Cremation was opposed and eventually became exceptional.

Opposition to cremation began to erode at the end of the 19th cent., and is now common; the prohibition against it among *Roman Catholics was lifted in 1963, and is now allowed provided it is not done for reasons contrary to the Christian faith.

Islam *Jināza/janāza* refers to the stretcher and to the corpse on it, and thus to the funeral itself. The *Qur'ān gives no detail, but much description occurs in *ḥadīth, and *fiqh is extremely detailed in its prescription. Generally speaking, burials should be carried out as speedily as possible. As soon as a Muslim is dead, he is laid on the stretcher with the head facing the *qibla. The *ghusl then takes place, and the body is covered in a shroud or shrouds (the number is disputed). *Ṣalāt is then said over the dead person, and if possible there should be recitation of the Qur'ān, or at least of *sūra 6. Mourning is restricted, because it disturbs the dead—though in practice lamentation (*niyaha*) occurs. Forty days later, a family commemoration is held (*al-Arba'ayn*, 'the Forty').

Hinduism see ANTYEṢṬI.

Buddhism Disposal of the body is preferably by cremation. An important feature is the interaction between officiants (e.g. *bhikṣus) and family, with gifts and transfer of *puṇya. The leave-taking and rituals may take place over several days (e.g., six in Sri Lanka). Observances follow on the completion of three, and of six months, and sometimes at the anniversary.

Sikhism When a Sikh dies prayers (especially *sukhmāni sāhib) are said for the deceased. The body, washed and dressed and wearing the *five Ks, is cremated. During cremation *Kīrtan *Sohilā (the bedtime prayer) is recited. At home or in the *gurdwārā verses about death are read from the *Ādi Granth and the service concludes with *Ardās, a *hukam, and *kaṛāh praśād. Sikhs are to accept death as God's will and as a stage in the progress to him. Elaborate displays of mourning or of grief are therefore discouraged.

Chinese Most dead exist in perpetuity in the rituals of the living family. Usually the dead gain immortality of memory in the family unit, periodic offerings, and possible assistance of the 'soul' (in Buddhist judgement); the family gains kinship cohesion by filial respect and blessings by the rites. Traditionally, the dead are buried with *ming chi* (spirit articles), a sustenance of some kind such as the urns and human sacrifices of the archaeological sites, or the burning of modern paper items of money and necessities. Thereafter, they are periodically offered incense and food in the family or hall shrines. The grave is carefully chosen according to the *yin and yang 'geomantic' influences of *feng shui, and the body is often buried in a coffin, later disinterred, the bones put in a pot in the open air, and finally buried in the pot. These rites and relationships vary considerably by location and historical period.

Fuqaha (Arab., pl. of *faqih), jurists possessing deep knowledge of *fiqh, such as the *ayatollahs and *'ulamā of the Muslim world.

Furqān. Generally translated as 'criterion' or 'distinction', sometimes 'deliverance'; an Arabic word of disputed origin. It is the name of *sūra 25 of the *Qur'ān, where it is a synonym for the Qur'ān itself. Elsewhere it would seem to signify 'deliverance', as in the case of *Moses (Qur'ān 2. 53, 21. 48). The battle of *Badr, the first significant victory for the Muslims, is described as a 'day of furqān' (8. 41).

Furyū monji (transmission outside the scriptures): see FUKASETSU.

Fusatsu. Jap., for *uposatha.

Fushimi Inari (Jap., *Fushimi*, a place-name, + *inari*, ' the rice deity'). The most famous of the shrines to the Japanese rice god, *Inari, located in the SE suburbs of *Kyōto.

Fushizen-fushiaku (Jap.). Not thinking good, not thinking evil. The transcendence in Zen Buddhism of discrimination and differentiation in evaluation. The phenomenological value may inhere in appearance: it is the attitude which is transcendent.

Fushō (Jap., 'unborn'). Zen Buddhist term for the true nature of reality, in which there is no beginning or end, birth or becoming, passing away or death. There is only what there 'is', which is manifestation, arising from, and bearing the nature of, *śūnyatā. It is usually translated as 'Unborn'.

Fusion of horizons (the relating of past text to present circumstance, thereby creating new meaning in lived experience): see HERMENEUTICS.

Futai (Jap., 'not falling back'; Skt., *avinivartanīya*). The stage in Buddhism of not falling back to a lower state.

G

Gabirol, Solomon ben Judah ibn (*c.*1020– *c.*1057). Jewish Spanish poet and philosopher. Solomon ibn Gabirol was the author of many Hebrew poems. Many of his religious poems have been preserved in the *Sephardi and *Ashkenazi *prayer books and in *Karaite *liturgy; he was regarded as the outstanding poet of his time. In addition, two philosophical treatises survive: *Mekor Ḥayyim* (The Source of Life) is a discussion of the principles of matter and form; and *Tikkun Middot ha-Nefesh* (The Improvement of the Moral Qualities) is concerned with ethics.

Gabriel (Heb., 'God is my warrior'). An archangel. He and Michael are the only angels named in the Jewish Bible (Daniel 8. 16; 9. 21; 10. 13; 12. 1; Raphael is mentioned in the *apocrypha, Tobit).

In Islam, Gabriel is Jibrīl or Jibrā'īl. He is one of the *angels (*malā'ika*), named three times in the *Qur'ān (2. 97, 98; 66. 4), once as the being who 'brought [the Qur'ān] down to your heart' (2. 97). Jibrīl has thus been identified as the one who transmitted the message.

Gaccha (Skt., *gacchati*, 'goes'). Name of breakaway Śvetāmbara Jain sects. Originally, *ascetic communities were known as *kula* ('family') or *guna* ('throng'). The two major gacchas are Kharatara Gaccha (see DĀDĀ GURŪS) and Tapa Gaccha, derived from Jagaccandra Suri (1228), but owing its strength to Dharmasagara, a fierce controversialist—not least against the Kharatara. The latter are now a small remnant, but the Tapa Gaccha has about 4,000 monks and nuns.

Gadaffi, Colonel (Libyan leader): see QADHAFFI, MUʿAMMAR.

Gadamer, H.-G. (philosopher): see HERMENEUTICS.

Gagaku (ceremonial music in Japan): see BUGAKU; MUSIC.

Gaki. Japanese term for restless or hungry spirits, Skt., *preta.

Galatians, Letter to the. An epistle of *Paul and book of the New Testament. It was prompted by news that Paul's converts were turning to a 'different gospel' (1. 6) which required adherence to the Jewish *Torah.

Gallicanism. The assertion of more or less complete freedom in the *Roman Catholic Church from the authority of the *papacy. This was affirmed particularly for the Church in France (the old Gaul, hence the name). The opposite is *Ultramontanism. The definition of papal infallibity at the first *Vatican Council made any further expression of Gallicanism impossible.

Galloping Girls (name for IBVM): see INSTITUTE OF THE BLESSED VIRGIN MARY.

Galut (Heb., 'exile'). The state of being uprooted from the Jewish homeland. By extension, Jewish mystics saw the evil inherent in the present world order as the result of the 'galut of the Divine Presence'. In contrast, trust in the providence and the promises of God is expressed in the hope, which underlies *Zionism, of *kibbutz galuyyot*, the ingathering of the exiles.

Gamaliel. Name of six Jewish sages, descendants of *Hillel, who filled the role of *nasi. Rabban Gamaliel ha-Zaken (the elder) (early 1st cent. CE) was responsible for many *takkanot. According to Acts 22. 3, he was the teacher of the apostle *Paul. Rabban Gamaliel II (late 1st cent.) succeeded *Johanan b. Zakkai as nasi and was one of the greatest scholars of his generation. Gamaliel III (early 3rd cent.), the son of *Judah ha-Nasi, pronounced invalid the method of ritual slaughter of the *Samaritans. Rabban Gamaliel IV was nasi in the late 3rd cent., while Rabban Gamaliel V presided in the late 4th cent. Rabban Gamaliel VI (d. 426) was the final nasi. He was deprived of his position in 415 because he had built a *synagogue without permission and had defended the Jews against the Christians.

Gampopa or **sGam-po-pa** (also known as Nyame Dagpo Lharje; 1079–1153). Tibetan monk and teacher, who drew on the *Kagyüpa and *Kadampa schools in establishing Dagpo Kagyu, and in the *lamrim work, *The Jewel Ornament of Liberation*. He held that the buddha-nature (*tathāgatha, *buddhatā, *bussho), or at least the capacity to become a *buddha is present in every sentient being, but that the human appearance forms the best base for this advance.

Gaṇadharas (Skt., 'leaders of the assembly'). In Jainism, the chief disciples of a *tīrthaṅkara who continued the teaching and organized the community after his death.

Ganapati (Hindu God): see GAṆEŚA.

Gāṇapatya (Hindu sect): see GAṆEŚA.

Gaṇas (Hindu God): see GAṆEŚA.

Gaṇḍa-vyūha (Skt.). The cone-shaped elevation on the crown of the *Buddha Śākyamuni, one of the thirty-two marks of a buddha (*dvātriṃśadvara-lakṣana).

Gandhabba (heavenly beings): see GANDHARVA.

Gandhāra. A region in the NW of India (S. Afghanistan/N. Pakistan) which was a major centre of Buddhist art and culture.

Gandharva (Skt., imbiber of song). 1. In Hinduism, sometimes a single god, who is the guardian of *soma. More often they are in the plural, described by the *Atharva Veda* as half-human, half-bird, and hairy. In later texts (e.g. *Mahābhārata*), they have become the musicians of the gods (with the *apsarasas*, the dancers) who also threaten to seduce *ascetics when they rival the gods.

2. In Buddhism, (Pāli, *gandhabba*) they continue as heavenly musicians, but they also have a role in sustaining the karmically governed accumulation of consequence from a previous life, through death, into a new appearance. They thus covered, mythologically, the 'gap' between death and new birth.

Gāndhī, Mohandās Karamchand (1869–1948). Called Mahātmā, 'great soul', spiritual and practical leader of India (especially in pursuit of independence from British rule). When asked for his message to the world, he said, 'My life is my message.' Born into the *Vaiśya caste, in a *Vaiṣṇavite family, with Jain friends (both of which influenced his later attitudes), he left a wife and infant son in 1888 to study law in London. He returned in 1891 to India, carrying with him Christian influences, but when he failed to establish his legal career in India, he went to S. Africa in 1893 (to assist a Muslim in a court case), where his experience of, and resistance to, racial abuse and oppressive government began. He founded the Natal Indian Congress, and began to develop his way of non-resistance, based on *ahiṁsā, *satyāgraha (lit., 'truth-insistence', a term which he coined and defined as 'soul-force'), *tapasya*, renunciation (cf. TAPAS), and *swaraj*, 'self-rule'. He was much influenced by (within his general Hindu perspective) the **Bhagavad-gītā*, and by such writings as the *Sermon on the Mount, *Tolstoy's *The Kingdom of God is Within You*, Ruskin's *Unto this Last*, Thoreau's *Civil Disobedience*.

But his inclusive style led to suspicion among orthodox Hindus, and he was shot on 30 Jan. 1948, uttering the name of *Rāma as he died.

Gan Eden (Garden of Eden; destiny of the righteous): see EDEN.

Gaṇeśa (Skt., 'Lord of the hosts'). Gaṇapati, Vināyaka (leader), Ekadanta (one-tusked), Lambodara (pot-bellied), Siddhadāta (the one who gives success), Vighnarāja (lord of obstacles), the elephant-headed god of wisdom and good fortune. Since early medieval times Gaṇeśa has been one of the most popular Hindu gods. He is invoked before all undertakings—from religious ceremonies (excluding funerals) to written compositions, and before the worship of other deities. Though his origins may be that of a tutelary village deity, today all sects claim him as their own. A few sectarians worship him exclusively, especially the Gāṇapatyas who produced the *Gaṇeśa-gītā* (a version of the **Bhagavad-gītā* in which Gaṇeśa replaces Kṛṣṇa) and the *Gaṇeśa-Purāṇa*.

Gaṇeśa Catūrthi (Hindu festival): see FESTIVALS AND FASTS.

Gaṅgā. The river Ganges, sacred among Hindus. Its waters are employed in *pūjā (worship), and if possible, a sip from them is administered to the dying.

Gaṅgeśa (Indian logician): see NYĀYA.

Ganjin (688–763). Japanese name of Chinese Buddhist master of *Vinaya school, Chien-chen, who went to Japan by invitation and founded the *Ritsu School. He lived in Tōdaiji, later in Toshodaiji, and gave formal instruction to many, including the emperor Shōmu and members of his family.

Gantō (Jap., 'the goose tower'). A tower built in Japan in honour of a *bodhisattva who had become manifest in the form of a goose, and who had sacrificed himself in order to instruct *Hīnayāna *bhikṣus. Thence it became a name in general for Buddhist towers.

Gaon (Heb., 'pride', Nahum 2. 3; pl. *ge'onim*). Honorific title of the heads of the Jewish *academies of *Sura and *Pumbedita. Between the 6th and 11th cents. CE, the geonim were recognized as the highest Jewish religious authorities. Pre-eminent among the geonim were *Yehudai, *Sa'adiah, *Sherira, *Samuel b. Hophni, and *Hai ben Sherira.

Gapat (acronym for gemara, perush, and tosafot): see TOSAFOT.

Garbhagṛha (Skt., 'womb-container'). In Indian religions, a conceptualization of the inner source of life and truth, the origin of the universe; more particularly, the inner sanctuary of Hindu temples.

Garden, gardens. The creation of order, beauty, and utility, out of what would otherwise be wildness and perhaps wilderness, has supplied both a metaphor and a practice to religions. This is particularly obvious in the landscape and the stone gardens of Zen Buddhism. Zen saw the garden as an extension of the same life which seeks to discern and realize the buddha-nature inherent in all things. Thus early Zen gardens (e.g. in *Kyōto) create places for the extension of contemplation. This led into *kare sansui*, the dry landscape, where meditation, both in the making and in the observing, is paramount. Famous examples are at Daisen-in (*c.*1513) in Kyōto and Ryōan-ji (*c.*1490). In the West, gardens reflect the Garden of *Eden (Gan Eden). In Islam, nostalgia was replaced by anticipation and foretaste, with Muslim gardens representing proleptically what the *Qur'ān says of the gardens of heaven—hence the strong emphasis on water; they tend also to be symmetrically ordered. A memorable example can be found at Granada in the Generalife above Alhambra. See also PARADISE.

Garden of Eden: see EDEN.

Gārhapatya (Hindu domestic fire): see AGNIHOTRA.

Gartel (Yid., 'girdle'). Girdle worn by Jewish *ḥasidim.

Garuḍa. A fantastic creature of Hindu mythology, usually depicted either as a crowned bird or as a bird with a man's head.

In Buddhism, the predatory aspects of Garuḍa are emphasized. He is also the vehicle of *Amoghasiddhi, so that in context garuḍa may be a synonym of *buddha.

Garvey, Marcus Mosiah (1887–1940). Leading advocate of black advancement, and a central figure in *Rastafarianism. He was opposed by the National Association for the Advancement of Coloured People, but pursued his own line, culminating (1920) in the 'Declaration of the Human Rights of the Negro People of the World'. After a two-year gaol sentence for fraud, he was deported to Canada in 1924. Taking literally the prophecy in Psalm 68. 31, he affirmed Ethiopia and Africa as the source of civilization.

Gasshō (Jap.). Placing the palms of the hands together in greeting, understood in Zen Buddhism as the reconciliation of the conflicting forces in the universe, in order to bring about (and invoke) peace and harmony.

Gatha (key verse in Buddhist text): see DHAMMAPADA.

Gāthās. The seventeen hymns of *Zoroaster, and thus texts of fundamental authority for *Zoroastrians, especially in the liturgy (*yasna). In Hinduism, gāthās are poems which do not appear in the *Vedas.

Gati (Skt., Pāli, 'mode of existence'). The various levels of existence in Buddhism, in which reappearance can take place through the process of *karma and *saṃsāra. There are six levels (three good, three bad), those of (i) gods (*devas); (ii) humans; (iii) spirits (*asuras); (iv) animals; (v) restless ghosts (*pretas); (vi) hell beings (*naraka).

Gauḍapāda. According to tradition, the author of the *kārikā* or commentary *Gauḍapādīyakārikā* (also known as *Āgama Śāstra*, or *Māṇḍūkyakārikā*) on the *Māṇḍūkya *Upaniṣad*, and the teacher of Govindapāda, *Śaṅkara's teacher. This commentary is the earliest extant work to set forth the basic teachings of *Advaita Vedānta in systematic form.

Gauḍīya (devotee of Kṛṣṇa): see CAITANYA (2).

Gautama (traditional founder of Nyāya): see DARŚANA; NYĀYA.

Gautama, Indrabhuti. Early and prominent disciple of *Mahāvīra, still much revered among Jains.

Gautama Siddhārta (Skt.; Pali **Gotama Siddhatta**). The family name, plus the first name, of the *Buddha Śākyamuni.

Gayā (Hindu sacred city): see BODHGAYĀ.

Gāyatrī. A Hindu metre of 24 syllables, variously divided, but often 3 × 8. Many hymns in the *Ṛg Veda* are in this metre, one verse being of outstanding importance, and often called simply 'gāyatrī' (*Ṛg Veda* 3. 62. 10). Gāyatrī is then personified as the Goddess who presides over the three castes.

Gedaliah, fast of. Jewish fast commemorating the death of Gedaliah. (2 Kings 25. 25–6; Jeremiah 41). A fast to commemorate this event is held on 3 Tishri.

Gedatsu (Jap., 'release'). In Zen Buddhism, release or liberation into enlightenment; hence also the equivalent of *zazen, the meditative way that leads to enlightenment.

Gedo (-zen) (Jap.). 'Outside' way of sharing Zen aims. see FIVE WAYS OF CH'AN/ZEN.

Geertz, Clifford (b. 1926). Influential American cultural anthropologist who advocates 'examining culture as an assemblage of texts'. The role of religion in organizing experience, in particular in providing responses to those experiences which lack 'interpretability', is explored in a number of works, including *The Religion of Java* (1960) and *Islam Observed* (1968).

Gefühl (feeling): see SCHLEIERMACHER, F.

Gehenna, Gehinnom (Heb., Valley of Hinnom). A valley south of *Jerusalem, used as a waste tip. It became a place where the wicked are abandoned with none to remember them, and where they are tormented after death. Gehenna is the Gk. form of the name.

Geiger, Abraham (1810–74). Leader of *Reform Judaism. In 1837 Geiger convened the first meeting of Reform *rabbis and as rabbi of the Berlin Reform congregation, he was director of the Hochschule für die Wissenschaft des Judenturms from 1872 until his death. He perceived Judaism to be solely a religion and was thus anxious to encourage *assimilation into the national life, as well as freedom of thought and enquiry. He summarized his view of Judaism in a popular series of lectures *Das Judenthum und seine Geschichte* (3 vols., 1865–7: Judaism and its History).

Gelugpa: see GELUK.

Geluk (dge.lugs.pa, 'Virtuous Way'). One of the four principal schools of Tibetan Buddhism and that to which the *Dalai Lama belongs. Established in 1409 with the founding of the Riwo Ganden ('Joyous Mountain') monastery by *Tsong Khapa, the Geluk was the last of the great schools to be formed, and is now the largest. That Tsong Khapa was at pains to differentiate his school from the others is revealed by his prescription of *Yellow Hats for his monks, while the other schools wore Red.

The head of the Geluk school is not (as is commonly supposed) the *Dalai Lama, but the Khri Rinpoche (or throne-holder), an office passed on by educational attainment, not by incarnation.

See Index, Geluk.

Gemāra (Aram., 'completion'). The discussions of the Jewish *amoraim on the *Mishnah. Both the Babylonian and the Palestinian *Talmud contain gemāra, which is traditionally printed around the relevant Mishnah passage.

Gematria (Heb., *gimatriyya*, from Gk., *geometria*). Use or study of hidden meanings through numbers, especially the numerical equivalence of letters. Gematria was much employed by the *kabbalists and was used to prove the *messiahship of *Shabbetai Zevi. Despite criticism, its use was widespread in both *Sephardi and *Ashkenazi circles.

In Islam, the equivalent techniques are known as *'ilm ul-ḥurūf*, based on *abjad (the numerical values of the letters). Thus Adam and Eve are specially related to God because their names = the Divine Name (of *Allāh).

Gemeinschaft (social ties of family and friendship): see IDEAL TYPE.

Gemilut ḥasidim (Heb., 'the bestowal of loving kindness'). The essential Jewish virtue of concern for one's fellow human beings. Gemilut ḥasidim is more than *charity in that it can be given to the rich as well as to the poor, and can involve personal service as well as the mere gift of money. It is one of the major characteristics of Jewish ethics.

Gempon Sōgen Shintō (school of shinto): see YOSHIDA SHINTŌ.

General Baptists. The name given to those *Arminian Baptists who believed in 'general' redemption for all humanity. This group united with the *Particular Baptists in 1891.

General providence: see PROVIDENCE.

Genesis. The first book of the *Pentateuch and opening book of the Hebrew Bible and Christian Old Testament. The Eng. title follows that of the Septuagint Gk. version, the Hebrew title *Bereshith* being the first word of the text.

Genesis Rabbah. Jewish *midrash on the book of *Genesis.

Geneva. City in Switzerland, associated with J. *Calvin. The Geneva Academy and the Geneva Catechisms expounded Calvinist views; the Geneva Bible (usually known as the Breeches Bible for its translation of Genesis 3. 7) was issued with Calvinist commentary, and was widely read. A Geneva gown is a black, full-sleeved gown, still worn by some *Protestant ministers, to make a deliberate contrast with *vestments and their association with the *sacrifice of the *mass.

Genizah (Heb., 'storing'). A place or receptacle for storing the Jewish books or ritual objects which can no longer be used.

Genjō (the wise and enlightened): see KENSHO.

Genjō (Jap. for Hsüan-tsang): see HSÜAN-TSANG.

Genjō-kōan. Text by Zen Buddhist master, *Dōgen Zenji, which became a part of **Shōbōgenzō*. It analyses the relation between *zazen and enlightenment, and is one of the most revered texts of the *Sōtō school.

Genkan (Jap., 'hidden gate'). The entrance to the guest rooms in a Zen Buddhist monastery, hence, metaphorically, the entrance to the path leading to enlightenment, according to the different methods of training.

Genku (founder of Jodo): see HŌNEN.

Gennep, C.-A. K. van: see RITES OF PASSAGE.

Gensha Shibi (Ch'an/Zen master): see HSÜAN-SHA SHIH-PEI.

Genshin or **Eshin Sōzu** (942–1017). Japanese Buddhist monk of the *Tendai sect. Genshin was one of the most brilliant Tendai monks of his age, and left many important works of Tendai Buddhist doctrines, including the *Ichjō Yōketsu*, (Essentials of the One Vehicle), which argued that all beings are capable of attaining buddhahood. However, he is most famous as the author of the seminal Pure Land text, the **Ōjōyōshū* (Essentials of Birth in Pure Land).

Gentile. A non-Jewish person. The term *goy*, although frequently used, is inappropriate, since the Heb. term means 'nation', and is used in the Bible of Israel. More accurate might be *nokhri*, a foreigner (or stranger), or *ger*, alien (see PROSELYTE). From early times, a distinction was made between *ger toshav* (lit., 'resident alien'), one who keeps the *Noachide laws, and *akum*, an acronym for those who worship stars and planets.

Genuflection (Lat., 'knee' + 'I bend'). Act of reverence performed by kneeling briefly on one knee.

Geomancy. *Divination based on patterns or shapes drawn (or appearing) on 'the land' (Gk.), particularly on sand. The term is also applied to *feng-shui (winds and waters), the ancient Chinese proto-science of siting human habitations (for the living or the dead) in locations that will take maximum advantage of the currents of vital breath (*ch'i) that circulate throughout the landscape.

Geonim (pl.) (title for heads of Jewish academies): see GAON.

George, St. *Patron saint of England (and of soldiers, knights, etc.) and *martyr. Very little is known of his life or death, but he probably died at or near Lydda in Palestine *c.*303. His cult and legends did not become popular until the 6th cent. In the E. he is known as the great martyr, *megalomartyros*. The slaying of the dragon (a standard symbol of strength) is first credited to him only in the 12th cent., but became widely known in the W. through the **Golden Legend*.

Georgian Orthodox Church. The *autocephalous church of Georgia, the republic situated in the Caucasus between Russia and Armenia.

Ger (a non-Jew living among Jews): see GENTILE.

Gereformeerde Kerk (Christian Protestant Church): see DUTCH REFORMED CHURCH.

Gerhardt, Paul (*c.*1607–76). German Christian hymn-writer. Apart from *Luther's own, his hymns are often held to be the finest of the Lutheran tradition. His hymns mark a transition from the objective orthodoxy of earlier Lutheran hymns to the personal piety of more modern compositions.

Gerizim. Mountain in *Israel. Mount Gerizim and Mount Ebal rise above the modern town of Nablus. Gerizim was the site of the *Samaritan *temple which was built about the time of *Nehemiah. It has remained the most sacred spot for the Samaritans.

Gerontius (poem by Newman): see NEWMAN, J. H.

Gershom ben Judah or **Me'or ha-Golah** ('light of the exile', *c.*960–*c.*1030). German Jewish *Talmudic scholar. Rabbenu Gershom was held in enormous reverence by later generations and *Rashi declared 'all *Ashkenazi Jewry are disciples of his disciples'. His grave in Mainz is still visited by the pious.

Gerson, Jean le Charlier de (1363–1429). French churchman and spiritual writer. All his life he was concerned for a true reform of the Church by a renewal of the spirit of prayer and sacrifice. He played a conciliatory role in the *Great Schism and was a supporter of conciliarism (see ANTIPOPE), attending the Council of *Constance.

Ger toshav (resident stranger): see GENTILE; NOACHIDE LAWS.

Gertrude of Helfta (Rhineland mystic): see RHENO-FLEMISH SPIRITUALITY.

Ge-sar (Tib., 'lotus temple'). A legendary hero in *Tibetan religion, who led the fight, in many dramatic episodes, against evil. He was adopted into Buddhism as the embodiment of *Avalokiteśvara, or of *Padmasambhava.

Gesellschaft (social bonds of a formal kind): see IDEAL TYPE.

Geshe (Professor in Tibetan school): see GELUK.

Get (bill of divorce): see MARRIAGE AND DIVORCE (JUDAISM).

Gethsemane. The garden to which Jesus went with his disciples after the *Last Supper. It lies in the valley between Jerusalem and the Mount of Olives.

Getig (materiality): see FRAVASI; FRASOKERETI.

Ge'ul(l)ah (Heb., 'redemption'). Title of several Jewish prayers. The prayers invoke God, as 'mighty Redeemer' to regard Israel's affliction and deliver his people.

Gezerah (Heb., 'edict'). Command of several different kinds in Judaism. In general, they are commands of an unusual kind. A gezerah, once (legitimately) enacted, cannot be rescinded.

Ghaiba (Arab., 'absence'). The state of one who has been withdrawn by God from visible appearance on earth, although he is still living invisibly on earth. The clearest example is the Hidden Imām (*al- Mahdī). It is also a *Sūfī stage on the way to *fanā', absent from self and present (*ḥaḍra*) only to God.

Ghaṇṭa. A bell, one of many objects used in Hindu ritual in association with *Śiva. The sound of his bell, or of his drum (*ḍamaru), encapsulates creation and is his 'form in sound' (*mantra (-svarūpa)). In the hands of Śiva's spouse, Ghaṇṭī (who is *Durgā), the bell is one of her twelve weapons to drive away threats and terrify enemies.

Ghāṭ. (Hindi; Skt., *ghaṭṭa*). A place of access, often by means of steps, to a river or lake, etc., for purposes of washing and for ritual cleansing (e.g. in *Gaṅgā). Some of these are reserved for dealing with the dead, especially for the dispersal of ashes.

Ghayba (hidden state): see GHAIBA.

Ghaz(z)ālī (Muslim philosopher and theologian): see AL-GHAZ(Z)ĀLĪ.

Ghetto. A compulsory urban residential area for Jews. The term 'ghetto' was probably first used for the Jewish quarter of Venice which was enclosed in 1516.

The phrase 'ghetto mentality' refers to the (alleged) internalization of the attitudes of the outsider—humiliation, rejection, and contempt, and the acceptance of isolation. The uprising of the Warsaw ghetto against the Nazis on 19 Apr. 1943, exhibits the reverse. It was put down by the destruction of the whole area.

Ghi or **ghee** (clarified butter, important in Hindu ritual): see GHṚTA.

Ghose, Aurobindo (Hindu philosopher and teacher): see AUROBINDO.

Ghost dance. The most famous *millennial movement among the N. American Indians, amongst the destitute tribes of the Great Basin and the Plains in 1889–90. The founder was Wovoka (*c.*1856–1932), a Paiute, also called Jack Wilson. After a mystic experience of visiting *heaven, he proclaimed the peaceful coming of a paradisal age in which the depleted buffalo and the ancestors (i.e. 'ghosts', hence the name) would return and the whites would depart. Its coming would be hastened by moral reform and the newly revealed round dance which, after several days of dancing, led to meeting the ancestors in a visionary trance. The movement among the Sioux was regarded by many whites as more militant; this culminated in the massacre of some 300 at Wounded Knee in Dec. 1890. With hopes thus crushed, the movement passed its peak by 1892; it lingers on among some tribes and provided the inspiration for the confrontation between Indians and government forces at 'Wounded Knee II' in S. Dakota in 1973.

Ghṛta (Skt.). Clarified butter, in modern Hindi *ghi*, often transliterated 'ghee'. It is a summary of the illumination which comes from *Indra, the light of divine knowledge become form.

Ghusl (Arab., 'to wash'). The major ritual of *ablution in Islam. It is commanded for major ritual impurity (*ḥadath), and consists in washing the whole body.

Ghwath-al-Aẓam (supposed founder of Sūfī order): see ABD AL-QĀDIR AL-JĪLĪ.

Giānī (Pañjābī, 'learned'). Scholar of Sikh scriptures. Sikhs use this title for any person regarded as proficient in expounding the teachings of the *Ādi Granth in the *gurdwārā.

Gideon. One of the biblical *judges. His activities are recorded in the Book of Judges (6. 11–8. 32).

Gifts: see ALMSGIVING.

Gijō. Jap. for **I Ching*.

Giku (Chinese Ch'an/Zen master): see I-K'UNG.

Gilbert of Sempringham (*c.*1083–1189). Founder of the Gilbertine Order of monks and nuns. While parish priest of his native Sempringham in Lincolnshire, he encouraged seven women of his congregation to form a community on the *Cistercian model. Other foundations followed. When the Cistercians refused to accept communities of nuns under their aegis, Gilbert arranged for the direction of his nuns by priests following the *Augustinian Rule, who together with the nuns, and the lay-brothers and lay-sisters, formed a double community, sharing their liturgical life. It was the only purely English medieval order.

Gilgit. An area between Chitral and Baltistan where *stupas of c. 5th/6th cents. CE have revealed the earliest known list of Buddhist magical formulae (*dhāraṇīs).

Gilgul (Heb., *gilgul neshamot*, 'transmigration of souls'). The Jewish doctrine of the transmigration of *souls. Although belief in the transmigration of souls was rejected by the major medieval Jewish philosophers, it was held by *Anan b. David, the founder of *Karaism, and it is expressed in many *kabbalistic texts. The purpose of transmigration was the purification of the soul.

Gill, Eric (1882–1940). Artist and type-designer. From 1907 to 1924 he was associated with the Ditchling community and with its press. In the last decade of his life he wrote a number of influential books defending the goodness of natural things, and, in life, even 'its Rabelaisian buffoonery and pig-style coarseness. All these things are good and holy.' His expression of this in his personal life created strain for those close to him.

Gilson, Étienne (1884–1978). French Roman Catholic philosopher and historian. His special interest was the philosophy of Thomas *Aquinas, particularly the influence of *Aristotle on his thought. Though he was later to be criticized for underestimating the strength of *Platonism in the Middle Ages, his interpretation of the scholastics had a great impact upon modern RC philosophers.

He held, with *Augustine, that 'the universe is a kind of unfolding, a *distensio*, which imitates in its flowing forth the eternal present and total simultaneity of the life of God'. Such a view of order and providence cannot be concerned with a more dispassionate estimate of the actual history of the Church and its restrictive attitude to the quest for truth.

Ginsberg, Asher Hirsh (Jewish Zionist leader): see AHAD HA-'AM.

Ginzberg, Louis (1873–1953). *Talmudic scholar, an important figure in the *Conservative movement. His major work was the 7-vol. *Legends of the Jews* (1909–38) in which he collected and combined hundreds of legends into a continuous narrative; and he was also the rabbinics editor for the *Jewish Encyclopaedia*.

Giotto di Bondone (1266/7–1337). Italian fresco painter, often regarded as 'the founder of modern art'. His stature was recognized especially by his attention to perspective, and by making recognizable human figures and landscapes the bearers of Christian meaning. His most famous (undisputed) work is in the Arena Chapel in Padua. The better-known frescos on the life of St Francis in Assisi may not be by him.

Giralda (Muslim dynasty in N. Africa and Spain): see ALMOHADS.

Girdle: see HABIT, RELIGIOUS.

Girsah (plain meaning): see PILPUL.

Gītā (Hindu text): see BHAGAVAD-GĪTĀ.

Gita. A *Maronite Christian veil, used to cover the paten, chalice, or oblation in the liturgy.

Gītāgovinda (Song of the Cowherd). A court poem by Jayadeva (12th cent. CE). Erotic in nature, it appears on the surface to be a straightforward account of the loves of *Kṛṣṇa for the gopīs. But the poem is also read (and dramatically acted), especially by *Vaiṣṇavas, as a poem on the longing of the human for the divine.

Gitanjali (poem by Indian poet Tagore): see TAGORE, R.

Glastonbury. In Somerset, one of the oldest English monasteries. Its history goes back to the 7th cent., but it became a famous Benedictine centre from *c.*940 under its abbot St Dunstan. About 1135 William of Malmesbury wrote its history, and in a 13th-cent. revision of this are the legends which associate it with *Joseph of Arimathea, King Arthur, and St *Patrick.

Glebe. Land which belongs to the endowment of a parish and which provides an income from farming by the priest himself or a tenant.

Gloria. The first word in the Latin, and hence the common name, of a Christian hymn. It begins with the words of Luke 2. 14. It is also known as the 'Greater *Doxology' or 'Angelic Hymn'. The 'Lesser Doxology', or *Gloria Patri*, is sung or said at the end of Psalms and *canticles.

Glossolalia (Gk., *glossa*, 'tongue', + *lalia*, 'speaking'). 'Speaking in tongues', the phenomenon, common in many religions, of a person speaking in words or word-like sounds which form a language unknown to the speaker. Related phenomena are *xenoglossolalia*, speaking in a foreign language unknown to the speaker but known to the hearer; and *heteroglossolalia*, speaking in a language known to the speaker which the hearer hears in his/her own language.

Gnosticism. A complex of religious movements, having at least some of its roots in Jewish and pagan thought but appearing in developed form as a Christian *heresy in the 2nd cent. Among the systems of that time, those of *Valentinus, *Basilides, and (somewhat apart from the rest) *Marcion are the best known.

Among points of difference from mainstream Christianity are (i) the distinction between the remote supreme Divine Being and the inferior *Demiurge or creator god responsible for the imperfect and perverted material world; (ii) the importance of *gnōsis* ('knowledge') as a means of redemption for at least some people (sometimes called the *pneumatikoi*, 'spiritual ones'); and (iii) a *christology of Jesus as the emissary of the supreme God in *docetic human form.

The *Manichaeans, *Mandeans, and *Cathars may be in various ways descendants of the gnostics. The autobiography of C. G. *Jung shows the influence of gnosticism on his thought.

See Index, Gnostics.

Gō. Jap. for *karma.

Go (Skt., 'cow'). *Bos indicus*, in Hinduism, revered as the source of food and symbol of life. The cow became associated with the sacrificial rituals through its designation as the appropriate gift (*dakṣinā) to the *brahmans, and thus its sacred and inviolable nature became established: to kill a cow is equal to killing a brahman. The five products (*pañcagavya*) of the cow (milk, curds, *ghṛta, urine, dung) are all used in *pūjā, worship.

The cultic worship of the cow takes place especially on the day of Gopastami, the 'cow holiday', when the cow is washed and decorated in the temple, and given offerings in the hope that her gifts of life will continue.

Gobind Siṅgh, Gurū (1666–1708 CE). Tenth Sikh *Gurū. Gobind Rāi was born on 26 Dec. 1666, in Paṭnā, to Mātā *Gūjarī, while her husband, *Tegh Bahādur, was travelling further east. Later, the family returned to *Anaṇḍpur Sāhib, where, in Nov. 1675, Gobind Rāi received the severed head of his martyred father. As his father's chosen successor, he was installed as Gurū. His poetry comprises the *Dasam Granth. Adoration of God's holiness and majesty is expressed in new epithets (e.g. *akāl* (timeless), *sarvloh* (all-iron), 'Sword', and 'Punisher of Evil', as well as 'Gracious' and 'Benign'). Pious Sikhs daily recite his *jāp, *savayye, and *chaupaī in *Nitnem. On *Baisākhī 1699 (according to tradition) he inaugurated the *khālsā, and initiated with *amrit the *pañj pyāre to be the nucleus of a pure, casteless community, characterized by the *five Ks and a code of conduct (*rahat). He in turn received initiation (*Khaṇḍe-dī-pāhul) from them, assuming the name Siṅgh. Thousands more accepted this initiation.

On *Auraṅgzeb's death in 1707 CE Gobind Siṅgh supported the succession of Bahādur Shāh. In an attempt to punish Wazīr Khān and other persecutors of the Sikhs. Gobind Siṅgh was fatally wounded by two Pathān assassins. He bade his Sikhs regard the Ādi Granth as Gurū (so ending the line of human gurus), and died 7 Oct. 1708.

See HOLĀ MAHALLĀ; NĀMDHĀRĪ; RAṄGHṚETĀ.

Gobutsu (Jap., 'five buddhas'). The five buddhas, distributed in the two *maṇḍalas, of Japanese esoteric Buddhism. They are *Dainichi in the centre, with, in the Diamond Realm mandala: Ashuku (east), Hōshō (south), *Amida (west), Fukūjōju (north); and in the Matrix Realm mandala: Hōdō (E.), Kaifukeō (S.), Muryōju (W.), Tenkuraion (N.).

God. The absolute and real who is, than which nothing greater can be conceived, the unproduced Producer of all that is, without whom nothing that is could be or could remain in being; or, alternatively, the *projection into supposed reality of human fears, neuroses, and abject needs (*Freud), or of human ideals which can never be realized (*Feuerbach), or of the requirements to perpetuate the conditions of alienation in the interests of some party (*Marx); in this second case, language about 'God' is a surrogate language about humanity or human persons ('Theology is anthropology'). The possibility of so wide a contrast between theistic realism and psychological unrealism arises because God (supposing God is) is not an object among objects in a universe, able to be discovered and/or explored, as are atoms, quasars, and the dark side of the moon. Nor is God the conclusion of an argument, although argument points to the probability of God, at least in the sense that the universe makes more sense if it exists as a consequence of one who produces and sustains it, than otherwise. For examples of such arguments, see QUINQUE VIAE. Since God cannot be produced as an object among objects, and since God is, whether this or any other universe happens to exist, it follows that God cannot be described in language, since God is far apart from humanly apprehended categories in time and space (i.e. is transcendent). In all theistic religions, this has led inevitably to *apophatic theology, to the recognition that we can only say with confidence what God is not, (e.g. *via negativa, *neti neti, *ein-sof).

Theistic religions have always been aware of the inadequacy of human language about God (hence the importance of *analogy). Even in the human affection of *worship, it is known that no words or images can contain or describe God, and yet the experienced consequence of God creates its own and continuing demand for, or invitation into, relationship. Religious and theological traditions then offer the inadequacies of language, sign, *symbol, *icon, etc. (or images in the case of Hindus), as a means of initiating an apprehension of God which is qualitatively *sui generis*—one which is capable of lifting life from the mundane to a point of balance and rescue where the entire universe is seen as a start and not as a conclusion.

In the terms, therefore, of a critically realistic theology, religions accept that anything which is said about God is approximate, provisional, corrigible, and mainly wrong; but the question still remains, Is it wrong about some One? Even those religions which are most secure in their confidence that God has overcome the epistemic gap of transcendence, by revealing his word and his will, accept that all *revelation is conveyed contingently through words which are not identical with that concerning which they purport to be about—in terms which are approximate. In the end, all religions are bound to issue the invitation, 'Taste and see'. The experience and procedures of relatedness to what has been described in those approximate ways as *El, Zeus, *Allāh, *Viṣṇu, *Amida, *Brahman, etc., have built up through the millennia an impressive reliability of reference and relationship—and a reliability which has encouraged constant correction as successive generations have learnt, with increasing security, something more of the nature of the One with whom they have to deal. At the same time, that which is God has seemed, unequivocally, to be, so to speak, 'dealing with them': it is in this way that the major transformations in the human understanding of God have been made. In ways (which humans have tested and winnowed through time, and in virtually all cultures) of *prayer, *worship, *sacrifice, *contemplation, *meditation, *art, *music, artefact, the reliability of the communities of faith has been tested. In each tradition, there emerge characterizations of God which impress themselves on the style in which its adherents live. In Judaism, the major emphasis is on holiness, in Christianity on the commitments of love which reflect a relatedness in the Godhead itself; in Islam on mercy and demand; among Hindus on the real presence of God in every circumstance.

The logic of God, therefore, remains, that if God does indeed turn out to be God, it is God that God will turn out to be. The ways and the words of human attentiveness to God leave such a mark on the possibilities of life now, that the nature of the future remains open: it is necessarily the case that All remains yet to be known.

For names, see Index, Names of God, Names of Goddess.

God, name of in Judaism. Because of God's exalted nature, his name is sacred. The *tetragrammaton is never pronounced, and *Adonai (the Lord) or Ha-Shem (the name) is substituted. In the Aramaic *targums, the name of God is often translated *memra* (word). Similarly, euphemisms are used by the *rabbis, such as *Rahmana* (the Merciful), *Ha-Makom* (the Place) or *Ha-Kadosh Barukh Hu* (the Holy One, blessed be He). The *Kabbalists called God *Ein-Sof (the infinite): there is nothing to be said about him, and he can only be known by his *Sefirot or emanations which are single facets of his revelation.

According to Jewish law, only the *high priest could pronounce the tetragrammaton once a year on the *Day of Atonement. The name of God cannot be erased or discarded from any document (see GENIZAH), and it is forbidden to use any of the biblical names of God in a secular context. Among very *orthodox Jews, it is even customary to avoid writing God in the vernacular, and G-d is preferred.

God, names of among Sikhs. The Name (*Nām) of God has particular importance for Sikhs. Many names are used for God, some familiar to Hindus (e.g. *Hari, *Śiv, *Brahmā, *Rām, Mohan) and others to Muslims (e.g. Rabb, *Allāh, Khudā, *Sāhib). Above all God's name is Truth (*sat(i)nām). He is the *Sat(i)gurū by whose *grace the way of *salvation from *rebirths is revealed. By the Gurū's grace and by devoted repetition of God's name (*nām simaran) he can be realized.

God, names of in Islam: see NINETY-NINE BEAUTIFUL NAMES OF GOD.

Goddess. The source of life and being, once prevalent in religious imagination, but much suppressed during the millennia of male control of religions. The same observations about the provisionality of language and symbol apply here as in the case of God: they are compounded in the case of feminine imagery of the divine by the insistence on their inadequacies in the major monotheistic religions: see FEMININE SYMBOLS.

Godianism. A Nigerian remodelling of African religions as a new modern faith, formed by amalgamation in 1963 between the Cult of Aruosa ('holy place' or 'altar') or Edo National Church and the National Church of Nigeria. Despite borrowing many external Christian forms, the movement repudiates Christianity as a foreign religion. It represents pride in Africa, rather than a dynamic religious development.

Godō (Jap., 'back hall'). Part of the meditation hall in a Zen monastery, and thus also the senior monk who has charge of the godō.

Godparents. The sponsors of a child to be *baptized. They undertake responsibility for the child's Christian upbringing.

God's Kingdom Society. A Nigerian sabbatarian movement resembling *Jehovah's Witnesses. It was founded in 1934 in the area south of Benin City by Gideon Urhobo, a former *Roman Catholic and ex-Jehovah's Witness, and by the 1960s had achieved over 2,000 members.

Goel ha-dam (in Judaism liability for punishment of those who have shed blood): see BLOODGUILT.

Gog and Magog. *Apocalyptic character and territory in the vision of *Ezekiel. According to Ezekiel 36–8, God would wage war against 'Gog of the land of Magog' at the end of time. In the New Testament (Revelation 20) the war of Gog and Magog takes place one thousand years after the first resurrection. They are represented in giant statues at the Guildhall in London, as porters of the royal palace and descendants of giants.

Gogyaku-zai (Jap., 'five rebellious sins'). The *five deadly sins in Japanese Buddhism: killing your father, killing your mother, killing an *arakan* (*arhat), causing the Buddha's appearance body to bleed, causing schism in the Buddhist order. Any of these leads to reappearance in hell (*jigoku), for torment of many *kalpas.

Gohei (Jap.), a wand-like implement used in Shinto observances to signal purification, or may be used to indicate the presence of a deity (*kami).

Gohonzon (tablet bearing Buddhist mantra): see DAIMOKU.

Go-i (Jap.). A classification in Zen Buddhism, first established by *Tung-shan Liang-chieh, of five degrees of enlightenment (*kenshō, *satori). They are laid out in pairs, each of which summarizes how the phenomenal is more truly to be understood: (i) *sho-chu-hen*, '*hen* in the midst of *shō*', the phenomena are immediate, but are understood as manifesting the underlying, true reality; (ii) *hen-chu-sho*, '*shō* in the midst of *hen*', non-differentiation is then achieved; (iii) *sho-chu-rai*, 'it coming out of *shō*', body and mind drop away as the realization of *śūnyatā obtains; (iv) *ken-chu-shi*, 'entering between the two', the realization of how śūnyatā itself vanishes (into phenomena); (v) *ken-chu-to* 'arrival in the midst of both', form and emptiness interpenetrate, in a realization of dynamic non-interaction.

Goi (non-Jewish person): see GENTILE.

Go-i-kōan (form of kōan in Rinzai): see KŌAN.

Goindvāl (Sāhib). Sikh place of *pilgrimage (*tīrath) 50 km. SE of *Amritsar. Every autumn a local *melā commemorates the death of Gurū Amar Dās.

Gökalp, Ziya (1875–1924). A Turkish liberal reformer who prepared his country's orientation towards the establishment of a modern secular state. Turkish authorities have on occasion revived the cult of Ziya Gökalp to check the rising tide of conservative Islam in universities.

Goke-shichishū (Jap., 'five-houses, seven-schools'). A classification of the seven Ch'an Buddhist schools, during the T'ang period, which derived from five lineages: (i) *Rinzai from *Lin-chi I-hsuan (Jap., Rinzai Gigen); (ii) Igyo from Kuei-shan Ling-yu (Jap., Isan Reiyū) and from *Yang-shan Hui-chi (Jap., Kyōzan Ejaku); (iii) *Sōtō from *Tung-shan Liang-chieh (Jap., Tōzan Ryōkai) and from *Ts'ao-shan Pen-chi (Jap., Sōzan Honjaku); (iv) *Ummon from *Yün-Men Wen-yen (Jap., Ummon Bun'en); (v) *Hogen from *Fa-yen Wen-i (Jap., Hogen Bun'eki). Rinzai then split, to make up seven: (vi) *Yōgi from Yang-ch'i Fang-hui (Jap., Yōgi Hōe); (vii) Ōryō from *Huang-lung Hui-nan (Jap., Ōryō E'nan).

Gokhalé, Gopāḷ Krishna (1863–1915). An Indian political leader, born near Chipḷooṇ in the W. Indian region of Konkaṇ. His influence on religious matters (via politics) was great, because he was a staunch advocate of constitutional methods and reforms for Indian Home Rule, and was of importance for *Gāndhī.

Gokuraku. Jap. for *Sukhāvatī.

Golden Book (mythology of Buddhist-influenced millennial movement): see TELAKHON.

Golden Calf. The golden statue made by *Aaron in Exodus 32.

Golden Legend (Lat., *Legenda Aurea*). A manual consisting of lives of the *saints and of episodes in the lives of *Jesus and *Mary, making connection with Christian festivals, in the order of the Church *calendar. It was written by the *Dominican Jacob of Voragine between 1255 and 1266.

Golden Lotus (form of religious Taoism): see CH'ÜAN-CHEN TAO.

Golden Rule. Epitome of ethical action, occurring, at least proverbially, in most religions, but associated particularly with Judaism and Christianity. In Judaism, it occurs most often in negative form: 'Whatever is hateful to you, do not do to another'. In the New Testament, it appears, unpacking Leviticus 19. 18, in the form: 'As you would that people should do to you, do likewise to them' (Matthew 7. 12; Luke 6. 31).

Golden Temple (Sikh holy place): see AMRITSAR; HARIMANDIR.

Golem (Heb., 'shapeless matter'). An embryo (Psalms 139. 16) or stupid person (*Avot* 5. 9), and eventually a creature brought into being artificially through the use of God's name. At the outset, they are created as useful servants, but they use their great strength malignantly and get completely out of control.

Golgotha (the place of Jesus' crucifixion): see CALVARY.

Goliath. *Philistine giant who was killed by young *David: see 1 Samuel 17.

Goloka (Skt., 'Loka of cows'). Kṛṣṇa's paradise on Mount *Meru. It was added to the original seven *lokas, and it became for the *Vaiśnavites a term for eternal bliss.

Goma (Jap. for Skt., *homa). A burnt offering. Fire rituals (*gegoma*) are of particular importance in esoteric Buddhism, both for averting disasters and for increasing *merit. They should be accompanied by interiorized ritual (*naigoma*), which is in effect meditation. Fire represents the burning out of evil desires, etc.

Gomel blessing (Heb., *ha-Gomel*, 'he who bestows favours'). Jewish blessing offered in thanksgiving to God by one who has lived through a dangerous experience.

Gomi(-no)-zen: see ICHIMI-ZEN.

Gongen (Jap., temporary manifestation). An incarnation, e.g. of a *Shinto deity, or of a *buddha or *bodhisattva.

Gonsen-kōan (form of kōan in Rinzai): see KŌAN.

Good Friday. The Friday before *Easter commemorating Jesus' crucifixion.

Good Samaritan. The *Samaritan in Jesus' *parable (Luke 10. 30–7).

Good Shepherd. A title of *Christ derived from his discourse in John 10. 7–18 and the '*parable of the good shepherd' in Luke 15. 3–7.

Gopastami (cow festival): see GO.

Gopī (Skt., 'keeper of cows'). The women cowherds at *Vṛndāvana, who are involved with *Kṛṣṇa in the love-affairs of his youth. They come to symbolize, both the soul's devotion (*bhakti) to God, and also the legitimacy of flouting convention in the service of God.

Gorakhnāth, Gorakṣa, or **Gorakṣanātha.** A Hindu yogin of *c*.10/11 cent. CE, of the Nātha *tantra cult, which claimed magical and occult powers through the practice of *yoga. He is said by some to have originated *Haṭhayoga, and to have founded the order of Kānphaṭa yogīs (so-called from 'ear' + 'split': they wear heavy earrings after initiation; they are also called Gorakhnāthis). Two works in Skt. are attributed to him (*Siddhasiddhāntapaddhati* and *Gorakśa sátaka*), together with various hymns, but all are doubtful.

Gordon, Judah (1831–92). Heb. writer. Through his poetry and journalism, Gordon inveighed against the rigidity of the *rabbinic leaders of his time. He was a prominent supporter of the *haskalah. Although not a committed *Zionist, he proposed the founding of a society for those going to Palestine.

Gore, Charles (1853–1932). Anglican theologian and bishop of Oxford. As first principal of Pusey House, Oxford, later, as canon of Westminster and as bishop (of Worcester, and then of Birmingham), his writings, especially on Christian apologetic (*Belief in God*, 1921; *Belief in Christ*, 1922; *The Holy Spirit and the Church*, 1924), were widely read. Of particular and far-reaching importance was his contribution to the establishment of the Community of the Resurrection, founded in 1892.

Gorinsotoba (Jap., 'sotoba [*stūpa] with five sections'). Tombs (which became common after the Kamakura period in Japan) with five stone sections, of different shapes, placed on top of each other.

Gosāla, Makkhali (founder): see MAKKHALI.

Gosan or **Gozan.** 'Five mountains' (Chin., *wu-shan*), the federation of Ch'an/Zen monasteries, in groups of five, especially of Hangchou, Ming-chou, and then in Japan of Kamakura and Kyōto. Because monasteries were often built on mountains, the word *shan* (Jap., *san* or *zan*) came to mean 'monastery'.

Gosan-bungaku (Jap., 'five-mountain literature'). Collective term for writings from the *gosan (federation) of Kyōto, during the Muromachi period (1338–1573).

Gose (Jap., 'the hereafter'). The afterlife in general; in particular, birth after death in the domain of *Amida.

Goseki (Jap.), 'Trace of enlightenment' in Zen Buddhism, of one who has had some experience of enlightenment, but still carries, 'the stench of enlightenment', i.e. has not yet learned to live as though he might or might not have had such experience, since he should be totally detached from it.

Goshichinichi mishiho. The annual Japanese *Shingon prayer ritual. Its purpose was prayer for the emperor, the state, peace and prosperity, etc., during the year to come. It was inaugurated by *Kūkai in 834, suspended during the *Meiji restoration, revived in 1883, and still continues.

Goso Hōen (Jap., for Wu-tsu Fa-yen): see KŌAN.

Gospel (Gk., *euangelion*; OE, *godspel*, 'good news'). 1. The content of Christian preaching.

2. A book containing sayings and stories of Jesus. Since there was only one Good News, the four separate gospels in the New Testament were distinguished as 'according to' *Matthew, *Mark, *Luke, and *John.

3. The reading from the gospels in the Christian *eucharist.

Gospel of Truth. A work on Christian life and salvation found among the Coptic texts of *Nag Hammadi. It is probably the work of this title by *Valentinus which *Irenaeus mentioned, in which case it must represent his early less unorthodox thought (before *c*.150 CE).

Gosvamins (Hindu group concerned with aesthetics and religious experience): see ABHINAVAGUPTA.

Gosvāmīs (disciples of Caitanya): see CAITANYA.

Gotama or **Gautama** (Pāli, Skt.). 1. The clan (Skt., *gotra*) to which the historical *Buddha belonged. It is hence the name by which his non-Buddhist contemporaries refer to him, and a name used when distinguishing him from other Buddhas.

2. The founder of the *Nyāya school of Hindu philosophy (*darśana), and author of a law book (*dharmaśāstra).

3. A Vedic *ṛṣi, to whom the composition of one of the finest hymns in the *Ṛg Veda* (1. 92) is attributed.

Gothic. An architectural style in N. Europe from early 12th cent. to 16th, and, as Gothic revival, in 19th cent. Thence it is applied to literature and religion to denote the opaquely mysterious—to some, grotesque.

Gotra. (Skt., 'cow-shed', 'assemblage', 'clan'). In India, the exogamous group of all persons (especially *brahmans) related by descent through the male line from a common male ancestor.

In *Mahāyāna Buddhism the term is employed to denote categories of religious practitioners on the basis of psychological, spiritual, and intellectual capacity.

Gott-trunckener mensch ('God-intoxicated man'): see SPINOZA.

Govinda (Skt., 'cow-finder'). In Hindu mythology, another name for *Kṛṣṇa or *Viṣṇu.

Govinda, Lama Anāgārika (1898–1985). Interpreter of Tibetan Buddhism to the W. and founder of Ārya Maitreya Mandala. He was born E. L. Hoffmann of Bolivian and German parents. He went to Śri Lankā in 1928, in pursuit of an interest in burial mounds, and was attracted by Buddhism. He became an *anāgārika. From a conference in Darjeeling, he felt a strong compulsion to go to Tibet, where he met his *guru, Tomo Geshe Rinpoche. He made many journeys in Tibet, and described both these and his reasons for transferring to Tibetan Buddhism.

Govindapāda. The teacher of *Śaṅkara, also known as Govindabhagavatpāda. Nothing is known about him apart from later traditional accounts.

Goy (non-Jewish person): see GENTILE.

Goyim (non-Jewish people): see GENTILE.

Gozan (Jap., 'five mountains'). The five major *Zen temples designated by the Japanese government, in order of precedence (though this order changed from time to time). Initially (14th cent.) they were in *Kamakura: Kenchōji, Engakuji, Jufukuji, Jōchiji, Jōmyōji. Later in the same century, five further temples were designated in *Kyōto: Tenryuji, Shōkokuji, Kenninji, Tōkufuji, Manjuji.

Gozan Zen (form of Zen Buddhism in Japan): see RINZAI-SHŪ.

Gozu (school of Ch'an Buddhism): see FA-JUNG.

Grace. 1. In Christian theology, the expression of God's love in his free unmerited favour or assistance.

'Grace' then becomes a category for describing free and uncoerced actions in other religions, especially of Kṛṣṇa in the **Bhagavad-gītā*: see e.g. PRASĀDA; RĀMĀNUJA (for *anugraha*); PRAPATTI. As a concept, grace is of great importance for Sikhs, in Gurū *Nānak's hymns and in all subsequent Sikh theology. Analogous to the benedictory glance of a human guru, this sense of God's loving favour is conveyed by the words *praśad*, *kirpā*, *nadar*, *bakhśīś*, *bhāṇā*, *daiā*, *mihar*, and *taras*. This concept of grace is not a denial of *karma, but God's initiative can override the result of bad actions. However, the individual must strive to improve.

2. Short prayers of invocation and thanksgiving, before and after meals. They are natural and characteristic in Judaism. The *Birkat ha-Mazon* (blessing after meals) is a central liturgical practice in the observant Jewish home.

Gradual (Lat., *gradus*, 'step'). The *antiphons, usually from the Psalms, sung after the first lesson from the Bible in the *mass.

Gradual enlightenment/sudden enlightenment. Schools within Ch'an Buddhism in China, derived from two pupils of *Hung Jen, Shen Hsiu, and *Hui-Neng. They correspond to the Northern and *Southern Schools.

Gradual Sayings. Common Eng. name for **Anguttara-Nikāya*.

Graham, Billy (William Franklin; b. 1918). American Christian evangelist. He was ordained a *Southern Baptist minister and became a local pastor (1943–5), then a college president (1947–52). The first of his big evangelistic 'crusades', in which he preached to a series of mass meetings, was in Los Angeles in 1948. Many others have followed, notably one attended by hundreds of thousands in London in 1954, which made him a world figure. Graham took his message to a worldwide audience via satellite TV in his 1989–90 'Mission World' campaign and the 1996 'Operation Matthew' and 'Billy Graham World Television Series', which had estimated viewing figures of 2.5 billion people across 160 nations.

Grahast(h)ī (Pañjābī, 'householder' = *grhasth āśram). The Sikh *Gurūs taught that God-realization is not to be sought by leading a reclusive life, but through fulfilling the responsibilities of family life. In the first verse of *Rām Dās' *Lāvān the grahastī state is affirmed (Ādi Granth 773).

Grail, The Holy, or **Sangreale** (perhaps Old Fr., from Lat., *gradale*, 'dish'). The legendary subject of several romances in the late Middle Ages. In some versions, (principally the *Estoire dou Graal* or *Joseph* of Robert de Boron, *c*.1200) the sacred object is the chalice or dish used at the *Last Supper which passed into the possession of *Joseph of Arimathea. The origin of the whole cycle of legends is obscure; it is not even clear whether the Christian elements are primary. In the 13th cent. it reinforced the ecclesiastical propaganda of *Glastonbury Abbey and later on was coupled with the legend of *Prester John.

Grail Foundation. A movement started in the 1920s by the German-born Oskar Ernst Bernhardt (1875–1941), later known as Abd-ru-shin (also as Son of Light). After undergoing a 'conversion' experience in 1919, Abd-ru-Shin, who claimed to be in a previous life (in the time of Moses) a prince of an Arabian tribe, began his mission, which was in essence to develop people's knowledge of creation as the means to resolving the problems of humanity. To this end *The Grail Message*, part of a series of public lectures, was published in 1923, to be followed by *In the Light of Truth*, consisting of 3 vols. of Abd-ru-Shin's lectures delivered between 1923 and 1937.

Grāmadevatā (Skt., 'local deity'). An image set up on the boundary of an Indian village to ward off evil. They also serve as guardians against disease. They are usually female (cf. the frightening aspects of *Kālī and *Durgā), but some are male (e.g. Iyenar among the *Tamils).

Grandmother Zen (gentle form of Zen): see RŌBA ZEN.

Granth (Pañjābī, 'book', from Skt., 'to knot together' since early books consisted of palm leaves strung together and tied). Sikh scripture. Granth refers primarily to the *Ādi Granth but see also DASAM GRANTH.

Granthī. Sikh who looks after the *Ādi Granth. A granthī should be skilled in reading the Ādi Granth and often acts as custodian of the *gurdwārā.

Gratian (d. not later than 1159). Author of the *Decretum Gratiani* and thus the major source of Roman Catholic *canon law. It became the basic text on which subsequent teaching and development were based.

Great Assembly. The supreme authority of the Jewish people in the time of the second *Temple. Traditionally it had 120 members, known as 'the men of the Great Assembly'. It was responsible for drawing up much of the text of the accepted *liturgy.

Great Awakening. A series of conversionary revivals of Christian religion in N. America, 1720–50. They were particularly associated with George *Whitefield, and proved divisive.

Great Bible: see COVERDALE, MILES.

Great doubt (of Dōgen): see DŌGEN KIGEN.

Great Entrance. In the *Orthodox liturgy of the *eucharist, the procession at which the bread and wine to be consecrated are carried in from the *prothesis table to the *altar.

Great Learning. The *Ta Hsüeh*, one of the group of **Four Books* in the *Confucian Classics. A small work extracted from the collection called *Records of Rituals* (**Li Chi*). It was singled out for special attention by *neo-Confucian philosophers of the Sung dynasty (960–1279), who found it a perfect expression of their own programme of self-cultivation to attain saintliness and save the world.

Great Perfection. Name given to the Tibetan tradition 'Great Perfection', i.e. *dzogchen.

Great Radiant Sūtra (Tantric Buddhist sūtra): see MAHĀVAIROCANA-SŪTRA.

Great sayings (of the Upaniṣads): see MAHĀVĀKYA.

Great schism. Either (1) the excommunication by Rome in 1054 of the *patriarch of *Constantinople, and the patriarch's excommunication of the *pope; or (2) the *schism in the W. Church, 1378–1417 when there were two, and for a time three, contenders for the title of pope.

Great synagogue. Perhaps better translated '*great assembly', a Jewish administrative council during the Persian period (538–331 BCE).

Great tradition, little tradition. Categories introduced by the sociologist, Robert Redfield (*Peasant Society and Culture*, 1956) to distinguish between the major, continuing components of a religious tradition and the appropriation of them at local or village level. An example is M. E. Spiro's distinction between nibbanic Buddhism as a religion of ultimate salvation and kammatic Buddhism as a religion of proximate salvation, which, in practice, is the highest that most people can aim for.

Great vehicle (the development of Buddhism): see MAHĀYĀNA.

Great vow (commitment to first limb of Hindu yoga): see YAMA (2).

Great vows (basic Jain commitments): see FIVE GREAT VOWS.

Great Western schism: see ANTIPOPE; GREAT SCHISM.

Greek Orthodox Church. 1. The *autocephalous Christian church found mainly in Greece, a part of the *Orthodox Church whose belief and practice it shares. The Church is particularly strong in N. and S. America, and numbers *c*.15 million.

2. Incorrectly, but widely used prior to 1914, for all Orthodox churches, e.g. in Baedeker's *Guide to Russia*, 1914.

Green Book (revolutionary text of Libyan leader): see QADHAFFI, MUʿAMMAR.

Gregorian calendar, new calendar, or **new style.** The Julian *calendar as adjusted by Pope Gregory XIII in 1582 to make it cohere better with the solar year. It was not accepted in most *Orthodox Churches until 1924.

Gregorian Chant: see GREGORY I.

Gregory I, 'the Great', St (*c*.540–604). *Pope from 590 and founder of the medieval papacy. As pope at a time of great unrest, Gregory had to deal with the invasion of Italy by the Lombards, and with threats to the position of the Church from the claims of the Byzantine Empire. He maintained the supremacy of the see of Rome, refusing to accept or recognize the title of *ecumenical patriarch, which the patriarch of Constantinople claimed. He made important changes in the *liturgy (though the 'Gregorian' *Sacramentary ia a later compilation) and promoted liturgical *music (hence the name 'Gregorian chant' for *plainsong). His many writings were mostly practical, including *Pastoral Care*, a *Commentary on Job* (expounding the literal, mystical and especially moral senses of the text), *Homilies on the Gospels*, and a collection of 854 letters. He was canonized by popular acclamation when he died, and is one of the *Doctors of the Church Feast day, 12 Mar.

Gregory VII, St (*c*.1020–85). Originally Hildebrand, Christian pope who provoked the Investiture Controversy. His *Dictatus Papae* (1075) not only emphasized the holiness of the pope in succession from *Peter, but also asserted the right of the pope to depose princes. He prohibited lay investiture (i.e. the right of laity to make appointments to certain church offices), which in effect envisaged the abolition of the royal control over bishops. Considerable unrest ensued, especially in France, England, and Germany. Henry IV continued to nominate bishops, convening a synod of German bishops at Worms and Piacenza in 1076 which deposed the pope. Gregory responded by excommunicating Henry and releasing his subjects from allegiance. Seeing the threat, Henry capitulated and sought absolution in penitent's attire at Canossa, near Reggio, in 1077. But this was the beginning, not the end, of conflict. When Henry seized Rome in 1084, Gregory fled to Monte Cassino, thence to Salerno where he died. He was canonized in 1606: feast day 25 May.

Gregory of Nazianzus, St (329–89). One of the *Cappadocian fathers, known in the Orthodox Church as 'the Theologian'. He shrank from the active life of a bishop, but in 379 he was summoned to Constantinople, where his preaching helped to restore the *Nicene faith at the council of 381. At this council he was recognized as bishop of Constantinople, but resigned the see almost at once. Gregory's writings include his forty-five *Orations*, of which nos. 27–31, the *Theological Orations*, are most important; the **Philocalia* of Origen; a collection of letters, some against *Apollinarius; and a number of religious and secular poems.

Gregory of Nyssa, St (*c*.330–*c*.395). One of the *Cappadocian fathers, and younger brother of *Basil. Gregory was the most profound and skilful writer of the Cappadocians. Apart from important polemical works his major writings are the systematic *Catechetical Orations*, a *Life of Moses* in which mystical exegesis is used, and ascetical works such as *On Virginity* in which he develops the thought that in virginity the soul becomes a spouse of Christ.

Gregory Palamas, St (*c*.1296–1359). Greek theologian and chief exponent of *hesychasm. Nobly born and well-educated, he became a monk, and *c*.1318 went to Mount Athos where he became familiar with hesychasm. With the advance of the Turks he fled to Thessalonica where he was ordained priest in 1326, and consecrated archbishop of Thessalonica in 1347. His fame stems from his controversy with Barlaam of Calabria, which began in 1337, over the nature of Christian contemplation. Against Barlaam's extreme statement of God's unknowability, he insisted, in his *Triads in Defence of the Holy Hesychasts* (*c*. 1338), that God really communicates knowledge of himself to humans, and that the experience of the uncreated light of the Godhead in contemplation, claimed by the hesychast monks, is veridical. Although initially Palamas was condemned, he was vindicated by councils at Constantinople in 1347 and 1351 and canonized in 1363. Feast days in E., 14 Nov. and the 2nd Sunday in Lent.

Gregory Thaumaturgus, St (miracle-worker): see THAUMATURGY.

Gregory the Illuminator, St (*c*.240–*c*.325). Apostle of Armenia. He converted the king Trdat (*c*.238–314) to Christianity, which was forthwith imposed as the official religion of the country. He was later consecrated the first bishop, and the episcopate remained for some generations in his family. The *Armenian Orthodox Church is sometimes styled 'Gregorian'.

Grey Earth monastery (school of Tibetan Buddhism): see SAKYA.

Gṛhastha (Skt., 'standing in the home'). In Hinduism, the householder life-stage (*āśrama) described in **Manusmṛti*. During the gṛhastha āśrama, a man establishes a household, raises a family, and pursues worldly goals such as acquisition of wealth. At age 50 the householder is to retire to the forest.

Gṛhyakarmani (home-based offerings or sacrifices): see SACRIFICES (HINDUISM).

Gṛhyasūtras (rules governing home rituals): see SŪTRA.

Griffiths, Bede, (1907–93). Christian monk and leading figure in the development of reinforcing spiritual practice from Christian and Eastern religious roots. Griffiths said that he went to India to find the other half of his soul. In 1968, he became prior of the then failing Saccidananda Ashram (*Āśrama), putting into practice his vision of (as he entitled one of his books) *The Marriage of East and West*. He died revered in India though still suspect to some in the Vatican for an implicit syncretism—which in fact he always denied as a destruction of both traditions.

Grodzinski, Ḥayyim Ozer (1863–1940). *Talmudic scholar. As *dayyan of Vilna, Grodzinski was one of the founders of the *Orthodox Keneset Israel Organisation. He also organized the Va'ad ha-*Yeshivot (council of the Yeshivot) for the support of Polish and Lithuanian yeshivot. The author of 3 vols. of *responsa, he believed 'the large and small yeshivot were the strongholds of Judaism'.

Groote, Geert, Gerard or **Gerard the Great** (1340–84), founder of the Brothers and Sisters of the Common Life. Born of a wealthy family in Deventer, he studied theology and law at Paris. After a somewhat worldly life, he spent three years in a *Carthusian monastery, and became attracted by the teachings of *Ruysbroek. He became a powerful preacher, attacking abuses in the Church. In 1380, he and his friend, Florentius Radewijns, established a group for the development of personal piety. From this group, the Brethren developed; and in 1383, he wrote a Rule for a similar community of women. In effect, this was the creation of the Devotio Moderna, the 'up-to-date devotion' which brought the practice of the presence of God into the midst of everyday life.

Grossteste, Robert (*c*.1175–1253). Scholar, reformer, and bishop of Lincoln. One of the most successful teachers in the early 13th cent., in 1224–35 he lectured at the *Franciscan house of studies in Oxford. In 1235 he was appointed to Lincoln, and undertook a thorough visitation and reform of his diocese —which included Oxford. He translated a number of Greek works, including two by Aristotle, although in his own considerable philosophical writings he leant more heavily upon *Augustine and *Neoplatonism.

Gshen rab mi-bo-che. In *Tibetan Bon religion, the Enlightened One of the present era and source of the ordering of Bon religion. Moved by the compassion witnessed also in *bodhisattvas, he entered this world as manifestation (*rgyal tshab*) of the heavenly being, *gShen*. He engaged in stupendous battles with demons and with gods—who feared his power. He conquered them all, and acquired from them as spoil the sacred syllables of their strength. Three biographies of him remain religiously important.

gterma (class of Tibetan Buddhist texts): see TERMA.

gter. ston (discoverer of Tibetan Buddhist texts): see TERMA.

gtum mo ('Heat Yoga'): see NĀRO CHOS DRUG.

Gufu-shogyō-zen (Jap., 'fool's way of Zen'). The limited forms of Zen meditation. They are distinguished from *zazen because they focus on conventional concepts, e.g. *śūnyatā, *anātman, *anicca, etc. They have a preliminary use, for an extreme novice, but only in order to clear the way for zazen.

Guide For the Perplexed (work by Jewish philosopher): see MAIMONIDES, M.

Gūjarī, Mātā (d. 1704 CE). Wife of Gurū *Tegh Bahādur and mother of Gurū *Gobind Siṅgh. In the fighting which followed the siege of *Anaṇḍpur, she and the surviving *sāhibzāde reached Sirhind where she died after they had been betrayed to the authorities and walled up alive.

Gūji (Jap.). The chief priest of a *Shinto shrine.

Guṇa (Skt., 'strand' or 'cord'). In Hindu *Sāṁkyha, the three components, qualities, or attributes (i.e. *sattva, *tamas, and *rājas) of material nature (*prakṛti). Everything mental and physical consists of these three guṇas in varying degrees; only pure consciousness (*puruṣa) is without attributes (*nirguṇa). Disturbance of the equilibrium of the guṇas is the cause of creation, and all of creation can be classified according to the predominance of one of the three guṇas.

In Jainism, guṇa is one of the qualities which apparent objects exhibit: any substance (*dravya) has certain guṇas which appear in different modes (*parāya*).

Gunasthāna. Fourteen stages of Jain progress toward emancipation of the *jīva (cf. the Eightfold Path of Buddhism, *aṣṭangikamārga): (i) *mithyātva*, having wrong belief; (ii) *sāśadana*, tending to right belief, but prone to backsliding; (iii) *miśra*, having a mixture of right and wrong belief; (iv) *avirata samyaktva*, having right belief but not acting upon it with a commitment through vows; (v) *deśa-vrata*, taking some vows; (vi) *pramatta-vrata*, taking all vows but impeded, e.g. by illness, from keeping them; (vii) *apramatta-vrata*, unimpeded vowkeeping; (viii) *apūrva-karaṇa*, new thought activity begins; (ix) *nirvṛtti-karaṇa*, is extended; (x) *sūkṣama-sāmparyāya*, only a residue of delusion remains; (xi) *upaśānta-moha*, delusion has subsided; (xii) *kṣīna-moha*, delusion is destroyed; (xiii) *sayoga-kevalī*, the jīva is omniscient in its last body; (xiv) *ayoga-kevalī*, the jīva passes through a brief stage of non-interactive omniscience, before its complete emancipation from *karma.

Gunavrata (supplementary Jain vows): see ANUVRATA.

Gunkel, Hermann (1862–1932). *Biblical scholar. Gunkel pioneered *form criticism of biblical study. He classified the *psalms according to their liturgical use and life setting, by the methods known as *formegeschichtliche* ('form-historical') and *gattungsgeschichtliche* ('type-critical'). Although his categories have been much amended, his cultic interpretation of the Psalms, as a general approach, has endured.

Gupta dynasty. Established in N. India in 3rd cent. CE, and later covering a much larger area. It flourished *c.*350–510 CE. Under this dynasty, great heights of Hindu, Jain, and Buddhist religion and culture were achieved.

Gurbāṇī (Pañjābī, 'utterance of the Gurū'). Usually, the words of the Sikh *Gurūs and *bhagats recorded in the *Ādi Granth, itself revered as Gurū; hence also a summary term for prayer.

Gurdās Bhallā, Bhāī, (c.1551–1637). Sikh writer contemporary with four *Gurūs. Bhāī Gurdās was the son of Gurū *Amar Dās' younger brother, and died unmarried. Although of varied literary quality, his compositions are highly regarded as the 'key to the *Ādi Granth'. They are not included in this, but, with the Dasam Granth and the poetry of *Nand Lāl 'Goyā', are approved for recitation in *gurdwārās.

Gurdjieff, Georgy Ivanovich (*c.*1877–1949). Writer and one-time director of the Institute for the Harmonious Development of Man, in Paris.

In his lectures, published posthumously as *All and Everything, or Beelzebub's Tales to His Grandson* (1973), Gurdjieff traced the development of the universe from its beginnings to modern times.

Gurdjieff, who sought to synthesize Christianity and his own philosophical notions, has had a considerable influence on the thinking of such *new religious movements as the *metaphysical and *new age movements, and *Rajneeshism.

Gurdwārā (Pañjābī, gurduārā, 'gateway of the *Gurū'). A building for Sikh congregational worship in which the *Ādi Granth is appropriately installed. A gurdwārā is characterized by its function of housing the Gurū, rather than by its architecture. An upstairs room in an ordinary house in which the Ādi Granth has been ceremonially installed can be a gurdwārā.

Most famous is the impressive *Harimandir, *Amritsar. Many gurdwārās have historical associations with the Sikh Gurūs e.g. *Rakāb Gañj, *Śīś Gañj, and the *takhts.

The gurdwārā is primarily the place where the *sangat gather daily for *kīrtan to worship in the presence of the Gurū as embodied in the Ādi Granth, and it has a vital social function. *Gurpurbs and family rites are often celebrated in the gurdwārā.

Inside the gurdwārā prayer hall, furniture is minimal. The scriptures are enthroned on cushions on a *mañjī beneath a canopy. The floor is carpeted for the congregation to sit, men on one side, women on the other, facing the Ādi Granth.

Gurmat. 'The teachings of the *Gurūs', the collective teaching and disciplinary instructions of the Sikh Gurūs, and thus the Sikh name for what in English is called 'Sikhism'.

Gurmatā (Pañjābī, 'Gurū resolution'). Decision affecting Sikh community, taken before the *Gurū—now in the presence of *Ādi Granth.

Gurmukh (Pañjābī, 'person oriented towards the *Gurū'). A pious Sikh responsive to the Gurū's word. In contrast to the *manmukh, the gurmukh embodies the living teaching of the *Ādi Granth.

Gurmukhī (Pañjābī, 'from the mouth of the *Gurū'). Sacred script of the Sikhs. The Gurmukhī alphabet consists of thirty-five letters and is simpler than, but closely related to, the Devanāgrī script used for Sanskrit and Hindī.

Gurpurb (Pañjābī, 'rising of a Gurū'). Sikh festival associated with an event in the *Gurūs' lives. The dates of Gurpurbs vary within twenty-eight days as they are lunar. In Britain, most gurdwārās celebrate Gurpurbs on the Sunday nearest the actual day. The most important Gurpurbs are Gurū *Nānak's birthday, celebrated on the full moon of Kārttika (Oct.–Nov.), Gurū *Gobind Siṅgh's birthday, celebrated in Pauṣa (Dec.–Jan.), and the *martyrdoms (*śahīd din*) of Gurū *Arjan Dev and Gurū *Tegh Bahādur, observed respectively in Jyaiṣṭha (May–June) and Mārgaśīrsa (Nov.–Dec.). The martyrdoms of the *Sāhibzāde are commemorated in Pauṣa. Many Gurpurbs are observed only or chiefly at the site of the original event—e.g. the birthday of Gurū *Har Krishan at Delhi (July) and the anniversary of the installation of the Gurū Granth Sāhib (*Ādi Granth) at *Amritsar (Sept.).

Guru (Skt., 'heavy'). A teacher, initially of worldly skills or knowledge, hence a parent or a schoolteacher; but more often a teacher of religious knowledge or conveyor of spiritual insight and liberation (*mokṣa) in Indian religions, especially among Hindus and Sikhs. The term is often synonymous with *ācārya, though the latter is also used for the teacher of a skill. Guru should also be distinguished from *paṇḍita, a scholar or learned man.

In *Vaiṣṇavism, *Śaivism, and *Tantrism the guru is the means whereby the tradition is conveyed through the generations and teachings are authenticated through the guru lineage (*paramparā). With the development of *bhakti, devotion to the guru as a means of liberation became a central practice, especially in the *Sant tradition.

Buddhism has perhaps laid less stress on the guru than Hinduism, though the idea of the teacher as the conveyor of spiritual insight is still important. The idea of the guru is now found in modern W. religious movements some of which have developed directly out of Indian traditions such as *Transcendental Meditation, the *Hare Krishna (*International Society . . .), and *Rajneesh movements.

Conceptions of the guru vary from that of one who is identical with God and conveys liberation (mokṣa), the *sat guru, to that of the guru as a guide, showing beings the way but not actually bestowing liberation. For example, in monistic *Kashmir Śaivism the guru is identical with God (*parameśvara), whereas in dualistic *Śaiva Siddhānta he is distinct from God (*Śiva).

See Index, guru.

Among Sikhs, the term refers primarily to Gurū Nānak and his nine successors, *Aṅgad, *Amar Dās, *Rām Dās, *Arjan Dev, *Hargobind, *Har Rāi, *Har Krishan, *Tegh Bahādur, and *Gobind *Siṅgh. All manifested the one divine light, just as one lamp is lit from another. This belief in the essential oneness of the Gurūs is central to Sikhism. On the death of Gobind Siṅgh, Gurūship was vested in the *Ādi Granth (Gurū Granth *Sāhib) and the *Khālsā community. Sikhs venerate the Ādi Granth as Gurū.

Gurū Granth Sahib. (Sikh Scripture): see ĀDI GRANTH.

Gurū-kā-laṅgar. Sikh free kitchen, refectory. In every *gurdwārā vegetarian food is cooked and served free to people of any *caste, race, and creed with no order of precedence, although men and women usually sit separately. In major gurdwārās thousands are fed daily.

Gurumantra. The *mantra passed on to a pupil by a *guru, during initiation, which the pupil makes his own (by constant repetition), but also keeps secret.

Guruparampara (lineage of spiritual teachers): see PARAMPARĀ.

Gush Emunim. Organization of the faithful, a Jewish religious and nationalist group of the 20th cent. It was led by Tzevi Yehudah Kook (1891–1982), the only son of Abraham Isaac *Kook. Gush Emunim took the initiative in establishing Jewish settlements in the Administered Areas of Palestine/Israel after the Six Day War in 1967.

Gute kvitl (Yiddish greeting): see BOOK OF LIFE.

Gutiérrez, G. (theologian): see LIBERATION THEOLOGY.

Guṭkā (Pañjābī, 'manual'). Book of devotions. Sikhs use this term to refer to the breviaries including the *Nitnem and the *Sukhmanī.

Gymnastics, Taoist. This refers to the Chinese Tao-yin, meaning literally 'to guide' or 'conduct': stretching and bending exercises to facilitate permeation of 'vital breath' (*ch'i) throughout the body. The version best known today is the formalized, adagio-dance-like *t'ai-chi-ch'üan* practised daily by millions of people in E. Asia, and nowadays elsewhere as well.

Gymnosophists. 'Naked philosophers', referred to by Greek historians from the time of Alexander's invasion of India (327–326 BCE) to the 5th cent. CE. Pliny's description of them sitting naked in one posture and inflicting hardships on themselves suggests that they were possibly *Digambara Jain monks.

Gyōgi or **Gyōki** (668–749). Hossō (*Dōshō) monk who popularized Buddhism through his selfless activities. He was a descendant of a Korean king, and studied Buddhism at the Yakushi-ji. But instead of remaining monastery-based, he travelled about, building roads, temples, and bridges—and performing magical signs. Knowing of his high regard among the people, the emperor Shōmu asked him to undertake the building of the *daibutsu at Todai-ji. He was also believed popularly to be the incarnation of *Mañjuśrī.

Gyō-jū-za-ga (Jap, 'walking, sitting, lying'). The Zen Buddhist emphasis that Zen attentiveness can and must be maintained, in all circumstances.

Gyulü ('Illusory Body' in Tibetan Buddhism): see NĀRO CHOS DRUG.

H

Ha-Ari (Jewish kabbalist): see LURIA, ISAAC BEN SOLOMON.

Ḥabad (Heb., acronym of Ḥokmah, Bīnah, Da'at: wisdom, discrimination, knowledge). A religious and intellectual movement within Jewish *ḥasidism. Founded by *Shne'ur Zalman and based on Isaac *Luria's *Kabbalah and the doctrines of the Baal Shem Tov (*Israel ben Eliezer), the terms Ḥokmah, Binah, Da'at (ḤBD) are understood as *sefirot (emanations) in the divine mind. The Ḥabad *Zaddik is essentially a spiritual leader, and the Ḥabad were the first ḥasidic group to found *yeshivot. Shne'ur Zalman was succeeded by his son, Dov Baer, who settled in Lubavich, with the consequence that Ḥabad and Lubavich are now interchangeable terms (though in fact there was a diffuse spread of Ḥabad movements). Today their main centres of activity are in Israel and the USA.

Central to Ḥabad is the belief that humans created in the image of God mirror the three sefirot within the divine mind.

Therefore a profoundly joyous experience must be expected when 'like meets like', hence the celebratory nature of Ḥabad assemblies. This emerges from *bittul ha-yesh*, 'annihilation of that which is'. This is the loss of the individual, grasping ego in the adoration of God, but it is, also, the belief that a part of the *Ein-Sof lies within human nature: through annihilation of all else that surrounds it, the one is left with the One, and there is no distinction between them.

Habakkuk, Book of (Vulgate *Habacuc*). One of the *Minor Prophets of the Hebrew Bible and Christian Old Testament. A commentary on Habakkuk is among the most important of the *Dead Sea Scrolls.

Ḥaber (member of Jewish group): see ḤAVER.

Habiru (*'prw* of the Egyptian Tel el-Amarna letters, *hab/hapiru* in correspondence of Amenophis III and IV). A group or groups of people mentioned in Middle Eastern documents from the 18th to 12th cents. BCE. There has been much scholarly speculation as to the connection between the Habiru and the Hebrews (Heb., *'ibri*), but identity between the two is unlikely.

Habit, religious. Distinctive dress worn by members of religious orders. In W. Christianity, these are usually white (*Cistercians), brown (*Franciscans), or black (*Dominicans). In addition to the main garment, it usually includes a girdle (often with three knots for the vows of poverty, chastity, and obedience), scapular (a long piece of cloth worn on the shoulders and hanging down back and front, symbolizing the yoke of Christ), and a hood (for men) or veil (for women).

In E. Orthodoxy, the different habits reflect different stages in the monastic life. A beginner wears the *proschema*, with an inner and outer *cassock-type garment (*rason*), with a leather belt, a round cap, and sandals. The next stage may substitute a cloak (*mandyas*) for the outer *rason*, which in any case will be fuller; a wooden cross is worn. The final stage introduces something like a scapular (*analavos*) which is decorated with representations of the instruments of the *Passion. There may also be a hood or cowl (*koukoulos*).

In E. religions, the equivalent of the religious habit appears with varying degrees of formality. In the Buddhist *saṅgha, a three-part dress was adopted: the lower body is clothed in the *antaravasaka* (a kind of sarong); the *uttarasaṅgha* or *cīvara* in Thailand (a length of woven cloth) surrounds the upper body; and the *saṅghati* or *kaṣāya* (a patchwork cloth to symbolize poverty) is worn over the left shoulder. *Kaṣāya* ('earth-coloured') refers to the 'impure' (aged or faded) colour of the cloth, in contrast to pure (bleached) white: it is the yellow dye used to create this effect which leads to the characteristic 'saffron robe'. For the Japanese habit, see SANNE.

Taoist ritual functionaries wear a cloak (*chiang-i*) which has on it symbols of the cosmos with which the ritual is making connection.

In Judaism, the specialized garments of the *Temple functionaries ceased with the destruction of the Temple. A rabbi has no specialized ritual role, and therefore wears the same 'religious habit' in the *synagogue as any other man in the assembly: *tallit (prayer shawl with *zitzit, tassels), *tefillin (phylacteries), and kippah or *yarmulke (skull-cap).

Among Sikhs, formal dress requirements apply only to *amritdhārī Sikhs (see FIVE KS), but some customs have also established themselves.

For Muslim veiling, see HIJĀB. See also Index, Dress.

Hachimaki (white cloth of samurai): see KAMIKAZE.

Hachiman (Jap., 'eight banners'). A popular Shinto deity, often associated with good fortune in war. The worship of Hachiman spread quickly in early Japan, and by the 8th cent. CE a distinctive Shinto cult devoted to Hachiman had developed.

In Japanese Buddhism, Hachiman was integrated as H. *Daibosatsu, the Great *Bodhisattva, the first Shinto deity to be so treated. He is regarded as the incarnation of *Amida.

Hadad. A god of the Amorites and *Canaanites.

Hadassah. The women's *Zionist organization of America. According to its constitution, Hadassah is dedicated to 'the ideals of Judaism, Zionism, American democracy, healing, teaching and medical research'. It was founded in the USA early in the 20th cent.

Ḥadath (Arab.). Ritual impurity for a Muslim, major or minor, which can only be eliminated by appropriate ablutions, *ghusl or *wuḍū'*.

Ḥadd (Arab., *hadda*, 'determine'; often in pl., *ḥudūd*). A boundary or limit set by God, in *Qur'ān of laws laid down, e.g. on fasting (2. 187), divorce (2. 229 f.). It came to mean unalterable punishments, especially stoning or beating for sexual intercourse outside the permitted relationships (*zinā'); beating for false accusations of adultery, or for drinking intoxicants; cutting off of the hand for theft.

Among *Sūfīs, ḥadd (but more often the part. *maḥdūd*) refers to the finiteness of humans in contrast to God.

Hadewijch of Antwerp (Christian mystical writer): see RHENO-FLEMISH SPIRITUALITY.

Ḥad Gadya (Aram., 'only one kid'). Folk-song chanted at the end of the Passover *Seder. It is a sequence poem.

Ḥadīth (Arab., 'narrative'). Muslim tradition—accounts of the 'words, deeds or silent approval' of *Muḥammad during the period of his preaching, but especially after the beginning of the *Qur'ān revelations. Although the plural is *ahādith*, Hadith is used in English as a collective for 'traditions', as well as the word for a single tradition.

A ḥadīth—a single item of tradition—consists of two parts: *matn* ('text') and *isnād* or *sanad* ('chain of authorities'). An elaborate science of ḥadīth criticism grew up, mainly to ensure the authenticity of any given ḥadīth. Of the major collections of Ḥadith, the best known and most quoted is the Ṣaḥīḥ (Sound Collection) of *al-Bukhārī (d. 870). A second important collection is the Ṣaḥīḥ of *Muslim b. al-Hajjāj (d. 875), and those two are known as the 'two Ṣaḥīḥ'. Next in importance are those of *al-Tirmidhī (d. 892), *al-Nasā'ī (d. 915), Ibn Māja (d. 886), and *Abū Dāwūd (d. 888). Together these form the 'six books' of reference.

The *Shī'a have their own collections of ḥadīth, which they accuse the *Sunnis of having deliberately ignored or concealed, which extol the virtues of *'Alī b. Abī Ṭālib and the Twelve *Imāms. The earliest authoritative collection is *Al-kāfī fī 'Ilm al-Dīn*, of Abu Ja'far.

See Index, Hadith.

Hadj (pilgrimage): see ḤAJJ.

Ḥaḍra (present only to God): see GHAIBA.

Haeceitas (idea of individual uniqueness): see DUNS SCOTUS, J.

Haedong Kosŭng Jŏn (Lives of Eminent Korean Monks). One of the most important sources dealing with the history of *Buddhism in Korea. The work was compiled by scholar-monk Kakhun in 1215.

Ḥafets Ḥayyim or **Israel Meir ha-Kohen Kagan** (1838–1933). Jewish writer and source of inspiration for *Orthodox Jews. Born in Lithuania, he settled at Radun in Poland, where a group gathered around him which was known as the Ḥafets Ḥayyim *yeshivah of Radun. The name (by which he was subsequently known) was taken from his first book, which he published anonymously, in 1873, under that title. He helped in the founding of an extreme Orthodox movement, *Agadut Israel.

Ḥāfiẓ (one who learns the Qur'ān by heart): see QUR'ĀN.

Ḥafṣa. Wife of *Muḥammad. Although divorced after a domestic quarrel, she was later taken back. She is said to have owned the first written version of the Qur'ān.

Haftarah (Heb., 'conclusion'). A *synagogue reading from the biblical *prophets. The second reading in the synagogue on *Sabbaths, *Festivals, and on the afternoons of fast days is taken from the prophetic books.

Hagar. The servant of *Sarah who was given as concubine of *Abraham and became the mother of *Ishmael (Genesis 16. 1–16).

In Islam, Hagar is the wife of Ibrāhīm (*Abraham), who was sent out by him, with their son Ismā'īl (Ishmael), into the desert. Hagar's running between two small hills, in search of water, is said to be the origin of the rite of *sa'y, 'running' between Ṣafā and Marwa, which is part of the ritual of *'umra.

Hagbahah, gelilah (Heb., 'lifting and rolling'). The ceremonial elevating and rolling up of the *Torah *scroll in the *synagogue.

Haggadah (Heb., 'telling'; equivalent to *aggadah, and often used in that general sense). The order of service prescribed for the Jewish *Passover *seder.

Extra songs, poetry, and elaborations have been added to the original Haggadah over the years and, since the time of *Rashi, commentaries on the text have been produced. The *progressive movements have produced their own versions, amending the text in accordance with their own theology, and there is also a *Karaite version.

Haggai. Post-*exilic Jewish *prophet. The prophecies contained in Haggai can be dated to 520 BCE (the second year of King Darius) and are concerned primarily with the reconstruction of the Temple.

Hag ha-keves (Doenmeh festival): see DOENMEH.

Hagia Sofia, Aya Sofya, or **Sancta Sophia** ('Divine Wisdom'). The mosque, originally basilica or church of the Divine Wisdom, in Istanbul. It was commissioned in the 6th cent. by the emperor Justinian after the second church on the site (founded in 452 by Theodosius II) had been razed to the ground in the Nika revolts of Jan. 532. In the late 16th cent. as part of a restoration process, minarets were added by the architect Sīhān (see SULAIMĀN THE MAGNIFICENT). The last extensive restoration was commissioned by Sultan Abdul Mecit in 1847, and the Aya Sofia continued to function as a mosque until 1932 when it was opened as a museum.

Hagiographa (third section of Jewish scriptures): see WRITINGS.

Hagiography. The writing of the lives of Christian *saints (hence a derogatory sense, 'full of praise for, without sufficient criticism of, the subject').

Ha-Gra (Jewish spiritual leader): see ELIJAH BEN SOLOMON ZALMAN.

Hahalis Welfare Society. A religious and economic development movement with some *cargo ideas on Buka Island, Papua New Guinea. In 1952, two former students in *Roman Catholic schools, John Teosin (b. 1938) and his brother-in-law, Francis Hagai, formed a family co-operative which in 1957 developed into a co-operative society involving half the Buka population in plantations, stores, transport, etc. In 1961, they set up their own 'church'.

Hai ben Sherira (939–1038). Jewish *gaon of *Pumbedita, hence also known as Hai Gaon. Hai succeeded his father as gaon and was regarded as a supreme *halakhic authority. Besides *responsa, he also wrote mystical *piyyutim, including five *seliḥot for 9 *Av, marked by a somewhat gloomy assessment of our present condition. He had considerable influence on the leaders of Spanish Jewry such as *Samuel ha-Nagid.

Haibutsu kishaku. Jap. slogan, 'abolish Buddhism, destroy Buddhist images', adopted during the *Meiji determination to establish Shinto as the state religion, in separation from Buddhism. The period of aggression lasted from 1868 to 1874.

Haiden (Jap.), The frontmost building in a Shinto shrine complex, used as an oratory or hall of worship.

Hai Gaon: see HAI BEN SHERIRA.

Haiku (Jap.). A verse form consisting of three lines: five, seven, and five syllables in length. Traditionally, each poem also contains an image or reference associated with one of the seasons in the year. Originally conceived as a form of amusement verse, the haikai utilized colloquialisms and words derived from Chinese, terms expressly forbidden in the more formal, high form of verse called *waka*. Only in the early 16th cent. did haikai come to be viewed as a legitimate poetic genre in its own right.

Mainly through the impact of Matsuo Bashō (1644–94) and his successors, the literary form assumed religious, specifically *Zen Buddhist, dimensions.

Hail Mary (tr. of Lat., *Ave Maria*). A prayer to the Virgin *Mary as follows: (*a*) Hail Mary, full of grace, the Lord is with you; blessed are you among women, and blessed is the fruit of your womb, Jesus. (*b*) Holy Mary, Mother of God, pray for us sinners now and in the hour of our death.

Hair. Hair is a visible and continuous sign of growth (or, in its cessation, of the approach of death), and as an indication of vigour, it lends itself to various statements of relationship to God or to other goals—e.g., the *Nazirite vow in Judaism. Christianity adopted a sign of dedication in the opposite direction, by introducing the tonsure, the shaving of the top of the head of priests and monks. Tonsure has taken different forms, from the shaving of the whole head to only a part, often leaving a fringe to draw out the symbolism of the crown of thorns.

In E. religions, comparable contrasts can be found. Thus among Hindus, *keśāntah*, the first shaving of the beard, is one of the *saṃskāras; but a Hindu *ascetic will leave his hair long and matted (*juṭā*): *Śiva, in particular, displays his contrasted modes of activity through the style of his hair. Among Sikhs, a *Khālsā Sikh is prohibited from cutting hair from any part of his body, and *keś* is one of the *Five Ks. Among *Rastafarians, a similar message of identity is sent through hairstyle, but this may be by 'dreadlocks' or by careful cutting (for the long locks of Jews see PEOT). A further extension can be seen in care taken to cover the head—for example, in the custom for some Jewish women of wearing a wig (*shaytl/sheitel*) in public (see HEAD, COVERING OF).

To bring order into this diversity, E. Leach ('Magical Hair'), *Journ. of the R. Anth. Inst.* 1958) argued that the treatment of hair denotes social responses related to ideal social categories. Thus long hair is related to unrestrained sexuality, short or tightly bound hair is related to restricted sexuality, closely shaved hair is related to celibacy. C. R. Hallpike ('Social Hair', *Man*, 1969) argued that hair rituals cannot be mapped on to sexual opportunity alone. In his view, the treatment indicates relation to the acceptance or rejection of social control.

Ḥajj (Arab.). Pilgrimage to *Mecca, specifically to the *Ka'ba, during the month *Dhū'l-Ḥijja. This is one of the *Five Pillars of Islam, a duty ordered in the *Qur'ān (3. 91/97). This is incumbent upon every adult free Muslim, of sound mind, with sufficient funds to cover his journey and the expenses of his family during his absence. *Women should be suitably escorted.

The general term ḥajj includes the *'umra (lesser pilgrimage) to the Ka'ba, which can be performed at any time of the year but does not itself fulfil the obligations of ḥajj.

The area around Mecca is designated *ḥarām (holy); the male pilgrim on reaching the boundary exchanges his usual clothes for two pieces of white cloth, covering the upper and lower parts of the body, and wears sandals; women, also in white, cover their whole body except face and hands. The pilgrim has now entered the state of *iḥrām, and until the end of the ḥajj ceremonies he must not put on other clothes, wear shoes, cut nails or hair, engage in sexual relations, take part in arguments, fighting, nor hunting of game. The *talbīyah is repeated frequently.

In Mecca itself the pilgrim goes first to the *Masjid al-Ḥarām for the rites of *ṭawāf, 'circumambulation' of the Ka'ba, and of *sa'y, 'running', and will if possible kiss the *Black Stone. The ḥajj proper begins on the seventh day, with a *khuṭba (sermon) at the *mosque. On the eighth day, all pilgrims move eastwards from Mecca, spending that night at Minā or, further on, at *'Arafāt. On the ninth day, the central and essential part of ḥajj takes place, the *wuqūf* ('standing') at 'Arafāt, before a small hill named Jabal al-Raḥma. Then pilgrims hurry back to the small town of Muzdalifa within the Meccan boundaries, to stay overnight. On the tenth day, which is *'Id al-Aḍḥā, they move to Minā, first to throw seven small stones (see RAJM) at a rock called Jamrat al-'Aqaba, then to perform the ritual *sacrifice. From Minā the pilgrims return to Mecca to perform another ṭawāf; then the head can be shaved, or the hair cut, and the state of iḥrām is over.

Ḥājjī Bektāsh Valī (founder of Turkish Derwish order): see BEKTĀSHĪYYA.

Ḥakham (Heb., 'wise'). *Rabbinic title. Originally the title ḥakham was used for scholars, especially in early days, who had not received rabbinic *semikhah. The title fell into oblivion at the end of the First World War.

Ḥakham Zevi (Jewish halakhist): see ASHKENAZI, ZEVI.

Hakhel (Heb., 'assemble'). The Jewish seventh year assembly (in Deuteronomy 31. 10–12). The practice has not been followed since the destruction of the *Temple, but since the establishment of the state of *Israel there has been an attempt to revive the ceremony.

Hākim (last and greatest of divine manifestations): see DRUZES.

Hakkafot (Heb., 'circuits'). Jewish ceremonial circular processions. This practice is continued in the *synagogue when the *Torah *scrolls are carried round on *Simḥat Torah. Hakkafot are also performed in some communities by brides encircling their husbands during the *wedding ceremony, and round the coffin before the burial (see CIRCUMAMBULATION).

Hakuin (c.1685–1768). Ordination name of Nagasawa Ekaku, a major Japanese *Zen master, painter, and poet. Hakuin is especially noted for his vigorous revitalization of *Rinzai-shū spiritual training and for his bold style of inkwash painting. His teacher, Dōkyō Etan, refused to recognize an early experience of *satori, and set him to more severe Zen training. In his own teaching, he emphasized the three pillars of Zen (see DAI-FUNSHI) and kōan practice: he is the source of the most frequently (in the W.) quoted kōan, 'What is the sound of one hand clapping?', which is known as *sekishu*. He was abbot of several monasteries, including Ryūtaki-ji, (active to the present day), and he emphasized disciplined meditation at all times (not just at chosen times) in order to achieve *kensho.

Hakushi (Jap., 'white paper'). The state of consciousness in Zen Buddhism attained through *zazen, which immediately precedes enlightenment.

Hakuun Ryōko Yasutani (1885–1973). Japanese Zen Buddhist master. He spent much time visiting the USA, and his instructions in Zen underlie P. Kapleau (ed.), *The Three Pillars of Zen* (1980).

Ḥāl (Arab., 'state', 'inner condition'; pl. *aḥwāl*). Among *Sūfīs, those thoughts and conditions which come upon the heart without intention or desire, such as sorrow, fear, pleasure, ecstasy, anger, or even lust. In their religious forms, they are such states, in relation to God, as confidence, peace, love, attentiveness, nearness, certitude.

Halāhala (poison drunk by Śiva): see CHURNING OF THE OCEAN.

Halakhah (Heb., from *halak*, 'he went'). A particular *law or the whole Jewish legal system. The halakhah is traditionally believed to go back in its entirety to *Moses. The halakhah is composed of the written law (the *six hundred and thirteen commandments of the *Pentateuch), the statements handed down by tradition (such as the words of the *prophets and the hagiographa (*Writings), the *oral law (which includes interpretations of the written law), the sayings of the *scribes, and established religious custom. Written law is *Torah she-bi-khetav*, oral law is *Torah she-be'al peh* ('... by mouth'). See Index, Halakhah.

Halal (released from prohibition): see AL-HALAL WA'L-HARĀM.

Halevi, Judah (Jewish philosopher and poet): see JUDAH HALEVI.

Ḥaliza or **ḥalitsa** (Heb.). 'Taking off the shoe', part of the ritual arising from *levirate marriage if the brother of a dead man (without male descendant) wishes to repudiate his obligation to marry the widow. The description is in Deuteronomy (25. 5–10).

Ḥallah. Type of dough or bread, or a portion, set aside for the *priest in ancient Judaism. The laws governing ḥallah are found in the tractate of that name in *Mishnah and the subsequent writings dependent on Mishnah.

Hallāj (Sūfī): see AL-HALLĀJ.

Hallel. Psalms 113–18. The full Hallel is chanted in *synagogue on the first day of *Passover, on *Sukkot and on *Ḥanukkah. It is also recited in two parts during the Passover *seder.

Hallelujah. Hebrew (biblical) expression of praise. Hallelujah occurs twenty-three times in Psalms and means 'praise the Lord' (*halelu-Yah*).

Hallelujah religion. A group of new movements among Amerindian peoples in the interior of Guyana and across into neighbouring states. The 19th-cent. origins are obscure, pointing to Christian mission contacts and including a Makushi, Bichy Wung, who is believed to have visited England where, in a dream, God gave him the new Hallelujah religion (so-named from the shouting of 'Hallelujah' in worship). After his death, it spread to the Akawaio whose own prophet Abel (d. 1911?), after visiting heaven and receiving prayer-songs, reformed the religion which had drifted back into traditional *shamanist forms. With Anglican assistance, Hallelujah became affiliated in 1977 to the Guyana Council of Churches and secured more recognition from the government.

Halloween or **All Hallows Eve.** A Christian festival on 31st Oct., the evening before All Saints, 1 Nov. It absorbed and adopted the *Celtic new year festival, the eve and day of Samhain; as such, it was a time of reversals associated with liminality (see RITES OF PASSAGES), and much of this character has persisted in the now secularized customs associated with Halloween, especially in the USA.

Halo. Circular symbol of holiness or enlightenment, surrounding the head of the person thus distinguished. In Buddhist iconography, halos surround *arhats, *buddhas, and *bodhisattvas, often infilled with designs borrowed from *maṇḍalas. They are found in Christian art from the 3rd cent. for Christ alone; then from the 5th cent. for Mary, saints, and angels also. In the Middle Ages Christ's nimbus was distinguished, usually with a cross. In the case of Christ and the Virgin Mary (and the Persons of the Trinity), the halo is extended to a gilt background, indicating glory, called the aureole. In early Byzantine art, it is of an oval shape and is known as *mandorla* (Ital., 'almond-shaped').

Ha-Maggid (Jewish ḥasidic leader): see DOV BAER.

Hamallism. A W. African Islamic brotherhood. It began from the attempt in Mali of a mystic within the *Sūfī and *Tijāniyya tradition, al-Akhdar (1909), to restore original Tijāni practices. In 1925 his saintly disciple, a half-Fulani, Hamahu'ullah ben Muhammad ben Seydina Omar (1886–1943), now known as Hamallah, formed a separate Tijāni brotherhood, whose aggressive reforming and missionary activities led to violent clashes with the Tijāniyya order and the French colonial regime. As a modernizing African Islam, Hamallism appealed to young élites as an ally against Arab and French influence, and was identified with the struggle for political independence, but has since gone into decline.

Haman. Evil opponent of Jews in *Esther. When his name occurs during the reading of Esther, at *Purim, it is shouted down, because the name of evil-doers must be 'blotted out'.

Ḥamdala (formula of blessing): see BASMALA.

Ḥamesh Megillot (five *books of Hebrew scripture): see SCROLLS, FIVE.

Ḥamez or **ḥamets** (raising agent forbidden to Jews in Passover): see LEAVEN.

Haṁsa. Wild goose (the bar-headed goose), which migrates to India from Central Asia. Its purity of colour and gracefulness in flight led to its becoming a symbol, in the *Upaniṣads, of the unity at the heart of all manifestation, e.g. one spirit in the midst of the world. It is also the vehicle (*vāhana) of *Brahmā.

Haṁsa. Indian *mantra, often repeated, *so'ham*, 'He am I' (while *breathing in), *hamṣaḥ*, 'I am He' (while breathing out). It expresses the unity of the devotee with God.

Ḥamza b. 'Alī b. Aḥmad. A founder of the *Druze movement, the details of whose life are uncertain. He lived in the 5th cent. AH (11th cent. CE). He is regarded by the Druzes as the last incarnation (*qā'im al-zamān*) of *'aql* (universal intelligence), and produced one of the two fundamental works of the movement, *Al-naqd al-Khafi* (copy of the Secret). For his seven precepts, see DRUZES.

Hanafi Muslims. A black American Muslim group, founded by Hamaas Abdul Khaalis in 1958, when he left the Nation of Islam (see ELIJAH MUHAMMAD; BLACK MUSLIMS). The movement aims to adhere to the *Ḥanafite school, regarding the parent movement as too much compromised by the American way of life.

Ḥanafites. The followers of a religious school named after the jurist *Abū Ḥanīfa, which grew out of the old Kufan and Basran law schools. Two of Abū Ḥanīfa's pupils, Abū Yūsuf Ya'kub (d. 795 (AH 182)) and Muḥammad b. al-Ḥasan al-Shaybānī (d. 805 (AH 189)) were more responsible for the authoritative development of the law school than Abū Ḥanīfa himself. The Ḥanafites are distinguished from the other law schools by recognizing that *Qur'ān and *ḥadīth are not sufficient for all issues, so that *qiyās and *ra'y* (personal opinion) are legitimate.

Nowadays this school prevails in Iraq, Syria, Turkey, USSR (Turkistan, Bukhara, and Samarkand), China, Afghanistan, India, and Pakistan.

Hana Matsuri (flower festival): see FESTIVALS AND FASTS (JAPANESE).

Ḥanbalites. One of the four main law schools of *sharī'a which developed from the teachings of the theologian Aḥmad *ibn Ḥanbal (d. 855 (AH 241)). Ḥanbal established no system of his own, but his pronouncements over legal problems were systematized by such followers as Abu Bakr al-Khallal (d. 924 (AH 311)). This school was an orthodox reaction against the excesses of esoteric *Sufism (though certainly not against all Sūfīs) and speculative theology. The Ḥanbalite school is characterized by its literal and dogmatic nature. It recognizes no other source than the Qur'ān and the *Sunna in Islamic law. At the present time, because of their proselytizing efforts in Africa and the East, and because of secularizing threats to Islam, the Ḥanbalites are becoming increasingly influential.

Hand of Fāṭima (Arab., *yad Fāṭima*, also known as *al-kaff*, 'the palm'). Decorated hand or palm, common in Islam as a *charm. It has no connection with *Fāṭima, the daughter of *Muḥammad.

Hands, laying on of. An action suggesting ideas of blessing, consecration, and the transmission of spiritual power. It is accordingly used in most Christian rites of *confirmation, *ordination, and *healing.

Hands, washing of: see ABLUTIONS.

Handsome Lake or **Longhouse Religion,** a movement embracing some 5,000 Iroquois on Indian reservations in New York state, Ontario, and Quebec. It is probably the oldest continuing tribal prophet movement in the world. It was founded by Ganioda'yo (Seneca, 'Handsome lake') (1735–1815). Ganioda'yo's teaching became fixed in a Code which is recited once in two years by authorized 'preachers', and helps maintain 'Indianness'.

Ha-nerot hallalu (prayer): see ḤANUKKAH.

Han Hsiang-tzu (one of the Eight Immortals in Taoism): see PA-HSIEN.

Ḥanīf (Arab., pl. *hunafā'*; probably from Syriac *ḥanpē*, 'pagans'). In the *Qur'ān, a believer in the One God; a seeker after truth; it is sometimes equivalent to *muslim* in the broadest sense of a worshipper of *Allāh.

Hannya (Jap.). Direct and immediate insight in Zen Buddhism, based on (Skt.) *prajña.

Han-shan (Jap., Kanzan). A Chinese layperson, who practised Ch'an Buddhism in his own style, in approximately the 7th cent. CE. He wrote poems on any surface available, some of which were later collected in *Han-shan-shih* (Poems from Cold Mountain). He undertook no formal training or discipline, but did consult Feng-kan (Jap., Bukan) in the monastery, Ku'o-ching, in *dokusan. A cook's assistant, Shih-te, supplied Han-shan with food, and together the two realized the buddha-nature (*buddhatā) more profoundly than most of the monks. The two have become symbols (extremely common in Zen art) of the lay approach to enlightenment; they are sometimes represented with Feng-kan and a tiger, all lying down in sleep together.

Han Shu (History of the Hạn): see HISTORIES IN CHINA.

Ḥanukkah (Heb., 'Dedication'). Jewish Festival of Lights. Ḥanukkah begins on 25 Kislev and lasts for eight days. According to 1 *Maccabees* 4. 36–59, Judas *Maccabee purified the *Temple after the *Hellenistic desecration and rededicated it on 25 Kislev. Celebrations lasted for eight days. The story of one day's supply of the holy oil miraculously lasting eight days is legendary and dates back to the days of the *tannaim. After the lamp is lit, a short prayer beginning, 'Ha-nerot hallalu' (These lamps) is recited. A short summary of the Ḥanukkah story is included in the *Amida and during the course of *grace after meals. Card-playing is traditionally associated with the festival, as is spinning the *dreidel* (spinning-top). The Ḥanukkah lamp or *menorah is a prominent ritual object in every Jewish household, and has become a vehicle for the display of artistic craftsmanship.

Hanumān, Hanumat, or **Sundara** (the beautiful). A major character in the **Rāmāyaṇa*, the monkey-king, or chief, Mahāvīra ('great hero'). He led a band of monkeys, or ape-like creatures, who gave vital assistance to *Rāma in the rescue of *Sītā from *Rāvaṇa's kingdom of Laṅkā. He is a symbol of strength and loyalty, and is patron of wrestlers.

For the *bhakta* (devotee to God, *bhakti), Hanumān is the symbol of *dāsya*, the servant in relation to the master.

Hanuman-nāṭaka or ***Mahānāṭaka.*** An epic play, in fourteen long acts, portraying the adventures of Hanumān.

Han Yü (786–824). Taoist writer, of exemplary prose style, who was a fierce defender of Confucianism, not simply against Buddhism, but also against the widespread and tolerant eclecticism which accepted Buddhism and Taoism as complementary to Confucianism. Although not effective in public life because of his uncompromising attitude, he was 'rediscovered' in the 10th-cent. Confucian revival, and became a hero of that movement. Han Yü ended his days in exile in S. China.

Ḥaqq (Arab.). The true, the real, that which is exactly opposite to *bāṭil*, the unreal, the transitory. Al-Haqq is thus supremely the title of God in the Qur'ān. He alone is absolute, all else is derived from him, and is dependent on him for each moment of its existence.

Hara (Skt., 'seizer'). A name of *Śiva. He is sometimes represented iconographically as Hari-Hara, appearing as a single god representing the two principal deities *Viṣṇu and Śiva.

Harai or **harae** (Jap., *harau*, 'to sweep or cleanse'). *Shinto rite of *exorcism or purification. It refers principally to ritual purification brought on by the waving of a sacred wand in order to prepare for worship. In other contexts, it may also refer to ritual cleansing (*misogi) or other acts of atonement.

Hara-kiri (Jap.). The means through which Japanese (Shinto and Zen) demonstrate mastery of death through *seppuku*, by cutting into the hara—the inner part of the body beneath the abdomen, which is believed to be the vital centre of life and control.

Ḥaram (Arab., not to be confused with *ḥarām). A sacred enclave, or territory, whose sanctity makes it immune from certain practices (e.g. hunting, tree-felling, trading), being set apart and hallowed for purposes of pilgrimage. The ḥaram at *Mecca is the supreme example.

In a wider sense, it is the term used for *women's apartments inaccessible to strangers—i.e. the harem (*ḥarīm*).

Harām (things prohibited in Islam): see AL-HALAL WA'L-HARĀM.

Harappā. Archaeological site and modern name of a city of the *Indus Valley civilization, on the left bank of the Rāvī River in the Pañjāb, in what is now Pakistan. Harappā was the first of two major Indus Valley cities to be discovered by archaeologists; hence the Indus Valley civilization is designated the 'Harappā culture'. The site of Harappā was first excavated, 1924–1931, and again after the Second World War.

Hardwār (Haridvāra, 'Viṣṇu's Gate'). One of the seven *sacred cities of Hindus. It is at the place where the *Gangā leaves the mountains and begins its transverse across the plains.

Haredim (Heb., 'those who tremble'). Jews who observe the tenets of their religion with care. The word is derived from Isaiah 66. 5. They do not constitute a distinct sect: the term, rather, covers those who seek to maintain traditional and *Orthodox Judaism in the midst, not only of a *secularizing world, but of those Jews who might be inclined to accommodate faith to modernity.

Hare Krishna (Hindu devotional movement): see INTERNATIONAL SOCIETY FOR KRISHNA CONSCIOUSNESS.

Harem (ḥarīm): see ḤARAM.

Hargobind, Gurū (1595–1644). Sixth Sikh *Gurū. Hargobind was born in *Amritsar to Gurū *Arjan Dev's wife, Mātā Gaṅgā, and survived *Prithī Chand's attempts on his life. In 1606 Bhāī *Buḍhā installed him as successor to his martyred father.

Hargobind's martial, princely style marked a new emphasis in Sikhism. He trained soldiers and built Lohgaṛh (castle of steel), a fortress in Amritsar, and the *Akāl *Takht where heroic feats were sung. Between 1628 and 1634 the Gurū was victorious in four engagements with Mughal forces. The Gurū died in Kīratpur 1644. Contemporary sources contain minor inconsistencies regarding his life, and Hargobind wrote no hymns, but a clear picture, reinforced by *iconography, emerges of his impact on Sikhism.

Hari. Divine manifestation, in Hinduism, especially in the forms of *Viṣṇu and *Kṛṣṇa, but of innumerable different figures also—including *ṛṣis and lawgivers. Because Hari is the means through which *Brahman becomes manifest (*Viṣṇu Purāṇa* 1. 22), he becomes equated with the personal form of God in general (*Īśvara).

Haribhadra (d. trad. 529 CE, perhaps later). Śvetāmbara Jain philosopher and teacher. Much about his life is uncertain, and indeed the accounts of other teachers of the same name may have been assimilated to him. He is said to have been a *brahman of great learning who was converted by a Jain nun, Yākinī, from whom he took the title of Yākinīputra ('spiritual son of Yākinī'). A second title (perhaps indicating a second person) is Virahāṅka ('having the mark of separation'), referring to his separation from two nephews who had undertaken surreptitious instruction from Buddhists. More than 14,000 works are attributed to him, and although many of these may be by others of the same name, the 'name' remains as a mark of the highest philosophical achievement and is still revered.

Haribhadra, also known as **Siṃhabhadra** (late 8th cent. CE). Indian Buddhist philosopher, a pupil of *Śāntarakṣita. A very important commentator on all aspects of *Mahāyāna *śāstra, his work presupposes knowledge of the *Pramāṇa school and of the **Abhidharma-kośa*. His school flourished during the reigns of the Pāla emperors Dharmapāla and Devapāla (*c.*765–850). His principal works are the *Small Commentary* (*Sphuṭārtha*) and the *Great Commentary* (*Āloka*) on the Abhisamayālaṁkāra of Maitreya, and commentaries on all the major works of the Prajñāpāramitā (*Perfection of Wisdom) corpus, all of which are still indispensable materials for study in Tibetan monastic institutions.

Haridās, Svāmī (16th cent.). Hindu devotee of *Rādhā and *Kṛṣṇa, and founder (or inspiration) of a cult bearing his name. He wrote a small amount of Hindī verse (e.g. *Kelimāl*, 'Garland of Divine Play', in which he imagines himself as the attendant of Rādhā), but was remembered also for his skill as a musician. The Haridāsas have made vital contributions to Indian music, and include Purandaradāsa (1480–1564), who laid the foundations for Karnatak/Carnatic music of the modern period. The cult divided into two sects in the 17th cent., the one being ascetic, the other remaining based on the household. The two continue in *Vṛndāvana to the present day.

Hari-hara. A combination of Viṣṇu (Hari) and Śiva (Hara), to make clear (at least to *Advaita) the non-duality of all appearance, including theistic appearance.

Harijans ('Children of God'): see UNTOUCHABLES.

Ḥarim (forbidden area): see ḤARAM.

Harimandir (Sāhib) (Pañjābī, 'temple of God'). Name of several Sikh shrines, including the *gurdwārā marking Gurū *Gobind Siṅgh's birthplace at Paṭnā, and, most notably, the Sikhs' principal shrine, the Golden Temple or Sāhib Darbār at *Amritsar.

Hari Oṃ. Hindu *mantra to call forth the presence of God.

Harivaṃśa (Skt., 'the dynastic history of Hari [= Viṣṇu]'). A Hindu mythological text in Skt. It is a work of considerable text-historical complexities, with early layers reaching as far back as the 1st or 2nd cent. CE. The bulk of the work is constituted by material derived from two main traditions: (i) the *Purāṇa-pañcalakṣaṇa*; and (ii) stories about the life of *Kṛṣṇa among the herdsmen of Vraja.

The Jains also produced, in various languages, Harivaṃśa (Purāṇa)s which deal with their version of the Kṛṣṇa story.

Harivarman. Buddhist scholar of the 3rd cent. CE, originally a member of one of the subschools of the *Great Assembly (Mahāsaṃghikas) and perhaps also the founder of the Nominalist school (*Prajñaptivāda). He composed a great *Abhidharma (scholastic) treatise entitled 'The Establishment of Truth' (*Satyasiddhi-śāstra*), which now survives in Chinese alone.

In this work, which is divided in accordance with the *Four Noble Truths, the author discusses a multitude of technical problems in Buddhist doctrine and rejects those opinions which are not sanctioned by scripture.

Har Krishan, Gurū (1656–64 CE). Eighth Sikh *Gurū. As his brother, *Rām Rāi, had incurred the disfavour of their father, Gurū *Har Rāi, Har Krishan succeeded as Gurū in 1661 at the age of 5. The emperor Auraṅgzeb summoned him to Delhi, where he stayed in the house of Mirzā Rājā Jai Siṅgh of Jaipur. Here he died of smallpox. The site is now marked by Banglā *Sāhib *gurdwārā (near Connaught Place, New Delhi).

Various stories are told of the boy Gurū's powers. In particular he indicated the provenance of his successor, Gurū *Tegh Bahādur, by saying, '*Bābā Bakāle', i.e. he would not be Rām Rāi or *Dhīr Mal, but would come from Bakālā.

Harmandir (Sikh shrines): see HARIMANDIR.

Harnack, Adolf Von (1851–1930). Christian theologian and historian. He gained his doctorate from Leipzig in 1873, and after a short period (1886–9) as professor at Marburg, he moved to Berlin where he remained until his retirement in 1921. The move to Berlin was challenged by the Lutheran Church because of the doubts expressed by Harnack in his *Lehrbuch der Dogmengeschichte* (History of Dogma, 1894–9) about the authorship of various New Testament books, *miracles, the *resurrection, and *Christ's institution of *baptism. Influenced by Ritschl, he regarded *hellenization as an intrusion into early Christianity, which had distorted the original, simpler gospel, whose content he summarized in *Das Wesen des Christentums* (The Essence of Christianity). Harnack was a particular target of his pupil K. *Barth, for allowing liberal thought to control his understanding of early Christianity and of dogma.

Ḥaroset. Paste eaten at the Jewish *seder meal.

Har Rāi, Gurū (1630–61). Seventh Sikh *Gurū. Gurū Har Rāi was the second son of Gurū *Hargobind's son, Gurdittā (d. 1638) and brother of *Dhīr Mal. He was chosen as successor by his grandfather and became Gurū on his death in 1644, but was soon compelled to leave his birthplace, Kīratpur, for a remote mountain village. Har Rāi returned to Kīratpur 1658 and aided *Dārā Shikoh, Emperor Shāh Jahān's eldest son. Gurū Har Rāi's words, that a temple or mosque can be repaired but not a broken heart, are indicative of his peaceable disposition.

Harris movement. A mass movement toward Christianity in the Ivory Coast and W. Ghana between 1913 and 1915, due to the itinerant ministry of a Grebo from Liberia, William Wadé Harris (*c.*1860–1929). Some 120,000 people of many tribes discarded traditional religious practices and magic, accepted his *baptism and elementary Christianity. Harris independent churches, include the largest under John Ahui (b. 1894) with perhaps 150,000 members by 1980, and the Church of the Twelve Apostles under Grace Thannie (*c.*1880–1958) in W. Ghana. One of the best-known figures in the Ivory Coast is Albert Atcho (b. 1903), an Ebrié prophet-healer operating within the Harris context from his own village of Bregbo.

Harrowing of Hell. Medieval Christian term for the belief that on *Holy Saturday, *Jesus descended into *hell and defeated the powers of the devil. In consequence, he was able to set free the souls of those who had been faithful to God (and conscience) before the *incarnation and its associated *atonement.

Hartshorne, Charles (b. 1897). American philosopher. His influence within religious thought has been mainly on those who call themselves '*process theologians'. This influence stems from his conception of God as 'dipolar': God encompasses such contraries as absoluteness *and* relativity, necessity *and* contingency, eternity *and* temporality. God is 'perfect being', not unchanging, but capable of being excelled by nothing other than himself: change, not permanence, is the fundamental nature of reality. This conception leads in Hartshorne's view to a panentheistic (see PANTHEISM) view of God–world relations: that is, one in which God is both world-inclusive *and* world-transcending.

Hārūn (name of Aaron in the Qur'ān): see AARON.

Hārūn al-Rashīd ('Abbāsid caliph): see 'ABBĀSIDS.

Haru no Higan (festival): see FESTIVALS AND FASTS.

Haru no Shanichi (festival): see FESTIVALS AND FASTS.

Harvest Festival (Jewish): see SUKKOT.

Harvest Festival or **Thanksgiving** (Christian festival): see LAMMAS DAY.

Hasan (Jap.). The 'interruption' of Zen Buddhist training which comes about with the experience of enlightenment (*kensho, *satori). One who rests in the experience rapidly falls back.

Hasan (son of 'Alī): see AL-HASAN.

Ḥasan al-Bannā' (1906–49). The founder and leader of *al-Ikhwān al-Muslimūn in Egypt. Ḥasan al-Bannā' studied at *al-Azhar and qualified as a teacher. In 1928, he founded the al-Ikhwān at Isma'iliyya. He attracted wide support for the Ikhwān among all classes. He believed that the sickness of Egyptian Islamic society could be cured 'only by a return to the regenerative springs of the *Qur'ān and the *Ḥadīth'. Increasing tension between him and the government culminated in his assassination in 1949.

Ḥasan al-Baṣrī (642–728 (AH 21–110)). One of the earliest and most influential of the *Sūfīs. He was a freed slave, who was born in *Madīna but settled in Basra in 658, where he attracted many students. Most of the Sūfī lineages (*silsilah, *tarīqa) claim to pass through Ḥasan, and he appears also as a link in many *isnāds of *ḥadīth. His sayings are frequently quoted, making clear that he regarded the world as an arena in which we are tested in our devotion to God. Sūfīs consider him the third master after *Muḥammad and 'Alī, and as the founder of 'the science of hearts', *'ilm al-qulūb*. He is perhaps the most frequently quoted of the early preachers, and his sermons are highly valued for their content and style.

Ha-Shelah ha-Kadosh (rabbi and kabbalist): see HOROWITZ, ISAIAH BEN ABRAHAM.

Ha-Shem (Heb., 'the name'). Way in Judaism of referring to the name of God without pronouncing it: it becomes a surrogate especially for the *tetragrammaton.

Hashemite or **Hāshimite.** A descendant of the clan (Banū Hāshim) to which *Muḥammad belonged. The term is sometimes restricted to those who are *shurafa* (*sharīf) descendants of the Prophet, as in the case of the recently-founded dynasty of kings in Jordan.

Hashkivenu (Heb., 'cause us to lie down'). Beginning of second *benediction after the *Shema' at Jewish evening *prayer. The prayer asks for God's protection during the night.

Ḥasidei Ashkenaz. 12th- and 13th-cent. movement within German Jewry. The Ḥasidei Ashkenaz, which was made up of many like-minded groups, originated in Regensberg and spread to Speyer, Worms, and Mainz, and then to the rest of Germany. It produced ethical works, such as *Sefer Ḥasidim* (Book of the Pious), and esoteric mystical works, such as *Sefer Ḥayyim* (Book of Life). Prominent leaders include Samuel b. Kalonymus he-Ḥasid (late 12th cent.). The movement was influenced by *merkabah mysticism and by the works of Abraham ibn Ezra and *Sa'adiah Gaon. It rejected all anthropomorphic descriptions of God and maintained that divine powers were immanent in all creation.

Ḥasidei ummot ha-'olam (Heb., 'the pious ones of the nations of the world'). *Gentiles perceived as righteous by the *rabbis (*Tos.Sanh.* 13. 2). *Maimonides defined the hasidei ummot ha-'olam as 'all who observe the Seven Commandments' (i.e. the *Noachide Laws). It is generally agreed that righteous gentiles have a place in the world to come. Since the Second World War, the term has been used to refer to those gentiles who helped Jews escape from Nazi persecution. Yad Vashem, the authority entrusted with the remembrance of national martyrs and heroes, includes a department to investigate and recognize those rescue activities, and it invites ḥasidei ummot ha-'olam to plant a tree in the Avenue of the Righteous in the Yad Vashem memorial in Jerusalem.

Ḥasidim (Heb., 'righteous'). Those described in Bible, especially Psalms, as close to God; the term was then used by the *rabbis to describe those leading particularly holy lives. See Index, Ḥasidim.

Ḥasidim, Sefer (Heb., 'Book of the Pious'). Medieval German Jewish book of ethics. The *Sefer Ḥasidim*, comprises the ethical lore of the *Ḥasidei Ashkenaz movement.

Hasidism (Heb., *ḥasidut*). Jewish religious movement which emerged in the late 18th cent. Hasidism first arose in S. Poland and Lithuania, with such charismatic leaders as *Israel b. Eliezer (Ba'al Shem Tov, the Besht), *Dov Baer of Mezhirech and Jacob Joseph of Polonnoye. These leaders drew groups of disciples around them, characterized by popular traditions of ecstasy, mass enthusiasm, and intense devotion to the leader, the *Zaddik. Hasidic groups travelled as far as *Erez Israel, and hasidic centres were to be found throughout E. Europe. With the great waves of immigration of the 1880s, Hasidism spread to the USA.

Initially there was considerable opposition to the movement from such figures as *Elijah b. Solomon Zalman, the Vilna Gaon. Early Hasidism was thought by opponents to be tainted with *Shabbateanism and Frankism (see FRANK, JACOB). Its mystical enthusiasm was also thought to detract from the sober study of *Torah. However, by the mid-19th cent., despite the different practices and rituals of the movement, the *Orthodox acknowledged Hasidism as a legitimate branch of Judaism.

Hasidic social life is centred on the court of the *zaddik who is seen as the source of all spiritual illumination (e.g. *devekut). Stories of past and present zaddikim are circulated as part of the mythology of the group. As in the root source, *Ḥabad, worship is characterized by joy, and is expressed in song and dance as well as prayer. A major goal is the individual *bittul ha-yesh* (the annihilation of selfhood) in which the worshipper is absorbed into the divine light. The best-known modern expositor of Hasidism is Martin *Buber whose *Tales of Rabbi Nachman* (Eng. 1962), *Tales of the Hasidim* (1947–8), and *Legend of the Baal Shem* (Eng. 1969) interpreted the movement in the light of existentialism.

Haskalah (Heb., 'enlightenment'). The Enlightenment movement of the late 18th and 19th cents. in Judaism. Those who espoused the Haskalah were known as Maskilim. Related to the secular Enlightenment, Moses *Mendelssohn is generally considered to be the 'father of the Haskalah'.

Prominent Haskalah thinkers included Naphtale Herz Wessely, the educationalist, who believed that Jewish children 'were not all created to become *Talmudists', and David Friedlaender who rejoiced in the decline of the *yeshivot. Throughout Europe, rich Jews rejected *Yiddish and taught their children the language of their host nation.

In their desire for acceptance and emancipation, the Maskilim were particularly patriotic towards their host countries, and the *messianic hope was weakened. Members of the Assembly of Jewish Notables, set up by Napoleon in 1806, described themselves as 'Frenchmen of the Mosaic religion'. The *diaspora was no longer seen as a punishment for *Israel's wickedness, but the result of historical and geographical factors. Judaism was understood as a spiritual and moral creed, and from this thinking grew the *Reform movement with its updated *Prayer Book and its rejection of the absolute claims of *halakhah.

Haskamah (Heb., 'agreement'). Either *rabbinic approval of *halakhic decision, or rabbinic recommendation of a particular book (cf. in Christianity, the *imprimatur). The first haskamah appeared in the *Agur* by Jacob Landau (1490). The haskamah is still in use. Among *Sephardi in the West, it is spelt Ascama.

Hasmoneans. Name given to the *Maccabees in the *Talmud. The Hasmoneans were a priestly family who led the rebellion against the Selucid kings in the 2nd cent. BCE and established an autonomous Jewish kingdom.

Haso (sect founder): see NICHIREN SHŌSHŪ.

Hasso (Jap., 'eight aspects'). The eight major events of the Buddha's life. These are in fact differently listed, but a typical list is: (i) *gōtosotsu*, his coming down from the *Tuṣita heaven; (ii) *takutai*, his conception; (iii) *shusshō*, his birth; (iv) *shukke*, his renunciation of the world; (v) *gōma*, his defeat of evil powers; (vi) *jōdō*, his enlightenment; (vii) *tenpōrin*, his teaching of *dharma; (viii) *nyunehan*, his attaining of *nirvāna. Hasso no kegi is the Buddha's way of converting people by his manifestation of eight aspects.

Hassu (Jap., 'dharma-successor'). A Zen Buddhist pupil who has reached at least the same level of attained enlightenment as his master, and who is therefore given the seal of recognition (*inka-shōmei). He can then become a dharma-successor.

Hasta. Hindu use of hand positions, especially to ward off evil.

Ḥatam Sofer (Jewish orthodox community leader): see SOFER, R. MOSES OF PRESSBURG.

Haṭha-yoga. Originally a part of *Rāja-yoga as taught by *Patañjali, but now frequently detached as a yoga to seek mental and physical health. Its purpose is to locate and activate the *cakras (centres of energy) and thus to raise the *kuṇḍalinī (dormant spiritual power) to life.

Haṭha-Yoga-Pradīpikā (A lamp for Hatha-yoga). A work on *Haṭha-yoga which shows how Haṭha-yoga prepares the foundations for *Rāja-yoga.

Ḥātim al-Aṣamm (Sūfī): see SŪFĪS.

Hatto (dharma-hall): see KYŌTO.

Haumai (Pañjābī, 'ego'). In the Sikh *Gurūs' teachings, something in human nature akin to self-centred pride, although there is no satisfactory English equivalent. It is the dominant force in the *manmukh (unregenerate person), obscuring the path towards union with God.

Haurvatat and Ameretat (two of the Holy Immortals): see AMESA SPENTAS.

Havdalah (Heb., 'separation'). *Blessings in Judaism recited at the end of *Sabbaths and *Festivals.

Ḥaver or **ḥaber** (Heb., 'member, companion'). Member of a group which observed the Jewish laws of *tithing and heave-offering. The laws of membership date back at least to the 1st cent. BCE, and differ according to the schools of *Bet Hillel and Bet Shammai. Later, in the geonic (see GAON) period, the term was used to describe important scholars, who were God-fearing but not sufficiently learned to be ordained as *rabbis.

Haviryajña (group of sacrifices): see SACRIFICES (HINDU).

Ḥavurah or **ḥaburah.** Mutual benefit society in Judaism. A ḥavurah is an association devoted to visiting the sick and burying the dead, or it may be simply a society for informal worship and fellowship. In the period during the 1960s and 1970s when there was a massive increase in *new religious movements, especially in the USA, ḥavurot were often the equivalent of communes.

Ḥawḍ (Arab., 'basin'). The place at which *Muḥammad will meet his *'umma (community) on the day of *resurrection. There is no reference to it in the *Qur'ān, but only in *ḥadīth.

Hawwā (wife of Adam): see EVE (Islam).

Hayagrīva. 1. A non-classical *avatāra of the Hindu god *Viṣṇu. He is worshipped in traditions influenced by the *Pañcarātra (e.g. among the *Śrī-Vaiṣṇavas). Envisaged as primordial teacher, he has absorbed features of the *Buddha.

2. A demon of Hindu mythology who stole the Vedas and was killed by Viṣṇu.

Hayon, Nehemiah Hiyya ben Moses (*c*.1655–*c*.1730). *Kabbalist Jewish scholar. Hayon spent much of his life in *Erez Israel and was a prominent kabbalist. He was accused of *Shabbateanism and was the source of controversy both in Israel and in Amsterdam, where he was *excommunicated. He was the author of *Oz le-Elohim* (Strength to God) and a commentary on the pamphlet *Raza de-Meheimanuta* (The Mystery of the True Faith) which was attributed to Shabbetai Zevi. Ultimately he was rejected by most European communities and died in N. Africa.

Ḥayyim Vital (Jewish kabbalist): see VITAL, ḤAYYIM.

Ḥazal (our Wise of blessed memory): see SAGES.

Ḥazzan (leader of Jewish prayer service): see CANTOR.

Head, covering of. In Judaism, the custom of men covering their heads as a sign of humility before God, and of married women covering their heads as a sign of modesty before men, practised throughout the *Orthodox Jewish community. Today, Orthodox men wear at least a skull cap (Heb., *kippah*; Yid., *yarmulke) at all times; *Conservative Jews cover their heads for prayer; and it remains a matter of choice for *Reform Jews. The increasingly common practice of gentiles wearing a head-covering in Jewish company (especially on e.g. official visits) somewhat confuses the matter, since head-covering seems to have begun as a deliberate contrast to gentile practices (see YARMULKE), but it is presumably a matter of courtesy.

In *biblical times, women kept their hair hidden (see Numbers 5. 18). Since the early 19th cent., some married women followed the custom by wearing a wig (Yid., *shaytl*), although this was opposed in some circles. Today, only strictly Orthodox women keep their heads covered at all time.

Healing. In the religious perspective, disease and dis-ease are never far removed from each other. Since an aim of religions is to offer the means through which health in body, mind, and spirit may be attained (unless countervailing causes supervene, such as *karma, the will of God, invasion by *demons, etc.). Thus *Augustine observed succinctly that 'all diseases of Christians are to be ascribed to demons'; and the contest with demons is familiar in the descriptions of the healing of particular disorders in the ministry of *Jesus, which was to him (and others) a demonstration that the *dunamis* (power or dynamic) of God is active in the world.

The contest against disease was continued in Islam, through which Greek medical knowledge was preserved and extended. *al-Ṭibb* ('medicine') became a major part of the Muslim commitment to *'ilm (knowledge)—e.g. *al-Rāzī (Rhazes).

Indian medical science is known as *Ayur veda ('the knowledge of longevity'), and is based on a theory of five elements (*bhūta) and three humours (*dośa*), wind, bile, and phlegm. Health consisted in maintaining all in balance and equilibrium, correcting imbalance by an array of herbal and other remedies. Thus health matters are not isolated from the general condition of life. *Carakasamhita* is a classic text on medicine (compiled in the 1st cent. BCE; *Suśrutu Samhita* is a slightly later text on surgery): it combines health and medical matters with general instructions for the achieving of a good and satisfactory life.

The same catholicity of attitude is evident in China, where the quest for immortality in religious Taoism (Tao-chiao/Daojiao) is not restricted to an endeavour to emancipate a self from society or a soul from a body. Taoists seek to relate the microcosm—which is present in the body in the three life-principles of breath (*ch'i/qi), vitality especially in semen (*ching/jing), and spirit (*shen)—to the macrocosm, so that the whole of life, internal and external, becomes an unresistant (*wu-wei) expression of that which alone truly is, namely, the Tao. It would thus be impossible to isolate some part of disease or disorder from its context.

Healing, therefore, in all religions takes place in a much larger context of life and its purposes, and remains closely related to modern insights into the psychosomatic unity of the human entity.

For the Buddhist 'Master of Healing', see BHAIṢAJYAGURU. See also Index, Healing.

Healthy, Happy, Holy Organization (3HO). A movement founded by Yogi Bhajan (Harbhajan Singh) in California in 1969. A Sikh-derived movement, 3HO aims at cleansing the subconscious mind and the whole person of all impurities principally through the practice of *kuṇḍalinī and *Tantric yoga, *meditation, and mantric chants, thereby preparing the individual for the reception of that 'pure consciousness' of which Yogi Bhajan is the vehicle.

Heart, Sacred (object of Christian devotion): see SACRED HEART.

***Heart Sūtra* (*Mahāprajñapāramitā-hridaya-sūtra*).** A short Buddhist text, which, like the **Diamond Sūtra*, may be regarded as a distillation of the essential teachings on emptiness (*śūnyatā). The *Heart Sūtra* may be dated at around 350 CE.

Heaven

Judaism The biblical understanding of heaven is restricted to a cosmology which envisaged a realm or domain above the earth, where (initially) the gods and (subsequently) God and his agents dwell. The Garden of *Eden is a controlling model, since this is *paradise lost—but able to be regained. In *kabbalah, a more elaborate series of heavens was envisaged through the effect of God's emanations. See also AFTERLIFE.

Christianity Heaven is held to be the domain of God and the *angels, and ultimately of all the redeemed, where they receive their eternal reward. Traditional Catholic doctrine holds that the souls of those who have died in a state of grace, which have been first purged of their stains in *purgatory, pass to heaven, where they enjoy perfect bliss; but, except for the Virgin *Mary, these souls still await reunion with their bodies at the general resurrection.

Islam The Arabic terms are *Janna*, 'garden', and *Firdaws*, 'paradise'. The Qur'ān mentions *jannāt al-na'īm* 'gardens of delight' (10. 9); *jannāt 'Adn*, 'gardens of Eden' (19. 62, 61. 12); 'gardens beneath which rivers flow' (3. 137, 61. 12). The delights of heaven and the punishments of *hell (*jahannam*, or *al-nār* = the fire) are vividly described in early *sūras of the Qur'ān.

Some theologians preferred allegorical interpretation for all the descriptions given in Qur'ān and ḥadīth. The *Mu'tazilites in particular denied any form of 'seeing' Allāh; the Ash'arites (*al-Ash'ari) allowed for some form of divine vision, interpreted *bi-lā kayf*, without asking 'how'. *Sūfīs taught that although the joys of paradise would be real, the greatest of all would be the vision of Allāh.

Other Religions for approximate equivalents see LOKA; SVARGA; TUṢITA; VAIKUṆṬHA (BAIKUNTH); PURE LAND; SUKHĀVATĪ; SACH KHAṆḌ; T'IEN; and Index, Heavens, Paradises.

Heaven and earth, sacrifices to. The most important rituals of the Imperial Cult in China from most ancient times down to the 20th cent. In the earliest historically known period (late Shang dynasty, *c.*1300–?1111 BCE), the high god was called *Ti, or *Shang-Ti. He dwelt in Heaven where he presided, so to speak, over the council of ancestors of the incumbent king. The high god of the succeeding Chou dynasty (?1111–256 BCE) was called *T'ien, which means Heaven. Shang-Ti and T'ien gradually became assimilated as the supreme ruler, by whose mandate (*t'ien ming) every ruling dynasty was legitimated. In Chinese philosophy Heaven was the embodiment of *yang*, one of the two basic forces (*yin-yang) in the universe. By the same token Earth, mother of all and source of their nourishment, as well as ultimate devourer of their physical forms, was the embodiment of yin.

In worshipping Heaven and Earth, therefore, the emperor was on the one hand acknowledging the subordination and dependence of all humans in relation to the supreme powers of the universe, and on the other hand demonstrating his own supremacy as ruler of all, who alone had the right to act as their intermediary with those powers. Hence, these rituals were the sole prerogative of the emperor.

Heavenly Master School (school of religious Taoism): see WU-TOU-MI TAO.

Heaven's Gate. A US cult which achieved notoriety in 1997, when 39 of its members committed *suicide. Marshall Applewhite persuaded his followers that the comet Hale-Bopp was the precursor of a space vehicle to which, after death, they would be taken. Several men had already begun to detach themselves by castration (cf. Matthew 19. 12, *Origen).

Hebraeus, Leo (alternative name of Jewish philosopher and poet): see ABRABANEL JUDAH.

Hebrews. Biblical term for those who became the Jews. The origin of the word and its connection with *Habiru are disputed, but the term subsequently became synonymous with 'Jew'.

Hebrews, Letter to the. Book of the New Testament. Hebrews was traditionally included among *Paul's letters, but it does not bear his name and nothing else points to him as the author.

Hebrew Union College—Jewish Institute of Religion. Oldest seminary in the USA dedicated to Jewish studies and the training of *Reform *rabbis. The Hebrew Union College was founded in Cincinnati, Ohio, by Isaac Meyer *Wise in 1875. The Jewish Institute of Religion was founded in New York by Stephen S. Wise in 1922, and the two schools were merged in 1950.

Ḥeder (Heb., 'room'). Traditional Jewish elementary school. The term ḥeder first occurred in the 13th cent. CE. These schools were much scorned by the Maskilim of the *Haskalah, leading to an attempt at modification (ḥeder metukkan, 'reformed ḥeder'), but the attempt failed.

Hefker. Ownerless property. According to Jewish law, ownerless property (whether it has never been owned, such as a wild bird, or whether its original owner has irretrievably lost it) is exempt from the law of *tithes and heave-offering.

Hegel, Georg Wilhelm Friedrich (1770–1831). German philosopher, the most influential and arguably most significant in the 19th cent. Hegel completed his formal education at Jena, where he also taught until the university was 'reorganized' by Napoleon (whom Hegel called 'the *Zeitgeist* on horseback') and where he wrote *The Phenomenology of Spirit* (1807). In this, his first major book, the dialectic of human experience is unfolded. Spirit as pure potentiality (*An-sich-sein*), through its self-alienation and self-objectification in nature (*Dasein*) and then through its progressive self-reconciliation in the history of human self-consciousness, comes finally to full awareness of itself as pure or absolute Spirit (*Für-sich-sein*). Hegel defined 'religion' with disarming simplicity as 'the consciousness of God'. Viewed *phenomenologically, 'consciousness of God' refers in Hegel's writings to a person's coming to be aware of essential unity with the divine Spirit. Viewed speculatively, however, 'consciousness of God' refers at the same time to God's own self-consciousness. The history of religions is likewise the means of God's coming to 'be-for-himself' in and through people's ever-developing consciousness of him.

Hegira (migration of Muḥammad): see HIJRA.

Hegumenos or **Igumen** (Gk., 'leader'). A title in E. Christianity for the leader of a *monastic community (equivalent of the W. *abbot or prior).

Heian Period (Japan, 794–1185): see BUDDHISM IN JAPAN; SAICHŌ.

Heifer, Red (animal used in Jewish ritual of purification): see RED HEIFER.

Heikan (Jap., 'closing the gate'). The Zen Buddhist ability to cultivate in *zazen an awareness of one's surroundings without involvement in them.

Heikhal (Sephardi name for the Ark): see ARK (3).

Heiler, Friedrich (1892–1967). Christian theologian and *phenomenologist of religion. He was originally a Roman Catholic, but became a Lutheran under the influence of Nathan *Söderblom. From 1922 until his retirement in 1960, he was professor of the comparative history of religions at Marburg. Pulled back in a more Catholic direction by the writings of von *Hügel, he founded an evangelical order of Franciscan tertiaries. His major work was *Das Gebet* (1918; Prayer: A Study in the History and Psychology of Religion, 1932). In this he put into practice his understanding of phenomenology as a way to discovering common truths at the heart of different religions, beneath the surface. He saw the study of religion in this way as a path that could lead to reconciliation between religions. At the outset of *Erscheinungsformen und Wesen der Religion* (1961), he summarized his understanding of the phenomenological method: it could not be 'value-free', since every science has its presuppositions; thus the historian of religion must be inductive, but the phenomenologist must be deductive, building on the foundations of history, philology, etc., working always with empathy.

Heilsgeschichte (Germ., 'salvation-history'). The attempt (made initially by Christians) to discern a unifying thread in human, and especially in biblical, history, that thread being the initiatives and actions of God in saving his people and the world.

Hekdesh (Heb., 'consecrated'). Among Jews, consecrated property. In the period of the *Temple, Jews were expected to consecrate property for the upkeep of the Temple, and, unlike secular gifts, consecration could be effected simply by word of mouth. After the destruction of the Temple, the term hekdesh was used for the dedication of property to a *synagogue or a *charity.

Hekhalot and merkabah. Early Jewish magic and mysticism connected with the palaces of heaven (hekhalot) and the chariot (merkabah) of *Elijah by which he was carried up to heaven. Contemplation of the chariot chapters of Ezekiel are at least as early as *Johanan ben Zakkai, and, following the discovery among the *Cairo Genizah Fragments of an early text describing Johanan's experience, it seems clear that Saul (who became *Paul) practised this mysticism, and that this was the foundation of his many reported experiences, including the vision on the Damascus road. The other surviving treatises date from the 3rd to 7th cents., of which five were of particular importance in subsequent Jewish mysticism: *Hekhalot Zutartei* (The Smaller Book of Palaces), describing the ascension of *Akiva to heaven; *Hekhalot Rabbati* (The Greater Book . . .), describing the ascension of R. Ishmael; *Ma'aseh Merkabah* (The Work of the Chariot), an anthology of hymns sung by mystics during their ascent; *Sefer Hekhalot*, known also as the Third Book of Enoch, in which R. Ishmael describes his ascension and meeting with *Metatron, *Sar ha-Panim*, the Prince of Countenances; and *Shi'ur Komah* (The Measurement of the Height), in which the vision of God is described in anthropomorphic terms derived particularly from Song of Songs. These early texts and practices profoundly influenced *kabbalah and such movements as *Ḥasidei Ashkenaz.

Hekigan-roku (Chinese Ch'an/Zen verses): see HSÜEH-TOU CH'UNG-HSIEN.

Hell

Christianity The word 'hell' in English Bibles translates both Heb. *sheol and Gk. *gehenna. Traditional theology holds that unrepentant sinners go to hell after this life, while the redeemed go either to *purgatory or directly to *heaven. According to *scholastic theology, souls experience in hell both the loss of contact with God (*poena damni*) and *poena sensus*, usually taken to be an agent tormenting them. But many theologians, if not critical of the whole notion of everlasting punishment (see UNIVERSALISM), are reticent about the doctrine of hell. See also JUDGEMENT; DESCENT OF CHRIST INTO HELL.

Islam Jahannam (cf. Heb., *gēhinnōm*, Gk., *gehenna) is mentioned frequently in the *Qur'ān. It has seven gates (39. 71; 15. 43), and different levels, the lowest being the tree Zaqqūm and a cauldron of boiling pitch and fire. Punishments are in accord with the gravity of sins—a theme much elaborated by later commentators. The Qur'ān does not make it clear whether punishments of Muslim sinners are for ever. In contrast, a *kāfir is generally held to be punished eternally.

Other Religions For Buddhist and Hindu hells see NARAKA (Pālī, *niraya*); Index, Hell.

Hellenism. Greek life and culture in the period from the conquests of Alexander the Great (4th cent. BCE) to the death of *Constantine. For both Judaism and (in different ways) Christianity, Hellenism offered both threat and challenge. On the one side, it offered opportunity to enhance the Jewish understanding of God's nature and action toward his creation (as in the philosopher *Philo or the historian *Josephus). On the other hand, the adoption of Hellenistic ways threatened the requirements of *Torah. For Christianity, Hellenism offered a vehicle of missionary extension and of theological (and *christological) reflection. Yet at the same time there were those who thought that the involvement of the gospel in classical thought was an erosion of it.

Helpers. The usual Eng. tr. of the Arab. *anṣār*, denoting those in *Madīna who had espoused Islam before and after the *Hijra of Muḥammad, and who helped or supported him. They were thus distinguished from the Muhājirūn (*Emigrants).

Helvetic Confessions. *Confessions of Christian faith drawn up by the Swiss Protestant Churches. The First Helvetic (Swiss) Confession (1536) was drawn up by *Bullinger (and others), with the help of *Bucer, in the hope of reconciling the Swiss and the Lutherans. The Second (1566) is a revision of Bullinger's personal Confession. It sought continuity in the Church, and has had a wide and continuing influence.

Hemacandra (1089–1172). Śvetāmbara Jain monk of great learning, who came to be known as 'the all-wise one of the degenerate age'. In 1108, he was made *suri*, teacher of a group of monks with authority to expound scripture and appoint a successor. From this moment, he became known as Hemacandra. His main surviving works recapitulate Jain history and principles, especially as exemplified in the past.

Triṣaṣṭiśalākāpuruṣacarita (The Deeds of the Sixty-Three Eminent Men) has a last section on *Mahāvīra which includes a kind of Jain utopia, in which the king will usually avoid prostitutes, and the queen will be chaste.

His *Yogaśastra* (Treatise on Yoga) takes *yoga in a very broad sense and becomes a compendium on appropriate Jain behaviour.

Hémādrī. A learned scholar and a minister of the Yādava kings of Deogirī near Auraṅgābād,

1260–71. He possessed great powers of organization and a wide outlook directed towards the many-sided improvement of the people. He employed many scholars to prepare a compendium of religious observances, entitled *Chāturvarga-chintāmaṇī*. He also wrote the history of the Yādava rulers, entitled *Yādava-Prashastī*. He was put to death by Rāmachandra Yādava about 1272 CE.

Hemkunt (Skt., *hemakuta*, 'golden peak'). Sikh shrine in N. India. Since the rediscovery of the site *c.*1930 it has become a place of summer *pilgrimage.

Hen-chū-shō (one of five degrees of enlightenment: Zen Buddhism): see GO-I.

Henotheism (Gk., 'one God'). The worship of, and devotion to, one God, while allowing that other gods exist. The term was introduced by Max *Müller. Kathenotheism is the worship of one god after another, but in the end Müller preferred the name 'henotheism'.

Henotikon (Gk., 'decree of unity'). The *christological formula sponsored by the Byzantine emperor Zeno in 482 to conciliate the *Monophysite party in the E. Empire. By the formula 'Christ was one and now two' it sought to avoid speaking of the number of 'natures' in Christ.

Henry Suso (Seuse, *c.*1295–1366). German mystic. Of noble birth, he entered a Dominican convent at Constance at the age of 13. He studied under *Eckhart at Cologne between 1322 and 1325, and became his disciple. His defence of Eckhart led to censure. His teaching, found especially in his life, and his *Little Books of Truth* and *Eternal Wisdom*, are expressed in vivid imagery. He called himself 'The servant of the Eternal Wisdom'.

Herbert, Edward (1583–1648). First Lord Herbert of Cherbury, religious philosopher and early advocate of the idea that there is a universal religion natural to human beings. He went to Paris as ambassador in 1619, where he published, in 1624, *De Veritate* ... laying the foundations for his views on a common or natural religion, which he developed further in *De Religione Laici* (1645) and *De Religione Gentilium* (1663). He held that there are five beliefs which are innate and which are common to all people: (i) that there is a Supreme Being; (ii) that he is worthy of our worship; (iii) that virtue is the true mode of that worship or relationship; (iv) that sin is to be recognized and repented of; and (v) that justice demands that we receive a due reward or punishment after death for what we have done during this life. Since these beliefs are innate and universal, there is no need for revelation, and for this reason Herbert has been called 'the father of the *Deists'.

Herbert, George (1593–1633). *Anglican priest and *Metaphysical poet. In 1630 he was ordained priest and became rector of Bemerton. His *Priest to the Temple* presents an ideal of Anglican pastoral ministry; his collection of poems, *The Temple*, depicts the inner engagement between his soul and God.

Here I stand (Luther's commitment): see WORMS, DIET OF.

Ḥerem (Heb., 'ban'). Excommunication from the Jewish community. Derived from the isolation of holy items in biblical times, the first reference to excommunication is in Ezra 10. 8. In the period of the *Talmud, four types of excommunication had developed: (i) *nezifah*, a rebuke, an expulsion for seven days; (ii) *shamta*, now of uncertain meaning; (iii) *niddui*, 'separation', thirty days in *Erez Israel, seven in the *diaspora, but renewable without reform of ways; (iv) ḥerem, isolation: such a person was forbidden to hear or teach *Torah, and had to observe the laws of mourning. It is now little used in that way except by the extreme *Orthodox in Israel.

Heresy (Gk., *hairesis*, 'choice'). The adoption of false views and practices. Basically, the Gk. word may mean simply the adoption of a particular opinion or school of thought (e.g. Acts 5. 17), but in religious terms it is usually a choice of belief which is held to be aberrant (i.e. heretical) by the main continuing body of believers. A heresiarch is the originator of a heresy or heretical movement. In Christianity, where the term is essentially located, *Roman Catholic theologians distinguish 'formal heresy' (the grave sin of wilful persistence in error) and 'material heresy' (the holding of heretical doctrines through no fault of one's own).

In other religions, the term is not formally appropriate, but similar considerations, derived from the necessity for systems to have boundaries, can be found. Thus in Judaism, neither Bible nor *Talmud present creeds or dogmas to which Jews must conform. However, Deuteronomy 17. 8–13 isolates the *zaqen mamre*, the obstinate teacher (*rebellious elder). Already in the *Mishnah serious aberrancy is recognized. Heresy now is belief in ideas condemned by the *Orthodox religious authorities. In Judaism, a heretic is still considered to be a *Jew, and is described by a number of terms such as *min, *apikoros, and *kofer* (cf. *kāfir).

The nearest equivalent in Islam is *ilḥād*, 'deviation'. Heretics are called *malāḥidah*. Right practice (*sunna) is as important as right belief, but in any case the heretic is, quintessentially, one who denies the reality of God. Thus the major offences in Islam are *shirk and *bid'a. One who forsakes Islam is an apostate (*murtadd), and if he turns against Islam in public attack, he should be executed.

In E. religions, it might seem, superficially, that there is little room for a concept equivalent to heresy. 'Hinduism' and 'Buddhism' contain diversities of an even more spectacular kind than Christianity. Hinduism as *sanātana dharma is able to include conceptually even those breakaway religious movements, such as the Jains and Buddhists, which are usually described as separate religions. They are interpretations (*darśana) of the revelation in the *Vedas, but unorthodox ones—*nāstika as opposed to *āstika. In a sense which is now eroded, the orthodox is defined geographically: it is the area in which *dharma can be observed. Thus **Manusmṛti*:

The land between the two sacred rivers Sarasvati and Drsadvati, this land created by divine powers, is the Brahmavarta. The customs prevailing in this land, passed on from one generation to another, constitute right behaviour (*sadācāra*). From a *brahman born and bred in this land all people should learn how to live.... Beyond is the land of the mlecchas: a *twice-born should remain in this land; a *śūdra may, to gain his livelihood, live anywhere.

Buddhism was not even confined to territory, since it was, at least in terms of teaching, opposed to caste, sacrifice, and dharma determined by Vedas and brahmans. However, it was not on trivial issues that the early schools divided (see COUNCILS (BUDDHIST)); and the subsequent elaboration into *sūtra-based Buddhism (i.e. *Mahāyāna) led to an immense proliferation of schools and traditions. But although there has been considerable hostility between Mahāyāna and *Hīnayāna (witness the latter name itself), the different forms of Buddhism have in general flourished in different geographical areas. The definition of the heretic has therefore been extremely local, leading to expulsion from communities, especially of monks (see EXCOMMUNICATION). The nearest equivalent to heresy is 'false views': see DIṬṬHI; Index, Heresy, Heretics.

Hermas. Second-cent. Roman Christian and author of a work called *The Shepherd*. This purports to have been written in consequence of a series of visions. It is divided into five 'Visions', twelve 'Mandates', and ten 'Similitudes'. In the E. Church it was widely regarded as scripture, and is found in the Codex Sinaiticus after the New Testament.

Hermeneutical circle: see HERMENEUTICS.

Hermeneutics (Gk., *hermeneutikos*, 'interpretation', from Hermes, the Greek messenger of the gods). The discipline arising from reflection on the problems involved in the transmission of meaning from text or symbol to reader or hearer. Since there is no privileged or 'correct' meaning of an utterance, hermeneutics has sometimes been summarized in the question, 'whose meaning is the meaning of the meaning?' —i.e., there are many possible and legitimate meanings to be found in any text.

The modern discussion of hermeneutics derives from the early Romantic movement. *Kant's emphasis on understanding was essential: *Verstand* (understanding) is the underlying human capacity for thought and experience, and *Verstehen* (acts of understanding), which are present in all thought and experience, are the expression of the distinctively human rationality. For *Schleiermacher (the key figure in the development of hermeneutics), hermeneutics could no longer be a matter of uncovering a single given meaning in a text by chipping away at the obstacles which at present obscure it. Rather, hermeneutics 'is an unending task of understanding'. Every utterance, verbal or nonverbal, belongs to a linguistic system (*Sprache*), but it belongs also to the lived experience (*Erlebnis*) of the one who utters. There is thus a hermeneutical circle which it is the task of hermeneutics, conceived of as the art of understanding, to close.

Wilhelm Dilthey (1833–1911) took what he understood of Schleiermacher much further. His *On the Construction of the Historical World in the Human Sciences* (1910) abandoned the view that understanding rests in human language-competence, and claimed instead that it rests in the whole life-process: it is a *Lebenskategorie* (a category of life). By this he meant that the process of life is a constant 'scan' of circumstances so that they can be understood and so that appropriate reactions can be initiated. What has to be 'understood', therefore, by the scientist of human behaviour is always a life-expression (*Lebensausserung*), which points back to a lived experience (*Erlebnis*) as its source. The expressed meaning (*Ausdruck*) can be apprehended only by relating the two, but that in itself is a 'lived experience' on the part of the one who apprehends, part indeed of a continuing 'lived experience' which constitutes a 'pre-understanding'. The closing of the hermeneutical circle now becomes the connecting of two culturally and historically embedded lives, not to achieve '*the* meaning', but to create a new horizon of meaning from the connection, the fusion of horizons. For Emilio Betti (1890–1968), this offered the best hope for a tolerant society, since there is no one meaning, closed to all revision, ever to be attained.

Against what may seem to be a steady drift toward subjectivism ('meaning is for me'), ontological hermeneutics (associated especially with the later Heidegger and Hans-Georg Gadamer, *Wahrheit und Methode* . . ., 1972, 'Truth and Method', 1975) has sought to integrate the truth which lies behind language and which alone makes intelligible utterance possible. While it seems obvious to say that 'what are true are sentences', Gadamer insists (as do critical realists in the natural sciences) that there is what there is 'over and above our wanting and doing'. Gadamer argues that 'the truth finds us'. Language is the surface where truth becomes visible.

While hermeneutics is thus an issue in many disciplines, it is central to the interpretation of religious utterance, and of religious and sacred texts. In the Christian tradition, there have in fact been many different styles of exegesis of the Bible. In the medieval period, scripture was expected to yield a fourfold meaning: the literal (letter) sense; the allegorical or *typological sense (the meaning in the context of the drama of salvation); the moral sense (the practical meaning in terms of conduct); the *anagogical sense (the meaning in relation to the purposes of God in eternity). For the Reformers, much of this had produced eisegesis (reading meaning into the text) rather than *exegesis. The fusion of horizons between text and reader reconciles these extremes by allowing the continuing creativity of the Holy Spirit to bring God's truth and the truth of God to the surface of a particular moment.

See Index, Hermeneutics.

Hermeneutics, rabbinic. The systems of biblical interpretation employed in rabbinic Judaism. The three best-known sets of rules are the seven rules of *Hillel, the thirteen rules of R. *Ishmael, and the thirty-two rules of R. Eliezer b. Yose ha-Gelili. In addition, Nahum of Gurrizo developed a system based on the assumption that the marking on every letter has a specific meaning, and this idea was subsequently developed by R. *Akiva. Later, *kabbalists interpreted scripture on the basis of *gematria or the numerical values of words.

Hermeticism. System of *gnostic thought known from the *Corpus Hermeticum*, a collection of philosophical and magical texts dating from the 2nd and 3rd cents. CE. The Egyptian God, Thoth, is identified with the Greek Hermes who is called 'Thrice Greatest', i.e. Trismegistus.

Hermeticism and the *Corpus* became immensely influential in the Renaissance when most of the texts were translated in Italy. The *Corpus* was correctly dated by Isaac Casaubon in 1614, and the texts rapidly waned in influence.

Herod. Several rulers of Jud(a)ea bore this name.

1. Herod I (73–4 BCE, the Great) was appointed by his father to be governor of Galilee and, after his father's death, was appointed initially tetrarch by the Romans and, by 37 BCE, king. During his reign he embarked on an extensive building campaign including the *Temple in Jerusalem. Despite this he was regarded by his Jewish subjects as a foreign agent and a destroyer of their institutions.

2. Herod II, grandson of Herod I and Mariamne, ruled as king of Chalcis, 41–8 CE. During this period, he had the right to appoint *high priests.

3. Herod Antipas, son of Herod I and Malthace, ruled as tetrarch of Galilee, 4 BCE–39 CE, until he was exiled by the Romans.

4. Herod Philip I, son of Herod I and Cleopatra of Jerusalem, ruled as tetrarch of Transjordan, 4 BCE–34 CE.

'That fox Herod' (Luke 13. 32) is thus Herod Antipas.

Herodians (Jewish party): see BOETHUSIANS.

Heruka (Skt.; Tib., *khrag.'thung*, 'Blood Drinker'). A class of *wrathful deity in Tibetan Buddhism who presides over *Tantric ritual. According to the texts, the Heruka serves not to 'protect' the ritual, but is rather a meditational 'tool' by which the *yogin, through identification with the Heruka, attacks his own egotistical grasping.

Hervomde Kerk (Christian (Protestant) Church): see DUTCH REFORMED CHURCH.

Herzl, Theodor (1860–1904). Founder of the Jewish World *Zionist Organization. As a newspaper correspondent, he attended the *Dreyfus trial in 1895 and became convinced that the only solution to the problem of *anti-Semitism was establishing a Jewish national homeland. In 1896 he published *Der Judenstaat* (The Jewish State) which went through eighty editions in eighteen languages. Although he himself was prepared to consider a homeland in Argentina, he began to realize from Jewish reaction to his book that only *Erez Israel had sufficient attraction as a Jewish state. In 1897, the first Zionist Conference was held in Basle. Herzl was in the chair and was elected president of the new World Zionist Organization. Herzl held the fourth Congress in London and tried to gain the support of the British Government for Jewish settlement in the British terrotories of Cyprus and the Sinai Peninsula. Again no support was forthcoming, but instead Uganda in E.

Africa was suggested. The Uganda scheme was rejected by the Zionist General Council in 1904. Herzl died of pneumonia later that year. After the foundation of the State of Israel, his remains were reburied in Jerusalem, and the anniversary of his death, 20 Tammuz, is kept as a national memorial day.

Herzog, Isaac Halevi (1888–1959). First *Ashkenazi *Chief Rabbi of Israel (though not of Palestine). After the Second World War, he travelled widely to try to find and rescue Jewish children who had been hidden with *gentile families. Besides several volumes of *responsa, he published *Main Institutions of Jewish Law* (1936, 1939). His son, Chaim Herzog, was 6th President of Israel.

Heschel, Abraham Joshua (1907–72). US Jewish scholar. He was born in Poland, descended from *Ḥasidic rabbis. A close associate of Martin *Buber, he became a refugee from Nazi Germany, first in London, then in the USA. There he taught at the *Hebrew Union College and the *Jewish Theological Seminary. He wrote important studies on *kabbalah and was a highly influential philosopher of religion. In *Man is not Alone* (1951) and *God in Search of Man* (1956), Heschel tried to define the existential question to which Judaism provides the answer. It lies in the true use of freedom. God longs for his creatures but will not coerce them. Judaism exhibits the response of love and devotion when the commands of God are accepted in that style. His strong emphasis on ethical behaviour as the demonstration of religion took him into the Civil Rights movement, and into *dialogue with other religions, especially in the discussions which led to the revised attitude of *Vatican II to Judaism.

Hess, Moses (1812–75). German socialist and *Zionist. As an ethical socialist, Hess believed, in the early part of his life, that Jews should *assimilate into the majority culture. By 1862, he had published *Rome and Jerusalem* (Eng., 1918) which recommended the 'founding of Jewish societies of agriculture, industry and trade in accordance with Mosaic, i.e., socialist principles'.

Hesychasm (from Gk., *hesychia*, 'quietness'). Tradition of contemplative prayer associated above all with the monks of Mount *Athos. Many antecedents can be found in the early *Fathers, but its full expression is found in the 14th cent. in Gregory of Sinai, Nicephorus of Mount Athos, and especially *Gregory Palamas. Its central feature is constant recitation of the *Jesus Prayer, combined with optional physical techniques of a crouched posture and synchronization of such recitation with *breathing, so that the mind is united with the heart, and the whole person is drawn into 'prayer of the heart'. This leads to a vision by the bodily eyes of the Uncreated Light of the Godhead, the light that surrounded Jesus at the Transfiguration, none other than the uncreated energies of the Godhead.

Heteroglossolalia (a form of speaking in tongues): see GLOSSOLALIA.

Hetu. In Buddhism, a 'root-condition', good or bad, which brings about a thought or action. The six root-conditions are *lobha, *dosa, and *moha and their opposites.

Hevra Kaddisha (Aram., 'holy brotherhood'). Jewish mutual benefit societies. By the late 17th cent. the term came to be used only for burial societies. The Hevra was celebrated annually on a specific day (often 15 Kislev) with a fast followed by a banquet.

Hexapla (Gk., 'sixfold'). An edn. of the Old Testament produced by *Origen in *c.*245 CE. In it the Hebrew text, the Heb. text in Greek. letters, and four Gk. versions were arranged in six parallel columns.

Hexateuch (Gk., *hex*, 'six', + *teuchos*, 'book'). A name given by J. *Wellhausen to the first six books of the Hebrew Bible, supposing that *Joshua was compiled from the same sources as the *Pentateuch.

Hicks(ites) (leader/followers of Quaker sect): see FRIENDS, THE SOCIETY OF.

Hidden Imām. A Shī'a Muslim belief that the last Imām in succession from *'Alī did not die, but disappeared, and is now in a hidden state (occultation) from which he helps believers and will return as *al-Mahdī at the end of time to return peace and justice to the earth. Different Imāms are identified as the Hidden Imām by different Shī'a groups. See AL-MAHDĪ; DRUZES; ITHNA 'ASHARIYYA; GHAIBA.

Hiden (Jap., 'field of compassion'). Buddhist actions of supporting the poor or needy. Since these produce *merit, they are compared to a field which brings forth a great harvest.

Hiei, Mt. (site of first Tendai temple): see MOUNT HIEI.

Hierarchy. A body of religious rulers organized in successive ranks. In Christianity, one may speak of the hierarchy of *bishops, *priests, and *deacons. For the 'heavenly hierarchy', see ANGEL.

Hierophany (Gk., *hieros*, 'sacred', + *phainein*, 'to show'). The manifestation of the divine or the sacred, especially in a sacred place, object, or occasion. Manifestations of some particular aspect may be named after the aspect revealed, e.g. theophany (of divinity), kratophany (of power).

High Churchmen. The group in the Church of England which gives a high place to the authority and antiquity of the *church, to the *episcopate, and to *sacraments. The title is first attested at the end of the 17th cent.

High Holy Days. The Jewish *festivals of *Rosh ha-Shanah and Yom Kippur (*Day of Atonement).

High Mass (Lat., *missa solemnis*). In W. churches the more ceremonial form of the *mass, in which the emphasis may be more on adoration than reception of communion.

High place. Place of worship. In biblical times, shrines were built on hills throughout *Erez Israel; though 'high place' may mean 'raised altar'.

High priest. The chief priest (Heb., *kohen gadol*) of the *Jerusalem *Temple. By the end of the second Temple period, when the land was under Roman rule, the high priest was often considered merely an arm of the secular administration and was under constant criticism from the *Pharisees and *Zealots. Once the Temple was destroyed in 70 CE the office lapsed.

Ḥijāb (Arab.). Any partition which separates two things (e.g. that which separates God from creation), but usually the veil worn by Muslim *women. The almost total covering of the *chaddor* is not required by Qur'ān, The Qur'ān requires a comparable modesty in dress for men. See also PURDAH.

Hijiri. 1. (Jap., 'holy person, wise person'). Buddhist title for a monk of lower rank. In general, it is an epithet for any wise or virtuous person, but especially for devotees of a particular *buddha, etc., as in Amida-hijiri; or for one who dwells in a particular place, as in *Kūya-hijiri.

2. (Jap., 'he who knows the sun'). Lay *ascetics in Japanese religion, often in opposition to, and conflict with, officials in religion.

Hijra (Arab.). The 'emigration' of *Muḥammad from *Mecca to *Madīna in July 622 CE. Those who accompanied him on this move, or who joined him shortly after, were known as *emigrants (*muhājirūn*). The hijra marks a stage in Muḥammad's own development, from a persecuted preacher to the leader of a socio-religious community with political and military power.

The Muslim calendar dates its years (H = *hijrīya*; AH = After the Hijra, or *Anno Hegirae* in W. usage) from the beginning of the lunar year in which the hijra took place.

Hilda, St (614–80). Abbess and founder of a Christian community at Whitby, to which both women and men belonged. She became a nun in 647, and in 649 she became abbess of a convent at Hartlepool. After she founded the community at Whitby, she remained there for the rest of her life. An Anglican community of nuns (Community of the Holy Paraclete) continues at Whitby at the present day. Feast day, 17 Nov.

Hildebrand (Christian pope): see GREGORY VII.

Hildegard (of Bingen), St (1098–1179). Medieval mystic and visionary. Brought up by a recluse, Jutta, in *c.*1116 she entered the Benedictine community that had gathered round her. In 1136 she succeeded Jutta as abbess. About 1150 she moved her community to Rupertsberg, near Bingen, on the Rhine. Encouraged by her confessor, she recorded some of her visions, and in 1147 Pope Eugenius III, under *Bernard of Clairvaux's influence, gave guarded approval to them. Gathered together in her *Scivias* ('Know Thy Ways'), her visions condemn contemporary vice and prophesy forthcoming disaster. But more importantly, they record an intelligent and direct seeing. Hildegard was immensely accomplished: as an artist, she illustrated her own books; as a healer, she wrote a *vade mecum* of medicine, *The Book of Simple Medicine*; as a musician, she composed a Symphonia with many song settings, and a morality play with eighty-two melodies. She was also a splendid correspondent, who saw women and men as equal in their work for God in the 'creative greenness' of his Spirit. Feast day in Germany, 17 Sept.

Hillel (late 1st cent. BCE–early 1st cent. CE). Leading Jewish *ḥakham* (*sage) of the second Temple period. He rapidly emerged as a prominent interpreter of *Torah, developing his seven rules of *hermeneutics. He became *nasi (president) of the *Sanhedrin, and, with *Shammai, formed the last of the pairs (*zugot) of scholars. In general, Hillel adopted the less rigorous interpretations of Torah, though *B.Shab.* 77a refers to six issues where Hillel was more rigorous.

Ḥillul ha-Shem (Heb., 'profanation of the name'). Description of any action that profanes the name of God. The phrase is used to denote any action which might bring disgrace to Judaism or to the Jewish community—the converse, in fact, of *Kiddush ha-Shem.

Hilton, Walter (d. 1396). English mystic. After a period as a hermit, he became an Augustinian canon at Thurgarton Priory, Notts. His principal work, widely read in medieval England, is his *Ladder of Perfection*, which traces the soul's ascent to God in terms of the reformation of the image of God in the soul in two stages: reformation in faith, and in feeling, the former being the correction of false notions, the latter appropriation of the truth at the deepest level.

Himālaya ('abode of snow'). A vast mountain range on the northern border of India, regarded as sacred by Tibetans and Hindus alike. According to the **Mahābhārata*, the gods sacrifice on the summits, and Mount *Meru, the axis of the world and the source of its vitality, lies at its centre.

Himorogi (Jap., 'sacred hedge or enclosure'). In ancient times a particularly sacred place, such as a hill, grove, or the area surrounding some other unusual natural phenomenon. The sacral nature of the site can be manifested in various ways, both spontaneously and through divinatory rites.

Contemporary groundbreaking ceremonies, known as *ji-(chin-)sai* or *koto-shizume no matsuri*, reflect in both form and intention the archaic ritual significance of himorogi. A derived usage refers to sacrificial offerings made at the sanctuary; a different Chinese ideogram is used for this meaning.

Hina matsuri (doll festival): see FESTIVALS AND FASTS.

Hīnayāna (Skt., 'small vehicle'). A name used by *Mahāyāna Buddhists for forms of early Buddhism, which they characterize as defective or preparatory in contrast to themselves, the 'Great Vehicle'—in particular because they regard adherents of Hīnayāna as being preoccupied, selfishly, with the advancement of their own aggregation of appearance towards the goal of *arhat, as opposed to that of *bodhisattva. A less aggressive name for the earlier forms of Buddhism is Theravāda, 'teaching of the elders', but this strictly is inaccurate, since Theravāda is the name of one particular school belonging to the *Sthavira group, itself one of the two parties into which early Buddhism split at the 3rd Council (see COUNCILS (BUDDHIST)) of Pātaliputra. An alternative name is 'Pāli school', because early Buddhism rested on the Pāli canon. More accurate, but unlikely to displace Theravāda, is Śrāvakayāna, the vehicle of the disciple (i.e. who seeks to become *arhat, not buddha, or who 'hears', *śrāvaka, in the mode of personal disciple).

Hinduism. The major continuing and connected religions of India, which have now spread throughout the world. About 80 per cent of India's approx. one billion people regard themselves as Hindu, and there are about 30 million Hindus elsewhere in the world. The word 'Hinduism' derives from the Persian *hindu* (Skt., *sindhu*, 'river'), belonging to the Indus Valley, hence 'Indian'. The term is misleading if it gives the impression of a unified system of belief and practice: it was replaced for a time in academic circles by 'Indian religion', but even that has now become 'Indian religions' in the plural (though that too is ambiguous, since Jains, Sikhs, and Christians are also religions of India, as for many centuries was Buddhism). The term 'Hinduism' is used here and throughout this work as a convenient shorthand. A name for the tradition which is in common use among Hindus is *sanātana *dharma, everlasting dharma; another with more specific focus on the *brahmanical system is *varṇaśramadharma* (see VARNA; ĀŚRAMA).

Historically, Hinduism is seen as unfolding through successive stages, but this again is misleading, since many beliefs and practices from earlier stages persist through to the present, often little affected by subsequent developments. The roots are set down in the traditions of the original stone-age inhabitants of India; the *Indus Valley civilization; the more developed Dravidian culture, related to the Indus Valley, and persisting especially among the *Tamils; and the *Āryan invasion leading to *Vedic religion (the religions based on the *Vedas).

The Vedas (eternal truth) are believed to be eternal (sanātana). They are made known through *ṛṣis, who received them by a kind of intuition (*dṛṣti*). The revealed scriptures are known as *śruti (revelation, that which has been perceived through hearing; for details see VEDA). *Āgama (scripture) denotes all writings which at least some Hindus regard as revealed, which may therefore extend beyond the core corpus. Revered by most Hindus is **Bhagavadgītā*, and the majority regard it as revealed. Gathering śruti material are many *sūtras, but since they do not contain new material they are not usually cited as authorities in debate.

The second major source of authority is found in the texts of *smṛti ('that which has been remembered', tradition) which are much more closely concerned with the details of everyday life; among these texts, **Manusmṛti* is held in particularly high esteem. Much of śruti and smṛti has been gathered into *itihāsa-purāṇa (ancient histories), of which the two great epics *Mahābhārata* and *Rāmāyaṇa* probably have far greater direct influence on the population than the scriptures as such.

The Vedas gave rise to the elaborate ritual instructions and explanations of the texts known as *Brāhmaṇas, and this ritual-based religion is often referred to as brahmanical religion. It gave rise also to reflections on the meanings and implications of the rituals, in the *Āraṇyakas and the *Upaniṣads. Based on the consummations of the Veda in *Vedānta, the major forms of philosophical religion were elaborated (see ŚAṄKARA, RĀMĀNUJA, and MADHVA). But philosophical systems had already been established, some of them atheistic or materialist. There are traditionally six ways of orthodox (*āstika) insight (*darśana, for list); there is a continuing debate about those which should be considered *nāstika (unorthodox: not just, from a Hindu point of view, the obvious aberrations of the Jains and Buddhists, but perhaps also e.g. *Sāṁkhya).

But for the majority of Hindus, religious life is a matter, not so much of philosophy, as of ordering one's life according to the principles and practices which will lead to a better rebirth or even to *mokṣa (release). This 'ordering of life' is to live it according to dharma, or, less usually, to live it according to particular vows or devotions (see SĀDHU; TANTRISM). Dharma has many meanings, but in this case it means roughly 'appropriateness': 'Hinduism' as sanātana dharma is the map of how to live appropriately. It is this 'mapping' of the ways to live appropriately which is expressed in the divisions of labour (*varna), and even more specifically in the *caste-system (*jāti). In general, Hindus can aim legitimately for four goals (*puruṣārtha): within the bracket of controlling dharma and of mokṣa, the aims of *kāma and *artha are wholeheartedly endorsed.

Although the Vedas do not reveal any lively expectation of a worthwhile life after death, the concentration on *prāṇa (breath) in the period of the Brāhmaṇas and Āraṇyakas gave rise to the belief that there is an underlying self or soul (*ātman) which persists through the process of living and dying, and which subsists through all the changing appearances of a body. By the time of the Upaniṣads, this had become a belief that Brahman, the unproduced Producer of all that is, pervades the fleeting appearances of this or any other universe as ātman, as the underlying guarantor of appearance, but not in any way identical with it. While ātman is entangled in desire for the world, it continues to be reborn (*saṃsāra), at many different levels of appearance, in heavens and hells, as animals or as humans: the outcome, for better or for worse, is governed by a natural moral law of *karma, as inexorable as that of gravity. To be born as a human is a rare opportunity to advance toward mokṣa, release from the round of rebirth.

The nature of that attainment is variously described. At the philosophical end, *advaita envisages a reunion of undifferentiated reality.

Theism, however, dominates Indian religion. Each person (or often region or village) is likely to have a particular focus of devotion (*iṣṭadevatā), but these will usually complement, not supplant the major deities. The sense of God as Lord (*bhagavān) is usually expressed as *Īśvara; but God may become manifest in many different forms, hence the (initially bewildering) proliferation of gods and goddesses from the Vedic period onward. The manifestation of these on earth (especially of *Viṣṇu) are known as *avatāra.

Amidst the myriad theistic devotions, three are of extensive importance: those to *Śiva (*Śaivism, regarded by some as the oldest continuing Indian religion), to Viṣṇu (*Vaiṣṇava, numerically the largest, though divided into many subdivisions), and to *Śakti (see also ŚĀKTISM), in whom, as Goddess and divine mother, are gathered all the functions that Viṣṇu has for the Vaiṣṇavites and that Śiva has for the Śaivites. But the breakdown of these into particular traditions is prolific in its diversity. The traditions of devotion and teaching are transmitted through *gurus and protected in organized systems (*saṁpradāya).

Worship of God is *pūjā (worship). The evocation of the real presence of God is particularly important also in the focus of *mantra/*maṇḍala and *yantra (sounds and diagrams); and in places or rivers closely associated with manifestations of God (see SACRED CITIES/SACRED RIVERS, SEVEN).

The three major paths (*mārga) of progress toward mokṣa are karmamārga (the way of works, following dharma), jñānamārga (the way of knowledge or of philosophical truth), and bhaktimārga (the way of devotion to God). *Bhagavad-gītā* makes an attempt to reconcile all three. All three are united also by being called *yoga.

At Independence (1947), India was designated a secular state with recognition of all religions: the eclectic genius of Indian religion (which does not mean that there cannot be sharp conflicts and divisions) makes this a natural outcome. However, the remarkable ability of Indians to put this into practice (e.g. with the possibility of a Muslim president; contrast the status of Islam in Pakistan) has already come under strain with a growing sense that Hindus should affirm their identity over against the separatist tendencies of Sikhs and (in some areas) Muslims—hence the emergence of specifically Hindu political movements and parties (see BHARATYA JANATA PARTY). The contrast between these two attitudes (of inclusive toleration and Hindu self-affirmation) were already apparent in the many 19th-cent. attempts to revive and restate Hinduism: see ROY, RĀM MOHAN; BRAHMO SAMĀJ; SEN, KESHUB CHANDRA; DAYĀNANDA SARASVATĪ; ĀRYA SAMĀJ.

For many, the purpose of Hinduism is summarized in the prayer of *Bṛhādāranyaka Upaniṣad* 1. 3. 27, 'Lead me from the unreal to the real; lead me from darkness to light; lead me from death to immortality.'

Hindu Sacred Cities: see SACRED CITIES, SEVEN.

Hindu Sacred Rivers: see SACRED RIVERS, SEVEN.

Hinin (non-persons): see BURAKU.

Hinnom, Valley of (*gey-hinnom*): see GEHENNA.

Hippolytus, St (*c.*170–*c.*236). Church *father. He was an important *priest in the Roman Church and an enemy of *Sabellianism. However, he criticized the lax policy of Pope Callistus (217–22) in readmitting penitents to *communion, and seems to have been elected by a party of right-wing dissidents as rival bishop of Rome. Probably he was reconciled to the pope's party before his death.

Hippolytus's principal work is his *Refutation of all *Heresies* (largely discovered only in the 19th cent.), whose object was to show that all heresies derived from pagan philosophy. Historically more important is his treatise *The Apostolic Tradition*; this was composed *c.*215, and contains detailed descriptions of the rites of *ordination, *baptism, and the *eucharist as practised at the time in Rome. Feast day, 13 Aug. (W.), 30 Jan. (E.).

Ḥirā'. The mountain near Mecca to which, according to *ḥadīth, Muḥammad withdrew to meditate, and where, towards his fortieth year, he began to receive heavenly words which he was commissioned to announce to the Meccans.

Hiraṇyagarbha or **Hiraṇyāṇḍa** (Skt., 'golden womb', 'golden embryo'). In early Hinduism, the source of all creation and life. In **Ṛg Veda** 10. 121. 1 ff., Hiraṇyagarbha becomes the unified source of the created order and is identified with *Prajāpati.

Hiraṇyakaśipu. In Hindu mythology, the son of *Kaśyapa and *Diti, and twin brother of *Hiraṇyākṣa.

Hiraṇyākṣa. In Hindu mythology, son of *Kaśyapa and *Diti, and twin brother of *Hiraṇyakaśipu.

Hirata Atsutane (exponent of Japanese Studies movement): see KOKUGAKU.

Hiravijaya (1527–95). Śvetāmbara Jain teacher. He belonged to the Tapa *Gaccha, becoming head (*suri*) in 1566. In 1587, *Akbar summoned him to court to give an account of Jain teaching. Hiravijaya singled out compassion to all forms of life, and as a result, Akbar ordered that caged birds should be freed and that animals should not be slaughtered on the Jain festival of *Paryūṣana.

Hirsch, Samson Raphael (1808–88). Prominent exponent of Jewish *orthodoxy in 19th-cent. Germany. His most important works, *Neunzehn Briefe ueber Judentum* (Nineteen Letters on Judaism) (1836; Eng. 1899) and *Choreb, oder Versuche ueber Jissroels Pflichten in der Zerstreuung* (Hobab-Essays on Israel's Duties in the *Diaspora) (1837; Eng. 1962), were designed for young adults as a defence of traditional Judaism. He strongly opposed the emergent *Reform movement, defending, both Hebrew as the proper language for prayer, and also the traditional *synagogue organization.

Hisbollah (party of God): see ḤIZBALLAH.

Historical Jesus: see QUEST FOR THE HISTORICAL JESUS.

Histories in China. The Chinese reverence for antiquity, ancestors, and precedent produced, as early as the Han dynasty (206 BCE–221 CE), not only Grand Historians as court officials, but also systematically organized histories which acquired a canonical status. *Shih chi* (Records of the Historian) set the pattern: it was begun by Ssu-ma T'an (d. 110 BCE) and completed by his son, Ssu-ma Ch'ien (145–90 BCE). The historical work was continued by Pan Piao (3–54 CE) and his son Pan Ku (32–92), in *Han shu* (History of the Han). In this, they extended the Discourses to include punishments and laws, state sacrifices, geography, drainage of land, and literature. Subsequent Grand Histories followed these basic patterns.

Hitbodedut (conversation with God): see NAḤMAN OF BRATSLAV.

Hitopadeśa (Indian collection of stories): see PAÑCATANTRA.

Ḥizb (Islamic prayers): see WIRD.

Hizballah or **Hisbollah** (Arab., *ḥizb Allah*, 'party of God'). Quranic term for Muslims as opposed to idolators, in the early struggle for Islam (5. 62, 58. 23). The term has been repeatedly adopted by movements within Islam (e.g. by Indonesian rebels in 1945), as, recently, by a radical group in the Lebanon, which retained links with Iran.

Ho. The ear-splitting shout of a Ch'an master, designed not only to startle into sudden enlightenment (*tongo*) but also to mark the line of transmission from teacher to pupil. The Japanese pronunciation of the Chinese character is *katsu*, and in Zen it is used in ways comparable to the *kyosaku, the 'wake-up stick'. It is also a manifestation of transmission without concepts, words, or symbols. It was introduced by *Ma-tsu, but established in teaching by *Huang-po Hsi-yün.

Ho (Chin., 'crane'). Taoist symbol of immortality and wisdom.

Ho. Jap., for *dharma.

Hoa Hao. A simplified neo-Buddhist religion in the Mekong Delta of Vietnam with *c*.1½ million followers. It arose in Hoa Hao village in 1939 when an infirm *Roman Catholic peasant, Huyan Phu So (1919–47), had a convulsive religious healing experience. He began vigorous teaching of the new faith in which he claimed to be the reincarnation of earlier religious leaders and uttered prophecies that were later fulfilled. As a militant and nationalist religion, it set up its own virtually autonomous government in the Delta and joined the independence struggle, but opposed the Viet Minh which captured and executed the founder in 1947.

Ho-ch'i (sexual union in Taoism): see FANG-CHUNG SHU.

Hodge, Charles (1797–1878). *Calvinistic theologian. Ordained into the *Presbyterian ministry (1821), he was educated at Princeton at which seminary he taught biblical studies, then theology, for most of his life. He wrote several New Testament commentaries as well as a 3-vol. *Systematic Theology*, and edited the *Biblical Repertory and Princeton Review* for over forty years. Firmly committed to the *Westminster Confession, he held to the verbal inspiration and infallibility of *scripture, though Hodge always remained tolerant to those who could not fully subscribe to his doctrinal position.

Hogen (Chin., Fa-yen-tsung; Jap., Hōgen-shū). Ch'an/Zen school, one of the *goke-shichishū, the revered early schools. It was founded by *Hsüan-sha Shih-pei (Jap., Gensha Shibi), so that it was originally called Hsüan-sha. But *Fa-yen Wen-i, in the next generation, far exceeded Hsüan-sha, so that the school became known as Fa-yen (Jap., Hōgen).

Hōgen Bun'eki (Chinese Ch'an Buddhist teacher): see FA-YEN WEN-I.

Hōge-sō: Zen Buddhist monks in Japan who renounced, not only worldly possessions, but also monastery-support (cf. *friars in Christianity). Because of their complete abandonment of the world, the term came to be used also for any wholly enlightened monk.

Hōgo (Jap., 'dharma word'). The sayings of Zen patriarchs and ancient masters in the Ch'an/Zen tradition. They are frequently the subject of *shodō* (way of the pen, *calligraphy).

Hoguk Sŭngdan. Monks' Militia for National Defence, organized by the national Chogye (see BUDDHISM IN KOREA) order in modern Korea. The participation of Korean monks in the military defence of their country has its roots in the constant threat of foreign invasion.

Ho Hsien-ku (one of the eight immortals in Taoism): see PA-HSIEN.

Hōjin (Jap., for Skt., *sambhogakāya*). Body of delight, part of the *trikāya.

Hōjō (Jap., 'ten feet square'). The cell of a monk in a Zen Buddhist monastery; also the abbot, or the senior monk.

Hōjō-e (Jap., 'life-releasing ceremony'). A Japanese ceremony during which captive birds or fish are released into their natural environment. It was first held in the 8th cent. CE, and after falling into abeyance, it was revived in 1679.

Hoke-kyo. Jap., for **Lotus Sūtra*.

Hokkai (constituents of appearance). Jap., for *dharmadhātu.

Hokkeshū (Jap. Lotus School): see TENDAI (-SHŪ).

Hokke-zanmai (ancestor rituals): see ZANMAI.

Hokkyō (Jap., 'dharma bridge'). A term for what, in the West, is called 'Buddhism'; cf. *Hinduism and sanātana dharma.

Hō koji goroku (Ch'an/Zen Buddhist text): see P'ANG YÜN.

Hōkyōin-darani (Jap., 'the treasure-casket seal *dhāraṇī'). One of three spells chanted daily in *Shingon and Tendai temples. It is of great efficacy, since if its forty clauses are recited seven times, an ancestor in torment in hell (*jigoku*) will be released into the domain of *Amida. It is also efficacious in relation to illness.

Holā Mahallā (Pañjābī prob. masc. of Holī + place of attack). Sikh *festival, the day after *Holī. It was established by Gurū *Gobind Siṅgh as a day for military training through mock battles, a custom maintained by the *Nihaṅgs who gather in thousands at *Anaṇḍpur.

Holdheim, Samuel (1806–60). German *Reform Jewish leader. He represented the extreme trend in Reform Judaism; he held *Sabbath services on a Sunday and defended the right of *uncircumcised children to be accepted as full *Jews. Abraham *Geiger thought that he had gone too far, but nevertheless gave the eulogy at his funeral.

Holī or **Holākā.** One of the important Hindu annual *festivals. Celebrated all over India at the beginning of spring, its precise form and motivation display enormous variety. On its basic level, it is a rural, agricultural festival of fertility.

Holiness (OE, *halignes*, 'without blemish'). The state of being set apart for God, or for religious purposes. For R. *Otto, the *Holy is *Ganz Andere*, the Totally Other, and all that relates to it must be separated from the profane and sinful. Holiness (Heb., *kedushah*) is a fundamental requirement of Jewish religion. (Leviticus 19. 2). What does it mean to be holy? According to *Maimonides, 'When the Bible says, "Be holy", it means precisely the same as if it had said, "Keep my commandments".' *Torah is thus the *syag* ('fence', a founding principle of rabbinic Judaism, *Pirqe *Avot* 1. 1, 'Be reflective in judgement, raise up many pupils, and build a *syag* around Torah') which prevents diffusion into randomness and uncertainty.

Christianity inherited the hope of holiness from Judaism, but no longer saw Torah as either a necessary or a sufficient condition. The *Holy Spirit is the source of the making holy (i.e. sanctification) of Christians, who become (or are meant to become) temples of the Holy Spirit (1 Corinthians 6. 11 and 20; 1 Peter 2. 9).

The word 'holiness' is then widely used for comparable vocations and goals in other religions, although it then loses its more specific constituents. In particular, it merges with considerations of *purity and *ablution: see also SACRED AND PROFANE.

Holiness Churches. Those churches which emphasize J. *Wesley's doctrine of perfection. Such groups usually teach that 'entire sanctification', involving the removal of inbred sin, follows conversion and is experienced instantaneously by faith. Following this crisis, the believer is empowered to live without deliberate sin, though not without 'weaknesses'.

Holiness Code. The collection of laws in Leviticus 17–26. The Holiness Code is so named because of the emphasis in the text that the Jewish people must be holy even as God is holy. However, some doubt whether these chapters constitute a separate Code, since they have a varied character and the word 'holiness' occurs only in 19–22 (and is in Leviticus outside this section).

Holocaust (Gk.). The burnt offering of Leviticus 1. 3, from which the word is applied to any offering which is consumed by fire.

Holocaust, Sho'ah (Heb., 'calamity'), or **Ḥurban** ('destruction'). The systematic destruction of European Jewry, 1933–45. In fact, the systematic extermination of other groups (e.g. homosexuals and gypsies) was also undertaken, but the term most often refers to the endeavour to make Europe 'Judenrein', free of Jews. From 1933 until war was declared in 1939, Jews were systematically eliminated from public office, intellectual and cultural life, and citizenship, and, from 1941 onwards, they were subjected to the 'Final Solution', systematic destruction in concentration camps (see AUSCHWITZ). It is impossible to know the exact number of Jewish victims of the Holocaust, but losses are estimated at six million. Since 1951, 27 Nisan is kept as a Holocaust Remembrance Day (Heb., Yom ha-Sho'ah) in *Israel and the *diaspora.

In the Holocaust, all theologians, including Jewish, are confronted with the problem of evil in its most acute form. A range of different responses has been made:

1. The third Ḥurban lies in the same providence of God which allowed the first two (the destructions of the two *Temples). I. Maybaum argued that Hitler could even be regarded as God's *messiah in the way that Deutero-*Isaiah interpreted Cyrus as 'God's messiah' (i.e. instrument of God's purpose) during the *Exile. For some, this is evidenced in the establishment of the State of Israel.

2. Suffering, even on so immense a scale, is a punishment for sin (a traditional Jewish understanding of suffering): in the words repeated in the liturgy, 'Because of our sins we were exiled from our land' (*mi-p'nei ḥata'einu* . . .). On this account, the abandonment of God by so many Jews in the *galut (exile from the Holy Land) brought about a just punishment.

3. Rejecting so grotesque a view of God's character, E. Berkowits argued that God nevertheless had to allow the camps: 'God is mighty, for he shackles his omnipotence and becomes powerless so that history may happen' (*Faith After the Holocaust*). He repudiated the Christian fascination with the Holocaust which was turning it into an intellectual game, even introducing university courses on 'The Holocaust': 'After

Auschwitz, leave us alone.' For Berkowits, the Jews have accepted the vocation of exile, in order to bear the pain of freedom on behalf of a world which abuses it, thereby becoming themselves a moral vocation to the world to turn and repent.

God is, but is beyond our understanding, as in the *Ein- Sof and *Deus absconditus traditions.

4. The presence of God in the Holocaust was affirmed also by E. Fackenheim (e.g. *God's Presence in History*, 1970) distinguishing between the two formative moments of Israel's origin, the Re(e)d Sea and Sinai, the saving presence and the commanding presence. God's saving presence was wholly absent from the camps, but his commanding presence was there.

This amounts to a 614th commandment (the total in Torah being 613): Thou shalt survive.

5. R. J. Rubenstein has been accused of making that posthumous surrender to Hitler because of his belief that 'God' as characterized in the tradition is clearly dead. Yet Rubenstein (e.g. *After Auschwitz*, 1966) has made a thoroughly religious and Jewish response by suggesting that Judaism is called to a far more radical understanding of its inheritance: it cannot rely on the obviously bankrupt dependence on a God who intervenes when called upon in prayer to do so: in that sense (for Rubenstein, also a cultural sense) God is dead. But the necessity for community is all the more imperative (cf. *civil religion), and for that purpose, Jewish rituals, festivals, observances, etc., are vital.

6. Elie Wiesel has offered an equally radical assessment of the Jewish tradition and belief in God. His sequence of three novels, moving from *Night*, to *Dawn* to Day (*Le Jour*, given the Eng. title, *The Accident*), marks the transition from the God-infused world which Wiesel had known as a child (born in 1928 in a Hungarian shtetl), through the camps (of which Wiesel was a survivor) where the search for God continues, to the world in which that God is dead: it is the transition from a world in which messianic redemption is 'around the next corner', to a world in which humans are clearly 'on their own'. Wiesel sees humanity after the Holocaust thrown into an abyss of non-meaning. Survival now means the forging of a new *covenant, no longer between Israel and God, because God has proved to be too unreliable a partner, but between Israel and its memories of suffering and death—of what *can* happen. Overall, the presence of God to the questioning *patriarchs is one of a silent and enigmatic tear. There is a comparable note at the end of A. Schwarz-Bart's novel, *The Last of the Just*. The Holocaust calls in question the legend that the presence of thirty-six just men will be sufficient to preserve a generation. If the covenant has been broken, it is not by God's people.

While there has been a wide variety of Christian responses, few have taken the measure of the opening words of A. L. and A. R. Eckhardt (*Long Night's Journey into Day: A Revised Retrospective on the Holocaust*, 1988): 'No event has made more clear the consequences of ideas than the German Nazi "Final Solution to the Jewish Problem". There could have been no "Jewish problem" to resolve had not almost two millennia of Christian teaching and preaching created it.' The absence of God from systematic *theology is nowhere more apparent than here. See also Index, Holocaust.

Holy. Term brought to prominence in the history of religions by N. *Söderblom and R. *Otto. For Söderblom, the distinction between the Holy and the Profane (cf. *Sacred and Profane) is the fundamental category of all religion. Otto saw the apprehension of the Holy through the operation of the religious *a priori* as the root of all religion: just as there must be *a priori* conditions which make possible such forms of human judgement as the scientific, the moral, and the aesthetic (and these different categories of judgement cannot be converted into each other, but give rise to different communities of human discourse), so, in Otto's view, there must be a priori conditions which give rise to the category of religious judgement, the human sense, different from the moral or the aesthetic sense, of a *mysterium tremendum fascinans et augustum*, an awe-inspiring depth of mysterious otherness, which attracts and yet terrifies. This is the *numinous. See also HOLINESS.

Holy fools. Figures who subvert prevailing orthodoxy and orthopraxis in order to point to the truth which lies beyond immediate conformity. The holy fool endeavours to express the insistence of all religions that detachment from the standards of the world is the *sine qua non* of advance into truth. Holy fools are also an important part of the reversals which are characteristic of the liminal stage of *rites of passage. Thus the Lord of Misrule (also known as the Abbot of Misrule) was elected in medieval Christianity to preside over Christmas festivities, often at the Feast of Fools. This was held at the New Year, and was so insistent in its reversals that it was repeatedly attacked by the official Church, but the traditional insights linger on in the figure of the clown. (For examples, see Index, Holy fools).

Holy Ghost (third person of the Holy Trinity): see HOLY SPIRIT.

Holy Innocents. The children of Bethlehem who, according to Matthew 2. 16–18, were slaughtered by the order of King *Herod the Great in a vain attempt to kill the infant Jesus. They are commemorated as martyrs on 28 Dec.

Holy Office. The Roman *congregation established in connection with the *Inquisition by Pope Paul III in 1542 as the final court of appeal in trials of *heresy. In 1965 *Paul VI reformed it and changed its name to 'The Congregation for the Doctrine of the Faith'.

Holy of Holies. Inner sanctum of the *Jerusalem *Temple. It was entered only once a year, by the *high priest on Yom Kippur (*Day of Atonment).

Holy Saturday. The Saturday in the Christian year between the *crucifixion and the *resurrection (i.e. *Good Friday and *Easter Day). Two contrasting themes characterize the day, that of waiting without knowledge of how grief is to be overcome, and that of the *harrowing of hell. It culminates in the Easter Vigil.

Holy see. A legal entity comprising the *pope and his *curia, recognized in international law as a sovereign body.

Holy Spirit

Judaism In *Tanach (Jewish scripture), *ruaḥ ha-Qodesh/Kodesh* is the breath of God, and thus the effective and inspiring consequence of God at work in his creation. The Holy Spirit is also known as *ruaḥ Elohim* and *ruaḥ Adonai*, indicating that no separate 'person' in relation to God is intended, but rather that this is the way in which God enables humans to do or say particular things.

Christianity Formally, the Holy Spirit (or 'Holy Ghost', especially in liturgical use) is the third person of the Holy *Trinity. The Spirit is distinct from but coequal with the Father and the Son, and is in the fullest sense God. This understanding was canonized in the 4th cent.

In the *fathers before the 4th cent., the Holy Spirit is variously identified with the Son, or with the *Logos, or with God's *wisdom. No particular activity of God is consistently said to be that of the Spirit, although *Origen held that the characteristic sphere of the Spirit's operation was the Church, as contrasted with the whole creation which was that of the Logos. But from 360 CE onwards the doctrine of the Spirit became a matter of controversy when the Pneumatomach(o)i ('spirit-fighters') denied the full divinity of the Spirit. The *Cappadocian fathers argued against them, e.g. *Basil in his *On the Holy Spirit*, and were victorious at the Council of *Constantinople (381). In the West this doctrine was elaborated by *Augustine in his *On the Trinity*, especially in his understanding of the Spirit as the bond of unity in the Trinity. For the later divergence between Western and Orthodox language about the Holy Spirit, see FILIOQUE.

Holy Synod. The supreme institution for the government of the *Russian Orthodox Church from 1721 to 1917. The governing body of the Church in Greece, a synod composed of bishops, is also called the 'Holy Synod'.

Holy war. Categorization of warfare in several religions (e.g. *jihād, *crusades), the war envisaged in the book of *Deuteronomy. It is distinct from the *just war, though they may overlap.

Holy water. In Christian usage, water which is blessed for use in certain rites, especially that which is blessed at the *Easter Vigil for baptism of *catechumens.

Holy Week. The week preceding *Easter, observed in liturgical churches as a period of remembrance of, and attachment to the *passion of Christ.

Holy Year. A year during which the pope grants, subject to particular conditions, a plenary *indulgence, the so-called Jubilee, to all those who visit Rome. A *bull specifies the particular purposes of the year and the conditions and benefits associated with it.

Homa. The making of an oblation, in Hinduism, to the gods by throwing *ghṛta and other offerings on the sacrificial fire. This is particularly important in the effecting of the major *saṁskāras, e.g. *marriage.

Homon (Jap., 'dharma gate'). The teachings of the *Buddha. In the Four Great Vows (*shiguseigan) of Zen, (part of the *bodhisattva vow), the third is: 'The dharma gates are manifold: I vow to enter them all.'

Homoousion (Gk., 'of one substance'). The word in the *Nicene Creed to express the relation in the one Godhead of the Father and Son. It was accepted as an anti-*Arian formula at the Council of *Nicaea at the urging of the emperor, although many bishops preferred the looser term *homoiousion*, 'of like substance'. Thus its sense may have been broadly 'of the same nature', rather than 'of the identical substance' as later theology took it. Homoousion was used again at *Chalcedon to express the relation of Christ to people; and it was extended to the *Holy Spirit during the 4th cent.

Homo religiosus (humans as religious beings): see ELIADE, MIRCEA.

Homosexuality. The attitude of religions to homosexuality is obscured by the extremely wide reference of the term (in some religions, for example, particular acts may be condemned, but not the disposition itself, and not all acts), by the ambiguities in the status of eunuchs, and by the uncertainty whether the term covers both males and females. In general, homosexuality is regarded as abnormal (standing outside the norms of nature and practice); there is then much difference concerning the 'normativeness of the norm'—i.e. how much it has to be covered by law. In Judaism, certain kinds of sexual activity are forbidden, including incest and adultery. The prohibitions against 'men lying with men as with a woman' occur in Leviticus (18. 22; 20. 13). According to the *rabbis, the prohibition is a part of the *Noachide Laws, and thus applies to all people (i.e. to gentiles as much as to Jews). The penalties are *karet* (being cut off from the people of Israel, Leviticus 18. 29) and death (Leviticus 20. 13). Very little is said about relations between women (known as *mesoleloth*). Christianity inherited the prohibitions and amplified them with the condemnations of homosexual acts in Romans 1. 26–7 (including women), 1 Corinthians 6. 9, and 1 Timothy 1. 10. While some Christian exegesis has drawn attention to a distinction between (i) context-dependent applications and the more fundamental context-independent command to love, and (ii) the condition of homosexuality which lies in nature and particular acts which would have to be assessed for morality just as heterosexual acts have to be, the Roman Catholic Church has moved strongly to maintain the condemnation, describing the homosexual orientation as 'an objective disorder' (*On the Pastoral Care of Homosexual Persons*, 1986); the *Catechism of the Catholic Church* recognized that homosexuality is basically not a matter of choice, but insisted that homosexual persons are called to a life of chastity. In Islam, homosexuals (*qaum Lut*, the people of Lot, or Lutis) are condemned in the story of Lot's people in the Qur'ān (e.g. 15. 73 f.; 26. 165 f.), and in the last address of *Muḥammad. Some argue that since penetration has to be involved, homosexual acts between women should be less severely punished. In any case, *shari'a is, as usual, concerned with public behaviour, so there is no strong condemnation of homosexuality if it is not displayed in public.

In India, the evaluation is more complex, because of the many strands of religious life. In general, it is clear that for *twice-born Hindus, 'homosexual acts' (*maithunaṁ puṁsi*) are condemned (e.g. **Manusmṛti* 11. 174 f., both men and women). But attitudes vary. The **Kāma Sūtra* specifically states that physical sex between two people of the same sex (as also of the opposite) 'is to be engaged in and enjoyed for its own sake as one of the arts'. The evaluation depends on the context and on what is appropriate (i.e. *dharma) for it. Among Buddhists, the issue is subsumed under the general dynamic of Buddhist societies, in which the choice is between monastic celibacy and lay life. While consideration is given to homosexual acts within communities, there seems to have been little isolation of homosexuality as such.

All these considerations were formed at a time when the 'natural nature' of homosexuality (and particularly of the genetic contribution to this widespread human condition) were not known. Religions which affirm the goodness of sexuality in its own right are adjusting more easily to new knowledge than those which hold that sexual acts must be open to life, and that the other functions of sex are always subordinate.

Hōnen (1133–1212). Founder of the *Jōdo (Pure Land) sect of Japanese *Pure Land Buddhism. At the age of 13, he became a monk of the *Tendai sect. At the age of 43, he converted to the Pure Land teachings upon reading Shantao's *Kuan-wu-liang-shou-fo ching shu*. Subsequently he preached that everyone without exception can be reborn in *Amida Buddha's Pure Land by simply reciting the *nembutsu, and insisted that the Pure Land teachings be considered an independent sect. The older established sects' opposition to Hōnen's teachings led to his exile from the capital of *Kyōto in 1207. Although he was soon pardoned and returned to Kyōto in 1211, he died the following year. Among his major works are the *Senchaku Hongan Nembutsu Shu*, an outline of his Pure Land teachings, and the *Ichimai Kishomon*, a one-page summary of his teachings written or dictated on his deathbed.

Hongan (Jap., 'original vow'). The initial vow of a *bodhisattva, or more specifically, the eighteenth vow of *Amida.

Honganji (Jap., 'Temple of the Original Vow'). The headquarters temple of the Otani Branch (*ha*) of *Jōdo Shinshū or 'True Pure Land School' of Buddhism in *Kyōto, originally established in 1272. Until the beginning of the 17th cent., there was only one Honganji. But Kyōmyo established a second temple bearing the same name, in 1602. Since this date, the original Honganji has been called Nishi ('West') Honganji and the newer temple Higashi ('East') Honganji.

Honi ha-Me'aggel (1st cent. BCE). A Jewish miracle worker. According to the *Talmud, Honi ha-Me'aggel ('the circle drawer') prayed for *rain in a time of drought and his prayer was fulfilled. Some have seen him as exemplifying the kind of activity in which *Jesus engaged, but virtually no indication of his teaching has survived, nor is there any reason why that context should have compelled Jesus to move from Galilee to Jerusalem.

Honjisuijaku (Jap., 'original substance manifests traces'). Principle whereby Buddhism is reconciled with Shinto. In its original form, it stated that the *kami and gods or goddesses of Japan are *avatars of *Vairocana. From the Middle Ages until the Meiji Restoration (1868), honjisuijaku was extensive. On occasion, Shinto asserted itself as the senior partner—e.g. after the *kamikaze had driven off the Mongol invasions of 1274 and 1281; or again, in the composition of the Five Classics at about the same time, which are mainly about the history of the Ise shrine, but which also give an account of Shinto philosophy and ethics (leading to Ise Shinto). The Five Classics were used by adherents of 'Primordial Shinto' (Yuiitsu Shinto) in the 15th cent. to reverse the relationship. Thus Yoshida Kanetomo (1435–1511; see YOSHIDA FAMILY) interpreted honjisuijaku as meaning that the Japanese gods were the original substance and the Buddha and *bodhisattvas the manifest traces.

Honrai-no-memmoku (Jap., 'original face'). An expression through which Zen Buddhists penetrate through the superficial appearances to the unchanging, uniform buddha-nature (*buddhatā) present in all things.

Honshi (Jap., 'root-master'). Any master or teacher in Zen Buddhism who is the root or source of *hō* (*dharma).

Hooker, Richard (*c.*1554–1600). *Anglican theologian. As the apologist of the Elizabethan religious settlement in England, he was a decisively important interpreter of Anglicanism. His *Treatise on the Laws of Ecclesiastical Polity*, also a classic of English prose, was only partly published in his lifetime (books i–v of eight books). Starting from a broadly conceived philosophical theology appealing to natural law, he attacked the *Puritans for regarding the *Bible as a mechanical code of rules, since not everything that is right (e.g. *episcopacy) finds precise definition in the *scriptures. Moreover, the Church is not a static institution, and the method of Church government will change according to circumstances. Hence the Church of England, though reformed, possesses continuity with the early Church.

Hopkins, Gerard Manley (1844–89). Poet and *Jesuit priest. Educated at Balliol College, Oxford, where he came under the influence of *Tractarianism, he became a Roman Catholic in 1866 and a Jesuit in 1868. He taught, latterly, as Professor of Greek in Dublin. His poetry was a search after style which would match his vision of God's creation. From the 13th-cent. philosophy of *Duns Scotus, he developed the view that all things bear the inward stress of their particularity (what Scotus called *haecceitas*) and of their own God-given meaning, which he called 'inscape'. In 1874, Hopkins was sent to St Beuno's in N. Wales as part of his training, and during his three years there, his poetry took off from theory into celebration. After he left Wales, he wrote little poetry until the final so-called 'black' sonnets/poems.

Hora'at sha'ah (Heb., 'ruling for the hour'). Legal ruling by Jewish authorities in an emergency, but not intended to have permanent validity.

Horin. Jap. for *dharmacakra.

Horner, I. B. (1896–1981). Pioneer of Pāli Buddhist studies in the West. She edited and translated many Buddhist texts, in particular, the *Vinaya Piṭaka, the **Majjhima Nikāya*, and *Milinda's Questions*. She became Honorary Secretary of the Pāli Text Society in 1942, and its President from 1949.

Horologion. In E. Christianity, a book of liturgical prayers and offices, somewhat like a *breviary.

Horowitz, Isaiah ben Abraham ha-Levi, also called **ha-Shelah ha-Kadosh** (The Holy Shelah, 1565–1630). *Rabbi and *kabbalist. His main work is the *Shenei Luḥot ha-Berit* (Two Tablets of the Covenant, 1649: the title is abbreviated as Shelah, hence his name above) which combines *halakhah, sermon, and *kabbalah in teaching how to lead the good life. As a mark of respect, he was buried close to *Maimonides.

Horrid thing (claims to special gifts from the Holy Spirit): see BUTLER, JOSEPH.

Horse-sacrifice (Hindu ritual): see AŚVAMEDHA.

Hōryū-ji (temple-complex): see NARA BUDDHISM.

Hosanna (Gk., from Heb., *hoshana*, 'save, we beseech you'). An acclamation used in Christian worship from an early time (**Didache* 10. 6).

Hosea. First of the twelve books known as the minor *prophets in the Hebrew Bible and Christian Old Testament. Hosea was almost certainly produced in the Northern Kingdom of

*Israel and, after the destruction of Israel in 721, subject to redaction in *Judah.

Hoshana Rabba (Heb., 'the great hoshana'). The seventh and last day of the festival of *Sukkot. Special willow branches (known as 'hoshanot') are cut for the festival and beaten on the ground, and Hoshana Rabba is described in the *Talmud as the 'Day of the Willow'.

Ho shang (Chin. transliteration, possibly from Turk., *Udin*, language of Khotan, or the Kashgarian dialect, *Hwa Shie*, of the Skt., *upadhyāya*, 'self-taught teacher', or *upasaka* 'the tutor of Rahula': Ho, 'Harmony or Peace', + Shang, 'in charge of or ascend'). Any religious figure; or a reverent form used for an *abbot, *fang-chang*, or *bhikṣu in charge of a *saṅgha.

Ho-shang Kung. A somewhat legendary Taoist figure, supposed to have written the commentary on the **Tao-te ching* which bears his name.

Hoshanot (willow branches): see HOSHANA RABBA.

Hospitallers (Knights of Malta): see TEMPLARS.

Hossen (Jap.; 'dharma contest'). Fundamental method in Zen Buddhism whereby a master and pupil move each other toward truth. The literal tr., 'contest', is inappropriate, since hossen is mutual encouragement, arising out of *zazen experience.

Hosshin. Jap., for *dharmakaya* in the three-body (*trikaya) understanding of the Buddha's manifestation.

Hosshin-kōan (creation of awareness of identity with Buddha-nature): see KŌAN.

Hossho (buddha-nature): see BUDDHATĀ.

Hossō school (Zen Buddhist school): see DŌSHŌ.

Hossu (Jap.). A small brush in Zen Buddhism, based on the brush used by Jains to sweep the path before them. It became a symbol of transmission. It was therefore passed on to a dharma-successor (*hassu).

Host (Lat., *hostia*, 'sacrifice, victim'). The bread of the *eucharist, especially the thin round wafer used by Roman Catholics and Anglo-Catholics (among whom the mass is most explicitly seen in relation to the death of Christ understood as *sacrifice).

Host, desecration of. Alleged profanation by Jews of the consecrated bread of the Christian eucharist. The accusation was made on many occasions throughout the Middle Ages and was revived in Romania as late as 1836.

Hotei (Chin., *Pu-tai*, 'cloth-bag'). A popular figure in the Ch'an or Zen Buddhist *iconography of China and Japan, as well as a popular deity in Chinese and Japanese folk religion. He is the Zen (and perhaps *Taoist) eccentric, wandering sage who bestows his spiritual goods on all he comes in contact with.

In Far Eastern folk religion he becomes associated with indigenous deities of happiness and good luck, all symbolized by obesity and a large (cloth) sack on his back.

Hōtoku (Jap., 'repaying virtue'). A popular syncretic religious movement of the Tokugawa period (1600–1868) in Japan. Hōtoku was founded by Ninomiya Sontoku (1787–1856), whose mission was to uplift morally the life of farmers, while, at the same time, encouraging economic productivity. Sontoku's creed emphasized the *Confucian doctrine of filial piety, the virtue of manual labour (which was the human counterpart of the creative activities of the gods, *kami), and the practice of husbanding agricultural surpluses to protect against times of famine.

Hotṛ (group of Hindu priests): see ṚTVIJ; SACRIFICES (HINDUISM).

Ho-tse Shen-hui (Jap., Kataku Jin'e; *c.*680–*c.*760). Chinese Ch'an master, pupil of *Hui-neng, and founder of the Kataku school. In contrast to his predecessors, Ho-tse maintained that enlightenment was not attained by a gradual process through long stages of training, but rather through disengagement from mind and mentality (*mushin*) which leads directly into awareness of one's true nature (*kensho) and thus to sudden enlightenment. Despite this important breakthrough, the school did not last long.

Hō Un (lay Ch'an/Zen Buddhist): see P'ANG YÜN.

Houris (beautiful maidens of Paradise in Islam): see ḤŪR.

Hours, canonical. The individual services of the divine *office. In both E. and W. Christianity, these have traditionally been reckoned as seven, following Psalm 119. 164: *mattins and *lauds (counted together as one hour), *prime, terce, sext, none, *vespers, and *compline.

House Churches (local and communal gatherings of Christains): see ECCLESIOLOGY.

Hou-t'u (generative force of the earth in China): see T'U-TI.

Hōyū (Ch'an Buddhist master): see FA-JUNG.

Hōza (seated fellowship): see RISSHŌ KŌSEI KAI.

Hōzo (Jap. name for the monk, Dharmākara): see AMIDA.

Hṛdaya Sūtra (Buddhist text): see HEART SŪTRA.

Hsi-an Fu. In NW China, site of the discovery in 1625 of a stele usually called the '*Nestorian monument'. It is inscribed in Chinese with a text including a history of the Nestorian Church (see CHURCH OF THE EAST) in China up until the time of its erection in 781.

Hsiang (incense): see INCENSE.

Hsiang-yen Chih-hsien (Jap., Kyōgen Chikan; d. *c.*900). Chinese Ch'an master; pupil and dharma-successor (*hassu) of *Kuei-shan Ling-yu. He is best known for the story of his breakthrough to enlightenment. After much text-based study and no progress, he went to Kuei-shan who asked him about his original face (*honrai-no-memmoku). According to Hsiang-yen, the human predicament is summarized in the story of a man hanging by his teeth from the highest branch of a tall tree, who is asked why *Bodhidharma came from the West.

Hsiao (Chin., 'old age' + 'son'). Filial piety, a virtue considered most important in E. Asian social ethics, influenced by the school of Confucius, and by the ancient cult of *ancestral veneration. *The Classic of Filial Piety* (**Hsiao Ching*) has been associated with Tseng-tzu, a direct disciple of the sage himself. See also ETHICS (CONFUCIANISM).

Hsiao Ching (Scripture of Filiality). A small text included in the *Confucian Classics. It purports to be a lecture given by the Master (*Confucius) to his eminent disciple, Master Tseng (Tseng-tzu), who was noted for his filiality. The text is likely to be no earlier than the late Chou or early Han (roughly 5th–3rd cents. BCE).

Hsien. Immortal beings depicted in Chinese art, literature, religion, and folklore since the 3rd cent. BCE. As bird-like people or wise old men lost in misty mountains, they could fly great distances or change their appearance at will. Among the most popular immortals is *Hsi Wang Mu, Queen Mother of the West, whose famous peaches of immortality ripen once every 3,000 years. Her orchards were once raided by another renowned hsien, Sun Wu-k'ung, the monkey king. A Taoist group of 'Eight Immortals' (*Pa-hsien) contains the famous Lu Tung-pen with his gourd of immortal *elixir.

Hsien-t'ien (Chin., 'before heaven'). Taoist concept of 'before time', i.e. the absolute condition before the creation of heaven.

Hsin (trust): see WU-CH'ANG.

Hsing (human nature): see HSÜN TZU.

Hsing-ch'i (Chinese breathing practice): see CH'I.

Hsin-hsing (founder of school of Chinese Buddhism): see SAN-CHIEH-CHIAO.

Hsin-hsin-ming (Buddhist poem): see SENG-TS'AN.

Hsi Wang Mu. One of the most popular of the Chinese *hsien (immortals). She is the Queen Mother of the West, whose peaches of immortality ripen once every 3,000 years. She has many cosmic powers, and became the focus of a cult seeking her aid in salvation at the opening of the Common Era.

Hsi-yün (Ch'an teacher): see HUANG-PO HSI-YÜN.

Hsüan-Hsüeh (Chin., 'secret teaching'). An early stage of neo-*Taoism, in the 3rd and 4th cents. CE. Important figures were Wang Pi (226–49), Hsiang Hsiu (221–300), Ho Yen (d. 249), and Kuo Hsiang (d. 312), all of whom wrote commentaries on **Tao-te ching*. They developed *Ch'ing-t'an, reflective conversation, by which name the 'movement' is also known. Against their predecessors, they held that *Tao, as non-being, is not an agent bringing things into being; things arise spontaneously within the totality of all existent being, which they took to be the meaning of *ti'en, heaven.

Hsüan-sha Shih-pei (Jap., Gensha Shibi; 835–908). A Ch'an/Zen master, the dharma-successor (*hassu) of *Hsüeh-feng I-ts'un, who began life as an illiterate fisherman. He received initial training in a monastery under *Vinaya rules, and lived an austerely ascetic life until he began pilgrimages to meet Ch'an masters. On one of these, he stubbed his toe against a stone in the road and experienced sudden enlightenment (*Ho-tse).

Hsüan-t'ien Shang-ti (Lord of the Dark Heaven). A Chinese deity. One of a family of five deities in antiquity, each in charge of a cardinal direction of the cosmos: Lord Green (East), Lord Red (South), Lord White (West), Lord Dark (North), Lord Yellow (Centre). Lord Dark has the power of driving away evil spirits. The religious Taoists, desirous of physical immortality, prayed to the stellar divinities for assistance for the making of the *elixirs. According to them, the North Pole Star (Plough or Dipper) is the central residence for the stellar deities headed by Hsüan-t'ien Shang-ti.

Hsüan-tsang, San-tsang, or **T'ang-seng** (*c.*600–64). A Chinese Buddhist monk and pilgrim, who was a major influence on the development of Buddhism in China through his translation of Skt. texts. He became a monk at the age of 13 and studied *Mahāyāna under several teachers. The discrepancies led him to travel to India in order to return to the sources of the teaching. His famous pilgrimage is described in *Ta-t'ang hsi-yu chi* (Record of the Western Journey, tr. S. Beal, 1906), which became the basis for the 16th cent. novel *Hsi-yu chi* (tr. A. C. Yu, 1980; cf. also A. Waley, *Monkey*). His pupil, K'uei-chi (636–82) wrote commentaries on many of the translations, using them to systematize the Fa-hsiang teachings.

Hsüeh-feng I-ts'un (Jap., Seppō Gison. 822–908). Ch'an/Zen Buddhist master, dharma-successor (*hassu) of *Te-shan Hsüan-chien, from whom derived (via his pupils) the *Yün-men (Ummon) school and the *Fa-yen/*Hsüan-sha (*Hogen) school. He experienced profound enlightenment in *mondō with his dharma brother, *Yen t'ou Chuan-huo. Against his initial wishes, many monks gathered around him on Mount Hsüeh-feng (hence his name), and through them, Ch'an spread extensively.

Hsüeh-tou Ch'ung-hsien (Jap., Setchō Jūken; 982–1052). Chinese Ch'an/Zen master of the *Yün-men (*Ummon) school, a great poet, who laid the foundations of the hundred verses of the *Pi-yen-lu* (Jap., *Hekigan-roku*; The Blue Cliff Record). Yüan-wu K'o-ch'in took up and extended the work, making it into the most important collection (along with **Wu-men-kuan*) of Zen *kōans. To the two basic texts (the cases of enlightenment experience, and the verses) Yüan-wu added notes and a commentary. Thus for each of the hundred examples, there are seven parts: introduction, case, notes, commentary, verse, notes, commentary.

Hsü Kao-seng chuan (Chinese Buddhist biographical text): see TAO-HSÜAN.

Hsün Ch'ing: see HSÜN TZU.

Hsün Tzu (Xunzi). An important work of early Chinese philosophy attributed to Hsün Tzu or Hsün Ch'ing (b. *c.*300 BCE). His interpretation of *Confucian teaching, which became canonical (to be studied by court officials) during the former Han dynasty (206 BCE–9 CE), remained largely dominant until the rise of the *Neo-Confucian movement in the 11th cent.

The book teaches that people are by nature 'evil'—not in any metaphysical way, but in the practical sense that without proper education people cannot rise to full participation in culture and society. At the root of this doctrine is a distinction between human 'nature' (*hsing*, 'that which cannot be learned or acquired by effort') and 'conscious activity' (*wei*, 'that which can be acquired by learning and brought to completion by effort', B. Watson tr., p. 158). *Hsün Tzu* stresses the importance of *wei*: people are not fully human until they have become imbued with a sense of moral and ritual propriety, and they are not born with that sense but must be taught it.

Hsün Tzu was influenced by the legalist school of his day, which stressed the necessity of law and coercion for maintaining social order.

Hsü-t'ang Chih-yü (Jap., Kidō Chigu; 1189–1269). Chinese Ch'an/Zen master of the *Rinzai tradition. He was the teacher of Shōmyō who took his *dharma teaching to Japan. His discourses are collected in *Hsü-t'ang ko-shang yü-lu* (Jap., *Kidō oshō goroku*), and contain *kōans still used in Rinzai training.

Hua-Hu Ching (Chin., On the Conversion of Outsiders). Taoist work, *c.*300 CE, describing the missionary work of *Lao-tzu 'to the west', i.e. in India. Its main polemic claim is that Lao-tzu instructed the *Buddha.

Huai-nan Tzu. Chinese work of the 2nd cent. BCE, written and compiled by scholars of the court of Liu-an, prince of Huai-nan. It summarizes the main philosophies and schools, but proclaiming the superiority of Taoism.

Huan-ching (Chin., 'allowing semen to return'). The control of semen, especially the prevention of ejaculation, as a redistribution of power in the body, a prelude to meditation in Taoism.

Huang-chin (yellow cloth worn by Tao group): see CHANG CHÜEH.

Huang-ch'üan (Chin., 'yellow springs'). The underworld to which, in Taoism, *yin-weighted souls descend after death. See further P'O.

Huang-lao Chün (Chin., 'ancient yellow Lord'). Taoist deity, and principal god of *T'ai-ping tao. Originally compounded from Huang-ti (one of the legendary emperors—the Yellow Emperor—and four founders of religious Taoism, *tao-chiao* and *Lao-tzu, he is the ruler of the world who appears in numerous incarnations of Taoist teachers to maintain the understanding of Tao.

Huang-lung Hui-nan (Jap., Ōryō E'nan, 1002–69). Ch'an/Zen master of the *Rinzai school. He was the dharma-successor (*hassu) of Shih-huang Ch'u-yüan, and founder of the Ōryō school of Zen within the Rinzai tradition. It was the first school of Zen to be carried from China to Japan and taught by way of the three barriers (Jap., *sankan*), in the style of *kōans.

Ōryō is one of the Seven Schools (*goke-shichishū) of Ch'an/Zen, but it died out in both China and Japan after a few generations.

Huang-po Hsi-yün, (Hsi-yün of the Huang-po mountain, Jap., Ōbaku Kiun; d. 850 CE). Ch'an/Zen master, dharma-successor (*hassu) of *Pai-chang Huai-hai and teacher of *Lin-chi I-hsüan, through whom he becomes one of the forefathers of the *Rinzai school. His teachings were gathered by P'ei Hsiu (Jap., Haikyū) under the (shortened) title *Chu'an-hsin-fa-yao*, a classic text of the Ch'an tradition, which expounds the teaching of universal mind.

Huang-ti (the Yellow Emperor): see HUANG-LAO CHÜN.

Huang-ti nei-ching (medical text): see BOOK OF THE YELLOW EMPEROR.

Huang-t'ing Ching (Chin., 'treatise on the yellow castle'). A Taoist work, *c.*3rd cent. CE, describing the deities of the body (*shen), and also the practices which lead to immortality (e.g. *ch'i and *fang-shih). The recitation of the title invokes the deities and wards off evil from the body.

Hua T'o (developer of Taoist exercises): see WU-CH'IN-HSI.

Hua-yen (Jap., *Kegon, lit., 'Flower Adornment' school). A major school of Chinese Buddhism, which derived its name from the title of the Chinese tr. of its main text, *Buddhāvatamsaka-sūtra* (see AVATATAṂSAKA). Its main organizer was *Fa-tsang (3rd Patriarch) (643–712), although its roots are earlier (e.g. *Tu-shun). Important teachers were Cheng-kuan (737–820), regarded as the incarnation of *Mañjuśrī, and Tsung-mi (780–841). Hua-yen was taken to Japan in 740 by Shen-hsiang, where it is known as *Kegon.

Hua-yen regarded itself as the culmination of the *Buddha Śākyamuni's teaching after his enlightenment. This teaching maintains the interdependence and equality of all appearance, the 'teaching of totality'. Appearances may be in different states, but they are necessarily interdependent in constituting the universe of phenomena, and in equally manifesting the Buddha-illumination of enlightenment. Thus when Fa-tsang was summoned by the formidable empress Wu to expound the sūtra, he took a golden lion in the room as illustration: the lion is the phenomenal world, *shih*, but it is constituted by gold, *li*, the underlying principle which has no form of its own. By analysis into *shih* and *li*, every manifestation is identical to every other, and is an expression of the buddha-nature (*buddhatā). This key perception of the interpenetration of all existences is expressed in Fa-Tsang's image of Indra's net, which spreads across the universe, with a perfect jewel in each of its links: each jewel reflects every other jewel in the whole net.

Hubbard, Lafayette Ron (1911–86). American science-fiction writer and founder of *Scientology. He became widely known with the publication in 1950 of his book *Dianetics: The Modern Science of Mental Health*, which is the basic textbook of Scientology. The Church of Scientology was founded in 1954. It has been involved in disputes about whether it is a religion or a psychotherapy, and over its methods of recruitment: in Australia, the High Court ruled in 1983 that it is a religion; in the UK, restrictions were placed (between 1968 and 1980) on those wishing to enter the country to work for, or to study, Scientology. Meanwhile, Hubbard withdrew increasingly from administration in order to write.

Hūd. A prophet, according to Qur'ān (in sūras 7, 11, 26, 46, 49), among the 'Ād, demonstrating that God has sent messengers to more peoples than Jews and Christians.

Hudnan Pesobay (leader of the faithful): see MAGI.

Ḥudūd (limits set by God in Islam): see ḤADD.

Hügel, Baron Friedrich von (1852–1925). Roman Catholic philosopher, theologian, and spiritual writer. He befriended A. *Loisy and G. *Tyrrell, and played an important role in the *Modernist movement. His major works include *The Mystical Element of Religion as Studied in St *Catherine of Genoa and her Friends* (1908), *Eternal Life* (1912), *Essays and Addresses in the Philosophy of Religion* (2 vols., 1921, 1926), and *The Reality of God* (1931).

Hugh, St (*c.*1140–1200). Bishop of Lincoln. Henry II of England, impressed by his talents, persuaded him to become prior of the first English Carthusian house at Witham, Somerset, in 1175. In 1186, at the king's insistence, Hugh became bishop of Lincoln. As bishop he was very able and much loved. His shrine at Lincoln was among the most popular in medieval England.

Hugh of St-Victor (*c.*1096–1142). Medieval theologian, of whom little is known. About 1115 he entered St-Victor, a house of *Augustinian canons in Paris. Together with other later members of the Abbey, notably Richard of St-Victor and Thomas Gallus, he represents the distinctive and influential 'Victorine' school of theology, which is marked by the influence of *Dionysius the Areopagite (on whose *Celestial Hierarchy* Hugh wrote a commentary), and sees the whole created order as a set of symbols manifesting the glory of God and drawing people to contemplation.

Huguenots. (poss. from the name Hugues, or Swiss Eidgnosse, 'confederate'). French Calvinists. As *Calvinism spread rapidly in France during the 1540s, so persecution increased, especially under Henry II (1547–59). On his death, a more confused political situation ensued, leading to civil war. Militant Catholics (above all the family of the Guises) refused compromise: the massacre of St Bartholomew's Day (1572) was made the more repugnant by the fact that Protestant leaders had been invited to Paris to celebrate the marriage of a Huguenot leader, Henry of Navarre, to a Catholic, Margaret, sister of Charles IX. The reconciliation which that event might have introduced was nevertheless brought near by the accession of Henry, who turned Catholic to gain the throne (hence the saying of himself or perhaps of his minister Sully, 'Paris vaut bien une messe', 'Paris is well worth a mass'). He ended the civil war, and by the Edict of Nantes, in 1598, he extended toleration to the Huguenots. In 1685, the Edict of Nantes was revoked. The ensuing Camisard revolt persisted for twenty years, but again was suppressed with great violence. The differing groups were largely united in 1938 in the Reformed Church of France.

Hui (brotherhoods): see SECRET SOCIETIES.

Hui-ch'ang persecution. Suppression of Buddhism in Korea by Emperor Wu-tsung of the T'ang dynasty during 842–5 in the Hui-ch'ang era (841–6).

Hui-k'o (Jap., Eka; 487–593). Second patriarch (after *Bodhidharma) of Ch'an/Zen in China. He was driven to S. China by other Buddhist monks, and may perhaps have been assassinated by them. In addition to menpeki (wall-gazing), much emphasis was placed on the **Laṅkāvatāra-sūtra*.

Hui-kuo (Buddhist master): see KŪKAI.

Hui-neng or **Wei-lang** (Jap., E'nō; 638–713). Sixth patriarch of Ch'an/Zen in China, and dharma-successor (*hassu) of *Hung-jen. With his name is associated both a new orientation of Ch'an/Zen, and the only Chinese work to be accorded the status of a *sūtra, the *Platform Sūtra* (see LIU-TSU-TA-SHIH FA-PAO-T'AN-CH'ING). But much is legendary, and the autobiographical part of the *Platform Sūtra* (2–11) summarizes the traditions as they had accumulated in the 8th cent. After the schism between the Northern and the *Southern schools, with the N. emphasizing gradual progress, especially through attention to scriptures (*zengyō), and the S. emphasizing sudden enlightenment (*tongyō), Hui-neng is represented in art tearing up the Sūtras.

Hui Shih (4th cent. BCE). Chinese philosopher and friend of *Chuang-tzu, who taught by paradox and the unification of opposites. Everything is relative to something else, and thus is not absolutely great or small, etc.; but that suggests a standard of the infinitely great outside which nothing can lie, and of the infinitely small within which nothing can be contained.

Hui-tsung (1082–1135). Sung dynasty emperor in China, who strongly promoted Taoism. He encouraged the formation of the Taoist canon (*Tao-tsang) and built many monasteries.

Hui-yuan (334–416). Buddhist monk of the early period of Chinese Buddhism. He was born into the Chia family in Yen-men (North Shansi). Although he studied the *Confucian Classics and *Taoist works in his youth, he became a disciple of *Tao-an (312–85), the most highly respected Buddhist monk of his time, at the age of 21. Hui-yuan wrote the treatise, *Monks Do Not Pay Obeisance to Kings* (to argue for the independence of the Buddhist community from political authorities) and *San-pao-lun* (a treatise on *karma).

Hukam (Pāñjābī, 'order' from Arab.). Sikh concept of divine order. For Gurū *Nānak and subsequent Sikh thinkers, hukam is a fundamental concept, recurring in the *Ādi Granth and prominent in the *Japjī *Sāhib, according to which nothing is exempt from God's hukam.

For Sikhs today hukam or *vāk* is the daily practice prescribed in the *Rahit Maryādā of consulting the scriptures. The Ādi Granth is opened at random and the portion appearing at the top of the left-hand page is read.

Hukamnāmā (Pañjābī, 'decree'). Historically the orders of the Sikh *Gurūs and *Bandā Siṅgh. Of the hundreds sent by the Gurūs and their families to congregations and individuals about one hundred are extant.

Ḥukkat ha-goi (Heb., 'custom of the *gentiles'). Idolatrous or heathen customs forbidden to Jews (Leviticus 20. 23).

Huligammā (Kannaḍa, *huli*, 'tiger', + Dravidian, *amman). One of the innumerable *grāmadevatās of S. India. One major temple of the Goddess is found in Raichur, Karṇāṭaka; it is associated with a special group of devotees —impotent or malformed men.

Humanae vitae. An encyclical written by Pope Paul VI in 1968 addressing the question of birth control, following the report of the commission set up by Paul's predecessor, John

XXIII, to study the question of artificial contraception, principally the recently developed contraceptive pill.

Paul repeats the traditional view that 'each and every marriage act must remain open to the transmission of life' (§ 11). This is so because of the inseparable connection willed by God between the unitive and procreative aspects of the conjugal act, which not only closely unites husband and wife but also enables them to generate new life 'according to laws inscribed in the very being of man and of woman' (§ 12).

The encyclical ends with an appeal to Catholics to follow and support its teaching on artificial contraception. However, its publication, while welcomed by some, was greeted with dismay and open dissent by many Roman Catholics, and its teaching on contraception has remained a matter of controversy, to the neglect of Paul's outline of the values of marriage and responsible parenthood.

Hume, David (1711–76). Philosopher, religious sceptic, historian, and leading figure of the Scottish Enlightenment.

His most important philosophical works were: *A Treatise of Human Nature* (1739–40), *An Enquiry concerning Human Understanding* (1748), and *An Enquiry concerning the Principles of Morals* (1751). In them Hume took the empiricism of *Locke and Berkeley a stage further, reaching sceptical conclusions about the foundations of our knowledge of the external world, about inductive reasoning and rational *ethics (he pointed to the logical gap between 'is' and 'ought'), and about the existence of the self and a necessary causal nexus in nature.

A similar scepticism is seen in his works on religion. His *Natural History of Religion* (1757) foreshadows later anthropological accounts of religion in its investigation of the psychological and environmental factors influencing religious belief.

His essay 'Of Miracles' argues that an appeal to *miracles cannot serve as the foundation of a religion, for it is always much more probable that our evidence for the universal and regular laws of nature will preponderate over the evidence for putative miracles, which Hume defines as violations of such laws.

Hume's most substantial work on religion is his *Dialogues concerning Natural Religion* (written in 1751–7, revised later, and published posthumously in 1779), much of which consists of a critique of Enlightenment *natural theology, especially the *teleological argument for the existence of God.

Thus already in the 18th cent. there is a radical questioning of the Enlightenment project of rational theism. Unlike many of the French *philosophes* of his own time, however, and also his own later followers, Hume did not claim to be an atheist, for he regarded *atheism too as going beyond the available evidence.

Ḥummash (Heb., 'five', = Gk., 'Pentateuch'). First five books of the Hebrew *Bible.

Hun. Constituent element in Chinese anthropology, one of two non-corporeal elements to make up the living human being (the other being *p'o). The two must interact harmoniously for life to continue; when they separate, death ensues.

For their destiny after death, see SHEN.

Hung-chih Cheng-chüeh (Jap., Wanshi Shōgaku; 1091–1157). Chinese Ch'an/Zen master of the *Sōtō school who clarified the distinction from *Rinzai Zen, in argument with his contemporary, Ta-hui Tsung-kao. Where Ta-hui advocated the way of *kōan, Hung-chih valued more highly the way of silent illumination (*mo-chao ch'an*; Jap., *mokushō zen*), and responded to Ta-hui in a brilliant work of only 288 characters, *Mo-chao ming*/*Mokushomei*, (The Seal of Silent Illumination). Ta-hui attacked this as false Zen (*jazen*). Hung-chih rejected Ta-hui's method as kōan-gazing Zen, *k'an-hua ch'an*/*kanna zen*, and the terms *mokushō zen* and *kanna zen* now designate the sides in this division; but the division is not absolute, and remains one of emphasis and of different understanding of the status of kōan and of *satori (enlightenment).

Hung Hsiu-ch'uan (ruler of Taiping's Heavenly Kingdom of Great Peace'): see TAIPING REBELLION.

Hung-jen (Jap., Gunin or Kōnin; 601–74). Fifth patriarch of Cha'n/Zen in China. He lived on Mount P'ing-jung, the East Mountain, hence his following were known as 'The Pure Gate of the East Mountain'. He did not exclude sudden enlightenment (*tongyō) but advocated progressive control of mind, especially by concentration on the figure one (Chinese character being a single horizontal line) as it merges in the horizon of perception. The One became a central concept in Ch'an/Zen, particularly in the realization by the mind of its buddha-nature (*buddhatā). *Tsui-shang-ch'en lun* (Jap., *Saijōjō-ron*) is attributed to Hung-jen, but doubtfully. His successor was *Hui-neng.

Hungry ghosts (deceased who have not received appropriate or due support): see PRETA; LI-KUEI.

Huntingdon, Selina, Countess of (1707–91). Founder of the 'Countess of Huntingdon's Connexion', an association of Christian evangelicals. Desiring to reach the upper classes, she opened chapels where the *Calvinistic preaching of her chaplains was combined with a liturgical form of worship. The Countess of Huntingdon's Connexion, formed in 1790, united her churches. In 1980, twenty-nine of these survived, with membership of 860.

Huppah (Heb., 'canopy'). Jewish marriage canopy. In the Jewish marriage service, the huppah represents the marriage chamber.

Ḥūr, pl. **ḥawrā'** (Arab., 'white ones'). The beautiful maidens of *paradise, who are described in the *Qur'ān e.g. 2. 25, 3. 15, 4. 57, 55. 56 ff. They are often transliterated as 'houris'. Not all commentators (e.g. *al-Baiḍāwī) take the passages literally, and the *Sūfīs spiritualize the huris.

Ḥurban (destruction): see HOLOCAUST.

Ḥurūfī. A *Shi'a movement founded by Fazl Allāh in the 14th cent. (8th cent. AH), later adopted by some *Bektāshīya. Their belief (summarized in *Maḥram-nāme*, AH 828) is that the universe moves in eternal cycles, from *Adam to the Day of *Judgement, with God becoming manifest through creation, especially in the human face which reflects the image of God. This manifestation is concentrated in the successive forms of prophet, saint, and (finally, in Fazl Allāh) the incarnation of God.

Hus, Jan, or **John Huss** (1373–1415). Bohemian Christian Reformer. An ordained *priest and popular preacher, he came to accept some of *Wycliff's teachings as they were disseminated in early 15th-cent. Bohemia. The propagation of these views about reform coincided with the *Great Schism, and it was agreed to hold a Council at *Constance in 1414 to settle the controversy. The Emperor Sigismund promised Hus safe conduct, but Hus was arrested and privately convicted of perpetrating Wycliffite ideas: extracts from his own *De Ecclesia* (1413) were used to accuse him of heresy. He was condemned and burnt at the stake on 6 July 1415. He has remained a vital figure of Czech identity and resistance to foreign domination, especially in the 20th cent.

Husain (son of 'Ali and Imām): see AL-HUSAIN.

Huss, John: see HUS, JAN

Husserl, Edmund (philosopher): see PHENOMENOLOGY.

Hutterites (radical Reformation group): see ANABAPTISTS.

Huyan Phu So (founder): see HOA HAO.

Hwarang Do (Korean, 'The Way of Flower Youth'). An indigenous institution of young aristocrats residing in the kingdom of Silla in Korea. The Hwarang corps, founded during the reign of King Chinhŭng (540–76), was composed of aspiring leaders, schooled in civil and military virtues through their devotion to Mirŭk (*Maitreya, the future Buddha), their observance of Wŏn'gwang's 'Five Precepts for Laity', and the adoption of various *shamanic, *Taoist, and *Confucian values.

Hyakujō Shingi (rules governing Ch'an/Zen monasteries): see PAI-CHANG-CH'ING-KUEI.

Hymn of Creation: see NĀSADĀSĪYA; COSMOLOGY (HINDU).

Hymns

Christianity The use of poetry, or metrical prose, in worship may be detected in the New Testament (e.g. Ephesians 5. 14, 19). A 3rd-cent. writer (perhaps *Hippolytus) refers to 'Psalms and odes such as from the beginning were written by believers, hymns to the Christ, the Word of God, calling him God' (*Eusebius, *History* 5. 28. 5).

Latin hymns appear later than Greek. The most famous of early ones, the *Te Deum, is written in rhythmical prose. Hymns were admitted into the Roman office in the 13th cent.

The *Reformation affected greatly the development of hymns. Many were written by *Luther (imitating the pattern of medieval secular music), by P. *Gerhardt, and others. Since *Calvinism resisted anything but the words of *scripture in its services, the *Psalms were converted into metrical versions.

The practice of hymn-singing was encouraged and developed by the *Methodists, and soon spread among the Evangelical party of the Church of England.

The 19th cent. saw the establishment of hymn-singing in all parts of the Anglican church. *Hymns Ancient and Modern* (1861) was an eclectic collection that set the pattern for most modern hymnals. In virtually all parts of the Church there has developed a wide use of chorus-type hymns in a modern idiom.

See also Index, Hymns.

Sikhism Sikh worship consists mainly of *kīrtan, singing the hymns comprising the *Ādi Granth. Gurū *Nānak is popularly represented singing his compositions to *Mardānā's accompaniment. See AṢṬAPADĪ; CHAUPAD; CHHANT; RĀG; RĀGĪ; ŚABAD; ŚALOK; SAVAYYE; VĀR.

Hypatia (Neo-Platonic philosopher): see CYRIL, ST.

Hypostasis (Gk.; pl. -ses). A technical term used in Christian formulations of the doctrine of the *Trinity and of *christology. In secular Gk. its most general meaning is 'substance', but it could also mean 'objective reality' as opposed to illusion (as in Aristotle), and 'basis' or 'confidence' (as in Hebrews 3. 14). In Christian writers until the 4th cent. it was also used interchangeably with *ousia*, 'being' or 'substantial reality'. The term also came to mean 'individual reality' hence 'person'. It was in this sense that it was enshrined, under the influence of the *Cappadocian fathers, in the orthodox doctrine of the Trinity as 'three hypostases in one ousia'.

From this technical use, the term is applied to the substantiation of a metaphysical reality—e.g. the (possible) hypostasization of *Wisdom in Jewish Wisdom literature.

I

I. A Chinese term often translated as 'righteousness'. It connotes that which is just, proper, in accord with moral and customary principles.

As a moral and philosophical concept, i is rooted in early *Confucian thought. For *Confucius himself, i seems to have been related to a more comprehensive value, *jen ('humanheartedness'). *Mencius placed greater stress on i, making it one of the four virtues each of which has a 'font' (*tuan*) in the heart or mind.

In early *Taoist thought, particularly in the **Chuang Tzu*, i is the condition in which all things, merely by following their nature, do the 'right' thing.

For early 'legalist' thinkers such as Han Fei Tzu, by contrast, i was seen as already a relic from the past. Jen and i no longer suffice to order society, despite the fact that they were taught and practised by the sage kings and teachers of old; only coercion by force is effective.

These early schools of thought set the parameters for most subsequent moral and philosophical thought on i.

ʿIbādāt (Arab., pl. of *ʿibāda*, 'service' or 'worship'). The rules governing worship in Islam. The singular is common in Qur'ān, e.g. 10. 29; 19. 65.

ʿIbādiy(y)a, ʿIbadites, or **ʿAbādites.** The only continuing branch of the *Kharijites, who are found particularly in Oman, and in N. and E. Africa. Their (probable) founder, ʿAbd Allāh b. ʿIbād (1st cent. AH) took a far more moderate line, not regarding non-Kharijites as *mushrikūn* (*shirk), and therefore rejecting political assassination as a weapon. Marriage with non-ʿIbādites was also allowed. It influenced other Muslim movements, of which the most enduring has been the *Wahhābīs.

Ibbur (transmigration of souls): see DIBBUK.

Iblīs (Devil in Islam): see DEVIL.

Ibn ʿAbd al-Wahhāb, Muḥammad (founder of conservative Muslim movement): see WAHHĀBĪYA.

Ibn (al-)ʿArabī, Muḥyi al-Dīn (1165–1240 (AH 560–638)). A great *Sūfī mystic and original thinker, called *al-shaikh al-akbar* (the Great Teacher, *Shaykh) by his followers. He profoundly influenced the development of Islamic mysticism and philosophy. He was generally well received, though in Egypt the *ʿulamā denounced him as a *heretic, and there was a movement to assassinate him.

Ibn al-ʿArabī synthesized Hellenic, Persian, and Indian systems of thought into his own particular system, emphasizing monistically *wahdat-al-wujūd* (Unity of Existence) and *al-Insān al-Kāmil (The Perfect Man). For him, Being is essentially one, and all phenomenal existence is a manifestation of the divine substance. For that reason he was suspected of pantheism.

More than 800 works have been attributed to him, and it is claimed by some that about 400 have survived. His major works are *al-Futūḥāt al-Makkīya* (The Meccan Revelations, a complete system of mystical knowledge in 560 chapters), *Fuṣūṣ al-Hikām* (The Bezels of Wisdom, tr. R. W. J. Austin 1981, A. A. al-Tarjumana 1980), *Kitāb al-Ajwiba* (The Book of Answers), and *Tarjumān al-Ashwāq* (The Interpretation of Divine Love).

Ibn Adham, Ibrāhīm (Sūfī): see SŪFĪS.

Ibn al-Fāriḍ (Sūfī poet): see SŪFĪS; OMAR KHAYYAM.

Ibn Daud, Abraham ben David ha-Levi (Rabad; *c.*1110–80). Jewish philosopher, historian, and physician. Ibn Daud worked for most of his life in Toledo where he eventually died as a martyr. His most important books were *Sefer ha-Kabbalah* (The Book of *Kabbalah, G. D. Cohen, 1967), which defends Judaism throughout history against the *Karaite heresy, and *Al-ʿAqida al Rafiʿa*, tr. into Heb. as *Ha-Emunah ha-Ramah* (The Sublime Faith), which defends the doctrines of Judaism using Aristotelian modes of thinking. Both books have remained influential down to modern times.

Ibn Ezra, Abraham (*c.*1089–1164). Jewish philosopher, poet, and biblical commentator. He wrote both secular and religious poetry, commentaries on all the books of the Bible (those to the early prophets, Chronicles, Proverbs, Jeremiah, Ezekiel, Ezra, and Nehemiah are no longer in existence), books on Hebrew grammar, and two short works on philosophy.

He may have been the model for R. Browning's 'Rabbi ben Ezra'.

Ibn Gabirol (Jewish Spanish poet): see GABIROL, SOLOMON.

Ibn Ḥanbal, Aḥmad (780–855 (AH 164–241)). The founder of a school of *sharīʿa of a highly conservative nature. His most famous work was the *Musnad*, a vast collection of traditions edited from his lectures by his son. He did not formally establish a school of *fiqh, but laid the foundations built on by others. Rigorous against *bid'a (innovation), his conservative theology made even fewer concessions than *al-Ash'arī (see also HANBALITES); yet on many matters of law, he held two opinions, giving to his school a degree of flexibility, albeit within bounds.

Ibn Hasdai, Abraham ben Samuel ha-Levi (early 13th cent.). Spanish Jewish translator and poet. A staunch supporter of *Maimonides, he translated, *inter alia*, *al-Ghaz(z)ālī, and the Arabic text **Barlaam and Joasaph*. Published as *Ben ha-Melekh ve-ha-Nazir* (The Son of the King and a Nazarite, 1518), in Ibn Hasdai's version went through many edns.

Ibn Ḥazm, Abu Muḥammad 'Alī b. Aḥmad b. Said (994–1064 (AH 384–456)). Spanish Muslim philosopher, theologian, poet, and jurist, the chief codifier of the *Ẓāhirīya (literalist) school of law and theology. An intellectual giant, his tongue was said to be as sharp as a sword. Ibn Ḥazm is said to have written 400 works.

Ibn Ḥazm's major work *Kitāb al-faṣl* (Book of the Harvest) dealt with the subject of God, his nature and attributes, freewill and predestination, faith, life after death, and the *Imamate. For Ibn Ḥazm the only union possible with God is the union of understanding (*fahm*) and obeying his commands. The emotional consequences of life lived in *islām* (allegiance to God) were explored by him in *The Ring* [or *Necklace*] *of the Dove*.

Ibn Isḥāq (author of life of Muḥammad): see MUḤAMMAD IBN 'ABD ALLAH.

Ibn Khaldūn, 'Abd al-Raḥmān ibn Muḥammad (1332–1402 (AH 733–808)). Muslim historian and philosopher who discerned recurrent patterns in the movements of social groups in Muslim (and other) history, and who has therefore been called 'the father of sociology'.

His greatest work is the *Muqaddima*, or *Prolegomenon*, to his *Kitāb al-'Ibar* ... (The Book of Examples and the Collection of Origins of the History of the Arabs and the Berbers). Going back to the biblical story of *Cain, ibn Khaldūn discerned a constant conflict between desert and town. The nomads, far removed from the decadence associated with towns, periodically move towards the easier, or more predictable life on the edge of the deserts, herding sheep and goats, and beyond that, herding cattle, which demands fixed pastures. This creates an interior pressure toward the conquest of towns, bringing in a new regime. The new rulers bring with them vigour and innovation, but after three generations the first vigour is dissipated. The fourth generation believes that it possesses power 'as of right', as a consequence of birth: they receive all and give nothing, and thus open themselves to a new wave of conquest.

Ibn Rushd (1126–98 (AH 520–95)). Spanish Muslim theologian, philosopher, *Qur'ān scholar, natural scientist, and physician, known in the West as Averroes.

He is known particularly for his commentary on Aristotle, and for other works dealing with many aspects of philosophy and theology. One concerns 'the convergence which exists between the religious law (*sharī'a) and philosophy (*ḥikma*)'. Another work considers the problem of predestination. One of his most famous writings, *Tahāfut al-tahāfut* (The Incoherence of the Incoherence), criticizes *al-Gha(z)zālī's work, *The Incoherence of the Philosophers*, and upholds the value of philosophy as a wisdom applied to God's creation.

Among Ibn Rushd's doctrines, *Neoplatonist in origin, were the eternity and potentiality of matter (the world is eternal but caused, the *natura naturata* of God who is eternal and uncaused, *natura naturans*), and the unity of the human intellect, i.e. the doctrine that only one intellect exists in which every individual participates, to the exclusion of an isolated personal immortality. When his theories became known in N. Europe *c.*1230, the contradiction with Christian doctrine was not at first clear, and there emerged a party of 'Averroists' at the University of Paris led by Siger of Brabant (*c.*1240–*c.*1284). A treatise of Thomas *Aquinas was directed against them in 1270, and they were later accused of saying that 'things are true according to philosophy but not according to the Catholic faith, as though there were two contradictory truths', i.e. the theory of 'double truth'. Ibn Rushd's own understanding of 'double truth' was one of reconciliation. It rested on *ta'wīl, understood as producing, not two contradictory interpretations or truths, but rather the same single truth under two different styles of presentation.

Ibn Sīnā, Abū 'Alī Ḥusayn (980–1037 (AH 370–429)). Muslim philosopher, scholar, theologian, physician, natural scientist, and statesman, known in the West as Avicenna.

Of his large number of written works, most are in Arabic, with a few in Persian. Among his best known are works on philosophy and metaphysics, such as *Kitāb al-Shifā'* (Book of Healing, i.e. for the soul), and *Ḥayy ibn Yaqẓān*, a symbolic narrative. His belief in God as creator was combined with theories derived from *Plotinus (as conveyed in the 'theology of Aristotle'), particularly the idea of *emanation through various spheres of being. God as first cause and prime mover produces a single intelligence, which is able in turn to give rise to others. Although he was sometimes accused by other Muslims of being an unbeliever and of contradicting Islamic teaching, Ibn Sīnā considered himself a Muslim attempting to show that philosophy was compatible with religious teachings.

His works were tr. into Latin under the name Avicenna, and had considerable influence in the later Middle Ages. Ibn Sīnā's medical encyclopaedia the *Qānūn*, latinized as *Canon Medicinae*, gave rise to many commentaries, influenced the development of European medicine, and was not superseded until the arrival of modern W. medical theories and discoveries.

Ibn Taimiy(y)a (Taymīyah), Taqī al-Din (1263–1328 (AH 661–728)). A Muslim theologian of conservative and literalistic views, who belonged to the *Ḥanbalite school, but so exceeded even them that he was considered by some heretical. Frequently imprisoned, he refused to compromise, and was an emphatic opponent of *bid'a. His views were important in the emergence of the *Wahhābīs.

Ibn Tufayl, Abu Bakr (d. 1185 (AH 581)). Muslim philosopher and physician, known in the West as Abubacer. Born near Granada in Spain, he became *wazīr and physician to the *Almohads, introducing *ibn Rushd to the court. He developed his philosophical views in *Ḥayy ibn Yaqẓan*, (Alive, the Son of the Awake): Ḥayy represents humanity and Yaqẓan God. Ḥayy grows up on a desert island, and using his powers of observation, reason and reflection, he arrives at the truth and experience in relation to God. The work was tr. into Lat. by E. Pococke in the 17th cent. (*Philosophicus Auotodidactus*) and was influential in the development of the idea of 'the noble savage' (Dryden) and of Rousseau's argument for a primitive simplicity which is corrupted by civilization. It may also have influenced Daniel Defoe's *Robinson Crusoe*.

Ibn Tumart (1077–1130 (AH 470–524)). A Muslim reformer in Morocco who was known as *al-Mahdī of the *Almohads. He grew up under the Almoravids who followed the *Mālikite understanding of *fiqh, in which reason is subordinate—a position contested by *al-Ghaz(z)ālī, whose works were burnt by the rulers. He was prepared to preach *jihād even against other Muslims, if their lax behaviour constituted, in effect, an attack on Islam. Gathering increasing personal authority to himself, he identified himself as al-Mahdi, calling his followers al-Muwaḥḥidūn (the Unitarians), hence the name Almohads.

Ibrāhīm: see ABRAHAM (ISLAM).

Ibrāhīm b. Adham (d. 777 (AH 160)). Born at Balkh in Central Asia into a royal family, he renounced his princely life after hearing a divine voice whilst out hunting. He became recognized as a great mystic. His views on meditation (*muraqaba*) and gnosis (*ma'rifa*) influenced the later *Sūfīs.

Iccā-mṛtyu (Skt., 'desired-death'). The Hindu ability to yield up life at a designated moment, not by suicide, but by concentration.

Ich'adon, also known as **Pak Yŏmch'ŏk, Yŏmch'ŏk,** or **Kŏch'adon** (503–27). A martyr during King Pŏphŭng's reign (514–40) in the kingdom of Silla, in Korea. When the king's desire to establish and propagate Buddhism was thwarted due to ministerial opposition, Ich'adon, the Grand Secretary to the king, offered to be executed in the hope that, by witnessing miraculous phenomena resulting from his death, the ministers might be persuaded to look favourably upon the disfavoured religion. Ich'adon's martyrdom did, in fact, immediately bring about Silla's official recognition of Buddhism, dated 527.

Ichien, also known as **Dōkyō,** or **Muju** (1226–1312). Japanese Zen monk of the *Rinzai school. He was primarily a student of *Ben'en, but he studied under several masters, and eventually produced an anthology of Buddhist stories, still used in training, *Shaseki-shu* (Collection of Sand and Stone).

Ichi-ensō (symbol in Zen Buddhism): see ENSŌ.

Ichigū o terasu undō (movement): see TENDAI SHŪ.

Ichiji-fusetsu (Jap., 'not a word said'). Zen term summarizing the fact that no teacher (including the *Buddha) has used a single word to describe ultimate truth or reality, since it is indescribable. For the elaboration of this, see FUKASETSU.

Ichiji-kan (Jap., 'one word barrier'). The culminating point (*wato) of a Zen *kōan when it consists in a single word.

Ichijitsu Shintō (one-truth Shintō): see TENDAI SHŪ.

Ichiji-Zen (Jap., 'one word Zen'). The use of a single word from a Zen teacher as a *kōan; cf. ICHIJI-KAN.

Ichimi-shabyo (Jap., 'one taste from bowl'). The authentic transmission of the buddha-dharma in Zen, from a master to his dharma-successor (*hassu).

Ichimi-Zen (Jap., 'one taste Zen'). The authentic Zen of the Buddha and the patriarchs (*soshigata), which consists in the experience of no distinction ('one taste') between form and emptiness. Its opposite (within Zen) is zen which relies on different types or goals of meditation (*five ways of Ch'an/Zen), known as *gomi (-no)-zen*.

Ichinen (Jap., 'one thought'). The instant moment of one thought in Zen, hence the exclusive 'thought' (i.e. without content) of true concentration.

Ichinen-fushō (Jap., 'a thought not arising'). The state of mind in Zen in which no distracting or wayward thought arises. It is attained through *zazen, and it is the 'mind' of a buddha.

Ichinen-mannen (Jap., 'one moment of *nen*, ten thousand years'). A summary of the Zen view that, in enlightenment, numerical sequences of endurance are irrelevant: if one is in a state of absolute enlightenment or bliss, it cannot be calculated whether it lasts a second or ten thousand (or more) years.

I-Ching (Jap., Gijō; 635–713). Chinese Buddhist monk and traveller. He entered the religious life when young, and travelled to India in 671. His journey took him through more than thirty countries, and he returned in 695 with relics and images, and also with texts which he set about translating, completing fifty-six works before he died. He also wrote a record of his travels, *Nankai-kiki-den*. He was given the title of *sanzō* (*san-tsang*), one well-versed in Buddhist teaching.

I Ching or ***Yi Ching*** (Scripture of Change(s)). One of the three pre-*Confucian Classics. It seems originally to have been a diviners' manual, built on the symbolisms of eight trigrams (each composed of broken and unbroken lines, standing respectively for *yin and yang). These trigrams were later expanded to give sixty-four hexagrams. Confucius is supposed to have added commentary, called the Ten Wings, which gave philosophical depth to the work.

Ichthus (Gk., 'fish'). An early emblem of Christianity, since the Gk. letters form the acronym of 'Jesus Christ, God [*theos*] and Saviour [*sōtēr*]'.

I-ch'uan (neo-Confucianist of the Sung dynasty): see CH'ENG HAO.

Icon (Gk., *eikon*, 'image' or 'picture'). Sacred pictures of the *Orthodox tradition. They are usually flat pictures, and painted in egg tempera on wood; but metal, ivory, and other materials may be used, and bas-relief and even high-relief icons are known, especially in Russia. They are used to decorate churches, where they are found on walls, ceilings, and stands (the *iconostasis separating the sanctuary from the nave being particularly prominent), and portable icons are used in private devotions. They depict *Christ, and the saints and mysteries of the Church. The symbolism of the icon is held to effect the presence of the saint or mystery depicted, and in that presence prayer and devotion are made. The painting (or 'writing') of the icon is itself a religious act, prepared for by prayer and fasting, and was usually reserved for monks: such was Andrei Rublev (*c*.1370–*c*.1430), the greatest of all icon-painters. Suspicion of icons as idols led to *iconoclasm.

The word 'icon' also appears as a technical term in semiotics, with a transferred use: see SYMBOLS.

Iconoclasm (Gk., 'image-breaking'). A movement which agitated the Church in the E. Roman Empire, *c*.725–843. The veneration of *icons had attracted an undercurrent of opposition for centuries (as early as *Epiphanius), but in the wake of a renewed Arab threat to Asia Minor it was widely blamed, especially in the army, for the weakness of the Christian empire. The opposition to icons was taken up by the emperors Leo III (717–41) and Constantine V (741–75). A fierce persecution, especially of monks, ensued. Under the empress Irene (from 780), however, the position was reversed: at the seventh *ecumenical council at Nicaea in 787 the veneration of icons was officially reintroduced and the degree of veneration to be paid to them was defined.

After a politically unsettled period the new emperor Leo V (813–20) reasoned that iconoclasm ought to be reinstated, but persecution was in general less severe in this second phase of the controversy. An iconophile patriarch, Methodios, was elected in 843, and a great feast (since kept as the Feast of Orthodoxy) was celebrated on the first Sunday of Lent to mark the victory of the icons.

Iconoclasm then becomes a general word for opposition to, and destruction of, visible representations of the divine, and, more colloquially, for the destruction of that which is traditionally revered.

Iconography (Gk., *eikon*, 'image', + *graphe*, 'writing'). The study of the representation of otherwise unseen realities through coded means: such realities may include anything from God or gods to ideas; and the means may include statues, pictures, buildings, charms, or indeed anything which can hold the 'charge' of such representation. Since religions have differing attitudes to the representation of the holy or the divine, each religion has a different iconographical style and content. See further ART; and also Index, Iconography.

Judaism Jewish iconography is dominated by the prohibition on idols. While recurrent symbols occur in *Torah and *synagogue decoration, they are mainly to be found in manuscripts.

Christianity The earliest Christian art was influenced by late Hellenistic realism, while in theme it was largely symbolic: *Christ represented by a fish (see ICHTHUS), or a young shepherd, etc. From the 4th cent., Christian art was influenced by Neoplatonic aesthetics which saw art as disclosing a higher, spiritual realm, and the highly conscious symbolism characteristic of *icons developed. Already one can detect a difference of emphasis between East and West, the E. stressing the liturgical function of the icon, while the W. saw images as pictorial illustrations of biblical events and religious doctrines. This came to a head in the 8th and 9th cents. with the *Iconoclastic Controversy. In the W., partly under the influence of a growing devotion to Christ's sacred humanity, a more realistic, less symbolic style of painting developed from the 12th cent., about the same time as the symbolic use of form and colour reached its apogee in the stained glass of, e.g., Chartres Cathedral. The development of art in the W. has broken any *tradition* of Christian iconography: W. religious artists combine an arbitrary dependence on current artistic techniques with personally adopted symbolic schemes. As with other religions, Christianity also developed elaborate codes associated with events (e.g. *baptism, *crucifixion, *resurrection, etc.) and people, esp. *saints.

Islam See CALLIGRAPHY.

Hinduism Of all religions, Hinduism is the richest and most complex in its iconographical materials. Its strong sense of *Brahman, not simply underlying and guaranteeing all appearance, but actually pervading, and able to become focally manifest, in all appearance, means that any object can be charged with the divine. To make an image, therefore, is to bring the divine into that image—equally, the image may become 'dead' when the particular concentration of the divine is withdrawn from it at the end of the act of *pūjā (worship). Iconography is therefore a matter of interaction and of the means to its achievement. The most important *locus* of the interaction is the *mūrti (lit., 'embodiment', hence 'image').

Buddhism Early Buddhist icons are by no means as prolific as those of Hindus: the Buddha had pointed away from relying on outside help (e.g. gods). Nevertheless, the centrality of the Buddha in leaving guidance evoked icons of recognition (e.g. images of the Buddha in the attainment of enlightenment). *Stūpas are iconographic representations of Buddhist truth in this way. However, in Mahāyāna Buddhism, the strong sense of the buddha-nature being present in all things (indeed, being all that there is of all things) led to developments comparable to those in Hinduism. In Mahāyāna, one is surrounded by a vast host of buddhas and *bodhisattvas, who are, so to speak, 'here' in order to assist those who reverence them. Each of these has an elaborate set of images and symbols, which reach a supreme height in Tibet.

Sikhism Although Sikh *gurdwārās are much plainer than most Hindu *mandirs, pictures of Gurūs *Nānak and *Gobind Siṅgh feature prominently. Gurū Nānak is typically depicted as radiant, white-bearded, and turbaned, gazing in benediction. Sometimes all ten Gurūs are portrayed in a single picture, illustrating their essential unity. A picture of *Harimandir Sāhib, *Amritsar, is popular and to be seen in many Sikh houses, as are paper calendar pictures of the Gurūs.

Iconostasis or **Eikonostasion** (Gk., 'a picture stand'). The screen in Eastern-rite churches separating sanctuary from nave. Since the 14th or 15th cents. the screen has been a wall of wood (a Russian innovation) or stone covered with *icons, which follow a prescribed arrangement. Through it are three doors, the central or Royal Door admitting to the altar, and those on the right and left respectively to the *diakonicon* (deacon's area) and *prothesis. The iconostasis conceals part of the liturgy from the view of the congregation.

Icons: see ICON.

'Īd (Arab., from Aram./Syriac, 'festival, holiday'). In Islam, feast or *festival. There are two main feasts, *'Īd al-Aḍḥā, the feast of *sacrifice, based on a part of the ceremonies of the *ḥajj; and *'Īd al-Fiṭr, the feast of the breaking of the fast (of *Ramaḍān).

Iḍā (Skt.). 1. Sacrificial food or libation in Hinduism. After the Flood, of which Manu was the only survivor, he collected from the waters butter, milk, whey, and curds, together called iḍā, which were then personified as his daughter (*Śatapata Brāhmaṇa* 1. 8. 1. 1 ff.) She asked Manu to allow her to assist at the sacrifices, since when she has been the mediator of benefits accruing through sacrifices.

2. One of the channels of subtle energy (*nāḍī) in the Hindu understanding of the body.

ʿĪd al-Aḍḥā, ʿĪd al-Qurbān or **al-ʿĪd al-Kabīr** (feast of the *sacrifice or the great feast). Muslim sacrifice of an animal—camel, sheep, or goat—forms part of the ceremony of *ḥajj, pilgrimage, and is carried out at Minā, near *Mecca, on the tenth day of *Dhū'l-Ḥijja. Muslims all over the world sacrifice an animal on this day, a ceremony which is intended to commemorate the sacrifice of Ibrāhīm (*Abraham).

ʿĪd al-Fiṭr or **al-ʿĪd al-ṣaghīr** (the small feast). Feast of the breaking of the fast (of *Ramaḍān), second in importance to *ʿĪd al-Aḍḥā. It is celebrated on the first two or three days of Shawwāl, the month following Ramaḍān.

Iḍā-pātra (Skt.). The vessel used in Hinduism for the *iḍā offering. It is placed at the head of a corpse when the body and the sacrificial implements of the dead person are cremated.

'Idda (waiting period in relation to divorce): see MARRIAGE (ISLAM).

Iddhi, ṛddhi (Pāli, Skt.: *ardh*, 'grow', 'increase', 'prosper', 'succeed'). Paranormal, psychic, or magic power in Buddhism, where it is one of the six kinds of higher knowledge (*abhiññā). Canonical writings contain a standard list of eight forms of iddhi: the power to (i) replicate and project bodily-images of oneself, (ii) make oneself invisible, (iii) pass through solid objects, (iv) sink into solid ground, (v) walk on water, (vi) fly, (vii) touch the sun and moon with one's hand, (viii) ascend to the world of the god *Brahmā in the highest heavens.

Iddhi-pāda (Pāli, 'ways of power'; Skt., *ṛddhi-pāda*). In Buddhism, the four components of concentrated power which result in supernatural powers (*iddhi), and bring about *samādhi (absorption in the object of contemplation): (i) intention (*canda*); (ii) will (*virya); (iii) mind (*cit); (iv) audacity in inquiry (*mīmāṃsā*). See also BODHIPĀKṢIKA-DHARMA.

Idealism (Buddhist school of): see VIJÑĀNAVĀDA.

Ideal type. A key concept and strategy in the study of religions, introduced by M. *Weber. Because of the complex and fluid nature of social (and thus of religious) phenomena, Weber realized that observations of actual instances have to be described through the isolation of characteristic features: examples are 'economic man', 'marginal man', *'sect', *'church', 'Gemeinschaft' (a group in which social bonds are based on close personal ties of kinship and friendship), 'Gesellschaft' (secondary relationships prevail, i.e. of a formal, contractual, specialized, impersonal, or expedient kind). Weber insisted that ideal types are never found in pure, uncontaminated form.

Ideology. The organization of ideas and related practices into a more-or-less coherent belief-system, carrying with it commitment. Although the term was first used by Destutt de Tracy in 1796 to apply to the study of the way in which ideas are related to their base in sensations, it has come to refer to belief-systems which aim to achieve goals, justifying particular actions or policies on the way and vigorously excluding others. 'Ideology' is most naturally understood of a political system, e.g. Fascism, totalitarianism, Maoism. Although the definition lends itself most naturally to such religious organizations as *Vatican Catholicism, it is nevertheless an issue whether religions can rightly be thought of as ideologies.

Far more loosely, ideology is used simply as a substitute for 'world-view', and in that general sense religions as ideologies are sometimes discussed in relation to *secularization—with secularization taken to be a contesting world-view. Popular though that usage is, it lacks rigour in dealing with the actual processes of change in belief-systems.

Idiorrhythmic. Following the pattern of one's own life: monastic communities, especially on Mount *Athos, where the monks pursue separate lives, meeting for *offices and perhaps for communal meals on great feast days.

Idolatry (Gk., *eidolon*, 'image', + *latreia*, 'worship'). The attributing of absolute value to that which is not absolute, and acting towards that object, person, or concept as though it is worthy of worship or complete commitment. In a religious context, this most usually means treating as God that which is not God; and in particular acting towards a representation of God as though it *is* God. Thus idolatry is associated with the worship of idols, as though these are the actuality of God. In that sense, idolatry is extremely rare, since most religious worshippers are well-aware that the signpost is not to be confused with that which is signified. Judaism is unequivocally opposed to idol worship as is evidenced by the *Ten Commandments (Exodus 20). *Rabbinic law deals with prohibitions concerning contact with an idolator (*Avodah Zarah*, passim).

Islam is comparably opposed to idols (Arab., *wathan*, pl., *wuthun*; *sanam*, *asnam*), which must necessarily detract from the absolute supremacy and oneness of God.

Idrīs (Muslim Enoch): see ENOCH.

Iglesia ni Cristo (Tagalog, 'Church of Christ'). The largest *Protestant church in the Philippines, founded in 1914 by Felix Manalo (1886–1963), the 'angel from the East' of Revelations 7. 12, sent to restore the true church among the chosen Filipino people. Based on a literal reading of the Bible, *unitarian in christology, and highly polemical in relation to other churches, it has expanded into other parts of the world since 1968.

Iglesia popular ('church arising from the people'): see LIBERATION THEOLOGY.

Ignatian spirituality: see IGNATIUS (OF) LOYOLA.

Ignatius, St (d. *c.*107). Bishop of *Antioch. Nothing is known of his life beyond his journey under guard across Asia Minor to Rome to be martyred. He was received along the way by representatives of five local churches (Ephesus, Magnesia, Tralles, Philadelphia, Smyrna), and sent a letter back to each. These five letters, with one to the church at Rome and one to *Polycarp, were early collected and venerated (and other spurious letters added to them). The letters witness to the emergence of the office of *bishop, to which Ignatius was passionately committed as the best safeguard of the unity of the *Church. The letter to the Romans also shows Ignatius's ardent desire for *martyrdom. Feast day, 17 Oct. or 17 Dec. (W.); 20 Dec. (E.).

Ignatius (of) Loyola (1491)/1495–1556). Founder of the Society of Jesus (*Jesuits). Born of a noble family, he became a soldier and was wounded during the siege of Pampeluna (1521). During a prolonged convalescence he read Ludolf of Saxony's *Life of Christ* and various lives of the saints which led him to abandon his military career. Upon recovery he went to Montserrat, made his confession, hung up his sword before a statue of the Blessed Virgin Mary, and exchanged clothes with a beggar. There followed a year (1522–3) of prayer and mortification at Manresa, the fruit of which profound experience is manifest in his *Spiritual Exercises*, probably written there. He then went on pilgrimage to the Holy Land, via Rome, and on his return studied for eleven years, first in Spain, then in Paris. In 1534, he and six companions (including *Francis Xavier) took religious vows. In 1540 the Society of Jesus was formally established, with Ignatius its first general. The Ignatian way in prayer, based on the *Exercises*, moves religion from the head to the heart, in absolute devotion to God. The claim of the *Exercises* is that the specific will of God for this person can be found, and that God will 'deal directly with the creature, and the creature directly with his/her Creator and Lord'. See also JESUITS.

Ignorance: see AVIDYĀ; INVINCIBLE IGNORANCE.

Igyō-shu (school of early Ch'an/Zen): see KUEI-YANG-TSUNG.

Ihai. Japanese Buddhist mortuary tablets with which the spirits of deceased ancestors are associated.

Iḥrām (Arab., 'making forbidden or sacred'). In Islam, the state of ritual purity necessary for carrying out the rites of *ḥajj and *ʿumra (greater and lesser pilgrimage).

IHS. Abbreviation of the name *Jesus by means of the first three letters in Greek (*H* being the uncial form of the letter *eta*). Later, however, attempts were made to understand the three letters as initials of words in Latin. Most popular was the interpretation *In Hoc Signo [vinces]*, 'in this sign [thou shalt conquer]', the inscription on the cross seen in a vision by the emperor *Constantine; or Iesus Hominum Salvator (Jesus, saviour of men).

I-Hsuan (Chinese master): see LIN-CHI I-HSÜAN.

Iʿjāz (Arab.). Inimitability or uniqueness of the *Qur'ān; literally 'incapacity', i.e. of others to imitate its style and content.

Ijmāʿ. Principle of development in Islamic law. The root verb means 'to cause to gather', or 'converge', and yields the noun for a *mosque as a gatherer (*jāmiʿa*) of the faithful. It is by consensus of the community that the *sharīʿa in *Sunni Islam can be enlarged to respond to new situations. Ijmāʿ is always subject to being consistent with the prior sources *uṣūl al-dīn: the *Qur'ān, *ḥadīth, and *qiyās, or applied analogy.

Ijtihād (Arab., 'exertion'). An independent judgement concerning a legal or theological question, based on the interpretation and application of the roots of Islamic law (*Qur'ān, *Sunna), as opposed to *taqlīd. The *mujtahid* (the one who makes and mediates such judgements) is particularly important in Shiʿa Islam, in contrast to the *ʿulamā.

Ikebana (Jap., 'living flowers'). The practice of flower-contemplation, often (but misleadingly) called the art of flower-arranging in Japan; also known as *kadō*, the 'Way of flowers'. By the 15th cent., informal traditions of floral arranging became formalized into distinct, stylistic 'schools'—each with their own oral and written teachings, and each with their own line of master teachers. These exist today as the Ohara, Ikenobo, and Sogetsu schools.

Ikeda Daisaku (b. 1928), Japanese third president of *Sōka Gakkai. With a strong missionary sense, he set out to raise the membership to three million, and to establish Sōka Gakkai International. In 1983, he received the UN Peace Award.

Ikhwān al-Muslimūn (Muslim Brotherhood): see AL-IKHWĀN AL-MUSLIMŪN.

Ikhwān al-Ṣafā' (Arab., 'Brotherhood of Purity'). A secret movement founded *c.*951 (AH 340) in Iraq. It had strong *Ismā'īlī connections and views, which were summarized in the fifty-one (or fifty-two) letters, *Rasā'il ikhwān al-Ṣafā'*, which deal, in encyclopaedic fashion, with sciences, theology, metaphysics, cosmology, etc., showing their relation to each other.

Ikkarim (basic principles of Jewish belief): see ARTICLES OF FAITH.

Ikkyu Sōjun (1394–1481). Zen master of the *Rinzai school in Japan. He experienced sudden enlightenment in 1418. He called himself 'the son of the wandering cloud', and although in later life he was appointed by the emperor abbot of *Daitoku-ji, he constantly and strongly rejected the decadent forms of Zen which he found around him. He expressed this critique in a highly unconventional lifestyle, and in his 'Mad Cloud' poetry, collected in *Kyōun-shu* (Germ. tr., Suichi and Thom, 1979). The many tales of his mocking style have made him one of the most popular figures in Japan—the holy madman, who frequented inns and brothels, and who danced down the street waving a skull. He was also noted for his dramatic *calligraphy.

Ikon (painted representation): see ICON.

Ik Onkar or **Ik Oaṅkār** (Pañjābi, 'one'; Skt., 'sacred syllable *oṃ'). Gurū *Nānak's statement that God is One. Ik Onkār is the Sikhs' most frequent statement about God, emphasizing the unity of the Primal Being. In its customary symbolic form the numeral stresses the divine singularity.

Iktisāb (acquisition of acts): see QADAR.

I-kuan Tao (Way of Pervading Unity). A Chinese Buddhist-*Taoist society, an offshoot of the *White Lotus Sect, founded by Wang Chüeh-i in the early 20th cent. Its main doctrine is *eschatological-*messianic: *Bodhisattva *Maitreya, at the command of Mother of No-birth (Wu-sheng Lao-mu), the creator-deity, will appear to the world imminently, at the end of the third and last *kalpa to save its members and all other human beings.

I-k'ung (Jap., Giku; 9th cent.). Chinese Ch'an/Zen master of the *Rinzai school, who was invited by the empress, Tachibana Kachiko, to bring Ch'an to Japan. Danran-ji in *Kyōto was built for him, but he found no apt pupils, and he therefore returned to China. No further attempts were made at this translation until the 12th/13th cents.

Ilā. One of three Hindu goddesses (*Ṛg Veda* 1. 13. 9) who bring delight. She was born from the horse-sacrifice (*aśvamedha) of Manu.

Ilḥād (deviation): see HERESY.

Illo tempore (that-ideal-time): see MYTH.

Illuminati. Either 16th-cent. Spanish mystical sects; or a German secret society founded in 1776. The Spanish illuminati or *alumbrados appear to have been founded by Antonio de Pastrana at the end of the 15th cent. They believed in a form of pure contemplation and absorption into God, practised severe mortifications, and claimed visions and the power of prophecy. The German illuminati, founded by Johann Adam Weishaupt (1748–1830), pursued progressive illumination through initiation into the successive stages of their society, involving the study of philosophy and the arts. They were also known as Perfectibilists. Though outlawed in 1784/5, the society re-emerged at the end of the 19th cent., only to disappear again under the Nazis.

Illuminationist (*ishraqi*) school: see SUHRAWARDĪ, SHIHĀB.

Illuminative Way. The second of the *Three Ways of the spiritual life. After being purified from sin in the *purgative way the soul is illuminated and enabled to attain a true understanding of created things ('natural contemplation') and thus prepared for the *unitive way.

Illuminism: see ALUMBRADOS; ILLUMINATI.

Illusion (in Advaita Vedānta philosophy): see MĀYĀ (2) and MITHYĀ.

'Ilm (Arab.). Knowledge, especially of *fiqh and *kalām. 'Ilm, of all kinds, has particularly high status in Islam, because a strong doctrine of creation (all things coming from God and potentially being revelatory of him, as *ayat) is combined with an absence of anything resembling *original sin (which might make humans incapable of appreciating God's self-revelation in the created order). The capacity for 'ilm is thus a gift from God.

Ilm-i Kshnoom. Path of Knowledge, a Parsi occult movement: see PARSIS.

Ilyas, Mawlānā (founder): see TABLĪGHĪ JAMĀ'AT.

Il-yŏn or **Iryŏn** (1206–89). Korean Buddhist scholar-monk. He compiled the *Samguk yusa*

(Legends and History of the Three Kingdoms), a treasury of the history of Korean Buddhism, in or about the year 1285. At the time when Confucianism was beginning to gather strength in Koryŏ (935–1392), he endeavoured to revitalize Buddhism through this literary effort.

Images: see ICONOGRAPHY.

Imago Dei (Lat.). The image of God, in which, says Genesis 1. 26–7, humanity was created, but which is now marred as a consequence of the *Fall.

In the *Qur'ān, man is created as the *khalīfa (caliph, or representative) of God on earth.

Imām, (Arab., in the *Qur'ān 'sign', 'pattern', 'leader'). The leader of the Muslim congregational *ṣalāt, who can be any man of good standing in the community, but is often a theologically educated man who is engaged by the *mosque. There is no ordination, nor is the imām like the Christian *priest: he is only imām while acting as such.

2. Among Shi'ites, the Imām has an incomparably higher status. Initially, it is almost synonymous with 'rightful caliph' (*khalīfa), i.e. *Alī and his descendants. The stress on succession led to the elaboration of the Imām as one who has received secret knowledge (*jafr), and who still receives (or may receive) direct divine guidance. There is dispute among Shi'ites whether the line ended with the seventh (*Seveners) or twelfth (Twelvers or *'Ithna 'Ashariyya) successor, complicated further by those who believe there is a Hidden Imām (see AL-MAHDĪ) whom the initiate can recognize, who may still give guidance, and who will become manifest at the End (see also ISMĀ'ĪLIYA). See Index, Imams.

3. Among *Sūfis (not always in distinction from (2)), the imām is the guide to true knowledge, and is thus equivalent to *pīr* (in Persian) or *murshid*.

4. The two larger beads in the *subḥa* (*rosary).

Īmān (Arab., 'be secure' 'trust'). The Muslim word for faith and trust in *Allāh, and in the Prophet *Muḥammad, and hence in the content of his message. In the *Qur'ān, therefore, īmān is sometimes the same as *islām* (allegiance to God). Does it follow, then, that īmān is all-important in relation to salvation, and that one who makes profession of īmān will be saved, no matter what his works? This was a deeply divisive issue in early Islam (cf. faith and works in Christianity), with the *Khārijites declaring that īmān accompanied by evil works designates such a person as no longer Muslim (and therefore to be treated as such) and the Murji'ites postponing the decision until Allāh reveals all secrets (and therefore treating as Muslims all who perform *ṣalāt facing the *qibla).

Imitation of Christ. Basic Christian practice, the attempt of a disciple to follow the example of the Lord. It is also the title of a widely influential book on the spiritual life attributed to *Thomas à Kempis (15th cent.).

Imitation of God. Jewish way of expressing the human obligation to imitate God in his actions (Deuteronomy 10. 12). The detail is found in Genesis 3. 21, Genesis 18. 1, Leviticus 16. 1, and Deuteronomy 34. 6.

Immaculate Conception. The *dogma that the Blessed Virgin *Mary was, from the first moment of her being conceived, free from all stain of *original sin. It and the feast of the conception of the Virgin Mary were a matter of controversy in the West from the 12th cent. The Feast of the Immaculate Conception is kept on 8 Dec.

Immanence (Lat., *immanere*, 'to inhabit'). The presence of actions, or of God, in the world, usually in such a way that the source of the action or presence remains distinct. At an extreme, the created order is understood to be the mode of God's self-manifestation, and thus to be the body of God. See also PANTHEISM; PROCESS THEOLOGY.

Immanuel or **Emmanuel** (Heb., 'God is with us'). The name of a son prophesied to be born of a young woman (or virgin) in Isaiah 7. 14. Christian tradition, starting with Matthew 1. 23, has interpreted the passage as a prophecy of the *virgin birth of Christ.

Immortality: see AFTERLIFE.

Immortality, Chinese: see HSIEN; CH'ANG-SHENG PU-SSU.

Impassibility of God. The belief that because God is immutable, unchanging, and unchangeable, he cannot suffer or be affected by what happens in, e.g., his creation. This view has dominated Christian theology for most of its history. However, this is far removed from the biblical picture of God as one who feels and responds, and who can hardly be unaffected by the crucifixion of Jesus, if Jesus is indeed the Son of the Father. *Process theology reversed this emphasis by insisting that becoming is a necessary condition of being. Others have retained the traditional emphasis on the unchanging/unchangeable nature of God, but have insisted that change, suffering, petition, intercession, etc., are consequential to God and evoke response, but to and from one whose nature it is to make such response without his own nature changing.

Impermanence (in Buddhism): see ANICCA.

Imprimatur (Lat., 'let it be printed'). The permission granted in *Roman Catholicism by the appropriate authority for the approved publication of certain religious works. *Canon law no longer requires any book on a religious subject to seek the imprimatur, but it encourages such books to be submitted for approval (cf. *haskamah in Judaism). The imprimatur requires the prior *nihil obstat ('nothing obstructs') of the officially appointed censor before it can be issued.

Imputation. The reckoning of qualities of one person as belonging to another. Traditional *Protestant theology emphasizes the imputation of *Adam's guilt at the *Fall to the whole human race, and in particular God's imputation of *Christ's righteousness to believers who have no righteousness of their own.

Inari (Jap., probably from a place-name). The most popular agricultural deity of Japan, especially associated with rice. In the Heian period, Inari was increasingly associated with the official mythology of *Shinto. Inari shrines especially feature the fox whose life-size statues usually flank the worship centre and whose phallus-like tails again reinforce the motif of sexuality and fecundity.

Incantation: see MAGIC.

Incarnation (Lat., *in carne*, 'in flesh/body'). The belief that God is wholly present to, or in, a human life and body. The term may be used to 'translate' the Hindu understanding of *avatāra, but is more commonly used of the belief that in *Jesus Christ, the divine and human natures were united in one person, and that God was, consequently, *in carne*, incarnated. See further CHRISTOLOGY.

For examples in different religions, see Index, Incarnation.

Incense (Lat., *incendere*, 'to burn'). Substances which produce a sweet scent when burned, and are thus used in worship. Among many such substances are aloe, sandalwood, myrrh, frankincense, balsam, cedar, and juniper. In China, incense (*hsiang*) was used to enhance appreciation and thus (especially in Taoism) to assist in the realization of the *Tao—though incense was also used to ward off evil spirits or disease. In India, incense is used as an act of homage to the divine manifestation, especially in a *temple. In early Judaism, incense may have been associated with the smoke of sacrifice: the Heb. *ketoret* is derived from √*ktr*, 'cause to smoke', which may be the smoke from a sacrifice (1 Samuel 2. 15). In Christianity, incense first appears in Christian worship *c*.500.

Incense is an important part of Hindu offerings, both in the home and in the temple. It forms a part of the daily ritual in invoking the presence of God in preparation for worship. In Buddhism, this ritual was transferred to the representations of the *Buddha (or *bodhisattvas) as a part of *dāna.

Inclination, good and evil. Instincts for good and evil in human nature, made formal in Jewish anthropology. The *rabbis taught that human beings were subject to two contradictory impulses, *yeẓer ha-ra'* (evil inclination) and *yeẓer ha-tov* (good inclination).

Independence Day (Israel): see YOM HAATZMA'UT.

Independents. Another name for the English *Congregationalists.

Index (type of sign in Pierce's analysis): see SYMBOLS.

Index Librorum Prohibitorum (Lat., 'list of prohibited books'). The 'Index', the official list of books which Roman Catholics were, in general, forbidden to read or possess. The first Index was issued by the Congregation of the *Inquisition in 1557. Its last edn. was in 1948, and in 1966 it was finally abolished.

Indian Ecumenical Conference. A movement for spiritual renewal among N. American Indians. The meetings began on the Crow Reservation, Montana, in 1970, with those attending coming from Alaska to Florida, and from many religions (*Catholic, *Protestant, *Bahā'ī, traditional and the new religions of Handsome Lake, and the Native American Church). Attitudes have ranged from emphasis on 'Red Power' and anti-white, anti-Christian feelings, to more positive and forward-looking relationships with Christianity and W. culture.

Indian Shaker Church. A new *syncretist religion among Indians of NW USA and British Columbia. (There is no relation to white *Shakers or *Quakers.) John Slocum (?1840–97?) was a Squaxin logger near Olympia, baptized as a Roman Catholic. In 1881, he claimed to have visited heaven during a coma and to have been given a new way. In 1882, his wife Mary's shaking paroxysm was regarded as God's Spirit and cured John of an illness. Together they founded the Shaker Church, with moral reforms and spiritual healing through shaking and dancing rites in place of *shamanism.

Indicative (form of absolution): see ABSOLUTION.

Indra. Supreme God of the Indo-Āryans, to whom (except for *Agni) more hymns are addressed in the **Ṛg Veda* than to any other. He is the dispenser of rain and source of fruitfulness, who is himself sustained by vast quantities of *soma. His strength is represented by his thunderbolt (*vajra*). He is found also in Jain and Buddhist mythology (as Sakka).

Indra's net (image of the interconnectedness of all things): see HUA-YEN.

Indriya (Skt.). 1. In Indian philosophical systems, especially Sāṃkhya-yoga, the indriyas constitute the sense organs. There are ten indriyas divided into two categories: the organs of perception (buddhindriyas), and the organs of action (karmendriyas).

2. In Buddhism, the controlling or directing powers in human life, often listed as the twenty-two physical and psychological capacities in humans, including the five roots which lead to the five powers (*bala), and culminating in the capacity of perfect knowledge—i.e. an *arhat. See also BODHIPĀKṢIKA-DHARMA.

Indulgence. In Roman Catholic practice, a remission by the Church of the temporal penalty due to sin, even when forgiven, in virtue of the merits of Christ and the saints. The granting of indulgences is now generally confined to the pope. The unrestricted sale, in the later Middle Ages, of indulgences by professional pardoners, was an abuse against which the Reformation protested.

Indus Valley civilization. Early civilization, known especially through the excavations of *Harappā and Mohenjodaro (both now in Pakistan), the religious characteristics of which continued into *Vedic religion after the *Āryan invasion. The civilization lasted *c.*2300–1750 BCE. The reconstruction of the religious beliefs is based mainly on the figures and images, and on scenes depicted on seals; the script has not been deciphered in a way that has met with universal assent. The worship of the Mother Goddess was prominent, in association with the tree of fertility.

Infallibility. Inability to err, predicated by Roman Catholics of the *Church or of some teaching office within it, e.g. the *papacy or an ecumenical *council, when expounding the Christian revelation. The term is a negative one, signifying preservation from error rather than inspiration, and it is predicated properly of people or institutions rather than of the statements they make.

In Islam, infallibility (Arab., *ʿiṣmah*) is predicated by all Muslims of the Prophet *Muḥammad when mediating God's revelation (i.e. the *Qur'ān), though otherwise he is an ordinary human, subject to error, etc.; by Sunni Muslims of the consensus of the community (*ijmaʿ), and by Shiʿa Muslims of the *Imāms.

Infancy Gospels. The *apocryphal gospels retailing stories about the birth and childhood of *Jesus. The best known are the *Protogospel of James* (2nd cent.), *Infancy Gospel of Thomas* (a little later?), and *Gospel of Pseudo-Matthew* (8th or 9th cent.).

Infant baptism: see BAPTISM.

Infralapsarians (relation of election to Fall): see PREDESTINATION.

Inga. The cause-and-effect nature of *karma (cf. *innen) in Zen Buddhism.

Ingathering of the exiles (Heb., *kibbutz galuyyot*). The return of Jewish exiles to the *Promised Land. Since the establishment of the modern State of Israel, the ingathering is often now understood as the immigration of Jews from over a hundred countries to the land of their forefathers, and is thus divested of the messianic character. See also GALUT.

Ingen (introducer of Ōbaku-shū to Japan): see ŌBAKU-SHŪ.

Initiation. The (usually *ritual) transfer of a person into a new state, and thus common in religions—either to bring a person into a new religious community, or to make transfers of status within such communities. Examples are *circumcision in Judaism, *baptism and *confirmation in Christianity, *bayʿat* ('pact') when a *Sūfī novice joins an order, *upanayana among twice-born Hindus, *abhiṣeka in Buddhism, *dbang.bskur* in Tibet (see ABHIṢEKA), *dīkṣa in all Indian religions, but of especial importance among Jains, *khaṇḍe-dī-pāhul among Sikhs. See Index, Initiation.

Injīl (Arab., from Gk., *euangelion*, 'gospel', via Ethiopic). In the *Qur'ān, the revelation given to ʿĪsā/*Jesus, or a book given to him, or the scripture in the possession of the Christians. The fact that the actual gospels do not correspond with the Qur'ān is explained by the theory of 'corruption' (see TAḤRĪF).

Inka (-shōmei). The legitimating seal of recognition, in Zen Buddhism, that authentic enlightenment has been attained, and that a pupil has completed his training.

Innen (Jap., 'cause and condition' *karma). The way, in Zen Buddhism, in which eventualities are brought into their being or appearance by constraints or causes. Innen is also the account of events in the past which explain a person's present state.

Inner Deity Hygiene school: see TAOISM.

Inner elixir (in Taoism): see NEI-TAN.

Inner light. In *Quaker vocabulary, the inward revelation of *Christ's will and presence. After years of intense searching, *Fox and his followers came to rely spiritually on 'the inner light of the living Christ' rather than external ceremonies, religious traditions, or even the *Bible itself. In second-generation Quakerism the term occasionally becomes synonymous with 'conscience'.

Innocent III (1161–1216). *Pope from 8 Jan. 1198. Innocent's pontificate is often held to be the zenith of papal power, and certainly the pope's training as a lawyer made him much in demand as arbitrator or judge. In 1208 Innocent put England under an *interdict, and four years later *excommunicated John, absolved his subjects from their allegiance, and handed the kingdom to the king of France. John capitulated. He made England a fief of the papacy, after which Innocent supported John, even against Langton over the Magna Carta. Innocent gave approval to the *Franciscan rule and summoned the fourth *Lateran council, but he also launched the campaign against the *Albigensians, and the disastrous fourth *crusade.

Inquisition. A Roman Catholic tribunal for the suppression of *heresy and punishment of heretics. Strictly speaking, one should speak of 'inquisitions', since there was no single institution. The Inquisition came into being under Pope Gregory IX in 1232, with papal inquisitors selected chiefly from among *Dominicans and *Franciscans because of their (theoretical) detachment from the world. In 1542 the Congregation of the Holy Office was established, being reorganized in 1587 into the Congregation of the Roman and Universal Inquisition to supervise faith and morals in the entire church. After a further reorganization in 1908, in 1965 it became the Congregation for the Doctrine of the Faith and its role in censuring wrong belief has again become prominent.

The 'Spanish Inquisition' was a separate national institution, set up in 1478 (endorsed by Sixtus IV in 1483) against the *Marranos and *Moriscos but later directed against Protestants. The number of persons burnt under the first Grand Inquisitor, *Torquemada, was *c.*2,000. It was finally abolished in Portugal in 1821 and in Spain in 1834. See Index, Inquisition.

Inquisition (Islam): see MIḤNA.

INRI. The initial letters of the Latin words *Iesus Nazarenus Rex Judaeorum* ('Jesus of Nazareth the King of the Jews'). These words, according to John 19. 19 f.), were written over the cross of Jesus in Hebrew, Latin and Greek.

Insān al-Kāmil (the Perfect Man): see AL-INSAN AL-KĀMIL.

Insang. Korean for *mudra.

Insh'Allah ('if God wills it'): see QADAR.

Institute of the Blessed Virgin Mary. Christian religious order for women, founded by Mary Ward (1585–1645) in 1611. She believed that the vocation of women cannot be confined to enclosed orders, and she therefore adopted the constitutions of the *Jesuits (Society of Jesus) as the basis for her Institute. It was known also as the Institute of the English Ladies, les Dames anglaises, or more dismissively as the Galloping Girls. They were strongly opposed by the papacy and were eventually suppressed. They did not receive papal approval until 1877.

Institutes, The. Short title of *Calvin's *Institutes of the Christian Religion*, a basic text of Christian Reformed theology.

Integral Yoga (Aurobindo's Yoga): see AUROBINDO, ŚRI.

Intention. A term in Catholic usage with several meanings:

1. The purpose of doing 'what the church does' in the *sacraments. Along with the right 'form' and 'matter', the right intention is held to be necessary for the validity of the sacrament.

2. The special object for which a prayer of intercession is made, or a *mass said.

In all religions, stress is laid on the importance of intention in the performance of religious duties or the pursuit of religious goals. For an example in Islam, see NIYYA.

Intentionality (Intentionalität): see PHENOMENOLOGY.

Intercession. *Prayer or petition on behalf of others.

Intercession (Islam): see SHAFĀʿA.

Interdict. A punishment in the Roman Catholic Church akin to *excommunication.

Interim ethic/Interims Ethik: see SCHWEITZER, ALBERT.

International Society for Krishna Consciousness (ISKCON). A Hindu devotional movement, commonly known as Hare Krishna, founded in the USA in 1965 by Bhaktivedanta Swami *Prabhupada (1896–1977), a devotee of *Kṛṣṇa. It is in the tradition of *Caitanya. The movement's principal aim is to lead people, living in this demonic age, the age of *Kali-yuga, to attain salvation in the form of permanent Krishna-consciousness by the Way of *Bhakti-yoga, the highest of the three Ways of Knowledge, Works, and Devotion. The Mahāmantra is: Hare Krishna, Hare Krishna; Krishna, Krishna, Hare, Hare; Hare Rama, Hare Rama; Rama, Rama, Hare, Hare. The devotees are vivid and obvious on the streets, in white or saffron robes (for men), and in coloured saris (for women), dancing and singing to traditional instruments.

Inter-Varsity Fellowship (IVF). Since 1974 the Universities and Colleges Christian Fellowship. It was established in 1927 to encourage links between student members of *evangelical Christian Unions. The International Federation of Evangelical Students unites similar groups throughout the world.

Intinction. A method of administering *communion, by dipping the eucharistic bread into the wine.

Introit (Lat. *introire*, 'go in'). The opening act in the *mass. It consists of a psalm or part of a psalm with *antiphon and *gloria Patri, sung as the celebrant enters the church.

Invention of the Cross. The legendary discovery (Lat., *inventio*) of the cross of Jesus at *Calvary by St Helena, the mother of *Constantine. The legend developed from the 5th cent. on. The feast is now called the *Exaltation of the Cross in both E. and W.

Investiture controversy (dispute about the right of laity to make certain Church appointments): see GREGORY VII.

Invincible ignorance. Ignorance according to Roman Catholic understanding, which cannot be eradicated, even by the utmost effort, being a consequence of circumstances which were not chosen.

Invisible religion. Religious beliefs and practices which are held in parallel with (or in association with) those of the official religion to which the person concerned belongs: it is thus closely associated with non-official religion. They include such items as superstition and the paranormal. More broadly, the 'Invisible Religion thesis' is the argument of T. Luckmann (in the book of that title in its Eng. tr., 1967) that *Durkheim and *Weber were correct in identifying religion as the key to understanding society and the place of individuals in society. In his definition, religion is that which enables individuals to transcend their biological nature, thus making religion virtually synonymous with *culture.

Inyon. Korean for *karma.

In-zo. Jap. for *mudra.

Ippen or **Yugyō Shōnin,** 'wandering holy man' (1239–89). Founder of the Ji (Time) sect of Japanese *Pure Land Buddhism; he called his followers, *Jishū, Followers of the Timely Teaching; the 'time' is the six-hour invocation of the *nembutsu each day. Ippen is a representative example of the *hijiri, itinerant Buddhist practitioners, who travelled throughout Japan during the medieval period spreading the Pure Land teachings. At the time of his death, Ippen burnt all of his writings, saying that they all revert to the phrase Namu Amida Butsu. Only a few of his writings, such as the letters and poems collected together in the *Ippen Shonin Goroku*, remain.

Iqbal, Sir Muhammad (1876–1938). Indian Muslim poet and philosopher. Iqbal's reinterpretation of Islam in the light of the *Sūfī heritage and W. philosophy (especially Bergson's creative evolution) gave a fresh stimulus to Indian Islam. His powerful poetry in Urdu and Persian inspired a new generation of Indian Muslims to shape and improve their condition of life, and was one of the chief forces behind the creation of Pakistan. The salient features of Iqbal's thought are the notion of reality as pure duration, with God and man interrelating dynamically in the universe; and the marriage of intellect and love in transforming humans to a higher being. Of his ten major works, *Bang-i-Dara* (1924), *Bal-i-Jibril* (1935), and *Zarb-i-Kalim* (1936) were well received by educated Indian Muslims. *The Reconstruction of Religious Thought in Islam* (1928) was a more systematic elaboration of Iqbal's Islamic vision, arguing for a return to *ijtihād and the establishment of *ijmāʿ through a legislative institution in the reformation of Islamic law.

Irenaeus, St (*c.*140–*c.*200). Church *father. He heard *Polycarp as a boy, so is generally supposed to have come from Asia Minor. He studied at Rome, then became presbyter and later (*c.*178) bishop of Lyons. The tradition that he was a martyr is late and unreliable. The most important work of Irenaeus is his *Detection and Overthrow of the Falsely Named 'Knowledge'* (usually known as *Against *Heresies*). This is a detailed attack on *gnosticism, especially the system of *Valentinus. With him is associated the notion of 'recapitulation': based on Romans 13. 9 and Ephesians 1. 10, the idea in Irenaeus is that Christ is the consummation and completion of God's purpose and design, summoning up all that God intended in creation and dealing in his own person with the defects which had entered in.

Irving(ites) (Christian movement): see CATHOLIC APOSTOLIC CHURCH.

Iryŏn (Korean Buddhist scholar-monk): see IL-YŎN.

'Īsā (Islamic name): see JESUS.

Īśa (Lord God): see ĪŚVARA.

Isaac. Son of the Hebrew *patriarch *Abraham by his wife Sarah. His name is derived from the fact that his mother laughed (*ẓahaka*) when told that she would bear a child (Genesis 18. 12). See also 'AKEDA.

In Islam, Isaac (Isḥāq) is listed in the *Qur'ān among the *prophets (e.g. 4. 163), and named as the son, a 'prophet, one of the righteous' (37. 112) promised to Ibrāhīm (Abraham) (cf. 6. 84, 21. 72). Later Muslim tradition held that the son demanded in sacrifice was Ismā'īl, though the Quranic account (37. 100–9) does not specify his name.

Isaac the Blind or **Sagi Nahor** (*c*.1160–1235). *Kabbalist. Isaac the Blind was the son of *Abraham ben David of Posquières. Described as 'the father of the Kabbalah', he was the author of several works including a commentary to the *Sefer* **Yezirah* (ed. G. Scholem, 1963).

Isaiah. Hebrew prophet of the 8th cent. BCE, and name of a prophetic book of the Hebrew Bible and Christian Old Testament. An early tradition relates his death as a martyr in the reign of Manasseh (*c*.690–*c*.640). He is called Sha'ya in Islamic tradition.

The book of Isaiah falls into three parts: chs. 1–35, 36–9, and 40–66. Chs. 40–66 take up the theme of the redemption of Israel and its mission in the world. Since the 19th cent. these chapters have been known as 'Deutero-Isaiah', on the recognition that they were written by a later author to encourage the Jewish exiles in Babylon shortly before their release in 537 BCE. Chs. 56–66 seem to presuppose that the *Temple had been rebuilt, and are therefore often distinguished as 'Trito-Isaiah'.

The *Ascension of Isaiah* is an *apocryphal work, originally Jewish, but now with Christian interpolations.

Īśā Upaniṣad. The shortest (eighteen verses) of the principal *Upaniṣads, so-called from its opening word, Lord, though also known from its full form as *Īśāvāsyam*. It is often regarded as containing the whole essence of the Upaniṣads.

Ise. City in Japan containing the Ise shrines. The Inner Shrine is dedicated to *Amaterasu, and the Outer to Toyouke Okami, in addition to which there are various other shrines. Under State Shinto, Ise became the shrine of the whole nation. Attempts were made here to absorb Buddhism (see HONJISUIJAKU) in Watarai Shintō, often known as Ise, or Outer Shrine, Shintō. The belief that pilgrimage to Ise can bring benefits to the nation can still be seen in visits of politicians to Ise. The pilgrimage is known as Ise Mairi.

Isḥāq (Muslim name for Abraham's son): see ISAAC.

Ishāq Ṣafī al-Dīn (Sūfī shaykh): see ṢAFAVIDS.

Ishida Baigan (1685–1744). Founder of the Japanese movement, Shingaku ('education of the heart'). Applying himself to meditation, he had several experiences of a total identity of mind and body. He set up his own class, teaching that the true and attainable goal is the overcoming of self-centredness by the deliberate appropriation of the *Confucian virtues. Two of his works have survived, *Toimondo* (Town and Country Dialogues) and *Seikaron* (On Household Management).

Ishin-denshin (Jap., 'transmitting mind through mind'). Zen recognition of the transmission of buddha-dharma from master to pupil and to dharma-successors (*hassu), especially in the lineages of succession (*soshigata, *inka-shōmei).

Ishmael. Eldest son of the Jewish *patriarch, *Abraham, by his maidservant, Hagar. After the birth of *Isaac, Ishmael and his mother were driven from the camp, because Isaac, rather than Ishmael, was the heir of the *covenant (Genesis 16. 21). According to the *Aggadah, Ishmael dishonoured women, worshipped *idols, and tried to kill his younger brother (*Gen.R.* 53. 11; *Tosef.Sot.* 6. 6). He was said to be the ancestor of the Ishmaelites and, by extension, all the Arab peoples.

In Islam Ishmael (Ismā'īl) is mentioned in the *Qur'ān as one of the *prophets (3. 84, 4. 163), and more specifically as a son of Ibrāhīm (*Abraham) (14. 39). The two are said to have rebuilt the *Ka'ba in *Mecca and instituted the rites of *ḥajj (pilgrimage). (2. 127–9).

Ishmael ben Elisha (early 2nd cent. CE). Jewish sage. The son of a *priest, Rabbi Ishmael was one of the chief spokesmen of the sages of *Jabneh. According to legend, he was one of the *martyrs who was killed in the persecutions following the *Bar Kokhba rebellion, but this is doubtful.

Ishraqi or **Ishrāqiy(y)a** (illuminationist school): see SUHRAWARDĪ, SHIHĀB.

Ishvara (God): see ĪŚVARA.

Isidore, St (*c*.560–636). Archbishop of Seville. He is known mainly for his encyclopaedic writings, which were freely used by innumerable medieval authors. The most important of them is the *Etymologiae*. He was made a *Doctor of the Church in 1722.

Isis and Osiris: see DYING AND RISING GODS.

ISKCON: see INTERNATIONAL SOCIETY FOR KRISHNA CONSCIOUSNESS.

Islam (Islām). The religion of allegiance to God and to his *prophet *Muḥammad, the religion (*dīn) which God always intended for his creation, but which is derived in its present form from the prophetic ministry of Muḥammad (*c*.570–632 CE), and from the *revelation mediated through him, the *Qur'ān. The verbal noun *islām* appears eight times in the Qur'ān: derived from the same Semitic root as Heb. *shālom* (peace), it means 'entering into a condition of peace and security with God through allegiance or surrender to him'.

Islam began historically in the quest of Muḥammad to find the absolute truth of God in the midst of the many conflicting claims which he encountered in his environment about the nature of God. Muḥammad went off for periods of increasing isolation during which he struggled in prayer to find *al-Haqq*, the true One; and in a cave on Mount *Ḥirā', there came to him the overwhelming sense of that reality pressing upon him, and the first of the utterances that later became the Qur'ān were spoken through him (96. 1). From this absolute sense of God, *Allāh, derived the insistence which is characteristic of Islam, that if God is indeed God, then there can only be what God is, the One who is the source of all creation and the disposer of all events and lives within it. The life of Muḥammad and the message of the Qur'ān then become a working out and application of that fundamental vision: all people (divided as they are from each other at present) should become a single *'umma (community), and every action and every aspect of life should become an act of witness that 'there is no God but God' and that 'Muḥammad is his messenger'.

Those latter affirmations, making up the basic witness (al-*Shahāda), form the first of the *Five Pillars of Islam. Muslim life and belief are derived directly from the Qur'ān, but since the Qur'ān does not deal with every issue or question which a Muslim might wish to ask, authoritative guidance is derived also from the traditions (*ḥadīth) concerning the words, deeds and silences of Muḥammad and his *companions. Even so, there remains much scope for application and interpretation. Methods of such interpretation emerged (see IJMĀ'; IJTIHĀD; QIYĀS), as also did major schools of interpretation, which drew up law-codes to govern Muslim life: see SHARĪ'A.

When Muḥammad died, no exact provision had been made for any successor to lead the new community. Those who looked for the most effective leader chose Abu Bakr, known as caliph or *khalīfa. Those who looked for the closest relative of Muḥammad supported *'Alī. Although there were four immediate successors (al-Rāshidūn; see KHALĪFA) before a final split, the strains were too great, and the party (*shī'a*) of 'Alī broke away from those who claimed to be following the custom (*sunna) of the Prophet, thereby creating the divide between Sunni and *Shī'a Muslims which persists to this day.

The spread of Islam was extremely rapid. Within a hundred years of the death of Muḥammad, it had reached the Atlantic in one direction and the borders of China in the other. It now amounts to about a billion adherents, and is found in most countries of the world. At one stage (from the 9th to the 13th cents. CE), the Muslim delight in creation led it into a passionate commitment to *knowledge (*'ilm), which in turn led Muslims into spectacular achievements in philosophy (*falsafa) and the natural sciences.

There were two major reactions to the achievements of Muslim philosophy and science. The first was a growing suspicion that perhaps the achievements of the human mind were taking priority over the revelation from God. 'The Incoherence of Philosophy' was exposed by *al-Ghaz(z)ālī (1058–1111 (AH 450–505)), and since that time the prevailing tendency has been one of giving priority to revelation (and the sciences associated with it of exegesis) and obedience.

The second major reaction was a reinforcement of that style of Muslim life and devotion which is known as *Sufism.

Islam is necessarily a *missionary religion, since entrusted to it is the revelation of God's word and will for the world. The world is divided into three domains (see DĀR AL-HARB), with the clear expectation that in due course all will be unified in the single *'umma of God's intent. In the mean time, that quest for community is much complicated by the imposition, during the colonial period of European expansion, of nation-states. The caliphate, which had created the great *dynasties of the past (e.g. the *Umayyads, the *'Abbasids, culminating in the *Ottomans) lingered on in Turkey, but was abolished in 1924 during the attempt to establish Turkey as a secular state. The resulting ambiguities in countries where Muslims are in a majority (e.g. over the extent to which sharī'a law should be introduced or extended), and the many problems for the recovery of authentically Muslim life in a world of rapid change, have not yet been resolved.

Islamic law: see SHARĪ'A; FIQH.

Islands of the immortals (blissful home of the immortals): see FANG-SHIH.

Ismā'īl (eldest son of Abraham): see ISHMAEL.

Ismā'īliy(y)a or **Ismā'īlīs.** An aggregation of Muslim groups, notable for esoteric teaching. They emerged historically from disputes following the death of the sixth Shī'a *Imām, Ja'far al-Sādiq. The succession should have passed to his eldest son, Ismā'īl, but he died before his father. Nevertheless, some maintained that the authority had been transmitted to him as the first-born (and beyond him to his son). Others held that the succession should pass to Ja'far's eldest surviving son (his third), Mūsā al-Kāzim. The Twelvers (*ithnā'ashariyya, majority Shī'a) chose Mūsā and his successors, while those following Ismā'īl came to be known as Ismā'īlīs—and also as *Seveners (*sab'iyya*), partly for having chosen the Seventh Imām in direct succession, but also because of their belief that prophets always come in cycles of seven. Out of the Ismā'īlīya there later arose many subsects e.g. *Qarmatians, Nizārīs (including *Assassins), Musta'līs, *Druzes, and Muqann'ah. During the early 10th cent. CE, the Ismā'īlīs established the powerful and prosperous Fāṭimid dynasty in N. Africa which extended its control, in the 11th cent., to Egypt, Palestine, Syria, Hijāz, Yemen, and Sind. The Fāṭimids were patrons of the arts and sciences and commerce, and they founded the first Islamic universities of *al-Azhar and Dār-al-Hikmah in Cairo. The feature which distinguishes Ismā'īlīs from other Muslim sects is their belief in seven (not five) *pillars of faith: belief, purification, prayer, almsgiving, fasting, pilgrimage, and struggle in Allāh's way.

At present the major Ismā'īlī sect is the Nizārīs, numbering *c.*20 million, in India, Pakistan, E. Africa, Iran, Syria, and Lebanon. In India, they are known also as Khojas, from the Hindu *caste originally converted by a Persian Isma'īlī, Ṣadr al-Dīn. Their Imām is the *Aga Khān.

Isnād. The chain of transmitters of a Muslim *ḥadīth.

Isra' (*al-Isra'*, Arab., 'the journey'). The miraculous journey of the Prophet *Muḥammad from *Mecca to Jerusalem. Qur'ān 17. 1 is taken as a reference to this journey, but no details are given. These are to be found in *ḥadīth, which tells of *Burāq, an animal 'smaller than a mule but larger than an ass'. Together they travelled through the sky to Jerusalem, from where, after prayer and worship, he made the Ascent (al-*Mi'rāj). See also AL-*MASJID AL-AQṢĀ'.

Israel. 1. Name given to the *patriarch *Jacob after he wrestled with an angel (Genesis 32. 28–9).

2. Name used for the descendants of Jacob, and so for all the Jewish people, in full: *bene Israel*, sons of Israel.

3. The Northern Kingdom of the Jews. With the division of the kingdom during the reign of Rehoboam (*c.*930 BCE), the Southern Kingdom, which remained faithful to the House of *David, was known as *Judah, while the Northern Kingdom was called Israel. It included the territory of all the tribes except Judah and *Benjamin. It was eventually captured by the Assyrians in 721 BCE, and its people were scattered.

4. The Jewish homeland established in 1948.

Israel ben Eliezer, Baal Shem Tov, or **Besht** (1700–60). Founder of E. European *Ḥasidism. Many legends are circulated about the life of Israel Ben Eliezer. On his thirty-sixth birthday, he is said to have revealed himself as a new charismatic leader. He worked as a teacher and a healer, travelling round the Jewish communities of E. Europe, attracting many followers by his charm and magnetism. His teachings were partly derived from the *Kabbalah, but his main emphasis was on individual salvation through which the world would be redeemed. He maintained that 'every Jew is a limb of the *Shekhinah', but some individuals have superior spiritual qualities (the *Zaddik). Not only should the Zaddik teach his people to worship God, he should help the sinner to repent and, through special acts, restore the souls of sinners who have died.

Israeli, Isaac ben Solomon (*c.*855–955). Jewish philosopher. Israeli was court physician in Kairouan, the capital of the Maghreb. He was the author of *Kitāb al-Hudūd* (The Book of Definitions) which attempts to define such concepts as the soul, wisdom, the intellect, and nature.

Israelite Mission of the New Universal Covenant. A new movement in Peru, founded by Ezequiel Ataucuzi Gamonal. As a result of what he claims were divine revelations, Ezequiel considers himself called to lead God's chosen people to a new obedience to the *Mosaic law. By the early 1960s, a group of followers were meeting in Lima, and after legal recognition in 1969, the movement spread rapidly throughout Peru.

Isserles, Moses ben Israel or **Rema** (*c.*1530–72). Jewish legal authority. Isserles was one of the great *halakhic authorities of the time. He founded a *yeshivah and gained a worldwide reputation for his *responsa, being known as 'the *Maimonides of Polish Jewry'. Although he aroused opposition for his emphasis on custom (*minhag) and his leniency (particularly when financial loss was involved), his rulings have become accepted as binding on *Ashkenazi Jews.

Isshi-injo (Jap., 'one vehicle'). The Zen insistence that a student can be taught (up to the level of the conferring of *inka-shōmei) by one master (*roshi) only. This is emphasized (especially in *Sōtō-shū) to stop students going from one teacher to another.

Isshin (Jap., 'one mind'). The universal mind which, in Buddhism, pervades all appearance—i.e. the Buddha-mind.

Issur ve-hetter (Heb., 'forbidden and permitted'). All Jewish legal rulings about forbidden food (see DIETARY LAWS).

Iṣṭadevatā (Skt., 'beloved' + 'god'). The chosen deity, in Hinduism, of a temple, family, or cult; or the deity, either chosen by a worshipper, or given to a devotee by a *guru (along with a personal *mantra). The form of the chosen deity is known as *lakṣya*.

Iṣṭamantra (Skt.). Personal or chosen *mantra in Hinduism. It may be allocated by a *guru, or it may be one of the many traditional mantras, e.g. *om namo Nārāyanāya*.

Istiḥsān (Arab.). A method of legal reasoning used in conjunction with *qiyās (analogy), especially by the *Ḥanafite law school. Istiḥsān can best be understood as juristic preference for a principle of law to promote the aims of the law. It is closely related to *istiṣlāh.

Istikhārā (Arab.). The prayer (*du'ā') in Islam of one who is uncertain or undecided for divine guidance.

Istiṣlāh (Arab.). In Islamic law, the concept (not accepted by all schools of *sharī'a) of discerning the intended good of *Qur'ān and *ḥadīth injunctions in relation to the demands of human welfare (*maṣlaḥa*).

Īśvara (Skt., *īś*, 'to have power'). The concept of a personal God as creator of the cosmos. In the *Vedas, īśvara is the power of a ruler, hence divine power (*Atharva Veda*, 7. 102. 1) and thus (19. 6. 4) a title of *Puruṣa as lord of immortality. In *Advaita Vedānta, Īśvara is *Brahman as Brahman is related to the manifest world of appearance. As, in effect, the personal god (i.e. the way in which God becomes personal to an individual), Īśvara evokes the attitude of *bhakti (devotion).

Īśvarakoti (Skt.). A perfected soul in Hinduism, which is reborn on earth to help others to realize truth; cf. AVATĀRA, or in Buddhism BODHISATTVA.

Īśvarakṛṣṇa (c.350–450). Author of the *Sāṃkhyakārikā*, a summary compilation of the *Sāṃkhya philosophy.

Ithnā 'Asharīy(y)a (Arab., *ithna'ashar*, 'twelve'). The Twelvers, majority *Shi'a Islam, the official Shi'a religion of modern Iran. This Shi'a sect follows the cult of Twelve *Imāms, in distinction from the smaller Sab'īyya sect (*Seveners, see also ISMĀ'ĪLIYYA). The series of Twelve Imāms is: *'Alī, *al-Hasan, *al-Ḥusain, 'Alī Zayn, al-'Abidīn, Muḥammad al-Bāqir, Ja'far al-Ṣādiq, Mūsā al-Kāẓim 'Alī al-Ridā, Muḥammad al-Taqī, 'Alī al-Naqī, al-Ḥasan al-'Askarī, and Muhammad *al-Mahdī. The Imāms are the chosen of God, who direct the destiny of humanity, and preserve and guide the world. Special prayers are reserved for each of the Imāms during weekdays, and it is believed that pilgrimage to their tombs brings special rewards, especially at *Karbalā' and *Mashhad.

I–Thou (in contrast to I–It). A distinction in ways of knowing, emphasized by M. *Buber: in the personal relationship, one subject, I, encounters or meets another subject, Thou; in connection with things, the subject observes or experiences an object, It. The relation with God may be I–It as a matter of discussion, but God can only be known in the I–Thou relationship.

Itihāsa (Skt., 'so indeed it was'). Early Hindu literature, comprising legends, myths, poems, etc., associated with epics and *purāṇas (especially the eighteen Mahāpurāṇas), which is then later called the fifth *Veda. More generally the great epics (*Mahābhārata*, *Rāmāyaṇa*) are termed itihāsa.

'Itikāf. 'Retreat' to a *mosque for a certain period of time, to engage in worship, fasting, and reading the *Qur'ān.

Itivuttaka (part of the Buddhist Pāli canon): see KHUDDAKA-NIKĀYA.

Itō Jinsai (1627–1705). A Japanese *Confucian scholar from the movement called Ancient Learning (*kokugaku). He opened his school in *Kyōto where he taught that the true message of the Confucian sages could only be apprehended by reading their ancient writings directly, without reliance upon the later Neo-Confucian commentaries of *Chu Hsi (1130–1200) and others. His school, known as the Kogidō or 'Hall of Ancient Meanings', was continued by his son, Itō Tōgai (1670–1736), with students drawn from all over Japan. See also Ogyū Sorai.

Ittai (Jap., 'one body'). The Zen experience of participating in (and indeed being) undifferentiated reality. It is thus the attainment of the goal of Zen.

Iwasaka (Jap.). Proto-*Shinto sanctuary. The word appears only twice, once in the **Nihongi*, once in the **Kogoshūi*. The texts infer that iwasaka stands for something to be set up, together with *himoroki* (meaning uncertain), for worship service, which implicitly suggests that it was not intended to be a permanent sanctuary.

Iyenar (Tamil tutelary deity): see GRĀMADEVATĀ.

Izanagi and Izanami. The paired 'male who invites' and 'female who invites' in Japanese mythology. They are of the seventh generation of gods who are required to undertake creation—including, in the **Nihongi*, *Amaterasu. They stand on the floating bridge of heaven and stir up the matter of creation with a spear thrust into the depth of the ocean. Izanami is destroyed in the making of fire and goes to the land of Yomi (death). Izanagi searches for her, and when he finds her, he disobeys her command not to look at her. He lights a torch and sees her decaying body. Yomi tries to catch him so that he cannot return to the living and warn them about death, but he escapes. Izanami threatens in her anger to kill a thousand beings every day, but Izanagi responds by promising to bring one and a half thousand to birth. So begins the process of life and death.

Izmirim (Doenmeh sect): see DOENMEH.

'Izrā'īl or **'Azrā'īl** (Arab.). In Islam, the *angel of death. *Ḥadīth and legend describe him as being of vast size and great strength.

J

J. The name given to a supposed source used in the composition of the *Pentateuch: it is an abbreviation of the Jahwistic (Yahwistic) source.

Jabneh (Yavneh, also known as Jamnia). Town to the east of *Jerusalem. It came to prominence after the Fall of Jerusalem in 70 CE, when R. *Johanan ben Zakkai was allowed by the Romans to establish a centre of learning—and, from the Jewish point of view, the *Sanhedrin. From here the continuity of Judaism in Israel was secured.

Jabriy(y)a (Muslim sect emphasizing God's control): see QADAR.

Jacob (Heb., Ya'akov). Third Hebrew *patriarch. Jacob was the younger twin son (with *Esau) of *Isaac and Rebekah. In the *aggadah, the story of Jacob is understood as symbolic of the later history of the Jews—so Esau struggling with Jacob in their mother's womb is interpreted as the conflict between Rome and Israel (e.g. *Gen.R.* 63. 8).

Jacob ben Asher or **Ba'al ha-Turim** (*c*.1270–1340). Jewish *halakhic authority. Jacob was the son of *Asher b. Jeḥiel. Working in poverty in Toledo, he compiled his halakhic masterpiece the *Arba'ah Turim* (Four Rows, 1475). The *Turim* is divided into four parts: (i) *Oraḥ Ḥayyim* (The Path of Life), the laws concerning religious life through the whole day, including conduct in *synagogue and on fast and festival days; (ii) *Yoreh De'ah* (The Teaching of Knowledge), on *issur ve-hetter, including food, family, mourning, usury, oaths; (iii) *Even ha-Ezer* (The Stone of Help), on women, marriage, and divorce; (iv) *Ḥoshen Mishpat* (The Breastplate of Judgement), civil law. The work went through many edns., evoking commentaries and epitomes.

Jacob Joseph of Polonnoye (*c*.1710–84), *Ḥasidic teacher and author, known as Toledot (from his book *Toledot Ya'akov Yosef*, 'The Generations of Jacob Joseph', 1780). Already a rabbi, he met and became a disciple of Ba'al Shem Tov (*Israel ben Eliezer) when he was about 35. He became a *zaddik, understanding the zaddik as 'the soul of the world'. His other major works (alluding to *Joseph in the title) were *Ben Porat Yosef* ('Joseph is a Fruitful Vine', 1781), *Tzafenat Pane'ah* (the name given to Joseph by Pharaoh in Genesis 41. 45, 1782), and *Ketonat Passim* ('Coat of Many Colours', pub. 1866).

Jacobson, Israel (1768–1828). Pioneer of *Reform Judaism. Jacobson worked for the emancipation of the Jews of the German states and was an enthusiastic supporter of Napoleon's Assembly of Jewish Notables. Jacobson himself summoned a similar assembly in Westphalia in 1808 and was instrumental in the founding of the first Reform *synagogues both in Westphalia and Berlin.

Jacopone da Todi (*c*.1230–1306). *Franciscan poet. A lawyer of a somewhat worldly life, he was converted after the death of his wife. He became a Franciscan laybrother in 1278, joining the 'Spirituals' who sought to live according to the original rigour of the rule. He is famed for his deeply emotional devotional poems (*Laude*), in Latin and the Umbrian dialect, which became very popular (amongst them, probably, the *Stabat Mater*).

Jaḍa-samādhi (Skt., 'insentient' + 'samādhi'). A defective condition in Hinduism, parasitic on two important goals: jaḍa, the highest state of yogin concentration, and *samādhi, the highest state of contemplation. But the two together refer to something more like 'dreamless sleep', a state of suspended consciousness.

Jade Emperor (Deity in Chinese folk religion): see YÜ-HUANG.

Jadid al-Islam (group of secretly practising Jews): see CRYPTO-JEWS.

Ja'far al-Sādiq (6th Shī'a Imām): see ISMĀ'ĪLIY(Y)A.

Ja'farī Shi'ites. Those Shi'ite Muslims (Ithnā 'Ashariy(y)a, Twelvers) who follow the codes of religious law associated with Ja'far al-Sādiq.

Jafr. The belief of *Shī'a Muslims that there is a secret tradition of esoteric knowledge passed on through the succession of Imāms.

Jagaccandra Suri (Jain sect): see GACCHA.

Jagadguru (Skt., 'world-teacher'). Title assumed by sect leaders, as e.g. among the *Liṅgāyats.

Jagannātha (Skt., 'Lord of the Universe': often Anglicized as 'juggernaut'). Local name of the Hindu god *Viṣṇu/*Kṛṣṇa worshipped in the temple of Purī, Orissa. The temple is famous all over India and attracts large numbers of pilgrims, particularly to its *festivals. The temple became notorious under colonial rule because of its festivals, during which period the wooden images are carried out in procession on huge wooden carts, under whose wheels some were killed, probably by accident, not suicide. However, 'Juggernaut' came to denote blind, religious frenzy. But with memories of the huge festival carts lingering on, a more recent application of the word is to large, heavy lorries.

Jagjīt Siṅgh. A *Nāmdhārī Sikh who became leader in 1959. Although based at Bhainī *Sāhib, *Pañjāb, his commitment to the order led to much travel, promoting improved dairy farming, vegetarianism, and world peace.

Jahāṅgīr (1569–1626). *Mughal emperor from 1605, whose full title was Nūr-ud-din Mohāmmad Jahāṇgīr Gāzī. He had four sons and many wives and concubines, but he loved Nūr-Jahān best and ruled with her advice and active support. Towards the end of his reign he was under the influence of opium, which rendered him emperor in name only, and the real power was with Nūr-Jahān which she wielded with the ministers of her choice.

Jahāṇgīr followed *Akbar's religious policy of tolerance.

Jahannam: see HELL (ISLAM).

Jāhilīy(y)a (Arab., *jāhil*, 'untaught'). The state of ignorance understood to have characterized Arabian society prior to Islam. The *jāhil* is the ignorant person with (because of lack of the truth) an accompanying wildness or uncouthness. In Islam today there are those who see in W. secularism a new jāhilīya and who anathematize some expressions of Islam itself by this term.

Jahnu. A Hindu prince who drank the Ganges (*Gaṅgā) when it flooded his sacrificial ground. The *ṛṣis and gods propitiated him, and he allowed the water to flow out of his ear, hence to be known in personified form as Jāhnavī, daughter of Jahnu. Hence also it is the name of the cave at the source of the Ganges.

Jaimal Siṅgh (founder of Hindu religious movement): see RĀDHĀSOĀMĪ SATSAṄG.

Jaimini. Name of several Hindu authors, the distinction between whom is not always clear. The *Mīmāṃsā-sūtras are attributed to a Jaimini (though they are from different dates), as is a Gṛhya Sūtra. Another Jaimini translated the **Aśvamedha parvan* of the **Mahābhārata* into Kanarese, and it is regarded as the finest example of poetry in that language.

Jainism. An ancient Indian *śrāmaṇic religious and philosophical tradition still vigorous today. The religion derives its name from the *jinas (spiritual victors), a title given to twenty-four great teachers or 'ford-makers' (*tīrthaṅkaras) whom Jains claim have appeared in the present half-cycle (*avasarpiṇī*) of time. In fact, Jain teaching is uncreated and eternal, being reactivated by the 'ford-makers' (as the *Three Jewels) in unending cycles. In the present cycle, historical evidence clearly reaches back to the last two of these teachers, *Mahāvīra (24th), who was a contemporary of the *Buddha, and *Pārśva (23rd), but it is evident that these teachers were reviving, restoring, and re-forming a thread of ancient śramaṇic teaching whose origins lie in Indian prehistory and may have links with the *Indus Valley Civilization (see ṚṢABHA). The aim of Jain spiritual endeavour is to liberate the soul (*jīva) by freeing it from accumulated *karma. Every soul is potentially divine and can aspire to *mokṣa by following a course of purification and discipline demonstrated by the tīrthaṅkaras. At the heart of Jainism lies a radical asceticism based on *five great vows which monks and nuns follow and which the laity attempt to the best of their ability. The major schism of Jainism between the *Digambara ('the atmosphere clad', i.e. naked) and Śvetāmbara ('white clad'), began to emerge as early as 300 BCE ostensibly over whether monks should go naked or wear a simple cloth; but the two schools came to embody differing views towards the scriptures (see AṄGA), women, and monastic practice.

In early years, the Jain movement diffused from its place of origin in the Ganges basin. The diffusion of Jainism accelerated the tendency to form separate groups (see GACCHA). Jain philosophy rejects the authority of the *Vedas, *caste, and the idea of a God who creates. It is characterized by a realistic classification of being and a theory of knowledge which has connections with *Sāṃkhya and Buddhist thought. Jain philosophers have made many distinctive contributions to Indian philosophy particularly in the kindred doctrines of *nayavāda and *syādvāda which together form the doctrine of the manysidedness of reality (*anekāntavāda). This enables a tolerance which may account in part for the remarkable survival of Jainism in India. Whilst accounting for less than 0.5 per cent of India's vast population, Jain influence on the religious, social, political, and economic life of the country has been and is quite out of proportion to their numbers. Until the last cent., Jainism was strictly an Indian phenomenon, but many Gujarati Jains, who had settled in E. Africa, migrated to Europe in the late 1960s and early 1970s as a result of pan-Africanization policies; so that today there are estimated to be 25,000 Jains in Europe, largely in the UK. Some estimates suggest a similar number may be found in N. America.

Jakoblar (Doenmeh, Islamic sect): see DOENMEH.

Jakugo or **chakugo** (Jap., 'words of arrival'). A summary statement in Zen of the true understanding of a *kōan.

Jakuhitsu Genkō (1290–1367). Japanese Zen master of the *Rinzai school. He became a monk at the age of 15 and was taught by Yakuō Tokken in *Kamakura. When he asked Yakuō for his *matsugo* (his final, dying word, and also the word which will lead to enlightenment), Yakuō slapped him and he immediately experienced enlightenment. He went to China, 1320–6, where he was acknowledged as a master of Ch'an. On his return to Japan, he became an itinerant, seeking realization of truth in mountains and solitude. When Eigen-ji was built in 1361, he became the first abbot, and contributed decisively to the *rinka* or *ringe* style of Zen monasticism, 'under the forest' or 'thicket', in which the ideal of simplicity and non-attachment was maintained.

Jakumetsu (Jap., 'stillness' + 'extinction'). Japanese pronunciation of the two Chinese characters which represent the Skt. for *nirvāna. It is thus an indefinable state of absolute attainment in which a buddha lives.

Jalāl al-Dīn Rūmī or **Mawlānā/ Mawlawī** ('our master', 1207–73 (AH 604–72)). A great mystic poet of Islam and founder of the *Mawlawīy(y)a (Mevlevi) *Sūfī order. He was born at Balkh, but his family migrated to Kōnya in Rūm, Anatolia, hence his surname. Rūmī's meeting with the Sūfī, Shams al-Dīn Tabrīzī, led him to abandon his teaching career and devote himself entirely to the mystic path. From then on, Rūmī, over a period of time, received divine illumination; and the love of God became the whole basis of his life. Contrary to general Muslim practice, Rūmī gave *music and *dance an important place in religious expression.

The best known of Rūmī's works are *Diwan-i-shams-Tabrizi* (The Poems of Shams-i-Tabriz) and *Mathnawī* (The Poem in Rhyming Couplets, tr. R. A. Nicholson, 1925–40), a great mystical poem considered by *Jāmī to be the essence of the Qur'ān rendered in Persian. He also wrote a prose treatise entitled *Fīhi mā fīhi* (What is within is within). His influence over the Sūfī orders of Turkey, Persia, Central Asia, and India reinvigorated Islam from within and helped it recover from the Mongol invasions (1258).

Jalwah (return to the world to help others): see MULLĀ ṢADR.

Jamaa (Swahili, 'family'). A large *charismatic movement among African *Roman Catholics in Zaire. It was founded in the early 1950s among urban workers attached to the copper mines in the Katanga area, by a Belgian Franciscan missionary, Placide Tempels. It expressed the ideas in his influential book *Bantu Philosophy* (1945), which interpreted RC teaching in terms of African culture. After a sympathetic beginning, relations with the RC hierarchy deteriorated, Tempels was withdrawn to Belgium in 1962, members were virtually *excommunicated from about 1970. In spite of this Jamaa has spread widely into Kasai and beyond, and produced deviant secessions known as Katete.

Jamā'at-i Islāmī (The Islamic Society). A highly disciplined and well-organized Muslim political party, founded in 1941 by Abul al-A'lā *Mawdūdī. It aims at establishing an observant Islamic state in Pakistan. The Jamā'at advocates that Pakistan should be a theocratic state, ruled by a single man whose tenure of office and power are limited only by his faithfulness to Islam. The ruler should be assisted by a *shura* (advisory council), with no political parties and no provision for an opposition. General Zia al-Haqq, the military leader after the overthrow of Z. Bhutto (1977), used the Jamā'at as a political prop for his 'back to Islam' campaign.

Jamāl al-Dīn al-Afghānī (Muslim modernist reformer): see AL-AFGHĀNĪ.

James. The name of two or three early Christian figures. St James, the son of Zebedee, was brother of *John, and one of *Jesus' inner circle of disciples. He was martyred in 44 CE (Acts 12. 2). He was claimed in the Middle Ages to have been the apostle of Spain, and was supposed to have been buried at Santiago de Compostela (see PILGRIMAGE). St James, 'the Lord's brother' (Mark 6. 3), became the leader of the earliest Christian church at Jerusalem after the departure of *Peter. Nothing is known of St James the Less (or 'the younger'; Mark 15. 40) unless he is to be identified with James the son of Alphaeus (Mark 3. 18) or Jesus' brother.

The Letter of James is the first of the *Catholic Epistles in the New Testament. It is almost entirely moral in content.

James, William (1842–1910). American scholar whose contribution to the study of religion derives from his refusal to treat physiology, psychology, and philosophy as separate disciplines. What remains a major contribution to the psychology of religion, James's *The Varieties of Religious Experience* (1902), also benefited from the fact that he was equipped with 'religious musicality'. Always tending to be individualistic, *The Varieties* dwells on personal religious life rather than on institutional or social expressions. He introduced the phrase, 'stream of consciousness', and described the nature of the stream. *The Will To Believe* (1897) is a commitment to struggle against evil and moral deficiencies, not an exercise in empty metaphysical speculation.

Jāmi. A Hindu goddess of maternity and feminine attributes.

Jāmī, Mawlānā Nūr al-Dīn 'Abd al-Raḥmān (1414–92 (AH 817–98)). Muslim *Sūfī poet of the *Naqshbandiy(y)a order, known as *khātam al-shu'arā'*, 'the seal of the poets'. He immersed himself in the teaching of *Ibn 'Arabī, but united this with the vision of *Jalāl al-Dīn Rūmī. His best-known poetic work (*Haft Awrang*, The Seven Thrones) explores, through classical examples, how human love is transformed into the symbol and vehicle of divine love.

'Jam.pa'i.dbyargs (bodhisattva): see MAÑJUŚRĪ.

Jan (spirit): see FRAVASI.

Janaka. Hindu king of Videha who was instructed by *Yajñavalkya, and who maintained that a pious *kṣatriya can perform sacrifices as much as the *brahmans. He remains an example of how to live serenely in the world after obtaining liberation.

Janamaśtami, also known as **Krishnajayānti.** Hindu *festival celebrating the birth of *Kṛṣṇa. It is held on the eighth day of the dark fortnight of the month of Śravana (Aug.).

Janam-sākhī (Pañjābī, 'birth-testimony, biography'). Collection of hagiographic stories about Gurū *Nānak.

Janārdana: (Skt., 'giver of rewards'). One of the twenty-four *avatāras (incarnations) of *Viṣṇu. He takes the form of the planets, and distributes the consequences of actions to living beings.

Jaṅgamas (Liṅgāyat officiants): see LIṄGĀYAT.

Janissaries (Turk., *yeni cheri*, 'new troops'). Corps of highly trained Muslim soldiers who were raised from the *devshirme*, Balkan boys who, by levy, were compelled to become Muslims. They existed from the 14th cent. (8th cent. AH) to the 19th (13th).

Janna (garden): see HEAVEN (ISLAM).

Jansenism. A Christian religious movement of 17th- and 18th-cent. France which drew its inspiration from the *Augustinus* (1640) of Cornelius Jansen (1585–1638). This study of St *Augustine's doctrine of *grace adopted his most rigid views, and was accused of reiterating the teaching of *Calvin and of Baius. Jansen's views were propagated by Saint-Cyran, from 1635 the spiritual director of Mère Angélique *Arnauld, abbess of Port-Royal near Paris, and he also had a considerable influence on Angélique's youngest brother Antoine, encouraging him to write his attack on the practice of frequent *communion (1642). While emphasis on *predestination, the fewness of the number of the elect, and the perfect state necessary to receive the *sacraments, remained central, Jansenist teaching became associated with *Gallicanism, and it attacked the *casuistry of the *Jesuits. It gained notable support from *Pascal and Quesnel.

Jāp (Pañjābī, 'repetition'). Hymn by Gurū *Gobind Siṅgh. The Jāp is the introductory invocation to the *Dasam Granth and is included in *Nitnem for daily repetition.

Japa (Skt., 'whispering', 'repetition'). The main constituent of *mantra yoga involving the repetition of a *bīja mantra, mantra, or series of mantras given by a *guru at initiation (*dīkṣa). Often a *mālā (rosary) of ṛudrākṣa berries, or of various seeds, shells, or stones, is used to count the repetitions. The practice of japa leads to enlightenment, and to superhuman powers (*iddhis).

Japamāla (rosary): see MĀLĀ.

Japanese religion. A brocade of religious traditions developed over 2,000 years and consisting of indigenous folk religion, organized *Shinto, various schools of Buddhism, *Confucian teachings, *Taoist practices, and even Christian influences. There are original strands and added strands in Japanese religious history, none discarded, always changing and growing. The various strands intertwine and permeate each other, and Japanese people typically participate at different levels in several of these religious traditions. There are certain characteristics common to all, such as a sense of intimate relationship with the sacred reality in nature, an emphasis on local cults and festivals, veneration of ancestors with strong attachment to familial groups, and a clear sense of the unity of religion and the nation.

The indigenous folk religion, later called Shinto or kami no michi, revolved in prehistoric times around a feeling of awe for sacred powers called *kami. The social unit was the clan (*uji*), each of which had a tutelary kami (*ujigami*). When the imperial clan became dominant, a sacred national community was forged with the emperor as the divine head, supported by the myths collected in the *Kojiki* and the **Nihonshoki*. The central myths tell of the sun kami *Amaterasu Omikami.

New dimensions came to Japanese religion starting in the 6th cent. CE, with the advent of Sino-Korean culture with its system of writing, political models, and above all Buddhism, Confucianism, and Taoism. The Japanese accepted all aspects of Chinese culture without discrimination: Confucian concepts such as filial piety and veneration of ancestors, Taoist divination and fortune-telling, and especially Buddhist rituals and teachings. At first Buddhism was more the domain of the court and the élite (see NARA BUDDHISM), but by the Heian period it developed into the religion of all Japanese people, especially in the *Tendai and *Shingon forms, that provided a theoretical basis for the Shinto-Buddhist amalgamation known as *Ryōbu Shintō and Sannō Ichijitsu, in which kami were understood to be manifestations of the Buddhas.

The most typically Japanese forms of Buddhism developed at the beginning of the feudal era in the Kamakura period, when classical Japanese court society was disrupted and people longed for security of faith and certainty of salvation in a time of confusion and degeneracy. New popular schools of Buddhism developed to meet their needs in this time of spiritual awakening: *Pure Land, *Nichiren, and *Zen Buddhism.

Western influences entered into Japanese religion with the introduction of Christianity by *Francis Xavier (1506–52) and other *Jesuit missionaries in the middle of the 16th cent. Within one century Christianity rose rapidly to be accepted by many feudal lords and their people and just as rapidly was destroyed, with some tenacious Christians forced underground to continue their faith as 'hidden Christians' (*kakure kirishitan*). In reaction to the foreign threat associated with Christianity, the Tokugawa rulers closed Japan to all foreign influences and gave to Buddhist temples the task of monitoring the religious practices of the people. As Buddhism became formalized and stagnant, a movement to restore Shintō arose, drawing on antecedents such as *Yoshida Shintō. Some used *neo-Confucian ideas, as in *Suiga Shintō and *Shingaku, but the scholars of the *Kokugaku ('national learning') movement such as *Motoori Norinaga (1730–1801) used a painstaking study of ancient philology in an attempt to return to the pure roots of Japanese culture and separate Shinto from Buddhism, thus creating *Fukko ('return to antiquity') Shintō. When pressure from the W. forced Japan to open up again in the 19th cent., the restoration government of Emperor *Meiji moved toward making State Shinto (*Kokka Shintō) the ritual and ideological support of the nation with the emperor as its symbolic head. New Shinto movements which had arisen in the turbulent days at the end of the Tokugawa era and beginning of the Meiji era were categorized as Sect Shinto (*Kyōha Shintō). While Buddhists, Christians, and Sect Shintoists had freedom of religion, allegiance to State Shinto was required of all.

With Japan's defeat in the Second World War came the disestablishment of Shinto and the formation of the Association of Shinto Shrines independent of the government. The Sect Shinto groups have continued to attract large numbers of adherents, and many New Religions (*shinkō shūkyō*) have developed and are flourishing, drawing on ideas and practices from the various Japanese traditions. Among many, however, there persists the sense that much of the spiritual heritage of Japan has been lost amid the *secularization of modern life.

See also BUDDHISM IN JAPAN; Index, Nichiren; Pure Land; Shinto.

Japjī (Pañjābī, 'recitation'). Major Sikh religious poem composed by Gurū *Nānak. The Japjī introduces and epitomizes the *Ādi Granth.

Jara. A Hindu *rākṣasī, able to change her form at will as she seeks flesh to eat. She is propitiated by being called Gṛhadevī (goddess of the household) and by being painted on walls surrounded by children.

Jaratkāru. A Hindu ascetic and *ṛṣi. According to the **Mahābhārata*, his austerity was so great that he travelled round the world living only on air and never eating.

Jaṭ. *Caste group dominant in Sikh *Panth. Although low in the Hindu caste hierarchy, the Jaṭs are economically powerful as landowners in *Pañjāb, with a martial and agricultural tradition.

Jaṭā. The state of *hair when a Hindu leaves it matted and uncared for, either as a sign of mourning, or as a mark of *asceticism. It is characteristic of *Śiva as the great yogin, whose jaṭā is also identified with Vāyu, the god of wind.

Jātaka ('birth-story'). A story of the previous incarnations of the *Buddha. Many of these stories exist, and it is thought that some may originally have been Indian, pre-Buddhist, fables and fairy tales. Some are found virtually unchanged in Aesop's collection. In the *Theravādin *Tripiṭaka, a collection of 547 Jātakas forms part of the *Khuddaka Nikāya*.

Jātakamāla. A collection of thirty-four stories dealing with assorted former lives of the *Buddha (*jātaka).

Jathā (Pañjābī, 'armed band'). Squad of Sikhs. In the 18th cent., the Sikh army divided into five jathās to counter Muslim aggression in *Pañjāb. In the 20th cent. Sikh jathās marched, demanding reform of *gurdwārā management and in protest at the partition of Pañjāb.

Jāti. The Hindu term for *caste. Its origin has been connected to the *varna classification, but whereas that was originally concerned with classification by occupation, jāti determines social status according to birth and lineage. Nevertheless, the two overlap, although the castes have now proliferated and no longer correspond to the original divisions. The protest of some modern Hindus against jāti has diminished its importance in urban areas, though everywhere it remains important in marriage. In the same way, although Gurū *Nānak set himself against caste, it has persisted among Sikhs, particularly in relation to marriage.

Jayadeva (Indian poet): see GĪTĀGOVINDA.

Jazen (false zen): see HUNG-CHIH.

Jehovah. Eng. vocalization of the four consonants that make up the *tetragrammaton. It is erroneous, since it took the vowels of *adonai* ('my lord') which were inserted into printed or written texts to prevent any attempt to pronounce the name of God.

Jehovah's Witnesses. A sect derived from Charles Taze Russell (1852–1916), emphasizing biblical literalism and the imminent coming of the kingdom of God. Jesus is not God but the son of God, the first of his creations. The fulfilment of the promise of God's kingdom will be inaugurated by the battle of *Armageddon, an event which was predicted for 1914—hence the saying of Rutherford, Russell's successor, that 'millions now living will never die'. 1914 is now interpreted as the establishment of the kingdom. Jehovah's Witnesses engage in persistent door-to-door proselytizing, endeavouring to sell *The Watchtower*, in which the movement's interpretation of world events is contained.

Jen (Chin., 'benevolence'). A central virtue in the *Confucian tradition, also commonly tr. as 'humanity', 'human-heartedness', 'love', 'altruism', etc. The Chinese character is formed by combining the elements 'human' and 'two', suggesting a reference to the quality of human relationships. In early Confucian texts, jen is employed in two senses: (i) as the particular human virtue of benevolence or goodness which is embodied to some extent in all people (but perhaps especially in the nobility); (ii), and more importantly, as the moral life ideally embodied.

Confucius freed jen from the exclusive possession of the nobility, rendering it a moral quality that can be pursued as a goal by human beings regardless of their social position. As a general term, jen, for Confucius, embraces both *i ('righteousness') and *li ('propriety').

In the thought and teaching of *Mencius, jen is made into one of the four cardinal virtues.

Other schools of thought quickly criticized the Confucian understanding of jen. *Mo Tzu saw the Confucian jen as socially divisive because of what he took to be its partiality, and taught 'universal love' (*chien ai*, literally, 'a love that does not make distinctions') in its stead.

Taoists such as *Lao-Tzu and *Chuang-Tzu challenged the Confucian understanding of jen on the grounds that it was part of *wei*, the sort of contrived action they sought to avoid.

Nevertheless, chen-jen (real or perfect person) is admired as the one who bears all things with equanimity.

In later neo-Taoist texts (*hsüan-hsüeh), jen refers to the universal extension of love, by which one forms mystically one body with Heaven and Earth.

Jeremiah. Second of the major Hebrew *prophets, after whom is named the prophetic book. Traditionally the Book of Lamentations is also ascribed to Jeremiah.

Jeremy, Epistle of. Jewish *apocryphal book. The date is uncertain (4th–2nd cent. BCE). It purports to be a letter of the *prophet *Jeremiah to the Jewish *exiles in Babylon.

Jericho (modern Tell esSultan). Ancient city which (according to the account in Joshua 6) succumbed to the conquest of Joshua and the Israelites with a dramatic fall of the walls at the sound of the trumpets, and with a complete destruction.

Jerome, St (*c*.342–420). Church *father. A native of Italy, he set out for Palestine in *c*.374 and spent four or five years as a hermit. Later (382–5) as secretary to Pope Damasus he successfully preached *asceticism in Rome. He eventually settled in Bethlehem in 386, where he devoted the rest of his life to study. Jerome's greatest scholarly achievement was the translation of most of the Bible into Latin (see VULGATE). He also advocated the Church's acceptance of the Heb. *canon of the Old Testament, excluding the *Apocrypha. He is often represented with a lion at his feet. This goes back to the legend that Jerome helped a lion by removing a thorn from its foot. The lion subsequently assisted Jerome, e.g. by recovering a stolen ass. Feast day, 30 Sept.

Jerusalem

Judaism The capital of the State of *Israel. Jerusalem was captured by King *David from the Jebusites (see 2 Samuel 5) and became his capital. It was the site of *Solomon's *Temple and the royal palace, and remained the seat of the Davidic kings during the period of the monarchy. The city was captured and largely destroyed by the Babylonians in 587 BCE. The city was rebuilt in the Persian period. Now began the brilliant imagination of Jerusalem, containing virtually all beauty, the site of all important events from Creation to End. The Temple was reconstructed and remained the centre of social and religious life under the *high priest and was greatly enlarged by *Herod the Great. The Jewish revolt against the Romans in 66 CE, however, led to a prolonged siege of the city and its eventual destruction. Of the Temple only the western wall (*wailing wall) remained. When the State of Israel was created in 1948, Jerusalem was partitioned. In 1967 Israeli forces captured the Arab quarter and the united city was declared the capital of the State of Israel. See also ZION.

Christianity The Christian history of the city is associated with Jesus' short ministry there and with his death and resurrection. The Jewish church there flourished at least until the war against Rome of 66–70 CE. The see of Jerusalem did not return to importance until the 4th cent. with the building of churches by *Constantine and the new fashion of pilgrimage to the Holy Places. The Christian centre of Jerusalem is the Church of the Resurrection, commonly known as the Church of the Holy Sepulchre.

Islam Jerusalem is not mentioned by name in the *Qur'ān, but 17. 5–7 is clearly referring to the two destructions of Jerusalem. On that basis, 17. 1 ties the Night Journey (*isra') and the Ascent (al-*Mi'rāj) to Jerusalem as the place of their occurrence. Originally the *qibla (direction of prayer) was toward Jerusalem, only later being changed to *Mecca. Jerusalem thus becomes in Islam third in holiness to Mecca and *Madīna. Known originally as Iliya (i.e. Aelia) Madīna Bayt al-Maqdis, it became known from the 4th cent. AH as al-Quds, the Holy. Two major buildings were erected on the Temple Mount, al-Masjid al-Aqsa, 'the furthest mosque' referred to (in anticipation) in sūra 17; and Qubbat as-Sakhrah, the *Dome of the Rock (piously, but unhistorically, also called 'the Mosque of *'Umar').

Jerusalem, Synod of. A *council of the Orthodox church, convened by *Dositheus, patriarch of Jerusalem, in 1672 to reject Cyril *Lucar's sympathy with some aspects of *Calvinism. It emphasized church and sacraments, and with the Synod of Jassy (1642) it resembled the reaction to the Reformation of Tridentine Catholicism.

Jerusalem Conference (1928): see MISSION.

Jesse. Father of King *David (1 Samuel 16). His importance in Christian tradition derives from the messianic prophecy of Isaiah 11. 1. This led in the late Middle Ages to an iconographical composition showing a tree springing from Jesse and ending in Jesus.

Jesuits. Properly called the Society of Jesus, a *religious order of clerks regular founded by *Ignatius Loyola. It received papal approval in 1540. The spirituality of the Society is based upon the *Spiritual Exercises* of Ignatius, a thirty-day series of retreat meditations which most Jesuits undertake twice during their training. The power of the Jesuits in the 17th and 18th cents. gave rise to considerable hostility in political circles of Europe, and also in some religious ones, particularly among the *Jansenists. In 1773 the Society was formally suppressed by Clement XIV, but restored again in 1814 by Pius VII. From then on the Society showed itself especially devoted to the Holy See. For individual Jesuits, see Index, Jesuits.

Jesus (d. 30 or 33 CE). Jewish religious teacher, and in traditional Christian belief the unique *incarnation of God. (For the name 'Jesus Christ' see CHRIST.)

Jesus was born before the death of King Herod (4 BCE), of pious parents Joseph and *Mary, of Nazareth in Galilee. According to Matthew and Luke, Mary conceived Jesus by the operation of the *Holy Spirit while remaining a virgin: see VIRGIN BIRTH. Jesus is once called a 'carpenter' (Mark 6. 3, unless the alternative reading referring to his believed father is preferred), but nothing is known of his life (apart from the fact that he had brothers and sisters) until he began to preach publicly. Probably his first work was alongside *John the Baptist in the Jordan valley (John 3. 22 ff.), Jesus himself having been baptized by John (Mark 1. 9). The gospels, however, place most of his career in Galilee and N. Palestine generally. Probably this career lasted only two or three years, before he was arrested and executed, having made a deliberate journey to Jerusalem for *Passover.

Jesus preached about the *kingdom of God, and specifically of its imminent approach. Jesus, however, speaks of it sometimes as future

(Matthew 6. 10), sometimes as already present (Matthew 12. 28, Luke 11. 20), and at other times as something which cannot be described except indirectly through *parables (Mark 4. 30). Jesus taught and acted (especially in healing) in a way which manifested the 'power' (*dunamis*) and 'authority' (*exousia*), not of himself but of God, whom he characterized as both king and father, addressing him as *Abba. This provoked the fundamental question of Mark 6. 2 which is the beginning of *Christology.

How Jesus thought of himself in relation to this coming kingdom is uncertain. Clearly he mediated through himself an effect of God which transfigured his own life and transformed the lives of others. From the well-attested fact that Jesus addressed God as Abba (Aramaic, 'father'), it could be inferred that he was Son of God; but Jesus did not use this expression as an exclusive title for himself. His most significant reference to himself seems to have been as 'the *son of man'.

Jesus selected an intimate band of twelve disciples (Mark 3. 14), but there are many sayings about the challenge of following him (e.g. Mark 8. 34) which seem to be addressed to his adherents generally. It is striking that there is no clear evidence that Jesus formed any kind of institution for his followers.

In his teaching, he often challenged the teaching of others, while remaining within the Jewish religion of the *Torah (e.g. in attending synagogue, Matthew 4. 23, 9. 35; Luke 4. 16 ff.; John 6. 59). Often where he appears to criticize the biblical commandments themselves (e.g. Matthew 5. 21–48) his own dictates are more rather than less exacting, or even on a different plane altogether. His summary of Torah (*kelal) was in effect a context-independent command (see ETHICS, CHRISTIAN).

The gospels record that Jesus was executed by *crucifixion by the Roman authorities in Judaea. Jesus clearly made his way deliberately to Jerusalem (the Gk. uses strong words of necessity concerning his determination to leave the relative security of Galilee and to go to Jerusalem), because it was only in Jerusalem that the issue could be resolved, whether his teaching was 'from God or men'. It is equally clear that the initial offence of Jesus had to do with his threat to the authority of the Temple in deciding the true interpretation of Torah (the same issue which was raised by Stephen, Acts 7. 11 f.). This (as an offence) goes back to Deuteronomy 17. 8–13, which states that an obstinate teacher (see REBELLIOUS ELDER), who insists on his own opinion against the majority, must be brought before 'the judge who shall be in those days' (i.e. the highest authority), and if he rejects the decision on his teaching, he must be executed—because two interpretations of Torah must necessarily destroy Israel. The so-called 'trial' of Jesus was initially an investigation to see whether he came into the category of an obstinate teacher who insisted on his own opinion. Whether it was necessary or simply convenient to hand Jesus over to the Romans for the punishment which Deuteronomy requires is uncertain; the charge then would have involved Jesus' threat to the Roman administration by his threat to the religious establishment which co-operated with the Romans.

There is good reason, therefore, to believe that Jesus anticipated his own death (the necessity of the journey to Jerusalem carries that implication, since Jesus knew that his teaching and actions came, not from himself, but from God, and that they were not subject to human authority). If the connection with Daniel 7 is correct, then he saw his death as the fulfilment of Israel's true destiny; and he saw it also as a *lutron* (ransom, in terms of a current dispute between Pharisees and Sadducees) for the sins of 'many' (Mark 10. 45). Such an interpretation is inherent above all in the *eucharistic words at the *Last Supper.

Jesus was executed and laid in a tomb on Friday; according to the gospels on Sunday morning his tomb was found to be empty. Beyond this point the three gospels Matthew, Luke, and John offer various and differing accounts of appearances of Jesus to his followers. These appearances are also mentioned by Paul (1 Corinthians 15. 5–8) as among the earliest traditions he knew, and (more than the empty tomb) lie at the basis of the Christian belief that Jesus had risen from the dead (see RESURRECTION OF CHRIST). See Index, Jesus.

In Islam Jesus is generally called 'Īsā ibn Maryam (Jesus, son of Mary) in the *Qur'ān. He is one of the *Prophets, a line which began with *Adam and ended with *Muḥammad. He is mentioned, together with Zakariyā, *John, and Elias, as one of the 'Righteous' (6. 85). Like Adam, he was created from dust (3. 59). The Qur'ān concentrates on the beginning and the end of 'Īsā's earthly life; his actual teachings are not reported. He is conceived through the power of Allah, the message being conveyed to the virgin Maryam by 'Our Spirit' (19. 17–22), later identified with the angel Jibrīl *Gabriel (cf. 3. 45–7). He speaks in the cradle, to vindicate his mother's reputation (19. 30).

His miracles are said to include making birds out of clay, healing the sick, blind, and lepers, and raising the dead, (3. 49, 5. 113). The strange story of his making a 'table prepared' appear from heaven is thought by some to be an echo of the miracle of the loaves and fishes, or of the Last Supper (5. 115–18; sūra 5 is named 'the

Table'). This is to be a 'solemn festival and a sign' (5. 117).

The crucifixion is apparently denied in the Qur'ān: 'They killed him not, nor crucified him, but so it was made to appear to them' (4. 157); but the Arabic can be taken to mean that the resurrection contradicted what they thought had happened.

'Īsā has several titles: 'Word' from Allāh, and a 'Spirit' from him, though neither term corresponds to the Christian concept; 'Servant', 'Prophet', 'Messiah', 'Messenger', and 'only a messenger' (4. 171, 5. 78). He is 'strengthened by the Spirit of holiness' (*rūḥ al-qudus*; 5. 113, 2. 253). His humanity is emphasized, and the Christians are severely rebuked for ascribing divine status to him. The Qur'ān, however, objects to ideas which are not orthodox Christian teaching. There is within Arabic a distinction between *ibn*, 'son', which can be used metaphorically or to denote a spiritual relationship, and *walad*, 'son' or 'offspring', in a more literal sense. It is this latter term which the Qur'ān employs in the verses just quoted, and the point is appreciated by some Muslim commentators.

Jesus People. A variety of groups which flourished in the 1960s, differing somewhat in social organization, doctrine, and ritual, but all committed to a literal, *fundamentalist interpretation of scripture. For these groups, sometimes referred to as 'Jesus Freaks' or 'Street Christians', worship centred on the person of *Jesus and emphasized the continuing, direct activity of the *Holy Spirit.

Jesus Prayer or **Prayer of the Heart.** The prayer 'Lord *Jesus Christ, Son of God, have mercy on me' (or 'on me, a sinner'). The continual repetition of this prayer is specially important in *hesychasm.

Jetavana (Skt., Jeta or Jetri + *vana*, 'wood'). A grove on the outskirts of Śrāvastī, the capital city of Kośala, often frequented by the *Buddha. In many of the important dialogues, the Buddha is described as residing in the Jetavana grove.

The Jetavana *dāgaba in Śri Lankā, 370 feet in diameter, is the largest dāgaba in existence. A splinter sect of the *Theravāda, the Jetavanīyas (formed 4th cent. CE, reabsorbed 12th cent.) take their name from this dāgaba.

Jew. A person descended from a Jewish mother or who has formally converted to Judaism. According to the *halakhah, Jewish descent is from the maternal line. Even an *apostate is counted as a full Jew. Gentiles who wish to identify with Judaism have to undergo full ritual conversion, including *circumcision for men, and *mikveh.

Jewel net of Indra (image of the interconnectedness of all things): see HUA-YEN.

Jewel Ornament of Liberation (Tibetan Buddhist text): see GAMPOPA.

Jewish Theological Seminary (JTS). The educational centre of *Conservative Judaism. The Jewish Theological Seminary was founded in New York in 1887. Today the Seminary trains *rabbis, cantors, teachers, and *synagogue administrators.

Jews' College. *Orthodox rabbinical seminary in London. Jews' College was founded in 1855 to train *rabbis and teachers for the English-speaking world.

Jhāna, dhyāna (Pāli, Skt., 'meditation', 'absorption'; Chin., *ch'an; Jap., *zen). In traditional Buddhism, the scheme of meditational practice which leads to *samādhi; the different stages within that scheme; any kind of mental concentration or effort.

The system of *meditation known as Buddhist Jhāna is composed of eight successive steps, called jhānas: the four lower jhānas or 'meditations on form' (*rūpajjhānā*) and the four higher jhānas or 'meditations on the formless' (*arūpajjhānā*).

Meditation proceeds with the selection of a suitable object (*kasiṇa) upon which to fix one's gaze. This object (parikamma-*nimitta, visual image) is then contemplated until one is capable of forming in the mind's eye a replica image as vivid as the sensation of the original object. The meditator continues to contemplate the idealized image until he finds that methods become a disturbance to him, and he eliminates them; by so doing he enters the second jhāna. He then enters the third jhāna by eliminating *pīti* (ecstatic joy). The fourth jhāna is attained when all forms of pain and pleasure, sorrow and joy are transcended and upekkhā and mindfulness (*sati) alone remain. He may now go on to develop the *brahma-vihāra meditations, or the *abhiññās, or make the transition to the higher jhānas of the formless realm. By now concentrating upon the infinite void or space left by the discarded image he is said to achieve the fifth jhāna. By shifting his concentration from the infinite space perceived to the act of infinite perception which does the perceiving, he enters the sixth jhāna. The seventh jhāna is marked by the removal of the act of perception itself, so that nothing at all remains. In the eighth and final jhāna the 'idea' of 'nothing' is removed and the meditator ceases conscious ideation altogether.

Jiba (plot of land where man was created, according to Shinto sect): see TENRIKYO.

Jibrīl (angel in Islam): see GABRIEL.

Jigoku. Jap. for *naraka, hell.

Jigme Lingpa ('Jigs-med gling-pa, Tibetan teacher): see KLONG-CHEN RAB-'BYAMS-PA.

Jihād (Arab., *jahada*, 'he made an effort'). More fully, *jihād fī sabīl *Allāh*, 'striving in the cause of God'. Jihād is usually translated as '*holy war', but this is misleading. Jihād is divided into two categories, the greater and the lesser: the greater jihād is the warfare in oneself against any evil or temptation. The lesser jihād is the defence of Islam, or of a Muslim country or community, against aggression. It may be a jihād of the pen or of the tongue. If it involves conflict, it is strictly regulated, and can only be defensive.

Jijñāsā (Skt., 'desire to know'). In Hindu philosophy, an investigation or enquiry regarding a qualified object of knowledge. See BRAHMA-JIJÑĀSĀ.

Jikaku Daishi (posthumous title): see ENNIN.

Jikishi ninshin (direct transmission of teaching in Zen): see FUKASETSU.

Jikkai. 1. Jap., 'the ten realms', i.e. the states of possible being: (i) *jigoku* of torment or hell; (ii) *gaki-dō, of hungry spirits; (iii) *chikusho*, of animals; (iv) *ashura*, that of *asuras; (v) *ningen*, of humans; (vi) *tenjō*, of heavenly beings; (vii) *shōmon*, of *śrāvakas; (viii) *engaku*, of *pratyekabuddhas; (ix) *bosatsu, of *bodhisattvas; (x) *butsu, of *buddhas.

2. Jap., 'ten precepts', the ten precepts undertaken by a Buddhist monk: see ŚĪLA.

Jīlānī, al- (Muslim theologian): see 'ABD AL-QADIR AL-JĪLĪ.

Jīlī: see 'ABD AL-KARĪM AL-JĪLĪ; 'ABD AL-QADIR AL-JĪLĪ/JĪLĀNĪ.

Jimmu. The first emperor of Japan, a direct descendant from *Amaterasu, and the ancestor of subsequent emperors down to the present.

Jina (Skt., 'spiritual victor'). In the Indian religious tradition, a title given to great teachers and ascetics, and in Jainism a synonym for the twenty-four *tīrthaṅkaras.

Jinacandra (Jain teacher): see DĀDĀ GURŪS.

Jinadatta Suri (Jain teacher): see DĀDĀ GURŪS.

Jinakuśala (Jain teacher): see DĀDĀ GURŪS.

Jinasena (9th cent. CE). *Digambara Jain writer. His major work was the *Mahāpurāṇa* (The Great *Purāṇa), an attempt at a universal history—Jinasena finished only the first part; it was completed by his pupils. The work gives an account of *Mahāvīra, but it serves also as a guide to kings. It also lays out the appropriate behaviours for laypeople, and as such it remains in use to the present day.

Jināza: see FUNERAL RITES (Islam).

Jineśvara (follower of Jain monk Vardhamana): see DĀDĀ GURŪS.

Jingikan (Jap., 'Department of *Shinto'). One of the two principal administrative branches of the centralized government, the so-called *ritsu-ryō state, of the pre-Nara (710–94) and Heian (794–1185) periods. The Dept. of Shinto had jurisdiction over all matters pertaining to the worship of the gods (*kami). It supervised the rites of enthronement (Daijōsai), the rites of national purification (Oharae), the festivals of the first fruits and harvest, as well as the upkeep of shrines and the discipline of shrine priests. The Dept. of Shinto was briefly revived with the *Meiji Restoration of 1868, only to be abolished in 1871.

Jinja (Shinto shrine): see KAMI.

Jinja Shinto (category of Shinto organization): see SECT SHINTO.

Jinn (Arab., *junna*, 'be mad, furious, possessed'). Fiery spirits in Islam (Qur'ān 55. 15), particularly associated with the desert. A person who dies in a state of great sin may be changed into a *jinnī* in the period of the *barzakh.

Jinsei wa gejutsu de aru (living life as art): see MIKI TOKUHARU.

Jippō (Jap., 'ten directions'). The ten directions which encompass all possible places, the four cardinal points, the four intermediate points, up and down. Hence jippō-butsu, the *buddhas of the ten directions, i.e. all buddhas throughout the universe.

Jiriki and **tariki.** Japanese expressions referring to opposing methods of attaining salvation, jiriki, or salvation through one's own efforts, and tariki, salvation depending upon another power. The common illustration of these concepts is the monkey and the cat. Infant monkeys cling to their mothers to be carried, but cats carry their young, lifting them by the back of the neck.

Jirinkan (Jap.). Meditation on Skt. letters. For an example, see A.

Jishū (Jap., 'the Time School'). A form of *Pure Land Buddhism founded by *Ippen in 1276. The main practice of Jishū is the constant repetition of the *nembutsu, as if, at each moment, one is on the point of death. Since Jishū originally had no temple, its adherents travelled about (like Ippen) encouraging the recitation of the nembutsu. For this reason, they are also known as Yugyō-ha, the school of wanderers.

Jisso (reality): see SEICHŌ NO IE.

Jīva (Skt., 'living'). In Hinduism, the living self which is engaged in the world and which identifies itself with mind and body as empirically real. The true self is *ātman, which is the One pervading all appearance. It is an issue in Hinduism whether jīvá and ātman are, in the end, identical or whether some distinction remains between them: see JIVĀTMAN.

In Jainism, jīva is one of two categories into which all existing things must fall, the living as opposed to *ajīva. The concept of jīva is central to an understanding of Jainism, because of the way in which it credits all human beings, animals, insects, vegetation, and even earth, stones, fire, water, and air with living souls (jīvas). The universe is seen as being vibrant with innumerable jīvas, each of which is real, independent, and eternal, and characterized by consciousness (*caitanya), bliss (*sukha*), and energy (*virya). The Jain path of purification offers a means of purifying the jīva through the pursuit of the *ratnatraya* (the *Three Jewels) of right faith, knowledge, and conduct; and with the help of strict ascetic discipline, the Jains believe that association with karma can be halted. This teaching accounts for the enormous respect for life in all its forms which characterizes Jainism and is expressed in the keystone of Jain faith, *ahiṁsā.

Jivanmukta: see JĪVANMUKTI.

Jīvanmukti (Skt., 'liberated in this life'). In Indian religions, the condition of having attained enlightenment (*kaivalya, *mokṣa, *mukti, *nirvāna, etc.). A jivanmukta (one who has attained the condition) is in a state of being in the world but not of it. He has reached the supreme goal and simply allows his life to run out like the fuel of a candle or the rotation of a potter's wheel after the potter has ceased to work.

Jīvanmukti-viveka. 14th-cent. Hindu work by *Vidyaranya, which describes, in five chapters, the path to liberation, based on the *Vedas.

Jivātman (Skt., the 'living-self'). The personal or individual soul as distinct from the *paramātman, the 'Supreme-self'. According to *Advaita Vedānta, the distinction is only an apparent one. However, other schools of Indian philosophy, such as the *Viśiṣṭādvaita-vedānta and the various devotional (*bhakti) movements, affirm the reality of this distinction.

Jizō (bodhisattva who helps children): see KṢITIGARBHA; KAMAKURA; ABORTION.

Jizya (Arab., *jazā*, 'reward, requite'). The poll tax levied on non-Muslims in Muslim countries, based on e.g. Qur'ān 9. 29. In return for jizya, the Muslim state has an obligation to protect those who pay it.

Jñāna (Skt., 'knowing').

Hinduism In the early period, jñāna was practical *knowledge or skill (e.g. of a warrior or farmer). But jñāna was rapidly extended to include all spiritual knowledge, and knowledge of the way to approach *Brahman or God. More technically, jñāna is the cognitive episode or event in which knowledge can occur.

Buddhism (Pāli, *ñāṇa*). According to Buddhists, perception and reason cannot be totally relied upon since they are conditioned and distorted by our subjective attitudes—likes (*ruci*), dislikes (*aruci*), desire (*chanda*), fear (*bhaya*), ill will (*dosa), and delusion (*moha). Consequently, true knowledge (*aññā*) can only come about as a result of eliminating unwholesome mental and psychological factors. Buddhism prescribes a programme for eliminating these factors: training in morality (*śīla), concentration (*samādhi), and understanding (*prajña). In terms of Buddhist doctrine, the true object of knowledge is to be found in the *Four Noble Truths and the law of causation (*paticca-samuppāda). On this basis, one can attain higher states of knowledge, but only if one's mind is purified of five impediments (pañcanīvaraṇa, see NĪVARAṆAS—covetousness, ill will, sloth and torpor, restlessness and worry, and doubt, *Majjhima Nikāya* 1. 181, 270, 276) and on attaining the fourth *Jhāna.

Jñānadeva: see JÑĀNEŚVAR.

Jñānakāṇḍa (Skt., 'knowledge section'). Those portions, whether individual sentences or longer passages, of Vedic revelation (*śruti) dealing with knowledge (*jñāna), in which significant and authoritative statements are made concerning the nature of *Brahman. The knowledge section of the *Vedas is contrasted with the 'action section' (*karmakāṇḍa).

Jñāna-mudra. The Hindu *mudra (hand symbol) encapsulating knowledge: the index finger and thumb are joined, with the fingers outstretched; the finger (*jīva) is united with the thumb (*ātman), in the truth which points (outstretched fingers) beyond itself to what is real.

Jñanapañcami (Jain festival): see FESTIVALS AND FASTS.

Jñāneśvar or **Jñānadeva** (1275–96). *Marāṭhī Hindu writer and *yogi.

Jñāneśvar was one of four children. The eldest brother, Nivṛattināth, became a yogi of the *Nāth sect (according to one tradition) and instructed Jñāneśvar, thus enabling him to be a yogi and attain knowledge. This tradition is mentioned in Jñāneśvar's composition on the *Bhagavad-gītā*, where he lists the previous gurus as Ādināth, Mīnanāth, Gorakshanāth, Gaininath, and Niv-ṛattīnath before himself.

In the year 1290, at the age of 15, Jñāneśvar composed his Marāthī commentary entitled *Bhāvārtha-dīpikā* (The Lamp of Plain Meaning) on the **Bhagavad-gītā*. It is the most revered work in Marāthī literature. Jñāneśvar is himself revered as a divine figure. Other important works attributed to him are *Amṛatānubhava*, *Yogavāsistha*, and *Advaitanirupana*. He gave up his life, following the yogic tradition, after burying himself alive in 1296. See also EKNĀTH.

Jñātradharmakatha-aṅga (Jain text): see AṄGA.

Jō (Jap., 'meditation'). Buddhist concentration and meditation; also (a different Jap. word), a vehicle, i.e. a means of carrying people to salvation or *nirvāna; *jōjō* is the highest teaching.

Joachim of Fiore (*c*.1132–1202). Christian mystic and prophetic visionary. As a young man he became a *Cistercian, but later left and eventually founded his own monastery at Fiore in Calabria. He saw history divided into three ages: the age of the Father, in the Old Testament; the age of the Son, the period of the Church; and the shortly-to-be-inaugurated age of the Spirit, in which new religious orders would convert the world and usher in the 'Spiritual Church'. His views were influential among the new orders of the 13th cent., especially the Spiritual *Franciscans. He wrote a harmony of the Old and New Testaments, a commentary on the Apocalypse, and *The Psalter with Ten Strings*.

Joan, Pope. Legendary female pope. The gist of the story is that about the year 1100 a woman in male disguise succeeded to the papacy. After reigning more than two years she gave birth to a child during a procession to the Lateran and died immediately afterwards. The tale is first attested in the 13th cent. and was widely believed in the Middle Ages.

Job, Book of. One of the books of *Writings (*Ketuvim*) in the Hebrew scriptures. It describes how the righteous Job was deprived by God of all his possessions including his children and was struck down with a vile disease (1–2). His three friends try to comfort him (3–26), but Job will not accept that he has sinned against the Lord (rightly, since he has been defined as innocent for the purpose of the book). Job laments his disastrous fate (29–31) and a fourth friend attempts consolation (32–7). Ultimately God speaks to Job (38–48) and all his fortune is restored.

In Islam Job is known as Ayyūb. Qur'ān 21. 83–4 and 38. 41–4 refer briefly to his calamities, his patience, and his restoration to prosperity.

Jōbutsu (Jap., 'becoming a buddha'). The realization in Zen of one's own buddha-nature (*bussho).

Jōdo (Jap.; Chin., *ching-t'u*). *Pure Land, Jap. equivalent of *Ching-T'u. See further PURE LAND SCHOOLS.

Jōdo Shinshū or **Shin-shu** (Jap., 'True *Pure Land School'). A school of Japanese Buddhism founded by *Shinran, and organized by Rennyo (1414–99). It is a lay movement, with no monks or monasteries, and it is based on simple but absolute devotion to *Amida, in which the *nembutsu (recitation of the name) is an act of gratitude, rather than one of supplicating trust. It split into two factions, Ōtani and Honganji, in the 17th cent. Both have their main temples in *Kyōto, and both remain powerful in Japan today.

Jōdo-shu: see PURE LAND SCHOOLS.

Joel, Book of. One of the books of *minor prophets of the Hebrew scriptures and Christian Old Testament.

Johanan ben Zakkai (1st cent. CE). Leading Jewish sage (*ḥakham) after the destruction of the second *Temple. As a teacher, Johanan is remembered for his precise examination of biblical texts and as the first sage known to have been engaged in *merkabah mysticism. During the siege of *Jerusalem, he managed to leave the city and was given permission by the Romans to join the sages of the *bet din at *Jabneh. Although he was not officially named *nasi, he raised the status of the Jabneh group. Thus despite the catastrophic loss of the Temple, the institutions of the Jewish faith continued to exist.

John, St. One of the twelve *Apostles and traditionally author of the fourth gospel, three epistles, and the book of *Revelation (attributions increasingly questioned). John was the son of Zebedee (Matthew 4. 21), one of *Jesus' inner circle of disciples (Matthew 17. 1), and one of the 'pillar' apostles (Galatians 2. 9). Traditionally, he settled at Ephesus, whence he was temporarily exiled to Patmos under Domitian, and died a natural death as an old man. Feast day in the E., 26 Sept. (also 8 May); in the W., 27 Dec.

The Acts of John belongs to the New Testament *Apocrypha. It is a 3rd-cent. work notable for the 'Hymn of Jesus' (set to music by Gustav Holst) and for colourful stories of John's later life in Ephesus.

John Climacus, St (*c*.579–*c*.649). Abbot of Sinai and Christian spiritual writer. The surname (Gk., *klimax*, 'ladder') comes from the work of his old age, the *Ladder of Divine Ascent*. The ladder has thirty 'steps' (chapters), leading to a God-centred life. The work has been very influential in E. Christian spirituality, e.g. among the *Hesychasts, and is prescribed for reading in Lent in *Orthodox monasteries.

John of Damascus, St (*c*.675–*c*.749). E. Christian theologian, known as Chrusorroas, 'gold-flowing'. After holding a high official position in the Muslim government in Damascus for ten or twenty years, he moved to the monastery of St Sabas near Jerusalem, and became a priest. He came to prominence there after 726 on account of his *Three Apologies against those who Attack the Divine Images* (see ICONOCLASM). His other most important work, the *Fount of Wisdom*, was an important source for subsequent writers, including *Aquinas. He was declared a *Doctor of the Church in 1890, with a feast day on 27 Mar.; 4 Dec. in the E.

John of God, St (1495–1550). *Holy fool and founder of the 'Brothers Hospitallers'. Born in Portugal and piously brought up, he became a soldier and abandoned religious practice. When he was about 40, he was converted and sought to atone for his former life. Unsuccessful in his bid for *martyrdom in Morocco, he returned to Spain and lived a life of sanctity marked by excesses of penitence and devotion. Under St John of Avila's influence, he diverted his energies to the care of the sick and poor. His order took shape after his death.

John of the Cross (1542–91). Poet, mystic, and joint founder of the Discalced *Carmelites. He entered the Carmelite Order in 1563 and studied at Salamanca (1564–8). Faced with what he regarded as laxity in the order, he considered becoming a *Carthusian. *Teresa of Avila persuaded him to stay and undertake her own kind of reform. He spent the rest of his life furthering the reform and suffering imprisonment and banishment from those opposed to his and Teresa's vision. Out of his suffering his great works of mystical theology were born. All take the form of commentaries on his own poems, amongst the greatest in Spanish.

The *Ascent of Mount Carmel* and the *Dark Night of the Soul* expound the *dark night, the *Spiritual Canticle* expounds the whole spiritual life through commentary on his long poem inspired by the *Song of Songs, and the *Living Flame of Love* is concerned with the *unitive way. He died on 14 Dec. (feast day), saying, 'Tonight I shall sing *mattins in heaven.' He was canonized in 1726 and declared a Doctor in 1926.

John Paul I (1912–78). *Pope from 26 Aug. to 28 Sept. 1978. He was made bishop of Vittorio Veneto in 1958, and patriarch of Venice in 1969. He was made *cardinal in 1973. He was elected pope on the third ballot and was acclaimed as 'God's candidate', and as one who would develop *Vatican II while conserving the tradition. He died of a heart attack while reading papers in bed. Subsequent theories (building in part on the absence of an autopsy) claimed that he was poisoned because of his determination to clarify the suspect dealings of the Vatican Bank. He wrote *Catechesis in Easy Stages* (1949) and *Illustrissimi* (1978), letters addressed to figures in the past. The hope that the papacy would continue to develop the vision of Vatican II and would be committed, not just in rhetoric but in reality, to a gospel of commitment to the poor, faded under his successor: see JOHN PAUL II.

John Paul II (b. 1920). Pope since 1978. Karol Wojtyla was a professor at Lublin University and archbishop of Cracow before becoming the first non-Italian pope since 1523. An energetic man of engaging personality, he has become a well-known figure throughout the world because of his wide travels. He survived an attempt to assassinate him in Rome 1981. Conservative on moral and doctrinal issues, he has been concerned for social questions and for the defence of human rights.

John the Baptist. A Jewish prophetic figure at the time of Jesus mentioned by *Josephus and frequently in the gospels. He preached on the banks of the Jordan demanding repentance and baptism in view of God's impending wrath (Matthew 3. 11). He denounced King Herod Antipas and was beheaded by him (Mark 6. 16–29). Jesus was among those baptized and it is possible that he belonged originally to John's circle (cf. John 3. 22–4). Feast days, 24 June (nativity; six months before Christmas according to Luke 1. 37) and 29 Aug. (death, or 'decollation').

In Islam, Yaḥyā is mentioned as a *prophet (6. 85, 19. 14 f.), and the prayer of his father, Zakariyya, for a child in his old age (21. 89) is held up as an example of prayer being answered.

John XXIII (1881–1963). *Pope from 1958. Because of his advanced age, he was expected to be only a stop-gap pope, but in fact he proved to be the most revolutionary pope of modern times. He announced the calling of the Second *Vatican Council in 1959, and presided over its first session in 1962–3. He established the Secretariat for Promoting Christian Unity in 1960. His encyclicals included **Mater et Magistra* and **Pacem in Terris* (addressed to all people of good will). His *Journey of a Soul* illuminates the underlying quest of his whole life.

Jojitsu (Buddhist sect): see NARA BUDDHISM.

Jokhang ('House of the Lord'). Tibet's holiest temple, sometimes called the Tsuglakhang ('the Academy') and generally referred to by W. commentators as the 'Cathedral of Lhasa'. It was built by the thirty-third king of Tibet, Songsten Gampo (*c.*609–50), to house the statue of the Buddha Akṣobhya. The statue of Akṣobhya was broken in two during the present Chinese occupation, and the upper half was transported to Beijing. In 1988 the lower portion was discovered in a Lhasa rubbish tip, and in 1989 the two halves were reunited and reconsecrated. The Jokhang's contents were more systematically destroyed in 1966, and throughout the cultural revolution it was used as the Red Guard headquarters. It was not until 1984 that it began to function as a temple and a monastery again. In 1990 it had over a hundred monks, but in common with other 'newly functioning' monasteries in Tibet these include a number of police, and its ruling committee consists of non-ordained political appointees.

Jonah, Book of. One of the twelve books of the *Minor Prophets of the Hebrew scriptures and Christian Old Testament. Although Jonah is classified as a *prophetic book, it is mainly concerned with the narrative story of Jonah.

In Jewish liturgy, the book is read in the afternoon service for Yom Kippur. Jonah's stay in the fish's belly was taken in Christian tradition as a *type of Jesus' death and resurrection (Matthew 12. 40). In Islamic tradition the prophet is known as Yunus.

Jonang-pa. A school of Tibetan Buddhism prominent from the 13th cent. but closed down by the Great Fifth *Dalai Lama, allegedly for heresy, in the 17th-cent. reformation. The founding of the Jonang is attributed to the 12th-cent. Yumo Mikyo Dorje, and the school took its name from the Jomonang monastery founded by Thukje Tsondru, whose student Sherab Gyaltsen (1292–1361) was the first to systematize its teachings. Their offending beliefs go back to Yumo Mikyo Dorje, who evolved the *zhen dong heresy during meditation on the Kālacakra and presented it supported by *sūtras 'indicating an essence' (*snying.po*; i.e. the *Tathāgatagarbha Sūtra*), but considered by other schools as 'requiring interpretation' (*neyārtha*) and not to be taken at face value (*nītārtha*). It is ironic that, given the charge of heresy as a reason for their repression, the offending zhen dong doctrine was reactivated to underpin the 19th-cent. *Rimé movement, and has since become prevalent in all schools except the Geluk.

Jones, Eli Stanley (1884–1973). Christian missionary. Born in Maryland, USA, he was ordained Methodist minister and sent to work at the Lal Bagh English-speaking church in Lucknow. He adopted a travelling ministry, based on Sitapur, where he wrote the widely selling *Christ of the Indian Road* (1925). His commitment to Christianity ceasing to be an imported 'European' religion, and becoming Indian, issued especially in the Sal Tat ashram (*āśrama). This was originally an annual event, but it and other ashrams became permanent. In 1964, he was awarded the Gandhi Peace Prize.

Jones, Sir William (1746–94). British jurist and orientalist, who began his broad linguistic studies at Oxford, where, in addition to European languages, he learnt Arabic, Persian, Chinese, and Hebrew. In 1774 he was called to the Bar, and nine years later was appointed judge at the Calcutta Supreme Court. He was Founder President of the Bengal Asiatic Society, which he headed until his death. Sir William Jones was one of the earliest European scholars to learn Skt., and his work was of major importance in enabling non-Indian academics to become aware of and appreciate the richness of the ancient Hindu contributions to Indo-European literature and philology.

Jones Church (Christian sect): see PEOPLES' TEMPLE.

Jon Frum (John Broom?). A *cargo cult in Vanuatu (formerly New Hebrides) which arose on Tanna Island in the late 1930s and has spread more widely and appeared intermittently ever since. A mysterious figure, Jon Frum (variously understood as an ancestor, the local mountain god, Karaperamun, or the 'King of America', after contact with affluent American troops in Second World War), was believed to be coming with a cataclysm that would sweep away the whites, unite Tanna and other islands, and introduce a world of plenty without need for farming or keeping pigs.

Jordanites or **White Robed Army.** A religious group located along the coast of Guyana. It traces its beginnings to Joseph MacLaren, an *Anglican Grenadian, who from 1895 preached 'pure *Protestantism' from the Bible in Guyana. This led to the establishment of the West Evangelist Millennial Pilgrim Church, but the main founder was E. N. Jordan (d. 1928), who was 'called' to join in 1917 through visions. Their beliefs combine Hindu (reincarnation), Jewish, Christian, African and occult elements.

Jōrei (technique of faith-healing): see SEKAI KYŪSEIKYŌ.

Jōriki (Jap., 'power of mind'). The power that arises from *zazen, which enables instantaneous reactions to be perfectly composed and correct. Since it also gives access to *iddhis, it is regarded with circumspection by most Zen teachers.

Joruri-ji (temple-complex): see NARA BUDDHISM.

Joseph. The favourite son of the *patriarch *Jacob, borne by his wife Rachel. His story is told in Genesis 37–47.

Joseph, St. The husband of the Virgin *Mary. In Matthew 1–2 and Luke 1–2 Mary is said to have been 'betrothed' to him when Jesus was born. According to Matthew 13. 55 he was a carpenter. From 1479, his feast day in the W. was on 19 Mar. Between 1914 and 1955 his feast day was on the third Wednesday after Easter. In 1955 it was transferred (as St Joseph the Worker) to 1 May, to align it with the secular holiday. It ceased to be obligatory in 1969. In the E. it is the first Sunday after Christmas.

Joseph of Arimathea, St. The 'councillor' (Luke 23. 50) who buried the body of *Jesus after the crucifixion. (Arimathea was perhaps Ramlah.) John 19. 38 adds that he was a secret disciple of Jesus. According to a 12th-cent. source, he came to England with the Holy *Grail, building a church (the first in England) at *Glastonbury. The Holy Thorn is said to have sprung from his staff. Feast day in E., 31 July; in W., 17 Mar.

Joseph of Volokalamsk, St: see POSSESSORS.

Josephus (1st cent. CE). Jewish historian. He recorded the events of the Jewish rebellion in *The Jewish War* in which he declared he was writing without bias. His other great work was the *Jewish Antiquities* in which he tried to explain Jewish history and customs to the gentiles. He also attempted to explain his own conduct in *The Life*, and he composed a defence against *anti-Semitism in *Against Apion*. Josephus' histories are the only extensive surviving source, and, without them, little would be known of the history of the second *Temple.

Joshua. Son of Nun, Hebrew/Israelite leader at the time of the conquest of *Canaan. The fact that his name is that of (the Gk.) *Jesus made Joshua a type of *Christ in early Christian exegesis (e.g. Hebrews 4. 8 f.). In Islam, *al-Tabarī records traditions about Yushaʿ/Joshua.

Joshua, Book of. The book in the Hebrew scriptures and Christian Old Testament which describes the conquest and settlement of the land of *Canaan.

Jōshū Jūshin (Ch'an Zen Master): see CHAO-CHOU T'SUNG-SHEN.

Josiah (640–609 BCE). King of *Judah. The reign of King Josiah was marked by religious renewal. According to the *Aggadah, Josiah was an example of a truly repentant person (*OR* 24) and he was killed by being pierced by 300 arrows (*B.Taʿan.* 22b).

Josippon. 10th-cent. CE Hebrew history of the second *Temple period. Written in Italy, the book starts by listing the nations and ends with the siege of Masada. It was much quoted in medieval Bible and *Talmud commentaries.

Joss. An idol; the word is a pidgin corruption of the Portuguese *deos*, taken back into European languages as a supposed Chinese word. Although it appears in various combinations (e.g. joss-house, a temple), it is most familiar now in 'joss-stick', a stick of incense used in temple ceremonies—or simply for its sweet smell.

Jōyō Daishi. Posthumous name of *Dōgen.

Jōzabu. Jap. for *Theravāda.

JPIC (Justice, Peace, and the Integrity of Creation): see COSMOLOGY.

JTS: see JEWISH THEOLOGICAL SEMINARY.

Ju (Jap., 'praise'). Eulogies of Zen masters often found attached to *kōan collections, e.g. *Pi-yen-lu*, *Wu-men-kuan*. The emotions of gratitude and reverence make these some of the finest examples of Buddhist poetry.

Ju. Jap. for *mantra.

Jubilee (Heb., *yovel*). Biblical law requiring the release of slaves and the restoration of family property every fifty years. The agricultural laws of the sabbatical year (i.e. the seventh year of seven) applied in the Jubilee year.

Jubilees, Book of. *Pseudepigraphic Jewish book. *The Book of Jubilees* dates from the second *Temple period and is supposedly the revelation of an *angel to *Moses. It consists of a recitation of the events of Genesis 1–Exodus 12, as dated according to *jubilee years. The *Falashas have based their *calendar upon its calculations.

Ju-chia. Chinese name for what is known in W. languages as *Confucianism. 'Confucianism' is also known as *ju-chiao* (*chiao* meaning those who belong to the same organization or social structure, e.g., a family, and who share common goals or interests; it is thus often translated as 'religion'). Since *chiao* involves educating or instructing a child, it became associated with those who belong to the same tradition. The later name Kung-chiao (tradition of *Confucius) is less common.

Ju-chiao (way of the followers of Confucius): see CHINESE RELIGION; CONFUCIANISM.

Judah. Fourth son of the Jewish *patriarch *Jacob and his wife Leah. Judah was the ancestor of the most prominent southern *tribe, and the name was used for the Southern Israelite kingdom which remained loyal to the *Davidic kingship.

Judah ben Samuel he-Ḥasid (*c.*1150–1217). Main teacher of the Jewish *Ḥasidei Ashkenaz movement. In *c.*1195, he moved to Regensburg, where he established an academy. Many legends were circulated about his life, but little for definite is known. His major works were *Sefer ha-Kavod* (Book of Divine Glory) of which only fragments survive, and *Sefer Ḥasidim*, to which he was only a contributor.

Judah Halevi (*c.*1075–1141). Jewish philosopher and poet. Judah spent much of his life travelling round the various Jewish communities of Spain. He was a close friend of Abraham *ibn Ezra who quoted his works of grammar and philosophy. Towards the end of his life, he travelled to *Erez Israel, but probably died on the way there in Egypt. According to legend, he was trampled to death in one of the gateways of Jerusalem.

About 800 of his poems have survived, including love poems, laments, lyric poetry, and songs of *Zion. His philosophy is contained in his *Kitab al-Hujja wa-al-Dalil fi Nasr al-Din al-Dhalil* (The Book of Argument and Proof in Defence of the Despised Faith), generally known as *Sefer ha-Kuzari* (The Book of the Kuzari, 1506). For both Abraham Isaac *Kook and Franz *Rosenzweig it was seen as a most faithful picture of the unique attributes of Judaism.

Judah ha-Nasi (late 2nd cent. CE). Jewish leader and legal expert. Judah ha-Nasi, a direct descendant of *Hillel, devoted his life as *nasi to building up the unity of the Jewish people in *Erez Israel and spreading the knowledge of *Torah. His name is particularly associated with the redaction of the *Mishnah.

Judah Loew ben Bezalel of Prague (**Der Hohe Rabbi Loew,** known as **Maharal mi-Prag,** *c.*1529–1609). Jewish leader and legal expert. Judah Loew served as *Chief Rabbi in Posen and Prague. He was the outstanding leader of his day, renowned for his piety, who produced highly influential works on ethics, philosophy, and homiletics. He was an early advocate of the view that 'the state' is an unnatural compromise, which will wither away when the true conditions of human freedom are realized. He regarded Israel's vocation to be the proleptic representation of the harmony which will, eventually, be the world's final condition. There has been a revival of interest in his work in the 20th cent., but the well-known legend that he was creator of the Prague *golem is unfounded.

Judah the Maccabee (2nd cent. BCE). Jewish warrior. Judah Maccabee was the third son of Mattathias, the *Hasmonean, who led the revolt against the rule of Antiochus Epiphanes in *Erez Israel. The story of his campaigns is told in the *Books of *Maccabees*.

Judaism. The name 'Judaism' emerged at around the opening of the Christian era (*2 Maccabees* 2. 21, 8. 1, 14. 38; Galatians 1. 13). Like other aggregating names of major religions, it is misleading if it implies that there is uniformity of belief and practice among all Jews. Yet it is appropriate if it draws attention to a shared genealogy (identified through having a Jewish mother, and going back to 'our fathers *Abraham, *Isaac and *Jacob'; see PATRIARCHS) and to a sense of being a people chosen to receive God's guidance in *Torah—though the emphasis on being a *chosen people has itself been questioned during the 20th cent. Today a distinction is frequently drawn between 'secular' or 'cultural' Judaism (denoting those who accept the history and values of Judaism, but who do not observe the details of Torah) and 'religious' Judaism, which implies acceptance of Torah. Even then, there are major differences in the ways in which Torah is brought to bear on life, among the major divisions of *Orthodox, *Reform, *Conservative, *Progressive, *Reconstructionist, and Liberal Judaism.

The origin of the Jewish people and of Judaism cannot be traced historically with any certainty. The major sources of information are contained in those books which came to be believed as having come from the initiative and inspiration of God, and which became *scripture, i.e. Torah, Nebi'im (*Prophets), and Kethubim (*Writings), hence the abbreviated name. *Tanach. From these books, it seems clear that a kinship group, the bene Jacob (descendants of Jacob) gradually ceased to be nomadic and settled in areas of Canaan. Different parts of the kinship group followed different histories (a dramatic part of which was an enslavement in Egypt and an escape now commemorated in *Passover; another was a covenant with a god Yhwh at Sinai). As the tribes began to settle, so they began more formally to unite in the defence, and later conquest, of territory, making a covenant, not only with each other, but also under the demand and protection of Yhwh (how this name was originally pronounced is unknown; conventionally it is transliterated as *Yahweh, but Orthodox Jews would not attempt to pronounce it at all: see HA-SHEM). Thus Israel is a proleptic community, established by God in the midst of time, to represent that harmony which was intended by God in creation, and which will in the end be the whole human case, 'when the knowledge of God shall cover the earth as the waters cover the sea' (Habakkuk 2. 14). Under David, *Jerusalem was captured, and there the Lord's anointed (*ha-Māsh-iach* = the Messiah) mediated between God and people; there too the *Temple was built where worship and *sacrifices surrounded the *Holy of Holies, the inner sanctuary where only the *high priest entered on the *Day of Atonement (Yom Kippur). Yet ritual action and kingly control were never self-sufficient: they were monitored by prophets who spoke directly from God, *koh amar Adonai*, 'Thus says the Lord . . . '. In this way the triple cord of Israel's religion (prophet, priest, and king) was woven together.

At the time when Jesus was alive, Judaism was a successful missionary religion, winning many converts to its ethical and obedient monotheism. During this period there were many conflicting interpretations of what it must mean in practice and in detail for Jews to fulfil the commands of the covenant. (e.g. *Sadducees, *Pharisees, *Dead Sea Scrolls). Nevertheless, there was a common sense that the final control and outcome of history is in the hand of God, and that God would send a messiah to restore the independent kingdom of the Jews, or of heaven; and this led to increasing restlessness under Roman occupation, culminating in two revolts against Rome, in 66–70/2 and 132–5 CE, which left the Jews a people no longer in possession of their holy land and places.

The reconstruction and continuity of Judaism was achieved by the *rabbis, beginning at *Jabneh. They sought and achieved a practice of Judaism which no longer possessed a Temple. The family and the synagogue became the centres of Jewish life. The period of Rabbinic Judaism saw a gathering together of the many interpretations of the original written Torah, which thus came to form a 'second' Torah, *Torah she be'al peh* (oral Torah): this produced *halakhah, that by which Jews can walk in knowledge that this is the received application of Torah to life. This voluminous interpretation was gathered first in *Mishnah, then in *Talmuds; and eventually it was organized in Codes (*codifications of Law), notably the Code of *Maimonides and Joseph *Caro's *Shulḥān Arukh*. At the same time, Judaism was graphically expressed and sustained through its stories, *Aggadah, and its biblical exegesis, *midrash. But the fact remained that Jews were now dispersed throughout the world (*diaspora): the two major communities (between whom many differences, especially of custom, persist) were the *Sephardim (from Spain after the expulsion in 1492, and in the Mediterranean) and the *Ashkenazim (originally in Europe, but after the many *pogroms, culminating in the *Holocaust, now scattered again, but numerous in the USA). Both communities and traditions are present in Israel.

Two other major developments were those of *Kabbalah and *Ḥasidism. At the same time, Jewish philosophers made important connections between the inherited faith and the quest for wisdom and truth (see Index, Philosophers: Jewish).

Throughout this whole period of *galut (exile) from the Jewish homeland, the memory of *Zion and the prayer for restoration and return (especially in the *liturgy) has been constant. The pogroms of 1881–2 forced many Jews to return to Palestine from where the *Zionist movement rapidly spread into Europe. Zionism received a major boost during the First World War, particularly through the *Balfour Declaration; and it became inevitable during and after the 'war against the Jews' waged by the Nazis and their followers from 1933 onward. *Anti-Semitism remains a real and vicious illustration of the depravity of the human herd; but marrying out of Judaism threatens a serious dissipation of its numbers; and assimilation jeopardizes the identity of Jews in a pluralist and pluralizing world. But the tenacity of Jewish faith, which has endured millennia of hatred and murder, remains undiminished.

Judaizers. Non-Jews and especially Christian groups who take up Jewish religious practices. Examples include the *Quartodecimans, the *Ethiopian Church, various descendants of English Puritanism including the Seventh-Day *Adventists, and a number of sects in Russia from the 15th cent. on. The term is also used of a group of Christian Jews in the earliest church of Jerusalem who insisted that gentiles embracing the gospel should also become Jewish *proselytes. They were defeated at the *apostolic council.

Judas Iscariot. The disciple who betrayed Jesus to the Jewish authorities (Mark 14. 10 f., 43 ff.; John 18. 2 ff., etc.).

Juddin (non-Zoroastrian): see PURITY.

Jude, St. One of the twelve *apostles ('Judas not Iscariot', according to John 14. 22). He is a popular saint in the Roman Catholic Church and is invoked in circumstances of special difficulty. Feast day in the E., 19 June; in the W., with St *Simon, 28 Oct.

The Letter of Jude is one of the *Catholic epistles of the New Testament.

Judenrein (free of Jews): see HOLOCAUST.

Judgement (of the Dead). Although religions differ in the extent to which they allow that humans are free in their choices and actions, they insist that humans are responsible and accountable for their thoughts and actions; and that in different ways their thoughts and actions now will affect their future outcome. In religions which believe in rebirth and *karma (Indian religions), a kind of judgement is always operating in and through this life, and the next form of rebirth may be in a *heaven or *hell, and in that sense there is not only judgement through life but also of the dead. *Yama is thus associated with that judgement.

In W. religions, the status and descriptions of the judgement of the dead have become increasingly precise. Initially (in biblical Judaism), the idea scarcely exists, since there was no belief in a personal and substantial life after death. The emphasis in later Judaism has been on the final eschatological judgement exercised by God on the world, especially in the return of the *messiah. Early Christianity absorbed the Jewish perspective, but made the theme of judgement far more prominent as a consequence of the belief that the messiah (i.e. Christ) had arrived in the person of *Jesus. Jesus becomes the agent of God's judgement, especially in his second coming, *Parousia (e.g. Acts 10. 42, 17. 31; 2 Corinthians 5. 10). The issue of this judgement turns partly on belief and recognition of Jesus as Christ and as the Son of the Father (e.g. John 5. 22 ff.), but also on actions which exemplify the nature of *agape (active and disinterested love). This is particularly apparent in the *parable of the sheep and the goats in Matthew 25. 31–46.

In Islam, the precision of judgement in relation to the works which people have done is even more exact. The events of the Day of Resurrection and the Day of Judgement are described in literal detail, in both Qur'ān and *ḥadīth: see YAUM AL-QIYĀMA and YAUM AL-DĪN.

Judges, Book of. The second book of the Former Prophets in the Hebrew Bible and of the historical books in the Christian Old Testament. It is named for the series of heroes ('judges') who ruled Israel between the death of Joshua and the beginning of the monarchy and whose exploits are described in turn in the book.

Judith, Book of. *Apocryphal Jewish book dating from the second *Temple period. The book was probably written to encourage the people during the *Hasmonean campaigns.

Juggernaut (name of Hindu god): see JAGANNĀTHA.

Jūgyū (-no)-zu. The Ten Oxherding Pictures, which portray the stages of Zen progress. There are several different cycles, all of great popularity.

Jujukai or **jujukinkai** (Jap.). The ten main precepts of Mahāyāna Buddhism. There are two sets, exoteric and esoteric. Exoteric: they forbid (i) taking life; (ii) stealing; (iii) unchasteness; (iv) lying; (v) trade in alcohol; (vi) gossip; (vii) praising self and deprecating others; (viii) reluctance in giving help to others; (ix) aggression; (x) slandering the *Three Jewels. Esoteric: one vows (i) not to abandon *dharma; (ii) not to abandon seeking enlightenment, (iii) not to covet; (iv) not to lack compassion; (v) not to slander any Buddhist teachings; (vi) not to be attached to anything; (vii) not to entertain false views; (viii) to encourage all to seek enlightenment; (ix) to instruct adherents of *Hīnayāna; (x) to practise responsive charity to *bodhisattvas.

Jujutsu: see MARTIAL ARTS.

Jukai. Receiving and granting the precepts (*kai), the formal initiation into the Zen Buddhist way.

Ju-lai. Chin. for *tathāgata.

Julian (332–63). Roman emperor from 361, known in Christian tradition as 'the Apostate'. His religious policy was to oppose Christianity and promote paganism. He also wrote *Against the Christians* (now lost). The story that he died with the words 'Vicisti, Galilaee' (Thou hast conquered, Galilean!') is a late invention.

Julian of Norwich (*c.*1342–after 1413). English mystic. Little is known of her life, except that she probably lived as an anchoress close to St Julian's church in Norwich. On 8 or 13 May

1373, while she was suffering from a severe heart attack, she had a series of fifteen visions relating to the Passion of Christ, followed the next day by a final vision. This she recorded in the shorter text of her *Showings*. More than fifteen years later she had a further revelation, after which she recorded a longer version in which she develops more deeply their significance. From her come the familiar words of consequent trust, 'All shall be well, and all shall be well, and all manner of thing shall be well'. She also laid great stress on the motherly nature and love of God: 'God is really our Mother as he is Father' (cf. FEMINIST THEOLOGY).

Jum'a (Arab., *jama'a*, 'collect, unite'). The Muslim assembly for the midday prayer (*ṣalāt) on *yaum al-juma'*, (day of assembly), Friday (*Qur'ān 62. 9). It is obligatory on free, adult males.

Junaid (Junayd): see AL-JUNAID (JUNAYD).

Jung, Carl Gustav (1875–1961). Psychiatrist and analytical psychologist, whose views have been thought by some to be more sympathetic to religion than those of *Freud. After an exchange of letters, Jung first met Sigmund Freud in 1907; they collaborated closely until 1913. By 1912, however, Jung could no longer conceal his differences from Freud. After his break with Freud, Jung suffered a psychotic breakdown during which he believed that he confronted his own unconscious. The first fruit of this exploration was his formulation of a general theory of psychological types. Jung's typology has been the subject of debate and application, for example in the Myers Brigg's type indicator (MBTI) which has been widely used in church and other circles in order to enable a dispassionate awareness of one's preferences to be developed.

Jung felt humans to be naturally religious, the religious function being as powerful as the instinct for sex or aggression. He was not a supporter of established religions but he was interested in religious philosophies. Jung could be said to have spent his whole life trying to relate human nature and beings to God. Jung distinguished between God and God-image. From his view that a collective personality is carried in the racial or collective subconscious, he claimed to have located the source which gives rise, not only to artefacts, but to dreams, myths, and religions.

Jung was not so much concerned with the ontological truth of religious assertions as with the role of religious symbols in enabling a healthy life.

Justification. In Christian theology, God's act in redeeming men and women from a state of sin, and discounting its deserved effect. How this act is conceived is a matter of fundamental difference between traditional *Catholic and *Protestant theology.

Catholic and Protestant theologies have now approached each other *ecumenically. Protestant views, however insistent on God's unconditional acceptance of sinners, do not necessarily tend to a disregard of good works (*antinomianism) and of holiness. Catholic views, although based on God's justice and the rewards and punishment which must accompany it, do not deny that merit itself may be a gift of God.

Justin Martyr, St (*c*.100–*c*.165). Early Christian apologist (see APOLOGETICS). A native of Samaria, he became a Christian after a long search for truth in pagan philosophies. According to an authentic record of proceedings, he and some of his disciples were denounced as Christians and, on refusing to sacrifice, they were beheaded. Justin's *First Apology* (*c*.155) argues that traces of the truth are to be found in pagan thinkers, since all share in the 'generative word' (*logos spermatikos*), but Christianity alone is rationally credible, because the *logos became incarnate to redeem as well as to instruct. *His Dialogue with Trypho* (R. Tarphon) *the Jew* is considered one of the more fair-minded of ancient Christian rebuttals of Judaism.

Just war. The belief that war is in some circumstances just, and that it must be conducted in ways limited by what is right. The two aspects of the Just War theory are called *ius ad bellum* and *ius in bello*. The classic form of the Christian theory, which had been consolidated by the time of the *Reformation, stated that *ius ad bellum* requires that there is (i) a just cause (of which three were recognized, to regain something wrongfully taken, to punish evil, and in defence against planned or actual aggression); (ii) a right authority initiating the war; (iii) a right intention on the part of those engaged; (iv) a proportional use of force, relevant to the issue and not doing more harm than good; and that the war should be undertaken (v) as a last resort, (vi) with the purpose of peace, and (vii) with a reasonable hope of success. *Ius in bello* limits warfare by the requirements of proportionality of means and discrimination of objects—often translated into non-combatant immunity.

In other religions, war can be regarded as 'just' (or at least as justifiable), but the criteria vary. In Islam and among Sikhs, the criteria are formal: see JIHĀD; DHARAM YUDH. In Indian-based religions, there is an overriding consideration of *ahiṁsā (non-violence). Nevertheless, in the long cycles of rebirth, there will always be those whose obligation (*dharma) it is to undertake warfare in certain circumstances (especially those of defence). This is the classic argument of *Kṛṣṇa to Arjuna in the *Bhagavad-gītā* (it must clearly be the dharma of a *kṣatriya to act as a warrior); but it is also found in Buddhism and among Jains. There is no religion in which the propriety of war in some circumstances is not admitted.

Jyeṣṭhā (Skt., 'elder sister'). Hindu goddess of misfortune. She is known also as Śītalā, the Goddess of smallpox.

Jyotir-liṅga(m). The limitless *liṅga(m) of light, the form assumed by *Śiva which compelled *Brahma and *Viṣṇu to acknowledge his supremacy.

Jyotiṣa. Astronomy in Hinduism, one of the six *Vedāṅgas (supplements to the *Vedas). It is of particular importance in determining the most propitious time and day for sacrifices and for such enterprises as war or marriage.

K

K (Sikh requirement): see FIVE KS.

Ka (Skt.). Interrogative pronoun, 'who?', used as a summary of the inadequacy of language to describe God.

Ka'ba(h) (Arab., 'cube'). The building, deeply revered by Muslims, in the centre of the great *mosque at *Mecca, in the eastern corner of which, about 5 feet from the ground, is embedded the *Black Stone. The Ka'ba, about 35 feet by 40 feet and 50 feet high, is called 'the house of *Allāh', and is the focus of the daily *ṣalāt (ritual worship) of Muslims throughout the world, (see QIBLA; ṢALĀT), and of the annual *ḥajj (pilgrimage).

Kabbalah or **Qabbalah.** Teachings of Jewish mystics. The term encompasses all the esoteric teachings of Judaism which evolved from the time of the second *Temple. More particularly, it refers to those forms which evolved in the Middle Ages. Kabbalah draws on the awareness of the transcendence of God, and yet of his immanence (e.g., through *Sefirot). God can most closely be perceived through *contemplation and illumination. God both conceals and reveals himself. Through speculation and revelation, the hidden life of God and his relationship with his creation can be more nearly understood. Because mystical knowledge can so easily be misinterpreted its spread should be limited to those of a certain age and level of learning.

Although the influence of kabbalah was limited in the area of halakhah, the kabbalists created fresh *aggadic material and completely reinterpreted much early *midrashic aggadot. The classic anthology of kabbalistic aggadah is Reuben Hoeshke's *Yalkut Re'uveni* (1660). Kabbalistic teaching and motifs entered the various *prayer books and thus spread to every *diaspora community. Popular customs were also affected by kabbalah, and kabbalistic ideas were absorbed as folk beliefs. These customs and beliefs were described by Jacob Zemah in *Shulḥan Arukh ha-Ari* (1661). Popular ethics were also influenced by kabbalism, as is evidenced by such works as Elijah de Vidas' *Reshit Hokhmah* (1579). From the 15th cent., attempts were made to harmonize kabbalistic ideas with Christian doctrines, and, although this tendency was derided by the Jewish kabbalists, it did serve to spread kabbalah beyond the Jewish community. K. von Rosenroth's version of kabbalah texts (*Kabbala Denudata*, 1677–84) led the way to a popular appropriation of kabbalah outside Judaism, at least in *Theosophy.

Kabhod (Kavod) (Holiness): see KEDUSHAH.

Kabīr (d. 1518). An Indian saint-poet. His birth and origins are uncertain. He may have been the son of a high-*caste *brahman girl who was brought up by a low-caste Muslim weaver (though this story may have been told to show his derivation from diversity). He is said to have been a disciple of the Vaiṣṇava sage, *Rāmānanda. Certainly the differences between Hinduism and Islam meant nothing to him: *Allāh and *Rāma are but different names for the same Godhead. He thus promulgated a religion of love in which all castes and classes would be seen to be wrong, and creeds would be unified. It was a religion of *bhakti (personal devotion to a personal God), in which the influence of *Sufism is apparent.

Kabīr was a sant (see SANT TRADITION), claiming to derive spiritual awareness from direct experience of the *śabad spoken by the Satgurū in the depth of the *soul. This alone transcends *death.

Sources for Kabīr's life include the Kabīrpanthī literature and Bhakta-mālā of Nābhājī.

Kachh (shorts): see FIVE KS.

Kada (Hagura) no Azumaro (Jap., 1669–1739). A *Kokugaku scholar and poet. At the age of 29 he taught poetry (*waka*, see HAIKU) at the court bureau of Prince Myōhōin, the son of the emperor Reigen. His writings were mainly the exegesis of the Japanese classics and of the works related to ancient rituals and laws. Among his many disciples, *Kamo no Mabuchi distinguished himself. Though the *Petition to Establish a School* may have been written by one of his disciples, there is no reason to doubt that he desired to establish an accredited institution for the exclusive study of Kokugaku.

Kadam (*bka'.gdams*, 'advice'). A school of Tibetan Buddhism which gave rise to the *Geluk school under *Tsong Khapa in the 15th cent. CE. The Kadam school was founded by Dromdon ('brom.ston), a pupil of *Atiśa, with the establishment of the Radreng monastery in 1056, in answer to a need felt by Atiśa and Dromdon for monastic reform and discipline. At this time the *saṅgha was not well ordered, and the interpretation of both 'new' *tantras flowing in from India, and of 'old' tantras already in Tibet, was not always well disciplined. The value of tantric practice was not denied by the Kadampas, but its students were given greater guidance as to the symbolic nature of the tantras and most importantly were taught to see them as founded upon the *sūtra tradition. The Kadam school became renowned not only for its discipline (which involved four major abstentions—from marriage, intoxication, money, and travel) but also for the magical power of its ritual.

Kaddish (Aram., 'holy'). *Aramaic doxology recited at the end of the individual sections of Jewish services. There are four different types of kaddish (or five, if an expanded form recited by some after a burial, is included).

The prayer is said standing, facing *Jerusalem. It is of ancient origin, being mentioned in the *Talmud as the concluding prayer at public *aggadic discourse. According to *Orthodox, kaddish can only be recited by men, but *Conservative and *Reform allow women also. The point can be critical, since it is necessary (*Soferim* 10. 7) for ten to be present if kaddish is to be recited.

Kado (flower arranging): see IKEBANA.

Kāfir (Arab., *kafara*, 'conceal, be ungrateful'). One who does not believe in *Allāh, or in the content of *Qur'ān, or in the prophetic status of *Muḥammad. *Kufr*, unbelief, is thus fundamental opposition to God and Islam, and will be punished in *hell for ever.

Kagan, Israel Meir ha-Kohen: see ḤAFETS ḤAYYIM.

Kagawa Toyohiko (1888–1960). Japanese Christian evangelist and pioneer social worker. Kagawa was perhaps the greatest leader in the development of Japanese Christian social-welfare work and reform in the 20th cent. At the same time he preferred to describe himself primarily as an evangelist.

Kagawa first encountered Christian faith in the middle school at Tokushima in Shikoku. He was befriended by a Japanese Christian teacher and by two *missionaries of the Presbyterian Church, USA. He read and reread the *New Testament until all the pent-up agony of his past burst forth in the prayer 'O God, make me like Christ'. From this developed a growing inner conviction that he had been given a divine commission to serve the poor.

On Christmas Day 1909, he carted his few belongings to his one room in the slums of Kōbe. There Kagawa committed himself to service and love of the lowliest of persons, in whom he came to be convinced that God dwells, in the whole person and circumstance. For this reason he became a *Christian Socialist, a social seer and reformer as well as a Christian evangelist.

He helped to form the Japan Federation of Labor and to organize the labourers of Kōbe into a branch of this national body. He was perhaps the leading figure in the great strike of the shipyard workers in Kōbe in 1921. For the next forty years he was prominent in almost every movement for constructive social reform in Japan.

In his methodology Kagawa was a thorough social evolutionist, a strict follower of the principle of non-violence. Kagawa has been called one of the three greatest Christians of this century. His ideals were expounded in many books, e.g. *Love, the Law of Life* (tr. 1930) and *Christ and Japan* (Eng. tr., 1934).

Kagura (Jap., originally 'seat [or site] of the *kami', though now written with the Chin. ideograms for 'sacred music'). Dramatic ritual events performed during seasonal festivals in Japan. Thematically associated with mythological exploits in the **Kojiki* and **Nihongi*, the performances represent one form of ritual entertainment which constitutes an essential element of all *matsuri.

Kagyü (*bka'.brgyud*, 'oral transmission'). One of the four principal schools of Tibetan Buddhism, taking its name from the mode of transmission of its teachings before their proper systematization by *Gampopa (1079–1153). To it, or to some of its sub-divisions, the name 'Red Hats' is often incorrectly given in the W. (for the use of that name, see RED HATS). Like the *Nyingma, the Kagyü have a strong identification with the Indian *siddha tradition, out of which they recognize two lineages culminating in *Marpa (1012–97). From Nāropa, Marpa inherited the 'Six Doctrines of Nāropa', Tantric practices of mastery over self and phenomena which are now recognized by all schools, and which constitute the heart of a Kagyü *lama's training. From Maitrīpa, Marpa inherited the philosophical doctrine of Mahāmudrā, in which the progression and culmination of the spiritual path are seen as the expression of a procreative *śūnyatā, in which bliss, luminosity, and wisdom are seen to coincide.

From Marpa, the philosophy of Mahāmudrā and the practices of Nāropa passed to *Milarepa, and from Milarepa to Gampopa, who had also studied in the *Kadam tradition. It is only with Gampopa that one can begin to talk of a Kagyü 'school', and this immediately split into four subschools, the Tshal, Baram, Karma, and Druk. Today there are many Kagyü subschools, the two most important of which are the Druk ('brug) Kagyü, founded by Yeshe *Dorje (1161–1211), which became the dominant tradition in Bhutan, even giving its name to that country, and the Karma Kagyü, established by Düsum Chempa (1110–93), the first Gyalwa Karmapa hierarch, and which is generally today the dominant Kagyü school. See Index, Kagyü.

Kahal (community leader): see MAʿAMAD.

Kai (Jap.). The Buddhist precepts: see ŚĪLA. Kai-gyō is the observance of the precepts ordered by the Buddha; and kai-dan is the platform from which the precepts are pronounced when an initiate takes them upon himself for the first time; kai-gi is the ritual for that purpose.

Kaibara Ekken (1630–1714). A Japanese *Confucian scholar of the early to mid-Tokugawa period. As an advocate of 'practical learning' (*jitsugaku*), Kaibara wrote many popular works encompassing a wide range of interests: philosophy, moral education, health and diet, and the natural sciences. Although originally a follower of the orthodox *Chu Hsi school of *Neo-Confucianism, he established his own independent, critical position, often compared to the school of Ancient Learning (*Kokugaku). For example, in his major work, the *Taigiroku* (Record of Grave Doubts), Kaibara attacks Chu Hsi's overreliance on Buddhist and *Taoist teachings. He saw an inherent unity between the Confucian ethics of the early sages and Japanese *Shinto, while rejecting Buddhist ideas, such as the application of *honjisuijaku.

Kaidan. The ordination hall in a Zen monastery, where monks are initiated into an order and receive the ten precepts (*jujukai). The Kaidan-seki is a stone tablet set in front of the monastery, saying, 'Meat, fish, and alcohol are forbidden.'

Kaigen (Jap., 'opening the eye'). A general Zen expression for the awakening of a true insight into the nature of reality; thus the insight of a master (*roshi) is often referred to as his *dharma eye. More particularly, it is the ceremony whereby a representation of a *buddha or *bodhisattva (in sculpture or painting) is consecrated and brought to life, by giving it eyes. It thereby gives expression to the buddha-nature (*bussho) within it.

Kailāsa (Skt., 'ice/silver mountain'). 1. Mountain range in Himālayas, but also one mountain in particular sacred to both Hindus and Tibetan Buddhists. It is the paradise of the gods, especially *Śiva. Ridges in the southern face resemble a *svastika, hence reference to it as 'the svastika mountain'.

2. A temple at *Ellorā, probably constructed by the king *Kṛṣṇa (d. *c.*773 CE), and dedicated to Śiva. The temple is constructed to translate the Himalayan mountain into architectural form.

Kaimyō (Jap., 'precepts name'). The name Japanese Buddhist monks and nuns are given when 'taking the precepts', at the time of their ordination, which replaces their secular name.

Kairos (time as opportunity): see TILLICH, P.

Kaisan (Jap., 'mountain founder'). The founder of a Zen monastery, or of a Buddhist school. The anniversary commemoration is called kai-san-ki.

Kaiten (turning of the heaven): see KAMIKAZE.

Kaivalya (Skt., 'alone, unique'). The state of the soul in Hindu *Rāja-yoga when it realizes that it is not dependent on such support systems as gods or material sustenance. Kaivalya-*mukti is thus freedom from all further rebirth.

Among Jains, kaivalya describes the *jiva (soul) emancipated from *karma, and regaining its original condition of isolation from *ajiva*: see KEVALA; KEVALIN.

Kaji (Jap.). The power of the *Buddha transferred to sentient beings, and the response to it. In particular, it is the transference of that power to those in need through prayer. Kaji-riki is the interaction between the Buddha and humans in activating this power.

Kakka food (acceptable from same or higher caste members): see FOOD AND RELIGION (HINDUISM).

Kakure Kirishitan (hidden Christians): see JAPANESE RELIGION.

Kakushin also **Shinchi Kakushin** (1207–98). Japanese Zen master who did much to establish *kōan practice in Japan, not least by introducing the *Wu-men-kuan* (see KŌAN). In 1249, he visited China and trained in (or perhaps established) the Fuke school (where playing the flute replaces *sūtra recitation), but settled with *Wu-men Hui-k'ai, of the Yōgi school of *Rinzai. He returned to Japan in 1254, and founded Saihō-ji (later called Kōkoku-ji). His teaching remained eclectic, but with concentration on kōans of the *Mumonkan* (*Wu-men kuan*) especially its opening kōan on 'nothingness'.

Kāla (Skt., 'time'). A general Hindu word for *time, displacing the Vedic *ṛtu*, which focused on the seasons. *Kal* means 'enumerate', or 'calculate' and moved the interest in time to the longer sequences of past, present, and future. Both *Viṣṇu and *Śiva are regarded as aspects of cosmic time. *Yama, death, is associated with kāla (and is sometimes called Kāla), and the kāladaṇḍa, the staff of death, is one of Yama's emblems. Kāla is also the bringer of, in addition to death, destiny from the gods (*daiva).

Kalā (limit on efficacy): see KAÑCUKA.

Kālacakra (Tib., *dus.kyi.'khor.lo*, 'Wheel of Time'). Perhaps the most revered *tantra in Tibetan Buddhism, which in addition to yogic teachings involves an esoteric world history and *eschatology. The introduction of the tantra into Tibet is often ascribed to *Atiśa, but it is hard to substantiate this. The Kālacakra teachings figured prominently in the old *Kadam and *Jonang schools due to its chief 14th-cent. promulgators, Butön and Dolpopa.

The Kālacakra Tantra has three aspects, 'outer', 'inner', and 'other'. The 'outer' is lore concerning the environment: astrology, history, eschatology; the 'inner' concerns the esoteric physiology of the 'subtle body'; the 'other' consists of the 'generation' and 'completion' stages of yoga, and aims to purify the 'outer' and 'inner' aspects. Of these, the 'generation' (*utpattikrama*) involves the *visualization of the 722 deities of the Kālacakra *maṇḍala, which has at its centre the *Ādibuddha in the form of the sexual union (*yab-yum) of Kālacakra and Vishvamātā. The 'completion' (*sampannakrama*) stage involves the manipulation of one's subtle energies to produce a consciousness with the capacity for enlightenment. Kālacakra is a member of the Anuttara (unsurpassed) class of tantras, and as such offers buddhahood through its mastery.

Kalām (Arab., *kalima*, 'word, discourse'). The science (*'ilm) of theology in Islam, developed in parallel with 'ilm ul-*fiqh (and was originally called *al-fiqh al-akbar*, the greater fiqh). Its roots lie in early attempts to deal with rational questions prompted (or provoked) by *Qur'ān—e.g., how can the *qadar (determining power) of *Allāh be reconciled with the freedom and accountability of humans? The earliest group to bring reason to bear on such issues were the *Mu'tazilites. But that inclination to give primacy to reason seemed to others to subordinate the Qur'ān. Kalām, therefore, for *al-Ash'arī and *al-Māturīdī became the elucidation and application of the Qur'ān as the absolute (and uncreated) Word of God. The dangers of Kalām to the uninitiated were signalled by *al-Ghaz(z)ālī, whose reconciliation of philosophy, theology, and simple faith in effect put an end to theological exploration. Those who study theology are known as *mutakallimun*. See Index, Theologians (Muslim); Theology (Muslim).

Kālāmukhas (Śaiva sect): see ŚAIVISM.

Kālarātri (Skt., 'the dark night'). One of a variety of names of *Devī. She is a Goddess of the night personifying Time, and at the end of each age assumes the form of Mahākālī, a dark destroyer born out of the wrath of *Śiva. She has tusks and wears a garland of skulls; also called Mahālaksmi, Mahāmāyā, Nidrā, Yoganidrā, etc.

Kālī or **Kālikā** (Skt. 'black'). A ferocious form of the Goddess (*Devī) in Hinduism, sharply contrasted with her benign aspects as *Śrī and *Lakṣmī. Kālī, the devourer of time (*kāla), is depicted as having a terrifying appearance, naked or wearing a tiger skin, emaciated, with fang-like teeth and dishevelled hair, a lolling tongue, and eyes rolling with intoxication. She is garlanded with human heads, sometimes girdled with severed arms; laughing and howling, she dances, wild and frenzied, in the cremation grounds with a sword and noose or skull upon a staff.

Human *sacrifices were made to her in the past (cf. *Kālīkapurāṇa*, ch. 71), but now goats have to suffice, and such sacrifices are made at the main temple of her cult, Kālīghāṭa (*Calcutta). The Thugs were devotees of Kālī, to whom they offered worship before committing murderous theft. Many Hindus see Kālī as representing the realities of death and time; she stands for the frightening, painful side of life which all who desire to progress spiritually must face and overcome.

In *Tantrism Kālī is depicted as dancing upon the ithyphallic corpse of Śiva, a form expressing the passive consciousness (*puruṣa) and dynamic energy (*prakṛti) which comprise the universe. Kālī is the central deity of the Kālīkula tradition in contrast to the Śrīkula whose followers worship the gentle Śri. The Kālīkula adept or 'hero' (vīra) will follow the 'left-hand' path (*vāmācāra), worshipping Kālī in the cremation grounds.

In the 18th and 19th cents. Bengali poets such as Rāmprasād (1718–75) and *Ramakrishna (1836–86) wrote devotional poems to her as the supreme deity.

Kālidāsa. A Hindu poet and dramatist. Nothing certain is known about his life and family. It is possible that he lived, between 350 and 460 CE. This period is suggested from internal evidence found in his books *Meghadūta* and *Kumārasambhava*. His most celebrated works are the three plays **Śakuntalā* (*Abhijñanaśakuntala*, 'The Recognition of Śakuntalā'), *Vikramorvashīyam*, and *Mālavikāgnimitra*. His epic compositions, *Raghuvaṃsha* and *Kumārasambhava*, are unsurpassed in Skt. poetry, and his genius is equally evident in *Rṛtusamhāra*.

Kālikā-purāṇa. A Hindu ritual and mythological work in Skt., belonging to the genre of the upa-*purāṇas. It is a fairly amorphous compilation of material connected with the worship of the Hindu Goddess (see KĀLĪ). In its present form (which may well be as late as the 13th or 14th cent., put together in Assam or a neighbouring part of Bengal), the text has as its central figure the Goddess *Kāmākhyā. Her temple in Assam is one of the pīṭhas, and is said to derive from *Satī's *yoni.

Kali-yuga. The fourth and final of the *yugas, of increasing disorder and distress. The world is at present in a kali-yuga, which began in 3102 BCE.

Kalki. In Hindu mythology, the tenth and last in the standard list of *Viṣṇu's *avatāras, who is to come in the future. He is usually described as a warrior *brahman who will arise to punish evil-doers at the end of the *Kali-yuga and thus usher in a new Kṛta-yuga.

Kallah, months of. The months in the Jewish year when scholars gathered to study *Torah in the Babylonian *academies. The custom has been revived in modern Israel.

Kallir, Eleazar (?6th cent. CE). Jewish liturgical poet. Kallir was one of the most prolific authors of liturgical *piyyutim. His poems were widely known, and today more than 200 are still extant in various rites.

Kalpa. In Hinduism, a day and a night in the life of *Brahmā, consisting of four *yugas, i.e. one *mahā* (great) *yuga*; or sometimes calculated as 1,000 yugas; in any case, an immense endurance of time.

In Buddhism (Pāli, *kappa*), the length of a kalpa is equally vast: through the four stages of a kalpa, a universe arises, continues, declines, persists in chaos. Within this mahākalpa, there are twenty small kalpas.

Kalpa Sūtras. Hindu texts which deal with details of life, especially ritual matters. Kalpa, dealing with ritual, is part of the *Vedāṅgas, i.e. the auxiliary disciplines which enable *brahmans to implement the Vedas in practice.

Kal va-homer (Heb. 'light and heavy'). Principle of determining Jewish *halakhah: it means that what applies in a less important case will certainly apply in a more important one. The phrase has come to mean an inescapable conclusion.

Kalyāṇa-mitta (Pāli, 'good friend', 'wise companion'; Skt., *kalyāna-mitra*). Teacher or mentor in *Theravāda Buddhism; one who advises and instructs in the choice and use of a meditation subject (*kammaṭṭhāna). The Buddha is regarded as the paradigmatic kalyāṇa-mitta.

Kalyāṇa-śraddha ('reliable faith'). One of the four perfections of the heart, developed in Integral Yoga by Śri *Aurobindo. The others are *prema-sāmarthya* (the power of love), *saumyatva* (gentleness), *tejas* (commitment).

Kāma (Skt., *kam*, 'desire'). Love, sexual pleasure, personified as the Hindu god of love. Kāma, erotic and aesthetic expression, is the third Hindu end of life (*artha), traditionally categorized as *preya* (pleasant) rather than *śreya* (good); but in *Mahābhārata* 12. 167, kāma is the source of both artha and *dharma, because without kāma, humans do not strive for anything. See also KĀMAŚĀSTRA.

In Buddhism, kāma is a major obstacle to progress toward enlightenment. It belongs to the lowest of the three domains (triloka), the domain of desire (*kāmaloka*). It is one of the five hindrances (*nīvaraṇas) and one of the defilements, āsrava (see ĀSAVA).

Kāmākhyā or **Kāmākṣī** ('wanton-eyed'). Hindu goddess, a form of *Durgā. Her cult was associated with human sacrifice until 1832, when animal sacrifice was substituted. Details concerning her cult were gathered in **Kālikā-Purāṇa*.

Kamakura. Major centre in Japan of Shinto shrines, and of Buddhist temples and monasteries. Due south of Tokyo, it was a fishing village which became the effective capital in 1185. The principal Shinto shrine, Tsurugaoka Hachiman-gu, is dedicated (as the name states) to *Hachiman. Among the Zen monasteries, Kencho-ji is of particular importance, because Zen monks are still trained there. It was founded by Tao-lung in 1253, and is built, like the classic monasteries of *Kyōto, on the single-axis design. *Engaku-ji (also Enkaku-ji), founded thirty years later, contains a Relic Hall in which one of the *Buddha Śākyamuni's teeth is preserved; several of its buildings were destroyed in an earthquake in 1923. Also of note is Zuisenji, founded by Soshi in 1327, recently rebuilt and surrounded by gardens of great beauty. Kamakura contains the second largest *daibutsu (image of the Buddha, the largest being in Todaiji). The *Jōdo school is represented by the Hasedera temple, which contains a massive image of Kannon (*Avalokiteśvara) carved from a single tree, and many shrines devoted to Jizō (see KṢITIGARBHA) by those who have lost infants.

Kamakura Period. The period in Japan of the Kamakura shoguns, 1192–*c.*1338. It was a period when Buddhism flourished. See BUDDHISM IN JAPAN.

Kamakura Schools (of Japanese Buddhism): see TENDAI-SHŪ.

Kamalaśīla (*c*.740–95 CE). Indian Yogācāra-*Mādhyamaka pupil of *Śāntarakṣita, who significantly determined the form of Buddhism in Tibet during its 'first diffusion' (*snga.dar*) there. During Śāntarakṣita's time in Tibet, many Ch'an teachers were arriving from China, whose 'sudden attainment' (*ston.min.pa.*) understanding of enlightenment contrasted with Śāntarakṣita's own 'gradualist' (*rtsen.min.pa*) approach to realization. On Śāntarakṣita's recommendation, King Trisong Detsen invited Kamalaśīla from India to debate with the Chinese Hua Shang Mahāyāna at *Samyé (792–4 CE), on the understanding that the teachings of whichever school won the debate would be established as the religion of Tibet. Although there are Chinese accounts to the contrary, there is little doubt that Kamalaśīla won. In 795 CE, however, Kamalaśīla was murdered, though whether by his defeated opponents or by followers of the native *Bön religion is not clear. It has been suggested that Ch'an Buddhism did not completely leave Tibet as a result of the debate, and that elements of it remain in present *Nyingma and Bön teachings.

Kamalaśīla was an illustrious scholar who also influenced the development of Tibetan Buddhism by his writings. His most important work, *Madhyamakāloka* (Light on the Middle Way), presents the Madhyamaka doctrine of emptiness (*śūnyatā) and incorporates *Tathāgata-Garbha (Essence of Buddhahood) theory perhaps for the first time in the Madhyamaka school; his commentary (Skt., *pañjikā*) on Śāntarakṣita's *Madhyamakālankāra* (Ornament of the Middle Way) remains an important assessment of Buddhist philosophy (though a few Geluk scholars doubt its authenticity); his commentary on Śāntarakṣita's *Tattvasaṃgraha* (Compendium of Reality, tr. G. Jha, 1937–9) contains the first known Buddhist consideration of the Indian *Advaita school. In addition to this, Kamalaśīla's three texts on meditation, the *Bhavanakrama* (Stages on the Meditative Path) represent his own position taken in the debate.

Kāmaloka: see LOKA (BUDDHIST).

Kāmaśāstra (Skt., *kāma*, 'love', + *śāstra*, 'teaching'). Any of a class of Skt. texts concerned with *kāma—love, sexuality, and sensual enjoyment.

Bābhravya is said to have condensed the tradition of Kāmaśāstra into a work of 150 chapters in seven *adhikaraṇa* (sections), forming the basis of a school of sexology. The *adhikaraṇa* are: general principles; courtship; sexual union; marriage; how to steal other men's wives; prostitutes; and potions, spells, aphrodisiacs, *mantras, and devices.

The most influential Kāmaśāstra texts are the *Kāmasūtra* of Vātsyāyana (*c*.450 CE), and the *Anaṅga-raṅga* (Theatre of the Love God), attributed to Kalyāṇamalla (?1460–1530 CE). Other classic Kāmaśāstra texts include Dāmodaragupta's *Kuṭṭanī-mata* (Lessons of a Bawd), Kṣemendra's *Samaya-māṭrikā* (The Harlot's Breviary), Koka's *Rati-rahasya* (Mysteries of Passion), and Jyotirīśa's *Pañcaśāyaka* (Five Arrows). Hundreds of popular Kāmaśāstra texts exist, in which the Hindu deities enact the various sexual postures as paradigms for human performance.

Kāmasūtra (Skt., *kāma* 'love', + *sūtra* 'aphorism'). A Sanskrit prose text concerning the art of love and sexual union. The *Kāmasūtra* of Vātsyāyana (*c*.450 CE) is the best-known Indian sexological manual, covering almost every aspect of human sexuality, with special attention to general principles.

Kami (Jap.). Sacred powers venerated by the Japanese, described in the *Shinto mythologies, and enshrined in Shinto shrines (*jinja*) as objects of worship. The etymology of kami is uncertain; the word is at once singular and plural, and while it often refers to personified beings, it also retains the sense of awesome sacred power. The kami are numerous, even innumerable, according to the traditional phrase *yaoyorozu no kami* ('vast myriads of kami'), implying that the cosmos is replete with divine powers in which all forms of existence participate. The kami are commonly divided into heavenly kami (*amatsukami*) and earthly kami (*kunitsukami*). But any form of existence that possesses some extraordinary, awe-inspiring quality could be called kami: mountains, seas, rivers, rocks, trees, birds, animals. Humans who have some extraordinary quality—people like emperors, family ancestors, heroes—could be referred to as kami.

The kami who are worshipped in the thousands of shrines in Japan are predominantly those mentioned in the Shinto mythologies.

Amaterasu-ō-Mikami is usually recognized at the head of the kami, but her position is not absolute or exclusive, for she pays her respects to the other kami, and ordinary people worship other kami as well as Amaterasu. There are also, of course, kami with negative, destructive powers (e.g. *magatsuhi-no-kami) who are the source of sin and uncleanness and who inflict calamities. But ultimately they too are manifestations of a power of life which requires reverence and worship.

Kamidana (Jap., 'kami-shelf'). In *Shinto, an altar or high shelf for enshrining a *kami in a quiet place in the house of a Shinto believer.

Kamigakari (Jap.). A state of trance in which a spiritual being (*kami) possesses (*kakaru*) the human body by entering and speaking through it. Kamigakari may be experienced spontaneously or induced through ascetic practices. Women experience kamigakari more often than men. Kamigakari has been a common feature of Japanese folk religion since ancient times.

Kamikaze (Jap., 'Divine Wind', so-called from the strong winds and storms which dispersed two Mongol invasions in 1274 and 1281). Japanese pilots during the Second World War who volunteered, from 1944 onward, to undertake missions against enemy targets in which they were 'flying bombs', and from which, therefore, they could not expect to return alive. Related to kamikaze were the *kaiten* (turning of the heaven), human torpedoes. They wore white scarves and also round their foreheads a white cloth, taken from the *hachimaki*, the cloths worn by *samurai warriors. In a Zen perspective (often referred to by volunteers who survived), death is of no greater importance (or less) than any other event or manifestation. In a wider Japanese perspective, the spirits of warriors who die in obedience to the emperor return in any case to Japan, and in particular to the Shinto Yasukuni (Country of Peace) shrine in Tokyo. This shrine was founded in 1879 as the Tokyo Shokon Jinja (shrine).

Kamimukae, Kamiokuri (Jap., 'summoning *kami', 'sending off kami'). In *Shinto, ancient ceremonies of summoning kami to be present in a *himorogi and sending them off again. The himorogi or temporary dwelling-place is set up outside the shrine buildings for special celebrations.

Kami no michi (Jap.), the native Japanese words meaning 'the Way of the *Kami', corresponding to the Chinese *shen-tao* (*Shinto) as the designation for the indigenous religion of Japan. This term is sometimes read as *kannagara no michi*, 'the way which accords to the kami'.

Kamma: see KARMA.

Kammaṭṭhāna (Pāli, 'working-ground', i.e. 'support'). In Theravāda Buddhism, a subject of meditation; specifically, one of those which serves as the basis for the practice of mindfulness (*sati) and concentration (*samādhi). *Buddhaghosa's *Visuddhimagga* lists forty kammaṭṭhāna. The meditator selects a topic or corpus of topics, on the grounds of their suitability to his own psychological disposition and character traits; in ideal circumstances he should be advised and guided in his choice by a teacher (*kalyāṇa-mitta).

Kamo no Mabuchi (1697–1769). A Japanese *Kokugaku scholar and poet. In 1733, leaving his wife and child behind, he journeyed to Kyōto to master classical Japanese studies and ancient Japanese. On the death of his master in 1736, he returned to Hamamatsu for a year and left home once again for Edo (modern Tokyo) to devote himself to the cause of Kokugaku. He became a prolific writer on the themes of Shinto studies, court customs, linguistics, and poetics, especially when these made evident the superiority of the Japanese tradition, in contrast to China, and his admiration for the ancient Japanese way of life became the main thrust of the Kokugaku Movement. His scholarship and thought attracted many able men such as *Motoori Norinaga, Kao Chikage, and Murata Harumi.

Kaṃsa. In Hindu mythology, *Kṛṣṇa's arch-enemy, identified with the demon Kālanemi.

Kamuy (spiritual powers): see AINU.

Kaṇāda (*c.*2nd cent. BCE). Hindu philosopher who according to tradition founded the *Vaiśeṣika system (*darśana). The *Vaiśeṣika-sūtra* is attributed to him. He is also known as Kaṇabhuj, etc., 'atom delighter', because of the atomic nature of the theory.

Kanada Tokumitsu (founder of a Japanese religion): see MIKI TOKUHARU.

Kanah, Book of. Jewish *kabbalistic book. Modelled on the **Zohar*, the book is a commentary on the mitzvot (sing. *mitzvah) with additional mystical interpretations. Of unknown authorship, it was probably written in Spain in the 14th cent.

Kan'ami Kiyotsugu (Nō writer): see NŌ.

Kāñcīpura (Conjeevaram). One of the seven Hindu holy cities, near Madras, a centre of pilgrimage, with mainly *Śaivite and *Vaiṣṇavite temples.

Kañcuka ('armour'). In *Kashmir Śaivism, the five ways in which *māyā covers over pure consciousness (*śuddha saṃvid*). The five are: *kalā*, limitation of efficacy; *vidyā, limited knowledge; *rāga, passion; *kāla, time; and *niyati*, fixed order or limitation relating to space and cause.

Kāṇḍa: see KARMA-KĀṆḌA.

Kangen (Japanese music not accompanying dance): see MUSIC.

Kaṅghā (comb): see FIVE KS.

Kangyur: see KANJUR.

K'ang Yu-wei (1858–1927). Leading figure in the Chinese Reform Movement which followed defeat in the Sino-Japanese war, 1894–5. His *Chronological Autobiography* shows that he was early dissatisfied with maintaining traditional ways and ideas. He had an enlightenment experience of the one nature of all appearances (including his own), and withdrew into isolation where a sense of mission formed to offer a way of salvation to the world. He wrote **Ta t'ung shu* and *K'ung Tzu kai-chih k'ao* (Confucius as a Reformer). In 1898 he was invited to take charge of government by the emperor. He set about reform, but his twenty-seven reform edicts provoked a conservative *coup d'état* in favour of the empress dowager, Tzu Hsi. Forced overseas, he continued to oppose the Republic, but lived circumspectly when he returned to China.

K'an-hua ch'an (kōan-gazing Ch'an). Chin. for *Kanna Zen; see HUNG-CHIH; TA-HUI.

Kaniṣka. 1. A king of the Śaka-Kūṣāna period (*c.*78–144 CE), who ruled over the west of N. India, and some parts of Central Asia, about 78–102. Buddhist tradition celebrates him as a great patron of Buddhism, a view borne out by historical and archaeological evidence.

Under his patronage, the Gandhara school of art flourished. His court included such Buddhist luminaries as *Aśvaghoṣa, *Nāgārjuna, Pārśva, and Vasumitra, as well as the physician Caraka, the politician Māṭhara, and the Greek engineer Agesilaus, who designed and built a famous *stūpa in Kaniṣka's capital of Puruṣapura (Peshāwar).

2. A class of Hindu deities of the fourteenth *manvantara* (cf. *Manu).

Kānji Svāmi Panth. Jain movement named after its founder, Kānji Svāmi, born in Gujarat of Śvetāmbara parents in 1889. When he was about 30, he read *Kundakunda's *Samayasāra* (Essence of Doctrine), which opened him to the possibility that the *Digambara way was the true one. In 1934, he renounced his status as a Śvetāmbara monk and became a Digambara layman. This took place at Songadh which remains the centre of the movement derived from him. He became an indefatigable preacher, mainly commenting on the works of Kundakunda and taking even further his stress on the primacy of the realization of the true soul (*paramātman) over all external observances, vows, and rituals. The Panth is a mainly lay movement, though there are some *brahmacharis (ascetics). The Panth is missionary and has adherents in many countries round the world.

Kanjur (*bka.'gyur*, 'translated word (of the Buddha)'). The primary part of the Tibetan Buddhist canon which comprises all *sūtras and *tantras attributed directly to the historical *Buddha *Śākyamuni, to his later revelation, or (in the case of some tantras) to another transcendent Buddha. The Kanjur numbers 100 or 108 vols. according to edn., and was largely systematized by the scholar and historian Butön, in the 14th cent. CE. See also TANJUR.

Kanna Zen (Jap.; Chin., K'an-huach'an). Zen based on the contemplation of words, a description of Zen in which the *kōan is pre-eminent. In time, it became virtually synonymous with *Rinzai, in contrast to *Sōtō, which was termed *mokushō zen.

Kannen (Jap., 'meditation'). Meditation in Japanese Buddhism, especially on the *Pure Land of *Amida.

Kannō-dōkō (Jap.). The direct and immediate connection and interaction between teacher and pupil in Zen (*dokusan, *mondō, *hossen).

Kannon (abbr. of Kanzeon, a bodhisattva): see AVALOKITEŚVARA.

Kannushi (Jap.). A Shinto priest, generally the guardian of a shrine.

Kāṇphaṭa yogis (sect founded by Gorakhnāth): see GORAKHNĀTH.

Kan-shiketsu (Jap., 'dry shit stick'). Zen description of a person attached to the world of appearance. It is the *wato of *kōan 21 in the *Wu-men kuan*.

Kant, Immanuel (1724–1804). German philosopher. He was born in Königsberg of devoutly Pietist parents, and spent all his life there, becoming Professor of logic and metaphysics at the university in 1770.

He wrote his most important books in his later years, especially the three Critiques. The *Critique of Pure Reason* (1781) deals with fundamental questions about human knowledge, understanding, and reason, and has been one of the most influential works of modern philosophy. In the later part of the *Critique* Kant criticizes the *ontological, *cosmological, and *teleological arguments for God's existence. He allows, however, that the ideas of God, the soul, and the world may have what Kant calls a 'regulative' role. Thus, although Kant attacked traditional *metaphysics and *natural theology, he allowed for the possibility of a 'rational faith'.

Kant's *Groundwork of the Metaphysic of Morals* (1785) is a significant work on moral philosophy, famous for its discussion of the 'categorical imperative', a test whereby we judge our moral principles at the bar of reason, to see if they are indeed universal rules valid for all people.

Kant's last substantial discussion of religious questions was his *Religion within the Bounds of Reason Alone* (1793), in which he further developed his idea of a 'pure, rational religion', rejecting 'false worship'. He discussed questions concerning divine commands, grace, the nature of Christ's redemption, the atonement, and the Church, stressing the primacy of the rational moral judgement and often criticizing traditional doctrines.

Kaṇva. 1. A Hindu *ṛṣi often referred to in the *Ṛg Veda*, to whom several of its hymns are attributed.

2. A demon of disease who destroys and devours embryos.

Kanzan: see HAN-SHAN.

Kanzeon: see AVALOKITEŚVARA.

Kao-Seng-Chuan (Biographies of Eminent Monks). Buddhist text compiled by Hui-chiao of the Liang dynasty (502–51 CE). It contains the biographies of 257 eminent Chinese and foreign Buddhist monks who lived in China from the 2nd cent. CE to the 6th cent.

Kāpāla (Skt., 'made of skulls'). Followers of *Śiva who worship him in his terrible (Bhairava) form: see KĀPĀLIKA.

Kāpālika (Skt., 'skull-wearer'). A sect of *Śaivism which flourished from the 7th to 14th cents. CE, also called the Somasiddhānta. The Kāpālikas were cremation-ground (*śmaśāna) dwellers who covered themselves with the ashes of corpses and carried a skull which they used as a bowl. The terrifying form of *Śiva as *Bhairava, *Mahākāla, or Kāpālabhṛt ('skull-carrier') was the central deity of the cult. Kāpālika practice aimed at a vision of, and possession (*aveśa*) by, a deity or power (*śakti), in order to achieve perfection (*siddhi). Practice included the consuming of corpse-flesh and scatalogical substances, meditation whilst seated on a corpse, sexual rites with low-caste women, and animal, human, and self-sacrifice. The Kāpālikas were scorned and feared by orthodox Brahmanism, and if a brahman saw one, he would stare into the sun to purify himself. The Kāpālikas were absorbed into the *Nāthas and *Aghorīs.

Kapila. A legendary figure, traditionally recognized as the founder of *Sāṃkhya. He is said to have lived during the late 7th or early 6th cent. BCE though these dates precede his supposed authorship of the *Ṣaṣṭitantra* (*c.*100 BCE–200 CE) and other texts. Today, thousands of pilgrims gather at the point by the island Sagar where the river *Gaṅgā is said to have come to earth, and here they visit the hermitage (*āśrama) of the sage Kapila.

Kapilāvastu, Kapilavatthu (Skt.; Pāli). The early home of the *Buddha. It lies between the foothills of Nepal and the Rapti river. It is one of the four major places of Buddhist *pilgrimage.

Kaplan, Mordecai Menachem (1881–1983). Founder of the Jewish *Reconstructionist movement. He was born in Lithuania, but was taken to the USA when he was 9. He studied at the *Jewish Theological Seminary, and was appointed *rabbi to an *Orthodox congregation. But the erosive power of so many ideas around him (*Durkheim, Darwin, *Freud, *Marx, and *Wellhausen in particular) led him to leave his congregation and work as a teacher at the JTS. His radical views led to a further break with *Conservative Jews, and in 1922, he initiated the Jewish Reconstructionist movement, although at that stage not wishing it to be a separate organization. The laws remained important, but as a means to an end. He thought that Jewish élitism was a mistake, and argued that all reference to 'the *Chosen People' should be dropped from the liturgy. He was a profound influence on generations of Conservative rabbis, although some extreme Orthodox repudiated him, excommunicating (*ḥerem) him and burning his revised Prayer Book. His views were expressed in his many books, the best known of which is *Judaism as a Civilization* (1934).

Kappa (period of time): see KALPA.

Kapparot (Heb., 'atonements'). Folk custom in Judaism, involving a cock or hen, to secure atonement before the *Day of Atonement, so that an adverse judgement would not be reached on that day. In Yiddish, a bad event is often met by the words, 'Oyf kapporos', may this be an atonement, i.e. a sufficient punishment to remove the need for any more.

Kaṛā (steel bangle): see FIVE KS.

Kaṛāh praśād (Pañjābī, *kaṛāh*, 'iron bowl', + *praśād* [= *prasadā]). Among Sikhs, sweet food offered to all attending worship in the *gurdwārā. After the service the kaṛāh praśād is distributed to all present as a sign of their equality and unity and to ensure that no one leaves the Gurū's presence empty handed.

Karaites (from Heb., 'readers', i.e. of scripture). Jewish sect basing itself on scripture, not subsequent interpretation. The name 'Karaite' was not used until 9th cent. CE. The sect is usually thought to have been founded by the ascetic *Anan b. David in the 8th cent., when his younger brother Hananiah was elected *exilarch. Their basic doctrine was that the Bible is the only source of law, and that scholars must study scripture for themselves and interpret it according to their own consciences. From the 12th cent., however, a process of systematization began under such scholars as Judah b. Elijah Hadassi (who summarized Karaite theology in his *Eshkol ha-Kofer*), Aaron b. Joseph ha-Rofe (who was an eminent biblical exegete and wrote *Sefer-Mivhar*, the classic Karaite commentary), and the codifier, Aaron b. Elijah the Younger, whose *Gan Eden* earned him the title of 'the Karaite *Maimonides'. They were perceived as Jews by their gentile rulers, and were in general subject to the same edicts. During the Second World War, the German government pronounced that the Karaites were not Jews and they were thus spared the horrors of the *Holocaust. In Israel, they have their own *bet din and they are not permitted either by *halakhah or by their own laws to intermarry with the rest of the population. See Index, Karaites.

Karakashlar (sect): see DOENMEH.

Karāmat 'Alī (d. 1873 (AH 1290)). Indian Muslim reformer, who contested the assimilation into Islam of Hindu customs, regarding them as *bid'a: his book against them is entitled *Radd al-Bid'a*. His differs from other conservative reform movements (e.g. *Wahhābīya) by accepting the value of spiritual guides (*pīr), and he could thus aim to reconcile *Sūfī movements with orthodox Islam.

Kāraṇa śarīra. The Hindu causal body which carries the effects of *karma into subsequent lives.

Karbalā'. The place where the Prophet *Muḥammad's grandson, *al-Ḥusain b. 'Alī, was killed and his headless body buried. The tragedy at Karbalā' marks an important point in the development of *Shi'ism, and therefore the place attracts many pilgrims. The shrine of the third Shī'a *Imām, al-Ḥusain, is enclosed in a beautiful sanctuary called Mashad al-Ḥusayn (tomb chapel of Ḥusain).

Kardec, A. (spiritualist): see UMBANDA.

Karelitz, Avraham Yeshayahu (1878–1953). *Talmudic scholar. Karelitz was an enormous influence on his generation. He was the author of over forty books, including *Hazon Ish* (1911), by which name he is often known. After he settled in *Erez Israel, in 1933, his house was a centre for teaching and guidance.

Kare sansui (Zen dry gardens): see GARDEN.

Karet (Heb., 'cutting off'). Punishment from God. Karet is defined as premature death (*Sifra, Emor* 14. 4) and more particularly as 'death at the age of fifty' (*BMK* 28a). The *Mishnah lists the thirty-six sins for which karet is the penalty (e.g. *idolatry, eating *leaven at *Passover, incest, and *adultery).

Karma, kamma (Skt., Pāli: 'action', 'deed'; Chin., *yin-yuan*; Jap., *innen*; Korean, *inyon*). Karman, the law of consequence with regard to action, which is the driving force behind the cycle of reincarnation or rebirth (*saṃsāra) in Asian religions. According to karma theory, every action has a consequence which will come to fruition in either this or a future life; thus morally good acts will have positive consequences, whereas bad acts will produce negative results. An individual's present situation is thereby explained by reference to actions in his past history, in his present or in previous lifetimes. Karma is not itself 'reward and punishment', but the strict law producing consequence.

In Hinduism, the word karma first appears in the *Ṛg Veda*, where it means religious action, specifically sacrifice; there is no hint here of its later meaning as the force driving beings through saṃsāra. There is some hint of this in the *Brāhmaṇas, but only with the *Upaniṣads do we really find karma in the sense of causality of action—e.g. **Bṛhadāranyaka Upaniṣad* 4. 4. 5.

Action creates impressions (*saṃskāras) or tendencies (*vāsanās) in the mind which in time will come to fruition in further action. The *subtle body (*liṅga or śūkṣma śarīra), in which the individual soul (*jiva) transmigrates, carries the seeds of karma; and the gross body (*sthūla śarīra*) is the field (*kṣetra*) in which the fruit (*phala*) of action is experienced, and which also creates more karma.

Vedānta and Yoga speak of three kinds of karma: (i) *prārabdha*, karma to be experienced during the present lifetime, (ii) *sañcita*, latent karma, or the store of karma which has yet to reach fruition, and (iii) *āgamin* or *sañcīyama*, the karma sown in the present life which will be reaped in a future life. Liberation (*mokṣa) is freedom from karma. When mokṣa is attained, the great store of *sañcita karma* is burnt up, but the *prārabdha* remains to complete its course. The liberated person (jivanmukta) creates no more new karma and at death, having no more karma, is no longer reborn.

In Buddhism, much of the same basic sense of a law of consequence is retained, but there is no 'self' to be reborn. Only intentions and actions free of desire, hate, and delusion are free of karmic consequence. Karma/kamma is neither fatalistic nor deterministic, since true insight enables one to direct the stream of continuity, or even to bring it to cessation.

Among Jains, karma is a kind of subtle

matter which attaches itself to the *jīva and weighs it down in bondage and rebirth. All actions, good as well as evil, cause karmic matter to attach to the soul. Therefore, the abandoning of action, in complete ascetic renunciation (even to the extent of voluntary starvation), is necessary.

For Sikhs, karma (Pañjābi, *karamu*) is accepted as consequential action, but against it is set karma (Arab., *karam*, 'favour') meaning the grace of God. Sikhs concentrate on bringing karma (*grace) to bear on karma, leading to union with God. See Index, Karma.

Karma Kagyü (Tib., *kar-ma bka'-brgyud*). One of the four main early subschools of *Kagyü (*bka'.brgyud*), founded by Düsum Chempa (Chos 'dzin dge 'phel Dus gsum mkhyen pa, 1110–93). Originally identified by Black Hats, made from the hair of *dākinīs who embody the good *karma of all the *buddhas, an early schism led to the Red Hats, with whom much conflict ensued. They contributed to *Rimé (*ris-med*), and have built up a considerable following in the West.

Karma-kāṇḍa (Skt.). The division, or practical part, of the *Vedas which refers to religious duties, *ritual, and actions; as opposed to the *jñānakāṇḍa of the *Vedānta which deals with philosophical knowledge. *Pūrvamīmāṁsā is concerned with karma-kāṇḍa.

Karman: see KARMA.

Karma-pa. Title of the highest spiritual authority in the Tibetan Buddhist school of *Karma Kagyü who is an embodiment of compassion.

Karma-yoga. One of the four main types of *yoga in Hinduism, leading to union with God. It consists of detachment, not from action as such, but from the fruits of all action, offering them instead as a sacrifice to God.

Karmendriya (Skt., *karma + *driya*, 'organ'). The five organs or means of action, those of speech, hands, feet, excretion, and reproduction.

Karṇa. In the **Mahābhārata*, the half-brother of the *Pāṇḍavas, who serves as the third general on the side of the *Kauravas in the *Kurukṣetra war.

More than any other *Mahābhārata* character, Karṇa brings out the ambiguities of *dharma pivotal to the epic. On the one hand, a mean and dreadful enemy, who must be defeated by the righteous Pāṇḍavas, Karṇa is, on the other hand, outstandingly loyal in his commitment to Duryodhana. Again and again, throughout the *Mahābhārata*, Karṇa is shown to be caught up in a web of curses, oaths, and promises, which, in fact, make his cause hopeless.

Karo: see CARO.

Kār sevā (Pañjābī, *kār*, 'work', + *sevā*, 'service'). Voluntary work undertaken by Sikhs for the good of the community. In particular, it has come to be applied to the work undertaken each fifty years of clearing silt from the pool of the *Harimandir (Golden Temple).

Kartārpur (Pañjābī, 'abode of the Creator'). Name of two historic Sikh sites.

1. Town founded by Gurū *Nānak in 16th cent. CE. Kartārpur lies on the Rāvī river in Siālkoṭ district, Pakistan, 3 km. from Dehrā Bābā Nānak on the Indian bank. Nānak died in Kartārpur, but his *samādhī* (tomb) was moved to Dehrā Bābā Nānak in the 17th cent. A *gurdwārā was built 1911–12.

2. Town founded by Gurū *Arjan Dev. Arjan founded Kartārpur in the Jalandhar (Jullundur) Doāb, *Pañjāb at the end of the 16th cent. CE. The original copy of the *Ādi Granth, compiled by Gurū Arjan Dev, is housed in a gurdwārā called Śīś Mahal in Kartārpur. Thousands flock to Kartārpur for *Baisākhī and on every Amāvas (darkest night of the month).

Kārt(t)ikeya. Hindu god of war and pestilence, son of *Śiva from seed which was thrown into fire, the ashes of which were then cast into the *Gaṅgā, from which he emerged. He rides on a peacock. He is also called *Skanda, Kumāra, and Murugan—see TAMIL NĀDU.

Karuṇā (Skt., 'compassion').

1. In Hinduism, all actions that diminish the sufferings of others.

2. In Buddhism compassion is a virtue which is of importance in all schools but which is particularly emphasized in *Mahāyāna. In early Buddhism, karuṇā figures as one of the four 'Sublime Attitudes', namely love or benevolence (*metta), compassion (karuṇā), sympathetic joy (*mudita), and equanimity (*upekkha).

In the Mahāyāna, karuṇā is emphasized as the necessary complement to wisdom (*prajña) and as an essential ingredient in the perfection of the fully enlightened. Hence the *bodhisattva of the Mahāyāna seeks to attain *nirvāna for the benefit of all, and vows that he will not cease from his efforts until all beings have attained liberation. In Mahāyāna iconography and art the embodiment of compassion is the great bodhisattva *Avalokiteśvara.

Kasatkin, Ivan (personal name of Niolai): see NICOLAI, PÈRE.

Kaṣāya (earth-coloured dress): see HABIT, RELIGIOUS; MONASTICISM (BUDDHIST).

Kasb (acquisition): see QADAR.

Kasher, kashrut, kosher (foods pronounced fit): see DIETARY LAWS.

Kashf (Arab., 'unveiling'). Comprehension of facts, events, and truths (mundane and spiritual) by inner sight or light. A *Sūfī term, it is used for a revelation of any secret truth to the mind and heart by the grace and power of God.

Kashmir Śaivism. An esoteric *Śaivism prevalent in Kashmir, N. India, from the 8th to the 11th cents. CE. It comprises a number of related Śaiva and *Śākta systems, namely the *Kaula ('relating to the family'), Krama ('gradation'), and Trika ('threefold'), though the term often refers only to the latter school, which is the most important, in that it integrated the Kaula and the Krama.

The literature of the Trika school is divided into three stages: (i) *Āgama Śāstra, revealed truth as embodied in the sixty-four monistic Śaiva āgamas and the *Śiva Sūtras*; (ii) Spanda Śāstra, a group of texts dealing with *spanda* ('vibration'), principally the *Spanda Kārikās*; and (iii) Pratyabhijñā śāstra, the philosophical systematization of the earlier material, which advocates a theology of the recognition (*pratyabhijñā*) of Śiva in all things. Somānanda's *Sivadṛṣti* first expounded this view, followed by Utpala's *Īśvarapratyabhijñā* (Tr. K. A. Subramaniya Aiyar and K. C. Pandey, *Bhāskarī* [1938]). The most famous Trika exponent was *Abhinavagupta who wrote the *Tantrāloka*.

The absolute (*parama* Śiva) of which there is nothing higher (*anuttara*), is regarded as the union of Śiva and Śakti conceived as *prakāśa* (light) and *vimarśa* (awareness). Acting from absolute freedom (*svātantrya*) equated with Śakti, Śiva manifests the cosmos as Śakti in the form of the thirty-six pure and impure *tattvas.

There are four ways to liberation (*mukti) or recognition (*pratyabhijñā*) of *parama* Śiva: (i) *aṇu upāya, direct liberation through grace or the descent of śakti (śaktipāta); (ii) *śāmbhava upāya, the absorption of the self in divine consciousness by the upsurge of pre-cognitive emotion which shatters thought construction; (iii) *śākta upāya, realization through the development of pure thought, such as 'I am Śiva'; and (iv) āṇava upāya, meditation on the body, mantra, and chosen deity (*iṣṭadevatā). See Index, Kashmir Śaivism.

Kashmir Sufism: see SŪFĪS.

Kashrut (food ritually fit for consumption): see DIETARY LAWS.

Kāśi. One of the seven sacred cities of India, an earlier name for Vārānasī (Benares). A centre of pilgrimage with many temples, it is especially important for devotion to *Śiva, who is worshipped (in a temple of this name) as Viśvanātha, Lord of the universe.

Kasiṇa (Pāli, derivation uncertain). A means in Buddhism of attaining *kammaṭṭhāna and *jhāna.

Kasiṇa devices are ten in number and are as follows: *paṭhavi* (earth), *āpo* (water), *tejo* (fire), *vāyo* (air), *nīla* (blue), *pīta* (yellow), *lohita* (red), *odāta* (white), *ākāsa* (space), and *viññāṇa* (*vijñāna, consciousness). These ten form part of the forty objects of meditation. See KAMMAṬṬHĀNA.

Kasogatan (local Javanese Buddhism): see WALUBI.

Kassapa (Pāli name): see MAHĀKĀŚYAPA.

Kaśyapa. In Hindu mythology, a divine seer, son of Marīci and grandson of *Brahmā.

Kataku (school of Ch'an): see HO-TSE.

Kataphatic theology: see AFFIRMATIVE WAY.

Kathak (N. Indian dance): see DANCE.

Kathākali (S. Indian dance): see DANCE.

Katha Upaniṣad. An *Upaniṣad sometimes assigned to the **Atharva Veda*, but more often to the Black **Yajur Veda*. It contains *Yama's instruction of Naciketas, including the granting of three wishes, the third of which was to know the nature of life in the hereafter.

Kathāvatthu (Points of Controversy): see MOGGALLIPUTTA TISSA.

Kathenotheism. The worship of successive gods, treated for the moment as the only god: see HENOTHEISM.

Katsu (Zen shout): see HO.

Kattō (Jap., 'clinging vines'). Zen description of those who use too many words to describe buddha-dharma, or of those who cling to the words of a teacher or *sūtra without penetrating their meaning. This is also known as *moji zen*.

Kaula (Skt.). Both an important school of *Tantrism whose adherents constitute the 'family' (*kula*) of *Śakti, and a theological term with many levels of meaning. The Kaula school reinterprets the teachings of the *Kula, rejecting the narrow sectarian bias of the Kula's *Kāpālika origins. The **Kūlārṇava Tantra* represents the Kaula as a distinct system which maintains the union of *Śiva and Śakti as the absolute reality, and advocates the secret ritual of the *pañca-makāra. Emphasizing secrecy, the text defines a Kaula as one who is privately a Śākta, outwardly a Śaiva and among people a *Vaiṣṇava. Among the meanings of Kaula as a theological term are śakti (as opposed to Śiva who is *akula*), *Kuṇḍalinī, 'body', and 'universe'.

Kaur. Sikh woman's second name, usually translated 'princess'. Kaur is the female counterpart of *Siṅgh.

Kauravas. In the **Mahābhārata*, the evil cousins of the *Pāṇḍavas, and their rivals for the throne; thus, the villains of the epic, whom the Pāṇḍavas eventually defeat in battle.

Kauṣitāki Upaniṣad. A short *Upaniṣad of four chapters, dealing with several topics, but especially with *prāṇa as the first principle, and with the interpretation of dreams.

Kauṭilya (attributed author): see ARTHAŚĀSTRA; PUROHITA.

Kavvanah (Heb., 'directed intention'). Concentration in Jewish *prayer and when performing a *mitzvah. *Maimonides taught that 'prayer without kavvanah is no prayer at all', and the **Shulḥān Arukh* insists, 'better a little supplication with kavvanah than a lot without it'. Kavvanah is also required of those performing mitzvot, but here there was more controversy: while all agree that kavvanah is desirable in fulfilling an obligation, is it necessary? In Ḥasidism and devotional Judaism, kavvanah is of such importance that it is deliberately cultivated in preparations before religious duties and prayer. In *kabbalah, kavvanah is also a special concentration on words and letters in order to discern an inner meaning. Cf. *niyya in Islam.

Kawate Bunjiro (1814–83). Founder of *Konkōkyō, a Japanese new religion. During a serious illness when he was 42, he encountered Konjin, a malevolent *Kami, in a healing ceremony, and from that time pronounced him to be beneficent rather than the opposite. He began to call him Kane no Kami ('the kami of gold'), Tenchi Kane no Kami ('the golden kami of heaven and earth'), and Konkō Daijin ('the great kami of golden light'). He began to receive direct communications from Konkō Daijin, and in 1859 he retired from farming in order to mediate between the kami and human beings. This date is regarded by adherents as the founding date of Konkōkyō, although it was not organized until 1885, after his death, being recognized by the government in 1900. After 1859, Kawate took the name of Konkō Daijin and met individuals who came to him, to act as a direct link between themselves and the kami.

Kederi (Sūfī order): see QĀDIRĪYA.

Kedushah (Heb., 'holiness'). In Judaism, set apart through holiness. The *biblical commandment, 'you shall be *holy, for I the Lord your God am holy' (Leviticus 19. 2) has consistently been understood by the *rabbis as requiring that the *Jews must be a people 'set apart'. The ultimate hope is that not only the Jewish nation, but the entire universe will be filled with the divine glory (*kavod*), and the *prophet *Zechariah looked to a time when even the bells on horses will be inscribed with 'Holy to the Lord' (Zechariah 14. 20–1). In rabbinic literature, holiness is of God's essence ('The Holy One, Blessed be he'). *Israel can only share in God's holiness through the performance of the mitzvot (sing. *mitzvah). More specifically, kedushah is applied to parts of the liturgy, especially the doxologies based on Isaiah 6. 3 and Ezekiel 3. 12 which echo the praise of the *angels.

Kedushta (morning piyyut): see KEROVAH.

Keep Sunday Special: see LORD'S DAY.

Kegi (Jap., 'teaching method'). The four ways of teaching in Japanese Buddhism, especially as classified in *Tendai: (i) *tongyo*, sudden and abrupt; (ii) *zengyo*, gradual; (iii) *himitsukyō*, secret (meaning that pupils are attaining understanding without awareness of it); (iv) *fujōkyō*, discriminate (pupils attain understanding while aware of it).

Kegon School or **School of the Flower Garland.** One of six schools of Buddhism established in Japan during the *Nara period (710–84)—see BUDDHISM IN JAPAN. The school originated in China where it was known as *Hua-yen, and was based on the massive *Avataṃsaka-sūtra* (see AVATAMSAKA LITERATURE). In doctrine the school presented a totalistic view of the universe wherein the Absolute (*ri*) is immanent in every individual entity (*ji*) and each entity mirrors the Absolute.

Keichu (scholar): see KOKUGAKU.

Keizan Jōkin (1268–1325). *Sōtō Zen master, the fourth patriarch (*soshigata) of the Sōtō-shu. He founded Sōji-ji, one of the two most important Sōtō monasteries (the other being *Eihei-ji), and after *Dōgen is regarded as one of the most important figures of the school. Among his writings, *Denkō-roku* (a collection of biographies and teachings) has had the most extensive influence—see KEIZAN OSHO.

Keizan Oshō Denkō-Roko (The Account by the Monk Keizan of the Transmission of the Light). A Zen Buddhist collection of stories concerning the transmission of the buddha-

*dharma in the *Sōtō school. The episodes have the enigmatic challenge of a *kōan.

Kekka-fusa (Jap., for Skt., *padmāsana). The lotus position in meditation. The legs are crossed, with right foot on left thigh, and left foot on right thigh, and hands, palms upward, on the heels of both feet.

Kelal (Heb., 'surround, include'). A summary in rabbinic Judaism of the essential meaning of *Torah, or of a series of halakoth in the *Mishnah. One of the ideals in teaching is to follow *derek qezarah*, the short(est) way. Rabbis, therefore, used to search for a statement, preferably a verse from Torah, which would summarize the purpose and meaning of the covenant. Thus *Aqiba called Leviticus 19. 18 'the great kelal in Torah'; Simeon b. Azzai identified Genesis 5. 1. Perhaps the best known examples are those of *Hillel ('Whatever you would not have people do to you, do not do to them') and of *Jesus (combining Deuteronomy 6. 4 f. and Leviticus 19. 18, in Mark 12. 28 ff.; cf. Matthew 7. 12, Luke 6. 31 for the Golden Rule in positive form).

Kelal Yisrael (Heb., 'the whole Jewish community'). The kinship of the Jewish community. See also *Keneset Yisrael.

Kemal, Mustafa: see OTTOMAN EMPIRE.

Kempe, Margery (*c*.1373–after 1433). Author of the *Book of Margery Kempe*. Born in Lynn, Norfolk, she married young and had fourteen children, but was increasingly drawn to a deeper religious experience. In 1413 she and her husband took vows of chastity. Sharply critical of contemporary religious corruption, she went on *pilgrimage and also visited *Julian of Norwich. Her life, as revealed in her *Book*, became one of an imaginatively close relationship to Christ, her heavenly spouse, expressed in visions and highly emotional (some say disordered) devotion, and also in auditions.

Kempis: see THOMAS À KEMPIS.

Kena Upaniṣad also ***Talavakāra Upaniṣad.*** One of the thirteen principal *Upaniṣads, belonging to the **Sāma Veda*. It deals with the longing of all living beings to transcend reason and become one with *Brahman.

Kencho-ji (monastery): see KAMAKURA.

Kendo (Jap., 'way of the sword'). The Zen way of attaining mastery over emotions, by swordplay and fencing.

Keneset Yisrael (Heb., 'the community of Israel'). The totality of the Jewish community. In *aggadic literature, 'Keneset Yisrael' is used as the personification of the Jewish people in the dialogue with God. The Keneset subsequently became the name for the Israeli parliament. Solomon *Schechter proposed the use of the term, translated as 'Catholic Israel', to pick out those elements on which the consensus of the Jewish people is agreed.

Kengyō (exoteric Buddhist teaching): see MIKKYŌ.

Kenite. A nomadic Middle Eastern tribe. Some scholars have maintained that the theology of *Moses was influenced by the Kenites through his father-in-law Jethro, and that this is the origin of the innovation of the god *Yahweh; this is the Kenite hypothesis.

Kenko, Yoshida (i.e., Yoshida Kenko): see YOSHIDA FAMILY.

Kenosis, kenotic theories. In Christian theology, formulas which seek to explain the *incarnation in terms of *Christ's self-'emptying' (Gk., *kenōsis*). The starting-point is Philippians 2. 5–11. Kenotic *christologies first appeared at the Reformation, but became current in the 19th cent. as a way of understanding how Jesus could have shared the limitations of human beings while remaining the omniscient, omnipotent Son of God.

Kensho (Jap., 'seeing nature'). The Zen experience of enlightenment, when one's own nature is seen for what it truly is, not to be differentiated from the buddha-nature. It is thus indistinguishable from *satori, but the latter is used of the *Buddha or of the Zen patriarchs, kensho of the initial experience of others which still needs to be deepened. The term also applies collectively to those who have attained this state, the wise (*genjo*).

Kenshō jōbutsu (realization of buddha-nature): see FUKASETSU.

Kensui (Jap., 'hammer and tongs'). The rigorous element in Zen training, the 'short, sharp, shock', much associated with *kōan method.

Kentan (Jap., 'looking at the *tan'). The morning survey by a Zen master of his pupils, to perceive their state of mind.

Kerbala (site of death of *al-Ḥusain): see KARBALĀ'.

Keriah. The rending of garments among the Jews as a sign of mourning.

Kerovah (pl. Kerovot). Jewish *piyyutim recited as part of the *'Amidah prayer. The kerovah recited in the morning service 'Amidah is known as the *kedushta*, while that said at the afternoon service is called the *shivata*.

Kerygma (Gk., 'preaching'). The basic Christian message of salvation through the death and resurrection of *Jesus, especially as preached by the earliest apostles (Acts 2. 14–39,

1 Corinthians 15. 3–11). It is contrasted to *didachē, 'instruction'.

Keś (uncut *hair): see FIVE KS.

Keśadhārī (Pañjābī, 'one who keeps long *hair'). Sikh whose hair (and beard) are uncut. One of the *Five Ks is the uncut hair (*keś*).

Keshub Chandra Sen: see SEN, KESHUB.

Keśin (Skt., 'long-haired'). Solitary *ascetics in early Indian religion, as in *Ṛg Veda* 10. 136. They were thus forerunners of the *śrāmaṇas, and important precursors of the ascetic emphasis among Jains.

Keswick Convention. An annual conference of *evangelical Christians. It began in 1875 with the conferences at Broadlands and Brighton. It transferred to Keswick, but 'Keswick' conferences may take place in other centres but will still have the purpose of trying to unify evangelical groups and teaching.

Ketav Rabbunat (letter of appointment): see RABBI.

Ket(h)er Malekuth (Heb., 'crown of royalty'). The mark of sovereignty of the Hebrew God. *Kether malekuth* is also the name of Solomon ibn *Gabirol's poem which is recited after the evening service on the *Day of Atonement.

Ket(h)er Torah (Heb., 'crown of Torah'). Jewish metaphor for learning. The term also refers to the ornament used to 'crown' the *Torah scroll in synagogues.

Ketubbah. Jewish *marriage document. The ketubbah sets out the financial obligations of the husband towards the wife. In the event of a divorce, it is stated that the woman will be given a certain amount of money.

Kevala (Skt.). 1. In Jainism, the kevala (-*jñāna), the absolute knowledge of isolation, the attribute of a *kevalin. Kevala refers to the state of isolation of the *jīva from the *ajīva, attained through ascetic practices which burn off one's *karma residues, releasing one from bondage to the cycle of death and rebirth.

2. In *Sāṁkhya-Yoga, an adjective meaning both 'isolated, exclusive, pure, uncompounded' and 'whole, entire, absolute, and perfect', referring to the state of *kāivalya and one who has attained it.

Kevalin (Skt.). 1. In Jainism, a saint or *tīrthaṅkara, one possessing the *kevala (-*jñāna), an *arhat.

2. In the Hindu *Bhāgavata-purāṇa*, a meditative ascetic devoted to the doctrine of the unity of *ātman and *brahman.

Ke-yi. Matching the meanings, a reference to the practice of Chinese Buddhist translators who matched Buddhist technical terms with Chinese concepts.

Khadīja. The first wife of *Muḥammad, and acknowledged as the first to believe in his message. She was a rich widow in *Mecca, who employed the young Muḥammad for several trading journeys, and subsequently married him, at which time it is said that she was about 40 and he 25. She bore him four female children, including *Fāṭima, and perhaps two sons, who, did not survive. The *ḥadīth inform us that Muḥammad declared her to be one of the four best women of Paradise, along with Maryam, Fāṭima, and the wife of Pharaoh.

Khafd (female circumcision): see CIRCUMCISION.

Khajurāho. Group of eighty-five temples in Madhya Pradesh, built from about 850–1150, dedicated to both Hindu and Jain devotions.

Khalīfa (Arab., *khalafa*, 'succeed'). A successor or representative, often transliterated as 'Caliph'.

1. In the Qur'ān, frequently used of those who enter into the blessings enjoyed by their ancestors (e.g. 6. 165; 24. 55; 27. 62); and specifically of *Adam as khalīfat *Allāh on earth (2. 20).

2. The successor(s) of the Prophet *Muḥammad. The first three Khulafā' were Abu Bakr, *'Umar, and *'Uthmān. But some thought that *'Alī, Muḥammad's nearest male relative, should have succeeded, and become the party (*shī'a*) of 'Ali. His claim prevailed briefly, and he was the fourth caliph; but other dynasties, 'Umayyad (661–750 CE), then 'Abbasid (750–1517) were established, and the Shī'a became minorities with their own rulers and successions (see IMĀM). The first four khulafā' are known as arRāshidūn, the upright or rightly guided. The Caliphate was assumed by the Ottoman Turkish rulers (sultāns) as a title, and it was abolished in the secularizing reforms of Kemal Atatürk in 1924.

Khālistān ('the land where the *khālsā rules', or 'the land of the pure'). The name given to the territory which some Sikhs would like to see established as a Sikh homeland. In some estimates, it would be greater than the present Puñjāb, and would include an outlet to the Indian Ocean.

Khālsā (Arab., 'khālis', 'pure'). Body of initiated Sikhs; also any true Sikh. The term denoted land in the Mughal emperor's direct possession, as opposed to lands owned by his lords. So, even before the time of Gurū *Gobind Siṅgh, khālsā could refer to groups of Sikhs whose loyalty was to the Gurū rather than to his *masands. However, according to tradition, the khālsā was instituted by Gobind Siṅgh on *Baisākhī (30 Mar.) 1699 CE, when the Gurū administered *khaṇḍe-dī-pāhul to the *pañj pyāre, followed by thousands more. He then enunciated a code of discipline (*rahit) to which all khālsā Sikhs must adhere. The khālsā was to be a casteless body of *Siṅghs and *Kaurs, outwardly distinguishable by the *five Ks. Khālsā Sikhs must be brave in battle and protect the needy. They must not commit adultery and must observe rules akin to those currently set down in the *Rahit Maryādā.

Following the death of Gurū Gobind Siṅgh, the khālsā struggled militarily for survival. With Mahārājā *Rañjīt Siṅgh's reign came the nearest realization of khālsā rule. In the late 19th cent. *Nāmdhārīs and *Akālīs reasserted the khālsā ideals which were challenged by moral degeneracy, Christian mission, and the *Ārya Samāj. The khālsā remain the guardians of orthodox Sikh principles.

Khamr (Arab., 'fermented drink, wine'). Intoxicants forbidden (*haram) in Islam. In Qur'ān 5. 90–1/93–4, wine is linked with gambling and divination with arrows as an abominable creation of Satan. Khamr was extended by *Muḥammad to include every intoxicant (not just wine), and trading in khamr is forbidden, as is its exchange as a gift. If it was proved that tobacco is always harmful, it would be prohibited; and many Muslims already regard it as in that category. In contrast, 47. 15/16 states that in the *Garden are 'rivers of wine, a joy to those who drink'. But in the Garden, those who are safe are beyond being diverted from their adoration of God. See also ALCOHOL; OMAR KHAYYAM.

Khanaqah (assembly place of derwishes; Fitzgerald's tavern): see OMAR KHAYYAM.

Khaṇḍ (Pañjābī, 'domain'). Stages of spiritual progress for a Sikh who is moving from *manmukh to *gurmukh: see SIKHISM.

Khaṇḍā (Pañjābī, 'sword'). Sikh symbol, two-edged sword. The khaṇḍā, bisecting a circle (*chakkar*) and flanked by two kirpāns, symbolizes the *khālsā, and appears on the *Niśān Sāhib.

Khandaka (division of Vinaya Piṭaka): see TRIPIṬAKA.

Khāṇḍava. In the **Mahābhārata*, the name of a forested tract of land given by *Dhṛtarāṣṭra to the *Pāṇḍavas; here the Pāṇḍavas built their splendid capital, Indraprastha.

Khaṇḍe-dī-pāhul (Pañjābī, 'sword initiation'). Sikh incorporation or initiation ceremony. On *Baisākhī day 1699 (according to tradition), Gurū *Gobind Siṅgh instituted khaṇḍe-dī-pāhul or initiation. When the original *pañj pyāre had volunteered their lives, Gobind Siṅgh stirred water with a khaṇḍā in an iron bowl, while reciting certain prayers (see below). His wife added *patāse* (sugar sweets). The Gurū then gave each of the pañj pyāre in turn five palmfuls of the *amrit (sweetened water) to drink and sprinkled it five times in their eyes and on their hair. Each time the initiate repeated, '*Vāhigurū jī kā *khālsā; vāhigurū jī kī *fateh'. The Gurū himself then received amrit from them in the same manner. He gave them and himself the new surname Siṅgh (lion) and instructed them as his khālsā to maintain the *five Ks and observe certain rules and prohibitions.

Sikhs who wish to follow their faith more strictly, those who have lapsed since taking amrit, and those adopting Sikhism are still initiated in this way by the pañj pyāre.

Khandha (aggregates of human composition): see SKANDHA.

Khaṇḍobā, Mallāri, Malhāri, Mārtaṇḍa, etc. A regional Hindu god, mainly worshipped in Mahārāṣṭra and Karṇāṭaka. His central shrine is the hill-temple of Jejurī (near Puṇe), but there are many other temples scattered over the whole area. His worship is performed by non-*brahman priests (*guruvas*), and his devotees also are predominantly non-brahman.

Kharatara Gaccha: see DĀDĀ GURŪS.

Kharijites (Arab., *kharaja*, 'go out'). Early schismatics in the Muslim community (*'umma). The details of their origin are obscure, but are connected by Muslim historians with the arbitration at the battle of Siffīn (see ʿALĪ B. ABĪ TĀLIB). Protesting that 'judgement belongs to God alone' (*lā ḥukma illā li-'llāhi*), they rejected both ʿAlī and *Muʿawīyya, and began a fierce and often brutal rebellion. Defeated by ʿAlī at Nahrawān in 658 (AH 38), they nevertheless persisted into the *ʿAbbāsid caliphate (and down to the present day as the ʿIbādiyya, a religious movement). Holding a strict view that a Muslim who sins grievously has become *murtadd (apostate), they reject all (so-called) caliphs (*khalīfa) except *Abu Bakr and *ʿUmar (and the first six years of *ʿUthmān), and believe that any Muslim recognized as irreproachable can become Imām, known as *Amīr al-Muʾminīn*, 'Leader of the Faithful'.

Khatm al-anbiyya/al-wilāyah: see SEAL OF THE PROPHETS.

Khatrī (cognate, 'Kshatriya'). A Pañjābī *zāt* (*caste). Gurū *Nānak was born to a Hindu

Khatrī family and married a Khatrī wife according to caste practice. Many Khatrī Sikhs are *sahajdhārī, and *marriage with Hindu Khatrīs is common.

Khazars. National group, originally of S. Russia, who professed Judaism. The Khazars were an independent nation of E. Europe between the 7th and 10th cents. CE. They converted to Judaism *c.*740 CE. The nation disappeared by the 11th cent., but as late as 1309, Hungarian Roman Catholics were forbidden to marry people described as Khazars. See also JUDAH HALEVI, who took the story of the conversion as the framework for his exposition of Judaism in *Sefer ha-Kuzari*.

Khemā (5th cent. BCE). The perfect or model Buddhist bhikhṣuni (nun; see BHIKHṢU) according to the Buddha. She was a queen of Bimbisāra, of great beauty; but through the Buddha's teaching, she realized the transience of the body and achieved the condition of *arhat.

Khenpo (abbr. for *mkhan-po*): see ABBOT.

Khiḍr. In Islam, the mystical guide. He is at once human and angelic, mundane and celestial. Authorities such as *al-Tabarī and al-Nawawī consider him immortal. He is associated with the colour green, the highest of colours in Islamic cosmology. The starting-point for traditions about Khiḍr is the account in the Qur'ān (18. 60–82), in which the prophet *Moses meets Khiḍr and they set out on a journey. According to the *Sūfīs, Khiḍr is the immortal guide possessing wisdom and powers beyond human understanding. He can manifest himself at many places at the same time, become invisible at will, and fly through the air.

Khirqa (Arab., 'rag'). A distinctive woollen or sheepskin garment worn by the *Sūfīs. It is conferred by the spiritual guide in token of his approval for an initiate to enter the mystic path.

Khitan (male circumcision): see CIRCUMCISION.

Khoja (Nizaris in India): see ISMA'ĪLĪYA.

Khomeini, Ayatollah (Shi'ite leader): see KHUMAYNI, RUḤ ALLAH.

Khomiakov, Alexis Stepanovich (1804–60). Russian lay theologian. He was at the centre of the Slavophil movement and was very influential, though his writings are mainly occasional. He saw the Orthodox Church as preserving the truest form of Christianity, finding its unity in *sobornost', a togetherness brought about in the Church by the *Holy Spirit, deeper than the authoritarian unity of the *Papacy or the individualist fragmentation of the *Protestants.

Khrafstras (evil agents): see ANGRA MAINYU.

Khsathra (one of the Holy Immortals): see AMESA SPENTAS.

Khuddaka-nikāya (Pāli, 'short collection'). The fifth part of the Sutta-, or Sūtra-piṭaka, in the Buddhist Pāli *canon, containing fifteen 'short' sections: (i) *Khuddaka-pātha*, rules for ceremonies, etc.; (ii) **Dhammapada*, 426 verses on basic teaching; (iii) *Udāna*, 80 sayings of the *Buddha; (iv) *Itivuttaka*, on moral questions; (v) *Sutta-nipāta*; (vi) *Vimānavatthu*, 83 legends of devas to show how to attain reappearance as a *deva; (vii) *Petavatthu*, on reappearance as a hungry ghost; (viii) *Thera-gāthā*, 107 songs (*gāthā*) ascribed to the monks of old; (ix) *Therī-gāthā*, 73 ascribed to nuns of old; (x) *Jātaka*; (xi) *Niddesa*, commentary on (v); (xii) *Patisambhidā-magga*, analysis of philosophical issues; (xiii) *Apadāna*, stories of renowned monks and nuns in previous appearances; (xiv) *Buddhavamsa*, stories of previous Buddhas; (xv) *Cariya-piṭaka*, *jātaka stories showing how the Buddha reached the ten perfections (*pāramitā).

Khul' (divorce initiated by woman): see MARRIAGE AND DIVORCE (ISLAM).

Khumayni, Ruḥ Allah (1902–89). Religious leader among *Ithna 'Ashariyya (Twelver) Shi'ite Muslims, and figurehead of the Islamic Revolution in Iran. He was born in Khumayn and followed a path of Islamic education in various centres including *Qom. He became both mujtāhid and *ayatollah. He was briefly arrested for opposing the Shah, and on his release continued to oppose the government, especially for its links with the USA and (he claimed) with Israel. In 1964 he was exiled, settling until 1978 in Najaf, in Iraq, when he was again expelled, settling this time in France. He returned to Iran in triumph on 1 Feb. 1979, after the flight of the Shah. He assumed the position of leader of the revolution. His strong understanding of authority had deep roots in the Shi'a understanding of the *Imām, and Khumayni pressed into new territory in his exercise of his powers (see AYATOLLAH). Despite the failures of the war with Iraq and his own disappointment at the ceasefire, his popularity remained to the end; and his *fatwā against Salman Rushdie and his book, *The Satanic Verses*, was accepted widely in the Muslim world.

Khurasani Sufism: see SŪFĪS.

Khuṭba (Arab., *khataba*, 'preach'). Sermon delivered in the *mosque during the Muslim weekly assembly (*jum'a), in celebration of the two festivals (*ʿĪd), and on other special occasions.

Khwāja Bāqī Bi'llah (Naqshbandi Shaykh): see AḤMAD SIRHINDĪ.

Khwarr (destiny): see FRAVASI.

Ki (Jap., 'potential'). One who is potentially able to receive the *Buddha's teaching; or to become a *bodhisattva or buddha; hence, 'a human being'.

Kibbutz. Voluntary agricultural collective in *Erez Israel. The first kibbutz to be founded was En Harol in 1921, and the founding of kibbutzim (pl.) has had an important part in the pioneering settlement of the land.

Kibbutz galuyyot: see GALUT.

Kiddush (Heb., 'sanctification'). *Prayer recited over a cup of wine to sanctify the *Sabbath or *festivals. It is forbidden to eat on a Sabbath or festival until the Kiddush has been recited.

Kiddush ha-Shem (Heb., 'sanctification of the divine name'). The glorification of the God of Israel, especially by remaining steadfast in faith. The *rabbis taught that God's name could be sanctified in three specific ways: *prayer, excellent conduct, and *martyrdom. Martyrdom has always been seen as the ultimate expression of Kiddush ha-Shem. Martyrdom in the Jewish tradition is obligatory, rather than break the laws of *idolatry, unchastity, or murder. The opposite is ḥillul ha-Shem, 'desecration of the Name', which involves consideration of how an action will be regarded in the gentile world. It includes the offence of erasing God's name following Deuteronomy 12. 3 f.). See Index, Martyrs (Jewish).

Kidō Chigu: see HSÜ-T'ANG CHIH-YÜ.

Kie (Jap. 'take refuge in'). The basic move of faith in Japanese Buddhism. It extends beyond *dharma (see THREE JEWELS), and may be a commitment to a teacher, *bodhisattva, etc.

Kierkegaard, Søren (1813–55). Denmark's best-known and widely influential contributor to modern religious thought. For his psychological and philosophical writings he is widely regarded as the father of *existentialism. A prolific and playfully elusive writer, Kierkegaard indicates in *The Point of View for my Work as an Author* that all his work is dominated by the single issue of how to become a Christian in Christendom, where one automatically assumes oneself to be a good Christian if one is simply a good citizen. In all his writings on the topic, Kierkegaard stressed that to become a (true) Christian entails personal decision and individual commitment, born of risk in the face of 'objective uncertainty'. He attacked the idea of Christendom at first indirectly and then, in the last year or so of his life, increasingly directly and publicly.

Kigen Kikō (Zen style of teaching): see MATSU.

Kikan-Kōa (type of kōan): see KŌAN.

Kilesa, Kleśa (Pāli, Skt., 'defilement'). In Buddhist doctrine, moral and intellectual faults. There is no formal list in the Suttas but the **Abhidharma* lists ten: greed (*lobha), ill will (*dosa), delusion (*moha), conceit (*māna), speculative views (*diṭṭhi), sceptical doubt (*vicikicchā*), mental torpor (*thīna*), restlessness (*uddhacca*), lack of shame (*ahirika*), and lack of moral dread (*anottappa*).

Kill the Buddha: see LIN-CHI I-HSÜAN.

Kimbangu, Simon: see KIMBANGUISM.

Kimbanguism. The largest independent Christian movement in Black Africa. It derives from Simon Kimbangu (1889–1951), a *Baptist mission catechist, whose preaching and healing in the lower Congo started a mass movement in 1921. His subsequent death-sentence for alleged sedition was commuted to life imprisonment, after British Baptist missionaries had appealed to the Belgian king. The new movement continued underground, despite mass deportations by the colonial government. In 1957 it secured toleration and in 1959 legal recognition as Église de Jésus-Christ sur la Terre par le Prophète Simon Kimbangu (EJCSK, The Church of Jesus Christ through the Prophet Simon Kimbangu), under the leadership of Kimbangu's son, Joseph Diangienda (b. 1918). N'kamba, Kimbangu's birthplace and final burial place, is a pilgrimage centre. There have been secessions and other Kimbanguist groups with different emphases, but all look to Simon Kimbangu as an idealized founder and martyr figure.

Kimḥi, David, or **Radak** (*c.*1160–1235). Jewish grammarian and exegete. Kimḥi was the author of the grammatical treatise *Mikhlol* (1532); he wrote commentaries on the books of Chronicles, Genesis, the prophetic books, and the Psalms. He was a strong supporter of *Maimonides, and the correspondence between Kimḥi and Judah ibn Alfakhar on Maimonides' philosophy has been preserved.

Kimō-tokaku (Jap., 'hair of a tortoise and horn of a hare'). Zen expression for belief in something that does not exist, especially in the existence of an independent self.

Kinah. Heb. mourning poem. Kinot (pl.) were traditionally spoken over the dead (e.g. Genesis 23.2) and at times of national calamity. Many anthologies have been produced over the years.

King, Martin Luther, Jr. (1929–68). American *Baptist minister and leader of the civil rights movement. He was born in Atlanta, Georgia, and attended Moorhouse College and Crozier Theological Seminary where he was in search of a theology commensurate with his understanding of society through sociology. He gained a Ph.D. at Boston University School of Theology, where he became acquainted with the writings of *Gāndhī. In 1954 he became pastor of a Baptist church in Montgomery, Alabama, where he became involved in the boycott of the city's segregated buses, taking leadership of the campaign. In 1955, such segregation was declared unconstitutional. King founded the Southern Christian Leadership Conference to draw together campaigns against discrimination, emphasizing non-violence. Somewhat disappointed at the general apathy, he wrote his 'Letter from Birmingham Jail' in 1963, when he was arrested during the massive demonstrations in Birmingham, Alabama.

King's campaigns culminated in the Washington march in 1963 and in his address, 'I have a dream'. He was assassinated in Memphis, Tennessee, in April 1968. The USA now observes 15 Jan. (his birthday) as a federal holiday.

Kingdom of God. A symbol or concept in ancient Judaism (though more usually 'kingdom of heaven') especially prominent in the preaching of Jesus. In rabbinic literature the idea of keeping the *Torah was likened to taking upon oneself the 'yoke of the kingdom'. In Jesus' preaching the kingdom of God (or equivalent 'kingdom of heaven') was a central theme (Mark 1. 15; John 3. 5) but its meaning is elusive. Usually it is said to belong to the future (e.g. Matthew 6. 10; Mark 14. 25); sometimes it appears to be already present (Luke 11. 20); most often it is spoken of in *parables ('The kingdom of God is as if a man should scatter seed . . .', Mark 4. 26 ff.).

The identification of the kingdom of God with the Church was made by *Augustine, who opposed it to 'the kingdom of the Devil'. Following him, medieval writers tended to equate it with the visible hierarchical church. Modern liberal theologians tend to speak of the kingdom of God generally as that state of human affairs in accord with God's will.

Kings, Books of. Two books belonging to the Former Prophets in the Hebrew Bible and to the historical books of the Christian Old Testament. In RC edns. of the Bible they are usually called 3 and 4 Kings, titles deriving from the *Septuagint.

Kingship, Chinese. Traditional Chinese concepts of kingship were sacralized, the political, moral, and economic powers of the emperor all having a religious dimension. The emperor was seen as pivot and sustainer of the cosmic order, ruler of the four quarters of the world and mediator between *Heaven and earth. As the 'Son of Heaven', he lived in a palace complex called the Purple Forbidden City, modelled on the Purple Protected Enclosure, where the God of Heaven (*Shang-Ti) dwelt in the circumpolar region of the sky.

Kingship, Sacral. In Judaism, the beliefs associated with the ruler chosen and supported by God. The king was God's chosen, his anointed one (*messiah), the man sanctified by God's spirit. The relationship between God and the king was perceived as that of father and son (see Psalm 89. 27), but at the same time there was no suggestion that the king was anything but mortal. With the destruction of the Northern Kingdom in 721 BCE and the Southern Kingdom in 587 BCE, kingship came to an end, and hopes vested in God's anointed one were transferred to a future Messiah. The positions, rights, and limitations of the king are elaborated in the *Mishnah (*Sanh.* 2. 2–5).

Kinot (lamentations): see KINAH.

Kippah: see HEAD, COVERING OF (JUDAISM); YARMULKE.

Kirchenkampf (Germ., 'church struggle'). The conflict between German churches and the Nazi state. The *Barmen Declaration of 1934 by the *Confessing Church rejected any outside control of the church, and succeeded in denying the government the docile collaboration of the church. The Confessing Church, however, was progressively weakened by disagreements in its own ranks about co-operation with the official Minister for Church Affairs; by tightening restrictions on church funds and paper for publishing and the conscription of pastors; and by the arrest of leaders like M. *Niemöller and D. *Bonhoeffer. Even so, the opposition mounted by the Protestant churches to Hitler seems small, a fact acknowledged in the 'Declaration of Guilt' made by Confessing Church leaders at Stuttgart in 1945.

The RC Church, seeing an ally against 'Bolshevism' in the Nazi government, quickly came to terms with it in a *Concordat of 1933. This was soon dishonoured (e.g. by the suppression of Catholic schools), and in 1937 Pope Pius XII issued a strongly anti-Nazi *encyclical *Mit brennender Sorge* (with burning anxiety). The Concordat was never rescinded, however, and no organized RC resistance emerged, although there were individual heroes.

Kirpā (help from God): see SIKHISM.

Kirpān (dagger/sword): see FIVE KS.

Kīrtan (Hindī, Pañjābī, 'devotional singing', from *kīrat* = 'praise'). Hindu and Sikh corporate hymn-singing, often to instrumental accompaniment. It is the second stage of *bhakti according to *Bhāgavata Purāṇa*.

Kīrtimukha. In Hinduism, the mask of a demon placed above the door of the temples of *Śiva to ward off intruders.

Kismet (Turkish from Arab., *qisma*, 'share, portion'). The allocation of whatever occurs, hence the acceptance in Islam that God determines all things: see QADAR.

Kissako (Jap., 'drink tea'). Zen saying, derived from *Chao-chou Ts'ung-shen, to emphasize that Zen is not divorced from the ordinary process of life.

Kiss of death: see DEATH, KISS OF.

Kiss of peace (Lat., *pax*). Mutual greeting during the Christian *eucharist, perhaps based on the command of Christ to make peace before bringing one's gift to the altar (Matthew 5. 23 f.).

Kiswa (Arab., 'clothing' or 'covering'). Curtain of cloth for the *Ka'ba, the central shrine of Islam, in *Mecca. The kiswa is prepared each year in Egypt.

Kitabake Chikafusa (1293–1354). Leading advocate of Shinto revival. He lived during the confused period of conflict in Japan when there were two rival courts in the north and south (1336–92). He wrote to express his vision of a legitimate imperial line ruling over all Japan, and to reinforce the view of Ise Shinto (see HONJISUIJAKU) that Shinto is superior to the invading religions from China and India. *Jinnō Shōtō-ki* (Records of the Succession of the Divine Rulers) begins: 'Japan is the land of the *kami. Our heavenly ancestor, Kunitokotachi, laid its first foundations, and *Amaterasu, the sun goddess, left the land to her descendants to rule over it for ever. This is true only of our country. Nothing like it can be found in foreign lands.'

Kitamura Sayo (founder of movement): see TENSHŌ KŌTAI JINGŪ KYŌ.

Kitawala. A widespread movement in Central Africa, especially 1908–30, based originally on contacts in S. Africa with *Jehovah's Witnesses, then known as the Watchtower Bible and Tract Society (hence *ki-tawala*, an Africanization of 'tower'). Elliot Kamwana Chirwa (1872–1956) brought the teachings to his native Malawi in 1908. His strong *millenarian and anti-colonial overtones soon led to his arrest and deportation. His followers took the movement to Zambia, where it was especially strong in the 1920s. The movement spread also into Zaïre and southern Tanzania.

Kit(t)el (Yid., 'gown'). White garment worn by some *Ashkenazi Jews for special services. White symbolizes purity, and at one time the kit(t)el was worn every *Sabbath.

Kiyomizu (temple): see KYŌTO.

Kleśas (Skt., 'pain', 'affliction'). In *Yoga philosophy, the five causes of human affliction. *Patañjali's **Yoga-sūtra* (ii. 3) enumerates the kleśas as: (i) *avidyā, 'ignorance', (ii) *asmitā*, 'egoism', (iii) *rāga, 'attachment', (iv) *dveṣa*, 'aversion', and (v) *abhiniveśa*, 'the fear of death'. These causes of human suffering are all rooted in the first kleśa, ignorance, which is defined (iii. 5) as 'seeing the impermanent as permanent, the impure as pure, the painful as joyful, and the not-Self as the Self'.

For the Buddhist equivalent, see KILESA.

Klong-chen Rab-'byams-pa (often simplified to Longchenpa, 1308–63). Major Tibetan scholar of the *Nyingma-pa. He was of particular importance in the transmission of *dzogchen (Great Perfection). After a thorough education in the existing traditions, he became disillusioned with this and sought enlightenment as a pupil of Kumārarāja (1266–1343), a renowned wandering ascetic who was a noted exponent of dzogchen. For a time, Klong-chen Rab-'byams-pa was abbot of *Samyé, but he could not avoid the political conflicts of the time and spent a period as an exile in (modern) Bhutan. He wrote many works, especially *The Seven Treasures* (*mdzod-bdun*) and *Trilogy on Rest* (*ngal-gso skor-gsum*). His own teachings were reorganized and promulgated by Jigme Lingpa ('Jigs-med gling-pa, 1730–98), whence they became widely influential and were transmitted especially through the *Rimé movement.

Knights of Malta: see TEMPLARS.

Knowledge. A valued, but somewhat ambiguous, human competence in most religions. *Gnosis* (Gk., 'knowledge') as insight into the deepest mysteries flourished in the Hellenistic world, leading to both mystery religions (with initiates alone gaining access to healing or saving knowledge) and to *gnostic religions. Christian history unfolds a tension between *fideism and the exploration of the universe as God's creation, out of which the natural sciences eventually emerged. In Islam, knowledge receives the highest endorsement (see ʿILM); yet even here, knowledge in contrast to behaviour in conformity with *Qurʾān and *sharīʿa is suspect.

In Indian religions, the tension is equally evident. *Vidyā is the all-important counter-availing value. Ignorance (*avidya) is the deepest fault and impediment which has to be dealt with if any progress is to be made toward a higher goal. Thus *jñāna-marga (the way of knowledge) is one of the three ways (*mārga) leading, in Hinduism, toward enlightenment and release (*mokṣa). Avidya is countered by *vidyā, *samjña*, *prajña. Yet it is clearly recognized that there are different levels of knowledge, of which the earlier (e.g. knowledge of texts) is necessary, but comes to be seen as a kind of ignorance, compared with direct knowledge of *Brahman.

Knox, John (1505–72). Leader of the *Reformation in Scotland. As preacher at St Andrews he was captured by the French, and whilst serving as a galley slave, used the time to produce an edn. of Henry Balnave's *Treatise on Justification by Faith*. He refused the bishopric of Rochester, and on Mary's accession fled to the Continent where he met the Swiss *Reform leaders. His *First Blast of the Trumpet against the Monstrous Regiment of Women* (1558) argued that female sovereignty contravened natural and divine law. In 1559 Knox returned to Scotland, devoting his time to preaching and writing. He drew up the *Scottish Confession*, shared in the compilation of *The First Book of Discipline*, and wrote his *Treatise on Predestination* (1560). He also took a major part in the compilation of the *Book of Common Order* (1556–64), the service book in use in Scotland until 1645. Knox's memoirs are preserved in his *History of the Reformation of Religion with the realm of Scotland*, first published in 1587 and immediately suppressed.

Kō. Jap. for *kalpa.

Ko. Korean for *dukkha.

Kōan (Chin., *Kung-an*; 'public announcement', or 'precedent for public use'). A fundamental practice in Zen training, challenging the pupil through a question, or a phrase or answer to a question, which presents a paradox or puzzle. A kōan cannot be understood or answered in conventional terms: it requires a pupil to abandon reliance on ordinary ways of understanding in order to move into or towards enlightenment. The origins of kōan are uncertain, but predate Nan-yüan Hui-yung (d. 930 CE) to whom the first use is attributed. The earliest surviving collection is in the writings of Fen-yang Shan-chao (*Fen-yang lu*; Jap., *Fun'yōroku*), including a series of 100 kōan questions (*chieh-wen*; Jap., *kitsumon*). Fen-yang was of the *Rinzai school, and the use of kōans is particularly associated with Rinzai (*kanna zen), but is not exclusive to it. Under Fen-yang's successor, Shih-shuang, Li Tsu-hsü produced *Tenshō Kōtōroku*, one of the five foundation chronicles of Zen in the Sung period, containing many kōans. Among Shih-shuang's pupils, Wu-tsu Fa-yen extended the short, sharp kōan to its height. Fa-yen's main pupil, *Yüan-wu K'o-ch'in (1036–1135) was a vital figure in developing kōan method in this period, completing the *Blue Cliff Record* (Chin., *Pi-yen-lu*; Jap., *Hekigan-roku*, for which see HSÜEH-TOU CH'UNG TSIEN).

The second largest collection of the Sung period is *Ts'ung-jung lu* (Jap., *Shōyōroku*), assembled by Wan-sung Hsing-hsiu (1166–1246). It was followed (1229) by the *Wu-men-kuan* (Jap., *Mumonkan*), edited by Wu-men Hui-k'ai (1183–1260). About 1,700 kōans survive, of which about 600 are in active use.

In Rinzai, five types of kōan are identified: (i) *hosshin-kōan*, to create awareness of identity with buddha-nature (*bussho); (ii) *kikan-kōan*, to create ability nevertheless to discern distinctions within non-distinction; (iii) *gonsen-kōan*, creating awareness of the deep meaning of the sayings of the masters; (iv) *nantō-kōan*, grappling with the hardest to solve; (v) *go-i-kōan*: when the other four have been worked through, the insight gained is tested once more. See Index, Kōans.

See also MU; WATO.

Kobō-daishi (posthumous title of Kūkai): see KŪKAI.

Kobutsu (Jap., 'old buddha'). Originally a *buddha of an earlier age, but also a Zen term, like *kobusshin*, for a deeply enlightened master.

Kōchi Sanzō. Title of *Amoghavajra.

Kōfuku-ji (temple-complex): see NARA BUDDHISM.

Kogidō ('Hall of Ancient Meanings'): see ITŌ JINSAI.

Kogoshūi (Gleanings from Ancient Stories). An account of Japanese mythology and early history according to the Imbe clan, a hereditary *Shinto priestly family. It was composed and presented to Emperor Heizei in 807 CE, by Imbe no Hironari as a protest against a rival priestly family, the Nakatomi, who had increasingly eclipsed the Imbe. The author's overall intention is to picture the ancestor of the Imbe as equal in dignity and importance with that of the Nakatomi. While containing much the same material as the *Kojiki and the *Nihongi*, the *Kogoshūi* preserves a number of interesting pieces of information that are not found elsewhere.

Koheleth: see ECCLESIASTES.

Kohen (priest): see PRIEST.

Kohler, Kaufmann (1843–1926). Prominent US *Reform *rabbi. Recommended by Abraham *Geiger, he became rabbi of Temple Beth El in Detroit in 1869, and in 1879 he took over Temple Beth El of New York from his father-in-law, David *Einhorn. His collection of sermons *Backward or Forward* (1885) led to the convening of the Pittsburgh Conference of Reform rabbis, and in 1903, he was appointed President of the *Hebrew Union College. His best known book was *Jewish Theology* (1918).

Ko Hung (*c.*280–340 CE). Chinese *alchemist (according to J. Needham, the most outstanding in this field), best known as the author of *Pao-p'u tzu* ([Book of the] Master Who Embraces Simplicity). This consists of two parts: (i) tells of 'gods and genii, prescriptions and medicines, ghosts and marvels, transformations, maintenance of life, extension of years, exorcising evils, and banishing misfortune' (Ware tr., p. 17), and belongs to the Taoist tradition; (ii) gives 'an account of success and failure in human affairs and of good and evil in public affairs', and belongs to the Confucian school. He also wrote the *Shen hsien chuan* (Records of Gods and Immortals) and many other works.

Kojiki (Records of Ancient Matters). The earliest account of Japanese mythology and early history in three books. Compiled in 712 CE, it focuses on the origin of kingship in the sacred history as narrated in myths, and on the 'smooth' transition from myth to actual history. Emperor Temmu (672–86) initiated the process of compilation. However, it was not until 712 that the work was compiled into the *Kojiki* by another scribe in the imperial court, Ō no Yasumaro, and presented to Empress Gemmei (707–15).

Book i unfolds what is usually known as Japanese myths.

Book ii opens with the story narrating how Jimmu, the great-grandson of Ninigi and Japan's legendary first emperor, establishes the imperial dynasty at Yamato in central Japan.

Book iii covers the period from the reign of Emperor Nintoku to that of Empress Suiko (593–628), presenting the genealogies of the emperors and their legendary stories. Cf. **Nihongi*.

Kokka Shintō (Jap., 'state Shinto'). In Japan, the system of state-supported Shinto shrines, ceremonies, and education which the government administered from the early Meiji period until the end of the Second World War. The Meiji government attempted to provide a sense of national and cultural identity by restoring the ancient ideal of 'the unity of religious rites and government (*saisei itchi*)'. Shrine Shinto was separated from Buddhism and combined with the Shinto of the Imperial House. At the core of Kokka Shintō was the belief in the divinity of the emperor and the uniqueness of Japan's national polity (*kokutai). Kokka Shintō was abolished by the Allied Powers in 1945 in their Shinto Directive which prohibited the control, support, and dissemination of Shinto by the government. This separation of government and religion was subsequently incorporated into the constitution of Japan.

Kokoro. Jap. reading of the Chin. character *hsin*, the fundamental and interior nature of a person, thus virtually equivalent to buddha-nature (*bussho, *buddhatā).

Kokorozashi (Jap.). The fundamental disposition of will and longing to find truth and enlightenment.

Kokugaku (Jap.), National Learning or Japanese Studies. Its foremost task was to study ancient Japanese literature by means of scrutinizing the exact meaning of ancient words, and for that reason, Kokugaku as an academic discipline can be defined as a school that relied on philology as its methodological tool to bring out the ethos of Japanese tradition freed from foreign ideas and thoughts.

The Hirata School in the late Tokugawa period reckoned *Kada no Azumaro (1669–1736), *Kamo no Mabuchi (1697–1769), *Motoori Norinaga (1730–1801), and Hirata Atsutane (1776–1843) as the four major exponents of the Kokugaku Movement. The honour as its founder, however, would go to Keichū, a Shingon priest and scholar, who introduced a new academic standard for the study of ancient Japanese literature. See Index, Kokugaku.

Kokushi: see KOKUTAI.

Kokushittsū (Jap., 'can of black paint'). The condition in Zen meditation of total darkness before the light suddenly breaks through.

Kokutai (Jap., 'national polity'). Among nationalists of the late 19th and early 20th cents., a term referring to the Shinto-Confucian idealization of the Japanese nation-state. Japanese society was compared to a large family, with the emperor at the head as the benevolent guiding hand and patriarch. As such, the imperial throne served as the focus for the patriotic, nationalist fervour of the period prior to the Second World War. *Kokushi* (Chin., *Kuo-shih*) 'teacher of the nation' is the title of a Buddhist who teaches the emperor, because the nation is summarized in his person. *Ben'en was the first to receive the title in Japan (posthumously in 1312).

Kol Bo (Heb., 'everything within'). Jewish book of *halakhic rulings. *Kol Bo* was probably composed at the end of the 13th cent. CE.

Kol Nidrei (Aram., 'all vows'). Prayer which begins the Jewish *Day of Atonement evening service. The prayer is customarily repeated three times, and declares that all personal vows made rashly to God which have not been fulfilled are now cancelled. The prayer has frequently been misunderstood by gentiles who have argued that it demonstrates that Jewish promises are worthless, but in fact the *halakhah imposes severe limitations on which vows can be cancelled.

Komagaku (Korean-derived music): see MUSIC.

Koma-inu (Jap., 'dog of Koguryô'). A legendary beast resembling a lion, said to have entered Japan from the ancient Korean kingdom of Koguryô (Koma). Statues of the animal, popularly conceived as a guardian figure, are commonly found in pairs at entrances to shrine and temple precincts and in front of or attached to buildings themselves to ward off evil.

Kōmei-tō (party of clean government): see SŌKA GAKKAI.

Komusō (Jap., 'emptiness monk'). A monk of the Fuke School (see KAKUSHIN) who wanders through the countryside playing the flute. They wear large hats, shaped like beehives, to hide their faces and preserve their anonymity, pointing to truth beyond themselves. In self-disregarding attitude, they are often regarded as *holy fools.

Konārak (temple): see SŪRYA.

Konchok Gyalpo (founder of Sakya): see SAKYA.

Kong. Korean for *śūnyatā, the void, that which is empty of characteristics.

Kongō-kai Mandara (Diamond Maṇḍala): see TAIZO-KAI MANDARA.

Kōnin (Jap. name): see HUNG-JEN.

Konkōkyō (Golden Light). A movement founded in Japan in 1859 by *Kawate Bunjiro (1814–83). Although registered by the Japanese government as a Shinto sect, it represents in many respects a departure from Shintoism. Not only does it place the emphasis on individual as opposed to group salvation, but also, unlike Shintoism, it believes in the existence of a mediator, in the person of its leader, between God (known as Tenchi Kane no Kami, the parent Spirit of the Universe) and humans. Moreover, it rejects such Shinto practices as exorcism and divination, and attaches great importance to social welfare activities.

Kontakion (hymn): see AKATHISTOS.

Kook, Abraham Isaac (1865–1935). First *Ashkenazi *Chief Rabbi of Israel. Kook emigrated to Israel in 1904 and became Ashkenazi Chief Rabbi in 1921. He maintained that the return to *Zion was a step towards the beginning of the divine redemption. He was a prolific writer, and his books combine learning with mystical insight. Among his books are *Orot ha-Kodesh* (3 vols., 1963/4), *Iggerot ha-Re'ayah* (3 vols., 1962/5), and *Orot ha-Teshivah* (1955; Eng., 1968).

Koran: see QUR'ĀN.

Korban. Jewish practice of *sacrificing (or dedicating) property to God. The practice of pledging all possessions to the *Temple is mentioned in the New Testament. It died out with the destruction of the Temple in 70 CE.

Korean religion. Korea, lying as it does between China and Japan, was of such importance in the transmission of Chinese culture to Japan that its own contribution is easy to overlook. Even now, after many conversions to various forms of Christianity (and the production of its own religion under Sun Myung *Moon), elements of its own, *shaman-based, religion persist. *Mudangs* (female shamans) are most common, but there are also some males, often blind, known as *paksus*. The Buddhist predominance in Korea began in 372. The second kingdom, that of Paekche (often in the later Japanese texts a synonym for Korea), sent to China for instructors, and in 545, the king sent the first missionary to Japan. The third kingdom, Silla, was the last to accept Buddhism but became the most stalwart. Of particular importance in the early centuries was *Wŏnhyo. The country was united by the Silla kingdom, and under the Koryŏ dynasty (935–1392), Buddhism attained its greatest influence. The great endeavour of creating a Korean version of the major Buddhist texts was undertaken: see KOREAN TRIPIṬAKA. Although many temples were built of wood and have been burnt, some remains of the building activity of this period have survived. Notable is the cave, Sŏkkul-am, at the summit of Mount Pulguk-sa, containing an image of the Buddha illuminated by the rising sun. Yi Sŏng-gye overthrew the Koryŏ dynasty, establishing the Yi dynasty (1392–1910), and blaming the decay of the previous period on the excessive reliance on Buddhism (despite the efforts of such reformers as *Chinul). He and his successors endorsed Confucianism, especially as taught by

*Chu Hsi, and reduced the status of Buddhism. In 1422, the many Buddhist sects were reduced to two schools, those of Sun (i.e. Ch'an or Zen) and Kyo (active in the world). Roman Catholicism entered Korea during the 18th cent., suffering considerable persecution. It was known as *Sōhak* ('Western Learning') and evoked *Tonghak* ('Eastern Learning'). This was founded by Ch'oe Che-u (1824–66), who had a vision of Sangche (i.e. *Shang-ti) which led to a miraculous cure. Although Ch'oe Che-u was executed, the movement grew and became known as Ch'ŏndo-gyo/Ch'ŏndo-kyo ('Sect of the Way of Heaven'). By 1893, the numbers were so great that they petitioned the king for official recognition. When no action was taken, they began campaigns for the removal of foreign influence; an appeal to the Chinese for help against them led to Japanese intervention against the Chinese, thus beginning the Sino-Japanese war (1894). Meanwhile, Protestant Christianity (especially *Presbyterians) had been growing even faster, and to some extent allied itself with Korean opposition to outside interference. Buddhism itself underwent a revival under Pak Chungbin who established *Won Buddhism. Despite the split of Korea and the pressures for each 'side' to outperform the other in secular terms, Korea remains a country in which religion plays a major part. See Index, Korean religion.

Korean Tripiṭaka or **Tripiṭaka Koreana.** A collection of Buddhist texts from the Koryŏ period (935–1392). Its first edition was completed during the reign of King Munjong (1047–82) but destroyed at the time of the Mongolian invasion of Korea in 1231. Under the patronage of King Kojong (1214–59) the woodblock carving of the second edition was undertaken in 1236 and completed in 1251; one of the most comprehensive collections of Buddhist texts up to that time, this is now stored at the Haein monastery on Mount Kaya.

Kośa (Skt., 'covering'). The five coverings of the *ātman in Hinduism—see e.g. **Taittirīya Upaniṣad*: (i) the outer and furthest from ātman, annamaya-kośa, the material covering of food; (ii) prāṇamaya-kośa, the vital covering, manifest as breath; (iii) manomaya-kośa, the mental covering; (iv) vijñanamaya-kośa, the intelligence covering; (v) ānandamaya-kośa, the bliss covering, where the human is closest to ātman.

Kosher (*Ashkenazi pronunciation of Heb. *kasher*): see DIETARY LAWS.

Kōshin (Sino-Japanese pronunciation of the signs for 'metal' and 'monkey' in Chinese sexagesimal system of calendrical reckoning). A Japanese folk deity whose original impetus was Chinese folk belief (loosely, Taoist), but which by accretion has taken on both Shinto and Buddhist associations. The Chinese believed in three malevolent deities (literally 'three worms') who inhabit every human body, inflicting it with various ailments, and who on the nights of the six Kōshin days each year would escape to heaven to report to the gods the moral transgressions of their hosts, thus shortening their lives. This idea was spread in Japan in the Heian period by wandering *Onmyō-ji* ('*yin-yang masters'). It was thought that by keeping awake on Kōshin nights, the worms would be unable to escape to make their reports, hence the aristocratic custom of keeping Kōshin vigils and whiling away the hours in poetry-writing, musical entertainments, and games.

Koshōgatsu (lesser New Year): see FESTIVALS AND FASTS, JAPANESE.

Kotani Kimi (co-founder): see REIYŪKAI.

[Ha-]Kotel ha-Ma'aravi: see WAILING WALL.

Koto-dama (Jap., 'word-spirit'). The traditional Shinto belief in spiritual power residing in spoken words.

Kotow or **kow-tow.** 'Knocking the head on the ground', the court ceremony of three kneelings and nine prostrations, which Chinese ritual of the Ch'ing period required of a foreign envoy when he was received by the emperor. From 1873 onward, the kotow was not required.

Kotsu (Jap., 'bones'). Also known as *nyoi*, the staff bestowed on a Zen master (*roshi) on his attaining that rank. It is used in teaching.

K'ou Chien-chih (*c*.365–*c*.448 CE). Taoist successor of *Ko Hung who did much to organize that tradition in Taoism and to make it the official religion of the Northern Way dynasty. He became celestial master (*t'ien-shih) of the northern Wei court from 425–8. He introduced extravagant Taoist ritual to affirm the emperor as Perfect Ruler; but he was murdered by a palace eunuch, and his successor re-established Buddhism as the state religion.

Kovazim (collections): see RESPONSA.

Kow-tow (obeisance): see KOTOW.

Kōya (Japanese Buddhist): see KŪYA.

Kōya, Mount (Jap., Kōyasan). Site of a Buddhist monastic complex of the *Shingon sect in Wakayama Prefecture, Japan. Long considered by ascetics as a sacred mountain, Mount Kōya was selected in 816 by *Kūkai as a site for establishing a monastic community and is currently home to over 110 associated temples.

Kōzen Gokoku-ron: see EISAI.

Kraemer, Hendrik (1888–1965). Dutch Christian missionary and missiologist. In 1928, he was part of the delegation to the Missionary Conference at Jerusalem which remained deeply critical of that Conference's attempt to find a new relation with non-Christian religions on the basis of shared values. In 1937, he became Professor of Comparative Religion at Leiden and prepared the discussion document for the successor Missionary Conference at Tambaram, in 1938. This 'document' is his classic work, *The Christian Message in a Non-Christian World*. Based strongly on the unequivocal theology of Karl *Barth, Kraemer argued that Christianity is a consequence of the act of God, issuing in biblical demand, whereas other religions are the consequence of the human religious quest. Between the two there is a radical discontinuity.

Kranz, Jacob, The Maggid of Dubno (1741–1804). Jewish preacher. Born in Lithuania, Kranz became famous as a preacher in the city of Dubno where he came in contact with *Elijah ben Solomon Zalman. Many of his sermons were printed posthumously in *Ohel Yā'akov* (The Tent of Jacob: 4 vols., 1830, 1837, 1859, 1863). He was a brilliant story-teller who was called by Moses *Mendelssohn 'the Jewish Aesop'—though few of his stories or parables involved animals.

Kratophany (manifestation of power): see HIEROPHANY.

Krishna: see KṚṢṆA.

Krishnamurti, Jiddu (1895–1986). Indian religious figure and claimed *guru. The *Theosophists, Charles Leadbeater and Annie Besant, proclaimed him the 'World Teacher', the vehicle of the Lord *Maitreya, who showed himself in human form every 2,000 years. In 1911 Krishnamurti was made head of the newly founded 'Order of the Star in the East' (later shortened to 'Order of the Star'). In 1929 Krishnamurti, tired of the role assigned to him, dissolved the Order, renounced all claims to divinity, and declared that he no longer wanted disciples. Today Krishnamurti Foundations are to be found in many parts of the world which aim to set people 'absolutely and unconditionally free'. Some of those close to him (e.g. M. Lutyens, *Krishnamurti: The Years of Awakening*, 1975; ... *The Years of Fulfillment*, 1983) adulate him; others (e.g. R. R. Sloss, *Lives in the Shadow with Krishnamurti*, 1991) observed a more fraudulent and cynical character.

Kristallnacht (Germ., 'night of glass'). The night, 9 Nov. 1938, on which Nazi *anti-Semitism in Germany moved onto a new level of ferocity: *synagogues were burned down and Jewish-owned shops were looted and destroyed (hence the name, because the streets were covered in glass). From this point on, the mass deportations to concentration camps began. See also HOLOCAUST.

Kriyatantra (division of tantric texts): see TRIPIṬAKA.

Kriyā-yoga: see YOGĀNANDA.

Krochmal, Nachman (ReNak; 1785–1840). A founder of the 'Science of Judaism' (Wissenschaft des Judentums): see also ZUNZ, LEOPOLD. As a leader of the *Haskalah movement, Krochmal's philosophy is summed up in his *Moreh Nevukhei ha-Zeman* (Guide to the Perplexed of Our Time, 1851). His main contribution was his attempt to study Hebrew literature, including the *halakhah, in terms of its history and development.

Krodha (Skt., 'anger, wrath'). In the *Mahābhārata*, one of the 'five sins' the *yogin must overcome: lust (*kāma), anger (krodha), greed (*lobha), fear (*bhaya*), and sleep (*svapna*).

In Hindu ethics, krodha is one of the six internal enemies against which all must be vigilant, the others being lust, greed, infatuation (*moha), pride (*mada*), and envy (*mātsarya*). The two basic sins from whence all others derive are kāma and krodha.

Kṛṣṇā (heroine of Mahābhārata): see DRAUPADĪ.

Kṛṣṇa or **Krishna** (Skt., 'black', 'dark'). A composite figure in Hinduism, becoming eventually the eighth and most celebrated *avatāra (incarnation) of *Viṣṇu. In the *Ṛg Veda*, the name appears, but is not connected with divinity. The transformation of Kṛṣṇa appears to have been a part of a longing (expressed in **Bhāgavata Purāṇa*) for a more personal than philosophical focus for religious devotion and progress: according to 1. 3. 27, *Kṛṣṇas tu bhagavān svayam*, 'Kṛṣṇa is *Bhagavan himself.' He is prominent in the **Mahābhārata*, and it is he who instructs Arjuna in the **Bhagavad-gītā*. The many legends told about him make him one of the most popular and accessible figures of Hindu devotion (*bhakti).

Initially, Kṛṣṇa was closely associated with Viṣṇu. His involvement with the *gopīs in amorous dance (*rasa līlā) becomes the model of passionate union with God; as the adviser to Arjuna in the *Bhagavad-gītā*, he transcends the action and evokes a comparable transcendence in those who attend to him. He is represented iconographically in sinuous dance, playing his irresistible flute to summon the gopīs (and his lovers); but he is also shown in images of power, raising Mount Govardhana above the floods unleashed by *Indra, or destroying the malevolent snake, Kāliya, who has poisoned the life-giving waters of the river *Yamunā. Kṛṣṇa is devoted especially to *Rādhā, and the two are often worshipped together.

See also VAIṢṆAVA; Index, Kṛṣṇa.

Kṛta-kṛtya (Skt.). The one in Hinduism who has fulfilled what has to be done, i.e. who has set his whole life to the realization of God and has attained liberation.

Kṛta-yuga: see YUGA.

Ks, Five: see FIVE KS.

Kṣanti (bodhisattva virtue): see PĀRAMITĀ.

Kṣatra (Skt., *kṣi*, 'have power over'). Sovereignty (abstract or concrete ruling power) in the Vedic and Hindu traditions. Kṣatra was initially the power associated with sacrifice.

Kṣatriya. The second classification in the four *varnas of Hinduism. In its strict sense, it means 'a warrior', but it embraces all those involved in *kṣatra.

Kṣitigarbha (Skt., 'womb of the earth'; Korean, Chijang). In Buddhism a *bodhisattva who is believed to help children (especially deceased children) and to be a saviour from the torments of hell (*naraka). In China he is known as Ti-ts'ang and is represented as a monk holding a staff with six bells (to indicate his power in the six realms of the Kamaloka (see LOKA). In Japan, he is known as Jizō, and is of particular importance.

Kṣudrakāgama (Indian division of Sūtrapiṭaka): see TRIPIṬAKA.

Kū. Jap. for *śūnyatā, the void, emptiness.

Ku, K'u. Jap. and Chin. for *dukkha.

Kuan (Chin., 'seeing'). Taoist monastery or nunnery, initially allowing celibates and married priests, but eventually insisting on celibacy.

Kuan-ti. Taoist god of war, who protects the kingdom from enemies, both internal and external. In folk religion he is also Fu-mo ta-ti, the great ruler who expels demons.

Kuan-yin: see AVALOKITEŚVARA.

Kubera. An Indian earth spirit, mentioned in *Atharva Veda* 8. 10. 28, who becomes an increasingly important figure in Hindu myths and legends, especially in *Rāmāyaṇa*, where he becomes an ally of *Rāma after his defeat by *Rāvaṇa.

Kubla Khan: see 'PHAGS-PA-BLO-GROS-RGYAL-MTSHAM

Kubo Kakutarō (founder): see REIYŪKAI.

Kubo Tsuginari (founder): see REIYŪKAI.

Kūḍalasaṅgamadēva (Lord of the Meeting Rivers): see BASAVA.

Kuei (Chin., 'spirit'). Component of human being in Taoism and Chinese thought, associated with *p'o and thus with *yin, or the dark and physical side. In later systematization, kuei are the spirits of those who have been killed out of time (e.g. in war, murder, accident), or who have been wrongly executed or improperly buried, or for whom the proper remembrances (*tzu) have not been observed. The *li-kuei* return in vengeance, and must therefore be placated. For further details, see SHEN.

K'uei-chi (pupil): see HSÜAN-TSANG.

Kuei-feng Tsung-mi: see FIVE WAYS OF CH'AN/ZEN.

Kuei-shan Ling-yu: see KUEI-YANG-TSUNG.

Kuei-yang-tsung (Jap., Igyō-shu). One of the *Goke-shichishū ('five houses, seven schools') of early (Tang period) Ch'an/Zen. Its name is derived from two mountains (Kuei and Yang) where the temples of its founders were located. Kuei-shan Ling-yu (771–853 CE) was appointed head of Ta-kuei monastery when *Pai-chang Huai-hai set a jug of water before his pupils: 'If you cannot call this a water-jug, what can you call it?' Kuei-shan kicked the jug over and walked away, demonstrating his enlightened state. His wordless action characterizes Kuei-yang-tsung, in which action and silence are connected to each other, to create the sudden and direct encounter with truth. Among Kuei-shan's important successors were *Hsiang-yen Chih-hsien and *Yang-shan Hui-chi.

Kufr (unbelief): see KĀFIR.

Kuga Sorta (Cheremis, 'big candle'). Popular name for a *syncretist movement among the Cheremis people of the Mari Republic in the USSR from about the 1870s. Although nominally Christianized before this, the threat of Russian acculturation led to an attempt at cultural survival as 'true Cheremis' (their own term for the movement) through a synthesis of traditional and Christian elements.

Kūkā (Sikh revivalist movement): see NĀMDHĀRĪ.

Kūkai (774–835). Known posthumously as Kōbō Daishi, the founder of the *Shingon school of Buddhism in Japan. In 804 Kūkai travelled to the Chinese capital of Ch'ang-an and sought out its foremost esoteric master,

Hui-kuo (746–805). Under him Kūkai received instruction in the two fundamental esoteric scriptures and underwent initiation (Jap., *kanjō*; Skt., *abhiṣeka) into the two related *maṇḍalas—the Womb Maṇḍala (Jap., *taizōkai*) and the Diamond Maṇḍala (Jap., *kongōkai*). After Hui-kuo's untimely death in 805, Kūkai decided to return to Japan and to establish esoteric Buddhism there. He arrived back in 806 with over 200 religious objects from China, including scriptures, ritual implements, icons, and maṇḍala.

Kūkai gradually emerged as one of two eminent Buddhist masters in Japan. The other was *Saichō (767–822), the founder of the *Tendai school. Kūkai's greatest benefactor was Emperor Saga (786–842) who, like Kūkai, was a master calligrapher. In 816 Saga granted Kūkai Mount *Kōya as a mountain retreat for the exclusive practice of esoteric Buddhism, and in 823 gave him jurisdiction over Tōji, an imperial temple in Kyōto. These became the centres of the Shingon school. By the time of Kūkai's death, in 835, Shingon was a fully recognized school of Buddhism, and esoteric ritual pervaded Japan's religious establishment.

Kula (Skt., 'family'). 1. The family lineage and home in Hinduism, of importance (along with *jāti and gotra, the original ancestor) in determining the exact position of a person in society.

2. *Tantric school originating in the *Bhairava-Kālī cults and *Kāpalika cremation-ground (*śmaśāna) dwellers. The aim of Kula practice, which involved consuming scatological substances and corpse-flesh, was possession (*aveśa*) by a female deity to achieve perfection (siddhi). These forces were also manifested in human form as *yoginīs. Kula practice still continues in certain parts of India.

Kulacēkaraṉ (one of the Aḻvars): see ĀḺVĀRS.

Kula-devatā. The god, or gods, chosen by a Hindu family for worship or for protection.

Kulārṇava Tantra (Skt., 'ocean of the family Tantra'). A text (1000–1400 CE) of the *Kaula tradition advocating various forms of *Tantric worship, including the five 'Ms' (*pañcamakāra).

Kumāra (youthful offspring of Śiva): see SKANDA.

Kumārāja (Tibetan ascetic): see KLONG-CHEN RAB-'BYAMS-PA.

Kumārajīva (*c.*344–413 CE). One of the greatest of Buddhist translators. Kumārajīva, who had grown up under the influence of the *Hīnayāna, became acquainted with the Mahāyāna teachings and was converted to them. Captured by Chinese in 383, he studied Chinese until he was liberated and welcomed to Chang-an in 401, where he spent the rest of his life teaching and translating. He rendered many of the most important Mahāyāna sūtras and treatises into elegant and accurate Chinese.

Kumārila Bhaṭṭa (7th cent. CE). A learned *brahman of Bihar and follower of the Mīmāṃsā school. He actively opposed the Buddhists and Jains. Author of the *Mīmāṁsā-vārttika* and also the *Ślokavārttika* (the latter an extensive argument against the existence and the necessity of God), he adopted the principle of non-duality (*advaita). For Kumārila, liberation was not *mokṣa, but rather the state of the self free from pain.

Kumāri pūjā (Skt.). In *Tantrism, the worship of a 12-year-old virgin girl who represents the Goddess (*Devī) or *Śakti. She is installed on a seat (*pīṭha) and worshipped through *mantra repetition. The rite is prevalent in Bengal, but is also found throughout India and Nepal.

Kumbha (Skt., 'pot'). The mark of a *sādhu's renunciation. The empty pot is also a symbol of the womb, and Kumbhamātā is the guardian deity of villages in Hinduism, especially prominent at marriages.

Kumbhaka. Suspension of breath between exhaling and inhaling, a part of Hindu *rāja- and *haṭha-yoga.

Kuṁbhamelā. Pilgrimage assembly of Hindu devotees, held every three years at four different places in turn. The places, *Hardwār, Nāsik, Prayāga, and Ujjain, are those where drops of *amṛta, the nectar of immortality, fell to earth during a heavenly conflict. Many millions of pilgrims are attracted to the kuṁbhamelās.

Kundakunda. Eminent *Digambara Jain teacher, writer, and philosopher of perhaps 2nd–3rd cents. CE. His prolific Prakrit writings form the most authoritative source of Digambara Jain teaching. Sixteen works are attributed to him, but these attributions are not secure; at most, only parts of some works are likely to have been written by him. However, Digambara Jains regard all these works as coming from him and as having authority. Major works are *Niyamasāra* (Essence of Restraint, tr. U. Sain, 1931), *Pravacanasāra* (Essence of Scripture, tr. B. Faddegon, 1935), and *Pañcāstinikayasāra* (Essence of the Five Entities, tr. A. Chakravarti, 1920). His *Samayasāra* (Essence of Doctrine, tr. A. Chakravarti, 1930; R. B. Jain, 1931) is of great importance since it is devoted to a discussion of the real nature of the soul, a central preoccupation for Kundakunda.

Kuṇḍalinī (Skt.). *Śakti (power) envisaged as a coiled snake at the base of the central channel (suṣumnā *nāḍī) in the mūlādhāra *cakra of *Tantric esoteric anatomy. Kuṇḍalinī *yoga is a means of attaining *samādhi and finally liberation in Tantric *sādhana. She is aroused by the arrest of breath and semen through *prāṇayāma and *mantra repetition (*japa). Kuṇḍalinī yoga is used by contemporary religious sects such as the 3HO and the Rajneesh movement.

Kundalini Research Institute: see KUṆḌALINĪ.

K'ung. In Buddhism, the Chin. tr. of *śūnyatā (Skt., 'emptiness') which supplanted the earlier term **wu* ('non-existence'), which was misunderstood as implying *nihilism.

Küng, Hans (b. 1928). Swiss RC theologian teaching at the University of Tübingen. His *The Council and Reunion* (1960; Eng. 1961) set out a programme of reforms for the Second *Vatican Council, many of which actually came about. After the council he wrote widely on *ecclesiology (especially *The Church*, 1967), *Christology, the existence of God, and many other topics. His questioning of some traditional RC doctrines in his *Infallible?* (1970; Eng. 1971) and *On Being a Christian* (1974; Eng. 1977) led to the intervention of the Sacred Congregation for the Doctrine of the Faith in Rome. In 1979 it was announced that he could no longer teach officially as a Catholic theologian.

Kung-an: see KŌAN.

K'ung-tzu: see CONFUCIUS.

Kunitokotachi (founding deity of Japan): see KITABAKE CHIKAFUSA.

K'un-lun. A mountain range in W. China, the abode of Hsi wang-mu and the immortals (*hsien), and thus the Taoist paradise.

Kuntī, also called **Pṛthā.** In the **Mahābhārata*, mother of the three oldest *Pāṇḍavas: Yudhiṣṭhira, *Bhīma, and *Arjuna.

Kuo Hsiang (early neo-Taoist): see HSÜAN-HSÜEH.

Kurahit (Pañjābī, 'misdeed'). Offences against the Sikh *rahit, the *khālsā code of discipline. They are removing or trimming *hair from any part of the body, eating halal meat, committing *adultery, and using tobacco. Transgressors have to be reinitiated.

Kūrma (Skt., 'tortoise'). In Hindu mythology an animal which is associated with *Viṣṇu in various ways. In the ancient fourfold cosmography of the *Purāṇas, it is said to be the form of Viṣṇu which supports Bhārata (India). In the earliest known versions of the myth of the Churning of the Ocean, the tortoise allows the gods and demons to use its back as a base for the mountain which serves as their churning-stick, and in later versions Viṣṇu himself takes the form of a tortoise in order to do this. Kūrma is the second in the standard list of Viṣṇu's ten *avatāras.

Kurozumikyō: see KUROZUMI MUNETADA.

Kurozumi Munetada (1780–1850). Founder of Kurozumikyō, a Japanese new religion. In 1812, both his parents died, and he contracted tuberculosis; as a result he was virtually bedridden for three years. Believing that his original goal of becoming a *kami in this life was now frustrated, he vowed that after death he would become a healing deity. However, in prayer to *Amaterasu, he awoke both to healing and to the realization that the divine and the human are inseparable, and that consequently there is neither birth nor death but only movement in eternal life. This transformative vision occurred on 11 Nov. 1814, a date which is now commemorated as the beginning of Kurozumikyō. He extended his own healing through healing others, and his own vision through itinerant preaching. Kurozumikyō was given government authorization as an independent Shinto sect in 1876. Its leadership is held by direct descendants of Kurozumi and numbers about a quarter of a million adherents.

Kursī (Arab., 'stool'). In Islam, the footstool of the throne (*al-'arsh*) of God, and often used as a synonym of 'throne'. It is thus central in debates about the literal or metaphorical sense of such terms in the *Qur'ān; metaphorically *al-'arsh* is the Being of God, al-kursī his non-formal manifestation. A kursī is also a support for a Qur'ān in a *mosque.

Kurukṣetra (Skt., 'field of the Kurus'). Site of a great war between the *Pāṇḍavas and the *Kauravas, the central action of the **Mahābhārata*.

Identified as being in the area of Delhi, Kurukṣetra has also served as a battlefield in other contexts, mentioned in the epic itself, and elsewhere.

Kuśa. A species of grass regarded by Hindus as the most sacred of grasses (and often called, more popularly, *darbha*). It was spread over the whole sacred and sacrificial area during ritual celebrations. It was also used as a substitute for *soma.

Kusala (Pali; Skt., *kuśala*). In early Buddhist texts, the skilfulness which enables one to abstain from committing those actions which retard or obstruct spiritual development and to limit oneself to doing only those actions which help and bring about spiritual development. The next and the more important step consists of deliberate involvement in the cultivation of the opposite positive qualities.

Thus, a kusala action consists of these two essential components, the negative and the positive, either of which complements the other. For the opposite, see AKUŚALA.

Kuṣāṇa (period): see KANIṢKA.

Kusha (Buddhist sect): see NARA BUDDHISM.

Kuśinagara. Town (in Uttar-pradesh) where the *Buddha passed on (parinirvāna). It remains one of the four most holy places in Buddhism.

Kusti (sacred cord): see NAUJOTE.

Kūya or **Kōya** (903–72). Founder of the Kuya Sect of the Japanese *Tendai (Chinese, *T'ien-t'ai) school of Buddhism. Born in *Kyōto, he became a novice monk in his infancy. He was also one of the early advocates of *Pure Land Buddhist teaching and practice in Japan, spending his career as an itinerant teacher urging the common people to place faith in *Amida Buddha (the Buddha of Infinite Light) through the constant invocation of the Pure Land *nembutsu *mantra, *namu amida butsu*, 'I take refuge in the Buddha of Infinite Light.' For this reason, he was popularly regarded as a *nembutsu-hijiri* ('nembutsu holy man'). Kūya was also famous for his social work activities, to demonstrate in practice (and to inculcate) Amida Buddha's compassion among the people. In 938, after an extensive period of itinerant teaching in the northern provinces, he settled in Kyōto and began spreading Pure Land teaching and practice there. In Kyōto he was also popularly known as *ichi no shōnin* ('first of the saints'), *ichi hijiri* ('first of the holy men'), and *amida hijiri* ('Amida holy man').

Kuzari (text by Judah haLevi): see JUDAH HALEVI.

Kwannon: see AVALOKITEŚVARA.

Kwatsu (Jap. pronunciation): see HO (1).

Kyabdro. The Tibetan understanding and adaptation of 'taking refuge' in the *Three Jewels. The Diamond Vehicle (*Vajrayāna) added a fourth refuge, the *lama; other schools added three, the lama, the *yidam (personal deity), and the *dākinī (sources of wisdom).

Kyō. Jap., for *sūtra.

Kyoge-betsuden (transmission outside formal teaching): see FUKASETSU.

Kyogen Chikan (Japanese name): see HSIANG-YEN CHIH-HSIEN.

Kyōha Shintō (Jap., 'sectarian *Shinto'). A group of independent Shinto sects which began their activities in the late Tokugawa and early Meiji periods. When the government created State Shinto (*kokka shintō), which embraced most of the Shinto shrines, it did not wish to incorporate these new groups but created the special category of Kyōha Shintō so that it could regard them as private religious organizations. These thirteen sects originated in close relation to peasant movements, devotional associations, magico-religious practices, and ideas about changing the world through religious practices. The thirteen traditional Shinto sects can be classified in several different groupings: pure Shinto sects (Shintō Taikyō, Shinrikyō, and Izumo Ōyashirokyō), Confucianistic Shinto sects (Shintō Shūseiha and Shintō Taiseikyō), purification sects (Shinshūkyō and Misogikyō), mountain-worship sects (Jikkōkyō, Fusōkyō, and Ontakekyō), and faith-healing sects (Kurozumikyō, Konkōkyō, and Tenrikyō). The Sect Shinto groups remain active with large numbers of adherents today. In addition, some forty-eight new Shinto sects that have sprung up since the war, with 2 million followers, are generally tabulated as 'New Sect Shinto' (*Shin Kyōha Shintō*).

Kyŏmik (fl. 6th cent. CE). Founder of the *Vinaya school of Buddhism in the kingdom of Paekche in Korea. Kyŏmik studied the Vinaya in India, returning home in 526 with the texts of the five-division Vinaya. Upon his return, he was commissioned by King Sŏngmyŏng (r. 523–53) to translate the Vinaya texts which, subsequently, became the foundation of Paekche Buddhism.

Kyōō-gokokuji (temple in Kyōto): see TŌJI.

Kyosaku also **Keisaku.** Zen 'wake-up stick', used by teachers to stimulate pupils and perhaps shock them into enlightenment. It represents the sword of *Mañjuśrī which cuts through all delusions.

Kyōto. Japanese city, of particular importance for its Buddhist temples and monasteries. Virtually every school and sect in Buddhism had or has its location in Kyōto. Of particular early importance are the Hosso (*Dōshō) temple Kiyomizu, with its elaborate scaffolding construction (to throw oneself from the scaffold of Kiyomizu is to launch oneself into the unknown), and the Byōdō-in, temple of equality, the 'Phoenix Hall' of which survived the fire in

1483 which destroyed all else; it was beautifully restored in 1957. The arrival of Zen brought back the simpler style of a single axis leading from a southern entrance, through the triple gate (*sammon*), the buddha-hall (*butsuden), to the dharma-hall (*hatto*). Among the earliest are Nanzenji (13th cent., see MUKAN FUMON), and the smaller, but related Eikan-do. Of equal importance is *Daitoku-ji, whose original 14th-cent. buildings burned down in the 15th cent., but which remains a classic example of a Zen monastery. *Pure Land temples are also prominent in Kyōto, especially Chion-in of Jodo-shu, and *Honganji where *Shinran was buried. Also at Kyōto is the famous rock garden at the Ryoanji temple, fifteen rocks so placed in groups of seven, five, and three, that from any aspect, one rock is hidden.

Kyoto School: see NISHIDA KITARŌ.

Kyōun-Shu: see IKKYŪ SŌJUN.

Kyōzan Ejaku (Jap. name): see YANG-SHAN HUI-CHI.

Kyrie (Gk., *Kyrie eleēson*, 'Lord, have mercy'). A brief prayer used in Christian liturgical worship. The Gk. words were kept untranslated in the Latin mass and often remain thus in English-language services.

Kyūdō (Jap., 'way of the bow'). The zen art of archery, in which control and mastery are cultivated.

L

Labarum. The military standard of the emperor *Constantine. Its design was that of the Roman cavalry standard with the pagan emblems replaced by the *chi-rho monogram.

Lady, Our. Designation of the Blessed Virgin *Mary. Lady Day is the feast of the *Annunciation, 25 Mar. A Lady Chapel is one dedicated to Mary.

Laestadianism. A Christian revival movement in northern Scandinavia founded by Lars Levi Laestadius (1800–61). This Swedish pastor of the *Lutheran church in Karesuando, near the Finnish border in Lappland, was more interested in botany than in souls until a deep personal awakening in 1844 led to a new preaching of the gospel, with emphasis upon repentance and the absolute forgiveness of sins within the congregation as the body of *Christ and through his atoning death. Emigrating Laestadianism Finns were responsible for the foundation of the Apostolic Lutheran Church in the USA in 1871.

Laetentur Coeli (Lat., 'let the heavens rejoice'). The title, taken from the opening words, of two unconnected Christian documents.

1. The Formulary of Reunion of 433 between the opposing parties after the Council of *Ephesus.

2. The *bull of 1439 decreeing the union agreed at the Council of *Florence of the E. and W. churches, that the Orthodox accept the *filioque and the primacy of the see of Rome.

Lag Ba-Omer (Heb., 'thirty-third of Omer'). A Jewish holiday. Lag Ba-Omer is celebrated on the thirty-third day of counting the *Omer, i.e. 18 Iyyar. Mourning customs are lifted, weddings may be solemnized, and music enjoyed. Customs associated with the festival include giving 3-year-old boys their first haircut, playing with bows and arrows, and lighting bonfires.

Laghiman (Skt., 'lightness'). Yogic ability in Hinduism to levitate. See also DARDURA-SIDDHI.

Laity (Gk., *laos*, 'people'). Baptized Christians who are not clergy or ordained to specific ministry (i.e. the majority). Since the New Testament envisages a priesthood of all believers, the place of the laity in the mission and life of the Church should be paramount. In fact, virtually the whole of mainstream Christianity is dominated by the ordained clergy, so far as control and decision-making is concerned. The term is now also applied to people in other religions who are not among the formally accredited personnel—e.g., in Buddhism, those who do not belong to the *saṅgha, the community of *bhikkhus, i.e. *upāsaka.

Lakṣaṇa (Skt., 'marks'). Marks on a body, auspicious for Hindus if they appear on the right (for a man) or the left (for a woman): see also ASHES. The term has also been used for the five characteristics of a complete *purāṇa: (i) creation of a cosmos; (ii) its dissolution and renewal; (iii) the origin and descent of gods and heroes; (iv) the work of the *Manus (lawgivers); (v) the work of their descendants.

Lakṣmaṇa. The half-brother of *Rāma and son of Daśaratha, king of *Ayodhyā. As Rāma's life-span was coming to an end, Lakṣmaṇa took upon himself the death-sentence that was Rāma's and committed suicide by drowning in the River Śarayū, whence his body was removed to heaven by the gods.

Lakṣmī (Skt., 'sign'). In the *Vedas a mark or indication, neither good nor bad unless so qualified (e.g. by *puṇya* if good). But at least from the time of **Mahābhārata*, Lakṣmī is personified as a Goddess of good fortune and the embodiment of beauty. In all manifestations, she is associated with fertility and good fortune, and her image is often put on doorposts to ward off evil. Śrī Lakṣmī is often known simply as *Śrī.

Lakṣya (form of chosen deity): see IṢṬADEVATĀ.

Lal Ded: see LALLĀ.

Lalitā. Indian goddess, also known as Mahādevi (see DEVI), important in Tantric Hinduism. She is also the personification of *Līlā, and thus her form is the universe: she is *Pārvatī when dancing, and is the writhing which precedes birth and manifestation.

Lalitavistara (Skt., *lalita*, 'played', + *vistara*, 'details'). A Buddhist text of about 2nd cent. CE, highly valued in *Mahāyāna. The *Lalitavistara* gives a poetical account of the early life of the *Buddha up to the beginning of his ministry.

Lallā or **Lal Ded.** 14th-cent. *Kashmiri Śaivite poetess. Little is known of her life apart from an immense proliferation of stories, which attest to her popularity, but cannot be verified historically. She composed verse sayings, known as *vakh*, which are often direct and simple. But many of them are in fact complex in their associations, so that translations cannot convey why they remain so deeply loved among Kashmiris, both Hindu and Muslim.

Lama (Tib., *bla.ma.*, 'Higher One'). An honorary title in Tibetan Buddhism conferred upon anyone accepted as a 'spiritual teacher' (corresponding to Skt., *guru), but generally only given to one who has completed particular scholastic and yogic training.

Lama dancing (Tib., *lha.'cham*, 'sacred dance'). Tibetan Buddhist *mystery play. A drama of great colour, costume, masks, and music, enacted predominantly by *lamas as a form of mime, in which every bodily movement carries a precise symbolic meaning. Such dances are normally performed at festivals, particularly those of the new year (*losar*) such as the Great Prayer held around the *jokhang, when they can double as *exorcism ceremonies, banishing evil from the community in order to begin the new year auspiciously.

Lama dancing should not be confused with a popular form of dance called *A che lha mo* ('elder sister-goddess') which is performed by travelling theatrical troupes and where the subject-matter is more profane.

Lamaism. A now antiquated term used by early W. commentators (as L. A. Waddell, *The Buddhism of Tibet, or Lamaism*, 1895) to describe Tibetan Buddhism. Although the term is not accurate (because not all Tibetan monks are *lamas), 'Lamaism' does at least convey the great emphasis placed on the role of the spiritual teacher by this religion.

Lamb. Christian symbol for *Christ. Its basis is the biblical *Passover lamb (Exodus 12. 1–13; 1 Corinthians 5. 7), the *suffering servant who was led as a lamb to slaughter (Isaiah 53. 7), and the words of *John the Baptist pointing out Jesus as 'the lamb of God' (John 1. 29–36). See also AGNUS DEI; AGNES, ST.

Lambeth Conferences. Assemblies of the bishops of the whole *Anglican Communion held about once every ten years under the presidency of the archbishop of *Canterbury (whose London residence is Lambeth Palace). The first one was convened in 1867.

The 'Lambeth Quadrilateral', approved at the conference of 1888, remains the Anglican statement of the fourfold essential basis for a reunited Church: (i) the Bible as the ultimate rule of faith, (ii) the *Apostles' and *Nicene creeds, (iii) the *sacraments of baptism and Lord's supper, and (iv) the 'historic episcopate'.

Lambeth Quadrilateral (basis for ecumenicism): see ANGLICANISM.

Lam Drey (siddha system): see SAKYA.

Lamed Vav Zaddikim (Heb., '36 righteous men', appearing in Yiddish as Lamedvovniks), according to Jewish legend, the minimum number of righteous men alive in any one generation required to prevent the destruction of the world. For the novel, *The Last of the Just*, based on this legend, see HOLOCAUST.

Lamennais, Hugues Félicité Robert de (1782–1854). French religious and political writer. In the newspaper *L'Avenir* (1830–1) and elsewhere he advocated a policy of 'liberal *Ultramontanism'. When his views were condemned by the pope, he retired to La Chênaie in Brittany (where he had established a centre for like-minded people) and wrote *Paroles d'un croyant* (1834). Condemned again, he left the Church and spent the rest of his working life in politics.

Lamentabili. Decree of the *Holy Office issued under Pius X in 1907, condemning sixty-five propositions drawn from the works of the RC *Modernists, especially A. F. *Loisy.

Lamentations, Book of (in Heb., *Ekah* or *Kinot*). One of the five *scrolls of the Hebrew *Bible. It is read in Jewish liturgy on the Ninth of *Av.

Lammas Day. 1 Aug. in the calendar of the *Book of Common Prayer. By etymology it derives from 'loaf' and 'mass', and in the early English church it was customary to consecrate bread from the first-ripe corn at mass on this day, probably in thanksgiving for the harvest. Since the 19th cent., the unofficial Harvest thanksgiving has been more prominent.

Lamotte, Etienne (1903–83). A renowned Belgian scholar of Buddhism, who was an ordained priest and prelate of the pope's household. He studied under his great compatriot Louis de *la Vallée-Poussin, and specialized in the tr. of Buddhist texts from Tibetan and Chinese where the Sanskrit original was no longer extant.

Lamrim (Tib., 'path stages'). Tibetan manuals describing stages on the spiritual path. Important examples are *Gampopa's *Jewel Ornament of Liberation*, *Tsong Khapa's *Graded Path to Enlightenment*, and (much later) Pältrül Rinpoche's *Instructions on All that Belongs to Good Teaching*.

Landau, Ezekiel (1713–93). Also known as Noda bi-Yehuda from the title of his book of *responsa, Jewish Talmudic scholar. He was born in Poland, where he served as a *rabbi, but he became well-known only when he became rabbi of Prague in 1755. His book of 855 responsa (*Noda Biyhudah*, Known in Judah) shows a tendency to lenient interpretations. He strongly opposed *Shabbateanism and any kind of *messianic speculation, and was suspicious of the emerging *Ḥasidic movement. But he attempted to mediate in the bitter dispute between *Emden and *Eybeschuetz, even though he was not convinced that the latter was innocent of connection with Shabbateanism, because he felt that the damage to the Jewish community must be contained.

Laṅgar ('anchor'). Communal partaking of food when visiting a *gurdwārā. The practice was instituted by Gurū *Nānak and endorsed by his successors. It is fundamental among Sikhs because it demonstrates the abolition of *caste: all eat together, and any Sikh may provide or prepare the food.

Language-games: see WITTGENSTEIN, LUDWIG.

Laṅkāvatāra-sūtra (The Descent into Laṅkā). An important *sūtra in the *Mahāyāna Buddhist tradition which sets out the teachings of Idealism or *Vijñāna-vāda. The text must have been in existence some time before 443 CE when the first Chin. tr. was made. Meditation based on the sūtra was emphasized by *Hui-k'o.

Lan Tsai-ho (one of eight immortals): see PA-HSIEN.

Lao-chun. The name of *Lao-tzu in his deified form, one of the highest deities in religious Taoism. He has been incarnated many times, and is deeply revered as the supreme focus of worship. The reverence of both Lao-tzu and the *Buddha led to a belief that Lao-tzu actually was the Buddha, who assumed that guise in order to convert all people to the way of Tao.

Lao-Tzu also **Lao Tan** (Chin., 'old master'). A founding figure (though perhaps legendary) of Taoism, and according to tradition a contemporary (and teacher) of *Confucius. His main importance is the tradition that he is the author of **Tao-te ching*, which is consequently also known as *Lao-tzu*; though again that claim cannot be historically true. He was later deified in religious Taoism (*tao-chiao).

Lapsi (Lat., 'the fallen'). Christians guilty in varying ways of *apostasy under persecution. Could such persons be readmitted to the Church? After the Decian persecution of 250–1, the Church, guided by the view of *Cyprian (expressed in his work *De Lapsis*), decided to do so after penance and a period of probation.

La-shanah ha-ba'ah bi-Yerushalayim: see NEXT YEAR IN JERUSALEM.

Last Gospel. A second *gospel reading which until 1964 came at the very end of *mass. It was usually John 1. 1–14.

Last of the Just: see HOLOCAUST.

Last Supper. The final meal of Jesus with his disciples before his death. In the *Synoptic gospels (Mark 14. 12–26 etc.) it is described as a *Passover meal. John 13. 1–11 mentions only a supper at which Jesus washed his disciples' feet, and places the crucifixion before the time of the Passover meal, which has the effect of relating the death of Jesus to the slaughter of the lambs for Passover.

Lateran Councils. A series of *councils of the Roman Catholic Church held at the Lateran Palace in Rome from the 7th to the 18th cents. Five are considered *ecumenical, of which the most important was the Fourth (1215), with a definition of the *eucharist in which the word 'transubstantiate' was used for the first time, and annual *confession for all Christians was prescribed.

Latihan (training, exercise): see SUBUD INTERNATIONAL BROTHERHOOD.

Latimer, Hugh (*c*.1485–1555). Bishop of Worcester and *Reformer. Ordained *priest in 1524, he was influenced by the conversion of Thomas Bilney and gradually became a zealous exponent of the reformed faith. In 1535 he was made bishop of Worcester, but in 1539 his convinced *Protestantism caused him to oppose Henry's Act of Six Articles. He was imprisoned in the Tower in 1546, but on the accession of Edward (1547) was released, becoming an increasingly popular preacher. Early in Mary's reign he was reimprisoned, excommunicated, and burnt along with *Ridley on 16 Oct. 1555.

Latitudinarianism. Anglican Christians who took a 'broad' view of the necessity for dogma and definition in matters of belief. They are naturally distinguished more by what they oppose than by what they propose as a consistent set of doctrines.

Latrocinium (Robber synod): see EPHESUS.

Latter-Day Saints: see MORMONS.

Lauds. The traditional morning *office of the W. Church, with the title *Ad Laudes Matutinas* (for morning praises). In the *Book of Common Prayer, *morning prayer embraces parts of lauds and mattins in a single service.

Laughing Buddha (Chin., *mi-lo-fo*). The depiction of the future buddha *Maitreya with stout belly, broad smile, and surrounded by children—symbolizing wealth and equanimity. He is identified with *Hotei (Chin., Pu-tai).

La Vallée-Poussin, Louis de (1869–1938). A renowned Belgian scholar of Buddhism who made a major contribution to the field, notably through the editing and translating of important Buddhist works in Sanskrit, Tibetan, and Chinese. His major contributions were in the fields of *Mādhyamaka philosophy and *Abhidhamma scholasticism.

Lāvān (Pañjābī, 'reverent circumambulation of sacred fire or scriptures'). For Hindus this refers to the central *marriage rite in which bride and groom, linked by a scarf, walk clockwise around the sacred fire. For Sikhs it means circling the **Ādi Granth* four times.

Lavater, Johann (opponent): see MENDELSSOHN, MOSES.

Lavra (Gk., *laura*, 'street' or 'alley'). In the early Christian Church, a gathering of *anchorites who lived in separate dwellings or cells, and assembled only on Saturdays and Sundays. The term has also become the name of important *coenobitic monasteries and especially to the 'Great Lavra' or simply 'Lavra' on Mount *Athos founded by St Athanasios the Athonite in 962.

Law, William (1686–1761). Christian devotional writer. He was fellow of Emmanuel College, Cambridge, until deprived of his fellowship as a Nonjuror (see DIVINE RIGHT ...) at the accession of George I. After a period as tutor to the father of the historian E. Gibbon, he retired in 1740 to his birthplace, Kings Cliffe, Northants., where he gave his remaining years to writing and local social concern, increasingly influenced by *Boehme and becoming much more idiosyncratic.

His most famous work, published in 1728, was *A Serious Call to a Devout and Holy Life*. The simplicity of its teaching and its vigorous style soon established the work as a classic, which has probably had more influence than any other *Protestant spiritual book except *Bunyan's *Pilgrim's Progress*.

Law (Jewish): see HALAKHAH; TORAH.

Law Code of Manu: see DHARMA.

Law of Return. The Israeli law which gives every *Jew the right to settle in *Israel as an immigrant. The Law of Return was passed by the Israeli Knesset (Parliament) in 1950. Various legal problems have arisen concerning who counts as a true Jew.

Law of the Fishes (political assumption): see ARTHAŚĀSTRA.

Laya (Skt., 'melting'). The merging of the soul with *Brahman in Hinduism; the dissolution of the cosmos at the end of a *kalpa.

Laylat al-Barā'ah (Muslim festival): see FESTIVALS AND FASTS.

Laylat al-Qadr (Arab., 'night of power'). One of the later nights—generally thought to be the 27th—of the month of *Ramaḍān. It is the title of sūra 97 of the *Qur'ān, which describes this night as 'better than a thousand months', since during it the *angels (*malā'ika*) descend to earth; it is 'peace until the rising of the dawn'. Many Muslims like to spend this night in prayer and retreat (*'Itikāf) in a *mosque.

Layman/person: see LAITY.

Leaven (Heb., *ḥamez*). Raising agent forbidden to Jews during the season of *Passover—hence this is sometimes called the festival of unleavened bread. Leaven must necessarily come from the preceding year's harvest, but the festival looks forward, in absolute trust in God, to the new year. The search for leaven (*bedikat ḥamez*) is based on the injunction in Exodus 12. 15 ff., to 'eliminate leaven from your houses'.

In the New Testament, leaven is a likeness of the potential for growth in the kingdom (Matthew 13. 33); but equally it is an illustration of the speed with which evil and corruption spread (1 Corinthians 5. 8; Luke 12. 1). Leavened vs. unleavened bread for the *eucharist became a matter of dispute between the E. and the W. Churches: see AZYMITES.

Lectio Divina (Lat., 'divine/holy reading'). Attention to the scriptures (or occasionally to a spiritual text) in an attitude of prayer and devotion, leading to communion with God.

Lectionary. A book containing, or listing, passages from the Bible appointed to be read at public worship.

Lee, Ann (founder): see SHAKERS.

Lefebvre, Marcel (1905–91). Former archbishop of Dakar and leader of a traditionalist movement within *Roman Catholicism. He rejected the changes brought about by the second *Vatican Council, proclaiming that 'our future is the past'. After an unauthorized ordination of thirteen priests in June 1976, he was suspended from the exercise of his priestly ministry by the *pope. Cardinal Ratzinger, whose extreme conservatism recognized virtue in Lefebvre's position, negotiated a protocol of reconciliation, which Lefebvre signed in 1988; but he withdrew his signature when he realized that a Commission of Inquiry would have a Vatican majority on it.

Left-hand Tantrism: see VĀMĀCĀRA.

Legate, Papal. A personal representative, in effect ambassador, of the *Holy See.

Legio Maria (in distinction from the Legion of Mary, a Roman Catholic lay organization): see MARIA LEGIO.

Leibniz, Gottfried Wilhelm (1646–1716). German philosopher and mathematician. He studied law initially (at Leipzig), but turned to philosophy and mathematics, making an independent discovery of the infinitesimal calculus. From a Protestant background, he espoused the cause of reconciliation between Protestants and Roman Catholics—and was invited to supervise the Vatican Library. In *Essays on Theodicy* (1710), he argued that the law of continuity (based on the consistency of the universe) points to a perfect Being (i.e. God), who would necessarily create the best of all possible worlds (a view satirized by Voltaire, especially in *Candide*). In *The Monadology* (1714) he advanced the view that everything is made up of simple monads. Arranged hierarchically, the soul is the ruling entechy of the body—offering an analogy of the relation of God to the world.

Lekhah dodi (Heb., 'Come, my friend'). Initial words and title of a Jewish *Sabbath hymn. *Lekhah dodi* is sung near the beginning of the Sabbath evening service to welcome the Sabbath.

Lenshina, Alice (founder): see LUMPA CHURCH.

Lent (Old Eng., *lencten*; Germ., *Lenz*, 'spring'). The forty-day *fast before *Easter. The length was presumably suggested by the forty days' fasts of *Moses, *Elijah, and *Jesus himself. Lent is observed as a time of penance by abstaining from festivities, by almsgiving, and by devoting time to prayer and religious study.

Leo I, St, known as **'the Great'** (d. 461). Pope from 440, who worked to enhance the preeminence of the see of Rome, claiming jurisdiction in Africa, Spain, and Gaul. Leo composed his *Tome*, expounding the *Christology of the Latin Church, according to which Jesus Christ is one person, the divine Word, in whom are two unconfused natures, the divine and human; each of these exercises its own particular faculties, but because of the *communicatio idiomatum it may be said that the Son of Man descended from heaven, and the Son of God was crucified. The *Tome* was given formal authority at the Council of Chalcedon in 451. Leo was declared a *Doctor of the Church by Benedict XIV.

Leo X (1475–1521). *Pope from 9 Mar. 1513. As pope he showed himself a patron of learning and of the arts, but wholly failed to appreciate the strength of *Luther's convictions (he issued the *bull *Exsurge Domine* in 1520) or the degree of hostility felt in Germany towards the taxes he had demanded to finance a *crusade against the Turks. His period of office plunged the papacy deeply into debt, through its extravagance.

Leo XIII (1810–1903). *Pope from 20 Feb. 1878. Born Giocchino Vincenzo Pecci, he was sent to Perugia as *archbishop in 1845. He immediately set about improving the education of his clergy, and encouraged the study of Thomas *Aquinas in the diocesan seminary (Thomism was later to be strongly advocated in the *encyclical, *Aeterni Patris*). He carried his support of neo-*scholasticism into his pontificate, and one of his first acts was to write the encyclical commending the study of Aquinas's philosophy. He was a considerable patron of learning, insisting that the Church had nothing to fear from the truth. He failed to reach an accommodation with the new kingdom of Italy, and his encyclical **Rerum Novarum* gave support to those wishing to restore the *ancien régime*, though his endorsement of the workers' movement was of great psychological importance as the first such act by an authority of international standing.

Leontopolis. A 2nd-cent. BCE Jewish settlement in Egypt. As a reward to Jewish soldiers, the ruler Onias IV converted an Egyptian temple into a *temple for the God of Israel which survived until its closure by the Romans in 73 CE.

Lessing, Gotthold Ephraim (1729–81). German poet, dramatist, and religious essayist who influenced theological and philosophical discussion both within Germany and beyond. He helped to arrange publication of some controversial essays by Hermann Samuel Reimarus (the *Wolfenbüttel Fragments*, 1774–8) in which then-novel methods of criticism were employed to undermine traditional aspects of Jewish and Christian scripture. Lessing's own religious views were broadly *deistic. He advocated complete toleration in matters religious in his play *Nathan the Wise*, a work modelled loosely on his close friend Moses *Mendelssohn.

Letter mysticism: see GEMATRIA.

Letter to Women (Apostolic Letter): see WOMEN.

Levi. Third son of *Jacob and Leah and ancestor of the Jewish tribe of Levi. During the period of the monarchy, the Levites became state officials in their administration of the cult; they became eventually the Temple singers.

Leviathan. A large sea animal. In the Hebrew scriptures, the leviathan frequently represents the forces of chaos which are opposed to God.

Levi ben Gershom, **Ralbag**, or **Gersonides** (1288–1344). Jewish philosopher and Bible commentator. He was an eminent *Talmudist who wrote a commentary on *Berakhot* (now lost) and probably a commentary on the thirteen *hermeneutical rules of R. *Ishmael (publ. 1800). He wrote several commentaries on Averroes' paraphrases and commentaries on Aristotle and on the Bible. His major philosophical work was the *Sefer Milhamot Adonai* (The Book of the Wars of the Lord), written between 1317 and 1329. Divided into six parts, it deals with the immortality of the *soul, *prophecy, divine knowledge, providence, the celestial spheres, and creation.

Levi Isaac [Yitsḥak] ben Meir of Berdichev (*c.*1740–1810). Jewish *Ḥasidic *zaddik. Levi Isaac was a pupil of *Dov Baer. He emerged as a Zaddik in the town of Zelechow, but was driven from there and from Pinsk by the *mitnaggedim. Finally he moved to Berdichev in 1785 where he lived until his death. He was recognized as a major Ḥasidic leader of his time and became a popular hero in Jewish fiction and poetry, in which he is regarded as an advocate for Israel before God. He wrote a two-part work, *Kedushat Levi*, which expounds Ḥasidic teaching in the form of a commentary mainly on *Torah.

Levinsohn, Isaac Baer, or **Ribal** (1788–1860). Hebrew author. Levinsohn's literary output was mainly polemical. He was one of the founders of the *Haskalah movement in Russia, and he was concerned with the position of the Jews in E. Europe. His best-known work, *Te'udah be-Yisrael* (Testimony in Israel, 1828), described the Hebrew language as 'the bond of religion and national survival', and he argued against the use of *Yiddish. He also wrote *Beit Yehudah* (House of Judah, 1838) which was an attempt to answer Christian questions about Judaism, and *Efes Damim* (No Blood, 1837) which was written to refute the *blood-libel.

Levirate marriage (*yibbum*). A Jewish custom which obliges a childless widow to marry her dead husband's brother. The obligation of levirate marriage is laid down in Deuteronomy 25. 5–6.

Lévi-Strauss, Claude (b. 1908). French anthropologist associated particularly with structuralism. Seeing himself as 'neolithic', Lévi-Strauss drew upon traditional societies, including their *myths and classificatory systems (taboos, etc.), to put the human imagination in its place. Collective representations are the product of the human mind. They are 'thought out' in a way which reflects their virtual identity with fundamental mental structures of the mind, rather than their being autonomous creations. Although some have seen Lévi-Strauss as a 'culture hero', his emphasis on cognition to the virtual exclusion of emotion, his pessimistic view of imagination and progress, the excesses of his structuralism, and the apparently self-verifying nature of his approach, are drawbacks increasingly attended to by critics.

See also MYTH.

Levitation: see DARDURA-SIDDHI; LAGHIMAN.

Levite: see LEVI.

Levitical cities. Cities in *Erez Israel prescribed in the Hebrew scriptures for the tribe of *Levi (Numbers 35. 1–8).

Leviticus. The third book of the Hebrew Bible and Christian Old Testament. The Eng. title follows the Gk. and Lat. versions, the Heb. title *Vayyiqra* ('and he called') being the first word of the text. The book is essentially a manual for priests (the *tannaim called it *Torat Kohanim*, 'Guidance for Priests'). In Judaism, Leviticus is, traditionally, the first book to be taught to school-children (Lev. R. 7. 3).

Lewis, Clive Staples (1898–1963). British scholar of English literature, writer and Christian apologist. As an Oxford don in the 1920s, C. S. Lewis moved from atheism to committed Christianity, specifically to an evangelical *Anglicanism. His most popular Christian works are *The Screwtape Letters* (1942), relating the advice given by a senior devil to his subordinate in luring a human subject away from salvation; *Mere Christianity* (1952, but originally a series of radio talks begun in 1941); and his spiritual autobiography *Surprised by Joy*. A science-fiction trilogy (1938–45) and the seven children's books known as the Chronicles of Narnia (1950–6) incorporate Christian themes allegorically. The death of his wife, Joy Davidson, evoked the searching record of his grief, *A Grief Observed* (first publ. under the name N. W. Clerk).

Lex talionis (law of retaliation): see TALION.

Lhan.cig.skyes.pa (innate enlightenment indwelling the body): see SAHAJA.

Lhasa (*lha*, 'abode of the gods'). Sometimes known as 'the forbidden city', former home of the *Dalai Lama and centre of Tibetan Buddhist life. It was made capital city of Tibet in the 7th cent. CE, and it remains the capital of the autonomous Xizang region (Tibet), and contains the Potala, a fortress of a thousand rooms, in which are kept many images of the Buddha. The *Jokhang temple in Lhasa was built in the 6th cent. CE. Drepung monastery, 5 km. away, is an active centre of *lama life (though much reduced since 1959).

Li. A Chinese word which 'on the most concrete level refers to all those "objective" prescriptions of behavior, whether involving rite, ceremony, manners, or general deportment, that bind human beings and the spirits together in networks of interacting roles within the family, within human society, and with the numinous realm beyond' (B. Schwartz, *The World of Thought in Ancient China*, 1985).

Li was first developed as a moral and religious concept by *Confucius and his followers, for whom li consists of a pattern of behaviour which, when performed correctly, of itself effects and expresses harmony among the various hierarchically ordered elements of family, society, and the cosmos.

*Mo Tzu, in contrast, attacked the Confucian understanding of li. It has nothing to do with the training of people or the 'regulation of their likes and dislikes'. It has a certain limited value as an expression of gratitude to the spirits (belief in which Mo Tzu views as performing an essential social-moral function), but if performed extravagantly it wastes precious resources and distracts people from the more pressing tasks of ordering society. Taoists saw li as a prime example of the sort of contrived practice (*wei*) characteristic of the fall from primordial simplicity.

Despite these attacks, the concept of li remained central to the Confucian tradition in China down to recent times.

Li (gold): see HUA-YEN.

Liberal Judaism: see REFORM JUDAISM.

Liberation Theology (perhaps more accurately in the plural, theologies), an understanding of the role of theology in moving from abstraction to praxis, in which the actual condition of the poor is the starting-point. It was defined by H. Assmann as 'teologia desde la praxis de la liberación' ('theology starting from the praxis of liberation'), and by G. Gutiérrez (b. 1928) as 'a critical reflection both from within, and upon, historical praxis, in confrontation with the word of the Lord as lived and experienced in faith'. Liberation theology arose in S. America out of 'an ethical indignation at the poverty and marginalisation of the great masses of our continent' (L. Boff), and it is theology both lived and written 'from the underside of history' (Gutiérrez). It is Christian community in action, arising from what Frantz Fanon called *The Wretched of the Earth* (his final work, publ. months before he died in 1961). From the start, liberation theology saw itself as different from the social gospel programme of the turn of the century, epitomized in W. Rauschenbusch (1861–1919). Liberation theology saw itself facing a different agenda from that of Anglo-Saxon theology: for the latter, the agenda, set by unbelievers, is of how to speak of God in an unbelieving world. For liberation theology, the agenda is set by the question of the non-person: 'Our question is how to tell the non-person, the nonhuman, that God is love, and that this love makes us all brothers and sisters' (Gutiérrez).

Major themes of liberation theology can be discerned in the titles of some of the leading books. *Jesus Christ Liberator* (L. Boff, 1972) points out that in Christ, not words, but the Word was revealed in act, to make 'the utopia of absolute liberation' a *topia*, a place here and now. *Church: Charism and Power* (L. Boff, 1981) contests the 'institutional fossilisation' of the centuries which has produced a hierarchical Church, oppressive and clerical, which cannot be amended by minor reform; in its place, Boff (and others) propose *Iglesia popular*, the church arising from the people by the power of the Holy Spirit (*desde el pueblo por el Espiritu*)—in which connection, the importance of base (ecclesial) communities is paramount. *We Drink from Our Own Wells: The Spiritual Journey of a People* (G. Gutiérrez, 1984) took the phrase and argument of St *Bernard that in matters of the spirit, one must draw first on one's own experience: whereas this has usually, in the past, been a matter of individual process, aimed at an improved interior life, in S. America the experience is communal, and often of solidarity for survival. *The Power of the Poor in History* (G. Gutiérrez, 1983) reflects 'the preferential option for the poor': by this is meant that 'the poor deserve preference, not because they are morally or religiously better than others, but because God is God, in whose eyes "the last are first" '—a mother with a sick child does not love her other children less just because she commits herself immediately to the child in need; it also allows the possibility that violence may be a necessary means of bringing about justice: 'We cannot say that violence is alright when the oppressor uses it to maintain or preserve order, but wrong when the oppressed use it to overthrow this same order.'

The response of the *Vatican to liberation theology was initially hostile, but became more circumspect. The second Latin American Episcopal Conference at Medellín (CELAM II) in 1968 condemned institutionalized violence and the alliance of the Church with it; CELAM

III at Puebla in 1979 endorsed the preferential option for the poor, commended base communities, and made 'a serene affirmation of Medellín'. The *Congregation for the Doctrine of the Faith, ignoring the more reflective findings of the International Theological Commission's Dossier of 1976, issued its *Instruction on Certain Aspects of the Theology of Liberation* in 1984, and it summoned L. Boff to Rome for investigation, forbidding him, as a result, to lecture or publish—a ban that lasted for a year. The poverty of the analysis, thought by many to amount to a caricature, led to a second *Instruction on Christian Freedom and Liberation* (1986). This was to be read in conjunction with the first *Instruction*, and was not to be taken as contradicting it, but it is a far more positive document; nevertheless, Gutiérrez was banned from lecturing in Rome in 1994.

Liberation theology has had extensive influence outside S. America. From the Detroit 'Theology in the Americas' Conference in 1975 (*Proceedings*, ed. S. Torres and J. Eagleson, 1976), the connections with black theology and with *feminist theology were so clear that the phrase 'liberation theologies' became preferred. In 1976, the Ecumenical Association of Third World Theologians (EATWOT) held its first meeting in Dar-es-Salaam, with a clear commitment to the struggle for a just society. Equally important has been the determination to require theology to arise from the context of experience (e.g. K. Koyama, *Waterbuffalo Theology*, 1974; C. S. Song, *Third-Eye Theology*, 1979; *minjung* theology in Korea, which takes the concept of people who are ruled and dominated, but who use the process of history to become free subjects).

Li Chi (Records of Rituals). One of the *Confucian Classics. Among the several collections of texts relating to secular and religious rituals, and the codes of behaviour for the privileged classes in general, the *Li Chi* is richest in material of a philosophical nature. The *Li Chi* is a voluminous anthology, its component texts are undatable, but presumably mostly come from the last few cents. of the Chou dynasty (?1111–1256 BCE) and possibly in some cases from early Han (2nd cent. BCE).

Lieberman, Saul (1898–1983), Jewish *Talmudic scholar. Lieberman was born in Belorussia, but first settled in *Jerusalem, and then from 1940 taught in the *Jewish Theological Seminary. A prolific writer, he produced a series of studies on the text of the Jerusalem *Talmud, a commentary on the entire *tosefta, and two important books on *Hellenism, *Greek in Jewish Palestine* and *Hellenism in Jewish Palestine*.

Lieh-Tzu (The Classic of Complete Emptiness). Taoist text attributed to *Lieh Yü-k'au, whose personal name was Lieh-tzu; but in fact the text is much later (*c*.3rd cent. CE).

Along with **Lao Tzu* and **Chuang-Tzu*, it is the third of the old texts to form part of the Taoist canon. It contains stories, parables, and legends, and discussions on the nature of life.

Lieh Yü-k'au (*c*.450–*c*.375 BCE). Taoist philosopher of whom little, if anything, is known, except for a tradition that he claimed that, after nine years of Taoist study, he was able to ride on the wind—'or is the wind riding on me?' The *Lieh-tzu* is attributed to him, but wrongly.

Lien-ch'i (Chin., 'melting the breath'). Taoist exercise in breathing, to allow the breath to flow to all parts of the body. See also CH'I.

Life after death: see DEATH.

Life as art: see MIKI TOKUHARU.

Lifnim mi-shurat ha-din (beyond the boundary of what the law requires): see ETHICS (JUDAISM).

Light: see NŪR.

Liguori, St Alphonsus (1696–1787). Christian moral theologian and founder of the Redemptorists. He intended to be a missionary in China, but was sent to the poor in Naples, where he soon built up a large following. He founded the Redemptorists with fellow-missionaries in 1732, stressing contemplation of the cross and the *eucharist. He sought a middle way between *Jansenist rigour and *Jesuit laxity—associated with *Probabilism, against which he set Equiprobabilism in discerning a course of action: this holds that a doubtful law does not oblige, and that a probable opinion may be followed, but that a law is doubtful only when the opinions for and against it are equally balanced. His views were set forth in *Annotationes* (1748) and more fully in *Theologia Moralis* (1753/5). He was beatified in 1813, made Doctor of the Church in 1871, and patron of confessors and moralists in 1950, when *Pius XII stated that he was 'a safe norm' in the Church.

Li Hongzhi (founder of Chinese movement): see FALUN GONG.

Li-Hsüeh (Chinese school): see CHU HSI.

Li-kuei. The *kuei in Chinese popular belief who return after death as vengeful spirits.

Līlā (Skt., 'play'). The 'joyous exercise of spontaneity involved [according to Hindus] in the art of creation' (S. *Radhakrishnan). Līlā is freedom of movement, as in the rush of water from a fountain. It represents an exuberance in creation, undertaken by the god(s) for sheer delight, and is thus the reason why there is something rather than nothing. Līlā is personified in *Lalitā. Līlā came also to refer to the acts of gods, so that dramatic re-enactments are called '-līlā', as e.g. *Ramalīlā* or *Kṛṣṇalīlā*.

Lilith. A female *demon in Jewish mythology. Isaiah lists Lilith among the beasts of prey which will devastate the land (34. 14). According to a *midrash, Lilith was the first *Eve who disputed with *Adam because she was unwilling to forgo her equality.

Limbo (Lat., *limbus*, 'border', *sc.* of hell). In Catholic theology, the place for the dead who have deserved neither the beatific vision nor the punishment of hell. These include the righteous before the coming of Christ, and also unbaptized babies (and some children) held to be in *original sin but innocent of actual sins.

Liminality (rituals negotiating thresholds): see RITES OF PASSAGE.

Lin-chi I-hsüan (Jap. Rinzai Gigen, *d.* 867 CE). Chinese master who founded the Zen Buddhist Lin-chi line (*Rinzai-shū in Japanese). Lin-chi was noted for his emphasis on shouting (*ho) and striking (*kyosaku) as techniques for spurring on the spiritual progress of his students. 'A type of Chinese Socrates' (Demiéville), he is one of the outstanding figures, not just of Buddhism, but of humanity.

The Lin-chi way is characterized by dialectical formulae, the three statements (*sanku*), three mysteries (*sangen*), and three essentials (*sanyō*); and the sets of four—four alternatives (*shiryōken*), four conversations, four types of shouting (*shikatsu*). The threefold formulae are dense and not explained.

His sayings and some biographical information are gathered in *Lin-chi lu* (tr. R. F. Sasaki, 1975; see also *Rinzairoku*), which includes the notable command: 'If you meet the Buddha, kill the Buddha; if you meet the patriarch, kill the patriarch', which summarizes the goal of independence from even the highest authority in the achieving of what they alone have the authority to teach.

Lindisfarne. 'Holy Island', off the coast of Northumberland in England. It became a missionary centre and episcopal see under St *Aidan in 635. The Latin manuscript known as the Lindisfarne Gospels was written and decorated *c.*698–9 by Eadfrith (afterwards bishop of Lindisfarne) 'in honour of St *Cuthbert'.

Lineages (Buddhist): see BUDDHIST SCHOOLS.

Ling (Chin.). A term used in Chinese religious, literary, philosophical, and medical texts to denote a wide variety of attributes and beings. The closest Eng. approximation is 'spiritual' or 'spirit'.

Liṅga(m) (Skt., 'symbol'). Hindu term for a mark or sign, especially the sign or symbol of generative energy. The liṅga and *yoni, the representations of the male and female sex organs, thus bring the issues of generation and fertility into a religious context. In *Śaiva temples, the liṅga stands on a pedestal (which represents the yoni), their union being the quintessential summary of creative energy. Important examples can be found in the Liṅgarāj, in the temple dedicated to Śiva as the Lord of the Three Worlds (Tribhuvaneśvar) in *Bhubaneswar (hence the name of the city in Orissa, the site of many Hindu temples); at *Elephanta; and at Ellora in the Kailāsa temple, dedicated to Śiva. Among the most ancient (still a centre for worship) is that in Guḍimally in S. India. The twelve *Jyotir-liṅga(m)s, made directly from light without human assistance, are each a centre of *pilgrimage. The **Liṅga Purāṇa* is devoted to the honour of Śiva. See Index, Liṅga.

Liṅga-purāṇa. Long *purāṇa concerned with the four goals of life: *artha, *kāma, *dharma, *mokṣa. It has little connection with the *liṅga.

Liṅga-śarīra or **Sūkṣma-śarīra.** The second, subtle sheath surrounding the *ātman. It supports the continuity from one life to another in rebirth, bearing the consequences of *karma.

Liṅgāyat (Skt., *liṅga, emblem of *Śiva). An ancient Indian *Śaivite sect believing in the One Undivided, or Non-dualistic, Being, *Brahmā, or Śiva-tattva, possessing latent creative energy in its aspect as pure 'existence' (*sthala*). Its adherents are also known as Viraśaivas. Once the creative principle is activated, this Being becomes two: Śiva made manifest who is worshipped (*liṅga-sthala*), and each individual worshipping soul (*aṅga-sthala*).

Before the 12th cent. the Liṅgāyats, termed Ārādhya (devoted), maintained many traditional *brahmanic practices, but a reform movement was initiated by *Basava (*c.*1106–67/8), a S. Indian *brahman who carried out systematic attacks on Jains, Buddhists, and *Vaiṣṇavas, while sponsoring Śaivism and, in particular, the Liṅgāyat sect.

The Liṅgāyats adopted many socio-religious reforms, some of which were later to be promulgated throughout Hinduism.

Liṅgāyat priests (*jaṅgamas*) are highly regarded; while some are allowed to marry, those in the most prestigious category are *celibate.

They have great influence in the community, and every Liṅgāyat, boy or girl, has to undergo initiation, at which the significance of the three types of liṅga is explained: the bhāva-linga of Śiva-tattva, the supreme, all-pervading, and eternal; the prāṇa-liṅga, that which a person may comprehend, the deity he worships; the ishṭa-liṅga, or 'desire'-liṅga, which may be seen and which fulfils all desire, and is therefore to be reverenced. All Liṅgāyats, after initiation, wear a stone liṅga in a silver casket; its loss is the equivalent of 'spiritual death': this is a reminder that the body is the true temple.

Liṅgāyats are found chiefly in Kanara, and much of the development of literary Kanarese is owed to them.

Ling-chih (herb of immortality): see CH'ANG-SHENG PU-SSU.

Ling-pao Ching (Writings of the Magic Jewel). Chinese *Taoist texts underlying *Ling-pao p'ai, a religious Taoist (tao-chiao) movement. They describe the Taoist pantheon and the rites by which they may be approached, and they contain instructions for rituals. See also SAN-CH'ING.

Ling-pao P'ai (Chin., 'School of the Magic Jewel'). A movement within religious *Taoism (tao-chiao), based on **Ling-pao Ching*. Influenced by Buddhist devotion to *bodhisattvas, it claimed that liberation or salvation depends on help from deities (*t'ien-tsun*). Of great importance is *chai (fasting) in projecting deities from within, and thus externalizing them for worship. The school is thus noted for its ritual.

Ling-pao t'ien-tsun (Taoist heavenly ruler): see SAN-CH'ING.

Li Po (**Li Pai, Li T'ai-pai**), (701–62). Chinese Taoist poet. Although he spent a short period in Ch'angan (*Sian/Xi'an) as a court writer (742–4), he spent most of his life wandering. Tradition makes him one of the 'eight immortals of the wine cup', and he himself interpreted his wild behaviour as arising from the fact that he was 'a banished immortal': these are immortals who do some wrong in heaven and are banished to earth for a life-time. Whatever the source, his poems express a strong ecstasy, as well as sympathy with the misfortunes of others. He remains a very popular poet.

Litany (Gk., 'supplication'). A form of prayer, often addressed to God, but also to the Virgin *Mary or to *saints, made up of a series of petitions.

Li T'ieh-kuai (one of eight immortals): see PA-HSIEN.

Li Tsu-hsu (Kōan collector): see KŌAN.

Little Brothers (order founded by): see DE FOUCAULD, CHARLES EUGÈNE.

Little Entrance. In the *Orthodox liturgy of the *eucharist, the procession with the book of the gospels at the beginning of the liturgy of the catechumens.

See also GREAT ENTRANCE.

Little Flowers of St Francis: see FRANCIS, ST.

Little Gidding. The early 17th-cent. Huntingdonshire community of about forty members led by the *Anglican *deacon Nicholas Ferrar (1592–1637). Often critically referred to as 'the *Arminian Nunnery', from the title of a scurrilous pamphlet published in 1641, the household ordered its life by a set pattern of spiritual devotion with daily services, also paying attention to the study of theology and the practice of daily work.

Little Office of Our Lady. A Christian devotion, modelled on a day of the daily *office, in honour of the Virgin *Mary.

Little Russians: see RUTHENIANS.

Little Spring Time: see TAIZÉ COMMUNITY.

Liturgical Colours. Christian practice, beginning to be regularized from about 12th cent., of specifying particular colours for vestments and altar hangings, according to the season in the W. Church's year, on the occasion of a particular day. Thus white is generally commended for the two festival periods, Christmas to the Sunday after Epiphany, and from Easter Day to Pentecost Week, for days celebrating saints, and for Trinity Sunday; red for Pentecost Week, Holy Week, days commemorating martyrs, and sometimes for *confirmation and *ordination; violet/purple during Advent and Lent, and (if black is not used) for funerals and the commemoration of All Souls; and green on other occasions.

Liturgical Movement. A 20th-cent. movement in W. Churches to revitalize liturgical worship and give the congregation a more active part in it. It began among RC religious communities (often dated from an address by *Benedictine L. Beauduin in 1909) with efforts to make assembly for worship the main place where people learn and grow in faith.

Liturgy (Gk., *leitourgia*, from *laos*, 'people', + *ergon*, 'work'). Worship according to prescribed forms, as opposed to private devotions; hence 'the liturgy', the form of such worship.

In Christian use the word may refer to all the services of the Church (but not usually to those of Protestant churches). Most specifically, however, and especially in E. Churches, it is a title of the *eucharist or of a particular text of this service (e.g. the Liturgy of St John *Chrysostom, of St Basil, of St James, etc.). See Index, Liturgy.

Liturgy of the Presanctified. Ancient form of Christian *liturgy (sometimes called the Liturgy of St Gregory Dialogos, i.e. *Gregory the Great), which continues particularly in E. Christianity. It is celebrated on Wednesdays and Fridays in *Lent and on the first three days of *Holy Week. There is no prayer of consecration: the congregation may receive the *antidoron and perhaps the reserved sacrament.

Liu-tsu-ta-shih (Jap., Rokuso Daishi). Honorific title for *Hui-neng, often used instead of his name in works about him.

Liu-Tsu-Ta-Shih Fa-Pao-T'an-Ching*/*T'an-ching (Jap., *Rokuso daishi hōbōdan-gyo, Dan-gyo*). The Sūtra of the Sixth Patriarch from the High Seat of the Dharma Treasure, usually known as the *Platform Sūtra*, a key Zen work in which the biography and sayings of *Hui-neng are collected. However, it exists in longer and shorter forms, and may have been developed (as tradition affirms) from a lecture given by Hui-neng and recorded by Fa-hai.

Livingstone, David (1813–73). Christian medical *missionary and pioneer of Central and Southern African exploration. His 30,000-mile missionary journeys, mostly under appalling conditions, gave him first-hand knowledge of slave-trade cruelties, and he constantly worked for its suppression. His work inspired many who later established dispensaries, clinics, and hospitals all over the African continent. He died in the village of Ilala; his body was buried in Westminster Abbey.

Lobha (Skt.). Greed, or avarice, an impediment to enlightenment in Hinduism and Buddhism. Lobha is also one of the five sins (*akuśala) cited in the **Mahābhārata*.

Locanā (goddess): see AKṢOBHYA.

Lo Ch'ing (1443–1527). Founder of an eclectic religion in China. From his writings, gathered in *Five Works in Six Volumes*, it seems clear that he attained enlightenment after a personal quest. His teaching attacks the vacuity of ritual and prayer, and stresses in contrast the importance of gratitude—for everything and everyone on whom one's being depends. His school has diversified into a number of different sects, including one, the Dragon Flower Way (Lung-hua) which has somewhat reversed his teaching and includes a ritual element.

Locke, John (1632–1704). English philosopher who became a major source for British empiricism and for liberal democracy, and who applied his thought to the support of Christian theistic belief. In addition to his *Essay Concerning Human Understanding* (1690), *The Letter on Toleration* and (anonymously) *Two Treatises on Government*, he wrote *Thoughts on Education* (1693), *Reasonableness of Christianity* (1695), and works which appeared later, *The Conduct of the Understanding* (1706) and *Miracles* (1716).

That things are 'well-ordered' was important for Locke. Far from being 'a blind, fortuitous concourse of atoms', we are able to make sense, from our senses, of the universe, in which 'Nature never makes excellent things for mean or no uses'. From this, the existence of God is able to be demonstrated; and given that demonstrable truth, Locke was able to argue that certain rights which humans possess by nature are God-given and cannot be taken away: toleration becomes a primary virtue, to be exercised everywhere except where the rights of others are threatened. Locke's views were thus influential in forming the attitudes of the founders of the USA.

Logia (Gk., 'sayings'). Any of various collections of sayings of *Jesus in circulation in the early church.

Logic. An activity both condemned and justified in the history of Buddhist thought. While the *Buddha discouraged vain philosophical speculation, there is no evidence that he disapproved of logic as such. The *Abhidhammic literature, with its listing of Buddhist concepts, is presented in a vaguely logical manner; and the *Theravādin *Kathāvatthu* is an attempt to refute logically more than 200 propositions held by opposing schools. See also TARKA.

Logos (Gk., 'word' or 'reason'). A term prominent especially in early Christian theology as a title or description of Christ. The Christian use depends on: (i) the popular Stoic idea (going back to Heraclitus, *c.*500 BCE) of a universal reason governing and permeating the world; and (ii) the Hebrew conception of God's word (as of his *wisdom) as having an almost independent existence (e.g. Isaiah 55. 11). The prologue to the gospel of *John (1. 1–18) identifies the Logos as incarnate in Jesus. To the *apologists of the 2nd cent. the duality of the term was a welcome means of making *Christology compatible with popular philosophy. Later on (e.g. by *Athanasius), it was used to refer generally to the second person of the *Trinity.

Logos spermatikos ('innate word/wisdom'): see JUSTIN MARTYR, ST.

Lo-han. Chin. term (Jap., *rakan*) for the Theravādin Buddhist *arhat, though in Chinese Buddhism they have developed in the direction of minor deities, or (in the case of Ch'an) those who have obtained enlightenment by their effort. They resemble the *Hsien, the mountain-dwelling, cloud-riding immortals of Taoism. Major cults and iconography developed.

Lo-han Kuei-ch'en, also known as **Ti-ts'ang** (Jap., Rakan Keijin or Jizō; *c.*865–*c.*928 CE). Ch'an/Zen master, successor (*hassu) of Hsuan-sha Shih-pei and teacher of *Fa-yen Wen-i. He is particularly known for his exchanges (*mondō) with Fa-yen.

Loisy, Alfred Firmin (1857–1940). French biblical scholar and RC *Modernist. An enthusiastic exponent of the historico-critical study of the *Bible, he was dismissed from the Institut Catholique in Paris in 1893. In 1902 he wrote *L'Évangile et l'Église*, a defence of Catholicism against A. von *Harnack. He denied that Christ founded the Church and established *sacraments; and he was sceptical about the possibility of recovering the words of Jesus, and about the traditional doctrines of the Church. His *Autour d'un petit livre* (1903) made his divergence from traditional Catholicism still clearer. Several of his books were put on the *Index in 1903, and Loisy was *excommunicated in 1908 after publishing a critique of **Lamentabili*. From 1909 to 1930 he was professor of the history of religions at the Collège de France.

Loka (Skt., 'world').

Hinduism The domains or regions which make up the cosmos. In origin there were three lokas (*triloka*), locations inhabited by beings appropriate to them: earth, atmosphere, and 'the yonder world' (of the gods, the sun, the moon, and the stars). But these were early related to domains pertaining to salvation (and its opposite). Thus *svar*, 'sky', is already synonymous in the *Vedas with *svarga, 'heaven', so that another triad was produced of svarga-loka, *bhūmi-* (earth), and *pātāla-* (underworld or hell).

Buddhism The primary sense is analytic, in which loka is the 'habitat' of gods and human beings. In these contexts, loka is explained as all the perceptible world, i.e. all that which comes within the spheres of the senses. Loka in its cosmographic sense includes the entire cosmos. A *lokadhātu* is a smaller unit within the loka, a unit which may be described as a solar system. Thus, the loka consists of myriads of such solar systems. Therefore, in its immensity, the loka is unlimited. It is not possible, therefore, to reach the end of the loka by travelling and its immensity cannot be grasped by thinking either. Hence, *lokacintā* is one of four unthinkables according to *Anguttara Nikāya* (2. 80).

Buddhism also has its equivalent to the triloka of Hinduism (in Pāli, *trailokya* or *traidhātuka*). They are (i) kāmaloka, the domains of desire and attachment, including those of hell (*naraka), humans, animals, the *devas, and the *asuras; (ii) rūpaloka, the domain of form without desire, the gods in the *dhyāna heaven, attained through the four dhyānas; (iii) arūpaloka, the domain of formlessness. They may also be known as Kāmadhatu, etc.

Lokācārya (Skt., 'teacher of the people'). A theologian of *Śrīvaiṣṇavism and regarded as the figure-head of the *Teṉkaḷai. To distinguish him from an older teacher in the same tradition, he is called Piḷḷai, 'junior' (his personal name was Vāraṇādrīśa). He died during the earlier part of the 14th cent. CE. Eighteen treatises are ascribed to him, all in a highly Sanskritized form of Tamil, of which the *Mumukṣuppaṭi*, *Śrīvacaṇabhūṣaṇam*, and *Tattvatraya* are the most important. Lokācārya emphasized the commitment of God to those who seek him with devotion and love.

Lokadhatu: see LOKA (BUDDHISM).

Loka-pāla (Skt., 'world protector'). In both Hinduism and Buddhism, guardians of the whole world.

Lokāyata. Hindu philosophy restricting truth and reality to this world (*loka) only, hence a name for the school of *Cārvāka.

Lokeśvararaja (a Buddha): see AMIDA.

Lokottara (Skt.; Pāli, *lokuttara*). The transcendental and supramundane in Jainism and Buddhism. In early Buddhism, it refers to all that leads beyond clinging (*taṇhā) and attachment to *nirvāna. In Mahāyāna, it applies especially to the Buddha conceived of as a transcendental being of limitless wisdom and power. The Lokottaravāda was a school maintaining that every utterance of the Buddha, even those which are apparently mundane, are in fact concerned with transcendental matters.

Lollards (etym. uncertain, poss. from Lat. 'tares', *sc.* growing amidst the good wheat, or 'one who mumbles'). Name (originally one of abuse) given to the followers of *Wycliffe, who took issue with the Church on a number of grounds, but especially the power of the papacy, *transubstantiation, and the privileges of the priesthood. Later the term was applied to those more generally dissatisfied with the Church. They co-operated in the distribution of *Tyndale's New Testament, and were broadly in sympathy with the changes associated with the Henrician reformation. Their distinctive protest did not survive, but merged into the wider spectrum of Protestant views.

Lonergan, Bernard (1904–84). Christian theologian of central importance in the development of *transcendental Thomism (see NEO-THOMISM) into new and daring territory. Born in Canada, he became a *Jesuit in 1922. He was ordained priest in 1936, and taught in both Canada and Rome. His major work is *Insight: A Study of Human Understanding* (1957), a detailed study of the conditions and levels of human understanding. Nothing could be more erroneous than the positivist assumption that 'knowing consists in simply taking a look'. In contrast, he argues that 'Insight' is *in*-sight, seeing into the observed object to discern it in various ways. There is thus created a relation between 'intelligent grasp and reasonable affirmation', which constantly pulls the intelligent mind to the realm of transcendent being. His approach was elaborated in *Method in Theology* (1972).

Longchenpa (Tibetan scholar): see KLONG-CHEN RAB-'BYAMS-PA.

Longmen/Dragon Gate Caves or **Lungmen.** Large complex of caves occupied by Buddhists and containing, or supporting, carvings, and wall-paintings. There are about 1,300 caves, innumerable niches and a number of *pagodas. The caves are 9 miles south of Luoyang (cf. *Pai-ma-ssu) in Honan province. The earliest carvings are from the end of the 5th cent. and the latest from the 8th cent. Unusual is the Medical Prescription Cave, which has inscriptions offering remedies for a variety of illnesses. Along with the caves at *Tun-huang and *Yun-kang, they are the most revered in China.

Loṅkā (Shah) (15th cent.). Jain reformer and influence on the Sthānakvāsi *Gaccha (sect). Being convinced that the Jain scriptures (see AṄGA) gave no warrant for image worship, he set out on a path of rigorous reform, emphasizing personal asceticism. The term Sthānakvāsi means 'those who reside in preaching halls', emphasizing their avoidance of temples and images. Although few in number, they remain a part of Jain life to the present.

Lord of Misrule: see HOLY FOOLS.

Lord of the Dance: see DANCE.

Lord's Day. Christian name for *Sunday, based on Revelation 1. 10 (which however may refer to the day of judgement; cf. Amos 5. 18). It nowadays has *sabbatarian overtones, as in Lord's Day Observance Society, or in the more politically campaigning Keep Sunday Special.

Lord's Prayer. The prayer taught by Jesus in the *Sermon on the Mount (Matthew 6. 9–13) or privately to his disciples (Luke 11. 1–4). The two forms reflect different Aramaic versions no doubt already in liturgical use.

Lord's Supper. A title for the Christian *eucharist now used especially by Protestants. It is based on the term in 1 Corinthians 11. 20. Some scholars distinguish the 'mass' and 'lord's supper' as two different forms of eucharist in the earliest Church.

Loricae (breastplate prayers): see CELTIC CHURCH.

Lossky, Vladimir (1903–58). Russian lay theologian. One of the greatest 20th-cent. exponents of *Orthodox theology in the W., he was opposed to the sophiological theories of *Bulgakov, and championed a renewal of the thought of the fathers interpreted in the light of *hesychasm. Among W. thinkers he was drawn to Meister *Eckhart, on whom he wrote an important study. He combined a profoundly *apophatic theology with a doctrine of the mystery of the human person created in the image of God. His works include *The Mystical Theology of the Eastern Church* (1944, 1957); *In the Image and Likeness of God* (1967; 1975), and *Orthodox Theology* (1964, 1978).

Lotus (Skt., *padma*). Religious symbol in Eastern religions.

Hinduism The lotus represents beauty, and also non-attachment: as the lotus, rooted in mud, floats on water without becoming wet, so should the one seeking release live in the world without attachment. More specifically, it represents centres of consciousness (*cakra) in the body.

Buddhism The lotus summarizes the true nature of those who float free of ignorance (*avidya) and attain enlightenment (*bodhi). It is therefore the throne or seat of a buddha; and in *Pure Land, it is the symbol of the Buddha's teaching.

See also PUṆḌARIKA.

Lotus Position: see PADMĀSANA.

Lotus School: see T'IEN-T'AI.

Lotus Sūtra (Skt., *Saddharmapuṇḍarikasūtra*, 'The *Sūtra on the True *Dharma [which resembles a] White Lotus'). An early (1st cent. BCE–2nd cent. CE) and most important *Mahāyāna sūtra. It is taught by *Śākyamuni *Buddha in his *Saṃbhoga-kaya (cf. *trikaya) form. The sūtra reveals a new interpretation of many traditional beliefs, particularly concerning the nature of the Buddha. In the *Lotus*, the Buddha is no longer regarded as a mere mortal but as a sublime being with supernatural powers who preaches in a mythological paradise surrounded by thousands upon thousands of followers.

The true dharma teaches that the buddhas pass into nirvāna after, not before, all sentient beings, and the true Buddhist unwearyingly labours along the bodhisattva path for the liberation of all beings.

Lourdes. In SW France, site of a shrine of the Virgin *Mary. In 1858 the 14-year-old peasant girl, *Bernadette Soubirous, had visions of the Virgin Mary who told her that she was the *Immaculate Conception (a dogma then recently defined). A spring appeared and miraculous healings began to be reported, with the result that increasing numbers began to visit Lourdes. In 1862, the pilgrimage was officially recognized, and the first of a succession of churches was begun. A recent building has been the vast underground basilica of St Pius X, dedicated by the future Pope John XXIII in 1958. Feast day of Our Lady of Lourdes, 11 Feb.

Love. The many facets of love have been given expression in religions in ways so diverse that they characterize priorities and attitudes. For examples of these characterizations, see AGAPE; BHAKTI; KĀMA; KARUṆĀ; MO TZU; PREMA; RAḤMĀNĪYA.

Love Feast: see AGAPE.

Low Churchmen. Christians who give a relatively 'low' place to the importance of the episcopate, priesthood, sacraments, and matters of ritual; specifically, the more Protestant (*evangelical) party in the Anglican Church.

Low Sunday. The first Sunday after *Easter, probably by contrast with the 'high' feast of Easter Sunday itself.

Loyola: see IGNATIUS (OF) LOYOLA.

Lubavi(t)ch. Movement within Jewish Ḥasidism, founded by *Shne'ur Zalman in the 18th cent. His descendants made Lubavici, in Russia, their main centre, hence the name. Their views are those of Ḥabad, so that the two are now synonymous (see ḤABAD for their beliefs), although there have been other and independent Ḥabad schools. As with other Ḥasidic groups, they revere the authority of the *zaddik. Since the headquarters of the Lubavich moved to New York, the zaddik, now known as Rebbe, has become much more than the one responsible for the spiritual well-being of the community. The Lubavich regard the conversion of Jews to Judaism (i.e. to observant Judaism) as a matter of high priority, since otherwise the full return of the messiah cannot occur.

Lucar, Cyril (1572–1638). Patriarch of Constantinople from 1620. His earlier experiences in church politics had turned him against Rome, and in correspondence with Dutch theologians he expressed more and more sympathy with the *Reformed churches. His *Confession of Faith* published in Geneva in 1629 was an attempt to strengthen the Orthodox Church against Romanizing tendencies and bring it into dialogue with other Churches. His theology was finally condemned at the Synod of *Jerusalem (1672).

Lucifer (Lat., 'light-bringer'). In the *Vulgate and *Authorized Version of Isaiah 14. 12 ('How art thou fallen from heaven, O Lucifer'), an epithet for the king of Babylon. By some of the *fathers it was taken in conjunction with Luke 10. 18 as a name for the *devil, so that the whole passage Isaiah 14. 12–16 became one basis for the myth (developed in *Milton's *Paradise Lost*) that the devil is a rebellious *angel cast into *hell.

Luis of Granada (1504–88). Spanish spiritual writer. Born in Granada, he became a *Dominican in 1525. His spiritual writings, influenced by the *devotio moderna*, especially the **Imitation of Christ* and *Erasmus' *Encheiridion*, stress the importance of inward devotion. His books were condemned in 1559 but in revised form were widely influential, in particular on Francis *de Sales.

Luke, St. Travelling companion of *Paul, and (according to tradition) author of the third gospel and *Acts of the Apostles. Luke was a physician (Colossians 4. 11) who stayed with Paul in his imprisonment. Later tradition made him a painter, and in the Middle Ages a picture in Rome of the Virgin Mary was ascribed to him. He is the patron saint of doctors and artists. Feast day, 18 Oct.

The Gospel according to Luke is the third book of the New Testament. It forms a two-part work with the book of Acts.

Lulav (Heb., 'a shoot'). A palm branch connected with the Jewish *festival of *Sukkot. The lulav is one of the *four species which are used in worship on the feast of Sukkot.

Lull, Raymond or **Ramón** (*c.*1233–1315). Christian missionary, mystic and philosopher. At the age of 30, following a vision of the crucified Christ, he gave himself wholly to Christ's service as a *Franciscan tertiary, and he sought in particular the conversion of Islam. He studied Arabic, went on various missionary journeys, and wrote. His system of thought is *contemplative and *Neoplatonic, and may owe something to *Sufism. Among those he influenced was *Nicholas of Cusa. *The Book of the Lover and the Beloved* describes how the lover (the faithful Christian) cannot reach the Beloved (God), except *through* love.

Lumbinī. One of four places especially sacred in Buddhism (with *Bodhgayā, *Kuśinagara, *Sārnāth), because it is believed to be the birthplace of the *Buddha. Lumbinī is in the W. Terai of Nepal, just over 400 km. SW of Kathmandu; now known as Rumindei.

Lumpa Church. The most widely known independent church in Zambia. It was founded by a Bemba, Alice Mulenga Mubusha (1924–78), a *catechumen in the Church of Scotland mission, who experienced a mystic death and resurrection in 1953, and was commissioned to deliver Africans from witchcraft and sickness. A mass response led to the foundation of her Lumpa ('best of all') Church about 1954, which gathered some 60,000 members by 1960 under herself as Alice Lenshina (i.e. 'Regina' or Queen), with a new Sione ('Zion') as headquarters and a strict ethic forbidding magic, divorce, polygamy, inheritance of widows, and beer-drinking.

Lung (Chin., 'dragon'). In Taoism, the dragon represents the *yang principle, and is thus often portrayed accompanied by representations of *yin—e.g. clouds or water. Dragons have important active roles in ruling and guarding the world. See also DRAGONS, CHINESE.

Lung-hua (sect): see LO CH'ING.

Lung-hu-shan ('Dragon Tiger Mountain'). Mountain in Chiang-shi province, regarded by Taoists as the home of the celestial masters (*t'ien-shih).

Lung-men ('Dragon Gate', Buddhist caves): see LONGMEN.

Lung-men (school): see CHÜAN-CHEN TAO.

Lung-t'an Chung-hsiu (Ch'an teacher): see TE-SHAN HSUAN-CHIEN.

Lung-wang ('dragon kings'). Taoist mythological figures who have immediate authority over life and death, in the sense that they are responsible for rain and funerals. Humans depend on them, but they in turn are accountable (annually) to the primordial lord who originates all things (Yüan-shih T'ien-tsun; see SAN-SH'ING). See also DRAGONS, CHINESE.

Lun Yü (the Dialogues or Conversations of Confucius): see ANALECTS.

L(u)oyang: see LONGMEN CAVES; PAI-MA-SSU (BAIMASI).

Luria, Isaac ben Solomon, Ha-Ari (1534–72). Jewish *kabbalist. Luria was brought up in Egypt and studied under *David b. Solomon ibn Abi Zimri. His early life is shrouded in legend, but he seems to have retired from communal life while a young man to study the *Zohar* and other mystical works, and during this time he wrote his commentary on the *Sifra Di-Zeniuta* (The Book of Concealment), a section of the *Zohar*. In *c*.1570 Luria settled in Safed and studied with Moses *Cordovero. In Safed, Luria drew round himself a group of disciples whom he instructed orally in the mysteries of the kabbalah. These teachings are preserved only in the descriptions of his students. He envisaged a 'contraction' (*tsimtsum*) in God to make space for creation in relation to himself. The term had formerly been used to account for God's presence in the *Holy of Holies, but Luria gave it a novel sense. There then followed, according to Luria, the process of emanation (*sefirot), but the vessels containing the emanation of light could not bear the weight of glory (or perhaps resisted: for surely, Luria's pupils asked, God could have created vessels strong enough for the task?) and disintegrated. This catastrophe is called *shevirah* or *shevirat ha-kelim*. Luria did not hesitate to accept that God is the source of both good and evil, since without his creative act, the manifestation of evil could not have occurred. However, set against *shevirah* is the work of repair, called *tikkun*, which was a particular responsibility for *Adam. His fall reinforced the powers of evil and weakened those of good. In consequence, God chose a people, the Jews, to shoulder the responsibility once more. Jewish history is the history of this struggle; and the detail of each biography is a contribution to it. In particular, the keeping of the law is essential, since even one failure delays the coming of the messiah when alone the final victory will have been won.

Luria, Solomon ben Jehiel (Rashal/Maharshal) (*c*.1510–74). Jewish *Talmudic commentator. Luria served as *rabbi and rosh *yeshivah at Ostrog, Brisk, and Lublin. His *halakhic rulings were independent and avoided *pilpul and were generally accepted. Only a proportion of his work has been preserved, including his *Yam shel Shelomo* (The Seal of Solomon) on the *Talmud (1616–18) and his *Hokhmat Shelomo* (The Wisdom of Solomon, 1582), glosses on the text of the Talmud, printed subsequently in most edns. His *responsa (1574/5) give valuable insight into the culture of 16th-cent. Polish Jewry.

Lu-shan. Mount Lu. Buddhist centre from 4th cent. CE on, in Kiangsi province. Here *Hui-yüan founded *Pai-lien-tsung (the White Lotus school).

Lü-Shih Ch'un-Ch'iu (Spring and Autumn of Master Lū). A Confucian work produced under the supervision of Lü Pu-wei (*c*.3rd cent.

BCE), which attempted to gather and systematize knowledge necessary for proper government.

Luther, Martin (1483–1546). Founder of the German *Reformation. In 1505 he entered an Augustinian monastery. Ordained *priest in 1507, he was sent for further study at the newly founded University at Wittenberg, later to Erfurt. In 1512 he was made Doctor of Theology and was appointed professor of scripture at Wittenberg, a post he held for the rest of his life.

Deeply troubled concerning personal guilt, he became convinced concerning *justification by faith alone, finding help in the study of the Bible, *Augustine's anti-Pelagian writings, John *Tauler's mysticism and the **Theologia Germanica*, as well as the sensitive counsel of his superior John Staupitz. In 1517, pastorally concerned about the propagation of the *indulgence traffic by the Dominican preacher J. *Tetzel, Luther protested in his famous ninety-five theses. In the inevitable controversy which followed their publication, Luther debated his views with Catholic opponents, and produced in 1520 some of his most influential writings, *On Good Works*, *The Babylonian Captivity of the Church*, *Address to the German Nobility*, and *The Freedom of a Christian*. In the same year the papal *bull, **Exsurge Domine*, censured his teaching as heretical, and the promulgation a few months later of *Decet Romanum Pontificem* declared him excommunicate. He returned to Wittenberg in 1522 in order to preach against the extreme views of Andrew *Carlstadt.

In 1525 Luther married Catharine von Bora, a former nun. The *Augsburg Confession (1530), mainly the more diplomatic work of *Melanchthon, gave moderate expression to his leading ideas; and his prolific writings, on average a book a fortnight, circulated his teaching (addressed to circumstances, rather than being systematic) throughout Europe. His leading ideas were treasured by the *Lutheran Churches who summarized Luther's essential message in their *Book of Concord* (1580). On major articles of faith (*Trinity, *Christology, *atonement, etc.) Luther adhered to the classic credal tradition. The distinctive Lutheran emphasis is on the authority of *scripture and *soteriology. Because scripture is the word of God, it is the truth of God, in relation to which innovations of the Church (esp. of the *papacy) must be judged defective. **Sola scriptura* (scripture alone) is the source of doctrine and practice. Through 'faith alone' (*sola fide*), a sinful person receives (but does not create, as though faith is a work of merit) all that Christ has done for the world. Justification through faith is thus a central Lutheran theme. See Index, Lutherans.

Lutheran Churches. Those churches formed in response to *Luther's teaching. Their doctrinal convictions are given expression in the *Book of Concord* (1580). Scripture is affirmed as the sole rule of *faith, and justification by grace alone is the principal tenet.

From its beginnings in Germany Lutheranism quickly spread throughout Europe, gaining dominance in Scandinavia, Iceland, Prussia, and the Baltic Provinces, but its energies were diverted in the late 16th cent. by internal conflicts. The Lutheran Churches have produced outstanding theologians, philosophers, biblical scholars, composers, and musicians. They now have a worldwide membership of over 75 million. See Index, Lutherans.

Lutis (homosexuals): see HOMOSEXUALITY.

Lutron (ransom, to avoid strict interpretations of *tallion): see JESUS.

Lü-tsung (school of discipline): see TAO-HSÜAN.

Lu tung-pen (Taoist immortal): see HSIEN.

Luwum, Janani (1922–77). Christian archbishop of Uganda and *martyr. Son of a Christian convert, he became involved for a time with Balokole (see EAST AFRICAN REVIVAL), but moved away to mainstream Christianity, and was ordained Anglican priest in 1955. He became bishop of N. Uganda in 1969. After the Acholi massacres under Idi Amin in 1972, he became an increasingly outspoken opponent of Amin's excesses and cruelties, until he was himself arrested and shot.

Luzzatto, Moses Ḥayyim (Ramḥal) (1707–47). Jewish *kabbalist. Luzzatto lived in Padua and was the leader of a group of Jewish students. In 1727 (and subsequently) he believed he heard the voice of a *maggid who revealed secret doctrines. He was, however, attacked as a magician and a *Shabbatean and made to denounce the maggid's revelations. His most important kabbalistic works were the *Kelah Pithei Hokhmah*, an exposition of *Lurianic kabbalah, and his *Zohar Tunyana*, written under the influence of the maggid: in this work, he offered rules of conduct which, if observed, would hasten the coming of the *messiah. His highly influential ethical works include *Mesillat Yesharim* (The Path of the Righteous, 1936) which was studied in the E. European *yeshivot; and he also wrote poetry and verse dramas.

Luzzatto, Samuel David, or **Shadal** (1800–65). Jewish *biblical scholar. In 1829 Luzzatto was appointed professor at the rabbinical college in Padua where he taught the Bible, philosophy, Jewish history, and philology. He was a traditionalist who was critical of Jewish philosophy, *kabbalistic speculation, and secular European civilization, while firmly maintaining his belief in tradition, *revelation, and the *chosenness of the Jewish people.

LXX: see SEPTUAGINT.

M

Ms, Five (polluting acts): see PAÑCA-MAKĀRA.

Mā (Skt., 'mother'). Hindu mother goddess; also incorporated in names as a title of respect.

Maʿamad, mahamad (Heb., 'stand'). Jewish *Sephardi community leader, the equivalent of the *Ashkenazi *kahal*. Derived from the orders of priestly duties, they took decisions which were binding on those affected.

Maʿamad har Sinai (revelation on Mount Sinai): see SINAI, MOUNT.

Maʿaravot. A series of *piyyutim (liturgical poems) which are added to the Jewish *maʿariv service on *festivals.

Maʿarekhet ha-Elohut (Heb., 'The Order of God'). A Jewish *kabbalistic book. It was written in about the late 13th cent. and is of unknown authorship. It is an attempt to present the teachings of the kabbalah systematically.

Maʿariv (Heb., 'he [God] who causes the evening to come'). The Jewish order of evening *prayer. The service, which requires a *minyan, includes the *Shemaʿ and the *ʿAmidah.

Maʿaseh (Heb., 'story'). A Jewish legal source. A maʿaseh is a particular factual circumstance, such as a legal judgement or a specific act of an established *halakhic scholar. Because 'what has been done is no longer open to discussion' (*BRH* 29b), halakhah derived from a maʿaseh has particular force.

Maʿaseh Bereshit (Heb., 'work of creation'). Jewish mystical exploration of creation and of the power of the Word of God and of language. So great was the power released that instruction in this mysticism was restricted to individuals who had attained earlier levels of experience. See also HEKHALOT AND MERKABAH.

Maʿaseh Book (Heb., 'Story Book'; Yid., *Mayse Bukh*). A collection of anonymous Jewish folk tales. The *Maʿaseh Book* was first publ. in *Yiddish in 1602 and contains 254 stories, including *Talmudic *aggadah, *midrash, legends, jokes, and oral traditions.

Maʿaser(ot) (tithes): see TITHE(S).

Macarius, St, of Egypt (*c*.300–*c*.390). One of the *Desert Fathers, also known as 'the Great'. At about the age of 30 he founded a settlement of monks in the desert of Scetis (Wadi al-Natrun), which became an important centre of Egyptian monasticism.

The *Macarian Homilies* traditionally ascribed to him seem to come rather from a writer in N. Mesopotamia in the 4th–5th cents. In modern times the *Fifty Spiritual Homilies* have been an influential mystical text (e.g. on John *Wesley, who translated twenty-two of them into English).

Maccabees, Books of. Jewish *apocryphal and pseudepigraphical works containing the history of Simon the *Hasmonean and Judah Maccabee. *1 Maccabees*, originally written in Hebrew, covers the period of Jewish history from the accession of King Antiochus Epiphanes (*c*.175 BCE) to the death of Simon the Hasmonean in 135 BCE.

Machpelah, Cave of. Burial place of the Jewish *patriarchs, *Abraham, *Isaac, and *Jacob. The site of the Cave of Machpelah is identified with Haram el-Khalil in Hebron.

Macumba: see AFRO-BRAZILIAN CULTS.

Mādhava (Skt., 'a descendant of Madhu'). 1. Any member of the tribe of Madhu, i.e. the Yādavas, whose kingdom and exploits are recounted in the **Mahābhārata* and the *Purāṇas. The most famous of the Yādavas was *Kṛṣṇa.

2. According to tradition, Mādhavācārya, the 'learned Madhāva' (also called Vidyāraṇya), was the name of one celebrated author who, along with his famous brother Sāyaṇa, the commentator on the *Vedas, was associated with the court of the kingdom of Vijāyanagara in the latter half of the 14th cent. CE.

Madhhab (Arab., 'direction'). A Muslim system of thought, but more specifically (and usually), a *school of law: see SHARĪʿA.

Madhu 1. (Skt., 'honey'). The favourite drink of Hindu warriors. It features in *madhuvidya*, 'honey-knowledge', and thus on ritual occasions.

2. A demon killed by the Hindu god *Kṛṣṇa/ *Viṣṇu, who thus is frequently called Madhusūdana. See also MAHIṢA.

Madhva or **Madhvacarya** (dates uncertain, ranging from 1199–1278 CE to 1238–1317). Founder of a Hindu *Vaiṣṇava school and philosophy whose adherents are known as Mādhvas. It is the third (with *Śaṅkara and *Rāmānuja) of three major related philosophical schools, and because it is opposed to the non-dualism of Śaṅkara and the qualified non-dualism of Rāmānuja, and because it maintains five irreducible dualities, it is known as *dvaita-vedānta. The five distinctions are between: God and the soul; God and matter; the individual soul and matter; between souls; between individual components of the material. The final union with God is not one of absorption, nor of a relation in which the constituent parts, while retaining identity, nevertheless constitute one reality, but rather of a distinction between lover and beloved which is eternal. He wrote many works, especially commentaries. He established his main temple (dedicated to *Kṛṣṇa) at Udipi, where his succession and school is still maintained.

Madhyamāgama (Sanskrit name): see MAJJHIMA NIKĀYA; TRIPIṬAKA.

Mādhyamaka ('middle way'; Chin., *San-lun; Jap., *Sanron; Korean, Samnon). The 'Middle School', a system of Buddhist philosophy founded by *Nāgārjuna in the 1st cent. CE, extremely influential within the *Mahāyāna. The school claims to be faithful to the spirit of the Buddha's original teachings, which advocate a middle course between extreme practices and theories of all kinds, and it applies this principle to philosophical theories concerning the nature of phenomena. Thus the assertion that 'things exist' or that 'things do not exist' would be extreme views and should be rejected; the truth lies somewhere in-between and is to be arrived at through a process of dialectic, as opposing positions are revealed as self-negating. The adoption of any one position, it was argued, could immediately be challenged by taking up its opposite, and the Mādhyamaka therefore adopted a strategy of attacking their opponent's views rather than advancing claims of their own (which is not to deny that they might none the less hold their own philosophical views).

The scene for the appearance of the Mādhyamaka was set by the debates among the schools of the Theravāda over such basic doctrines as that all phenomena (*dharmas) are impermanent (*anicca) and without self (*anātman). This gave rise to philosophical difficulties concerning questions such as causation, temporality, and personal identity. The scholastic solution was to posit a theory of instantaneous serial continuity according to which phenomena (dharmas) constantly replicate themselves in a momentary sequence of change (*dharmakṣaṇikatva*). Thus reality was conceived of as cinematic: like a filmstrip in which one frame constantly gives way to the next, each moment, none the less, being substantially existent in its own right.

The Mādhyamaka challenged this notion of the substantial reality of dharmas, arguing that if things truly existed in this way and were possessed of a real nature or 'self-essence' (*svabhāva), it would contradict the Buddha's teaching on no-self (anātman) and render change impossible. What already substantially exists, they argued, would not need to be produced; and what does not substantially exist already could never come into being from a state of non-existence. Thus real existence cannot be predicated of dharmas, but neither can non-existence, since they clearly present themselves as having a mode of being of some kind. The conclusion of the Mādhyamaka was that the true nature of phenomena can only be described as an 'emptiness' or 'voidness' (*dharma-śūnyatā*, i.e. 'emptiness of self'); and that this emptiness of self-nature is synonymous with the principle of dependent origination (see PATICCA-SAMUPPĀDA) as taught by the Buddha. This process of reasoning is fully set out in Nāgārjuna's concise verses in the **Mūla-Mādhyamaka-Kārikā*, the root text of the system.

There were implications also for *soteriology: since emptiness is the true nature of what exists there can be no *ontological basis for a differentiation between *nirvāna and *saṃsāra. Any difference which exists must be an epistemological one resulting from ignorance and misconception. Accordingly, the Mādhyamaka posits 'two levels of truth': the level of Ultimate Truth (*paramārthasatya*), i.e. the perception of emptiness of the true nature of phenomena (the view of the enlightened); and the level of 'relative' or veiled truth (*samvṛtisatya*), i.e. the misconception of dharmas as possessing a substantial self-existent nature (the view of the unenlightened). The gaining of enlightenment is the passage from the latter to the former.

After Nāgārjuna the work of the school was carried forward by his disciple Āryadeva, but subsequently two schools divided, the Svatantrika, led by *Bhāvaviveka; and the *Prāsaṅgika, championed by *Candrakīrti, which adhered to the negative dialectic of the founder. The Mādhyamaka system was transmitted from India to Tibet and China (where it flourished, particularly in Tibet, as a central school of Mahāyāna philosophy), and to Japan, where it is known as *Sanron. See also SAN-LUN.

Madhyamā-pratipad (Skt. for): see MIDDLE WAY.

Mādhyamika. An adherent of *Mādhyamaka.

Madīna, al-. Yathrib, 'the town' to which *Muḥammad made the *hijra at the invitation of its inhabitants. It is situated in the Ḥijāz, and is the place where the earliest organized forms of Islam could take root (hence the fact that the Madinan *suras of the *Qur'ān deal increasingly with practical issues of individual and social life). The so-called Constitution of Madīna gathers several different agreements drawn up with Jewish and other tribes. Muḥammad was buried in Madīna (as were *Abū Bakr and *'Umar, and also *'Uthmān, but in a place apart), so it has been a place of *pilgrimage for Muslims.

Madonna (Ital., 'my lady'). A Christian designation of the Blessed Virgin *Mary, common especially in artistic representations.

Madrasa. Islamic school, for children, and for adult studies.

Mae chii (buddhist nuns): see BUDDHISM IN SOUTH-EAST ASIA.

Ma-fa (in Buddhism, period of decline): see MAPPŌ.

Māgadhā or **Māgadhi.** An ancient Indian language. It is chiefly important as the language employed by the Mauryan court of *Aśoka and particularly in the rock edicts of that king. Māgadhī is a Prakrit, its most widespread script being Brāhmī.

The kingdom of Māghadā was one of sixteen N. Indian states mentioned in Buddhist sources. It was in an area centred in what is now Bihar.

Magatsuhi-no-kami (Jap., '*kami of misfortune-force'). In Shinto, divine beings which bring about sin, pollution, disaster, and evil. They belong to the land of Yomi, the netherworld. Related terms are Ōmagatsuhi-no-kami which means 'Great Magatsuhi Kami' and Yasomagatsuhi-no-kami which means 'Countless Magatsuhi Kami'.

Ma.gcig Lab.sgron (10th/11th cent. CE). Prominent Tibetan Buddhist yogin and teacher, who formalized the *Chöd (Gcod) meditational practice. She was early noted for her lack of regard for personal appearance, an attitude which she encouraged in practitioners of Gcod. When she explored Indian yogic methods, she was attacked for repudiating her vows, and after moving with her family, she then went into retreat for the rest of her life.

Gcod ('cutting') has the aim of cutting through the apparent dualities created by the process of thought. The purpose of Gcod is to bring about the complete realization that nothing in reality exists. The path to this realization is one of making the five aggregations (*skandha) of one's appearance into a sacrificial offering to the best of one's hopes and the worst of one's fears in personified forms, passing in one of the rituals through four stages: (i) *dkar 'gyed*, 'white sharing', imagining one's body as sweet honey offered to the *Three Jewels; (ii) *khra 'gyed*, 'multicoloured offering', imagining one's body as desirable objects like gardens and gifts; (iii) *dmar 'gyed*, 'red sharing', imagining the flesh and blood of oneself offered to the demons; (iv) *nag 'gyed*, 'black sharing', the gathering up of one's own faults and the faults of others into oneself and the offering of it to the demons as an act of reparation. Of course, neither she nor the demons have any reality outside the construction of the mind: the purpose of Gcod is to visualize the best and the worst in order to cut off one's belief that they have some reality: hence the importance of vivid pictures and rituals.

Magdalen (follower of Jesus): see MARY MAGDALENE.

Magen David (Heb., 'Shield of *David'). Six-pointed star which has become the symbol of Judaism. It was employed by the Nazis as a badge of shame and was the symbol chosen for the *Israeli flag. A red magen David is used as an equivalent of the Red Cross.

Maggid (Heb., 'one who relates'). Jewish popular preacher; or, a spirit which conveys supernatural teachings to Jewish scholars. In the *kabbalistic tradition, the term maggid was also used to describe a spirit who passes supernatural secrets to worthy students of the kabbalah.

Maggid of Dubno (founder of Jewish sect): see KRANZ, JACOB.

Maghreb (i.e. Arab., *al-maghrib al-'arabi*, the Arab West). The region comprising Libya, Tunisia, Algeria, Mauretania, and Morocco.

Magi. Originally a Median tribe (according to Herodotus, the Magoi were one of six Median tribes) responsible for all ritual activity regardless of religious boundaries, e.g. to which god a sacrifice was offered. As *Zoroastrianism spread across the Iranian plateau so it became part of their responsibility. In this way, it is thought, *Zoroaster's teachings were integrated into the general traditions of the region. It was the magi who thereafter carried Zoroastrianism through the Empire. During the Achaemenid era, Babylon was a major administrative centre, and it is likely that it was there that the magi became involved in the beliefs and practices subsequently named after them, *magic, and also astrology. It was this reputation which motivated the writer of Matthew's Gospel (see below) to relate a story about magi (the word used in the Gk. is *magoi*, and so the later Christian legend of kings does not do justice to the text). Zoroaster himself used two different terms to refer to a priest: *zaotar*, an officiating priest, and a *manthran*, who composes sacred *manthras*. As Zoroastrianism developed, the magi became ever more important in the work of the Zoroastrian 'church'. Naturally words change with time, *magus* (singular) became *mobed*, under a supreme head, the *Mobedan Mobed*. In post-Sasanian Iran, the high priest took the title *hudnan pesobay*, leader of the faithful, a title recalling Muslim titles. In modern times a high priest, *dastur*, is generally associated with a 'cathedral' fire temple (Atash Bahram, *Atas) whose liturgical life he oversees with a team of priests, *mobeds*, under him. There are two initiatory rites for priests, *navar* and *maratab*. A priest who has undertaken the first of these, and is therefore qualified to perform some of the minor rites, is known as an *ervad*. The *mobeds* and the *ervads* have essentially liturgical roles, with little sense of any teaching or pastoral duties. Purity is necessary so that the duly empowered priest can, in devotion, through concentration on the ritual, generate ritual power (*amal*) so that the heavenly forces are present. Because of the centrality of the concept of purity, one term for priest is *yozdathrager*, 'Purifier'.

The Christian appropriation of the Magi reveals little knowledge of the above. According to Matthew 2. 1–12, they were guided by a star to Bethlehem, bearing gifts for the new-born *Jesus. Acts 13. 6 ff. uses the word to mean magic-workers, and *Ignatius of Antioch understood the word in that sense, arguing that magic yielded up its power when Jesus was born. *Origen inferred that they were three in number from the gifts, and *Tertullian suggested that they were kings. By the 6th cent., they were named Gaspar, Melchior, and Balthasar. What were claimed to be their *relics were taken to Europe and are now in Cologne Cathedral.

Magic. The production of effects in the world by actions, often ritualized, whose source of power is not open to observation; or by words, especially by incantation: chants of formulae, which may sound nonsensical to the outsider, may summon the relevant power, or may themselves effect the consequence: they may also be *apotropaic. Attempts to define the relation of magic to religion have formed part of the modern study of religion since its inception at the end of the 19th cent., often utilizing the Melanesian concept of *mana*, power of a supremely effective kind—not simply 'cause', but the reason why particular things happen. Thus E. *Evans-Pritchard (*Witchcraft, Magic and Oracles among the Azande*, 1937) held that magic belonged to an interactive world in which it is possible to ask questions which a Westerner would not ask. Thus the Azande are interested in 'cause-and-effect', but also ask why events have happened to one person rather than another: magic is a means of interrogation as well as of finding answers.

More recently, this view has been developed further, seeing magic as embedded in religion, where it acts as an organization of context and meaning. In this perspective, magic offers the transformation of circumstances without guaranteeing effects: one consequence or its opposite will still be a demonstration that magic 'works', because it confirms the entire context in which a person lives. See Index, Magic.

Magic Jewel School (Taoist movement): see LING-PAO P'AI.

Magisterium, the teaching office of the RC Church, to which *infallibility attaches.

Magnificat. *Mary's song of praise in Luke 1. 46–55, from the Latin *Magnificat anima mea Dominum* ('My soul doth magnify the Lord').

Mahābhārata. A great epic of India. It comprises 100,000 verses (in all, seven times the Iliad plus the Odyssey in length), divided into eighteen books, supplemented by a nineteenth, the **Harivaṃśa*. The epic recounts the events before, during, and after the great battle for kingship fought at *Kurukṣetra between the *Pāṇḍavas and *Kauravas, branches of the Kuru lineage and descendants of *Bharata (whence the Skt., *Mahābhārata*, 'the great [tale of] Bharata's descendants'). Also included is didactic material of encyclopaedic proportions (particularly in books 12 and 13, the **Śānti-* and *Anuśāsanaparvans*), along with elaborate genealogies and much myth and legend (especially in books 1 and 3).

The *Mahābhārata* in its present form grew up over a long period of time, *c*.400 BCE–400 CE. The action of the *Mahābhārata* proceeds at several levels at once. First is the typically Indo-European heroic tale of the battle of good against evil. From this point of view, the Kurukṣetra war is visualized as a gigantic sacrifice conducted by semi-divine epic heroes. Mixed with this semi-mythical material is consideration of the human-centred issue of the decline of *dharma at the onset of the *Kaliyuga, the present degenerate age of history. One high point of human uncertainty in the epic is the episode of the **Bhagavad-gītā*, in which the Pāṇḍava hero *Arjuna casts down his weapons before the war begins, dismayed at the prospect of having to fight against his relatives and elders on the other side. In the *Bhagavad-gītā* and throughout the *Mahābhārata*, it is a 'Hindu' element, revolving particularly around the character of the god *Viṣṇu, incarnate as *Kṛṣṇa, and his alliance with the Pāṇḍavas, which resolves the tension. The stage production by Peter Brook (1985) was filmed in 1989.

Mahābhūta (Skt., 'great' + 'element'). The five elements in Hinduism: air, fire, water, earth, and aether; also a synonym for *dhātu.

Mahābodhi Society: see DHARMAPĀLA (2).

Mahābodhi-vaṃsa ('the great bodhi-tree chronicle'). Buddhist work which relates the story of the *bo(dhi) tree under which the *Buddha attained enlightenment. It is attributed to Upatissa, in *c.*11th cent. CE.

Mahābrahmā ('Great Brahmā'). Buddhist name for the creator deity of the Hindu religion, as known to the Buddhists of the 6th cent. BCE. According to the *brahmans, the world was created by the Great Brahmā, and he was conceived of as a personal, masculine deity: the 'Great Brahmā' (*Mahābrahmā*), the 'Supreme One' (*Abhibhū*), the 'Unconquered' (*Anabhibhūto*), the 'Ruler' (*Vasavatti*), the 'Overlord' (*Issaro*), the 'Maker' (*Kattā*), the 'Creator' (*Nimmātā*), the 'Greatest' (*Seṭṭho*), the 'Assigner' (*Sañjitā*), the 'most Ancient' (*Vasī*), the 'Father of all that are born and are to be born' (*Pitā-bhūtabhavyā-naṃ*), the 'Steadfast' (*Nicco*), the 'Immutable' (*Dhuvo*), the 'Eternal' (*Sassato*), and the 'Unchangeable' (*Aviparināmadhammo*).

The belief in a creator deity of such or any other description was not acceptable to Buddhism, as the world according to Buddhism is not the product of such creative activity, but of an on-going evolutionary process.

The Buddhist reinterpretation of the Hindu belief in the creator deity Mahābrahmā was designed not only to deny this belief, but also to build the case against it.

Mahādeva (Skt., 'great Lord'). 1. In Hinduism, a name of *Śiva.

2. In Buddhism, Mahādeva is associated with the first major schism in Buddhist history, the division into *Mahāsāṃghika and *Sthaviravāda which led to *Theravāda. Five theses are attributed to him concerning the exact attainments of the *arhat. Nothing certain is known of him or of his life.

Mahādevī (the Goddess in India): see DEVĪ.

Mahākāla (Skt., 'great-time'). A name of *Śiva in his destructive aspect; he also represents death. Mahākāla is one of the eight deities known as the Terrible Divinities, also venerated by the Mongols as 'protector of the tent' (*gur-gyi-mgnon-po*). In the Buddhist pantheon Mahākāla is reduced to being a doorkeeper of Buddha's temple.

Mahākāśyapa (Skt.; Pāli, [Mahā]kassapa). Prominent follower of the *Buddha. He was rigorous in self-discipline, and took over the leadership of the *saṅgha (community of monks) after the Buddha's death. He is the first of the Zen patriarchs (Ānanda being the second), and his image usually stands beside that of the Buddha in Chin. monasteries.

Mahalā (from Skt., *mahilā*, 'woman', or Arab., *mahal*, 'place'). Followed by the appropriate numeral, this word is used in the *Ādi Granth to designate the compositions of the Sikh *Gurūs, e.g. Mahalā II or M. II = Gurū *Aṅgad.

Mahāmāyā. The great power of creating appearance in Hinduism. This power to make the universe appear as though it is real is exercised (in personified form) by Mahāmāyā, the goddess identified with *Durgā.

Mahāmudrā (Tib., *Phyag.rgya.chen.po*, 'Great Symbol'). Principal religious and philosophical teaching of the *Kagyü school (appearing also in Gelugpa, see GELUK) of Tibetan Buddhism. Obtained by Marpa Lotsawa from the 11th-cent. yogins Maitrīpa and Nāropa, Mahāmudrā has two aspects—*sūtra and *tantra. The sūtra aspects contain the teachings that the ultimate nature of reality is coincident wisdom and luminosity, bliss and emptiness (*śūnyatā), while the tantra aspects concern the active realization of this truth through spiritual practices. As a teaching, Mahāmudrā falls in the *zhen dong perspective of Tibetan thought, and is related also to *dzogchen, especially in the realization of the three kayas (*trikāya).

Mahānāma (Buddhist historian): see MAHĀVAṂSA.

Mahānārāyaṇīya Upaniṣad. 1. An early work, not commented on by *Śaṅkara, which explains the hymns addressed to *Nārāyana.

2. A late work forming the tenth book of the *Taittirīya Āraṇyaka*. It celebrates *Prājāpati and an extensive pantheon, including *Durgā.

Mahānavamī. Hindu *festival of nine days, celebrating the Goddess, usually as *Durgā.

Mahant (Hindī, Pañjābī, 'head of certain religious establishments'). Hereditary 'priests' who often appropriated the property of *gurdwārās under their control.

Mahāparinibbāna-sutta (The Discourse on the Great Decease). The sixteenth discourse in the Long Collection of Discourses (*Dīgha Nikāya) of the Buddhist *Pāli canon. The text describes the events leading up to the Buddha's death and his travels during the last few months of his life, and records his final utterance: 'Decay is inherent in all composite things: work with diligence.'

Mahāparinirvāna-sūtra. A Skt. rescension of the Pāli **Mahāparinibbāna-sutta*. It is also a collection of Mahāyāna *sūtras, taking its name from the first of them, which has survived in Chin. tr.

Mahāpātaka. Great *sin in Hinduism, classified into five: (i) *brāhmaṇahatyā*, the killing of a *brahman—or of an unborn child or of a pregnant woman; (ii) *surāpāna*, drinking intoxicants (see ALCOHOL); (iii) *steyam*, theft, but the circumstances are limited; (iv) *guruvaṇganāgama*, relations with a *guru's wife, guru being variously understood; (v) *mahāpātakasaṁsārga*, associating in any way with one who has committed one of the great sins. Minor sins are known as *upapātaka*, and are not so formally classified.

Mahāprajāpati Gautami. Stepmother of the *Buddha, who brought him up after the early death of his mother.

Mahāprajñapāramitā-Hridaya-Sūtra: see HEART SŪTRA.

Mahāprajñapāramitā-Sūtra: see PERFECTION OF WISDOM LITERATURE.

Mahāpralaya (Skt., 'great' + 'dissolving'). The complete dissolution of a universe at the end of a *kalpa, when all the *lokas and everything within them, including *Brahmā, disappear.

Mahapurāṇa ('great purāṇa'): see PURĀṆA.

Maharaji (founder of movement): see DIVINE LIGHT MISSION.

Maharal (acronym): see JUDAH LOEW.

Maharam (acronym): see MEIR BEN BARUCH.

Mahāratnakūṭa (Sūtra collection): see RATNAKŪṬA.

Maharishi Mahesh Yogi. Proponent of *Transcendental Meditation. A disciple of Guru Dev, he held the office of Shankarcharya of Jyotir Math in Badarinath in the Himalayas, 1941–53. After leaving his place of seclusion in 1955, Maharishi began to tour India, Burma, Singapore, N. America, and Europe giving lectures on Transcendental Meditation, maintaining that both the ideas about and the practice of this ancient meditative technique, based on Vedic wisdom, had become confused.

According to Maharishi, the correct practice of Transcendental Meditation can only be taught by a qualified teacher, and to this end he established teacher-training centres in many parts of the world (e.g. Maharishi International University in Iowa, USA; Maharishi Univ. of Natural Law at Mentmore, UK). In Jan. 1975 Maharishi, from on board the flagship *Gotthard* on Lake Lucerne, Switzerland, inaugurated the dawn of the Age of Enlightenment, followed in Jan. 1976 by the inauguration of the World Government of the Age of Enlightenment.

Maharsha (Talmudic commentator): see EDELS, SAMUEL ELIEZER BEN JUDAH HALEVI.

Maharshal (acronym): see LURIA, SOLOMON BEN JEHIEL.

Mahārṣi: see ṚṢI; MAHARISHI MAHESH YOGI.

Mahāsāṃghikas (the 'Great Assembly'). A body which broke away from the Elder (*Sthavira) tradition of Buddhism after the Council of Pāṭaliputra in 350 BCE (see COUNCILS). The Mahāsāṃghikas distinguished themselves from the Sthaviras doctrinally in their conception of the Buddha as supramundane (*lokottara), and socially by their acceptance of popular religious beliefs and practices, allowing a greater role to the laity.

Mahāsaṃnipāta (sūtra collection): see TRIPIṬAKA.

Mahāsatipaṭṭhāna-sutta. Section 22 of the Dialogues of the *Buddha (*Dīgha Nikāya* 2. 290 ff.), occurring also in **Majjhima Nikāya*, dealing with the cultivation of *sati (see also SATIPAṬṬHĀNA).

Mahāsiddha (Skt., great masters of powers, *iddhis).

Hinduism Traditionally, there are eighty-four mahāsiddhas, mainly in the *Tantric tradition. Some are of legendary character, and are usually depicted in fearsome form, but others were teachers and prominent people.

Buddhism The eighty-four mahāsiddhas were adopted from Hinduism, and celebrated in stories and songs (*doha*). But the mahāsiddhas were then greatly extended in number, especially in *Vajrayāna, where a mahāsiddha is one who has acquired the teachings of the Tantras and demonstrates this through great powers (iddhis).

Mahāsthāmaprāpta ('One of great power'). A Mahāyāna Buddhist *bodhisattva, who opens people's sight to their need for liberation. He is especially associated with Amitābha (*Amida); with *Avalokiteśvara, the two appear frequently in representations as the helpers of Amitābha, a kind of *trinity of compassionate grace and liberation.

Mahāśūnya (Skt., 'great' + 'emptiness'). Hindu *vedānta understanding of the complete emptying of duality when it is realized that there are no self-subsistent objects to create a dual relationship, e.g. of seer and seen. Cf. also the Buddhist development of *śūnyatā.

Mahat (Skt., 'the great one'). In *Sāṁkhya (and other non-theistic) philosophy, the first evolution of *mūlaprakṛti*, synonymous with *buddhi ('intellect'). Mahat contains all individual buddhis and all potential matter of the gross universe in its cosmic extent as the first manifest principle (*tattva). Mahat in turn produces *ahaṁkāra, the ego principle.

Mahātman or **Mahātma** (Skt., *mahā*, 'great', + *ātman*, 'soul').

1. In Hinduism, one having a great soul, any exceptionally distinguished, magnanimous, or wise person; also a particular group of deceased ancestors mentioned in the *Mārkaṇḍeya* **Purāṇa*. Mohandas *Gāndhī was considered a Mahātma by many.

2. In the *Upaniṣadic tradition, the supreme principle or great soul of the universe.

Mahāvairocana-sūtra (Sūtra of the Great Radiant One). A *Tantric Mahāyāna Buddhist *sūtra, of importance in both China (e.g. *Mi-tsung) and Japan (e.g. *Shingon).

Mahāvākya (Skt., 'great saying'). Any one of several great sayings which occur in the *Upaniṣads and which are held to reveal the unity of the Self (*ātman) and Ultimate Reality (*Brahman). The number of these is generally said to be four, but five are commonly encountered in the later literature: **tat-tvam-asi* ('That Thou art'), *ahaṁ brahmāsmi* ('I am Brahman'), *sarvaṁ khalvidaṁ brahma* ('All this indeed is Brahman'), *ayam ātmā brahma* ('This Self is Brahman'), and **prajñānam brahma* ('Pure Consciousness is Brahman').

Mahāvaṃsa (Pāli, 'great' + 'story'). Pāli Buddhist chronicle of Sinhalese history from the time of the *Buddha Śākyamuni to the 4th cent. CE. *Cūlavamsa* (Little Story) is an appendix which carries the story down to the 18th cent. The main chronicle was written *c.*5th cent. CE, and it is attributed to Mahānāma, though nothing certain is known of him.

Mahāvastu (Skt., 'The Great Event'). A composite work of the *Lokottara(vāda) Buddhist school, dealing with previous existences (*jātaka) of the *Buddha. All the episodes of his life are designed to help those whom he meets at their own level; he himself is never other than transcendent.

Mahā-Vibhāṣā (Buddhist teaching commentary): see SARVASTIVĀDA.

Mahāvidyas (Skt., 'great' + 'knowledge'). Ten Hindu goddesses who represent the ten forms of transcendent knowledge and *tantric power, through the worship of whom one can gain knowledge of *Brahman, since they are all personifications of Brahman's *Śakti. They are *Kāli/*Lalitā; *Tārā (an emanation of Kāli); Soḍaśī (a girl of 16, the number of perfection, thus the perfection of the cosmic whole); Bhukaneśvari (the material world); *Bhairavi (the infinite variety of desires and the inevitability of death); *Chinnamastā/Vīrarātrī (eternal night, depicted naked drinking blood from her own self-severed head); Dhūmāvatī (the destruction, *pralaya, of the cosmos, when only smoke, *dhūma*, remains); Bagalā (emotional forces of hate, jealousy, etc.); Mātaṇgi (power and domination); Kamalā (the girl of the *lotus, pure consciousness). The Mahāvidya cult was prominent in medieval Bengal.

Mahāvīra (Skt., *mahat*, 'great', + *vīra*, 'hero'). In Jainism, the honorific title given to Vardhamāna Jnātṛputra, the 24th *tīrthaṅkara. The *Digambara and Śvetāmbara sects recount two divergent accounts of his life. Both agree that he was born the son of a *kṣatriya couple, Siddhārtha and *Triśalā, at Kuṇḍagrama just north of modern Patna (Bihar State, India) in 599 BCE. The Śvetāmbara Jains date his life 599–527 BCE (the Digambara hold that he died in 510), but some modern scholarship suggests 549–477 BCE. Śvetāmbara tradition claims that Mahāvīra married a princess Yośodā, who bore him a daughter, Priyadarśanā; but Digambara tradition rejects this. At the age of 30, Mahāvīra renounced family life to become a wandering ascetic in the tradition of *Pārśva—for a time in company with *Makkhali Gosala. After twelve years of severe fasting to cleanse his body, of silence to improve his speech, and of meditation to clear his mind, he gained omniscience (*kevala jñāna) and became a *jina. For the next thirty years he travelled throughout NE India, teaching by word and example the path of purification. Mahāvīra died and passed to *mokṣa at the age of 73 at Pāvāpurī, near Patna, leaving (tradition claims) 14,000 monks, 36,000 nuns, 159,000 laymen, and 318,000 laywomen to continue his teaching. Jains today look back on Mahāvīra as the greatest of all their teachers.

Mahāvrata (a 'great vow'): see YAMA (2); for Jains, see FIVE GREAT VOWS.

Mahāyāna (Skt., 'Great Vehicle'; Chin., Ta-ch'eng; Jap., Daijō; Korean, Taesūng). The form of Buddhism prominent in Tibet, Mongolia, China, Korea, Vietnam, and Japan. It regards itself as a more adequate expression of the *dharma than what it calls *Hīnayāna (Skt., 'Lesser' or 'Inferior Vehicle'). The absence of the later teaching in early texts is variously explained. Tibetan Buddhism ascribes, within the *Trikāya of the Buddha, the Hīnayāna to the historical Nirmāṇakāya and the Mahāyāna to the *Sambhoga-kāya; whereas *Zen claims a special wordless transmission that could not by its very nature have a literary witness. In any case, such teaching is now recorded in many *sūtras. The distinctive teaching of the Mahāyāna is that of compassion for all sentient beings such that the practitioner delays his own *nirvāna until all other beings shall have been liberated. The ideal practitioner is the *bodhisattva, i.e. one who has given birth to the *bodhicitta (Skt., 'enlightenment-mind') which strives to manifest Great Compassion. The two main philosophical schools of Mahāyāna are *Mādhyamaka and Yogācāra/*Vijñānavāda (for the lineages, see BUDDHIST SCHOOLS). Also of importance are the forms of devotion, e.g. to the Buddha Amitābha (*Amida) with the promise of rebirth in the paradise of *Sukhāvatī; the emphasis on sūtras containing the developed teaching of the Buddha (according to *upāya-kauśalya, his early teaching was adapted to the simple-minded); the recognition of the buddha-nature (*Tathāgata-garbha, *buddhatā) in all things.

Mahāyānaśraddhotpāda-śastra (Treatise on the Awakening of Faith in the Mahāyāna). A Mahāyāna Buddhist text, attributed to *Aśvaghoṣa, though it comes in fact from *c*.4th/5th cent. CE. It is a *sūtra which was also of importance in *Zen.

Mahdī (the awaited Imām): see AL-MAHDĪ.

Maḥdūd (finiteness of humans, in Islam): see ḤADD.

Mahendra ('Great Indra'). A name applied in Hinduism to *Indra, *Viṣṇu, and *Śiva.

Maheśāna (Skt., 'great ruler'). In Hinduism, one of the older names of *Śiva; the sun as a form of Śiva.

Maheśvara (Skt., 'Great Lord'). Epithet of Śiva (also sometimes of *Viṣṇu). He is the source of knowledge (*jñāna), will (*iccha), and action (*kriya*).

Maheśvara-sūtra. A *Śaivite work, attributed to *Śiva. It deals with the four ways leading to ultimate insight—*yoga, *vedānta, language, and music.

Maheśvari (Skt.). A name of *Śakti; also one of the goddesses created by *Śiva who constitute the Divine Mothers (*Mātṛkās*); consort of *Maheśvara.

Mahfouz, Naguib (b. 1911). Egyptian author of novels, short stories, and film-scripts. His early works were set in Pharaonic Egypt; then followed novels of social realism, set in Cairo, culminating in the *Cairo Trilogy*. In 1959, after a long silence, his religious allegory, *Awlad Haratina* (tr. as *Children of Gebelaawi*), was serialized in the newspaper *Al-Ahram*. It caused offence to many readers by its familiar treatment of figures representing *Adam, *Moses, *Jesus, and *Muḥammad, and by allowing the death of the old man thought by many to stand for God. Publication in book form has never been permitted in Egypt, but the author has always claimed it to be a deeply religious work. Controversy was revived by the award of the Nobel Prize for Literature in 1988 and, in the wake of the *fatwā against Salman Rushdie (see SATANIC VERSES), a hostile opinion was expressed in a Kuwaiti newspaper by Sheikh Omar Abdul-Rahman. Some interpreted this as a fatwā against the author, although the Sheikh himself has vigorously denied it. Mahfouz survived an attempted assassination in Oct. 1994.

Mahinda Festival. Buddhist (Śri Lankan) festival, better known as Poson, which celebrates the mission of the monk Mahinda who brought Buddhism to Śri Lankā.

Mahiṣa, Mahiṣāsura (Skt., 'water-buffalo'). 1. Name of a demon (*asura, thus also frequently Mahiṣāsura) in the shape of a buffalo, in Hindu mythology. The classical version of the myth about the Goddess killing the demon was told in the *Devīmāhātmya* of the *Mārkaṇḍeya-Purāṇa*, and from there acquired pan-Indian popularity. In the text itself, the Goddess is most frequently referred to as Ambikā ('little mother', see AMBĀ) or Caṇḍikā ('fierce woman'), but later iconographic traditions usually call her Mahiṣāsuramardini, 'she who crushed the Buffalo demon', while in religious contexts she is called Mahā-*Lakṣmī.

2. By no means all images depicting a female figure associated with a water-buffalo signify this Goddess or refer to this myth. Among many images, a water-buffalo is the *vāhana, 'vehicle', of the Hindu god *Yama, the god of death, and in Mahārāṣṭra we find a goddess Yamāī riding on (or killing?) a buffalo.

3. From ancient times until recently, when for economic reasons the custom became curtailed, buffaloes have been killed in Indian villages as part of sacrifices and for the sake of eating their meat.

Mahr (dowry): see MARRIAGE.

Maḥzor (Heb., 'cycle'). Jewish festival prayer book. The term maḥzor distinguishes between the prayer book for festivals as opposed to the *siddur, which is the daily *prayer book.

Maḥzor Vitry. Jewish *halakhic-liturgical book. The *Maḥzor Vitry* was composed by Simḥah ben Samuel of Vitry, a pupil of *Rashi, in the late 11th cent. CE. The book gives the halakhic rulings of the *liturgy for the annual cycle of weekdays, *Sabbaths, and *Festivals.

Mai Chaza's Church. Church founded, among the Shona-speaking Manyinka in Zimbabwe, by Mai (Shona, 'mother') Chaza (d. 1960), after a mystical experience of death and resurrection while in a coma early in the 1950s. Initially remaining within *Methodism, development as a separate body began in 1955, based on her new village, Guta Ra *Jehovah ('city of Jehovah'), as the first of a series of holy cities which served as famous faith-healing centres, especially for barren women. Her works and teachings, as related to those of *Jesus, have been collected in a Guta Ra Jehovah Bible. The movement's adherents have declined to no more than 3,000.

Maimon, Solomon (1753–1800). Jewish philosopher. He was the author of *Versuch ueber die Transzendentalphilosophie* (1790), *Streifereien im Gebiete der Philosophie* (1793), three works on the history of philosophy, a philosophical lexicon, and a commentary on *Maimonides' *Guide of the Perplexed*. He was condemned as a heretic and denied burial in a Jewish cemetery, mainly as a consequence of his evident subordination of revelation to reason.

Maimonidean controversy. Jewish controversy (in fact, more than one) centring on the themes discussed by the philosopher *Maimonides. Scholars such as Meir *Abulafia were appalled by Maimonides' apparent rejection of the doctrine of the *resurrection of the dead. A *ḥerem (excommunicatory ban) was pronounced on Maimonides' philosophical work. In the West, the controversy was halted by the burning of Maimonides' books by the Christian *Dominicans in 1232. It was continued in the East by Maimonides' son, Abraham, although the desecration of Maimonides' tomb in Tiberias was a profound shock to all concerned. This tension between the anti-rationalists and the rationalists continued through the Middle Ages and is to be seen in such disputes as that between Moses *Isserles and Solomon b. Jehiel *Luria in the 16th cent.

Maimonides, Moses, Moses b. Maimon, or **Rambam** (1135–1204). Jewish philosopher and codifier. Maimonides grew up in Cordova, but as a result of persecution, the family eventually moved to Fez in N. Africa after years of wandering. During this period he wrote treatises on the Jewish calendar, logic, and *halakhah. In 1168, he completed his commentary on the *Mishnah. In 1170–80, he worked on his great code, the *Mishneh Torah* (The Repetition of the Law, sometimes known as 'The Strong Hand'). The purpose of this work was 'so that the entire *Oral Law might become systematically known to all'. This codification of the Law was fiercely criticized by such as *Abraham b. David of Posquières (see MAIMONIDEAN CONTROVERSY). His great philosophical work, The *Guide of the Perplexed* (Heb., *Moreh Nevukhim*) was influenced by Aristotle and the *Hellenistic commentators Alexander of Aphrodisias, Themistius, and Averroes, and also by the Muslim philosopher *al-Fārābī. The *Guide* shows 'the perplexed' how scripture can be interpreted spiritually as well as literally, and Maimonides aimed to reveal to his readers 'the science of the Law in its true sense'. To this end, he discussed God, creation, the nature of evil, divine providence, and morality. He also formulated his *thirteen principles of the Jewish faith which he believed every Jew was bound to accept. He is also remembered as a significant physician and astronomer.

Maimuna. Celebration among some Jews (especially in or from N. Africa) of the last day of *Passover. Maimuna is celebrated in many eastern Jewish communities with special foods and picnics. Traditionally it is also the anniversary of the death of Moses *Maimonides' father.

Maithuna (Skt.). Sexual intercourse; in Indian religions, particularly *Tantrism, a vehicle for and metaphor of liberation (*mokṣa).

Although maithuna as a means of liberation is not found in the *Upaniṣads, the cosmic symbolism of the sexual act found there anticipates the *tantras.

The sexual act as a metaphor of divine union is found in the *Bhakti tradition, particularly the erotic (*sṛṅgāra*) bhakti to *Kṛṣṇa of the Gaudiya *Vaiṣṇavas, in which the bhakta identifies himself with the *gopīs, especially *Rādhā, and their adulterous love (*parākiya*) for Kṛṣṇa. Sexual love is here a symbol for the soul's love of God.

Maithuna as a means of liberation is found *par excellence* in Hindu and Buddhist *Tantrism, in the left-hand (*vāmācāra) traditions of the *Kaula-Kāpālika cults and the *Sahajīyās. Through ritual maithuna, sexual energy is transformed into spiritual energy, and desire is destroyed by desire. Human sexuality reflects the cosmic male–female polarity, and human copulation reflects the cosmic union (*yāmala, *yuganaddha*, *yab-yum) of *Śiva and *Śakti, in Hindu Tantra; and *Prajñā and *Upāya or *Śūnyatā and *Karuṇa in Buddhist Tantra. The rhythmical movement of maithuna also reflects the rhythmical vibration (*spanda*) of the cosmos.

The Tantras give details of rituals (*pūjā) involving maithuna (the *strī pūjā*), stressing their secrecy and the danger of *hell for one who performs these rites with desire.

Maitreya (Skt., 'loving one'; Pāli, Metteyya; Chin., Mile-fo; Korean, Mitūk; Jap., Miroku).

One of the five earthly buddhas, the embodiment of all-embracing love, who is expected to come in the future as the fifth and last of the buddhas. In early Buddhism, Maitreya dwells in the *Tuṣita heaven (the realm of the fully delighted gods), waiting for the decline and eclipse of Buddhism, when he will become the next Buddha—in about 30,000 years time. This belief was further developed in all Mahāyāna countries, and above all in Tibet, where he is known as *byams pa* (*champa*). It is a particular commitment of *Gelugpa to prepare for his coming. He is depicted usually with feet placed firmly on the ground, ready to step into the world.

Maitreyanātha. Buddhist teacher of uncertain status. He is held to be a founder of Yogācāra/*Vijñānavāda because of the statement that *Asaṅga was taught by Maitreyanātha. But this may be a reference to *Maitreya.

Maitri (Skt., 'kindness'; Pāli, *metta*). A major virtue in Buddhism. It is generous benevolence to all, which is free from attachment or calculation of reciprocal interests. Its cultivation is a specific *Theravādin meditation-practice, and its nature is explored in the *Metta-sutta*. That sutta is recited daily by monks, and often by laypeople.

Maitrī-karuṇā. Kindness and compassion linked in Buddhism as the supreme characteristic of a *bodhisattva.

Maitri Upaniṣad. A late work written in the prose style of a *brāhmaṇa. Its contents are varied, but it is valued particularly for its discussion of the distinction between the two forms of *ātman: the eternal ātman 'abiding in its own greatness', and the bhutātman, the elemental self entangled in change, as a bird is caught in a snare.

Majjhima nikāya (Skt., Madhyamāgama). The Middle Length (second) Collection (*nikāya) of the Sutta/*Sūtra-*piṭaka of the *Pāli (Buddhist) canon (see also BUDDHIST SCRIPTURES). The Pāli canon contains 150 sutras, the Chin. tr. of the (lost) Skt. 222; 97 are found in both.

Majjhimapātipadā (way taught and practised by the Buddha): see MIDDLE WAY.

Majlisī (Shi'ite theologian): see AL-MAJLISĪ, MUḤAMMAD BĀQIR.

Makara. A sea-beast, resembling a crocodile, on which the Hindu god *Varuṇa rides. A makara is believed to increase fertility, and is the emblem of *Kāma.

Makāra. The performance in *Tantra of the Five Ms—see PAÑCA-MAKĀRA.

Makiguchi Tsunesaburō (founder): see SŌKA GAKKAI.

Makkhali Gosala or **Maskarin Gosala** (Pāli, Skt.). Sectarian teacher and leader of the *Ājīvaka sect who was criticized by the Buddha for his doctrine of determinism.

Makyō (Jap., 'devil' + 'phenomenal appearance'). The deceptive appearances which arise for a Zen Buddhist in *zazen. Provided they are ignored or put aside, they are harmless.

Māl (name of god): see TAMILNADU.

Mālā (also **japamālā**). A *'rosary' for Hindus, Buddhists, and Sikhs.

Hinduism Basically, mālā is a garland made of beads and/or berries, presented to honoured guests, and to symbolize victory. They consist (usually) of 108 berries, and are then used in the practice of *japa. 108 is the number of evil passions to which humans are subject.

Buddhism The number of beads is the same, and they are used to count repetitions in the recitation of *dhāraṇīs, *mantras, and the name of a buddha (*nembutsu).

Sikhism It is usually made of wool, and has 108 knots, though smaller ones of twenty-nine knots are also used. They are used to aid concentration on the name (*nām) of God.

Malabar Christians. The Christians of the state of Kerala on the Malabar (SW) coast of India. They number over 2 million, now divided into several communities (see SYRIAN CHURCHES). They are known as 'Thomas Christians' from their claim—taken seriously by some W. scholars too—that their ancestors were evangelized by St *Thomas. In any case, by the 6th cent. there was a Church in the region using Syriac in its liturgy and dependent for bishops on the (*Nestorian) catholikos of Baghdad. After heavy-handed missionary work by the Portuguese, the Church was formally purged of Nestorianism, brought under Roman obedience, and thoroughly Latinized at the synod of Diamper (Udayamperur, near Cochin) in 1599. Latin government of the Church continued as a source of tension down to the 20th cent. There was a defection of a large body eventually to the Syrian Orthodox in the 17th cent.; this schism gave rise to another in the 19th cent. with the creation of the *Mar Thoma Church. The Catholics are now styled the 'Syro-Malabar Church', having been granted their own metropolitanate of Ernakulam with Indian bishops in 1923.

Malabar rites. The customs and rites adopted from Hindu customs by *de Nobili in India, to enable converts to Christianity not to feel estranged from their culture.

Malachi, Book of. Last of the books of the Jewish *minor prophets. Malachi is of anonymous authorship, but was probably written early in the post-exilic period.

Malāḥidah (heresy in Islam): see HERESY.

Malak/malā'ika ('messengers with wings' in Islam): see ANGEL.

Malankara Church: see UNIAT(E) CHURCHES; SYRIAN CHURCHES.

Malcolm X (1925–65). Leading figure in the Nation of Islam (see ELIJAH MUHAMMAD) and civil rights activist in the USA. He was born in Nebraska as Malcolm Little, and after an early life of petty crime (somewhat exaggerated later), he was converted through the Nation of Islam programme. His appearance on the TV programme, 'The Hate that Produced Hate', projected him into national prominence, leading to a rift with Elijah Muhammad. He opposed civil rights movements, looking for direct action, and he contrasted 'true' with 'compromise' Islam. He left the movement, and, while on pilgrimage (*ḥajj) to *Mecca, he was converted to *Sunni Islam. He took the new name of el-Hajji Malik el-Shab(b)az(z). He failed to establish himself as an independent leader, and was assassinated by black Muslim loyalists in 1965. A popularizing film led to a revival of his influence in the 1990s.

Mālik b. Anas (d. 795 (AH 179)). Author of *Kitāb al-Muwaṭṭa*, one of the earliest surviving Muslim lawbooks. It records Islam as practised in *Madīna. Mālik was sensitive to the untrustworthy ways in which sunna was being produced, and for that reason allowed *istiṣlāh to overrule a deduction from *Qur'ān and sunna. Mālikites are therefore intermediate between Hanifites and Shāfi'ites.

Mālikites. Muslim school (*schools) of law, deriving its name from *Mālik b. Anas, though not established in a formal sense by him. Its main strength is in N. and W. Africa (i.e. the Muslim West).

Malines Conversations. Meetings of Anglican and Roman Catholic theologians held at Malines (Mechelen) in Belgium between 1921 and 1925, reaching agreement on some matters, and anticipating *ARCIC.

Malinowski, B.: see MAGIC.

Malka or **Malca** (Heb., *melek*, 'king'). The 'royal' or holy leaven, used by *Nestorians in the preparation of bread for the *liturgy. It goes back in an unbroken line to the bread used by *Jesus at the *Last Supper.

Malkhuyyot (Heb., 'kingships', i.e. 'sovereignty'). The first part of the *musaf prayer for the Jewish *festival for *Rosh ha-Shanah (New Year).

Mamlukes (dynasty): see SLAVERY (ISLAM).

Mamzer (Heb., 'bastard'). Jewish person conceived as the result of an illicit union. A mamzer is a child conceived by a married woman with a man other than her husband, or as the result of incest. Illegitimate children in the usual sense are not mamzerim.

Man. A primordial and cosmic figure, occurring in several religions, but with different emphases. In Hinduism, see NARA.

Man (Hindī, Pañjābī, 'one's total being'). Mind, heart, and soul. In Sikhism this bears the connotation of human capriciousness.

Māna (Pāli, Skt.). Pride, conceit; a moral fault in Buddhism. It takes three forms: thinking of oneself as inferior to, equal to, or better than others.

Mana (inherent power): see MAGIC.

Manas (Skt., 'mind'). In Skt. literature, the mind, the co-ordinating organ of intelligence, thought, understanding, perception, and will. In Vedic times manas meant the individual spirit and the basis of speech (*vāc). In the Upaniṣadic period manas is variously treated: sometimes it is closely associated with speech and *breath as a triple entity, sometimes considered more as the intermediate link between the Self, *ātman, and the senses.

In the *darśanas, manas is seen as a special additional sense organ by which thoughts and sensations have access to the ātman. In *Sāṃkhya philosophy, the principle (*tattva) of manas together with intellect (buddhi) and ego (*ahaṃkāra) makes up a threefold 'inner instrument' (*antaḥkarana*).

In Buddhist psychology, manas is the rational or intellectual faculty of the mind. In the Pāli canon it is said to be synonymous with *citta and *vijñāna (2).

Manasā. A Goddess of folk Hinduism worshipped in Bengal and neighbouring areas by middle and lower strata of society. From *c.*14th cent. onward, she played an important role in Bengali literature, but failed to reach the same level of popular veneration as *Caṇḍī, *Durgā, and *Kālī in this region.

Manasseh ben Israel (1604–57). Jewish scholar. He founded the first Hebrew printing-press in Amsterdam. He himself was the author of several theological works, including *Piedra Gloriosa* which was illustrated with engravings by Rembrandt who also painted his portrait. He dedicated his *Esperanca De Israel* to the English Parliament in 1650 and was closely involved in the negotiations to readmit Jews to England in the Commonwealth period.

Manasseh, Prayer of. Jewish *psalm included in the *Apocrypha. It was probably written at the end of the 1st cent. BCE, and is put forward as Manasseh's supposed words.

Mānava-dharmaśāstra (laws of Hindu lawgiver Manu): see MANUSMṚTI.

Mandaeans: see MANDEANS.

Maṇḍala (Skt., 'circle'; Chin., *man-ta-lao*; Jap. and Korean, *mandara*; Tib., *dkyil.'khor*). A symbolic pictorial representation of the universe, originating in India but prominent in *Tibetan Buddhism. It is *visualized in the context of *Tantric ritual. Although maṇḍalas are commonly found on scrolls or as wall-paintings, for important rituals the maṇḍala is traced onto consecrated ground using coloured powders which may be erased upon termination of the ritual. In meditation, they can be visualized without external representation.

All maṇḍalas follow a precise symbolic format.

In Hinduism, maṇḍalas are described in great detail in the Tantras and *Āgamas. For example, the *Pañcarātra text, *Lakṣmi Tantra* (37. 3–19), describes a maṇḍala of nine lotuses.

In liturgy (*pūjā) a maṇḍala is the place where a deity is invoked by *mantra. The placing of mantras upon the maṇḍala (*nyāsa) gives it life, and the maṇḍala is then regarded, like mantra, as the deity itself (and not a mere representation of the deity). A maṇḍala is also visualized (*dhyāna) by the yogin who aims at merging with the deity. Visualization is accompanied by mantra repetition and the practice of mudrā for the control of mind, speech, and body. See also CAKRA; YANTRA; Index, Mandala.

Mandalah. Islamic derivation from the Hindu *maṇḍala, consisting in the drawing of an inkspot surrounded by verses of the *Qur'ān (one of which is always 50. 22) on the hand of a boy. After incantations, he is enabled to see the answer to questions about things unknown.

Maṇḍala-nṛtya. An Indian *dance performed in a circle. It is based on the dance of *Kṛṣṇa with the *gopīs, in which he moved so rapidly around them that they did not notice a moment when he was absent from any one of them. In the same way, God is available for full union with any one of his devotees in *bhakti at any time.

Maṇḍala of the Five Jinas or **Tathāgatas.** A basic type for Buddhist maṇḍalas, the maṇḍala of the five jinas (Tib., *rgyal.ba*, 'eminent ones') is a representation of the psyche and the world in fivefold symbolism.

The basic form of this maṇḍala consists in the five jinas who have each become assigned a series of qualities as follows: (i) *Vairocana, white, in the centre, represents the element ether, the *skandha of consciousness, the ignorance of delusion and the wisdom of the *dharmadhātu; (ii) Akṣobhya, blue, in the east, represents the element water, the skandha of form, the ignorance of hatred and the mirror-like wisdom; (iii) Ratnasambhava, yellow, in the south, represents the element earth, the skandha of feeling, the ignorance of arrogance and the wisdom of equality; (iv) Amitābha, red, in the west, represents the element fire, the skandha of perception, the ignorance of craving and the wisdom of all-knowing; (v) Amoghasiddhi, green, in the north, represents the element air, the skandha of volition, the ignorance of jealousy and the wisdom of all-accomplishing.

Whether the maṇḍala or other forms of intentional meditation are used, it is never *simply* a symbolic representation, but a blueprint accompanying Tantric instructions for the effective transmutation of the mundane personality into Buddhahood.

Maṇḍapa. Any kind of canopy or tent, a ceremonial building, but especially the main area of a Hindu temple. It is transferred into Buddhism in relation to *paritta ritual.

Mandara. Jap. and Korean for *maṇḍala.

Mandara. The mountain on which, according to Hindus, the gods and giants stood for the *Churning of the Ocean.

Mandāra. The coral tree (*erythrina indica*) which stands in *Indra's heaven, and which, when someone smells it, summons up remembrance of times past.

Mandate of Heaven (transcendent order in China): see T'IEN MING.

Mandeans (from *manda*, 'knowledge'). Religious group in S. Iraq and the only surviving representative of *Gnosticism. Important in an extensive literature are *Ginza Raba* (Great Treasure) and *Drasha ed Yahia* (Book of John). The appearance of *John the Baptist in Mandean texts suggested to some that the Mandeans were descendants of John's own disciples. In their own estimate, their religion is much older. They have a hierarchy of Malki (King), Reesh Amma (leading people), Ganzebra and Termithy (supplying priests). They are strongly pacifist, and believe in redemption being effected by a series of messengers beginning with one known as 'Gnosis of Life'. They may be the

Sabeans mentioned in the *Qur'ān, and today are called by Muslims Subbas.

Mandir(a) (Skt., 'dwelling'). Hindu temple. Because the divine pervades appearance and can be realized in any place or object, temples were not prominent in early Indian religion, and are not an obligation (as is, e.g., assembly in the *mosque for Muslim men). Yet they are important because they are supremely the place where the image (*murti) of God is housed and can be brought to life, and are therefore known also as *devagṛha* ('house of God') and *devālaya* ('abode of God'). The image is only alive when appropriate rituals make it so. Thus the 'awakening' of God is a part of the daily ritual: in the morning, there are chants (*bhajana*) and washings, as well as offerings of food in worship (*pūjā). Temples are built according to strict rules of design and measurement: the ground-plan is a *yantra (cosmic diagram), with the central square dedicated to *Brahmā or some other prominent deity, at the centre of the universe. The image is housed in the *garbhagṛha, the 'womb-chamber', symbolizing a dark cave. Above it rises the structure of the temple leading up to the summit of the symbolic mountain which it is: the line is the *axis mundi, up which the worshipper ascends. Temples are protected by many other deities, spirits, and signs, beautifully and elaborately carved. They may also have protective walls which are pierced by cow-gates (*gopuram*). See ART (HINDUISM).

Mandorla (almond-shaped aureole): see HALO.

Māndūkya Upaniṣad. An *Upaniṣad belonging to the **Atharva Veda*. It deals with the sound *Oṃ and the four states of consciousness: waking, dreaming, deep sleep, and *turīya, which alone is real.

Maṇi (Skt.). Jewel in the shape of a tear-drop, powerful in removing the causes of sorrow or of evil.

Manichaeism. Religion founded by Mani in 3rd-cent. Iran and later very widely established.

Mani was born in 216 near Seleucia-Ktesiphon, the Iranian capital. At the age of 12 he had his first vision of his heavenly twin (identified later with the *Paraclete), who instructed him. Thereafter he disputed with the community, and after a second vision, calling him to be an 'apostle', he separated from them, with his father and two disciples, sometime after the age of 25. Mani's later life is not well known. After preaching in India he returned to Iran *c.*242 where his patron was the new Sassanid ruler Shapur I. His religion prospered until the accession of Bahram I (274–7), who at the instigation of Kartir imprisoned and executed him in 276.

Although suppressed in Persia, Manichaeism spread west and east. In central Asia it had more lasting success, even being made the state religion of the Turkish Uigur Empire in 762. It also reached China in 694 where, known as the 'religion of light', it seems to have persisted, in spite of official opposition at various periods, almost down to modern times.

Mani's teaching was fundamentally *gnostic and *dualistic, positing an opposition between God and matter. There was an elaborate cosmological myth: this included the defeat of a primal man by the powers of darkness, who devoured and thus imprisoned particles of light. The cosmic process of salvation goes on as the light is delivered back to its original state. Saving knowledge of this process comes through 'apostles of light', among whom Mani, a self-conscious syncretist, included various biblical figures, *Buddha, *Zoroaster, and *Jesus. He himself was the final one.

The Manichaean 'church' was divided into the 'elect' (or 'righteous') and 'auditors' ('hearers'). The burden of Manichaean ethics, to do nothing to impede the reassembly of particles of light, was on the elect. Obviously the elect, not even able to harvest their own vegetables, could only survive with the support of the auditors. These could apparently lead quite unrestricted lives. The calendar contained one major festival, the Bema feast on the anniversary of Mani's 'passion'. Fasting was enjoined on two days each week, plus a whole month before the Bema feast.

Māṇik(k)avācakar ('the ruby-worded saint', 8th or 9th cent.). Tamil poet and holy man, a *Saivite devotee, one of the *Nāyaṇmārs. He became one of the greatest of the poets of devotion to *Śiva. His most celebrated work, *Tiruvācakam* (Sacred Utterances), is included in *Tirumuṛai*, a virtual *'canon' of *Tamil Śaivism.

Maniple. A Christian *eucharistic *vestment, worn over the left arm, or carried. The corresponding Orthodox vestment is the *epigonation*.

Manī Siṅgh, Bhāī (d. 1738 CE). Sikh scholar and *martyr. Manī visited Gurū *Gobind Siṅgh, remained with him, and was later initiated by him. He remained celibate, devoting his life to the Gurū's service.

After the death of Gurū Gobind Siṅgh, Manī Siṅgh remained as *granthī in *Amritsar. He was a learned exponent of the Ādi Granth, and to him are attributed *Gyān Ratanāvalī*, a *janam-sākhī, and *Bhagat Ratanāvalī*, a list of famous Sikhs up to the time of Gurū *Hargobind.

In 1738, Manī Siṅgh obtained permission from the Governor of Lahore, Zakariā Khān, for a *Divālī celebration in the *Harimandir on condition that he paid a large sum. This he was unable to pay from the anticipated offerings, as the Sikhs were prevented from coming. Consequently, as he refused the option of accepting Islam, he was tortured to death and cremated in Lahore.

Mañjī (Pañjābī, 'string bed'). 1. Sikh area of jurisdiction.

2. The small 'bed' on which the Ādi Granth is installed in the *gurdwārā is called the Mañjī Sāhib.

Manjushri Institute. Religious and educational foundation established at Conishead Priory in Britain in 1976 by students of the *Geluk Tibetan Buddhist tradition.

Mañjuśrī (Jap., Monju, Tib., 'Jam.pa'i.d-byangs). A great *bodhisattva of the *Mahāyāna tradition of Buddhism closely associated with learning, knowledge, and transcendental wisdom (*prajñā). Mañjuśrī is prominent in Buddhist *Tantra and is frequently invoked in ritual and depicted in mystic diagrams and *maṇḍalas. In iconography he is portrayed with the sword of wisdom in his right hand and a book to his left-hand side. In Tibet, great teachers are often regarded as incarnations of Mañjuśrī, e.g. *Tsong Khapa. He also appears in angry form, and as a *yidam of that sort, is especially important in *Gelugpa.

Mañjuśrī's name means Gentle Holy One, yet he has a terrifyingly wrathful form as the bull-headed Yamāntaka (Slayer of Death), who as Vajrabhairava has been chief protector of the *Geluk since his *sādhana (ritual practice) was institutionalized by Tsong Khapa. Vajrabhairava—the most common form of Yamāntaka—is blue-black in colour with eight wrathful heads surmounted by a ninth, peacefully smiling Mañjuśrī. That Mañjuśrī as the wisdom-overcoming-death should be wrathful is understandable by the nature of the task, but that a certain amount of wrathfulness is necessary in simply dealing with one's own ignorance is also suggested by the symbolism of the sword in his peaceful aspect.

Manmukh (Pañjābī, 'person guided by inclination'). According to Sikhs, a self-willed, perverse individual who, in contrast to the *gurmukh, is controlled by the impulses of *man, rather than by the dictates of the *Gurū. See also FIVE EVIL PASSIONS.

Manna. Food from *heaven described in the Jewish book of *Exodus. During the period of wandering in the wilderness after the exodus from Egypt, the Israelites were fed on manna (16. 26–36).

Mannheimer, Isaac Noah (1793–1865). Rabbi and author of a *Reform Jewish *liturgy. Mannheimer served as leader of Reform Jewish communities in Copenhagen, Berlin, Leipzig, and Vienna. In contrast to the move of some congregations to other languages, his prayers continued to be in Hebrew, the prayer for *Zion was retained, and no organ music was permitted. His books include a German tr. of the *prayer book. He also worked for Jewish civil liberties, and, as an elected member of the Reichstag, he succeeded in abolishing the 'Jews' Tax'.

Manning, Henry Edward (1808–92). Roman Catholic *cardinal. Initially an Anglican and *archdeacon of Chichester, he became attracted to the *Oxford Movement and wrote Tract 78 of *Tracts for the Times*. Following the Gorham Judgement in 1851, he became a convert to Roman Catholicism, and (his wife having died in 1837) he was ordained priest. He founded the Oblates of St Charles Borromeo, and became archbishop of Westminster in 1865. He was *ultramontane in his sympathies and a strong defender of papal *infallibility. In 1889, he mediated successfully in a dock strike. He was buried in Kensal Green cemetery, but was reburied in Westminster Cathedral which he had helped to found.

Manseren and Koreri. Millennial *cargo cults in N. Irian Jaya. These derive from the myth of Manseren. In a typical version, an ugly culture hero, Manamakerei, secured a wife and son by magical means, called himself Manseren Manggundi ('the Lord himself') and created the local peoples. They rebelled against him so he departed westwards but will return to begin a golden age or Koreri ('we replace our old skins by new ones').

Mansukh (abrogation): see NASKH.

Man-ta-lao. Chin. for *maṇḍala.

Manthra (sacred chant): see MAGI.

Manthran (composer of sacred chants): see MAGI.

Mantra (Skt., 'instrument of thought'; Chin., *chou*; Jap., *ju*; Korean *chu*). A verse, syllable, or series of syllables believed to be of divine origin, used in a ritual or meditative context in Indian religions. Mantras are used for the propitiation of the gods, the attainment of power (*siddha), and identification with a deity or the absolute, which leads to liberation from *saṃsāra. First appearing in the *Vedic *Saṃhitās

(2nd millennium BCE), mantras take on a central role in sectarian Hinduism, and Buddhist and Hindu *Tantrism, especially in the Buddhist Mantrayāna school (7th/8th cents. CE).

There are three kinds of mantra: linguistically meaningful, such as *namaḥ śivāya*, 'homage to Śiva'; linguistically meaningless, the *bīja or 'seed' mantras, such as *oṃ aḥ huṃ*; and combined, such as the Buddhist *oṃ mani padme huṃ, 'om jewel in the lotus huṃ'.

Mantras are only endowed with transformative power if given in initiation (*dīkṣa) from the mouth of a *guru. It is not so much correct pronunciation, but rather the power with which the mantra is endowed that gives it transforming capability. See Index, Mantra.

Mantrayāna (Skt., 'path of mantra'). A term used synonymously with *Vajrayāna or *Tantric Buddhism, but which perhaps misleadingly suggests that incantation is the fundamental Tantric practice; in fact, practices of body (*yoga) and practices of mind (*visualization) are equally as important as practices of speech (*mantra), although in some early forms of Vajrayāna, mantra may well have been the dominant practice.

Mantra Yoga. The practice of *mantra repetition (*japa) as a means of liberation (*mokṣa), especially in *Tantrism.

Manu. Hindu lawgiver to whom is attributed **Manusmṛti* (The Laws of Manu). If historical, he may have been of the *Kṣatriya *varṇa, and was probably the compiler of legal traditions antecedent to him.

Manu (Skt., √*man*, 'think'). In Hindu mythology, a semi-divine patriarch who is progenitor of humanity and ruler of the earth. Each Manu rules over an aeon, or *manvantara*, each of which is shorter than the preceding. Accounts of the number and length of *manvantaras* vary greatly, but the Manus are generally numbered fourteen.

Manual of Discipline: see DEAD SEA SCROLLS.

Manusmṛti (Skt.). The Laws of Manu, a Hindu *dharmaśāstra attributed to the mythical lawgiver *Manu; also known as *Mānava-dharmaśāstra* or *Manu-saṃhitā*. *Manusmṛti* is the most authoritative of Sanskrit legal texts. Although having the authority of *smṛti, this authority is rejected by some lower-caste Hindus who regard the *Laws of Manu* as brahman propaganda. The present compilation is no older than 100–300 CE.

Mao-shan (religious movement): see TAOISM.

Mao Tzu-yuan (developer of school of Buddhism): see PAI-LIEN-TSUNG.

Mappō (Jap.; Chin., *mo-fa*, 'last *dharma'). In Buddhism, especially *Pure Land, the period of decadence and decline at the end of a time-cycle. According to Tao-ch'o, 2nd patriarch (562–645 CE), the year 549 was 1,500 years after the *Buddha's death and marked the beginning of mappo-ji, the period of 'latter-day dharma' predicted in the **Lotus Sūtra*, when no one can achieve enlightenment by their own effort, but must rely on Amitābha/*Amida. It is the third of three periods after the Buddha's death, for which see SHŌZŌMATSU.

Maqām (unintentioned but stable states of emotion, etc.): see ḤĀL.

Māra. A Hindu god of pestilence and mortal disease, lord of the *kāma-dhātu: it is the attraction of sensual pleasure which makes humans reckless in what they do. Māra is better known in Buddhism, being the opponent of the *Buddha. He is also known as Namuci, the tempter. A collection of stories about Māra is in the *Māra-Saṃyutta* of *Saṃyutta Nikāya.

Marabout (Arab., *murābiṭ*). Name given (especially in N. Africa) to holy Muslims, or to their descendants. The acquisition of holiness may be by any of many different paths—i.e. there is no formal school, nor restricted process of beatification.

Maraṇa. Death in Buddhism, not of the bodily aggregation, which is *cuti*, but of all phenomena as they rise into appearance and pass away.

Maranant'a or **Mālānanda.** A Serindian Buddhist missionary to Paekche (Korea). Maranant'a travelled from Eastern China to Paekche in 384, during the first year of the reign of King Ch'imnyu (384–5); this event is traditionally regarded as the official introduction of Buddhism to the kingdom of Paekche.

Maranatha. An Aramaic Christian formula in 1 Corinthians 16. 22, probably to be translated 'O Lord, come!' (cf. Revelations 22. 20). It may reflect the urgent expectation of the *parousia in the earliest Church, or it may be an invocation to reinforce a threat.

Maranke, Johane (founder of Christian movement in Africa): see AFRICAN APOSTLES.

Maranke Apostles (independent Christian movement in Africa): see AFRICAN APOSTLES.

Marāṭhī. A language which is a direct descendant of the literary Prākrit language called Mahārāshtrī. The Maratha confederacy at its height (at the end of the 18th cent.) covered most of central India.

Marburg, Colloquy of. The meeting of *Protestant leaders in October 1529 at the Castle of Marburg-on-the-Lahn to discuss theological differences. Fourteen articles were formulated expressing basic agreement on major doctrines, but in the debate concerning the fifteenth article it proved impossible fully to reconcile the divergent eucharistic views of *Luther and *Zwingli.

March of a Million Men (rally in Washington): see ELIJAH MUHAMMAD.

Marcion (d. *c*.160). Founder of a Christian movement which was a rival to *Catholic Christianity in the 2nd and 3rd cents.: he was excommunicated in 144. By the end of the 3rd cent. most Marcionite communities had been absorbed by *Manichaeism.

Notable in his teaching (e.g. in his (lost) *Antitheses*) was the absolute opposition between the Old Testament with its wicked God and the God of Love revealed by Jesus. He therefore rejected the Old Testament, and from the New Testament admitted to his canon only the letters of Paul and an edited version of the gospel of Luke.

Mardānā (d. *c*.1535 CE). Companion of Gurū *Nānak. Mardānā was a Dom (Dum or Mirāsī), i.e. a musician of low-*caste Muslim background. According to tradition Mardānā played the *rabāb*, a stringed instrument, to accompany Gurū Nānak's spiritual teaching, travelling with him to Indian centres of pilgrimage and to Arabia. Three *śaloks of the *Ādi Granth are attributed to Mardānā, one of the five Muslim contributors.

Maréchal, J. (neo-Thomist philosopher): see RAHNER, KARL.

Mārga (Skt., 'path'; Pāli, *magga*). In Hinduism and Buddhism, the way or path to release or enlightenment.

Mari. A Mesopotamian centre of the 3rd millennium BCE. Important documentary finds at Mari have added extensively to our understanding of the organization of early Israelite society, including indications of functionaries resembling *prophets.

Maria Legio or **Legio Maria.** The largest independent church with *Roman Catholic origins in Africa. It arose in Kenya from a heavenly visit experienced in 1962 by a Luo farmer and Roman Catholic catechist, Simeon Ondeto. In 1963, he was joined by a 20-year-old Roman Catholic Luo woman, Gaudencia Aoko after an experience of death and resurrection. Called at first 'Legion of Mary', it grew rapidly to over 50,000 members, with several thousands more among Luo migrants in Uganda and Tanzania.

Maria Lionza. A complex of informally organized spirit-possession cults in Venezuela. Beginning among rural Indians of Yaracuy in the 18th cent., it has expanded in this cent. across Venezuela, especially among the urban poor of all racial origins, and by adding African spirits from immigrant Cubans and Trinidadians, it has come to resemble *Shango, etc. Maria Lionza was a legendary Indian princess in the Sorte mountains of Yaracuy, who is now often assimilated to the Virgin [*Mary] of Coromoto, patroness of Venezuela, honoured with Roman Catholic rites and besought by practising Roman Catholics. There is a pilgrimage centre in the Sorte mountains and the movement is still developing many new forms.

Mariology. The study of the Blessed Virgin *Mary in Christianity. In *Vatican II, *The Dogmatic Constitution on the Church*, ch. 8, offers a summary of the basic constituents of Mariology.

Maritain, Jacques (1882–1973). French neo-Thomist philosopher. After he and his wife Raïssa became Roman Catholics in 1906, he devoted most of his life to studying and writing about the works of St Thomas *Aquinas and their application to life, society, art, and politics. His achievements include his elucidation of the different forms of knowledge (*The Degrees of Knowledge*, 1932; Eng. 1937), outlining a new form of Christian humanism (*True Humanism*, 1936; Eng. 1938) and developing a philosophy of art (*Art and Scholasticism*, 1920; Eng. 1923). He also helped to foster interest in Christian democracy. Shortly before he died, he exemplified that simplicity which he believed to be at the heart of a good life by becoming a Little Brother (see DE FOUCAULD) in Toulouse.

Maritain argued that confusion has arisen because *'knowledge' and 'empirical knowledge' have been regarded as synonyms: empirical knowledge is one way of knowing amongst many others (including perhaps *mysticism); consequently, there is a hierarchy of ways of knowing, each of which arises from, and opens up, a different perspective on what is real. Human beings, as ensouled essences, depend constantly on the creative work of God for their existence, with the 'gap' between humans and God to be closed by grace: 'Grace, while leaving us infinitely distant from pure Act [i.e. God] in the order of being, is still, in the order of spiritual operation and relation to its object, a formal participation in the Divine Nature.' This is 'knowledge by connaturality', and can only be attained by the very act of knowing in this mode.

Māriyamnam (in Tamil, etc.; in Marāthī she is Māri-ai; and there are other forms). A Goddess of folk Hinduism worshipped by the lower *castes in a wide area, from Mahārāṣṭra down to *Tamilnadu. Her name consists of 'mother, goddess' (*ammaṉ, āī) and the doubtful 'killing' (from Skt., *mārī*?). She is envisaged as violent, bloodthirsty, and creating havoc (outbreaks of epidemics), if not properly worshipped. This worship includes animal sacrifice, rites of possession, and sometimes fire-walking. Some connection with, or interference from, the mythology of *Mahiṣa is possible here.

Mark, St. One of the four *Evangelists. He is traditionally identified with the cousin of *Barnabas who accompanied him and *Paul (Colossians 4. 10; Acts 12–15). According to *Papias he was the 'interpreter' of *Peter in Rome (cf. 1 Peter 5. 13). By the 4th cent. he was credited with founding the church of Alexandria. His relics were removed from there to Venice in the 9th cent. Feast day, 25 Apr.

The Gospel according to Mark is the second book in the New Testament.

Markan Apocalypse: see APOCALYPSE.

Mārkaṇḍeya-Purāṇa. A Hindu mythological text in Skt., belonging to the genre of the *purāṇas. It is included in all lists of the eighteen mahā-purāṇas (major purāṇas) and can be regarded as an old representative of that tradition. The bulk of the work deals with ancient Indian cosmography and cosmology, with the structure of the world, and the history of its ancient kings (the descendants of *Manu) during past and future *manvantaras* (see *Manu). This core may well belong to the 3rd cent. CE.

Marks of perfection, thirty-two (of a great man or Buddha): see DVĀTRIṂŚADVARA-LAKṢANA.

Maronites. *Uniat *Syrian Christian body whose homeland is Lebanon. Maronite scholars trace their origin to a monastery founded by the disciples of a 4th-cent. Syrian *anchorite, called Maro. It seems certain, however, that they became a separate body only in the 7th cent., with their adoption of *Monothelite doctrines and subsequent excommunication in 680. Following the Arab conquest, their monastery on Mount Lebanon was destroyed. They formally united with Rome at the time of the Crusades (1182), and since then have maintained relations with the West.

As a Uniat body they have their own liturgy (mostly Syriac) and their own hierarchy of patriarch and ten bishops. Outside Lebanon and Syria there are also churches in Cyprus, Egypt, and N. and S. America.

Maror (Heb., 'bitter herb'). The bitter herb the Jews eat at the *Passover festival. According to Exodus 12. 8, the Israelites were commanded to eat maror with unleavened bread (*mazzah) and the Passover offering, and it is one of the *foods displayed and eaten at the *seder table.

Mar-pa (Mar-pa Chos kyi blo gros) (*c.*1012–*c.*1098). Tibetan *yogi, who journeyed three times to India and returned with the teachings of *mahāmudrā and *Nāro Chos Drug. He taught *Milarepa, and was the key link in the transmission lineage of *Kagyupa.

Marranos (from Span., 'swine'). Baptized Jews of Spain and Portugal, i.e. *anusim, or forced converts. Jews in Spain were forced to convert to Christianity in 1391 and in Portugal in 1497. These 'new Christians' were always suspected of harbouring their original faith and were renowned for their reluctance to eat pork. Particularly after the introduction of the *Inquisition into Spain in 1481 and into Portugal in 1536, many Marranos fled abroad. Marranos lived undisturbed in many *Protestant states. In *Roman Catholic countries, their situation was far more precarious, and in most places they had to maintain the semblance of Catholicism.

Marriage and divorce. Marriage is the union between at least two people (in *polygamy and polyandry it may be more), in which commitment is made and responsibility undertaken. It is recognized and controlled in society, because of its obvious relation to the procreation and nurture of the next generation. Because of the profound consequences of the institution of marriage (yielding experience including, but going far beyond, the pleasure of sexual satisfaction), marriage is a frequent metaphor in religions for union with God. But it is recognized that not all marriages are realized in relation to the goals, however described. Divorce is regarded in general as at least a matter of regret, more often as a matter of defeat and fault. The facilities for divorce therefore differ between religions.

Judaism According to the Hebrew scriptures, marriage is a state instituted by God because 'it is not good that the man should be alone' (Genesis 2. 18). Although various biblical figures (such as *Jacob, *Saul, *David, etc.) had more than one wife, monogamy seems to have been the general rule, and the prophets used marriage as an illustration of God's relationship with Israel. Certain marriages, particularly between close relatives, were forbidden, and marriage between Jew and *idolater was strongly condemned (see EZRA). Although a continuing marriage was much to be desired, divorce was permitted (Deuteronomy 24. 1–4). The actual marriage ceremony was in two parts, the *kiddushin* or *erusin* (betrothal) and the *nissuin* (marriage proper). In the Middle Ages, the two parts were combined. The ceremony is performed under a *huppah. The bridegroom has previously undertaken the obligations of the *ketubbah (marriage contract) and is led to the bride. *Blessings are recited over wine and the couple drink from the same cup. The bridegroom places a ring on the bride's finger and recites in Hebrew the formula, 'Behold you are consecrated to me with this ring according to the Law of Moses and Israel'. The ketubbah is read out; seven *benedictions over wine are recited; and, in most communities, the bridegroom crushes a glass with his foot.

Although divorce is a matter of great regret, it is possible. According to Jewish law, if both husband and wife agree, a husband may give a get ('bill of divorce') to his wife. Both husband and wife can demand a divorce if the spouse has a physical defect, or because of unsatisfactory conduct. It is, however, in a post-ghetto society notoriously difficult for the community to compel a husband to give a divorce, and if he refuses, the wife is tied; she cannot marry again, and any subsequent children will be *mamzerim.

Since the husband is the one who must give the get, he must, necessarily, be found; otherwise, the wife remains *agunah ('tied woman') and cannot remarry. In *Conservative Judaism, a *takkanah (1953) allows a clause to be inserted in the ketubbah whereby both parties agree to abide by a decision of the bet din if there is conflict. Reform Judaism has dropped the practice of the get. The law of divorce is covered in *B.Gittin*.

Christianity Marriage, in the words of the **Book of Common Prayer*, 'is an honourable estate'. The causes of marriage are three (for the procreation of children and their nurture, for a remedy against sin and to avoid fornication, and for the mutual society, help, and comfort that the one ought to have of the other, both in prosperity and adversity). In *Roman Catholic understanding, marriage is a *sacrament which creates a *vinculum*, an unbreakable (metaphysical) bond; it can only be brought to an end by a recognition, on various specific grounds, that it never happened in the first place, i.e. by annulment. Among other Christians, there is a more serious wrestling with the vision of Jesus Christ that marriage recreates the lost and disturbed conditions of the Garden of Eden. Uncertainty about the NT texts has led to a divergence of practice among Christians, some allowing remarriage after divorce (with a previous partner still living) in some circumstances, while others do not.

Islam Marriage in Islam does not have to take place in a specifically religious context. It is thus a civil matter (so far as such distinctions can be drawn in Islam). Nevertheless, it is one of the signs (*ayā) of God. The word for a pair or a mate is *zawj*, which is a term used for marriage (*al-zawaj*), as also is *nikāḥ*, the marriage contract. There is debate in the schools of *sharīʿa about whether marriage is a compulsory obligation. In general it is for those who can pay the dowry (*mahr*), who can support a wife and children, who is healthy, and who fears that otherwise he will commit fornication (*zinā'); for women it is compulsory for those who have no other means of maintaining themselves and who fear ẓinā'. Marriage is a contract between the two parties, often under the initiative of fathers or guardians. According to 2. 228, men have a degree or rank (*darajah*) over their wives, and in 4. 38 are 'standing over them' (*qawwumun*, which *may* mean 'standing beside in support'). Marriage with non-Muslims, who might be suspected of *shirk, is forbidden, but Muslim men are allowed to marry women who belong to *ahl al-Kitāb (the people of the Book). The mahr is given by the groom to the bride, and it remains hers even in the event of a divorce (half of it if the marriage is dissolved before consummation). The amount of mahr is not stipulated in sharīʿa. Polygamy (up to four wives) is allowed in Qur'ān 4. 3, provided they can be treated equitably (some believe that this condition can never be attained, and that in practice monogamy is required); Muḥammad himself married eleven wives. Divorce (*ṭalāq*, 'to set an animal free') is permitted, but 'of all things that are permitted, divorce is the most hated by God'. A statement of divorce should be followed by a waiting period (*'idda*) of three menstrual cycles, to ensure that no child has been conceived, and to offer the chance of reconciliation. *Talāq ḥasan* requires three successive pronouncements of divorce to be made, during three consecutive periods of purity (*ṭuhur*); it is not permissible to pronounce the three repudiations all at one time. Divorce may be initiated by the wife (*khulʿ*), but if she does so without identifiable cause, she must abandon the dowry. For the early (and disputed) temporary marriage, see MUTʿA.

Hinduism Marriage is an expected norm for all Hindus except those who become renouncers and adopt a community or *ascetic life. For a woman, the ritual of marriage (*vivāha*) is in itself a route to *mokṣa. Marriages are generally a matter of arrangement between families, attempting to ensure compatibility of (obviously) *caste, but also of such things as education and wealth. The ritual is one of the most important of the *saṃskāras (rites of passage), and involves great expense, with gifts passing between the families. The details of the ritual differ from place to place, but some elements are constant. Although celebrations may last for several days, the actual ceremony is simple. It begins with the formal giving away, by the father, of the bride. Songs of blessing are then sung, followed by oblations to the sacred fire, *homa, before which the couple are sitting. They then take seven steps (*satapadi*) round the fire, with the groom leading the bride. If evening has fallen by this time, the couple will go out to see the star Dhruva (the Pole Star), and the bride vows to be as constant as that star. The festivities then continue.

According to classic theory (e.g. *Arthaśastra), a marriage brought into being by the proper rituals cannot be dissolved. It follows that a widow should not remarry—and in a case of absolute devotion, a widow should follow her late husband into death (*satī). Nevertheless, before death mokṣa (release) is possible on various grounds (the exact grounds are debated). Defects in bride or groom (especially lack of virginity and absence of virility) are usually accepted as sufficient grounds, as may be prolonged absence, or desertion, or cruelty. The Hindu Marriage Act, 1955, allows divorce, but for traditional Hindus it is still, in general, unacceptable.

Buddhism In the long process which leads eventually to enlightenment, the Buddha espoused the wisdom of addressing teaching and practice to the levels attained by different people (*upāya-kauśalya). In this perspective, marriage properly undertaken is a legitimate step, even though sexuality will be transcended in due course. In the *Sigālovāda Sutta*, the Buddha laid out the responsibilities of lay Buddhists which embrace the duties involved in a householder's life. Paramount (and one of the Five Precepts, *śīla) is the avoidance of sexual impropriety. If a marriage fails, there may be a contribution of *karma to the failure, but in any case the dismantling of the marriage must attempt to avoid hurt to either of those involved.

Sikhism The 1909 Anand Marriage Act legalized the Sikhs' Anand Karaj ceremony, following pressure from reformers—though many weddings are still influenced by Hindu practice. Although, according to *Rahat Maryādā, *caste is immaterial, marriages are usually arranged within caste. Astrological considerations should not decide the date. Often betrothal (Pañjābī, *mangaṇī*, *kūrmāī*) is elaborate, with the bestowal of gifts. Subsequently a *chunni* (scarf) and other gifts are presented to the bride-to-be. For the marriage ceremony the bridegroom, his family, and friends come to the *gurdwārā as guests of the bride's family who make the arrangements. In front of the congregation, the couple sit before the *Ādi Granth, the bride to the groom's left. She generally wears red and his turban is often pink. *Ardās is said. The officiant (any approved Sikh) explains the ceremony's significance, reminding them to show love and loyalty. Bride and groom bow in assent to the Ādi Granth. A pink scarf (*pallā*) now links them. Four times the bride follows the groom clockwise around the Ādi Granth. Before each circumambulation, one stanza of the *Lāvān is read and the *rāgīs sing it as the couple walk around. They are garlanded and given money. The service concludes with six verses of *Anand *Sāhib, the Ardās, and distribution of *kaṛāh praśād. A reception follows.

Chinese The married state, one of the five relationships, is essential in this life and afterlife for the purposes of uniting families and assuring descendants. Traditionally, marriage is arranged by a matchmaker and based on the eight character horoscopes. While keeping her family's surname, the wife is bodily, spiritually, ritually, and juridically transferred to the husband's family, subordinate first to the husband then to the eldest son, and remains in that family after death. By marriage, a husband assures his place in the ritual continuity of generations by assuming responsibility for his wife. See Index, Marriage, divorce.

Marsiglio (Marsilius) of Padua (*c*.1275–1342). Political philosopher who called in question the primacy of Church over State in the political order. His *Defensor Pacis* (1324) was held to be antipapal and led to his expulsion from Paris. He argued that the State, not the Church, is the unifying bond in society, and that the task of a ruler is to maintain peace.

Mārtāṇḍa (misshapen foetus who is shaped as the sun): see ĀDITYAS.

Martel, Charles: see UMAYYADS.

Martha, St. The sister of Mary and Lazarus who according to Luke 10. 38–42 received, and cooked a meal for, Jesus in her house. She is commonly regarded as typifying the active Christian life as contrasted with Mary, who typifies the contemplative. Feast day in E., 4 June; in W., 29 July.

Mar Thoma Church. Christian body of *c*.300,000 in Kerala, S. India. It originated from a party of *Syrian Orthodox who came under the influence of the *CMS in the mid-19th cent. and were known as 'Reformed Jacobites'. See also MALABAR.

Martial arts in Japan. They were formerly called *bugei* (martial arts) or *bujutsu* (martial skills), but the word *budō* (martial ways) is commonly used today, though they are not identical in details. The budō, which evolved from bugei, aim at the self-realization of aspirants through discipline and training.

There is no standard list of martial arts. An expert enumerates thirty-four *bugei*, whereas the traditional list counts eighteen (*bugei juhappan*, the eighteen martial arts). In the Tokugawa period warriors had to master sword-play, spear, archery, horsemanship, *jujutsu* (proto-judō), and firearms, together with academic subjects.

Buddhism, Taoism, and Confucianism provided the basic rationale by which warriors resolved the question of death as well as improved their skill in handling weapons. The principle, '*Bushido means the determined will to die' (*Hagakure*), was fundamental to every generation of warriors, and in this regard, the *Zen doctrine of No-mind (*mushin*) or No-thought (*munen*) had an important role to play in martial arts, summarizing indifference to, or transcendence of, the events or accidents of life, including death.

Martyr (Gk., *martus*, 'witness'). One who suffers death on behalf of his or her faith, often for refusing to renounce it. See Index, Martyrs.

Judaism See KIDDUSH HA-SHEM.

Christianity The Gk. word was only gradually restricted to those whose witness to their faith had led to their death in persecutions. From the 2nd cent. martyrs were specially honoured in churches, and the anniversaries of their deaths, as (heavenly) 'birthdays', were kept as feasts. They were venerated as intercessors in heaven, and their relics sought after. Accounts ('Acts') of martyrdom form an important class of *hagiography.

Islam See SHAHĪD.

Sikhism Many Sikhs have died for their faith, particularly under the Mughal emperor, Auraṅgzeb, and during the conflicts of the 18th cent. Martyrs (Pañjābī, Hindī *śahīd*) are remembered daily in *Ardās, and pictures of martyrdoms are displayed in the *gurdwārās. Of the *Gurūs, *Arjan Dev and *Tegh Bahādur were martyred.

Ma'rūf al-Karkhī (d. 815–16 (AH 200)). A *Sūfī master of the Baghdād school, who emphasized sobriety in life and religion. He emphasized that Sūfī attainment cannot be achieved by effort, but only by God's gift. His tomb, on the west bank of the Tigris in Baghdad, is still a centre of pilgrimage.

Maruts (etym. uncertain: perhaps *mṛ* + *ut*, 'immortal'; or *mā rud*, 'do not weep'). A collection (*gaṇa*) of *Vedic storm gods, who work in the service of *Rudra, and who are therefore also known as Rudriyas (though in some accounts the Rudriyas are separate and different).

Marx, Karl (1818–83). German social and political theorist. He advocated a form of humanism and is widely regarded as an important critic of religion, although he himself attached little importance to this aspect of his thought. Marx was primarily interested in religious life as a symptom of a more general self-estranged and unfulfilled human existence. Marx thus extended the *Feuerbachian critique of religion into a more general critique of society by extending analogically the idea that God is alienated human nature into a general theory of social alienation.

Mary, Blessed Virgin. The mother of *Jesus, counted pre-eminent among the *saints. She is prominent in the 'infancy stories' in Matthew 1–2 and especially Luke 1–2. According to both gospels, she conceived Jesus while a virgin (see VIRGIN BIRTH OF CHRIST). She appears in the background during his career (Mark 3. 31; Luke 11. 27–8; John 2. 1–11), then at the foot of the cross (John 19. 25), and with the apostles after Easter (Acts 1. 14).

By the earliest *Church fathers Mary is mentioned rarely and usually in contrast with *Eve. *Mariology (devotion to Mary) probably owed much of its impetus to two currents of early and medieval Christian thought: (i) the predilection for celibacy and virginity as a style of life superior to marriage; and (ii) the removal of Jesus from the human level, particularly in breaking the entail of sin (see ORIGINAL SIN). The first of these was congenial to the tradition of Mary's 'perpetual virginity' (i.e. even after giving birth to Jesus), which was current by the time of *Athanasius, and later to the doctrine of the *immaculate conception, according to which Mary was without stain of original sin from the moment of her being conceived. The second current of thought may be observed in the canonization of the title *Theotokos ('Mother of God') for Mary at the council of *Ephesus (431). She eventually became known in the W. Church as 'co-redemptress' and 'mediator of all graces', the latter title being popularized by St Alphonsus *Liguori. The doctrine of her bodily *assumption into heaven was first formulated in orthodox circles by Gregory of Tours (d. 594), and was defined as Catholic dogma in 1950.

At the Reformation there was a strong reaction against Marian devotion, partly owing to the rejection of the cult of saints, and partly in keeping with a more positive view of sex and of the married state. The main feasts of Mary are the Assumption (15 Aug.), Nativity (8 Sept.), Annunciation (25 Mar.), Purification (2 Feb.; *Candlemas), and Visitation (2 July; in the RC Church now 31 May).

In Islam, Maryam is the mother of 'Īsā (*Jesus); the name is probably derived from Syriac-Christian usage. Sūra 19 of the *Qur'ān, 'Maryam', relates a version of the *annunciation, followed by an account of Maryam's giving birth, alone, at the foot of a date palm (19. 17–33; cf. 3. 45–51, a slightly different version of the annunciation). The *ḥadīth relate that Maryam and 'Īsā were preserved from the 'touch of Satan' which affects all children at birth, i.e. were free from sin; further, she is considered one of the four best women of Paradise, along with *Fāṭima, Āsiyā (Pharaoh's wife), and *Khadīja.

See Index, Mary.

Maryam: see MARY, BLESSED VIRGIN.

Mary Magdalen(e). A follower of Jesus out of whom he cast seven devils, who ministered to him in Galilee (Luke 8. 2). She remained close to the *Cross (Mark 15. 40) with other women (when the male disciples had fled), and she was the first to meet the risen Christ, being charged to proclaim the resurrection to the eleven. For that reason, she was called (first by Hippolytus of Rome, early 3rd cent.) 'the apostle to the apostles'. However, *Gregory I merged Mary Magdalene with two other Marys, the sinner who anointed Jesus (Luke 7. 37) and Mary of Bethany who also anointed him (John 12. 3), thus producing the composite figure of the sexually aberrant penitent. From this, 'Magdalens' became a term for prostitutes who had turned to Christ, and for the Houses which took them in, sometimes as specific religious orders. There is, however, no ground for Gregory's identifications, and they have been abandoned even by the *Roman Catholic Church where they had great emotional importance.

Mar Zutra (Jewish exilarch of 5th cent.): see ZUTRA, MAR.

Masada. Prominent rocky site in Israel/Palestine, where *Herod the Great built a palace and refuge. According to *Josephus, it was here that the last defenders against Rome at the end of the first Jewish revolt committed *suicide rather than surrender. Despite the emotional importance of this in the state of Israel, archaeology throws doubt on Josephus' account.

Masand (Hindī and *Pañjābī corruption of Persian *masnad-ī-ālā*, lofty throne, title of courtiers). Agent of Sikh *Gurūs, originally appointed to organize the worship of the *sangats and to collect their offerings. The masands were instructed to come annually on *Baisākhī day to present the Sikhs' contributions. The masands appointed were devout, informed men who could instruct the increasing saṅgats.

Unfortunately, the system degenerated as individual masands supported rival claimants to Gurūship. Consequently Gurū *Gobind Siṅgh dismissed the masands and in successive *hukamnāmās bade the Sikhs to ignore them and bring their offerings direct to the Gurū.

Mashal (Heb., 'likeness, fable'). Short Jewish moral tale normally with animal characters. In their earliest form, among the *rabbis, they resemble the *parables of *Jesus, including many of the form, 'To what can the kingdom of God be likened?'

Mashhad or **Meshed.** Capital of the Iranian province of Khurāsān and the most important place of pilgrimage for Persian Shi'ites. It is here that the eighth Imām of the *Ithna 'Asharīiyya (Twelvers) 'Alī al-Riḍā b. Mūsa (d. 818 (AH 203)) is buried. Around his tomb grew a large town. Mashhad contains a sacred area, called *Bast, which can only be entered through two gates, and is strictly forbidden to non-Muslims.

Since mashhad means 'a place where one has borne witness', i.e. died as a *martyr, the word may be used of any place where this has occurred. Notable examples are *Karbalā', *Najaf, Kazimain (near Baghdad, with the tombs of the 7th and 9th Imams of the Twelvers, Ithnā 'Asharīyya, namely Musa al-Kazim and Muḥammad al-Jaurad), and Samarra (10th and 12th, 'Ali al-Hadi and Hasan al-Askari).

Masjid (Muslim place of assembly): see MOSQUE.

Masjid al-Aqsa, al- ('the furthest mosque'). The Muslim *mosque built in the 7th cent. CE, on the Temple Mount in *Jerusalem (al-Quds). It is the mosque associated with the Night Journey (*isrā') and the Ascent (*mi'rāj) of *Muḥammad, based on Qur'ān 17. 1. It is a building distinct from the *Dome of the Rock.

Masjid al-Ḥarām, al-. The *mosque at *Mecca, closely associated with the *Ka'ba and *Zamzam.

Maskilim (proponents of the Haskalah, enlightenment): see HASKALAH.

Maslow, Abraham Harold (1908–70). Psychologist and theorist of human personality. He proposed 'a hierarchical prepotency of basic needs', goals to which we address ourselves in roughly the same order, with one desire rapidly succeeding another when the first is satisfied: physiological, safety, love, esteem, self-actualization. The self-actualized person exhibits unusual degrees of detachment and self-dependence. S/he also achieves peak-experiences in greater number, which take the individual far beyond the ordinary levels of striving to achieve more proximate goals. He argued that religions derive from founders who have sustained extended peak-experiences.

Masorah. The rules and practices of reading certain books of the Hebrew Bible in Jewish public worship. Among *Ashkenazi Jews, a tradition of cantillated reading of the *Torah and *liturgy developed which was recorded by special accents and marks placed in the texts. These conventions were developed in the 6th–9th cents. CE by scholars known as the masoretes whose aim was to preserve the authentic Hebrew text. The accepted text is that determined by Aaron ben Asher of the Tiberias School of Masoretes.

Masoret (tradition): see TRADITION (JUDAISM).

Masowe Apostles (Independent Christian movement in Africa): see AFRICAN APOSTLES.

Mass (Lat. *missa*, from the words *Ite, missa est*, 'Go, you are dismissed' at the end). In the *Roman Catholic Church, and among *Anglo-Catholics, the usual title for the *eucharist. Outside Catholic circles, the word has come to be associated in theological contexts with the doctrine of the eucharistic *sacrifice.

Massacre of St Bartholomew's Day (massacre of French Calvinists): see HUGUENOTS.

Massekhet (Heb., 'a web' and 'a tractate'). A subdivision of one of the six orders (*sedarim) of the Jewish *Mishnah.

Mastema. The *devil's name in the Jewish *Book of *Jubilees*. Mastema is portrayed as the chief of the evil spirits and the enemy of righteousness.

Mater et Magistra. An *encyclical issued by *John XXIII on 15 May 1961 to mark the 70th anniversary of **Rerum Novarum*. It began to break the ties between the Roman Catholic Church and socially conservative groups, approving a greater role for the State in national life than earlier papal statements had countenanced.

Maṭha (Jain centres): see BHATTARAKA.

Mathurā, Mattra, or **Muttra.** Ancient city on the river Yamunā in Uttar-Pradesh. As the birthplace of *Kṛṣṇa, it is one of the seven *sacred cities of India. It is a major centre of pilgrimage, and the site for the enactment of *Rāslīlā*, a series of plays based on the life of Kṛṣṇa.

Mātikā (heading in Abhidhammapiṭaka): see TRIPIṬAKA.

Matriarch: see PATRIARCHS AND MATRIARCHS.

Mātṛkas (divine mothers): see MAHEŚVARI.

Matsah (unleavened bread): see MAZZAH.

Ma-tsu (Chinese Goddess): see T'IEN-SHANG SHENG-MU.

Matsuo Bashō (Japanese poet): see HAIKU.

Matsuri. Japanese festivals. Derived from a verb meaning 'to attend to', 'to entertain', or 'to serve the *kami', the souls of the deceased, or a person of higher status, matsuri implies 'the mental attitude of respect, reverence, and the willingness to listen, serve, and obey' (J. M. Kitagawa). Always there is an element of revelation, whereby sacred beings manifest their wills to the human community, which responds in matsuri.

Given the immanental Japanese world-view, every act can be considered an act of matsuri, which in this sense is a ritualization of everyday life. Since the function of government under the imperial system was to actualize the sacred will, the ancient word for government was *matsurigoto* or 'matsuri affairs'. Matsuri, or its sinocized pronunciation (*-sai*), came to refer to special ceremonies at court or at Shinto shrines which involve formal procedures, from the invocation and arrival of kami, through the phase of festive communion (*naorai*), to their final dispatch. Some form of sacred entertainment always accompanies the communal feast.

In modern Japan, as in the West, the essential context of the festival is often disregarded, resulting in strictly commercial or civil celebrations also known as matsuri.

Ma-tsu Tao-i (Jap., Baso Dōitsu; 709–88). Third-generation leader of the Ch'an/Zen school of *Hui-neng, who, with Shih-t'ou, established the two main characteristics of Ch'an, issuing eventually in *Rinzai and *Sōtō. He is the first known to use the abrupt methods of Ch'an/Zen, e.g. the shout (*ho) and the stick (*kyosaku).

Since there is only one undifferentiated nature of all appearance, it has to be realized as already being the only truth that there is; it cannot be attained as something not yet realized. His style is summarized in the phrase *kigen kikō*, 'strange words and extraordinary actions', which became a model for other Zen masters.

Matsya (Skt., 'fish'). The leading character, a fish, in an important Hindu myth, who rescues *Manu, the ancestor of humanity. Matsya is the first *avatāra of Viṣṇu in the standard list of ten.

Matthā ṭekṇā (Pañjābī, 'to bow the forehead'). Upon entering the *gurdwārā, Sikhs kneel before the *Ādi Granth, touching the floor with their foreheads as a sign of respect to it as *Gurū. This is also the custom when greeting an elderly relative.

Matthew, St. One of the twelve *Apostles and of the four *Evangelists. In Matthew 10. 3 he is described as a tax collector. According to *Papias he made a collection in Hebrew of the sayings of Jesus, and since the time of *Irenaeus he has been credited with the authorship of the gospel bearing his name. In art he is depicted with a sword, a money-bag, or a carpenter's square. Feast day in the E., 16 Nov.; in the W., 21 Sept.

The Gospel according to Matthew is the opening book of the New Testament.

Matthias, St. The *apostle chosen to fill the vacancy in the twelve left by the treachery of *Judas, according to Acts 1. 15–26. Feast day in W., 14 May (24 Feb. in Anglican churches); in the E., 9 Aug.

Mattins or **Matins.** The West Christian *office for the night, derived from the *vigils of the primitive church and so called until the 11th cent. In the *Rule* of St *Benedict it was prescribed for 2 a.m. 'Mattins' is also an unofficial name for Anglican *morning prayer.

Māturīdī, Maturidites: see AL-MĀTURĪDĪ.

Matzah, Matzo (unleavened bread): see MAZZAH.

Maudūdī: see MAWDŪDĪ.

Maundy Thursday. The Thursday before *Easter. It celebrates Jesus' institution of the *eucharist at the *Last Supper on that day. The English name 'Maundy' derives from a Latin *antiphon *Mandatum novum* ('a new commandment', John 13. 34) sung on this day. The royal Maundy Ceremony in the UK, in which the reigning sovereign distributes Maundy money to twelve deserving and (relatively) poor people, has lost all contact with the original commemoration.

Maurice, Frederick Denison (1805–72). Christian clergyman and social reformer. He was the son of a *Unitarian minister, and was unable to graduate from Cambridge University because he could not subscribe to the *Thirty-Nine Articles. Influenced by the writings of *Coleridge and by a profound conversion experience, he became an *Anglican and was ordained in 1834. After a curacy, he became chaplain to Guy's Hospital in London in 1836, when he published *The Kingdom of Christ*. In this he argued that since Christ is the head of every person, all people are bound in a universal fellowship which life in all its aspects should make manifest. In 1853, he published *Theological Essays*, which included a rejection of eternal punishment determined at the moment of death. He had 'no faith in man's theory of a Universal Restitution' (i.e. *universalism), but maintained that the quest for the return of the prodigal would have no end.

This cautious view was nevertheless taken to be a subversion of the necessary foundation for moral life, and he was therefore dismissed from the College (although the real animus against him lay in his connection with Christian Socialism.

Maurya dynasty. The first unifying, imperial dynasty in India, *c.*321–180 BCE. Its founder was Chandragupta (d. *c.*297); his grandson was *Aśoka.

Mauss, M. (sociologist of religion): see SACRIFICE.

Mawdūdī, Sayyid Abū al-Aʿlā, usually known as **Mawlānā Mawdūdī** (1903–79). Founder of the political party Jamaat-al-Islam (i.e. *Jamāʿat-i Islāmī) in India and Pakistan. He wrote 138 major works in Urdu (much translated), the most influential being *al-Jihād fi'l-Islam* (1927), and *Tafhīm al-Qur'ān* (Urdu version of the Qur'ān, 1947–72). He advocated a return to pure Islam, considering Islam to be a total system and rejecting anything extraneous.

Mawla (Arab.). In early Islam, a 'client' or protected person, who was a convert to Islam and by this procedure was integrated into the existing Arab tribal and family system. Mawla also means 'master', and al-Mawla is a term for God.

Mawlawīy(y)a. A Derwīsh order, known colloquially as 'whirling dervishes'. The name is derived from *mawlānā* ('our master'), a title of *Jalāl al-Dīn al-Rūmī. The dance induces trance- and ecstatic-states, and is undertaken by pivoting on the right foot, while engaging in *dhikr (concentration on God). The name of the Order is often transliterated as Mevlevi.

Mawlid, Mawlūd (Arab., *walada*, 'give birth'). The celebration of a birthday, but especially of the Prophet *Muḥammad, 12 Rabīʿ I.

Maximus the Confessor (*c.*580–662). Greek theologian, mystic, and ascetical writer. After a distinguished secular career, he became a monk *c.*612 in Chrysopolis, fleeing to Africa before the Persian advance in 626. A strong opponent of *monothelitism, he secured its condemnation in Africa and Rome (649). In 653 and again in 661 he was brought to Constantinople, where he refused to submit to monothelitism, was condemned as a *heretic, mutilated, and died shortly afterwards in exile.

Māyā. 1. The mother of Gotama who became the *Buddha. She died within a few days of his birth. Later accounts (e.g. *Buddhacarita*) recount many miracles, including a virgin birth.

2. (Skt., 'supernatural power'). In the early Vedic literature, māyā generally means supernatural power or magic. It also carries the connotation of deceit or trickery. In the **Bhagavad-gītā*, māyā is the power to bring things into apparent form.

In *Advaita Vedānta philosophy, *Gauḍapāda used the term māyā for the power of the apparent creation of the world as well as the world so created. *Śaṅkara extended the term by associating it with *avidyā (ignorance). For Śaṅkara, avidyā, ignorance of the Ultimate Reality (*Brahman) produces the illusory world of name and form, or māyā, through superimposition. It is usually misleading to translate māyā as 'illusion'. Nevertheless, soteriologically the power of māyā is wisely treated as such; and in later Hinduism, māyā as Cosmic Illusion is sometimes personified and identified with the great goddess *Durgā.

In *Mahāyāna Buddhism, māyā means a delusion or an illusion such as that produced by a magician. The phenomenal world is illusory, māyā, with the *Mādhyamaka arguing that the separate dharmas themselves are conditioned and have no being of their own, and the Yogācāra/*Vijñānavāda school regarding the dharmas as merely ideas or representations.

Among Sikhs, the teaching of the *Gurūs is that māyā is a real part of God's creation. However, the attractions of māyā (i.e., wealth, physical love, etc.) are also, in the end, delusory and cannot accompany a person beyond death.

Māyādevī. Name of the Hindu Goddess as personified delusion. Other names include Mahāmāyā, Yogamāyā, Viṣṇumāyā.

Maybaum, I.: see HOLOCAUST.

Mayoi (Jap., 'error'). Zen understanding of delusion, whenever the phenomenal world wrongly understood appears to be real and substantial.

Māyōṉ. S. Indian name of the Hindu god *Kṛṣṇa/*Viṣṇu. The name derives from a Tamil adjective meaning 'a person of black complexion'; synonyms are: Māyaṉ, Māyavaṉ, Māl, Mālavaṉ, and Tirumāl. Some sporadic references in the Tamil *caṅkam* literature (1st cent. BCE to 3rd cent. CE?) indicate a knowledge and veneration of the N. Indian god Kṛṣṇa also in the extreme South. During the next centuries, more extensive sources allow us to catch glimpses of a developed temple culture which envisages Māyōṉ predominantly as *Nārāyaṇa/Viṣṇu. Thus (in contrast to the **Bhagavad-gītā*) Māyōṉ = Kṛṣṇa is not envisaged as an *avatāra of Viṣṇu. Only with the *Śrīvaiṣṇavism institutionalized by *Rāmānuja in the 12th cent. does Viṣṇu emerge as the central god-figure.

Mayse Bukh: see MAʿASEH BOOK.

Mazal tōv (Heb., 'good planetary influences'). Traditional Jewish greeting, wishing someone 'Good luck!'

Mazhabī (Pañjābī, 'religious'). Sikh of sweeper *caste. Members of the *Harijan Hindu Chuhṛā caste who became Sikh were frequently termed Mazhabī.

Mazzah. Unleavened bread eaten by Jews during the *Passover Festival. When the Israelites left Egypt, they took mazzah with them because they could not wait for the dough to rise (Exodus 12. 39). Mazzah is described in the Passover *seder as 'the bread of affliction', based on Deuteronomy 16. 3. See also AFIKOMEN; PASSOVER; SEDER.

MBTI (Myers Briggs Type Indicator): see JUNG, CARL GUSTAV.

Mean, doctrine of the (book in Confucian Classics): see DOCTRINE OF THE MEAN.

Mecca (Makka). The birthplace of the Prophet *Muḥammad. Muḥammad's initial preaching made little impression, and indeed evoked increasing opposition, esp. from the ruling clan, the Quraish. He therefore made the *hijra to *Madīna, only recapturing Mecca near the end of his life. He immediately established the *ḥajj practices, thus ensuring the centrality of Mecca to Muslim life, even when the centres of political power under different *dynasties of caliphs (*khalīfa) moved far away. The *mosque at Mecca is al-*Masjid al-Ḥarām; and the two towns, Mecca and Madīna, are known as *al-Haramain* (Arab. dual, 'the two holy places'). Muslims turn toward Mecca in prayer (*ṣalāt, *qibla), and make the obligatory pilgrimage (ḥajj) to it.

Mechtild of Magdeburg (Beguine nun): see RHENO-FLEMISH SPIRITUALITY.

Meddlesome Friar: see SAVONAROLA, GIROLAMO.

Medellín: see LIBERATION THEOLOGY.

Medical Prescription Cave: see LONGMEN/DRAGON GATE CAVES.

Medicine: see HEALING.

Medicine Buddha: see BHAIṢAJYAGURU.

Medīna: see MADĪNA, AL-.

Meditation. A form of mental prayer. In Christianity, the term has been used since 16th cent., in distinction from *contemplation, as a discursive activity, which involves thinking about passages from scripture and mysteries of the faith with a view to deeper understanding and a loving response. Many methods of meditation were taught, especially by the *Jesuits. Outside this historical context, the term meditation is used more widely, embracing contemplation; and in this wider sense, is applied to practices of many different kinds in virtually all religions: see Index, Meditation.

Judaism The Heb. terms *hitbonenut*, *kavvanah, and *devekut all refer to concentration on the spiritual world; they were much used by the *kabbalists. The *merkabah mystics strove for a contemplative vision of the merkabah, and the later kabbalists attempted to commune with the world of the *sefirot (emanations from God). The meditative practices of the *ḥasidim were influenced by the kabbalists of Safed, whose doctrines were largely handed down orally.

Hinduism See DHYĀNA.

Buddhism Meditation in Buddhism is the process of training, developing, and purifying the mind, which is likened to an animal (especially an elephant or an ox) which is dangerously destructive when wild, but supremely useful when tamed. It is the third element in the triple training (Skt., *triśikṣā*) along with conduct or ethics (Skt., *śīla) and knowledge or wisdom (Skt., *prajñā), and as such is essential to Buddhist practice. General terms for it include *dhyāna/*jhāna (Skt., Pāli, 'thinking'), concentration (Skt., *samādhi), and mindfulness (Skt., *smṛti). There are two aspects, calming the mind (Skt., *śamatha) and using the calm mind to see reality clearly (*vipassanā). These are distinguishable but not distinct.

Medujigore: see PILGRIMAGE.

Meera (Hindu devotional poetess): see MĪRĀBĀĪ.

Megasthenes. Greek ambassador at the court of Chandragupta Maurya at *Pāṭaliputra, *c.*302 BCE. His account of his travels throughout N. India, *Indica*, is an important historical resource on *Mauryan India.

Megillah (Heb., 'scroll'). Each of the 'five scrolls' in the Hebrew Bible. The books of *Ruth, Song of Songs, *Lamentations, *Ecclesiastes, and *Esther are all referred to as 'megillot' (pl.), but later, Megillah came to refer to Esther alone. The term also refers to the tenth tractate in the Order *Mo'ed* in the *Mishnah.

Megillat Ta'anit (Heb., 'Scroll of Fasting'). An Aramaic 1st/2nd cent. CE work listing days prohibited for fasting for the Jews. The list contains thirty-six days on which victories or happy events occurred.

Meher Baba ('compassionate father', 1894–1969). An Indian spiritual master and founder of the Meher Baba movement. Baba claimed to be the final *avatāra or manifestation of God, who unfolded his truth in the form of three fundamental precepts—good thoughts, good words, good deeds—through *Zoroaster, *Rāma, *Kṛṣṇa, *Buddha, *Jesus, and *Muḥammad, all of whom were avatāras of a previous age. Baba declared, and his disciples or 'Baba lovers' believe, that his love sustains the universe. In 1924, he established a community at Meherabad, near Ahmednegar, with shelter and health care for the poor. In 1925, he announced that he was entering 'the Silence'; by 1954, all communication had been reduced to gestures.

The Baba's tomb at Meherabad is now a centre of pilgrimage. While it has attracted several thousand people in the West since the 1950s, the overwhelming majority of 'Baba lovers' are still to be found in India.

Mehizah (Heb., 'partition'). Partition screen between men's and women's seating in Jewish *synagogues. In synagogues, either women sit in a separate gallery which is screened off, or a partition is placed between the front seats and the back seats. The *Progressive movement has abolished the mehizah.

Meiji. Throne-name of the Japanese emperor under whom imperial rule was restored in 1868, after the overthrow of the Tokugawa shogunate; hence the name of the era, 1868–1912 (when Meiji died). The era is characterized by the slogan, 'Enrich the nation and strengthen its arms'. The leaders pursued a policy of ambitious innovation combined with vigorous adherence to the traditions and values of the past. Among the military leaders of the overthrow of the Tokugawa shogunate was Saigō Takamori (1827–77), who advocated aggressive policies (especially against Korea), and who revived the *samurai ideals—in ways that led eventually to the *kamikaze (winds of the *kami) pilots of the Second World War, who, like Saigō, were prepared to die without hesitation.

Meir, Rabbi (2nd cent. CE). Jewish *tanna. R. Meir was a student of *Akiva, *Ishmael, and *Elisha b. Abuyah. After the renewal of the *Sanhedrin, Meir was appointed *ḥakham, but, as a result of a conflict with the *nasi, *Simeon b. Gamaliel, it was decreed that all Meir's later statements quoted in the *Mishnah should be introduced anonymously. None the less, Meir made considerable contributions to the halakhah.

Meir ben Baruch of Rothenburg (Maharam) (*c*.1215–93). Jewish scholar and community leader. Meir was born into a prominent scholarly family. As a young man, he witnessed a public burning of the *Talmud in France which prompted him to write a poem of mourning that is included in the *Ashkenazi *liturgy for 9 *Av. Reputed as the greatest scholar of his generation, he acted as supreme arbiter in community disputes in Germany. His *responsa were sent throughout W. Europe, and about a thousand still survive. As well as his responsa, he wrote *tosafot to eighteen tractates of the Talmud, commentaries on two orders of the *Mishnah, and compendia of laws for special purposes.

Meister Eckhart: see ECKHART, MEISTER.

Mekhilta of R. Ishmael (*mekhilta*, Aram., 'a measure'). Jewish *halakhic *midrash on *Exodus, with the final redaction taking place in *Israel at the end of the 4th cent. CE.

Mekhilta of R. Simeon ben Yohai. Jewish *halakhic *midrash on *Exodus. Like that of R. *Ishmael, the *Mekhilta of R. *Simeon ben Yohai* interprets much of the Book of Exodus verse by verse. It probably dates from the beginning of the 5th cent. CE.

Melā (Hindī). 'Fair', particularly one held in India to celebrate a local Hindu *festival or, among Sikhs, a *Gurpurb.

Melanchthon, Philipp (1497–1560). German Reformer. After studying at Heidelberg, Tübingen, and Wittenberg, he was appointed Wittenberg's Professor of Greek at the age of 21, becoming *Luther's keen follower and closest friend. In 1519 he participated in the Leipzig Disputation and also defended in his Wittenberg BD thesis the conviction that the *Bible alone is authoritative, not papal decrees or conciliar decisions (see COUNCILS). During Luther's 1521 confinement in the Wartburg he led the *Reformation movement and in the same year published his *Loci Communes*, the first systematic exposition of Reformed doctrine and its repudiation of *scholasticism. Occasionally too hesitant for Luther, he was a man of conciliatory spirit whose skill as a negotiator and influential writings were an outstanding contribution to the Reformation.

Melchites: see MELKITES.

Melchizedek (Heb., 'my king is Zedek/righteous'). Biblical king of Salem. According to Genesis 14. 18–20, Melchizedek welcomed the *patriarch *Abraham after he defeated the four kings, and he is described as 'a priest of God Most High'. In Psalm 110. 4, it is written, 'the Lord has sworn and will not repent, you are priest for ever after the manner of Melchizedek'. It seems likely, therefore, that David adopted a sacral *kingship when he captured *Jerusalem, and that these passages reflect a positive assessment of this move against those who protested against it as innovation.

Melek Taus (name for Satan amongst Yezīdīs): see YEZĪDĪS.

Melito, St (d. *c*.190). Christian *father. He was bishop of Sardis in Asia Minor. The most important of his few surviving works is a sermon 'On the *Pasch' in rhythmic prose, which expounds the Passover as a *type of the work of Christ.

Melkites or **Melchites** ('Emperor's men', from Syriac *malkaya*, 'imperial'). Christians of Syria and Egypt who accepted the Council of *Chalcedon and remained in communion with *Constantinople. After the rise of Islam their liturgical language became Arabic. Today the term embraces all Arabic-speaking Christians of the Byzantine *rite, whether *Orthodox or *Uniat, in the patriarchates of Antioch, Jerusalem, and Alexandria. The Orthodox number about 750,000, while the Uniats (for whom there has been a separate hierarchy since 1684) number *c*.400,000.

Melville, Andrew (1545–1622). Scottish Reformer and theologian, concerned especially with educational reform. Entrusted in 1575 with the responsibility of compiling the *Second Book of Discipline*, he vigorously opposed *episcopacy and so incurred the displeasure of James VI of Scotland (I of England). Imprisoned in the Tower of London for four years, he was released in 1611 to become professor of biblical theology at the University of Sedan.

Memento mori (Christian remembrance of death): see FOUR LAST THINGS.

Memra (Aram., 'word'). The Word of God by which the universe was created. The term 'memra' occurs in the *Targum literature with similar connotations to the Gk. term *logos*, understood by *Philo to mean the mind of God as revealed in creation.

Menander: see MILINDAPAÑHA.

Mencius (Chin., *Meng Tzu/Mengzi*; *c*.391–*c*.308 BCE). Early *Confucian thinker. Mencius' ideas appear in a book bearing his name that contains sections, often unconnected, which range from brief aphorisms to long dialogues. Perhaps written by Mencius and his disciples, it was edited, with parts discarded, in the 2nd cent. The book became extraordinarily influential: *Chu Hsi (1130–1200) declared it one of the *Four Books, and the Mongol court in 1315 included it in the civil-service exams; from that time forward its impact continued to grow.

*Neo-Confucians read Mencius in terms of their own pursuit of the 'enlightenment' that occurs through contact with a moral and omniscient mind. But Mencius's own concern is to show Confucianism's superiority to (especially) two positions: one, the proto-utilitarianism of *Mohism, aiming to replace traditional norms with rational judgements about what will benefit most people; the other, exemplified by *Yang Chu, counselling people to reject social responsibility and pursue individual satisfaction. Against these ideas, Mencius argues that Heaven (*T'ien) produces in human beings four potentials that define human nature, making it good, giving birth to four central virtues when actualized: benevolence (*jen), propriety (*li), practical wisdom (*chih*), and *i, 'duty' or 'proper behaviour'. The cultivation of these potentials is a person's most significant task. After his death, he was dubbed the Second Sage, and his spirit tablet (*ancestral cult) was placed next to that of Confucius in the Confucian temples.

Mendelssohn, Moses (RaMbeMaN) (1729–86). Jewish Enlightenment philosopher. His original interest was in the development and spread of German culture—the Christian writer, G. E. *Lessing, was a close personal friend; but after 1769, when he became involved in a dispute on the Jewish religion, he confined his writing to Jewish matters. His early philosophical works dealt with aesthetics and human psychology. In 1763, his *Abhandlung ueber die Evidenz in Metaphysischen Wissenschaften*, on the philosophy of religion, won the first prize of the Prussian Royal Academy of Science, but as a Jew, he was rejected for membership of the Academy. He became involved in a religious dispute with the Swiss clergyman, Johann Lavater. His response to Lavater's attack was published as *Schreiben an den Herrn Diaconus Lavater zu Zuerich* (1770). This prompted widespread debate and caused Mendelssohn to concentrate his activities on improving the civic status of the Jews and on devising a philosophical justification for his belief in Judaism. His *Jerusalem: Oder, verber religioese Macht und Judenthum* (1783) summarized his thoughts. In that spirit, he prepared Jews to live in the midst of German life, translating the *Pentateuch into German (transliterated into Hebrew letters) and adding to it a rationalizing Hebrew commentary. He is regarded as the forerunner of *Reform Judaism.

Mendicant friars (literally, 'begging' brothers). *Religious orders which renounced the right to own income-producing properties. The term is now largely meaningless, since most if not all of the originally mendicant orders have been given the right to own capital.

Meng Tzu: see MENCIUS.

Mengzi: see MENCIUS.

Mennonites. Christian denomination. It derives from followers of the 16th-cent. *radical Reformer Menno Simons (1496–1561), a Dutch *Roman Catholic priest who joined the *Anabaptists in 1536. Simons's leadership was an inspiration to them. His teaching about believers' *baptism, Church discipline, pacificism, and the non-participation of Christians in the magistracy gained wide support in many congregations, amongst whom he exercised an itinerant leadership ministry for twenty-five years. Today there are about 700,000 Mennonites in various parts of the world, mostly in America where their ranks have been occasionally fragmented by division.

Menorah (Heb., 'candelabrum'). Jewish seven-branch candlestick, which from early times became a symbol of Jewish identity. According to the Hebrew scriptures, the menorah was an important furnishing of the *tabernacle in the wilderness and of the *Temple in *Jerusalem. In 1948 it became the official symbol of the State of *Israel. See also MAGEN DAVID.

Menpeki or **Mempeki** (Jap., 'facing the wall'). Zen description of the nine years which *Bodhidharma spent 'facing the wall', i.e. in profound meditation at Shao-lin. It became a virtual synonym for *zazen.

Men-shen (Chin., 'gods of the doorway'). Deities in Chinese folk religion who protect the doorways of public or private buildings. They appear to have been promoted *euhemeristically from two generals of the T'ang dynasty, Ch'in Shu-pao and Hu Ching-te. Their fearsome figures are painted on doorposts.

Menstruation. The periodic loss of blood from the womb: as such, it has evoked in all religions responses of caution, since blood, connected as it is with life and death, is regarded as potentially threatening, and therefore polluting.

Even in a religion, Christianity, which is supposed to have transcended the detail of the law, the tenacity of this fear has persisted, especially in those parts of the Church dominated by male celibates (e.g. the *Roman Catholic refusal until very recently, 1992, to allow girl servers into the sanctuary). The dissonance now set up, in law- or custom-based religions, between modern knowledge and religious requirement is an increasing point of stress.

Me'or ha-Golah: see GERSHOM BEN JUDAH.

Mercersburg theology. Movement in American theology in the 19th cent. Its principal figures were John W. Nevin (1803–86) and Philip Schaff (1819–93), colleagues at the German Reformed seminary in Mercersburg, Pennsylvania, from 1844 to 1851. Opposing what Nevin called 'Puritanic' in American Protestantism, the movement decried *revivalism, accorded Christian *tradition an importance complementary to that of *scripture, affirmed the *Church as an article of faith, asserted a *Calvinist sacramental view of the *eucharist, and championed *liturgical worship.

Merit. In Christian thought, the recognition by God that certain works are worthy of reward. In Catholic teaching—deriving ultimately from statements about reward in the New Testament (e.g. Matthew 5. 46; Romans 2. 6; 1 Corinthians 3. 8)—merit has a central place, although it is emphasized that merit *de condigno* ('of worthiness') must be acquired in a state of *grace and with the assistance of actual grace. Protestant theology denies or limits merit as efficacious in salvation: created beings can never establish any claim upon God or earn any reward from him; otherwise salvation is a matter of works and not God's grace. Merit *de congruo* is merit based on equity.

In Buddhism, merit and its transfer form one of the most important parts of the dynamic of society. The acquiring of merit and its transfer to others is an important way in which monks and laypeople interact. For details, see DĀNA; PUṆYA (Pāli, puñña); KUŚALA (kusala).

Among Jains, there are seven types of activity which are conducive to progress in rebirth (*puṇyakṣetra*): donating an image, or a building to house an image, paying for the copying of holy texts, giving alms to monks, or to nuns, assisting laymen, or laywomen, in their religious activities or other needs.

Merits of the Fathers (Heb., *zekut aboth*). Jewish doctrine of benefits secured for children by the good deeds of their ancestors.

Merkabah mysticism (Heb., 'Chariot' mysticism). Jewish speculations on God's throne. Later Jewish mystics speculated on the prophet *Ezekiel's vision of God's chariot, and such study was recognized to have particular dangers to untutored minds. *Johanan ben Zakkai was a practitioner of merkabah mysticism, and early accounts of his experience (e.g. in a *Cairo Genizah fragment) so closely resemble the accounts of Saul/*Paul's *Damascus road experience (with the obvious exception of the perception of Jesus) that it seems virtually certain that Saul had been an adept also. See also HEKHALOT AND MERKABAH.

Merton, Thomas (1915–68). *Trappist monk and writer. Born in France, he went to school in England and university in the USA, where, after a confused adolescence, he became a *Roman Catholic and in 1941 joined the Trappists at Gethsemani Abbey in Kentucky. His autobiography, *The Seven Storey Mountain* (1946), portrayed a traditional conversion story to traditional Catholicism. But Merton's way, recorded in his immense literary output, echoed the changes in modern Catholicism, leading to a greater openness to other traditions, and a deep concern for the moral dilemmas of the contemporary world.

Meru, also **Sumeru.** Mythological golden mountain, axis or centre of the world, recognized in both Hinduism and Buddhism. In Hinduism, it appears in many myths in the *purāṇas, where it is placed in the *Himālayas. *Gaṅgā (Ganges) springs from it. In Buddhism, Meru is important in a diagrammatic visualization of the process toward (or away from) enlightenment.

Meshed: see MASHHAD.

Meshullaḥ (emissary): see SHALI'AḤ.

Mesrob, St (361–439). Armenian Christian *father. He succeeded Sahak as patriarch in 440 but died in less than six months. He invented the Armenian alphabet *c*.406. Thereafter, gathering around him a band of scholars, he directed a programme of theological translations into Armenian, starting with the Bible (*c*.410–44). This activity succeeded in starting a national literature, and helped free the Armenian Church from dependence on Greek and Syriac institutions.

Messalians. A Christian sect of the 4th–7th cents. Their name derives from Syriac *mṣallyane*, 'praying people'; they were also known by the cognate Gk. name *Euchites*. They lived ascetically and by begging, in order to give themselves entirely to prayer. The Messalians were attacked by *Orthodox writers including *Epiphanius, and were condemned finally at the Council of *Ephesus in 431.

Messiah (adaptation of Heb., *ha-mashiaḥ*, 'the anointed one', also transliterated *haMashiach*).

Judaism Anointed descendant of the Jewish king *David who will restore the Jewish kingdom. The idea of the messiah did not exist before the second *Temple period, but grew out of the biblical hope that the House of David would again rule over the Jewish people. As a result of the Roman occupation of *Erez Israel, various messiahs emerged, including Jesus (as interpreted after his death by his followers), Judas the Galilean (mentioned in *Josephus), and Simeon *Bar Kokhba (see MESSIANIC MOVEMENTS). The *rabbis taught that, with the coming of the messiah, the climax of human history would be achieved and God's *kingdom would be established on earth. From the 13th cent., messianic expectations were centred on *kabbalistic thought and culminated in the *Shabbatean movement (see MESSIANIC MOVEMENTS, MESSIANIC SPECULATION).

Christianity Although at an early date the followers of *Jesus were marked out as those who believed that Jesus was the promised messiah/*christ, Jesus appears to have resisted any attempt to interpret what he was doing and saying in his God-derived way through that category—to such an extent that it gave rise to the theory of the messianic secret—see SCHWEITZER, ALBERT. Some aspects of his life (e.g. the entry into Jerusalem) were clearly open to the interpretation that he was acting as the descendant of David, but it was only after his death and resurrection that the appropriateness of interpreting him as messiah was developed. The New Testament reveals a certain amount of scripture-searching to find ways in which Jesus fulfilled messianic prophecies in *Tanach (Jewish scripture), but it remains a Jewish objection to Jesus as Christ that few of the biblical signs of the messiah were fulfilled.

Islam In Islam, al-Masīḥ is a description (almost a name, except that the Arabic article is never dropped) for 'Īsā/*Jesus.

Messianic movements. Movements centred on the Jewish hope for the coming of the *messiah. Jesus of Nazareth was believed by his Christian followers to be the messiah. According to Josephus, at the end of the 1st cent. BCE, Judas the Galilean condemned the people for 'consenting to pay tribute to the Romans and tolerating mortal masters after having God for their Lord'. Slightly later, other claimants came forward, e.g. Theudas and a Jew from Egypt 'who gained for himself the reputation of a *prophet'. The revolt against Rome in 66 CE must be seen in the context of messianic aspiration, and in the uprising of 132 CE, the great Rabbi *Akiva recognized Simeon *Bar Kokhba as the king-messiah. Further claimants arose, both in Muslim lands (such as the 7th-cent. Abu Isa), and in Christian Europe (e.g. the *Karaite Kohen Solomon in the 12th cent.). The 12th cent. in particular saw many messianic movements, possibly induced by Crusader violence. One claimant, Moses Al-Dari, was even admired by *Maimonides, and David Alroy persuaded the sophisticated Jews of Baghdad of his authenticity. Abraham b. Samuel *Abulafia saw himself as the forerunner of the messiah in the 13th cent. and Hasdai *Crescas believed that the messiah had been born in Castile. Messianic expectations continued to be aroused in the late Middle Ages until the time of the great *kabbalistic claimant, *Shabbetai Zevi, in the 17th cent. See also MESSIAH; Index, Messianic speculation.

Messianic secret: see MESSIAH (CHRISTIANITY); SCHWEITZER, ALBERT.

Metaphysical movements. Groups that share a common definition of metaphysics as a practical religious philosophy and that seek to relate spiritual and psychic phenomena to everyday life. Among the groups classified as metaphysical are the older ones—*Spiritualism, *Theosophy, and *Anthroposophy—and a number of newer ones such as the Spiritual Frontiers Fellowship. They tend to blend an occult with a metaphysical stream of thought.

Metaphysical(s) Poets. Term applied by Samuel Johnson to a group of 17th-cent. Christian poets (especially J. *Donne, G. *Herbert, T. *Traherne, H. *Vaughan). He intended it as a term of dismissal, but they have come to be recognized as, collectively, one of the finest expressions of Christian poetry.

Metaphysics. The study of the most fundamental constituents of reality. The term was given by a later editor to a series of treatises by *Aristotle, because the topics covered came after (*meta*) the philosophy of nature (*physics*). In those treatises Aristotle dealt with topics which do not belong to any particular science, both the analysis of fundamental concepts like 'substance', 'cause', 'form', and 'matter', and theological questions, especially that of the 'Unmoved Mover'.

The Logical Positivists dismissed metaphysical claims as meaningless, because unverifiable (A. J. Ayer, *Language, Truth and Logic*, 1936). More recently, P. F. Strawson has distinguished between 'descriptive' metaphysics, which is content to describe the actual structure of our thought about the world, and 'revisionary' metaphysics, which aims to produce a better structure (*Individuals*, 1959). The former at least remains a lively and respected branch of philosophy today.

Metatron. *Angel mentioned in Jewish *apocalyptic literature. The *kabbalists noted that his name could be spelt (in Hebrew) either with seven letters or with six. They identified the seven-letter Metatron with the supreme emanation from the *Shekhinah, while the six-letter Metatron was *Enoch.

Metempsychosis. The passing of some quintessential part or consequence of a person (e.g. soul or spirit) from one body to another through the process of death. It is frequently known as 'rebirth', especially in Indian religions, but in Buddhism there is no 'self' being reborn, only the process of caused and causal change.

Methodism. A Christian denomination, itself made up of several parts, deriving from the preaching and ministry of John and Charles *Wesley, and initially of George *Whitefield. The term 'methodist' was in origin used derisively by opponents of the Holy Club at Oxford, but Wesley used it from 1729 to mean the methodical pursuit of biblical holiness. The rapid success of Methodism, reaching places and people that the established Church did not, soon set up a tension, since the class system seemed to be setting up a 'parish' within a parish, especially when those converted wanted no connection with the parish church. In any case, Wesley was compelled by the shortage of ordained preachers in America (after the war of Independence) to ordain his fellow presbyter, Thomas Coke (1747–1814), as Superintendent over 'the brethren in America', who became the Methodist Episcopal Church; the title of Superintendent became that of Bishop in 1787. Many divisions occurred in the 19th cent.: the Methodist Episcopal Church divided in 1844 over the issue of slavery; before that, two black Churches had been established, the *African Methodist Episcopal (1816) and the African Methodist Episcopal Zion (1820), which now number over 4 million. Among many groups in Britain, the Wesleyan, Primitive, and United Methodists came together in the Methodist Church of Great Britain and Ireland, in 1932. In the USA, a similar process brought into being the United Methodist Church in 1968. The World Methodist Council was set up in 1951, not only to draw Methodists together, but to seek transconfessional actions and unions. Methodists number about 60 million in 100 countries.

Methodius: see CYRIL AND METHODIUS.

Metrical psalms: see PSALMS, LITURGICAL USE OF.

Metropolitan. Christian *bishop of a province, who presides over all the other bishops in the province.

Metta (Pāli). Buddhist virtue of generous kindness and goodwill. It is one of the four *brahma-vihāras.

Metta(-sutta): see MAITRI.

Metteyya (future Buddha): see MAITREYA.

Metz, J. B.: see POLITICAL THEOLOGY.

Mevlevis (Sūfī order): see DERWĪSH; MAWLAWĪY(Y)A.

Mezuzah (Heb., 'doorpost'). Parchment scroll attached to the doorposts in Jewish houses. According to Deuteronomy 6. 9, Jews are commanded to write the words of God upon the doorposts of their houses. This commandment is fulfilled by fixing a small container, with the words of Deuteronomy 6. 4–9 and 11. 13–21 written on parchment inside, to the right-hand doorpost of every room or gate in the house.

Mīān Mīr, Hazrat. *Sūfī who, according to one tradition, laid the foundation-stone of *Harimandir Sāhib, *Amritsar. The Muslim Mīān Mīr was a friend of the Sikhs' fifth Gurū, *Arjan Dev.

Micah. Sixth book in the collection of *Minor Prophets in the Hebrew Bible and the Christian Old Testament. The prophet was a native of the Southern Kingdom and is probably referring to the political events occurring in the reign of King Hezekiah.

Michael. Archangel mentioned in the Hebrew scriptures. With *Gabriel, he is the only *angel mentioned by name in the Bible (Daniel 10. 13).

Michi (spiritual path): see DŌ.

Mida. Abbr. of *Amida.

Middle Way 1. (Skt., *madhyamā-pratipadā*; Pāli, *majjhimapātipadā*). General term for the way taught and practised by the *Buddha, which avoids extremes; the name also of the system derived from *Nāgārjuna known as *Mādhyamaka.

2. In the Latin form, **via media*, it is used to describe the *Anglican Church, which is both Catholic and Reformed; neither papalist nor dissenting.

Midnight Vigil. The practice of observing a special time of prayer during the night.

Midrash (Heb., 'interpretation'). Type of Jewish literature mainly concerned with the interpretation of *biblical texts. The *aggadic midrashim seek to derive a moral principle or theological concept from scriptures, while the *halakhic midrashim aim to explain the full meaning of a biblical law.

Miḥna (Arab., *maḥana*, 'prove, examine'). Examination in Islam of those whose religious orthodoxy is suspect. The miḥna is sometimes referred to as a Muslim *inquisition.

Miḥrāb (directional niche): see MOSQUE.

Mikagura (Shinto music): see MUSIC.

Miki Tokuharu (1871–1938). Founder of the Japanese religion Hito-no-michi, and indirectly of PL Kyōdan. He was a Zen Buddhist priest who joined a movement called Tokumitsukyō. This had been founded by Kanada Tokumitsukyō (1863–1924), who had identified the sun as the source of all appearance. He introduced a form of faith-healing called *ofurikae*, through which he would take on himself, like a *bodhisattva, the afflictions of all who came for help. When Kanada died in 1924, it looked as though the movement would disappear. But Miki Tokuharu followed the instructions of Kanada and planted a memorial tree at which he worshipped for five years, experiencing the presence of Kanada. As a result, he and his son, Tokuchika, re-established the movement with the name Hito-no-michi Kyōdan ('The Way of Man Society'), which was renamed again after the Second World War as P(erfect) L(ife) Kyōdan. The twenty-one precepts revealed by Kanada remained the basis of belief, but the central practice of life now became summarized in the words, *jinsei wa gejutsu de aru*, 'living life as art', or 'life is art', which means that any activity honestly undertaken can be converted into a work of art and beauty. PL Kyōdan not only sponsors art extensively, but also encourages a wide range of activities, from sports to medicine, all of which exemplify the human possibility of converting life into art.

Mikkyō (Jap., 'secret teaching'). Esoteric Buddhism (as opposed to *kengyō*, 'exoteric teaching', all other forms of Buddhist teaching), a Japanese term also for *Vajrayāna and *Tantric Buddhism. This form of Buddhism came to Japan in the 9th cent. CE, with *Saichō (founder of *Tendai) and *Kūkai (founder of *Shingon). Both established monasteries in *Kyōto, which became the main centres.

Miko, more fully **Kamiko.** Women in Shinto who are dedicated to the service of the *kami.

Mikoshi (Jap., *mi* (honorific) + *koshi* ('palanquin'), homophonously, *mi* ('sacred') + *koshi*). A large portable shrine used in festive processions in Japan.

Mikveh (Heb., 'a collection', i.e., of water). Jewish ritual bath. A mikveh is used for ritual cleansing after contact with the dead or after menstruation (see NIDDAH). It can also be used for immersing vessels and as part of the *initiation ceremony for *proselytes.

Milam (*rmi-lam*, 'dream'). One of the six teachings of Nāropa (*Nāro chos drug), also known as 'dream yoga'. By the cultivation of particular dreams, awareness grows that the waking state is equally a constructed dream.

Milan, Edict of. A declaration made in 313 by the emperors *Constantine and Licinius to tolerate all religions and give legal status to Christianity.

Milarepa (Mi-la Ras-pa) (1043–1123). Tibetan Buddhist who remains exemplary to many Tibetans, and who was instrumental in founding *Kagyü. He was recognized by *Marpa as his chief disciple. He entered on a mainly isolated life, often walled up in caves for months or years at a time. Nevertheless, disciples came to be near him from many parts, and the lineage of *yogins derived from him continues to the present, well-adapted to the persecutions inflicted by the Chinese on Tibetan religious practitioners. Two collections of songs are attributed to him.

Mile-fo. Chin. for *Maitreya, the future Buddha.

Milindapañha (Pāli, Milinda + *pañha*, 'question'). A Pāli Buddhist text (also in Chin. tr.) concerning a debate between a Buddhist monk, *Nāgasena, and a disputatious king, Milinda. Milinda is probably Menander, a Yavana king of Śākala (Siālkot, E. Puñjab) who ruled in the 2nd/1st cent. BCE.

During the dialogue the king puts eighty-two separate dilemmas to Nāgasena which are successfully countered. At the conclusion of the contest, Milinda becomes a Buddhist lay disciple.

Millennialism or **Millenarianism.** In the narrowest sense, the belief in a future millennium, or thousand-year reign of *Christ. The main source of the belief is Revelation 20. Its adherents are pre- or post-millennialists, according to whether they conceive Christ's second coming (*parousia) as coming before or after the millennium. Millenarian groups since the Reformation include *Anabaptists, Bohemian and *Moravian Brethren, early *Independents, 17th–18th cent. *Pietists, *Catholic Apostolic Church, *Plymouth Brethren, and *Adventists.

In a more general sense, millenarian movements are those which envisage a coming age (usually imminent) in which a faithful group will be particularly rewarded on this earth. Such movements are extremely common. Some are derived from Christianity (e.g. some elements of *T'ai-ping, *Adventists), but others have no such connection.

Millet (non-Muslims): see DHIMMA.

Mi-lo-fo: see LAUGHING BUDDHA.

Milton, John (1608–74). Poet and controversialist. Hostile to Archbishop W. Laud's *high churchmanship and the 'hireling shepherds', he supported the parliamentarians in the Civil War and served as Latin Secretary under the Commonwealth. Favouring the disestablishment of all Churches, he came to disagree with Cromwell's later ecclesiastical policy. Difficult relationships with his first wife probably occasioned his sympathetic approach to marriage problems in *The Doctrine and Discipline of Divorce* (1643). A prolific writer, he published works against *episcopacy and wrote vigorously in support of the freedom of the press (*Areopagitica*, 1644). He became totally blind in 1651. His monumental *Paradise Lost* (1667) undertakes to 'justify the ways of God to man' and to show the cause of evil and injustice in the world.

Mīmāṃsā: see PŪRVA-MĪMĀṂSĀ.

Mīmāṃsā-paribhāṣa (Clear Presentation of Mīmāṃsā). Exposition of Mīmāṃsā by Krishna Yajvan.

Mīmāṃsā-sūtra. Work attributed to *Jaimini, which forms the basis of *Pūrva-mīmāṃsā. The interpretations of Vedic rituals are summarized, and the sources of Vedic knowledge are assessed.

Mimi shehui (Jap.): see SECRET SOCIETIES.

Min (Heb., 'heretic'). Hebrew term for *heretic or sectarian. A min can be a Jewish heretic or a *gentile. It was Samuel ha-Katan in the late 1st cent. CE who composed the '*benediction' (i.e. imprecation) against the minim found in the *Amidah, and this seems originally to have been directed against the Judaeo-Christians: see BIRKAT HA-MINIM.

Mīṇā (Pañjābī, 'a bull with horns inclined down along its face', 'deceitful'). Name given by *Bhāī *Gurdās to followers of *Prithī Chand, *Soḍhī Miharbān, and the latter's son, Harijī. The Mīṇās, whose significance faded in the late 18th cent. CE, disputed the succession of Gurū *Arjan Dev.

Minaret (tower): see MOSQUE.

Minbar (pulpit): see MOSQUE.

Mindfulness of death. Buddhist meditative practice to reinforce the sense of impermanence (*anicca) in all things, including one's own brief appearance. It is usually combined with meditation on the transient nature of the body, and both are summarized in *Buddhaghosa's *Vissudhimagga* 8. 1–144.

Mind-only (Buddhist school): see VIJÑĀNAVĀDA.

Ming 1. (Chin., 'light-bearing'). Taoist enlightenment. According to Lao-tzu, it is attained by realization and acceptance of the return of all things to their proper root (*fu). It is to live according to *Tao, as rhythm and return.

2. The celestial mandate in Confucianism, the will of heaven (*t'ien). Subsequently it came to mean the constraints in the universe which set limits on human action because they are non-negotiable (e.g. what might be called 'natural laws').

Ming chi (sustenance): see FUNERAL RITES (CHINESE).

Ming-tao: see CH'ENG HAO.

Ming-ti (58–75 CE). Chinese emperor of the Han dynasty, who, according to legend, was instrumental, as a consequence of a dream, in establishing Buddhism in China.

Minhag (Heb., 'custom'). Customs which have become binding on various Jewish communities. Minhag is an important ingredient of *halakhah. Some have taken the force of commandment and have become part of the written law for the entire Jewish community, while others have only local force (e.g. 'the custom in *Jerusalem', *BBB* 93b).

Minḥah. Jewish afternoon *prayer service. The Minḥah can be recited up until sunset and, in modern times, the *Ma'ariv service is recited shortly afterwards.

Minim (pl.): see MIN.

Minjung theology: see LIBERATION THEOLOGY.

Minor Prophets (Aram., *terei asar*, 'twelve'). The collection of twelve shorter *prophetic books in the Hebrew scriptures. It includes the books of *Hosea, *Joel, *Amos, *Obadiah, *Jonah, *Micah, *Nahum, *Habbakuk, *Zephariah, *Haggai, *Zechariah, and *Malachi.

Minucius Felix. Christian *apologist of the 3rd (or perhaps 2nd) cent. He is known as the author of the *Octavius*, a Latin treatise refuting the common pagan charges against Christianity, arguing for monotheism and providence, and attacking mythology.

Minyan (Heb., 'number'). Quorum necessary for public Jewish services. According to the Talmud, if ten men pray together, the divine presence is with them (*B.Ber.* 6a). Occasionally a 'minyan man' is paid to make up the quorum, and in the *Reform movement, women as well as men are counted as part of the minyan.

Mi-p'nei ḥata'einu ('on account of our sins'): see HOLOCAUST.

Mīqāt (times of Muslim worship): see ṢALĀT.

Mīrābāī or **Meera.** Hindu saint-poetess (a Rajasthani princess) in the *bhakti tradition of perhaps 15th–16th cent. CE. It is difficult to construct any accurate biography from the many stories which relate, e.g., how she flouted all convention by refusing to accept her Rajput husband, acknowledging only Lord *Kṛṣṇa as her true bridegroom. After refusing to commit *satī on the early death of her husband, she was persecuted by his family and became a wandering mendicant singing *bhajans* (chants) to Kṛṣṇa until finally being absorbed into his image in the Kṛṣṇa temple in Dvārakā.

The grace, melody, and simplicity of her songs have been preserved in Hindī and Gujarati, and her songs are still popular in many parts of India.

Miracle. A striking event brought about (usually by God) for a religious purpose, against the usual course of nature; for example, the *resurrection or the instantaneous healings recorded in the Christian gospels. The modern mind (post-*Hume tends to ask of miracles, did they really happen; and, if so, what do they show? But religiously, miracle stories have also to be evaluated in the contexts in which they are told, in order to discern their meaning for those transmitting them: they are usually regarded as signs of God's power, or as vouching for the authority of a revelation, prophet, or holy person.

Among Jews, belief in miracles rests on the biblical descriptions of the interventions of God, beginning with creation itself. In the Hebrew Bible, such events as the Ten Plagues and the parting of the Red Sea are understood as interventions by God. The medieval Jewish philosophers found it difficult to accept the supernatural element in the biblical understanding of miracles, but this way of thinking has been condemned as *'Hellenism' by such thinkers as S. D. *Luzzatto.

In Islam the *Qur'ān speaks of the 'signs' of Allāh (*āyāt*, singular **āyā*) as proofs of the divine power: natural phenomena, and extraordinary events. The term used in Islam for 'miracle', though not occurring in the Qur'ān, is *mu'jiza* (that which could not normally be achieved; cf. **i'jāz*, from the same root). This is a sign given by Allāh to prove the authenticity and truthfulness of a *prophet, in particular *Muḥammad. Although the sole 'miracle' of Muḥammad is said to be the Qur'ān, yet in the *sīra, *ḥadīth, and legend many miracles are attributed to him, some of which are reminiscent of New Testament narratives.

In E. religions, miracles are extremely common—so much so that they almost cease to be objects of wonder (Lat., *miraculum*). They surround the births of teachers or holy people, and are particularly associated with *siddha and *iddhi powers. Such powers would be expected of a living manifestation of the divine (*avatāra), as, e.g., in the contemporary case of Satya *Sai Baba. The Sikh Gurūs condemned appeal to miracles, mainly because they saw them as exploitation of the credulous. Nevertheless, many miracles are told of the Gurūs themselves.

See Index, Miracles.

Miracle Plays: see THEATRE AND DRAMA.

Mi'rāj (Arab., 'ascend'). The ascension of *Muḥammad to heaven on a night journey, which becomes connected to the night journey to Jerusalem (see ISRA'), so that the ascension takes place, not from *Mecca (as perhaps in some early *ḥadīth), but from Jerusalem. Muḥammad travelled on *Burāq, and, accompanied by *angels, visited the seven *heavens, finding paradise in the seventh. Before the throne of *Allāh, he conversed with God about *ṣalāt. Despite some discussion about whether these events were in a dream, or in a spiritual experience (and *Sūfīs often take them as symbols of the soul's ascent to God), Muslims in general regard them as matters of fact.

Mirghadab (Shi'ite policing force): see BIHBAHĀNĪ, VAHID.

Mīrī and pīrī (Pañjābī, 'temporal' + 'spiritual'). Sikh affirmation that belief and commitment relates to all aspects of life: there can be no distinction between secular and religious, or between spiritual and political; all aspects of life must be governed by the teaching of the Gurū Granth Sāhib (*Ādi Granth).

Miroku. Jap. for *Maitreya.

Mīrzā Ghulām Aḥmad Qādiyānī (founder): see AḤMADĪY(Y)A.

Miserere (Nobis) (Lat., 'have mercy on us'). A prayer in common use in Christianity, derived from such *Psalms as 51. 1, and often used as a response (*Kyrie eleison).

Mishnah (Heb., 'teaching'). The Jewish *oral law, and in particular, the collection of oral law compiled by *Judah ha-Nasi. The Mishnah is divided into six *sedarim* (Heb., 'Orders') known as *Zeraim* (Seeds), *Mo'ed* (Festivals), *Nashim* (Women), *Nezikin* (Damages), *Kodashim* (Holy Things), and *Tohorot* (Purities): the *Talmuds are based on these sedarim. The final text contains many different styles as well as an enormous variety of opinion. See also TALMUD; ORAL LAW.

Mishneh Torah (Heb., 'repetition of *Torah'). A name for *Deuteronomy; but more usually, the collective name for the code of *Maimonides.

Mishpat ivri (Heb., 'Hebrew law'). That portion of the Jewish *halakhah which parallels the legal systems of secular nations. According to Article 46 of the Israeli constitution, in the event of a lacuna in the existing law, Jewish sources of law must be explored, and thus the heritage of the Jewish legal tradition is preserved in a modern, largely secular, state.

Misl (Arab., 'alike', 'file', 'record'). Late 18th-cent. band of Sikh fighters. Traditionally twelve misls emerged in the mid-18th-cent., following the confusion after *Bandā Siṅgh's death, to defend *Pañjāb from Afghan attacks.

Misogi (Jap., 'pouring water [over] the body'). An act of ritual purification. A form of *harae, misogi is technically (though now not restricted to) a ritual performed at a river or seashore for the purpose of cleansing pollution from the body, often as part of preparations for a larger religious ceremony.

Misrule, Lord of (medieval subversive): see HOLY FOOLS.

Missal. The book (in full *Missale Romanum*) containing introductory documents and everything to be said at the celebration of the *mass (Lat., *missa*), together with the major ceremonial directions.

Mission (Lat., *missio*, 'sending'). The sense of obligation in all religions to share their faith and practice with others, generally by persuasion, occasionally by coercion (see e.g. MARRANOS). The emphasis on mission varies from religion to religion. Thus in the case of Judaism, there was a strong practice of mission in the period of the second *Temple. But after the failure of the two Jewish revolts, Judaism reconceived its vocation, and understood it to be the development of a holy community which is preparing the way for the coming of the *messiah. Thus converts (who mainly come through marriage) are almost discouraged by being reminded of the burden of *Torah-observation which they will have to carry.

Christianity, in contrast, believes that the messiah has come, that he is *Jesus Christ, and that he has commanded his disciples to go out into all the world, proclaiming the good news (i.e. *gospel), and baptizing all who believe. The 19th cent. was one of immense missionary expansion, somewhat contradicted by its own multiple divisions, often conducted with extreme rivalry and animosity. To overcome this, the Edinburgh Conference was convened in 1910, which became the origin of the modern *ecumenical movement. Further Conferences (e.g., Jerusalem, 1928) were convened by the new International Missionary Council (IMC, 1921), which itself amalgamated with the World Council of Churches in 1961.

Islam is necessarily missionary (see DAʿWA) because it is derived from *Muḥammad's absolute and unequivocal realization that for God to be God, there cannot be other than what he is. Thus other religions are assessed in terms of their description of God and attitude to him: on the one hand, there are 'peoples of the Book' (*ahl al-Kitab), who have received their own *Qur'ān, even though they have not preserved it without corruption, and they are the closest to God; on the other, there are those who are far from God, above all those who continue in any form of idolatry. There is to be 'no compulsion in religion' (Qur'ān 2. 257/6), but there is to be zeal in defending the honour of God.

It is sometimes felt that Eastern religions are less inclined to mission than Christianity and Islam, but that is only partially true. The process of rebirth will eventually bring all to the opportunity of *mokṣa (release) without a necessity being imposed on Hindus to go out and accelerate the process. Nevertheless, in the 19th cent. societies were formed to propagate Hinduism (or rather, movements within the Hindu way); and in the 20th cent. some of the fastest growing *new religious movements have been Hindu-based, attracting many converts.

In the case of Buddhism, the same consideration of rebirth obtains, but there was originally a far greater emphasis on making disciples. Within a few centuries, through the work of such figures as *Bodhidharma and *Kumārajīva, Buddhism had spread through China to Korea, and thence eventually to Japan. There have been a few societies formed with the intention of winning others to the Buddha's way, but these have not been so influential as have individuals in the West. See further, Index, Missionaries.

Mitama-shiro (Shinto spirit symbol): see SHINTAI.

Mithra. God worshipped in four different religions: in Hinduism (as *Mitra); in Zoroastrianism (Mithra); in Manichaeism (Mithra), and in the Roman Mithraic mysteries (Mithras). Why this Zoroastrianized Indo-Iranian deity was the focus of a cult in the enemy empire of Rome remains something of a historical puzzle. The reconstruction of Mithraic belief and practice is difficult, because no specifically Mithraic texts have survived, only inscriptions and accounts by outsiders, notably *Porphyry. The main source of evidence is hundreds of excavated temples (Mithraea) and their statuary. The cult explicitly claimed to have been founded by *Zoroaster and became known as the Persian mysteries. There were seven grades of initiation. The main cult relief (tauroctony) depicted

Mithras slaying the bull, a scene thought to have soteriological significance, understood at least in part in astrological terms. The death of the bull appears to have been thought of as a unique inimitable act of the god himself, who is described in one inscription as having saved the initiates by the shedding of the eternal blood. Mithraism appears from the inscriptions to have been a very respectable cult, inculcating a disciplined, ascetic, and arduous life.

Mithuna (ritual sexual intercourse in Indian religions): see MAITHUNA.

Mithyā (Skt., 'false'). According to the philosophy of *Advaita Vedānta, the phenomenal world perceived by the senses, which is 'false' (*mithyā*). The world cannot be determined as either existent or non-existent. According to Advaita Vedānta, the illumined sage sees the world as the Absolute, *Brahman, undifferentiated consciousness, existence, and bliss. Yet the world, *qua* world, is perceived by the unillumined. Hence the phenomenal world is 'false', and its ontological status is indeterminable (*sadasadbhyām anirvacanīya*).

Mitnaggedim (Heb., 'opponents'). Designation of the Jewish opponents to *ḥasidism. *Elijah b. Solomon Zalman, the Vilna *Gaon, led the opposition to ḥasidism and created an alternative pattern of Judaism which rested on intellectual discipline, study, and *Orthodox practice. His followers, the mitnaggedim, opposed the Ḥasidim and the *Haskalah (Enlightenment).

Mito school. A school (of Tokugawa period, 17th–19th cent.), of neo-Confucian and neo-Shinto thought in Japan. Initially inspired by the writings of the Chinese neo-Confucianist *Chu Hsi (1130–1200 CE), the school produced an influential book called *The History of Great Japan* (*Dai nihon shi*) which stressed the divine origins of the nation and Japan's history as a sacred tradition.

Mitra. Hindu Vedic god, one of the *Ādityas, 'he who awakens people at daybreak and prompts them to work' (*Ṛg Veda* 3. 59. 1). Because *mitra* means 'friend', Mitra is usually associated with another god in partnership, especially *Varuṇa.

Mitre (Gk., *mitra*, 'turban'). The head-dress of a Christian bishop, worn on liturgical or ceremonial occasions.

Mi-tsung. 'School of Secrets', *Tantric school of Chinese Buddhism. It was brought to China from India in the 8th cent. CE, by three masters, including Śubhākarasimha who translated the **Mahāvairocana-sūtra*, which became the basic text. The teaching was transmitted orally, to protect it, and was taken to Japan by *Kukai, where it is known as *Shingon.

Mitūk. Korean for *Maitreya, the future Buddha.

Mitzvah (Heb., 'commandment'). Jewish commandment, ritual duty, or good deed. The *rabbis categorized the mitzvot (pl.) into *mitzvot de-oraita* ('the biblical commandments') and the *mitzvot de-rabbanan* ('the rabbinic commandments'). All male Jews are expected to keep the mitzvot from the age of 13, while females are exempted from time-bound affirmative commandments. There are 613 mitzvot in *Torah (*taryag mitzvot*), of which 365 are prohibitions (one for each day of a solar year), and 248 are positive (one for each limb of the human body). To these E. Fackenheim added a 614th: see HOLOCAUST.

Mitzvot (de-oraita/de-rabbanan): see MITZVAH.

Mixed marriage. In Judaism, a *marriage between a *Jew and a *gentile. Mixed marriage is forbidden under Jewish law. Therefore, in Jewish law, a mixed marriage has no legal validity. In the case of *divorce, no *get is required and the wife has no right of maintenance. However, the children of a Jewish woman are regarded as Jewish even if their father is a gentile. The children of Jewish men are not accepted as Jews unless their mother is Jewish (an exception has been made to this in the *Reform movement). Mixed marriage is seen as a very real threat to the Jewish people.

Mizrachi movement (from Heb., *merkaz ruhani*, 'spiritual centre'). A Jewish movement which emphasizes that *Zionism and the establishment of the State of Israel must be spiritual as well as political. The Mizrachi movement underlies the National Religious Party of Israel, i.e. Mafdal.

Mizraḥ (Heb., 'East'). Direction to be faced by Jews during prayer; also, ornament on *synagogue or house wall to mark the easterly direction. In *Orthodox households a mizraḥ is often placed to mark the east, and this is often a highly artistic object.

Mizugo (unborn child in Japan): see ABORTION.

Mkhan-po (senior Tibetan Buddhist): see ABBOT.

Mleccha (foreigner): see HERESY (E. RELIGIONS).

Mobed (Zoroastrian priest): see MAGI.

Mo-chao ch'an (Chinese Ch'an/Zen master): see HUNG-CHIH CHENG-CHÜEH.

Mo-chia (Chin.): see MOHISM.

Modalism. The more important kind of *monarchian doctrine in Christianity of the 2nd–3rd cents. Its most sophisticated form was *Sabellianism. See also PATRIPASSIANISM.

Modernism. The attempt, especially in the *Roman Catholic Church at the beginning of the 20th cent., to reformulate doctrine in the light of contemporary philosophical and scientific research. Exegetes, the most distinguished of whom was Alfred *Loisy, argued that the scriptures had to be treated simply as historical documents, and studied without reference to tradition or to the *magisterium of the Church. Modernism was condemned by the *Holy Office in the decree *Lamentabili* of July 1907, and by Pius X's *encyclical *Pascendi* the following Sept. The ensuing purge in the Church has been known as 'the anti-modernist terror', requiring as it did the anti-Modernist oath. Outside the RC Church modernism may be generally identified with theologically liberal Protestantism; and with the movement in *Anglicanism which issued in the Modern Churchmen's Union.

Mo'ed (Heb., 'season'). One of the orders of the Jewish *Mishnah. *Mo'ed* is composed of twelve tractates dealing with *Sabbaths, *Festivals, and *Fasts.

Moggallāna (Pāli, Maudgalyāyana). Second (after *Sāriputta) of the *Buddha's two leading disciples. Despite this, he died a violent death as a consequence of *karma from a previous life. He is represented iconographically as standing at the left hand of the Buddha.

Moggaliputta, Tissa (3rd cent. BCE). Leading Buddhist monk and scholar. He is said to have presided over the 3rd *Council in the reign of *Aśoka, when the final part of the Buddhist *canon, the *Abhidhamma, was closed. At the end of the Council, Moggaliputta composed the *Kathavatthu* (The Book of Controversies). The work is of importance in reviewing the Vibhajjavādin/Theravādin objections to other schools of early Buddhism.

Mog(h)ila, Peter/Petr (1596–1646). Russian Orthodox theologian and *metropolitan of Kiev. He became metropolitan (in 1633) at a time when many Ukrainians were attracted by Roman Catholicism. In some respects he seemed to concede ground to Roman Catholicism. But overall he defended Orthodoxy against both Catholicism and Protestantism. He wrote the *Orthodox Confession of the Catholic and Apostolic Eastern Church*, which was amended before it was endorsed in 1643 and at the Synod of Jerusalem in 1672. His own teaching he maintained in the *Little Catechism*.

Moha (Pāli, Skt.). 'Delusion', which prevents discernment of truth in Hinduism and Buddhism. In the latter, it is one of the three 'unwholesome roots' (*akuśalamūla*) which, together with craving (*lobha)—or attachment (*raga)—and hatred (*dosa) leads to rebirth and suffering in cyclic existence (*saṃsāra).

Mohel. The one who carries out the operation at the Jewish ceremony of *circumcision.

Mohinī. In Hinduism, *Viṣṇu's female form. He assumed this beautiful form in order to entice the *asuras and get from them their share of *amṛta (the nectar of immortality) after the *Churning of the Ocean. He also assumed this form in order to test *Śiva when Śiva was in his *ascetic mode.

Mo(h)ism. W. term for the teaching associated with *Mo Tzu. The Chinese equivalent is mo-chia.

Moji Zen (word-dependants): see KATTŌ.

Mo-kao/Mogao Caves (Buddhist shrines): see TUN-HUANG.

Mokṣa (Skt., from *muc* or *mokṣ*, 'release', 'liberation'). The fourth and ultimate *artha ('goal') of Hinduism, release from the round of death and rebirth (*saṃsāra). This is attained when one has overcome ignorance (*avidyā) and desires.

For Jains, mokṣa is emancipation from the impediment of karma, and this lies beyond enlightenment (which provides the means for rooting out the remaining traces of karma): see also KEVALA.

Mokṣa Dharma. A text which forms part of the **Mahābhārata*, dealing with philosophical issues.

Moku-funi (Jap., 'silent not two'). Zen belief that the realization of the one, undifferentiated buddha-nature (*bussho) in all appearances can only be expressed in silence. This is the 'thundering silence' of Vimalakīrti, a lay Buddhist praised by *Mañjuśrī in the *sūtra bearing Vimalakīrti's name.

Mokusa (part of Buddhist ordination): see MOXA.

Mokushō Zen (silent illumination Zen): see HUNG-CHIH CHENG-CHÜEH.

Molcho, Solomon (1500–32). Jewish *kabbalist and pseudo-*messiah. Of *Marrano stock, Molcho converted to Judaism. Fulfilling the Talmudic legend that the messiah would suffer, Molcho fasted in Rome dressed in rags. He secured the protection of the Pope, but was eventually burnt at the stake by the Emperor

Charles V for his refusal to convert to Christianity. Many of his followers did not believe he had really died, and messianic legends grew up round his name.

Molinos, Miguel de (Christian quietist): see QUIETISM.

Moloch Worship. Ancient Middle-Eastern cult. According to Jeremiah 7. 31, an altar was built to Moloch near Jerusalem even though passing sons and daughters through fire was forbidden specifically in the law of Moses (Deuteronomy 18. 10).

Monarchianism. A Christian understanding of God, of the 2nd–3rd cents. Concerned to uphold monotheism and the unity ('monarchy') of God, it was condemned as heretical for threatening the independence of the Son. The *modalist monarchians held that within the Godhead there was no difference of persons, only a succession of transitory modes of operation. Modern scholars also speak of those *adoptianists who held that Christ was a mere man, endued with God's power at his baptism, as 'dynamic' monarchians.

Monasticism

Christianity The Gk., *monachos*, underlying 'monk', points to someone being 'on their own'. It may originally have meant *'celibate' and only later 'solitary'; but monasticism came to refer to those who withdraw from society (in a celibate state) in order to devote themselves with greater intensity to God through prayer, austerity, and discipline. In its extreme form, it is *anchorite (living alone), but it may also be *coenobitic (living in community). Monasticism began to emerge in Egypt in the 3rd cent.; St *Antony is regarded as the 'father' of Christian monasticism, although *Pachomius had begun to organize communities before him. *The Sayings of the Fathers* (*Apothegmata Patrum*), brought together by *Evagrius of Pontus, did much to popularize the 'spirituality of the desert', affecting especially *Palladius and John *Cassian. Monasticism received its major impetus and order from St *Benedict. Monasticism subsequently divided into a myriad of different orders and styles, among which the Benedictines, *Dominicans, *Cistercians, and *Carthusians have been prominent. In the Eastern Church, the influence of *Basil the Great has been acknowledged as supreme, along with the desert fathers. Of particular importance is Mount *Athos, where monks from many different parts of *Orthodox Christianity live.

Islam Rahbānīya (monasticism, derived from *rāhib*, 'monk') is taken to be opposed in Qur'ān 57. 27. Muslim opposition to monasticism is strong, not least because it seems to denigrate (by vows of poverty and celibacy) the good things of God's creation.

Buddhism The monastic lifestyle arises quite naturally out of the general Indian tradition of the homeless wanderer as a private option on the periphery of society, and develops into an institution at the heart of the religion so much so that to take refuge in the *saṅgha (the Buddhist community, but also the community of monks) is one of the *Three Jewels. Śākyamuni Buddha is taken as the model monk. He is said to have composed the monastic regulations (Skt., Pāli: *Vināya) and ideally a monk can trace his ordination lineage back to the Buddha. Renunciation (see ASCETICISM) is moderate by Indian standards: clothing is worn, made originally from discarded material, yellowed (Skt., *kaśāya*, 'earth-coloured') with age, and pieced together. The modern habit in *Theravāda is three strips of yellow, brown, or orange cloth, normally cotton, wound around the body so as to cover it for reasons of modesty and protection against the weather. The upper toga-like robe (Pāli, *cīvara*) has a patchwork pattern which is a formalization of the primitive piecing together of rags. Monastic buildings were at first simple shelters for the retreat (Pāli, *vassa) conducted during the monsoon, and have developed into elaborate centres of culture. Generally, monasticism is more central to Buddhism than it is to Christianity, and there is often a lively spirit of co-operation between monks and laypeople, which is the social dynamic of many Buddhist communities.

Because of the general resemblances of community and at least partial separation from society, the term 'monk' is widely used in English with reference to Buddhism. In its purest form, 'monk' refers to one who has taken the full vows of a bhikkhu or *bhikṣu, and 'nun' to a bhikkhunī or bhikṣuṇī. But given the many other forms, it would be better to abandon the English term monk and use terms such as bhikkhu, *lama, *sensei, and *rōshi as appropriate.

See Index, Monasticism; Monks.

Mondō (Jap.; Chin., *wen-ta*). 'Question and answer', the exchange between teacher and pupil in Zen Buddhism, which evokes from a pupil, not so much an answer as an expression of the pupil's deepest disposition (*kokoro). Many mondōs were recorded later as *kōans. See also HOSSEN.

Monica, St (*c*.331–87). Mother of St *Augustine of Hippo. A cult of St Monica began in the Middle Ages. In 1430 her relics were transferred to Rome, to the church of S. Agostino. She is frequently patron saint of associations of Christian mothers. Feast day, 27 Aug.

Monism. The belief that only one substance exists, in contrast to pluralism. Monistic religions are therefore those which maintain that there is only one underlying substance (Lat., *substantia*, standing under) despite the multiplicity of appearances. *Advaita Vedanata is thus monistic, in contrast to *Dvaita.

Monji-hōshi (Jap., 'dharma master of scriptures'). Zen teacher who adheres to the literal sense of the Buddha's teaching in the *sūtras. As such, he is unlikely to develop wisdom or insight.

Monju (Japanese): see MAÑJUŚRĪ.

Monk: see MONASTICISM.

Monkey king, the (Chinese immortal): see HSIEN.

Monna (Jap., 'question word'). The question posed by a Zen student to his teacher in a *mondō (exchange).

Monomyth: see MYTH.

Mono no aware (sensitivity, a key Shinto virtue): see MOTOORI NORINAGA.

Monophysites. The party who maintained, against the definition of *Chalcedon (451) that in *Christ there was but one (Gk., *monos*) nature (*physis*). They flourished in Syria and Egypt under leaders like Severus of Antioch and were alternately conciliated and persecuted by the imperial government until the Arab invasions of the 7th cent. Their direct modern descendants are the *Oriental Orthodox churches.

According to Monophysite doctrine, the union of God the Word (*Logos) with the flesh at the *Incarnation was such that to speak of distinct divine and human natures thereafter is wrongly to separate what was united. In 1984 the Syrian Orthodox *patriarch (Mar Ignatius Zakka II) and the *pope (John Paul II) signed a declaration affirming agreement, and declaring that the apparent differences arose from cultural and linguistic inadequacies.

Monotheism (Gk., 'only' + 'God'). Belief that there is one God (and only one), in contrast to *henotheism or polytheism.

Monotheletes or **Monothelites.** Adherents of the doctrine that in Christ there were two natures but only one (Gk., *monos*) will (*thelēma*). The matter was settled by the second Council of *Constantinople (680) which condemned the Monothelete formulas and affirmed the existence of two wills in Christ.

Monsignor (abbr. Mgr., from Ital., *monsignore*, 'my lord'). In the *Roman Catholic Church, a title given to members of the 'papal household'. In most cases, however, the holder is a 'supernumerary' and the title is only honorary. All *archbishops and *bishops are entitled to it.

Monstrance (Lat., *monstrare*, 'to show'). A vessel used for containing and displaying the *sacrament at *exposition and *benediction.

Montanism. An early Christian *heresy. In the latter half of the 2nd cent., *Montanus, claiming the inspiration of the *Holy Spirit (or *Paraclete), prophesied that the Heavenly Jerusalem would soon descend near Pepuza in Phrygia. His followers were led by *prophets and prophetesses, through whom the Paraclete spoke, and embraced a severe *asceticism, marked by fasting, forbidding of second marriages, and an enthusiastic attitude to *martyrdom.

Montanus (2nd cent. CE). A self-proclaimed *prophet, who attracted followers to his message that the end of the world was imminent. Initially the movement had the support of *Tertullian, but it came to be vigorously opposed, until, at the Synod of Iconium, its baptisms were held to be invalid.

Montefiore, Claude (1858–1938). English leader of *Progressive Judaism. He founded in England a radical form of *Reform Judaism, known as Liberal Judaism, which was centred on the Liberal Jewish *Synagogue in London. He espoused the 'many paths, one goal' view of religions, and also the view that *Paul was the source of the Christian hatred of the Jew.

Montefiore, Sir Moses (1784–1885). Anglo-Jewish leader. Montefiore was sheriff of London in 1837–8 and was knighted by Queen Victoria. He received a baronetcy in 1846 for his humanitarian efforts for the Jewish community.

Months of Kallah (Jewish months for study of Torah): see KALLAH, MONTHS OF.

Moody, Dwight Lyman (1837–99). American *revivalist preacher. A tour of Britain in 1873 met an enthusiastic response, and Moody, along with his organist and song leader Ira D. *Sankey, became internationally famous. Moody's meetings were characterized by respectability and lack of hell-fire sensationalism. Moody was a *Congregationalist, but like other evangelists to follow, he worked mainly outside denominational boundaries.

Moon (emblem of Islam): see CRESCENT MOON.

Moon, Blessing of the. Jewish prayer recited at the time of the New Moon. In the *mishnaic period, the proclamation of a new month (Rosh Hodesh) was made by the *rabbinic court and it was celebrated with rejoicing.

Moon, Sun Myung (b. 1920). Founder of the Unification Church, whose members are popularly known as Moonies. He was born in N. Korea, and when he was 10, his family converted to Christianity. On Easter Day 1936, Moon experienced a vision of *Jesus Christ who commissioned him to particular work. For the next nine years, he prepared for this, communicating with other religious leaders, such as the *Buddha and *Moses. The revelations which he received form the basis of Unification theology. He founded his Church after the Second World War, and after much opposition and persecution from the Communists, he established the Holy Spirit Association for the Unification of World Christianity in 1954. *The Divine Principle* teaches that the *Fall was the result of Eve having a spiritual relationship with Lucifer before a sexual one with Adam, with the result that their children and descendants have been born with defective natures. By his own marriage in 1960, Moon has begun to effect a more complete redemption, transmitted through mass wedding ceremonies, as a consequence of which the children of participants are born without fallen natures.

Moral argument for God's existence. A type of theistic argument which became common in the 19th and early 20th cents. Typically, such arguments contend that the binding character of moral obligation can only be explained in terms of God's will.

Morality plays: see THEATRE AND DRAMA.

Moral Majority. Organization in the USA which aims to exert political pressure in favour of traditional 'moral' values (family life, free enterprise, strong national defence) and against such causes as homosexual rights and freer abortion. Moral Majority, Inc. was founded in 1979 by the Baptist pastor and television evangelist Jerry Falwell (b. 1933), and rose to prominence in the presidential election campaign of 1980. Although it is 'pluralistic' and 'not based on theological considerations', the organization's support comes mainly from conservative Protestant Christians.

Moral Re-Armament (i.e., MRA). Before 1938 the Oxford Group Movement, founded by Frank *Buchman. Its largest organizations are now in the USA, Britain, Japan, and Switzerland. Its message, at home among conservative evangelical Christians, is the need for a moral awakening to reconvert the world.

Moravian Brethren. The Church of the United Brethren, a Christian body which renewed the declining Bohemian Brethren, after refugees from the Thirty Years' War took refuge on the estates of Count Zinzendorf (1700–60), who presided over a great spiritual revival. As a 'unity of brethren' (*Unitas Fratrum*), they did not seek to become a separate church, but saw themselves as a leaven in existing churches. Nevertheless, survival dictated organization (it was recognized as a church, e.g. in Britain in 1749), and it was vigorously missionary throughout the world. It is strongly *evangelical, regarding the Bible as the sole rule of faith and conduct.

More, Henry: see CAMBRIDGE PLATONISTS.

More, Thomas, St (1478–1535). Chancellor of England and *martyr. Born in London, he went to Oxford University but was called home and sent to Lincoln's Inn in 1496, being called to the bar in 1501. He was a man of notable learning, and a friend of scholars such as *Fisher and *Erasmus. He wrote what is perhaps his best-known book, *Utopia*, in 1516. He strongly opposed the rise of *Protestantism in England, and Henry's divorce from Catherine of Aragon. He was Lord Chancellor from 1529, but resigned in 1532 over the king's opposition to the *papacy. Like Fisher he refused to take the oath attached to the Act of Succession, though ready to accept the succession itself, and was imprisoned in the Tower of London, where he wrote his best spiritual work, *Dialogue of Comfort against Tribulation*. He was put on trial in 1535 for opposing the Act of Supremacy, and was executed on 6 July. He was canonized in May 1935. Feast day, 22 June.

Moreh Nevukhim (philosophical work): see MAIMONIDES, MOSES.

Moriscos. Muslims who remained in Spain after the fall of Granada in 1492. Although many outwardly conformed to Christianity, under pressure of persecution, the majority maintained Muslim practice and belief in private. Most were expelled from Spain in 1619.

Mormons or **The Church of Jesus Christ of Latter-Day Saints.** Religious movement derived from Joseph Smith (1805–44) and the *Book of Mormon*. In 1822, the angel Moroni revealed to Smith where gold tablets were to be found, on which were written God's words. The texts tell of a post-resurrection appearance of Christ in America to establish religious order and truth. The authenticity of the text has been called in question because of its grammatical errors, its reminiscences of the *Authorized Version, its resemblance to an unpublished novel, etc., but for Mormons, its authenticity is not in doubt. Under persecution and opposition, the Mormons made several moves, until Joseph Smith was arrested in Carthage, Illinois, and was killed by a mob. Schisms resulted, partly over leadership, partly over doubts about polygamy. Plural marriage after the order of Abraham had been introduced by a special revelation in 1843. Most Mormons followed Brigham Young (1801–77), who led the movement to the Salt Lake area of Utah, where Zion in the Wilderness was constructed. Central to Mormon belief is the Restoration: the Churches have apostasized, but true Christianity has been restored by Joseph Smith.

Morning Prayer. The morning *office of the *Anglican Church. It was composed, for the Prayer Book of 1549, on the basis of medieval *mattins with supplements from *prime.

Moroni (Mormon angel): see MORMONS.

Mortal sin. According to Christian (mainly Catholic) teaching, a deliberate act of rejecting God as one's final end in favour of some lesser desire. It is held to involve both the loss of sanctifying *grace and eternal damnation. See also VENIAL SIN.

Mortification (Lat., *mortificare*, 'to kill'). The 'killing' or subduing, especially through *ascetic practices, of unruly or disordered appetites which militate against spiritual advance.

Moses (*c.*13th cent. BCE). Jewish leader and lawgiver. According to the Book of Exodus, Moses was born in Egypt to Amram and Jochabel, who hid him in the reeds of the river Nile to escape Pharaoh's order to slaughter all Jewish male babies. He was rescued by Pharaoh's daughter: 'From the water I drew him' (Exodus 2. 10), *meshitihu*, hence the name Mosheh (Eng. Moses). While keeping his father-in-law's sheep on Mount Horeb, he encountered God in a *burning bush. He was commanded to liberate the Hebrew slaves in Egypt and lead them to the *Promised Land. He guided them for forty years in the wilderness, and, on Mount *Sinai, he received God's revelation of *Torah, including the *Ten Commandments. Before his death, he appointed *Joshua as his successor. In the Jewish tradition, Moses has a unique status. In Christianity, he appears with *Jesus at his transfiguration (Mark 9. 2–8) and, according to the Qur'ān, where he is known as Mūsā, he prophesied the coming of Muḥammad (7. 140).

Moses, Assumption of. Jewish *apocryphal text. The *Assumption of *Moses* probably dates from the 1st cent. CE. It consists of a prophecy by Moses for his successor *Joshua, concerning the future of the Israelites and the last days.

Moses, blessing of. *Moses' blessing of the Israelite tribes as described in Deuteronomy 33.

Moses ben Joshua of Narbonne (1300–62). French Jewish philosopher. Among other works, his commentary on *Maimonides' *Guide to the Perplexed* was well known and was printed with the original text (ed. I. Euchel, 1791).

Moses ben Maimon (Jewish philosopher): see MAIMONIDES, MOSES.

Moses ben Shem Tov de León (*c.*1240–1305). Jewish *kabbalist. Moses Ben Shem Tov taught his version of the kabbalah in his *Midrash ha-Ne'elam* (Mystical *Midrash) which became the foundation of the **Zohar*. Following his death, a controversy broke out about the role of Moses de León in the composition of the *Zohar*. Since the *Zohar* was ascribed to R. Simeon b. Yoḥai of the 2nd cent. CE, the issue initially was whether Moses de León had been copying from the original manuscript which was now lost, or whether, as his widow maintained, he had composed the work. Modern scholars (e.g. G. Scholem) tend to the view that he composed the work making use of earlier material.

Moses of Narbonne (French Jewish philosopher): see MOSES BEN JOSHUA OF NARBONNE.

Mosheh (Hebrew form): see MOSES.

Mosque or **Masjid** (Arab., *masjid*, from *sajada*, 'he bowed down', Egypt. dial., *masgid* > Fr., *mosquée*). The Muslim place of assembly (*jum'a) for *ṣalāt. While a special place is not necessary for ṣalāt (*Muḥammad built the first masjid in *Madīna, not in Mecca), it is certainly desirable, and should be attended where possible. Masjids (masājid) are 'houses which God has allowed to be built, that his name may be spoken in them' (Qur'ān 24. 36). Masjids in general have a minaret from which the call to prayer (*ādhān) can be made by the *muezzin (*mu'adhdhīn*), a large hall or halls for the assembly, in which a niche (*miḥrāb*) is placed in a wall indicating the direction of *Mecca (the *qibla), and in which there is a pulpit (*minbar*). There may also be a platform (*dakka*) from which further calls to ṣalāt are made, and a stand (*kursī*) for the Qur'ān.

The masjid soon became associated with education (see MADRASA), and it also became the centre for administration and justice.

The Mosque of the Prophet (Masjīd al-Nabī) is a mosque in Madīna, the second most venerated in Islam (after Masjīd al-Ḥarām in Mecca). It contains the tomb of Muḥammad, as also of *Abū Bakr and *'Umar. The Mosque of the Two Qiblas (Masjīd al-Qiblatayn) is also in Madīna: it is the mosque where Muḥammad turned for the first time from facing Jerusalem for prayer, and faced Mecca instead.

Mosshōryō (Jap., 'unsayable'). The true nature of reality according to Zen Buddhism, which cannot be described or spoken of. Cf. *fukasetsu, *moku-funi.

Mosshōseki (Jap., 'leaving no trace'). The condition, according to Zen Buddhism, in which one who has experienced enlightenment should live. As a fish leaves no trace in water, nor a bird in the air, so the enlightened one should live naturally with no evidence of his enlightenment.

Mother Earth: see PṚTHIVI (Hindu).

Mothering Sunday. A derivative from Refreshment or Laetare Sunday, during *Lent: the first words of the opening prayer of the *mass are 'Laetare Jerusalem', 'Rejoice Jerusalem . . .', and honour is given to Mother Church. The extension to actual mothers was gradual, and much influenced Anna Jarvis who (*c.*1900) proposed a day (in May) of thanks to mothers. The two have now merged, and have become a single commercial exploitation.

Mo Ti (Chinese philosopher): see MO TZU.

Motoori Norinaga (1730–1801). Leading scholar of the New Learning (*Kokugaku) movement in the Shinto revival (*Fukko Shintō). Motoori was a pupil of *Kamo no Mabuchi, who had insisted that the Manyōshū poetry of the 8th cent. (and earlier) had been free of foreign influence and thus expressed the genuine Japanese spirit without adulteration. Motoori pushed this quest for the genuine Japanese spirit into other areas, especially in rescuing the **Kojiki* from relative neglect in comparison with the **Nihongi* (*Nihonshoki*). The adoration of the Sun (*Amaterasu) indicates that Japan gave birth to the Sun (Nippon means 'origin of sun'), from which it follows that Japan and its people are 'closer to God' than any other people. Motoori took other classic Japanese works and set them in the foundation of the true and pure spirit which should inform life—e.g. *Shinkokinshū* (The New Collection of Poetry Ancient and Modern, compiled *c.*1205) and Murasaki Shikibu's *Tale of Genji*. He took the latter to be portraying the sensitivity of a good life—what he called *mono no aware*, which becomes the key virtue in the Shinto revival.

Mott, John Raleigh (1865–1955). American *Methodist layman and *ecumenical pioneer. He was instrumental in convening the first International Missionary Conference at Edinburgh in 1910, devoting himself tirelessly to the *ecumenical movement through the International Missionary Council, 'Life and Work', and the World Council of Churches, of which he became co-president in 1948.

Motu Proprio (Lat., 'on his own initiative'). A papal ordinance emanating from the *pope himself (rather than the *curia) and bearing his signature. It deals with matters of discipline less important than in an 'apostolic constitution'.

Mo Tzu (honorific title, 'Teacher Mo', given to Mo Ti, *c.*470–*c.*380 BCE). Leading philosopher among the 'hundred philosophers' of early China. He was educated in the classic texts, and may for a time have followed *Confucius; but he strongly opposed Confucianism for its agnosticism about heaven (*t'ien) and spiritual beings, and its preoccupation with ritual. He advocated an attitude of love (*ai) to all beings, not just toward family or those from whom reciprocal favours can be expected. This love, which is central to Mo Tzu's teaching, means regarding all as equally deserving of it. Extravagant activities, and above all warfare, should be abandoned. All this is in accord with the will of T'ien, now personified as actively seeking the practice of love.

Mount Athos (centre of Orthodox monasticism): see ATHOS, MOUNT.

Mount Hiei. The site in Japan, north of Kyōto, where *Saichō established his first *Tendai (Chin., *T'ien-t'ai, hence the alternative name for Mount Hiei, Tairei) temple, Enryakuji. The early buildings were destroyed in 1572. The Hall of Study (Daikodo) and the Main Hall (Konpo-chudo) were rebuilt in the 17th cent.

Mount Sinai (mountain where Moses was given Torah): see SINAI, MOUNT.

Mourides or **Muridiyya** (Arab., *murīd*, 'aspirant' or 'disciple'). An innovative Muslim brotherhood in Senegal. It derives from Amadu Bamba (*c.*1850–1927), a saintly, scholarly *marabout within the *Sūfī and *Qadariy(y)a tradition, and Ibra Fall (1858–1930), an aristocratic Wolof. Together they founded new agricultural villages and a new holy city, Touba, which became the centre for the Magal, an annual pilgrimage which attracted half a million pilgrims by 1975. Deviations from orthodox Islam include rejection of the duty of holy war (*jihād) and of the Meccan pilgrimage (*ḥajj), reduction of almsgiving to tithes to the marabout, and giving more attention to the latter than to Islamic law, and to Amadu Bamba than to *Muḥammad.

Mourners of Zion (Jewish group): see AVELEI ZION.

Mourning rites. One among several kinds of rites performed by a community (or an individual) upon the death of one of its members. Mourning rites characteristically function initially to separate those related (in various ways) to the deceased from the rest of the living community. They also constitute a process of transition through which the mourners are finally reintegrated into their community. Mourning rites are thus a kind of *rite of passage undergone in almost all societies by those in some way connected to one who has died. They are to be distinguished from funeral rites, which concern the disposition of the remains of deceased. Through them, the living in many cultures express a mixture of affection for the deceased, fear of the corpse, and self-protection against the return of a malicious ghost or spirit.

During the biblical period, Jewish mourning customs included the rending of garments (Genesis 37. 34), wearing sackcloth (Psalm 30. 12), sitting on the ground (Jonah 3. 6), placing dust on the head (Jeremiah 6. 26), fasting (Ezekiel 10. 6), and abstaining from washing (2 Samuel 12. 20). In contemporary practice, the mourning period begins after the *funeral. The bereaved put on special clothes, stay at home for seven days (*shivah*), receive visitors sitting on a low stool, and only attend *synagogue on the *Sabbath. No work may be done and sexual relations are forbidden. Modified mourning continues for a year after the burial. A *yahrzeit lamp is kindled during the mourning period and *kaddish is said every day. Subsequently the lamp is lit and kaddish recited on the anniversary of the death. In Christianity, mourning adapts itself to the customs of the country or community, while bringing them under the control of belief in the efficacy of Christ's atoning death and of the resurrection. The former has made prayers for the dead controversial, when or if it implies that the prayers of the living can add to the benefits of the *atonement. However, some Christians (especially Catholics) maintain that after death those who have not wholly alienated themselves from God but who fall short of perfection enter *purgatory. Here they may be aided by the prayers of the faithful, so that mourning may include such prayers, including requiem masses. These are made annually on All Souls' Day.

In Islam, death belongs to the order and will of God, so that mourning should not be excessive. According to Jabir b. Atik, *Muḥammad allowed lamentation for the sick until the moment of death, but not after. Tears and weeping are believed traditionally to disturb the dead during 'the period in the grave'. Yet in fact *niyaha* ('lamentation') occurs throughout the Muslim world, an instance of local custom and human sentiment overcoming doctrinal correctness and religious injunction.

In Indian religions, the understanding of death is controlled by the understanding of rebirth (or of release). Thus mourning is made practical by rituals which sustain the dead, bring merit to them, and ward off evil. The extreme of these is *satī on the part of a Hindu widow, but short of that, there are obligations on the part of the living to the dead which convert mourning into action. In Japan, this is also the case, though set in the context of different beliefs about the status of *ancestors. On the seventh day after death, the dead soul may receive a posthumous name (*kaimyō), in a ceremony which draws a line on this world and gives the soul new identity in the next. See also DEATH; FUNERAL RITES.

Movement of the Wondrous Law of the Lotus Sūtra (Japanese Buddhist movement): see NIPPONZAN MYŌHŌJI.

Moxa (*mokusa*). Part of Buddhist ordination ceremony, especially in China. It involves burning marks on to the head of the monk or nun. This became a more general practice for developing reliance on the help of a *bodhisattva, in overcoming pain.

Mozarabic rite. The form of Christian liturgy (*rite) which was in use in Spain before the Islamic conquest of the 8th cent. It is the only non-Roman rite still in use in the *Roman Catholic Church, though it survives in regular use only in one chapel in the cathedral of Toledo.

Mṛtyu. Death, the Hindu personification of death. In the Vedic period, there was no belief in an immortal life beyond death. *Prajapati made his body 'undecaying' through sacrifice and by practising *tapas (austerities), and he then taught the remaining gods how to do the same (*Śatapatha Brāhmaṇa* 10. 4). Mṛtyu complained that he would have no food if this skill was passed on to humans, and he pointed out that heaven would become overcrowded. The gods decreed that only those humans who surrender to Mṛtyu voluntarily will attain immortality; the rest will remain 'the food of death'.

Mṛtyuñjaya-siddhi (Skt., 'death' + 'conquest' + 'power'). One of the Hindu powers (*iddhi) which lead to supernatural attainment, in this case, victory over death.

Ms, Five (ritual ingredients): see PAÑCA-MAKĀRA.

Mu (Jap.; Chin., *wu*). Zen emptiness of content, nothingness, closely related to *śūnyatā. From this arises the first *kōan of the *Wu-men-kuan* (*Mumonkan*), which introduces the Zen student to 'the world of mu': 'A monk asked master *Chao-chou respectfully: "Does a dog actually have a Buddha-nature or not?" He replied: "Mu" '. The opposite is *U.

Mu'addhīn (caller of Muslims to prayer): see MUEZZIN.

Mu'āwiyya(h) ibn Abi-Sufyān (d. 680 (AH 80)). Founder of the *Umayyad dynasty. He was a late convert to Islam, but was immediately appointed as 'personal secretary' by the Prophet *Muḥammad. Upon 'Uthmān's murder, he politically outmanœuvred 'Alī. After 'Alī's death in 661 (AH 61), Mu'āwiyya easily persuaded *Hasan, the Prophet's eldest grandson, with a grant of a large sum, to step down in his favour.

As khalīfa, Mu'āwiyya pursued a policy of pragmatism. In politics he insisted on rapprochement. His approach to dissidents was through persuasion and monetary gifts. It was Mu'āwiyya who changed the character of the Caliphate to one of hereditary monarchy (*mulk*).

On the question of succession Mu'āwiyya tried to secure a peaceful transfer of power to his son Yazīd. Upon his death, however, these plans backfired and led to the beginning of the Second Civil War in Islam.

Mu-chou Ch'en-tsun-su (Jap., Bokushū Chinsonshuku; *c*.780–877). Ch'an dharma-successor (*hassu) of *Huang-po Hsi-yün, whose abrupt methods he developed even further. Thus *Yun-men attained enlightenment when he went to Mu-chou, who followed his practice of listening to the footsteps of approaching students, and of admitting them only if their steps expressed a prepared state of mind. Mu-chou's teaching was short and abrupt, and he appears in example 10 of *Pi-yen-lu* (see KŌAN).

Mudalavan (name of god): see TAMILNADU.

Mudangs (female shamans): see KOREAN RELIGION.

Muditā (Skt., Pāli, 'empathy'). One of the Buddhist *brahma-vihāras, a state of joy over the rescue and liberation of others from *dukkha. It is aspired to as a practice, by entering into the joys of others, and refusing to take pleasure in their misfortunes. See also UPEKKHA.

Mudra (Skt., 'seal', 'sign'). In both Hinduism and Buddhism, a sign of power, through the body, especially the hands.

In Hinduism, the mudras of ritual worship (*pūjā) are an outward and visible sign of spiritual reality which they bring into being. Thus mudras frequently appear in Hindu sculpture (as they do in Jain and Buddhist), especially *dhyāna (meditation, hands linked in front of body with palms upward), abhaya, cf. *abhaya-vacana (fear-repelling, hand lifted, palm outward), and *varada* (hand held out, palm upward, bestowing bounty). The *añjali* mudra is the best-known to the outsider, since it is the 'palms together', at the level of the chest, greeting in India. As a mudra, it expresses the truth underlying all appearance.

In Buddhism (Chin., *yin-hsiang*; Jap., *in-zō*; Korean, *insang*), a mudra is a particular configuration of the hands accompanying a *mantra and associated with a *visualization or other mental act.

See Index, Mudra.

Muezzin (Arab., *mu'adhdhin*). The one who gives the *ādhān (call to prayer) to the Muslim community before the five daily times of *ṣalāt.

Muftī (Arab.). In Islamic law, one qualified to give a *fatwā, legal opinion on a disputed point of law. Such a person had to be a Muslim, of upright character, with appropriate knowledge and experience in legal matters. The office of muftī was elaborated in the *Ottoman Empire.

Mughal or **Mogul empire.** A Muslim dominion in India, lasting from 1526 to 1857. It was founded by Babur (d. 1530), and reached its height of power under *Akbar, Jehangir (1605–27), Shah Jehān, who built the Taj Mahal (1627–58), and *Auraṇgzéb. By the time of the Indian mutiny, it had diminished to a small area around Delhi.

Muhajirun (followers of Muḥammad in the hijra): see EMIGRANTS.

Muḥammad 'Abduh: see 'ABDUH, MUḤAMMAD.

Muḥammad Aḥmad b. 'Abd Allāh (*c*.1834–85 (AH 1258–1302)). *Al-Mahdī of the Sudan. After early religious experience, he believed himself called to cleanse the world from corruption and wanton behaviour. His first target was the Turkish Empire. He made his first public appearance as Mahdī in 1881, and resisted all attempts of the Sudanese and Egyptians to defeat him. The extension of his campaigns took him to Khartoum, where, in 1885, General Gordon was killed. He himself died not long after, and the incipient Mahdīya movement was ended by Kitchener in 1898 at the battle of Omdurman.

His Islam was austere in practice, and he substituted his own teaching for much of the accumulated tradition and commentary.

Muḥammad al-Mahdī (12th Imām): see AL-MAHDĪ.

Muhammadans, Mohammedans, Mahotmetans. Westernized terms for Muslims, both inaccurate and offensive, because they suggest that Muslims are followers of *Muḥammad, rather than worshippers of God; and also because *al-Muḥammadīya* ('Muhammadians') are members of sects regarded as heretical by mainstream Islam (though in Indonesia it is the name of an orthodox reforming movement, which has adapted Western institutions, e.g. Boy Scouts, to Muslim ends).

Muḥammad b. Ismāʿīl (Shīʿite Imam): see ISMĀʿĪLIYA.

Muḥammad ibn 'Abd Allah (570–632). The last of the *Prophets, from whose proclamation of *Qur'ān Islam derives. Muḥammad was born in *Mecca in the 'Year of the Elephant' (i.e. when an Abyssinian army attacked Mecca). At an early age, he had an experience of a visitation by two figures (later identified as angels) who 'opened his chest and stirred their hands inside'. It was the first of several unusual experiences which led Muḥammad increasingly to search for the truth of God and religion on his own. By now he was under the protection of his uncle, *Abu Tālib, and at the age of 25 he married *Khadījah; they had two sons who died and four daughters. Muḥammad was increasingly influenced by the *Ḥanīfs (pl., *ḥunafā'*), those who were seeking to preserve a monotheism which they traced back to *Abraham (Ibrāhīm); Arabia was an important refuge for Jews and unorthodox Christians when they came under persecution, and their beliefs are clearly reflected in the Qur'ān. Mecca was polytheistic, with revered idols, and Muḥammad recognized the contrast as extreme. He went with increasing frequency into isolation in a cave on Mount Hira in order to struggle with the truth of God lying behind the bewildering conflict of idols and religions. On one occasion, he had the strong sense of a presence (later identified with *Gabriel/Jibrīl) pressing on him and insisting three times, ''Iqra', read (or recite). He resisted, but then felt words being impelled through him, the first words of what became many revelations, collected eventually in the Qur'ān; the opening words of *sūra 96.

At first Muḥammad believed that he had gone insane and thought of killing himself. But Khadījah found him and told him to test the truth of what he was certain he had experienced. There followed some further revelations, but then a break which was equally testing. He began preaching, but encountered great hostility. From his initiating vision he saw with absolute clarity that if God is God, then there can only be what God is: there cannot be a God of the Christians, a God of the Jews, still less can there be the many deities of Mecca. It followed that the idolatry of Mecca was deeply wrong about God and must be abolished. In a sense, the whole of Islam is a footnote to this simple observation: there is only one God and all creation is derived from him. Therefore all humans should live in a corresponding unity (i.e. community, *'umma); and Islam is the quest for the realization of 'umma, under God. Not surprisingly this message was violently resisted by the Meccans. As the crisis and persecution grew worse, Muḥammad was invited to Yathrib to make his way of unity a practical reconciliation between the two contesting ruling families there. He made this move, the *Hijra, in 622 (to become later the first year of the Muslim *calendar) and began to establish the first community under the rule of God's revelations as they continued to be given.

At Yathrib, now to be known as al-*Madīna ('The City'), Muḥammad was joined by some seventy other emigrants, the Muhājirūn (see EMIGRANTS). The opposition from Mecca did not cease, partly because Muḥammad took to raiding their caravans. At the battle of *Badr, in 624, a small army of Muslims defeated a much larger army of Meccans; but in 625, the Meccans reversed this defeat at the battle of Uhud: both battles remain epitomes of faith and lack of trust. In 627, the Quraysh failed to win a siege with numbers overwhelmingly in their favour (the battle of the Trench), and subsequently Muḥammad took the fight to his enemies, capturing Mecca in 630 and purifying it from idols. Meanwhile he had been organizing not only life in Madina, but also the relations of the new community with surrounding tribes: some of these endeavours are gathered together in the so-called Constitution of Madīna, a kind of 'anthology' of early treaties with different surrounding tribes. When Muḥammad died in 632, there was no obvious successor, and from this uncertainty the division of Islam between *Sunni and *Shīʿa became an embittered fact within a generation of Muḥammad's death.

As the Seal of the Prophets, Muḥammad has brought the revelation of God which is the same as that mediated through previous prophets, but before Muḥammad, all communities had corrupted revelation for their own purposes. After Muḥammad, there can be no further prophet or revelation, because now the pure and uncorrupted revelation exists in the world. The first connected life of Muḥammad is that of Ibn Ishaq, edited by Ibn Hisham. See Index, Muḥammad's life.

Muḥammadīya, al- (Muslim sectarians): see MUHAMMADANS.

Muḥarram. First month of the Muslim calendar, the first ten days of which are observed by *Shī'a Muslims as a period of mourning for the death of *Al-Husain. For *Sunni Muslims, 10 Muḥarram is celebrated as a day of blessing.

Muḥāsibī (Shāfi'ite theologian): see AL-MUḤĀSIBĪ.

Mu-ichimotsu (Jap., 'not one thing'). A Zen extension of *mu, emphasizing that no phenomenon has any substantial, underlying, permanent foundation—as *śūnyatā also affirms.

Mu'jiza (Islamic): see MIRACLE.

Mujōdō-no-taigen (Jap., 'the embodiment of the unsurpassable way'). The embodiment of Zen enlightenment (*satori, *kensho) in the midst of everyday life.

Mujtāhid (judge of Islamic law): see IJTIHĀD; 'ULAMĀ.

Muju (Zen monk): see ICHIEN, DŌKYŌ.

Mukan Fumon (1212–91). Zen pupil of [Enni] *Ben'en, who was summoned by the emperor Kameyama to exorcise the ghosts who were disturbing his new palace in *Kyōto, the traditional priests having failed. Mukan and his monks sat in silent meditation and the spirits disappeared. The emperor converted the palace to a Zen monastery, Nanzen-ji, and Mukan became the first abbot.

Mukasa, Reuben (founder): see AFRICAN GREEK ORTHODOX CHURCH.

Mukhaliṅga. A *liṅga in Hinduism on which faces are depicted, the number depending on the purpose of the ritual; thus the two-faced liṅga is used in rituals for the destruction of enemies.

Mukta (Skt., *muc*, 'release', 'liberation'). In Hinduism, one who has attained *mokṣa or *mukti. One whose liberation from attachment and desire occurs during one's life is a *jivanmukta; one whose liberation occurs in the discarnate state after death is a videha-mukta. A jivanmukta, though released, remains in this world due to unripened karmic residues (*karmāśayas*), as a potter's wheel continues to turn once the potter's hand is removed.

Mukte (Hindī, Pañjābī, 'liberated ones'). 1. Those who have achieved salvation (cf. MUKTA).

2. Five Sikhs who received *initiation immediately after the *Pañj Pyāre.

3. Forty Sikhs who died fighting at Chamkaur.

4. See MUKTSAR.

Mukti (Skt., from *muc*, 'release', 'liberation'). In Vedic Skt., mukti meant release from the limitations of the body and mind, effected by ritual action. Later the term became identified with *mokṣa. This is the term used by Sikhs for liberation from successive rebirths.

Muktsar (Pañjābī, 'lake of *salvation'). Historic Sikh site in Ferozepur District, Pañjāb. Originally called Khidrāṇā, the place was renamed after forty Sikhs, who had earlier deserted Gurū *Gobind Siṅgh, but who returned to die fighting against the men of the local governor, Wazīr Khān. The Gurū forgave their perfidy, pronouncing them liberated ones (*mukte*). They are commemorated daily in *ardās and by an annual *melā on 1 Māgha (Jan.–Feb.).

Mukyokai (Japanese Non-Church movement): see UCHIMURA KANZŌ.

Mūla-Mādhyamaka-Kārikā (*The Root Verses on the Mādhyamaka*). The major work of *Nāgārjuna in which he laid the foundation for the development of Mādhyamaka philosophy. In the 445 short verses which comprise the treatise, Nāgārjuna examines twenty-seven topics and demonstrates that the concepts and categories with which the intellect normally operates are inadequate to grasp the true nature of phenomena and the manner in which they are related. The breakdown of reason at this point means that reality can only be described as inexpressible or 'void' (*śūnyatā).

Mula Saṅgha (The Root Assembly). The central organization of *Digambara Jain ascetics. Jains developed into innumerable sects and groups, maintaining lineage, but splitting like the delta of a river.

Mūla-sarvāstivāda. Name adopted by the Buddhist *Sarvāstivāda school some time in the 7th cent. CE, to distinguish it from three subschools which had detached themselves. The three subschools, of the Dharmagupta, Mahīśāsaka, and Kāśyapīya, became established in Central Asia.

Mūlavijñāna (Skt., *mūla*, 'root', + *vijñāna*, 'consciousness'). A doctrine characteristic of the *Mahāsāṃghika school of early Indian Buddhism. As a consequence of the centrality of the teachings on impermanence (*anicca), and not-self (*anātman), it was felt necessary in the developing Buddhist systems to account for mental continuity in individuals, particularly between one existence and another, and after deep meditational trances, without committing the essentialist fallacy of *Upaniṣadic teachers who posited a permanent soul (*ātman). The notion of a basic consciousness (*mūlavijñāna) is the solution arrived at by the Mahāsāṃghikas. It is an anticipation of the distinctive Yogācāra/*Vijñānavāda idea of a 'store-consciousness' (*Ālaya-Vijñāna).

Mulla (Arab., *mawla*, 'master'). A Muslim (man or woman) who has studied the basic disciplines. In *Ithna 'Ashariyya Shi'ism, a mulla is a teacher and preacher, who leads the congregational prayer; Persian *akhun(d)* is the equivalent.

Mulla Nasruddin. Character in Muslim folktales, also known as Juha and Nasruddin Khoja. He views the whole world (especially its officialdom) with humour.

Mullā Ṣadr al-Dīn Muḥammad ibn Ibrāhīm Shīrāzi (known as **Mullā Ṣadrā**) (1571–1640 (AH 979–1050)). Shi'ite philosopher. During his life, there was contest between those who did and did not want a philosophized account of *Shi'a Islam. Mullā Ṣadra was clearly of the former, achieving a profound reconciliation of Islam with *Aristotelianism and *gnostic systems—though as a result he underwent periods of forced and voluntary exile. In ... *al-Asfār al-Arba'ah* (The Four Journeys), he described the process by which a spiritual journey can be made back to the Source without becoming fused with it: (i) detachment from the world and the body; (ii) penetration of the divine names (and attributes) of the *Qur'ān; (iii) *fanā' (annihilation of one's own attributes as a self-possessed individual); and (iv) the return in utter independence (because wholly dependent on God) to bring guidance to others (*jalwah*).

Müller, Max (1823–1900). Historian of religions and pioneer of the comparative study of religions. His main interest was in Indian religions, and after translations of *Hitopadeśa* (see PAÑCATANTRA) and *Kalidasa's *Meghaduta*, he moved to Oxford where he became professor of comparative philology, and where he remained for the rest of his life. He was a prolific author, with interests ranging from the production of both editions and translations of Eastern religious texts (he edited the series *Sacred Books of the East*, 1879–94, and began the series *Sacred Books of the Buddhists* in 1895) to arguments about the origins of religion and *mythology. In his view, mythology began in the human sense of the overpowering might of natural phenomena (hence the name for those who followed his views, 'nature mythology'), with these powers early being personified and deified. He held that religion is the human capacity to perceive the infinite, and that all religions consequently contain to some degree the eternal truths of belief in God, in the immortality of the soul, and in a future retribution.

Mul Mantra (Pañjābī, 'basic sacred formula'). Concentrated and essential Sikh teaching, one of the first compositions of Gurū *Nānak, which is placed at the head of the Gurū Granth Sāhib (*Ādi Granth), preceding even the *Japjī. It contains the essence of Sikh theology.

Mumonkan (Zen text): see KŌAN.

Mumukṣutva (Skt., 'serious for liberation'). One of the four prerequisites in Hindus for those who aspire to *mokṣa (liberation). *Śaṅkara describes the others as the power to discriminate between what is real and unreal (*viveka), natural capacity and willingness to grow away from worldly things (*vairāgya), and the six great virtues (*ṣatkasaṃpatti).

Munāfiqūn, al- (Arab.). Term in the *Qur'ān denoting those who pretended allegiance to Muḥammad's cause but in bad faith. Sūra 63 is named for them, and there are evidences elsewhere of their 'hypocrisy'.

Muṇḍaka Upaniṣad. One of the eighteen principal *Upaniṣads, considered the most poetical. The name means 'shaven', and perhaps reflects the emphasis on the life of *saṁnyāsa.

Mundāvaṇi (Pañjābi, 'seal', some suggest 'riddle'). The passage at the end of the Sikh *Ādi Granth which indicates that nothing further is to be added. The whole is likened to the offering dish of the Hindu sacrifices: it contains the three treasures of truth, wisdom, and satisfaction.

Muni (Skt., etym. uncertain; perhaps from √*man*, 'think', 'be silent'; or *mud*, 'intoxicated ecstasy'; or *muka*, 'dumb'). In Hinduism, Jainism, and Buddhism, one who has progressed far on the way to enlightenment. In Hinduism, a muni in the Vedic period is one who possesses magical powers (*Ṛg Veda* 136. 2), a wise *ascetic, especially one who has taken a vow of silence. In the *Upaniṣads (e.g. *Katha Upaniṣad* 1. 4), a muni is one who has transcended attachment to this world and life by the realization of *ātman.

In Buddhism, it is used of one who has achieved tranquillity (*santi*; cf. ŚANTI) as a result of emancipating himself from views (see DIṬṬHI) and passions (*rāgā) and who therefore advocates the doctrine of tranquillity (santivāda—*Sutta Nipāta* 5. 845). In later canonical and post-canonical Buddhist literature the word is used to mean one who practises restraint in the triple activity of thought, word, and deed. In Jainism, it has become the common word to denote the avowed *ascetic.

Munkar and **Nakīr.** The two *angels, in Islam, who examine the dead in their graves, asking their opinion of *Muḥammad. Martyrs (*shahīd) are exempted from this interrogation.

Münzer, Thomas (*c.*1490–1525). German *radical Reformer. He was born in Saxony and was educated at Leipzig and Frankfurt. He was ordained and spent four years (1516–20) as an itinerant priest. At the Leipzig Disputation (1519) he met *Luther and created a good impression, but later developed revolutionary views, asserting as authority for his radical message a form of Spirit-inspired direct revelation. He was in repeated conflict, and after the defeat of the peasants in the Peasant's Revolt, he was captured and executed: according to Luther, it was 'a just and terrible judgement of God'.

Muratorian canon. The oldest surviving list of New Testament books, discovered by L. A. Muratori (1672–1750) in an 8th-cent. Latin manuscript at Milan. It mentions all the books except Hebrews, James, and 1–2 Peter, and includes (though cautiously) the Apocalypse of *Peter and *Wisdom of Solomon.

Murji'a (Murji'ite; Muslim movement): see ĪMĀN.

Murtadd (Arab., 'one who turns away', hence *ridda). An apostate from Islam. The ultimate punishment for an apostate, according to Qur'an 3. 86–9/80–3; cf. 2. 161–2/155–6, lies in the next world after death. There are, however, penalties in this world, including restrictions on inheritance and annulment of marriage. In accord with the fundamental principle, 'There is no compulsion in religion' (2. 257/6), no physical pressure may be put on those who seek to change their religion, though in practice this happens, even to the extent of death. The penalty of death is not mentioned in the Qur'an, but comes from a *ḥadīth transmitted through *al-'Abbās, 'Whoever changes [*badala*] his religion [*dīn], kill him.' But even here the issue is debated. According to some Muslims, the hadith includes the provision that the one who changes religion must also subsequently attack Islam, so that the death penalty is then an act of *jihād, in defence of Islam (see SATANIC VERSES); othewise, those who are overzealous are themselves liable to account for their actions on the Day of Judgement (for varying opinions, see J. W. Bowker, *What Muslims Believe*, 1998, 100–5). It is also a matter of dispute whether a murtadd should be given time to repent or reconvert.

Mūrti (Skt., 'embodiment'). In Hinduism, the embodied form of the infinite deity, the Indian way of bringing the all-pervasive divine into particular focus and concentration (see ICONOGRAPHY (HINDUISM)). The making of a divine image is controlled by extremely detailed rules, but remains inert until it is consecrated through the installation ceremony of *pratiṣṭhāpana*. Mūrti-pūjā is of great importance, not just in the temple, but also in the home.

Murtipujaka (image-worshipper): see TEMPLE (JAINISM).

Murugan (name of Tamil god): see TAMILNADU.

Murukaṉ (name of Tamil god): see TAMILNADU.

Mūsā (Muslim form of Moses): see MOSES.

Musaf. Additional Jewish service for *Sabbaths and *Festivals. After the destruction of the Temple, the Musaf prayer was formalized into the *synagogue service and was considered by the *rabbis to be as important as the normal morning service (*B.Ber.* 30b).

Musalmān. Turkish and Persian form of Muslim, from which derive the Fr. *musulmane* (for Muslim) and the (now rare) Eng. Mussulman.

Musama Disco Christo (Fanti, 'Army of the Cross of Christ'). An independent Ghanaian Church, founded by a highly *charismatic Fanti *Methodist teacher, Joseph Appiah (1893–1948). In 1923, he formed his own Church after dismissal from the Methodists for *pentecostal-like deviations, changed his name by revelation to Jehu-Appiah, and established a holy city, Mozano ('God's own town'), which was moved to New Mozano near Gomoa Eshiem after his death. The polity draws on both the Akan state system and some Methodist structures, and further Methodist influences are seen in orthodox and biblical doctrinal beliefs, the layout of churches, infant *baptism, *holy communion (held before dawn), a strict ethic, and the Fanti hymnal.

Musar (Heb., 'ethics'). Jewish moral instruction. In biblical Hebrew, the term 'musar' was used variously to mean 'punishment' or 'instruction'. Later, in *Talmudic times, it came to mean ethics or moral instruction. A distinct branch of Musar literature grew up in the Middle Ages which dealt with ethical matters.

Mushrik (offender, by association of less-than-God with God): see SHIRK; DHIMMA.

Music. Since music has charms to do much more than soothe the savage breast, it has been a major part of all religions. It has powers to alter and match moods, to sustain and evoke emotion, to induce trance or *ecstasy states, to express worship, and to entertain. At the same time, it is supremely a corporate activity: it not only binds together performers and audience, it is an activity in which many people can be engaged at once—people, for example, can chant together (not necessarily in unison) in a way which would become noise and babble in ordinary speech—facts which were much developed and exploited in oratorio and opera. At moments of despair and of triumph, humans sing, and sing together.

In India, sound itself (*śabda, *Om) is the sacred source of all appearance: music therefore has the capacity to articulate the order and ordering of the cosmos. The characteristic musical form of the *rāga is said to resemble in its gradual construction the building of a temple (see ART). In the *Vedas, music is embedded in the chants of the *Sāma Veda. While many of the sacrifices, of which the chants (*sāman*) once formed a part, are no longer practised, the protection of the chants themselves still continues. Music is also integrated into the religious occasions and purposes of *dance, as classically formulated in the *Nāṭyśāstra*, which pays particular attention to the ways in which religious and other sensation (*rasa) can be produced. Although Indian music divided into two major traditions (the Hindustani and Carnatic), the underlying religious perceptions remain the same.

In China, music received official recognition and support at an early date (at least by 1000 BCE) as an instrument of education and court ceremony. Ritual music of this kind was later called *ya-yüeh* (*yayue*, 'elegant music'), in distinction from 'popular music', *su-yüeh* (*suyue*). When *Confucius emphasized ethics and education as the basis of government and society, music formed a natural part in sustaining appropriate rituals and attitudes. *Shih Ching* (*Shijing*, The Book of Odes) became one of the *Confucian Classics, but no music from it survives. Music was equally central in Taoism: poetry-writing and the playing of the *ch'in* (*qin*, a kind of zither-like instrument) were regarded as avenues to the realization of the *Tao.

In Japan, music was early connected with *shamanistic rituals, but later music was much affected by 'imports' from Korea, China, and Central Asia. Thus *gagaku* (elegant music; cf. China above) is the traditional court music developed during the *Nara period, and codified during the Heian period (794–1185), which includes *mikagura* (music for the Shinto cult in relation to the court). *Mikagura* is divided formally between *komagaku* derived from Korea, and *tōgaku*, derived from China. If *gagaku* is music for the purpose of accompanying *dance, it is known as *bugaku, if not, as *kangen*. In 701, a department of court music (Gagaku-ryō) was established employing hundreds of musicians, often for specific state rituals and occasions. During the Heian period, the Buddhist practice of chanting *sūtras, known as *shōmyō*, became widespread, and was of particular importance for *Shingon and *Tendai. Music is also important in *theatre, with its continuing religious connections, as e.g. in Kabuki and *Nō.

Buddhist music has undergone a comparable transformation in Tibet. Ritual chanting of myths and formulae seems to have been a part of *Bön religion. But the advent of Buddhism led to the development of music, both vocal and instrumental, partly to accompany the rituals, but even more to prepare those present for *visualization and *meditation. Ritual drama (e.g. *'cham*) was also an important occasion of public music.

Jewish music is clearly rooted in the biblical traditions which speak of the Temple music and of the powerful music of *David. But none of this has survived, and the most important continuity of Jewish music is secured in the *synagogue. From the earliest period, synagogue music included the sung recitation of *Psalms, *cantillation (recitation of the *masoretic text of *scripture according to accent marks written in the text, led by the ḥazzan or *cantor, or by a member of the congregation, in cadences indicated by gestures of the hand—hence 'chironomy', the traditional instruction of these techniques), and the chanting of prayers. To these were added a large number of hymns and *piyyutim, and among the Ḥasidim *niggunim*, sung to nonsensical words, or to no words at all, in order to induce the desired state of ecstatic joy.

Christians from the outset were enjoined to 'sing psalms and hymns and spiritual songs' (Colossians 3. 16; Ephesians 5. 19), and they have not stopped doing so since. The biblical text underlay the development of Christian music, with especial emphasis on the Psalter. Plainchant (*plainsong) is a monophonic chant in free rhythm, which developed in various traditions (e.g. Ambrosian, Gallican, Gregorian, Mozarabic, Armenian, Byzantine, etc.). But plainchant led into polyphony, introduced in about the 11th cent., but coming to maturity from the 14th cent. on. The opportunity this afforded to the Reformation of telling the biblical story led to the astonishing achievements of Heinrich Schütz (1585–1672), whose major works, *Cantiones Sacrae*, *Symphoniae Sacrae*, *Psalmen Davids*, *The Resurrection History*, *The Christmas History*, and *The Seven Last Words from the Cross*, indicate how important the biblical text was. Even more spectacular was the development of the oratorio by J. S. Bach (1685–1750): although written for church settings, his Passions according to St Matthew and St John can still convey a religious sense of occasion, even in concert performances. In the Church, during this whole period, there had been developing the early Greek custom of singing *hymns, some early examples of which are still in use. Hymns have also spread their skirts a little into the related forms of motet, canticle, anthem, and cantata.

In Islam, music is related to the chanting of the Qur'ān which is highly technical and stylized, and to the *mosque, where the *ādhān (call to prayer) is taught and adjudged musically. The power of music to affect moods has led to its extensive use in *Sūfī movements. Although no body of religious music has been developed in Islam, Muslims have taken a great interest in music as a part of God's creation, and early works on music (especially that of *al-Fārābī) were translated into Latin, thereby extending their influence into Europe.

See Index, Music.

Music of the Spheres. The perfect harmonies created by the friction between the moving spheres of Greek (and later Christian) cosmology. It was originally a Pythagorean theory, expounded by Plato (*Republic* 10. 11) but rejected by Aristotle (*On the Heavens* 2. 9. 12). *Boethius (*On the Principles of Music*) laid out the relations between the music of the spheres which is inaudible to human ears (*musica mundana*), the harmonies of a correspondingly well-ordered human life (*musica humana*), and the music of instruments (*musica instrumenta constituta*): humans mediate between the perfect harmonies of the heavenly spheres and the potential chaos and disorder of the lower worlds. Although the Copernican revolution destroyed the cosmology, the underlying idea of attainable harmonies persisted, as can be seen, e.g., in Thomas Browne (1605–82), *Religio Medici*.

Muslim: see ISLAM.

Muslim b. al-Ḥajjāj al-Qushayri (817–75 (AH c.202–61)). Muslim scholar. His collection of *ḥadīth is, with *al-Bukhārī's *Ṣaḥīḥ*, the most highly esteemed amongst Muslim holy books. He was born at Nishāpūr in Persia, and after completing his formal education, travelled widely to collect the traditions of the Prophet *Muḥammad. His Ṣaḥīḥ (Sound) collection was composed out of 300,000 traditions. It differs from other ḥadīth collections in two ways: the books are not subdivided into chapters, and he pays special attention to the *isnād for the sake of accuracy.

Muslim Brotherhood: see AL-IKHWĀN AL-MUSLIMŪN; ḤASAN AL-BANNĀ'.

Musō Soseki, also known as **Shōkaku Kokushi** and as **Musō Kokushi** (1275–1351). A leading Zen monk of the *Rinzai school during the Five Mountain, Ten Temple period, based on *Kyōto and *Kamakura. In a time of conflict, seven emperors bestowed the title of *kokushi* on him, and he did much to integrate Buddhism into Japanese culture, especially in Kyōto. Nevertheless, much about his own life is obscure. He travelled widely, until, in 1305, he was walking on a dark night, and stopped to think: he leant against a wall that was not there, and as he fell, so did his darkness. Eventually (and reluctantly) he was appointed abbot of Nanzen-ji in Kyōto, and although he still moved on several occasions, he remained close to the reform and rebuilding of Rinzai Zen, a legacy from which remains in his rules for monasteries, *Rinsen kakun*, *San'e-in yuikai*, and *Saihō yuikai*.

In his teaching, he refused to endorse the growing division between *sūtra and *kōan methods, believing the means are determined by the capacity of the student. He employed the term *shōgyoku* as a virtual equivalent to *upāya.

Among many works, his *Muchū-mondō shū* (Dialogue in a Dream) explains Zen Buddhism in response to questions from the Shogun.

Mussulman (archaic name for Muslims): see MUSALMĀN.

Musubi (Jap., from *musu*, 'to produce', + *bi*, 'spiritual power'). The mysterious power and source of creativity producing all things in the universe. The word appears originally in the 'Age of Gods' section of the *Nihongi* (720). But it is also found in other early works, such as the *Kojiki* and *Kogoshūi*, as part of the names of the creative gods (*kami); for example, Takamimusubi no kami and Kamimusubi no kami. In the Shinto revival of the 18th cent., *Motoori Norinaga and other scholars of national learning (*kokugaku) emphasized the uniquely Japanese character of the idea.

Mut'a (Arab., *matta'a*, (of God) 'let one enjoy something'). Temporary marriage in Islam, a contracted marriage for a limited period. Based on Qur'ān 4. 24, this became a divisive issue between *Sunni and *Shī'a Muslims. Sunnis take this to refer to marriage in the ordinary sense, Shi'ites that it authorizes mut'a. The latter hold that the original text (suppressed by Sunnis) added, *ilā ajalin musamman*, 'for a definite period'. Both parties agree that the Prophet *Muḥammad allowed mut'a in the early days, when Muslim men were engaged in campaigns which took them far from home for long periods. Sunnis then refer to *ḥadīth in which Muḥammad makes it *harām, appealing to the principle of 'gradualism' through which the true *sunna became established (cf., *badā'); and *'Umar was explicit in forbidding it. However, the Shi'ites do not accept that 'Umar had authority to prohibit what Muḥammad allowed.

Mutakallimūn. Those who engage in *kalām (theology in Islam).

Mutawwi'ūn (enforcers of obedience): see WAHHĀBĪYA.

Mu'tazilites (Arab., *'itazala*, 'separate from'). An early theological school in Islam, which espoused the use of reason in finding a middle way between unbelief and naïve *fideism. The 'intermediate state' may have political origins, neutrality in the conflict between *'Alī and his opponents, and separation from it. The founding of the theological school is attributed to *Wāṣil b. 'Aṭā' and 'Amr b. 'Ubaid, AH *c*.105–30. Theologically, the Mu'tazilites were characterized by five principles (*uṣūl*): (i) *Aṣl al-*tawḥīd*, strict monotheism and repudiation of anthropomorphism; (ii) *Aṣl al-'adl*, the absolute justice of God, which led to emphasis on the freedom and accountability of humans, and to the reality of God's 'promise and threat' of heaven and hell (which, on a strong view of *qadar, could have no effect on human decisions, because God knows and determines the outcome); hence (iii) *Aṣl al-wa'd wa' l-wa'īd*, the promise and the threat, which have real consequence in the forming of belief (*īmān); (iv) *Aṣl al-manzila baina 'l-manzilatain*, the state between the states (of Sunnis and Shi'ites) in relation to the caliphate (*khalīfa); (v) *Aṣl al-amr bi 'l-ma'rūf*, commanding the good and forbidding the evil, appropriate action in spreading the faith, and in establishing a Muslim society. The Mu'tazilites were opposed by those who gave primacy to the Qur'ān over reason, especially *al-Ash'arī and *al-Māturīdī.

Myers Briggs Type Indicator: see JUNG, CARL GUSTAV.

Myōchō Shūhō (Zen master): see SHŪHŌ MYŌCHŌ.

Myōgō-renga (Jap.). A Japanese linked verse in which each line contains the name of a *buddha or *bodhisattva. They were often composed as a memorial for a dead person to accrue merit to him.

Myōkōnin (Jap.). One who practises Shin Buddhism (*Jōdo Shinshū) in exemplary fashion, and who is likened to a lotus flower. Biographies of myōkōnin were first compiled by Gōsei (1720–94) and followed by others of Jōdo Shinshū tradition. They were relatively unknown until D. T. *Suzuki (1870–1965), the *Zen scholar, drew attention to them as exemplifying Japanese spirituality.

Myōō (protective deities): see FUDŌ.

Mysterium Tremendum: see NUMINOUS.

Mystery plays (Christian): see THEATRE AND DRAMA.

Mysticism. The practices and often systems of thought which arise from and conduce toward mystical experience. Mystical systems are distinguished from other metaphysical systems by their intimate connection to a quest for salvation, union, or liberation realized through distinct forms of mental, physical, and spiritual exercise. In a classic definition:

> Mysticism, according to its historical and psychological definitions, is the direct intuition or experience of God; and a mystic is a person who has, to a greater or lesser degree, such a direct experience—one whose religion and life are centred not merely on an accepted belief or practice, but on that which he regards as firsthand personal knowledge (E. Underhill, *The Mystics of the Church*).

But mysticism need not be theistic. *Theravāda Buddhism, for example, is more conducive to mystical thought, experiences, and practices than Islam in general; yet *Sufism emerged in Islam giving priority to the mystical apprehension of God. Mystical experiences bring a serenity or bliss to the mystic. Such experiences may have some relation to the spontaneous experience of the unity of the world ('panenhenic' experience) and with certain kinds of chemical- and drug-induced experiences; but the connections are much disputed. See also BIOGENETIC STRUCTURALISM; Index, Mysticism.

Mysticism (Jewish): see KABBALAH.

Myth (Gk., *muthos*, 'story'). Narrations through which (amongst much else) religious affirmations and beliefs are expressed. In popular usage, especially in the media, myth has become synonymous with falsehood. Yet in religions, myths are simply the means whereby individual biographies are located in stories of a more extensive kind—e.g. concerning the nature of time, space, and place. Because many myths appear to be about putative matters of fact (e.g. about the origins of the cosmos, or of death) and are often aetiological (giving an account of the reasons why events or objects, etc., came into being), it has seemed obvious to the modern mind that, if the explanations are shown to be false, so also myths have been shown to be in error: myths are defective (category-mistaken) accounts of putative matters of fact which can now be improved upon.

The truth is far more complex. Myths are frequently distinguished from legends and folktales by the way in which they offer explanations. But while myths *may* be both intended and understood as factual, it is clear that more often they are stories which point to truths of a kind that cannot be told in other ways, and which are not disturbed if the apparent 'facts' of the supposed case are shown to be otherwise (so that the purported explanation strictly fails: but the value of the story does not fail with it). That is why a religion may, for example, have many myths of creation which are strictly incompatible with each other (see COSMOLOGY), without seeking to reconcile them. No matter how remote from history myths may be (though some are clearly rooted in historical events; and historical events can take on the heightened characteristics of mythology—e.g. the myth of the Kennedy era), they supply the means through which the meaning of experience can be affirmed, and through which history is converted from threat of unpredictable chaos and change to stability. In particular, myth places individual biographies and local events in a larger context which supplies them with meaning and significance. Myth endures because it engages human attention at the extremes of terror and delight; and also because it illuminates, and is illuminated by, *ritual.

Myth is so pervasive and recurrent that it is clearly a human universal. In what way it is a universal and is thus able to bear, as it does, the weight of human biography, is open to widely different interpretations—of which only some examples can be given here. Perhaps most obviously, *Jung was fascinated by the recurrence of stories, symbols, etc., in all ages and places. He concluded that myths arise from the universal and underlying collective unconscious, biologically inherited and born anew in each individual. These profound, brain-stored archetypes are dynamic, not passive, manifesting timeless patterns and dramas of human existence in individual experience.

*Freud equally set myth in the formation of the psyche, but related it to the recapitulation of those primordial situations of conflict which made sexuality so dominant in his theory. Beyond that, he regarded myth as related to dream: in dreams, we can escape the constraints of hard reality, and become as poets or artists, for whom all things are possible. Art is a public dream, and myth is verbalized art.

*Lévi-Strauss also maintained that the meaning of myth must be sought behind the level of surface-content in the universal structure of the human mind: while different circumstances may have evoked different developments and applications, everywhere particular motifs reappear in myth. To him this suggests that, although the contents of myth may seem to us to be absurd or fanciful or arbitrary, nevertheless they represent a quest for order and logic—the logic of the concrete, 'which is constructed out of observed contrasts in the sensory qualities of concrete objects, e.g., the difference between the raw and the cooked, wet and dry, male and female'. Lévi-Strauss maintained that the elements of myth (mythemes) are chaotically meaningless if taken in isolation. They become meaningful only in relation to other elements. Structure reveals itself at many different levels, but Lévi-Strauss was particularly interested in the ways in which myths mediate the binary oppositions which arise in experience (as above).

Others, however, have felt that it is the content of myth, not some underlying structure, which reveals universal human preoccupations. For *Eliade, myth places events *illo tempore*, 'in that (great) time' of primordial origins, a sacred and ideal time radically separated from the present. Myths make connection with this real and sacred time: myths are themselves sacred for that reason; they are exemplary, offering models of approved (and disapproved) behaviour; and they are significant, pointing out similarities in existential situations and exhibiting the meaning of otherwise random events. Joseph Campbell also emphasized the importance of content in understanding myth. He argued that myth serves four functions: mystical (evoking awe and gratitude), cosmological (providing models of the cosmos which are coherent with the sense of the *numinous), sociological (supporting the existing social order), and psychological (initiating individuals into their own potentialities, especially in the domain of the spirit). Myth, far from returning to the past, transforms the present. Campbell also sought to discern a central 'monomyth' associated with the fortunes of the primordial hero which recurs in all mythologies and is available for recapitulation in subsequent lives.

In the 19th cent., the knowledge of mythology, especially Norse and Indian, was greatly extended (the term 'myth' was itself coined), and for some it offered a way of telling truth which lay outside the boundary and ambition of post-Newtonian science and technology. Myth was thus a positive term for *Strauss; and, as the culmination of this process, Wagner sought to create (especially in *Parsifal*) a myth which would bear the weight of human questions beyond those which physics can answer, and beyond (though incorporating) the impoverished or inadequate myths of existing religions. Theologians can consequently talk of 'the myth of God incarnate' and imagine that they are giving a positive evaluation of *Jesus; but to the popular mind, myth is now irredeemably associated with falsehood, so that such claims suggest a subversion of historical truth.

See Index, Mythology.

Mythemes (elements of myth): see MYTH.

Myth of secularization: see SECULARIZATION.

N

Naasenes (Heb., *naḥash*; a gnostic sect): see OPHITES.

Nabī (Arab., 'prophet', cf. Heb., *nabhi*). A *prophet, the basic description, with *rasūl (apostle), of *Muḥammad's role and status. According to the *Qur'ān, prophets have been sent to all peoples, conveying the same guidance and warning from God. Thus *Moses, *Jesus, *Hūd (to give only three examples) are recognized equally as prophets in the Qur'ān. But Muḥammad is the *khātam*, 'seal', of the prophets. Prophets are characteristically persecuted by the people to whom they come, and Muḥammad was no exception; but 'Īsā/Jesus alone was exempted from death. In later Islam, considerable effort was made to relate the work of the prophet (whose word by definition comes from God) to that of the philosopher (who relies on intellect, and may therefore be unnecessary to the discovery of the truth that matters).

Nachi sennichi no gyōja. An *ascetic in Japanese religion (usually Buddhist) who completes the practice of standing naked for a thousand days beneath the Nachi falls, near Katsu-ura. The falls drop in a narrow band of water for about 130 m. At the base of the falls is the Hirō-ō (Flying Dragon) shrine. The Nachi shrine is above the falls, an ancient site, but the present buildings are recent (1848).

Nachmanides (Spanish Jewish philosopher): see NAḤMANIDES.

Naciketas. Son of Vājaśravas, who appears in *Taittrīya Brāhmana* and in **Katha Upaniṣad*, where he learns from *Yama the secret of immortality.

Nāda (Skt., 'sound'). In Hinduism (especially *Tantrism) cosmic sound: *Brahman conceived as sound underlying all phenomena. Through *yoga, especially *mantra yoga, the senses are withdrawn (*pratyahāra) and the yogin becomes aware of the nāda reverberating in the central channel (*suṣumna *nādī*) of his subtle body (*liṅga/sūkṣma śarīra). The vocalized sound of mantra becomes the unvocalized, inner sound of God. See further OṂ; ŚABDA; VARṆA; VĀC; and Index, Sound.

Nadar (help from God): see SIKHISM.

Nāḍī (Skt., 'channel' or 'vein'). A channel of the subtle body (*sūkṣma śarīra) connecting the *cakras, along which life-energy (*prāṇa) flows to regulate bodily functions. There are said to be 72,000 nāḍīs, though some texts, such as the *Śiva Saṃhita* (2. 13), say that there are 350,000.

Nāfila (Arab.). A work of *supererogation in Islam, based on *Qur'ān 17. 79: 'Perform vigils during a part of the night, reciting the Qur'ān, as a nāfila for yourself.' The most obvious nawāfil (pl.) are additional *ṣalāts; see also ROSARY.

Nafs (Arab.; cf. Heb., *nephesh*). The individual self or soul in Islam, which exists in conjunction with *rūḥ* (see below). In the *Qur'ān, nafs is sometimes nothing more than a reflexive pronoun ('you yourself'). But it also has stronger content as 'living person' (21. 35 f.), and as the self or soul removed by God at death (39. 43). It is the subject of accountability at the Day of Judgement (*Yaum al-Dīn) (2. 281). *Rūḥ* (cf. Heb., *ruaḥ*) is the breath breathed into humans by God to create living beings, and is thus less individualized, but it carries the consequential meaning of a speaking being, hence something like 'spirit'. Nafs is frequently the lower self, the self with appetites and passions, 'the soul which incites to evil' (12. 53). *Rūḥ Allah* is the name of *Jesus/'Īsā in Qur'ān 4. 169, and by implication of *Adam (15. 29), perhaps reflecting the first Adam/second Adam symmetry of *Paul.

Nāga (Skt., 'snake'; the *Nāgās are derived from a different root). 1. In Indian mythology nāga is both snake and elephant, but especially mythical serpents. Sometimes nāgas are half-human and half-snake.

2. Devotees of an Indian snake cult, especially in the south, Bengal and Assam.

3. In Buddhism, Nāga is a half-human, half-divine figure. Mahānāga (Great Nāga) is an epithet of the *Buddha and all who have passed beyond rebirth. In Tibetan Buddhism, nāgas are water deities who protect Buddhist scriptures until humans are ready to receive them.

4. A people and their country, in E. Assam, never fully assimilated into Hindu culture.

Naganuma Myōkō (co-founder): see RISSHŌ KŌSEI KAI.

Nāgapañcami (Hindu festival): see FESTIVALS AND FASTS.

Nāgārjuna (*c.*150–250). The founder of the *Mādhyamaka school of Buddhism and author of the **Mūla-Mādhyamaka-Kārikā* and other important works. As a philosopher he has few equals in the history of Buddhism, yet the details of his life are obscure and surrounded by mythological accretions.

He is regarded by many Buddhists of the *Mahāyāna tradition as a 'Second Buddha', and his philosophy of emptiness (*śūnyatā) was of enduring significance for later Buddhist thought.

Nāgārjuna reached this position through a dialectic of oppositions. The initiating recognition of *anātman (no Self in the human appearance) still left an awareness that the human appearance sustains activities with characteristic natures (*dharma natures). Nāgārjuna argued that these too are empty of self (*dharma-nairātmya*), and are not independent constituents of appearance: they depend on each other and have no more reality than their interdependence. All dharmas are *māyā (dreamlike appearance).

However, appearances have at least that much existence—they appear to be. Thus Nāgārjuna charts the Middle Way between substance and solipsism. The 'thusness' (*tathatā) of what is cannot be described but only realized, as undifferentiated in nature. Therefore even *nirvāna and *saṃsāra have the same nature ('there is not the slightest difference between the two')—they are not other than each other, since all is empty of self. In that sense, all oppositions between nirvāna and saṃsāra, heaven and earth, icon and index, disappear.

The purpose of a wise life, therefore, is not to strive to attain some goal or target (heaven, enlightenment), but to uncover and discover what one already is, and has been all the time: the buddha-nature which is the same nature of oneself and all appearance (see BUDDHATĀ; BUSSHO; TATHĀGATA; Index, Nāgārjuna.).

Nāgās (from Skt., *nagna*, 'naked'). A Hindu sect of naked *ascetics. They were recruited mainly from non-*brahman *castes, and became well-known for their belligerence in defending their tradition.

Nāgasena. A Buddhist sage who lived probably in the present-day Pañjāb, in the early 2nd cent. BCE. He appears in a 1st-cent. CE Pāli text, **Milinda-pañha*. In a *Sarvāstivādin version of the same text, he is given the name Dhītika.

Nag Hammadi library. A collection of thirteen texts, written on papyrus, found in 1945 buried near Chenoboskion (Nag Hammadi) near the Nile, in Egypt. The books contain fifty-two short tractates in Coptic, of which most are *gnostic works translated from Greek. They have titles such as the **Gospel of Truth*, the *Apocalypse of Adam*, *Gospel of *Thomas*, and *Trimorphic Protennoia*.

Nagid. The head of the Jewish community in a Muslim country. In Islamic countries, a head of the community was appointed by the head of the state. In the Middle Ages, there were negadim (pl.) in Yemen, Egypt, Kairourian, and Spain, and in the 16th–19th cents., there were negadim in Algeria, Morocco, and Tunisia. The office was discontinued in the 19th cent.

Naḥmanides, Moses ben Naḥman, or **Ramban** (1194–1270). Spanish Jewish philosopher and Talmudic scholar. Naḥmanides earned his living as a physician. He founded a *yeshivah in Gerona and among his students was Solomon ben Abraham *Adret. He had enormous prestige during his lifetime and was referred to as *ha-rav ha-ne'eman* (the trustworthy *rabbi). In the *Maimonidean controversy, he tried to reach a compromise, on the one hand condemning the way *Maimonides' writings had been used; on the other, arguing against the *ḥerem that the French rabbis had declared. About fifty of his works survive, including prayers, *piyyutim, theological works, biblical commentaries, and novellae on the *Talmud and *halakhah. His *Commentary on the *Torah* (publ. 1480) was written 'to appease the minds of the students, weary through *exile and trouble'.

Naḥman of Bratslav (1772–1811). Jewish *ḥasidic leader. A direct descendant of *Israel b. Eliezer (Ba'al Shem Tov), he emerged as a *zaddik in Podolia and the Ukraine. Naḥman believed he was destined to be at the centre of controversy, by his vocation to contest insincere leaders among the Ḥasidim. Between 1800 and 1802, he was in dispute with Aryeh Leib, a popular ḥasidic leader who accused him of *Shabbatean and *Frankist leanings. Subsequently, in Bratslav, where he lived between 1802 and 1810, he came into conflict with all the local zaddikim. He left Bratslav for Uman, in the Ukraine, and died there of TB.

His disciple, Nathan Sternhartz, wrote his biography, *Hayyei Moharan* (1875), and organized his followers after his death. Groups of Bratslav Ḥasidim still follow Naḥman's teachings in Israel and elsewhere.

Naḥman placed great emphasis on daily conversation with God in which the ḥasid pours out his feelings to God (*hitbodedut*). He promised that he would continue to lead his Ḥasidim after his death—hence his followers are called by other Ḥasidim 'the dead Ḥasidim', because they have no living rebbe. He was a strong opponent of philosophical religion (with *Maimonides as a particular example of error), stating that 'where reason ends, faith begins'.

Sternhartz, as well as writing his biography, collected many of Naḥman's words and works in several volumes, of which the best-known is *Sippurei Ma'asiyyot* (Tales of Rabbi Naḥman).

Naḥman of Horodenka. Jewish *ḥasid. Naḥman was a disciple of *Israel b. Eliezer (Ba'al Shem Tov) and the grandfather of *Naḥman of Bratslav. In 1764, Naḥman led a group of ḥasidim to *Israel and settled in Tiberias.

Nahn (purification): see PURITY.

Nahum, Book of. One of the *Minor Prophets of the Hebrew Bible and Christian Old Testament. Nahum seems to have been active in the late 7th cent. BCE, probably just before the final destruction of Nineveh.

Naigoma (interiorized fire ritual): see GOMA.

Naiṣkarmya-Siddhi. A work of four chapters expounding *Advaita Vedanta, by one of Śaṅkara's pupils, Sureśvara. It warns against reliance on prayer or meditation (since these imply duality) and expounds the meaning of *Tat tvam asi.

Najaf, al-. Town of pilgrimage in Iraq, 6 miles west of al-Kūfa, the traditional burial-place of *Adam and *Noah, and site of the tomb of Imām *'Alī b. Abī Ṭālib.

Najah (salvation): see SALVATION (ISLAM).

Nakagawa Sōen, also **Sōen Roshi** (1908–83). A leading Zen master of the *Rinzai school, dharma-successor (*hassu) of Yamamoto Gempo. He was abbot of Ryūtaku-ji, and was much concerned to spread understanding and practice of Zen in the West. He was characterized by his ability to convert everyday occasions into Zen practice (e.g. a coffee-break could be as much an occasion as the traditional tea-ceremony). In this, he extended the example of a revered predecessor, *Musō Soseki.

Nakayama Miki (Japanese visionary): see TENRIKYŌ.

Nālandā. The site of a ruined Buddhist monastery and *stūpa in Bihar, N. India.

The Chinese traveller *Hsuan-Tsang described Nālandā during the 7th cent., when it was visited by pilgrims from all over the Buddhist world. Despite being fortified, it was destroyed, probably by Muslim armies, sometime in the late 12th cent.

Nālandā is also a significant holy site for Jains since it is associated with the life of *Mahāvīra.

Nāl-āyira-divya-prabandham, Nāl-āyira-ttiviya-ppirapantam, or ***divya-prabandham.*** A collection of hymns and poems in Tamil by the S. Indian *Āḻvārs. The title (mixed Tamil and Sanskrit.) means 'the Sacred Composition in 4,000 [stanzas]'. This collection was compiled around 900 CE, allegedly by the *Vaiṣṇava *brahman (Śrī-Raṅga-) Nāthamuni who is also said to have composed the music for the hymns. As in the case of the roughly contemporary *Śaivite *Tirumuṟai*, this is a codification of vernacular *bhakti literature which began in the 6th cent. CE.

Nām (Hindī, Pañjābī, 'name'). Name of God. For Hindus and Sikhs, God's name is a formula (*mantra) encapsulating divine reality. Through meditation (*nām simaran), this takes root in the devotee.

Beyond the devotional, the sense of Nām takes on for Sikhs a profound theological importance. It is the means of God's self-manifestation.

Nāmajapa: see NĀMAKĪRTANA.

Nāmakīrtana. The constant repetition of the name of a god, which may lead to a trance or ecstatic state. More modestly, the repetition is a means of adoration and of identifying oneself with the god. As *nāmajapa* (see JAPA), the repetition becomes a *mantra, encapsulating the nature of the god.

Nāmarūpa (Skt., 'name' + 'form'). 1. In Hinduism, the way in which *māyā, the power of all appearance to become apparent, achieves characteristic and identifiable properties.

2. In Buddhism, the description of the characteristic form of appearance, able to be named (even though there is no Self conferring persistent or subsistent identity). It thus summarizes the aggregation of the five *skandhas (components of human appearance), with nāma standing for the last four, and rūpa for the first. Nāmarūpa is the fourth link in the chain of the conditioned arising of appearance (*paticca-samuppāda).

Namaskār, namaskāra mudrā (In Hinduism and Buddhism, hand signs), cf. *mudra.

Namaskāra-mantra. In Jainism, a much-repeated, reverent salutation of the five holy beings. Its repetition is often the first and the last act of the day, and it is chanted in the final hours of life.

Nāmdev. A Hindu poet from Mahārāṣṭra, to whom at least 2,000 *abhaṅgs* in Marāṭhī are attributed; in Hindī a smaller corpus of poems is included in the Sikh *Granth Sāhib. This material is closely related to the temple tradition of Paṇḍharpur in Mahārāṣṭra where Viṭhobā (Viṭṭhala) is worshipped. Many of these *abhaṅgs* deal with legends about the saints associated with this cult.

The poems attributed to Nāmdev proclaim

the oneness and omnipresence of God and the need to realize this *nirguṇa God by 'dying' to the world.

Nāmdhārī or **Kūkā** (Pañjābī, 'adherent of divine name'). A Sikh movement which others regard as a sect, although Nāmdhārīs regard themselves as a revival of Sikh orthodoxy. The Nāmdhārī movement was founded in the 19th cent. by *Bālak Siṅgh's disciple, *Rām Siṅgh, who based himself at Bhainī Sāhib, Pañjāb. Bālak Siṅgh's insistence on the importance of repeating God's name (*Nām) gave his followers their title. The alternative name, Kūkā, resulted from the ecstatic cries (Pañjābī, *kūk*) of Rām Siṅgh's followers during worship.

Nāmdhārīs regard their belief in an indispensable, ever-living *Gurū, apart from the scriptures, as consonant with the *Ādi Granth, but this tenet is rejected by other Sikhs. According to Nāmdhārīs, Gurū *Gobind Siṅgh did not die at *Nandeṛ, but continued to travel, finally bestowing the Guruship on Bālak Siṅgh. While awaiting the return from exile of Rām Siṅgh, Nāmdhārīs look upon *Jagjīt Siṅgh as their Gurū.

Under Rām Siṅgh's leadership the movement aimed at social uplift, particularly of *women, at ending British rule, and protecting the cow from Muslim butchers. The Nāmdhārīs' life is strictly disciplined. They must rise early, bath, then meditate upon a *mantra confided to each by the Gurū. A woollen *rosary of 108 beads is used. Their diet is vegetarian and dress must be simple, with the *turban tied flat across the forehead as in portraits of Gurū *Nānak.

Name of Jesus. A subject of Catholic devotion. Reflection on the Holy Name derives ultimately from the New Testament (e.g. 1 Corinthians 6. 11), but the devotion was popularized by the *Franciscans in the 15th cent. The feast, the second Sunday after *Epiphany, was prescribed for the whole Church in 1721, but suppressed in 1969. A feast day on 7 Aug. is found in Anglican calendars.

Names of God (in Islam): see NINETY-NINE BEAUTIFUL NAMES OF GOD.

Naming. Although many Sikhs do not name their children in this way, the distinctive religious practice is as follows. About forty days after birth, the parents take the baby to the *gurdwārā, where the *granthī prepares *amrit and puts some on the baby's tongue with the tip of a *kirpān, the mother drinking the remainder. The *Ādi Granth is opened at random and usually the first word of the *śabad which ends at the top of the left-hand page is read. The parents choose a name beginning with the same initial or commencing with another letter from that word. The granthī announces this to the congregation, adding *Siṅgh for a boy and *Kaur for a girl. His cry of 'Jo bole so nihāl' is answered by the congregation's '*Sat Srī Akāl'. The first five and last *paurīs of the *Anand *Sāhib are read, and after *Ardās and a *hukam, *kaṛāh praśād is distributed.

Nammāḻvār (Tamil, 'Our Saint'). The most important among the twelve Hindu *Āḻvārs. His real name was Caṭakōpaṉ, and he may have lived during the 7th or earlier 8th cent. Mystic and theologian, he created a novel poetic style of *bhakti poetry of great sophistication, and contributed almost one-third of the **Nāl-āyira-divya-prabandham*. His poems exhibit a profound devotion to *Viṣṇu and his *avatāras, especially *Kṛṣṇa.

Nampo Jōmyō (also Shōmyō, also **Daio Kokushi)** (1235–1308). Major figure in establishing *Rinzai Zen in Japan. He started training under Lan-hsi in Kamakura, and in 1259 travelled to China where he studied under *Hsü-t'ang Chih-yü, from whom he received the seal of recognition (*inka-shōmei) in 1265. He returned to Lan-hsi, and then took charge of Kōtoku-ji, followed three years later by Sōfuku-ji. His teachings in this period are gathered in *Kōtoku-ji goroku* and *Sōfuku-ji goroku*, and emphasize that Zen is not a 'foreign' import: it is timeless and not confined to one place, since *Bodhidharma is constantly 'coming from the west'.

Nām Simaran, Nām Japan (Pañjābī, 'remembrance of the name', 'repetition of the name'). Remembrance of God, a term common to Hindu and Sikh devotion. Whether silently or aloud, through singing *hymns or with the help of a *rosary, God's name must be consciously repeated. Sikhs focus their mind in *meditation on the word *Vāhiguru. By continuous concentration upon the Nām, one absorbs God's qualities.

Namu (Jap., 'praise'). Adoration and homage in Japanese Buddhism, hence equivalent to, 'I take refuge in' (see THREE JEWELS). It is therefore found in many combinations, e.g. the *nembutsu, namu-*Butsu, namu-Kanzeon, namu-Miroku, etc.

Namuci (the tempter): see MĀRA.

Ñāna: see JÑĀNA (Buddhism).

Ñāṇadassana ('knowledge and insight'). Buddhist *knowledge as an act of 'seeing'. *Dassana* indicates 'seeing or sight'. When combined with *ñāṇa* it gives the special meaning, 'insight arising from knowledge'. Thus the *Buddha is described as one who 'knows and sees' (*tam ahaṃ jānāmi passāmi*, *Majjhima Nikāya* 1. 329). The central truths of Buddhism are 'seen' (*Saṃyutta Nikāya* 229). Even nirvāna is 'seen' (*Majjhima Nikāya* 1. 511). According to the Nikāyas this 'knowledge and insight' is a result of mental concentration (*samādhi), and it is said that there is a causal relation between the attainment of mental concentration and the emergence of this knowledge and insight (*Dīgha Nikāya* 1.75).

Nānak, Gurū (1469–1539 CE). First *Sikh *Gurū, and founder of the Sikh religion. The sources of his life are limited: there are some hints in the *Ādi Granth, otherwise the first *vār of *Bhai Gurdas and the hagiographic *janam-sākhīs contain information.

At Sultānpur, probably in 1499, Nānak experienced God's call while bathing in the River Bein. After a mystical experience, reputedly of three days' duration, he reappeared, gave away his possessions and repeated, 'There is neither Hindu nor Muslim', probably meaning that the majority were not truly religious. He then devoted his life to preaching.

Nānak set out with Mardānā on a series of travels to many places (*udāsī), including notable *pilgrimage centres. In each place he taught the people, sang his hymns, discussed religion with Hindu and Muslim divines, and established a *dharmsālā* as a centre of worship.

Eventually Nānak settled in *Kartārpur where followers gathered and observed a daily regimen of bathing, hymn-singing, and eating together in the *Gurū-kā-laṅgar. Among these devotees was Lehṇā, later Gurū *Aṅgad, whom Nānak designated his successor as Gurū, in preference to his sons. Thus the Sikh movement continued with a succession of human Gurūs beyond his death, which probably occurred in Sept. 1539.

Gurū Nānak's teachings, as recorded in the *Ādi Granth, form the basis of Sikh theology. The *Mūl mantra encapsulates Nānak's assurance that God is one, the creator of all, and immune from death and *rebirth. He is formless and immanent as realized in the mystical union to which human *bhakti (devotion) is directed. To refer to God, Nānak used many Hindu and Muslim names (e.g. *Hari, *Rām, Khudā, *Sāhib), but especially *Sat(i)nām, i.e. his Name is Truth, as opposed to illusion.

By meditating upon God's name (nām japan, *nām simaran) the individual can master the wayward impulses of the *man (mind) and so conquer *haumai (egoism) and the *five evil passions. But above all one must trust to the Gurū—the guide to salvation from the *karmic cycle of rebirth—who discloses the *śabad (word of divine manifestation). Nānak stressed the irrelevance of *caste. Inner purity was what counted—not *asceticism but purity amid impurity, spiritual detachment while shouldering the family responsibility of a *grihasth (householder).

The Ādi Granth contains 974 hymns (including *pauṛīs and *śaloks) composed by Gurū Nānak. Of these, the most famous compositions are *Japjī, *Āsā kī Vār, Sodar, *Āratī, and *Sohilā, all repeated daily, and the *bārah-māhā* (in Tukharī, *rāg).

Gurū Nānak's birthday is celebrated annually on the full moon of Kārttika (Oct.–Nov.) in accordance with the *Bālā janam-sākhī, although scholarly opinion, based on the other janam-sākhīs, sets his birth in Baisākh (Apr.–May).

In popular iconography Nānak is represented as a robed figure with radiant face and flowing white beard, wearing a *turban, and holding a *rosary. See Index, Gurū Nānak's life.

Nan-ch'uan P'u-yuan (Jap., Nansen Fugan; 748–835). Ch'an/Zen master, dharma-successor (*hassu) of *Ma-tsu Tao-i. From a study of Buddhist philosophy, Ma-tsu pointed him to enlightenment. In 795, he retired to a hut on Mount Nan-ch'uan (hence his name), but after thirty years he was persuaded to settle in a monastery and to teach students who never numbered less than a hundred.

Nandeṛ. Sikh place of pilgrimage, *c.*320 km. NW of Hyderabad, India. In July or Aug., 1707 CE, Gurū *Gobind Siṅgh arrived in Nandeṛ, now in the S. Indian state of Mahārāṣṭra, on the banks of the river Godāvarī. Here he met the *bairāgī (Hindu renunciant) Madho Dās, who became his follower, taking the name *Bandā Siṅgh. At Nandeṛ, Gurū Gobind Siṅgh was stabbed by a Pathān, and, although at first the wound apparently healed, he died on 7 Oct. 1708. In Nandeṛ there are several sites revered by Sikhs.

Nandi. The bull vehicle of the god *Śiva. His image often has a shrine of its own at the entrance to temples dedicated to Śiva. The bull image is usually shown kneeling, facing the temple entrance, implying that Nandi gazes always at his Lord. Because of this his expression is gentle and smiling, full of joy at being in the presence of Śiva.

Nand Lāl 'Goyā' ('one who speaks', *c.*1630–1712). Eminent contemporary of Gurū *Gobind Siṅgh. Nand Lāl 'Goyā' composed predominantly philosophical works in Persian, notably *Dīvān* and *Zindagī-nāmā*.

Nan-hua chen-ching (name of *Chuang-tzu*): see CHUANG-TZU.

Nanjiō (Nanjō) Bunyū (1849–1927). Japanese Buddhist scholar who was one of the first to study in Europe and introduce W. methodologies in Buddhist studies to Japan. He edited the Skt. texts of *Pure Land *sūtras, the **Lotus Sūtra*, and compiled *A Catalogue of the Chinese Translation of the Buddhist Tripiṭaka* (1883).

Nansen Fugan (Ch'an/Zen master): see NAN-CH'UAN P'U-YUAN.

Nantes, Edict of: see HUGUENOTS.

Nanto (Jap., 'the southern capital'). The Japanese city and its environment of Nara, associated with *Nara Buddhism. Nanto Rokushu are thus the Six Sects (for list, see NARA BUDDHISM), and Nanto no shichidaiji are the seven great temples of Nara.

Nanto-kōan: see KŌAN.

Nanto Rokushu (six sects): see NANTO.

Nan-yang Hui-chung (Jap., Nan'yō Echū; 8th cent. CE). Prominent Ch'an/Zen master, one of the 'five great masters' of the school of *Hui-neng, whose pupil he was. After training, he retired to Mount Pai-ya in Nan-yang (hence his name) for about forty years. When about 85, he responded to the emperor's invitation to become his instructor (as also of Tai-tsung, his successor). As a result, he was called 'National Teacher of Two Emperors', the beginning of the tradition of the honorific titles *kuo-shih* (Jap., *kokushi*: see KOKUTAI). Thus Nan-yang is also known as Chung-kuo-shih (Jap., Chū Kokushi). Several *kōans of his survive, but he is more usually associated with 'the seamless pagoda'. The emperor asked Nan-yang how he could honour him on his 100th birthday. Nan-yang replied, 'Build the old monk a seamless pagoda'. When the emperor asked for advice about the construction, Nan-yang told him that his pupil, Tan-yüan, would lead him out of his ignorance. Tan-yüan supplied the 'explanation'.

Nan'yō Echū (Ch'an/Zen master): see NAN-YANG.

Nan-yuan Hui-yung (originator of kōans): see KŌAN.

Nan-yüeh Huai-jang (Jap., Nangaku Ejō; 677–744). Ch'an/Zen master, pupil and dharma-successor (*hassu) of *Hui-neng. From him, the second main lineage of the Ch'an tradition in China developed, and he remains best-known as the teacher of *Ma-tsu Tao-i.

Nanzenji (Buddhist temple): see KYŌTO.

Naorai (communion with kami): see MATSURI.

Naqshbandiy(y)a. *Sūfī order (*tarīqa) named after Khwāja Muḥammad Bahā' al-Dīn Naqshband (1317–89 (AH 717–91)). It originated in Central Asia, but soon spread to India, and eventually to China and Egypt. It adhered strictly to *sunna and *sharī'a, and sought to 'Islamicize' the state through its influence on rulers. The *Vedas could be regarded as revealed scripture (thereby making Hindus 'people of the book', *ahl al-Kitāb), with the many gods understood as childish pictures of the attributes of *Allāh—though this attitude was itself disputed. Outstanding among later members of the order were *Jāmī and Shaykh Aḥmad Sirhindī, in the Pañjāb. The latter reorientated the order by dropping the doctrine of *waḥdat al-wujūd*, the unitary nature of all being, so important to *Ibn 'Arabi, and replacing it with *waḥdat al-shuhūd*, the unitary nature of consciousness. He also rejected any seeming accommodation between Islam and other religions if that compromised the absolute supremacy of Allāh, and he repudiated *Akbar's eclectic explorations. The order remains active in Afghanistan, Turkey, and Russia, resistant to all political or secularizing erosions of Islam, and it has established a number of centres in Europe and the USA.

Nara. In Vedic Hinduism a general word for 'man', but in later texts, primordial *Man, the agent through whom the creation of humanity is effected. Nara and *Nārāyana are also depicted as *ṛṣis.

Nara Buddhism. The place and period (709–84) in which Buddhism was enduringly introduced into Japan. The prince-regent Shōtoku Taishi (574–622) became a devout follower of Buddhism, accepting Korean emissaries and sending to China for further support and instruction. In 604 he promulgated the 'Seventeen Article Constitution' which included (Art. 2) the instruction to reverence the *Three Jewels. Most of the emperors and empresses in the 8th cent. were Buddhist, and the court patronage led to a profusion of sects and building, especially in the capital, Nara, founded by the emperor *Shōmu (701–56) in 710. The proliferation of sects was such that an alternative title for the period is that of 'The Six Sects' (Nanto Rokushu), of which the most important and enduring were *Sanron, Hossō, and *Kegon, the others being *Ritsu, Kusha, and Jojitsu, all *Hīnayāna-based. The Buddhism which flourished as a state religion was concerned with the 'nation-protecting' qualities of sūtras, *bodhisattvas, and other guardians. The emperor Shōmu gave particular impetus to the building of many temples, particularly in Nara. He founded Temples of Golden Light and of the Four *Devas in all the provinces, and he planned and built the *daibutsu (large image of Birushan/*Vairocana) in Tōdai-ji, so that the power of Birushan would emanate to the local temples from the centre. The Great Buddha Hall, said to be the largest wooden structure in the world, was restored in 1980. Other important temple complexes are Jōruri-ji (*Shingon Ritsu), founded 1047, with *Amida images from the Heian period; Kōfuku-ji, founded *c.*670 (Hossō); Shinyakushi-ji (Shingon Ritsu), founded 745; Tōshōdai-ji (Ritsu), founded 759, notable for the Fan Festival (Uchiwamaki), held on 16 May; Yakushi-ji (Hossō), founded in 680, notable for the portrait on hemp of Kichijoten, on view once a year from the end of Oct. to the beginning of Nov. Hōryū-ji, founded by Shōtoku Taishi in 607, is the oldest temple complex surviving and is 12 km from Nara.

Nārada. One of the seven great *ṛṣis in Hinduism, to whom a number of hymns in the Veda are ascribed.

Naraka (Skt.; Pāli, *niraya*). In both Hinduism and Buddhism, states of punishment and torment, the equivalent of 'hell'. In neither case can the torment be 'everlasting', since rebirth or reappearance is always continuing.

Nara period (709–84): see NARA BUDDHISM; BUDDHISM IN JAPAN.

Narasiṃha (Skt., 'man-lion'). In Hindu mythology, the fourth in the standard list of *Viṣṇu's *avatāras. Although the figure of Narasiṃha is the most bloodthirsty of Viṣṇu's avatāras, he is often portrayed in yogic posture, and in some *Pāñcarātra contexts he is associated with the tranquillity of meditation.

Nārāyana. The personification, in Hinduism, of the creative energy of *Viṣṇu, associated, therefore, with the sun. It is Nārāyana, as the solar energy, moving on the face of the waters, which produces creation. He is also closely associated with *Nara, so that nara-nārāyana constitute the union man–god, i.e. ātman is *brahman.

Narmadā, Nerbuddha. Sacred river to Hindus, second only to the *Gaṅgā. Its pebbles which resemble the symbol of *Śiva (*liṅga svayambhū) are especially treasured.

Nāro chos drug, Chödrug. Six Doctrines of Nāropa. One of the principal bodies of teaching of the *Kagyü school of Tibetan Buddhism, so-called because they passed from Nāropa (1016–1100) to the Kagyü founder, Marpa Lotsawa. Nāropa had received them from his *guru *Ti-lo-pa (988–1069), who in turn had obtained them from their ultimate source Vajradhara, a *dharmakāya* (see TRIKĀYA) form of Buddhahood itself. They consist of:

1. *Tummo* (*gtum.mo*, Heat Yoga), by which the indivisibility of bliss (*bde.ba*) and emptiness (*stong.pa.-nyid*) are realized.

2. *Gyulü* (*sgyu.lus*, Illusory Body), by which the insubstantiality of all phenomena is realized.

3. *Milam* (*rmi.lam*, Dream Yoga), where the knowledge gained in gyulü is extended into the maintenance of consciousness in the dream state.

4. *Osal* (*'od.gsal*, Clear Light), by which the natural luminosity of emptiness is apprehended.

5. *Phowa* (*'pho.ba*, Ejection), in which the ability to separate the consciousness from the body is attained.

6. *Bardo* (*bar.do*, Intermediate State between death and rebirth), in which the yogin re-enacts his experiences in that state and obtains control over his bardo passage and rebirth.

Nā-ro-pa/Nāropa or **Nāḍapāda/Nāroṭapa** (1016–1100). Pupil of *Ti-lo-pa, and teacher of *Marpa, through whom his teachings (and Six Doctrines, *Nāro chos drug) passed into Tibet. Nā-ro-pa was born in Bengal, but received a Buddhist education in Kashmir and at *Nālandā. In 1057, he set out in search of a teacher whose name, Ti-lo-pa, had been given to him in a dream. When Ti-lo-pa appeared, the great instruction began. In this, a great severity of discipline continued, and Ti-lo-pa passed on the (mainly) yogic practices which were in turn passed on to Nā-ro-pa's followers. His teaching is contained in a number of works attributed to him.

Nāsadāsīya. Skt. title of the Hymn of Creation, *Ṛg Veda* 10. 129:

Neither not-being nor being was, at that time. There was no air-permeated space, nor sky beyond. What enfolded all? Where? Under whose protection? Was there deep, unfathomable water? ... Who knows for certain? Who can state it, when was it born, and whence came this creation? The gods appeared later, after this world's creation, so who can know whence it has evolved? ... He who surveys it in the highest heaven, He only knows—or perhaps even He does not know.

Nasā'ī (Muslim collector of ḥadīth): see AL-NASĀ'Ī.

Naṣārā (Arab., Christians (singular Naṣrānī), possibly derived from al-Nāṣira (Nazareth) but most likely from Syriac *naṣrāyā* (Nazaraioi of Acts 24. 5)). In modern Arabic, Christians are generally called Masīḥiyyūn, i.e. followers of the Masīḥ (Messiah). The name Naṣārā is used in the *Qur'ān for the various Christian communities at the time of *Muḥammad.

When the Naṣārā would not accept the teachings of Muḥammad, the Qur'ān began to declare the independence of the Muslims.

With the fairly sizeable community of Christians in Najrān, a treaty was made, in which Muḥammad allowed them freedom to practise their religion and to keep their property; treaties were similarly made with Christian tribes in the Arabian peninsula. Later, however, *'Umar had the majority of the Najrān Christians exiled to Iraq.

Nashim (Heb., 'women'). The third order of the Jewish *Mishnah. *Nashim* deals with matrimonial law and sexual morality, and also includes the tractates *Nedar* (*Vows) and *Nazir* (The *Nazirite).

Nasi (Heb., 'ruler'). Jewish leader. The failure of kings (*kingship) led to their 'demotion' in the restoration after the *Exile. The term 'king' was largely reserved for a future *messiah, and Jewish rulers from the second *Temple period used the term 'nasi'. The title persisted in different communities through the post-*geonic period, and the *Karaites described their leader as 'nasi' until the 18th cent.

Nāsik. The main city (pop. *c.*80,000) of the district by the same name in Mahārāṣṭra state and 20 miles from the famous Trymbakéshver temple built by the Peshwās.

It is a holy city where one of the four Hindu orthodox Dharmagurus has a seat, the other three places being Shṛṇgeri, Purī, and Dwārakā; it is also one of the four cities where a *kuṁbha-mela is held once every twelve years. The pious consider Nāsik as the *Kāśī of the South.

Naskh (Arab., 'deletion'). The Muslim procedure whereby certain verses of the *Qur'ān modify or abrogate others. The verses so modified are known as *mansukh*. The general principle is that the Qur'ān remains absolute and unqualified, but *Allāh in his mercy makes its application bearable in particular situations. A second sense refers to the cancellation of verses insinuated by *Satan/Shaitān: see 22. 52/1 f. The best-known example is that of the *Satanic Verses. The doctrine of abrogation is known as *al-nasikh wa'l-mansukh*.

Nasruddin (character in folktales): see MULLA NASRUDDIN.

Nāstika (Skt., 'atheistic'). Hindu term for heterodox systems of Indian religion and thought, which deny the authority of the *Vedas. They include *Carvaka, Jainism, and Buddhism.

Nāṭarāja (Skt., 'Lord of the dance'). Śiva, the cosmic dancer, especially in the Tāṇḍava *dance. His dance manifests creation, sustenance, destruction, balance, and liberation. Śiva as Nāṭarāja appears in his familiar dancing form from the 5th cent. CE onwards, at e.g. *Ellora and *Elephanta.

Nāth or **Nātha** (Skt., 'Lord'). A medieval *yoga tradition of India, influenced by *Tantrism, *Śaivism, and Buddhism. The tradition traces its origin to Matsyendranāth, one of the eighty-four *siddhas, who is regarded as its *adiguru*, and his pupil *Gorakhnāth (*c.*1200 CE). Originating in N. and NE India, the tradition became pan-Indian, tending to adopt the religious forms of a particular region. Thus most Nāths follow Śaiva practices, though in W. India Nāths tend towards *Vaiṣṇavism, and in Nepal towards Buddhism.

The aim of Nāth yoga is liberation in this life (*jīvanmukti) which is attained in a perfected or divine body (siddha/*divya deha*). The practice of developing the body (*kāyā* *sādhanā) under the guidance of a *guru, involves a long process of purification, *Haṭha, and *Kuṇḍalinī yoga which creates a ripe (*pakva*) body out of an unripe (*apakva*) one.

An oral tradition of songs in the vernaculars, especially Bengali and Hindī, praises the Nāth saints, and a written literature in Skt. describes yoga practice. Gorakhnāth is credited with writing the *Haṭha Yoga*, now lost, and the *Gorakṣa Sataka*. Other important texts of the Nāths are the **Śiva Saṃhitā*, the *Gheranda Samhitā*, the *Haṭhayogapradīpika*, and the *Siddha Siddhānta Paddhati*, which deal with yoga and the attaining of perfection in a perfected body.

The Nāth tradition still exists in India and has influenced other forms of Hinduism such as the *Sant tradition, the *Sahajīyās, and Indian *alchemy (*rasayāna*).

Nāthamuni or **Nātamuni** (10th cent. CE). Collector of the important *Vaiṣṇava anthology of hymns and poems, **Nāl-āriya-divya-prabandham*. He is said also to have composed music to them. Nothing certain is known of his life.

Nathan. Hebrew biblical *prophet. According to 2 Samuel 7, Nathan prophesied the postponement of building the *Temple; he rebuked *David for his behaviour with Bathsheba (2 Samuel 12); and with *Zadok the *priest, anointed David and Bathsheba's son, *Solomon, king.

Nathan of Gaza (1643–80). A leader of the Jewish *Shabbatean movement and *kabbalist. Nathan studied the kabbalah of Isaac *Luria and in 1665 had a vision of the divine world. As a result of this, he was convinced that Shabbetai Zevi was the *messiah and that he was his *prophet. Many legends were told of him, and his grave became a place of *pilgrimage. His letters were much copied and circulated, and his kabbalistic system was explained in his *Sefer ha-Beriah*, written in 1670.

National Covenant (Scottish Presbyterian commitment): see COVENANTERS.

National Learning School/Movement (School studying antiquity in Japan): see KOKUGAKU.

Nation of Islam (African-American movement): see ELIJAH MUHAMMAD.

Nats. Spirit beings (often to be propitiated) originally so-called in Burma, though the term has now spread. There are two sets of thirty-seven overlords among them, the Inner Nats (so-called because they were allowed inside sacred buildings as Hindu or Buddhist deities) and the Outer Nats, more variously listed, but also more significant, because they represent the spirits of figures in Burmese history or legend, and appear frequently in Burmese art, dance, music, and sculpture. They resemble *Yakkhas, and permeate the world as lived and experienced.

Natural law (Lat., *lex naturae*, *ius naturale*). The view that there is an intelligible and consistent order which exists independently of human opinion or construction, and that this order is a source of moral constraint and command for human beings. It is particularly prominent in E. religions, as, for example, in the understanding of the *Tao, or in the Indian understanding of *ṛta and *dharma. In the W., the Stoics conceived of a universal reason ordering and providing law for the cosmos and for human beings (and this was expressed in Roman law as a distinction between *ius gentium* and *ius naturale*); and, for the Christian tradition, there is an allusion to the natural discernment of right and wrong in Paul's Letter to the Romans. But the first major elaboration occurs in *Aquinas. The eternal law of God is conveyed to humans, partly through revelation (especially the Decalogue (see TEN COMMANDMENTS) of the *lex vetus* and the *gospel ordinances of the *lex nova*) and partly through what is open to human discernment in natural law. By obedience to natural law, humans put into effect their responsibility to be secondary causes in the action of God in relation to the universe.

Natural theology. Knowledge of God obtainable by human reason alone without the aid of *revelation. Exponents of such theology claim that God's existence and at least some of his attributes can be known through reason (e.g. by philosophical argument). The traditional arguments for God's existence are a central part of such theology (see COSMOLOGICAL; MORAL; ONTOLOGICAL; PHYSICO-THEOLOGICAL; and TELEOLOGICAL ARGUMENTS).

Natural theology continues to be an important part of the philosophy of religion; and the traditional theistic arguments are still vigorously debated.

Natura naturans/naturata (the relation of God to creation when both are held to be eternal): see IBN RUSHD.

Nāṭya Śastra (text relating to Hindu dance): see DANCE.

Naujote (generally interpreted as 'new birth'). The *Zoroastrian initiation ceremony. The central conviction behind Zoroastrian ethics is the emphasis on human free will. Initiation, therefore, cannot take place until a child is old enough to choose for him/ herself, usually seen as just before the age of puberty. Prior to the ceremony, the initiate has a ritual bath (*nahn*) inwardly cleansed by a sip of *nirang* (consecrated cow's urine). Fundamentally the rite consists of the investiture by the priest (*magi) with the sacred shirt and cord, the *sudre* and *kusti* (sometimes referred to as the 'armour of faith') and the first ritual recital of the associated prayers which the initiate should henceforth offer five times daily.

The *sudre/kusti* prayers are one of only two compulsory religious duties in Zoroastrianism. The other is observance of the *gahambar* (*festivals). The *sudre* is made of cotton and is worn at all times next to the skin, like a vest. It is white to symbolize purity and has a small pocket at the front of the 'V' neckline in which the faithful are exhorted to store up good thoughts, words, and deeds. The *kusti* is a long lamb's wool cord, tied around the waist (unlike the brahman cord, both of which presumably originated in Indo-Iranian religion).

Nautch dancers (Hindu): see DANCE.

Navarātri (nine days of Hindu observance): see FESTIVALS AND FASTS.

Nava Vidhāna (New Dispensation proclained by K. C. Sen to supplant Christianity): see SEN, K. C.

Nāyaṇmār (sing., *nāyaṇār*, 'leader'). Title bestowed on a claimed sixty-three saints in the Tamil *Śaivite tradition. The hymns (especially of Ñāṉacampantar, Cuntaramūrti, and *Appar) are regarded by Tamil Śaivas as equal in worth to the *Vedas. They are gathered in the *Tēvāram*, part of the Tamil Śaiva canon. Their lives (in *hagiographical style) are contained in Cekkilār's *Periya Purāṇam* (12th cent. CE), building on earlier works, especially that of Suntarar (Nampiyārūrar). Cekkilār includes an account of Suntarar in his own work, tracing his life from his abode with *Śiva to his earthly manifestation, which he undertook, with Śiva's permission, in order to marry—provided he worshipped Śiva on earth.

Nayavāda (Skt., *naya*, 'viewpoints'). In Jain philosophy, the doctrine of viewpoints, sometimes called the doctrine of relative pluralism. This doctrine is a unique instrument of analysis which asserts that all viewpoints are only partial expressions of the truth. No statement can be absolutely true because it is a view arrived at from only one angle or one particular standpoint. When combined with the kindred teaching of *syādvāda, this doctrine results in the distinctive Jain teaching of *anekāntavāda, in which Jain philosophers delineate seven *nayas*. The seven possible points of view (*saptabhaṅgī*) are figurative, general, distributive, actual, descriptive, specific, active (see e.g. **Tattvārthasūtra* 1. 31 f.), and they are abstracted from what a thing may be in itself (*pramāṇa*). These doctrines have helped the Jains avoid extreme and dogmatic views, and have bred an intellectual toleration and a breadth and realism to their thinking which acknowledges a complex and subtle world.

Nazarene. Term used in various senses.

1. It is an epithet for Jesus, usually understood to mean 'of Nazareth' (e.g. Acts 10. 38), but its origin and meaning are obscure.

2. 'Nazarenes' (or Heb., *Noṣerim*) appears as a Jewish term for Christians in early times.

3. Jewish Christian groups called 'Nazarenes', perhaps related to the *Ebionites, are mentioned by some 4th-cent. writers.

4. The *Mandeans are described as 'Nasoreans' in some of their early writings.

Nazarene, Church of the. An international holiness denomination which, in the early 20th cent., united various American groups which taught John *Wesley's doctrine of 'perfect love'. In the British Isles the churches formerly associated with the International Holiness Mission were united with the Church of the Nazarene in 1952, whilst in 1955 a further union took place with the Calvary Holiness Church.

Nazarite Church (Zulu, *ama-Nazaretha*) or **Shembe's Church.** The largest independent movement among the Zulu, later including other peoples. It is named from the biblical *Nazirites, and represents an Old Testament form of religion—sabbatarian, and with two main festivals, Tabernacles (see SUKKOT) and the *New Year, focused on their holy city Ekuphakameni, near Durban, and their holy mountain Nhlangakazi, 130 km north. The founder, Isaiah Shembe (1870–1935), a black *Baptist church member, was a *charismatic prophet-healer who composed a great corpus of hymns in Zulu.

Nazirite (Heb., *nazar*, 'dedicate'). A Jewish ascetic who vows to abstain from grape products, from cutting hair, and from touching a corpse. The rules for Nazirites are described in Numbers 6. 1–21 and in the tractate 'Nazir' in the order **Nāshim* of the *Mishnah.

Neale, John Mason (1818–66). *Anglican *high churchman and *hymn-writer. He was one of the founders (1839) of the Cambridge Camden Society, which stimulated interest in church architecture and Catholic worship, thus contributing to the *Ritualist movement in the Church of England. Besides his own hymns he also produced fine translations from the Latin (e.g. 'Jerusalem the golden').

Neasden temple (Hindu temple in London): see SVAMINARAYAN.

Nedavah (vow): see VOWS (JUDAISM).

Neder (vow): see VOWS (JUDAISM).

Negative way: see APOPHATIC THEOLOGY; VIA NEGATIVA.

Nehan. Jap., for *nirvāna.

Nehemiah. Governor of *Judah after the Babylonian *exile. Nehemiah restored the walls of *Jerusalem and established order within the community. In the *aggadah he is identified with *Zerubbabel. See also EZRA.

Nei-ch'i: see NEI-TAN.

Nei-kuan or **Nei-shih** (Chin., 'inner viewing'). A Taoist practice of visualizing the interior of the body, in order to facilitate the distribution of vitality (*ch'i) and to contact the inner powers/deities. It also produces great mental calm.

Nei-tan. Interior *alchemy or inner elixir. Contrasted with Wai-tan (exterior alchemy), or techniques of concocting the elixir of immortal transcendency by cooking certain substances in a cauldron. In Nei-tan the 'substances' are the basic elements of life—*ch'i (vital breath), *ching (generative essence), and *shen (spirit)—and the 'cauldron' is the practitioner's own body. Important in the development of Nei-tan was Chang Po-tuan (984–1082), who shifted the emphasis away from chemical transmutation to interior achievement of immortality (see his *Wu-chen p'ien*, Essay on the Awakening to the Truth).

Nembutsu (Jap.; Chin., *nien-fo*). The foremost religious practice in the *Pure Land Schools of Buddhism. Nembutsu literally means 'Mindfulness of the Buddha'. It was thus originally a meditational practice with the Buddha and his innumerable merits 'kept in mind', i.e. as an object of contemplation. In the earliest period of Pure Land development it was interpreted as a form of meditation in which the Buddha *Amida (Jap.; Chin., O-mi-t'o; Skt., Amitābha/Amitāyus) and his transcendent Pure Land are visualized. In China and Japan it was reinterpreted to mean invoking the name of the Buddha in the form *Namu Amida Butsu* (Jap.; Chin., *Na-mo O-mi-to fo*), 'I take refuge in the Buddha Amida'. This interpretation was most forcefully enunciated by Shan-tao in China, and by *Honen in Japan.

Neminātha or **Ariṣtanemi.** The 22nd of the Jain *tīrthaṅkaras, who ruled over Dvaraka, the place where *Kṛṣṇa ended his days on earth. Consequently, popular stories are told about the contests between the two which presumably reflect contests between the two communities.

Nenbutsu (Jap., 'thought' + 'Buddha'). The deliberate recollection of the *Buddha, and meditation on the Buddha. It is more often transliterated *nembutsu.

Nenge mishō (Jap.). The wordless transmission of the truth from *Buddha Śākyamuni to *Mahākāśyapa. From this paradigmatic interaction, *Zen developed the key notions of transmission from heart to heart or mind to mind (*ishin-denshin) and the special transmission outside the scriptures (*kyoge-betsuden*; (see FUKASETSU).

Nenju or **juzu** (Jap., 'thought beads'). A Japanese Buddhist *rosary. The name of a *Buddha, especially *Amida, is recited with each bead.

Nenjū gyōgi (annual festivals): see FESTIVALS AND FASTS (JAPANESE).

Neo-Catechumenate. *Roman Catholic movement for the renewal of traditional faith. The movement was founded in 1964 by K. Arguello, in order to resist the increasing *secularization of society and the erosion of traditional understandings of faith and practice. Reverting to the practice of the early Church of training *catechumens before *baptism, the Neo-Catechumenate, more simply called 'The Way', establishes teams of trained people who are dispersed into parishes in order to train others. They in turn move into other parishes to continue the movement. While some (including the pope, *John Paul II) welcome this as a renewal of informed commitment, others see it as destructive of parish community, because it creates an élite with its own structure (including separate activities and *masses) in the midst of what might otherwise be regarded as a united church.

Neo-Confucianism. The revived form of *Confucianism which became dominant in China especially after the 10th cent. CE, under the leadership of a succession of great philosophers of the 11th cent., including Chou Tun-yi, *Ch'eng Hao, Ch'eng Yi (see CH'ENG HAO), and Chang Tsai, as well as the later synthesizer *Chu Hsi (1130–1200), all of the Sung dynasty. Neo-Confucianism attempted to offer certain explanations of the problems of the universe and of human existence, developing a cosmology of the Great Ultimate (*T'ai-chi, Chou Tun-yi), a doctrine explaining the rise of evil in human nature (Chang Tsai and Ch'eng Yi), grounded in the metaphysics of *li (principle) and *ch'i (matter-energy), and a practical teaching of cultivation which regards as important intellectual pursuit as well as moral progress (Ch'eng Yi and Chu Hsi). As a philosophical movement, it is usually described as having at least two principal branches, the 'realist' school of Chu Hsi with its emphasis on li or principle, and the 'idealist' school of *Wang Yang-ming (1472–1529), with its preference for the subjective *hsin* (mind-and-heart). Neo-Confucianism spread from China to Yi Korea and Tokugawa Japan, which also witnessed local developments of the Chu Hsi schools (and, in the case of Japan, of the Yang-ming school also).

Neo-Orthodoxy. 1. A modernist faction among the *Orthodox Jewish community. As a movement, Neo-Orthodoxy was established in the late 19th cent. under the leadership of Samson Raphael *Hirsch. He taught the principle of **Torah 'im derekh erez* ('Torah [in harmony] with the way of life') i.e. careful observance of *mitzvot (commandments) and customs combined with a positive attitude to secular life where no conflict obtained.

2. A Protestant Christian reaction against 19th-cent. liberalism in theology. The reaction was not organized, and is particularly associated with K. *Barth. Quintessentially, Neo-Orthodoxy rejected the liberal belief that it is possible to argue from experience to God, or, more extremely, that theology is disguised anthropology. For Neo-Orthodoxy, the word and revelation of God constitute a disjunctive act which cannot be subordinated to human judgement: this self-revelation is uniquely embodied in *Jesus Christ, the Word of God made flesh.

Neo-Paganism. A variety of *witchcraft and other movements such as the *Pagan Pathfinders that have emerged in recent times to revive and spread what is called the pagan way of being, to protect pagan sacred places and more generally Mother Earth.

Neoplatonism. The philosophy of *Plotinus and his followers, derived (remotely) from Plato. After Plotinus, its most outstanding proponents were *Porphyry, Iamblichus (3rd/4th cent. CE), Eunapius of Sardis, and *Proclus. The major aim of Neoplatonism was to provide a satisfactory account of the relationship of the One to the many. Between the One at the summit of the hierarchy of beings and the material world, it proposed a series of intermediaries. The progressively less perfect intermediaries are constituted by procession from their respective sources. Through abstractive thought, the soul can return to its source and be mystically united with it.

In this way, God is abstracted into absolute transcendence, and is protected from involvement in the material and evil; and human beings (who have in them some aspect of the divine) can return upwards to God, the 'flight of the alone to the Alone'.

In Islam, *falsafah* (philosophy) made no particular distinction between Plato, Aristotle, and Neoplatonism, since it was concerned only with the opportunity of philosophy, not its history. The translation of what was taken to be Aristotle began in the reign of al-Ma'mūn (d. 833 (AH 218)), and through these endeavours, Greek philosophy and its texts were effectively rescued for the world, with many texts surviving only because of this Muslim interest. Neoplatonism entered Muslim thought in this way, though often attributed to Aristotle (e.g. when books iv and vi of Plotinus' *Enneads* were translated); al-Kindī and *al-Farābī were key figures in the establishing of this way of thought, though the major figures were *ibn Sīnā and *ibn Rushd, and *ibn 'Arabī on the mystical side.

Neo-Taoism: see HSÜAN-HSÜEH.

Neo-Thomism. The application and development of the work of Thomas *Aquinas. Somewhat improperly, 'Neo-Thomism' is used to refer to the revival of interest in Aquinas in the 16th and 17th cents., which was inspired by the writings of *Cajetan (see also THOMISM). More accurately, Neo-Thomism refers to the revival after *Vatican I reinforced by *Leo XIII. One approach has been to emphasize the opinions of Aquinas' commentators, explicating and systematizing these. Another (and more influential) has been to abandon *scholastic method in favour of reformulating Aquinas' thought in more discursive and historical ways. Notable exponents of this latter approach have been J. *Maritain and E. *Gilson. Both approaches have shared Aquinas' point of departure that reason can know *that* God is, but that revelation is needed to know *what* God is. The term 'neo-Thomism' is also sometimes applied to those who are more usually known as Transcendental Thomists. Notable exponents of neo-Thomism in this sense have been B. *Lonergan and K. *Rahner.

Ner tamid (light burning before the Ark in synagogues): see ARK (3); ETERNAL LIGHT.

Neshāmah yeterah (Heb., 'additional soul'). Popular Jewish belief that each Jew is given an additional soul for the duration of the *Sabbath.

Nestorianism. The Christian *heresy that within the incarnate *Christ there were two separate persons, the one divine, the other human. It is named for Nestorius (d. *c.*451), patriarch of Constantinople from 428, who rejected the title *Theotokos ('God-bearer') for the Virgin *Mary as suggesting *Apollinarianism.

The so-called Nestorian Church is the ancient church of the Persian empire, now most properly called the *Church of the East.

Neti, neti (Skt., 'not this, not this'). The phrase (*Brihadāranyaka Upaniṣad* 4. 2. 4) through which, in Hinduism, the reality of appearances in the universe is rejected. Instead (ibid. 4. 5. 15) appearance is superimposed on *Brahman, giving the appearance of duality. But *ātman, which *is* Brahman, is not to be identified with appearance: 'That Self (ātman) is not this, not this.'

Neturei Karta (Aram., 'guardians of the city'). Ultra-religious Jews who, for religious reasons, do not recognize the State of *Israel.

New Age movement. A diverse set of organizations united by their enthusiasm for the creation of a new era of enlightenment and harmony in the 'Aquarian Age' (in *astrology the era or cycle of *c.*2,150 years when the constellation and zodiacal sign of Aquarius will coincide, following on from the 'Piscean Age' during which the same is true for Pisces).

New Age 'teachings' are characterized by an emphasis on monism, relativism, individual autonomy, and the rejection of the Judaeo-Christian emphasis on sin as the ultimate cause of evil in the world. Instead, New Age posits lack of knowledge and awareness as the root of humanity's problems. It is eclectic in style, gathering in a wide range of people and teachings if they reinforce the central concern.

New Apostolic Church. Christian denomination deriving from the *Catholic Apostolic ('Old Apostolic') Church in Germany. It began in 1860 with the ordination of three apostles to succeed those who had died and thus perpetuate the apostolate. New Apostolics number *c.*2 million, including a sizeable branch in the USA.

New Christians (forced Jewish converts): see MARRANOS.

New (Jerusalem) Church: see SWEDENBORG, E.

Newman, John Henry (1801–90). Christian theologian and leader of the *Oxford Movement, also a writer, poet, and historian, whose genius lay in the combination of these talents.

In the early 1840s he withdrew from leadership of the Oxford Movement and, in 1845, converted to Roman Catholicism. For Newman, Rome offered that assurance Anglicanism seemed to lack and for which he longed. In 1848 he founded the Birmingham *Oratory. He spent the rest of his life there, save for a period in Dublin, between 1854 to 1858, to which he went as rector of the new Catholic university. He also helped to found the London Oratory, and was made a *cardinal in 1879.

His published works are substantial. They include his autobiography, *Apologia pro vita sua*, published in 1864 in response to an attack from Charles Kingsley; a treatise on education *The Idea of a University* (1852); numerous theological texts, including *An Essay on Development of Christian Doctrine* (1845); *An Essay in Aid of a Grammar of Assent* (1870); the novel *Loss and Gain*, and *The Dream of Gerontius* (1865).

New Moon: see MOON, BLESSING OF THE.

New quest for the historical Jesus: see QUEST FOR THE HISTORICAL JESUS.

New religions in Japan (Jap., *shinkō shūkyō*). While *new religious movements are a common and recurrent phenomenon, the strength and importance of new religions in Japan is such that it makes them distinct. They are made up of movements which have emerged during the last two cents., and which may have connections with Buddhism, Shinto, or Christianity, or may be entirely independent. They are 'new' in relation to shrine Shinto and temple Buddhism, both of which carried with them the control of vital rituals.

Early examples of new religions in the 19th cent. are Nyoraikyō (cf. *nyorai), Kurozumikyō (see KUROZŪMĪ MUNETADA), *Tenrikyō, *Konkōkyō, and *Ōmotokyō. All of these emphasized the importance of lay members (over against the exclusive role of the priests in traditional religions), and made healing available outside the traditional rituals. In the 20th cent., important examples are *Reiyūkai, *Sōka Gakkai, and *Seichō no Ie.

New religious movements. A generic term referring to the literally thousands of religious movements (and occasionally secular alternatives to religion) that have emerged world-wide, but especially in Africa, Japan, and the West during this cent. Their adherents are to be estimated in millions. While for the most part highly syncretistic, the ritual and content of many of these new religions have been influenced, to a greater or lesser degree, by Buddhist, Christian, and Hindu spiritual techniques and perspectives. There is also a sizeable number of Islamic- and Jewish-oriented new religions, and numerous esoteric, *metaphysical, and *neo-pagan movements.

Although classification is difficult, one of the more successful is that of R. Wallis, using 'response to the world' as the principal distinguishing criterion: this separates two main types: world-denying and world-affirming movements—and a third, relatively minor category, the world-accommodating type. The first type emerged as participants of the *counterculture, somewhat disillusioned with its approach and objectives, began to turn to religions such as Hare Krishna (see INTERNATIONAL SOCIETY ...), the *Divine Light Mission, the Unification Church (see MOON, SUN MYUNG), and the *Children of God, which shunned the world and stressed the importance of the expressive, experiential approach to religious truth over against reason and reflection.

For a time these movements, highly authoritarian, rigid, demanding, and communalistic, exercised most appeal, sometimes rivalled by the world-affirming *Scientology and *Transcendental Meditation. More recently, however, world-affirming movements as a whole (embracing among others *metaphysical movements such as the *Spiritual Frontiers Fellowship, such 'self-religions' as *Exegesis and *Silva Mind Control, African and Japanese new religions, for example the Aladura churches and *Sōka Gakkai respectively) have experienced considerable growth.

The world-affirming movements (or self- or psycho-religions) aim to transform the individual by providing the means for complete self-realization, in the sense of becoming fully aware that the real or inner self is divine and that the ultimate goal of the religious quest is not to know but to become God.

Other common characteristics include a strong *millennial dimension, the use made of contemporary language and symbols, eclecticism, and an egalitarian emphasis which in theory permits all to attain the highest levels of spiritual growth. The world-accommodating movements (such as the growth of Christian house churches, and the various restoration and renewal groups) are more concerned with personal holiness and the revitalization of the established religions than with the wider society.

New Sect Shinto: see SECT SHINTO.

New Testament. The collection of books which in addition to the Jewish scriptures make up the Christian Bible. The Greek word *diathēkē*, 'covenant, testament', in the sense of writings goes back to *Paul (2 Corinthians 3. 14).

New Thought. A loosely structured movement that emerged in the USA in the last quarter of the 19th cent., which includes a variety of *metaphysical, occult, healing sects, schools, and groups such as *Christian Science, Divine Science, The Unity School of Christianity, and Science of Mind. It was strongly influenced by Phineas Parkhurst Quimby, who practised a form of mesmeric healing with the aid of a medium and advanced the idea that by positive or right thinking it is possible to realize one's highest ideals in the here and now, especially in the realm of healing where prayer is a central part of the process. Since the 1950s there has been a revival of interest in these movements in the USA and W. Europe.

New Year. There are four dates for New Year in the Jewish tradition: 1 Nisan is reckoned as New Year for the religious *calendar and for calculating the reigns of Jewish kings; 1 Elul is the New Year for *tithing; 1 Tishri: see ROSH HA-SHANAH; 1 Shevat is the New Year for trees (according to Bet Shammai): see TU BI-SHEVAT.

Next Year in Jerusalem (Heb., *la-shanah ha-ba'ah bi-Yerushalayim*). Traditional phrase expressing the Jewish hope for the coming of the *messiah and for their return to Jerusalem. For those in Jerusalem or in *Erez Israel, the word *ha-benuyah*, 'rebuilt', is added.

Nezifah (rebuke): see ḤEREM.

Nezikin (Heb., 'damages'). Fourth order of the Jewish *Mishnah. Nezikin is concerned with civil law and legal procedure, especially in cases of damage. It also includes the tractate **Avot*.

Neziv (Jewish Talmudic scholar): see BERLIN, N. Z. J.

NGK (Nederduitse Gereformeerde Kerk): see DUTCH REFORMED CHURCH.

Ngor (sect of Sakya): see SAKYA.

Nibbāna: see NIRVĀNA.

Nibbuta (Pāli). 'He who is cooled', i.e. from the fever of attachment, clinging, and desire (*taṇhā, thirst).

Nicaea, Council of. The first *ecumenical council of the Christian Church, held in 325. The site is modern Iznik in NW Turkey. It was an assembly of bishops called by the emperor *Constantine to deal with the *Arian controversy and secure the unity of the church in the East. A creed was promulgated by the council which contained the *homoousion formula and to which anti-Arian *anathemas were attached. The council also promulgated canons and reached decisions on the Melitian schism in Egypt, the calculation of the date of *Easter, and the precedence of the major Christian sees. See also NICENE CREED.

Nicene Creed. A Christian statement of faith used in both E. and W.

Although it contains the *homoousion, the creed does not originate from the council of *Nicaea, nor probably from the later council of Constantinople (381) as traditionally held. It was, however, current as part of the *eucharist by the 5th cent. All liturgical churches now use it.

Nichikō (Japanese movement founder): see NICHIREN SHŌSHŪ.

Nichiren (1222–82). Japanese Buddhist monk who was the founder of *Nichiren Shū, and whose name literally means 'Sun Lotus', 'sun' standing for Japan and 'lotus' for the **Lotus Sūtra*. While young, he travelled to various temples in search of a form of religious teaching and practice which he could regard as 'true Buddhism'. In Kamakura, he studied the teachings of *Pure Land school (Jōdo Shū) and *Zen. Later, after a brief return visit to Seichōji in his home village, he enrolled in the monasteries of Mount Hiei and began an intensive study of Tendai teaching and practice. Because of his radical ideas, he was driven out of Mount Hiei, and so he moved on to Mount Kōya to study the esoteric teachings and practice of the *Shingon ('True Word') school of Buddhism. It was during his study on Mount Kōya that he finally concluded that the only true form of Buddhism was that taught by *Saichō (Dengyō Daishi, 'great teacher Dengyō'), who had established the Tendai (Chin., **T'ien-t'ai*) School of Buddhism in Japan in the 8th cent. Saichō taught the superiority of the *Lotus Sūtra* over all Buddhist sūtras. Nichiren, after discovering the *Lotus Sūtra* for himself, returned to his home village and began preaching to the common people that enlightenment was available to every human being through simple trust in the truth (*dharma) expressed in this sūtra.

The act of faith which Nichiren taught was the invocation of a specific *mantra which he called *daimoku*, 'sacred title': *namu myōhō renge kyō*, 'I take refuge in the Lotus of the Wonderful Law Sūtra.'

In Feb. 1260, Nichiren wrote his well-known essay, *Risshō ankoku-ron* (Treatise on the Establishment of Righteousness to Secure the Peace of the State).

Because of the radicalness and outspokenness of his criticism of the government and his attacks against other schools of Buddhism, Nichiren was arrested in 1261 and exiled to the Izu Peninsula for two years. He was pardoned in 1264. However, Nichiren did not recant. He returned to Kamakura and began publicly denouncing the government in sermons he preached on the streets of the city. Nichiren was again arrested, this time receiving the death sentence. According to tradition, the executioner's sword was struck by lightning just at the moment he began to strike at Nichiren's neck. Whatever happened, the execution was stayed, and he was again sentenced to exile, this time on the isolated island of Sado in the Sea of Japan.

During the three years of his second exile on Sado Island (1271–4), Nichiren wrote *Kaimokushō* (Treatise on Opening the Eyes) and *Kanjin Honzonshō* (Treatise on Contemplating the True Object of Worship).

Together with *Risshō Ankokuron* and two later works, *Senjishō* (Selection of the Time) and *Hōonshō* (Repaying Kindness), these two treatises comprise Nichiren's major writings. Along with 230 letters collected in his *Gosho* (Sacred Writings) these serve as scripture for Nichiren Buddhism. Nichiren is also believed to have created the original Object of Worship, the *gohonzon*, a calligraphic inscription on wood of the invocation, *namu myōhō renge kyō*. The Nichiren Shū claims it is enshrined at their headquarters temple at Mount Minobu, while the Nichiren Shōshu claims it for theirs at Taisekiji.

Again Nichiren was pardoned on 13 Mar. 1274. During this final stage of his career, he set out to establish 'Vulture Peak', the mythical mountain where the historical Buddha, Śākyamuni, is said to have delivered the teachings of the *Lotus Sūtra*. Nichiren believed the earthly form of Vulture Peak was in Japan, and he selected Mount Fuji (*Fujisan) as the site, and established a temple, Kuonji, nearby on Mount Minobu.

Nichiren died on 13 Oct. 1282, at the home of a patron named Uemondayū Munenaka Ikegami. According to Nichiren Shū teaching, Nichiren's remains are now enshrined at Mount Minobu. For subsequent developments, see NICHIREN SHŪ. See also Index, Nichiren.

Nichiren Shōshū. Japanese Buddhist religious movement. When *Nichiren died, his followers agreed that the guardianship of his tomb should circulate among his six senior disciples. When the turn came of Nikō (1253–1314, priest of the Kuonji temple) he declared that he and his successors would take the responsibility permanently. Nichikō (1246–1332) broke away and founded the Daisekiji temple at the foot of Mount Fuji to defend the true teaching of Nichiren. Against the other five, he maintained that the two halves of the **Lotus Sūtra* are not equal in importance: the second half (the Honmon, fourteen chapters which reveal the eternal nature of the *Buddha) are a superior wisdom to the first half (the Jakumon, fourteen chapters which deal with the form taken by the Buddha in order to accommodate himself to human understanding). The Nichiren Shōshū reveres Nichiren as the religious founder (*shūso*) but Nichikō as the true sect founder (*haso*). It believes that in the *mappō (degenerate age), only Nichiren can provide any help (thus relegating the historical Buddha to second place), and that the government should endorse Nichiren Shōshū and establish it as the state religion—a principle known as 'politics united with Buddhism', *ōbutsu myōgō*. As with other Nichiren movements, the *nembutsu is central and of paramount importance.

Nichiren Shū. A collection of Japanese Buddhist sects in the *Mahāyāna tradition which trace their origins to the 13th-cent. *Tendai monk *Nichiren, who sought to restore what he considered to be the orthodox teachings of the historical *Buddha, *Śākyamuni. Next to the *Jōdo Shū (Pure Land Schools), the Nichiren tradition has the largest numbers of devotees of all religions in Japan today. There are currently, according to the *Shūkyō Nenkan* (Yearbook of Religions), eighteen Nichiren Buddhist sects and nineteen Nichiren-related 'new religions' such as *Reiyūkai, *Risshō Kōseikai, Myōshikai Kyōdan, *Sōka Gakkai, *Nichiren Shōshū.

Nicholas (Nikolaos) Cavasilas (Greek Orthodox theologian): see CAVASILAS.

Nicholas of Cusa or **Cusanus** (*c*.1400–64). German Christian philosopher. He was made a *cardinal and was briefly *vicar-general of Rome. As a philosopher he was a late *Neoplatonist, indebted to Meister *Eckhart. The two fundamental principles of his thought are *docta ignorantia* ('learned ignorance'—the furthest the human mind can reach) and the *coincidentia oppositorum* ('coincidence of opposites'), which is found in God who is at once transcendent and immanent, the centre and circumference of the universe, the infinite and the infinitesimal, and therefore beyond the grasp of the human intellect. This position was defended in his most famous work, *De Docta Ignorantia*. He is often regarded as a precursor of the Renaissance.

Nicodemus of the Holy Mountain, the Hagiorite (*c*.1749–1809). Greek monk and spiritual writer. Born in Naxos, he became a monk on Mount *Athos in 1775. He was immensely prolific in editing and publishing traditional monastic texts on spiritual, ascetic, and liturgical subjects, and a great advocate of the *Jesus prayer and frequent *communion. His most important work, with Macarius of Corinth, was the **Philokalia* (1782), an anthology of spiritual texts treasured by the *hesychasts.

Nicolai, Père (1836–1912). Russian *Orthodox pioneer *missionary to Japan, raised to *archbishop in 1906. Nicolai, whose personal name was Ivan Kasatkin, was the pioneer leader in what has been called the most spectacular achievement in the long history of Russian missionary work. The unique aspect of this work lay in Nicolai's making an almost complete separation from Russian political aims or interests its basic working principle.

Nicolai arrived in Japan on 2 June 1861 to serve as chaplain of the Russian consulate in Hakodate. His proficiency in Japanese and growing understanding of the people and their culture enabled the Orthodox Mission to become indigenized quickly and to raise up Japanese leaders of distinction. By these methods Nicolai and his colleagues, Russian and Japanese, were able to hold together the growing Japanese Orthodox Church even through the intense strains of the Russo-Japanese War of 1904–5.

Nidāna (link in chain): see PATICCA-SAMUPĀDA.

Niddah (Heb., 'menstruating woman'). The Jewish laws relating to menstruating women. Seventh tractate of the order Tohorot of the *Mishnah. The laws are numerous and complicated, but are considered essential to a pure family life. The *Reform movement has rejected the laws of Niddah in their entirety.

Niddesa (part of Buddhist Pāli canon): see KHUDDAKA-NIKĀYA.

Niddui (Separation): see ḤEREM.

Nidi dhyāsana (Skt., 'contemplate'). Third and culminating component of meditation in *Vedānta, leading to spiritual knowledge. The first is *śravaṇa*, hearing and reading scripture; second is *manana*, reflection and assimilation of the first; third is the integration of both through meditation.

Niebuhr, Reinhold (1892–1971). Christian theologian, reflecting especially on social and political issues. After twenty-three years in a Detroit working-class church, he moved to Union Theological Seminary in New York, where he became professor of Christian ethics, remaining there until his retirement. *Moral Man and Immoral Society* (1932) already anticipated his Gifford Lectures, *The Nature and Destiny of Man* (1941–3). What he looked for was 'a combination of moral resoluteness about the immediate issues with a religious awareness of another dimension of meaning and judgement', thereby grounding politics in realism about human frailty.

Nieh-pan. Chin. for *nirvāna.

Niemöller, Martin (1892–1984). German pastor and *Confessing Church leader. He was a submarine commander in the First World War, and later a pastor in Dahlem, a suburb of Berlin. He formed the Pastors' Emergency League to resist the Nazi takeover of church life, and this formed one basis for the Confessing Church. As an outspoken preacher against the regime, Niemöller was arrested by the Gestapo in 1937 and only freed from concentration camps in 1945. Into his 80s he remained an active leader of the Christian peace movement.

Nien-fo (Chin.; Jap., *nembutsu*). The foremost religious practice in the *Pure Land schools of Buddhism: see NEMBUTSU.

Nietzsche, Friedrich Wilhelm (1844–1900). Philosopher and literary figure who, although German, preferred to be called a 'European'. He indicted Christianity as 'the one great curse, the one intrinsic depravity, the one immortal blemish upon humankind'. He attacked on several fronts: (i) like all religions, it is a narcotic to protect people from fear of unknown forces; (ii) theistic explanation has been made unnecessary by the rise of science, and theistic belief has become 'unbelievable'; (iii) Christian values are anti-human and hostile to life, being fit only for slaves or the weak and inadequate. I will say to Death, "Right on! The same again!" ' His major works are *The Birth of Tragedy* (1872), *Human, All Too Human* (1878), and *Beyond Good and Evil* (1886).

Nigama (dialogue in Tantra): see TANTRA.

Niggunim (Ḥasidic chants): see MUSIC.

Night Journey (of Muḥammad): see MIʿRĀJ.

Night of power (night in month of Ramaḍān): see LAYLAT AL-QADR.

Nigoda. Minute, single-celled, living beings which, according to Jains, pervade the universe. Their presence makes the Jain commitment to *ahiṁsā (non-violence) even more scrupulous than in other Indian religions.

Nihaṅg (Pañjābī, 'without anxiety'). Militant core of Sikh *Khālsā. Nihaṅg *Siṅghs arose in the time of Gurū *Gobind Siṅgh whose *Dasam Granth they particularly revere. Nihaṅgs are distinguishable by their dark blue shirt and tall, tightly tied *turban, surrounded by a steel ring. As well as the *Five Ks they carry steel weapons. For Nihaṅgs iron/steel symbolizes God's might. Cannabis is used to aid meditation.

Nihilism (Lat., *nihil*, 'nothing'). The view that positive claims (in metaphysics, ethics, epistemology, religion, etc.) are false; or (in its own way more positively) that oblivion awaits humans after death and the cosmos in due course. 'Nihilism' is used of a belief refuted by Buddhism. In *Theravāda, it is the false belief that the self is identical with the body-mind continuum and therefore perishes completely at death (Pāli, *uccheda-diṭṭhi*). In *Mahāyāna it is the false belief that nothing exists at all (Skt., *uccheda-dṛṣṭi*) or that reality is an illusion (Skt., **māyā*). The opposite is *Eternalism.

Nihil obstat (Lat., 'nothing obstructs'). The approval in *Roman Catholicism granted by the officially appointed censor to books requiring permission before being published. The nihil obstat precedes and is required for the *imprimatur.

Nihongi or ***Nihonshoki*** (Jap.). Chronicle of Japan, the first of the six histories (*rikkokushi*). In 681 the emperor Temmu appointed Prince Kawashima, his nephew, and eleven men to compile an official version of the imperial genealogy and ancient records, and it is commonly believed that this was the initial stage of the making of the *Nihongi*. The work, written in Chinese, was compiled in 720.

The *Nihongi* seems to have been written in response to the need for an official chronicle equal to the Chinese historical records. The Chinese view of the sage king became a model for instituting the Japanese monarchic system with a major modification. The Japanese monarchic system was based on the continuance of the imperial lineage, which excluded the Chinese view of changing rulership by means of revolution. The unbroken imperial lineage was extended far into the mythological age by historicizing myth.

Nihon Jōka Ryōhō. Early form of *Sekai Kyūseikyō.

Niiname-sai (Jap., 'festival of new food'). In *Shinto, an important annual rite celebrated by the emperor in the eleventh month in which he makes an offering of the newly harvested rice to the *kami of heaven and earth and partakes of the rice offering in communion with the kami. In recent times the day on which the niiname-sai is held, 23 Nov., has been designated as a new national holiday, Labour Thanksgiving Day (*Kinrō Kansha no Hi*). A popular expression of the imperial niiname-sai is the widely celebrated autumn festival (*aki matsuri*) in which the people gather at the shrines to offer thanks to the kami for an abundant harvest.

Nijūshi-ryu (Jap., '24 currents'). The twenty-four Zen schools or traditions in Japan. They include the three major divisions, *Rinzai, *Sōtō, and *Obaku, and also the divisions of Rinzai usually named after the monastery where they began.

Nikāḥ (marriage contract): see MARRIAGE (ISLAM).

Nikāya (Pāli, 'body'). A collection of works within the 'baskets' (*piṭaka*) of the Buddhist Pāli canon. Thus the *Sūtra-piṭaka contains five nikāyas: Dīgha, Majjhima, Saṃyutta, Aṅguttara, and Khuddaka. It may also be a 'body' of *bhikṣus (monks), and is so used of sects or schools in the *saṅgha.

Nikō (Japanese leader of sect): see NICHIREN SHŌSHŪ.

Nikodemos of the Holy Mountain: see NICODEMUS.

Nikolai (Kasatkin), Père (Russian Orthodox missionary): see NICOLAI, PÈRE.

Nikon or **Nikita Minin** (1605–81). Orthodox patriarch of Moscow, 1652–8. He was a married parish priest, with three children. But when the children died, he went, with the agreement of his wife, into monastic solitude. He was drawn back into ecclesiastical life by the support of the Tsar, but continued the pursuit of reform when he was made patriarch, thereby creating the fierce resistance of the *Old Believers. He fell out of favour with the Tsar and resigned. He made an attempt to return to office, but was imprisoned. When at last he was invited to return to Moscow, he died before he could get there. He remains deeply respected (except by descendants of the Old Believers) as one of the greatest of the patriarchs for his reforms.

Nil(us) Sorsky, St (leader of Non-Possessors movement): see POSSESSORS.

Niʿmat Allāh Walī, Shāh Nūr al-Dīn (*c*.1331–1431 (AH 731–834)). Founder of the Niʿmatullahi *Sūfī order, one of the few *Shiʿite Muslim orders which has had a continuing history. He was dissatisfied with his traditional education and set off in search of an enlightened teacher, whom he found in Shaykh Yāfiʿī. He remained with him for seven years. He then set out on extensive travels, recognized as the *qutb (spiritual centre) of his age. He settled in Kirman in Iran, where he died and where his tomb is a centre of pilgrimage. At the heart of his way was his instruction to keep the name of God constantly in mind, since this would lead to actions imitative of God, especially mercy and generosity.

The Niʿmatullahi Order has houses in the USA, and in London. It continues to see contemplation as a basis for ethical action and reconciliation in the world.

Niʿmatullāhi (Sūfī order): see NIʿMAT ALLĀH WALĪ, SHĀH NŪR AL-DĪN.

Nimbārka (11th/12th cent. CE). Indian philosopher of the near-*dvaita (Bhedābheda) Vedānta tradition, and founder of the *Vaiṣṇava sect devoted to Rādhā-Kṛṣṇa; followers are known as Nimbārkas. Nimbārka's own views are preserved mainly in his commentary on the *Vedānta Sūtra*, *Vedānta-Parijāta-Saurabha*.

Nimbus: see HALO.

Nimitta (Pāli, Skt.). In Buddhism, variously translated as 'outward aspect', 'general appearance', 'perceived object', 'mark', 'image', 'sign', 'omen'. Its five most significant usages are as follows.

1. In canonical Buddhism, the outward aspect or general appearance of an object; that aspect which we find attractive (*abhijjhā*) or repulsive (*domanassa*) when our senses perceive things.

2. In meditation, the perceptual objects used for contemplation (*kammaṭṭhāna) are referred to as nimitta because they function as a mark, sign, or image on which the eye and mind focus their attention.

3. According to the Pāli Commentaries (*Aṭṭhakathā*), at the last moment of consciousness before death the sign of previous *karma (*kamma-nimitta*) together with the sign of future destiny (*gati-nimitta*) arise as mental objects, as an indication of that person's impending rebirth.

4. It is the term for the 'signs' or 'omens' of old age, sickness, death, and the wandering mendicant which, according to legend, convinced the Buddha to leave home and lead the ascetic life.

5. In the Yogacārya (*Vijñānavāda) branch of Buddhism, it is the term for the perceived object, which has no existence independently of the perceiver but is merely a representation of his inner consciousness.

Ninety-nine beautiful names of God. The names of *Allāh in Islam, most of which are taken or derived from the *Qur'ān. There are several different lists, and while each list contains ninety-nine names, there are variations in the lists. The names are called *al-asmā' al-ḥusnā*, from 7. 179. The names are divided into two categories, those of essence (*al-dhat*) and those of quality (*al-ṣifāt*). They are also divided into the names of mercy and the names of majesty (or judgement), *al-jamāl wa'l-jalāl*.

Ninigi. The grandson of the *Shinto deity *Amaterasu, and an important figure in the mythologies of the founding of Japan. He also represents an important motif of descent in Shinto: throughout Shinto, the kami are thought to descend from high places (sky, mountains, etc.) in order to bring their power, authority, and benefits.

Ninomiya Sontoku (founder of Japanese religious movement): see HŌTOKU.

Ninth of Av (Heb., *Tishah be-Av*). Jewish fast day, which commemorates the destruction of the first and second *Temples in 586 BCE and 70 CE.

Nippon (origin of the sun): see MOTOORI NORINAGA.

Nipponzan Myōhōji. A Japanese Buddhist revival movement, founded in 1917 by Fujii Nichidatsu (1884–1985), based on the teachings of *Nichiren. It is therefore also known as the Movement of the Wondrous Law of the Lotus Sūtra. Its basic practice is the repetition of the name of the *Lotus Sūtra*. It organizes marches for peace, and builds peace *pagodas throughout the world (in the UK at Milton Keynes and in Battersea Park). Fujii's book, *Beating Celestial Drums*, reflects the practice of beating the drum of heaven to extend the reverberations of peace.

Nirang (ritual cow's urine): see NAUJOTE.

Nirañjan (Pañjābī, 'without darkness, untinged'). Sikh epithet for God. The *Gurūs so describe God to show his total purity and freedom from *māyā.

Niraṅkār (Pañjābī, 'formless one'). Sikh name for God.

Niraṅkārī. Sikh reform movement, regarded as a sect by mainstream Sikhs. Niraṅkārīs emphasize reliance on the will of God, *Niraṅkār. Despite the injunctions of their founder, Dayāl Dās (1783–1855), he and his successors, Darbārā Siṅgh, Hārā Siṅgh, and Gurbakhsh Siṅgh, are venerated as *Gurūs in succession to *Gobind Siṅgh. Like the *Nāmdhārīs, the Niraṅkārīs originated as a 19th-cent. renewal of true Sikhism. Dayāl Dās called Sikhs to worship Niraṅkār, rejecting idol-worship, *brahmanical birth- and death-ritual, and pilgrimage to *Hardwār. Sant Niraṅkārīs are a separate movement often confused with Niraṅkārīs. In 1978, following clashes between Sant Niraṅkārīs and followers of Jarnail Siṅgh *Bhindrānawāle, a *hukamnāmā was issued from the *Akāl Takht, bidding all Sikhs to boycott the Sant Niraṅkārīs.

Niraya (state of punishment and torment): see NARAKA.

Nirbīja (without seed, a stage in samādhi): see ASAMPRAJÑĀTA.

Nirguṇ (Pañjābī, 'without qualities'). In the *Ādi Granth, *Brahman (God) is described as nirguṇ, i.e. abstract, lacking attributes. However, as creator, the immanent source of all qualities, he is also *saguṇ, endowed with attributes.

Nirguṇa-Brahman (Skt., 'Brahman without qualities'). The term in Vedānta Hinduism for the Absolute and indescribable nature of *Brahman, in contrast to *saguṇa Brahman. For explication, see ŚAṄKARA.

Nirmalā (Pañjābī, 'spotless, pure'). A learned, *quietist Sikh group. They are *celibate, follow distinctive rules, and live in *monasteries called *akhāṛās* (literally, 'wrestling arenas').

Nirmāṇa-kāya (Buddha in human form): see TRIKĀYA.

Nirodha (Skt., *ni* + *rodha*, 'obstruction'). 1. In Hinduism, the state of intense concentration in which the distinction of subject and object is destroyed, so that the mind attains realization of non-duality.

2. In Buddhism, the cessation of *dukkha (the third of the Four Noble Truths); it is thus also equated with *nirvāna.

Nirodha-samāpatti. In Buddhism, the cessation of mental activity as a consequence of *meditation practices of specific and well-tested kinds.

Nirṛti. Evil, misery, dissolution and decay, personified in Hinduism as a Goddess.

Nirupadhiśeṣa-nirvāṇa (Skt.; Pāli, *anupadisesa-nibbāna*). *Nirvāna with no lingering conditions remaining—as opposed to nirvāna which is attained, but with residual shadows of previous existence still continuing. The latter condition means that the *Buddha can be completely enlightened, but his bodily appearance continues, so that he can, for example, teach others. *Parinirvāṇa* is then the attainment of complete nirvāna at death (though *parinirvāṇa* can also mean nirvāna before death, hence the present term). Cf., but contrast, the *Mahāyāna *pratiṣṭhita-nirvāna.

Nirvāna (Skt., 'extinction'; Chin., *nieh-pan*; Jap., *nehan*; Korean, *yŭlban*). The final goal and attainment in Indian religions.

In Hinduism, nirvāna is the extinguishing of worldly desires and attachments, so that the union with God or the Absolute is possible. In *Bhagavad-gītā*, it seems to be contrasted deliberately with the Buddhist understanding, because it is described as the attainment of *Brahman, and the yogin is described, not (as in Buddhism) as a candle blown out, but as 'a candle flame away from a draught which does not flicker' (6. 19). The attainment of nirvāna is thus *mokṣa.

In Buddhism there is no Self or soul to attain any state or union after death. Nirvāna (Pāli, *nibbāna*) therefore represents the realization that that is so. It is the condition of absolute cessation of entanglement or attachment, in which there is, so to speak, that state of cessation, but no interaction or involvement. Thus *nibbuta* (past participle) is 'he who is cooled', i.e. from the fever of clinging and thirst (*tanhā). It does not mean 'extinction', a view which the Buddha repudiated (*nihilism). That is why nirvāna can receive both negative (what it is not) and positive (what it is like) descriptions. The so-called 'Nirvāna School' of early (5th-cent.) Chinese Buddhism, stressed the positive aspects of nirvāna, and regarded it as an eternal and blissful condition. The final attainment of the state of nirvāna, with no residues remaining (of involvement in the appearance of this world) is pari (complete) nirvāna.

Nirvāna school: see NIRVĀNA.

Nirvikalpa-samādhi: see VIKALPA.

Niśān Sāhib (Pañjābī, 'flag' + 'respected'). Flag indicating a Sikh *gurdwārā. The Niśān Sāhib is triangular and usually saffron-coloured, bearing a black *khaṇḍā in the centre.

Nishida Kitarō (1870–1945). Leading Japanese Buddhist philosopher and founder of the Kyōto school of philosophy. He assimilated W. philosophy and created his own distinctive philosophical system based largely upon Buddhist religious thought. In 1911 he published his first work, *A Study of Good* (*Zen no kenkyū*), which was to become the most widely read philosophical book written by a Japanese. Then with his work, *Hataraku mono kara miru mono e* (From the Acting to the Seeing, 1927), Nishida began systematically building up his concept of 'place' (*basho*), the self-identity of 'absolute Nothingness' from which the individual reality of everything could be derived. In the world of human reality, through religious experience we enter into 'absolute nothingness', the final determination and field of everything.

Nishkam Sēwak Jathā. Sikh reform movement. It was founded by Sant Puran Siṅgh (who lived at Kericho in Kenya, hence his other name, Kerichowale Bābā, d. 1983). He encouraged a return to the elementary conditions of *gurmat, especially the avoidance of alcohol and the practice of *nām simaran.

Nīti-śāstras. Indian *śāstras that concern *ethics and wise or prudent behaviour. They are told mainly through stories and narratives, but particularly important maxims are encapsulated in verse.

Nitnem (Pañjābī, 'daily rule, prayer'). Sikh daily prayer. They are available in *guṭkās (manuals).

Nitya (Skt., 'enduring'). In Hinduism, the Absolute. One united with the Absolute is known as nitya-*mukta; one who is thus united but returns to birth for the sake of others (cf. *bodhisattva) is called nitya-siddha (an example is *Nārada). Nitya is the Absolute at rest, in contrast to *līlā, through which manifestation occurs.

Nīvaraṇas (Pāli, 'hindrances'). In Buddhism, mental and emotional factors which hinder the acquisition of knowledge and insight. There are five: (i) sensuous desire (*kāmacchanda*); (ii) anger (*vyācada*); (iii) sloth and torpor (*thīna-middha*); (iv) excitability and anxiety (*uddhacca-kukkucca*); (v) doubt (*vicikicchā*).

Nivedita, Sister (1867–1911). Hindu nationalist and nun, originally Miss Margaret Noble. As Sister Nivedita, she became a disciple of Swami *Vivekānanda after meeting him in London. On moving to India, she joined the Ramakrishna Mission, and devoted herself to social work, notably in Calcutta. Immediately after the death of Swami Vivekānanda she left the Ramakrishna Mission, in order to be free to devote herself to the service of India.

Nivṛtti (Skt.). Return, rest, especially in Hinduism the return of manifestation to its source in *Brahman.

Niwano Nikkyō (co-founder of RKK): see RISSHŌ KŌSEI KAI.

Niyama (Skt., 'restraint'). 1. In Hinduism, the second 'limb' of 'eight-limbed' (*aṣṭaṇga) or *rāja *yoga concerning self-discipline to help purify the mind of impediments (*kleśa).

2. In Buddhism, the constraints which control eventualities into their outcomes: (i) *bīja-niyama, biological or hereditary constraints; (ii) mano- or *citta-niyama, unwilled operations of the mental order; (iii) *karma-niyama, the consequences of volitional dispositions; (iv) uti-niyama, constraints in the physical environment; (v) *dharma-niyama, constraints derived from the transcendental order. From these, it will be seen that events cannot be construed as the simple working out of karma, as though all eventualities must have a preceding karmic cause.

Niyya (Arab., 'intention'). The 'intention' which must be pronounced before carrying out a religious observance, in order to make it valid in Islamic religious law.

Niẓām al-Mulk (ruling Muslim adviser): see WAZĪR.

Nizārī (Ismāʿīlī sect): see ISMĀʿĪLĪYA; ASSASSINS.

Noachide laws. The seven laws believed by Jews to be obligatory for everyone. The Noachide laws are based on those given to *Adam (Genesis 2. 16) and *Noah (*Gen.R.* 34). They are prohibitions against *idolatry, *blasphemy, sexual sins, murder, theft, and eating from a living animal, as well as the injunction to formulate a legal system. According to the *sages, a Jew is obliged to keep the whole *Torah, while every *gentile who keeps the Noachide laws is a *ger-toshav* ('resident stranger'). Maimonides taught that such a *ḥasid (righteous person) has a share in the world to come.

Noah. Survivor of the great flood in the Hebrew scriptures. According to Genesis, Noah was commanded to save himself, his family, and a breeding pair of each animal species in a wooden *ark. After surviving the flood, Noah offered sacrifices to God who blessed him and made a *covenant (see NOACHIDE LAWS) with him (Genesis 6. 9–9. 17).

Nobili, Roberto de (Christian Jesuit missionary): see DE NOBILI, ROBERTO.

Noble savage (Rousseau's concept of 'primitive simplicity'): see IBN TUFAYL.

Nō drama (Jap., *nōgaku*, *nohgaku*; 'skill music' or 'skill entertainment'). A highly sophisticated dance, music, dramatic form with important religious connections to all the religions of premodern Japan (from *c.*14th cent. when most plays in the classical repertoire were written).

Nō attained its classical form through the work of Kan'ami Kiyotsugu (1333–84) and his son, Zeami Motokiyo (1363–1443), who also wrote a number of treatises concerning the art of Nō. Many of Zeami's aesthetic categories and his conception of artistic discipline are linked with Buddhist notions and practices. Plays are roughly classified into five categories: (i) god plays, (ii) warrior plays, (iii) woman plays, (iv) madness plays, and (v) demon plays. The plays are typically dramatizations of pilgrimages or journeys to temples, shrines and other sacred places.

Noh (type of Japanese drama): see NŌ DRAMA.

Nominalism and realism. A philosophical debate with implications both for theology and religion. In the West, the debate goes back to Greek philosophy: what is truly real, individuals or universals? Nominalism argued that individuals are real (this particular book before me) and that universals (the idea of 'books') are concepts abstracted from our experience of individuals. Realists held that particular books come and go, but that the idea of 'books' endures while particular individuals do not; thus the idea is more real than the items illustrating it. Theological nominalism (see e.g. WILLIAM OF OCKHAM) held that the pure Being of God is real, and that attributes are equivalent to universals, being conceptual abstractions which organize our limited apprehension of God (enabling us to say *something*, however inadequate), but having no corresponding reality in God. This position reinforces *apophatic theology. Theological realism accepts the approximate and limited nature of human language, but argues that the perfections of God are revealed in the ways in which God is related to the universe of his creation, and to humans in particular. But for that revealed relatedness not itself to be simply a human construction, the inference must be drawn that the ground for the possibility of God being revealed in that way lies in the nature of God *a se* (in himself, i.e. in his aseity): the perfections endure even when the creatures who dimly apprehend them come and go. In E. religions, the issue arises out of *avidyā, ignorance. Is the appearance of reality something which humans superimpose on that which is the cloak of what alone is truly real, or do the particulars have some enduring reality (see e.g. ŚANKARA; RĀMĀNUJA; MADHVA)? Is there some reality in the particulars of this (albeit transitory) cosmos, or is every manifestation devoid of characteristics, being simply a manifestation of the only nature that there is, i.e. the buddha-nature (see ŚŪNYATĀ)?

Nomothetic ambition. The attempt (characteristic of work in the 19th cent.) to find laws, comparable to those of the natural sciences, governing social and individual behaviour, including religion.

Non-Church movement (Japanese Protestant movement): see UCHIMURA.

Nonconformists. Members of *Protestant churches in England outside the *Church of England. They are otherwise known as *Free Churches.

Non-Jurors: see DIVINE RIGHT OF KINGS.

Non-official religion: see FOLK RELIGION.

Non-violence (in Indian religions): see AHIṀSĀ.

Norito (Jap., probably 'words stated with awe'). In *Shinto, sacred words and prayers expressed in elegant ancient Japanese and addressed to the *kami in Shinto worship. The use of norito is related to the traditional belief in spiritual power residing in beautiful and correctly spoken words (*koto-dama). The earliest norito texts are in *Engi-shiki*, a law book compiled in the 10th cent. CE. Typical norito give praise of the kami, make reference to the origin of the specific rite or festival, express thanksgiving to the kami, report to or petition the kami, enumerate the offerings presented, identify the persons on whose behalf the prayers are recited and the priests who are reciting them, and finally add some parting words of respect and awe.

North end. The end of the communion table from which in some Anglican churches the priest celebrates the *eucharist, eliminating any hint that the celebrant is a sacrificing *priest.

Northern Kingdom: see ISRAEL.

Northern school (of Zen Buddhism): see SOUTHERN AND NORTHERN SCHOOLS.

Notarikon. System of exegetical abbreviation used by Jews. Either each letter in a word is thought to stand for a whole word, or a word is divided into shorter components with separate meanings.

Not-returner (Buddhist on third stage of path to attainment): see ANĀGĀMIN.

Novatian (d. 257/8). Leader of a *schism in the Latin Church. He was a Roman presbyter and author of an important work *On the Trinity*. He joined the rigorists who rejected concessions to the *lapsi, and was consecrated rival bishop of Rome. He was martyred in the persecution under Valerian.

Novena. In the *Roman Catholic Church, continuous prayer, private or public, either on nine consecutive days, or once a week for nine weeks.

Nubūwah (Arab.). The office of prophecy (i.e. of being a *nabī) in Islam.

Nü-kua. Chinese female deity, who created human figures from yellow earth, but when she grew bored with this activity, she dipped a rope in the mud, swung it about and thus produced the poor (in contrast to the rich and well-endowed). She also instituted marriage.

Numbers (hidden meanings): see GEMATRIA; Index, Numbers.

Numbers, Book of. Fourth book of the *Pentateuch in the Hebrew scriptures and in the Christian Old Testament. Numbers is known in Hebrew from its first word *Be-Midbar*, 'in the wilderness'.

Numinous (derived by R. *Otto from Lat., *numen*, 'divinity'). The non-rational elements in what is experienced in religions as the 'Holy'. Experience of the numinous is of a *mysterium tremendum fascinans et augustum*. As *mysterium*, the *numen* is revealed as a 'wholly other'. As *tremendum*, it generates boundless awe and wonder in the person who experiences it. As *fascinans*, it entrances and captivates the individual. It is of supreme subjective value for humans and possesses in itself objective value (*augustum*).

For Otto, the whole course of the history of religions is determined by an evolving apprehension of the fundamental elements of the numinous. It is therefore held to be the core of all religion.

Nun. A member of a religious order of women. The term is technically used of Christian women who belong to a religious order with solemn vows, but it is used more loosely in practice, and is applied at times to women in orders in other religions—e.g. to bhikṣunīs in Buddhism (see BHIKṢU).

Nunc Dimittis. The song of the old man Simeon (Luke 2. 29–32). The name comes from the opening words in Latin.

Nuncio or **apostolic nuncio.** A representative (with status of ambassador) of the *pope, appointed initially to the countries which were signatories to the Convention of Vienna in 1815. He is usually a titular archbishop.

Nūr (Arab.). Light, and especially *Allāh as the source of light (Qur'ān 24. 35). The cultivation of the vision of God through the contemplation of light became a widespread practice, particularly among *Sūfīs.

Nūrbakhshīy(y)a. Religious movement in Islam, named after its founder, Muḥammad b. Muḥammad b. ʿAbd Allāh, who was known as Nūrbakhsh ('gift of light'), and who lived 1393–1465 (AH 795–869). He was proclaimed caliph (*khalīfa) and *al-Mahdī by his followers. He maintained a *Sūfī understanding of the world as manifestation of God, and a *Shiʿite insistence on the necessity for the true *Imām to be a descendant of *ʿAlī.

Nūr Muḥammadī (Pers. abbr. of Arab., 'light of Muḥammad'). The essential nature of *Muḥammad which was created before the creation of the world, and is thus something akin to 'the pre-existent prophet'. For the Shiʿites, the belief lent itself to the continuing inspiration of the *Imāms, who share in the nature of the Prophet through the dispensation of his illumination.

Nusaḥ or **nosaḥ** (Heb., 'arrangement'). Musical term in Jewish *liturgy. The term is used both in the sense of 'traditional tunes', and as signifying a particular musical mode.

Nuṣairī or **Alawī.** An extreme *Shıʿa sect, strongly influenced by *Ismāʿīlīs and Christianity. Mainly found in N. Lebanon, Syria, and S. Turkey, they number over a million, maintaining a tribe-like lineage system. The Nuṣairī believe that *ʿAlī is the supreme manifestation of God, that the *Qur'ān is an initiation to devotion to ʿAlī, and that ʿAlī, *Muḥammad, and *Salmān al-Farsī (identified with the archangel *Gabriel) are a trinity. Their tenets are mostly secret, for they practice an initiatory rite which lays importance on *ta'wīl (allegorical interpretation) of Qur'ān. The Nuṣairī employ *taqīya (dissimulation). Since the 1980s the Nuṣairı have become powerful in Syrian politics. Hafez Assad, a Nuṣairī, rose to become leader of Syria over a *Sunnī majority.

Nyāntiloka (1878–1957). A German Buddhist scholar and translator. Apart from editions and translations, his most influential works were a *Buddhist Dictionary*, *The Word of the Buddha*, and *Path to Deliverance*.

Nyāsa. The ritual placing of *mantras or letters on the body through touch and visualization, thereby making the body divine and filling it with power (*śakti).

Nyāya (Skt., argumentation, that by which the mind is led to a conclusion). Logical proof or demonstration, the third (in addition to *śruti and *smṛti) means of religious *knowledge in Hinduism. More particularly, Nyāya is one of the six philosophical systems (*darśana) of Hinduism, based on logical argument and analysis. It is therefore also known as Hetuvidyā (the knowledge of causes), Vādavidyā (the knowledge of ways of demonstration), Pramāṇaśastra (discipline of logic and epistemology), etc. Its founder is held to be Gautama (known also as Gotama and Akṣapāda) to whom is attributed the major work of the school, *Nyāya-Sūtra* (*c*.3rd cent. BCE). Nyāya extends and develops *Vaiśeṣika (producing the form Nyāya-Vaiśeṣika), which is classed as *samānatantra*, a similar philosophy. Both accept that life is burdensome and full of pain and suffering, and that the true goal is liberation (*mokṣa) which can only be gained through right understanding—hence the stress on valid argument and demonstration. The purpose remains unequivocally religious: logic serves to lead to truth and thus to mokṣa, since the major impediment is *avidyā (ignorance). In the 12th cent., Nyāya was developed further into Navya-nyāya (New Logic), especially in the 14th-cent. *Tattvacintāmaṇi* of Gaṅgeśa. He reinforced the means of valid cognition (pramāṇa), resting on the four means of ascertaining truth: (i) *pratyakṣa*, sense perception; (ii) *anumāna*, inference, from cause to effect, from effect to cause and from common characteristics; (iii) *upamāna*, analogy; (iv) *śabda, verbal testimony from a reliable authority.

Nyingma (rnying.ma, 'ancient'). One of the four major schools of Tibetan Buddhism, so-called because its adherents trace their tradition to the first diffusion of Buddhism in Tibet, and particularly to the figure of *Padmasambhava, whom they consider their founder.

The Nyingma are noted for their separate canon, consisting of *terma literature and the *Compendium of Old *Tantras* (rnying.ma'i.rgyud.'bum). While the **Tibetan Book of the Dead* is the best known, the most important Nyingma text is the *Heart-Drop* (snying.thig); a terma text discovered in the 12th cent. by Zhangtön and commentated upon by Longchenpa, it contains teachings on Dzogchen (rdzogs.chen; 'Great Perfection'), the primary Nyingma system of meditation.

The Nyingma has produced several great scholars, such as Longchenpa (1308–63) and Mipham (d. 1912), who was influential in the 19th-cent. *Rimé movement. A recent supreme head of the order, Dujom Rinpoche (1904–87) was considered an incarnation of Dujom Lingpa. See Index, Nyingma.

Nyorai (Jap.; Skt., *tathāgata*). Synonym of *Buddha and one of his ten titles. The original Skt., *Tathāgata, can be analysed as 'coming' (*āgata*) from 'suchness' (*tathā*) or 'going' (*gata*) to 'suchness', suchness referring to truth or reality. Nyorai is the translation for the former, literally meaning 'coming from suchness', and, because of its dynamic connotation, it is preferred over its synonym, Buddha. Thus, in Japan people make reference to *Amida Nyorai, *Dainichi Nyorai, Shaka Nyorai, and so forth. Nyoraikyo is a Japanese *new religion, founded in 1802.

Nyūdō (home-living Buddhist under rule): see SHŌMU TENNŌ.

O

Oaths. A self-curse in Judaism which would be fulfilled if certain conditions were not met. Oath-taking was common in Ancient Israel. In *Talmudic law, oaths were used as a means of judicial proof in civil cases and could not be sworn by known liars, minors, the deaf and dumb, or the insane. Taking an oath involved holding the *Scroll of the Law and swearing by God or one of his attributes (*B.Shevu*. 38b). See also CURSING.

In Christianity, Matthew 5. 33–7 has been taken by some (e.g. *Baptists, *Mennonites, *Quakers, *Waldensians) to preclude any kind of oath-taking; but more generally it has been understood as a prohibition on swearing.

Obadiah, Book of. *Minor Prophet of the Hebrew scriptures and Christian Old Testament, the shortest book therein. The rabbis identified Obadiah with King Ahab's servant (1 Kings 18. 3–4), but this is unlikely.

Ōbaku Kiun (Ch'an/Zen master): see HUANG-PO HSI-YÜN.

Ōbaku-shū (Jap. pronunciation of 'Huang-po', a religious mountain in China where the school originated + *shū*, 'tradition', 'school', or 'teachings'). One of the three major schools of Japanese Zen Buddhism originating in China. Ōbaku-shū was introduced in the 17th cent. by Yin-yüan (1592–1673, Ingen in Japanese) and reflects the syncretism between the Zen and *Pure Land *nembutsu traditions characteristic of Ming China. Although not popular religiously, Ōbaku-shū has influenced Japanese culture by introducing late Ming artistic forms.

Oberammergau (Passion play): see PASSION.

Ōbutsu myōgō (politics united with Buddhism): see NICHIREN SHŌSHŪ.

Occam/Ockham (Ockham's Razor): see WILLIAM OF OCKHAM.

Occasionalism. The view that God is the direct creator by way of cause of all occasions (as held, e.g., by some Muslims); or that God is the occasioning intermediary between soul and body: when the soul consents to an action, God moves the body, and when the body makes a demand of any sort, God makes the soul aware of it.

Occultation: see HIDDEN IMĀM.

Oceanic experience. The experience, usually brief and completely unexpected, of being at one with the entire universe, and of feeling a deep meaning and purpose to every part of existence. It is often accompanied by feelings of compassion and love for all beings. See also BIOGENETIC STRUCTURALISM.

Oceanic religion. The religion of the Pacific region. The term is imprecise, but at least draws attention to the fact that migration and trade have produced some common features in the life and culture of the Pacific region, the main part of which is water, in which is set a large number of widely scattered islands. Generalizations about religion in so vast an area, with so many cultural variations, are impossible. G. W. Trompf observed of Melanesia: 'Melanesia has been revealed as the home of about one-third of mankind's languages, and that means —considering how languages are so crucial in defining discrete cultures—just as many religions' (*Melanesian Religion*, 1991). Nevertheless, the area has thrown up concepts which have been mediated via the *anthropology of religion into the study of religion in general: see e.g. MAGIC (for *mana*); TABOO.

Ocean of breath (location of human life energy according to Chinese religion): see CH'I.

Ockham (Christian philosopher): see WILLIAM OF OCKHAM.

Octave. The period of eight days beginning with a Christian feast (i.e. until the same day of the next week), during which it may continue to be celebrated.

Odium theologicum (Lat., 'theological hatred'). Phrase drawing attention to ill-tempered passions to which theological argument frequently gives rise.

Oecumenical. Archaic spelling of *ecumenical, now used almost exclusively in the title of the Oecumenical *Patriarch of Constantinople.

Offertory. In the Christian *eucharist the worshippers' offering of the bread and wine to be consecrated; also of gifts, especially of money.

Office, Divine (Lat., *Officium Divinum*). The daily prayers prescribed in liturgical churches in Christianity.

In the W., the arrangement of the monastic office goes back to St *Benedict, who named it the 'work of God' (*opus Dei*): in his Rule the offices comprise the 'day hours' (*lauds, *prime, terce, sext, none, *vespers, and *compline) and the 'night office' (*mattins); the whole Psalter was recited each week. In the Middle Ages this office became obligatory for secular clergy as well.

In the E., there is a similar sequence of hours to that of the W., of which the most familiar is Orthros (lauds). The whole office is of great length, and is abbreviated by all except monks in choir.

Office of Readings. An *office prescribed for Roman Catholics which may be said at any hour of the day. It includes two readings, one from the Bible and a second from the *fathers or from some other Christian writing. It replaced *mattins in the 1971 revision of the *Breviary.

Ofurikae (transference of affliction): see MIKI TOKUHARU.

Ogyū Sorai (1666–1728). Japanese Confucian scholar who laid, indirectly, the foundations for the School of National Learning (*Kokugaku). When 25, he started to give free lectures in Edo, in front of the temple of Zōjō-jī. *Itō Jinsai (1627–1705) had already argued for a return to the classic Confucian sources, in a school known as *Kogidō*, 'School for the Study of Ancient Meaning'. Ogyū followed him at first, but concluded that Itō had not gone far enough in making his study of the past serve the needs of society: he was right in criticizing the neo-Confucians, but he had remained, like them, too concerned with individual ethics and self-improvement. In his view, *Hsun Tzu was a better guide. Ogyū had a profound effect, because it was realized by his pupils that the antiquity of Japan could equally be studied and established as a court of appeal against the domination of Chinese thought.

Ōjo (Jap., 'birth'). Rebirth, especially in the *Pure Land of *Amida, but found also in many combinations, for example, ōjo-ko, a prayer-meeting for the practice of *nembutsu.

***Ōjōyōshū*.** A collection of scriptural quotations outlining religious practices that lead to birth in *Pure Land. It was compiled in 985 by the Japanese Buddhist priest *Genshin (942–1017) of the *Tendai school.

Okada Mokichi (founder of a Japanese religion): see SEKAI KYŪSEIKYŌ.

Oker Harim (uprooter of mountains): see RABBAH BAR NAḤMĀNĪ.

Ōkuninushi no Mikoto (Jap., 'great lord of the land'). An important *Shinto *kami. Originally a major local kami of Izumo Province (now Shimane Prefecture), he was incorporated into the national Shinto mythology by the time of the compilation of **Kojiki* (712), in which he plays a prominent part. The *Izumo no Kuni fudoki* (Gazetteer of Izumo Province, 733) shows that he was viewed in Izumo as the creator of the world and as an agricultural kami. The chief shrine to Ōkuninushi is the Izumo Taisha in Taishamachi, Shimane Prefecture, one of the oldest shrines in Japan.

'Olam ha-Ba (Heb., 'the coming world'). In Judaism, the hereafter, in contrast to *'olam ha-zeh*, 'this world'. See also AFTERLIFE.

Olcott, Henry Steel (co-founder of Theosophical Society): see THEOSOPHICAL SOCIETY.

Old Believers. Dissident groups of Russian Orthodox Christians. Because they have been in *schism (*raskol*) since 1666, they are known also as Raskolniki. The schism began when Nikon, patriarch of Moscow, introduced reforms of ritual. Penal laws remained in force until 1903. Under such continuing pressure, there were several divisions, but two main groups: the *popovtsy* (those with priests) and the *pezpopovtsy* (those without priests who resorted to less formal organization).

Old Catholics. Christians who adhere (according to the declaration of their *bishops in 1889) to the *Vincentian Canon, not in order to resist all change, but in order to guard against unwarranted innovation. The roots of the separation of Old Catholic Churches go back to the post-Reformation debates in the Netherlands: the *Jansenist Church of Utrecht retained the *apostolic succession after its separation from Rome in 1724 and was later able to supply valid consecration of bishops. The major breach occurred as a consequence of the *Vatican I proclamation of papal *infallibility. In 1889, the newly called Old Catholic Churches united in the Union of Utrecht. Old Catholics recognize the seven ecumenical *Councils and the teachings of the undivided Church before the *Great Schism of 1054.

Old Man of the Mountain (name for ruler of Syrian sect): see ASSASSINS.

Old Testament. Christian name for the Jewish scriptures (see TANACH) which form the first part of the *Bible. In Roman Catholic usage the *deuterocanonical books are included.

Olympian religion: see CHTHONIAN RELIGION.

Oṃ or **Auṃ.** The most sacred syllable in Hinduism, which first appears in the *Upaniṣads. It is often regarded as the *bija (seed) of all *mantras, containing, as it does, all origination and dissolution. It is known as *praṇava* ('reverberation'), and it is the supreme *akṣara* (syllable). See also ŚABDA.

OM.AH.HUM (Buddhist chant): see ĀDI BUDDHA.

O-mamori (Jap., *o* (honorific) + 'protection'). A Japanese amulet (*charms). The o-mamori is an object, often a small placard, emblem, or card in a talismanic case, obtained from shrines and temples for protection from evil and misfortune.

Omar Khayyam. Anglicized version of 'Umar al-Khayyām (1048–1125 (AH 439–*c*.519)). Muslim mathematician and astronomer who made important contributions to the development of algebra, but who is perhaps best known as a poet. He composed four-line verses (i.e. *rubā'iyyāt*, 'quatrains') which became known through the Eng. version of Edward Fitzgerald as *The Rubaiyat of Omar Khayyam*. Fitzgerald does not appear to have realized that the terms of the original verses are *Sūfī. Thus 'wine', far from being the one compensation which God has allowed in a hard world, is a common symbol of the recollection (*dhikr) of God (the most spectacular example is *al-Khamriyya*, the Wine Ode of the Sūfī, Ibn al-Fāriḍ; the tavern (*khanaqah*) is the assembly place of *derwishes.

Omega point: see TEILHARD DE CHARDIN; PROCESS THEOLOGY.

O-mei, Mount: see SAMANTABHADRA.

Omer (Heb., 'sheaf'). An offering brought to the *Temple on 16 Nisan in the Jewish religion. By extension 'Omer' became the name of the period between *Passover and *Shavu'ot. Traditionally the days of the omer are ones of semi-mourning which is associated with a plague that struck the disciples of R. *Akiva (*B.Yev.* 62b). *Lag Ba-Omer is celebrated on the thirty-third day, but the origins of this minor festival are obscure.

O-mi-t'o (Chin. for Amitābha): see AMIDA.

Oṃ maṇi padme hum (Tib. pron.: *Om maṇi pehme hung*). The *mantra of *Avalokiteśvara (Tib., Chenrezig). In spite of being the most well-known and commonly recited mantra of Tibet, where it is to be found inscribed everywhere, from homes to mountain passes and roadside rocks, it has been greatly misunderstood. Usual translations, such as 'Oh, the jewel is in the lotus' or 'hail to the jewel in the lotus', are misconceived. *Oṃ and hum are invocation syllables which require no translation; *maṇi ('jewel') is not a word but a stem, and therefore joins *padme* ('lotus') to make a single word, *maṇipadme* ('jewel-lotus') which is feminine and locative. This suggests a female deity being invoked, called Maṇipadmā, the problem being that no such deity is recorded anywhere. The usual translations may have no linguistic accuracy but they do closely express through the separation of the words jewel (male, form) and lotus (female, emptiness) a sense of the symbolism of opposites at the heart of manifestation in *Mahāyāna Buddhism. The possibility of the present form of the mantra being a corruption of its original Sanskrit cannot be dismissed.

Omnipotence. A characteristic of God in all theistic religions. It is especially prominent in Islam, where the power of God cannot be frustrated and where everything that is or that happens can only be or do so because he wills it. Theologians have introduced some qualifications in their attempts to define the extent of God's power: nearly all would rule out God's being able to do something self-contradictory, whilst many would say that God not only does not but also *cannot* do evil. God's omnipotence does not preclude his limiting or abdicating from his power on occasion. The so-called 'paradoxes of omnipotence' concern whether God can make a stone so heavy that he cannot lift it, can make a creature which he cannot subsequently control, and so on.

Ōmoto-kyō or **Omoto** (Teaching of the Great Origin and/or Foundation). A Japanese 'new religion'. The group traces its history from 1892 when its foundress, *Deguchi Nao (1837–1918), was possessed by the folk deity Ushitora-no-Konjin. Through this and later experiences of *kamigakari, she articulated a radical *millennarian world-view centred on this god. Following the failure of her *eschatological prophecies in 1905, her cult was reorganized by her son-in-law and co-founder, Deguchi Onisaburō (1871–1948). Onisaburō rejected Nao's more radical teachings in favour of his own nationalistic Shinto doctrines, modernization theories, and spiritualistic practices. Today, the group maintains headquarters at Kameoka and Ayabe in W. Kyoto prefecture and claims a national membership of 163,000. Although non-proselytizing, Ōmoto-kyō supports charitable activities abroad and participates in the international ecumenical and peace movements.

Oṃ tat sat (Skt., 'Oṃ That Being'). Hindu sacred formula (*mantra) often uttered at the beginning and the conclusion of prayers, or the recitation of a passage from the *Vedas and other religious literature.

Onanism. Coitus interruptus, unnatural sexual intercourse or masturbation. In the Jewish tradition, onanism is associated with the biblical figure Onan who was condemned by God for spilling his seed 'on the ground' (Genesis 38. 7–10).

Once-returner (Buddhist close to enlightenment): see SAKADĀGĀMIN.

One hand clapping: see HAKUIN.

One-pointedness (of mind): see EKĀGRATA.

One word barriers (single-word answers): see YÜN-MEN WEN-YEN.

Onias. Four Jewish *high priests of the second *Temple period. Onias I (4th cent. BCE) is mentioned in 1 *Maccabees* 12. 20–3; Onias II (late 3rd cent. BCE) was involved in the war between Ptolemy III and Queen Leodice; Onias III (2nd cent. BCE) was deposed by Antiochus IV; and Onias IV, son of Onias III, erected a temple in *Leontopolis.

Onkelos. Translator of the Hebrew *Bible into *Aramaic. Onkelos stays close to the Hebrew text, but its choice of words etc., shows that it is related to the Palestinian targum tradition with its incorporation of exegesis.

Onmyō-ji (yin-yang masters): see KOSHIN.

Ontic theories: see ONTOLOGY.

Ontological argument. An argument for God's existence, first formulated by *Anselm (1033–1109) in his *Proslogion*, chs. 2–3. Anselm argued that since anyone can think of 'a being than which no greater can be conceived', such a being must exist at least in the understanding; but if it existed only in the understanding, we could conceive of an even greater being, namely one existing both in the understanding and in reality; therefore, the being than which no greater can be conceived must exist both in the understanding and in reality. In ch. 3 he went on to argue that this being must exist necessarily.

Ontology (Gk., *ōn*, 'being', + *logos*, 'reflection'). Reflection in philosophy and metaphysics on what truly exists, or on what underlies appearance by way of existent reality. The term was introduced in the 17th cent., when the study of being as being was also called *ontosophia*. In the continuity of *scholasticism, ontology was the term applied to the study of the properties of being as such, in contrast to special metaphysics which studied aspects of being open to experience. W. V. O. Quine made a distinction between *ideology and ontology, and between meaning and reference: he argued that what one takes to be existing depends on the values required or allowed by the variables of the language in use, so that there is a necessary relation between language and ontic commitments—hence his claim that 'to be is to be the value of a variable'. While this might seem to allow virtually any belief to have an ontological correspondent, in fact metaphysical systems (which he called 'ontic theories') are tested by their compatibility with science which interacts publicly (and by various other criteria) with the world and universe around us. It then becomes obvious that ontology is intricately related to epistemology (roughly, how do we know what we know?).

Ontologism was a system of philosophy which, applied to theology, claimed that humans know God immediately and directly through natural cognitive abilities: the first act of human cognitive powers is the intuition of God. It was condemned (on the grounds that our knowledge of God can only be *analogical) in 1861 and again by *Vatican I.

Ontosophia: see ONTOLOGY.

Oomoto (Japanese new religion): see ŌMOTO-KYŌ.

Ophites (Gk., *ophis*, 'serpent'). A group of *gnostic sects. According to them the wise serpent (Genesis 3. 14 f.) symbolized a higher god, who acts to liberate humanity and give illumination. Some sects worshipped the serpent, regarding the *fall as God's denying of promised wisdom. They were also known as Naasenes.

Oppenheimer, Samuel: see COURT JEWS.

Option for Options: see SECULARIZATION.

Option for the Poor: see LIBERATION THEOLOGY.

Opus Dei (Lat., 'work of God'). Either the divine *office, especially as sung in choir; or (and now more commonly) a *Roman Catholic religious association founded in Madrid in 1928 by José Maria Escrivá de Balaguer, known more fully as the Priestly Society of the Holy Cross and the Work of God. Its status since 1982 has been that of a personal prelature, its superior exercising over members a similar authority to that of a *bishop, though not on a territorial basis. It has evoked criticism of its authoritarian style and control. Its founder was declared blessed by Pope John Paul II in 1992, despite widespread criticism in the Church of the style and speed with which this was done.

Oracle bones. Usually the scapula and split leg bones of cattle which the Chinese of the Shang dynasty used for divination purposes. Priests wrote out on the bones questions which the king or aristocrats wished to have put to the gods. They are by far the oldest examples of the Chinese writing system and furnish the only reliable information on the religion and social culture of the first Chinese *dynasty known to archaeology. A number of gods are mentioned, most notably the high god *Shang-ti and the gods of wind and of millet, of various heavenly bodies, of mountains and rivers. But the most important personages questioned in the Shang oracle bones were the *ancestors.

Oral law (Heb., *torah she-be'al-peh*). The (in origin) orally transmitted interpretation of the Jewish written *law. According to the *rabbis, there are two parts of *Torah 'one written and one oral' (*ARN* 15. 61). Traditionally both Torahs were given to *Moses on Mount *Sinai. Oral Torah was studied in the *academies and eventually collected together and written down by *Judah ha-Nasi in the 2nd cent. CE (see MISHNAH). Subsequently, commentary and interpretation of the Mishnah were recorded in the *Talmud (6th cent.). In the modern era, the *Progressive movements have largely rejected the belief in the divine origin of Jewish law and are therefore ready to disregard any *halakhic provisions which conflict with modern secular values.

Oral tradition (in Islam): see ḤADĪTH.

Orangemen. Members of the *Protestant fraternal Orange Order, prominent in N. Ireland, concerned to defend Protestant ascendancy. The order was founded in 1795, named from William III, William of Orange. (Orange is a town on the river Rhône, once capital of a small principality from which William's ancestors took their name.) The marches of the Orangemen in N. Ireland are a public manifestation of what the *Roman Catholic population perceives as a determination of at least some Protestants to remain dominant and a part of the United Kingdom.

Orange People (Indian-based religious movement): see RAJNEESH, BHAGWAN SHREE.

Orange/saffron robes: see MONASTICISM (Buddhist).

Oratorio. The setting of a religious (usually Christian) text to music; the setting is extensive, with soloists, chorus, and instruments. It is not, however, like opera, in that it is not staged or acted out.

Oratory, Oratorians (Lat., *oratorium*, 'place of prayer'). *Roman Catholic place of worship other than a parish church, and the name of those belonging to a community based on an Oratory. From the oratory of S. Girolamo in Rome came the Oratory of St Philip Neri, a community of priests whose constitution was ratified by Pope Paul V in 1612. Oratories spread rapidly: they are congregations of secular priests living in community without vows, the more wealthy, therefore, being expected to support themselves.

Order of Ethiopia. A semi-independent, mainly Xhosa, section within the *Anglican Church in S. Africa. James M. Dwane (1851–1916), an ordained *Methodist minister, seceded in 1894 to the Ethiopian Church (see ETHIOPIANISM) and drew this Church into the orbit of the black African Methodist Episcopal Church in the USA, through which he became ordained as 'vicar-bishop'. He was ordained deacon in 1900 and priest in 1909. The Order retained a peculiar extra-parochial position, with its own synod and finance, and a provincial, but no bishop. Periodic negotiations failed to find a solution until 1983, when Siggibo Dwana, principal of an Anglican theological college, was consecrated as bishop, and he and the Order, now with some 50,000 members, have full diocesan rights within the Church.

Order of the Cross. A religious movement or fellowship founded in England in 1904 by J. Todd Ferrier. The movement proclaims 'the brotherhood of man', the essential unity of all religious quests and the unity of all living beings in the divine.

Orders. The various grades of Christian ministers. In the W. Church until 1972 these were *bishop, *priest, *deacon, *subdeacon, *acolyte, exorcist, reader, and doorkeeper (though sometimes 'bishop' was not considered a distinct order from 'priest').

In 1972 the Roman Catholic orders of subdeacon, exorcist, and doorkeeper were suppressed; the other two minor orders which had formerly been nominal steps to the priesthood, were called 'ministeria' and allowed to be conferred on laymen. In most E. churches the major orders are bishop, priest, and deacon, and the minor orders subdeacon and reader. (Other titles like *chorepiscopus and *archpriest are not usually considered separate orders.)

Ordinal (Lat., *ordinale*). Originally a Christian manual giving details of the variations in the *office according to changes in the ecclesiastical year.

Ordinary. In *canon law, an ecclesiastic having the spiritual jurisdiction over a particular area as part of his office. Thus the ordinary of a diocese is the *bishop, etc.

Ordinary of the Mass (Lat., *ordo missae*). The (almost) invariable parts of the *mass, comprising the preparatory prayers, *Kyrie, *Gloria and *Creed, the *Preface and *Sanctus, the *canon, *Lord's Prayer, *fraction and *Agnus Dei, and part of the communion and post-communion devotions. It is distinguished from the *proper.

Ordination. The conferral of office in a formal, often ritualized manner. For Judaism, see SEMIKHAH. Among Christians, in Catholic and Orthodox practice, priests and deacons are ordained by a bishop, acting as minister of Christ and successor of the apostles (for the doctrine see APOSTOLIC SUCCESSION).

The term 'ordination' has then been applied to the formal and ritualized admission procedures in other religions, especially of the admission of women and men to the Buddhist *saṅgha.

Oriental Orthodox Churches. The *Syrian, *Coptic, *Ethiopian and *Armenian Orthodox churches. They have in common their historic rejection of the Council of *Chalcedon and its *christology of two natures in Christ. They are therefore sometimes called the 'non-Chalcedonian' Churches (although properly this term includes the *Church of the East also). They should not be confused with the ('Eastern') *Orthodox churches, which are Chalcedonian. Since the 1960s the Oriental Orthodox have held conferences together, and, aiming at theological reconciliation, with the Orthodox and *Roman Catholic Churches.

Oriental Rite Catholics: see EASTERN RITE CATHOLICS.

Origen (*c*.185–*c*.254). Christian scholar and theologian. He was brought up in Egypt by Christian parents, and became head of the catechetical school in Alexandria after *Clement. He led a strictly ascetical life and even (according to *Eusebius, and on the basis of Matthew 19. 12) castrated himself. He travelled to Rome, Arabia, and in 215 and 230 to Palestine. On the latter visit he was ordained priest by bishops there, and in consequence of this breach of discipline (and no doubt other disagreements) his own bishop Demetrius sent him into exile. He took refuge in 231 at Caesarea in Palestine where he established a famous school. He was tortured in the persecution of Decius in 250. Origen's works are mostly preserved in fragments and translations, owing to their great length (e.g. his **Hexapla*) and the later condemnations of his views. Origen wrote commentaries and homilies on much of the Bible; theological treatises, nearly all of which are lost except *On First Principles*; a defence of Christianity *Against *Celsus*; and *On Prayer* and *Exhortation to Martyrdom*.

The term Origenism refers to the views of (or at least attributed to) Origen which gave rise to two later controversies. These include the pre-existence of souls and the distinction between the mortal and the resurrection body. The anti-Origenists were victorious at a synod convened by the emperor Justinian in 543, and Origenism was finally condemned at the 2nd Council of *Constantinople (553).

Original sin. In Christian theology the state of sin into which everyone is born as a result of the *fall of Adam. The basis of this in the Bible is *Paul's teaching that 'through one man [Adam] sin entered the world', so that 'by the trespass of the one the many died' (Romans 5. 12). It was developed by the early Greek *fathers, but became most precise in Latin writers of the 2nd–5th cents., culminating in *Augustine's formulation. According to this, Adam's sin has been transmitted from parent to child ever since. The human race has thus become a 'lump of sin' (*massa damnata*). In the *Pelagian controversy Augustine's view prevailed, although his extreme views were not adopted in the East. Since the 18th cent. the influence of Old Testament criticism, combined with natural science, has changed the emphasis to one of describing human inability to rescue itself from its condition out of its own strength or resources: genetic endowments, combined with social, cultural and historical circumstances, precede the birth of all individuals and are not chosen by them; yet they form both character and action in ways that are inevitably disordered.

Orthodox Church. Major grouping of Christian churches, constituting, by full communion with each other, a single Church. The Orthodox Church claims direct descent from the Church of the *apostles and of the seven ecumenical *councils. The name 'Eastern Orthodox' (to be distinguished from *'Oriental Orthodox') arose from accidents of history and geography which led to a separation from 'the West'; but Orthodoxy has in fact spread throughout the world.

The Orthodox Church comprises a number of *autocephalous bodies in communion with one another: the ancient *patriarchates of *Constantinople, *Alexandria, *Antioch, and *Jerusalem, and the Orthodox Churches of *Russia, Serbia, Romania, Bulgaria, *Georgia, *Greece, Czechoslovakia, Poland, Cyprus, and Albania. In addition, there are autonomous churches (whose *primate is under the aegis of one of the autocephalous churches) in Finland, Crete, Japan, and China, and missions yet to become autonomous in Korea and Africa. The oecumenical patriarch of Constantinople has a primacy of honour, but no universal jurisdiction to correspond to that of the *pope.

The Orthodox Church traces its history back to the missionary work of *Paul, and itself became missionary, achieving notably the conversion of the Slavs through the 'apostles of the Slavs', *Cyril and Methodius. Russia became a Christian kingdom under St *Vladimir in 988.

There was a progressive estrangement between Rome and Constantinople, partly on account of divergent liturgical usages and also because of the claims of the Roman *papacy. There was a temporary schism under patriarch *Photius, then a final one under Michael Cerularius in 1054. Attempts at reunion, notably at the Council of *Florence (1439), have been ineffective.

After the fall of Constantinople (1453), the Church came under Muslim rule.

Orthodox doctrine proceeds from the Bible, the formulae of the seven *ecumenical councils, and broadly from the writings of the Greek *fathers. Many doctrines of more recent definition in the W., e.g. the nature of *sacraments and the *Immaculate Conception, are not laid down. On the other hand, constant and exclusive appeal to ancient authorities makes Orthodox theology inherently conservative.

The Orthodox liturgy (*eucharist) is longer than the Western, and typically celebrated with greater ceremonial. *Baptism is by immersion, and is followed by chrismation (see CHRISM). *Icons are an essential part of the furnishing of a church building, and in houses are a focus of private prayers.

Parish priests are usually married, but may not marry after their ordination as *deacon. Bishops, however, are always celibate, and therefore do not come from the parish clergy but from the ranks of monks. Besides providing bishops, monasticism has also provided the intellectual and spiritual centre of Orthodoxy, specifically in modern times at Mount *Athos, but many theologians today are laypeople. See Index, Orthodox Church.

Orthodox Judaism. Traditional Judaism. The term 'Orthodoxy' was first applied in Judaism in 1795 as a distinction between those who accepted the written and *oral law as divinely inspired and those who identified with the *Reform movement. The Orthodox believe that they are the sole practitioners of the Jewish religious tradition and regard non-Orthodox *rabbis as laypeople and non-Orthodox *proselytes as *gentiles. Orthodoxy involves submission to the demands of *halakhah as enshrined in the written and oral law and in the subsequent codes (see CODIFICATIONS OF LAW) and *responsa. Notable institutions and organizations are or have been: Torah Umesorah, which organized schools and yeshivot from 1944 onward; the Union of Orthodox Jewish Congregations of America (which certifies, internationally, reliable kosher *food); Yeshiva University and the Hebrew Theological College in Chicago; the Union of Orthodox Rabbis and the Rabbinical Alliance.

Orthopraxy (Gk., *orthos*, 'correct', + *praxis*, 'action'). Right action, in addition to (or sometimes in contrast to) orthodoxy, 'right belief'. Many religions are characterized by an emphasis on orthopraxy—e.g. 'Hinduism', whose concern is with *sanātana dharma (everlasting dharma, with dharma meaning, roughly, appropriate ways to live) or Islam, where the account to be rendered on the day of judgement (*yaum al-Din) is one of works.

Ōryō E'nan (Japanese name of Ch'an master): see HUANG-LUNG HUI-NAN.

Ōsal (Clear Light): see NĀRO CHOS DRUG.

Ostrich eggs. Often found in E. Christian churches where they are regarded as a symbol of the *resurrection, as a breaking open of the tomb.

Otto, Rudolf (1869–1937). Philosophical theologian and professor of systematic theology at the University of Marburg, 1917–29. He is most renowned for *Das Heilige* (1917, The Idea of the Holy), a *Kantian analysis of the non-rational core of religion—the *numinous experience—and its relation to the rational.

Ottoman empire (13th cent. CE–1924 (AH 7th cent.–1342)). Extensive Muslim empire, whose disintegration has contributed greatly to the complexities of Middle East politics, not least through the demise of the office of caliph (*khalīfa). 'Uthman (also spelt Othman, hence the name) founded a principality in Asia Minor which, in 758, began to expand into Macedonia, Serbia, and Bulgaria (where Muslim populations remain strong). By 1453 (AH 857) they were strong enough to take *Constantinople. In 1517 (AH 923) Selim I (Yavuz, 'the Grim') conquered Egypt, claiming that the last *'Abbāsid caliph, al-Mutawakkil III, had relinquished the caliphate to his family. The first signs of decline came in 1571 (AH 979) at the battle of Lepanto, when the Ottomans lost control of the W. Mediterranean. The 19th-cent. attempts at revival by the assimilation of W. ideas and technology in fact hastened the move to a secular state, established under Mustafa Kemal, Atatürk ('father of the Turks'): the sultanate was abolished in 1922, the caliphate in 1924.

Ōuchi Seiran (supporter of Sōtō): see SŌJI-JI.

Our Lady. Christian reference to Mary, the mother of Jesus, equally familiar in French, Notre Dame.

Outcastes. The gravest punishment for a member of any one of the four **varṇa* was to be declared an outcaste, and, in former times, this outcasting would be ritually performed against anyone who seriously offended against caste laws. This effectively cut the offender off from social intercourse, religious ritual, economic gain, even home and family. This almost amounted to a sentence of death in some cases. For other categories of outcaste, and for Harijans, see UNTOUCHABLES. For those sometimes called 'the untouchables of Japan', see BURAKU(MIN).

Outer elixir (*wai-tan*, techniques in quest of immortality): see NEI-TAN.

Outer Shrine Shinto: see ISE.

Oxford Movement. A movement in the *Church of England, beginning in the 19th cent., which had a profound impact on the theology, piety, and liturgy of *Anglicanism. Its acknowledged leaders, John Keble, J. H. *Newman, and E. B. *Pusey, were all Oxford dons, and it is Keble's 1833 sermon on 'National Apostasy' (attacking the government's plan to suppress, without proper reference to the Church, ten Irish bishoprics) which is conventionally seen as the moment when the movement came to birth.

The movement reacted against decline in church life, the threat posed by liberal theology and rationalism, and the fear that the government was, in the words of Keble, intent on making the Church of England 'as one sect among many'.

The organ of the movement was the series of Tracts for the Times (1–90; 1833–41) from which its supporters derived the name *Tractarians. Although aimed against both 'Popery and Dissent', they were viewed with increasing alarm by those outside the movement who saw in them evidence of creeping Romanism. Newman's *Tract Ninety*, which attempted to square the *Thirty-Nine Articles with Roman Catholicism, was condemned by many bishops, and a crisis was reached in 1845 when Newman and some of his supporters converted to Rome.

The heart of the movement's renewal of Anglicanism lay not so much in the ritual of worship, as in the impetus it gave to more godly living worked out through the revival of religious communities and a deep commitment to parish and mission work, especially among the poor and deprived.

Ox-herding pictures (depicting stages of Zen progress): see JŪGYŪ-(NO)-ZEN.

Oyf kapporos ('may this be an atonement'): see KAPPOROT.

P

Pabbājita or **paribbājaka** (Pāli; Skt., *parivrājaka*, 'homeless one'). One who has left home for religious purposes. In early Buddhism, it is a name for one who has joined the *saṅgha (community).

Pacceka-buddha (solitary Buddha): see PRATYEKA-BUDDHA.

Pacem in Terris. An *encyclical letter of Pope *John XXIII, dated 11 Apr. 1963, on the achievement of peace through the establishment of justice. It argues that peace can be established in the world only if the moral order 'imprinted by God on the heart' is obeyed.

Pa-chiao Hui-ch'ing (Jap., Bashō Esei; *c*.10th cent. CE). A Korean Zen master of the Igyō school (see KUEI-YANG-TSUNG), who travelled to China and became the dharma-successor (*hassu) of Nan-t'a Kuang-jun. He is best remembered for his *kōan (*Wu-men-kuan* 44): 'If you have a staff, I will give you a staff. If you do not have a staff, I will take your staff away.'

Pachomius, St (Coptic, Pakhom; *c*.290–346). Founder of *coenobitic Christian monasticism. In 313 he became a disciple of the hermit Palamun, and in 320 founded a monastery at Tabennisi on the Upper Nile. Other foundations followed, and at his death he was head of nine monasteries for men and two for women. The *Rule of Pachomius* influenced *Basil, *Cassian, and *Benedict.

Pactum Callixtinum (agreement between Papacy and Holy Roman Emperors): see CONCORDAT.

Padma (symbol in E. religions): see LOTUS.

Padma-purāṇa. One of the eighteen Vaiṣṇavite Mahāpurānas, telling of the earliest times when the world was a golden *lotus (*padma*). It is exclusivist in tendency.

Padmasambhava ('Lotus-born'; Tib., Padma-'byuṅ-gnas). Prominent member of the Indian *siddha tradition associated with the introduction of Buddhism to Tibet and founder of the *Nyingma school. He is more commonly known by Nyingmapas as Gurū Rinpoche (Precious Teacher) and sometimes as the 'second Buddha'. According to legend, Padmasambhava was born in Oḍḍiyana (possibly the Swat Valley in Pakistan) eight years after the Buddha's death, which would make him over a thousand years old when he visited Tibet. He took up the practice of *Tantra, studied with many teachers including Ānanda, was ordained as a monk and achieved many *siddhis (superpowers). For several hundred years Padmasambhava wandered, giving teachings and performing miracles, until receiving the invitation to Tibet. His intervention there successfully cleared the way for the introduction of Buddhism. Accounts vary as to how long he stayed in Tibet. Some say he left soon after Samyé was completed, others that he stayed for fifty-five years. All accounts say that Trisong Detsen's ministers conspired against him, and whenever he did leave, he did so in appropriate fashion by riding his horse through the air.

Padmāsana. The Lotus position, adopted for meditation, in which Hindu and Buddhist gods, *bodhisattvas, etc., are often depicted. For details, see ĀSANA.

Padyab (purification): see PURITY (ZOROASTRIAN).

Paekche (Korean kingdom): see KOREAN RELIGION.

Pagan Pathfinders. A *neo-pagan movement, established in Britain in the 1970s. Combining pagan and occult techniques with practical psychology, it aims to achieve altered states of consciousness and quicken the pace of personal growth.

Pagoda (poss. from *dāgaba*, 'relic-container', via Portuguese). Buddhist structure, developed from the Indian *stūpa, and often a name for a stūpa. Its many variations contain characteristic features in common: they are usually raised and narrow structures, with four or eight sides, with several levels and prominent eaves. On the top is a post with many rings encircling it. Pagodas, like stūpas, contain *relics (*śarīra) of a/the Buddha, or of a famous teacher/master. They express the Buddhist cosmos in symbolic form. A pagoda is thus a *maṇḍala in its own right.

In the history of Buddhist architecture, the placing of the pagoda is the issue which then dominates the overall layout and design of Buddhist temple areas and monasteries. The geographical solutions to the problem are diverse, but always provide a clue to the religious priorities of the community and age involved.

Pahlavi ('Parthian'). Term used in Islamic times to debate earlier Iranian (*Zoroastrian) material. It is also referred to as 'Middle Persian' to distinguish it from the Old Persian (cuneiform) of the royal inscriptions and the New Persian of modern times. It was a language used between approximately 300 BCE–10th cent. CE. It encompasses secular work, poetic, historical, and epic material, but most extant works are religious and include the books from which Western scholars reconstruct 'traditional' Zoroastrian teaching (though most modern Zoroastrians consider this literature with the same hesitations many modern Christians view their medieval literature). The largest work is the *Denkard* which in six books is a compendium of Zoroastrian knowledge from many epochs and of diverse types. Two brothers, Zadspram and Manuscihr produced a number of important works in the 9th cent., the *Wizidagiha i Zadspram* (Selections) and the *Dadistan i denig* (Religious Judgements—in response to ninety-two questions) being among the most important for the reconstruction of Zoroastrian (and *Zurvan) teaching. Important also are *Skand-Gumanig Wizar* (Doubt-Destroying Exposition), *Arda Viraf Namag* (The Visions of the Righteous Viraf) and *Zand-i Vohuman Yasn* (Commentary on the Bahman Yast).

The term 'Pahlavi' was adopted by the 20th-cent. Iranian royal dynasty of Reza Shah as a marker of the importance it attached to the pre-Islamic culture of Iran.

Pa-hsien (Chin., 'eight immortals'). Taoist figures ('perfected persons', *chen jen) associated symbolically with good fortune. They are also associated with the 'eight conditions of life': youth, age, poverty, wealth, high rank, *hoi polloi* (general population), feminine, masculine. They are frequently portrayed in art and literature: (i) Li T'ieh-kuai (also known as Ti Kuai-li), Li with the iron crutch, a bad-tempered eccentric who nevertheless carries a gourd containing magic and healing potions; (ii) Chang Kuo-lao, a historical figure of the T'ang dynasty, but better known through legends; his symbol is a fish drum; (iii) Ts'ao Kuo-chiu (d. 1097 CE), usually symbolized through a pair of castanets; (iv) Han Hsiang-tzu, the epitome of the peaceful mountain-dweller, the patron of music, portrayed with a flute, flowers, and a peach; (v) Lü Tung-pen (b. 798 CE), who received from a fire dragon a sword which enabled him to hide from death; (vi) Ho Hsien-ku, the only female immortal (but see vii); (vii) Lan Ts'ai-ho appears in rags, with a boot on only one foot, carrying a basket of flowers: he is a type of 'holy fool'; he is sometimes portrayed with female features; (viii) Chung-li Ch'üan (also Han Chung-li), a stout man with only wisps of remaining hair, but with a beard reaching his waist; his symbol is a fan, indicating power to raise the dead.

Pai-Chang-Ch'ing-Kuei (Jap., *Hyakujō Shingi*). A manual of rules governing Ch'an/Zen monasteries (*tera), associated with *Pai-chang Huai-hai, but subsequently reworked at least by Te-hui.

Pai-chang Huai-hai (Jap., Hyakujō Ekai; 720–814). Ch'an/Zen master, dharma-successor (*hassu) of *Ma-tsu Tao-i. His major achievement was to establish a rule of life for Ch'an monasteries, thereby securing their independence and self-identity in relation to other Buddhist schools—hence his title, 'The patriarch who created the forest' (i.e. the communities of many monks). His rule was first practised in the monastery he founded, Ta-chih shou-sheng ch'an-ssu (Jap., Daichijushō-zenji), where the vital addition of a monks' hall (*sōdō*) was first made, allowing the Zen monk's 'life on a straw mat' during periods of ascetic training—i.e. the mat on which he would sleep, eat, and meditate.

Pai-lien-tsung. 'White Lotus School', a school of *Pure Land Buddhism, founded by *Hui-yüan in 402 CE, and developed by Mao Tzu-yuan, of the T'ien-t'ai school, in the 12th cent. CE. It was devoted to Amitābha (*Amida) but regarded the Pure Land as the attainment of a mental construct and state.

Pai-ma-ssu/Baimasi. White Horse Monastery/Temple, Buddhist monastery and temple near Luoyang in China. It was founded in 75 CE by two Indian monks, Matanga and Chu-fa-len, who arrived on a white horse. It remains a working centre for Ch'an Buddhists.

Pai-yün Kuan (Baiyun Guan). Monastery of the White Clouds, a Taoist 8th-cent. monastery (*kuan) in Beijing, rebuilt in 1167. It is the only surviving Taoist temple on this scale in Beijing.

Pakka food (i.e. acceptable from a wide range of people): see FOOD (HINDUISM).

Pak Subuh (founder): see SUBUD.

Pa-kua. Eight trigrams, the eight signs which form the basis of **I Ching*, and from which the sixty-four hexagrams are constructed.

Palamas (Greek theologian): see GREGORY PALAMAS, ST.

Palestinian Talmud: see TALMUD.

Paliau Maloat (*b.* 1907). Leader of a development and religious movement on Manus (Admiralty Islands), Papua New Guinea. Stimulated by his experiences in the war with Japan, he returned to his native village in 1946, believing he was sponsored by *Jesus to set up a New Way that would unite the area, with co-operatives and new villages, a fund for development, and a Western lifestyle. His version of Christianity was expressed in the Baluan Native Christian Church, modelled on the Roman Catholic mission. The expectations he aroused led to two *cargo-cult outbreaks, the first called 'The Noise' in 1946–7, which he repudiated at the time, and the second in 1953–4; in effect these opened the way for Paliau's changes.

Pāli Canon. The earliest collections of Buddhist authoritative texts, more usually known as Tipiṭaka (*Tripiṭaka), 'Three Baskets', because the palm-leaf manuscripts were traditionally kept in three different baskets: Vinaya, (Monastic) Discipline; Sutta, Discourses; Abhidhamma, Further Teachings. The Sutta-pitaka consists of five *Nikāyas (Collections): *Dīgha* (thirty-four 'long' discourses/dialogues); *Majjhima* (150 'middle length' discourses); *Saṃyutta* (7,762 'connected' discourses, grouped according to subject-matter); *Aṅguttara* (9,550 'single item' discourses); *Khuddaka* (fifteen 'little texts', listed under *Khuddaka). Much has been tr. by the Pali Text Society.

See also BUDDHIST SCRIPTURES; and for further detail, TRIPIṬAKA.

Palladius (*c*.365–425). Historian of Christian *monasticism. His *Lausiac History* (*c*.419) is of great importance for the history of early monasticism in Egypt, Palestine, Syria, and Asia Minor.

Pallium. The symbol of the *archbishop's office in the *Roman Catholic and *Uniat Churches. It is a circular band of white wool with two hanging pieces, front and back, and is now marked with six black crosses.

Palm Sunday. The Sunday before *Easter which thus commences *Holy Week. Palms are blessed and carried in procession, representing Jesus' 'triumphal entry' into Jerusalem in the last week of his life. The service may also include the chanting of the passion story from one of the gospels, and for that reason is also known as Passion Sunday (a name which is also given to the preceding Sunday: *Vatican II attempted to combine the two).

Pañcadaśi ('the fifteen'). A major Hindu work so-called from its fifteen chapters. It was written by *Vidyāranya, a follower of *Śaṅkara. It is an *advaita exploration, of great complexity, of the elements surrounding *ātman (*śarīra), the great precepts (Mahāvākyas), and the nature of bliss.

Pañca-makāra or **pañca-tattva.** Five ritual ingredients whose first letter is 'm': *madya* (wine or alcoholic beverage), *maṃsa* (meat), *matsya (fish), *mudrā* (parched grain), and *maithuna (sexual intercourse). The five Ms are central to *Tantric liturgy, and are interpreted, either literally by left-hand (*vāmācāra) sects such as the *Kaulas and *Kāpālikas, or symbolically by right-hand (*dakṣinācāra) sects. The left-hand groups seek perfection and power (*siddhi) through the use of prohibited substances.

Pañca-mārga (Skt., 'five paths'). Five stages in Buddhist progress (cf. *bhūmi): (i) sambhāra-marga, path of accumulation; (ii) prayoga-marga, path of preparation; (iii) darśana-marga, path of seeing; (iv) bhāvanā-marga, path of meditation; (v) aśaikṣa-marga, path of not-learning any further.

Panca namaskāra (five Jain homages): see FIVE SUPREME BEINGS.

Pañcānana (Skt., 'five-faced'). A Hindu epithet of *Śiva, representing any of the fivefold characteristics of his nature—e.g. the elements; the four quarters + Sadaśiva—the most complex of the faces, invisible even to the advanced yogin. The contemplation of the five faces is a central focus for meditation.

Pañcanīvaraṇa (five kinds of higher knowledge): see NĪVARANA.

Pañca parameṣthin (five exemplary modes of being for Jains): see FIVE SUPREME BEINGS.

Pañcarātra. An early *Vaiṣṇava tradition and sect with a large number of texts called *Saṃhitās, of which the 'three gems' (the *Pauṣkara*, *Sāttvata*, and *Jayākhya Saṃhitās*) are the most important and earliest (5th–6th cents. CE). The *Jayākhya Saṃhitā* is the *locus classicus* of Pañcarātra religious practice, which consists of the divinization of the body through the assimilation of a divine *mantra body by *nyasa and *visualization. *Bhakti and grace are also important. Other topics dealt with are outer worship (*bāhya yoga*), temple building, initiation, *śraddha, and funeral rites.

Pañca-śila (Buddhist obligations): see ŚĪLA.

Pañcatantra. A collection of stories and legends, in five (*pañca*) books (*tantra*), compiled by Viṣṇuśaram in the early cents. CE. The original is lost, but it continues in at least three different lineages, and in many adaptations or imitations, of which *Hitopadeśa* is the best-known. The stories teach moral and pragmatic lessons for rulers, but they extend beyond that into the realms of entertainment. As a 'story-book', it passed into many other cultures and languages.

Pañca-tattva: see PAÑCA-MAKĀRA.

Pañchama (lowest category of Hindu society): see UNTOUCHABLES.

Panchen Lama (abbr. *Pandita Chen.po*, 'Great Teacher'). Holder of the Tibetan Buddhist monastic throne of Tashilhunpo in Shigatse, the religious nature of which has become inseparable from Sino-Tibetan political history. The office had been established by the third *Dalai Lama as a position attainable by merit, until the Great Fifth Dalai Lama—who had become close to his contemporary Panchen Lama (Chokyi Gyaltsen, 1570–1662) who was also his tutor—predicted that the throne would be retained by reincarnation, from which time Chokyi Gyaltsen has been considered the 'first' Panchen Lama. In 1944 the seventh Panchen Lama, Chokyi Gyaltsen (whom the Chinese reckon as the tenth, thus increasing his status), was declared by the Chinese to have been discovered in China. It was not until 1951 that Chokyi Gyaltsen was recognized by the Tibetans, and only then as part of the seventeen-point agreement (signed with false Tibetan seals by a deserter and collaborator, Ngapo Ngawang Jigne, who held office in the Chinese government) forced on them after the 1950 invasion while the Dalai Lama was in exile. 'Discovered' by the Chinese, brought up in China, and given a Chinese education, Chokyi Gyaltsen toed the Chinese line until, in 1960, his seat at Tashilhunpo was ransacked and his entire corpus of 4,000 monks was either executed or sent to labour camps. In 1964, in a speech to 10,000 citizens of Lhasa, he asserted Tibet's right to independence. He was imprisoned, released in 1978, until, in 1988, at a speech in Tashilhunpo, he declared that 'the detriments of Chinese rule in Tibet outweighed the benefits'. Three days later he suffered a fatal heart attack. The search for the Panchen Lama's reincarnation was then set in motion, and in 1995 the Dalai Lama recognized him in a 6-year-old boy, Gedhun Choekyi Nyima. The Chinese authorities refused to recognize him. They held their own procedures at *Jokhang at the end of 1995, producing a 5-year-old boy, Gyancain/Gyaltsen Norbu.

Pāṇḍavas. Five *kṣatriya 'brothers' of the Kuru lineage, Yudhiṣṭhira, *Bhīma, *Arjuna, and the twins, Nakula and Sahadeva, the heroes of the epic **Mahābhārata*, which recounts their battle for sovereignty against their cousins, the *Kauravas.

Paṇḍita, paṇḍit, or **pundit** (Skt.). A Hindu scholar, learned man, teacher, or philosopher. Paṇḍitas are those who conserve the Sanskrit tradition, specialists in memorization of the classical traditions of Indian philosophy and literature. Paṇḍitas are often associated with particular philosophical schools, and attempt to live as a separate community of literati, cultivating the Sanskrit language as a *lingua franca* for communication with paṇḍitas from all of India.

Panentheism: see PANTHEISM.

P'ang Yün or **P'ang-chu-shih** (Jap., Hō Un/Hō Koji; 740–808). A lay Ch'an/Zen Buddhist, regarded in his time as 'a second *Vimalakīrti'. He remains a model of how Zen attainment is possible to laypeople, and not just to monks. His sayings were collected after his death in *P'ang chü-shih yü-lu* (Jap., *Hō Koji goroku*).

Panikkar, Raimundo (1918–). Christian promotor of Hindu–Christian dialogue. He was brought up to read the *Veda as well as the *Bible. In 1968 he published, on the basis of his experience of *dialogue, *The Unknown Christ of Hinduism*. Along the lines that led to the formulation of the concept of anonymous Christians (see RAHNER), he argued that Christ is universal and that his presence and reality can be articulated in Hindu terms. This book led to the correction by M. M. Thomas that Christ has already been acknowledged in Hinduism by various people in various ways, which he proceeded to review, in *The Acknowledged Christ of the Indian Renaissance*. Panikkar also wrote *The Trinity and the Religious Experience of Man* (1973), and *The Vedic Experience* (1977).

Pāṇini. Author of *Aṣṭādhyāyi*, the earliest surviving work on Sanskrit grammar, written at some time between the 7th and 4th cents. BCE. The religious importance of grammar lay in the necessity to transmit and interpret sacred and ritual texts correctly, in order to relate adequately to *śabda.

Pan-Islam. Movements to unify the Muslim world, particularly in reaction against Western threats of encroachment. Theoretically, Pan-Islam is a natural expression of the fundamental and necessary Muslim concept of *'umma, but its realization in practice is elusive.

Pañjāb (Pers., 'five, water', i.e. land of five rivers). Punjāb, homeland of the Sikhs. The present NW Indian state of Punjāb was created in 1966, excluding former areas which now comprise Himachal Pradesh and Haryana. The state language is *Pañjābī, and Sikhs outnumber Hindus. In 1947 the much larger British Punjāb had been partitioned between Pakistan and India, with the boundary dividing *Amritsar from, e.g., Nānkāṇā *Sāhib (*Talvaṇḍī Rāi Bhoī dī). Thousands of Sikhs moved from east to west but remain anxious for free access to holy places in a relatively (or completely) autonomous homeland: see KHĀLISTĀN.

Pañjābī or **Punjābī.** 1. Person whose family originates from *Pañjāb, often referring to its pre-1947 boundaries.

2. Mother tongue of Pañjābīs, regardless of their religion. Pañjābī, in *Gurmukhī script, is the official language of Indian Pañjāb, and has been especially respected by Sikhs.

Pañj kakke (five marks of a khālsā Sikh): see FIVE KS.

Pañj Piāre: see PAÑJ PYĀRE.

Pānj Pīr (Pañjābī, 'five guides'). Popular Hindu cult of Five Saints, who may be *any* five the devotee may remember or worship. The cult includes Muslim figures, such as the Prophet *Muḥammad, *'Alī, *Fāṭima, *al-Ḥasan, and *al-Ḥusain. Another popular 'quintet' is Ghazi Miyan, Baba Barahna, Palihar, Amina Sati, and Bibi Fāṭima (the last two being most obviously Hindu–Muslim hybrids). The Panj Pir cult is followed by some fifty-three Hindu castes.

Pañj pyāre (Pañjābī, 'five beloved ones'). 1. Five men who volunteered their heads for Gurū *Gobind Siṅgh on *Baisākhī 1699. All were renamed Siṅgh. They subsequently fought bravely for the Gurū. The pañj pyāre are remembered daily in *Ardās, and a portion of *kaṛāh praśād is taken out in their memory before general distribution.

2. Five baptized Sikhs who administer *khaṇḍe-di-pahul. They are normally men and must be *amritdhārī, physically whole, and known to observe the Sikh code of conduct (*rahit).

3. The central and final authority for all Sikhs, located at *Amritsar.

P'an-ku. Taoist creator of the world, and also the first human. From the original chaos in the form of an egg, P'an-ku emerged. At his death, his body was allocated to the creation of different parts of the world.

Pañña (wisdom): see PRAJÑA (2).

Pansil. Abbreviation of pañca-sila (*sīla), the five precepts which should be expressed in the life of every Buddhist.

Panth (Pañjābī, 'way, sect'). Religious community in E. religions, but especially among Jains (see e.g. KĀNJĪ SVĀMI PANTH) and Sikhs. Among the latter, Panth denotes the whole Sikh community.

Pantheism, panentheism. A family of views dealing with the relation between God and the world. In contrast to *theism's stress on the total transcendence of God, both terms reflect an emphasis on divine *immanence. In pantheistic views, God and the world are essentially identical; the divine is totally immanent. In panentheistic views, the world exists in God (all reality is part of the being of God), but God is not exhausted by the world; the divine is both transcendent and immanent. Such views are often closely related to *mysticism.

Pantisocracy (egalitarian society): see COLERIDGE, S. T.

Pāpa (Skt.). In Hinduism, evil, *sin, misfortune. Like its synonym, *adharma, pāpa includes both moral and natural evil, which are considered aspects of the same phenomenon. An absolute distinction between moral evil (or evil willed by humans) and natural evil (or an 'act of God'), is not present in Hindu thought. One can sin unintentionally by unknowingly eating a prohibited food or making an error in ritual. One's sin, whether intentional or unintentional, may have consequences, not only for oneself, but for others, so that one must pray for deliverance from the sins of others as well as from one's own sins.

In Buddhism, the connotation of evil and immorality is applied particularly to states of mind and actions. Pāpa is considered evil because it takes one away from the path of spiritual development, the path of *nirvāna.

Pāpa is what ensues from an *akuśala action.

Papacy. The office of the *bishop of Rome as leader of the *Roman Catholic Church. Claims to some form of leadership over the churches seem to be implicit in Roman documents from the end of the 1st cent. onwards, but were made more explicit in the century between popes Damasus and Leo. Acceptance of the papal fullness of authority ('plenitudo potestatis') over other churches has varied with the personal standing of the bishops of Rome and other historical circumstances, but is generally held to have been at its height during the pontificate of *Innocent III. At *Vatican I the bishops asserted the pope's 'ordinary and immediate' authority over all churches and members of churches, and his *infallibility when defining matters of faith or morals to be held by the whole church. See Index, Papacy.

Papal aggression. Popular name for the action of Pope *Pius IX in 1850 making England and Wales an ecclesiastical province of the *Roman Catholic Church (with an archbishop and twelve *suffragans with territorial titles), referring with evidently calculated contempt to the Church of England as 'the *Anglican schism'.

Papias (*c*.60–130 CE). Christian bishop of Hierapolis in Asia Minor. His work *Exposition of the Sayings of the Lord*, known only from quotations in *Irenaeus and *Eusebius, contained oral traditions and legends. The most important of these concern the writing of the *gospels: *Matthew 'composed the sayings (*logia*) in Hebrew, and everyone translated them as best he could'; *Mark was 'the interpreter of Peter' who set down 'accurately though not in order' Peter's memories of Jesus' words and activities.

Para. Skt., 'supreme, highest', found in conjunction with many Hindu words to express the superlative state—e.g. *para-*bhakti* and see under VIṢṆU. Unless some special sense is created, the meaning will be carried within the basic word, and will not be listed separately here.

Parable (Gk., *parabolē*). A story or illustration of important teaching, used by *rabbis and by *Jesus, more direct than *allegories, and, in the case of Jesus, usually making a demand on the hearers. Jesus' insistence on teaching in parables, implies something about the nature of the *kingdom of God. Most of the thirty to forty gospel parables are found in Matthew (e.g. the clusters in chs. 13, 25) and Luke (among the best-known, 10. 25–42, 15. 11–32). For Jewish parables, see MĀSHAL.

Paracelsus (Theophrastus Baumastus von Hohenheim, 1493–1541). *Alchemist and physician. He was born in Switzerland and travelled extensively throughout Europe, gaining a reputation as the leading figure in the Renaissance quest for interior meanings and transformations of nature.

Paraclete. A figure mentioned by Jesus in the gospel of John (chs. 14–16), as coming after his own departure, to be with his disciples. The Gk. word *paraklētos* may mean 'comforter', 'counsellor', 'advocate', but none of these translations entirely matches the range of functions ascribed to him. He is once identified with the *Holy Spirit (14. 26), and it is easy to see why Christian tradition took up this identification. In Islam, the (Arab.) *faraqlīt* is identified with Muḥammad as the one who was promised (John 16. 7).

Paradise (Gk., possibly from Pers. *pardes/pairidaeza*, 'enclosure, park', hence 'garden'). Idyllic state in the presence of God, especially after death, hence often a synonym for heaven. The *Septuagint uses the word of a literal *garden (Ecclesiastes 2. 5; Song of Songs 4. 12), but the reference is more often the Garden of Eden (Paradise Lost) or the restored Garden (e.g. Ezekiel 36. 35, 47. 12; Isaiah 51. 3—Paradise Regained).

Parah adummah (red heifer): see RED HEIFER.

Pārājika-dhamma. The four most serious offences against the Buddhist monastic code of discipline (*prātimokṣa), the penalty for which is lifelong expulsion from the Order (*saṅgha). They are (i) sexual intercourse, (ii) serious theft, (iii) murder, and (iv) falsely claiming to have attained supernatural powers.

Parakīya (woman, one outside ordinary bounds): see SAHAJĪYĀ.

Paramahaṃsa (Skt., 'highest flyer'). The highest of four categories of Hindu ascetics seeking *mokṣa; also the followers of a school derived from Śaṅkara.

Paramātman (Skt., 'Supreme Self'). The Supreme Spirit, i.e. *Brahman. In the *Pañcadaśī, the paramātman is defined as 'the substratum on which the individual souls (*jīvas) are superimposed'.

Among Jains, paramātman takes on a comparable significance, especially after the work of *Kundakunda. The self, freed from all impediment of *karma, in its unconditioned and absolute state, is realized by liberated *jīvas. Since this paramātman pre-exists all manifestations and is unaffected (however much impeded) by them, the paramātman becomes an object of reverence for Jains: it can be revered in all beings, but especially in the *tīrthaṅkaras (ford-makers).

Parameśvara (Skt., 'the highest god'). In *Kashmir Śaivism, the highest Reality, conceived to be either beyond all thirty-six *tattvas or as the thirty-seventh. All reality, both mystical and material, emanates from Parameśvara, also called Paramaśiva, through a process of 'shining forth' (*ābhāsa*).

Pāramitā (Skt., 'that which has crossed over'). In Mahāyāna Buddhism, the six (or later ten) virtues developed by *bodhisattvas: (i) *dāna-paramitā, generosity; (ii) *śīla-paramitā, correct conduct; (iii) kṣānti-paramitā, patient acceptance of injuries received; (iv) *vīrya-paramitā, exertion; (v) *dhyāna-paramitā, meditation; (vi) *prajña-paramitā, wisdom; (vii) *upāya-kauśalya-paramitā, skill-in-means; (viii) pranidhāna-paramitā, the bodhisattva vow; (ix) bala-paramitā, manifestation of the ten powers of knowledge; (x) *jñana-paramitā, true wisdom. Of these, (vi) is often considered paramount, the others relating more to means than to the end. Consequently, there developed the *Perfection of Wisdom literature and school (Prajñāparāmitā).

Paramparā (Skt., 'succession'). A lineage of spiritual teachers (*guru/*acārya) in Hinduism. The paramparā is thought to be the means of channelling spiritual power through time, passed on from one guru to his successor. The guru's teaching is thus authenticated by the lineage (hence the frequent form, *guruparamparā*). Each paramparā has a founder (*ādiguru) who is often thought to have received teachings directly from a divine source.

Parapsychology. Literally the scientific study of what lies beyond (Gk., *para*) those properties of the mind which are accepted by current scientific research. However, since there is very considerable debate as to whether or not paranormal (or 'psi') phenomena actually exist, it is better defined as the scientific investigation of a possibility. The main psi candidates which have been advanced for research purposes can be classed under two headings: ESP (extrasensory perception) which covers paranormal cognition, as with telepathy, clairvoyance, and precognition, and PK (psychokinesis) which covers paranormal action, such as influencing electronic and atomic randomizers.

Parāśara. A *ṛṣi who is said to have been one of the four law-givers. *Ṛg Veda* 1. 65–75 and 9. 97 are attributed to him.

Paraśurāma (Skt., 'Rāma with the axe'). In Hindu mythology, a *brahman of the *Bhṛgu clan, destined from birth to lead a warrior's life. He is chiefly known as the hero of two myths. In many ways Paraśurāma is a puzzling figure: although the *Purāṇas identify him with *Viṣṇu and he becomes the sixth *avatāra in the standard list, he is also presented as a protégé of *Śiva, who gives him his celebrated axe.

Parāvṛtti (Skt., *parā* + √*vṛt*, 'turn away'). A revolution, according to Buddhists, in one's understanding of reality. The term is not found in the Pāli *Tripiṭaka but is used frequently in the writings of the Yogācāra (*Vijñānavāda) and of Buddhist *Tantrism. Through parāvṛtti the bodhisattva attains the body of a *Tathāgata (*tathāgatakāya*) and is beyond the reach of the illusory world. This is *nirvāna.

Pardes (Pers., 'garden', perhaps underlying Gk., *paradeisos*). It appears in scripture three times (see PARADISE, plus Nehemiah 2. 8). In *B.Ḥag.* 14b, it is used of the Divine Wisdom; and in medieval Judaism, it was taken to be an acrostic of the four major styles of biblical interpretation: *Peshat (literal); Remez (allusive); Derash (homiletical); Sodh (esoteric or mystical).

Pardon. Forgiveness; hence a name for an *indulgence. The attempt to sell such pardons by 'pardoners' was attacked by Chaucer and Langland, long before the *Reformation and its own attack on indulgences.

Paribbājaka (one who joins a community): see AÑÑATITTHIYA PARIBBĀJAKA; PABBĀJITA; PARIVRĀJAKA.

Pariṇāmavāda. The Hindu *Saṃkhya teaching of evolution: effects exist latently within causes (since otherwise eventualities would be random and inconsistent in relation to similar causes); all that is required is the appropriate 'trigger' to release the latent effect. However, such latency may mean that the direction of unfolding (*udbhāva*) can run backwards with equal consistency (*anudbhāva*).

Parinirvāṇa or **parinibbāna** (passing into nirvāna at death): see NIRUPADHIŚEṢA-NIRVĀṆA; MAHĀ-PARINIBBĀNA SUTTA.

Parish (Gk., dwelling near). A geographically designated area having its own church and minister; hence the people and work of that area. From this derives the (usually pejorative) sense of 'parochial', being too narrowly or locally concerned.

Paris worth a Mass: see HUGUENOTS.

Paritta (Pāli, Sinhalese, *pirit*, from Skt., *pari* + √*trā* to protect). A formula which is to be recited for protection or blessing; the non-canonical collection of such formulae; and the *ritual at which the collection of this formulae or specific portions thereof are recited. Paritta is a Buddhist healing and blessing rite. Originally adopted to cater to the extrareligious needs of the new converts to Buddhism, both from the *brahmanic and the non-brahmanic religious followings, it has absorbed into itself many features of the protective, healing, and blessing rites of those religions.

The Pāli texts used in the paritta rites form a separate text consisting of twenty-nine *sūtras of mixed length. While all these belong to different texts of the five *Nikāya collections, the majority are associated with individual instances of healing or blessing. All such texts may have been incorporated into a single text after the paritta attained ritual significance.

Parivāra (division of Vinayapiṭaka): see TRIPIṬAKA.

Parivrājaka (Skt., *pari* + √*vraj*, 'to wander about'). A wandering religious mendicant. Although this term occurs in the early Brahmanic tradition of the *Upaniṣads, it is also applicable to *Buddhist and *Jain monks, as well as to Hindu *saṁnyāsins. The Pāli equivalent is *paribbājaka*.

Pariyatti. The entire teaching of the *Buddha: it is thus one of the Buddhist meanings of *dharma.

Parker, Matthew (1504–75). Archbishop of Canterbury from 1559. His main objective as archbishop was to preserve the Elizabethan religious settlement which sought to safeguard Protestantism while retaining some of the moderation placed on it by the experience of the past. He sought to find the proper doctrinal and historical basis for the Church of England, and to this end he accumulated a library with many Anglo-Saxon and medieval manuscripts (which can be seen in Corpus Christi College, Cambridge).

Parliament of Religions: see WORLD'S PARLIAMENT OF RELIGIONS.

Parochet or **parokhet.** The curtain that separated the 'holy place' in the sanctuary from the *Holy of Holies (Exodus 26. 31–3). Nowadays the term is used by the *Ashkenazim to refer to the curtain hanging before the *Ark in the *synagogue.

Parousia (Gk., 'presence' or 'arrival'). The final establishing of the Kingdom of God, associated with the coming of the Lord (God, often identified with *Christ, hence the 'Second Coming') to judge the living and the dead. Belief in an imminent parousia was widespread in the earliest church (cf. 1 Corinthians 16. 22) but quickly faded (2 Peter 3. 3–10). It has been revived from time to time in various Christian and *extra*-Christian circles (*Adventists), often accompanied by belief in a *millennium, or thousand-year reign of Christ on earth.

Parsis. *Zoroastrians who (in the 8th cent. CE), in unknown numbers, decided to leave their Iranian homeland in the face of ever greater Muslim oppression and seek a new land of religious freedom. The story of that migration is contained in the text the *Qissa* (or *Tale*) *of Sanjan* (see S. H. Hodivala, *Studies in Parsi History*, 1920). The *Qissa* was written in 1600 by a Parsi priest on the basis of oral tradition.

The generally accepted date of the Parsi settlement on the western coast of India is 937 CE. Little is known of their history for the next 700 years. With the arrival of the European trading powers in the 17th cent., especially the British, they prospered as middle men in trade. As a result they grew also in political importance; e.g. they were at the heart of the Indian National Congress from its inception in 1885 until the radical takeover in 1907.

The transformation of the community from a tiny obscure group into a major force in Indian life has inevitably had its effect on their religion. Although daily prayers are still said at home, many of the important moments of worship are now located in a place set apart for that purpose. Large *baugs*, public places, were set up for splendid functions for initiations, weddings, and public religious feasts (*gahambars*). There was, in short, a considerable degree of institutionalization of community religion.

There were also significant developments in faith. At the end of the 19th cent., many Parsis, like a number of Westernized Hindus, sought to legitimate traditional practices in terms of *Theosophy and the occult interpretations that the Western-originated movement propounded. When Theosophy became more closely associated with Hinduism and the Independence movement, then a Zoroastrian occult movement grew, Ilm-i Kshnoom (Path of Knowledge). Instead of turning to the Tibetan Masters invoked by Theosophists, Khshnoomists follow the teaching of Behramshah Shroff who claimed to have been given his esoteric message by a secret race of Zoroastrian masters in Iran. This movement shares the Theosophical ideals of vegetarianism and teetotalism, the doctrine of rebirth, the belief in the occult power of prayers recited in the sacred language, and in a personal aura. Thus in the 19th cent. Parsi doctrine became polarized between the Liberal Protestants and the Orthodox who have inclined more towards the occult. There are now *c*.60,000 Parsis in India. Numbers in Karachi have dropped from *c*.5,000 in the 1950s to 2,000 in the 1990s.

An unknown number, but a substantial proportion, of the Parsi population has migrated, first to Britain (initially in the 19th cent., but more particularly from the 1960s, *c*.3,000), then America and Canada, also from the 1960s (*c*.7,000), and from the 1980s to Australia (*c*.1,000).

Pārśva. Twenty-third *tīrthaṅkara in Jainism. Accepted now as a historical figure, born in the 9th cent BCE (*c*.250 years before *Mahāvīra), tradition claims that he became a wandering ascetic for seventy years, teaching the law of fourfold restraint: *ahiṃsā (non-injury); *asatya* (not lying); *asteya* (not taking anything not given); *aparigraha (non-attachment to people, places, or things). According to 11th-cent. Jain commentators, this latter restraint included *brahmacharya (chastity), the fifth vow in Mahāvīra's *mahāvratas* (see FIVE GREAT VOWS). Jain scriptures describe him as 'the Best', 'the Awakened', and 'the Omniscient', and claim that he gained a large following in his travels through Bihar and W. Bengal, where Jains today give him special honour, particularly on Mount Sammeta where he attained *nirvāna and died. Numerous excavations in N. India have uncovered images of

Pārśva seated under a canopy of cobras, the symbol associated with this *jina.

Particular Baptists. Those *Baptists committed to the *Calvinistic doctrine of 'particular' redemption for the elect only. The term distinguishes them from the other main group of English Baptists with 17th-cent. origins, the *General Baptists, who adhered to an *Arminian theology.

Pārvatī (Skt., 'daughter of the mountain'). Also called *Umā or Gaurī. A beautiful benign Goddess in Hinduism, the wife of *Śiva and daughter of the mountain *Himālaya whose mythology is found in the *Mahābhārata* and the *Purāṇas. Their marriage is a model of male dominance with Pārvatī docilely serving her husband, though this is also a model of the way a mortal should serve the god. Although at one level subservient, there is behind Pārvatī the power of the Goddess (*Devī) who is thought to be beyond the gods.

Parveh or **pareveh** (Yid., 'neutral'). Food which is classified by the Jewish authorities as neutral. It is neither milk nor meat and therefore under the rules of *kashrut* can be eaten with either. See DIETARY LAWS (JUDAISM).

Paryūsana. Jain *festival of repentance, fasting, self-discipline, and universal goodwill, held over an eight (*Śvetāmbara) or ten (*Digambara) day period in the months of Shrāvana/Bhādrapada (Aug./Sept.) when Jain monks and nuns are in retreat for the monsoon season. It is the most distinctive and important of Jain festivals, when the laity seek forgiveness for any misdeeds of the previous year and spend time with their ascetic leaders performing *sāmāyikas, listening to regular sermons and attending rituals in the temple.

Pascal, Blaise (1623–62). French mathematician and philosopher. From 1646 he was closely involved with the *Jansenists and the convent of Port-Royal. On 23 Nov. 1654 he experienced a conversion, recorded in his *Mémorial* (but found stitched into his coat, known as Pascal's amulet), in which he discovered 'the God of Abraham, God of Isaac, God of Jacob, not of the philosophers and the men of science'. When the Jansenist, Arnauld, was condemned in 1655, he wrote his *Lettres provinciales* in which he satirized the laxity implicit in *Jesuit theories of grace and moral theology. In his *Pensées*, published posthumously from his notes, Pascal saw Christianity as lying beyond exact reason and apprehended by the heart which dares to risk. He is associated also with his 'wager': if we believe God exists and he does, the reward is eternal happiness; if he does not exist, we lose nothing; and the same is true if we disbelieve and he does not exist; whereas if we disbelieve and he does exist, we have lost eternal life. On the mathematics of probability (see further, G. Schlesinger, *Religion and Scientific Method*, 1977), the wager should be taken up *unless* the existence of God can be conclusively disproved —which it cannot.

Paschal (Aramaic, *pasḥa*, 'Passover'). Of or relating to the Jewish *Passover or more usually the Christian *Easter. 'Paschaltide', or Eastertide, is the period in the Christian year from Easter to *Pentecost. The 'paschal candle' is a large candle used in W. churches during Paschaltide.

Paschal lamb. The lamb sacrificed in the Temple as part of the Jewish *Passover festival. The paschal lamb was sacrificed on 14 Nisan, roasted whole and eaten by the community (Exodus 12. 1–28; Deuteronomy 16. 1–8). In Christianity, *Jesus became identified with the paschal Lamb.

Paschal mystery. The Christian understanding of human salvation concentrated in Christ, dead, risen from the dead, and ascended to heaven, who is the *paschal Lamb of the new Passover.

Pasha. Turkish military and civil title denoting someone of high rank. The title persists in some Arab countries for more local authorities.

Passion (Lat., *passio*, 'suffering'). The events of *Jesus' last days as recounted in the *gospels, culminating in his crucifixion. From at least the 4th cent. the passion was recited with musical settings in churches during *Holy Week; by the Middle Ages, the chant was *plainsong, with motet choruses added in the 15th cent. The *St John Passion* (1723) and *St Matthew Passion* (1729) of J. S. Bach are among the most familiar of these Passions.

Passion Sunday is the 5th Sunday in Lent, a week before *Palm Sunday, but Passion Sunday is now fused with Palm Sunday.

Passion plays are enactments of the suffering, death, and resurrection of Jesus which served, originally, important didactic purposes. The best known of these is a late example, the play at Oberammergau in Bavaria. According to tradition, the village was spared from plague in 1633, and vowed, in gratitude, to perform a passion play once every ten years. The term 'passion play' is also used of dramatic reenactments, by Shī'a Muslims, of the martyrdom of *al-Husain (and *al-Hasan): see TA'ZIYA. For a text, see L. Pelly, *The Miracle Play of Hasan and Husain* (1879).

Passion plays (in Shī'a Islam): see TA'ZIYA.

Passion Sunday: see PALM SUNDAY.

Passover (Heb., *pesaḥ*). Jewish Festival of Unleavened Bread (*mazzah), one of the *Pilgrim Festivals. The festival begins on 15 Nisan and lasts seven days in *Israel and eight in the *diaspora. During this time, the *exodus from Egypt is commemorated. It is so called because God 'passed over' the houses of the Israelites during the tenth plague of Egypt (Exodus 12). Traditionally the *paschal lamb was sacrificed in the *Temple on Passover eve (14 Nisan), and both *Josephus and the *Talmud record Passover celebrations in the second Temple period. After the destruction of the Temple, the celebrations of the festival reverted to being home-based.

Pastoral Epistles. The three letters, 1–2 *Timothy and *Titus in the New Testament, so-called because they contain instructions for church officers and organization.

Pāśupata (Skt., *paśu*, 'beast', + *pati*, 'lord'). An early *Śaiva sect worshipping *Śiva as Pāśupati. Their name is derived from the threefold Śaiva doctrine of Lord (*pati*), soul (*paśu*, 'beast'), and bondage (*pāśa*). Accounts of them are given in the **Mahābhārata*, the *Vayu *Purāṇa* and the *Atharvaśiras *Upaniṣad*. Their doctrines are known from the later *Pāśupata Sūtra* and the commentary by Kauṇḍīnya (5th or 6th cent. CE). The Pāśupatas maintained that Śiva is transcendent, and is the instrumental, not the material, cause of the world. The aim of Pāśupata practice, which comprised *yoga, *asceticism, and *mantra repetition, was freedom from suffering, which comes about only through grace (*prasāda). The Pāśupatas were celibate (*urdhvā retas*, ones who 'keep their semen up'), and ascetic (*tapasvin). They also practised anti-social behaviour, such as snoring in public, acting as if mad, and talking nonsensically, in order to court abuse, whereby the *karma merit of the abuser would be transferred to the abused. They went naked, with matted hair, covered in ashes, and frequented cremation grounds.

Paśupati (lord of cattle). *Śiva as the lord of all creatures.

Pāṭaliputra. The capital of the ancient kingdom of Magadha (near present-day Patna in N. India). After the reign of *Aśoka, who expanded the city and held the third Buddhist *Council there (247 BCE), Pāṭaliputra fell into decline.

Patañjali. 1. The reputed author of the **Yoga Sūtra* (2nd–3rd cents. CE), in which classical yoga is given systematic presentation.

2. An Indian grammarian of the 2nd cent. BCE who wrote *The Great Commentary* (*Mahābhāṣya*), an explanation of grammar based on the *Aṣṭadhyāya* of *Pāṇini. His text is concerned with various philosophical and grammatical problems such as the relation of word to meaning. He has sometimes been collated with Patañjali (1), but whether the two are really one person is still uncertain.

Paten. The dish on which the bread is placed at the Christian *eucharist.

Pater noster. Lat. for 'Our Father'. See LORD'S PRAYER.

Pāṭh (Hindī, Pañjābī, 'reading'). For Sikhs, a reading of the entire *Ādi Granth. This may be an uninterrupted reading (*akhaṇḍ pāṭh) or may take about ten days or longer (sahaj pāṭh, sadhāran pāṭh).

Paticca-samuppāda (Pāli; Skt., *pratītya-samutpāda*). A key concept in Buddhism, variously translated—e.g. 'dependent origination', 'conditioned genesis', 'interconnected arising', 'causal nexus'. It states that all physical and mental manifestations which constitute individual appearances are interdependent and condition or affect one another, in a constant process of arising (*samudaya*) and ceasing to be (*nirodha). The analysis is laid out in, e.g., **Saṃyutta Nikāya* 2. 1–133 and **Dīgha Nikāya* 2. 55–71. The 'knitting-together' which constructs appearances and activities in the realm of *samsāra is the twelve-link (*nidāna*) chain of paticca-samuppāda, which leads inevitably to entanglement and *dukkha (the cessation of dukkha being the unravelling of the chain in reverse order): (i) ignorance, *avidyā leads to (ii) constructing activities, *samskāra, to (iii) consciousness leading into another appearance/birth, *vijñāna, to (iv) *nāma-rūpa, name and form of a new appearance, to (v) the sense awareness of the six object realms, to (vi) contact with those environments, to (vii) sensation and feeling, *vedanā* (see SKANDHA), to (viii) craving, *tṛṣṇa, to (ix) clinging on to life and further life in a new womb, *upādāna, to (x) further becoming and appearance, *bhāva, to (xi) birth, *jāti*, to (xii) old age, senility, and death.

Pāṭihāriya (Pāli, 'wonder', 'marvel', 'phenomenon'). A device that could be put to use in winning converts to Buddhism. Canonical Buddhism acknowledges three: the wonder of magic power (*iddhi-pāṭihāriya), of mind-reading (*ādesanā-pāṭihāriya*), and of instruction (*anusāsana-pāṭihāriya*). The use of displays of the first two to impress and convert laypersons was severely criticized by the Buddha, because they were feats which non-Buddhist ascetics could also perform and because they played upon people's credulity. He stressed the absolute sovereignty of the third device, instruction in the *dharma, because it was a means of communicating truths that were intelligible and beneficial to its audience and not a form of exhibitionism like the others.

Pātimokkha (Buddhist moral code): see PRĀTIMOKṢA.

Paṭipatti. The practice of Buddhist truth, and thus one of the many meanings of *dharma.

Patisambhidāmagga (part of Buddhist Pāli canon): see KHUDDAKA-NIKĀYA.

Patit (Pañjābī, 'fallen'). Lapsed Sikh. Any *amritdhārī Sikh who breaks the *khālsā's code of discipline (*rahit), most often by hair-cutting and removal of *turban, is termed 'patit'.

Paṭivedha. The realization of Buddhist truth through stages, leading up to *nirvāna, and thus one of the many meanings of *dharma.

Patriarch. 1. Title from the 6th cent. for the presiding *bishops of the five main sees of Christendom (Rome, Alexandria, Antioch, Constantinople, and Jerusalem), corresponding to provinces of the Roman Empire, who had authority over the *metropolitans in their territories. In addition to these, the heads of some *autocephalous Orthodox churches, the heads of *Uniat Churches, and the heads of the *Oriental Orthodox and *Assyrian Churches also have the title of patriarch.

2. The term is also used as an English equivalent of *soshigata, the founder of a Buddhist, especially Zen, school, together with his lineage successors.

Patriarchs and matriarchs. The ancestors of the Jewish people. The *rabbis designated *Abraham, *Isaac, and *Jacob and their wives Sarah, Rebekah, Leah, and Rachel as the patriarchs and matriarchs of Israel. Their stories are told in *Genesis.

Patrick, St (*c*.390–*c*.460). Christian missionary bishop of Ireland.

The only certain information about St Patrick's life comes from his one surviving letter and from his autobiographical *Confession*. His authorship of the ancient Irish hymn 'The Breastplate of St Patrick' is unlikely. In later legends, he becomes a miracle-worker who drove the snakes out of Ireland. The same legends, concerned to make him the sole 'apostle of the Irish', exaggerate the scope of his missionary work. His place of burial was not known, allowing *Glastonbury to claim possession of his relics. Feast day, 17 Mar.

Patripassianism (Lat., *pater*, 'father', + *passus*, 'suffered'). The Christian doctrine, usually held to be *heretical, that God the Father was the subject of Jesus' sufferings. See also IMPASSIBILITY OF GOD.

Patristics. The study of Christian writers, specifically the *Church Fathers, in the period from the end of New Testament times to *Isidore of Seville (d. 636) in the W. and *John of Damascus (d. *c*.749) in the E. The term 'patrology', synonymous in older books, now usually refers to a handbook on the patristic literature.

Patrology: see PATRISTICS.

Patronage (nominating to a benefice): see ADVOWSON.

Patron saint. A *saint who is recognized, or has been chosen as the special protector or advocate in heaven of a particular place, church, organization, trade, etc.

Pa-tuan-chin. A series of eight Taoist physical exercises, dating from the 12th cent. CE, to which others were added at a later date. They exist in two forms, northern (harder) and southern (easier).

Paul, St (d. *c*.65 CE). The most important early Christian *missionary *apostle and theologian.

The main source for Paul's biography is *Acts, which however must be tested against the sparse data in Paul's own letters. Paul (originally 'Saul') was a Jewish native of Tarsus in Cilicia. He was brought up as a *Pharisee and probably studied in Jerusalem. He opposed the Christian movement, but while on a mission to Damascus (*c*.33 CE) to arrest Christians he was converted by an encounter with the risen *Christ (described in Acts 9. 1–19), probably while practising *merkabah mysticism. Paul's main missionary work appears to have begun fourteen or seventeen years later (Galatians 1–2). According to Acts it took the form of three missionary journeys beginning and ending at *Antioch: 13–14, 15. 36–18. 23, 18. 23–21. He thus established congregations in south and central Asia Minor, Ephesus, and Greece. These were largely Gentile congregations, although he continued to preach in *synagogues. He was constantly harassed by local authorities and Jewish communities (2 Corinthians 11. 24–7). He was at last arrested in Jerusalem, and sent for trial to Caesarea, and then (on his appealing to Caesar) to Rome (Acts 21–8). An early tradition holds that Paul was acquitted, and then preached in Spain before being re-arrested and put to death by the sword under Nero. The church of St Paul Outside the Walls in Rome was built over the site of his burial. Feast days: with Peter, 29 June; conversion, 25 Jan.

Of the thirteen letters in Paul's name in the New Testament (*Hebrews makes no claim to be by Paul), scholars generally, but not unanimously, distinguish seven as certainly genuine (*Romans, 1–2 *Corinthians, *Galatians, *Philippians, 1 *Thessalonians, *Philemon) and six as 'deutero-Pauline'. The latter (*Ephesians, *Colossians, 2 *Thessalonians, 1–2 *Timothy, *Titus) reflect Paul's thought more or less weakly, but are by no means certainly not written by Paul. The genuine letters date from the period from *c.*51 (1 Thessalonians) to *c.*58 (Romans). Philippians, Colossians, Philemon, and Ephesians, known as 'captivity epistles', if from Paul, may have been written later in Rome, or from an earlier time in prison in Ephesus or Caesarea.

Although they are not systematic writings, Paul's letters laid the foundations for much of later Christian theology. Paul's doctrine, starting from the traditions he 'received' (1 Corinthians 15. 3–11), was further worked out in controversy with right-wing Jewish Christians, against whom Paul held that sinful humanity is redeemed and justified by God's *grace through *faith in Jesus Christ, independently of keeping the Jewish *law. Christ's death had abrogated the Law and ushered in the new era of the *Holy Spirit. Christians therefore form a new *'Israel of God' (Galatians 6. 16) and inherit the promises of God to Israel (see especially Galatians and Romans). The local congregation is likened to a body by Paul, and in Colossians 1. 24 the whole church is called the body of Christ. Paul expected a speedy return of Christ to judge the world (e.g. 1 Thessalonians 4) but this theme recedes in the later letters.

Paul III (1468–1549). *Pope, 1534–49. He received a humanist education and was made cardinal deacon by pope Alexander VI in 1493 (his nickname was 'cardinal petticoat', because his sister was the pope's mistress). He was not ordained priest until 1519, but he nevertheless held benefices and bishoprics. As bishop of Parma (1509), he put the reforms of the Fifth Lateran Council into effect, and began to reform his own life. Elected pope unanimously, he became 'a renaissance pope', encouraging artists and architects. He also undertook reform of the Church (he is sometimes called 'the first pope of Catholic reform') to meet the threat of *Protestantism. He supported Charles V in his campaign to destroy the alliance of Protestants known as the Schmalkaldic League, and he excommunicated Henry VIII in 1538.

Paul VI (1897–1978). *Pope from 21 June 1963. Born Giovanni Battista Montini near Brescia, he entered the papal secretariat of state in 1924 and served there until appointed archbishop of Milan in 1955. As pope he pledged himself to continue the policies of *John XXIII: he continued the Second *Vatican Council, instituted a regular *synod of bishops to assist in governing the church, reformed the *curia and the diplomatic service, legislated for revised *liturgical rites, and abolished the *Index. In 1967 he published **Humanae Vitae* which reiterated the traditional RC rejection of artificial means of birth control, and this overshadowed his more progressive actions, such as the 1975 Apostolic Exhortation *Evangelii Nuntiandi* with its implicit endorsement of some elements of *liberation theology.

Paulicians. Christian sect prominent in the 7th–11th cents. in Armenia and the east of the Byzantine Empire. According to Gk. sources they were *Manicheans, and by modern scholars they have often been considered a link in the chain between the early *gnostics and the Manichees of the Middle Ages. Apart from a period of favour under the *Iconoclast emperors of the 8th–9th cents., the Paulicians were persecuted in the Empire, and allied themselves with the Muslim power.

Paul of Samosata (3rd cent.). Christian *heretic. He became bishop of Antioch *c.*260 but was deposed by a synod there in 268 on account of his *Christological teaching, little of which has survived. The best-attested accusation against Paul is that he taught that Christ was a mere man.

Pauṛī (Pañjābī, 'ladder'). Sikh verse. The *padās* (sections) of longer poems in the *Ādi Granth are called pauṛīs.

Paytanim. Jewish liturgical poets (e.g. Eleazar *Kallir): see PIYYUT.

Peace (exchange of greetings): see KISS OF PEACE.

Peacock Angel (Yezīdī term for Satan): see YEZĪDĪS.

Peak-experiences: see MASLOW, A. H.

Peculiar People. A small *Free Church denomination taking its title from the description in 1 Peter 2. 9. They were initially called the 'Plumstead Peculiars' from the place of their origin in 1838. Most of these congregations no longer use their original title and have now become affiliated to the Fellowship of Independent Evangelical Churches.

P'ei Hsiu (Jap., Haikyu): see HUANG-PO HSI-YÜN.

Pelagianism. The Christian *heresy which holds that a person can come to salvation by her or his own efforts apart from God's grace; or in co-operation with grace. It is named from the British theologian Pelagius, who taught in Rome in the 4th–5th cents. Pelagius' teaching was ascetic and moral, arguing that human nature is created by God in such a way that individuals are free to choose good or evil. Pelagianism was finally condemned at the Council of *Ephesus in 431. Its influence continued, especially in the S. of France in the form of a movement now called 'semi-Pelagianism'. First expounded by John *Cassian, this was a doctrine midway between Augustine and Pelagius, mainly in opposition to Augustine's extreme views of predestination. It held that the first steps toward the Christian life were taken by the human will, God's grace supervening only later. After its condemnation in 529, Augustine's teaching on grace and free will prevailed everywhere in the Christian West.

Pelican. A bird, employed as Christian symbol. Because of the false belief that the pelican feeds her young with her blood by piercing her breast with her beak, the pelican became a popular medieval symbol for Christ's redemptive work, especially as mediated through the *eucharist.

Penance. In Christianity, punishment (Lat., *poena*) for sin. By the 3rd cent. the system had emerged in which the sinner, after public confession, was placed, once only in his or her life, in an order of 'penitents', excluded from communion and committed to a severe course of prayer, fasting, and almsgiving for a specified time. This scarcely workable system gave place to another, originally *Celtic, in which confession was made privately. Public penance continued for notorious offences. From all this developed the Catholic practice of *confession, *absolution, and light penance.

P'eng Lai. Taoist 'isle of the immortals' (*hsien), first referred to in *Lieh-tzu*. Many stories are told of expeditions to reach it and find the mushroom of immortality. All fail, because if the hazards of shipwreck, etc., are overcome, the island sinks as the sailors approach. The story becomes in later Taoism an allegory of the spiritual quest.

P'eng-tzu. Mythological figure in China, representing long life. In religious Taoism, he is said to have introduced *fang-chung shu (sexual exchange of power) for that purpose.

Penitence, Ten Days of. The period of ten days from *Rosh ha-Shanah to Yom Kippur in the Jewish *Calendar. According to tradition, individuals are judged at the *New Year (1 Tishri) and the judgement is announced on the *Day of Atonement. Clemency can be obtained through sincere repentance during the Ten Days of Penitence.

Penitential prayers (Jewish): see SELIḤOT.

Penn, William (1644–1718). *Quaker leader and founder of Pennsylvania. Frequently imprisoned for his writings, he used his confinements to produce further apologetic works, notably *No Cross No Crown* (1669), and assisted the Quaker pursuit of religious and political freedom by obtaining from Charles II a charter for Pennsylvania. His later years were saddened by ill health, poverty, and imprisonment.

Pentateuch (Gk., *penta*, 'five', + *teuchos*, 'book'). The first five books of the Hebrew *Bible, also known as *Torah (for Hebrew names see each book): *Genesis, *Exodus, *Leviticus, *Numbers, and *Deuteronomy. The Pentateuch contains the history of the Jewish people from the creation of the world until the death of *Moses. Traditionally it was believed to be a single document revealed by God to Moses and written down by him. According to the 'documentary hypothesis', it is composed of four major sources: J (Jahwistic) which uses in Genesis the *tetragrammaton as the divine name; E (Elohistic) which refers to God as *Elohim until Exodus; P, the *Priestly source; and D, the *Deuteronomic. J and E, which have been combined by a later editor are thought to have been written during the period of the united kingdom (i.e. 10th cent. BCE), while Deuteronomy was produced in the 7th cent., and the Priestly source is dated to the time of *Ezra and *Nehemiah. However, the precision of these claims has more recently come under attack. Greater emphasis is placed on kinship and sanctuary traditions which have been more deliberately and creatively drawn together. The entire Pentateuch is divided into fifty-four sections (*Sedarot) and one section is read each week in the *synagogue, concluding on Shemini Atzeret. The text is written on a *Scroll which is dressed and kept in the Synagogue *Ark. The Pentateuch, as the written law of the Jewish people and the ultimate source of the *oral Law, is often known as the Torah, and thus the Scroll as the Torah Scroll.

Pentecost. The Jewish feast of Weeks, i.e. *Shavu'ot, held fifty days (hence the name) after *Passover. The Greek name occurs in (e.g.) Tobit 2. 1; *Josephus, *Antiquities*, 17. 10. 2. In Christian use, 'Pentecost' refers specifically to the occasion at the conclusion of the Jewish festival when, according to the account in Acts 2, the *Holy Spirit descended on the *apostles 'with the noise of a strong driving wind' in the form of tongues of fire, so that they began to speak in foreign languages.

Pentecostals/Pentecostalism. Groups of Christians who emphasize the descent of the *Holy Spirit on the *apostles at the first (Christian) Pentecost (Acts 2) and the continuing post-conversion work of the Holy Spirit. The modern movements date from the ministry of Charles Parham (1873–1929) in the USA, in 1900/1901. He linked baptism in the Spirit with *glossolalia (speaking with tongues), and saw the revival as a restoration of the gifts promised in the latter days. Because experience outweighs formal ministry, there have been many Pentecostal churches. There are at least 130 million Pentecostals worldwide, with particularly rapid expansion in S. America. See also CHARISMATIC (MOVEMENT).

People of God (Russian sect): see DOUKHOBHORS.

People of the Book (those whom Muslims accept have received revelation from God): see AHL AL-KITĀB.

Peoples' Temple. Movement founded by the Reverend Jim Jones, a Christian socialist, in Indianapolis during the early 1950s. Having moved to California in 1965, Jones then established Jonestown, Guyana (1977). The Jonestown tragedy occurred in Nov. 1978, when 913 followers and Jones himself died, a sizeable number by drinking cyanide-laced 'Flavor-Aid' (the remainder were murdered). The tragedy was triggered by an investigation by Congressman Les Ryan and a party of journalists, seen as demonic agents.

Peot (Heb., 'corners'). The growth of *hair by Jews in accordance with the command of Leviticus 19. 27. By the *Talmudic period, it was interpreted to mean that some hair must be left between the back of the ears and the forehead, and for many Jews in the present the command is obeyed by taking care not to remove all the hair by the ear. Ḥasidim encourage the long twisting locks which mark them off from gentiles (and from other Jews), although there is no specific commandment for them.

Perek Shirah (Heb., 'Chapter of a Song'). An anonymous Jewish tract containing hymns of praise. It is sometimes recited as a private prayer after the morning service.

Perennial philosophy: see PHILOSOPHIA PERENNIS.

Perfection. A term meaning 'completeness', in which sense it is only absolutely appropriate to God, though the Gk. term (*teleiosis*) can also mean 'consecration'. Whether perfection is possible in this life, even through grace, has been disputed amongst Christians, *Protestants being mainly doubtful, though *pietists and *Methodists see it as the normal consequence of conversion. For the Buddhist perfections see BHŪMI.

Perfection of Wisdom literature (Prajñāpāramitā). This Buddhist literature was composed over a long period, the nucleus of the material appearing from 100 BCE to 100 CE, with additions for perhaps two cents. later. There followed a period of summary and restatement in the form of short sūtras such as the **Diamond* and **Heart Sūtras*, *c*.300–500 CE, followed by a period of *Tantric influence, 600–1200 CE. The oldest text is *Aṣṭasāhasrikā-prajñāpāramitā-sūtra* (Perfection of Wisdom in 8,000 Lines).

The Prajñāpāramitā literature was innovative in two principal ways: (i) it advocated the *bodhisattva ideal as the highest form of the religious life; and (ii) the 'wisdom' it teaches is that of the emptiness (*śūnyatā) and non-production of phenomena (*dharmas), rather than their substantial, albeit impermanent, mode of being.

Other important developments in the Perfection of Wisdom literature are the concept of 'skilful means' (**upāya-kauśalya*) and the practice of dedicating one's religious merit to others so that they are assisted in realizing śūnyatā in their own case. The major exponent of the Perfection of Wisdom school was *Nāgārjuna.

Perfect Life Society/Kyōdan (Japanese religious movement): see MIKI TOKUHARU.

Pericope (Gk., 'section'). A passage of scripture; specifically, one that is a self-contained product of oral tradition, or one prescribed for liturgical reading.

Periyâḻvār (one of the Āḻvārs, group of Hindu poets): see ĀḺVĀR.

Persecution. Adherents of virtually all religions have suffered persecution for their faith at some point in their history, and such persecution has generally been held to forge a more resilient faith. Thus the pressure on *Muḥammad during the Meccan period made him more determined, so that *martyrs (*shahīd) became highly favoured and revered in Islam. That 'the blood of the martyrs is the seed of the church' (see TERTULLIAN) arose as a belief from the early cents. of Christianity, when Christians were sporadically persecuted as a non-conformist minority: there was only formal imperial persecution under the Emperors Decius (250), Valerian (257–8), and Diocletian (304–11). The 20th cent. has seen persecution of Christians on an unprecedented scale—by atheistic communism, by fascism, and by militant Islam in certain countries. See also ANTI-SEMITISM; HOLOCAUST.

Perushim: see PHARISEES.

Pesaḥ (Jewish festival): see PASSOVER.

Peshāt. The literal meaning of a Jewish text. Peshāt is generally contrasted with *derāsh, the non-literal interpretation.

Pesher (Heb., 'interpretation'). An inspired application of the Hebrew *prophecies to the historical events of the end of time. The term is used with that implication in Daniel 4. 16.

Pesikta (Aram., 'section'). Jewish *midrashic homilies. The best-known pesikta are *Pesikta de-Rav Kahana* and *Pesikta Rabbati*.

Peta (form of the dead): see PRETA.

Petavatthu (part of Buddhist Pāli canon): see KHUDDAKA-NIKĀYA.

Peter, St. In Christianity, foremost of the *apostles. His name was Simon but according to the gospels *Jesus called him from his work as fisherman and gave him the name 'Cephas', the Aramaic equivalent of Greek 'Peter' (*petra*, 'rock'). According to early tradition Peter visited Rome where he was martyred (*1 Clement* 5, etc.); but the claim that he was its *bishop is an anachronism. According to the 2nd-cent. *Acts of Peter*, the apostle, while fleeing from Nero's persecution, met Jesus on the road. Peter asked, 'Domine, quo vadis?' ('Lord, where are you going?'). When Jesus answered 'I am coming to be crucified again', Peter turned back to the city to face his *martyrdom. His tomb in St Peter's basilica may be authentic. Feast day, 29 June.

The two Letters of Peter are found among the *Catholic Epistles of the New Testament. 2 Peter is a warning against false and corrupt teachers; 2. 1–3. 3 seems to be borrowed from *Jude; features such as the treatment of Paul in 4. 15–16 suggest a date well after Peter's death.

Other 2nd-cent. books attributed to Peter include the *Gospel of Peter* (a *docetic retelling of Jesus' death and *resurrection based on the four New Testament gospels) and *The Apocalypse of Peter* (a description of heaven and hell put into the mouth of Christ after his resurrection).

Peter Damian, St (1007–72). *Monk and *cardinal. In 1035 he entered on an ascetic life in the *Benedictine hermitage at Fonte Avella. About 1043 he became prior and was active in monastic reform and as a preacher against the worldliness of the *clergy. Made cardinal bishop of Ostia (against his will) in 1057, he played a prominent part in the reform movement that heralded the Hildebrandine Reform. He was influential too as theologian and spiritual writer. In 1828, he was pronounced Doctor of the Church.

Peter Lombard (*c*.1100–60). Christian theologian. Born in Lombardy, after studying in Italy, he went to Reims, and then to Paris where he taught from *c*.1134. In 1159 he became bishop of Paris. His chief work, the *Sentences*, was written 1155–8. It became the standard textbook of theology during the Middle Ages, commented on by nearly every theologian of repute.

Peter (Petr) Moghila (Russian Orthodox theologian): see MOGHILA, PETER.

Petiḥah (Heb., 'opening'). The Jewish ritual of opening the *Ark of the *synagogue. Petiḥah is performed during the course of services to take out the *Torah scrolls or to recite prayers of particular importance.

Petits Frères. French (and proper) name for the Little Brothers, a *Roman Catholic order derived from *de Foucauld, characterized by long training, especially in prayer, and by absolute commitment to the places (usually poor) where they are sent. Notable among them have been René Voillaume (see especially his *Seeds of the Desert*) and J. *Maritain.

Petrine texts. Those New Testament texts which are held by *Catholics (mainly, but not exclusively, *Roman Catholics) to establish the supreme authority of *Peter over the *Church, whose foundation, after *Christ, he is. The major text is Matthew 16. 18 f., but others are Mark 3. 16, Luke 24. 34, 1 Corinthians 15. 5. On these texts, the *papacy in fact and theory is founded.

Peyote. A hallucinogenic cactus and the basis of an inter-tribal religion among N. American Indians. It grows only in the Rio Grande valley and N. Mexico, and has long been central in local rites. Peyote brings peace and healing, resists alcoholism, and gives visions of the Peyote Spirit who is regarded either as *Jesus or an Indian equivalent.

Pezpopovtsy ('without priests' group among Old Believers): see OLD BELIEVERS.

'Phags-pa Blo-gros-rgyal-mtshan (*c*.1235–80). One of the five leading figures of the Sa-skya order of Tibetan Buddhism. He was a prolific author who addressed a wide range of topics, engaging also in correspondence with Mongol princes in which he summarized Buddhist teaching. In 1244, when his uncle, Sa-skya Paṇḍita, was summoned to serve in the Mongol court, 'Phags-pa went with him. As a result of this, the Sa-skya order was delegated to rule over Tibet, but 'Phags-pa was kept by the emperor of China, Kubla (Qubilai) Khan, to ensure Tibet's submission to Mongol rule. He so impressed the emperor with his *Tantric skills (which eclipsed those of the court *shamans) that he was made instructor of the court and ruler (in absence) of Tibet. The pattern of relationship between China and Tibet was thus established which is known as *yon mchod*, 'patron and priest', and which was overthrown by the Chinese annexation of Tibet. The emperor is protector of the *lama and through him, by extension, of the land, and the leading lama of Tibet (in due course, the succession of *Dalai Lamas) is the spiritual advisor and guarantor of rites to the emperor. For the complexity of this relationship, see also PANCHEN LAMA.

'Phags-pa-lha (leading exponent of Buddhist Mādhyamaka): see ĀRYADEVA.

Pharisees (Heb., *perushim*, 'separatists' or 'interpreters'). Members of a Jewish religious sect of the second *Temple period. The Pharisees emerged *c*.160 BCE, after the *Hasmonean revolt. They believed themselves to be the inheritors of the traditions of *Ezra and were scrupulous in their obedience to the *oral law as well as to the written *Torah. In some sense, they were the predecessors of the *rabbis. Despite the strong anti-Pharisaic bias of the New Testament, there is no doubt that the Pharisees set high moral standards for themselves and through their devotion sustained the people through the trauma of the destruction of the Jerusalem Temple and the loss of the sacrificial cult.

Phenomenology (Gk., *phainomenon*, 'that which appears', + *logos*, 'reflection'). The study of the ways in which appearances manifest themselves. The phenomenology of religion is thus the study of religious appearances; it may also embrace reflection on the nature of what gives rise to them. The term is used of endeavours to study religion, without commitment to the truth or otherwise of what is being studied, and with the suspension of value-judgements about the worth or otherwise of what is being studied. Such a wide understanding of the term allows many different styles of the study of religion to be called 'phenomenological'. Whether any such value-free study is possible remains a matter of doubt—or at best of dispute.

The term was first used by J. H. Lambert in 1764, but with the completely different sense of the theory of appearance as one of four philosophical disciplines. As a term it appears e.g. in *Kant and *Hegel. In its more modern sense, it is particularly associated with the work of Edmund Husserl (1859–1938). He was a pupil of Franz Brentano, and therefore began his work on the foundations of mathematics. Husserl began to realize not only that philosophers had failed to resolve the issue between solipsists and realists, but that it would make no practical difference to the lived and experienced world if they did so. Clearly, philosophical doubt must be driven further back: *Descartes had thought that he had secured a foundation of certain knowledge in his *cogito, ergo sum* ('I think, therefore I am'); but Husserl pointed out that the conclusion is not entailed; therefore he proposed that the only secure foundation of knowledge lies in the cogito: all that we can be sure of (and from this it is clear that Husserl remained a foundationalist despite some interpretations of his thought to the contrary) are *cogitationes*, appearances in consciousness.

In his later works (the most accessible of which are *Cartesian Meditations*, 1931, and *The Paris Lectures*, 1950), he argued that transcendental phenomenology 'brackets out' (*epoche*) all assumptions about existence, truth, and value, and analyses the *cogitationes* in terms of the stream of consciousness. But since consciousness is directed to what it takes to be an external world (or to its own past and future, etc.) through its *Intentionalität* (intentionality), it is legitimate to consider, perhaps even to infer, what may be a ground, in independence from consciousness, sufficient to give rise to the particular appearances in consciousness which happen to arise—especially when these arise with consistency. In this way, Husserl was able to return those degrees of reality to the world which the consistency of the data in consciousness seemed to require. Thus 'you' may appear in my consciousness with the consistency of a person whom I can label and name; I do not have to resolve the argument about solipsism before extending the intentionality of my consciousness toward 'you' as a consistent appearance in my own consciousness (i.e. I can bracket out the issue of whether you are truly there or not, or in what sense). Moreover, 'you' appear in my consciousness with the characteristic of marking off other appearances with an equal consistency, so that together we can label a world of appearances and name it—that is why Husserl called people 'walking object indices'.

Through this process, it is possible to build up a world of intersubjective reliability without solving first the contentious philosophical issues of existence. An obvious candidate was the world of the natural sciences. At the very end of his life, Husserl realized that there is an extensive reliability in the world of theology (or more exactly of *prayer and *worship, etc.), and that his method required him to return a corresponding degree of reality to God.

Husserl's thought proved immensely fertile, both in philosophy (leading directly into *existentialism) and in the study of religion. Virtually no phenomenologist of religion has ever followed a strictly Husserlian programme: words and indications are picked up from his thought, and are brought to bear in largely novel ways. Thus the early phenomenologists of religion were attracted by the prospect of identifying essences (understood loosely as identifying essential characteristics in religions or in religious beliefs and practices). This proved largely unilluminating, since it tended to squeeze an ocean into a thimble. Others seized on *epoche* and understood phenomenology to be description on the basis of which one might be able to enter empathetically into the phenomena being described. The most sophisticated attempt was made by Gerardus van der Leeuw (1890–1950), in *Phänomenologie der Religion* (1933, tr. as *Religion in Essence and Manifestation*); he achieved brilliant insights, especially in the relation of religion to power, but in fact he made little attempt to bracket out his own assumptions.

Thus phenomenology has been a powerful influence, but the phenomenology of religion remains to be undertaken. As matters stand, phenomenology has transformed the study of religion in schools, colleges, and universities *at the first level*: it has ushered in the dispassionate (as opposed to confessional) teaching of religion, in a way which brackets out questions of whether e.g. God or gods 'exist': religions are studied as an important expression of human life. But the second level (as Husserl envisaged it, albeit in dense language) is always demanded by the first: given that these are the phenomena, what in reality has given rise to them, or brought them into being? The integration of the two levels has not yet been achieved.

Philaret (Theodore Nikitich Romanov, *c*.1553–1633). *Patriarch of Moscow and founder of the Romanov dynasty. Imprisoned by the Poles in 1610, he was only freed in 1619, by which time his son, Michael, was Tsar. He became patriarch and was virtual ruler of Russia until his death. A zealous reformer, he encouraged the study of theology and the establishment of seminaries in each diocese.

Philaret Drozdov (1782–1867). Russian theologian. In 1818 he became a member of the *Holy Synod, and in 1821 *archbishop of Moscow, receiving the title *metropolitan in 1826. He was an exemplary *bishop—a wise administrator and popular preacher. Among his many theological works, his *Christian Catechism* (1823) was most influential, despite the alleged influence in it of *Lutheran ideas.

Philemon, Letter to. An *epistle of *Paul. It is a private letter carried by Onesimus (a runaway slave who had met Paul) back to his owner. It is a tactful plea for Philemon's forgiveness.

Philip, Gospel of. A *gnostic treatise preserved in the *Nag Hammadi Library. It contains reflections on the quest for salvation, understood in a *Valentinian way.

Philippians, Letter to the. An epistle of *Paul and book of the New Testament. The addressees are Paul's first congregation in Europe, at Philippi in Macedonia. It was written from prison, either in Rome *c*.60–2, Caesarea *c*.56–8, or Ephesus *c*.53–5. Paul sees himself balanced between life and death (1. 19–26). Among the ringing exhortations in ch. 2 is the important passage verses 5–11, a hymn which speaks of *Christ's 'self-emptying' (*kenōsis). This has traditionally been taken as a basic statement of incarnational *christology, though some argue that it refers to Jesus' willingness to accept a shameful death.

Philippine Independent Church. This stems from Gregorio Aglipay (1860–1940), a Filipino *Roman Catholic priest, who first formed the Filipino National Catholic Church after the revolution; this languished for lack of papal recognition, and in 1902, Isabelo de los Reyes proclaimed a new Philippine Independent Church with Aglipay as Supreme Bishop. This soon acquired nearly half the RC population, but after the Supreme Court returned its properties to the RC Church it gradually declined and affiliated with *Unitarians in 1931. Since then there has been a remarkable renewal by division between unitarian and conservative groups.

Philistines. The people occupying S. Palestine who were in conflict with the Israelites at the time of the *Judges. Contrary to the colloquial English usage, whereby 'Philistine' means 'antagonistic to culture', the Philistines had a sophisticated culture.

Philo (*c*.20 BCE–50 CE). *Hellenistic Jewish philosopher. His writings were preserved by the Christian Church in their original Gk. Mainly dealing with the *Pentateuch, they include *De Opificio Mundi* (On the Creation), *De Vita Mosis* (On the Life of *Moses), *Legum Allegoriae* (*Allegorical Interpretation), *De Somniis* (On Dreams), *Quaestiones et Solutiones in Genesin* (Questions and Answers on *Genesis). In addition, he produced various philosophical treatises on such subjects as providence and the eternity of the world. He also wrote works (of great historical importance for understanding the situation of the Jews in Alexandria) against the oppression of Jews by Flaccus, and concerning the cruelty of the Roman emperor Gaius.

Philocalia (Gk., 'love of what is beautiful'). The title of two Christian works: (i) the *Philocalia* of *Origen, an anthology from his writings compiled by *Basil and *Gregory of Nazianzus; and (ii) the *Philocalia* of Sts Macarius Notaras and *Nicodemus of the Holy Mountain, first publ. in Venice in 1782, a collection of ascetic and mystical writings of the 4th–15th cents.

Philosophia perennis (Lat., 'perennial philosophy'). Originally introduced as a term (by Steuchen) in 1540 to describe what the school of Padua and *scholasticism had in common. The term since then has had various technical applications, e.g. to what Greek and medieval philosophy have in common, or to *Thomism as a whole. But a looser sense was introduced by *Leibniz (1646–1716) to pick out those elements of philosophy which had endured through time—his own philosophy being, in his own view, the proper continuation and development of it. Even more loosely, the term has come to refer to a fundamental core of truth to be found at the heart of all religions.

Philosophical Taoism: see TAOISM.

Philosophicus Autodidactus (text by Ibn Tufayl): see IBN TUFAYL.

Philosophy, six schools of (Indian): see DARŚANA.

Philosophy of religion. Philosophical thought about religion. The term was first used in Germany in the late 18th cent., for the philosophical investigation of the origin, essence, and content of religion, and for the critique of its value and truth. Modern philosophy of religion is much concerned with assessing the reasons for religious belief, especially arguments for God's existence (see NATURAL THEOLOGY), investigating the nature of religious language, and considering the philosophical problems raised by religion. These problems include the coherence of the concept of God, the problem of *evil, *miracles, *prayer, immortality, and the nature of religious truth. For philosophy in Islam, see FALSAFA. See also Index, Philosophers, Philosophy.

'pho ba (one of Six Doctrines of Nāropa): see NĀRO CHOS DRUG.

Phoenix. A mythical bird of great splendour, which after a long life was said to burn itself to ashes and then rise to life again. It was regarded by Christian writers, and occasionally by Christian artists, as a symbol of the *resurrection.

Photius (sometimes called 'The Great', *c*.810–*c*.895). Patriarch of *Constantinople. A high official at the Byzantine court, Photius succeeded the patriarch Ignatius who was deposed by the emperor in 858. His election, at first endorsed by the legates of Pope Nicholas I, was then (863) annulled by the pope and a schism ensued. Divisions were sharpened by an encyclical of 867 in which Photius attacked the *filioque in the W. creed, and by the rival claims of Rome and Constantinople to the newly evangelized territory of Bulgaria. The Photian schism anticipated the final East–West schism of the 11th cent., and Photius is remembered in the E. Church as a champion against Rome.

Photius' learning was amazing. His most important work, his *Biblioteca*, describes several hundred books and is a mine of information.

phowa (one of Six Doctrines of Nāropa): see NĀRO CHOS DRUG.

phyagchen. Short form of Tib., *phyag-rgya-chen-po*, i.e. *mahāmudrā.

phyag-rgya chen-po (teaching of Kagyü school of Buddhism): see MAHĀMUDRĀ.

Phylacteries (containers for Jewish commands): see TEFILLIN.

Physico-theological Argument. Type of argument for God's existence, from determinate experience of the natural world, especially of its order, purposiveness, and beauty. It is the third kind of theistic argument discussed by *Kant, after the *ontological and *cosmological arguments. Nowadays such arguments are referred to as '*teleological'.

The argument has been revived in the 20th cent., but it is often presented as an argument from analogy which seeks to establish the probability rather than the certainty of divine existence.

Pi-ch'iu. Chin. for *bhikṣu.

Pico della Mirandola, Giovanni (1463–94). Christian mystical and humanistic writer. A considerable linguist, he regarded *kabbalah as illuminating Christianity. The created order emerges in hierarchies of emanation, with humans mediating between the spiritual and the material, able to know God as a friend rather than a fact (cf. *I–Thou). This amounts to an assertion of Christian humanism which he argued in *De Hominis Dignitate* . . . (1492).

Pietà (Ital., 'pity'). Representation (often in sculpture) of the Blessed Virgin *Mary lamenting over the dead and recently deposed body of *Christ, after the *crucifixion.

Pietism. A movement in Protestant Christianity which reacted against too rigid a confessional orthodoxy, and emphasized good works and a holy life. It began soon after the Thirty Years War (1618–48), led by Jakob Spener (1635–1705). Invited to write a preface to a book of sermons, he wrote a short tract, *Pia Desideria* (1675; tr. T. G. Tappert, 1964), which became a kind of 'manifesto', laying down six 'simple proposals' (*einfältige Vorschläge*) for a more godly life: individual study of the Bible; the exercise of the priesthood of all believers (i.e. including the laity); the importance of good works; the control of charity in controversy; the better training of ministers, with training conforming to life; and the reformation of preaching to serve all these purposes. Spener was widely influential (though also opposed, as all reformers are), affecting especially A. H. Francke (1663–1727), who committed himself to the poor of Halle. Among many influenced by Pietism were Count Zinzendorf (who brought together the *Moravian Church) and John *Wesley.

Pigu (Buddhist monk). Korean for *bhikṣu.

Pikku'aḥ nefesh (Heb., 'regard for human life'). The Jewish obligation to save human life in situations of danger, if necessary overriding the law. According to the *Talmud, pikku'aḥ nefesh supersedes even *Sabbath law (*Yoma* 85a). The principle is derived from the commandment in Leviticus 19. 16.

Pi-ku. Taoist practice of abstaining from eating grain, in order to attain immortality: as the five types of grain are the staple diet of life, so they are the food of worms which threaten life and consume the body. Detachment from the former signals escape from the latter.

Pilate, Pontius. The governor ('prefect') of Judaea under whom *Jesus was crucified. The gospels may show him in an unduly favourable light in their insistence on blaming the Jewish mob for Jesus' death.

The apocryphal text known as the *Acts of Pilate* (4th cent. at the earliest) can hardly derive from any official records of Jesus' trial.

Pilgrimage. The literal or metaphorical movement to a condition or place of holiness or healing. Pilgrimage may be interior or exterior. Interior pilgrimage is the movement of a life from a relatively abject condition to the goal (ultimate or proximate) in a particular religion: John *Bunyan's *The Pilgrim's Progress* is a classic Christian expression of this theme, particularly as expressed in its full title, ... *from this World to That which is to Come: Delivered under the Similitude of a Dream, wherein is Discovered the Manner of his Setting Out, his Dangerous Journey, and Safe Arrival at the Desired Country.* Life becomes metaphorically a pilgrimage. Interior pilgrimage is stressed by Sikhs. Exterior pilgrimage is a journey to some place which is either itself associated with the resources or goals of a religion, or which is the location of objects which may assist the pilgrim—e.g. *relics. The reasons for pilgrimage are extremely varied. They may, for example, be for healing, holiness, cleansing, penance, education, gratitude, in response to a vow, to recapitulate an event which occurred at the pilgrimage centre (as, for example, to see for oneself a reported vision; or, somewhat differently, to re-enact events in the past, as in the Muslim *ḥajj, or in the Christian retracing of the *Via Dolorosa in Jerusalem). Pilgrimage frequently, and not surprisingly, takes on the character of a *rite of passage; and as such, the stage of liminality exhibits the inversion of values and status; pilgrimages may then take on the character of a holiday, in which everyday life and its values are suspended—as in Chaucer's *Canterbury Tales*. See Index, Pilgrimage.

Judaism The major practice is that of making *'aliyah to *Jerusalem, as required in Deuteronomy 16. 16. According to the *Torah, all male Jews should go up to Jerusalem three times a year, on *Passover, *Shavu'ot, and *Sukkot (Exodus 34. 23). Since the Six Day War and the reunification of the city, the remaining wall of the Temple (*Wailing Wall) has become the centre of Jewish pilgrimage. The tradition of going up to Jerusalem for the pilgrim festivals has been, to some extent, resumed, particularly during the intermediate days of Sukkot. Because there is no temple, no sacrifices are performed.

Christianity There is no record of the earliest Christian pilgrimages, but the practice of journeying to the Holy Land received much impetus from the visit of the empress Helena, mother of *Constantine, in 326. *Peregrinatio Etheriae* (The Pilgrimage of Etheria) is a vivid account of a pilgrimage to the Holy Land at the end of the 4th cent. Rome became a centre of pilgrimage because of its connection with Sts *Peter and *Paul; and other centres proliferated through the connection with other saints. Notable was the supposed burial place of St *James, Santiago at Compostela in NW Spain: it became the goal of the famous 'pilgrims' route' to Compostela (see J. S. Stone, *The Cult of Santiago* ..., 1927). The association of pilgrimage with *indulgences and credulity (especially in relation to relics) made pilgrimage highly suspect to the *Reformation; but it has revived in the 20th cent., not least as a consequence of the lucrative tourist trade. Devotion to *Mary has led to increasing claims of visions of Mary, with consequent pilgrimages, e.g. to *Lourdes, *Fatima, and Medjugorje.

Islam See ḤAJJ; ZIYARA.

Hinduism See TĪRATH; TĪRTHA. Pilgrimage is supremely important in Hinduism, both in an interior and exterior sense. The interior pilgrimage is epitomized in the *yogi who 'visits' the seven *sacred cities while remaining motionless in a specific kind of meditation. The exterior pilgrimage is dramatically obvious in the constant movement of people in every part of India, but especially to the seven cities. Prayāga (renamed by the Muslims Allahābad), Gāyā (i.e. *Bodhgāyā to Buddhists), and *Kāśi are the major sites on the Gaṅgā (Ganges); and of these, Kāśi exceeds all. Indeed, to make pilgrimage and die in Kāśi means that the burden of karma and the necessity for rebirth are removed by *Śiva himself. Places of pilgrimage are called in India tīrthas ('fords'), and the pilgrimage is tīrtha-yatra. In the *Tīrtha-yatra* section of *Mahābhārata*, a description is given of the whole of India as a place of pilgrimage, mapping out an itinerary in a clockwise direction.

Buddhism and **Jainism** Buddhist pilgrimage is common, in both Theravāda and Mahāyāna forms. Of particular importance are sites where relics are held, e.g. of the Buddha's tooth at Kandy (in Śri Lankā); or where there are associations with the Buddha, especially the places of his birth, first sermon, enlightenment, and *parinibbāna, and of his presence, e.g. of his footprint (notably in Śri Lankā on Mount Siripāda, 'Adam's Mount', since Muslims revere the footprint as that of *Adam, though for Hindus it is that of Śiva). Equally important are sites where cuttings derived from the *bo tree (the tree under which the Buddha attained enlightenment) are growing. In China and Japan, mountains are extensively sites of pilgrimage. In China, the Five Peaks are thought to be important for the protection of the country. One, Mount Tai, is Taoist, the other four are associated with four *bodhisattvas: Emei is linked with *Samantabhadra, Wūtai with *Mañjuśrī, Putuo with *Avalokiteśvara, and Chiu-hua with *Kṣitigarbha. A new emperor was required to make pilgrimage to Mount Tai; to the other four mountains (remote though they are) both monks and laypeople make pilgrimage, known as 'journeying to a mountain and offering incense'. In Japan, the major Buddhist centres are Saikōkū, dedicated to Kannon (Avalokiteśvara) and Shikōkū. For Japan, see also ISE and FUJISĀN (Fujiyama).

Among Jains, places associated with tīrthaṅkaras or other holy *ascetics, or with images of the tīrthaṅkaras, are places of pilgrimage—as indeed may be a living and revered ascetic: particularly revered are places where someone has undertaken *sallekhanā (death by fasting). For the *Digambaras, the White Lake of the Ascetics (Śravana Belgola), in the state of Karnataka, is of great importance, with its hill on which stands the image of Bahubali, the first person of this world cycle to attain liberation. Of corresponding importance for the Śvetāmbara (see DIGAMBARA) is Mount Śatrunjāya ('The conqueror of enemies'). It is one of five holy mountains, standing near Palitana in Gujarat. To organize a pilgrimage is an act of great merit for Jain laymen—the equivalent, according to some, of undertaking initiation as a monk. The organizer is called *saṅghapati*, 'the lord of the community' (cf. *saṅgha).

Pilgrim Fathers. English Christian Dissenters who set sail in 1620 to cross the Atlantic (in the *Mayflower*) and who established Plymouth Colony. They numbered 102, though a baby was born at sea. The name was based on Hebrews 11. 13.

Pillars of Islam: see FIVE PILLARS OF ISLAM.

Pilpul (derived from *pilpel*, 'pepper'). A method of Jewish *Talmudic study. Traditionally pilpul meant the logical distinctions by which contradictions in the texts could be explained. Pilpul was distinguished from *girsah* (the cursory straightforward meaning of the words) and it served the functions of resolving contradictions, making the text relevant to changing circumstances, and providing a constant changing intellectual challenge.

Piṇḍa. A ball of rice offered, in Hindu funeral rites, to the *pitṛs (ancestors). Five piṇḍas are placed on the corpse with the words from (*Ṛg Veda* 10. 17. 3).

Piṅgalā. In Hinduism, the solar channel which runs through the body, through which (in conjunction with its counterpart *iḍā) connection is made with *kuṇḍalinī energy. See also PRĀṆA.

Pippalāda (wise man): see PRAŚNA UPANIṢAD.

Pīr (Sūfī spiritual guide): see IMĀM.

Pīr-i-Anṣār (Sūfī poet): see SŪFĪS.

Pirit (Buddhist healing rite): see PARITTA.

Pirke de Rabbi Eleazar or ***Eliezer*** (8th cent. CE). Jewish *aggadic work. The book clearly reflects the *halakhic customs prevalent in *Israel at the start of the *geonic period. First published in 1514, it has been reprinted many times.

Pirqe Avot (treatise of Jewish Mishnah): see AVOT.

Piśācas. Demons in Hinduism who eat flesh and are ranked even lower than *rākṣasas. They dwell in cremation grounds, and can assume any form—even that of invisibility. They can enter into (and possess) anyone who yawns without covering the mouth.

Piṭaka (Pali, 'basket'), gathered collection of Buddhist texts. The 'three baskets', i.e. *Tripiṭaka, form a fundamental collection, equivalent to a *canon of scriptures.

Pitha (post-Vedic, possibly from *pi sad*, 'sit on', hence seat or throne), an important centre, especially for pilgrimage. Four major pithas became associated with the points of the compass, and represented the presence of *Devi (the Goddess).

Pitṛ (Skt., 'father'). The ancestors (pl., pitaras), who dwell in the pitṛ-loka, which is sometimes identified with heaven (*svarga). Funeral rituals (*śrāddha) are essential to maintain the pitṛs in their proper state—and for that purpose, a son is necessary. In the *Brāhmaṇas, the pitṛyāna becomes a place of judgement.

Pittsburgh Platform (statement of principles): see REFORM JUDAISM.

Pius IX (1792–1878). *Pope from 16 June 1846. As Bishop of Imola he instituted a series of reforms, but he was no liberal in temperament, and his refusal, after his elevation to the *papacy, to accept a leading role in Italian politics turned many away from him. In 1854 he had, on his own authority, defined the *dogma of the *immaculate conception of Mary. Other aspects of his pontificate bolstered his authority and the First *Vatican Council defined the dogma of papal *infallibility without having the opportunity to situate it within a wider decree on the church. Pius' rejection of many of the changes in the modern world were listed in his **Syllabus Errorum* of 1864.

Pius XII (1876–1958). *Pope from 2 Mar. 1939. Born Eugenio Pacelli he came from a family with a long history of service to the *papacy. He became secretary of state in 1930, and negotiated a number of *concordats, most notably that with Hitler in 1933. He has been accused of being insufficiently active in opposition to Nazi policy towards the Jews, and this inactivity may have sprung from his search for a diplomatic settlement of the war. In the later part of his pontificate he vigorously opposed the spread of communist régimes in E. Europe. Within Roman Catholicism he did much to encourage scholarship, and instituted a number of *liturgical reforms. He spoke frequently on major topics of the day, in a manner which reflected his elevated view of the papal office. In the definition of the *dogma of the *assumption of Mary he was the last pope (to date) explicitly to invoke papal *infallibility.

Pi-yen-lu (Chinese verses): see HSÜEH-TOU CH'UNG-HSIEN.

Piyyut (perhaps from Gk., *poiētēs*). A Jewish poem intended to embellish community or private prayer. Originally piyyutim (pl.) were composed as substitutes for the established *liturgy. Texts of piyyutim can be found in *Talmudic sources, but the earliest known composer of piyyutim was Yose b. Yose who worked in *Erez Israel in the 6th cent. CE, with a great period of composition, 9th–13th cents. The *paytanim* ('poets') employed different systems of rhyme and rhythm. Initially there were no fixed collections and each cantor followed his own choice, but over the years, anthologies were compiled for the various occasions.

Plainsong or **Plainchant.** The traditional *music of the Latin Christian *rite. It is generally known as 'Gregorian' chant, though its exact connection with St *Gregory the Great is debated.

Platform Sūtra (key Zen work): see LIU-TSU-TA-SHIH FA-PAO-T'AN-CHING.

Platonism. The philosophical system found in Plato's writings or derived therefrom. Fundamental to Platonism is the conviction that truth cannot be found in everyday life and sensible reality, but in a (more real) ideal realm (of the 'Forms'). To attain that, purification, both moral and intellectual (through dialectic and becoming accustomed to abstract thought), is necessary. Middle Platonism (1st cent. BCE–2nd cent. CE) developed a religious cosmology from the *Timaeus*, whereas *Plotinus found inspiration for his doctrine of the One in the *Parmenides*. In addition to the ideal realm (of intellect) and the realm of ordinary life (of soul), Plotinus posited the One from which all else proceeds, which is unknowable except in ecstatic union. Such *Neoplatonism was developed in particular by *Porphyry, Iamblichus, and *Proclus and had a great influence on later thought, Christian, Jewish, and Muslim.

PL Kyōdan (Japanese religious movement): see MIKI TOKUHARU.

Plotinus (*c*.205–70). Founder of *Neoplatonism and mystic. His works were published after his death by his pupil *Porphyry in six 'Enneads' (Groups of Nine). The major theme of Plotinus' thought is the relation of the One (*to hen*) or the Good at the summit of the chain of beings to the realm of multiplicity. Beneath the undifferentiated One is the intelligible world of ideas (*nous*) and, beneath it, the World Soul (*psyche*). This latter is the creator and orderer of the material world. The aim of the Plotinian scheme is to attain knowledge of the One by a return to it through *contemplation.

Plumstead Peculiars (Free Church sect): see PECULIAR PEOPLE.

Plymouth Brethren. See BRETHREN, PLYMOUTH.

P'o. Component in Chinese anthropology, one of two spiritual elements in the human (the other being *hun). P'o is associated with the dark and passive side, i.e. *yin; and at death, the p'o returns to the earth. With the p'o is associated the *kuei, which represents the unsettled and vengeful element of p'o in some circumstances of death: for details see SHEN.

Pocomania or **Pukkumina** (possibly from Span., 'a little madness'). Afro-Jamaican cults descended from surviving forms of African religion mixed with *Protestant elements from the time of the Great Revival in Jamaica in 1860–2. They take the form of small local 'bands' led by a 'Captain', 'Mother', or 'Shepherd/ess' who lives at and rules over the band's Yard. Pocomania passes over into ancestor-spirit cults on one side, and into *Revival Zion on the other, and some adherents belong to the Christian churches.

Pogrom (Russ., *gromit*, 'destroy'). An attack involving looting, murder, and rape by one sector of the population on another. More precisely, the term pogrom has been used to describe attacks against the Jews, specifically between 1880 and 1920 in Russia and Poland.

Pole, Reginald (1500–58). *Cardinal and last *archbishop of *Canterbury (to date) in communion with Rome. After the accession of Mary Tudor to the English throne, Pole was sent as papal legate. He arrived in 1554, received the country back into communion with Rome, and instituted a number of reforms, though his desire to restore church lands aroused great hostility. In 1556 he was appointed to Canterbury. He died just twelve hours after the death of Queen Mary.

Political theology. A Christian concern to explore the implications of theology for political life and thought. The term has an uneasy history, being associated, for example, with the endorsement by Carl Schmitt of Hitler and the rise of German nationalism. However, the term is now usually associated with the work of Johann Baptist Metz (who sometimes uses the phrase 'the new political theology') and Dorothee Sölle. In contrast to what it takes to be the traditional concentration of theology on the individual and on personal holiness, allowing the support of virtually any political system or party (or none), Metz sees 'the deprivatising of theology as the primary critical task of political theology'. *Orthopraxy becomes the mark of true discipleship more than the traditional orthodoxy. The connections with *liberation theology are clear.

Polycarp, St (*c.*69–*c.*155). Christian bishop of Smyrna in Asia Minor. His *Letter to the Philippians* is preserved, as well as one of *Ignatius' letters addressed to him. According to the contemporary *Martyrdom of Polycarp* he was arrested during a pagan festival and, on his refusing to recant his faith, burnt to death. Feast day, 23 Feb.

Polygamy. Marriage in which a person may have more than one spouse at the same time (in contrast to monogamy). Polygyny is the marriage of a man to more than one wife, polyandry the marriage of a woman to more than one husband. Polyandry is relatively rare (e.g. the Nayar and Toda of India), polygyny more common, especially in Africa. In Islam, marriage to more than one wife is allowed (see MARRIAGE), but in general, religions have moved toward monogamy or have endorsed it from the start. The *Lambeth Conference of 1888 declared polygamy to be 'inconsistent with the law of Christians', but the Conference of 1988 allowed baptism to those who undertook not to enter into further (polygynous) marriages, and it asked that the consent of the local Anglican community should be sought (resolution 26). *African Instituted Churches are divided on the issue.

Pŏmnang (fl. 632–46). The Korean monk credited with introducing Sŏn (Ch'an/Zen) to Korea. Pŏmnang studied Sŏn under Tao-hsin (580–651), fourth patriarch of the Ch'an sect in China, during the reign of King Sŏndŏk (632–46), and transmitted his lineage to the kingdom of Silla. Among his disciples was Sinhaeng (d. 779) who introduced Northern Ch'an to Korea.

Pongyi (Burmese Buddhist monk): see BUDDHISM IN SOUTH-EAST ASIA.

Pontifex Maximus (Lat., *pontifex*, 'bridge-maker', of uncertain significance). Title of the *pope. It was originally the title of the chief pagan priest at Rome. In English it is rendered 'supreme pontiff'.

Pontifical. The liturgical book in the *Roman Catholic Church which contains the prayers and ceremonies for rites involving a bishop.

Poor Clares. The 'Second Order' of St *Francis, founded by him and St Clare some time between 1212 and 1214. Clare was moved by the preaching of Francis to abandon her possessions and to join a Benedictine house. In 1215, she became abbess of a new and separate community, living under a severe rule—later ameliorated for some convents. Nevertheless, Poor Clares are regarded as the most austere religious order in the *Roman Catholic Church.

Poor men of Lyons (followers of Waldenses): see WALDENSES.

Pōp. Korean for *dharma.

Pope (Gk., *pappas*, 'father'). In the *Roman Catholic Church a title applied exclusively to the *bishop of Rome since the 11th cent., though used earlier of all bishops. The *Coptic patriarch of *Alexandria is also known as the pope, and in the Greek *Orthodox Church the title is commonly used of all priests. For examples, see Index, Popes.

Pope of Taoism: see T'IEN-SHIH.

Popovtsy ('with priests' group of Old Believers): see OLD BELIEVERS.

Popular religion: see FOLK RELIGION.

Pormalim. A *messianic religion among the Batak of Sumatra. It derived from the tradition of Singa Mangaradjas (Skt., 'Lion King'), legendary priest-kings, the last of whom, Ompu Pulo Batu, was killed in 1907. He allegedly founded the Pormalim (Batak, *malim*, 'be independent') religion, after which it was developed by a *guru, Somailung, in resistance to Christian missions and Dutch control. Pormalim was at its height between 1910 and 1920 but still exists, scattered across the Toba highlands.

Porphyry (*c*.232–*c*.303). *Neoplatonist philosopher and anti-Christian writer. His philosophical works include an *Introduction to the* Categories *of Aristotle* which became a standard medieval textbook; he wrote a *Life* of his teacher *Plotinus, and the treatise *Against the Christians*. This was condemned to be burnt in 448 and survives only in quotations in works of refutation.

Port Royal Logic (writing of Antoine Arnauld): see ARNAULD, ANTOINE.

Porvoo Declaration (ecumenical agreement between some Anglican and some Lutheran Churches): see ANGLICANISM.

Posal. Korean for *bodhisattva.

Posek. A Jewish scholar who is concerned with practical *halakhah. For an example of a much revered 20th-cent. posek, see FEINSTEIN, MOSHEH.

Poson (Buddhist festival): see FESTIVALS AND FASTS.

Possessors. Party in a monastic controversy in *Russian Orthodoxy. St Joseph of Volokalamsk (1439–1515) argued that monks should live lives of poverty and *asceticism, but that monasteries should accumulate wealth in order to serve and support the Church. His followers were enthusiastic patrons of musicians, builders, and *icon-painters. He and they were also severe against *heretics. In contrast, the Non-Possessors, led by St Nil(us) Sorsky (*c*.1433–1508) believed that the whole Church is called to poverty, and that heretics should be treated with understanding and patience. Both were canonized by the Council of 1551, but the position of St Joseph was endorsed. However, the view of St Nil was kept alive, first by the 'holy fool' tradition (*salos/yurodivy*), along with mystical teachers and hermits, and then by the *Old Believers.

Potala (Tibetan Buddhist fortress): see LHASA.

Potlatch (N. American Kwakiutl ceremony): see ALMSGIVING.

Prabhākara (*c*.7th cent. CE). Philosopher in the Hindu *Pūrva-Mīmāṁsā system. His major work was a commentary on *Sābara-bhāsya* (itself a commentary on the *Mīmāṁsā Sūtras* attributed to *Jaimini) entitled *Bṛhati* (ed. S. K. R. Sastri, 1931).

Prabhavana. The Jain custom of offering a sweetmeat to those who have participated in a religious ceremony. In origin, it refers to the eight ways in which the Jain way is commended and exalted: through knowledge of the scriptures; through debating; through preaching; through mastery of *astrology; of *magic; of invocation; through writing; through *asceticism.

Prabhupada, Bhaktivedanta Svami (1896–1977). Founder (i.e. *ācārya) of the *International Society for Krishna Consciousness. He was born Abhay Charan De in Calcutta. He undertook translation work until he retired in 1959, when he took the *saṃnyasin vow which set him free for his mission. In 1965 he went to Boston and established ISKCON. In 1967 he moved to California where the movement began to grow rapidly. In contrast to some other Hindu-based new religions, he discouraged his followers from regarding him as an *avatāra, but rather presented himself as one who, like them, was endeavouring to be a servant of God.

Pradakṣina. Hindu rite of circumambulation, to express reverence to an object (or to the deity or Brahman within it), or to protect it, or to secure safety if it contains potential for evil.

Pradhāna (Skt.). Nature in its undeveloped state, the equivalent in Hindu Sāṃkhya of *prakṛti.

Pradyumna (manifest power of Viṣṇu): see VIṢṆU.

Praemunire. The title of statutes (first passed in 1353, 1365, and 1393) which were designed to resist papal encroachment on the rights claimed by the English crown. The Criminal Law Act of 1967 repealed all the statutes.

Prajāpati (Skt., 'Lord of creatures/creation'). A conceptual development in the late Vedic period of Hinduism drawing together the many manifested forces of nature into a single source of creation, and often, therefore, made synonymous with *Indra and *Sāvitrī. In relation to the thirty-three gods of the classical system, Prajāpati was reckoned the thirty-fourth, embracing and including the others.

Prajña (Skt., 'wisdom', 'consciousness'). 1. In Hinduism, the competence of *ātman to realize itself for what it is, and thus to abide in this state as in a dreamless sleep.

2. In Buddhism (Pāli, *pañña*; Jap., *hannya*), prajña is the third heading of the three into which the eightfold path is divided (see AṢṬANGIKA-MĀRGA)—i.e. right thought and right view constitute wisdom. In Mahāyāna, prajña is the direct awareness of *śūnyatā (emptiness of self) in the case of all appearance. See further PERFECTION OF WISDOM LITERATURE; NĀGĀRJUNA.

Prajñānam Brahma (Skt., 'consciousness is *Brahman'). One of the five Hindu *mahāvākyas (great precepts): 'All that is is guided by prajñānam, is founded on prajñānam. Prajñānam is Brahman' (*Aitareya Upaniṣad* 3. 5. 3).

Prajñāpāramitā (Buddhist literature): see PERFECTION OF WISDOM LITERATURE.

Prajñaptivāda (Skt., *prajñapti*, 'designation', + *vāda*, 'way'). An early school of Buddhism. Having originated in the late 3rd cent. BCE as an offshoot of the *Mahāsaṃghikas, the Prajñaptivāda claims a line of descent from one of the Buddha's disciples, Mahākātyāyana. No texts of the school are extant but both Paramārtha and Vasumitra claim that the Prajñaptivāda had a special *Abhidharmic text which differentiated between two levels of statement in the *Buddha's teachings; those acceptable for non-initiates and therefore requiring further elaboration, and those aimed at adepts. Such a distinction closely corresponds to the *Mahāyānist doctrine concerning conventional (*saṃvṛti*) and ultimate (*paramārtha*) *sūtra utterances; and for this reason the Prajñaptivāda is sometimes held to be a proto-Mahāyānist school.

Prajñāvimukta (arhat who has attained supreme wisdom): see ARHAT.

Prakṛti (Skt., 'making first'). In Sanskrit literature, primordial material nature. In mythology prakṛti is personified as a goddess of cosmic creative energy, *Śakti, the female counterpart of every god. In *Vedānta, prakṛti is synonymous with cosmic manifestation, hence as appearance, *māyā. In *Sāṃkhya-yoga prakṛti plays an important role as the ultimate material reality juxtaposed with *puruṣa, the ultimate spiritual reality. Here prakṛti is the matrix of the universe, the material cause of all manifest matter and energy. As such, prakṛti is composed of three balanced *guṇas (Skt., 'strands') or constituent modes which, in disequilibrium, combine to generate all other material principles (*tattvas).

Pralaya or **laya** (Skt., 'dissolution'). The Hindu understanding that all appearance is subject, not to destruction, but dissolution —leading to re-creation. It is especially used of the ending of a *kalpa (cosmic cycle).

Pramāṇa (Skt., 'measure', 'authority'). 1. In Hinduism, proof, the means for attaining true knowledge.

2. In Buddhism generally, a school of thought established by Dignāga. In its more technical sense, however, pramāṇa refers to differing means of knowledge.

The Pramāṇa school appears to have centred on Nālandā; its other important exponent, a pupil of Dignāga, was *Dharmakīrti. The works of both authors are still studied by Tibetan Buddhists.

Prāṇa (Skt., 'breath'). In Hinduism, the vital force which differentiates the living from the dead. By the *breath from his mouth, *Prajāpati created the gods. The essential characteristic of breath as life-bestowing, was eventually identified with *Brahman present as *ātman. See PRĀṆĀYĀMA.

Prāṇapratiṣṭhā (Skt., 'endowing with breath'). The ritual acts in Hinduism through which life is endowed on a representation of God, so that the divine reality becomes active in and through the image.

Prāṇāyāma (Skt.). Breath (*prāṇa) control in *yoga; the fourth limb of *Patañjali's eight-limbed (aṣṭāṅga) or *rāja yoga. In the **Yoga Sūtra* (2. 49) Patañjali defines it as the 'cutting off (*viccheda*) of the flow of inhalation and exhalation' which is achieved after the attaining of 'posture' (*āsana) and prepares the mind for concentration (*dhāraṇā).

*Haṭha Yoga texts connect prāṇāyāma with the physiology of the subtle body (*sūkṣma-śarīra, *liṅga-śarīra).

Praṇava (reverberation): see OṂ.

Praṇidhāna (Buddhist vow): see BODHISATTVA VOW.

Prapatti (Skt., 'seeking refuge'). A key-concept of *Śrīvaiṣṇava theology. Synonyms are the Skt. *śaraṇāgati* ('arriving for protection'), *nyāsa* ('placing down [one's responsibilities]' and the Tamil *aṭaikkalam* ('resorting [for protection]'). As a technical term, prapatti does not yet occur in the theological works of *Rāmānuja, although its existence in the related traditions of the *Pāñcarātra and Vaikhānasas is earlier. Post-Rāmānuja theologians, belonging both to the *Teṉ- and Vaṭa-kaḷai, employ it as a central term in their discussion. It now denotes the acceptance of *Viṣṇu's grace which has been made available universally through the scriptures, his temple incarnations (see AVATĀRA), the hymns of the *Āḻvārs, the teaching of Rāmānuja, etc. Thus it is *the* 'means' of achieving salvation. Ultimately prapatti is the realization (in both senses of the word) of a factually given situation—total human dependence on Viṣṇu—which has been obscured by a separate self-awareness (ignorance) due to past *karma.

Prasāda or **prasad.** 1. In Hinduism, the sense (especially in the *Upaniṣads) of the free action of favour or *grace, coming to the assistance of individuals and helping them toward *mokṣa (release). 'Grace' is thus opposed to 'works' (i.e. the strict working out of *karma). See further, S. Kulandran, *Grace in Christianity and Hinduism* (1964); and for its importance among Sikhs see SIKHISM.

2. Food offerings, which are then shared among worshippers, carrying with them spiritual effect.

3. Peace of mind received, without effort, as a gift.

Prāsaṅgika. A branch of the *Mādhyamaka school of Buddhist philosophy which regards itself as adhering most faithfully to the methodology of *Nāgārjuna, the founder of the Mādhyamaka system. It adopts the strategy of criticizing the views of its opponents by deriving undesired consequences (*prasaṅga*) from them, rather than setting out a positive thesis of its own. Main proponents of the Prāsaṅgika method were *Buddhapālita and *Candrakīrti, while the Svatantrika cause was championed by *Bhāvaviveka.

Praśna Upaniṣad. An Upaniṣad belonging to the **Atharva-Veda*. It deals with six questions posed to the wise man, Pippalāda.

Praśnavyākarana-aṅga (Jain text): see AṄGA.

Praśnottara (Skt.). In Hinduism, the process of 'question and answer', through which teaching proceeds.

Prasthānatraya (Skt., 'system' + 'threefold'). The three authoritative sources, in *Advaita Hinduism, of *Vedānta, the *Upaniṣads, the **Bhagavad-gītā*, the **Brahma-sūtras*.

Prātimokṣa (Skt.; Pāli, *pātimokkha*). Part of the Buddhist *Vinaya-pitaka, containing the rules for *bhikṣus (monks) and for bhikṣunis (nuns). It is recited at every *uposatha ceremony. Originally, public confession of fault against the code was made, but this became an individual confession prior to the ceremony, with a silent assent at its conclusion. Three codes survive: *Theravādin (227 rules for bhikṣus, 311 for bhikṣunis), Mula-*Sarvastivādin (258 and 366), and Dharmaguptaka (250 and 348).

Pratiṣṭhita-nirvāna. In Mahāyāna Buddhism, the attainment of final *nirvāna, with no remaining connection with the world of appearance. A *bodhisattva postpones this attainment to help others (*pranidhāna*), though in fact, since all is of the same nature, empty of self (*śūnyatā), he is in the condition of nirvāna while helping still in the domain of appearance (*saṃsāra). Thus although the concept seems the equivalent of the *Theravāda *nirupadhiśeṣa-nirvāna, the two are radically different.

Pratītya-samutpāda (the causal nexus of interconnected appearance): see PATICCA-SAMUPPĀDA.

Pratyāhāra (Skt., 'withdrawal'). 1. In Hinduism, sense-withdrawal, the fifth 'limb' of 'eight-limbed' (*aṣṭaṅga*) or *rāja yoga, referring to the contraction of consciousness from the external world and senses, as a tortoise contracts its limbs.

2. A technical sense in Sanskrit grammar meaning the compression to one syllable of a series of letters or affixes, by combining the initial letter with the final.

Pratyekabuddha (Skt.; Pāli Pacceka). In Buddhism, one who attains the condition next to that of *arhat entirely on his own. He has no teacher and does not belong to the *saṅgha, and he makes no attempt to communicate his way or his attainment to anyone else. He is therefore known as the Solitary or Silent Buddha, and is described as 'a lonely rhinoceros'.

Pratykṣa (perception): see RĀMĀNUJA.

Pravrajya. 'Going forth' from home, the determination to renounce the world and undertake an *ascetic way. It is characteristic of Jains, but applies also to Hindus.

Pravṛtti (Skt., 'origin, arising'). The unfolding or emergence of a new cosmos, after its dissolution (*pralaya).

Praxis (Gk., 'activity'). Action which arises from true belief, the manifestation of religion in practice. This is of particular importance in *liberation theology.

Prayāga or **Prag.** 'Place of sacrifice'. Hindu place of *pilgrimage (*tīrtha), later called by Muslims Allāhābād, at the meeting point of *Gaṅgā and Yamunā rivers, and the subterranean Sarasvatī. It is therefore called *triveṇī*, 'triple-thread'. Even its soil is so sacred that a small part of it can cleanse from sin. It is one of the seven *sacred cities, and one of the four sites of the *kuṁbha-mela, which takes place every twelve years. To avoid the Muslim name, Hindus usually call it Ilāhābād, the abode of Ilā, the mother of a solar dynasty king.

Prāyaścitta. In Jainism, the practice of making vows in repentance for sins committed.

Prayer (from Lat., *precare*, 'to beg, entreat'). The relating of the self or soul to God in trust, penitence, praise, petition, and purpose, either individually or corporately. Some of these aspects of prayer have been isolated (e.g. petition as intercession), as have some of the ways of being before God (e.g. *contemplation, *meditation, recollection), so that the term 'prayer' may cover more, or less, in each tradition. See Index, Prayer.

Judaism See TEFILLAH; PRAYER BOOK (JUDAISM).

Christianity Prayer is the acknowledgement of God as the source of all goodness and therefore the One who can meet human need and longing. It is thus an expression of wonder and a cry for help. A. Tanquerey (*The Spiritual Life . . .*, 1930) defined prayer as 'an elevation of our soul to God to offer Him our homage and ask for His favours, in order to grow in holiness for His glory'. Christian prayer is prayer in Christ, sharing in the prayer of the Son to the Father through the Spirit, who in prayer exposes our deepest need (cf. Romans 8. 14–27). The model is Jesus' prayer to his Father, joyful, intimate, trusting, and obedient; the pattern is the prayer he gave to his disciples, the *Lord's Prayer, which moves from adoration of the Father, through surrender to his will, to petition for sustenance, recognition of the need for forgiveness in the darkness of the world, and a cry for deliverance.

Islam There are three major forms of prayer in Islam: *ṣalāt, the obligatory prayer five times a day; *dhikr, remembrance of God, developed especially in *Sūfī Islam; and *du'ā', a more personal calling on God, of which the prayers based on *yā Laṭīf*, 'O Gracious One', are an example, based on Qur'ān 42. 19: 'O Gracious One, . . . as you were generously kind in creating the heavens and the earth, and to me in the darkness of the womb, so be generously kind in your unswerving decree [*qadar], and in your decisions concerning me.' Prayers, or blessings, on the Prophet are also important.

Hinduism Prayer permeates Hindu life, but not in so formal or detached a style as it does e.g. for Muslims. Great merit (*puṇya) is accrued from the saying of prayers, many of which are derived from the Vedic hymns. Prayer is highly devotional, especially in *bhakti, and often merges into *mantra.

Sikhism Prayer is rooted in *nām simaraṇ, the calling to mind of God, brought about by meditation. Formal and informal prayer both begin and end with *ardas. Praise is expressed through *kirtan. Out of all this, petition flows.

Zoroastrianism There are two main types of Zoroastrian prayer: private and more public liturgies. Every Zoroastrian is expected to recite the *kusti* prayers (*naujote) at least five times daily having first cleansed himself or herself physically (by washing). The duty of prayer is common to all, high or low, male or female. There is a series of Avestan prayers which each Zoroastrian is expected to learn by heart, the *Yatha Ahu Vairyo* (Pahlavi, *Ahunavar*), thought to have been composed by Zoroaster himself: as the greatest of all Zoroastrian prayers, it can, where necessary, replace all other acts of devotion; *Asem Vohu* in praise of truth or righteousness; the *Yenhe hatam*, in praise of holy beings which is recited at the end of litanies; and the *Airyema ishyo* especially recited at weddings and which will be recited by the saviours at *Frasokereti.

There are also the formal liturgies performed mainly in a temple, though some are still performed in the home.

Prayer Book

Judaism These are books containing the texts of daily and festival prayers. The book containing regular prayers is known as the *Siddur*. The earliest known Jewish prayer book is the 9th-cent. *Seder Rav Amram *Gaon*. Other famous *siddurim* include the 10th-cent. *Siddur *Sa'adiah Gaon* and the 11th-cent. **Maḥzor Vitry* compiled by Simḥah b. Samuel, a pupil of *Rashi. The *Ashkenazim use four types of prayer book: *Ha-Maḥzor ha-Gadol* (*Kol Bo) containing all the yearly prayers, the *Maḥzor* which contains the prayers for each particular festival, the small *Siddur* for individual use, and the fuller *Ha-Siddur ha-Shalem*. The *Sephardim use the *Tefillat ha-Hadesh* which contain daily and *Sabbath prayers, *Mo'adim* which contain the prayers for the pilgrim festivals *Rosh ha-Shanah* containing *New Year prayers, *Kippur* for the *Day of Atonement, and *Ta'aniyyot* which has prayers for *Av 9. The *Ḥasidim and the *Progressive movements have produced their own prayer books reflecting their own customs.

Christianity See BOOK OF COMMON PRAYER; BREVIARY; MISSAL.

Prayer Book society: see BOOK OF COMMON PRAYER.

Prayer mat (Muslim): see SAJJĀDA.

Prayer of the heart: see JESUS PRAYER.

Prayer shawl (Jewish): see TALLIT.

Prayer wheel. A cylinder, used in Tibetan Buddhism, inscribed on the outside with a *mantra (often *Oṃ mani padme hum), and containing scrolls on which this and other mantras, as well as sacred texts, are written. Turning the wheel (clockwise, never anti-clockwise, except among adherents of *Bön) releases the power inherent in the texts and prayers.

Prayopaveśana. The Hindu devotion of lying prostrate before a representation of the divine/god, fasting and praying for some particular goal.

Preaching: see Index, *ad loc.*

Prebendary. A member of a cathedral *chapter whose living came from a share ('prebend', Lat., *praebere*, 'furnish') of its endowment.

Precatory (form of absolution): see ABSOLUTION.

Precentor. The cleric responsible for the direction of the choral services of a *cathedral or chapel.

Precepts, Ten/Five (undertaken by Buddhists): see ŚĪLA.

Precious blood. The *blood of *Jesus as an object of Catholic devotion. Apart from the veneration of particles of Christ's blood as *relics, devotion to the precious blood was most of all a product of the medieval spirituality of the *passion. The period of its greatest cultivation was the 19th cent., when Pope *Pius IX proclaimed its *feast day as part of the calendar of the whole Church (1859).

Predestination. The theological view that God foreknows and predetermines the outcome of all things, including an individual's life and eternal destiny; predestination is sometimes used of foreknowledge alone; and in Christianity it may apply to salvation alone or to condemnation as well (single and double predestination). Predestination is usually discussed in relation to the fierce and unending controversies in Christianity, but the term is also applied to similar doctrines in other religions, especially to *qadar in Islam, but also to *kāla, *karma, *daiva, and *astrology in Hinduism, and to the (heavenly) mandate (*ming) in China. The Christian doctrine became associated particularly with *Augustine, who held that humans are so subverted by *sin that they do not have the capacity even to seek for salvation, let alone find it: he thus doubted the ability of humans to produce works of worth in the sight of God. If any are saved, it can only be because the sovereign will of God so decrees it—although even so, it remains the case that all are still justly condemned. *Pelagius, in contrast, held that humans had the freedom to choose or deny God (semi-Pelagians held that God's *grace was a necessary initiative, but that works had status thereafter), but Augustine maintained that the will is enslaved to sin, that grace is needed to make the choice for God, and that this grace is given to those whom God has predestined to receive it. To say less than this is to limit the omniscience and omnipotence of God. However, the Augustinian position, while it gave adequate emphasis to the grace of God, raised problems about the responsibility of humans in their decisions, and about the justice and severity of God in predestining so many to damnation—the doctrine of reprobation. The *Reformers led to a renewed stress on the Augustinian position, that since the will is wholly enslaved (as *Luther held against *Erasmus), even the assent of faith which admits to the community of the elect must be enabled by the grace of God, wholly and completely unearned and unmerited. But if the gift is entirely gracious, it can of course lie within God's predestined intention. *Melanchthon attempted to rescue a place for the worth and validity of the human will, in the so-called 'Synergistic' ('working together with') controversy; and in *Calvinism, which held strongly to predestination, comparable controversies broke out (and continue) over the scope of what God willed (and foresaw) in relation to the *Fall. The argument was between those who were later called sublapsarians (or infralapsarians) and supralapsarians: did God always know, when he created, that some would be saved and some not, so that he allowed the Fall (*lapsus*) in order to bring this about (as the supralapsarians held); or (since, as the sublapsarians held, this seemed to make God the author of sin), did he create with a foreknowledge of the possibility of the fall, and, when it happened, then elect some to salvation, leaving the rest in a condition of enmity (but that seemed to suggest a lack of control on the part of God, and also that Christ's *atonement had reference only to a few)? The Synod of Dort (1618–19) upheld the sublapsarians, whose position is expressed in the Westminster Confession (1647). Various attempts (see e.g. ARMINIUS; SUAREZ for Congruism) were made to ameliorate the most severe forms of the doctrine, attributing, as it seems to do, a character to God which would be prosecuted if exhibited by a human father to his children. More recently, therefore, *Barth shifted the emphasis by taking *Paul's argument to be pointing to the absolute centrality of Christ as the one who experienced in himself both election and reprobation for the sake of all humanity.

Preface. In Christian liturgies the words introducing the *eucharistic prayer, in between the *Sursum Corda and *Sanctus. The preface is an ascription of praise to God.

Preferential option for options: see SECULARIZATION.

Preferential option for the poor: see LIBERATION THEOLOGY.

Prelate. A church official of high rank. In the Church of England the term is used only of bishops. In the Roman Catholic Church it is also applied to a variety of officers attached to the Roman *curia. The evident delight of such dignitaries in hierarchy, authority, and self-adornment led to the adjective 'prelatical', a style which many bishops now try to avoid, not all with equal success.

Prema(-bhakti). The highest form of the love of God in Hinduism, comparable to para-*bhakti, described as the desperate longing as of a drowning person for air. However, this condition is permanent and cannot be taken away.

Presanctified, liturgy of: see LITURGY OF THE PRESANCTIFIED.

Presbyter. In the Church from the 2nd cent. on, a Christian minister of the second rank in the hierarchy of *bishop–presbyter–*deacon. It corresponds to the modern office of *priest.

Presbyterianism (Gk., *presbuteros*, 'elder'). Forms of Christian Church order and doctrine which emerged from the *Reformation (although in their own estimate they are in direct continuity from the New Testament), relying on the ministry and governance of elders. When the Swiss reformation reached Scotland, the quest for a Church order which would be both scriptural and open to constant reformation (the principle of *semper reformanda*, 'always to be reformed') led to Presbyterianism (the government by *presbyters, parity of ministers and the participation of all church members) and beyond Scotland to Congregationalism (the autonomy of congregations). Reformed/Presbyterian Christianity has been characterized by constant division, to such an extent that the myriad Churches cannot be listed here. In the opposite direction, various alliances have been made, culminating in the formation in 1970 of the World Alliance of Reformed Churches (Presbyterian and Congregational).

Prester John. Legendary king of the orient. Stories of a Christian king who had defeated the Muslim powers in central Asia (possibly based on a real victory of a Turkish or Mongol chief) were known in Europe in the middle of the 12th cent. In 1165 a letter from 'Prester [i.e. Presbyter] John', who ruled 'from the Tower of Babel to the sunrise' began to circulate. It was an obvious fabrication of Western origin, but was wishfully believed at a time of ebbing Christian fortunes in the Holy Land.

Preta (Skt., 'deceased'; Pāli, *peta*). In Hinduism, the condition of the dead between death and joining the ancestors (*pitṛ). Their state is that of a kind of *purgatory; and the correct funeral rites (*śrāddha) are essential if the transition is to be effected, since otherwise the preta may threaten the living. The pretaloka is the sphere where they remain until the rites are completed.

In Buddhism, their domain constitutes one of the three undesirable forms of existence (*gati). Their *karma is good enough to keep them from the hells (*naraka) but not sufficient to project them to *asura. If they do not receive appropriate support from the living, they can become vengeful. Their condition is described in *Petavatthu* (*Khuddaka-nikāya).

Priest

Judaism The *kohanim* (sing., *kohen*) are a hereditary class whose special responsibility was the performance of the cultic ceremonies of the Jerusalem *Temple. The Hebrew scriptures indicate in some places that only the descendants of *Aaron have the right to priesthood (Leviticus 8) and in others that the entire tribe of *Levi has a priestly role (Deuteronomy 33. 8–10); to these were added the Zadokites (perhaps predecessors of *Sadducees) when *David captured Jerusalem and assimilated the cult of Zadok. After the destruction of the Temple in 70 CE, the sacrificial system came to an end. Knowledge of priestly descent can no longer be proved. None the less supposed Kohanim enjoy certain privileges in the *synagogue. Because of the doubt entailed in priestly ancestry, the *Progressive movements disregard all the laws applying to Kohanim.

Christianity In Roman Catholic, Orthodox, and Anglican Churches, the priest is the minister who is typically in charge of a *parish. The English word is ultimately derived from Gk.

presbyteros, as the office is derived from that of the early Christian *presbyter. The idea of 'priesthood', in the sacrificial sense continuous with the Jewish office, only gradually attached to this order of minister. At first, the *sacrifice of the *eucharist was the function of *bishops only, but with the spread of Christianity to country districts priests were allowed to consecrate the eucharist themselves. This opened the way for a doctrine that priestly powers were conferred in *ordination, especially when in the 11th cent. the practice spread of ordaining priests who had no benefice. The priest thus became the normal celebrant of the eucharist and after 1215 the one who heard *confessions. He remained, however, subordinate to the bishop, who alone could ordain and *confirm.

The tendency of medieval theology to see the priesthood of the clergy in terms of the *mass led to its rejection by the *Reformers. Protestant Christians thus take the view that priesthood belongs only to Christ and, derivatively, to 'all believers' (1 Peter 2. 5, 9).

The term 'priest' is then sometimes applied to functionaries in other religions, as e.g. to *mullahs in Islam, or to *granthi or *mahant among Sikhs, to *hotṛ and *brahmans among Hindus, to *tao-shih among Taoists, to *magi among *Zoroastrians, but the differences in order, duties, appointment, and role are extreme. See Index, Priests.

Primate. The *metropolitan of the 'first see' (Lat., *prima sedes*) of a whole nation or people. Anomalously, the archbishop of *Canterbury is 'Primate of All England' and the archbishop of York 'Primate of England'.

Prime, terce, sext, none. The 'little hours' of the divine *office of the W. Church, appointed to be read at the first, third, sixth, and ninth hours (i.e. 6, 8, 11 a.m., and 2 p.m.) respectively.

Primitive Methodist Church. A branch of early 19th-cent. *Methodism. In N. Staffordshire Hugh Bourne and William Clowes engaged in open-air preaching. The Liverpool *Wesleyan Conference (1807) condemned their 'highly improper' meetings as 'likely to be productive of considerable mischief'. Once expelled by the parent body, Bourne and Clowes officially formed the Primitive Methodist Connexion in 1811. In 1932 the denomination joined with the Wesleyan and United Methodists to form the Methodist Church of Great Britain and Ireland.

Primordial Shinto (Yuiitsu Shinto): see HONJI SUIJAKU.

Primus. The presiding bishop in the Scottish Episcopal Church. He is elected by the bishops in Scotland to preside over the synod, but does not have the powers of a *metropolitan.

Principles of Faith (Ikkarim): see ARTICLES OF FAITH.

Priscillianism. Christian *heresy of the 4th–5th cents., so-named from Priscillian, bishop of Avila in Spain. Priscillian was exiled for a time in 381, and executed for sorcery together with several of his adherents in 386. The Priscillianists taught a *modalist doctrine of the Trinity and denied the pre-existence of Christ as well as his real humanity; they condemned marriage, the procreation of children, and eating meat. How much of this was taught by Priscillian himself is uncertain.

Prithī Chand (16th cent. CE). Claimant to succession as Sikh *Gurū. Prithī Chand (or Prithīā) was Gurū *Rām Dās' eldest son. He opposed the succession of his younger brother, *Arjan Dev, turned Emperor Jahāṅgir further against him, and unsuccessfully attempted to kill the young *Hargobind.

Probabilism. A moral theory conceding to the individual the right to act in accordance with a probable opinion about the rectitude of that act, even though there may be a more probable opinion, apparently supported by law, against the action. The theory which insists that the more probable opinion must be followed is probabiliorism (Lat., *probabilior*, 'more probable').

Procession of the Holy Spirit. A disputed issue between E. and W. Churches. See FILIOQUE.

Process theology. A Christian theological system emphasizing the fluid rather than static nature of the universe, and finding God within the process of becoming, rather than as the transcendent source of being. Process theology owes much to the metaphysical thought of A. N. Whitehead (1861–1947) which culminated in *Process and Reality* (1929). Everything is 'in God', but God is more than the sum of the parts (panentheism; see PANTHEISM)—just as I am my body, and yet I am more than the sum of the parts of my body. God is not apart from the universe, but is the comprehension of the whole process. This entire cosmic process is God, and God works like an artist attempting to win order and beauty out of opportunity. God is thus 'the great companion—the fellow-sufferer who understands'. This metaphysic was developed in a theological direction by Charles Hartshorne (e.g. *Man's Vision of God and the Logic of Theism*, 1941), and in a *Christological (and applied) direction by John Cobb (e.g. *Christ in a Pluralistic Age*, 1975; *Process Theology as Political Theology*, 1982; *The Liberation of Life*, 1981). Christ is interpreted as the one who embodied the most perfectly obedient response to the 'lure' of God. The possible connections with Buddhist thought have not been overlooked: see e.g. J. B. Cobb, *Beyond Dialogue: Towards a Mutual Transformation of Christianity and Buddhism* (1982).

Proclus (*c*.410–85). *Neoplatonic philosopher. His many works expound a systematization of the form of Neoplatonism derived from *Plotinus via Iamblichus and Syrianus. In line with this tradition, he set considerable store by *theurgy ('divine action'), a kind of white magic that exploited the sympathy between elements and processes underlying the unity of the cosmos, to further the ascent of the soul to the One.

Progressive Judaism. A collective term to refer to non-*Orthodox movements within Judaism. Although usually applied to *Reform or Liberal Judaism, it may sometimes be used to include the very different *Conservative and *Reconstructionist movements. See Index, Progressive Judaism.

Projection. The theory that God and gods are merely objectifications of human needs, ideals, or desires. With few exceptions, the theory in modern Western thought forms part of reductionistic accounts of *theistic belief. These accounts are in general built on the thought of L. *Feuerbach and K. *Marx, on the one hand, or of S. *Freud and the psychoanalytic school, on the other.

In Eastern religions, projection takes on a different and more fundamental significance. In Hinduism, it implies the basic ignorance (*avidyā) which superimposes reality on to *Brahman, as though appearances have independent existence.

In Buddhism, the projection of reality on to the unreal world of appearance arises equally from ignorance; and in *Mahāyāna, especially Ch'an/*Zen, it involves a failure to realize that all appearances are equally empty of self (*śūnyatā).

Promise and threat (Islamic philosophical issue): see MU'TAZILITES.

Promised Land. The land promised to the Jewish *patriarch, Abraham. The phrase does not appear in scripture, though 'land of promise' refers in Hebrews 11. 9 to the faith of Abraham.

Promotor fidei: see DEVIL'S ADVOCATE.

Proofs of the existence of God: see QUINQUE VIAE.

Propaganda. The 'Sacred *Congregation for the Evangelization of Peoples or for the Propagation of the Faith'. It is concerned with Roman Catholic missions in non-Christian territories and the administration of the Church where there is no established hierarchy.

Proper. The part of the Christian *eucharist and *offices which changes with the season of the *calendar or festival.

Prophet, Prophecy

Judaism In the Jewish Bible, a prophet (*nabi*; pl., *nebi'im*) is one who speaks on behalf of God. In origin, they were a part of a Near Eastern phenomenon (e.g. at *Mari), cultic functionaries who make known the unknown. Among these functionaries were also the *ḥozeh* ('seer') and *ro'eh* ('seer'), and *'ish ha-Elohim* ('the man of God'). The relationship between these is unclear, 1 Samuel 9. 9 simply affirming that he who is now called a prophet was in former times called a seer.

The classical or literary prophets are those whose oracles were preserved in writing, i.e. Isaiah, *Jeremiah, *Ezekiel, and the twelve *Minor Prophets. Like the pre-classical prophets, some at least were subject to ecstatic seizures (e.g. Hosea 9. 7), they performed symbolic acts (e.g. Isaiah 20. 2 ff.), and they were intimately involved in the current affairs of the nation. The prophets constantly pleaded with Israel to repent (e.g. Amos 5. 4). The later classical prophets realized that humanity could not by its own efforts return to God and they looked forward to a time when God would initiate a 'new *covenant' when 'I will write my law upon their hearts ...' and 'I will remember their *sin no more' (Jeremiah 31. 33–4). In that day, the faithful *remnant of Israel would live in peace and God's glory would again be manifest through all the earth (Isaiah 40. 5). It was generally agreed that prophecy had ceased in the time of the second *Temple: after the *Exile, authority was transferred to the Temple and its priests, interpreting *Torah (to ensure holy behaviour and thus no repetition of the Exile).

Christianity Early Christians experienced the consequences of the *Holy Spirit, and believed that this 'return' of the Holy Spirit in visible gifts was a mark of the redemptive will of God. Thus in addition to accepting the earlier Jewish prophets (who were seen to have been foretelling the coming of Christ and events surrounding and arising from that advent), prophets returned as functionaries in the early Church. However, the problem arose of what control Church leaders could have over the inspired (or claimed-to-be inspired) utterances of an individual. The problem became acute in relation to *Montanism; and prophets ceased to have a major role, until the revival of their importance in African Christianity.

Islam See NABĪ; RASŪL.
See also Index, Prophets.

Prosbul (from Gk.). Jewish legal formula for reclaiming debts after the *Sabbatical Year. A prosbul was signed by witnesses before a *bet din and would entitle the creditor to collect his debts despite the intervention of the Sabbatical Year (*Shev.* 10. 2).

Proselytes. Converts to a religion, and especially (because formally defined and controlled) to Judaism. Proselytism was widespread in the second *Temple period. Once converted, the proselyte is given a new name and is described as 'Ben' or 'Bat' Avraham (son or daughter of *Abraham). He is cut off from his previous family and must observe all the precepts which bind Jews. A female proselyte may not marry a *priest (*B.Yev.* 60b), but may marry a *mamzer (*B.Kid.* 4. 7); and a male proselyte may not be appointed to any Jewish public office (*B.Yev.* 45b). However, once the canons of the Christian Church had forbidden 'Judaizing', proselytism became increasingly rare.

Prostitution, sacred. The sense of union in the sexual act became in many religions a powerful expression of religious union. This is most familiar in Indian practice (see DEVDĀSĪ), but it was clearly a common practice elsewhere.

Protestant ethic: see WEBER, MAX.

Protestantism. Generic term for manifestations or expressions of Christianity arising from the *Reformation. Although the Lat., *protestari*, means 'to protest' (sc., against the errors of Roman Catholicism), it also means 'to avow' or 'to affirm'. Thus Protestants were, and are, not simply negative, but seek to return to a faith and order based on scripture, and in continuity from the early apostolic Church. They stress the sovereign majesty of God, who as Father entrusts Lordship over creation to his Son. They hold strongly to *justification by faith and the *priesthood of all believers. They reject the claims of papal supremacy, at least as so far practised and expressed, and also the seven *sacraments of Catholicism, adhering to the two which have dominical (i.e. from the Lord) warrant, *baptism and the *Lord's Supper. Protestantism has proved highly fissiparous, and embraces extremes of conservatism and radicalism. There are, in extremely approximate terms, about 500 million Protestants in the world.

Prothesis or **proskomide.** The ceremonial preparation of the bread and wine which takes place at a table apart within the sanctuary before the beginning of the *Orthodox *eucharist.

Protocols of the Elders of Zion. An *anti-Semitic forgery of the 19th cent., written to demonstrate a Jewish conspiracy to achieve financial and political power world-wide. Despite their evident falsity, they were used by the Nazis, and have resurfaced as anti-Jewish propaganda during the conflict over Palestine/Israel.

Proverbs, Book of. One of the three *wisdom books in the Hebrew scriptures. Traditionally ascribed to '*Solomon, son of *David, King of *Israel', it is generally dated in the post-*exilic period, but obviously contains much earlier material.

Providence (Lat., *providere*, 'to foresee'). The belief that all things are ordered and regulated by God towards his purpose. A distinction is usually made between general providence (which occurs through the laws of nature) and special providence (which is related to individuals).

Providence Industrial Mission. The first independent church related to *Ethiopianism in Malawi (formerly Nyasaland), founded in 1900 by John Chilembwe (*c.*1870–1915). Chilembwe was educated in the USA, and supported then and later by the National *Baptist Convention. He organized an abortive rising in 1915. Chilembwe was killed and the rising easily suppressed, but he remains a national hero in Malawi today. His 'New Jerusalem' church, built in 1913 at Chiradzulu, was demolished by the authorities. His followers were allowed to reorganize in 1926, under the leadership of Dr Daniel S. Malekebu (also educated in the USA). The Church split in the 1970s. One branch, the Independent Baptist Convention, claims a following of 25,000–30,000, and is a member of the Christian Council of Malawi.

Proximate salvation (attainment of immediate, not ultimate, goals): see GREAT TRADITION, LITTLE TRADITION.

Pṛthivi ('the extended one'). The Hindu manifestation of the earth, the womb of *Agni (*Śatapatha Brāhmana* 7. 4. 1. 8), the Mother in whose womb the embryonic earth is formed. She is sometimes joined with the sky as Dyāvā-Pṛthivi, and remains associated with agriculture. In later Hinduism, she is Bhūdevī, the consort of *Viṣṇu.

Psalms, Book of (Gk., *psalmoi*, 'songs accompanied by string music'). The first of the *Writings in the Hebrew Bible and nineteenth book in the Christian Old Testament. The Hebrew title is *Tehillim* ('songs of praise'), from the same root as the common refrain *Alleluia. The 150 Psalms are numbered differently in Protestant (following the Hebrew) and Roman Catholic (following the *Septuagint/Greek and *Vulgate) Bibles.

Psalms, liturgical use of. Use of *Psalms in the Jewish and Christian *liturgical services. Their regular use in Christian liturgy is at least as early as the 4th cent. (though in fact probably as early as Christianity itself). The introduction of Gregorian chant (see GREGORY I) universalized the style of their use; and St *Benedict made it a requirement in his *Rule* that the whole *psalter should be said or sung each week—an observance still followed by many religious orders. The increasing disappearance of morning and evening prayer as liturgical services has led to a marked decline in the use of the psalter, though metrical psalms (psalms translated into metrical hymns) remain popular; and some modern forms of chant (e.g., Gelineau and *Taizé) have kept parts of psalms in use.

Psalter. The book of *Psalms in a form for use in devotion or worship.

Pseudepigrapha. Jewish and Christian books whose purported origin or authorship is not as claimed by themselves. Thus books are attributed to Moses, Baruch, Solomon, Peter, Thomas, etc. Famous examples include the *Book of *Enoch, *Jubilees, The Ascension of *Isaiah, The Assumption of *Moses, The Book of *Adam and Eve*, and *The *Testament of the Twelve Patriarchs*. See also APOCRYPHA.

Pseudo-Dionysius (author of corpus of spiritual and theological writings): see DIONYSIUS.

Psychodynamic theory. A dynamic model of the self which concentrates in particular on emotions and drives. This is perhaps the most widely used theory in the *psychological study of religion.

Good examples of psychodynamic theory applied to religious phenomena are provided by the study of *witchcraft (the witch providing an outlet for repressed emotions), the study of rituals of rebellion (providing cathartic release), and those studies which hold that religious institutions serve to compensate for social or other deprivations. Victor *Turner's *The Forest of Symbols* (1967) contains good illustrations of modified psychodynamic theorizing.

Psychology of religion. The field of study which employs psychological techniques and theories to explore and explain religious phenomena. In the W., various schools of psychology have given birth to different treatments of religion. Theories have been taken from associational psychology (J. G. *Frazer's *The Golden Bough*, 1890–1937), from psychoanalysis (S. *Freud, C. G. *Jung), from social psychology (as surveyed by M. Argyle and B. Beit-Hallahmi in *The Social Psychology of Religion*, 1975), and from cognitive psychology (see L. Festinger, *When Prophecy Fails*, 1956, and D. Sperber's *Rethinking Symbolism*, 1975). The most influential of these approaches has been psychoanalytic theory, specifically in the *psychodynamic form.

In most cultures, however, psychologies are less 'of' religious life than they are integral to it. Since religions must address participants as well as whatever is taken to be ultimate, they contain their own psychologies. The most sophisticated, and, it appears, efficacious indigenous psychologies appear in the great Eastern traditions (see e.g. Rama *et al.*, *Yoga and Psychotherapy*, 1976), but there are countless other examples (e.g. V. *Turner on rites of passage and curing rituals).

The most frequently met aim of indigenous psychologies 'of' religion is transformative. The aim of Western, supposedly more scientific psychologies of religion is explanatory.

P'u (Chin., 'rough block'). Taoist understanding of the original innocence and simplicity of human nature, like that of raw silk or a newborn child.

Pudgala (person): see PUDGALAVĀDINS.

Pudgalavādins (Skt., *pudgala*; Pāli, *puggala*). 'Personalists', a school of Buddhist philosophy which began 3rd cent. CE, and which posited the existence of a self or soul over and above the five aggregates (*skandhas). This school, also known as the Vātsiputrīya, regarded the pudgala or 'person' as an entity which continued through each life in the cycle of rebirths, carried along in some manner by the skandhas, but which disappeared when liberation was gained. It was thus a kind of impermanent or temporary soul, unlike the Hindu *ātman which was thought of as eternal.

The doctrine of the pudgala was accepted by no other school and was actively criticized, with the result that it died out in the medieval period. See also ANĀTMAN.

Puebla: see LIBERATION THEOLOGY.

Puggala: see PUDGALAVĀDINS.

Pugio Fidei (text against Jews): see ADRET, SOLOMON BEN ABRAHAM.

P'u-hsien (Bodhisattva): see SAMANTABHADRA.

P'u-Hua (Jap., Fuke; d. 860). Ch'an/Zen master, dharma-successor (*hassu) of P'an-shan Pao-chi. Well-known for his unconventional style, he was important in the founding of the Fuke school which made non-*sūtra activities important, e.g. flute-playing: see KAKUSHIN; KOMUSŌ. P'u-hua remains a model of the *ḥoly fool style of Zen.

Pūjā (Skt., Pāli, 'respect, homage, worship', perhaps early Dravidian 'flower' + 'offer'). Immensely varied acts, in Eastern religions, of offering, devotion, propitiation, etc., but often including the offering of flowers. In early (Vedic) Hinduism, pūjā began to replace yajña (*sacrifice) as 'invocation, reception and entertainment of God as a royal guest' (Gonda). According to S. K. Chatterji, pūjā developed in the non-Aryan culture: *homa was exclusively Aryan, requiring animal *sacrifice (*paśu-karma*), but pūjā was open to all and required flowers (*puspa-karma*). Certainly in later Buddhism the offering of flowers (*puppha-pūjā*) has become the main pūjā ritual.

For Hindus, pūjā relates humans to the domain and action of the deities in all their many ways of sustaining or threatening the cosmos and life within it, and thus it takes a vast number of different ritual forms, of which the simplest is *darśan, looking on the image of the deity (or in the case of Jains, on the image of a *tīrthaṅkara; among the Jains, an ascetic can only look at an image, never act toward it; such interior devotion is known as *caityavandana*, and is one of the six obligations). Pūjā is mentioned in the early *Gṛhya Sūtras*, with focus on home rituals (which remain central). In the *Sūtras, the reception of, and hospitality for, *brahmans in the home to preside over rites for ancestors is called pūjā, and it may be that *devapūjā* (worship of deities) developed from this: *devapūjā* is described in the *Purāṇas only in sections added later; but it then becomes fundamental in *bhakti.

Among Jains, that understanding of prasad is impossible (the tīrthaṅkaras cannot consume anything). Instead, the offering of food is understood as a gesture of renunciation. Equally, pūjā addressed to the tīrthaṅkaras with expectation of response is inappropriate, because they have given all that they can, 'instruction in faith, knowledge and behaviour' (Vattakera); but expressions of gratitude and love are natural, and increase merit. In general, the *Digambaras do not touch images themselves, but employ a priest (*upadhye*) to do so, whereas the Śvetāmbaras perform the rituals and employ temple servants (*pujārī*) to clear up after them.

In Buddhism, pūjā may be offered to the deities (as Buddhism understands them), but it is also translated in a non-theistic direction (as in the case of *dāna). It then becomes a basic form of religious observance, through recitation of the threefold 'Refuge Formula' (*triśarana), etc., but even more through offerings of thanksgiving, food, and flowers to the *Buddha.

Pujārī: see PŪJĀ.

Pu-k'ung Chin-kang (teacher of Buddhism, 8th cent.): see AMOGHAVAJRA.

Pul. Korean for *buddha.

Pumbedita. Centre of Jewish learning, 2nd–4th cents. CE. The *academy at Pumbedita and the academy at *Sura were together the centres of Jewish scholarship in Babylon.

Puṃsavana. A Hindu ritual (*saṃskāra) to ensure the birth of a male child—vital for the proper performance of funeral (*śraddha) rites.

Punabbhava (Pāli 'again-becoming'), the Buddhist understanding of rebirth. Since there is no self or soul being reborn, 'rebirth' suggests too strong an understanding of what continues. Re becoming simply affirms that there are continuities of consequence, in which a consciousness of what is happening (as in the case of humans) is a part of the process.

Punarājāti (Skt., 'rebirth'). Hindu belief that the process toward release (*mokṣa) requires many rebirths—perhaps as many as 84 million.

Punarāvritti (Sanskrit term): see REBIRTH.

Punarjanman (Sanskrit term): see REBIRTH.

Punarmṛtyu. Repeated death, the predicament for Hindus which is brought about by *karma through the process of *saṃsāra.

Punarutpatti (Sanskrit term): see REBIRTH.

Puṇḍarika ('white lotus'). Water plant unfolding above the surface, symbolizing attainment of purity, and also the appearance of a manifest world.

Pundit (Hindu learned man): see PAṆḌITA.

Puṇḍra (marks in Hinduism made on the body): see TILAKA.

Punjāb: see PAÑJĀB.

Puñña (merit): see PUṆYA.

Puṇya (Skt.; Pāli, *puñña*). The accumulation of beneficial consequence (loosely, *merit) in Eastern religions, through the process of *karma. In Buddhism, the transfer of puṇya to the dead is an important function of *saṅgha and other monastic rituals.

Punyaksetra (Jain acts of merit): see MERIT.

Purāṇa (Skt., 'ancient'). Any of a class of Sanskrit verse texts which contain mythological accounts of ancient days. Purāṇas are considered *smṛti or non-*Vedic Hindu scripture. They were probably compiled between 500 and 1500 CE, although they contain much earlier material from the *itihāsa (epics) and other sources.

The Purāṇas have their origin in texts for the Vedic edification of lower *castes and women.

A proper Purāṇa should expound the *pañcalakṣaṇa* (five subjects): *sarga* (creation), *vaṁśa* (genealogy of gods and *ṛṣis), *manvantara* (the reigns of the *Manus), *pratisarga* (destruction and recreation, together with the history of humanity), and *vaṁśānucarita* (legendary history of the Solar and Lunar dynasties).

The Purāṇas are divided into two categories, Mahāpurāṇas (major) and Upapurāṇas (minor), each category having eighteen members.

Purāṇas stress bhakti (devotion) and miraculous manifestations of divine grace. Although many Hindu reformers such as *Dayānanda have attacked puranic religiosity, it remains the dominant form of Hinduism.

Purandaradāsa (Hindu musician): see HARIDĀS, SVĀMĪ.

Puran Siṅgh, Sant (founder of Sikh reform movement): see NISHKAM SĒWAK JATHĀ.

Puraścaraṇa (Skt., 'preparation'). Preparing the way in Hinduism for meditation by repeating a *mantra, and by performing the appropriate rituals. The repetition of a mantra may extend over many days (often from new moon to new moon) and thus produce a large number of repetitions.

Purdah (Pers., *pardah*, 'curtain'). The Muslim seclusion of women from strangers, related to *hijāb (the veil). The basis is in Qur'ān 33. 53.

Pure Gate of the East Mountain (group of followers of Hung-jen): see HUNG-JEN.

Pure Land (Skt., *sukhāvatī*; Chin., *ching-t'u*; Jap., *jōdo*). An untainted transcendent realm created by the *Buddha Amitābha (*Amida), to which his devotees aspire to be born in their next lifetime. Since all the conditions in Pure Land propel one toward enlightenment, anyone born there will attain *nirvāna quickly and easily. According to *Mahāyāna doctrine, there are countless Pure Lands or Buddha Lands (Skt., *buddhakṣetra*; Chin., *fo-t'u*; Jap., *butsudo*), each produced by a different Buddha. In addition to Amitābha's, the one created by the Buddha *Akṣobhya is frequently mentioned in Buddhist writings. None the less, only the Pure Land of Amitābha ever achieved widespread popularity in E. Asian Buddhism. Hence, in China, Korea, and Japan the expression 'Pure Land' came to be used as a proper noun signifying Amitābha's transcendent realm rather than as a generic term for any Buddha Land.

Detailed descriptions of the Pure Land are contained in three Pure Land sūtras (*Sukhāvatīvyuha Sūtras*) revered by E. Asian Buddhists: *Wu-liang-shou ching* (Jap., *Muryojukyo*; Larger Pure Land Sūtra); *O-mi-t'o ching* (Jap., *Amidakyo*; Smaller Pure Land Sūtra); *Kuan wu-liang-shou-fo ching* (Jap., *Kanmuryōjukyō*; Pure Land Meditation Sūtra). According to them, Amitābha's realm is located in the western direction, and it is known by the name *Sukhāvati (Skt.; Chin., *chi-lo*; Jap., *gokuraku*), meaning 'Utmost Bliss'. The chanting of Amitābha's name, known in Japan as the *nembutsu, emerged as the most common practice.

Pure Land schools. A devotional form of Buddhism centring on the Buddha Amitābha (Skt.; Chin., O-mi-t'o; Jap., *Amida) and his transcendent realm known as *Pure Land. Everything in Pure Land is conducive to Buddhist enlightenment; hence, persons born there in their next lifetime will attain *nirvāna without fail. Pure Land Buddhism originated in India, but it gained its largest following in E. Asia once Pure Land scriptures were translated into Chinese. One of China's early Pure Land adherents was *Hui-yuan (334–416). The spread of Pure Land Buddhism to the general populace occurred a century or two later as a result of the evangelistic efforts of several Pure Land masters. The first of these was T'an-luan (476–?560). He embraced the Pure Land teachings at the urging of the Indian priest Bodhiruci, a famous transmitter and translator of Buddhist scriptures. Tao-ch'o (562–645), who carried on T'an-luan's work, added a historical dimension to the Pure Land teachings. Tao-ch'o's successor, Shan-tao (613–81), was the great systematizer of Pure Land thought. He encouraged believers in five types of religious practice: reciting scripture, meditating on Amitābha and his Pure Land, worshipping Amitābha, chanting his name, and making praises and offerings to him. Among these he emphasized the invocation of Amitābha's name as the paramount act leading to birth in Pure Land. The simplicity of this practice, known as the *nien-fo (Chin.; Jap., *nembutsu), made Pure Land an appealing form of Buddhism to those unable to perform more rigorous religious devotions.

Pure Land Buddhism passed into Japan as one of many cultural imports from China. From *c.*10th cent., Pure Land increased in popularity with the publication of a handbook on Pure Land practice by the *Tendai priest *Genshin (942–1017), entitled the **Ōjōyōshū*. Pure Land did not emerge as an independent school of Japanese Buddhism until *Hōnen (1133–1212). Under Hōnen's leadership a formal Pure Land school known as the *Jōdo school came into existence. Among his followers *Shinran (1173–1262) stressed faith in Amitābha as the essence of the nembutsu and as the true cause of salvation. His followers, drawn primarily from the peasant class, went on to establish the *Jōdo Shinshū school of Buddhism. The other major Pure Land school to arise in Japan was the Ji school founded by *Ippen (1239–89). He also inherited Hōnen's teachings, but he advocated simple repetition of Amitābha's name whether undergirded by faith or not. All of these schools made Pure Land one of the dominant forms of Buddhism in Japan. See Index, Pure Land.

Pure Land sūtras: see PURE LAND.

Pure Yang (form of Taoism): see CH'ÜAN-CHEN TAO.

Purgative Way. The first of the *Three Ways of the mystical life. This triadic division was popularized by *Dionysius the Areopagite. See also ILLUMINATIVE and UNITIVE.

Purgatory. According to Catholic teaching, the place or state in which those who have died in the grace of God expiate their unforgiven *venial sins, by undergoing due punishment before being admitted to the *beatific vision. Scriptural warrant is claimed in 2 Maccabees 12. 39–45; Matthew 12. 31 f.; 1 Corinthians 3. 11–15. The doctrine of purgatory was openly rejected at the *Reformation, and Protestants deny it as unscriptural and a denial of the complete forgiveness of sins through faith in Christ's saving work.

For a Buddhist equivalent, see YAMA.

Puri. Hindu pilgrimage centre in Bengal, site of the *Jagannātha temple, and one of the seven particularly holy places of India (see SACRED CITIES, SEVEN).

Puril Pojo (Korean reformer): see CHINUL.

Purim (Heb., 'lots'). Jewish feast commemorating the deliverance of Jews, as recorded in the book of *Esther. The feast is celebrated on 14 Adar; it was established by the 2nd cent. CE, and the *Mishnah tractate *Megillah* discusses its observance.

Puritans. Those members of the late 16th-cent. church in England who were dissatisfied with the Elizabethan Settlement of Religion. The term was one of abuse coined in the 1560s to describe 'a hotter sort of *Protestant'. These included people who had returned to England after exile under Queen Mary (1553–8), some of whom refused to be *bishops, and who held strong views about worship, as well as others who pressed vigorously for the purification of the Church. The term 'Puritan' thus describes attitudes to the Church of England which changed through time. In the early 17th cent., the lines separating Puritans and English Protestants became more blurred as they continued, in the main, to worship in the same churches and espouse the same basic theology. The appointment by Charles I of a number of bishops who were *Arminian in much of their theology, together with the seeming alliance of court and church in promoting *high church practices, alienated many: it raised questions about the *episcopate, the *liturgy, and the proper way of life for the elect (cf. *election), which had largely lain dormant for half a century. Not so by 1642, when these issues figured in the English Civil War, the so-called Puritan Revolution. After the restoration, some Puritans became Separatists, believing in a *Congregational form of church government. Several of these Separatist leaders were executed, whilst others were compelled to leave the country (e.g. the Pilgrim Fathers) in order to enjoy religious liberty.

Under the auspices of the Massachusetts Bay Company, Puritans settled in all the new colonies, but especially in New England and Virginia. Until the end of the 17th cent., the strong Puritan sense of holding authority under God (as God's elect) created a kind of 'holy commonwealth', with strong religious control.

See Index, Puritans.

Purity

Judaism Purity (Heb., *tohorah*) involves the state of being ritually acceptable. According to Leviticus 11–17 and Numbers 19, the three major causes of ritual impurity are leprosy, sexual emissions, and contact with the dead. In the *halakhah, the laws of ritual purity and impurity are laid out in twelve tractates of the *Mishnah and the *Tosefta. Human beings, utensils, and food can all become impure, and purification involves the performance of particular rituals, although many have fallen into disuse in modern times. See also MIKVEH; NIDDAH; TOHORAH.

Islam See ABLUTION.

Hinduism See ŚODHANA.

Zoroastrianism Purity and pollution are central concerns in *Zoroastrian thought and practice. In Zoroastrian theology (**Bundahišn*) *Ahura Mazda is wholly good and all that leads to death and decay is the work of the evil *Angra Mainyu. The ultimate pollution is a corpse, especially that of a righteous person, for their death represents a greater triumph for evil than that of a sinner. But anything leaving the body (urine, spittle, blood, cut hair, etc.) is also thought of as dead, and therefore polluting.

The purity laws affect most aspects of life for all Zoroastrians, from the obligation to clean the home; to observing laws which are nowadays seen as hygienic; to acts of worship (*Atas); funerals (*daxma); even to rules against intermarriage or in strict priestly homes against commensality with anyone who does not observe the purity laws, especially non-Zoroastrians (*juddins*).

There are various rites of purification. For minor pollutions, the *padyab*, washing and saying the *kusti* prayers (*Naujote), is all that is necessary. On special occasions, for example before initiations or weddings, the *Nahn* is necessary. This begins with the *Padyab-kusti*; the symbolic eating of a pomegranate leaf and drinking of *nirang* to cleanse spiritually; the recital of the *Patet*, the prayer of repentance, and finally a bath.

Pūrṇa-yoga. The Integral Yoga of Śri *Aurobindo.

Purohita. Early functionary in Aryan India, who counselled the ruler, especially through ritual techniques. The best-known purohita in post-Vedic times was Kauṭilya, to whom **Arthaśastra* is attributed. See also VASIṢTHA. In the Vedic period, the purohita was also an advisor at all levels of sacrifice, and could be the officiant.

Puruṣa (Skt., 'man', 'person'). A spiritual concept variously understood in Hindu religion and philosophy. The famous **Puruṣa-sūkta* (*Ṛg Veda* 10. 90) celebrates puruṣa as a cosmic demiurge, the material and efficient cause of the universe, whose sacrifice and division gave rise to the *Veda and all of creation. The early *Upaniṣads and the **Bhagavad-gītā* use the term to mean an individual's spirit, psychic essence, or immortal Self. In *Sāṃkhya philosophy, puruṣa is the first principle (*tattva), pure contentless consciousness, passive, unchanging, and witness to the unconscious dynamism of *Prakṛti, primordial materiality.

Puruṣārtha. The four legitimate goals of life for high-caste Hindus. The first is *dharma, which controls the others, since it embraces appropriate belief and behaviour. The second is *artha, material goods and wealth. The third is *kāma, which is enjoyment of the senses. The fourth transcends the others, since it is *mokṣa, liberation.

Puruṣa-sūkta. The famous creation hymn of *Ṛg Veda* 10. 90, attributed to *Nārāyaṇa. This hymn celebrates *puruṣa (Skt., 'person') as the primordial Cosmic Man. The hymn represents the earliest myth of secondary creation. The sacrifice of Puruṣa by the gods becomes a model for all Vedic sacrifice, generating the metres and hymns of the *Veda, animal life, and the socio-economic divisions of humankind.

Puruṣottama (Skt., 'the highest person'). A perfected soul, the nearest Indian equivalent to a *saint. Puruṣottama is the supreme Lord, i.e. God.

Purva (Skt., 'aboriginal'). 1. Hindu term, in combination with other words, to express chronological priority, but also greater depth, profundity, etc. It contrasts with *uttara* to express later and higher realities.

2. Jain texts of great authority, now lost (but their 'resonance' continues through oral teaching: see DIGAMBARA).

Pūrva-mīmāṁsā (Skt., *pūrva*, 'earlier' + *mīmāṁsā*, 'investigation'). One of the six orthodox systems of Indian philosophy, usually referred to simply as Mīmāṁsā. It is concerned with the interpretation of the ritualistic and ceremonial portion (*karma-kāṇḍa) of the *Vedas. It is to be distinguished from the later *Uttara Mīmāṁsā, also called *Vedānta, which deals with the teachings of the *Upaniṣads.

Mīmāṁsā, extant perhaps as early as the 3rd cent. BCE, was later formulated by *Jaimini in the **Mīmāṁsā-sūtra* (*Mīmāṁsādarśana*) which is the oldest and basic text of the Mīmāṁsā school. The Vedas are held to be eternal, uncreated, and need no further authority; any discrepancy within them, therefore, is only apparent.

After the 8th cent., two schools developed as a result of disputes over the interpretations of the commentaries of *Kumārila and *Prabhākara, noted teachers of Mīmāṁsā.

P'u-sa. Chin. for *bodhisattva.

Pūṣan (prosperity): see ĀDITYAS.

Pusey, Edward Bouverie (1800–82). Leader of the *Oxford Movement. As Regius Professor of Hebrew he lent his prestige and erudition to the Tractarian cause, which even became known, to its opponents, as 'Puseyism'. His most influential activities were preaching and polemical writing, as well as spiritual counselling and acting as confessor to a wide range of people.

Pu-tai (popular figure in Zen iconography): see HOTEI.

P'u-t'i-ta-mo (Chinese name): see BODHIDHARMA.

P'u-t'o-shan. A mountain island in the E. China Sea, the holy place of Kuan-yin (*Avalokiteśvara), and a place of particular importance for Chinese Buddhism.

Pyx (Gk.). A box used for holding the *reserved sacrament, and specifically a small silver box used for carrying the sacrament to the sick, when the pyx is wrapped in a small corporal (linen cloth) and carried in a pyx-bag around the priest's neck.

Q

Q (prob. an abbreviation of Germ. *Quelle*, source). A symbol denoting a (hypothetical) document used by the authors of the *gospels of *Matthew and *Luke. Its existence is inferred from parallel passages in those gospels, containing substantially the same material, which do not come from *Mark (see SYNOPTIC GOSPELS). Thus the Q hypothesis proposes a second written source beside the gospel of Mark for Matthew and Luke. It normally envisages that Luke did not use Matthew, and is therefore the main rival to the view that Luke knew and used Matthew (within either a Mark–Matthew–Luke or a Matthew–Luke–Mark sequence).

Qabbalah (Jewish mystical exploration): see KABBALAH.

Qabd (Arab. 'contract'). In *Sūfī Islam, a technical term (in contrast to *basṭ) describing fear and desolation, akin to 'spiritual dryness'

Qadar (Arab., *qadara*, 'have strength for, gain mastery over'). The decree of *Allāh which, in Muslim belief, determines all eventualities. The *Qur'ān reiterates constantly the power of God, who is the sole creator of all that is, and the One who knows all that is to be. Nothing can happen unless God wills it—hence the popular recognition of this in the phrase, *insh'Allah*, 'if God wills it'. How strong is this determinism? If God determines everything that happens, how can humans be held responsible on the Day of Judgement (*yaum al-Dīn)? This was a major and divisive issue in early Islam. At one extreme (eventually excluded from orthodox Islam), the Jabriy(y)a (Jabariy(y)a) emphasized the power and authority of God to such an extent that it implied absolute predestination. At the other extreme, the Qadariy(y)a, who became identified with the *Muʿtazilites, held that humans, as the caliphs (*khalīfa) of God on earth, have the delegated power to create their actions. The mediating positions of the Maturidites (*al-Māturīdī) and the Ashʿarites (*al-Ashʿarī) held that all possibilities are created by God, but that humans have the responsibility to 'acquire' (*kasb, iktisāb*) actions out of the possibilities, thus becoming accountable (hence 'the doctrine of acquisition').

Qadariy(y)a (Muslim school of thought defending free will, not to be confused with *Qādiriy(y)a): see QADAR.

Qaddish (sanctifying doxology): see KADDISH.

Qadhaffi, Muʿammar (b. 1938). Libyan leader, founding his revolution (and *Green Book*) on Islamic principles. In 1975, he began to publish the *Green Book*. His basic aim was to return to the original Islam of the 7th cent., with direct, not representative, democracy, 'partners, not wage-earners', and respect for natural ways of life.

Qāḍi. 1. A Muslim judge appointed by a ruler or government because of his knowledge of Muslim law.

2. A name sometimes given to an adherent of *Ahmadīy(y)a.

Qādiriy(y)a. A *Sūfī order (*ṭarīqa) founded in the 12th cent. by *ʿAbd al-Qādir al-Jīlī, who was revered as a teacher and also as a worker of miracles. His tomb in Baghdad is a place of *pilgrimage. The order makes use of music and dance, particularly to encourage trance states. It is widespread from Morocco to India.

Qajars (Persian dynasty): see AL-MAJLISĪ.

Qalandar. Eastern name for holy beggars, perhaps *derwishes. The name occurs in the *Thousand and One Nights*, as though the Qalandars are a particular sect; but although they have been associated with the *Bektāshīy(y)a, it seems more probable that they were unorganized and simply took to begging as a way of life.

Qal va-homer ('light and heavy' principle of exegesis): see KAL VA-HOMER.

Qarmatians (Arab., *al Qarāmiṭah*). Members of a broad, often revolutionary, movement in Islam, which sought social reform and justice during the 9th–12th cents. CE, in Khurāsān, Syria, Yemen, and Egypt. The Qarmatians were named after their 9th-cent. leader, Hamdān al-Qarmaṭ. They emerged from the *Ismāʿīli *Seveners, accepting Muḥammad b. Ismāʿīl as the final *Imām. Their teaching was kept as a secret *'gnosticism' among initiates.

Their most notorious act was the abduction, in 930 (AH 317), of the *Black Stone, refusing offers to ransom it. They threw it back into the mosque in Kufah in 951 (AH 340), saying, 'By command we took it, and by command we return it'—now in seven pieces, perhaps to affirm the seven Imāms? Although they disappeared as a sect, their influence continued in other movements, e.g. perhaps the Alawis (see NUṢAIRI).

Qawwāli (Indian Sūfī singers): see CHISHTI.

Qaynuqa. An ancient Jewish tribe of the city of *Madīna. The Banu Qaynuqa (a tribe of metal-workers) was the first Jewish group to be persecuted by Muḥammad.

Qedushah (holiness): see KEDUSHAH.

Qibla. Direction of *Mecca, more specifically the *Kaʿba, towards which each Muslim must turn in order to perform the *ṣalāt validly. In a *mosque, the qibla is marked by the *miḥrāb*.

The word 'qibla' is then also used more loosely for a fixed direction of prayer in any religion.

Qin Shihuangdi: Ch'in Shih Huang Ti. See BURNING OF BOOKS.

Qiṣāṣ (Arab., 'retaliation'). The principle, in Islam, of limited retaliation for harm inflicted. In contrast to the blood-feuds of pre-Islamic Arabia (often lasting for years and generations), the *Qur'ān commends a substitutionary compensation (5. 45)—though where victim and perpetrator are of equal status, *talion is admitted in strict relationship to the perpetrator alone. Where a life has been taken, the life of the killer may be taken (2. 179), but no further revenge-killing is allowed: in effect, retribution replaced revenge.

Qissa-i-Sanjan (story of Zoroastrian migration): see PARSIS.

Qiyāma (resurrection): see YAUM AL-QIYĀMA.

Qiyās (Arab., 'measure'). 'Deduction by analogy' whereby *Qur'ān and *Sunna can be brought to bear on novel issues or circumstances. It is a reasoned opinion, based on the similitude of circumstances with basic reference to the Qur'ān and Sunna, and must not run contrary to an established law.

Qizil Bash (Turkish Ṣafavis): see ṢAFAVIDS.

Qoheleth (alternative name for Biblical book): see ECCLESIASTES.

Qom. Iranian town, south of Teheran, a major centre for the training of Shīʿa Muslim teachers and leaders. The tomb of Hazrat-i-Fātima, the sister of the eighth *Imam, 'Ali al-Rida, is located here, and it is the most important place of *pilgrimage after his own tomb at *Mashhad. In 1978 the first outbreak of protest against the Pahlavi rulers occurred in Qom.

Qorbān, qurbān: see SACRIFICE (JEWISH); VOWS.

Quadragesima (Lat., 'fortieth [day]'). Another name for the forty days of *Lent, or for the first Sunday in Lent, six weeks before *Easter.

Quadragesimo Anno. An *encyclical issued on 15 May 1931 by *Pius XI on the fortieth anniversary of *Leo XIII's **Rerum Novarum*, an encyclical concerned with the ordering of society and of economic relations, giving rise to 'a true Catholic social science'. *Quadragesimo Anno* addresses, more than its predecessor, questions of ownership and of wages.

Quakers. Usual name for the Society of *Friends. It was first given in the mid-17th cent. to the followers of George *Fox. Its derivation is uncertain: it may be derived from an occasion when, in 1650, Fox told a judge in Derby to 'tremble at the Word of the Lord'; or from an existing women's sect; or from the 'spiritual trembling' experienced at meetings.

Quartodecimans. Early Christians who observed *Easter on 14 Nisan, the same day as the Jewish *Passover, rather than the following Sunday.

Qubbat al-Ṣakhra: see DOME OF THE ROCK.

Quds, al- ('the Sanctuary'). Muslim name for Jerusalem; by extension it may also refer to Palestine as a whole.

Queen Anne's Bounty. A fund established by Queen Anne of England in 1704 to receive *tithes and other payments formerly diverted to the crown by Henry VIII, so as to improve the endowments of poorer parishes.

Quest for the historical Jesus. The attempt to recover from the New Testament, especially the *gospels, an account of *Jesus disentangled from the confessional presentation of him in those documents of faith. The 'Quest' is associated with A. *Schweitzer and his review of previous attempts (mainly of the 19th cent.) to write 'lives of Jesus'; its impossibility was strongly argued by R. *Bultmann (see also KERYGMA). *A New Quest of the Historical Jesus* (1959) was initiated by J. M. Robinson, who argued that 'Jesus' understanding of his existence, his selfhood, and thus in the higher sense his life, is a possible subject of historical research.'

Questions of King Milinda (title tr. of Pāli Buddhist text): see MILINDAPAÑHA.

Quicunque Vult (Christian statement of faith): see ATHANASIAN CREED.

Quietism. Used broadly of any spirituality that minimizes human activity and initiative, leaving all to the will of God. More strictly, it is applied in Christianity to the teaching of certain 17th-cent. writers, especially Miguel de Molinos (condemned in 1687), but also Mme. Guyon and Archbishop *Fénelon. In its essence, it takes teaching about the importance of simple surrender to God's will (characteristic of *contemplation) out of its context as the end-result of a life of moral discipline and participation in the sacraments. Christian perfection is attained by *contemplatio passiva infusa*, in which the powers of the self are suspended, to be replaced by God himself.

Quinquagesima (Lat., 'fiftieth [day]'). The Sunday before *Lent, seven weeks before *Easter.

Quinque Viae (Lat., Five Ways). Five classical arguments pointing to the existence of God, summarized by *Aquinas at the opening of the **Summa Theologica*:

The first way is the argument from motion [which requires a first Mover] ... The second is from the nature of efficient cause [the chain of causation requires an uncaused Cause] ... The third way is taken from possibility and necessity [roughly, 'why there is something rather than nothing' requires a necessary being] ... The fourth way is taken from the gradation to be found in things [comparisons, e.g. 'hotter', relate to a perfect standard, 'hottest', so overall to God as the cause of perfection] ... The fifth way is taken from the governance of the world [that things are evidently designed to an end, requiring a Designer]. (*ST* I, qu. 2, art. 3).

The first four are related to the *Cosmological Argument, the fourth remotely to the *Ontological Argument, the fifth to the *Teleological Argument.

Quires: see CHOIR.

Qumran community. Jewish monastic community which lived near the shores of the Dead Sea. Major archaeological excavations have taken place in the area. Khirbet Qumran is the site of a building complex which includes a large cemetery. It has been suggested that it was the site of the *Essene community described by Pliny the Elder (but see further DEAD SEA SCROLLS). The occupants of the site clearly aimed at self-sufficiency with large storerooms and an elaborate system of customs. These have been connected to the elaborate cleansing prescriptions laid down in the *Manual of Discipline* in the *Dead Sea Scrolls. The buildings were destroyed and burnt *c.*70 CE, presumably by the Romans during the Jewish war (see JOSEPHUS).

Quo vadis? (whither are you going?): see PETER, ST.

Qur'ān. The scripture of Islam, believed by Muslims to be the word of *Allāh, revealed to *Muḥammad between the years 610 and 632 CE, recited by him, and subsequently recorded in written form.

In the Qur'ān itself, the word *qur'ān* means primarily the action of reciting; it can also in some places indicate an actual passage of scripture, or a part of the whole revelation, or the book; it is also mentioned together with the *Tawrāt and *Injīl (3. 3; 9. 111). The word *kitāb* (book) is also used as a synonym (e.g. 4. 105). The Qur'ān is thought to 'confirm', but also supersede, former scriptures (10. 37). It is taken from *umm al-kitāb, the pre-existent scripture preserved in heaven.

The Qur'ān in its present form consists of 114 chapters (*sūras) composed of varying numbers of verses (*ayāt*; sing., **ayā*), and roughly arranged in decreasing order of length. The first sūra, of only seven verses, is the *Fātiḥa. In general, the earlier sūras are the shorter ones, and thus are found towards the end of the book.

The generally accepted belief among Muslims, although there has been criticism of the details is that during Muḥammad's lifetime portions of the Qur'ān were written down, at his dictation, but that the first collection was made during the caliphate of *Abū Bakr (632–4 (AH 11–13)), by Muḥammad's scribe Zayd b. Thābit. Subsequently, under *'Uthmān, a recension was made by Zayd and a few others. Any other written versions of single parts were ordered to be destroyed. Thus within some thirty years of Muḥammad's death a definitive text was established, which has remained virtually unchanged down to the present day.

The Qur'ān is divided into the sūras revealed in *Mecca, and those revealed in *Madīna.

Although the Qur'ān describes itself as a 'clear book' (2. 2), and a clear 'Arabic Qur'ān' (12. 2), some of its passages are acknowledged to be obscure and in need of interpretation. The science of commentary and interpretation (*tafsīr and *ta'wīl) has given rise to a large body of literature.

As the speech (*kalām*) of Allāh, the Qur'ān is considered one of His attributes (*ṣifāt*), and also as co-eternal with him. Muslim teaching in general has been that the Qur'ān is eternal, uncreated, and perfect. Its inimitability (*i'jāz) is an article of faith (10. 38, 11. 13) and a proof of its divine origin. The intense respect for the words of the Qur'ān has led to an eagerness to recite portions frequently, and to learn the whole book by heart, one who has so learnt being known as a *ḥāfiẓ*. There has also been some reluctance to translate it into other languages. Any version other than *Arabic is considered as, at best, an 'interpretation'.

Qurayza, Banu. Ancient Jewish tribe in the city of *Madīna. The Banu Qurayza believed themselves to be of priestly descent and were primarily engaged in agriculture. By order of Muḥammad, the men were massacred and the women and children sold into slavery in 627 CE.

Qutb (Arab., 'pole, axis'). In Islam, especially among *Sūfīs, the idea of a central axis around which the interests of the world revolve. The centrality is that of God's will and word, manifested through a great saint or caliph (e.g. the first four). Thus it is not held that the individual is without fault or flaw, but rather that at certain moments the qutb is manifest through him.

R

Ra'av: see BERTINORO, O.

Rabad (acronym): see IBN DAUD, ABRAHAM . . .

Rabbah bar Naḥmānī (*c*.270–330 CE). Babylonian Jewish *amora. Rabbah was head of the *Pumbedita academy for twenty-two years during its time of greatest influence. Because of his skill in argument, he was known as Oker Harim, 'uprooter of mountains'. His death was described as 'being summoned to the heavenly academy', thenceforth a synonym for the death of a learned person.

Rabbanites. Name used to designate the opponents of the *Karaites in the Jewish religion. From *c*.10th cent., the Rabbanites were those Jews who accepted the *oral law in contrast to the Karaites who rejected it.

Rabbi, Rabbinate (Heb., 'my master'). Hence 'Rabbinic Judaism'. Jewish learned man who has received ordination (see SEMIKHAH). The term rabbi was not used as a title until the time of *Hillel. In *Talmudic times, this was not granted outside *Erez Israel, so that the Babylonian sages bore the title of 'Rav'. During this period rabbis were interpreters and expounders of the scriptures and *oral law. It was not until the Middle Ages that a rabbi became the spiritual leader of a particular Jewish community. Originally rabbis were not paid. By the 14th cent. there is evidence of payment, not for teaching the law, but as compensation for loss of time taken up with rabbinical duties. In order to serve, the *Ashkenazim in particular insisted that rabbis should have a diploma of *Semikhah; and his duties were laid down in a letter of appointment (*ketav rabbanut*). As community leader, he was asked to give *responsa on legal problems and ambiguities, and to serve in Jewish courts; later, in E. Europe, the office was frequently combined with that of 'rosh *yeshivah' (head of the yeshivah). Nowadays the role of the rabbi varies from community to community. Among *Reform congregations, he (and since 1972 possibly she) performs a function analogous to that of a Christian minister. The *Orthodox rabbi has also taken on these duties, but has retained his role as legal consultant and interpreter of the written and oral law. For individual rabbis, see Index, Rabbis, Teachers etc.

Rabbinical conferences. Synods held by Jewish *rabbis to provide authoritative guidance. From the mid-19th cent., the need was felt for rabbinical conferences to give definite rulings. This was firmly attacked by the *Orthodox, who argued that no one could abrogate the least of the religious laws. None the less, *Reform conferences were held at Wiesbaden in 1837, Brunswick in 1844, Frankfurt-am-Main in 1845, Breslau in 1846, Leipzig in 1869, and Augsburg in 1871. In the USA, the Reform movement adopted its Pittsburgh platform in 1887, which was partly reversed in 1937 at Columbus at its annual convention. In 1961, the Federation of *Reconstructionist Congregations laid down its guidelines at a conference. Among the Orthodox, there has been some agitation for the restoral of the *Sanhedrin.

Rabbinical seminaries. Seminaries for the training of Jewish *rabbis. Traditionally, rabbis were trained in *yeshivot, but under the influence of the *Haskalah, it was felt that the old *Talmudic curriculum was not adequate for the modern professional rabbi. In the USA, the *Conservative Jewish Theological Seminary was founded in 1886, the Reform *Hebrew Union College in 1875, and the Elchanan Theological Seminary (later a unit of *Yeshiva University) in 1897.

Rābiʿa al-ʿAdawiyya (*c*.713–801 (AH 95–185)). An outstanding *Sūfī and one of the few women in Islam to be considered the actual equal of men. Her name Rābiʿa means 'fourth'; she was the fourth daughter of a poor family, and while still a child sold into slavery, but later freed. She devoted herself to a life of prayer, poverty, and seclusion. She combined extreme asceticism with a purely disinterested love of God, and is generally acknowledged as the first Sūfī to teach this aspect of piety which later became prominent in Sufism. Miracles were attributed to her, and her sayings and teachings were handed down from one generation to another of Sūfīs.

Rachel. Wife of *Jacob and one of the matriarchs of Israel. Her tomb is a place of *pilgrimage, especially for barren women, since Rachel was barren for many years.

Racovian Catechism (statement of faith of

rationalist Christian movement): see SOCINIANISM.

Radak (acronym): see KIMḤI, DAVID.

Radbaz (acronym): see DAVID BEN SOLOMON.

Radcliffe-Brown, A. R. (British social anthropologist): see EVANS-PRITCHARD, E.

Radewijns, F. (fellow-worker): see GROOTE, G.

Rādhā, Rādhikā. A consort of the Hindu god *Kṛṣṇa, one of the *gopīs. It is only in secular poetic sources, not religious ones, that Rādhikā (later mostly Rādhā) was first described as Kṛṣṇa's favourite gopī and mistress. Apart from conventional episodes dealing with infatuation, love-making, jealousy, and quarrels of the lovers, nothing further is said about Rādhā till 12th cent. CE. The *purāṇas ignore her till an even later date, and a variety of Kṛṣṇaite traditions knows of a different favourite or female associate of Kṛṣṇa. Yet from the 14th or 15th cent., the figure of Rādhā begins to dominate Kṛṣṇaite literature and religion, perhaps as a result of Jayadeva's **Gītagovinda*, a highly erotic poem written in Bengal *c.*1185 CE. Although it deals with Kṛṣṇa's and Rādhā's love-making in terms of the secular poetic conventions, later mystics and religious movements have treated it as a religious, mystical work.

A second factor in the evolution of Rādhā as central religious figure was evidently the teaching of the theologian *Nimbārka (14th/15th cent.?). By him Kṛṣṇa is regarded as identical with *Brahman, and Rādhā as co-natural with him. Similar ideas are expressed by many subsequent theologies.

The poetry about Kṛṣṇa's love for Rādhā cannot avoid describing Kṛṣṇa as totally devoted and subservient to Rādhā, due to his love and passion for her. At least in the case of the Rādhāvallabhīs, this is not just seen as denoting an ultimate unity of Kṛṣṇa and Rādhā as Brahman, but has been developed into a form of 'Rādhāism': theologically speaking, Kṛṣṇa is dependent on Rādhā as the Absolute.

Radhakrishnan, Sarvepalli (1888–1975). Hindu philosopher and President of the Indian Republic. After various professorial posts in India, he became the first Spalding Professor of Eastern Religions and Ethics at Oxford, 1936–52. He was Vice-President of India, 1952–62, and President, 1962–7. Radhakrishnan held strongly that all religions are different paths leading to the same goal, and that beyond the differences of credal formulations and practices there is an essential unity, since 'the signpost is not to be confused with that to which it points'.

He wrote many books, including *Indian Philosophy*, *The Hindu View of Life*, *Eastern Religions and Western Thought*, and translations with commentary of the *Upaniṣads and of the **Bhagavadgītā*.

Rādhāsoāmī Satsaṅg (Hindī, 'pious congregation of the supreme being, Lord of Rādhā'). Religious movement originating in N. India. Since Soāmījī Mahārāj (Shiv Dayāl Siṅgh) of Āgrā (1818–78) founded this movement in 1861, it has divided into two main groups, each with its own succession of Masters and organization, and many smaller followings. One *āśram has continued in Dayālbāgh (Garden of the Merciful) near Āgrā, UP, India, with Satgurūs Rai Saligram, known as Hazūr Mahārāj (1829–98), Mahārāj Sāhab (1861–1907), Sarkār Sāhab, Sāhabjī Mahārāj, and Mehtājī Sāhab. The other centre is Beās, near *Amritsar, *Pañjāb, founded in 1891 by Soāmījī Mahārāj's follower, Jaimal Siṅgh, whose successors were Sawan Siṅgh (1858–1948), Jagat Siṅgh, Charan Siṅgh (d. 1990), and Gurinder Siṅgh Dhillon. There are now branches throughout India and in other countries.

Radical Reformation. In Christianity, the 'left wing' of the 16th-cent. *Reformation, whose leaders maintained that the 'magisterial' Reformers were not sufficiently radical in their quest for a renewed Church life. *Luther, *Calvin, *Zwingli, and *Bucer asserted that reformation must be effected either under the direction, or at least with the approval, of the secular rulers or civil authorities, whereas more radical Reformers were persuaded that the implementation of necessary changes in doctrine and practice were matters for the Church and did not require the co-operation of the State.

The Radical Reforming groups defy neat classification and include revolutionaries claiming direct inspiration of the *Holy Spirit (*Carlstadt, *Münzer, and the Zwickau prophets), evangelical *Anabaptists, *adventists, mystics, and anti-trinitarian rationalists.

Rāfiḍites (Arab., *al-Rāfiḍah* or *al-Rawāfiḍ*, 'the repudiators'). A name given by *Sunni Muslims to the *Shī'a in general, as a term of disapproval or abuse. They are called 'repudiators' because they reject the first three of the four al-Rāshidūn, the first four caliphs (*Khalīfa) after *Muḥammad, holding that the fourth of them, *Alī, should (as Muḥammad's son-in-law) have succeeded in the first place.

Rāg, rāga (Skt., 'colour', a melodic sequence). In Indian music, combinations of notes associated with certain moods and times. The division of the Sikhs' *Ādi Granth is by rāg.

Rāga (Pāli, Skt.). In Eastern religions (for Hinduism, see ASMITA), the form of attachment identified with lust, greed, and passion. According to Buddhists, it is one of the most basic characteristics of human nature, having the pleasures of the senses as its object; but it also exists as attachment to more subtle pleasures at higher levels of spirituality (*saññojanā*) and is not finally disposed of until *nirvāna is reached.

Rāgī (Pañjābī, 'musician'). Sikh devotional music (*kīrtan), sung in *gurdwārās.

Rahirās or **Sodar Rahirās.** Sikh early evening prayer, repeated daily by devout Sikhs.

Rahit, Rahat (Pañjābī, 'code'). Rahit Maryādā, Sikhs' code of discipline. In 1945 the *Shiromaṇi Gurdwārā Parbandhak Committee approved the Rahit Maryādā (Code of practice), published 1950 (*Rehat Maryādā*).

After defining a Sikh, the Rahit Maryādā prescribes conduct expected of the individual and the Panth.

Raḥmānīya. Muslim religious order (*ṭarīqa), mainly in Algeria, named after its founder Muḥammad b. 'Abd al-Raḥmān (d. 1793 (AH 1208)). Originally a missionary in India for another order (Khalwatī), he received visions of the Prophet *Muḥammad, which prompted him to claim immunity from *hell for those who adhered to him and his way.

Rahner, Karl (1904–84). Christian philosopher and theologian. He was born in Freiburg im Breisgau and entered the N. German province of the Society of Jesus (the *Jesuits) in 1922. He studied philosophy and then theology, and was ordained priest in 1932. From 1934 he undertook research at Freiburg. His dissertation on *Aquinas' metaphysic of judgement was rejected for its explorations away from traditional interpretation into the direction of transcendental Thomism. He moved to Innsbruck where his dissertation was accepted, later published as *Geist im Welt* (Spirit in the World). His work dominates 20th-cent. philosophical theology, made up of densely laid foundations and sparkling raids on many different problems (some gathered in the long series, *Theological Investigations*), dominated by his pastoral concern that Christian truth must not be divorced from human living. He was influenced early on by Joseph Maréchal, who laid the foundations of neo-Thomism. Maréchal drew out the implications of the Thomist epistemology: knowledge is based on sense-data; the mind directs itself to sensory images; the mind therefore penetrates reality in the sense that it enters into the ontological nature of other things in its movement toward them of comprehension. Maréchal argued that the unity of sense and intellect, in the act of a unitary human subject *knowing*, required necessary conditions for its possibility, namely, that the knower and the sensible objects of knowledge be composed of matter, form, and existence, since otherwise the act of knowing (as it *is* known) could not occur.

In this way, Maréchal set the stage for neo-Thomism as the working out of its detail. Rahner set out to establish what he called 'a transcendental Thomism' and 'theology taking a transcendental turn'. Rahner grasped that philosophy and theology must start with the human subject as the one who constitutes the world of possible knowledge. The human subject constantly seeks to transcend itself and its existing points of departure, aspiring to the infinite while rendering the world intelligible. The latter is only possible because humans have a prehension (*Vorgriff*) of the former—a genuine 'pre-grasp' of Infinite Being as the true horizon of the world as lived.

On this philosophical foundation, Rahner insisted that theology must begin 'at the human end', not with *a priori* dogmas handed out as though self-evidently true. This 'theological anthropology' investigates human being in so far as it is turned toward God —which is, at once, on the basis of his previous argument, transcendental anthropology. In this way, the otherwise largely remote doctrines of Christianity are firmly located in the actual conditions of human knowing and living. Life experienced as spiritual and full of grace leads to the proposition that the world is exactly that (notwithstanding the human experience of fallenness as well). In that case, all human beings are participants in the grace of God which seeks to redeem the fallen, and thus all are 'Anonymous Christians', and within the salvific purpose of God, whether they are baptized or not. At the centre of all Rahner's thought remains the unequivocal pastoral demand, how can we help each other to attain the unlimited horizon of God?

Rāhula. The son of Gautama, the *Buddha. He was born at about the time that Gautama decided to leave his home in search of enlightenment. The Buddha later visited his son who was ordained as a novice (*sāmaṇera), and who received teaching from the Buddha.

Raidās (Indian saint-poet): see RAVI DĀS.

Raigō (also raikō) **Raikō** (Jap., 'welcome'). The welcome given by *Amida and the attendant company of the *bodhisattvas to those who enter the *Pure Land. Raigo-in is the manual sign of welcome.

Rain (Heb., *geshem*). A recurrent theme in Jewish liturgy (see esp. the tractate **Ta'anit*), perhaps reflecting the agricultural base of life in the biblical period. It was a mark of the *messiah's connection with God that he would mediate rain to the land.

For the rainy season in Buddhism, see VASSA.

Rai Saligram (Hazūr Mahāraj, guru): see RĀDHĀSOĀMĪ.

Rāja (Skt.). A ruler or revered (because authoritative) figure, also used of a dancer, musician, sculptor, etc., who is skilled in his art or craft.

Rāja- (Skt., 'royal') or **aṣṭāṅga-** (Skt., 'eight-limbed') **yoga.** Classical yoga as developed in *Patañjali's **Yoga Sūtra* and in the commentarial literature.

Patañjali defines yoga as the 'cessation of mental fluctuations' (*cittavṛtti *nirodha) (Yoga Sūtra 1. 2). This cessation is the distinguishing of ordinary awareness (*citta) from the real conscious self (*puruṣa). This is achieved by practising the 'eight limbs' (aṣṭāṅga) of yoga: restraint (*yama), discipline (*niyama), posture (*āsana), breath-control (*prāṇāyāma), sense-withdrawal (*pratyāhāra), concentration (*dhāraṇā), meditation (*dhyāna), and enstasy (*samādhi). Samādhi itself is categorized into samādhi 'with support' (*samprajñāta) and 'without support' (asamprajñāta), the latter being the stage at which Īśvara is revealed.

Rājacandra, Śrīmad (1867–1901). Jain spiritual reformer. He was born Raichandbhai Mehta, his later name being a title bestowed on him by his followers. In his youth, he reviewed all religions and came to the conclusion that Jainism was the truest, given that all religions contain corruptions and imperfections. He continued to study texts more closely, especially those of the *Digambaras, and came to believe that his vocation was to found a new religion as a reformed version of Jainism. In *Atmasiddhi* (Self-Realization, 1896), he maintained that true religion consists of six principles: (i) the soul exists; (ii) the soul is eternal; (iii) the soul is the agent of its own acts; (iv) the soul experiences what it enacts; (v) the state of deliverance exists; and (vi) the means to attain deliverance exists.

Rājacandra is well-known for the influence he had on *Gāndhī, not least for his emphasis on *ahiṁsā and for persuading him not to go any further on the path toward Christianity.

Rājagriha, Council of: see COUNCILS, BUDDHIST.

Rajas (Skt.). In *Sāṃkhya one of the three strands (*guṇas) of material nature (*prakṛti). It is present in varying degrees in all things except pure consciousness (*puruṣa). In the external world, rajas is manifested as force or movement: that which moves has a predominance of rajas. In the individual, it is ambition, effort, and activity; it is also anxiety, passion, wickedness, and all forms of suffering. Through interaction with the other guṇas all varieties of creation arise.

Rāj karegā Khālsā (Pañjābī, 'the Khālsā shall rule'). Rallying cry of the Sikhs, introduced during the 18th cent. The first line concludes the *Ardās at the end of communal worship.

Rajm (Arab., 'to stone', 'to curse'). 1. The punishment of stoning to death for adultery or sexual intercourse outside the permitted relationships (*zinā'). The punishment appears in *ḥadīth, not in *Qur'ān, and is surrounded by careful conditions, e.g. four competent male witnesses must report the incident in detail, and if their evidence breaks down, they are themselves liable to severe punishment.

2. The casting of seven small stones during al-*ḥajj. The original meaning is obscure (the rite is not mentioned in the Qur'ān). Traditionally, it is associated with the driving away of *Satan (Shaitan, known as *rajīm* in Qur'ān).

Rajneesh, Bhagwan Shree (1931–90). Founder of an Indian-based movement known variously as the Orange People (from their dress), Sannyasins or neo-Sannyasins, Rajneeshees, or followers of Bhagwan. He was born Mohan Chandra Rajneesh of a Jain father. He became enlightened, by his own account, in 1953. In 1981, having temporarily disappeared, he moved to Oregon in the USA, where a new city was planned, called Rajneeshpuram. Rajneesh took a vow of silence until 1984, so the foundation was run (increasingly autocratically) by his personal assistant, Ma Anand Sheela. In 1985, she absconded (and was later arrested), and Rajneesh was expelled from the USA. He resettled in Poona, where he became known as Osho. After his death, his followers continued to offer courses in his teaching.

In the Bhagwan's monistic interpretation of the world, there is only one source of energy and that is bio-energy, called 'life' or 'love' or 'light'. Awareness of one's inner life enables one to stand at a distance from it, and eventually to become an impartial observer and witness—the *sashi* of classical Indian *yoga. Thus, if one is 'aware', then whether one enters into or renounces sexual relationships, the end result is the same.

Rajputs. Rulers in Rājputana (now Rājasthan) in India. They were *Kṣatriyas who rose to prominence before and during the *Gupta dynasty.

Rakʿa. Unit of movements during the Muslim *ṣalāt (obligatory worship). These are: *rukūʿ*, bending forward; *sujūd*, prostration; *julūs* (half-sitting, half-kneeling); a second *sujūd*.

Rakāb Gañj Gurdwārā. Sikh shrine in New Delhi. In 1675 Gurū *Tegh Bahādur was beheaded in Chāndnī Chauk, Delhi. The present *gurdwārā, opposite Parliament House, is a two-storeyed marble building with several domes and similar frontage on all four sides.

Rakan (Jap. for Theravādin Buddhist arhat): see LO-HAN.

Rakan Keijin (Ch'an/Zen master): see LO-HAN KUEI-CH'EN.

Rakhi Bandhan (Hindu festival): see FESTIVALS AND FASTS.

Rākṣasa. A class of demons or evil spirits in India, hostile to humans. They can appear in many forms, including those of animals, and they operate mainly at night.

Ralbag (acronym): see LEVI BEN GERSHOM.

Rāma, also **Rāmacandra.** The hero of the major Hindu epic, **Rāmāyaṇa*. The initial core of the epic portrays Rāma as a courageous prince following the example of his ancestor Raghu (hence his epithet Rāghava). But in the full epic and the *Purāṇas, Rāma is an *avatāra (manifestation) of *Viṣṇu, the seventh and almost equal in importance to *Kṛṣṇa. Rāma and his wife *Sītā are the model spouses for Hindus. *Vālmīki traces the spiritual path of Rāma in **Yoga-vasiṣtha*, and to him also is ascribed the central part of *Rāmāyaṇa*. The present work is in seven *kāndas*, sections, of which (ii)–(vi) tell of Rāma's birth (celebrated in the festival Rāma Navami) and childhood; his life in *Ayodhyā and his banishment; his life in the forest and Sītā's abduction by *Rāvaṇa; Rāma's life with his monkey allies; his crossing over the bridge to Śri Lankā; the battle, the defeat of Rāvaṇa (celebrated in the *festival of Daśarā) and the rescue of Sītā; his life in Ayodhyā, Sītā's banishment and return, their death and ascent to heaven. (i) and (vii) contextualize the narrative by glorifying Rāma as an avatāra of Viṣṇu. To read the epic is to be associated with Rāma. The same is effected by repeating Rāma's name in the ear of a dying person. Rām as a *mantra is held, especially by *Vaiṣṇavites, to contain the universe, and from that mantra all languages have emerged. See also Index, Rāma.

Ramabai, Pandita (1858–1922). Indian Christian reformer. Born into a *brahman family, she lost both her parents during a pilgrimage in 1874. Because her parents had encouraged her in a classical education, she was able to support herself and her brother by becoming a wandering reciter of Hindu scriptures. She so impressed *pandits in Calcutta that she was given the title 'pandita'. She met Christians in Bengal, and was helped by the Wantage Sisters (an *Anglican religious order) to go to England for further education. There she and her young daughter were baptized. She went to America and secured financial support for her work, then returned to India, where she established a school especially for child widows.

Ramaḍān. The ninth month of the Islamic year, and the period of *ṣawm (fasting). It is mentioned in the *Qur'ān as a blessed month, 'in which the Qur'ān was revealed' (2. 185). It is a time also of greater prayer and devotion, and during the last ten days and nights many of the pious practise retreat (*iʿtikāf) in a *mosque. One of these nights, generally believed to be the 27th, is *Laylat al-Qadr (the 'Night of Power'), holiest in all the year. The month of Ramaḍān ends with *Īd al-Fiṭr, feast of the breaking of the fast.

Ramah (acronym of Rabbi Meʿir ha-Levi): see ABULAFIA, MEʿIR.

Ramakrishna (Gadādhar Chattopadhyāya; 1836–86). Hindu *ascetic and mystic. Born in a Bengali village, at 19 he became the priest of *Kālī at Dakshineśwar, near Calcutta, and lived there for almost all the rest of his life, exploring a wide range of religious experiences. Ramakrishna drew around himself a band of English-educated young Bengalis, who saw in him a living symbol of their ancient religious tradition and a sign of its renewed vitality in the modern world. He came to be regarded by some as an *avatāra (manifestation) of God. To these disciples he expounded his teaching, mainly in stories and short sayings. After Ramakrishna's death, his disciple, *Vivekānanda, drew together many of his other followers in a movement which is now world-wide, the Ramakrishna Mission, basing it upon his own interpretation of his master's teaching.

Ramakrishna Mission: see RAMAKRISHNA.

Rāmana Maharishi (*māhā-ṛṣi*; 1879–1950). Hindu *ṛṣi who attained union with *Brahman at the age of 17, without the help of instruction or a *guru. This realization of *ātman as Brahman remained with him as a constant condition, first in absolute silence on a hill in Tiruvannāmalai, later in dialogue with seekers, concentrating on the question, 'Who are you?'

An *āśrama developed around him at Tiruvannāmalai, which remains a place of pilgrimage.

Rāmānanda (?1360–?1470). Founder of the *Vaiṣṇavite Rāmānandī sect. A *saṁnyāsin who was originally a devotee of *Rāmānuja, he was offended by his fellow-disciples when, after years of preaching throughout India, they forced him to sit apart at meals for fear of the pollution he might have acquired through eating with others during his journeys. As a result of this he established his own sect, preaching against *caste and urging the equality of all people in the sight of God (thereby admitting *women to his order). His first twelve disciples were of varied castes, and included the Muslim *Kabīr, and a woman. Rāmānanda urged worship of one deity, *Rāma, with *Sītā, his consort, through *bhakti. His teachings spread widely and gave rise to a religious fervour which is still alive today. Later disciples of note were *Mīrābāi and *Tulsīdās, as well as the poets Malukdās and Nābhāji. His followers are devoted to Sītā and Rāma, sometimes wearing women's clothes and jewellery to indicate the indifference of gender. When they become members, they may burn the name of Rāma into their skin, and often add *dāsa* ('slave') to their names. Their main centre is *Ayodhyā, where their devotion to Rāma is intense.

Rāmānuja (11th/12th cent.). Hindu philosopher, theologian, and source of the school known as *Viśiṣṭādvaita-vedānta. He was a *Śrivaiṣṇavite, who sought to give the devotional attitude implicit in that allegiance a more reflective and philosophical foundation. He accepted three means of knowledge: *pratykṣa* (perception), *anumāna* (inference), and *śabda or *śāstra* (verbal testimony). He accepted the basic texts of *Vedanta philosophy (the *Upaniṣads, the **Brahmasūtra*, and the **Bhagavad-gītā*), but he also allowed the authority of the hymns of the *Āḻvārs, the Pāñcarātra-Āgamas, and the *Viṣṇu-* and *Bhāgavata-purāṇas*.

The major works attributed to him are *Śrībhāsyam*, *Vedāntadīpah*, and *Vedāntasārah* (all commentaries on the Vedanta Sūtras), a commentary on the *Gīta*, *Vedārthasamgrahah* (an exposition of his viewpoint), *Śaraṇāgatigadyam* (on self-surrender to God), *Śrīrangagadyam* (on the devotions and praise evoked by the Śrīrangam temple and its presiding deity), *Vaikuṇṭhagadyam* (on the nature of the liberated state), and *Nithyagranthah* (on worship).

Rāmānuja agreed with *Śaṅkara that *Brahman is that which truly is, without distinction (*advaita), but did not agree that there is nothing else that is real, and that all else is *māyā (appearance), the projection of *avidyā (ignorance). He held that individual selves and the world of matter (described in terms derived from *Sāṃkhya) are real, but that they are always dependent on Brahman for their existence and functions—hence his view is known as qualified non-duality, viśiṣṭādvaita. Selves and matter are the instruments of Brahman in a relationship like that of souls and bodies (*śarīra-śarīrī-bhāva*). Although God is beyond description, nevertheless much can be inferred and attributed analogously to God from his manifestations in the world as *avatāra (incarnation). He is thus the source of grace (*anugraha*), seeking the salvation of those who turn to him, in a general way through revelation (*Veda), and in particular to his devotees.

Rām(a)prasād (18th cent.). Bengali Hindu saint and poet. He was devoted to *Kālī.

It is said that when he was working as a bookkeeper, he was so preoccupied with Kālī that he entered, not figures, but poems in her honour. His employer provided him with a pension so that he would no longer need to work.

Rāmāyaṇa (The Exploits of Rāma). One of two major Hindu epics (the other being **Mahābhārata*), ascribed to *Vālmīki. For further details, see RĀMA.

Rambam (acronym): see MAIMONIDES.

Ramban (acronym): see NAḤMANIDES.

Ramcaritamānasa (work by Indian poet Tulsīdās): see TULSĪDĀS.

Rām Dās, Gurū (1534–81 CE). Fourth Sikh *Gurū. Rām Dās ('God's servant') was the name assumed by Jeṭhā ('first-born') on becoming Gurū in 1574.

As Gurū, Rām Dās is best remembered for founding *Amritsar, variously known as Gurū kā Chak, Chak Rām Dās, and Rāmdāspur. Reputedly the land was granted by emperor *Akbar to Bībī Bhānī. Rām Dās organized preaching through a network of *masands based in *mañjīs*. The *Ādi Granth contains 679 of his hymns (including *pauṛīs and *śaloks). His *Lāvān is central to Anand marriage.

Rāmdāsī or **Rāmdāsiā.** Sikh of the leatherworker *caste. People of *Chamār caste who became Sikhs were frequently called Rāmdāsī.

Rāmgaṛhīā or **tarkhāṇ.** Sikh *caste (*zāt*, *jati). Many *gurdwārās bear this name, indicating their establishment by members of the local Rāmgaṛhīā community.

Rāmgaṛhīā Sikhs take their name from the 18th-cent. *misl leader, Jassā Siṅgh Rāmgaṛhīā. After playing a key role in relieving the besieged Rām Raunī fort near *Amritsar, he was appointed its governor. The fort was renamed Rāmgaṛh and from this he took his new title.

Ramḥal (acronym): see LUZMATTO, MOSES ḤAYYI.

Rāmlīlā (the playful delight of *Rāma). The dramatic exposition of the story of Rāma's exploits. It is enacted during the *Daśahrā festival, and is based on the work of *Tulsīdās.

Rām Mohan Roy (Hindu apologist and reformer): see ROY, RĀM MOHAN.

Rām Rāi (17th cent. CE). Son of Sikh Gurū *Har Rāi. Rām Rāi is regarded as an apostate. He incurred his father's displeasure by changing one of Gurū *Nānak's lines in the *Ādi Granth to satisfy emperor Auraṅgzeb at whose court he was detained. Rām Rāi disputed the succession of his younger brother Har Krishan and great-uncle *Tegh Bahādur. His followers, the Rāmrāiyās, were hostile to subsequent Gurūs and their disciples.

Rām Siṅgh (b. 1816). Founder of *Nāmdhārī Sikh movement. Rām Siṅgh, a carpenter from Bhainī *Sāhib, Pañjāb, was a disciple of *Bālak Siṅgh. He made Nāmdhārīs distinguishable from other Sikhs by their white turbans, tied in the manner of Gurū *Nānak's, their woollen *rosaries, style of worship, and greeting. He led resistance to the British authorities, prophesying a Sikh revival. Nāmdhārīs await his return to herald a new age, and thus, although non-Nāmdhārīs believe he died in 1885, Nāmdhārīs do not believe he has died.

Rānadé, Mahādev Govind (1842–1901). Indian lawyer and judge, who because of his keen powers of perception and analysis, became the leader of many social, political, industrial, and religious movements in Mahārāṣṭra. He regarded much in traditional Hinduism as destructive and enervating. He supported the Hindu widow's remarriage movement and started Prārthanā Samāj at Bombay (Prayer Society, modelled on *Brahmo Samāj). He was a pioneer of reforming Hinduism, and of finding the inspiration within Hinduism for the reform of itself.

Rang dong (*rang.stong*, 'Emptiness of Self'). The central doctrine of *Prāsaṅgika *Mādhyamaka, the doctrine that all objects are empty of inherent existence. It is a statement about ultimate truth (*paramārtha satya*) from which standpoint the folly of conventional truth (*saṃvṛti satya*—that objects do have inherent existence) is realized. The doctrine of rang dong, held chiefly by the *Geluk who assert it to be the teaching of *Nāgārjuna, requires that only Prāsaṅgika logic can cut through the apparent distinction, and that only in Buddhahood can form and emptiness be simultaneously comprehended.

Raṅghṛetā (Raṅghar kā beṭā, i.e. child of a Raṅghar, Muslim outcaste group). Any *Mazhabī Sikh, who traces family association with Sikhism to Gurū *Gobind Siṅgh's period.

Rañjīt Siṅgh, Mahārājā (1780–1839). Sikh ruler of *Pañjāb, 1799–1839. Rañjīt Siṅgh, son of Mahān Siṅgh, headed the Śukerchakīā *misl. He eventually gained overall supremacy between the Sutlej River and the Khyber Pass, ending Afghan influence in Pañjāb. After recapturing *Amṛitsar, he had the *Harimandir rebuilt and covered with gold leaf. Ranjīt Siṅgh's reign was the only period of *khālsā political sovereignty in Pañjāb. After his death, the kingdom disintegrated and was annexed by the British. His son, Duleep Siṅgh, the first Sikh to live in Britain, has achieved a symbolic importance in the community.

Ransom. It is recognized in Judaism that compensation can be paid to avoid punishment, slavery, or death. In ancient Israel, it was common to pay ransom as an alternative to corporal punishment except in the case of murder (Numbers 35. 31–4). The issue of whether a ransom is possible, or whether exact retribution must be made, was disputed between *Sadducees (who maintained that no ransom by way of payment is possible) and their opponents (who held that substitution by way of payment is possible except in cases of wilful murder). This means that the remark attributed to Jesus in Mark 10. 45 is more likely to be authentic than not, since there are other instances of Jesus using the current debates to make his own creative interpretation.

Ranters. A loosely organized mid-17th-cent. radical group with *antinomian tendencies. Its leaders substantiated their individualistic teaching by appealing to revelatory experiences of the *Spirit or the indwelling *Christ. Jacob Bauthumley's *The Light and Darker Sides of God* expounds their *'inner light' teaching. The movement died out in the 17th cent., but the term was later used colloquially to describe the *Primitive Methodists.

Rantō (Jap., 'egg-shaped tower'). The tower which surmounts the tomb of a Zen monk.

Raphael (Heb., 'God is healing'). An angel recognized in Judaism and Christianity. Raphael appears in the *Apocrypha (*Tobit* 12. 15 and 1 *Enoch* 20. 3).

Rapture (Lat., *raptus*, 'seized'). The action in which believers will be 'caught up' (1 Thessalonians 4. 17; *Vulgate, *rapiemur*) to meet Christ in the air at his second coming (*parousia). In mystical Christianity, rapture is the carrying away of the believer by the overwhelming power of God, a 'flight of the spirit'.

Rasa (Skt., 'relish', 'passion'). Hindu state of spiritual ecstasy in union with the divine. In a more general way, it then refers to the eight different sentiments or emotions, e.g. *raudra (see also ART).

Rashal (acronym): see LURIA, SOLOMON.

Rashba (acronym): see ADRET, SOLOMON BEN ABRAHAM.

Rashbam (acronym): see SAMUEL BEN MEIR.

Rashi (acronym of Rabbi Solomon ben Isaac; 1040–1105). Jewish biblical and *Talmudic commentator. He wrote commentaries on all the books of the Bible with the exception of *Ezra, *Nehemiah, *Chronicles, and the final chapters of *Job. The commentaries as they have been handed down include annotations by his students. His biblical commentaries were enormously popular, and he was influential on Christian as well as Jewish scholars. His commentary on the *Pentateuch was the first Hebrew book to be printed (1475).

Rashīd Riḍā (d. 1933). A Syrian Muslim, supporter of reform and an influential Muslim scholar. He championed *al-Afghānī and *'Abduh's vision of a dynamic Islam. He saw the important need for modification of the existing *sharī'a: Islamic law had to face the realities of the modern world. In this matter Riḍā adopted a very controversial position. He refused to admit that the four recognized law schools, *Mālikite, *Hanafite, *Shāfi'ite, and *Hanbalite, were binding upon the modern *'umma. Instead, Riḍā advocated that Islamic law be redrafted, based on the Qur'ān and sound *ḥadīth, in accordance with the light of changing times.

Rāshidūn (first four successors of Prophet Muḥammad): see KHALĪFA (2).

Rashtriya Svayamsevak Sangh (Indian political militia): see BHARATYA JANATA PARTY.

Raskolniki (dissenting groups of Russian Orthodox Christians): see OLD BELIEVERS.

Ras Shamra. Site of the ancient city of Ugarit. Archaeological discoveries at Ras Shamra have added greatly to our knowledge of ancient *Canaanite customs and beliefs, especially through the Ugaritic texts.

Rastafarians. Members of a *messianic religio-political movement originating among unemployed, landless, young men in Jamaica in the 1930s. It began under the influence of the Jamaican black nationalist, Marcus Garvey, and his 'Back to Africa' movement, which identified blacks as the true biblical *Jews, superior to whites, and surviving either in Ethiopia (see ETHIOPIANISM) or in Jamaica, where they had been exiled as a divine punishment. When Crown Prince (Ras) Tafari was crowned Ethiopian emperor in 1930 as Haile Sellasie, this was a sign that the sentence was completed, the *millennium was at hand, and the return to Africa would begin. In 1955 he gave 500 acres of land for black people wishing to return, but in 1970 there were only twenty people living there. His dethronement in 1974 and death in 1975 had little effect on Rastafarians. Deputations touring Africa in the early 1960s, seeking acceptance, were unsuccessful, and more recent tendencies have been to find 'Africa' in Jamaica and replace repatriation by rehabilitation.

The movement first became visible in the 1930s when members formed peaceful communities living on the Kingston garbage dumps, and established distinctive modes of language, music, dress, 'dreadlock' hair forms, crafts, and lifestyle. European culture and Christian churches were rejected as 'Babylon'. They made their own selections from the Bible, eliminating the distortions introduced by its white translators, and adopted ganja (marijuana) as the sacramental herb for healing and meditation experiences. By the 1970s middle-class youth had begun to identify with the Rastafarian ideology and with the reggae music that carried this around the world, especially through singer Bob Marley and his band. Despite its wider influence, it is essentially a Jamaican movement.

Rasūl (Arab., *rasala*, 'send'). One whom God sends, a messenger or apostle, and supremely, in Islam, the Prophet *Muḥammad (cf. *nabī). Each *'umma has received its rasūl (Qur'ān 10. 47; 16. 36), but Muḥammad was sent to a people who had not yet received a rasūl. Previous rasūls (*rusul*) in Qur'ān are Nūḥ (Noah), Lūt (Lot), Ismā'īl (Ishmael), Mūsa (Moses), Shu'aib, Hūd, Ṣāliḥ, and 'Īsā (*Jesus). They are regarded as being free from sin.

Ratana Church. The largest independent movement and the third largest religious group among the Maoris of New Zealand, with headquarters at Ratana Pa ('village') near Marton. It was founded by Tahupotiki Wiremu Ratana (1873–1939), a *Methodist farmer who in 1918 received a visionary call to destroy

Maori religion and return to *Jehovah. In the 1918 world epidemic of influenza, he discovered his healing powers, and by 1919 crowds sought healing at Ratana Pa which developed into a model village. Ratana members have held up to all four Maori seats in New Zealand's parliament and have exercised considerable political power. A secession, less political and with a strict ethic, formed in North Island in 1941 as the Absolute Established Maori Church of Aotearoa, and has remained very small.

Ratnākaraśānti. A Buddhist philosopher of the 11th–12th cents. CE. He was a member of the *Pramāṇa school of *Dignāga and *Dharmakīrti, and a pupil of Ratnakīrti. Ratnākaraśānti is also known as Śānti. His important works include commentaries on the 8,000- and 25,000-line *Prajñaparamitā Sūtras* (*Perfection of Wisdom), the *Hevajratantra*, and the work of *Śāntarakṣita.

Ratnakūṭa or **Mahāratnakūṭa** (Skt., *ratna*, 'jewel' + *kūṭa*, 'mountain'). Collection of Buddhist *Mahāyāna scriptures. Although only four works are now extant in the original Skt. (*Ratnakūṭasūtra*, *Rāṣṭrapālaparipṛcchā*, *Sukhāvatīvyūha*, and *Aṣṭasahāsrikāprajñāpāramitā*), both Tibetan and Chinese sources assign forty-nine short titles to this collection.

Ratnasaṃbhava (Skt., 'jewel-born one'). One of the five transcendent *Buddhas. He is linked to the earthly Buddha Kaśyapa and to the *bodhisattva Ratnapani. He is usually represented with the *mudra (hand gesture) of granting wishes.

Raudra (Skt., 'furious'). In Indian literature one of eight prevailing sentiments, *rasas. Raudra is based in turn on the complementary 'emotion' (*bhāva) of anger, *krodha*. The term raudra may also denote a follower of the god *Rudra or a class of evil spirits.

Rauschenbusch, W. (19th-cent. exponent of social gospel programme): see LIBERATION THEOLOGY.

Rav (Babylonian equivalent to Rabbi): see RABBI.

Rav (3rd cent. CE). Abba b. Arikha (i.e. 'the tall'). Jewish Babylonian *amora. Rav was the founder of the *academy at *Sura. He was called Rav (see RABBI) because he was 'the rav of the entire *diaspora' (*B.Bezah* 9a). Ordained by *Judah ha-Nasi in *Erez Israel, he was so respected that his independent authority was universally accepted. He defined 'the true Jew' as one who has compassion on all people, since those lacking in mercy have not inherited the compassion of *Abraham.

Rava (4th cent. CE). R. Abba b. Joseph b. Ḥama. Jewish Babylonian *amora. The discussions of Rava and his companion *Abbaye are found throughout the Babylonian *Talmud. In general, the *halakhah follows Rava's opinion. His *academy at Mahoza attracted many students and his pupils took no satisfaction in the teachings of other sages (*B.Ta'an*. 9a).

Rāvaṇa. The demon king of Lanka and leader of the *rākṣasas. He is the antagonist of *Rāma, and is represented in *Ramāyāṇa* as the embodiment of evil.

Ra(v)i Dās or **Raidas** (14th–15th cent.). Indian saint-poet. Nothing is known of his life except that he was a Banāras leatherworker and reputedly, but implausibly, a disciple of *Rāmānanda. The *Ādi Granth contains forty of his *hymns. For the 20th-cent. Ād *Dharm or *Ravidāsī movement, Ravi Dās, venerated as *Gurū, is a focal, cohesive symbol.

Ravi Dās' poetry advocates total surrender to an absolute God beyond all attributes (*nirguna), whose grace and love save all kinds of beings, not just those who practise austerities (*tapas) and repetition (*japa). This grace comes through the guru or saint.

Ravidāsī. Religious movement among Pañjābīs of the leatherworker *caste. The memory of *Ra(v)i Dās survived with a loose network of shrines (*dehrās*) serving as focal points for *chamār devotion. However, the Ravidāsī movement only took shape in the early 20th cent., as members of lower castes, especially urban, educated chamārs, sought religious and political identity. They called their religion Ād *Dharm (the original religion). In 1907 *Sant Hirān Das established a Ravi Dās Sabhā, soon followed by other *dehrās* in *Pañjāb.

Despite affinity to Sikhism, Ravidāsīs frequently have Hindu names and are clean-shaven. Their major festival is Gurū Ravi Dās' birthday.

Rawḍa khānī or **rawẓah-khvānī.** Ritual recitation in Iran by Shi'ites of the sufferings and martyrdoms of *Imams, and especially of *al-Ḥusain. These are particularly prominent on 10 Muḥarram, when public processions take place with many emulating the sufferings of the Imāms with self-laceration and beatings. See also TA'ZIYA.

Raychandbhai Mehta: see RĀJACANDRA, ŚRĪMAD.

Rāzī: see AL-RĀZĪ (Abū Bakr; and Fakhr al-Dīn).

Raziel, Book of. Jewish mystical collection, which, on its own account, was conveyed to *Adam by the angel, Raziel. The *Book of Raziel* was first printed in 1701, and ownership of it was believed to protect the owner's house from danger. *Sefer ha-Razin* is a related book, conveyed to *Noah, which contains comparable material on mysticism and magic.

Ṛddhipāda (four components of power in Buddhism): see IDDHI-PĀDA.

rDzogs-chen (Atiyoga): see DZOGCHEN.

Reading of the Law: see TORAH, READING OF.

Realism: see NOMINALISM.

Real presence. In Catholic and some *Protestant teaching, the presence of the body and blood of Christ in the *eucharist. The specifically Catholic aspects of the doctrine are: (i) its understanding in terms of *transubstantiation, and (ii) its consequences for eucharistic devotions such as the *exposition of the sacrament.

Rebbe (Yid., 'teacher'). Jewish teacher. It is the title given by the *Ḥasidim to their spiritual leader. See also LUBAVI(T)CH; ZADDIK.

Rebecca (Rebekah). Wife of Isaac and one of the matriarchs of Israel. According to *aggadah, while she was pregnant, whenever she passed a house of *Torah study, Jacob struggled to get out, but when she passed a temple containing idols, Esau struggled to get out. She was buried in the cave of *Machpelah.

Rebellious elder (Heb., *zaqen mamre*). A stubborn, qualified teacher in Judaism who insists on his own opinion, even though the majority opinion is against him. Such a person, according to Deuteronomy 17. 8–13, must be taken through the whole range of available courts, culminating in whatever is the highest authority, 'the judge who shall be in those days'. If the teacher persists in his own opinion, he must be executed, because, as the *rabbis later put it, he is creating two *Torahs (*toroth*) in Israel, which destroys the *raison d'être* of Israel. Since *Jesus was investigated for a threat to the *Temple authority (cf. also Stephen, Acts 6. 13), and since he was eventually taken before the highest judge of the time, it is likely that Jesus was being investigated to see whether he came within the category of *zaqen mamre*, which would unquestionably have been an offence deserving the death penalty.

Rebellious son (Heb., *ben sorer u-moreh*). Jewish Commandment which was not counted in the 613 commands of *Torah, on the ground that it could never be applied. It is the command in Deuteronomy 21. 18–21.

Rebirth. The belief (also transmigration, *metempsychosis, reincarnation, etc.) common in Eastern religions, that there is a continuity from one life to a next, either of a self or soul (see e.g. ĀTMAN), or, in the case of Buddhism, of the process itself. Buddhism teaches a *karmically controlled continuity of consciousnesses between lives but denies that there is an ātman or inherently existing self which is the bearer of these consciousnesses (see *punabbhāva). There are six realms of rebirth: three are pleasant (peaceful deities (*deva), wrathful deities (*asura), and humans), and three are unpleasant (animals, hungry ghosts (*preta), and hell-beings).

In Hinduism also, rebirth may be in many forms, including those of animals, and on many levels of heavens and hells (see e.g. NARAKA). Terms for rebirth in Skt. include *punarājātī, *punarāvritti*, *punarutpatti*, *punarjanman*, *punarjīvātu*. Among Jains, for whom karma is an accumulated impediment, rebirth of the *jīva is immediate and instantaneous, 'leaping like a monkey' (*Viyahapannatti Bhagavai*), which eradicated the need for *ancestor rituals, and for speculation about what supports the soul or process as it awaits rebirth (as in Hinduism and Buddhism). Ideas of rebirth have appeared in Western religions, but have remained marginal: see DIBBUK; GILGUL; ORIGEN; TANĀSUKH. See also TIBETAN BOOK OF THE DEAD; Index, Rebirth.

Recapitulation (Lat. *recapitulatio*; Gk., *anakephalaiōsis*, 'summing up, summary'). In the writings of the Christian *fathers, the restoration of fallen humanity to communion with God through the obedience of Christ. The concept derives from Ephesians 1. 10, where God is said to sum up all things in Christ, and was first elaborated by *Irenaeus.

Rechabites. A Jewish religious sect mentioned by *Jeremiah. It seems clear that they are an early instance of 'tradition-fundamentalists', who adhered to what had been established in the Wilderness period of the *Exodus, and who refused innovations (e.g. wine, since vines could not be planted and harvested in that period).

Recollection. The concentration of one's mental powers, especially the will, on the presence of God, perhaps best known as one of *Teresa of Avila's states of prayer.

Reconstructionism. A modern movement within Judaism. Reconstructionism was inspired by Mordecai *Kaplan who argued that Judaism was an evolving religious civilization. The movement became formal with the founding of the Society for the Advancement of Judaism in 1922, in New York. In 1945 the Reconstructionist **Sabbath* **Prayer Book* appeared. It included neither the idea of *Chosenness of the Jewish people, nor that of God's revelation to *Moses on Mount *Sinai, nor that of a personal *messiah. In 1968, a *rabbinical college was established in Philadelphia. See also CONSERVATIVE JUDAISM; Index, Reconstructionist Judaism.

Rector. The title of certain Christian priests: (i) in the Church of England, an incumbent of a parish whose *tithes were in the past not appropriated by anyone else (cf. VICAR); (ii) in the Roman Catholic Church a priest serving certain churches other than parish churches; (iii) the head of a Catholic seminary or university.

Recusancy (Lat., *recusare*). Refusal to attend *Church of England services as required by the 1559 Act of Uniformity. *Nonconformists were therefore also recusants, but the term is more usually reserved for *Roman Catholics. The offence of recusancy was abolished by the Catholic Relief Act of 1791.

Redeemer liveth (mistranslation): see REDEMPTION.

Redemption

Judaism The Heb. words *padah* and *ga'al* were used originally of commercial transactions, implying the existence of prior obligations (for examples, see Leviticus 25, 27). *Ga'al* is also used of the brothers of someone who has died childless: they are under obligation to 'redeem' the name of the deceased (Ruth 4. 1–10; Deuteronomy 25. 5–10). The *go'el* is the blood-avenger of Numbers 35. 12–29; in Job 19. 25 (translated, of old, 'I know that my redeemer (*go'el*) liveth') it is a legal term: 'I know that my advocate is active'. These basic meanings were all transferred as metaphors of God's activity, nature, and commitment.

In modern times, the emphasis has become more 'this-worldly', and redemption tends to be understood as the triumph of good over evil in human history or in the individual's personal life.

Christianity In Christian theology the term is inherited from the New Testament, where it is associated with the death of Christ (e.g. Ephesians 1. 7). For this conception and its later developments see ATONEMENT.

More loosely, redemption is then applied to salvific processes and achievements in other religions—e.g. the work of *bodhisattvas in Mahāyāna Buddhism.

Redemptorists (Christian missionary order): see LIGUORI, ALPHONSUS.

Red Hats. A loose term used by early W. commentators on Tibetan Buddhism to refer sometimes to the *Nyingma school, sometimes to the students of the Zhamar ('Red Hat') *Rinpoche as if these constituted a subschool within the Karma *Kagyü, and sometimes to refer to all Tibetan Buddhist schools collectively, in contradistinction to the *Geluk school who are colloquially called *Yellow Hats. The term 'Red Hats' is not used among Tibetans themselves.

Red Hats (Turkish adherents of the Şafavis): see ŞAFAVIDS.

Red Hats (rebels in China): see RED TURBANS.

Red heifer (Heb., *parah adummah*). The animal used in Jewish ritual purification of persons or objects defiled by contact with a dead body (Numbers 19. 1–22). The tractate *Parah* in the *Talmud discusses the laws of the red heifer.

Red letter day. Important feast or saint's day (in Christianity), printed in *calendars in red.

Red Sea, crossing of (Heb., *keriyat yam suf*; possibly 'reed' rather than 'red'). The miraculous event which enabled the Israelites to escape from the pursuing armies of the Egyptians at the beginning of the *Exodus.

Red Turbans. Rebel and millenarian bands, associated with the *White Lotus, which appeared during the Yuan dynasty (1260–1367) in China. The 'turbans' were in fact sashes, but were sometimes worn round the head. They believed in the imminent return of *Maitreya, and went before him to prepare his way.

Reformation, the. Movements for reform in the Christian Church in the West, in the early 16th cent. This was arguably the greatest crisis in Christendom before the challenges of the present time. Modern scholarship no longer seeks to spell out the causes of a reformation movement in simplistic terms, and it is very important to think of *reformations* in the plural. In some quarters critiques of Roman *papal orthodoxy and the Catholic *status quo* were referred to as the search for 'a new divinity'; and when the original protestors gained a following, they were known eventually as 'protestants'. Orthodoxy in the late medieval parish was dominated by what has aptly been described as 'the mechanics of ritualised religion', which put faith into non-verbal language. This was deeply affected and called in question by the invention of the printing press.

Prominent in the critical appraisal of the debate, with its distance from pastoral involvement, was Desiderius *Erasmus (*c.*1466–1536). He sought a textual basis for faith. His *Colloquies* popularized the need for Church reform 'in head and members'. In his aim to secure religious, moral, and social reform, he anticipated much of the programme later adopted by *Luther (1483–1546), and by the Swiss and other 'protestant' theologians. His influence was also felt throughout the Catholic Church, not least in his work on the *New Testament, writing a critical exposition of the received text. He wanted lay people to read the Bible. In this he was helped by the invention of printing. But it was for others to work out what the pastoral and theological consequences would be of accurate, widely available Bibles, especially when translated into the vernacular.

The lead from university to parish was made by Luther. He is usually remembered for his outburst against the selling of *indulgences, and for his challenge to Johann *Tetzel (*c.*1465–1519), Luther's understanding of *justification by faith *alone* (*justificatio sola fide*) he held out as a 're-discovery' of the gospel. Moving away from *Augustine, he understood justification as the instantaneous realization that sinners are forgiven and made righteous by the work of the crucified Christ. By imputation, fallen humanity had been reconciled in Christ to God the Creator. The unmerited grace of the Almighty is conveyed to sinners because of the atoning work of Christ on the Cross (*Sermon of the Threefold Righteousness*, 1518). Luther's stand as a reformer is far clearer in the *Christocentric* emphasis of the Heidelberg Disputation (Apr. 1518), with its theology of the Cross, its contrast of 'law' and 'gospel', and its departure from scholasticism, than in the notoriety he gained by circulating *Ninety-Five Theses* (Oct. 1517) in order to debate the indulgence controversy.

Nothing in W. Christendom was quite the same again. Already threatened with excommunication (**Exsurge Domine* gave Luther sixty days to recant), the Edict of Worms (May 1521) outlawed him and placed him under ban for seeking to 'disseminate errors and depart from the Christian way'. He was saved by another of the key factors in the reformations: the lay ruler of his country, Friedrich, Elector of Ernestine Saxony (from 1486 to 1525), smuggled him into exile. Kidnapped, he was taken to Wartburg, and there, in a seclusion which he called 'my Patmos', he worked out the full implications of his stand, with profound consequences. In two tracts of 1520, he had already sought to recruit both secular authority and sympathetic clergy. A third, the celebrated *Treatise of the Liberty of a Christian Man* (1520), commended the new faith to those who would know Christ. With the aid of *Melanchthon (1497–1560), he masterminded a visitation of Saxon churches, and by his *Catechisms* (1529) he sought to instruct 'common people'. Embattled in controversy with *both* radicals *and* 'holy Rome', he proved a natural leader and pastor.

Luther was protected in his 'reformation' by a prince. Another reformer, Ulrich *Zwingli (1484–1531), addressed himself to a very different task in his Swiss City State, with different results: Zwingli in Zurich illustrates the way a people's priest (*Leutpriester*) might work with the civic authorities and, by public disputation, defeat the bishop and his representative in debate. The argument that popular demand could legitimately accomplish the will of God (*vox populi* being accounted *vox Dei*) enabled Zwingli to abolish the Mass in Zurich (1525) and to secularize convents and monasteries to fund the common chest.

Again distinct but of huge consequence for the W. Church was the work and ministry of John *Calvin (1509–64), who promoted John *Knox (the reformer in Scotland, *c.*1505–72) to proclaim *Geneva 'the most perfect school of Christ that ever was in earth since the days of the apostles'. Calvin, just after he had published *The Institutes* (*Christianae Religionis Institutae*, 1536), was diverted to Geneva because of troop movements in the Italian Wars. Recognized by the fiery Farel (1489–1565), he was prevailed on to help those who had only 'a little while before expelled the papacy' from their midst. By 1538, when the authorities reacted again and repudiated the reform party, he reached Strasburg, enjoying an influential three-year stay with Martin *Bucer (1491–1551). The pause was not to last. In 1541 the Magistracy of Geneva invited him to fill a preaching role at the Cathedral of St Pierre. For the next twenty-five years he became a prophet of Christian order, denouncing the religion of Rome as a legal tyranny and as entirely false by the standards of The *Acts of the Apostles and of the organization of the primitive Church. His *Ecclesiastical Ordinances* (1514) repudiated the role of bishops and priests, arguing instead for the oversight of ordained 'pastors' and 'doctors' (teachers), and the new lay offices of 'elder' and 'deacon'. The influence of Calvin was direct through his College of Geneva, founded in 1559 to prepare pastors to promote biblical theology throughout Europe (and later, via England, Scotland, and Holland, to evangelize the New World). The definitive edition of *The Institutes* was published in that year and adopted as a training text. Calvin succeeded in reaching a measure of agreement with Zwingli in 1549 (*Consensus Tigurinus*) and thus did something to correct the divisive effects of the number of different Protestant reformations.

Unlike the Protestant reformation in Europe, the reformation in England focused first on the needs of the ruler and only secondly on a desire to change theological formulae and lay piety. The earlier protests of John *Wycliffe and of the Lollards, and the movement toward vernacular Scripture, tended to be confined to an area and to be successfully persecuted as 'heresy'. The desire of Henry VIII (1491–1547, r. 1509–47) to annul his marriage with Catherine of Aragon obliged him to repudiate the restrictions of Roman canon law and ultimately the papacy itself. He used the Parliament of England to help him, and he put in positions of strategic importance Thomas Cromwell (*c.*1485–1540) and Thomas *Cranmer, the former as Secretary and Vicegerent, the latter as Archbishop of Canterbury. They steered a largely reluctant king toward the dissolution of the monasteries, a number of restatements of doctrine, and (most importantly) the order that a Bible in English should be put in every church (1539).

By the time Henry died a *Litany in English had been produced, but under his son, Edward VI, liturgical reform began in earnest, with the **Book of Common Prayer* of 1549, revised in 1552. Had the boy-king lived, reformation in England would have been different: his death in 1553 illustrates the crucial importance of supportive secular authority.

Edward was succeeded by the daughter of Catherine of Aragon, Mary. She reinstated the power of the papacy and a medieval liturgy in Latin. Cranmer was burned, and the stage was set for the restoration of Catholicism. It was not to be. In 1558 Mary was succeeded in England by Elizabeth (1533–1603, r. 1558–1603). Elizabeth owed her birth to her father's repudiation of Rome, and she knew the pain that religious upheaval caused. Under her, with the help of Parliament and of Matthew *Parker, her able Archbishop of Canterbury, a Protestant settlement of religion was established by law. The *Book of Common Prayer* of 1552 was adopted with emendations; the Church was to be episcopally governed under the Queen and Parliament. The theological enquiry and defence of the settlement resumed, notably at the hands of John Jewel (1522–71) and Richard *Hooker (1553–1600). Gradually parishes in England came into step.

Throughout the 16th cent., the Catholic Church also underwent reformation. This spontaneous movement to reform the religious life, to re-evangelize Protestant countries, and to convert the newly discovered peoples of America and of the East, was associated with the emergence of the new religious Order of *Jesuits, under *Ignatius of Loyola. Other Orders were reformed, especially in Spain with St *Teresa of Avila and St *John of the Cross, with an influence still felt today. The attempts by the Council of Trent (1545–7, 1551–2, 1562) to heal the rifts in Christian unity were a failure, but the Council achieved new definitions of justification and a revised liturgy. Papal sovereignty became more firmly entrenched, with permanent status being given to Congregations (committees of *cardinals) such as those which formed the *Inquisition (1542) and *Index (1566) to safeguard Catholic faith and practice.

The resulting transformation of Europe at the hands of different reformers was the rending of the seamless robe. This was the price paid for a Catholic Church no longer as corrupt in its head and members as it had been when Erasmus surveyed it. All the reformations, Protestant or Catholic, needed to use education to their own advantage: schools were founded and refounded, and the advance of literacy meant that reason ultimately replaced indoctrination. The Reformation also did much to awaken social conscience, although not with immediate effect. Philanthropy was on both sides of a great divide—no mean harvest yielded by those whose new-found commitment resulted in lives of thank-offering after the assurance of salvation.

Cultural achievement is more difficult to estimate. There were advances in portraiture and *music, as with Cranach (1472–1533) and the Bach family. Above all else, the revolution in printing, a process updated with moveable type and new paper, promoted a quite different spirituality, to give heart and transforming faith that must ultimately symbolize the magnitude of this significant crisis in Christendom.

See also RADICAL REFORMATION; Index, Reformation.

Reformed Churches. Term loosely applied to *Protestant churches, but specifically those which hold *Calvinistic, as opposed to *Lutheran, theology. See further PRESBYTERIANISM for the distinctions among Reformed Churches.

Reformed Ogboni Fraternity. A Nigerian equivalent to a Masonic lodge, deriving mainly from the efforts of an educated Yoruba *Anglican clergyman, J. A. T. Ogunbiyi, who had been chaplain to the Masonic lodges in Lagos. In 1914 he established a Christian Ogboni Society, both as a Yoruba version of Christianity modelled on the traditional Ogboni secret society, and as an alternative to imported freemasonry.

Reformed Scholasticism (Calvinistic movement): see BEZA, THEODORE.

Reformers (Christian): see REFORMATION.

Reform Judaism. A modern post-Enlightenment interpretation of Judaism. Initially there was an attempt to make Judaism more relevant by abbreviating the traditional *liturgy and introducing choral singing and prayers in the vernacular (see JACOBSON, I.). As a result of various *rabbinical conferences in the middle years of the 19th cent., many aspects of the liturgy were reformed, but these changes were justified by reference to the *Talmud and the Codes (see CODIFICATIONS OF LAW). In Great Britain, the Reform movement initially distinguished between the Bible and the Talmud, regarding only the former as authoritative. Subsequently it became more traditional, and a more radical movement, entitled 'Liberal Judaism', was founded in 1901. In Germany, reform liturgies became widespread, but the congregations generally remained theologically conservative. In the USA, the reform platform was established at Pittsburgh in 1885.

This position was modified in Columbus in 1937, and the Reform movement has since abandoned its anti-*Zionist stance. Reform congregations are united in the World Union for Progressive Judaism, and rabbis are trained at the *Hebrew Union College in the USA and the Leo Baeck College in the UK. Reform Judaism has no official status in Israel (though it has a few congregations and *kibbutzim), because only *Orthodox rabbis are recognized; and the Orthodox repudiate such Reform innovations as the ordination (*semikhah) of women as rabbis. See also CONSERVATIVE JUDAISM; RECONSTRUCTIONISM; Index, Reform Judaism.

Refuge. Characteristic attitude of Buddhists, summarized in the Three Refuges, a formula repeated three times: *Buddhaṃ saraṇaṃ gacchāmi, Dhammaṃ saraṇaṃ gacchāmi, Saṅgham saraṇaṃ gacchāmi*: I take refuge in the *Buddha, the *dharma, and the *saṅgha. See THREE JEWELS (*triratna*).

Regensberg Colloquy (meeting in 1541 between Roman Catholics and Protestants to reunify the Church): see CONTARINI, GASPARO.

Reigenki (Japanese stories): see DENSETSU.

Reincarnation: see REBIRTH.

Reiyūkai (Jap., 'friends of the spirit association'). A movement within *Nichiren Buddhism, founded in Tōkyō in 1925 by Kubo Kakutarō (1890–1944) and his sister-in-law Kotani Kimi (1901–71). It came into being *c.*1925 as an informal association. It stresses the importance of the **Lotus Sūtra* and of reverence for *ancestors. It was the most successful of the 'new religions' (*shinshū kyō*) after the Second World War, when, unlike most other *new religious movements, it was freed from governmental supervision. But because Reiyūkai was always prone to schism, it has been weakened by frequent defections, the most important of which is *Risshō Kōsei Kai, the 'Society for the Establishment of Righteousness and Friendly Relations'. Under the presidency of the founder's son, Kubo Tsuginari, Reiyūkai has been modernized and has experienced a regeneration by an influx of young people.

Relaxati (party in Franciscan controversy): see ZELANTI.

Release of the burning mouths (Chinese Buddhist ceremony): see FANG YEN-KOU.

Relics

Christianity The word is applied to material remains of a *saint after death, and to sacred objects associated with Christ or with saints. In the W. Church the cult of relics increased enormously, especially during the *Crusades when quantities of spurious relics were brought to Europe. They were kept in reliquaries (often elaborate, decorated vessels of formalized shape), carried in procession, and believed to have miraculous powers. Relics of martyrs were placed under the altar stones of all Roman Catholic churches until 1969.

Buddhism The earliest Buddhist relic (*śarīra) was the *bo tree (of enlightenment): trees grown from cuttings or seeds (taken from the original tree under which *Gotāma achieved enlightenment) became objects of veneration. This reverence involves *circumambulation (indicating the centre of one's life) and the offering of flowers or water. The development of the *stūpa included the placing of relics.

See Index, Relics.

Religion: see INTRODUCTION.

Religion as story: see INTRODUCTION.

Religionless Christianity: see BONHOEFFER, DIETRICH.

Religions: for individual religions, see Index, Religions.

Religionsgeschichtliche Schule (History of Religions School). A method developed originally at Göttingen (hence sometimes called 'the little Göttingen faculty') for attempting the study of religions as part of an unfolding historical development. Its main focus was to set the study of early Christianity firmly in the context of Jewish and Hellenistic religion, making it in effect 'one among many'; but the method was applied to the Old Testament, and eventually, more ambitiously, to a general history of religions.

Religious habit: see HABIT, RELIGIOUS.

Religious Orders. The organization of groups of men or women living in accordance with a common rule, and owing obedience to a single superior. In W. Christianity such orders are distinct from monastic congregations, which are associations of independent monasteries, although the earliest orders were those of Cluny and Citeaux (the *Cistercians), groups of monks living a particular interpretation of the Rule of St *Benedict, who recognized a common abbot general and met in general congregations to determine matters of common policy. Although outside the RC Church religious orders disappeared at the *Reformation, they were revived to some extent in *Anglicanism in the 19th cent.

The phrase is also used, by application, for organized communities in other religions, e.g. *tarīqa among *Sūfīs, *saṃpradāya among Hindus, *saṅgha among Buddhists.

For examples, see Index, Christian Orders.

Religious Taoism: see TAOISM.

Rema (acronym): see ISSERLES.

Remak (acronym): see KIMḤI, DAVID.

Remey, C. M. (claimant to as Bahā'ī guardianship): see SHOGHI EFFENDI RABBĀNĪ.

Remnant (of Israel; Heb., *she'erit Israel*). The few faithful Jews who are believed to survive calamitous punishment. The prophet *Isaiah in particular developed this theme; his son was called Shear-Jashub ('a remnant shall return'), and in ch. 6 it is promised that, despite the complete devastation of the land, a 'holy seed' shall remain. Similar doctrines can be found in *Micah, *Jeremiah, and *Joel. To this day in the daily prayers are included the words, 'Guardian of Israel, guard the Remnant of Israel and suffer not Israel to perish.'

Remonstrants: see DUTCH REFORMED CHURCH.

Renan, Joseph-Ernest (1823–92). Historian of Jewish and Christian religion. He prepared for the *priesthood in France, but felt unable to proceed to ordination. His work in Semitic languages led to his appointment as professor at the Collège de France. After an expedition to Syria and the Holy Land, he published, in 1863, *Vie de Jésus*, which won immediate fame (or notoriety). Renan attempted to rescue Jesus from the later impositions on his story made by enthusiastic disciples. *Miracles, in particular, were either legends or embellishments of natural events. Renan was expelled from his post, not to be reinstated until the fall of the Second Empire in 1870. He continued to work on *Histoire des origines du christianisme* (1863–82, tr. 1897–1904), culminating in a study of Marcus Aurelius.

Rending of garments: see KERIAH.

Rennyo (Japanese Buddhist): see JŌDO-SHINSHŪ.

Repentance: see PENANCE; PENITENCE; TESHUVA.

Reproaches (Lat., *improperia*). A set of responses sung at the *veneration of the cross on *Good Friday.

Reprobation: see PREDESTINATION.

Requiem (Lat., 'rest'). A *mass offered for the dead. The opening words of the *introit, which until recently began all such masses in the Roman rite, are: Requiem aeternam dona eis, Domine ('Lord, grant them eternal rest'). The 1970 *missal embodies a complete revision of these masses, and many of their previously distinctive characteristics, e.g. the requirement of black *vestments, have disappeared.

Rerum Novarum. Papal *encyclical issued on 15 May 1891, 'On the Condition of the Working Classes'. It represents the response of *Leo XIII to problems created by the Industrial Revolution, and formulates a doctrine of work, profit, industrial relationships, social justice, and the necessity of a proper wage. A principal aim was 'to keep under all strife and all its causes'.

Reserved sacrament. Bread (occasionally wine) consecrated at the Christian *eucharist and kept for devotion (see BENEDICTION) and for *communion, especially for the sick. The practice is similar in the *Orthodox Church, except that the reserved sacrament consists of the host with a drop of consecrated wine on it, and there are no extra-liturgical devotions.

Resh Kallah. Title of leading Jewish sages of the Babylonian *academies. Only two are mentioned by name in the *Talmud, R. Naḥman b. Isaac (*BBB* 22a) and R. *Abbahu (*B.Hul.* 49a).

Responsa (Heb., *she'elot u-teshuvot*, 'questions and answers'). Exchanges of letters primarily on Jewish *halakhic matters. From the *geonic period, the *oral law was largely disseminated throughout the *diaspora by means of responsa. The geonic responsa were copied and sometimes collected into *kovazim* ('collections'). Unlike the geonim, the *rishonim sometimes indicated doubt and used such expressions as 'in my humble opinion' or 'requires further thought'. *Orthodox rabbinic authorities have continued to give responsa to this day (*aharonim*), and the responsa literature provides an important source for the social history of the various Jewish communities through the ages.

Restoration movements. A tendency, in Christianity, to turn away from established churches and to seek to 'restore' what is taken to be primitive or original Christianity. Frequently associated with *charismatic gifts and *millennial expectations, examples are the Church of the *Latter Day Saints, or the House Church movement.

Resurrection (Lat., *resurgo*, 'I arise'). The destiny of the dead in the restoration to them of bodies through which their continuing identity can be expressed. The belief occurs especially in Judaism, Christianity, and Islam. In Judaism, the belief that people will ultimately be raised from the dead is not found in the Hebrew scriptures until the end of the biblical period. However, by the *rabbinic period, the doctrine had become a central tenet of the Jewish religion. In rabbinic thought the doctrine involved reward and punishment for the whole nation, and a belief that body and *soul are indivisible and both will be resurrected. Later Jewish philosophers continued to disagree on the details. In general, *Progressive Judaism has abandoned the doctrine of the resurrection of the body in favour of belief in the immortality of the soul, but it remains a basic tenet of *Orthodoxy.

In Christianity, the belief in resurrection rests partly in the teaching attributed to *Jesus and in the debates in the Jewish context of the time, but much more in the *resurrection of Christ. This produced the traditional teaching that at the *parousia of Christ departed souls will be restored to a bodily life, and the saved will enter in this renewed form upon the life of heaven.

For Resurrection in Islam (Arab., *ba'th*, *nushūr*), see YAUM AL-QIYĀMA; YAUM AL-DIN.

Resurrection of Christ. Fundamental tenet of Christianity, that *Jesus was raised from the dead by God 'on the third day' after his crucifixion. It was part of the earliest Christian preaching (the *kerygma). All four gospels record that Jesus' tomb was found empty on Easter Sunday morning, but no one would have come to believe that he had been raised from the dead on that basis alone. According to Paul and the gospel writers (except *Mark?) the cause of the belief was Jesus' appearances to his followers (beginning with *Peter: Luke 24. 34). Scholars who discount the appearances of Jesus as the cause of the Easter belief usually hold a 'theological theory' instead: the disciples, reflecting on Jesus' death, believed that it could not have been the end, and came to faith that God had raised him up; but in the Jewish context, and in the context of the fact of the crucifixion, there is no serious possibility that theological theories of this kind are correct.

Already in the New Testament the theological significance of the resurrection is variously expressed: as God's vindicating Jesus and raising him to his right hand in heaven (Acts 2. 34–6); as an anticipation of the general *resurrection (1 Thessalonians 4. 14); as Christ's victory over death (1 Corinthians 15. 57); and as the basis of the new life of Christians (Romans 4. 24).

Muslims deny the resurrection of Christ, believing that he did not die on the cross at all; and the *Aḥmadīyya maintain that he went on to preach in India, and believe that they can identify his tomb.

Retreat. A period of days spent apart from the world, in pursuit of religious ends. In Christianity, retreats are formally part of the life of *Jesuits (*Ignatius' *Spiritual Exercises* being a retreat plan), and it was the Jesuits who promoted the retreat as a formal practice. In the 17th cent. retreats became popular, and retreat houses were set up.

The term is used, in application, in other religions for withdrawal from the world, e.g. the time spent by *Muḥammad in isolation on Mt. Hira (which led to the revelation of the first words of the *Qur'ān); *vassa in Buddhism.

Retrogressive rituals. *Rituals which enable people to bring the past into the present, or to 'visit' the past in order to deal with events that lie in the past. The former bring into effect past events so that they are of consequence in the present (as in recapitulating dramatic moments of salvation, e.g. *Passover, *Good Friday); the latter are particularly important in enabling people to deal with offences or sins in the past which might otherwise seem to be literally 'past redemption'—hence rituals of *penance, *confession, *atonement, *absolution, etc.

Reuben. One of the twelve sons of *Jacob and forefather of one of the *tribes of *Israel.

Reuchlin, Johannes (1455–1522). *Gentile defender of Jewish scholarship. Reuchlin's *De Rudimentis Hebraicis* (1506) was a pioneering attempt at an understanding of Judaism by a Christian scholar. He also studied the *kabbalah, and his *De Arte Cabalistica* (1517), which was dedicated to the pope, did much to spread knowledge of Jewish mysticism to Christian readers.

Reuveni, David (d. 1583). Jewish adventurer who evoked *messianic expectation. At the age of about 40, he appeared in Venice in 1523 and was received by the pope in 1524. He visited

Portugal in 1525, where he was greeted as the herald of the messianic age by the *Marranos, but was subsequently imprisoned. After shipwreck off the coast of France, he returned to Italy where he was again imprisoned in 1532. Although inspiring messianic fervour, he himself stressed he was merely a military commander trying to raise an alliance against the Muslims and recapture *Erez Israel for the Jews.

Revelation (Lat., *revelare*, 'to unveil'). The disclosure or communication of truths which would not otherwise be known, at least in the same way. A distinction is often made between, on the one hand, 'natural revelation' or 'general revelation', whereby such truths are discerned within the natural order (either by reason or by conviction that absolute value, especially beauty, has invaded a contingent moment or object or circumstance); and on the other hand, special or supernatural revelation, which comes from a source other than that of the human recipient, usually God. The method of supernatural revelation is variously understood, ranging from direct dictation (in which the limitations of a human author are overridden) to concursive activity (in which the source is God, or the *Holy Spirit, working with the human author—a view which, in the Jewish and Christian case, recognizes the contingency of the words produced, but raises difficulties for traditional claims of inerrancy in revealed words).

Muslims hold a strong doctrine of revelation, believing that 'the mother of the book' (*umm al-Kitāb) is with God in heaven. The *Qur'ān, therefore, is sent down to prophets as they and their circumstances can bear it—and consummately so through *Muḥammad, whose recipient community preserved it without corruption or loss. The major terms for 'revelation' are tanzīl and *waḥy.

Whereas in W. religions revelation is usually related to particular persons and occasions, in Hinduism the concept is more subtle and diffused. The *Veda is believed to have no human author, and in some sense is revealed—the exact sense is not agreed. *Śabda (sound) is a source of knowledge with many different aspects. Within the context of sound, *anubhūti* (direct experience of *Brahman) arises from meditation on texts from the *Upaniṣads as they are *heard*—not simply as they are read in silence. But this experience is possible only because the Upaniṣads themselves arise from the Vedas which are the constant (or in some views eternal) revelation of the truth about *dharma and Brahman. In *Vedānta, the Vedas are no more real than anything else (*māyā), but they serve to point beyond themselves to what is real, much as a picture points to that which it endeavours to portray.

See Index, Revelation.

Revelation, Book of. The last book and the only *apocalypse in the *New Testament. The book is a series of visions, prefaced (chs. 1–3) by letters to seven churches in Asia Minor. The hostile attitude to Rome suggests a date during Nero's persecution, *c.*64, or later under Domitian (81–96). In Christian history the book has become important in times of persecution and in the context of *millenarian movements.

Revival Zion or **Revivalism.** Afro-Jamaican cults resembling *Pocomania in their hierarchical and authoritarian organization, in their Yards, and in their concern with healing by diverse means and with spirit possession.

Revivalism may also be a more general description of movements within Christianity which lead to a renewal of fervour and commitment. Examples are *Pietism, the *Great Awakening in N. America, the *Wesleys and the origins of *Methodism, 19th-cent. *mission meetings.

Revolutionary Guards (Shi'ite religious police): see BIHBAHĀNĪ.

Reza, Imām Ahmad (founder): see BARELVI.

Ṛg Veda (Skt., 'knowledge in verse'). The oldest of the *Veda collections of hymns (*c.*13th cent. BCE) and the most important for its scope and originality. It consists of sung strophes (*ṛc*) arranged into hymns (*sukta*) by the *hotṛ priests. Altogether the collection includes 1,028 hymns (or 1,017 excluding Vālakhilya hymns attached to the 8th *maṇḍala) divided into ten maṇḍalas (circles or schools). Maṇḍalas 2 to 7 are family collections, and are the oldest core of the *Ṛg Veda*. These are arranged according to the gods they address and according to decreasing length. Maṇḍala 8 collects hymns from a number of families. Maṇḍala 9 is devoted exclusively to the god *Soma. Maṇḍalas 1 and 10 preserve late hymns for the most part, including the more speculative hymns and those to figures otherwise unmentioned in the *Ṛg Veda*. In tone the *Ṛg Veda* is generally devotional and laudatory. The sacrificer calls upon the gods through his singing and asks for some blessing.

rgyal tshab: see GSHEN RAB MI-BO-CHE.

Rhazes (Muslim philosopher and physician): see AL-RĀZĪ, ABŪ BAKR MUḤAMMAD.

Rheno-Flemish spirituality. A style of Christian mystical devotion of the 13th cent., which developed in Belgium and the Rhineland. The Rhineland mystics emphasized the seeking and finding of God within, rather than in outward devotions. They were rooted in the practice and experience of the Beguines (and their male counterparts, the Beghards), who were lay religious groups seeking the simplicity of the early Church in communal association with each other (they were condemned, especially for their use of the vernacular Bible and private interpretation of scripture, but their descendants survive to the present). One major figure was Mechtild of Magdeburg (1210–*c*.1290), who lived most of her life as a Beguine, but retired to a convent when her writings were attacked; her main work, *Das fliessende Licht der Gottheit* (The Flowing Light of the Godhead), is a compendium of her own experiences and of medieval mysticism.

Gertrude of Helfta (1256–1301/2), often called 'the Great', experienced, at the age of 25, a bond of love with Jesus, a kind of 'nuptial mysticism' (*Brautmystik*), and from that time entered a life of contemplation; she wrote the much-admired *Legatus Divinae Pietatis* (The Herald of Divine Love, parts of which were written later from her notes), and was one of the first to develop devotion to the *Sacred Heart. Hadewijch of Antwerp (early 13th cent.), whose *Visions* develop the same theme of a union with God of ecstatic love (*minnemystiek*), Jan van *Ruysbroeck, and *Hildegard of Bingen are often associated with this group; and the *devotio moderna* of Gerard *Groote is usually regarded as a direct successor.

Rhineland mysticism: see RHENO-FLEMISH SPIRITUALITY.

Rhys Davids, C. A. F. (née Foley, 1857–1942). An important editor, translator, and commentator on Pāli Buddhist texts. After her marriage to T. W. *Rhys Davids in 1894, she worked as Honorary Secretary to the Pāli Text Society until her husband's death in 1922, when she became President.

Her major writings include translations of the *Saṃyutta Nikāya* (2 vols.), *Dhammasaṅgaṇi*, *Therīgāthā*, and an important early study of the Buddhist conception of mind, *Buddhist Psychology* (1914).

Rhys Davids, T. W. (1843–1922). Influential promoter of Pāli Buddhist studies in England.

Though not the first scholar of Pāli, he did much to introduce Buddhist ideas to the British public, and in his Hibbert Lectures of 1881 announced the foundation of the Pāli Text Society, of which he was the first chairman.

His vast output of work can be conveniently classified under the three headings of translation, history, and philology. The principal translations include *Vinaya Texts*, with H. Oldenberg (1881–5), *Dialogues of the Buddha*, with his wife C. A. F. Rhys Davids (1899–1921), and *Questions of King Milinda* (1890–4). His historical works include *Buddhism* (1878) and *Early Buddhism* (1908), while the great labour of his final years was the compilation of a Pāli–English Dictionary, completed by W. Stede.

Ri. This may be spelt Ṛ or ṛ; check at appropriate alphabetical order.

Ribā (Arab., 'increase'). The taking of interest on capital investment, which is prohibited in Islam (e.g. Qur'ān 2. 278 f.). The Qur'ān allows profit through trade, but if there is investment, it must be on a profit-sharing basis.

Ribal (acronym): see LEVINSOHN, ISAAC BAER.

Ribusshō (Jap.). The buddha-nature (*busshō) as the inherent and only constituent of all living beings, especially in Hossō (see DŌSHŌ).

Ricci, Matteo (1552–1610). *Jesuit missionary in China. He gained the attention of Chinese intellectuals by displaying and explaining to them European clocks, a map of the world, etc., planning thereby to bridge the difference in cultures and convert the country from the official classes downwards. His missionary success also owed much to his accommodation of Christianity to Chinese religion (cf. *de Nobili). In 1603, he prescribed the observance of traditional honours to *Confucius and the cult of *ancestors in Jesuit churches in China. These rites, however, gave rise to a protracted controversy after his death, and were pronounced by the *Holy See in 1704 and 1715 to be incompatible with Christianity.

Ridda (Arab., *'irtadda*, 'retrace one's steps'). Apostasy from Muslim belief (cf. MURTADD), especially al-Ridda, the wars of apostasy which immediately followed the death of *Muḥammad. The penalty is death if the apostate (murtadd) speaks against Islam (see also BLASPHEMY). The penalty is not stated in the Qur'ān, and is based on *ḥadīth.

Ridley, Nicholas (*c*.1500–55). English *Reformation *bishop. Consecrated bishop of Rochester in 1547, he was, on Bonner's deprivation, made bishop of London (1550). A memorable preacher, he gave forceful publicity in his diocese to his revised *eucharistic views by replacing the stone altar with a wooden *Communion table. On Mary's accession he was arrested and later burnt with *Latimer at Oxford. He exerted a great influence on Cranmer who always regarded him as of superior ability, especially in controversy.

Riḍvān (Paradise). Place outside Baghdād of great holiness to Bahā'īs. In 1863, *Bahā'u'llāh was summoned (at the instigation of the Persian government) to Constantinople. Bahā'u'llāh moved to the garden of Najīb Pāsha to prepare for the journey, and on 21 Apr. announced that he was the one whose coming had been foretold by the Bāb (see BĀBĪS). The garden was named Riḍvān, and the twelve days spent there are commemorated in the feast of Riḍvān.

Rif (acronym): see ALFASI.

Righteous gentiles (Heb., *ḥasidei 'umōt ha-'olām*). Gentiles who keep the *Noachide laws. They will have a share in the world to come (*'Olam ha-Ba) when the *messiah comes. More specifically, the term is used of those gentiles who risked their lives to save Jews during the *Holocaust. There is an Avenue of the Righteous Gentiles in the Holocaust Memorial, Yad Vashem, in *Jerusalem.

Right-hand tantrism: see DAKṢINĀCĀRA.

Right mindfulness (Pāli, *sati*). Part of the Buddhist eightfold path (*aṣṭaṇgika-marga), which consciously endeavours to look on all things in the true perspective—including aspects of the body of which usually one is not conscious, e.g. breathing. This brings insight into the equally transitory (*anicca) nature of all phenomena. These are the four awakenings of mindfulness, *satipaṭṭhāna. See also SATI.

Rig-Veda (collection of hymns): see ṚG VEDA.

Rikam (acronym): see KIMḤI, DAVID.

Rimé (*ris.med*, 'without partiality'). 19th-cent. Tibetan eclectic movement, initiated in 1864 by the publication of the first of Jamgon Kongtrul's 'five treasuries', the *Treasury of All Knowledge* (*Shes.bya.mdzod*). In its attempt at a reconciling inclusiveness, what had been a heresy—the *zhen dong doctrine—became the bedrock of a major national movement, which sought to harmonize all teachings in the light of an ontologically positive ultimate reality which is essentially beyond definition. Rimé was at its strongest in its own province of Khams and its effects were felt strongly everywhere but, perhaps because of the importance attached by all schools to their respective lineages, it never looked like dissolving the distinctions fully. The *Geluk indeed stayed well apart from it as a school, unflinching in their condemnation of the zhen dong heresy.

Rimpoche (precious one): see RINPOCHE.

Ringatu (Maori, *Ringa-tua*, 'upraised hand'). The oldest continuing prophet movement in New Zealand. It was founded by Te Kooti Rikirangi (?1830–93) among prisoners captured during the Anglo-Maori wars, with whom he had been unjustly deported to the Chatham Islands in 1866. His earnest Bible study established a new Maori religion which spread after their escape home in 1868. He is now revered as *saint and *martyr, and creator of the Ringatu *liturgy.

Rinka monasticism (style of Zen monasticism): see JAKUHITSU GENKŌ.

Rinpoche (Tib., *Rin po che*, 'Precious One'). A title of respect given to all *lamas in Tibetan Buddhism. A monk who becomes a lama for the first time (i.e. in this incarnation) will be accorded the title equally with a 'reincarnate lama' (*tulku). The *Dalai Lama, for example, may also be called 'Gyalwa Rinpoche' (Precious Eminence).

Rinzai Gigen (founder of Zen Buddhist Lin-Chi line): see LIN-CHI I-HSÜAN.

Rinzairoku. Abbreviated title of *Chinjū Rinzai Eshō zenji goroku*, Chin., *Chen-chou Lin-chi Hui-chao ch'an-shih yü-lu*, a major and classic work of Zen Buddhism. Its present form dates from the 12th cent. CE, and it is in three parts: (i) Discourses (*goroku*); (ii) Dialectic (*kamben*), questions and answers addressed to true existence; (iii) record of pilgrimages (*anroku*), which includes an account of Lin-chi's enlightenment, and a memorial inscription.

Rinzai-shū (Jap. pronunciation of 'Lin-chi', the Chinese founder of the line, + *shū*, Jap., 'tradition', 'school', or 'teachings'). With *Sōtō-shū, one of the two dominant forms of *Zen Buddhism widely practised in Japan. This tradition, founded by the Chinese master, *Lin-chi I-hsüan (d. 867), is usually considered to have been introduced into Japan by Yōsai, also known as *Eisai (1141–1215). In fact, however, it did not crystallize as an independent Japanese school until two or three decades after his death. The modern Japanese tradition owes much of its spiritual development to the revitalization of the practice brought about by *Hakuin Ekaku (1685–1768).

Rinzai-shū is noted for its emphasis on the more audacious forms of Zen training, including shouting, striking, and the dynamic exchanges between master and disciple centring on the *kōan. According to Hakuin, the master's role is to bring about a crisis in the student called the 'Great Doubt' or the 'Great Death' so that, in a moment of realization (*satori), the student makes a spiritual breakthrough.

When the Rinzai school was officially recognized by the state, it was organized in a tripartite system of *gozan* (Five Mountains), *jissetsu* (Ten Temples), and *shozan* (the remaining larger temples). The list of Five Mountain temples changed many times (though it remained based on *Kyōto and Kamakura), but this structured and state-recognized form of Rinzai is often called Gozan Zen.

Rishi (Indian seer): see ṚṢI.

Rishis (Sūfī order): see SŪFĪS.

Rishonim (Heb., 'first ones', i.e. early authorities). Jewish scholars of an earlier period. Nowadays, the term is used to indicate the authorities that succeeded the geonim until those of the mid-15th cent. after rabbinic *semikhah was revived.

Rishon le-Zion (Heb., 'First of Zion'). Hebrew title of the *Sephardi head of the *rabbis of *Israel. From 1920, the Rishon le-Zion was given the additional title of *hakham bashi* (*Chief Rabbi) of *Erez Israel.

Risshō Kōsei Kai ('Establishment of Righteousness and Friendly Intercourse'). New religion, derived from *Nichiren, started in Japan in 1938 by Naganuma Myōkō (1889–1957) and Niwano Nikkyō (b. 1906). Placing its own version of the *bodhisattva ideal at the centre of its teachings, this movement stresses that everyone can travel the road to Buddhahood by leading a life of moral and spiritual wisdom and by foregoing *nirvāna in order to be of service to weak and suffering humanity.

The word *risshō* alludes to Nichiren's injunction in 1260, *risshō ankoku ron*, 'establish authentic Buddhism to secure peace in our land'; *kōsei* points to a faith-oriented fellowship of those seeking the Buddha's goal; *kai* means 'association' or 'society'. RKK is highly organized, from the network of districts throughout Japan, down to the most local level, where people gather for *hōza*, i.e. seated (*za*) to share problems and solutions related to Buddhist principles (*ho*).

Rita (cosmic order): see ṚTA(M).

Rite: see RITUAL.

Rite. Term in Christian use. 1. A form of liturgical worship.

2. Any of the major local types or families of ancient *liturgies, e.g. the Latin, Byzantine, and *Mozarabic rites, and the churches where these were practised and their modern descendants.

3. In *Catholic use, a division of Catholic Christendom.

Rites controversy. A conflict among *Roman Catholic missionary orders in China in the 17th and 18th cents. It centred on the issue of whether Chinese converts could continue with some pre-Christian practices (especially *ancestor rituals), and whether *T'ien could be regarded as the equivalent of God. The *Jesuits were in favour, the *Dominicans and *Franciscans against (on grounds of syncretism and dilution of the faith). On appeal to the *pope, the Jesuits were overruled in 1704; the order against integration was repeated in 1715 and 1742. The Chinese court regarded this as interference in internal religious matters, and issued countermeasures, banning missionary preaching unless it accepted the so-called Matteo *Ricci regulations—i.e. following his example in approving the rites. The virtual eclipse of Christianity in China was the result of the papal ruling.

Rites of passage. Rituals which mark major transitions in human life (and death). A. van Gennep (*The Rites of Passage*), drew attention to a recurrent pattern in such rituals of one distinction, two categories, and three stages: for example,

death; dead/alive; alive → dying → dead
marriage; married/single; single → engaged → married

R. Hertz (*Année Sociologique*, 10 (1907)), argued that these rituals move the person in question over a *limen*, 'a threshold', so that they are in a condition that society can know and cope with. The central importance of liminality in rites of passage was taken even further by Victor *Turner, who recognized many more rites of passage than those which have to do with obvious transitions (indeed, nearly all rituals have this characteristic of moving those involved from one state to another); and in these rituals, he stressed 'the autonomy of the liminal': it is the liminal state which is both threatening and at the same time the only route to change—hence the centrality of focus on liminality in religious life.

For examples, see BAPTISM; CIRCUMCISION; FUNERAL RITES; MARRIAGE; PILGRIMAGE; SAṂSKĀRA.

Ritroma (Tib., *ri khrod ma*, 'the lady of the mountain ranges'). A Tibetan female deity, who is an object of meditation. She is associated with healing, and is one of the *wrathful deities.

Ritsu (Jap.; Skt., *vināya*). Codes of discipline which govern the Buddhist monastic life. The *vinaya were compiled about 100 years after *Śākyamuni Buddha's death and transmitted orally until they were put down in writing in the 1st cent. BCE, forming the Vinaya-piṭaka of the *Tripiṭaka. The version that prevailed in E. Asia was the *Ssu-fen lü* (Vinaya in Four Parts), translated into Chinese between 410 and 412 by Buddhayaśas (no Sanskrit original or Tibetan translation exists). There were several other vinaya texts translated and utilized, all of

Hīnayāna origin, but the *Ssu-fen lü* became standard, and became the basis of the Ritsu school in Japan, one of the six schools of the Nara period, based on Lu-tsung (see BUDDHISM IN CHINA), and introduced by *Ganjin. When the compound, kai-ritsu is used, ritsu (vinaya) refers to an objective code of disciplines, and *kai (*śīla) denotes precepts to be undertaken voluntarily, such as the Five Precepts. Thus monks and nuns observe both kai-ritsu, whereas lay believers take on only the kai. Two main schools survive: Ritsu, whose centre is the Tōshōdaiji; and Shingon-ritsu, whose centre is the Saidaiji.

Ritsu and **ryō.** The written criminal and civil codes that were the foundation for the imperial bureaucracy of Japan from the early 7th to the 12th cents.

The ritsu were essentially disciplinary sanctions of a penal character. The ryō were prescriptive regulations for the organization of governmental administration. A distinctive feature of the Japanese bureaucracy, however, was the establishment of a second branch with prestige superior to that of the Department of State. This was the *Jingikan or 'Department of Shinto' with jurisdiction over the cult of the national gods (kami). The ritsu-ryō government dissolved in the 12th cent., being replaced by shogun military rule.

In Japanese *music, ritsu and ryō are scales drawn from Buddhist chant.

Ritual (Lat., *ritus*, 'structure', 'ceremony'). Actions repeated in regular and predictable ways, both in religious and secular contexts, serving so many purposes that summary is impossible. Ritual is clearly an integral part of religious life, but it is common and persistent outside the domain of religion: consider the ordered expectations in different kinds of parties, for New Year's Eve, retirements, pre-wedding nights, etc. Religious ritual is usually thought to comprise repetition, commitment, intention, pattern (especially of movements), tradition (often by linkage with *myth which is regarded by some as supplying the meaning of the ritual), purpose, and performance. At the very least, public ritual is social drama, which makes unsurprising the origin of *theatre in religious ritual, for example in Greece, India (where ritual and drama are still closely linked), and Japan (see NŌ DRAMA). Beyond that elementary point, definitions and explanations of ritual proliferate. A. F. C. Wallace (*Religion: An Anthropological View*, 1966) suggested five main categories of ritual: (i) technological, including rites of divination, of intensification (to obtain such things as food or alcohol), and of protection; (ii) therapeutic (and anti-therapeutic); (iii) ideological (for the sake of the community as a whole), including rites of passage, of intensification (to ensure adherence to values), of taboos, ceremonies, and courtesies, and of rebellion (leading to catharsis); (iv) soteriological, aimed at repair of communal and individual damage, including rites of possession and exorcism, of new identity, and of ecstasy; and (v) revitalizing. From this it can be seen that ritual is at least the recognition in the midst of time of the ways in which the sequential passage of time affords the possibility of reassertive and significant action.

See also RITES OF PASSAGE; RETROGRESSIVE RITUALS; Index, Rituals.

Ritual bronzes: see BRONZE VESSELS.

Ritualism. A movement in the Church of England in the late 19th cent., to adopt the ritual and Gothic ornament of the Roman Catholic Church. Attempts to repress it in the secular or church courts (on the basis of the Ornaments rubric) from 1869, and through an act of Parliament (1874), were not ultimately successful.

Ritual slaughter: see SHEḤITAH; AL-HALAL.

Rituals of retrogression: see RETROGRESSIVE RITUALS.

Rivers: see SACRED RIVERS, SEVEN.

Rizalistas. Members of religious movements in the Philippines which honour José Rizal y Mercado (1861–96) as divine, as the power of the *Holy Spirit, as a second *Christ, or as a new *messiah who will return. Rizal was an intellectual, physician, novelist, and nationalist who was shot by the Spanish after the Philippines revolution broke out. Although not himself especially religious, he has become a national *martyr and symbol of Philippine independence. Among the larger movements are Bathalismo (*Bathala*, 'God') claiming to antedate the arrival of the Spanish; Banner of the Race Church (Watawat ng Lahi) which resembles *Roman Catholicism and awaits the return of Rizal; Sacred Church of the Race (Iglesia Sagrada ng Lahi) with its own ancient 'bible' kept secret until Rizal appeared as God on earth; Philippine Church or Adarnistas (after 'Mother Adarna' the founder) for whom Rizal was not executed but lives as true God and man; Patriotic Church of our Lord Jesus Christ.

Rmi.Lam (dream yoga): see MILAM; NĀRO CHOS DRUG.

Rnying-ma-pa: see NYINGMA.

Rōba Zen. 'Grandmother Zen', so-called because it adopts a gentle method of training.

This arises from the character of either the pupil or teacher or both.

Robinson, John A. T. (1919–83). *Anglican theologian. Formerly a New Testament scholar at Cambridge, it was as bishop of Woolwich in SE London (1959–69) that he became a public figure. His book *Honest to God* (1963), which admitted difficulties in traditional understandings of God and prayer, sold 3½ million copies, but also brought accusations of *heresy and atheism. His scholarly work was also controversial, particularly that which defended the earliness (pre-66 CE) date of the New Testament documents, particularly the gospel of John.

Rock garden: see KYŌTO.

Rogation days. In W. churches, days of prayer and fasting in the early summer, associated with *intercession (Lat., *rogare*, 'ask'), especially for the harvest.

Roger (Schutz), Brother (founder of Christian community): see TAIZÉ.

Rokkakudō (Jap., hexagonal hall). The common name for a *Tendai temple in Kyōto, otherwise known as Chōhōji. It was built by Shotoku to enshrine an image of Nyorin Kannon, and it became the emperor's prayer hall in 822.

Rokudō. Jap. for the six realms of existence (*gati); see also SHŌBŌ-NENJO-GYŌ.

Rokusō (Jap., 'six aspects'). The six features which, according to *Kegon teaching, can be found in all appearances: (i) *sōsō*, able to undertake a variety of functions; (ii) *bessō*, able to focus on one particular function; (iii) *dōsō*, possessing a function which is also held in general by other appearances; (iv) *isō*, having a distinctive feature of its own; (v) *jōsō*, having the power to form or construct in combination with other appearances; (vi) *esō*, persistence through destruction. *Rokuso en'yu* is the ability of those trained in Kegon to see the six elements as being undifferentiated, whereas the untrained see these features as disparate.

Rokuso daishi hōbōdan-gyo (key Zen work): see LIU-TSU-TA-SHIH FA-PAO-T'AN-CHING.

Rolle, Richard (*c*.1300–49). Christian hermit and mystic. Born near Pickering in Yorkshire, he became a hermit as a young man, latterly near the convent of Cistercian nuns at Hampole, where he died, perhaps of the Black Death. His writings, both in Latin and English, give expression to a highly affective mystical experience of 'heat', 'sweetness', and 'song'.

Roman Catholic Church. Those churches in communion with the Church of Rome, recognizing the leadership of the *pope. The word '*Catholic' means 'universal', and thus the addition of 'Roman' seems to some contradictory, since they regard the Church under the successor of *Peter (see PETRINE TEXTS) as the one, universal Church; other Christians (i.e. those who are baptized and 'honoured by the name of Christian', *Lumen Gentium*, 15) are held to be 'in a certain, although imperfect, communion with the Catholic Church' (*Unitatis redintegratio*, 3). To be in complete communion with the Church of Rome is to belong to the Catholic Church. However, the addition of 'Roman' has become more common during the recent decades of *ecumenicism, not least in recognition of the status of *uniate Churches and of other uses of the world 'Catholic'; 'Roman Catholic' is therefore used in this article and throughout the *Dictionary*.

Central government is exercised by the pope and *curia (usually referred to as 'the *Vatican).

It is by far the largest of the Christian denominations, with approaching a billion members. Serving the Church's members are just over 400,000 priests, 68,000 male religious, and just short of one million female religious. There are rather more than 2,000 *dioceses or equivalent administrative areas, but a quarter of these are in Europe.

The Roman Catholic Church insists on its continuity of belief, liturgy, and structure from the pre-*Reformation church, and upon its right, as (in its own view) the one church founded by *Christ, to hold *councils of its own bishops which are regarded as *ecumenical and, doctrinally, of the same standing as the councils of the early church. It has held three since the Reformation, those of *Trent, Vatican I, and Vatican II. At Vatican I the bishops asserted the primacy and *infallibility of the pope, but at Vatican II the RC Church made an effort to come closer to other Christian churches, and formulated no firm doctrinal statements—setting, for example, Mariological (see MARY) devotion (so typical of Catholicism) firmly within its ecclesial framework. In the subsequent years, *Paul VI did much to put into effect the programme of Vatican II, but began also to express a caution which became also a marked feature of the policy of John Paul II—culminating in *Catechism of the Catholic Church* (1993/4): in this, for example, the Bible is used as though a-historical, as though its embeddedness in history has no effect on the application of the text to current issues.

Throughout its history, the Roman Catholic Church has placed great emphasis on the offering of life, through the Church, to God in obedience and holiness. It has thus given special importance to the *monastic life, which epitomizes the choice of God rather than the world. At the same time, the radical choice for God has led to a constant acceptance of *martyrdom, which the outreach of evangelism (not least in the 20th cent.) has repeatedly brought about; the strong emphasis on being the only Church has equally led Roman Catholics to be zealous in their persecution of others, and evangelism often accompanied conquest, as in the policy of Spain (between the 16th and 18th cents.). In this context, the prayer of the faithful was, until the 15th cent., apt to be of a verbal and repetitive nature. The Latin liturgy and Bible (*Vulgate) increased the problems for the laity in understanding the faith. Since Vatican II, the change to vernacular liturgies and Bibles, together with the transformation of the penitential rites (*confession) and the move of the altar to the centre of the church, has increased the active participation of all in worship. It remains the case that strict rules govern membership of the Church, e.g. concerning who may communicate at *Mass, or the status of divorced people; celibacy is a requirement for priests (even though in some parts of the world this means that the celebration of the Mass is infrequent); and the laity are under obligation not to use artificial contraception (see HUMANAE VITAE). The latter arises from definitions of the meaning of 'the person', and of when the life of any particular person begins. The same consideration underlies the absolute opposition to *abortion. Control (through licensing) is also exercised over those teaching in Catholic schools and universities, and while many such institutions are now under the direction of lay professionals, publications and lectures may still occasion discipline, which many include the silencing of so-called progressive theologians. Conformity has not in the past meant a repetitive *theology: theology and philosophy have had a high place in Roman Catholicism, by no means confined to *scholasticism.

The central place, both of the Mass in worship, and of the Church in the community, has contributed to the inspiration of enduring *art, architecture, and *music, as well as many kinds of literature. The Church as patron has had immense consequences for civilization as a whole. So also has the absolute requirement to be generous to those in need (a requirement which goes back to Christ). As a result, schools, hospitals, places where the needy and dying can find refuge, and a wide range of aid programmes have multiplied. This tradition is also expressed in 100 years of teaching on social justice issues, from **Rerum Novarum* to the *Constitution of the Church in the Modern World* (*Gaudium et Spes*) in 1965, and subsequent encyclicals. The financial cost of the Vatican is great and falls heavily on the Church in the USA, where the majority have a vision of the Church in the service of the world which has been increasingly at variance from the official Vatican line (though, they would say, in line with the vision of Vatican II). The resulting tension can be seen particularly in the radical divide over the opportunities open to women to have a voice comparable to that of men in the Church. Roman Catholicism is highly clericalized, and the refusal to allow the possibility that women can be ordained means that they can never be a serious part of the leadership or decision-making of the Church.

See Index, Roman Catholicism and further references there.

Romanos the Melodist, St. (d. ?556). The greatest of Greek hymn-writers (although only a few—80 out of 1,000—of his hymns survive). A Syrian by birth, after a time as deacon at Berytus, he found his way to Constantinople under Patriarch Anastasius I (d. 518). Hardly any of his hymns are still used in the liturgy, though the famous *Akathistos hymn is widely regarded as his. Feast day, 1 Oct.

Romans, Letter to the. A book of the *New Testament and the longest of *Paul's epistles. It was written *c.*58 CE from Corinth. Romans is the most systematic of Paul's letters, and since the 4th cent. it has stood first among them in the Bible. It has powerfully affected Christian doctrine on such questions as *original sin, *merit, and justification.

Rome. 'The eternal city', capital of modern Italy (embracing the Vatican City since the Lateran Treaty in 1929 between the *pope and the Italian government of Mussolini), and major centre of Christianity since the arrival of *Paul and *Peter (the presence of the latter having sometimes been disputed). Both *apostles are believed to have been martyred in Rome: St Peter's Basilica stands on the traditional site of Peter's burial.

Romero, Oscar Arnulfo (1917–80). Christian archbishop of El Salvador, assassinated in 1980. He studied theology in Rome, 1937–43, became a parish priest and bishop of Santiago de Maria in 1974. Thought to be a conservative bishop, he was appointed archbishop in Feb. 1977, in the expectation that he would not disturb the political *status quo*. Three weeks later, the *Jesuit Rutilio Grande, together with two others, was gunned down in his jeep. The event was, for Romero, a conversion. He began a ministry of outspoken commitment to those who had no voice of their own. *Paul VI gave him encouragement, but the accession of *John Paul II, with its cult of the pope and movement away from the vision of *Vatican II, led to an increasing campaign against Romero in Rome. The details of this are disputed. The Vatican appointed an apostolic administrator to oversee his work, but Romero was killed before this could be put into effect. He returned from his last visit to Rome to the slogan painted on walls, 'Be a patriot, kill a priest'. He was killed as he said mass in the chapel of the Divine Providence Hospital where he lived.

Romuald (Christian monk): see CAMALDOLESE.

Rosary. In Christianity, a *Catholic devotion which consists in reciting fifteen 'decades' (groups of ten) of Hail Marys (*Ave Maria), each decade preceded by the *Lord's Prayer and followed by the *Gloria Patri. A string of variously numbered (e.g. 55 or 165 'beads', Med. Eng., *beda*, 'prayer') are used to count the individual prayers. Each decade represents one of the 'fifteen mysteries' (five 'joyful', five 'sorrowful', five 'glorious'), each an event in the life of *Jesus or his mother.

Prayer beads are also used in other religions (e.g. Hinduism and Buddhism: see MĀLĀ; Jap. Buddhism: see NENJU), and are referred to in English as 'rosaries'. Thus, many Sikhs use a rosary (*mālā*) to assist meditation. See also NĀM SIMARAN. In Islam, the *subḥa* (Arab., *sabbaḥa*, 'praise God', cf. *subḥān Allāh*, 'Glory to God!') is the Muslim string of prayer beads, in three groups, divided by two larger beads (*imām*), with a larger piece serving as a handle. By different reckonings, the total is always 100—Allāh + his *Ninety-nine Beautiful Names. See NĀFILA.

Rosenzweig, Franz (1886–1929). German Jewish theologian. He was born into an *assimilated family, and, as a young man, he was much influenced by a relative, E. Rosenstock-Huessy, with whom he conducted a correspondence, later published in part. Under this influence, Rosenzweig contemplated converting to Christianity, but in 1913, after attending a *High Holy Day Service, he resolved to remain faithful to Judaism. Influenced by Herman *Cohen and Martin *Buber, and while still a soldier in the First World War, he wrote *Der Stern der Erloesung* (1921; tr. W. W. Hallo, *The Star of Redemption*, 1971). After the War, Rosenzweig founded the Freies Juedisches Lehrhaus ('The Free Jewish House of Learning') for assimilated Jews to study the Jewish classics. From 1921, he was afflicted with progressive paralysis, but he continued to work translating *Judah Halevi's poems, and, with Martin Buber, he started translating the Hebrew scriptures. This project was completed by Buber after the Second World War.

Rosh (acronym): see ASHER BEN JEHIEL.

Rosh ha-Shanah (Heb., 'New Year'). The Jewish *New Year. Rosh ha-Shanah is celebrated on 1 Tishri (and 2 in the *diaspora). The four names of the festival in the Jewish tradition reflect the various themes of the day: Rosh ha-Shanah, Yom Teru'ah ('Day of Blowing the Horn' (*shofar)), Yom ha-Din ('Day of Judgement'), and Yom ha-Zikkaron ('Day of Remembrance'). On the first afternoon, the *Tashlikh ceremony is often performed, although there is no reference to this in the *Talmud.

Rosh ha-Shanah. A tractate of the Jewish *Talmud. The tractate deals with the laws and customs of the various *New Years in the Jewish *Calendar.

Rosh Ḥodesh (new month): see MOON, BLESSING OF THE.

Roshi (Jap., 'old master'). Title of a Zen master. Initially, the title was hard-earned, being bestowed by people at large on one who was recognized as having realized the *dharma of the Buddha by direct experience, and as having sustained it in everyday life (*mujōdō-no-taigen). 'Roshi' has now become a more general title of a Zen teacher, who may be monk or lay, man or woman; and it has degenerated even further into a term of respect for any old or venerated monk.

Rossi, Azariah ben Moses Dei (1511–78). Jewish scholar. Rossi was born into an eminent Jewish family. He was the author of *Me'or Einayim* (Enlightenment to the Eyes, 1573–5), which shows his familiarity with Greek and Latin authors, the Church Fathers, and *Philo. It was the source of some controversy, as he questioned the historicity of *Talmudic legends.

Rota Sacra Romana. The 'Sacred Roman Rota', the usual tribunal for judging cases brought before the *Holy See. Its jurisdiction in civil matters ended along with the temporal power of the papacy in 1870. It is the court to which appeals in nullity and other matrimonial cases are referred.

Roy, Rām Mohan (1772–1833). Hindu apologist and reformer. He was widely read in both religious and political philosophy, and from his knowledge of Muslim, Hindu, and Christian religious writings he developed into one of the foremost reformist intellectuals of early 19th-cent. India. In 1828 he founded the Brāhmo Sabha, a monotheistic form of Hinduism with no images, which stressed the One True Formless God who alone was worthy of worship. It led to the forming of the *Brahmo Samāj. Rām Mohan Roy denied the role of prophets and the exclusivist concept of Son of God, and so drew upon himself attacks not only from traditionalist Hindus but Muslims and Christians as well. He was opposed to caste, polygamy, suttee (see SATĪ), the prohibition of widow remarriage, the lack of education for ordinary people, and the seclusion of and institutionalized discrimination against women. He was one of the first to sow the seeds that flowered in the Indian National Congress.

Rām Mohan Roy, invested with the title of *Rāja* by the titular Moghul emperor Akbar II, visited Britain in 1830 to present the emperor's grievances to the British king and parliament. He died at Bristol on 27 Sept. 1833, but his influence lived on in the many subsequent Hindu progressive movements.

Ṛṣabha (Skt., 'bull'). In Jainism, the first *tīrthaṅkara of our present *avasarpiṇī*, who is also given the title *Ādinātha. An extremely popular figure in Jainism, he is credited by Jains with having founded the organization of human society, establishing *caste, law, monarchy, and agriculture. Ṛṣabha is mentioned in the Hindu **Bhāgavata-purāṇa* as a minor incarnation of *Viṣṇu, which probably reflects the popularity of his cult in the medieval period.

Ṛṣi (Skt., 'seer'). In Skt. literature, a patriarchal poet-sage. The ṛṣis are the visionary authors of the Vedic hymns (and other sacred literature) 'heard' within the silent depths of the heart and preserved in the orthodox *brahman *gotras of which they are the founders. Such ṛṣis were known as maharṣis, 'great seers', or brahmarṣis, 'priestly seers'. Of these the saptarṣis, 'the seven seers', identified with the constellation Ursa Major (their wives with the Pleiades), are particularly prominent.

According to legend the ṛṣis were men of extraordinary creativity and magical power. Much of Skt. literature is devoted to accounts of their supernatural powers (e.g. flying, creating celestial worlds) and command over nature. The term ṛṣi or maharṣi survives today in contemporary usage as a title for certain 'holy men', such as Ramana Maharṣi and Maharṣi Mahesh Yogi.

RSS (Indian political party): see BHARATYA JANATA PARTY.

Ṛta(m) (Skt., 'fixed order, rule'). In Hinduism, the sense of fundamental order and balance which obtains in the universe and must be observed and sustained through appropriate sacrifices, rituals, and behaviours. Ṛta as a word is related to *ṛtu*, the seasons, which recur with regularity out of the control of humans—or for that matter, of gods. *Mitra and *Varuṇa are invoked in the *Vedas as guardians of ṛta, but they are never regarded or described as its creator or controller. Ṛta is deeper and more fundamental than the gods, and anticipates the impersonal law of *karma, and the pervasive rule of *dharma.

Ṛtu (Skt.). A point in time: in Hinduism, it is the time appointed for ritual occasions which is determined by *astrological calculations.

Ṛtvij. The Hindu priests employed in sacrificial rituals. In origin four, they extended to seven: Hotar, Potar, Neṣṭar, Agnīdh, Praśāstar, Adhvaryu, and Brahman. By the time of **Śatapatha Brāhmaṇa* (3. 6. 2. 1), they are called 'seven *Hotṛs', Hotṛ having become the chief.

Ruaḥ ha-Qodesh (the Holy Spirit): see HOLY SPIRIT.

Rubā'iyyat (quatrains): see OMAR KHAYYAM.

Rubenstein, R. L. (Jewish commentator and writer): see HOLOCAUST.

Rublev, A. (icon-painter): see ICON.

Rubric (Lat., 'red'). A directive in printed forms of Christian *liturgy. The name derives from the fact that these instructions and guides were printed in red in the *Missal, to distinguish them from the text of the liturgy.

Ru-chia: see CONFUCIANISM.

Rudra (Skt., 'roarer', or 'the ruddy one'). A Vedic storm god. Rudra is sometimes identified with *Agni or *Indra, especially in connection with the monsoon rains. Like rainstorms, he has two aspects, one associated with fertility, healing, and welfare, the other associated with destruction, rage, and fear.

In post-Vedic times Rudra gradually becomes identified with the great god *Śiva. In the *Veda, *śiva*, 'the auspicious one', is one of Rudra's epithets. In later times, *rudra* is an epithet of Śiva, referring to his destructive aspect.

Rudra Cakrin (final king of Shambhala): see SHAMBHALA.

Ruether, Rosemary Radford. A *Roman Catholic theologian at the forefront of *feminist theology. Ruether has written extensively on the question of Christian credibility, addressing issues of *ecclesiology and its engagement with Church–world conflicts; Jewish–Christian relations; *christology; politics and religion in America; feminism and feminist theology; and God and creation. Two of her books, *Sexism and God-Talk* (1983), and *Womanguides: Readings Towards Feminist Theology* (1985) have served as key texts in her own teaching. She has been involved in writing over twenty-two books and at least 500 articles. Her other most notable works are *Gaia and God* (1992); *Women-Church* ... (1986); *New Woman, New Earth* ... (1975).

Rūḥ (spirit): see NAFS.

Rumālā (Pañjābī 'cloth'). The cloth which covers the Sikh scriptures. It measures about 1 metre by 1.25 metres, and covers the open *Ādi Granth when it is not being read.

Rūmī (mystic poet of Islam): see JALĀL AD-DĪN RŪMĪ.

Rūpa (Skt., 'form'). The means in Eastern religions through which the accidental and transitory flux of appearance achieves identifiable shape. By means of rūpa, appearance becomes an object of perception.

In Buddhism, rūpa is associated with nāma, as in *nāma-rūpa, in the analysis of human appearance, to denote corporeality; see also KHANDHA.

Rūpa Gosvāmī (disciple of Caitanya): see CAITANYA.

Rūpaloka: see LOKA (BUDDHISM).

Rural Dean. The head of a group of parishes (rural deanery).

Rushdie, Salman: see SATANIC VERSES.

Russian Orthodox Church. The *Orthodox *Patriarchate of Moscow. Although Christianity spread into Russia early (1st cent.), it was insignificant until the 10th cent. St *Vladimir of Kiev proclaimed Greek Christianity the faith of his realm in 988, and *baptism was ordered. In the 14th cent., leadership moved from Kiev to Moscow, and independence from *Greek Orthodoxy was established. *Monasticism played a key role during the Mongol invasion and rule (13th–15th cents.) especially notable being St *Sergius of Radonezh, whose Monastery of the Holy Trinity became particularly famous. After the fall of Constantinople (1453) and the defeat of the Mongols (1480), the powerful Russian state under Ivan IV ('the Terrible') enhanced Moscow's claim to be the 'Third Rome'. A close alliance (eventually subservience) between Church and State ensued, reinforced by the *Possessors controversy.

In 1727, Peter the Great abolished the patriarchate, (established in 1589) and set up a Holy Synod of twelve members nominated by the Tsar, so that the church became a department of state. Its institutional subservience was counteracted by the religious renewal initiated by a monk, Paissy, who emphasized continual prayer and obedience to a *staretz (elder). In the period of the startsi, St Seraphim of Sarov (1759–1833) was especially revered.

The Patriarchate of Moscow was re-established in 1917 by a Council which met between the February and October Revolutions: however, after the October Revolution, the Church's status in the USSR became very precarious. After an easier period during the Second World War, in which the church was encouraged to promote the patriotic efforts of the people, a determined programme of closing churches and seminaries followed under Khruschev between 1959 and 1964. The church had been guaranteed its freedom to worship by art. 124 of the Constitution of 1936, but activities and 'propaganda' outside regular worship were forbidden. *Glasnost* and *perestroika* led to a remarkable resurgence of Christian confidence, allied to the role of other Christian churches (notably the *Roman Catholic) in overthrowing Communist regimes in E. Europe.

The largest body of Russian Orthodox in America, the 'Orthodox Church in America' was declared autocephalous and independent of Moscow in 1970. There is also an independent 'Paris jurisdiction' in W. Europe, under the direct control of the *Oecumenical Patriarch.

Rustenburg Declaration (against apartheid): see DUTCH REFORMED CHURCH.

Ruten (Jap., 'drifting'). The process of rebirth or re-appearance (*saṃsāra). Ruten-no-go is the *karma which brings about rebirth.

Ruth, Book of. One of the Five Scrolls of the Hebrew *Bible. Ruth tells the story of the Moabite Ruth who stays with Naomi, her Israelite mother-in-law, and subsequently meets the prosperous farmer Boaz, a kinsman of her former husband. They make a marriage of redemption and become the ancestors of King *David.

Ruthenians or **Little Russians** (in distinction from Great Russians, those based on Moscow). Catholic Slavs. They come from SW Russia, Poland, the old Czechoslovakia, and Hungary, but are dispersed now throughout the world, especially in the USA.

Ruysbroek (Ruusbroec), Jan van, St (1293–1381). Flemish Christian mystic. Born in Ruysbroek and educated in Brussels, in 1343 he retired with two others to a hermitage at Groenendael, near Brussels, later an important centre of the *devotio moderna* (see THOMAS À KEMPIS). In the growing controversy over mysticism, he was critical of the 'Brethren of the Free Spirit', but his principal work, *The Spiritual Espousals*, was itself attacked by Gerson. His many, mainly short, writings in Flemish betray the influence of *Eckhart in particular, but develop within a clearly defined trinitarian framework. He is known as the Ecstatic Doctor; feast day, 2 Dec.

Ruzhin, Israel (1797–1850). Jewish *ḥasidic leader. A great-grandson of *Dov Baer, he succeeded to ḥasidic leadership at the age of 16. He set up court in Ruzhin, but in 1838 he was imprisoned for being instrumental in the deaths of two Jewish informers. Subsequently, he moved from town to town until he finally settled near Sadgora. Thousands of ḥasidim streamed to his court, and after his death, six of his sons established ḥasidic dynasties.

Ryō: see RITSU AND RYŌ.

Ryōbu Shintō (Jap., 'dual Shinto'). The pattern of *Shinto-Buddhist coexistence which developed in Japan. As a general term, it refers to the various forms Shinto took in the course of Shinto-Buddhist syncretism. More specifically, Ryōbu Shintō refers to the Shingon Shinto tradition under the influence of *Shingon Buddhism. The *Tendai Buddhist amalgamation with Shinto is called Sannō Ichijitsu ('Mountain-king one-truth'). In the early period of Buddhist influence on Shinto, the *kami were considered to be protectors of the Buddha's law and were enshrined in Buddhist temples. Later, the kami were felt to be in need of salvation through the help of the Buddha, and Buddhist scriptures were chanted before altars of the kami. After the middle of the Heian period, the idea developed that the kami's original nature was really the Buddha essence, and thus the kami were regarded as worthy objects of worship and adoration as manifestations of the Buddhas. The Tendai Buddhist theory that all Buddhas are really only 'one reality' (*ichi-jitsu*) was used to support the view of Tendai Shinto that the various kami are Japanese historical appearances that correspond to Buddhas—all subsumed in the 'one reality'.

Ryōkan Daigu (1758–1831). Monk of the *Sōtō school, and one of the greatest Zen poets. He sought simplicity, rejecting 'poems by poets, calligraphy by calligraphers and cooking by cooks', and preferring to play with children—the highest form of Zen was playing ball with children. Much influenced by the works of *Dōgen, he eventually settled in Gogō-an, where he lived as a hermit. It was here that most of his poetry was written, with about 1,400 poems surviving. Many express his way of acceptance which obliterates anxiety or distress. Everything is of the same nature (*śūnyatā), so every occurrence is an intriguing exploration into that nature. In his last years, Teishin became his pupil, and they communicated in poems written to and for each other. When he died, she collected his poems in an anthology, *Dew-drops on a Lotus Leaf*. Koji Nakano, *Philosophy of Honest Poverty*, made Ryōkan a cult hero in Japan in the early 1990s.

Ryū (Jap., 'dragon'). A deity which protects Buddhism. It is the equivalent of *nāga, a snake-like creature with power to cause rain.

S

Sa'adiah Gaon (882–942). Leader of Babylonian Jewry in the *geonic period. Sa'adiah grew up in Egypt, but eventually settled in Baghdād. From 921, he became involved in a struggle between the *Jerusalem *academy and the Babylonian authorities on the dating of the *festivals—in his *Sefer ha-Mo'adim*, he gives an account of the affair. In 928, he became head of the academy at *Sura. With extraordinary energy he revived the academy, but he quickly came into conflict with the *exilarch David b. Zakkai, who deposed him. Sa'adiah in his turn appointed an alternative exilarch. Ultimately the two were reconciled, but not until a bitter and long-drawn-out quarrel had taken place. Sa'adiah is remembered as a *halakhist, a philosopher, a grammarian, and a *liturgist. He wrote several halakhic books, most of which are still in manuscript. Those in print were collected and edited by J. Mueller (1897). His major philosophic work was his *Kitab al-Amanat w'al-I'tiqadat* (*The Book of Beliefs and Opinions*, 1948). The Hebrew translation by Judah ibn Tibbon, *Sefer ha-Emunot ve-ha-De'ot* (1562) was extremely influential and was drawn on by the opponents of *Maimonides.

Śabad (Pañjābī from Skt., **śabda*, 'word'). The divine word. Sikhs generally use this term for the *hymns of the *Ādi Granth. For *Nānak, it was the Satgurū's revelatory Word. Śabad also signifies the mystical 'sound' experienced at the climax of *Nāth *Yoga and the authoritative Word in the *Vedic tradition.

See also ŚABDA.

Sabaeans (a people of the Book in Islam): see MANDEANS.

Sabaoth (Heb.). 'Hosts' or 'armies', as in the biblical title 'Lord of Hosts'. It is often retained untranslated.

Sabbatai Z(e)vi (Jewish messianic claimant): see SHABBETAI ZEVI.

Sabbath (Heb., *shabbat*; Yid., *shabbas*). The seventh day of the week, on which Jews abstain from work. According to the Bible, God worked for six days in creating the world and on the seventh day he rested. Therefore he blessed the seventh day and made it holy (Genesis 2. 1–3). Re *rabbis classified thirty-nine main classes of work to be avoided (*B.Shab*. 7. 2), and required that, as it is a festive day, three meals should be eaten (*B.Shab*. 119a). It is the custom for the mother of the household to light two candles before the start of the Sabbath, and, before the special Sabbath *Kiddush is recited (*B.Pes*. 106a), the parents bless the children. The reason for two Sabbath lights is to fulfil the two commandments, 'Remember the Sabbath day' (Exodus 20. 8) and 'Observe the Sabbath day' (Deuteronomy 5. 12); and there are generally two loaves of bread to commemorate the double portion of *manna (Exodus 16. 22–6). The articles used for Sabbath ritual (candlesticks, Kiddush cups etc.) are frequently extremely artistic. Certain Sabbaths are regarded as 'Special Sabbaths', either because of the readings allocated to them, or because of their place in the calendar, especially when a Sabbath falls during a festival.

The Sabbath has been of paramount importance for Jews and Judaism: 'More than the Jews have kept the Sabbath, the Sabbath has kept the Jews' (*Aḥad ha-'Am). The Sabbath takes Jews back to the condition which God originally intended in the Garden of *Eden, but even more it anticipates the final state.

Since Christianity emerged as an interpretation of Judaism with Jesus accepted as messiah, many early 'Christians' (the name first appeared at Antioch, according to Acts 11. 26) observed the Sabbath and attended synagogue. The transfer of 'rest' from the Sabbath to Sunday began from about the 4th cent., but the reason given was to enable people to worship God, rather than to revive the abstention from work in imitation of the sabbath rest. The phrase 'the Christian sabbath' dates from about the 12th cent. The early Reformers (e.g. *Luther, *Calvin, *Cranmer, *Knox), insisted on the day of rest, though not in imitation of the Sabbath. The *Evangelical Revival reinforced strict sabbath observance in 19th cent. Britain (the Lord's Day Observance Society was founded in 1831), but the influence of Sabbatarian movements on the Continent was more limited. The erosion of 'sabbath observance' is now extensive. Seventh-Day *Adventists believe that the churches have been in error in abandoning the observance of the Sabbath on the original day and have reverted to that practice.

Sabbatical Year (Heb., *shemittah*). The year in which, according to Jewish law, the land lies fallow. According to Exodus 23. 10–11 and Deuteronomy 15. 1–11 on the Sabbatical Year, all agricultural work must be suspended and all debts remitted. The seventh Sabbatical Year (or possibly the year after the close of seven Sabbatical cycles) was designated the *Jubilee Year.

Sabbatthivādins (school of early Buddhism): see SARVĀSTIVĀDA.

Śabda (Skt., 'sound'). Indian, and especially Hindu, recognition that 'sound' has levels of meaning, and is not mere noise: (i) *sphoṭa, arising from the eternal, unmoving principle with illuminating power (*śakti); (ii) *nāda, perceptible only to a poet or *ṛṣi; (iii) *anāhata*, potential (e.g. a thought) but not expressed; (iv) *āhata*, sound of all kinds, whether humans can hear it or not. Śabda has power in its own right, not just in speech, especially in *mantras or in bells and drums: *Śiva's drum (*ḍamaru) manifests creation. Śabda-brahman is the ultimacy of sound devoid of attributes, the realization of *Brahman. Initially, this was equated with the *Vedas, but in the *Upaniṣads it is Brahman.

For the particular Sikh understanding of śabda, see ŚABAD.

Sabellianism. Christian *heresy according to which the Godhead consists of a single person, only expressing itself in three different operations. It belongs to the school of *modalist *monarchianism.

Sabīja (state of suppressed consciousness in Rājā yoga): see SAMPRAJÑĀTA.

Sab'iy(y)a (Seveners, a Muslim, Shī'a-related movement): see ISMĀ'ĪLIY(Y)A; SEVENERS.

Ṣabr (Arab.). Characteristic Muslim virtue of patient acceptance, often linked with *shukr* ('thanksgiving'), Ṣabūr is one of the *Ninety-nine Beautiful Names of *Allāh.

Saccidānanda or **sat-cit-ānanda** (Skt., 'being', + 'consciousness' + 'bliss'). In *Vedānta, a three-fold characterization of *Brahman, the Absolute, as that which is pure being, consciousness, and bliss. Sat-cit-ānanda characterizes the essence of brahman as it is grasped in human experience (*anubhava). Sat, 'being' or 'truth', emphasizes the unchanging nature of Brahman as pure unqualified existence with ontological priority over all other experience. Cit, 'consciousness', emphasizes the conscious nature of Brahman experience: Brahman is the epistemological ultimate, the self-luminous essence of knowing which is the witness of all other experience. Ānanda, 'bliss', emphasizes the sublime value of the experience of Brahman. Brahman is the axiological ultimate, the highest and most fulfilling human experience, the goal of human experience. However, sat, cit, and ānanda are not to be understood as qualities attributed to brahman which is *nirguṇa, beyond all relative qualification. Rather sat, cit, and ānanda are each the very essence of Brahman known through the experience of ecstasy.

Sach Khaṇḍ. The Sikh 'realm of truth', the fifth and final stage of spiritual ascent. It is the abode of the One without form, where the believer enters into union with God, and as such, the term can sometimes be a synonym for 'heaven'.

Sacrament. Any of certain solemn religious acts, usually associated with Christianity. The Lat., *sacramentum* (in secular usage, 'oath'), acquired this technical sense by its use to translate the Gk., *mystērion*, in the Latin New Testament. The exact reference has varied. *Augustine defined it as the 'visible form of invisible *grace', picked up in the *Anglican *catechism as 'an outward and visible sign of an inward and spiritual grace . . . ordained by *Christ himself'. He applied it to formulae such as the *creed and *Lord's Prayer; and this wide application was maintained into the Middle Ages. However, by the time of *Peter Lombard, seven particular sacraments have become traditional and are enumerated: *baptism, *confirmation, the *eucharist, *penance, extreme *unction, *orders, and *marriage; in E. Christianity, they retain their Gk. names, i.e. *baptisma, chrism, koinōnia* (as well as *eucharistia*), *metanoia, euchelaion, hierosunē, gamos*.

The traditional Catholic theology of the sacraments holds that they are channels of God's grace to the recipient. The right 'matter' (bread and wine for the eucharist, etc.), the right 'form', and the right *intention are essential for the sacrament to be 'valid'. In addition, the recipient must be in a proper state of faith and repentance for it to be 'efficacious'.

In Anglican tradition (Art. 25 of the *Thirty-Nine Articles) baptism and the eucharist are distinguished as having been ordained by Christ (i.e. Dominical sacraments), from the other five so-called sacraments. *Protestant theology generally speaks of these two sacraments only.

'Blessed Sacrament' (or 'Sacrament of the altar') refers specifically to the eucharist, or the bread and wine consecrated at it.

The term 'sacrament' is then applied to actions and substances in other religions where fundamental meaning is expressed through non-verbal languages (even if accompanied by words). The term is thus commonly applied to the Hindu *saṃskāras.

See Index, Sacraments.

Sacramentals. In Christianity, acts or objects resembling (but less important than) the *sacraments. Their number is not agreed, but they include the sign of the cross, grace at meals, *stations of the cross, *litanies, the *angelus, *rosary, etc.

Sacrament of the present moment (realization of God in all circumstances): see CAUSSADE, J. P. DE.

Sacred and profane. A distinction in human experience of the world which to *Durkheim seemed to be the essence of religion, and from which he derived his definition of religion:

A religion is a unified system of beliefs and practices relative to sacred things, that is to say, things set apart and forbidden—beliefs and practices which unite into one single moral community called a Church, all those who adhere to them. The second element which thus finds a place in our definition is no less essential than the first; for by showing that the idea of religion is inseparable from that of the Church, it makes it clear that religion should be an eminently collective thing. (*The Elementary Forms of the Religious Life* (1912; tr. 1961), 52, 62 f.)

The human inclination to organize the experienced world in terms of this distinction (between sacred and profane) was taken much further in the development of structuralism, especially by *Lévi-Strauss, since it was argued that the human mind is under an innate and universal obligation to perceive binary oppositions (up/down, male/female, night/day, etc.), not just in the case of the sacred and the profane, but in general. However, these classifications are bound to leave anomalous or ambiguous cases, so that religion is better understood by attending, not only to the classification systems, but also to the ways in which the anomalous is dealt with, since this will disclose why communities find some things abhorrent and others acceptable. This methodology was applied influentially by Mary Douglas (*Purity and Danger*, 1966), showing that 'dirt' as a concept leads to pollution rules which are not primarily concerned with hygiene. The binary opposition between wholeness (holiness) and imperfection (uncleanness) underlies the biblical laws concerning holiness: to be wholly attached to God brings blessing, to be removed from God brings a curse. Creatures designated as unclean according to the food laws are those which are anomalous or on a borderline between categories (e.g. if they are not clearly domesticated or wild, or belonging to air or sea). In *Implicit Meanings* (1975) she argued further that pollution beliefs (understood in this way) serve a social function, because they protect society at its most vulnerable points, where ambiguity would erode or undermine social structure.

Sacred cities, seven. Places where Hindus can attain *ānanda (bliss): (i) *Ayodhyā; (ii) *Mathurā; (iii) Gayā (*Bodhgaya); (iv) *Kāśī (Vārānasī, Benares); (v) *Kāñci; (vi) Avantikā (Ujjain); (vii) Dvārakā.

Sacred cow (in Hinduism): see GO.

Sacred Heart. The physical heart of Jesus as a subject of Catholic devotion. The devotion has been officially defined only since the 18th cent., though it can be traced back to the mystics of the Middle Ages (e.g. *Bonaventura) and ultimately to meditation on Jesus' wounds at his crucifixion. The feast is observed on the Friday of the week after *Corpus Christi.

Sacred rivers, seven. Among Hindus, all water is sacred, and rivers especially so; but seven rivers are particularly revered: *Gaṅgā (Ganges), Yamuna, Godavari, Sarasvatī, Narmada, Sindhu, Kaveri.

Sacred thread (rite in Hinduism through which a boy makes the transition to student life, i.e. brahmacarya): see UPANAYANA.

Sacrifice (Lat., 'that which is made sacred'). The offering of something, animate or inanimate, in a *ritual procedure which establishes, or mobilizes, a relationship of mutuality between the one who sacrifices (whether individual or group) and the recipient—who may be human but more often is of another order, e.g. God or spirit. Sacrifice pervades virtually all religions, but it is extremely difficult to say precisely what the meanings of sacrifice are —perhaps because the meanings are so many. Sacrifice is clearly much more than technique: it involves drama, ritual, and action, transforming whatever it is that is sacrificed beyond its mundane role: in general, nothing that is sacrificed has intrinsic worth or holiness before it is set apart; it is the sacrifice that gives it added value. Sacrifice has been understood as expiation of fault or sin; as propitiation of an angry deity; as *apotropaic (turning away punishment, disaster, etc.); as purgation; as an expression of gratitude; as substitutionary (offering to God a substitute for what is rightly his, e.g. the first-born); as commensal, establishing union with God or with others in a community; as *do ut des* ('I give in order that you may give', an offering in order to evoke a gift in return); as maintaining cosmic order (especially in Hindu sacrifices); as celebration; as a means of coping with violence in a community; as catharsis; as a surrogate offering at the level of power and its distribution.

Amongst many particular theories, that of H. Hubert and M. Mauss, *Sacrifice, Its Nature and Function* (1898), has been influential. The purpose of sacrifice can be discerned, not in the analysis of beliefs, but in the social function served by sacrifice, i.e. the connection made between the *sacred and profane worlds. Through sacrifice they interpenetrate and yet remain distinct, thereby allowing (or requiring) self-interest to be subordinated to the service of the social group. The methodology was extended by Mauss in the even more influential *The Gift* (1924; Eng. tr. 1954): gift-giving practices (especially potlátch: see ALMSGIVING), including extravagant feasts, seem at first to work against self-interest, but they establish social bonding and stability.

See Index, Sacrifice.

Judaism The general Heb. term, *qorbān*, has been taken to mean 'bringing close', sc., of humans and God. In ancient Israel, sacrifices were of various kinds. *Sin-offerings (*ḥatat*) could be made by individuals, or collectively at the sacred festivals, and were offered in propitiation for sin; guilt offerings (*asham*) were a particular kind of sin-offering, to be made when, e.g., someone had defrauded another or when lepers were cleansed. Dedicatory offerings expressed dedication to God. Burnt offerings (*'olah*) were offered twice daily in the *Jerusalem *Temple as part of the regular ritual, with two additional lambs offered each *Sabbath. Besides animal sacrifices, offerings of grain or loaves (meal offerings) accompanied burnt offerings and a libation was also poured out. In addition there were extra free-will offerings and peace offerings at *Shavu'ot. Full details of the Temple ritual are preserved in the *Talmud, tractates *Tamid* and *Zevaḥim*. After the Temple was destroyed by the Romans on 9 *Av, 70 CE, the sacrificial system came to an end. Prayer took its place.

Christianity Ideas of sacrifice are attached primarily to Jesus' death, probably going back to his own words at least at the *Last Supper. The writer to the *Hebrews gives an elaborate treatment of Christ's once-for-all sacrifice as superior to the Old Testament cult. The *fathers took up the biblical theme, stressing that Christ was a voluntary victim; a victim of infinite value; and also himself the *priest. (See also ATONEMENT.)

Islam The Arabic words *aḍḥā*, *dhabaḥa*, and *naḥara* refer to the slaughter of animals; *qurbān* (cf. Heb., *qorbān*) comes from the verb meaning 'to draw near' and implies an offering without slaughter. The major Muslim sacrifice occurs at al-*'Īd al-Aḍḥā ('the feast of the sacrifice', also known as 'Īd al-Kabīr, 'the great feast') which commemorates the offering by Ibrāhīm (*Abraham) of a ram instead of his son. In addition, sacrifice may be performed at any time with the intention of drawing closer to God, and is particularly expected when a child is born (*al-'aqīqah*).

Hinduism Sacrifice (*yajña*) is deeply involved among Hindus in the maintenance of cosmic order, and although it obviously has reference to the gods, it is distinct from the approach to God in *pūjā (worship). In the early *Vedic age, sacrifice was relatively simple, a way of bringing the power inherent in the natural order to bear in relevant ways. Hence there were also sacrifices at regular moments, such as morning and evening, new and full moon, etc. For these ceremonies, the *gṛhapati* (householder) is usually the officiant, though he could call on a *purohita if necessary. These offerings are known as *gṛhyakarmāṇi*, and are usually performed by the casting of milk, *ghī* (*ghṛta), grain, etc., into the fire. In the later Vedic period, sacrifices became elaborately detailed, and a distinction was made between *gṛhya* sacrifices (which rested on *smārta, i.e. oral tradition and memory) and śrauta sacrifices (those based on *śruti). The **Sāma Veda* and **Yajur Veda* were composed for the purposes of sacrifice, and the *Brāhmaṇas were compiled with a major purpose of explaining the meaning of the sacrifices. Whereas in the earlier sacrifices there had been a strong element of *do ut des* (see introductory paragraph), there now developed a sense that the gods were dependent on sacrifices and to an extent under the control of humans (or more specifically, of priests). The śrauta sacrifices are traditionally divided into two groups of seven, Haviryajñas (including *Agnihotra, animal sacrifices, and *Piṇḍapitṛyajña) and Somayajñas. Four groups of priests were required (headed by four chief priests): (i) Hotṛ, who invokes the gods by reciting verses from the **Ṛg Veda*; (ii) Udgātṛ, the chanter of *sāmans*; (iii) Adhvaryu, the performer of the sacrifice; (iv) the *brahman, who supervises the whole procedure, making sure that no errors are made. Śrauta sacrifices also became prohibitively expensive, and only vestigial remains of them survive in practice, confined to symbolic acts like the pouring of a glass of water or the giving of a handful of rice. Occasionally, a larger sacrifice is organized (e.g. against the menace of nuclear war in 1957), but only a few brahmans now maintain the daily ritual and study which underlie the larger occasions.

Sacrilege (Lat., the theft of sacred objects). The violent, contemptuous, or disrespectful treatment of persons or objects associated with religious reverence or dedicated to God. In Judaism, the violation of sacred things is a deep offence. In Christianity, the notion of sacrilege is extended to include receiving the *sacraments unworthily or in a state of *mortal sin.

Sadācāra (right behaviour in Hinduism): see HERESY (E. religions).

Ṣadaqa (Arab.). Almsgiving, voluntary charity. The word is sometimes used as a synonym of *zakāt, the official alms tax (as in Qur'ān 9. 58, 104); but ṣadaqa (pl. ṣadaqāt) is considered a pious duty, the details of which are not laid down.

Saddhā (faith): see ŚRADDHĀ.

Saddharmapuṇḍarīka sūtra (early Mahāyāna sūtra): see LOTUS SŪTRA.

Sadducees. Jewish sect of the second *Temple period. The Sadducees were made up of the more affluent members of the population. As Temple *priests, they dominated Temple worship and formed a large proportion of *Sanhedrin members. The name Sadducee is perhaps derived from King *Solomon's *high priest *Zadok. They stood in opposition to the *Pharisees in that they rejected the *oral law and only accepted the supreme authority of the written *Torah. After the destruction of the Temple in 70 CE, the Sadducees ceased to exist.

Sādhaka (Skt.). In a general sense the practitioner of a spiritual path (*sādhana), though the term has a more precise technical meaning in the *Āgamas and *Tantras as one who has undergone a certain kind of initiation (*dīkṣa) and who follows a certain path. The sādhaka's practice comprises *mantra repetition (*japa), *visualization (*dhyāna) of his chosen deity (*iṣṭadevatā), and observance of certain daily rites. After repeated practice he becomes one with his *mantra and deity, and so gains power.

Sādhana (Skt., √*sādh*, 'complete'). The spiritual practice of Hindu and Buddhist *Tantrism; a path to liberation (*mokṣa) and power (siddhi/ *iddhi) distinct from orthodox Vedic practice, which aims to unite the male–female polarity within the body, or to merge the individual self (*jivātman) with the highest self (*paramātman). Tantric sādhana consists of worship (*pūjā) and *yoga. The term has also been linked to God-devoted practices, not much more austere or *ascetic than self-denial and voluntary suffering.

Sādhāran Brahmo Samāj (reforming Hindu movement): see SEN, KESHUB CHUNDER; BRAHMO SAMĀJ.

Sādh saṅgat (Pañjābī, 'saintly association'). Sikh congregation. The term refers generally to the congregation gathered for worship in the *gurdwārā, and strictly speaking to those who meditate upon God's name (*nām).

Sādhu (Skt., √*sādh*, 'accomplish'). One who has controlled his senses, a Hindu holy person who has renounced the world, and seeks Brahman or God. The female equivalent is sādhvī. They are also known as *sant or 'saint'. Their lifestyles and practices are extremely diverse.

In its most general sense, a sādhu is one who follows a *sādhana (path): while he is still on the path, he is known as sādhaka; when he reaches the goal, he becomes a *siddha.

Sadmaya-kośa. The sheath of *sat (Being) which surrounds and sustains *ātman. In Hinduism, the approach to the realization of *Brahman requires this sheath, since otherwise it could not be imagined. But without this sheath, ātman is one with Brahman.

Ṣafavids. Persian dynasty which ruled 1501–1732 (AH 907–1145). It derived from Shaykh Isḥāq Ṣafī al-Dīn (d. 1334 (AH 735)), who was the leader of a *Sūfī order named after him, the Ṣafavis—hence the name of the dynasty. The order became associated with the *Ithnā 'Ashariy(y)a Shi'as (Twelvers), and for that reason the Turkish adherents wore a red hat with twelve tassles on it, and became known as Qizīl Bash, 'red hats'.

Saffron robe (of Buddhist bhikṣus): see HABIT, RELIGIOUS; MONASTICISM (Buddhism).

Sagdid (Zoroastrian death ritual): see DAXMA.

Sages (Heb., *hakhamim*, sing., *hakham*). Jewish scholars and biblical interpreters, often translated as 'the Wise'. The sages were the active leaders and teachers of the Jewish religion from the beginning of the second *Temple period until the Arabian conquest of the East. They are also known as Ḥazal, an acronym for *Ḥakhameynu zikhronam li-berakhah*, 'our sages of blessed memory'.

Sagga (Pāli, derived from Skt., *svarga*, 'heaven, the next world'). In Buddhism, the pleasant conditions of reappearance (*punabbhāva) which result from a life of moral, religious living.

According to the Pāli canonical texts, sagga is not 'heaven' in spatial terms, in keeping with the early Buddhist non-cosmographical conceptions. It is described as a condition or state of birth: the beings reborn into heavenly conditions are described as *devas (gods) and they are in the same spatial dimension as are human beings. The names of the different heavens, given as fourteen (consisting of the six lower heavens and the eight higher heavens) do not describe separate mini-worlds or compartments in space, but only different conditions of spiritual attainments by which alone they come to be distinguished.

Sagi Nahor (Kabbalist): see ISAAC THE BLIND.

Saguṇa-Brahman. 'Brahman with qualities', in contrast to *nirguṇa-Brahman. In the perspective of *Advaita, the latter is the highest, essential nature of Brahman, but in order that Brahman may become knowable, it manifests itself with qualities (*guṇa, upādhi), though these are always superimposed on Brahman and do not have ontological independence. In personified form, saguṇa-Brahman becomes *Īśvara, God, and by application *iṣṭa-devatā, the personal god of a devotee.

Ṣaḥāba. The Companions of the Prophet *Muḥammad. They have high status in Islam, because of their role in establishing *ḥadīth—in two senses: (i) their own sayings and actions are recorded; and (ii) they were the witnesses of what Muḥammad said and did.

Sahaj (Pañjābī, 'easy'). Ultimate, blissful state experienced by the spiritually disciplined. Gurū *Nānak frequently used 'sahaj', a term employed by the *Nāth yogīs, for the inexpressible mystical union reached through devoted *nām simaran.

Sahaja (Skt., 'innate'). In Buddhist *Tantrism and the *Vaiṣṇava *Sahajīyā cult, the absolute which exists within the body, the essence of everything, the unmoving, ineffable state beyond thought construction (*vikalpa) and beyond sin (*pāpa) and merit (*puṇya). It is therefore a synonym for *nirvāna, *mahā sukha (great bliss), and the perfected essential body (*svabhāvika kāyā*). The Tibetan is *Lhan.cig.-skyes.pa.*

Sahajdhārī (Pañjābī, 'gradual adopter'). A Sikh who accepts the *Gurūs' teachings without observing the *five Ks or taking amrit (as an *amritdhārī).

Sahajīyā (Skt., from *sahaja). A sect of *Tantrism preponderant in Bengal, whose practice involved ritual sexual intercourse (*maithuna). The origins of the sect are in the Sahaja-*yāna of the Buddhist *Siddhas (8th–12th cents. CE).

The Vaiṣṇava Sahajiyas adopted the theology of the Gauḍiya Vaiṣṇavas who maintained that the soul is both identical with and distinct from *Kṛṣṇa or *Rādhā-Kṛṣṇa. This doctrine is known as unthinkable difference-in-identity (*acintya bedhābheda*). The purpose of Sahajīyā ritual sex is to transform desire (*kāma) into pure love (*prema). Ritual sex was performed with a *parakīya* woman, unmarried or 'belonging to another'. As in other *Tantric sexual rites, semen is not ejaculated but directed 'upwards' through the suṣumṇa *nāḍī to the *sahasrāra padma where the bliss of Rādhā and Kṛṣṇa is enjoyed. For a further development, see BĀUL.

Sahasrāra (Skt., 'thousand'). The *lotus (*padma*) or circle (*cakra) which exists at or above the crown of the head, at the top of the suṣumnā *nādī in the *Tantric esoteric anatomy of the *subtle body. It is the place where *Śiva and *Śakti are united enjoying perpetual bliss. The sahasrāra is attained through the yoga of *Kuṇḍalinī.

Sāhib (Pañjābī, 'sir', from Arabic, 'lord, master'). A title appended to names of religious significance for Sikhs. In the *Ādi Granth, God is called Sāhib. As it is regarded as the living voice of the *Gurū, the Ādi Granth is usually called the Gurū Granth Sāhib. Individual compositions, such as *Japjī and *Anand, are also given this title, as are famous *gurdwārās and places of religious importance (e.g. *Harimandir Sāhib, *Anaṇḍpur Sāhib).

Sāhibzāde (Urdū, Pañjābī, 'Master's sons'). Gurū *Gobind Siṅgh's four sons, Ajīt, Jujhār, Zorāwar, and Fateh. Ranging in age from 18 to 7 years, all died at Mughal hands in Dec. 1704 CE, and are thus *martyrs.

Ṣaḥīḥ (Arab., 'sound'). Title (al-Ṣaḥīḥ) given to the two major collections of *ḥadīth, of *al-Bukhārī and *Muslim.

Sahl al-Tustarī, Abū Muḥammad (818–96 (AH 203–83)). *Sunnī theologian and mystic, of strict and ascetic standards. He wrote nothing, but his 'thousand sayings' were collected and edited by his pupil, Muḥammad ibn Sālim, and formed the basis for a theological school, the Sālimīya. An eclectic in his views, he agreed with *al-Ash'arī that a Muslim is anyone who prays facing the *qibla (see IMĀN), but he accepted the Shī'a claim of *jafr. Faith must nevertheless be demonstrated in works ('to love is to obey'), while the true lover of God is constantly detaching himself from the world.

Sai Baba. 1. Hindu spiritual guide and miracle (*siddha/*iddhi) worker. He died in 1918, and was recognized as one who had direct experience of reality and truth—so much so that many regard him as a manifestation (*avatāra) of God. He is known as Sai Baba of Shirdi to differentiate him from the following.

2. Sai Baba (b. 1926) of the *āśrama Prasanti Nilayam, who is believed by his followers (now worldwide) to be a reincarnation of the first Sai

Baba. He too is well-known for his miraculous powers.

Saichō (also known from his posthumous name as Dengyō Daishi, 767–822). Japanese Buddhist monk and founder of *Tendai. Together with *Kūkai, he was one of the two leading figures in the Heian ('peace and tranquillity') period in Japan. In 804, he went to China, to study *T'ien-t'ai, and to gain sanction for the new foundation on Mount Hiei. He did not intend to introduce, still less found, a new school, and for some time he applied himself to esoteric Buddhism as much as to T'ien-t'ai. When he returned to Japan in 805, he endorsed both as a kind of middle way between the Nara sects, *Sanron and *Hossō. His endeavours to incorporate esoteric Buddhism were overshadowed by the brilliance of *Kūkai, and after an early friendship, relations between the two deteriorated. The incorporation of esoteric Buddhism was accomplished by Saichō's disciples, Enchin and *Ennin. Saichō spent the last six years of his life trying to establish Tendai as the true *Mahāyāna, and as the 'protector of the nation'.

During this last period, Saichō composed his major works (including *Shugo-kokkai-shō* (Treatise on the Protection of the State), *Hokke-shūku* (Superlative Passages of the Lotus Sūtra), and *Kenkai-ron* (Treatise on the Precepts), in which he argued that Tendai was superior to other forms of Buddhism. He regarded his time as the period of Spurious Dharma (*zōmatsu*), and that only in Tendai would the people find guidance. A complex of many temples was established on Mount Hiei, but most (along with the major temple) were destroyed in 1571/2. Enryaku-ji was rebuilt on the mountain-top in the 17th cent. The main hall (Konpo-Chudo, 1643) is the third largest wood building in Japan.

Said Nursi (1873–1960). An influential religious scholar who led the defence of orthodox Islam against the forces of secularism in Turkey. His ambitious project for establishing an Islamic University to reconcile the religious sciences with modern science was thwarted by the government and never realized. Despite official opposition (continual harassment and imprisonment), he produced his greatest work *Risāla-i-Nūr* (The Treatise of Light), said to have been written after his Divine Illumination, an attempt to demonstrate the spiritual dimension of the *Qur'ān to an age under the sway of scepticism and materialism. Since the recent resurgence of Islam in Turkey, Said Nursi's *Risāḷa-i-Nūr* has played a prominent role in the Islamic revival.

Saigō Takamori (Japanese military leader): see MEIJI.

Saikōkū (Japanese centre): see PILGRIMAGE.

Sain Sāhib (Sikh reformer): see SIKHISM.

Saint (Lat., *sanctus*, 'holy'). The title is given to exemplary Christians who are venerated and invoked in prayer—as also to the *angels *Raphael, *Gabriel, and *Michael. (For individual saints, see under name, and see also the Index under Saints.) In the New Testament the word 'saint' is synonymous with 'Christian'. The first Christians to receive special veneration were *martyrs, beginning with *Polycarp whose followers treasured his *relics and celebrated the 'birthday' of his martyrdom. From the 4th cent., devotion to the saints increased and included 'confessors' (those who suffered but did not die in persecutions) and ascetics. From the 6th cent. onward, *diptychs of martyrs and confessors began to have a place in the liturgy, and from the 8th cent. the lives of saints were read at *matins. At an early date saints were also believed to effect *miracles after their death. At the *Reformation the cult of saints was rejected.

The modern cult of the saints in the Roman Catholic Church is regulated by *canon law, which recommends the veneration of the saints and especially of *Mary. The attitude of Eastern churches is akin to that of Rome. See also CANONIZATION; PATRON SAINT. Major saints are commemorated on particular feast days; the commemoration of All Saints occurs on 1 Nov.

In Islam, there is a veneration of holy people who are often referred to in English as 'saints'. The 'friends of God' (*walī) are important (cf. Qur'ān 10. 63), as are the pure and blessed ones (*ṭāhir*) and many *Sūfī teachers. The veneration of saints and of their tombs, while widely popular, is resisted by conservative Muslims. For a remote resemblance in Judaism, see ZADDIK. 'Saint' is then used widely of holy and revered persons in all religions: see e.g. NĀYAṆMĀRS; SANT TRADITION.

Saint-Cyran, Abbé de (French Augustinian monk): see JANSENISM.

Śaiva: see ŚAIVISM.

Śaiva-Āgama. Authoritative texts of *Śaivism, the earliest being written between 400–800 CE. The texts deal with Śaiva liturgy which involves *nyāsa, *mudrā, *mantra, the construction of *yantras or *maṇḍalas and *visualization (*dhyāna), the construction of shrines and *temples, and *festivals. Interest in philosophy is somewhat limited and is mainly concerned with speculation on the power of speech and the *tattvas. Initiation (*dīkṣā) is important in the texts. The Āgamas theoretically follow a fourfold structure of *jñāna, *yoga, *kriya*, and *carya padas*, though this pattern is seldom strictly adhered to.

Śaiva Siddhānta. A dualistic school of *Śaivism prevalent in S. India. The canon of this school is made up of the twenty-eight *dualist *Śaiva-Āgamas and Upāgamas, though, unlike in *Kashmir Śaivism, the authority of the *Vedas is also acknowledged. Two currents can be discerned in the school, the one gnostic, the other devotional.

The gnostic tradition emphasized knowledge (*jñāna) and used Skt. as its medium of expression. Its dualist theology is summarized in the *Tattvaprakāśa* (Light on the Tattvas) of Bhojadeva (*c.*11th cent.) and expounded in *Aghorasiva's commentaries on dualist Āgamas.

The devotional tradition, which used Tamil as a medium of expression, emphasized *bhakti and surrender to the Lord *Śiva. It revered the twenty-eight dualist Āgamas, but equally important if not more so was the devotional Tamil poetry of the *Nāyaṉmārs (4th–9th cents. CE).

The most important theological text of the school is the Tamil *Civañāṉapotam* (Skt., *Śivajñānabodha*) by Meykaṇṭatēvar (Skt., Meykaṇḍadeva) (*c.*1220 CE) which is said to be the quintessence of the Vedas and Āgamas.

Śaivism. One of the major theistic traditions of medieval Hinduism, worshipping *Śiva or one of his forms or symbols such as the *liṅga. Although difficult to generalize about, because of its diversity, Śaivism tends to be more ascetic than *Vaiṣṇavism. The origins of Śaivism are probably non-Vedic and its roots may lie in the pre-Aryan culture of the Indus Valley, where seals have been found depicting an ithyphallic, horned god, in a yogic posture and surrounded by animals. This may be a precursor of Śiva who is lord of yogis and animals. However, Śaiva literature only flourished with the Śaiva Purāṇas (4th–9th cents. CE) which are mainly concerned with mythology, and the *Śaiva-Āgamas, which are primarily concerned with initiation, ritual, *yoga, *mantra, and temple-building.

Various Śaiva sects developed, ranging from those who adhered to *Smārta orthodoxy to those who flouted it. The following sects can be distinguished: (i) *Pāśupatas, the earliest Śaiva sect, along with a subsect, the Lakulīśa Pāśupata, who took an 'animal' vow (*vrata) of asceticism, bathing in ashes, and engaging in anti-social behaviour; (ii) *Kāpālikas, cremation-ground dwellers who carried a skull and performed antinomian practices; (iii) Kālāmukhas, ascetics closely associated with the Pāśupata; (iv) Vīraśaivas or *Liṅgāyats, who may have developed out of the Kālāmukhas, and who worshipped Śiva in the form of the liṅga; (v) *Kashmir Śaivism or *Trika, so called because of its threefold category of God (Śiva), energy (*śakti), and individual (*aṇu); (vi) *Śaiva Siddhānta, a dualist system which became *bhakti-oriented with the Tamil bhakti poets, the *Nāyanṃārs; (vii) Smārta, orthodox Śaivism which adhered to the *varnāśrama-dharma advocated in the *smṛti literature, such as the law books of *Manu and Kalpa Sūtras, and regarded Śiva as one of the five central deities to be worshipped (*pañcayatana-pūja*); and (viii) *Nātha or Kanphata yogis, a sect traditionally founded by *Gorakhnātha, combining Pāśupata Śaivism with Tantric and *Hatha yoga.

Śaivism spread throughout India: Trika in Kashmir, Śaiva Siddhānta in the Tamil-speaking south, Vīraśaiva in the Kannada-speaking south, and Pāśupata in Gujarat. Today Śaivism is especially prevalent in Madras State. Śaiva ascetics are distinguished by their long matted hair, sometimes piled on top of their heads, three horizontal marks smeared on the forehead, the trident which they carry, and the ashes in which they are often covered. Śaiva temples and pilgrimage sites are found throughout India from the Amarnāth cave in Kashmir where there is an ice liṅga, to the Viśvanāth temple at Vārānasi and the Rauleswaram temple at the southernmost tip of India.

Saiyid (Arab., 'Lord, owner'). A title of respect, and in particular, the title/name of a direct descendant of *Muḥammad through his daughter *Fāṭima and *Alī ibn Abī Ṭālib.

Sajjāda (Arab., *sajada*, 'bow down', 'worship'). The prayer mat on which *ṣalāt is performed. The design in the carpet is not symmetrical, but leads to a point on one of the short sides which is placed in the direction of the *qibla. The word underlies *masjid*, mosque, the place of prostration.

Sakadāgāmin (Pāli; Skt., *sakṛdāgāmin*). A 'Once-Returner': in Buddhism, one of the Four Noble Persons (*ariya-puggala*), who is distinguished by having only one more rebirth to experience before gaining enlightenment.

Śākhā (Skt., 'branch'). A branch or school of the *Veda, especially any one of the particular recensions of one of the four *Vedic collections (*saṁhitās) as represented by a brahmanic lineage (*caraṇa*) entrusted with its preservation. According to Śaunaka there are five śākhās of the Ṛg Veda Saṁhitā (namely, Śākala, Bāśkala, Āśvalāyana, Śānkhāyana, and Māṇḍukāyana). Of these five, only the Śākala śākhā is extant.

Sākhī (Pañjābī, 'witness'). A section of a *janam-sākhī narrative. The term is also used for the couplets (otherwise called *dohā* or *śalok) of *Kabīr.

Sakīna (peace from God): see SHEKHINAH.

Sakka. Buddhist form of *Indra, who dwells in the Tāvatiṃsa heaven: see COSMOLOGY (Buddhist).

Sakkāya-diṭṭhi. 'Personality Belief': in Buddhism a basic misconception concerning the nature of personal identity in relation to the five aggregates (*skandhas). Sakkāya-diṭṭhi is the first of the 'Ten Fetters' (*saṃyojana). For the error, see also PUDGALAVĀDINS.

Śakra (courage): see ĀDITYAS.

Sakṛdāgāmin: see SAKADĀGĀMIN.

Śakti (Skt., 'power'). Creative power in Hinduism manifested as Goddess and consort of *Śiva. She is venerated under many aspects (e.g. each *cakra is governed by a particularization of Śakti) and many names (e.g. *Durgā, *Kālī, *Ambā). Devotion to Śakti is thus extremely diverse: see ŚĀKTISM. As the creative power, able to bring things into appearance, Śakti resembles *māyā; for that reason, goddesses in their role as śakti are often referred to as Māyā.

See Index, Śakti.

Śāktism (Skt., *śakti*, 'power'). A Hindu tradition or current of thought with *śakti, divine female power, as the focus of its worship. This power is either the supreme being conceived as female or a consort of one of the Hindu gods.

The origins of Śaktism as Goddess worship can probably be traced to the Indus Valley culture, and iconographical evidence dates back to the pre-Christian era. The goddess *Durgā appears as a powerful deity in the sixth book of the **Mahābhārata* and the fifth book of the **Viṣṇu *Purāṇa* (5th cent. CE), but it is in the Devīmāhātmya portion of **Mārkaṇḍeya Purāṇa* (7th cent. CE) that the Goddess (*Devī) is worshipped as supreme. In texts called *Tantras and Śākta *Upaniṣads we find a developed Tantric form of worship of the Goddess as Śakti.

The Śākta Tantras are closely allied to monistic or *Kashmir Śaivism and adhere to a nondual theology with either Śakti or the union of Śiva and Śakti as absolute. Most Śākta Tantras declare themselves to be of the *Kaula or *Kula school and can be divided into two main categories: (i) the *Śrī Kula*, which advocates worship of the benign and beautiful goddess *Śrī/ Lakṣmī as Tripurāsundarī; and (ii) the *Kālī Kula*, which advocates worship of the fierce goddess *Kālī. A smaller third category advocates worship of the Goddess *Tārā. The Śākta *sādhaka (practitioner) will follow one or other cult prescribed for him by the *guru according to his personality.

Śaktism developed, and is still practised principally, in Bengal and Assam, though worship of the goddesses at village level is found throughout India, especially in the south. Śaktism exalts the position of women by regarding them as incarnations of the Goddess; it is a mistake, however, to regard Śaktism as a force for improving the social conditions of women or low castes. Equality is only in ritual, and the role of woman is to act as a partner (śakti or *dūtī*) for the male sādhaka.

See Index, Śakti.

Śakuni. In the **Mahābhārata*, the evil maternal uncle of the *Kauravas, a master gambler, said to be an incarnation of the demon Dvāpara, named for a throw of dice. On behalf of Duryodhana, he plays a dice game against Yudhiṣṭhira, which he wins by trickery. The game leads to the great *Kurukṣetra war, in which Śakuni fights on the Kaurava side, and is killed by the *Pāṇḍava Sahadeva.

Śakuntalā. The title character of the play *Abhijñānaśakuntala* (Śakuntala Recognized), by the Indian poet and playwright *Kālidāsa, probably of the Gupta period (3rd cent. CE). The play is often called simply *Śakuntalā*. The story is taken from the first book of the **Mahābhārata*.

Sakya (Sa.skya, 'Grey Earth'). One of the four principal schools of Tibetan Buddhism, taking its name from the Grey Earth monastery founded by Konchok Gyalpo in 1073 CE. Konchok Gyalpo had been a *Nyingma follower until meeting the traveller, translator, and *yogin Drokmi, from whom he learnt the Hevajra cycle of *tantras and the system known as Lam Drey (lam.'bras, 'The Way and its Fruit'), which is attributed to the Indian *Siddha Virupa. Konchok Gyalpo's son Kunga Nyingpo formally systematized the Sakya teachings from the writings of Drokmi, with Lam Drey at the centre relating tantra to *sūtra and offering enlightenment in a single lifetime. The Sakya school has always hosted a wide variety of views, producing two subsects, the Ngor (15th cent.) and the Tshar (16th cent.). The Ngor and the Tshar appoint their own heads on a merit basis. A *tulku system is recognized in the Sakya, but it is not always connected with the transmission of major posts.

Sākyamuni (Pāli), **Śākyamuni** (Skt., '*muni of the Sākyas'). A title of the *Buddha denoting that he stemmed from the Śākya tribe which inhabited a region of present-day Nepal.

Sakyapa (an order in Tibetan Buddhism): see ’PHAGS-PA.

Saladin: see SALĀḤ UD-DĪN.

Salaf al-Ṣāliḥīn (virtuous/exemplary ancestors): see SALAFIY(Y)A.

Salafiy(y)a. Movement founded by Jamal al-Din *al-Afghānī and Muḥammad *ʿAbduh, which sought to reconcile Islam with the advances of Western science and rationality. It received its name from the phrase *salaf al-ṣāliḥīn*, ‘the virtuous ancestors’, but it was not regarded by its opponents as preserving the essence of the past, but rather as subverting it.

In contrast, the same word is now used to translate *‘fundamentalism’.

Salāḥ ud-Dīn or **Saladin** (1138–93 (AH 532–89)). A Kurdish soldier who recaptured *Jerusalem from the *crusaders. By 1187 (AH 583) he had captured Jerusalem, but he did not succeed in expelling them from their last stronghold in Tyre. Salāḥ ud-Dīn earned a reputation for chivalry which long outlasted his political empire.

Salām (Arab.). Peace, used in greeting. The Hebrew equivalent is *shālōm.

Ṣalāt. The ritual worship of the Muslim community.

One of the *five pillars of the faith, it is frequently mentioned in the *Qur’ān as a duty. Believers are ‘those who perform the Ṣalāt and give the *Zakāt (alms)’. Times (*mīqāt*) and regulations for ṣalāt are given in detail in the *ḥadīth, and were eventually fixed at five times: Ṣalāt al-Ṣubḥ or Ṣalāt al-Fajr (Dawn), Ṣalāt al-Ẓuhr (Noon), Ṣalāt al-ʿAṣr (Afternoon), Ṣalāt al-Maghrib (Sunset), Ṣalāt al-ʿIshā’ (Night). According to tradition, Muḥammad was given these instructions by Allāh on the occasion of his *Isrā’ (Night Journey) to heaven.

Ṣalāt should be performed in common, in a *mosque, especially the Noon prayer on Friday (*Jumʿa). But the Muslim may pray individually or in small groups, when one member is chosen as the *Imām, and this may be in any ritually clean area, marked off by *sutra. A prayer mat, *sajjāda, is commonly used. Ṣalāt must be performed facing the *qibla, the direction of *Mecca, which in a mosque is indicated by the *miḥrāb* (see MOSQUE).

Ṣalāt is preceded by ritual ablution (*wuḍū’*, *ghusl, or *tayammum*) as appropriate. It is divided into distinct movements, accompanied by formulae. First, in a standing position facing the qibla, is the pronouncement of the *niy(y)a (intention) to perform the ṣalāt; then the *takbīr (Allāhu Akbar), followed by the *Fātiḥa and a verse or two from the Qur’ān. The movements then are: *rukūʿ*, bending till the palms are level with the knees; kneeling; a prostration, *sujūd*; back again into *julūs* (between sitting and standing); another sujūd. At most movements, the takbīr is repeated. This set of movements, from the standing position to the end of the second *sujūd*, constitutes one *rakʿa, the number of which is fixed for each prayer time. After the final rakʿa, in a sitting position, the worshipper pronounces the *tashahhud* (profession of faith, *shahāda); the prayer upon the Prophet Muḥammad; finally the *taslima*, greeting, ‘Al-Salām ʿalaykum’ (‘Peace be upon you’), even when he is alone. Extra rakʿas may be added by the individual. The ritual may vary slightly according to the *madhhab.

Sales/Salesian (Christian spiritual director/style): see DE SALES, FRANCIS.

Ṣaliḥ. *Prophet and *rasūl who, according to the *Qur’ān, was sent to the Thamūd. Nothing is known of him apart from the Qur’ān, where he appears, like other prophets, as a warner, who was rejected by most of his people.

Sālimīya (Muslim theological school): see SAHL AL-TUSTARĪ.

Sallekhanā. In Jainism, ritual death by fasting. Through gradual fasting in accordance with detailed prescription and under close supervision of mendicant teachers, Jains can meet their death in a controlled and peaceful manner. Jains insist that this is a noble act, and not common suicide, because the vow to take sallekhanā is made publicly and the consent of the *ācārya or family must first be given.

Salmān al-Fār(i)sī (‘the Persian’). Close companion of the Prophet *Muḥammad and a central figure of many Muslim legends. *ʿUmar appointed him as governor of al-*Madā’in and he is said to have died there during *ʿUthmān’s reign. Salmān’s tomb at al-Madā’in is a place of pilgrimage for *Shiʿites returning from *Karbalā’. According to many *Sūfī orders, Salmān is a leading mystic and teacher in their *silsilah (chain of transmission). The *Nuṣairī raise him to their trinity of ʿAlī, Muḥammad, and Salmān, in which he is considered to be the figure who, under the name of *Gabriel, taught the Qur’ān to Muḥammad.

Śalok (Pañjābī, from Skt., ‘śloka’, ‘verse’). Short verse of two or more lines interspersing longer verses in the *Ādi Granth.

Salvation (Lat., *salus*, ‘sound, safe’). The act or state of being safe in ultimate terms. Although all religions have some sense of a condition which might appropriately be called by this name, the state and the way to it are very differently understood. Thus in Judaism, there is concern to achieve deliverance from sin and for a final *messianic victory, but no word or phrase in general use that summarizes the idea of 'salvation'. Again, in Islam, there is much concern with the day of judgement (*yaum al-Din) and with the mercy of God, who is constantly invoked *b'ismi-Llāhi rahmāni warahīm*, 'in the name of God, merciful and compassionate'. But the most common word for 'salvation', *najah*, is used only once in the *Qur'ān Again, in Buddhism, there is strong emphasis from the Buddha that he is only a physician who can diagnose ills and suggest the path to a cure, but that each person must be his or her own saviour. It is only in Mahāyāna Buddhism that figures akin to saviours (especially *bodhisattvas) enter in. In Hinduism, the notion is more clearly expressed through terms derived from *muc*, 'release from pains or penalties', such as *mukti (mukta) and *mokṣa. Help from a 'saviour', especially an *avatāra of Viṣṇu, and above all from *Kṛṣṇa, is acknowledged. It is in Christianity that great emphasis is laid on salvation, deriving from the centrality of Christ. The Christian doctrine has several aspects: (i) the work of Christ in the *atonement (and, broadly, in the *incarnation generally); (ii) the *justification and sanctification of men and women by God's *grace; and (iii) the outcome of death and of history (see JUDGEMENT; ESCHATOLOGY).

Salvation Army. Christian denomination. Founded in 1865 by W. *Booth for evangelism, and for social work, it is now established in about 100 countries. From the beginning, its organization has been along military lines. Its *Arminian doctrinal convictions, embodied in its *Orders and Regulations* (1878), reflect the *Wesleyan background of its founder, particularly in universal *redemption, human free will, and a post-conversion sanctification experience. Music has always played an important role in the Army's worship and witness.

Salvation history (Germ., *Heilsgeschichte*). In Christian theology, the history of God's saving work among men and women. More usually it is supposed to denote a distinctive concept in the Bible itself, according to which God is essentially one who acts in history, and Christ is the midpoint of a continuum from creation to consummation.

Sāma (chant): see SĀMA VEDA.

Śama (the six virtues according to Śaṅkara): see ṢATKASAMPATTI.

Samā' (Arab., 'hearing', 'listening'). *Sūfī practice of making and listening to music to encourage attention to God, and the states ensuing therefrom. The common human experience of mood alteration through music, leading at an extreme to trance and other ecstatic states, was developed among Sūfīs, especially in association with *dance, and both music and dance may now be referred to through the term *ḥaḍra* ('presence'; see GHAIBA), i.e. that which brings one into the presence of God.

Samādhi (Skt., 'putting together', 'union'). Enstasis, intense concentration or absorption of consciousness in a variety of higher mental states in Hindu, Buddhist, and Jain *yoga, in which distinction between subject and object is eliminated; the eighth 'limb' of 'eight-limbed' (*aṣṭāṅga*) or *rāja yoga. Samādhi is the consequence of meditation rather than the state of meditation itself.

In Hinduism, samādhi is achieved through yoga in which the yogin's consciousness (*citta) is absorbed in the object of meditation and there is no awareness of the physical or material world.

Other Hindu traditions such as *Vedānta, *Śaivism, *Vaiṣṇavism, and *Tantrism accept the idea of samādhi as a consequence of yoga practice, while adhering to a diversity of metaphysical systems and practices. Tantrism accepts samādhi as found in classical yoga, but emphasizes the attainment of samādhi and liberation (*mokṣa) through *Kuṇḍa-linī and *mantra yoga.

In Buddhism, samādhi is produced through the practice of that aspect of Buddhist meditation concerned with mind-development (*citta-*bhāvanā), involving tranquillity (*samatha) and the absorptions (*jhāna), as distinct from insight-development (*vipassanā-bhāvanā). It is therefore used as a synonym for these meditations.

Unlike insight (vipassanā), samādhi can be realized by non-Buddhist as well as Buddhist ascetics, and it is through its practice that supernormal powers (*iddhi) are achieved. Samādhi is generally regarded as an indispensable component of Buddhist practice and forms one of the links of the Eightfold Path (*aṣṭangika-marga) as well as part of the threefold dimension of the Path, together with *śīla (morality) and *prajñā (wisdom). It is listed as one of the seven factors of enlightenment (*bojjhanga), the five spiritual powers (*bala), and six perfections (*pāramitas).

In Zen Buddhism, samādhi (Jap., *sanmai*, *zenmai*) is the overcoming of a dualistic, subject–object, awareness, through concentration on a single object and experiencing unity with it.

Among Jains, samādhi is a virtual equivalent of *dhyāna or *bhāvanā, the meditation which seeks to destroy the accumulation of *karma in order to release the *jīva. It is the interior preparation for, and exercise of, increasingly severe *asceticism (*tapas).

Samael. The name of *Satan in Judaism from the *amoraic period. It first appears in the Ethiopic *Book of *Enoch*. He appears in later sources as the consort of *Lilith, and he is a prominent character in the *Zohar* and in *kabbalistic literature.

Samān (chant): see MUSIC.

Samaṇas. Hindu wandering philosophers of the Upaniṣadic period, who rejected Vedic tradition and family ties, and depended on alms for sustenance. Jain and Buddhist ascetics were in origin akin to samaṇas; Buddhist assessment of them occurs in *Sāmañña-phala Sutta*, part of *Dīgha Nikāya*.

Sāmaṇera (Pāli; Skt., Śrāmaṇera). One who is making a first approach to full membership of the Buddhist saṅgha (community)—i.e. the equivalent, in Western terms, of a novice monk.

Samantabhadra (Skt., 'he who is all-pervadingly good'; Chin., P'u-hsien; Jap., Fugen; Tib., Ādi Buddha). A *bodhisattva of great importance in Mahāyāna Buddhism. He is the protector of all who teach *dharma, and he is the embodiment of the realization that sameness and difference are a unity. He rides a six-tusked elephant, the tusks representing the conquest of attachment to the six senses. He rode on the elephant to China, settling on Mount O-mei, where he is venerated as one of the four great bodhisattvas. He is also closely associated with *Vairocāna. For the Tibetan development, see ĀDI BUDDHA.

Samaritans. A tribe descended from Israelites who were regarded as heretics by Jews. The Samaritans themselves believe they are descended from the tribes of *Ephraim and Manasseh and, until the 17th cent. CE, their *high priest was a direct descendant of *Aaron. After they were rejected by the returning *exiles in the Persian period, Sanballat, the Samaritan ruler, built a rival *temple on Mount *Gerizim (Nehemiah 13). This was destroyed by John Hyrcanus in 128 BCE, but it was said to have been rebuilt by the Romans as a reward for Samaritan help against the *Bar Kokhba revolt. By the 19th cent. only a very small community remained in Shechem. In 1842, they were recognized by the *Jerusalem *Chief Rabbi as 'a branch of the Jewish people that confess to the truth of the *Torah', and, after the establishment of the State of *Israel, they were recognized as citizens under the *Law of Return. The Samaritans have their own version of the *Pentateuch, and they claim that their most ancient *scroll dates back to the thirteenth year of the Israelite settlement of *Canaan. They have their own *liturgy and various expositions and commentaries on the Pentateuch. They keep all the *festivals mentioned in the Torah. *Passover, *Shavu'ot, and *Sukkot involve *pilgrimage to Mount Gerizim, and *sacrifices are made at Passover.

Samaritans (organization): see SUICIDE.

Samatha (Skt., Pāli śamatha, 'tranquillity', 'calming-down'). The form of Buddhist *meditation whose purpose is mind-development (*citta-*bhāvanā) and which is defined in terms of the end that it achieves—mental tranquillity. It is to be distinguished from the other form of Buddhist meditation, *vipassanā, whose purpose is insight into Buddhist doctrinal truth. It is thus an alternative designation for *samādhi.

Sāmavasarāna (Jain assembly hall): see ART (Jainism).

Samavāya-aṅga (Jain text): see AṄGA.

Sāma Veda (Skt.). The Vedic collection of chants (*sāman*) used by the Udgātṛ priests in the sacrificial rites with the belief that proper tone and pitch gave creative power to the singer of the chant. All but seventy-five of the verses of the *Sāma Veda* are found in the *Ṛg Veda*.

Sāmāyika (Skt., 'attaining equanimity'). In Jainism, a 48-minute period of *yogic meditation and restraint practised by both ascetics and the Jain laity, and (according to Jain texts), the highest form of spiritual discipline. It can be observed at any time, but is often practised at dawn or sunset (before or after the day's activities) when the Jain can sit unmoved and undisturbed, forgiving and seeking forgiveness.

Sambatyon. A river in Jewish legend. After the Assyrian conquest of 721 BCE, the ten Northern *tribes were said to have been *exiled across the river Sambatyon. It was said to flow with a huge current six days of the week, but to rest on the *Sabbath (*Gen.R.* 11. 5).

Śambhala (semi-mythical kingdom in Tibetan Buddhist cosmology): see SHAMBHALA.

Sambhoga-kāya. 'Enjoyment Body', one of the Buddha's 'Three Bodies' (*Trikāya), and the intermediate form in which he manifests himself in the heavens or celestial paradises.

Sambō. Jap., Mahāyāna, and Zen term for the *Three Jewels (*triratna*), i.e. 'three treasures', the foundation for all Buddhist life. In Mahāyāna, the significance of the three is greatly extended by exploring (i) how the three are nevertheless one, ittai-sambō; (ii) how they manifest themselves, genzen-sambō; (iii) how they are verifiable and verified.

Sambō-ekotoba. Three scrolls of paintings and explanations of *Sambō, composed by Minamoto Tamenori (d. 1011). They contain, in addition, outline biographies of famous Buddhists.

Sambō-ji (Buddhist monastery): see DAINICHI NŌNIN.

Saṃcita-karma. In Hinduism, the accumulation of *saṃskāras (acquired characteristics) which have been created and transmitted via *karma from previous lives.

Saṃdhinirmocana-sūtra (The Explanation of Mysteries, or The Unravelling of the Hidden Meaning). An important text in the Buddhist school of *Vijñānavāda (Yogācāra), and the source (2nd-3rd cent.) upon which many of the exponents of the school based their teachings. The work forms a bridge between the speculative *Perfection of Wisdom (Prajñāpāramitā) literature and the mind-only philosophy of the Vijñānavāda which was developed in the treatises it inspired.

Saṃdhyā (Skt., 'juncture'). The interval between light and dark (dawn, evening), manifested in Hinduism as a wife of *Śiva and daughter of *Brahmā. It is the moment of daily devotion.

Saṃgha (religious communities in India): see SAṄGHA.

Saṃghabeda (divisions in Buddhism): see SCHISM.

Saṃhitā (Skt., 'joined', 'collected'). The collected arrangements of hymns, chants, etc., constituting the *Vedas, and thus the basis of Hindu scripture. In origin, the term referred to the connected and continuous style of recitation, and was then applied to the collections of the hymns and chants thus recited.

Śaṃkara (Indian religious philosopher): see ŚAṄKARA.

Saṁkarṣana (manifest power of Viṣṇu): see VIṢṆU.

Sāṃkhya. One of the six orthodox schools of interpretation (*darśana) in Hinduism. Its founder is said to have been *Kapila. Sāṃkhya posits a fundamental contrast between *puruṣa and *prakṛti. Puruṣa is the conscious, intelligent self or essence, prakṛti the eternal, unconscious potentiality of all being or appearance. In itself, prakṛti rests in a state of perfect equilibrium, composed of three strands (*guṇas), *sattva (the subtle principle of potential consciousness), *rajas (the principle of activity), and *tamas (the principle of passivity). The unfolding or evolution of prakṛti from its state of equilibrium occurs when puruṣa becomes present to it, creating the duality of subject and object. By the light of the consciousness of puruṣa, humans are able to become aware of prakṛti. If puruṣa forgets its true nature and regards the body or mind as the true self, then it remains attached to prakṛti. Freedom is obtained by discriminatory knowledge (sāṃkhya), which is practical as well as theoretical; and that is why yoga became attached to Sāṃkhya, producing the so-called Sāṃkhya-yoga of *Patañjali. Potentially, and often actually, Sāṃkhya is a non-theistic system. However, gods are easily incorporated as products of prakṛti; or God as Puruṣa.

Sammana (members of male communities in E. religions): see ŚRĀMAṆA.

Sammā-padhāna (Pāli; Skt., *samyak-prahānāni*). The four perfect efforts in Buddhism, designed to eliminate obstacles in the present and future: (i) the effort to avoid obstacles; (ii) the effort to overcome them; (iii) the effort to cultivate the seven contributions to enlightenment (*bojjhanga); (iv) the effort to maintain them. They are the sixth step on the Eightfold Path (*aṣṭangika-marga).

Sammāsambuddha (Pāli), **Samyaksaṃbuddha** (Skt.). Perfectly Enlightened One, Supremely Awakened One; the proper title of *Gotāma the Buddha, marking him out from all other beings, including the other variety of enlightened person, the *paccekabuddha* (*prateyaka-buddha).

Sammeta, Mount (Jain centre): see PĀRŚVA.

Sammon (triple gate entrance to Buddhist temples and monasteries): see KYŌTO.

Samnon. Korean for *Mādhyamaka.

Saṁnyāsa (Skt., 'putting or throwing down', 'renunciation'). In Hinduism, the formal and final renunciation of all ties to family, caste, and property. It is a way of life outside the normal duties and rewards of society, dedicated solely to the goal of liberation (*mokṣa). According to the Hindu law books, saṁnyāsa is the fourth and last stage in life (*āśrama) of twice-born Hindus, and may be entered upon when one has seen the birth 'of the eldest son's son'.

The full ritual process by which one formally renounces may extend over two or more days. Following these rites it is customary for the newly initiated saṁnyasin to make his first round of begging alms (*bikṣā*).

Besides the normative description of the life

of renunciation found in the Dharmaśāstras and their later commentaries, there exists a whole class of minor *Upaniṣads, the Saṁnyāsa Upaniṣads, which extol the ideals of renunciation. Saṁnyāsins are often associated with the doctrines and practices relating to *Śiva, and many saṁnyasins are members of the *Daśanāmī order. See also ASCETICISM.

Sampai (Jap., 'three' + 'prostration'). Threefold prostration in Zen Buddhism, probably in honour of the Three Jewels (*sambō).

Saṁpradāya (Skt., from *saṁ-pra da*, 'to give completely up', 'to hand down by tradition'). In Indian religions, any established doctrine and set of practices transmitted from one teacher to another. From this it has come to mean any sectarian religious teaching or a religious sect. In the *Mahābhārata (Anuśāsanaparvan* 141), the four (supposedly) original saṁpradāyas are listed more as styles of increasing *asceticism through which *tapas is generated. For Jains, see MULA SANGHA.

Samprajñāta (Skt., 'differentiated') or **sabīja** (Skt., 'with seed'). A stage of *samādhi in *rāja *yoga following from *dhyāna and preliminary to *asamprajñāta samādhi. It is a state of suppressed or controlled consciousness.

Saṃsāra (Skt., Pāli, Prkt., 'wandering'). Transmigration or rebirth; in Asian religions, the cycle of birth and death as a consequence of action (*karma). Liberation (*mokṣa, *nirvāna, *kaivalya) is release from samsāra, conceived as either going beyond samsāra or realizing it to be an illusion (*māyā). The idea of samsāra, like karma, is possibly of non-Vedic or heterodox origin, though the matter is contentious.

The word *samsāra* does not appear in the *Vedas, but the idea of redeath (*punarmṛtyu) does, and the *śrāddha and *sapindakarana* rites may have been to prevent the dissolution of the deceased in the next world, which is contrary to later Hindu views of the need to prevent rebirth.

The basic pattern of release or continued transmigration is found in later Hinduism, transmigration being regarded as undesirable. Indian theism such as *Śaiva Siddhānta, regards samsāra as a means for the dispensation of grace (*anugraha*), the ultimate reason for samsāra being the liberation of souls: thus *Śiva both conceals himself (*tirobhāva*) and reveals himself (*anugraha*).

In Buddhism, samsāra is the cycle of continuing appearances through the domains of existence (*gati), but with no Self (*anātman) being reborn: there is only the continuity of consequence, governed by karma.

Among Jains, the whole universe depends on the conscious and unconscious (*jīva, ajīva) elements. Saṁsāra is the process through which souls are able to be disentangled from the material.

Samsin. Korean for *trikāya.

Saṃskāra (Skt., *saṃ*, 'together', + *kr*, 'make'). 1. The saṃskāras are the rituals through which high-*caste or twice-born Hindus mark their transitions through life (and death), and may thus be regarded as *rites of passage. The saṃskāras differ in number, depending on how many of the lesser moments which are marked by ritual (e.g. a child's first outing) are included. However, a fairly standard list of sixteen rites includes (i) *Garbhādhāna*, the securing of conception; (ii) *Puṃsavāna*, the securing of the birth of a male child; (iii) *Sīmantonnayana*, parting the hair of the pregnant woman to secure her from evil spirits (this again has reference to the birth of a male child; in W. India it is known as *Dohada*, and men cannot be present); (iv) *Jātakarma*, the securing and celebration of safe delivery; (v) *Nāmakaraṇa*, the giving of the name to the child on the twelfth day after birth; (vi) *Niṣkramana*, the making auspicious, by seeing the sun and going to a temple, of the child's first outing; (vii) *Annaprāśana*, the first feeding with solid food; (viii) *Cauḍakaraṇa*, shaving of the head during the first or third year; (ix) *Karṇavedha*, the piercing of the ear or nose between 3 and 5; (x) *Vidyārambha*, the learning of the alphabet; (xi) *Upanayana, the sacred thread; (xii) on the day following, for those deemed competent, *Vedārambha*, the beginning of the study of the *Vedas; (xiii) *Keśānta*, the first shaving of the beard; (xiv) *Samāvartana*, the end of student life; (xv) *Vivāha*, *marriage; (xvi) *Antyeṣṭi, funeral rites.

2. In Hinduism the formations in consciousness which accumulate from thoughts and actions in earlier lives, and which constitute individual character. In Buddhism, see SANKHARA.

Samson (Heb. Shimshon). An Israelite *Judge. The story of Samson is to be found in Judges 13–16.

Samu (Jap., 'work-service'). The Zen practice of physical work, at set times, in monasteries. It is understood as work in service of the Three Jewels (*sambō), and was stressed by *Pai-chang.

Samudramathana (Hindu myth): see CHURNING OF THE OCEAN.

Samuel (*c.*11th cent. BCE). Israelite *prophet and *judge. Samuel's activities are to be found in 1 Samuel 1–16. His (traditional) tomb on

Mount al-Nabi Samwīl, overlooking *Jerusalem, was a place of *pilgrimage in the Middle Ages.

Samuel, Book of. The eighth book of the Hebrew scriptures. Originally a single work, it was subdivided in the *Septuagint and *Vulgate (which has four Books of Kings).

Samuel ben Hophni (d. 1013). Jewish *gaon of *Sura. Samuel was descended from generations of scholars. He was a prolific writer, although most of his works are now lost. Among his writings mentioned by later authorities were an introduction to the *Talmud, a book of precepts, and an Arabic translation and commentary on the *Pentateuch.

Samuel ben Meir (Rashbam, *c.*1080–*c.*1174). Jewish biblical and *Talmudic commentator. A grandson and student of *Rashi, Samuel lived in France. He produced a commentary on the Bible which is notable for its preference for the literal meaning of the text (*peshāt), even when this opposes *halakhah. He also supplemented Rashi's commentary on the Talmud and wrote *tosafot on various tractates. He was a noted composer of *piyyutim and wrote a grammatical work, *Sefer Daikut*.

Samuel ha-Nagid (Isma'īl ibn Nagrel'a, 993–1055). Jewish vizier (*wazīr) of Granada. Samuel had a distinguished career as a public servant to King Habbus and King Badis of Granada which included commanding the army. His victory against the army of Almeria was the origin of a special *Purim among the Granadan Jews. He was a poet as well as a soldier, and three collections survive: *Ben Tehillim*, *Ben Mishlei*, and *Ben Kohelet*.

Samurai (Jap., derived from *saburau*, 'to serve'). Warriors. Originally the word was applied only to noble warriors with good family lineage, but this became the common designation for warriors in the Tokugawa period. The appearance of warriors as a distinct class coincided with the development of the *shōen* system dealing with private proprietary land management. The inability of the central government to control the various provinces and districts allowed them to develop their own defence force, from which the warrior class evolved. The medieval tales of warriors, though highly idealized, glorified heroism, courage, honour, and loyalty to one's lord, which became the core of *bushidō, the ethical code of the samurai class. Religion helped warriors resolve the question of life and death; see further MARTIAL ARTS; BUSHIDŌ.

Samyak-prahānāni (four perfect efforts in Buddhism): see SAMMĀ-PADHĀNA.

Samyaksaṃbuddha (perfectly enlightened one): see SAMMĀSAMBUDDHA.

Saṃyama (Skt., 'restraint'). Inner discipline, the three final stages in Hindu *rāja yoga, as analysed by *Patañjali: *dhāraṇā, *dhyāna, *samādhi. See *Yoga-Sūtra*, ch. 3. Among Jains, it is the key practice in the ascetic way, along with the generation (in counterbalance) of *tapas.

Samyé (*bsam.yas*). The first monastery in Tibet and scene of the great debate in which *Kamalaśīla defeated the Chinese emissary Mahāyāna, thus ensuring that Indian rather than Chinese Buddhism would be the model for the development of religion in Tibet. The Samyé monastery was commissioned by King Trisong Detsen (790–858) and its building begun by *Śāntarakṣita, formerly abbot of Nālandā, and completed with the assistance of *Padmasambhava. The building itself, said to have taken seven years before Padmasambhava's arrival and five years after, was architecturally important for having set the pattern for all future monasteries in Tibet. Modelled after Odantapurī in Bihar (itself destroyed by Muslims in 1193), it contained one large and twelve small temples, four large and 108 smaller *chörtens, all surrounded by a high wall, thus representing in *maṇḍala form the ideographic Buddhist universe. During the cultural revolution it was completely destroyed by the Chinese.

Samyé-Ling Centre (Tibetan Buddhist centre in Scotland): see TRUNGPA, RINPOCHE.

Saṃyojanas (Pāli, *sam-yuj*, 'to bind to'). In Buddhism, bonds or fetters that tie a being to the Wheel of Becoming. Traditionally there are ten: belief in self (*sakkāya-diṭṭhi), doubt (*vicikicchā*), attachment to works and ceremonial observances (*sīlabbata-parāmāsa), attachment to sense-desire (*kāma-rāga*), anger (*vyāpāda*), attachment to the world of form (*rūpa-rāga*), attachment to the formless world (*arūpa-rāga*), pride (*māna), excitability (*uddhacca*), and ignorance (*avijjā). The first five are named the 'lower fetters' (*orambhāgiya-samyojana*) as they bind a person to rebirth in the world of desire (*kama-loka*), the last five are named the 'higher fetters' (*uddhambhāgiya-samyojana*) because they tie a person that has escaped the world (*loka) of desire to the upper regions of the Wheel of Becoming. Therefore a being must escape all the fetters to achieve *nirvāna.

Saṃyuktāgama (Indian division of Sūtrapiṭaka): see TRIPIṬAKA.

Saṃyutta Nikāya. The 'unified collection', the third collection (*nikāya) of the *Sūtra/Sutta-pitaka, containing more than 7,000 discourses.

Sanātana dharma (Skt., *sanātana*, 'eternal', + *dharma*, 'law'). In Hinduism, the absolute and eternal law (*dharma) as opposed to relative duty (*svadharma). Sanātana dharma applies to everyone, including *outcastes. According to *Yājñavalkvasmṛti*, absolute dharma includes purity, good will, mercy, and patience. Later texts such as *Vāmana *Purāṇa* list the ten limbs of the eternal dharma as non-injury, truth, purity, not stealing, charity, forbearance, self-restraint, tranquillity, generosity, and asceticism.

In modern Indian usage, sanātana dharma is often equated with 'Hinduism' as a name, stressing the eternal foundation of it.

Sāñchī. A Buddhist religious centre in Central India, consisting of a number of *stūpas, *vihāras, and temples. It is also known as Caityagiri. The most important building in terms of size and artistic merit is the Great Stūpa, the core of which dates from the time of *Aśoka. The remains of an unusual free-standing *caitya hall dating from Gupta times (320–630 CE) has recently been found at Sāñchī.

San-chiao (Chin., 'three ways'). The three major religions/philosophies of China: Confucian, Taoist, and Buddhist.

San-chieh-chiao ('*School of Three Stages'). School of Chinese Buddhism during the Sui and T'ang periods, founded by Hsin-hsing (540–94). It portrayed the process of Buddhism as one of degeneration through three stages: (i) the period of true *dharma, which lasted for 500 years after the *Buddha Śākyamuni's translation from earth, during which the teaching was observed; (ii) 1,000 years of corrupted dharma, with many innovations; (iii) 10,000 years, most yet to come (beginning 550 CE), of increasing disintegration. Against this, Hsin-hsing set a rule of radical observance of *śīla, *dāna, and asceticism, eschewing monasteries, although willing to support them.

San-ch'ing (Chin., 'the three pure ones'). The three Taoist heavens (*t'ien) and those who inhabit them.

1. Yü-ching, the heaven of pure jade, inhabited by Yüan-shih t'ien-tsun, one of the highest deities of religious Taoism (*tao-chiao*). He created heaven and earth, and at the start of each new age, he gives **Ling-pao ching* to subordinates who instruct humans from it in the way of Tao.

2. Shang-ch'ing, the heaven of purity, ruled by Ling-pao t'ien-tsun. He is the guardian of *Ling-pao ching*, and regulates time and the balance of *yin and yang.

3. T'ai-ch'ing, the heaven of highest purity, ruled by Tao-te T'ien-tsun, the guardian of *tao and *te. He is identified with *Lao-tzu.

Sañci (Buddhist centre in Central India): see SĀÑCHĪ.

Sancita-karma (transmitted characteristics): see SAṂCITA-KARMA.

Sancta Sophia (church, later mosque): see HAGIA SOFIA.

Sanctification: see HOLINESS.

Sanctuary (Lat., *sanctuarium*). A holy place, especially in Christianity the part of a church containing the altar (or high altar). The right (or benefit) of sanctuary was recognized in Roman law, limited by Justinian in 535 to more serious crimes. *Canon law allowed sanctuary for a limited period so that compensation might be agreed (sacrilege and treason were excepted).

Sanctus (Lat., 'holy'). A hymn of adoration based on Isaiah 6. 3 and used in Christian liturgies near the beginning of the *eucharistic prayer.

Sandak. The one who holds the baby on his knee at a Jewish *circumcision ceremony. It is considered a great honour to be the sandak at the rite and it is customarily bestowed on the grandfather of the child.

Sandhya (time of Hindu daily devotion): see SAṂDHYĀ.

Sangai. Jap., for *triloka* (*loka), the realm of desire (Skt., *kāmadhatu*, Jap., *yokkai*), of form (*rūpadhātu*, *shikkai*), of non-form (*ārūpyadhātu*, *mushikikai*).

Sangai(-yui)-isshin (Jap., 'three worlds, (only) one mind'). Zen belief that the three worlds of desire, form, and no-form arise from unenlightened awareness (*kokoro, heart-mind), and have no objective reality: all is projection.

Sangat, Satsang, or **Sadhsaṅgat.** A Sikh group or association, often the local congregation of a *gurdwārā. The whole Sikh community is known as Sikh Panth.

Sangen (three mysteries in Lin-chi Zen Buddhism): see LIN-CHI.

Saṅgha or **saṃgha** (Skt./Pāli, 'gathering, community'). Religious communities in India, e.g. the Jains, but most often used of Buddhists. In general, it means 'those who follow the teachings of the *Buddha', i.e. the four groups of Buddhists (Skt., *pariṣad*; Pāli, *parisā*), monks and nuns (*bhikṣus, bhikṣunīs), laymen and laywomen (*upāsaka, upāsikā); but again, the reference is usually more precise, to the community of monks and nuns alone, or to those of advanced spiritual attainment as distinguished from beginners (Skt., *aryasaṃgha* or *savaka-saṃgha*, 'holy community'), or to the entire Buddhist community at a particular place. To take refuge in the saṅgha is one of the *Three Jewels (*trīratna*) of Buddhism.

The rules governing the life and organization of the saṅgha (in the restricted sense) are found in *Vinayapiṭaka. The saṅgha is basically mendicant, and it has no hierarchical organization (apart from a senior monk, Skt., *sthavira*; Pāli, *thera). The development of *Mahāyāna did not diminish the importance of the saṅgha, even though routes to enlightenment/salvation were opened up outside the saṅgha. The vinaya traditions persisted, and only in Japan did the organization of schools diminish the importance of the monastic saṅgha. In 1966, the World Buddhist Saṅgha Council was established.

Saṅghapati (organizer of pilgrimage): see PILGRIMAGE (Jain).

Sangjwabu. Korean for *Theravāda.

Saṅgrānd or **sankranti** (Pañjābī, 'first day of Hindu month'). The saṅgrānd is the day when the sun enters a new zodiac sign. Every saṅgrānd is marked in *gurdwārās with a service.

Sanhedrin (Heb. loan from Gk., *sunhedrion*). When or if it existed, the supreme political, religious and judicial body in *Erez Israel during the Roman period. There is much scholarly discussion therefore as to the composition and function of the Sanhedrin, especially whether there were two or more 'sanhedrins', or councils, from which the impression of a single Sanhedrin was formed—in other words, the assimilation of councils into Sanhedrin would mean that *the* Sanhedrin as such never existed in the period of the second *Temple.

San-hsing (Chin., 'three stars'). Three Chinese figures (variously identified in each case) who became gods because of their virtues: (i) Fu-hsing, Lucky Star, portrayed usually with a child, or as a bat; (ii) Lü-hsing, Highly Honoured Star, often portrayed as a stag; (iii) Shou-hsing, Star of Long Life, usually holding the staff or support of life in one hand, and the peach of immortality in the other. All are important in folk religion.

San-i (Chin., 'the three ones'). Threefold action of the one *Tao, derived from *Lao-tzu* 42. The creative three may be personified as the guardians of the inner fields of human life and energy; or they may be the Supreme One (*T'ai-i), the Earthly One (Ti-i), and the Heavenly One (T'ien-i); or they may be mind (*shen), vitality (*ch'i), essence (*ching).

Sañjaya Belaṭṭhiputta (Pāli). The leader of a sect of sceptics (*Amarāvikkhepikas), and one of the six heretical teachers whose doctrines are described in the *Sāmañña-phala Sutta* (see SAMAṆAS). As a way of indicating his total scepticism, he is said to have used the method of denying truth-claims in any logical form they could be presented.

Sankan ('three barriers' of Zen Rinzai teaching): see HUANG-LUNG HUI-NAN.

Śaṅkara or **Śaṅkarācārya** (trad., 788–820, but perhaps earlier). The pre-eminent philosopher and proponent of *Advaita Vedānta, and one of the most influential thinkers in the entire history of Indian religion.

Although the traditional biographies disagree in many details, the main outlines of the saintly life portrayed in them are clear. He was born of a *brahman family in S. India, probably at Kālaḍi in the modern state of Kerala. His father died while Śaṅkara was a child, and while still a boy, Śaṅkara left his mother in the care of some relatives, and set out on the life of a wandering mendicant. At a cave on the banks of the Narmadā River he met the sage *Govindapāda, the disciple of *Gauḍapāda, and remained there long enough to become his pupil, to study *Vedānta philosophy with him, and receive from him formal initiation into the life of a renunciant (*saṁnyāsa).

Leaving Govindapāda, Śaṅkara walked to Vārāṇasī (Benares) where he began to write, teach, and attract disciples of his own. From Vārāṇasī he journeyed north to Badarīnātha near the source of the Ganges in the foothills of the Himālayas. There, he composed his famous commentary on the *Brahmasūtra*. The last years of his short life were spent wandering the length and breadth of India proclaiming the philosophy of Advaita Vedānta and taking on all rivals in debate. This period is called the 'Tour of Victory' (*digvijaya*), during which Śaṅkara defeated Maṇḍana Miśra and many other worthy proponents of rival schools of religious philosophy, including Buddhists, Jains, and various sectarian *Śaivas.

One of the most widely accepted accounts of the end of his life is that at the age of 32 he left Kedārnāth in the Himālayas travelling northward toward Mount Kailāsa, the abode of *Śiva, and was seen no more.

For a description of his religious teaching see ADVAITA VEDĀNTA; ṢATKASAMPATTI.

Śaṅkarācārya (teachers in the tradition of Śaṅkara): see DAŚANĀMĪ.

Śaṅkaradeva (*c*.1449–1569). Hindu religious leader who was primarily responsible for the spread of the *Vaiṣṇava movement in Assam. He emphasized the recitation of the name *Hari, and set up a formal structure for the spread of devotion to God. The *sattras* were monasteries in which attention was paid to the ancilliaries of *music, *dance, and drama (*theatre); the *nāmagharas* were set up in villages to co-ordinate religious life, but eventually became centres of social and economic life as well. Śaṅkaradeva composed many songs, narrative poems, and dramas to encourage participation in bhakti, and to bring the presence of God immediately before the participants.

Sankey, Ira D. (1840–1908). Singer and composer of gospel *hymns. He joined Dwight L. *Moody in 1870 and became his regular organist, singer, and musical director. He composed a number of tunes, most to be found in his compilation *Sacred Songs and Solos* (many edns. since 1873).

Sankhara (Pāli; cf. Skt., *saṃskāra). In Buddhism, the fourth of the *skandhas/khandhas, the aggregations which constitute human appearance. Sankharas are the constructing initiatives and activities, which set life forward and give individual character to a life.

Sankhya (philosophical school in Hinduism): see SĀṂKHYA.

Sanki (Jap., 'the three refuges'): see THREE JEWELS.

Sanku (three statements, of Zen Buddhist Linchi line): see LIN-CHI.

San-kuan (Chin., three rulers). Three Taoist deities, rulers of heaven, earth, and water.

San-lun. School of the Three Treatises, established in China by *Kumārajīva (344–413 CE), the Kuchean monk who translated the three treatises—Treatise on the Middle, Treatise on the Twelve Gates, Treatise in One Hundred Verses—into Chinese. The school was instrumental in introducing the teachings of the Indian philosopher *Nāgārjuna (2nd cent. CE) concerning the concept of emptiness (*śūnyatā) to the Chinese. A major exponent of San-lun was *Chi-tsang.

Sanmai (state of attainment through meditation in E. religions): see SAMĀDHI (Zen); ZANMAI.

Sanmotsu (Jap., 'three things'). The Zen ceremony of recognition of a *rōshi who has also attained the rank of *shōshi.

Sanne (Jap., 'three robes'). The three robes used by a Japanese Buddhist monk: (i) *sōgyari*, made of nine to twenty-five pieces of cloth, worn for appearance in public, e.g. for begging; (ii) *uttarasō*, made of seven pieces and worn at ceremonies, lectures, etc.; (iii) *andae*, for ordinary use. See HABIT, RELIGIOUS.

Sannyāsa (renunciation of all ties with family etc. in Hinduism): see SAṀNYĀSA.

San-pao (Chin., 'three treasures'). Taoist virtues derived from *Tao-te ching* 67; mercy/love; no excess/frugality; modesty.

Sanron-shū. 'Three treatises' (Jap.) of *San-lun, brought to Japan by the Korean monk Ekwan in 625. From his followers derived Jōjitsu. Sanron was not an independently organized school, but its teachings, mediating *Mādhyamaka and *Nāgārjuna, were much studied.

San-Shen. Chin. for *trikāya.

San-sheng Hui-jan (Jap. Sanshō Enen), *c*.9th cent. CE, dharma-successor (*hassu) of *Lin-chi I-hsuan, to whom the compilation of **Rinzairoku* (*Lin-chi-lu*) is ascribed; but this is uncertain.

Sanshin. Jap. for *trikāya.

Sant: see SANT TRADITION.

Śāntarakṣita (Skt.; Tib., Zhi.ba.tsho; *c*.705–88 CE). Indian philosopher and chief exponent of the *Vijñavāda-*Mādhyamaka synthesis, who played a significant role in the 'first diffusion' (*snga.dar*) of Buddhism in Tibet (see TIBETAN RELIGION). A central feature of Śāntarakṣita's system is his doctrine that the mind's capability of self-awareness (Skt., *svasaṃvedana*) is the primary differentiation to be made between the mind and the objects of its awareness, which are said to be 'inert' (*jaḍu*).

Śāntarakṣita first visited Tibet in 763 CE and a second time in 775, staying until his death. It was he who, according to *Padma.ka'i.thang.yig* (The Clear Decree of Padma; a 15th-cent. *terma), advised King Trisong Detsen (Khri.srong.lde.brtsan) to invite *Padmasambhāva to Tibet on the basis of the latter's supernatural powers, because of magical opposition to Buddhist teaching from the native *Bön religion. Śāntarakṣita's major works are *Madhyamakālaṅkāra* (Ornament of the Middle Way) with his own commentary, and *Tattvasaṃgraha* (Compendium of Reality), an assessment of the Indian schools.

Santa Sophia (church, later mosque): see HAGIA SOFIA.

Santería (Cuban, 'the way of the saints'). A complex of religious cults in the Afro-Cuban population, combining Yoruba African and Spanish Catholic traditions, especially concerning the *saints (*santos*) who are identified with the spirits (*orisha*) of the Yoruba pantheon.

Worship features prayers and songs in Yoruba, drumming which may speak for the spirits, and sacred stones of power, associated with the spirits, kept under the altar, and 'baptized' and fed annually with herbs and blood.

Śanti (Skt., 'tranquillity'). Interior peace, personified in Hinduism as a daughter of Śraddha (faith); also a ritual for averting curses, adverse stellar or planetary influences, and bad *karma.

Śānti (Buddhist philosopher): see RATNĀKARAŚĀNTI.

Santiago (pilgrimage centre): see PILGRIMAGE (CHRISTIAN).

Śāntideva (8th cent. CE). Buddhist poet and adherent of the *Prāsaṅgika branch of the *Mādhyamaka school. He composed two important works, the 'Compendium of Discipline' (*Śikṣā-samuccaya*), and 'Entering the Path of Enlightenment' (**Bodhicāryāvatāra*). In 'Entering the Path', Śāntideva describes the various steps to be taken by one pursuing the *bodhisattva path to enlightenment from the production of the thought of enlightenment (*bodhicitta) through the practice of the Perfections (*pāramitās) to full enlightenment.

Sant Niraṅkārī (Sikh movement): see NIRAṄKĀRĪ.

Sant tradition. In Indian religions, a sant is a holy or dedicated religious person. He or she is thus equivalent to a *sādhū (fem., *sadhvī*). More specifically, Sant traditions are those in which a succession of styles and teachings have been developed and transmitted. Of these, one is the Vārkarī movement of Paṇḍharpur in Maharaṣṭra. But more usually the Sant tradition refers to a succession of religious teachers and devotees in N. India whose influence was extensive from the 15th to 17th cents., and persists to the present day. The Sant tradition also refers to itself as Nirguṇa Saṁpradāya (see NIRGUṆA; SAṀPRADĀYA), or Nirguṇa Pantha. This Sant tradition was a coalescence of different religious strands, of which *Vaiṣṇava bhakti, especially as associated with *Ramananda, was particularly important. Major figures among the Sants include *Nāmdev, *Ravi Dās, and *Kabīr; but the most dramatic influence was exercised on Gurū *Nānak, and thus on the formation of the Sikh tradition. See NIRAṄKĀRĪ.

The term 'sant' is also an honorific title given to revered teachers (cf. *sādhu). See Index, Sants.

Sanusis/Senusis (Sūfi movement): see AL-SANŪSĪ.

Sanyo (three essentials of Zen Buddhist Lin-chi line): see LIN-CHI.

Sanzen (Jap., 'going to Zen'). Going to a Zen master (*rōshi) to receive instruction. For *Dōgen, it means the correct practice of Zen. For *Rinzai, it is a synonym of *dokusan.

Sapir–Whorf hypothesis (role of language in creating cultural diversity): see CULTURAL RELATIVITY AND RELIGION.

Saptarṣi (visionary authors of Vedic hymns): see ṚṢI.

Sarah (wife of Abraham, ancestress of the Jewish people): see PATRIARCHS AND MATRIARCHS.

Saraṇa (refuge): see TRĪSARAṆA.

Sarasvatī. 1. In Hinduism, consort of Brahmā, and patron of learning and the arts. Sarasvatī is widely revered, and particularly attracts the worship of *brahmans and students.

2. The legendary river of NW India, personified as Sarasvatī.

Sardār (Pañjābī, 'chief'). Usual form of address for Sikh men, corresponding to 'Mr'. Sardārjī conveys more respect. The chieftains of the Sikh *misls were termed sardār or *misldār*.

Sari. The traditional dress of Hindu women, now frequently worn by women of other religious groups in India as well. It consists of a 4-foot-wide length of cloth, generally varying in length, 5–9 yards, though for daily wear a 6-yard length is favoured. Saris for daily wear are generally of cotton or, these days, nylon, but beautiful silken ones are worn for festivals or religious ceremonies.

Sāriputta or **Sāriputra.** 1. One of the two principal followers of the *Buddha (with *Moggallāna). He is represented iconographically on the Buddha's right hand.

2. A 12th-cent. leader of the Buddhist *saṅgha (monastic communities), and a highly revered commentator on the *Pāli canon. His work is marked by a quest for inclusion and reconciliation, and he was called 'the ocean of wisdom'.

Śarīra (Skt., 'husk'). 1. In Hinduism, the three surrounding protections or supports for the *ātman (undying self): (i) sthūla-śarīra, the apparent body; (ii) sūksma-śarīra, also liṅga-śarīra, the subtle body, not evident to direct sight; (iii) kārana-śarīra, the body that supports the possibility of the attainment of bliss (*ānanda). Because the ātman is thus protected, it can be carried from death to rebirth.

2. In Buddhism, the relics of the *Buddha

Śākyamuni, or of any other prominent Buddhist, usually preserved in a *stūpa or *pagoda.

Sārnāth. North of the Ganges (*Gaṅgā), near Vārāṇasī (*Kāśi), the place where the *Buddha delivered his first sermon. The exact spot in Sārnāth where this took place is known as the Deer Park (Iṣipataṇa) and the event is called 'the turning of the Wheel of Dharma' (*dharma-cakra-pravartana*).

Sārnāth has continued to be an important *pilgrimage site.

Sarum Use. The plainchant and ritual developed in Salisbury Cathedral from the 13th cent. to the *Reformation.

Sarvamedha. Hindu sacrifice of universal or power-creating efficacy. It is described in **Śatapatha Brāhmaṇa* 13. 7. 1 ff. It lasts ten days, and consists in the self-offering of the creator Svayambhu on behalf of his creation.

Sarvaṅ khalvidam Brahma. 'All this is truly *Brahman', one of the Hindu *mahāvākyas (great sayings). It appears in *Chandogya Upaniṣad* 3. 14. 1.

Sarvāstivāda (Pāli, Sabbatthivāda, from *sabbam atthi*, 'everything exists'). One of three systematic schools of early Buddhism which derived from the *Sthaviravāda of the first schism, the others being *Pudgalavādins and *Vibhajjavādins. They became the most prominent non-Mahāyāna school in N. India, whence they moved into China. Their main works on *Abhidharma survive in Chinese and Tibetan. They are distinguished, in their teaching, by their view that *dharmas have real existence, not only in the present but in the past, since they must exist as causes of *karma. Thus they made dharmas into reified entities, indivisible constituents of reality. Each has its own nature (*svadharma), and they are bound together in forms of appearance without constituting a self. Conflicts among Sarvastivādins led to a Council, c.100 CE, under Kaniṣka I, which produced a commentary of agreed teaching, *Mahāvibhāṣā*. Mainstream Sarvāstivādins, following this, were also called Vaibhāṣikas; dissenters split off to form the *Sautrāntika school.

Sarvodaya ('The Awakening and Welfare of All'). Buddhist-based rural self-development movement, initiated in Śri Lankā and mainly found there. The movement is based on *śramadāna*, community work projects, and is sometimes known as Sarvodaya Shramadana. The concept was endorsed by *Gāndhī, but the specifically Buddhist movement began in 1958, when a young teacher, A. T. Ariyaratne, encouraged his pupils to engage in a fortnight's holiday work camp, starting from the needs as perceived by the destitute villagers themselves. Many other schools and colleges followed this example, and before long *bhikṣus were involved. As the movement grew and became formalized, it took care to keep decision-making decentralized, establishing Village Awakening Councils (*samhiti*) which administered their own budgets and decided their own programmes. About a third of all Śri Lankā's villages became involved; and in 1981, Sarvodaya Shramadana International was instituted, with a concern, not only for Third World development, but for errors in developed societies as well.

Sāsana (Pāli) or **śāsana** (Skt.). Teaching, instruction, message of the *Buddha; however, the term by custom has come to mean the Buddhist religion (Buddha-sāsana) or tradition itself, especially with respect to the period of its duration as a historical phenomenon. So sāsana refers to the 'dispensation' of the teaching. When a *sammāsambuddha discovers and imparts the *dharma, his message and its impact on society and the world endures for a limited period of time only. The circumstances or fortunes of the dharma change, being subject, like all things, to the law of impermanence (*anicca), although the dharma itself, of course, never changes. Gradually Buddhist tradition wanes until it eventually disappears from the earth altogether. It remains lost until the next sammāsambuddha appears and introduces dharma to the world again.

Śāsanadevatā. Jain spiritual beings who serve the *jinas but who also respond as gods, at a popular level, to the devotion and prayers of humans. Frequently they are Hindu deities, and thus have afforded a way in which not only the natural human desire for God is satisfied, but also respect for those deities is made manifest in a Hindu context. Of particular importance are Śri *Lakṣmī, *Sarasvatī, and *Amba, the guardian of the jina *Nemināthа. Under the name of Sachika, *Durgā, the slayer of *Mahiṣa, is revered (mainly in Rājasthān). Yakṣadampati, pairs of attendant *yakṣas and yakṣis, are often found in carvings without any further identity beyond that of the jina whom they serve.

Sa-skya (order of Tibetan Buddhism): see 'PHAGS-PA.

Sassatavāda (Pāli) or **śāśvatavāda** (Skt.). Eternalism, the doctrine of an immutable soul or self which survives death and continues everlastingly. Both eternalism and its opposite view, annihilationism, are versions of the so-called soul heresy (*sakkāya-diṭṭhi) and represent, according to Buddhism, the two alternative directions which misrepresentations of reality take.

Śāstra(s) (Skt., 'command, rule'). 1. Hindu treatise or treatises on particular topics, amounting to law books or codes. The *sūtra manuals of the priests are extended and better organized. The best known examples are the *Dharmaśāstras (e.g. **Manusmṛti*, *Yajñavalkyasmṛti*), *Arthaśāstra, and Kāmaśāstras (e.g. of Vātsyāyana).

2. In Buddhism, Mahāyāna commentaries on philosophical issues in the *sūtras.

Sat (Skt., 'being', 'essence', 'right'). Absolute, unqualified Being in Hinduism, and thus identical with *Brahman. In ethics it means 'good', in epistemology 'true'. It is combined with *cit and *ānanda in the basic formula *saccidānanda.

Satan (Heb., 'adversary'; Arab., *al-Shaytan*). In Jewish, Christian, and Islamic tradition, the chief enemy of God.

Judaism In the older books of the Hebrew Bible, the word *sātān* is a common noun (e.g. 1 Samuel 29. 4), and is a human adversary (1 Kings 11. 14, 23, 25). Apart from the figure of the serpent in Genesis 3, there is no figure to correspond to the later tradition. This begins to emerge after the *Exile, perhaps under *Zoroastrian influence. In *Job, 'the Satan' is a heavenly figure who tests Job, but always with God's permission (e.g. chs. 1 and 2). In the *amoraic period, he becomes a significant individual. He is said to have been responsible for all the sins in the Bible (*PdRE* 13. 1), and the reason for blowing the *shofar on *Rosh ha-Shanah is 'to confuse Satan' (*BRH* 16b). In later Judaism (especially *kabbalah) he becomes known by other names, e.g. *Samael.

Christianity The cognate term 'the devil' (Gk., *diabolos*), which has become the usual word in Christian tradition, alternates with 'Satan' in the New Testament (see also BEELZEBUB). Here the Jewish picture is elaborated.

The identity of Satan as a fallen angel is asserted by Revelation 12. 7–9. The devil, *'Lucifer', fell through pride, because he would not submit to God. Satan's defeat by Christ on the cross led to 'Christus Victor' theories of *atonement, revived and made important in the 20th cent., by G. Aulén: the conquest of personified evil reinforced many Christians in their resistance to totalitarian dictators.

Islam Al-Shaytān is, in the *Qur'ān, the adversary. The term describes Iblīs (Gk., *diabolos*, 'devil') and his descendants as they cease to be simply rebellious *jinn, and become subverters or tempters of humans (eighty-eight times in thirty-six chapters).

Satanic Verses. Verses insinuated into the *Qur'ān by al-Shaytān (*Satan), when *Muḥammad was uttering authentic verses. But God cancels (*naskh) anything that Satan throws in.

The phrase has become notorious as the title of a novel by Salman Rushdie (1988), which elicited a *fatwā from the Ayatollah *Khumayni, placing the author under sentence of death—in effect for *apostasy, followed by the bringing of Islam into ridicule—though more colloquially for blasphemy.

Satapadi (seven steps): see MARRIAGE (Hinduism).

Śatapatha Brāhmaṇa. The 'Brāhmaṇa of a Hundred Paths', is the longest and fullest *brāhmaṇa. It is attached to the White **Yajur Veda*, and its *āraṇyaka is the *Bṛhadāranyaka Upaniṣad*. It describes the five great sacrificial ceremonies, *vājapeya*, *rājasūya*, *aśvamedha, *puruṣamedha*, and *sarvamedha*, and it reveals much of the political and religious condition of late Vedic times.

Sat cakra bheda (Skt., 'piercing the six wheels'). In *Tantrism, the movement of the *Kuṇḍalinī up the suṣumṇā *nāḍī, passing through the six *cakras to the thousand-petalled lotus (*sahasrāra). This is also called *laya yoga.

Sat-cit-ānanda (three-fold characterization of Brahman): see SACCIDĀNANDA.

Sat Gurū. For Sikhs, the supreme *Gurū, i.e. God. God is called by other names, e.g. *Akal Purukh, *Vāhigurū, but Gurū *Nānak used the term Sat Gurū more than 300 times in the *Ādi Granth, as the only source of true guidance. The term may also be used as an honorific title for gurus.

Satī. The wife of *Śiva who committed suicide when her father insulted Śiva.

The term (anglicized as 'suttee') was used for the self-immolation of Hindu widows, either by joining the dead husband on his funeral pyre, or by committing suicide later on a pyre lit by embers from that pyre. Not even pregnancy could save a woman from this fate; the ceremony was merely postponed until two months after her child's birth. The custom continues, but infrequently and illegally.

Hindu law books of the 1st and 2nd cents. CE see the act as gaining spiritual merit; 400 years later it was considered that for a woman to survive her husband was sinful.

It is unlikely that many widows went voluntarily to the flames, though it is certain that some did. Many were forcibly burnt; even sons would be deaf to their mothers' pleas, in order to protect family honour.

Not until 1829, under Lord Bentinck's Regulation, did satī become legally homicide, after pressure was brought to bear on the British authorities by Christian missionaries and Hindu reformers, notably Rām Mohan *Roy.

Sati (Pāli) or **smṛti** (Skt., 'mindfulness'). A form of mental application which lies at the very heart of Buddhist meditational practice, whose object is awareness, lucidity, true recognition. It is concerned with the bare registering of the objects of our senses and minds as they are presented to us in our experience, without reacting to them in terms of the behaviour of the ego—i.e. in terms of our likes and dislikes, passions and prejudices. Only then can the true nature of things become illumined.

Satipaṭṭhāna (Pāli, *sati-upaṭṭhāna*, 'the establishing or setting up of mindfulness'; Skt., *smṛti-upasthāna*). The system of meditation based on mindfulness (*sati), set forth by the Buddha in a discourse (*sutta*) of that name (*Dīgha Nikāya* 2. 290–315; *Majjhima Nikāya* 1. 55–63), and regarded as the one scheme of practice indispensable to the realization of *nirvāna. It consists of mindfulness directed successively upon the four objects which together represent the total range of the individual's experience of himself: his body (*kāya*), feelings (*vedanā*), mind (*citta), and mental concepts (*dhamma).

The practice of satipaṭṭhāna counteracts the tendency to confuse the ego with the body, feelings, mind and mental concepts by disclosing just 'the body in the body, feelings in feelings, mind in mind, and mental concepts in mental concepts'. Consequently, traits of the ego's behaviour resulting from this confusion, such as discontent (*domanassa*), dissolve away. They are replaced by a correct comprehension (*jñāṇa) and recollection (*paṭissati*) of the way things are.

Sati Srī Akāl: see SAT SRĪ AKĀL.

Sat-kārya-vada (Skt., 'theory of existent effect'), in *Sāṁkhya, the concept that any effect pre-exists in its cause; there is no creation of a thing previously nonexistent.

Everything that occurs exists potentially in its cause. Creation is produced simply through a recombination of the constituents of the uncreated (*avyakta*). By analogy, a statue pre-exists in the stone; curds in milk. Specifically, creation involves a re-organizing of the three *guṇas which exist in perfect equilibrium in the primal 'stuff' (*mūlaprakṛti*) of creation. All change occurs through the interaction of these three guṇas.

Ṣatkasampatti (Skt., 'six attainments'). The six great virtues which, in *Śaṅkara's Hindu system, must be fulfilled as one of the four prerequisites by a student of *Vedānta—the others being *mumukṣutva* (striving for liberation), *viveka (discrimination), and *vairagya (detachment). The six virtues are (i) *śama*, concentration and control of the mind, directed towards an object of meditation; (ii) *dama*, control of the organs of sense; (iii) *uparama*, quieting of the mind, especially by the fulfilment of one's duty of *dharma; (iv) *titikṣa*, the patient balance between opposing dualities; (v) *śraddhā, faith, trust in what scriptures teach; (vi) *samādhāna* (cf. SAMĀDHI), the concentration which enables one also to transmit truth to others.

Satnām (Pañjābī, 'whose name is true'). Distinctively Sikh appellation for God. Sikhs frequently invoke God with the words 'Satnām Śrī *Vāhigurū'.

Satori (Jap.; Chin., *wu). Zen term for the experience of awakening or enlightenment. It is derived from *satoru*, 'know', but it has no connection with knowledge in any ordinary sense. Retrospectively, satori is the enlightenment experience of the *Buddha (Chin., *wu*; Skt., *bodhi), but in Zen it is more often used prospectively, of the enlightenment to which the disciple or pupil is now aspiring. A first enlightenment experience is known as *kenshō, which may be followed by a small, then great, satori. The essence of satori remains the same, but the one who attains it gains in profundity within it.

Śatrunjāya, Mount (holy mountain): see PILGRIMAGE (JAINISM).

Satsamga (Skt., 'good' + 'company'). The virtue in Hinduism of seeking the company of good people so that the 'spark' of wisdom can pass from one life to another.

Satsang (Sikh association): see SANGAT.

Sat Srī Akāl (Pañjābī, 'True is immortal God'). Sikh greeting. This replaced the earlier 'sat kartār'. In battle 'Sat Srī Akāl' was the Sikhs' war-cry.

Sattva (Skt.). In *Sāṁkhya, one of the three strands (*guṇas) of material nature (*prakṛti). It is present in varying degrees in all things except pure consciousness (*puruṣa); it is luminosity. In the material world sattva is manifested as buoyancy or lightness: bright colours, air, light foods, etc. In the individual psyche it is expressed through intelligence, virtue, cheerfulness, etc. It is a predominance of sattva over the other guṇas which begins the creation process in prakṛti. Through sattva, puruṣa is most accurately reflected in prakṛti.

Sattyasiddhi: see SAUTRĀNTIKAS.

Satyāgraha (Skt., 'truth force'). The power of truth without force or violence to change political and other circumstances. It was developed by M. K. *Gāndhī, drawing on an association of *sat with *satya* ('truth'), and *agrah* ('grasp firmly'). It puts together the power associated with *tapas and the tradition of *ahiṃsā, and is often equated with non-violence as such.

Satya Sai Baba (Hindu spiritual guide and miracle worker): see SAI BABA.

Saul. The first king of the Israelites. 1 Samuel contains several stories about Saul's accession (see 9. 1–10. 16; 10. 17–27; 11), some indicating conflict about the propriety of so great an innovation.

Sautrāntikas. Members of a Buddhist school seceding from the *Sarvāstivādins (*c.*200 CE) on the grounds that only *sūtra and not *abhidharma is the authoritative word of the Buddha—hence their name, Sautrāntika (*sūtrānta* + *ika*). Their doctrines anticipated developments in the *Vijñāpti-mātra school. In China, they were continued by Ch'eng-shih (Jap., *Jōjitsu*), the Sattyasiddhi school.

Savayye or **Swayyā** (Pañjābī, 'type of verse'). Panegyric; Sikh hymn. In *Nitnem, are recited after *Japjī and *Jāp by devout Sikhs each morning.

Savitar (Vedic sun god): see SURYA.

Savitṛ (one of the Ādityas, the power of words): see ĀDITYAS; SŪRYA.

Sāvitrī. Hindu Goddess, daughter of the Sun (Savitar). She is known as the mother of the *Vedas, and is often identified with *Gāyatrī (thus seen as a personification of *Ṛg Veda* 3. 62. 10, the Gāyatrī *mantra, addressed to Savitar). A lengthy poetic reworking of the Sāvitrī legend by Śri *Aurobindo Ghose follows the careers of the various characters in the story as an allegory of the divinization of human life, a concept central to Aurobindo's philosophy. In the West, the composer Gustav Holst (1874–1934), having learnt Sanskrit in order to write *Choral Hymns from the Rig Veda* (1908–12), composed the chamber opera *Savitri* (1908, first staged 1916).

Savonarola, Girolamo (1452–98). Christian reformer and preacher. He was born at Ferrara in Italy, and entered the *Dominican Order in 1475. In 1482, he went to Florence, where he began to develop his programme of *ascetic morality. This he based on *apocalyptic preaching, emphasizing the final judgement and the possibility of eternal damnation. After three years in Bologna, he returned to Florence, where he preached against corruption in high places, and gave prophetic warnings, some of which appeared to come true. When Charles VIII invaded Italy, Savonarola averted the threat to the city, and the people made him their ruler. He attempted to establish a theocratic state with severe standards of behaviour: in the 'bonfire of vanities', the people burnt frivolous or lewd items. He denounced Pope Alexander VI and his corrupt court, and was summoned to Rome to account for his actions as 'a meddlesome friar': he refused to go and was excommunicated. A *Franciscan challenged him to ordeal by fire, which he refused. He was seized, tortured, and executed.

Savoraim (Aram., 'explainers'). Jewish Babylonian scholars between the time of the *amoraim and the *geonim. Traditionally the era of the amoraim ends in 499 CE, and the era of the Savoraim ends either in 540 CE or, according to Abraham *ibn Daud, in 689 CE.

Savupadisesa-nibbāna (in Buddhism, nirvāna while still in the condition of this life): see SOPADHIŚEṢA-NIRVĀṆA.

Ṣawm or **ṣiyām.** Fasting, the fourth *pillar of Islam. Fasting is obligatory on Muslims, during the whole month of *Ramaḍān, and at other times in compensation for days then missed; it can also be practised in fulfilment of a personal vow, or as a pious action. Ṣawm must be preceded by the *niy(y)a, 'intention'.

During Ramaḍān, any adult Muslim of sound mind and in good health must abstain from food, drink, smoking, and sexual relations during daylight hours, which are estimated as beginning when 'the white thread becomes distinct to you from the black thread' at dawn (Qur'ān 2. 187). It is customary, and recommended, for the Muslim to have a final meal (*saḥūr*) shortly before daybreak; in the evening the first food (*fuṭūr*) should be of water or dates, with a large meal following.

Saʿy. The part of the Muslim *ḥajj which comes after the circumambulation of the *Kaʿba. The pilgrim leaves the *masjid, left foot first, ascends the steps of al-Ṣafā and makes an invocation, looking toward the Kaʿba. He then descends and crosses the valley at a run until he reaches al-Marwa where again he prays.

Sayadaw (Burm., 'teacher'). Burmese title for a Buddhist monk. Strictly it applies to the head of a monastery, but it is used as a general honorific.

Sayers, Dorothy L. (1893–1957). British writer and Christian lay theologian. Her radio plays on the life of *Jesus, *The Man Born to be King* (broadcast 1941–2) were remarkable for their character study, especially of *Judas. In *The Mind of the Maker* (1941) she expounded the doctrine of the *Trinity by analogy with a creative artist's Idea, Energy, and Power.

Sayings of the Fathers (text commending the spirituality of the desert): see MONASTICISM (CHRISTIANITY).

Sayings/Chapters of the Fathers (Jewish text): see AVOT.

Sayyid (title of descendant of Muḥammad): see SAIYID.

Sayyid al-Shuhadā' (leader of martyrs): see AL-ḤUSAIN B. ʿALI.

Scapegoat. Jewish *sin-offering let loose on the *Day of Atonement. The Day of Atonement Temple ritual included casting lots between two goats. One was *sacrificed to God, while the other was dedicated to *Azazel. It was released into the wilderness and cast over a cliff: see Leviticus 16.

Scapular (Lat., *scapulae*, 'shoulder blades'). Part of the Christian religious *habit consisting of a piece of cloth worn over the shoulders and hanging down in front and behind. It represents the yoke of Christ (Matthew 11. 29 f.).

Schechter, Solomon (1847–1915). Jewish scholar. Schechter came from an *ḥasidic background. Through his efforts, the manuscripts and fragments of the *Cairo Geniza were recovered and brought to England. From 1902, he was President of the *Jewish Theological Seminary, and his *Studies in Judaism* (1896–1924) and *Some Aspects of Rabbinic Theology* (1909) are classics of *Conservative Judaism. He defended traditional ways and values against what he took to be *assimilationist tendencies in *Reform Judaism.

Schism (Gk., *schisma*, 'tear, rent'). A formal division of a religious body into separate parties. In Christian usage the word refers to sects or churches separating from communion with one another where *heresy is not involved. Early schismatic bodies (i.e. from the *Catholic Church) included the *Novatianists and *Donatists. The Orthodox and Catholic churches have been divided by schism (the 'East–West schism') since 1054. See also GREAT SCHISM. Schism appeared early in the history of Buddhism, due in part to the Buddha's refusal to appoint a successor as leader of the Order and his reluctance to impose a rigid discipline in matters of monastic practice.

A schism (*saṃghabheda*) is defined as occurring when nine fully ordained monks leave a community together, as a result of dissent, and perform their own communal services apart. If the number is less than nine, there is 'dissent' rather than schism. To cause a schism maliciously or from selfish motives is considered a grave offence and one destined for swift retribution (*anantārya*).

Schleiermacher, Friedrich (1768–1834). Christian *Protestant theologian, sometimes called 'the father of modern protestantism'. He followed his father into the *Moravian Brethren in 1783, and attended a Moravian school. He went to the university at Halle, and in 1794 was ordained into the ministry of the Reformed Church, and became a chaplain at the Charité Hospital in Berlin. Here he associated with an intellectual circle which included the two von Schlegel brothers, and in which there was much criticism of prevailing religion. In response, he wrote *Über die Religion: Reden an die Gebildeten unter ihren Verachtern* (On Religion: Speeches to its Cultured Despisers, 1798). He shared the distaste of the cultured despisers for the arid philosophy of religion which issued in *Deism, and even more for the petty and futile divisions of the Church over dogma and outward form. But this, he argued, is not truly 'religion'. Thus 'true religion is sense and taste for the Infinite'. This sense of the Whole, not (as in Newtonian physics) as a passive arena of inert forces, but as an active movement toward the human, evoking a certain feeling (*Gefühl*), is the origin of religion, 'raised above all error' because it is primordial and inescapable—it precedes the organization of church and doctrine. But a feeling of what? Schleiermacher here pointed to its relation to the commonly experienced human feeling of dependence (*Abhangigkeit*), but in the religious case, this is a feeling of absolute dependence ('das Gefühl der schlechthinigen Abhangigkeit').

In 1800, he applied his understanding to ethics in *Monologen* (Soliloquies). In *Der Christliche Glaube* ... (The Christian Faith), every religion is seen as the consequence of the feeling of absolute dependence, but Christianity derives from 'the Ideal Representative of Religion', i.e. from Jesus of Nazareth whose consciousness was entirely taken up with this awareness of God.

Schneur Zalman of Lyady (founder of movement in Judaism): see SHNE'UR, ZALMAN.

Scholasticism. A Christian intellectual movement which endeavoured to penetrate, and perhaps to bring into a single system, the fundamental (especially revealed) articles of faith by use of reason. It flourished in the 13th cent., and is characterized by the production of *Summae* (i.e. summations) of theology and philosophy. The best known of these are the *Summae* of Thomas *Aquinas. The method of scholasticism was that of disputation, in which problems were divided into parts, objections were raised and answered, and a conclusion was reached. Scholasticism was thus an assertion of the responsibility of reason in relation to revelation.

School of the Three Stages. A Chinese Buddhist school founded by Hsin-hsing (540–94 CE) during the Sui dynasty (581–618). The three stages were based on the idea that the teachings of the *Buddha may be divided into three periods; pure *dharma, duration 500 years; counterfeit dharma, duration 1,000 years; decay of the dharma, said to last 10,000 years. Hsin-hsing taught that his age was already the third stage. The school advocated the performance of altruistic deeds and almsgiving. To carry out these deeds, the school relied mainly on the income of the Inexhaustible Treasury established in the Hua-tu Monastery in Ch'ang-an. The income of the Treasury was divided into three portions, one for the repair of the temples and monasteries, one for social welfare, and one for ceremonies to the Buddha. Because the school insisted that it taught the sole formula for salvation during the age of decay, it met with opposition from other schools of Buddhism.

Schools of Law, Muslim (Arab., *madhab*, pl., *madhāhib*, 'direction'). Muslim life is founded on *Qur'ān, which itself was first expressed in the lives and words of the Prophet *Muḥammad and his *Companions. Their words and actions were collected in aḥādith (*ḥadīth), and these become exemplary in Muslim life. Even so, not every circumstance was covered, so application of these sources to life became necessary. These eventually issued in (among *Sunni Muslims) four major schools of law (*sharī'a), named after their founders: (i) Mālikite (*Mālik ibn Anas), which relies on the customary interpretations of *Madīna, and puts less reliance on methods of exegesis such as *ijmā' (consensus) or *ra'y* (informed opinion); (ii) *Hanīfite (*Abū Ḥanīfa), seeking consensus, and prepared to use methods of exegesis to make sharī'a readily applicable; (iii) Shāfi'ite (Muḥammad b. Idrīs *al-Shāfi'ī), seeking rules to govern the methods of exegesis, which is thus kept under control, the school mediating between innovative and conservative; (iv) *Hanbalite (Aḥmad *ibn Ḥanbal), conservative and defensive of early patterns of observation. In the Muslim world, (i) is strong in W. Africa and the Arab west, (ii) in the former *Ottoman Empire and the Indian subcontinent, (iii) in the far East, (iv) in Saudi Arabia and Qatar. Each school regards the others as legitimate, but a Muslim is expected to live within the pattern of one of them: eclecticism (*talfiq*) is discouraged. There is also a number of *Shī'a schools, though by its nature, Shī'a Islam is less strongly organized in a centralized sense.

Schopenhauer, Arthur (1788–1860). German essayist and philosopher who developed a closely knit system in which was emphasized the primacy of the will over both reason and sensation. Schopenhauer was greatly influenced by Indian thought, which he held paralleled Kant in every key respect. He attributed this parallelism to the indirect influence of ancient Eastern thought on modern Western thought through the mediation of Christianity, whose founder—he deduced—must have been familiar with Hindu and Buddhist ideas. His major work was *Die Welt als Wille und Vorstellung* (1819; tr. 1883, *The World as Will and Idea*).

Schütz, H. (composer of Christian works): see MUSIC.

Schweitzer, Albert (1875–1965). Christian theologian and mission doctor. A superb musician and organist, he made a name in academic circles when he published *Das Messianitats- und Leidensgeheimnis* (1901; *The Mystery of the Kingdom of God*, 1925). In this he argued that 'Jesus' is embedded in the interests and presuppositions of the *gospel writers, and to an extent, therefore, remains to us as 'One unknown'. What at least can be said is that Jesus shared the *apocalyptic expectations of his contemporaries, and that he saw himself as the one who was to inaugurate the Final Kingdom, not least through his sacrificial suffering. This 'messianic secret' was not divulged to any until the so-called 'Confession at Caesarea Philippi'. His extreme call for moral perfection was unrealistic if understood as a programme for life and history, but not if it was intended as an 'interim ethic', to be maintained in the short interval before the inauguration of the kingdom.

Schweitzer developed this perspective further in *Von Reimarus zu Wrede* . . . (1906; *The Quest for the Historical Jesus*, 1910), and in *Geschichte der Paulinischen Forschung* . . . (1911; *Paul and his Interpreters*, 1912). These works set an inescapable agenda for subsequent work on the New Testament; yet his most enduring work was *Die Mystik des Apostels Paulus* (1930; The Mysticism of Paul the Apostle). Meanwhile a profound experience of the unity of all life, evoking reverence for life, led him to establish a mission hospital at Lambaréné in Gabon, where he based himself for the rest of his life. Although criticized for his stern paternalism, his commitment and his work for reconciliation were recognized with the award of the Nobel Peace Prize in 1964.

Science and religion. The relationship between science and religion has been described in various ways, falling between two extremes. At one extreme, the relationship is seen as one of warfare. At the other extreme, the relationship is seen as one of convergence and confirmation, in which the insights of religion (albeit expressed in pre-scientific languages) are seen to point to the same truths as those claimed in contemporary sciences. Between the extremes are many different ways of evaluating the possible relationship between science and religion. Ian Barbour (*Religion in an Age of Science*, 1990) classified them in four groups: conflict, independence (as enterprises they are so different that there is no connection between them), dialogue, and integration. All these can be exemplified in any religion.

In the field of science and religion, a weakness of much work is its assumption that there is some 'thing' called science and some 'thing' called religion whose relationship can be discussed. Science changes, both in content and in methodologies, and religions have changed greatly through the course of time (for the consequent problem of defining religion, see Introduction). Religions are systems for the protection and transmission of human achievements and discoveries. For the most part, they arise from goals, methods, and objectives which are very different from those of the sciences, hence the impossibility of reducing the one to the other. But this means that religions can hardly be in competition with the sciences as comparable *systems*, even though the sciences will frequently challenge the content and methodologies of religious exploration, and religions will challenge the dehumanizing applications of science where they occur. For that reason particular issues will constantly arise, as notoriously in the case of Galileo and Darwin. But there neither was, nor is, only one way in which religions respond to such challenges. There are, and have been in the past, many different ways in which achievements in the sciences have been evaluated, ranging from denial to appropriation. Different (and strictly speaking incompatible) strategies have been adopted in order to maintain authority and control. Thus while there will always be propositional and conceptual issues between science and religion, and while they are often both interesting and important, they are second-order issues. Of primary concern are the issues of power, authority and control.

Science of hearts (Sūfī description of the work of one of the earliest Sūfīs): see ḤASAN AL-BAṢRĪ.

Scientology. The creation of L. Ron *Hubbard, who in the early 1950s, using his theory of lay psychotherapy (Dianetics) as its basis, developed a religious philosophy which was then incorporated into the Church of Scientology. While Dianetics deals in the main with the 'reactive mind' (the subconscious), Scientology is concerned with the 'Thetan' or everlasting spirit.

The movement has been accused of aggressive and on occasion unlawful methods in its ways of recruitment and its methods of defence against critics, so that its short history has been surrounded by controversy.

Scillitan Martyrs. Seven men and five women of Scillium in N. Africa who were put to death in 180 when they refused to renounce Christianity and swear by the 'genius' of the Roman emperor.

Scofield, Cyrus I. (1843–1921). American biblical scholar, and editor of the *Scofield Reference Bible* (1909; new edns. 1919, 1967). Its good typography and tacit rejection of all 'higher criticism' made it enormously popular in conservative Protestantism, and so secured an audience for its *dispensationalist teaching.

Scopes trial (for teaching of Darwinism): see CREATIONISM.

Scotus (medieval Christian philosopher): see DUNS SCOTUS.

Scotus Eriugena (neoplatonic philosopher): see ERIUGENA.

Scribe (Heb., *sofer*). Copier of Jewish documents, also a recognized transmitter and scholar of Jewish law. In the *rabbinic period and subsequently, scribes were professional inscribers of *Torah *Scrolls, *tefillin, *mezuzot, and *gittim* (bills of divorce). *Masseketh* or *Hilkoth Soferim* is one of the Minor Tractates in the *Talmud dealing with scribal matters. The decrees transmitted by scribes are known as *dibre soferim* ('words of the scribes'), *tikkune soferim* ('corrections of the scribes'), and *dikduke soferim* ('minutiae of the scribes').

Scripture. Texts regarded as sacred (usually revealed: see REVELATION), having authority and often collected into an accepted *canon. Despite the origin of the word (Lat., *scripto*, 'I write'), most religious scriptures began as recited texts, being preserved in orally transmitted forms: the *Vedas of the Hindus were written down only because the world moved into the degenerate *Kāli yuga; *oral law (*Torah she be'al peh*) was as much revealed on *Sinai as was written Torah; the *Qur'ān was not written down until after the death of *Muḥammad; and the Pāli canon was not committed to writing until (theoretically) the First *Council, though in fact much later. When scriptures were eventually written down, it often remained a primary religious act to recite (rather than read) scripture. The definition of scripture may be a long (and sometimes contested) process: thus the canons of Jewish and Christian scripture took many centuries to achieve; and in the Christian case, agreement has not yet been reached. The historical embeddedness of scripture (i.e. the fact that however eternal the Word may be, it is manifested in a language in the midst of time) gives a natural bias to at least a species of *fundamentalism, since it relates present-day life to a supreme moment of revelation.

For different scriptures, see Index, Canonical Collections.

Scroll of the Law (Heb., *sefer torah*). The scroll on which the Jewish *Pentateuch is inscribed. The Scroll of the law is always used for public reading in the *synagogue. It is written by a qualified *scribe and, when not in use, it is kept in the *synagogue *Ark. It is the most revered of ritual objects. *Sefer Torah* is the title of a Minor Tractate in the Talmud, concerned mainly with guidance for scribes.

Scrolls, Five (Heb., *Ḥamesh Megillot*). The five shortest books of the Hebrew scriptures. The Five Scrolls are the Books of *Ecclesiastes, *Esther, *Lamentations, *Ruth, and the *Song of Songs.

Seal of Confession. The obligation and commitment that nothing said in *confession will be revealed to any other person.

Seal of recognition (mark of succession in Zen Buddhism): see INKA-SHŌMEI.

Seal of the Fathers (Patriarch of Alexandria and Church Father): see CYRIL, ST.

Seal of the Prophets/prophecy (Arab., *khatm al-anbiyya, khatm al-nubuwwah*). Title of the prophet *Muḥammad, indicating that he is the last prophet whose message supersedes that of earlier prophets (e.g. *Moses, *Jesus).

Seamless pagoda, the (part of a kōan): see NAN-YANG.

Sebastian, St. Roman Christian martyr who is believed to have died in the persecution of Diocletian (late 3rd cent.). As a young man transfixed by arrows he was an extremely popular subject for Renaissance artists. Feast day, 20 Jan.

Second Coming (of Christ to earth): see PAROUSIA.

Second days. Additional holy day or days observed by Jews living in the *diaspora at the *festivals of *Passover, *Shavu'ot and *Sukkot. The need for them arose from the problem of securing the observation of the New Moon, on which the date of the festivals (and subsequent festivals or fasts) depend. When a fixed *calendar was introduced in the 4th cent. CE, Jews in Babylon asked the authorities in the land of Israel whether these 'two festivals of the Exile' (*yom tov sheni shel galuyyot*) should be discontinued. They were told that so long-standing a custom should be continued even though the reason for it had disappeared.

Second diffusion (of Buddhism in Tibet): see TIBETAN RELIGION.

Second Rome. *Constantinople, which, after the sack of *Rome in 476, became the capital of the Christian world. When Constantinople fell to the Turks in 1453, Moscow claimed to be the Third Rome, as in the letter of Philotheus of Pskov to the Tsar, Basil III, 'Two Romes have fallen, but the third stands, and there will not be a fourth.'

Secret societies, Chinese. Unlawful associations in China were of two main kinds, the brotherhoods (*hui*) of sworn association, pursuing secular ends, often of a criminal kind, and the religious (*chiao*) associations pursuing healing and salvation by unorthodox means. Membership could often overlap, and the current term, *mimi shehui* (adopted from Japanese) covers both. The Triads are not a single society, but a number of branches, each of which shares a common system of signs, initiation rites, etc., engaging in activities outside the law, and often characterized by anti-government activities. See also SOCIETIES, CHINESE; Index, Secret Societies.

Secrets of Enoch (apocalyptic text): see ENOCH.

Sects. Groups, usually religious, which are set up with their own organization in distinction from, and often in protest against, established religions. Sects featured in *Troeltsch's *Church–Sect typology. Sects are characterized by: depending on volunteers (to be born into a sect indicates that it is on the way to stability); *charismatic authority; strict discipline with clear rules of conduct; sense of élite privilege (of being the only ones in a true, or enlightened, or saved state); restriction on individuality. In addition, R. Wallis (*Salvation and Protest*, 1979) suggested that sects are either world-affirming (seeing power, value, etc., emerging from within the universe) or world-denying (seeing the world as evil and requiring rescue by God). For examples, see Index, Sects, movements, etc.

Sect Shinto. Official (i.e. registered with the Ministry of Education) Shinto organizations in Japan. They are assigned (chronologically) to one of three categories: jinja Shinto (Shrine Shinto, founded before the modern era), *kyōha Shinto (Sect Shinto, autonomous organizations authorized between 1868 and 1945—i.e. *Meiji to end of the Second World War), and shin kyōha Shinto (New Sect Shinto, post-1945). All of these very many movements have been discussed academically as *new religions, but some are clearly newer than others. For lists, addresses, and some brief descriptions, see *Japanese Religion*, a survey issued by the Agency for Cultural Affairs.

Secular clergy. Christian priests who live in the world (Lat., *saeculum*), as distinguished from members of religious communities who live according to a rule ('regular clergy'). They are not bound by vows and may possess property, and they owe obedience to their bishops.

Secular institutes. Organizations among *Roman Catholics whose members, lay or ordained, are committed to common rules while living in the world, without making public vows or wearing distinctive dress (*habit). They received papal approval in 1947.

Secularization (Lat., *saeculum*, 'age' or 'world', i.e. this world). The (supposed) process whereby people, losing confidence in otherworldly or supernatural accounts of the cosmos and its destiny, abandon religious beliefs and practices, or whereby religion loses its influence on society. Secularization is an elusive and much-debated concept. In origin, the term referred to the alienation of Church property to the State, and thence to the loss of temporal power by the Church. It referred also to the process whereby ordained clergy reverted to the lay state. It then came more loosely to refer to the transition from the religious to the non-religious world. At this preliminary level, it is possible to treat religion and the secular at the level of *ideology (despite the fact that ideology is itself a complex concept), and to understand the process as one in which one ideology is compelled to give way to another. This is the account offered by D. Cupitt in a widely read book, *The Sea of Faith* (1984).

The weakness of this account is that it fails to recognize the fact that religions in novel circumstances react in vastly different ways, ranging from adaptation to resistance, but more frequently by failing to act as ideology at all, and by doing complementary, not competitive things. More responsibly, therefore, Bryan Wilson proposed the 'secularization thesis' (e.g. *Religion in Secular Society*, 1966). Defining secularization as 'the process whereby religious thinking, practices and institutions lose social significance', he argued, not that people have necessarily lost interest in religion, nor that they have adopted a new ideology, but more restrictedly that religion has ceased to have any significance for the working of the social system. Many problems in this position have been exposed, ranging from the measures and methods of social significance (in the past as much as in the present) to the relevance of a contingent observation about the distribution of power to the understanding of religion. Religions clearly duck and weave through the vicissitudes of history, and are not in some single and invariant conflict with a reality which can be defined as 'secularization'.

For these (and other) reasons, T. Luckmann argued that 'the notion of secularisation offers a largely fictitious account of the transformations of religion in Western society during the past centuries' (*Life-World and Social Realities*, 1983), and called this spurious account 'the myth of secularisation': its basic mistake is to tie religion to the institutional forms it has happened to take, and then to measure religion by the fortunes (or misfortunes) of those institutions. It may be, therefore, that the phenomena which have evoked the term 'secularization' would be much better considered as a consequence of roughly three centuries of often bitter struggle to maximize the autonomy of individuals and (increasingly in contradiction) of markets. In political terms, the consequence of the struggle is referred to as 'democracy'. It is a commitment to the maximum freedom of choice for individuals and groups within the boundary of law. It is, in brief, a preferential option for options. But quite apart from its pressure to disentangle Church from State, it also has had the consequence of making religion optional, where once it was less so. But this understanding of secularization, while it does indeed raise problems for institutions, and may drive them to 'market' themselves as though a commodity, does not threaten the basic 'religiousness' of humanity; for the supposition that *Weber's 'shift to rationalisation' will leave religions behind has proved already to be false.

Secularization Thesis: see SECULARIZATION.

Sedarim. The six orders (or divisions) of the Jewish *Mishnah.

Sedarot. Portions of the *Pentateuch read in the Jewish *synagogue on the *Sabbath. Each sidrah (sing.) has a distinctive name taken from the first important word in the text. The Pentateuch is divided into fifty-four sedarot so that the entire work is read each year.

Seder (Heb., 'Order'). The order of a Jewish service, especially the home ceremony normally used at the festival of *Passover.

Seder 'Olam (Order of the World). Two Jewish chronicles. Written in Hebrew, the *Seder 'Olam Rabbah* is mentioned in the *Talmud and is a *midrashic chronology from the Creation of the world to the *Bar Kokhba revolt. The *Seder 'Olam Zuta*, written in a mixture of Heb. and Aramaic, traces the chronology of the generations from *Adam until the end of the Babylonian *exilarchate. Scholars disagree on its date of composition.

See. The seat (Lat., *sedes*) of a Christian *bishop; hence the town or district surrounding the cathedral (where the bishop has his *cathedra*, or throne), is known as the see.

Seed mantra/syllable (power underlying appearance in Indian religions): see BĪJA.

Sefer ha-Aggadah (Book of Aggadah): see AGGADAH.

Sefer ha-Bahir (Jewish Kabbalistic work): see BAHIR, SEFER HA-.

Sefer ha-Ḥayyim (Jewish heavenly book containing names of the righteous): see BOOK OF LIFE.

Sefer Ḥasidim (The Book of the Holy Ones). A popular Jewish text describing the way of the *Ḥasid. It is attributed to Judah the Ḥasid of Regensburg of the 13th cent., but it is a compilation of stories, maxims, and expositions coming from different hands.

Sefer ha-Jashar (Israelite book of poetry): see BOOK OF JASHAR.

Sefer Torah (scroll on which Pentateuch is inscribed): see SCROLL OF THE LAW.

Sefirot. Jewish *kabbalistic term meaning God's emanations. There are ten sefirot that emerge from *Ein Sof. Each one points to a different aspect of God's creative nature, and together they compose the world of divine light in the chain of being. All ten together form a dynamic unit, sometimes portrayed as a tree, by which God's activity is revealed. The three highest sefirot are the Supreme Crown, *Wisdom, and Intelligence. The seven lower are Love, Power, Beauty, Endurance, Majesty, Foundation, and Kingdom. The whole concept is influenced by *gnostic thought and is an attempt to explain how a transcendent God can interact with the world.

Seichō no Ie (Jap., 'House of Growth'). A Japanese religion founded by Taniguchi Masaharu (1893–1985) in 1930. Central to the teachings of this movement, an offshoot from *Ōmotokyō, is the belief that all human beings are divine and equal in that they are all children of God. 'The life of reality' (*jisso*) involves the realization that sin and illness have no reality in themselves. The movement is eclectic, drawing on many religions and regarding them as preparatory to itself.

Seigan (vows in Zen Buddhism): see SHIGU-SEIGAN.

Seirai-no-i (Jap.). The coming of meaning from the west, the arrival of *Bodhidharma from India to China, and thus of the buddhadharma with him.

Seiza (Jap., 'sitting in silence'). Zen position of meditation, kneeling on one's heels with straight back. In *zazen, it is an alternative to the lotus position (*padmāsana).

Sekai Kyūseikyō (Jap., 'The Religion for World Salvation'). Japanese religion founded by Okada Mokichi (1882–1955). Okada originally belonged to *Ōmotokyō, until in 1926, it was revealed to him in a state of divine possession that he was the *messiah of the present age. He established Dainihon Kannonkai, focused on the *bodhisattva Kannon (see AVALOKITEŚVARA), with the purposes of establishing communion with Kannon and of healing. Required by the government to choose one or the other, he chose healing, and the movement was renamed Nihon Jōka Ryōhō. After the Second World War, he reverted to the two goals, calling the movement Nihon Kannon Kyōdan, but after a schism, he arrived at the present name. Faith-healing is central in the movement, under the name and technique of *jōrei*: this involves transmitting healing divine light through cupped hands. Equally important is *shizen nōhō*, agriculture that follows the way of nature. Sekai Kyuseikyo believes that heaven on earth (*chijō tengoku*) can be established on earth at its centre at Atami. Museums and gardens exhibit the importance of harmony and beauty.

Sekishu (name for the koān, 'what is the sound of one hand clapping?'): see HAKUIN.

Sekisō Soen (Jap., for Shih-shuang Ch'u-yuan): see KŌAN.

Self-Realization Fellowship. Founded by the Indian *guru Paramhansa Yogananda (1893–1953) in Boston, Mass., in 1920. Yogananda taught specific yoga techniques to develop soul awareness and a form of meditation which heightens consciousness to the point where it becomes one with that of the guru.

Seliḥot. Penitential prayers seeking forgiveness (Heb., *seliḥah*), forming in effect an additional Jewish prayer-service for fast days and the penitential season. The *Sephardim usually recite seliḥot for forty days from Rosh Ḥodesh Elul (see NEW YEAR) to *Yom Kippur, while the *Ashkenazim begin on the Sunday before *Rosh ha-Shanah. Seliḥot are also recited on all official fast days.

Semikhah (Heb., 'laying on' (of hands)). The Jewish rite of *ordination. In biblical times, leaders were ordained by the laying on of hands (e.g. Numbers 27. 22; 11. 16–17). Membership of the Great *Sanhedrin required ordination, and it was agreed by the time of *Judah ha-Nasi that religious decisions could only be made by those qualified (*B.Sanh.* 5b). The formula for Semikhah was 'Yoreh Yoreh. Yaddin Yaddin' ('May he decide? He may decide! May he judge? He may judge!'); and in the early days any ordained teacher could ordain his students.

Semiotics (study of signs): see SYMBOLS.

Semi-Pelagians (Christians who believe that God's grace is a necessary precondition, but that works have status thereafter): see PREDESTINATION.

Semper reformanda (always to be reformed): see PRESBYTERIANISM.

Sen, Keshub (Keshab) Chunder (Chandra) (1838–84). Indian reformer, and third leader of *Brahmo Samāj. He joined the Brahmo Samāj in 1857, working with Debendranāth *Tagore to promote its aims, and lecturing widely in English on theistic doctrine and Brahmo philosophy, establishing branches of the Samāj in Bombay, Madras, and other centres.

Throughout his life Sen claimed to have had mystical experiences. He almost became a Christian in 1866, the only obstacle being an inability to accept the uniqueness of *Christ, though he turned against the philosophical system of Hinduism, including *Vedānta, supporting widow remarriage and repudiating the wearing of the sacred thread (*upanayana), finally breaking with Debendranāth Tagore in 1865. In 1866 he established the Bhāratvarshīya Brahmo Samāj, which preached the brotherhood of all under the Fatherhood of God, a teaching enshrined in the *Śloka-saṁgraha* scriptures.

Sen later adopted still more social reforms. He relied increasingly on direct inspiration, which enabled him, despite his previous opposition to child-marriage, to marry his 13-year-old daughter to a Hindu prince. Many of his followers abandoned him for this, setting up in 1878 Sādhāran (General) Brahmo Samāj. In 1879 he proclaimed a New Dispensation (Nava Vidhāna) to supplant Christianity. He chose twelve disciples, promulgated the Motherhood of God, revived the *āratī* and *homa ceremonies, the *Durgā Pūjā festival, and the religious dance of *Caitanya, while urging that *idolatry and polytheism were forms of *theism.

Sengai Gibon (1751–1837). Outstanding Zen artist and calligrapher. He became a monk at 11, and went on wandering pilgrimage (*angya) when 19. He became dharma-successor (*hassu) of Gessen Zenji, and was appointed abbot of Shōfuku-ji in 1790. He was noted also for his humorous instruction.

Senge (Jap., 'entering transformation'). Zen Buddhist term for death which stresses its transition-nature, and its inherent unimportance.

Seng-ts'an (Jap., Sōsan). Third patriarch (*soshigata) in the Ch'an Buddhist lineage in China, and dharma-successor (*hassu) of *Hui-k'o. He died in 606 CE, but nothing certain is otherwise known of him. He is said to have been attracted by **Laṇkāvatāra Sūtra*, which he received from Hui-k'o, and also to have written the poem *Hsin-hsin-ming* (Jap., *Shinjimei*, 'Inscribed on the Believing Mind'), but its union of Taoist and Mahāyāna ideas make this unlikely. It (especially its opening) is much quoted in Zen writings.

Sengyo (Jap., 'fish-run'). Zen expression derived from **Chuang-tzu* 31: 'A fish-run is constructed to catch fish: we should keep the fish and forget the run. A snare is to catch rabbits: we should keep the rabbits and forget the snare. Words are to transmit meaning: we should keep the meaning and forget the words.'

Senju-Kannon (Skt., *Sahasrabhuja-sahasranetra*, 'a thousand arms and a thousand eyes'). Kannon (see AVALOKITEŚVARA) with a thousand arms growing from the palm of each hand, each arm having an eye: this enables him to see all distress and act to alleviate it.

Senkō Kokushi. Posthumous title of *Eisai.

Sennin (Jap.). Immortal beings. The idea is of Chinese origin (*hsien-jen), associated with religious *Taoism and *alchemy. With the spread of knowledge in religious Taoism among the Japanese gentry in the Nara period, the legends of Japanese sennin, like Kume no Sennin, possessing supernatural powers and riding clouds, began to appear. In Buddhism, the word sennin is one of the translations for the Sanskrit *ṛṣi.

En no Gyōja, the supposed founder of *Shugendō, was also called a sennin.

Sen no Rikyū (formulator of tea ceremony): see CHADŌ.

Sensei (Jap., 'teacher'). In the Japanese tradition, a general term of respect accorded to, amongst others, university lecturers, instructors in the martial arts, priests of *Jōdo Shinshū Buddhism, and priests of *Zen Buddhism below the rank of *Rōshi.

Senshō-fuden (Jap., 'unable to be told by a thousand of the wise'). Zen insistence that truth cannot be carried or conveyed by words, but has to be recognized by an individual awareness or enlightenment. See also FUKASETSU.

Senusis (members of the Sanūsiya order): see AL-SANŪSĪ, SĪDĪ MUḤAMMAD.

Sephardim. Jews descended from those who lived in the Iberian Peninsula before 1492 (hence the name, Heb., *Sefarad*, Spain). However, the term 'Sephardim' is often also used to indicate all non-*Ashkenazi Jews. The Sephardi language is Ladino, a type of archaic Spanish; and Sephardic literature includes works in Hebrew and Spanish as well. The Sephardim, like the Ashkenazim, base their religious practice on the tenets of the *Talmud. However, they follow Joseph *Caro's **Shulḥān Arukh* without the amendments of Moses *Isserles, and thus their interpretation of the law tends to be more liberal. As a result of worsening conditions, there have been large-scale emigrations from the communities in Muslim countries to *Israel since 1948, where there is a dual *Chief Rabbinate. In general, Sephardim have felt themselves to be put in second place by Ashkenazim, and only slowly have come to positions of authority in government. A Sephardi, Leon Tamman (1927–95) founded Ta'ali, the World Movement for a United Israel, to reconcile the two communities, and progress was made as a result.

Seppō Gison (Japanese name): see HSÜEH-FENG I-TS'UN.

Seppuku (ritual suicide): see HARA-KIRI; SUICIDE.

Septuagesima. The third Sunday before *Lent, nine weeks before *Easter. See also QUINQUAGESIMA.

Septuagint (often written LXX, the Latin numerals). The early Greek translation of the Hebrew scriptures inherited by the Christian Church. It is so-called because it was supposed to have been translated by seventy scholars (according to the *Letter of *Aristeas*, it was 72).

Sequence. A hymn, usually in couplets, sung in the *mass on certain days after the *epistle. In medieval times a large number of sequences (*c.*150 melodies and 400 texts, with at least 5,000 having been written) were in regular use, but in the *missal only five are now printed.

Seraph. Either a species of serpent mentioned in the Hebrew scriptures, or a type of *angelic being.

Seraphim of Sarov (1759–1833). Russian monk and *staretz. Born in Kursk, he entered the monastery at Sarov *c.*1779. From 1794 he lived as a hermit, first in the nearby forest, later in a cell in the monastery. From 1825 he engaged in spiritual direction of his many visitors. He also founded a community of nuns. Severe in his personal asceticism, he was gentle with others.

Serendib. An old name for *Śri Lankā. It was derived from the Arab. version of the Skt. name Sinhala-dvipa (Pāli, Sihala-dvipa). The name was used during the Roman Empire. From it, Horace Walpole coined the word, 'serendipity', in *The Three Princes of Serendib* (1754).

Sergius (Sergii) of Radonezh, St (*c.*1314–92). Russian monastic reformer. Born at Rostov, as a boy he fled with his family to Radonezh near Moscow, where he founded with his brother the monastery of the Holy Trinity (and afterwards many others), thus reviving monasticism which had collapsed during the Tatar aggression. He was a great influence for peace, supporting Prince Dmitri in resisting the Tatars, thereby saving Russia. In 1378 he refused to become metropolitan of Moscow. He is regarded as one of the founders of Russia and the greatest of Russian saints. Feast day, 25 Sept.

Sermon on the Mount. A collection of sayings of *Jesus presented in Matthew 5–7 as a single discourse given 'on the mountain' (5. 1). It includes the *Beatitudes, *Lord's Prayer, *Golden Rule, and other ethical sayings. The 'sermon on the plain' in Luke 6. 20–49 is somewhat parallel though shorter.

Servant songs. Poems about a faithful servant of the Lord found in the Hebrew Book of *Isaiah. The Servant songs are located in Isaiah 42. 1–4; 49. 1–6; 50. 4–9; 52. 13–53. 12. The songs either have been interpreted collectively (see 49. 3)—the servant represents the Jewish people, the ideal *Israel, or the faithful *remnant—or have been understood to refer to a particular individual (e.g. the writer of the songs, Hezekiah, *Josiah, Zerubbabel, Cyrus, *Ezekiel, *Moses, *Job, etc.). In the Christian tradition, the songs are thought to point forward to the sufferings of Jesus. The question has been raised more recently whether it is correct to think of a group of Servant Songs at all.

Servetus, Michael, or **Miguel Serveto** (1511–53). Christian theologian. He was born in Spain and studied at Saragossa, Toulouse, and Paris. He turned from law to medicine which he practised intermittently throughout his life. During his travels he met *Bucer and perhaps some other *Anabaptist leaders. His interest in theology led him to produce *De Trinitatis Erroribus* (1531, On the Erroneous Understanding of the Trinity), in which he argued that the Son and the Holy Spirit are modes in which God manifests himself in creation, redemption, and sanctification, and that the Trinity is not made up of 'persons'. He reiterated these arguments in *Christianismi Restitutio* (1546, The Restoration of Christianity), by which time he had also argued against *predestination and infant baptism. He was arrested, first by the *Inquisition, and then (when he escaped to Geneva) by the Protestants. He was convicted and burnt to death, his death provoking debate about the bounds of tolerance.

Śeṣa (Skt., 'remainder'). In Hindu mythology, the serpent which forms *Viṣṇu's couch and canopy during the periods between destruction and creation. Śeṣa is also called Ananta (Skt., 'endless').

Sesshin (Jap., 'collecting the heart-mind'). Days in Zen monasteries of particularly concentrated practice.

Sesshu Tōyō (1420–1506). A major Japanese Zen painter, considered by many the greatest master. He entered a Zen monastery when 12 and was trained at Shōkokuji in *Kyōto. The control of his brush and line are a perfect expression of Zen control. 'The Four Seasons' is usually singled out as his masterpiece, but 'Landscape in the Broken Ink Style' (ibid. 129) is an equally superb achievement.

Sesson Yubai (1288–1346). Japanese Zen master of the *Rinzai school. In 1306/7 he went to China, where he was imprisoned for ten years, but also sought instruction from different masters, before returning to become abbot of Engaku-ji and Nanzen-ji. He was a writer of considerable care and style who is considered one of the founders of the *gosan-bungaku.

Setsubun (Jap.), the day before the beginning of spring, now celebrated on the 3 or 4 February. Setsubun, which means 'seasonal division', originally referred to the day before the beginning of the 24 divisions of the calendrical year, but it has become synonymous with the last day of the last division called *daikan* (great cold) which starts on the 20 or 21 January. On the eve of the beginning of spring (*risshun*) the evil spirits are expelled by the bean-throwing rite. This *exorcism is called *tsuina* (Chinese, *chui-no*).

Setsuwa (Jap., 'explanatory stories'). Japanese stories of miraculous happenings which carry a moral message. They are frequently Buddhist. Important collections are *Nihon Ryoiki* (9th cent., written by a Buddhist monk, Kyokai, *Konjaku Monogatari* (12th cent.), and *Uji Shui Monogatari* (13th cent.). See also DENSETSU and SHINWA for other kinds of Japanese story.

Se'udah (Heb., 'meal'). A Jewish festive meal. According to the *Talmud, there are two sorts of festive meals. *Se'udah shel reshut* has nothing to do with religion, and scholars are discouraged from participating (*B.Pes.* 49a); *se'udah shel* **mitzvah*, on the other hand, is a meal held in conjunction with religious rejoicing, as at a *circumcision, a wedding, the *Sabbath, the *Passover *seder, etc. It is a religious duty to share in and to enjoy such feasts.

Sevā (Pañjābī, 'service'). Sikh ideal of service. Service rendered in accordance with God's will and without expectation of reward counteracts *haumai (egoism). A sevā panthi is a Sikh who has spent a life in service to the *panth; or more specifically, a member of a group which serves others, founded in memory of Bhāī Kanayhā who tended the wounded in battle on both sides.

Seven Churches. The recipients of seven letters incorporated into chs. 1–3 of the New Testament book of *Revelation.

Seven deadly sins. In Christianity (more accurately, 'capital' or 'root' sins): pride, covetousness, lust, envy, gluttony, anger, and sloth (*accidie). The traditional number is first found in *Gregory the Great (although with *tristitia*, 'gloom', instead of *accidie*). For five deadly sins, see GOGYAKU-ZAI.

Seven dimensions of religion: see Introduction.

Seveners. *Ismā'īlī sect (or sects; from Arab., *sab'īya*) which holds that the legitimate line of *Imāms ended with the seventh (hence the name). The sixth Imām was Ja'far al-Ṣādiq: his eldest son, Ismā'īl, died before his father, leading to a complex contest of claims to legitimate succession. The Seveners held that Ismā'īl was the true (and perhaps, because of the significance of the number 'seven', the final) successor. Two of the many sects became prominent, the *Fāṭimids, whose rulers were Imāms of the sect, and the *Qarmatians. All groups placed emphasis on esoteric teaching, and were therefore known as *Batinis (*bāṭinī*).

Seven false views (wrong seeing in Buddhism): see DIṬṬHI.

Seven gods of luck (Japanese deities): see DAIKOKU.

Seven holy cities (Hindu): see SACRED CITIES, SEVEN.

Seven holy rivers (Hindu): see SACRED RIVERS, SEVEN.

Seven precepts (basic rules of Druze life): see DRUZES.

Seven Sacred Cities (Hindu): see SACRED CITIES, SEVEN.

Seven Sages of the Bamboo Grove (Taoist philosophers): see TAOISM.

Seven Sleepers of Ephesus. The heroes of a romance which was popular among both Christians and Muslims in the Middle Ages. In the story, seven Christian young men take refuge from the persecution of the emperor Decius (249–51) in a cave near Ephesus, fall asleep and reawaken under the Christian emperor Theodosius II (408–50). They become proof of the *resurrection of the dead. The grotto of the Seven Sleepers in Ephesus was an important Christian pilgrimage place until the Islamic conquest of Asia Minor in the 15th cent. Muslims located the story and tomb in various places, including a different Ephesus (Afsūs) which was within Arab territory from the 7th cent.

Seven Sorrows of the Virgin Mary. According to the Roman *Breviary: (i) at the prophecy of *Simeon (Luke 2. 34–5); (ii) at the flight into Egypt (Matthew 2. 13–15); (iii) at the loss of the holy child (Luke 2. 41–52); (iv) on meeting *Jesus on the way to *Calvary (Luke 23. 27–31); (v) at standing at the foot of the cross (John 19. 25); (vi) at the taking down of Christ from the cross (Luke 23. 53); (vii) at his burial (Matthew 27. 59–60, etc.). The seven sorrows are commemorated on 15 Sept., the feast of Our Lady of Sorrow.

Seventeen Article Constitution (Shōtoku's reform which gave support to Buddhism): see NARA BUDDHISM.

Seventeenth of Tammuz (Jewish fast day): see TAMMUZ, FAST OF.

Seventh Day Adventists (members of Christian sect who believe in the literal Second Coming of Christ): see ADVENTISTS.

Seventh Heaven. The highest of all the spheres in the created order, hence the nearest that humans can approach to God. The theory of seven heavens/spheres is widespread in religions, e.g. in *kabbalah.

Seven Virtues. In Christian tradition: faith, hope, charity, prudence, temperance, fortitude, justice. The first three are the 'theological virtues', grouped together by Paul in 1 Corinthians 13. 13. The last four are the 'cardinal virtues', a classification taken over by the chief Christian *moral theologians, e.g. *Ambrose, *Augustine, and Thomas *Aquinas, from Plato and Aristotle.

Seven Words from the Cross. Sayings of Jesus on the cross used as subjects of Christian meditation, especially on *Good Friday. They are: (i) Luke 23. 34; (ii) Luke 23. 43; (iii) John 19. 26 f.; (iv) Matthew 27. 46; Mark 15. 34; (v) John 19. 28; (vi) John 19. 30; (vii) Luke 23. 46. A musical interpretation was written by Haydn in his Sonatas on the Seven Last Words.

Sevorah (Jewish Babylonian scholars): see SAVORAIM.

Sexagesima. The second Sunday before *Lent, eight weeks before *Easter. See also QUINQUAGESIMA.

Sex and religion. Since both sex and reproduction are fundamental in human and other life, it is not surprising that religions give central importance to both (the two are not synonymous, as will be seen). At the most basic level, religions have been in the past, and to a great extent still aspire to be, systems which protect gene replication and the nurture of children. It was not possible in the past to have any knowledge of genetics, but that, from an evolutionary point of view, is irrelevant. Natural selection operates on the heritable differences which occur between individuals whether those individuals are aware of it or not. The evolution of sex has therefore carried with it a vast range of different strategies through which the chances of successful reproduction are maximized (e.g. a mating pair might produce the maximum offspring in the minimum time with no nurture, so that a few individuals survive, e.g. herrings; or they might produce few offspring with long gestation and maximum nurture so that the few individuals survive, e.g. elephants—or humans). There is no suggestion that organisms make conscious decisions about the strategies they adopt; rather, the strategies adopted are winnowed impersonally by the test of whether they produce fit individuals to continue the process.

In the human case, however, consciousness *is* introduced. Thus although humans are carried by the same process of natural selection, they can also enhance the process by the creation of cultural defences and controls. It is in this sense that gene replication in the human case is protected by *both* the body *and* culture.

It is here that religions have been so important: they are the earliest cultural creations of which we have evidence which supply contexts of security and controls over human behaviours and evaluations of them. Sexual variance may thus be harnessed—or prohibited (e.g. *celibacy or *homosexuality may serve the community, or they may be regarded as aberrant): as always, religions produce a bewildering variety of different strategies. The resulting religious control has produced high degrees of stability: it has produced moral codes, designations of who may mate with whom (including prohibited relationships), techniques and rituals for producing offspring (often of a desired gender), education, protection of women, assurance of paternity (by restricting access to women) and thus of heredity and continuity in society. The consequence has been strong male control of women, in which have been combined reverence for women and subordination of them (see further WOMEN).

At the same time, religions have made much, in different ways, of the distinction between sex and reproduction. Even before the relation between sexual acts and reproduction was better understood, the potential of sex for pleasure and power was well-recognized. This, in itself, reinforced the male control of women, since promiscuous or unlicensed sexual activity would clearly subvert that ordering of families in particular and of society in general which was rewarded in natural selection. Within that context of restriction, the nature of sexuality and sexual feelings have evoked widely differing responses in religions, ranging from a fear of being enslaved to the passions (leading to a dualistic subordination of sexuality, as in *Manichaeism) to a delight in sexuality as a proper end in life, as among Hindus: see *puruṣārtha, *kāma. In any case, the exploration of sexuality has been religiously important. In Eastern religions, in particular, the nature of sexual energy was explored in many directions. Since sexual arousal seems to make its own demands, what might be the consequence if that energy is brought under human control? In China this lent itself to the quest for immortality and the gaining of strength (see e.g. *breath, *ch'i, *fang-chung shu, *hsien, *Taoism), in India to the acquisition of power (see *Cakra Pūjā, *Dūtī Pūjā, *kālacakra, *Kāpālika, *maithuna, *pañca-makāra, *Sahajīyā, *Śaktism, *Tantrika, *Tantrism). In Christianity, the issue of control led in a different direction. In so far as human sex transcends both reproduction and biological imperatives, it is no longer an end of that kind in itself. How, then, does it relate to the end of salvation and the vision of God? One answer is to say, Extremely well: the union of a man and a woman, transcending the union of male and female in a biological sense, has seemed religiously to be the nearest one can come on earth to the final union with God. But another answer has been to say that sex is of lesser value than the final end of God, and is among those things which may have to be given up if the unqualified love of God is to flourish. This *ascetic option gives the highest value to *celibacy, chastity, and virginity, and it became the dominant voice of the official Church, especially in the West. Male resistance to the erosion of male control has produced in all religions vigorous defences of the status quo, along with a deriding, as 'political correctness', of attempts to implement the recognition that women are no longer at the disposal of men. The *Vatican resistance to the courtesy of gender-inclusive language is an obvious example of this. Contraception (see BIRTH AND POPULATION CONTROL) has been known to all religions and has been differently evaluated, but in general it has always been linked to the priority of reproduction, especially of male children who will continue the line of descent. In the last century, the development of simpler and more effective contraception has broken the link: sex and reproduction are no longer synonymous. The problems this is causing for male-dominated religious systems, intent on preserving the *status quo*, are great.

See Index, Sexuality.

Sforno, Obadiah ben Jacob (*c.*1470–1550). Italian Jewish biblical commentator. After settling in Bologna, he practised medicine and set up a *bet-midrash* ('house of study'). He wrote commentaries on the *Pentateuch, the *Song of Songs, and *Ecclesiastes (1567), on the *Psalms (1586), on *Job (1589), and on *Jonah, *Habakkuk, and *Zechariah (1724). In general, he kept to the literal meaning of the text; although he sometimes used *allegory, he avoided *kabbalistic interpretation. He also produced a work of philosophy, the *'Or Ammim* (Light of Nations, 1537), the Lat. tr. of which was dedicated to Henri II of France.

SGPC (authoritative elected Sikh body): see SHIROMAṆĪ GURDWĀRĀ PARBANDHAK COMMITTEE.

sgyu lus ('Illusory Body' in Buddhist doctrine): see NĀRO CHOS DRUG.

Sh. May be spelt ś; check in appropriate alphabetical order.

Shabbat. The first tractate of the Jewish *Mishnah, *Tosefta, and the two *Talmuds of the order of *Mo'ed*. *Shabbat* deals with the laws of the *Sabbath.

Shabbat (seventh day of the week for Jews when they abstain from work): see SABBATH.

Shabbateanism: see SHABBETAI ZEVI.

Shabbat ha-Gadol (Heb., 'The Great Sabbath'). The Sabbath preceding the Jewish *Passover. It is possibly called the 'great Sabbath' because the *haftarah reading is from *Malachi and refers to the 'great and terrible day of the Lord' (3. 23).

Shabbetai Zevi (1626–76). Jewish *messianic leader. Shabbetai Zevi was *ordained as a *ḥakham after a thorough *Talmudic and *kabbalistic education. In 1665, he travelled to Gaza to meet *Nathan of Gaza 'in order to find *tikkun and peace for his soul'. Nathan was convinced that *Shabbetai was the *messiah and on 17 Sivan, Shabbetai so declared himself. He appointed representatives of the twelve tribes and circled *Jerusalem on horseback like a king. Rumour spread throughout Europe. Shabbetai was *excommunicated in Jerusalem and returned to Smyrna, and the entire community was thrown into a state of messianic fervour. A division arose between the believers (the *ma'aminim*) and the 'infidels' (the *koferim*), but so hysterical was the excitement that many of the infidels were forced to flee from the city. After appointing counterparts to the ancient kings of *Israel, Shabbetai sailed for Constantinople, where he was arrested and held in moderately comfortable imprisonment. Meanwhile, news of the advent of the messiah produced enormous excitement throughout the diaspora, and broadsheets and pamphlets were circulated throughout Europe. In some instances support was given to the movement by Christian millenarians who believed that the world would come to an end in 1666. From prison Shabbetai continued his activities, abolishing the fasts of 17 *Tammuz and 9 *Av, and signing his letters as 'the firstborn son of God' and even 'the Lord your God Shabbetai Zevi'. In Sept. 1666, he was taken to the Sultan's court where he was given the choice of death or conversion to Islam. Shabbetai agreed to *apostasy, took the name of Aziz Mehmed Effendi, and accepted a royal pension. Shabbetai himself continued to act as before among his secret followers in Adrianople and was finally exiled to Albania where he died in 1676. Although repressed by the *rabbis, Shabbatean ideas, particularly in the realm of the kabbalah, continued to circulate, especially in Turkey, Italy, and Poland, and continued to inspire popular movements such as the *'aliyah of 'the holy society of Rabbi Judah Ḥasid' to Jerusalem in 1700. Such scholars as Moses *Luzzatto, Jonathan *Eybeschuetz, and Nehemiah Hiyya *Hayon provoked controversy because of their continued Shabbatean ideas. For later developments see DOENMEH; FRANK, JACOB.

Shadal (acronym): see LUZZATTO, SAMUEL DAVID.

Shādhiliy(y)a. A Sūfī order founded by al-Shādhilī (1196–1258 (AH 593–656)) who left, not written works, but many sayings and chants. The best-known collection is *Ḥizb al-Baḥr* (Incantation of the Sea), which effected many *miracles. He strongly emphasized *ṣabr (acceptance) and *shukr* (thanksgiving). He insisted on observance of *Sunnī orthodoxy, hence avoiding conflict as the movement spread, mainly into N. Africa. From the Shādhiliy(y)a derived many other orders, e.g. the 'Alawiy(y)a, the Darqawiy(y)a. The influence of the Shādhiliy(y)a was extended in the 20th cent. beyond the Muslim world through the writings of René Guénon, also known as Shaykh 'Abd al-Wāḥid Yaḥyā, who sought to identify comparable spiritual and cosmological principles underlying all the great religions; and through the work of Frithjof Schuon.

Shadkhan. Jewish *marriage broker. Traditionally all marriages were arranged in Judaism.

Shadow-boxing: see T'AI CHI CH'ÜAN.

Shadow theatre: see THEATRE AND DRAMA.

Shadrach, Meshach, and Abednego. Babylonian names for Hananiah, Mishael, and Azariah, the three Jewish exiles who were cast into the fiery furnace for their refusal to worship idols (Daniel 3).

Shafā'a (Arab., *shafa'a*, 'double, repeat a prayer'). *Intercession in Islam. The *Qur'ān insists that no intercession will be possible on the Day of *Judgement, which will evaluate a strict balance of good and evil works. However, the efficacy of *Muḥammad's intercession becomes a matter of *ijma' (agreed belief by consensus), making him something much closer to a redeemer. To Muḥammad were then added many other intercessors, e.g. angels and martyrs (*shahīd), and, among the *Shī'a, *Imāms (especially for *Ithna 'Ashariy(y)a, *al-Mahdī), and *Fāṭima.

Shāfi'ites. School of Muslim law derived from *al-Shāfi'ī. The school was founded by his pupils and followers. It is characterized by his own adherence to *Qur'ān and *ḥadīth as the absolute sources of law. Great importance is therefore attached to the methodology of exegesis. The school is characterized by its continuing openness to interpretation and application on this basis.

Shahāda. Profession of faith in *Allāh and his messenger; the first *Pillar of Islam, proclaiming the uniqueness of Allāh, and the centrality of *Muḥammad as his prophet. Pronouncing the shahāda implies acceptance of Islam in its totality, and is the only formal requirement for entry into the *'umma (community).

(Ashhadu aina) lā ilāha illā Allāh
wa-Muḥammad rasūl Allāh
(I bear witness that) there is no god but God
and Muḥammad is the messenger of God.

The shahāda is included in the *ādhān (call to prayer) and is pronounced during the *ṣalāt, as part of the tashahhud, which, however, contains extra phrases.

Shaḥarit. The Jewish daily morning service. Traditionally believed to have been instituted by *Abraham (Genesis 19. 27), it replaces the *Temple morning *sacrifice (*B.Ber.* 26b).

Shaheed (Sikh martyr): see SHAHĪD.

Shahīd (Arab., 'a witness'). In the *Qur'ān, one who bears witness, as God bears witness to human deeds. Its subsequent use for one who bears witness to God by dying in his cause—i.e. as a *martyr—is based on the Qur'ān (e.g. 3. 156, 166; 4. 69; 47. 4–6), although the word is not found in the Qur'ān. In *ḥadīth, the martyr who dies in battle against the *kafirun (infidels) is promised great rewards: he passes through the *barzakh, is exempted from the examination in the grave by *Munkar and Nakīr, and goes to the highest rank in *paradise, nearest to the throne of God. Because they are already pure, they alone are not washed before burial, and may be buried in their bloodstained clothes—though those last points have been disputed. The shahīd eventually makes effective intercession (*shafā'a).

The concept was subsequently extended to include those who die during the performance of a godly action (e.g. during al-*ḥajj, or while building a mosque), or while fulfilling one's God-given obligation (e.g. during childbirth). It could also include violent death (e.g. in a shipwreck or a storm) when accompanied by *islam* or trust in God.

Martyrdom is of particular importance in *Shī'a Islam. *al-Ḥusain is *shāhi shuhadā*, king of the martyrs. Ritual participation in his sufferings includes self-flagellation, often of a severe kind, and also the performance of *ta'zīya (condolence, expressed through re-enactments of the life and death of al-Ḥusain). It is moderated by *ṭaqīya, the concealment of faith under persecution or pressure—perhaps even as an obligation.

The word and the concept of martyrdom were adopted by the Sikhs (though usually transliterated as 'shaheed').

Shahrastānī, Abu-'l-Fath Muḥammad ibn 'Abd al-Karīm (1076–1153 (AH 469–548)). Muslim scholar, especially of the relation of religions to Islam. He was a *Sunni and an Ash'arite (*al-Ash'ari), who wrote a work on the limitations of philosophy in relation to theology (*Nihāyat al-Iqdām fi 'Ilm al-Kalām*), but he is remembered particularly for *Kitāb al-Milal w'al-Nihal* (The Book of Religions and Systems). Islam is placed at the centre, as the recipient of the uncorrupted *Qur'ān, and other religions (including Islamic sects) are then placed in varying degrees of positive or negative relation to Islam.

Shah Waliullah (1702–62). An Indian Islamic reformer, who was a *Sunni and a leading *Naqshbandī *Sūfī. He lived at a time when the Indian Muslims were bitterly divided and were suffering a decline in political power. He wrote fifty-one major works in Arabic and Persian. His *magnum opus, Hujjatullah-ul-Balaghah* (covering *Qur'ān, *sharī'a, *tasawwuf, politics, and philosophy), is a restatement of Islam allowing rational and empirical arguments on a much broader basis than the traditional line. His vast influence can still be perceived in such reform movements as *Jamaat-al-Islam, Tableeghi Jamaat, *Iqbal's neo-modernism, the *Ahl-al-Hadith, the *Barelvi, and *Deoband, all of which invoke Shah Waliullah's authority in support of their views.

Waliullah, an eminent Sūfī himself, also began the task of reforming Sufism which had declined extensively into a commercial exploitation of superstition.

On political and socio-economic matters, Waliullah upheld the principle of unity and toleration, condemning sectarianism and Sunni/Shī'a polemics.

Shaikh al-Islām or **shaykh.** Honorific title for Muslims who achieve eminence in various ways, but especially in *kalām or *fīqh. It became, under the *Ottomans, a formal institution, associated with the *muftī of Constantinople. Among *Sūfīs, a shaikh is one who has attained spiritual mastery (Pers., *pir*) by submitting to the discipline and instruction of another shaikh.

Shaikhī. Followers of *Shaykh Aḥmad Aḥsā'ī (1753–1826), a *Shī'a Muslim who lived in Persia. They reject what they regard as the excesses of *Sufism, especially the view that the essence of God becomes manifest in all that he creates (because essence cannot be divided into parts), but equally they are more rationalistic than many Shiʿites would allow. Thus they reject the resurrection of *this* body, saying that it goes to dust, but affirm a subtle body which subsists and is resurrected; and they interpret such miracles as the *miʿrāj (ascension) metaphorically.

Shaitān (the devil in Islam): see DEVIL.

Shaiva, Shaivism, etc. (major tradition of Hindu practice and devotion to Śiva): see ŚAIVISM.

Shakers. Popular name for the United Society for Believers in Christ's Second Appearing. The *sect was founded by Ann Lee (1736–84). She was converted to the Shaking Quakers (so-called because of their trembling and ritualistic dancing) in 1758. She then, as Mother Ann, received revelations that she was the female counterpart of Christ, and that she was to take the small group that had begun to form around her to the New World to await the millennium (see MILLENNIALISM). The community was to be strictly *celibate and was to hold all things in common. By about 1840, they had reached around 6,000 in number, in twenty communities, but have now virtually disappeared: the 'Mother Church' at Mount Lebanon in New York was sold in 1947, and membership was declared closed in 1965. Nevertheless, there is a small continuing community in Maine.

Shakkyo (Jap., 'the teaching of Śāk(yamuni)'). A term for what in the West is called 'Buddhism'. Other such terms include *Shakumon*, 'Buddha's gate', and *Shakushi no oshie*, 'Śākyamuni's teaching'.

Shakti (creative power in Hinduism): see ŚAKTI.

Shakubuku (breaking and subduing): see SŌKA GAKKAI.

Shakumon (Buddha's gate): see SHAKKYO.

Shali'aḥ (Heb., 'messenger'). Jewish emissary. The term is a synonym for Meshullaḥ. In the *rabbinic period emissaries were sent from *Erez Israel to communities in the *diaspora, often to raise funds for charitable institutions.

Shālōm (Heb., 'peace'). Common Hebrew greeting. 'Shālōm' indicates security, contentment, good health, prosperity, friendship, and tranquillity of heart and mind. The Arabic equivalent, also used in greeting, is *salām.

Shamans. Inspired, ecstatic, and *charismatic individuals, male and female, with the power to control spirits, often by incarnating them, and able to make journeys out of the body, both to 'heaven' and 'hell'. The word is traced to the Tungu in Siberia (where shamanism is common), though the claim is also made (but not universally accepted) that the origin is in the Skt. *śrāmaṇa, reaching China in the form of *shamen* and Japan of **shamon*. The word is now used of a wide variety of people who enter trance and ecstatic states, and make 'out of the body' journeys. The inducing of ecstatic states is accomplished in many ways, including exclusion of general sensory stimuli through drumming, concentration on a mirror, etc., and through tobacco, alcohol, and hallucinogens (see M. J. Harner (ed.), *Hallucinogens and Shamanism*, 1973). The spirits involved are not regarded as inherently either good or evil: the outcome depends on context and on whether they are controlled. The shaman removes threat to an individual or community by incorporating potentially destructive spirits into his or her own body and thereby neutralizing them. The ability to make journeys to upper or (more often) lower worlds is a part of the protective role of the shaman extended from its main focus on this earth.

Careful observations of shamanism make the analysis of M. *Eliade (*Le Chamanisme et les techniques archaiques de l'extase*, 1951) improbable, although it has had wide influence. He attempted to separate two forms, regarding the ascent as a survival of archaic religion, to be called 'pure shamanism' (but by other writers 'white shamanism'), with the descent and contest against malevolent spirits as innovations ('black shamanism'). There is no serious warrant for these distinctions in the practice of shamanism as observed.

See Index, Shamanism.

Shambhala (Skt., obscure: 'happiness giving'? Tib., bde.'byung, 'source of happiness'). A semi-mythical kingdom in Tibetan Buddhist cosmology; 'the only *Pure Land which exists on earth' (Birnbaum). While playing an important part in the *Kālacakra cycle of *tantras, Shambhala is also a popular myth in its own right. Located 'somewhere north of Tibet', Shambhala is governed by a line of thirty-two wise and powerful kings—who guard the true doctrine of Buddhism through a period of world history which sees a decline in religious values. When this decline is at its lowest depth, the final king of Shambhala, Rudra Cakrin, will emerge from his kingdom with a great army, subdue the forces of evil, and establish a golden age. See also SHANGRI-LA.

Shamen: see SHAMANS; ŚRĀMAṆA.

Shammai (*c*.50 BCE–*c*.30 CE). Jewish rabbinic leader. Shammai was a contemporary of *Hillel and together they were the last of the *zugot (pairs). He was the founder of the great school of Bet Shammai which was known for its stringent attitude towards the law, but Shammai himself does not always seem to have taken a hard line in the *halakhot transmitted in his name.

Shammash. Jewish salaried official attached to a *synagogue or *bet din. The duties of a Shammash vary according to the institution.

Shamon. Jap. for *śrāmaṇa, a world-renouncer; a Buddhist monk; sometimes (dubiously) linked to *shaman.

Shams al-Dīn Tabrīzī (Sūfī): see JALĀL AL-DĪN RŪMĪ.

Shang-Ch'ing (Taoist heaven): see SAN-CH'ING.

Shang Ch'ing (writings revealed through Wei Hua-tsun): see TAOISM.

Shango. Yoruba god of thunder and focus of a cult mainly in Trinidad and Granada, which is primarily of 19th-cent. African origin, and resembles Jamaican *Pocomania, Cuban *Santería, and the *Afro-Brazilian cults. Animal sacrifices may be made to the particular deity whose practical help is sought through possession of his devotee or through simple forms of divination or by dreams and prophecy; healing and *exorcism of evil spirits are also prominent.

Shangri-la. A fictional hidden valley created by James Hilton in his novel *Lost Horizon* (1933). Hilton's image of Shangri-la has some parallels with the Tibetan myth of *Shambhala, of which he had at least a little knowledge from sources such as the missionary Abbé Huc and possibly the author-explorer Nicholas Roerich.

Shang-ti (Lord of Heaven). In China, a collective name for gods, perhaps representing one supreme god or overlord. Ti were worshipped as deified ancestors of the Shang *dynasty, and the Shang rulers worshipped Shang-ti—but the absence of a plural form makes it uncertain whether Shang-ti was one or many. He or they had overarching functions of control (e.g. over natural phenomena and plagues). Shang-ti was regarded as the Ancestor of the royal house of the Chou dynasty (*c.*1123–1221). In later history Shang-ti or *T'ien (Heaven) became semi-monotheistic; the worship of him was primarily an imperial cult confined to the royal houses and their supporters—the *Confucian official class.

Shang-ti in later times was often referred to, in abbreviation, as Ti (Lord). But Ti was also commonly used in later history to refer to an emperor; his origin is divine because his First Ancestor is Shang-ti. Christian missionaries adopted Shang-ti as the name of God, though T'ien-chu (Lord of Heaven) was also used.

Shang-tso-pu. Chin. for *Theravāda.

Shankara (pre-eminent Indian philosopher): see ŚAṄKARA.

Shan-tao (founding master): see PURE LAND SCHOOLS.

Shao-lin-ssu (Jap., Shōrin-ji). Chinese Buddhist monastery, built in 477 CE, by the emperor Hsiao-wen. It was to here that *Bodhidharma moved from S. China when he saw that the time was not ripe for the reception of *dharma there. Shao-lin-ssu is associated with the development of *kung-fu*, an aspect initially of ch'i-kung (see CH'I). *Kung-fu* was initially concerned with control of interior fears and thoughts, but developed in different directions in Japan in association with other *martial arts.

Sharīʿa (Arab., 'the path worn by camels to the water'). The path to be followed in Muslim life. The term goes back to Qur'ān. It became the description of the systematic organization of how Muslims should live, wherever there is no permitted freedom (see AL-HALAL WA'L-ḤARĀM). This especially applies to the four classic *schools, *Ḥanafite, *Ḥanbalite, *Mālikite, and *Shāfiʿite. They are rooted in Qur'ān and *ḥadīth, the *sunna of the Prophet, but with different attitudes to what else is legitimizing (see further SCHOOLS OF LAW). Sharīʿa is constantly extended in the present, since Islam cannot be a reproduction of life in 6th-cent. Arabia. The extension of sharīʿa is made particularly by *ijmaʿ, qiyās and *ijtihād, and in practice through *fatwā. It is also modified by local custom (*adat).

Actions are classified in sharīʿa into five categories (with detailed sub-divisions in each case: (i) obligatory (*fard or *wājib*); (ii) meritorious; (iii) indifferent; (iv) reprehensible; (v) forbidden (*ḥarām*: see AL-HALAL WA'L-ḤARĀM). Fundamental to all are the *Five Pillars.

Sharīʿatī, ʿAlī (1933–77). Iranian thinker whose writings and lectures represent the ideology that precipitated the 1979 Islamic revolution in Iran. From 1964 until his death, he attracted vast audiences, mainly university and college students, at the Husayniya-i-Irshad, a religious centre in Tehran. During this time he produced his greatest work, *The Desert* (Pers., *Kavir*): 'Seeking refuge in history out of fear of loneliness, I immediately sought out my brother Ayn al-Quzat [12th-cent. Persian Sūfī] who was burned to death in the very blossoming of his youth for the crime of awareness and sensitivity, for the boldness of his thought. For in an age of ignorance, awareness is itself a crime.'

The government closed the centre and imprisoned Sharīʿatī for eighteen months, during which time he was tortured. Upon his release he was allowed to go to England, where shortly after his arrival he died in mysterious circumstances.

Sharīf (Arab., 'noble'). Title of honour, but in Islam especially of those descended from the Prophet *Muḥammad's family, among the banu Hāshim. The most prominent in the post-Second-World-War years has been King Hussein of Jordan, hence the Hashimite dynasty.

Shas. Acronym of Heb., *shishah sedarim*, i.e. the six *seders (orders) of the *Mishnah or *Talmud.

Shaṭḥ (Arab.). An ecstatic or divinely inspired utterance, especially among *Sūfīs. Since they often express extreme claims, the *Sunnīs rapidly contested their validity and authority.

Shavuʿot (Heb., 'weeks'). The Jewish festival of Pentecost. The festival is celebrated on 6 Sivan (and 7 in the *diaspora) and is one of the three pilgrim festivals (see Deuteronomy 16. 16). It falls fifty days after the first day of *Passover, and it originally marked the end of the barley and the beginning of the wheat harvest. The *first fruits were brought to the *Temple (Deuteronomy 26. 1–11), and in *rabbinic times the festival also became the anniversary of the giving of the *Torah to *Moses on Mount *Sinai.

Shaybānī (influential figure in development of one of the schools of sharīʿa): see ḤANAFITES.

Shaykh (Arab.). Old man, chief, or elder; a title of respect in Islam, especially for religious leaders, usually transliterated *shaikh.

Shaykh Aḥmad Ibn Zayn al-Dīn al-Aḥsāʾī (1753–1826). Shīʿa Muslim who founded the Shaykhīs. He was born in Arabia, but moved to Iran, where he became a teacher and prolific writer. His belief that he received, in dreams and visions, direct and infallible communications from the *Imāms, combined with suspect teaching on other matters, led to his condemnation in 1822. He died on pilgrimage to *Mecca, but his teaching was continued by Sayyid Karīm Rashtī (d. 1843 (AH 1259)) who organized the Shaykhīya/Shaikhīya order more formally. Many Shaykhīs/*Shaikhīs became followers of the Bāb (see BĀBĪS).

Shaytan (the devil in Islam): see SATAN (ISLAM).

Shaytl: see HEAD, COVERING OF (Judaism).

Shebu'ah (vow): see VOWS (Judaism).

Sheḥitah. Jewish method of slaughter for food. The principle behind sheḥitah is that the animal must be killed as swiftly and painlessly as possible by cutting horizontally across the throat in a firm uninterrupted movement.

Sheikh (eminent Muslim): see SHAIKH.

Shekalim. A tractate in the order of Moʿed in the Jewish *Talmud. *Shekalim* deals with the laws concerning the half shekel *Temple tax.

Shekhinah (Heb., 'dwelling'). The divine presence as described in Jewish literature. The Shekhinah is sometimes used to refer to God himself , but generally it signifies God's presence in this world. It is frequently associated with light. Later Jewish philosophers were concerned to avoid *anthropomorphism and therefore tended to maintain that the Shekhinah does not refer to God himself, but is an independent created intermediary. Thus *Saʿadiah Gaon argued that the Shekhinah is the same as the glory of God which was seen by the *prophets in visions.

In Islam, *sakīna* is supreme peace sent by God to dwell in human lives (e.g. Qur'ān 48. 4). In 2. 248, it refers to the Ark of the Covenant. But in general Islam resisted any localization of the transcendent power of God.

Sheli'aḥ Zibbur (Heb., 'messenger of the community'). Leader of communal worship in a Jewish congregation.

Shem, ha- (Heb., 'The Name'). Hebrew term for God. When reading, or speaking, the term 'ha-Shem' is used to avoid pronouncing the *Tetragrammaton. It is found in such phrases as *Barukh ha-Shem* ('Blessed be the name') and *'Im yirtze ha-Shem* ('God willing').

Shemaʿ (Heb., 'hear'). Declaration of God's unity in the Jewish *liturgy. The Shemaʿ consists of three *Pentateuchal passages: Deuteronomy 6. 4–9, 11. 13–21, and Numbers 15. 37–41.

It is recited twice daily in the evening and the morning, and the practice dates back at least to the 2nd cent. CE.

Shembe, Isaiah (founder): see NAZARITE CHURCH.

Shembe's Church (Zulu movement): see NAZARITE CHURCH.

Shemini Azeret (Jewish festival): see SIMḤAT TORAH.

Shemoneh Esreh (Heb., 'eighteen'): see ʿAMIDAH.

Shen. Chinese word for spirits. In antiquity, it refers to the spirit of the *ancestor who enjoys an afterlife because of the continuing and periodical sacrifices offered to him by the members of his offspring. Shen is not immortal; it is contingent upon the continuing offering of the sacrifices. Ancient China had a composite concept of the 'soul' in the body composed of *hun and *p'o. After death, hun becomes shen and partakes of the ancestral offerings. P'o, after death, becomes *kuei and goes to the Yellow Spring—the underworld. But in later times, shen and kuei refer to the two alternative designations of the spirit of the deceased: it is called shen when continuing sacrifices are offered to it, and it is called kuei when such sacrifices are denied to it. Shen blesses and kuei harms the family.

Sheng(-jen). In China, one who hears the way of Heaven (*T'ien) and develops understanding, often translated as 'sage'. Sheng-*jen is therefore the ideal wise person who penetrates the hidden meaning of all things and lives accordingly.

Shen-hsiang (teacher of Huo-yen who took the school to Japan): see HUA-YEN.

Shen-hsiu (Ch'an/Zen Buddhist teacher): see SOUTHERN AND NORTHERN SCHOOLS.

Shen-hui (responsible for establishing Ch'an/Zen Buddhist school in China): see SOUTHERN AND NORTHERN SCHOOLS.

Sheol. The dwelling place of the dead in Jewish thought. Mention is made in the Bible of the dead going down to Sheol. It was neither heaven nor hell, but something like 'the primitive grave' (Pedersen).

Sherira ben Ḥanina Gaon (*c.*906–1006). Jewish *gaon of *Pumbedita. Sherira claimed descent from King *David, and both his father and grandfather preceded him as gaon. Under Sherira, for a short time, the Pumbedita *academy regained its prestige.

Shevirah (destruction): see LURIA, ISAAC BEN SOLOMON.

Shevirat ha-kelim (destruction of the vessels): see LURIA, ISAAC BEN SOLOMON.

Shewbread. The bread laid out in the Jerusalem *Temple (Leviticus 24. 5–9).

Shīʿa (Arab., 'party'). Those Muslims who believe that *ʿAlī was the legitimate successor (*khalīfa) to *Muḥammad and that ʿAlī, *al-Ḥasan, and *al-Ḥusain were cheated of their right to succeed and fell (as *martyrs) victims to tyranny. Close to the *Sunni majority in most respects, their most important differences are: the Shīʿa community's suffering is consecrated by the suffering (regarded as martyrdom) of the founding *Imāms; the office of Imām is bestowed by God on a chosen person from Muḥammad's family; these Imāms are a spiritually perfect élite and are therefore infallible; the *hidden Imām's return will bring victory over an unjust political order, against which true believers have always been in opposition; meanwhile, the Shīʿa community is guided by the *mujtāhids* (religious specialists in the Shīʿa context). The importance of the *mujtāhid* (e.g. Imām *Khumayni) produces a radical notion of personal authority and a model of action. The idea of suffering, divine leadership, and of personal involvement come together in the re-enactment in passion plays (*taʿziya) of the tragic drama of Imām Ḥusain at Karbalāʾ, and also appears in the custom of self-beating in the mosque and public processions that occur on 10 Muḥarram. In addition, the Shiʿites identify as issues between themselves and the Sunnis: *mutʿa (temporary marriage), *taqīya (dissimulation in face of danger), *rawḍa khānī (recitation and memorial of Imāms), *ziyāra (pilgrimage to tombs), and above all the nature and identity of the Imām. Because of their strict allegiance to Imāms, Shiʿites have divided into many sects, of which the following are or have been important: *Ithnā-ʿAsharīya (Twelvers), Zaydis (*Seveners, see ISMA-ʿĪLĪS), *Bātinites, Nizāris (now called *Aga Khanids), and the *Druzes. Shīʿa communities are found as majorities in Iran and parts of Iraq, and as sizeable minorities in India, Pakistan, Lebanon, Yemen, Persian Gulf States, and E. Africa.

See Index, Shiʿa beliefs; Shiʿa Muslims.

Shibli (Sūfī mystic of Baghdād): see AL-SHIBLI.

Shichi-fuku-shin (Japanese seven gods of luck): see DAIKOKU.

Shiddukhin (Aram., tranquillity). A formal promise, in Judaism, to marry at some future date. The promise is generally confirmed in writing, and the date of the *marriage and the size of the dowry would be specified. The betrothal is an important stage in marriage, and some authorities, such as *Elijah b. Solomon, consider that it is better to marry and divorce immediately than to break a betrothal.

Shiguseigan (Jap.). 'Four great vows' in Zen Buddhism. They are part of the *bodhisattva vow as recited three times at the end of *zazen: (i) *shujō muhen seigando*, 'beings are countless, I vow to save them all'; (ii) *bonnō mujin seigandan*, 'passions are countless, I vow to eradicate them'; (iii) *homon muryo seigangaku*, '*dharma gates are many, I vow to enter them all'; (iv) *butsudō mujō seiganjo*, 'the way of the Buddha is unsurpassable, I vow to actualize it'.

Shih. 1. Phenomenal world: see HUA-YEN. 2. Song Lyrics: see SHIH CHING.

Shih Chi (Records of the Historian): see HISTORIES IN CHINA.

Shih-chieh (Chin.). 'Separation from the corpse', Taoist explanation of how an immortal (*hsien) appears to have died before ascending to heaven (*fei-sheng). When the coffin is opened, it is found to be empty, or to contain some emblem of an immortal.

Shih Ching. *Scripture of Song Lyrics* (also rendered as *Odes*, *Poems*, or *Songs*), one of the three pre-*Confucian Classics. *The Lyrics* are songs of court and countryside, some dating back perhaps as far as the 8th or 9th cent. BCE. They were the fountainhead of all Chinese poetry in the form called *shih* (poems to be sung). Beyond their intrinsic value, they are of importance in understanding archaic Chinese society and its religion.

Shih-i (Chin., 'ten wings'). The commentaries (*i-chuan*) on the Taoist *I-Ching*, Book of Changes: (i) *Tuan-chuan* (2 parts); (ii) *Hsiang-chuan* (2 parts); (iii) *Ta-chuan* or *Hsi-tz'u* (2 parts); (iv) *Wen-yen*; (v) *Sho-kua*; (vi) *Hsü-kua*; (vii) *Tsa-kua*.

Shihō (Jap.). Dharma transmission in Zen Buddhism: see HASSU; INKA-SHŌMEI; SOUTHERN AND NORTHERN SCHOOLS.

Shih-shuang Ch'u-yuan (chronicler of Zen and collector of kōans): see KŌAN.

Shih-te (lay Ch'an Buddhist and poet): see HAN-SHAN.

Shiʿism, Shiʿite: see SHĪʿA.

Shikan (T'ien-t'ai meditation methods): see CHIH-KUAN.

Shikantaza (Jap., 'nothing but simply sitting'). A form of the practice of *zazen in Zen Buddhism, in which none of the supports (e.g. attention to breathing) are used. It was advocated by *Dōgen as the purest form of zazen.

Shikatsu (Zen shouting): see LIN-CHI I-HSÜAN.

Shiko (Jap., 'four kalpas'). The four periods of change in Japanese Buddhism: (i) *jōkō*, *kalpa of creation; (ii) *jūkō*, kalpa of continuing existence; (iii) *ekō*, kalpa of destruction; (iv) *kūgō*, kalpa of destruction.

Shimenawa (Jap., etymology uncertain; perhaps 'forbid-rope'), in *Shinto, a sacred rope stretched before the presence of a *kami or around a sacred area. It is often used to mark off sacred areas for special rites, and it encircles sacred objects such as trees or rocks. It may be used also in private homes.

Shimʿon: see SIMEON.

Shinbutsu-shugō or **Shinbutsu-konkō** (Jap.). Syncretism of *Shinto and Buddhism. The *Tendai school formulated Sannō-ichijitsu Shinto and the Shingon school, *Ryōbu Shintō, approximately at the end of the Heian period. The merger of Buddhism with Shinto, however, goes back to the Nara period. The earliest appearance of *jinguji*, a Buddhist temple associated with a Shinto shrine, was in the early part of the 8th cent. When the great image of the *Buddha (*Daibutsu) was made, the Buddhist priest Gyōki visited the *Ise shrine, and the *kami of the Usa Hachiman in Kyushu was enshrined in the compound of the Todaiji Temple. In 781 the Buddhist title of *bosatsu (*bodhisattva) was conferred on the kami of the *Hachiman, and since then, this kami has been known as Hachiman Daibosatsu.

The union of Buddhism and Shinto was done on the basis of a *Mahāyāna doctrine, *honjisuijaku, which explains the relation of the Absolute Buddha to the Historical Buddha. Aided by this doctrine, the theory assumes that the Japanese kami are Buddhas/Bodhisattvas who reveal themselves for the sake of sentient beings.

Shingaku. A popular religious movement, sometimes known as 'Education of the Heart', started in 1729 in Japan by *Ishida Baigan (1685–1744), a self-taught scholar and chief clerk for a Kyōto commercial house. Shingaku appealed mainly to the urban merchants, but it also attracted devotees from the peasant and *samurai classes who listened to Baigan's public lectures or were acquainted with the movement's many popular tracts and house codes (*kakun*). The teachings of Shingaku were an eclectic blend of *Confucian moral precepts, Buddhist meditational practices, and worship of the national gods (*kami).

Shingon (Jap. pronunciation of Chin., *chen-yen*, 'true word', which represents Skt., **mantra*). A school of esoteric Buddhism established in Japan by *Kūkai after his learning experience in China, especially from Hui-kuo. The 'School of the True Words' (Skt., *mantrayāna*, Jap., *shingon*) emphasizes three mysteries or secrets which all possess, and through which the buddha-nature can be realized: body, speech, and mind. The secrets of the body include *mudrās and the handling of the *lotus and the thunderbolt (*vajra). The secrets of speech include *mantras and *dhāraṇīs. The secrets of mind are the five wise ways of perceiving truth. These skills are transmitted orally from teacher to pupil, never in writing, and not as public teaching. The esoteric mysteries were expounded by the cosmic buddha, *Vairocana/Dainichi Nyorai, for his own delight. In so far as its truth can be expressed at all, it can only be done in representational, above all *maṇḍala, form. Central are the two maṇḍalas, Vajra (Diamond) and Garbha (Womb). The first is active, with Vairocana seated on a white lotus surrounded by four transcendent Buddhas; the second is passive, with Vairocana on a red lotus, surrounded by eight buddhas and bodhisattvas. An initiate throws a flower on to the maṇḍalas and becomes the devotee of the buddha on which the flower falls. In Kūkai's case, it fell on Vairocana in both the Diamond and the Womb maṇḍalas.

Shingon remains a large Buddhist school in Japan, in six main branches, with more than 10,000 temples.

Shinje (Tibetan Lord of Death): see TIBETAN WHEEL OF LIFE.

Shinjimei (Ch'an Buddhist poem): see SENG-TS'AN.

Shinkokinshū (Collected Poetry, Ancient and Modern): see MOTOORI NORINAGA.

Shinkō Shūkyō (new religions): see NEW RELIGIONS IN JAPAN.

Shin Kyōha Shinto (Shinto organization in Japan): see SECT SHINTO.

Shinnyo. Japanese pronunciation of the Chinese character for the Skt., *tathatā.

Shinran (Shōnin Shinran; 1173–1262). Founder of *Jōdo-shin-shū, a major school of Japanese Buddhism, a pupil of *Hōnen. When Hōnen was exiled in 1207, Shinran rejected the necessity of monastic rules and residence. He married and fathered children. He was pardoned in 1211, and began to establish a community of followers. His belief that the buddhas and bodhisattvas fulfil their commitments and vows to help all in need led him to reject all 'ways of effort' (*jiriki) and to rely on 'the power of the other' (*tariki*; see JIRIKI), concentrated on the Buddha *Amida. Not even repeated calling on Amida's name (*nembutsu) was strictly necessary: one plea sincerely meant will bring Amida's help. He spent the remainder of his life working on his *Kyogyo-Shinshō* (True Teaching, Practice and Realization of the Way).

Shinrikyo (Japanese religious movement): see AUM SHINRIKYO.

Shinsei (founder of Tendai Shinsei-shu): see TENDAI SHŪ.

Shinsen (Jap.). In *Shinto, the food offerings made to the *kami as part of a worship festival (*matsuri). These food offerings vary at different shrines.

Shin-shu (true school): see JŌDO-SHIN-SHŪ.

Shintai (Jap., 'kami body'). In *Shinto, the symbol of the *kami or object in which the spirit of the kami is believed to reside, used as the object of worship in a shrine. Also called *mitama-shiro* ('august spirit symbol'), it is housed within the innermost chamber (*honden*) of the shrine sanctuary.

Shinto (Jap., 'the way of the kami'). The indigenous Japanese religious tradition. The term Shinto was coined in the 6th cent. CE, using the Chin. characters *shen* ('divine being') and *tao* ('way'); in the native Japanese reading it is *kami no michi or *kannagara no michi*. The origins of Shinto are clouded in the mists of the prehistory of Japan, and it has no founder, no official sacred scriptures, and no fixed system of doctrine. As the imperial (Tennō) clan gained supremacy, its myths also gained ascendancy, providing the dominant motifs into which the myths of the other clans were integrated to some extent. These myths were collected in the two 8th-cent. collections of mythology and early history, the **Kojiki* of 712 (Records of Ancient Matters) and the **Nihongi/Nihonshoki* of 720 (Chronicles of Japan), and they established the basic themes of Shinto, such as the cosmological outlook consisting of a three-level universe, the Plain of High Heaven (*takama-no-hara*), the Manifested World (*utsushi-yo*), and the Nether World (*yomotsu-kuni*); the creation of the world by *Izanagi and Izanami; the forces of life and fertility, as also of pollution and purification; the dominance of the sun kami *Amaterasu Ōmikami; and the descent of the imperial line from Amaterasu. The mythology also established the basic Shinto worship practices, dances, and chanting of *norito.

In the history of Japan, Shinto has gone through many transformations: the imperial edicts prescribing the national rituals in the 7th cent.; the stratification of the Shinto priesthood; the Institutes of the Engi Era (**Engi-shiki*) regulating Shinto in the 10th cent.; Buddhist influence which resulted in the Shinto-Buddhist amalgamation (*Ryōbu-shintō and Sannō ichijitsu); the influence of *neo-Confucianism on Shinto; and finally the resurgence of Shinto stimulated by the 'National Learning' (*kokugaku) movement in the 18th and 19th cents. which returned Shinto to its former position as the guiding principle of Japan and provided a theoretical framework for Shinto thought. There still exist in modern Japan several different types of Shinto. The Shinto of the Imperial Household (kōshitsu shintō) focuses on rites for the spirits of imperial ancestors performed by the emperor. Shrine Shinto (jinja shintō) is presently the form of Shinto which embraces the vast majority of Shinto shrines and adherents in Japan, administered by the Association of Shinto Shrines (jinja honchō), State Shinto (*kokka shintō) was created by the Meiji government and continued until the end of the Second World War to control most Shinto shrines and rituals in accordance with the ideological aims of the government. New Shinto movements were designated by the government as Sect Shinto (*kyōha shintō). Sect Shinto groups continue today, joined by a group of 'New Sect Shinto' (shin kyōha shintō) movements which have developed in the post-war period. Folk Shinto (minkan shintō) is a designation for the extremely wide-ranging group of superstitious, magico-religious rites and practices of the common people. The typical setting for the practice of Shinto is the shrine (*jinja*) precinct, which is an enclosed sacred area with a gate (*torii), ablution area, and sacred buildings including the main sanctuary (*honden*) which houses the symbol of the kami (*shintai) and a worship area (*haiden). The natural surroundings are also regarded as permeated with the kami presence; in fact, occasionally a mountain or sacred forest may take the place of the sanctuary. At special times through the year, shrines become the focal point for community *festivals (*matsuri), held according to the tradition of each shrine at stated times in honour of its own kami, although there are many common festivals. For the devout Shintoist, daily life itself is matsuri or service to the kami, and one worships before the home altar (*kamidana). Mortuary rites are usually conducted by Buddhist priests, even though Shinto lays great emphasis on veneration of the ancestral spirits.

Shinto is a 'this-worldly' religion, in the sense that it is interested in tangible benefits which will promote life in this human world.

See Index, Shinto.

Shinwa (Jap., 'stories of the kami'). Japanese stories about the actions of the *kami, more closely resembling *myth than *densetsu or *setsuwa. The most important collections are **Kojiki* and **Nihongi* or *Nihonshoki*.

Shinyakushi-ji (temple-complex): see NARA BUDDHISM.

Shiqquz shomen (idolatrous object set up in the Jerusalem temple): see ABOMINATION OF DESOLATION.

Shirk (Arab.). The most heinous of sins in Islamic reckoning, the alienation from God, to some pseudo-deity, of what only and properly is God's. Shirk is the antithesis of *tawḥīd. The root verb has to do with 'sharing' or 'association'. Shirk violates the exclusive sovereignty of God, as idolatry does. To worship what is not divine is shirk al-'Ibāda. But there is also shirk al-ma'rifa when knowledge, possessed only by God, is attributed to another. To commit shirk is to be a mushrik, one who is not *muslim (submitted) to God.

Shiromaṇī Gurdwārā Parbandhak Committee (Pañjābī, 'Chief Temple Management Committee'). Authoritative, elected Sikh body. The SGPC was established in 1920 during the *Akālī movement for reform of *gurdwārā management, and was legally recognized in 1925 by the Sikh Gurdwārās Act.

Shiryōken (four alternatives of the Buddhist Lin-chi line): see LIN-CHI.

Shishōtai. Jap. for the *Four Noble Truths.

Shi-tennō (four world protectors in Buddhism): see CELESTIAL KINGS.

Shiva (major Hindu deity): see ŚIVA.

Shivah (Jewish rite): see MOURNING RITES (JUDAISM).

S(h)ivānanda (1887–1963). Indian spiritual leader, influential in establishing the World's Parliament of Religions. He founded the Divine Life Society and the Yoga-Vedānta Forest Academy, both of which were dedicated to extending spiritual truth without reference to the boundaries of religion, and to offering all seekers food, medicine, and knowledge. Among many works, *Yoga for the West* (1951) and *Self-Realisation* (1954) express his developed views.

Shiva Sharan (musician and scholar of Indian religions): see DANIÉLOU, ALAIN.

Shivata (afternoon Piyyut): see KEROVAH.

Shiv Dayal Siṅgh: see RĀDHĀSOĀMĪ SATSAṆG.

Shizen nōhō (agriculture following nature): see SEKAI KYŪSEIKYŌ.

Shne'ur Zalman of Lyady (1745–1813). Founder of the *Ḥabad *Ḥasidism movement in Judaism. A student of *Dov Baer, he was set to compose an up-to-date **Shulḥān Arukh* (publ. 1814). He became the Ḥasidic leader of Reisen in 1788. By 1801 he was settled in Lyady and known as the '*Rav of Lyady'. His *Likkutei Amarim* (Collected Sayings) is the principal text of the movement. The work is also known as *Tanya* and is, unlike most Ḥasidic works, a systematic exposition. It is often referred to as the 'written law of the Ḥabad'; and Shne'ur Zalman is known as Ba'al ha-Tanya.

Sho (Jap., 'nature'). Fundamental or essential character. It appears usually with other terms, as *kensho, realizing one's own nature, or *bussho, buddha-nature.

Sho'ah (calamity): see HOLOCAUST.

Shōbō (Jap., 'true *dharma'). 1. The teaching of the *Buddha, hence *shōbō-shū*, 'Buddhism' in Eng.

2. 'Appropriate reward', main reward for *karma in previous lives, i.e. this body and life—in contrast to *ehō*, 'dependent reward', i.e. secondary consequences such as house, place, and possessions.

Shōbō-genzō (Treasure Chamber of the Eye of True Dharma). A major work of *Dōgen, and one of the supreme works of Japanese Zen. It is a vast and difficult work, written and compiled during the last decade of his life. Dogen intended 100 books but completed only 92—75 unrevised, 12 revised, and an appendix of 5. Much of it, including the title, is untranslatable.

Shōbōgenzō Zuimonki. A record of brief talks, comments, and exhortations of *Dōgen. It was compiled between 1235 and 1237, and was first published in 1651. The standard (*rufubon*) text was established in 1769. It contains basic instruction.

Shōbō-nenjo-gyō. Sūtra of the Mindfulness of True Dharma, tr. by Pajñaruci, *c*.540 CE. It expounds the causes leading to the six lower domains of appearance (*rokudō): hell, hungry spirits, animals, *asuras, humans, heavenly beings. It encourages escape from them.

Shodō (calligraphy): see ART (Ch'an/Zen).

Shofar. An animal horn (now traditionally a ram's horn) blown during Jewish rituals. The shofar is first mentioned in Exodus 19. 16 at Mount *Sinai. Today, it is blown daily from 2 Elul until the end of Rosh ha-Shanah and again at the end of the last service on Yom Kippur (*Day of Atonement). According to *Maimonides, the reason for sounding the shofar is to 'arouse you from your slumbers, to examine your deeds, to return in repentance and to remember your Creator'.

Shōgatsu (Japanese New Year): see FESTIVALS AND FASTS.

Shoghi Effendi Rabbānī (1897–1957). Guardian (*valī*) of the *Bahā'ī Faith (1922–57), eldest grandson of *'Abdu'l-Bahā, and his appointed successor. He effectively established the modern system of Bahā'ī administration with its locally and nationally elected Spiritual Assemblies (1922–3) and its separate branch of advisory leaders (from 1951). He instituted a series of plans for the expansion of the religion which eventually extended to most parts of the world. By his own voluminous writings, he provided authoritative interpretations of Bahā'ī scripture and doctrine. His main writings include his early letters on *Bahā'ī Administration* (1922–9), his delineation of the goals and characteristics of the *World Order of Bahā'u'llāh* (1929–36), and his interpretative history of *Bābī and Bahā'ī history, *God Passes By* (1944). He died unexpectedly, 4 Nov. 1957, in London. No new guardian was appointed, and only a tiny minority of Bahā'īs followed the American claimant, Charles Mason Remey.

Shōgyoku (skill in means): see MUSŌ SOSEKI.

Shōji. 1. (Jap., 'birth and death'). The cycle of birth and death in Japanese Buddhism: transmigration and reappearance, often referred to as *shōji no rōgoku*, 'the prison of birth and death'.

2. (Jap., 'superior person'). A person of outstanding virtue and wisdom.

Shōjō. Jap. for *Hīnayāna.

Shōjō Daibosatsu. The great *bodhisattva worshipped at the Shōjō shrine at Kumano in Japan. He is an incarnation of *Amida (*gongen), who demonstrates (*shōjō*, 'prove and bear witness') the effectiveness of Amida's route to salvation.

Shokaku Kokushi (leading Zen monk): see MUSŌ SOSEKI.

Shōkan or **Shōken** (Jap., 'seeing one another'). The meeting (*dokusan) of a Zen student with his teacher (*rōshi), when he is accepted as pupil; hence, attaining the same spiritual level as one's teacher.

Shōken. Jap., for 'right view', one of the steps on the Eightfold Path (*aṣtangika-marga).

Shoko Asahara (i.e., Asahara Shoko, Japanese cult leader): see AUM SHINRIKYO.

Shokon Jinja Shrine (Shinto shrine to those who died in battle): see KAMIKAZE.

Shōmu Tenno (701–56). Japanese emperor and patron of Buddhism in the *Nara period. He reigned 724–49, and sought to make Buddhism a foundation for the peace and order of the state. In 728 he ordered that *Konkōmyō-kyō* (The Golden Splendour Sūtra, Skt., *Suvarṇaprabhāsa-uttama-sūtra*) should be distributed and recited for the protection of the nation. In 745, he ordered the setting up of the *daigedatsu in Tōdai-ji. He inaugurated and dedicated the image, making a personal commitment to the *Three Jewels (*sambō). After his abdication, he became a home-living religious (*nyūdō*), i.e. one who shaves his head and wears the Buddhist religious *habit, but does not join a community.

Shōmyō (chanting sūtras): see MUSIC.

Shōmyō (major figure in establishing Rinzai Zen in Japan): see NAMPO JŌMYŌ.

Shōrin-ji (Chinese Buddhist monastery): see SHAO-LIN-SSU.

Shoshi (Jap., 'true master'). The recognition which a Zen student (who has already received the seal of recognition, *inka-shōmei) receives from his master that he too is competent to train others.

Shōshū (Jap., 'small school'). Jap. name for *Hīnayāna.

Shōtoku Taishi (Japanese prince): see NARA BUDDHISM.

Shou (Chin., 'Long life'). The extension of life via Taoist practices, as a preliminary to immortality (*ch'ang-sheng pu-ssu).

Shou-i (Chin., 'preserving the One'). Taoist meditation practice, in which the deities (*shen) within the body are *visualized, and thus prevented from leaving the body. The controlling or supreme One is visualized in such a way that it may lead to union.

Shou-lao. Popular name of Taoist god of long life, Shou-hsing: see SAN-HSING.

Shou-shan Sheng-nien (Jap., Shuzan Shōnen; 926–93). Ch'an/Zen master of the *Lin-chi succession of the *Rinzai school. He was dharma-successor (*hassu) of Feng-hsueh Yen-chao who regarded him as the saviour of the line. Shou-shan was the master of Fen-yang through whom the revival of Rinzai began.

Showbread (bread laid out in Jerusalem Temple): see SHEWBREAD.

Shōyōroku (Japanese title of collection of kōans): see KŌAN.

Shōzōmatsu (Jap., *shōbō + *zōbō* + *mappō). The three periods, especially in *Pure Land Buddhism, following the *Buddha's death, of true *dharma, semblance dharma, last dharma.

Shraddha (supplementary funeral rite): see ŚRĀDDHA.

Shri Chinmoy Centre. Founded by Shri Chinmoy Kumar Ghose (b. 1931), a Hindu *guru from Bengal who arrived in the USA in 1964 to teach his 'path of the heart' towards union with God. Appointed Director of the United Nations Meditation Group in 1970, Shri Chinmoy's New York Center (the main one of many that now exist in the West) received accreditation as a non-governmental organization in 1975.

Shrine Shinto (Shinto classification): see SECT SHINTO.

Shromaṇī . . . (authoritative Sikh body): see SHIROMAṆĪ.

Shroud of Turin. Christian *relic venerated as the burial shroud of *Jesus (mentioned e.g. in Matthew 27. 59). It is a strip of linen, 4.3 × 1.1 m., bearing the shadowy image of the front and back of a man's body, as if it had been folded over him at the head and the image somehow transferred. The shroud has reposed since 1578 in Turin cathedral. It seems likely that it came to Europe from Constantinople at the time of the Fourth *Crusade, but the theory which attempts to trace its history further back, by identifying it with the image of Christ known as the mandylion of Edessa, has not won acceptance.

By 1988 tests on the material had made it clear that the shroud itself (i.e. the material) could not be dated earlier than 1260. The way in which the image was produced is still unknown.

Shrove Tuesday. The day before *Ash Wednesday, so named from the 'shriving', i.e. *confession and *absolution, of the Christian faithful on that day.

Shtetl (Yid., 'small town'). Jewish communities in E. Europe, 16th–early 20th cents. The life of the Jewish community centred round home, *synagogue (*shul), and market. The values of *Yiddishkeyt* ('Jewishness') and *menshlikhkeyt* ('humanness') were all-important. Life in the shtetl is now well-known in the West through the paintings of Marc Chagall and the stories of Sholom Aleichem. The pattern of life was eroded in the 20th cent. through pogroms, economic depression, emigration, and ultimately the *Holocaust.

Shtibl (Yid., 'little room'). Ḥasidic *synagogue; developed as a centre of prayer, study, and social life when Ḥasidim were excluded by *mitnaggedim (their opponents) from their own synagogues.

Shtible (Yid.). Small Jewish village in E. Europe; see also SHTETL.

Shu (reciprocity): see ETHICS (Confucian).

Shu Ching. Scripture of Historical Documents of Archaic Times, or Book of History, one of the three pre-*Confucian Classics. Among many important ideas given religious sanction by this collection, that of the Mandate of Heaven (*T'ien ming) was perhaps most influential.

Shugendō. Japanese Buddhist mountain devotion. The sect was founded by En-no-Ozunu (born *c.*635 CE), hence it is also known as En-no-gyōja. From the age of 32, he devoted himself for thirty years to esoteric Buddhism on Mount Katsuragi until he attained miraculous powers. He developed ascetic mountain Buddhism by teaching ways of entering into the strength of mountains. He was exiled in 699, pardoned two years later, and died shortly after. Mountain Buddhists develop esoteric powers, and are known as *yamabushi* or *shugenja*.

Shūhō Myōchō, also known as **Daito Kokushi** (1282–1338). A Zen master of the *Rinzai school, dharma-successor (*hassu) of *Shōmyō, and one of the founders of the Ō-tō-kan lineage. He was the founder and first abbot of Daitoku-ji in *Kyōto, where he insisted on strict and rigorous observance.

Shūjō (Jap., 'teaching of a school'). The teaching of a Buddhist school or movement, and in particular that of *Zen.

Shul (Yid., 'School'). Yiddish term for *synagogue, common among *Ashkenazi Jews in Europe. It was a community meeting-place, in which local politics were as prominent as prayer.

Shulḥān Arukh (Heb., 'the prepared table'). Code of Jewish *halakhah (law) written by Joseph *Caro. The *Shulḥān Arukh* is a synopsis of *Jacob b. Asher's *Arba'ah Turim*. Its four parts deal with the daily and *Sabbath *Commandments, laws governing everyday life (e.g. *dietary laws, *purity, *mourning), laws of *marriage and divorce and, finally, civil and criminal law. It was first printed in 1565, and after amendments for the *Ashkenazim had been added by Moses *Isserles, it became accepted as the most authoritative code of Jewish law.

Shushi-gaku. Japanese term for the orthodox *neo-Confucian teachings of *Chu Hsi (1130–1200) and his followers. The major advocates of Shushi-gaku in Japan were Hayashi Razan (1583–1657), who served the shōgun and established a school staffed throughout the Tokugawa (1600–1868) period by his descendants, and Yamazaki Ansai (1618–82), who stressed the more religious aspects of neo-Confucianism.

Shushogi (text summarizing Sōtō): see SŌJI-JI.

Shūso (religious founder): see NICHIREN SHŌSHŪ.

Shusse (Jap.). One who has transcended an existing state. The application is various, e.g. to one who has renounced the world to become a Buddhist monk, to a *bodhisattva who appears in this world to save sentient beings, to a *Zen monk who undertakes the headship of a community or temple, etc.

Shuzan Shōnen (Ch'an/Zen master): see SHOU-SHAN SHENG-NIEN.

Shwedagon Pagoda. Major *pagoda in Burma. It is set on a hill in Rangoon, and its present form is a consequence of many extensions and rebuildings after earthquakes. Many of the additional buildings, and the elaborate gold decoration, are a result of *merit-seeking gifts, especially from the rulers of Burma.

Shylock (Jewish character in Shakespeare): see USURY.

Sian (Xi'an, 'Western Peace'). Major Chinese city (capital of Shaanxi province), frequently the capital of China, near which (30 km. to the east) the vaults of the Terracotta Warriors were discovered in 1974. When the Emperor Qin Shi Huangdi unified China in 221 BCE, he established his capital to the east of Sian and began to build a magnificent palace on the site of present-day Sian: it was then known as Chang'an. The warriors were discovered in his tomb —more than 8,000 in number. Sian also contains the Big Wild Goose Pagoda, in imitation of a pagoda of the same name in India: the name is derived from a time when some starving Buddhist monks prayed for food and a wild goose fell out of the sky. In gratitude, they buried the goose instead of eating it, and built a temple on the spot. It is one of the oldest (originally built in 652) buildings in China (restored during the 1950s). The Little Goose Pagoda (707–9) was early destroyed in war; the rebuilt Pagoda was damaged by earthquake in the 16th cent., but was repaired and reopened in 1977.

Sibylline Oracles. A collection of prophetic oracles in fourteen books by Jewish and Christian authors. Their dates are disputed, but probably range from the late 2nd to the 4th cents.

Sicarii (Lat., 'men armed with curved daggers'). Jewish resistance fighters against the Romans in the 1st cent. CE. According to *Josephus, the Sicarii assassinated the *high priest, Jonathan, and held the fortress of Masada in 70 CE.

Sicilian Vespers. A massacre of 3,000–4,000 French in Sicily, 30 Mar. 1282, initiated when the bell for *vespers was rung. It marked the end of the plans of Pope Martin IV and Charles of Anjou to reconquer Constantinople, and led indirectly to the decline of papal power. The theme supplied (remotely) the libretto for Verdi's *I vespri siciliani*.

Siddha (Skt., 'perfect, complete'). In E. religions, one who has attained the supreme goal, who may also have acquired the siddhi powers. The siddhi powers of a *yogi include becoming invisible, leaving the body and re-entering it at will, reducing the size of one's body to that of a seed, or increasing it to that of a mountain. For Śaivites, *Śiva is the supreme Siddha, Ādinātha, of whom all other siddhas are incarnations. In Buddhism the *iddhi powers are comparable. For Tantric Buddhism, see SIDDHA TRADITION. Among Jains, siddhas are souls (*jīva) which have attained release from *karma and attained the goal. See also FIVE SUPREME BEINGS.

Siddharta (personal name of the Buddha): see SIDDHATTA.

Siddhasena Divakara ('The Sun', *c*.4th/5th cent. CE). Jain logician. He appears to have been a *brahman who was converted after losing a debate with a Jain monk, Vṛddhavādin, who then performed many miracles disclosing the truth of his new faith. The major works attributed to him are *Nyāyāvatāra* (The Descent of Logic) and *Sammatitarka* (The Examination of True Doctrine, tr. S. Sanghavi and B. J. Doshi). He also wrote verse compositions of a more devotional kind, e.g. *Dvātriṃśika*.

Siddha tradition (Skt.; Tib., *grub.thob*, 'person of achievement'). A tradition in Indian Tantric Buddhism which had great influence on the development of Buddhism in Tibet. While *siddha generally signifies a *yogin (Hindu or Buddhist) who has achieved psychic powers (siddhi/*iddhi), Tibetan Buddhism recognizes a canon of eighty-four principal siddhas whose achievement is enlightenment itself: their magical powers are a display of the achievement. Eminent in the tradition are Virūpa, who prevented the sun from moving for two days and a night in order to continue drinking wine, and who originated the *Sakya *Lam Dré* system of relating *sūtras and *tantras; *Padmasambhava, who as Sakara ended a twelve-year famine by causing rains of food, water, and jewels, and who founded the *Nyingma school; Bhusuku, the Nālandā monk who levitated, cured blindness, and as *Śāntideva wrote the *Bodhicaryāvatāra* (Entering the Path of Enlightenment), a seminal *Geluk text; and *Nāropa, whose Six Doctrines (*Nāro Chos Drug) embody the very nature of siddhahood and still delineate the training of a *Kagyü *lama.

Siddhattha (Pāli) or **Siddhartha** (Skt.). Personal name of the *Buddha. It means 'he whose aim is accomplished'.

Siddha Yoga Dham. A movement founded by Swami Muktananda which practises a form of *Kuṇḍalinī yoga. In this, a force referred to as *śaktipat* ('descent of power') is said to activate the spiritual energy within the central nervous system.

There are few strict rules apart from daily meditation and vegetarianism.

Siddh Goṣṭ (Pañjābī, 'discourse with siddhs'). Gurū *Nānak's discourse with *siddhs* (*Nāth *yogīs). The *janam-sākhīs provide a context of religious debate for the unified composition attributed to Nānak in the *Ādi Granth (938–46). The Siddh Goṣṭ summarizes Nānak's teaching in answer to wide-ranging questions.

Siddhi (yogic powers): see SIDDHA.

Siddur (Jewish prayer book): see PRAYER BOOK.

Sidrah (part of the Jewish Pentateuch read in synagogue): see SEDAROT.

Siffin (battle): see ʿALĪ B. ABĪ TĀLIB.

Sifra (Aram., 'a book'). *Halakhic midrash to *Leviticus. *Sifra* was probably compiled in *Erez Israel in the 4th cent. CE.

Sifre(i) (Aram., 'books'). *Halakhic midrash on *Numbers and *Deuteronomy. *Sifrei* was probably compiled in *Erez Israel in the 4th cent. CE.

Sifrei Zuta. A *halakhic midrash to *Numbers. *Sifrei Zuta* was extensively quoted, but the original text was lost until it was rediscovered in the *Cairo Genizah. It should be dated in the 4th cent. CE.

Sigālovāda (discourse from Pāli canon): see DĪGHA NIKĀYA.

Siger of Brabant (Averroist philosopher): see AVERROISM.

Signs: see SYMBOLS.

Śikara (symbolic mountain): see ART (Hinduism).

Sikh (Pañjābī, 'learner, disciple'). One who believes in one God (*Ik Onkar) and is a disciple of the *Gurū. For further detail see SIKHISM.

Śikhā. The tuft of hair, also called *choṭī*, left unshaven by orthodox Hindus at the place (*brahmārandra) where the *ātman leaves the body at death or cremation. It is cut off, or plucked out, by anyone becoming a *saṁnyāsin.

Śikhaṇḍin. In the *Mahābhārata, a Pāñcāla prince, son of Drupada, and brother of *Draupadī and Dhṛṣṭadyumna, whose character is determined by his previous incarnation as a princess of *Kāśi named Ambā. In *Mahābhārata* legend, Śikhaṇḍin is best remembered for his transsexuality. He/she is also said to be the incarnation of a *rākṣasa.

Sikhism. The religion and life-way of those who are Sikhs. The word *sikh* (Pañjābī; cf. Skt., *śikṣya*) means 'a learner', 'a disciple'. Sikhs are those who believe in one God (*Ik Onkar) and are disciples of the *Gurū. In Indian usage, *gurū* can apply to any religious teacher or guide, but for Sikhs it is restricted to God as *Sat Gurū (true teacher), the ten Gurūs (listed under *Gurū) from Gurū *Nānak (b. 1469 CE) to Gurū *Gobind Siṅgh (d. 1708), and to the *Ādi Granth (Sikh scripture), known as Gurū Granth Sāhib and revered as such. Sikhs accept *initiation with *amrit, according to the *rahit maryādā which gives detailed requirements. Together Sikhs make up the *panth in which it is believed that the guidance of the Gurū is also present, but in a more limited way. Fully committed and initiated Sikhs belong to the *khālsā. There are *c.*14 million Sikhs in India, four-fifths in *Pañjāb. In a wide *diaspora, the largest community (*c.*300,000) is in the UK.

Sikhism began in the context of the Muslim–Hindu confrontation in N. India, when some (e.g. *Kabīr) were seeking reconciling truth. It was a time also of vivid and moving devotion to God (*bhakti), all of which (especially the *Vaiṣṇavites) was influential on Gurū Nānak, though even more so was his own profound experience of God. He did not attempt to merge Hinduism and Islam, but simply insisted on the worship of the True Name (*Nām), God who can be found within and does not require the rituals and doctrinal controversies of existing religions. God does not become present in the world (in contrast to Hindu understandings of *avatāra), but makes his will and his way known. In discerning this, *meditation (*nām simaran) on *śabda ('sound') is of paramount importance, especially through repetition of the Name, or on the hymns of the Guru Granth Sāhib. *Karma and *saṃsāra are accepted: the way to release or liberation is to move one's life against one's own wilful and disordered inclination (*haumai) into alignment with the will (hukam) of God. This is only possible because of the help of God, the equivalent of *grace, described in many words, e.g. *kirpā, nadar,* *praśād. Those who do so pass through stages (*khaṇḍ): dharam khaṇḍ (living appropriately; cf. *dharma); giāñ khaṇḍ (deeper knowledge); saram khaṇḍ (effort or joy); karam khaṇḍ (effort or joy); *sach khaṇḍ (bliss beyond words and beyond rebirth, merging with the divine as a drop in an ocean or as a spark in a flame). Sikhs remain *grihasth* ('householders'), in contrast to the four *āśramas of the Hindus, for whom *gṛhastha is only one stage, to be followed by progressive renunciation.

Under the first four Gurūs, there was no conflict with the surrounding majority religions, but marks of identity were further developed—e.g. Sikh days in the religious calendar. Under *Rām Dās, 'the tank of nectar', *Amritsar, was built, leading to the *Harimandīr (Golden Temple), the centre of Sikh identity. Always more at ease in general with Hindus, Sikhs found tensions with Muslims and the Mughal emperors increasing; this led to the forming of the *khālsā under the tenth Gurū, Gobind Siṅgh. The khālsā is the community of Sikhs who have received *khaṇḍe-dī-pāhul, and are distinguished by the *Five Ks. Various reform movements emerged, notably that of Dyāl Dās (1783–1855) whose *Niraṅkārīs (the formless) resisted the use of images, even of the Gurūs; Sain Sahib (d. 1862) whose *Namdhāris attacked all reversion to Hinduism and held that a continuing Gurū is necessary; and Sant Niraṅkārī Maṇḍal (the Universal Brotherhood, not to be confused with the Niraṅkārīs), which has modified traditional practices and was banned or boycotted by the *Akal Takht in 1978. In response to Christian missionaries, the *Siṅgh Sabhā was formed. The British recognized with some gratitude Sikh assistance during the Mutiny, and reinforced their spiritual independence. Partly from this encouragement, the *Akāli movement emerged, which secured the return of *gurdwārās to Sikh control and remains committed to Sikh autonomy in the Puñjāb (*Khālistān).

The communal nature of the Sikh religion is greatly emphasized by its institutions, with *sevā (community service) being highly valued. Gurū Nānak had established the *dharmsālā* as a place of assembly, in distinction from Hindu temples, not least by including the *langar as a basis for communal meals. The *dharmsālā* led to the gurdwārā (though Namdhāris retain the older name). Worship is simple compared with Hindu ritual, and *kīrtan is prominent.

Śīla (Skt.; Pāli, *sīla*). 'Precepts', the basic obligations which Buddhists undertake, ten for *bhikṣu/bhikṣunis, five for laypeople (or the first eight on *uposatha days): the undertaking, in the rule of training, is to abstain from (i) harming any living being, (ii) taking anything not given, (iii) misconduct involving sense-pleasure, (iv) false speech, (v) losing control of mind through alcohol or drugs, (vi) solid food after midday, (vii) frivolous entertainments, (viii) perfumes and jewellery, (ix) raised, soft beds, (x) involvement with money or other valuables. These are understood, not so much as 'ten commandments', as promises that Buddhists make to themselves at the start of each day.

Sīlabbata-parāmāsa (Pāli) or **śīlavrata-paramārśa** (Skt., 'cleaving to rules and rites'). According to Buddhism, the mistaken view that adherence to rules and rites is sufficient to bring about holiness and purity. The view is rejected as one of the four kinds of clinging (*upādāna) to existence and one of the ten fetters (*saṃyojanas).

Silsilah (Arab., *salsala*, 'make a chain'). The chain of transmission in *Sūfī Islam from the initial blessing (*baraka) of God, running down in succession to the present *shaykh. Most silsilahs are traced back to *Muḥammad, one (the *Tijāniy(y)a) claiming to be derived from a direct vision of Muḥammad to the founder. The Khāḍiriy(y)a claim to be founded directly by *Khiḍr. It is an initial obligation on joining an order to learn the silsilah in order to understand how the baraka has been transmitted.

Silva Mind Control. Established by Jose Silva in Mexico and the USA in 1966, this is a method for increasing the powers of the mind. The claim is to provide 'the science of tomorrow—today'. 'Dynamic meditation' is held to provide contact with the 'Alpha dimension', a level of consciousness belonging to the spiritual world.

Silver-tongued Smith (Christian preacher): see CHRYSOSTOM.

Sīmā (bounded space in Buddhism): see VINAYA.

Simeon, Charles (1759–1836). Second-generation leader of the *Evangelical Revival. Appointed Vicar of Holy Trinity Church, Cambridge, in 1782, he gave himself to expository preaching, and to a long ministry to undergraduates. His Simeon Trust was formed to purchase livings for evangelicals. His loyalty to the Church of England never wavered and he insisted on the primacy of parish work over itinerancy.

Simeon Bar Kokhba (leader of Jewish revolt): see BAR KOKHBA, SIMEON.

Simeon Bar Yoḥai (2nd cent. CE). Jewish *tanna. Simeon bar Yoḥai was a student of R. *Akiva, and was vigorous in his opposition to the Romans. Surviving the *Bar Kokhba revolt, he 'revived the *Torah at that time' (*B.Yev.* 62b). He was betrayed to the Romans and was forced to live in hiding for twelve years. After he emerged, he established a *yeshivah in Tekoa. He is traditionally credited with the authorship of the *Zohar*. *Kabbalists remember his death on the festival of *Lag Ba-Omer.

Simeon ben Gamaliel I (1st cent. CE). *Nasi of the Jewish *Sanhedrin. He presided over the Sanhedrin during the period of the Roman destruction of Jerusalem, and is remembered for his moderate leadership. He is traditionally included among the *Ten Martyrs.

Simeon ben Gamaliel II (early 2nd cent. CE). Jewish *nasi. Simeon ben Gamaliel II was the son of Rabbi *Gamaliel I and father of *Judah ha-Nasi. After the *Bar Kokhba revolt, he went into hiding, but was appointed nasi at the second meeting of the *Sanhedrin after the revolt. He was known for his humility (*BBM* 84b), and many *halakhot are preserved in his name in the *Mishnah.

Simeon the New Theologian (Byzantine mystic): see SYMEON.

Simeon the Stylite, St (*c*.390–459). First of the Christian *stylites. He began as a monk in the monastery of Eusebona near Antioch, then moved to Telanissos, where after several years as an *anchorite, he mounted a pillar; this was at first close to the ground, but the height was eventually raised to 18 m. He lived there until he died, occupied in prayer and worship. Feast day, 1 Sept. in the E., 5 Jan. in the W.

Siṃhabhadra (Indian Buddhist philosopher): see HARIBHADRA.

Simḥat Torah (Heb., 'rejoicing in the *Torah'). The last day of the Jewish *festival of *Sukkot. This is the day on which the cycle of Torah readings is completed and a new beginning made. In *Israel, it is celebrated on the same day as Shemini Azeret, but in the *diaspora it is the following day. There are Torah processions, hymns of praise are sung, and the *bimah is circled seven times.

Similitudes of Enoch (part of pseudepigraphical book): see ENOCH.

Simon, St. One of the twelve *apostles; 'the Less', called 'the Cananean' or 'the Zealot' (Mark 3. 18; Luke 6. 15). In W. churches he is traditionally paired with St *Jude in the ecclesiastical calendars and in dedications of churches. Feast day, 10 May in the E.; 28 Oct. in the W.

Simon Magus. An opponent of St *Peter, later identified as a heresiarch (see HERESY). According to Acts 8. 9–24 he was a sorcerer known as 'that Power of God which is called Great', who practised in Samaria. His career is elaborated in the *Clementine Homilies* and *Recognitions*, and also in other legends from which, perhaps, that of *Faust evolved.

Simons, Menno (Dutch priest and radical reformer): see MENNONITES.

Simony. From the action of *Simon Magus in Acts 8. 18–24, the purchase or sale of spiritual things, and specifically of an ecclesiastical benefice or preferment.

Sin

Judaism In the Hebrew scriptures there are three main categories of sin. *Ḥet* indicates a failure of mutual relations, *Pesha* indicates a breach in the relationship between two parties. The verb *awah* (*avah*) expresses the notion of crookedness. The *rabbis used the term *averah* (passing over), so sin is a passing over or rejection of the will of God. The primary cause of sin is the *evil inclination. See also SACRIFICE; TESHUVA; FORGIVENESS.

Christianity In the New Testament there are distinctive treatments of sin in (i) Paul, for whom sin is a ruling power in the world (Romans 5. 12; Galatians 3. 22) and in people (Romans 6. 6, 7. 14–20); (ii) the *Johannine writings, where 'sin' is the opposite of 'truth' and is related to disbelief in *Christ (John 9. 41, 15. 24); and (iii) *Hebrews, where it is a disorder atoned for by sacrifices (2. 17, 5. 1). Otherwise the word and its cognates are used without great precision, particularly in expounding the saving work of Christ.

Of later elaborations of the understanding of sin, the most important is probably the concept of *original sin. Also important was the development of the penitential system. Social sin has been increasingly recognized as amounting to far more than the sum of individual sins and sinners, as e.g. in *Liberation Theology. See also SEVEN DEADLY SINS.

Islam There are more than ninety words in the *Qur'ān for sin or offence against God or one's fellow human beings; it is therefore impossible to summarize the many nuances of sin in Islam. But from that fact alone, it is obvious that the mission of *Muḥammad was addressed to humans who are in grave danger because of their propensity to sin. There is no trace of an ab-original fault which affects all subsequent humans. Nevertheless, there are many ways in which humans fall into sin or error, and the Qur'ān offers guidance so that there can be no doubt what behaviour God requires. The Day of Judgement (*yaum al-Din) is decided on an exact balance between good and evil acts—though evaluation takes account of *niy(y)a (intention). But God is merciful and compassionate, and the way of repentance (*tawbah*) is always open. Even so, there were those in early Islam who held that a Muslim who sins has become an apostate and therefore no longer belongs to the community (see KHARIJITES).

Hinduism As in other E. religions, the most radical fault which has to be overcome is not so much sin as ignorance (*avidyā). Nevertheless, it is perfectly well recognized that there are behaviours (and thoughts) which are wrong and which might well be called sin, for which the most usual word is *pāpa. The foremost of these (pāpātama) is *moha. Closely associated are *lobha and *krodha* (anger). The classic texts of *dharmaśastra develop an elaborate casuistry, dividing sins into *mahāpātakas (great offences) and upapātakas (lesser offences). There are five greater offences: killing a *brahman (*brāhmaṇahatyā*; killing an *outcaste is a lesser offence than killing a cow, since there is no *dharma of religious consequence in relation to those without caste); drinking intoxicants (*surāpāna*); stealing (*steyam*, not in general, but in specified ways); sexual relations with the wife of a *guru (*guruvaṅganāgama*; sometimes interpreted as 'father', i.e. against incest); associating with a known sinner (*mahāpātakasaṁsārga*). The lesser offences are far more varied and differently listed. The way to deal with offences is to undertake penance and make atonement. Penance may range from *prāṇāyāma and *tapas (to burn out offence) to gifts to brahmans and pilgrimage.

Buddhism Buddhism does not accept the existence of an omnipotent deity and has no concept of sin as the offence against such a being by the contravention of his will as expressed through revelation or deduced by reason. It does, however (in terms of the doctrine of *karma), distinguish clearly between good and evil deeds.

A wrongful thought, word, or deed is one which is committed under the influence of the 'Three Roots of Evil' (*akusalamūla), namely greed (*lobha), hatred (*dosa), and delusion (*moha). Wrongful actions are designated in various ways: as evil (*pāpa), bad (*akusala*), demeritorious (*apuñña*), or corrupt (*sankiliṭṭha*), and all such deeds lead inevitably to a deeper entanglement in the process of suffering and rebirth (*saṃsāra) and away from the fulfilment and enlightenment of *nirvāna.

See Index, Sin, offence, etc.

Sinai, Mount. The mountain on which *Moses was given the Jewish *Torah. Mount Sinai is also referred to as Mount Horeb (Exodus 33. 6). According to Exodus, Moses was given the *Ten Commandments on Mount Sinai; he also received the tablets of the law after remaining there for forty days. In recent times the acceptance of the doctrine of *Torah mi Sinai* ('Torah from Sinai') is the primary criterion of *orthodox belief. Jews have not been much concerned to identify the mountain, since it adds nothing to the revelation which occurred there (*ma'amad har Sinai*) by which they are required to live. Jubal or Jebel Musa, the mount of Moses, in southern Sinai is an old (Christian) identification: the Monastery of St *Catherine was built on orders of the emperor Justinian in the 6th cent. at the foot of Jubal Musa, at the traditional site of the burning bush.

Sīnān (Ottoman architect): see SULAIMĀN THE MAGNIFICENT.

Siṅgh (Skt., *simha*, 'lion'). Second name of male Sikhs. According to tradition, Gurū *Gobind Siṅgh (hitherto Gobind Rāi) took this surname on *Baisākhī Day 1699 CE. He gave to the *pañj pyāre and to all males subsequently initiated into the *khālsā the name Siṅgh, to emphasize their equality, regardless of *caste, and their courage in battle. See also KAUR.

Siṅgh Sabhā (Hindī, Pañjābī, '*Siṅgh Assembly'). Sikh movement to defend the *panth against incursions by missionaries. The Siṅgh Sabhā was formed in 1873, with the intention of extending education, publishing, and reforming the management of the *gurdwārās. The first president was Thakur Siṅgh Sandwalia, and the first secretary Giana Gian Siṅgh. The leading writer was Vīr Siṅgh, who also founded the first Pañjābī newspaper, *Khālsā Samāchār*. Khalsa College in *Amritsar was established in 1892, followed by a proliferation of other Khalsa Colleges. As awareness of political oppression grew, the movement gave rise to the *Akali Party.

Sion (hill given sacral significance in Jerusalem): see ZION.

Sīra. 'Life', in Islam of the Prophet *Muḥammad. No connected biography of the Prophet was written, but *ḥadīth (traditions) of what he said and did were already being collected during his lifetime. The earliest work on the biography of Muḥammad was by 'Urwa b. al-Zubayr, but the dominant work became that of Muḥammad ibn Isḥāq whose Sīra survives in a recension by ibn Hishām. Also of importance are the works of al-Wāqidī, especially his *Kitāb al-Maghāzī*.

Sirach (book of the Apocrypha): see BEN SIRA.

Sirhindī, al- (Indian Sūfī teacher): see SŪFĪS.

Śīś Gañj Gurdwārā (*śīś*, Pañjābī, 'head'). Sikh shrine. 1. This *gurdwārā marks the place in Chandnī Chauk, Delhi, where Gurū *Tegh Bahādur was beheaded in 1675 CE, on the orders of the Mughal emperor, Auraṅgzeb.

2. Shrine in Anaṇḍpur Sāhib. See RAKĀB GAÑJ GURDWĀRĀ.

Śiśupāla. In the *Mahābhārata* and *Purāṇas, *Kṛṣṇa's evil cousin, king of the Cedis, destined to be killed by Kṛṣṇa. The story of the killing of Śiśupāla, later turned into a classical poem by Māgha, is told in full in book ii of the *Mahābhārata*. The *Viṣṇu* and *Bhāgavata Purāṇas* see Śiśupāla as a reincarnation of the earlier demons *Hiraṇyakaśipu and *Rāvaṇa, both of whom were pitted against incarnations of Viṣṇu.

Sītā (Skt., 'furrow'). Consort of *Rāma and considered therefore to be an incarnation of the Goddess *Lakṣmī. She is the heroine of the epic poem *Rāmāyaṇa*. She was born as a result of her father's prayers, and is said to have sprung from a furrow ploughed by him; she is thus closely associated with the 'mother-earth' concept and is the Vedic patron of agriculture.

Śītalā. Goddess of pustular diseases, dominant in Bengal. Her *līlā (play) is to sweep through the countryside with her companion Jvarāsura, the fever demon. Śītalā means 'cool one', perhaps a euphemism to ward off her fury. Worship of her, and writing poems to her, tend to follow upon an epidemic, thus belonging to the cults of *affliction.

Situation ethics (ethics which arise from evaluation of particular circumstances): see ETHICS (CHRISTIANITY).

Sitz im Leben (Germ., 'place' or 'setting in life'). In historical criticism of religious traditions, the supposed circumstances in which a particular story, saying, etc., either originated, or was preserved and transmitted. See also FORM CRITICISM.

Śiva (Skt., 'auspicious'). Major deity in Hinduism, the third in the Hindu trinity (*trimūrti), along with *Brahmā and *Viṣṇu. In the *Vedas, *śiva* appears as an epithet of *Rudra, not as separate manifestation of divine power. The joint form, Rudra-Śiva appears in the *gṛhya* (household) rites, which suggests that there was a gradual process of assimilation, and that Śiva has roots and origins in the pre-Vedic period. By the 2nd cent. BCE, Rudra was waning in significance, and Śiva began to obtain a powerful separate identity. In *Rāmāyaṇa*, he is a mighty and personal god, and in *Mahābhārata* he is at times the equal of Viṣṇu, perhaps even the creator of Viṣṇu and Brahmā, worshipped by other gods. He became associated with generation and destruction, especially in conjunction with *Śakti, and is therefore worshipped through the power of the *liṅga. The Mahādeva image in the *Elephanta caves already depicts Śiva in the threefold guise of creator, destroyer, and preserver: in this and other such images, the two faces on either side represent (apparent) opposites—male and female (*ardhanārī); terrifying destroyer (*bhairava) and active giver of repose; mahāyogi and *gṛhasta—while the third, serene and peaceful, reconciles the two, the Supreme as the One who transcends all contradictions. The three horizontal marks which Śaivites put on their foreheads represent the triple aspect of *Śiva. As a personal god (*iṣṭa-deva), he is worshipped in many forms of manifestation, important examples being *Nāṭarāja (lord of the *dance) and Dakṣiṇāmūrti, spiritual teacher. His *mantra is 'sivo 'ham'. Śiva is particularly associated with the river *Gaṅgā (Ganges) which flows through his hair and with Mount *Kailāsa in the *Himālayas.

See Index, Siva; Śaivism.

Śivabhuti. A Jain who, according to the Śvetāmbara, caused the eighth, and major, schism among Jains.

Śiva-Jñāna-Bodha (Skt.; Tamil, *Śivañāṉapōtam*, 'realization of the knowledge of Śiva'). An important theological text of *Śaiva Siddhānta written by Meykaṇḍadeva (Tamil, Meykaṉtartēvar; 13th cent. CE). The *Śiva-Jñāna-Bodha* is a concise, systematic exposition of Śaiva theology, which maintains that God (*Śiva) is transcendent and immanent, and souls are wholly dependent on him. To attain union with Śiva through his grace, one should offer devotion (*bhakti) to him.

Śivananda (1887–1963). Hindu founder of the Divine Life Mission. In 1923, he entered on the path of renunciation, becoming a *saṁnyāsin in 1924. After twelve years of *ascetic preparation, he founded the Śivananda *āśram and the Divine Life Society. This is basically *advaitin, involves a form of *Hatha yoga, and aims to be non-sectarian. The Mission now has branches worldwide.

Śivarātri (Hindu festival): see FESTIVALS AND FASTS.

Śiva Saṃhita. A Sanskrit text of the *Nātha yoga school (13th–15th cents.), a mixture of *advaita philosophy, *Hatha and *Tantric yoga. The last chapter enumerates obstacles to yoga, and also the four kinds of yoga which are, in ascending order, *mantra, *hatha, *laya, and *kriya*. The latter involves closing off the senses and listening to inner mystical sound (*hāda).

Śiva-tattva (the supreme being in Indian sect): see LIṄGĀYAT.

Six Doctrines of Nāropa (body of teaching in school of Tibetan Buddhism): see NĀRO CHOS DRUG.

Six Gosvāmīs (disciples of Caitanya): see CAITANYA.

Six heretical teachers. The six sectarian teachers who were contemporaries of the Buddha and who were castigated by him for their false teachings, principally their denial of the doctrine of *karma. The fullest exposition of their views is to be found in an early discourse entitled 'The Fruits of the Religious Life' (*Sāmaññaphala-Sutta*), the second discourse of the *Dīgha Nikāya*.

Six hundred and thirteen commandments. The laws found in the Jewish *Pentateuch. There are 248 positive commandments and 365 negative ones. The first classification was made by Simeon Kayyara, and *Maimonides later set them out in his *Sefer ha-*Mitzvot*. They are known as Taryag Mitzvot, because *taryag* has the numerical value in Hebrew of 613. For the 614th, see HOLOCAUST.

Six principles of Nāropa (six doctrines of Nāropa): see NĀRO CHOS DRUG.

Six realms (six states of possible rebirth): see TIBETAN WHEEL OF LIFE.

Six schools of philosophy (Indian): see DARŚANA.

Six sects (of Buddhism): see NARA BUDDHISM.

Six ways (classification of Chinese religions/philosophies): see CHINESE RELIGION.

Six yogas of Nāropa (six doctrines of Nāropa): see NĀRO CHOS DRUG.

Ṣiyām (fasting in Islam): see ṢAWM.

Skaṁbha (Skt., 'pillar, support'). Vedic Hindu term for a pillar, known in post-Vedic times as staṁbha. In the *Vedas, it is the scaffolding (metaphorically understood) supporting creation—e.g. *Atharva Veda* 10. 7 and 8. It is also the *axis mundi. In practice, skaṁbhas were set up for many reasons, and with elaborate decoration. Central are those associated with the *liṅga, but others are devoted to virtually any god. The classic work on architecture, *Mānāsara* 15, analyses the types of skaṁbhas.

Skanda. Hindu deity, offspring of *Śiva (conceived without the assistance of a female being), who became a notable warrior. He was suckled by the six Kṛttikas (Pleiades) and developed six faces for this purpose. From this derives the name *Kārttikeya by which he is commonly known and worshipped. He is depicted as young and chaste (i.e. as Kumāra), clothed in red, with a spear (which always hits its target and returns to his hand). His cult, of great antiquity, used to cover India, but is now mainly in the south: in *Tamilnadu, he has merged with Murukañ/Murugan. *Skanda Purāṇa* is one of the eighteen classical Purāṇas (the longest of them) and contains what purports to be his teaching.

Skandha (Skt., 'group'; Pāli, *khandha*). In Buddhism, the five aggregations which compose or constitute human appearance (*nāma-rūpa): (i) *rūpa, material composition; (ii) *vedanā*, sensing, including sensing through the sixth sense of mental impressions; (iii) *samjña* (Pāli, *sañña*), perception; (iv) *saṃskāra (Pāli, *sankhāra*), mental formations producing character; (v) *vijñāna (Pāli, *viññāna*), consciousness. They are constantly in the process of change, and do not constitute a self (*anātman).

Skete (Gk., 'dwelling'). A small monastic community, especially associated with Mount *Athos.

Skilful means, skill in means (skill in adapting teaching to the aptitude of those who are taught): see UPĀYA-KAUŚALYA.

Slaughter, ritual (Jewish): see SHEḤITAH.

Slavery

Judaism The institution of masters owning their servants is accepted in the Hebrew scriptures. A Hebrew could become a slave to redeem his debts (Leviticus 25. 35) or to make restitution for theft (Exodus 22. 2). According to Leviticus 25. 44–5, it was permissible to take slaves of 'the nations that are round about you'. The extent of the practice of slavery among the Jews in the *Talmudic period is debatable. *Maimonides summed up the *rabbinic laws of slavery by saying, 'It is permissible to work the slave hard; but while this is the law, the ways of ethics and prudence are that the master should be just and merciful.'

Christianity Slavery in the New Testament period is not questioned as an institution. A slave can fulfil his duty as a Christian by serving his master as Christ (Ephesians 6. 5–8), though the owner must realize that the slave is his brother in Christ and must treat him accordingly. Perhaps, even, he should set him free (Philemon 14–21). The more important point is that the age is being inaugurated when all divisions of this kind will be abolished, when there will be 'neither Jew nor Greek, slave nor free, male and female' (Galatians 3. 28), because all are one in Christ. Nevertheless, inequalities continued to be regarded as a consequence of the *Fall (e.g., by *Augustine), even though slavery gradually gave way in Europe to serfdom. The biblical warrant for slavery was appealed to in the development of the slave-trade (which, after fierce struggle, was formally ended at the Congress of Vienna, 1814–15) and in the perpetuation of slavery in America. Slavery ended in America after the Civil War through the Emancipation Proclamation (1863) and the Thirteenth Amendment (1865).

Islam Slavery is taken for granted in the *Qur'ān and in *ḥadīth—where the subject of slavery is mainly a concern with manumission and its consequences. Legally, slaves could only be obtained as a consequence of war, or as the children of existing slaves. Slaves were able to rise to positions of considerable responsibility, even seizing power in the case of the Mamlukes (the word means 'owned one', and refers to a dynasty derived from Turkish and Circassian slave soldiers, which held power in Egypt, 1250–1517 (AH 648–922)). Since Qur'ān and ḥadīth cannot be abrogated, it is not possible for slavery to be abolished, at least as a theoretical possibility, in Islam.

Hinduism Slavery appears to have existed in early India (Dev Raj, *L'Esclavage dans l'Inde ancienne*, 1957), but it did not continue as an institution extensively. Instead, forms of obligatory service developed through *dharma and the *caste system.

See Index, Slavery.

Śloka (epic metre): see VĀLMĪKI.

Sloka-saṁgraha (collected teachings): see SEN, KESHUB CHUNDER.

Smārta Sūtra. Any Hindu sūtra based on *smṛti, understood as traditional law. They include those concerned with family and household rituals (*gṛhya*) and the Dharma Sūtras. Smārtas are also those who compose such texts, and those *brahmans who integrate devotional theism into *dharma. The smārta movement was a syncretistic movement connected in origin with *Śaṅkara, who recognized five deities in particular (*Viṣṇu, *Śiva, *Pārvatī, *Gaṇeśa, and *Sūrya) as the guarantors of dharma and social order in harmony with the order of the cosmos.

Śmaśāna. Hindu cremation ground. Normally (i.e. according to the norms of *dharma) abhorrent and defiling, for Tantric cults of the left hand they are important as the place of testing detachment in the domain of the repellent. Śmaśāna *sādhana also includes rituals to control malevolent spirits.

Smith, Joseph (founder): see MORMONS.

Smṛti (Skt., 'recollection'). In Hinduism, the second part of 'scripture', less than *śruti, but possessing authority. Smṛti, passed on orally by tradition, gains validity by being derived from śruti. It extends to a wide range of works, including *Vedāṅgas, *Smārta Sūtras, *Purāṇas, *Itihāsa, including *Mahābhārata* and *Rāmāyaṇa*, Nīti-śastras.

In Buddhism, smṛti is the Skt. equivalent of *sati, 'mindfulness': it is the meditational practice which observes closely and continuously what is going on in the interior life of the practitioner, especially the four mindfulnesses, the body (*kaya*), sensation (*vedanā*), mind (*citta), and the Buddha's way (*dharma).

Smṛti-upasthāna (system of mediation in Buddhism): see SATIPAṬṬHĀNA.

Snake-handling. A practice in certain *Pentecostal churches mostly in the mountains of the SE USA. It is inspired by the words in Mark 16. 17–18. Handling snakes while in an ecstatic state thus becomes a sign of one's faith and possession of the *Holy Spirit. The American Civil Liberties Union has defended snake-handling religion as a test case of the constitutional right to freedom of religious belief.

Snapping (serial conversion): see CONVERSION.

Sober Sufism (style of Sūfī practice): see ʿABD AL-QADIR AL-JĪLĪ; AL-JUNAID; SŪFĪS.

Sobornost'. A Russian word derived from the Slavonic *soborny*, which translates 'catholic' in the *creed, and related to the word for a council (*sobor*). Its etymological root is the verb *sbrat'*, 'to gather together', and since its use in *Khomiakov's *The One Church* (1850), the term, understood to mean 'togetherness', has been used to characterize the *Orthodox understanding of the unity of the *Church, an organic unity of free persons brought about by the *Holy Spirit, in contrast to the authoritarianism of *Roman Catholicism and the individualism of *Protestantism.

Societies, Chinese religious. An important feature of the Chinese religious tradition. They have been particularly important for those without a secure place in the family and clan system. Such communities have usually been organized around religious ideals and symbols, sometimes including special revelations, in writing or through oral media. The state has often been suspicious of them because of their liminal social position and deviant loyalties, and sometimes with good reason, since many rebellions were inspired and led by such groups. The Taoist-led Yellow Turban rebellion in the Han (see CHANG CHÜEH), the nationalistic White Lotus revolt (see WHITE LOTUS SOCIETY) which helped to overthrow Mongolian rule and restore a Chinese ruler to the throne at the outset of the Ming, the millenarian *Eight Trigrams uprising in N. China in 1813, and the *T'ai-p'ing rebellion later in the same century, are only four of the most prominent examples. The Societies may be Taoist or Buddhist, but most are deliberately syncretistic.

Many Chinese religious societies, however, have been smaller than these, and without explicit political goals or reformist militancy. They have remained locally organized at the village level; others have joined in regional and national federations, though in most cases the degree of central control is minimal. See also SECRET SOCIETIES.

Society of Jesus (RC religious order founded by Ignatius of Loyola): see JESUITS.

Socinianism. A rationalist movement within Christianity, leading in a *Unitarian direction. It developed from the ideas of Lelio Sozzini (1525–62) and his nephew Fausto (1539–1604). Followers of the Sozzinis, i.e. Socinians, hoped to restore a primitive Christianity, rejecting the accretions of Rome. A basic statement of faith was drawn up in Fausto's revision of the Catechism of Racov (i.e. the Racovian Catechism), and more generally in his *De Jesu Christo Servatore* (1578). Persecution in Poland led to a wide diffusion throughout Europe. The influence of Socinianism can be seen in such figures as Isaac Newton and John Locke, and among the *Cambridge Platonists.

Sociobiology and religion: see Introduction; SEX AND RELIGION.

Sociology of religion. The study of religion in its social aspects and consequences, undertaken in all parts of the world. Emerging as part of the 19th-cent. *nomothetic ambition sociologists of religion have in general been committed to a would-be scientific analysis of the role played by religion in the emergence, persistence, and evolution of social and cultural systems. In the main, they subscribe to two fundamental propositions: (i) that the study of religion is absolutely essential to the understanding of society and (ii) that the investigation of society is an indispensable prerequisite to the comprehension of religion.

The sociology of religion reflects the main theoretical and methodological divisions among professional sociologists, including functionalism, *Marxism, *Freudianism, symbolic-interactionism, *phenomenology, structuralism, and post-modernism, together with rational-choice, market, world-systems, and globalization theories, all coexisting more or less peacefully. As a creation of the Enlightenment, sociology has characteristically conceptualized religion in Judaeo-Christian terms, and has largely restricted its investigations to a Christian (mostly Protestant) context despite the monumental comparative initiative of Max *Weber.

Although usage of the term tends to follow a number of basic formulae, there is no explicit or universal consensus among sociologists of religion regarding what 'religion' *is*. The problem of defining religion (see further, Introduction), and of doing so in a manner which adequately addresses its profoundly social character, is one which still periodically surfaces to challenge scholars anew regarding the fundamentals of their enterprise.

*Durkheim and Weber may justifiably be regarded as the founding fathers whose divergent approaches still supply the main axes of intellectual tension within subdisciplinary theoretical discourse. Durkheim's primary concern with religion's role in social cohesion, group stability, and the reproduction of sociocultural forms is strategically complemented by Weber's preoccupation with its part in radical, large-scale social and cultural transformation. Thus, for a broad range of current research topics (including *sectarianism, *millennialism/millenarianism, *civil religion, *invisible religion, *new religious movements, and *secularization), they remain influential.

The issue of whether modern religious (or irreligious) reality can still be analysed within a classic framework or whether, on the contrary, it requires radical reconceptualization is nowhere more pertinent than in the perennial 'secularization debate', for which see SECULARIZATION. Whatever the ultimate fate of the concept of secularization, the richness of current research cannot be denied. A new generation of sociologists of religion is profitably engaged in a wide variety of investigations into topics as diverse as Latin American *Pentecostalism, *New Age ideology, early Christianity, spiritual *healing practices, Islamic *fundamentalism, and the prospects of religion in former iron-curtain countries. For more than twenty years, considerable empirical and theoretical attention has been devoted to the beliefs, practices, composition, organization, and influence of so-called *new religious movements (NRMs), more popularly known to the mass media as *'cults' (obvious examples are the Moonies (*Moon), *Rajneeshis, *Scientologists, *Transcendental-Meditationists, Hare Krishnas (see INTERNATIONAL SOCIETY FOR KRISHNA CONSCIOUSNESS), and Wiccans (see WITCHCRAFT)). Despite their own exaggerations and the moral panic on the part of outsiders which so often accompanies their activities, such groups represent a minuscule proportion of religious believers in their host societies. Sociological rationales for their study thus tend to stress their embryonic character, evolutionary potential, and capacity for revealing, in microcosm, wider truths about religion and society.

Continuing their examination of religion's myriad mutual relationships with other social institutions (e.g. the family, the economy, the polity, and the law), sociologists of religion are increasingly alert to its elusive, problematic, and precarious contemporary character. In circumstances where commitment appears to have acquired the fragmentary, syncretic, consumerist qualities of *bricolage, belief is increasingly divorced from belonging and religion becomes less a social institution than a broad, pliant cultural resource at the disposal of autonomized individuals. Whether religion's heightened privatization or individualization will continue or whether its old capacity as a source of authoritative meaning will inspire new, lasting, and significant forms of collective and public spiritual expression remains to be seen.

Söderblom, Nathan (1866–1931). Christian *archbishop of Sweden and pioneer of the Christian *ecumenical movement. He was appointed archbishop in 1914, and he committed himself to the task of reconciliation between nations that had been at war, involving the Churches in working for peace and justice. This led to a necessary quest for common ground in this 'work of the Kingdom'. This work was recognized by the award of the Nobel peace prize in 1930.

Sodh (Heb., 'secret'). A Jewish esoteric method of exegesis, based on the biblical understanding that prophets enter into the sodh of God. Sodh extends the belief that the *Torah has more than one level of meaning. It was used particularly to interpret the Creation account in *Genesis and *Ezekiel's vision of the chariot (see MA'ASEH).

Śodhana. Hindu purification. Cleansing from impurity may be necessary on different levels, and for different reasons. Physical purification is a part of daily ritual, which may, in the case of *sādhus, be very elaborate. It is necessary also if *caste rules have been broken, and before *pūjā. Interior purification is an important part of *Hatha yoga. Spiritual purification involves setting the self free, as through the exercise of the restraints (*niyama).

Soḍhī. Pañjābī family to which belonged most of the Sikh *Gurūs. Present-day Soḍhīs of *Kartārpur own the Kartārpur *Ādi Granth.

Sodom and Gomorrah. Two cities near the Jordan river. According to Genesis 18 and 19, Sodom and Gomorrah were destroyed by God despite the pleas of the *patriarch *Abraham because of their extreme wickedness. The biblical understanding of the offence of the cities seems to have been that it is one of disregarding the obligations of hospitality.

Soelle, D. (Christian theologian): see POLITICAL THEOLOGY.

Sōen Roshi (Zen master): see NAKAGAWA SŌEN.

Sofer, R. Moses of Pressburg (Ḥatam Sofer, 1762–1839). Jewish *halakhic authority and *orthodox community leader. Sofer served as *rabbi of Pressburg, Hungary, for the last thirty-three years of his life. He founded a large and successful *yeshivah, and he firmly opposed the *maskilim* (see HASKALAH) in their attempts to adjust Judaism to the spirit of the times. After his death, his *responsa (in 7 vols., *Ḥiddushei Teshuvot Mosheh Sofer*, known from the initials as *Ḥatam Sofer*), sermons, and letters were published, all of which reflect his devotion to the orthodox cause and his encouragement of Jewish settlement in *Erez Israel.

Soferim (transmitters of Jewish documents): see SCRIBE.

Sōgō. Those in authority in Japanese Buddhism who have responsibility for maintaining the rules (*gō*) of a community.

Sŏhak (Western learning): see KOREAN RELIGION.

Sōhei (warrior-monks): see AKUSŌ.

Sohilā (Pañjābī, 'hymn of joy'). Sikhs' late evening prayer, taking its name from a word in the second line. The Sohilā is repeated during *cremation of the deceased.

Sōji-ji. One of the two major *Sōtō Zen monasteries in Japan (along with *Eihei-ji). It was founded in the 8th cent. CE, by Gyōgi as a *Hossō monastery, but it became Zen under Keizan Jōkin in 1321. When it was destroyed by fire in 1898, it was moved to Yokohāma, its present location. By the religious laws promulgated at the outset of the Edo period (1615), the two were accorded exactly equal status, and other Sōtō temples were made subordinate to them. Nevertheless, Sōji-ji had, by the 18th cent., 16,179 branch temples, compared with 1,370 of Eihei-ji. Not until 1879 was a formal agreement (*kyōwa meiyaku*) reached that both were to have equal say in Sōtō. The establishing of a central office (Sōtōshūmukyoku) and the determination to re-establish monastic training on the foundations of *Dōgen led to the revival of the 20th cent., assisted by lay well-wishers (e.g. the journalist and publisher, Ōuchi Seiran, 1845–1919, who promulgated the summary of Sōtō, *Shushōgi*.

Sōka Gakkai (Jap., 'Association for Creating Values'). Religious movement deriving from *Nichiren Shōshū and closely related to it. In 1930, Makiguchi Tsunesaburō (1871–1944) and Toda Jōsei (1900–58) founded the Sōka Kyōiku Gakkai. It became Sōka Gakkai (and a specifically religious movement) in 1937. Through aggressive proselytization and through its journal, *Kachi Sōzō* (The Creation of Value), the group disseminated Makiguchi's philosophy.

In 1943, the government tried to unify all Nichiren sects, but this was resisted by Makiguchi and Toda. They were arrested, ostensibly on the charge of advising their followers not to purchase amulets from the national *Ise Shrine. Makiguchi died in prison, but Toda deepened his faith greatly through his reading in prison. When released, he reconstructed the organization, and in 1952 it was incorporated as an independent religious institution. It rapidly became a multi-million-member organization, extending beyond Japan to other parts of the world, especially the USA and France. It possessed what was at the time of its building the largest temple on earth, on the slopes of Mount Fuji. Under *Ikeda Daisaku, Sōka Gakkai established a political party, Komei-to, the party of clean government. Initially, Sōka Gakkai had strongly exclusivist attitudes, following Nichiren in regarding other religions as false and other Buddhist sects as heretical. It was accused of forced conversions through its technique of *shakubuku*, breaking and subduing. However, since the 1970s, there has been a moderation of its extreme views.

Sōka Kyōiku Gakkai: see SŌKA GAKKAI.

Sŏkkul-am (cave): see KOREAN RELIGION.

Sokushin jobutsu (Jap., 'becoming a Buddha in one's existing body'). The *Shingon Buddhist belief that the buddha-nature can be realized now, and in this present appearance.

Sola Scriptura (Lat., 'by *scripture alone'). The belief that the truths of Christian faith and practice can and must be established from scripture alone, without additions from, e.g., tradition or development. It is thus in contrast to *Roman Catholicism and *papal definitions of truth in matters of faith and morals (see INFALLIBILITY), although theoretically such definitions are said to be rooted in scripture.

Solemn League and Covenant (in defence of Scottish Presbyterianism): see COVENANTERS.

Sölle, D. (Christian theologian): see POLITICAL THEOLOGY.

Solomon (Heb., Shelomoh, 10th cent. BCE). King of *Israel. Solomon was the son of King

*David and Bathsheba. According to the biblical account, he was anointed king by *Nathan the *prophet and *Zadok the *priest, he reigned *c.*967–*c.*928 BCE and his kingdom stretched from the borders of Egypt to the Euphrates (1 Kings 5. 1). He was, however, condemned in the *aggadic tradition for his toleration of the *idolatry of his wives.

Solomon, Ibn Gabirol (Jewish Spanish poet and philosopher): see GABIROL, SOLOMON.

Solomon, Odes of. A collection of forty-two short hymns in *Syriac linked in manuscripts to the Psalms. Their date must be earlier than the time of Lactantius (3rd–4th cents.) who quotes them, but their unorthodox imagery and indirect reference to Christ make them difficult to place.

Solomon, Psalms of. A collection of *pseudepigraphical psalms ascribed to the Israelite King *Solomon. Originally written in Hebrew, the eighteen psalms now exist only in Gk. and Syriac versions. They probably date from the 1st cent. BCE.

Solomon, Song of (part of Hebrew scripture): see SONG OF SONGS.

Solomon, Wisdom of (book of the Apocrypha): see WISDOM OF SOLOMON.

Soloveichik, Joseph Baer of Volozhin (1820–92). Jewish *Talmudic expert. Joseph was the son of Isaac Ze'ev, the *rabbi of Kovno, who was himself the descendant of a line of eminent rabbis. He was the head of the *yeshivah at Volozhin from 1849, although he fell out with his co-head, Naphtali *Berlin. His grandson, Isaac Ze'ev ha-Levi Soloveichik (1886–1959), was regarded as a supreme *halakhic authority in Jerusalem. Another grandson, Moses (1876–1914), was rosh-yeshivah at *Yeshiva University; his eldest son, also Joseph Baer (Joseph *Solovei(t)chik), was a leading figure in the interpretation and application of *halakhah in the USA. Although various *responsa of the Soloveichiks have been preserved, there was a family tradition against publication.

Solovei(t)chik, Joseph (1903–93). Jewish *Orthodox *rabbi and *Talmudic expert. He emigrated from Poland to the USA in 1932, and became Orthodox rabbi in Boston. He established an institute for advanced Talmudic studies, meeting the needs of the flow of refugees from Europe; but he became widely known and revered when he began to teach at Yeshiva University in New York. His commitment to teaching was in line with his view on the importance of halakhah and its oral transmission, and in consequence he did not put his interpretations into published form.

Soloviev, Vladimir (1853–1900). Russian poet and philosopher. From 1873 he was a friend of *Dostoevsky. As a poet, he was a leader of the Symbolists; as a philosopher, he was influenced by German idealism and *gnostic occultism; as a theologian, he was a proponent of visible unity with Rome, after initial sympathy with the Slavophils. Underlying all was a vision of Sophia (Wisdom), the creative and redemptive feminine principle, providing a fragile coherence increasingly threatened by apocalyptic disaster.

Solzhenitsyn, Alexander Isayevich (b. 1918). Russian novelist. Born in Rostov-on-Don, he studied mathematics at Rostov University. During the Second World War he served in the army. In 1945 he was arrested and spent the next eight years in labour camps. Released on Stalin's death in 1953, he was exiled for three years. On his return he taught and began to write. His first novel, *One Day in the Life of Ivan Denisovich* (1962), was an immediate success. After increasing tension with the Soviet authorities, he was expelled in 1974, having received the Nobel Prize for Literature in 1970. His voice is a voice from the Gulags, the labour camps, where he was converted to Christianity: the voice of profound faith in God and in his image in human beings, equally critical of Soviet inhumanity, Western lack of values, and ecclesiastical frailty. He returned to Russia in 1994.

Soma (Skt., *su*, 'to press'). 1. Intoxicating or hallucinogenic juice or substance, offered in Hinduism to the gods, and ingested by the *brahmans and other participants in sacrificial rituals. The identification of the plant is uncertain and contested. All 114 hymns of *Ṛg Veda* 9 are addressed to Soma. The ways of preparing and drinking soma are carefully described, and it is said to make one acquire the eight powers of the god.

2. Hindu moon god who protects herbs and rides in a chariot drawn by white horses or antelopes. The moon is the cup of soma (above).

Sōma Sēma (the body a tomb): see CREMATION; SOUL (Christianity).

Somatic exegesis: see CULTURAL RELATIVITY AND RELIGION; Introduction.

Somayajña (group of sacrifices): see SACRIFICE (Hinduism).

Sŏn (Korean). Ch'an/Zen in Korea. During the latter half of the Silla dynasty (668–935), the nine Sŏn traditions ('Nine Mountains'), which comprise Sŏn Buddhism, were founded, seven of them being derived from the lineage of Matsu Tao-i (709–88) of the southern school of

Chinese Ch'an. These nine traditions were integrated into the Chogye sect by *Chinul (1158–1210), and it is this Chogye tradition that became dominant at the end of the 16th cent. and continues to this day to be the most influential Buddhist sect in Korea.

Song of Songs. One of the five *scrolls of the Hebrew scriptures. In the hagiographa (*Writings), it follows Job and precedes *Ruth. Song of Songs consists of a series of love songs of an entirely secular nature. It has, however, been interpreted as an *allegory of the love of God for his people, either the Israelites or the Christian soul.

Song of the Three Children. An *apocryphal addition to *Daniel in the Hebrew scriptures. The *Song of the Three Children* was inserted between Daniel 3. 23 and 3. 24. It dates back to the 2nd or 1st cent. BCE. In Roman Catholic bibles it forms 3. 24–90; the Christian canticle known as the *Benedicite comes from vv. 35–66.

Son of man, a (Heb., *ben Adam*). Phrase used in Jewish scripture (especially Psalms and once in Job) in parallel to other words for 'man'. Since it is literally 'son of Adam' (i.e. descendant of the one who, with his descendants, is subject to the penalty of death, Genesis 3. 1–19), the phrase is used most often in contexts where it means 'humans subject to death' (a point already noticed and understood by the *Targums, early translations of scripture). It carries with it the association of 'humans subject to frailty and death'. In Daniel 7 (in an Aramaic passage), the phrase 'a son of man' is used of a figure seen in a vision as vindicated before a heavenly tribunal and awarded an everlasting kingdom. This probably epitomizes Jewish martyrs, vindicated by their obedience (which they have taken to the point of death), as the true kingdom of Israel. The phrase does not occur in scripture as a title.

Son of man, the (Gk., *ho huios tou anthropou*). A phrase (not title) used in the New Testament which occurs exclusively in the sayings of *Jesus (and once elsewhere, Acts 7. 56), the anarthrous (i.e. without the definite article *the*) form in John 5. 27 being the only exception. The definite form in the singular (otherwise found only in the plural, 'the sons of men') has not yet been found in any pre-Christian Hebrew literature, except once in the *Dead Sea Scrolls (*1QS* 11. 20, and there apparently as an afterthought, since the article is added above the line). On the other hand, the definite form is found in Aramaic, so that if Jesus spoke Aramaic it is a natural expression. The conclusion is inescapable that the phrase was used deliberately and with specific intent by Jesus to convey 'the son of man, the one you all know about'.

It seems probable, therefore, that Jesus used the phrase to draw together the two major uses in what was already becoming scripture by his time, namely, that he was teaching and acting among them with direct authority from God, not as a superhuman figure (e.g. an *angel or a *messiah or a *prophet) but as one who is as much subject to death as anyone else, who believes nevertheless that he will be vindicated by God despite death. When it seemed on the cross that the vindication had not happened, the cry of dereliction ('My God, my God, why have you forsaken me?') was real indeed; which makes the actual vindication in the resurrection all the more compelling, since it appears to have taken his followers very much by surprise. The allusion to Daniel 7 (and *Josephus, *Antiquities* 10. 267 implies that the passage might have been widely known) would also have carried with it a sense of his own obedience constituting the true vocation of Israel and the only ultimate basis for kingship—an obedience to which he called his followers also (however little they comprehended it at the time).

Sons of Light. Hebrew phrase used in the *Dead Sea Scrolls. The 'sons of light' are contrasted with the 'sons of darkness', and are presumably to be identified with members of the *Qumran community.

Sopadhiśeṣa-nirvāṇa (Skt.; Pāli, *savupadisesa-nibbāna*). In Buddhism, *nirvāna while still in the condition of this life.

Sorskii/Sorsky, Nil(us) (leader of Non-Possessors Russian monastic group): see POSSESSORS.

Sōsai. Japanese Shinto funeral services. Uncommon since 17th cent., due to over two centuries of government proscription, these rites are now chiefly performed for shrine priests and their families. In contrast with Buddhist cremation, the corpse is buried.

Sōsan (patriarch in Ch'an Buddhist line): see SENG-TS'AN.

Soshi. The Elder or Patriarch, Zen Buddhist title of *Bodhidharma.

Soshigata. The elders or patriarchs in Ch'an/Zen Buddhism, the great masters, practitioners, and teachers who stand in lines of direct transmission of *dharma—ultimately, from the *Buddha Śākyamuni.

Sōšyant (expected saviour): see ZOROASTER; FRASOKERETI.

Sotāpanna (stream-enterer, one who has entered the Buddha's path): see ŚROTĀPANNA.

Sotaranzō. Jap. for *sūtra/sutta piṭaka.

Soteriology. The doctrine of *salvation (Gk., *sōtēria*). In Christian theology this means the saving work of God in the *incarnation and especially the *atonement, and through *grace. The doctrines of the *Fall and of *sin are presuppositions. See also REDEMPTION; Index, Soteriology.

More widely, the term is used of any discussion of salvation or its equivalent in other religions.

Sotoba. Jap. for *stūpa; also the tablet set up on the grave of a dead person, bearing the name and a sacred formula to assist the spirit of the deceased.

Sōtō Shū (Chin., *Ts'ao-tung*). One of the two major schools of *Zen (Chin., *ch'an* or 'meditation') Buddhism and one of the thirteen traditional Japanese Buddhist schools. The name *sōtō* is derived from the names of two places in China: Ts'ao (Jap., Sōkei), where the Sixth Patriarch, *Hui-neng (Jap., Enō) lived; and Tung-shan (Jap., Tōzan), where Liang-chieh (Jap., Ryōkai), the Chinese founder of the Sōtō school lived. Among the Japanese schools of Zen, only the *Rinzai (Chin., Lin-chi) and the Sōtō schools have prospered.

The Sōtō school was brought to Japan from China by *Dōgen Kigen (1200–53). Doctrinally, the Sōtō and Rinzai schools maintain quite similar interpretations of Buddhism. The major areas of difference between them occur in the matter of practice. Whereas Rinzai Zen teaches *kanna zen* (*'kōan introspection'), emphasizing 'seated meditation' (*zazen) focused on a kōan in order to achieve a first enlightenment experience (*kenshō), the Sōtō school refers to itself as *mokushō zen*, 'silent illumination Zen', because of its sparing use of the kōan and its identification of zazen itself with enlightenment (*shikan taza*, 'zazen only').

In Japan, the history of Sōtō is bound up with the two major monasteries, *Eihei-ji and *Sōji-ji.

See Index, Soto.

Soul

Judaism In the Hebrew scriptures, the soul and the body are not sharply distinguished. The words *ru'aḥ* ('breath', 'wind'), *nefesh* (that which locates the animate as opposed to the dead—as e.g. 'the waters have come up to my *nefesh*', i.e. neck), and *neshāmah* ('vitality') have no independent, ontological status: they refer to that which gives life and which, if it is absent, leads to death. The *rabbis of the *Talmudic period recognized some separation. The soul was understood as the guest of the body during the body's earthly life (*Lev.R.* 34. 3). Jewish philosophers, such as *Philo, *Sa'adiah Gaon, and Solomon ibn *Gabirol, were influenced by Platonism in their teachings on the immortality of the soul, while the *kabbalists taught that the soul was a divine entity that evolved downwards to enter the body. It has its origins in the divine emanation and its ultimate goal is its return to the world of *sefirot.

Christianity The New Testament writers inherited the biblical terminology (though in Greek), together with the undecided contest about the basic human composition and about whether any part of it might continue after death. Roughly, *nephesh* became *psyche* and *ruaḥ* became *pneuma*; but both these were transformed by the resurrection of Jesus and by the experience of the *Holy Spirit in the early Church. Thus early Christianity came to believe that the *psyche* must be surrendered to God with complete commitment and trust, even to the extent of, so to speak, losing it (Matthew 6. 25, 16. 25; Mark 8. 35; Luke 9. 24; John 12. 25) and thus securing it. The soul was then associated with a belief that there will be an embodied resurrection. In the Hellenistic world, an application of the *dualism of Plato nevertheless seemed spiritually attractive, since the sense of a soul imprisoned in a body (*sōma sēma*, 'the body a tomb') led to a heroic spirituality in which *ascetic efforts might be made to ensure the soul's escape and safety.

Islam See NAFS.

Indian Religions See ĀTMAN; ANĀTMAN; JĪVA.

Soul-friend (counsel in the spiritual life): see CELTIC CHURCH.

Sound: see Index, Sound.

Sounding brass (emptiness of life without agape): see CHARITY.

South-East Asian Buddhism: see BUDDHISM *ad loc.*

Southern and Northern Schools. An early division of Ch'an/Zen Buddhism in China. Both schools agree in accepting the first four successors or patriarchs after *Bodhidharma: *Hui-K'o, *Seng-ts'an, *Tao-hsin, and *Hung-jen. They divide over the next successor. The division is reinforced by basic issues concerning the way to enlightenment. Thus, contrary to the titles, the division was not so much one of geography as of emphasis. Roughly, South is associated with sudden enlightenment, North with gradual approaches—hence the summary formula, *nan-tun pei-chien* (Jap., *nanton hokuzen*), 'suddenness of south, gradualness of north'. The history of the schism is obscured by the fact that it is mainly told by the eventual 'winners', the South. But the North had a central part in the transmission from Bodhidharma via Fa-ju (638–89), who addressed his teacher, Hung-jen, as 'patriarch' (indicating for the first time formal transmission), and who is regarded as the founder of the North. He was succeeded by Shen-hsiu (667–730), although Southern accounts replace him with *Hui-neng. But Shen-hsiu received the seal of recognition from Hung-jen (*inka-shōmei), and was widely recognized for his wisdom and powers of meditation. He systematized the earlier teachings which he had received, in *Kuan-hsin lun*, harmonizing *sūtras and meditation practices, and transmitting the foundations laid by Bodhidharma into China. According to his epitaph, 'he cut off the flow of ideas and put a stop to the rush of imagination, and with all his energy concentrated his mind', and he was able to go 'to that domain where there is no longer any distinction between sacred and profane'.

All that is far removed from the dominant Southern accounts, which in their tendentiousness are like Roman Catholic histories of Protestantism (or *vice versa*). The South was established by Shen-hui, a disciple of Hui-neng, at the Great Dharma Assembly on 15 Jan. 732, in Hua-t'ai. Of Shen-hui's earlier life, little is known apart from his disputes with pupils of Shen-hsiu, P'u-chi and I-fu. According to the Tun-huang text, Shen-hui argued that Bodhidharma is the authentic source of Zen: he stopped the futile activity of building temples, carving images of the Buddha, and copying sūtras. The dharma seal of recognition and the robe were transmitted to Hui-K'o, from whom they were transmitted in unbroken line to Hui-neng. The Northern protagonist refused to confine transmission to one line, via the robe. Shen-hui replied: 'The robe authenticates dharma, and the dharma is the doctrine [confirmed by] the robe . . . There is no other transmission.' True enlightenment, according to Shen-hui, is a sudden breakthrough to no-mind: 'Our masters have all grasped enlightenment at a single stroke [Jap., *tantō jikinyū*], with no concession to steps or progressions.'

North persisted for several more generations, but the Southern view prevailed and became what is now recognized as Zen. But the different emphases between *Sōtō and *Rinzai indicate that the issue was never wholly resolved.

Southern Baptist Convention. The largest organization of *Baptist churches in the USA. It was formed in 1845 following serious division among US Baptists over slavery. Since the 1940s, however, it has spread to all the states (partly on account of its membership among US military families) and has lost a little of its regional identity. In view of its numerical strength and resources, the Convention has considerable influence among Baptists, especially through the Baptist World Alliance.

Southern Kingdom (of Israel): see ISRAEL (3).

Sōzan Honjaku (co-founder of Ch'an school): see TS'AO-SHAN PEN-CHI.

Sozzini, Lelio, and Fausto (source of Socinianism): see SOCINIANISM.

Spartas (founder): see AFRICAN GREEK ORTHODOX CHURCH.

SPCK (Society for Promoting Christian Knowledge). British missionary society and publisher, founded in 1698. Its main work outside the UK is now through grants to churches to publish and distribute their own literature.

Special providence (God's action in relation to particular circumstances and individuals): see PROVIDENCE.

Special sabbaths (particular sabbaths in the Jewish calendar): see SABBATH.

Spector/Spektor Isaac Elchanan (1817–96). Lithuanian Jewish religious leader. Spektor served as the *rabbi of a number of communities, ultimately of Kovno. Because of the deteriorating situation of Jews in Russia, he supported the Hovevei *Zion (Lovers of Zion) movement, and publicly proclaimed the religious duty of settling in *Erez Israel. Many of his letters and *responsa have been published. Two yeshivot were founded in his memory in 1897, one of them in New York—the Rabbi Isaac Elchanan Theological Seminary. This developed into Yeshiva University, one of the largest Jewish institutions of higher education in the USA.

Spener, Jakob (leader of Protestant movement): see PIETISM.

Spheres, Music of (perfect harmonies in the moving spheres of cosmology): see MUSIC OF THE SPHERES.

Sphoṭa (Skt., 'a boil'). In Hindu understanding, the capacity of meaning to burst forth (as from a lanced boil) from the sound (*śabda) of words, because all sound has the potential to manifest the source of sound, namely, *Brahman.

Spinoza, Baruch (1632–77). Jewish philosopher. Despite his traditional education in Amsterdam, he associated with free-thinkers in his youth, and was *excommunicated from the community in 1656. His *Tractatus Theologico-*

Politicus (1670, published anonymously) was a work of biblical criticism which questioned revealed religion, opposed persecuting churches (including *Calvinism), and argued for religious freedom. His major work, *Ethics*, was not published until after his death. His *pantheistic, impersonal God was completely alien to the Jewish community and he remained under a ban (*ḥerem) for the rest of his life, once the edict had been issued.

In contrast, Novalis called him *Gott-trunckener Mensch* ('God-intoxicated man'), and there is no doubt of the centrality of God in his understanding of all things.

Spinoza began with axioms which had to be true because they could not logically be denied. But looking at it, so to speak, backwards, and tracing the chain of propositions back to deductions back to axioms, everything is logically and actually dependent on an absolutely infinite Being whose existence cannot be denied, and this is what Spinoza called God, though equally it is Nature—understood in this way; hence his saying, *Deus sive Natura*. Clearly this is far from the personal creator outside and apart from his creation. Spinoza allowed a small space for human endeavour (*conatus*) within the strictly determined, and that was in the human effort to raise its life above all that seeks to destroy it, including passions and emotions. This effort to become 'the captain of one's soul' and to rise above passion through reason is called 'the concept of positive freedom', and has been an important goal in other systems of ethics.

Spirit: see HOLY SPIRIT.

Spiritual. A type of American folk hymn of the 18th–19th cent. 'White' spirituals appeared on the American frontier, in the forms of religious ballads and camp-meeting choruses, characterized by repetitions and refrains. 'Black' spirituals, the religious songs of slaves, are better known, partly on account of their musical idiom, and partly because of the intensity of feeling.

Spiritual Baptists. A group, known as 'Shouters' in Trinidad and Granada, and as 'Shakers' in St Vincent, representing an Afro-Protestant *syncretism within autonomous congregations mainly of African descent. This started on St Vincent in the late 19th cent. Although outlawed 1912–65, it survived underground and is now publicly accepted.

Split-ear yogis (Kānpaṭha yogis, derived from Gorakhnāth): see GORAKHNĀTH.

Spurgeon, Charles Haddon (1834–92). Christian *Baptist minister. In 1851, he became a Baptist. He began preaching, and was appointed to a chapel at Waterbeach, near Cambridge. In 1854 he moved to New Park Street Chapel in London, where the crowds who came to hear him were so great that the Metropolitan Tabernacle was built for him in Newington Causeway, completed in 1861: he ministered there to the end of his life. The printed sermons (in the end amounting to 63 vols.) enabled him to reach an even wider audience. He was firmly *Calvinistic in doctrine, and he withdrew from both the Evangelical Alliance and from the Baptist Union.

sPyan-ras-gzigs (Tibetan name of Avalokiteśvara): see AVALOKITEŚVARA.

Śrāddha (Skt.). In Hinduism, a supplementary funeral rite involving daily offering of water and occasional offerings of food (*piṇḍa) to the three immediately preceding generations of paternal and maternal ancestors.

The śrāddha rite is a source of merit for those who perform it with faith (*śraddhā).

Śraddhā (Skt.). 'Faith', personified as a goddess in Hinduism. She kindles in worshippers the faith to approach *Agni (and other gods) without which offerings are in vain.

In Buddhism (Pāli, *saddhā*), śraddhā is devoted commitment to the *Buddha and his *dharma: it underlies as a prerequisite the first two stages of the Eightfold Path (*aṣṭangika-mārga). In Mahāyāna, it is a fundamental trust, especially in the help of *bodhisattvas. From its devotion to Amitābha (*Amida), *Pure Land is sometimes known as 'The Way of Faith'.

Śrāmaṇa (Skt.; Pāli, *sammana*; Chin., *shamen*). In Eastern religions, the name given to members of male communities (usually translated as 'monks') or *ascetics; the feminine ('nuns') is śrāmani. The śrāmaṇas were numerous at the time of the *Upaniṣads, and may have been precursors of Jains and Buddhists.

Śrāmaṇera (fem., *śramaṇerika*). Buddhist novices who have undertaken, through preliminary ordination, to observe the ten precepts (*śīla). The minimum age is 7.

Śrauta sacrifices: see SACRIFICE (HINDUISM).

Śrautasūtras (texts detailing sacrificial procedures): See SŪTRA.

Śrāvaka (Skt., 'one who hears'). In Eastern religions, a layperson with religious commitment. In Buddhism, it referred originally to personal disciples of the *Buddha, or to students in general, but in *Mahāyāna, it refers to those who, in contrast to *bodhisattvas, seek personal enlightenment to the level of *arhat.

Śrāvakayāna (the way of the disciple, a less derogatory name for Hīnayāna): see HĪNAYĀNA.

Śrī (Skt., 'prosperity, splendour'). An honorific title in Hinduism, but also personified as a goddess, emerging from *Prajāpati after his creation of all other beings. The association of Śrī with good fortune led to her assimilation with *Lakṣmi.

Sri Aurobindo (Hindu teacher): see AUROBINDO.

Srī Chand (1494–1612 CE). Elder son of Gurū *Nānak, founder of *Udāsīs. Gurū Nānak disappointed his celibate son by appointing *Aṅgad as successor.

Srid.pa'i 'khor.lo (pictorial representation of saṃsāra cycle in Tibetan art): see TIBETAN WHEEL OF LIFE.

Śrī Harṣa (1125–80 CE). A Hindu philosopher of the *Vedānta tradition and arguably the greatest Indian logician. His main work is the *Khaṇḍanakhaṇḍakhādya*, in which he rejects the *pramāṇa (means of knowing) system as a way of gaining knowledge. To refute his opponents—he employed the *vitaṇda* method of argument which refutes a thesis (*pratijñā*) by *reductio ad absurdum*, but offers no positive counter-thesis. This parallels the *prasaṅga* method of the Buddhist *Nagārjuna.

Srī Pada (sacred mountain): see ADAM'S PEAK.

Śrī-Vaiṣṇavism. Hindu devotion to *Viṣṇu with his consort *Śrī, one of the six major movements devoted to Viṣṇu. In early sources, there is no mention of Śrī as the consort of Viṣṇu, and indeed it seems clear that there was originally an independent cult of Śrī, which was absorbed into the worship of Viṣṇu. Once the cults were united, Śrī became inseparable from Viṣṇu, who now wears on his body the mark of Śrī (*śrīvatsa*). Not surprisingly, Śrī became identified with *Rādhā. The particular cult of Śrī-Vaiṣṇavism is strong in S. India, where it draws on the traditions of the *Āḻvārs. Thus they adhere to 'the theology of the two scriptures', i.e. *Vedānta and the Āḻvār hymns, especially *Tiruvāmoḻi*, which is held to be equal to the *Upaniṣads. It is characteristic of Śrī-Vaiṣṇavas that having made a ritual act of total surrender to God, they ask for nothing more. They practise *darśana, the 'seeing' of the Lord through or in his image. Among major teachers, Puruṣottamācārya emphasized the ethical consequences of this *bhakti.

Śrīvatsa (mark of Śrī): see ŚRĪ-VAIṢṆAVISM.

Śrī Yantra or **Śrī Cakra** (Skt.). In Hinduism, especially *Tantrism, the best known sacred diagram (*yantra) charged with power. It commonly comprises nine intersecting triangles, five 'female' triangles representing *Śakti pointing downwards and four 'male' triangles pointing upwards representing *Śiva, though in some forms the order is reversed.

Within the Śrī Kula tradition of Tantrism, the Śrī Yantra is the visual equivalent of the Śrī Vidyā, a *mantra of fifteen syllables. Each syllable represents a goddess who is located within the Śrī Yantra.

Śrotāpanna (Skt.; Pāli, *sotāpanna*). 'One who has entered the stream', the beginning of the Buddhist way. A 'stream-enterer' is free from the three fetters (*saṃyojana), but not yet from the passions (*kleśa). He will have to be born in a new appearance at least seven more times, but these will always be in the higher domains (*gati), and not in *hell, or as an animal, etc.

Sṛṣṭi (Skt., 'sending forth'). Hindu understanding of creation as an emanation or re-emergence of the cosmos after its period of rest.

Śrutapañcami (Jain festival): see FESTIVALS AND FASTS.

Śruti (Skt., 'that which is heard'). In Hinduism, sacred and eternal truth, now in the form of revelation. As the word implies, this revelation was 'heard' (or alternatively 'seen') by seers (*ṛṣis) in a mythical past and transmitted orally, now by *brahmans. It is completely authoritative because śruti is believed to be eternal, unmarked by human redaction, and only written down in the age of disorder. Thus it is distinguished from *smṛti, 'that which is remembered', this latter being sacred and of divine origin, but imperfect because it is an indirect form of revelation. Śruti is synonymous with the *Veda. Smṛti in its widest application includes the *Vedāṅga, the ritual *sūtras, the lawbooks, the *itihāsas, the *Purāṇas, and the Nītiśāstras.

Ssu-hsiang (combinations of heaven and earth in Chinese philosophy): see T'AI-CHI.

Ssu-ma Ch'ien (son of Ssu-ma T'an, both historians): see HISTORIES IN CHINA.

Ssu-ming (Chin., 'Lord of fate'). A Taoist version of Tsao-chün, the 'lord of the hearth'. Tsao-chün watches over a household from his vantage-point, and is therefore of great importance in folk religion.

Ssu Shu (group of Confucian texts): see FOUR BOOKS.

Stabat Mater Dolorosa. Opening words ('The sorrowful Mother was standing...') of a

Latin hymn describing the sorrows of the Virgin *Mary at the cross of Jesus. Its author and date are unknown, though it is sometimes attributed to Jacapone da Todi (d. 1306). Its beauty and popularity are reflected in the many English translations (e.g. 'At the Cross her station keeping') and musical settings, some of which are performed at concerts rather than in *liturgy (e.g. Rossini, Liszt, Dvořák, Verdi).

Stages of life (Hindu): see ĀŚRAMA.

Staṁbha (Hindu pillar): see SKAṀBHA.

Staniloae, Dumitru (1903–93). Romanian Orthodox theologian and guide to the Church during decades of political turmoil—leading to his book on Church–State relations in the particular setting of Romania. He became editor of a church paper, and then moved in 1949 to Bucharest. He began his long task of translating the **Philocalia*, which was interrupted when he was arrested, in 1958, during a clamp-down on the Orthodox Church. He was pardoned in 1964, and continued his work in Bucharest until his retirement in 1973.

Stanisław or **Stanislaus, St** (1030–79). Patron *saint of Poland. As *bishop of Cracow he came into conflict with King Bolesław II and was put to death. Stanisław was implicated in a plot to oust the king in favour of his brother, and his execution was ordered, with whatever admixture of other motives, for treason. His remains were buried under the main altar of Cracow cathedral in 1088, and he was canonized in 1253. Feast day, 11 Apr.

Staretz (Russ. tr. of Gk., *geron*, 'an old man'). A spiritual father in Russian Orthodoxy. The *geron* was originally a senior monk, priest or lay, to whom other monks (and others) turned for spiritual direction. Famous startsi (pl.), such as Amvrosy of Optina (1812–91), were eagerly sought out. One of Amvrosy's visitors was *Dostoevsky, and the staretz Zossima, in *Brothers Karamazov*, is a partial reminiscence of him.

Starhawk (proponent of Wicca): see WITCHCRAFT.

Star of David (symbol of Judaism): see MAGEN DAVID.

Station days. Certain days on which the pope formerly celebrated mass in the 'stational' churches (Lat., *statio*, 'assembly') in Rome. They became a part of *Lent devotion, with processions headed by a *relic of the True Cross. Today, a list of stational churches is published at the beginning of Lent, with the day of observance. Outside Lent, important 'stations' are St John Lateran for *Easter, and St Mary Major for the Christmas midnight mass.

Stations of the Cross. A series of fourteen incidents in the *passion of Jesus. They are: (i) he is condemned to death; (ii) he receives the cross; (iii) he falls; (iv) he meets his mother; (v) Simon of Cyrene is made to carry his cross; (vi) his face is wiped by *Veronica; (vii) he falls a second time; (viii) he meets the women of Jerusalem; (ix) he falls a third time; (x) he is stripped of his garments; (xi) he is nailed to the cross; (xii) he dies on the cross; (xiii) his body is taken down; (xiv) it is laid in the tomb.

In Roman Catholic and some Anglican churches, pictures or carvings of these incidents are arranged around the walls, and are the subject of public and private devotions in *Lent and Passiontide.

Stcherbatsky, F. I., later **Theodore** (1866–1942). Russian scholar of Buddhist philosophy.

He is chiefly remembered today for his work on *Mahāyāna Buddhist philosophy, and in particular the first detailed treatment of the Logical or *Pramāṇa school of *Dignāga and *Dharmakīrti. His most influential writings are *The Central Conception of Buddhism* (1923), an examination of the *Abhidharma notion of *dharma; an exposition of the thought of *Nāgārjuna, *The Conception of Buddhist Nirvana*; and his magisterial *Buddhist Logic*, 2 vols. (1932).

Steiner, Rudolf (founder): see ANTHROPOSOPHICAL SOCIETY.

Steinheim, Salomon Ludwig (1789–1866). German Jewish poet and philosopher, Steinheim argued that religious *revelation is of its very nature non-rational. He alienated the advocates of *Reform Judaism by his supra-naturalism, and the *Orthodox by not identifying revelation with the Jewish holy books. His major work was *Die Offenbarung nachdem Lehrbegriffe der Synagoge* (4 vols.), but it had little influence on his contemporaries. He is now regarded as a forerunner of existentialism.

Stephen, St (d. *c.*35). The first Christian martyr. He was one of 'the seven' appointed 'to serve tables' (traditionally the first *deacons) in the Jerusalem church. On account of his preaching and miracles he was brought before the *Sanhedrin, and after making a defence denouncing Israel's perennial hardness of heart, was put to death by stoning (Acts 6. 1–8. 2). As with *Jesus, the basic offence appears to have been a refusal to accept the final authority of the *high priest and Temple (cf. Deuteronomy 17, and see REBELLIOUS ELDER). Feast day, in the W. 26 Dec., in the E. 27 Dec.

Sthāna-aṅga (part of Jain text): see AṄGA (2).

Sthaviravāda. One of two early Buddhist schools into which the community split at the Buddhist Council of *Pātaliputra, the other being *Mahāsāṅghika. The cause of the split is uncertain, but probably concerned proposals to extend the *vinaya rules, so that traditional practices could be formalized as obligatory. The conservative majority, Mahāsāṃghikas, resisted innovation. Traditionally, the split was over the exact status of *arhat. According to the Mahāsāṃghika, he is still subject to temptation, can still make progress, has not overcome all ignorance; according to Sthaviravāda, he is no longer 'human' in those ways. But this account seems to reflect later debates.

Sthūla-śarīra (in Hinduism one of three protections for the undying self): see ŚARĪRA.

Sticharion (Gk.). A liturgical *vestment worn by *Orthodox priests and bishops. It corresponds to the Western *alb, but may be coloured (especially dark red) as well as white.

Stigmata. The wounds of *Jesus at his crucifixion reproduced on the body of a Christian. The first saint known to have received the stigmata is St *Francis of Assisi, but the official attitude of the Roman Catholic Church has been guarded. More than 400 cases are known, and some instances have occurred outside Roman Catholicism.

Stole. A Christian eucharistic *vestment, hung round the neck (or, by a deacon, over the left shoulder). It is coloured according to season. The equivalents for the *Orthodox are *epitrachelion* (for priests) and *orarion* for deacons.

Storefront Church: see AFRICAN-AMERICAN RELIGION.

Storehouse consciousness (the continuum of subjective consciousness in Buddhism): see ĀLAYA-VIJÑĀNA.

Story-telling in religions: see Introduction.

Strange words, extraordinary actions (style of Zen teaching): see MA-TSU TAO-I.

Strauss, David Friedrich (1808–74). German Protestant theologian and biblical critic. In 1835 he produced *Das Leben Jesu Kritisch Bearbeitet* (The Life of Jesus Critically Examined, tr. 1846). This, it has been said, produced both fame and ruin: its radical ideas prevented any future employment (he was appointed to a chair at Zurich but could not actually exercise the post). His *Christliche Glaubenslehre* (1840, Christian Faith) was a hostile account of the unfolding of Christian doctrine; and *Der alte und der neue Glaube* (1872, The Old Faith and the New) expressed more of his disillusion and unhappiness, rejecting, for example, any hope of immortality. When he died, he was buried according to the instructions of his will, without any religious ceremony. In his *Life of Jesus*, Strauss exploited Hegel's distinction between 'idea' and 'fact', with 'idea' being the significance which transcends mere occurrence. Religions are communities of 'meaning-making', or, to use Strauss' own term, of myth-making. *Myth did not mean (as it has come to mean colloquially) something false, but rather a way in which significance and meaning can be shared. *Whatever* happened in the case of Jesus, incomparably more important than his biography is the way in which his followers used the mythological opportunities in the Bible to expound his significance. Thus he was not 'explaining away' the supernatural, as he is often accused of doing; he was trying to show how the life of Jesus is embedded in the mythological codes of the time as a language of explication.

Stream-enterer (one at the start of the Buddhist way): see ŚROTĀPANNA.

Street called Straight: see DAMASCUS.

Stūpa (Skt.; Pāli, *thūpa*). A reliquary (*relics) monument ubiquitous throughout the Buddhist world and which, as an object of formal devotion and as a symbol of Buddhahood itself, has been compared in role to the *cross in Christianity. The stūpa originated in India from the earlier *caitya, a funeral mound commemorating regional kings. Instructions from the *Buddha that he himself should be so commemorated—in order to remind people of the possibility of *nirvāna—are contained in the *Hīnayāna *Mahāparinirvāṇa Sūtra*.

The earliest form of the stūpa (e.g. from the 1st cent. CE, at Sañci, C. India) consisted of a simple base supporting an egg-shaped dome (*aṇḍa*) which contained the relics, and a spire with three rings—a combination in meaning of the ceremonial parasol and the *Three Jewels. The whole was surrounded by railings which circumscribed the stupa as a sanctified area. From this basic form eight theoretical types were developed of which only two were commonly built. These were the Enlightenment Stūpa, which follows the above description, and the Descending Divinity Stūpa, commemorating the descent of the Buddha to teach his mother (after a *Jātaka tale), which has steps leading to a raised walkway around the dome. *Mahāyāna variations of these types could have five or seven 'umbrellas' to represent stages on the path to Buddhahood, and a multiple base to represent the five elements, thus greatly aligning the stūpa with the *maṇḍala as a cosmogrammatic representation. The stūpa continued to evolve outside India, producing the *pagoda in E. Asia, and reaching the height of its symbolic richness in the Tibetan *chorten.

See Index, Stupas.

Stylite (Gk., *stulos*, 'pillar'). An early Christian *ascetic living on top of a pillar. They were mainly located in the Middle East. These pillars varied in height and size—some of them having a small shelter. Their main preoccupation was prayer, but they also gave instruction, and participated in theological controversy. The first stylite, *Simeon, was regarded as their founder. There were many stylites from the 5th to the 10th cents., after which they have become infrequent.

Suárez, Francisco de (1548–1617). Christian theologian and philosopher. He was born in Granada, in Spain, and became a *Jesuit in 1564. He was ordained in 1572, and, apart from five years in Rome, spent his life teaching in Spanish universities. In philosophical theology, he developed a position (especially in *Disputationes Metaphysicae*, 1597, Disputed Issues in Metaphysics), which is sometimes called after him 'Suarism' or 'Suarezianism'. He maintained, with the Jesuits against the *Dominicans, that God does not create the acts of individuals, but rather gives them the special graces (*gratia congrua*, from which this position is known as 'congruism') which, by his foreknowledge, he knows they will need. He was called by Paul V 'doctor eximius et pius'.

Subbas (Mandeans): see MANDEANS.

Subdeacon. An *order of Christian minister below *deacon. It was originally a minor order, and remains so in Eastern churches; in the Roman Catholic Church it became a major order in the 13th cent., but was suppressed altogether in 1972.

Subḥa (prayer beads in Islam): see ROSARY.

Sublapsarians (relation of election to fall): see PREDESTINATION.

Subordinationism. View in Christianity of the Triune Godhead which regards either the Son as subordinate to the Father, or the *Holy Spirit as subordinate to both, in contrast to the co-equality of all three Persons. It was condemned at the Council of *Constantinople in 381.

Subtle body (Skt., *liṅga śarīra* or *sūkṣma śarīra*). In Indian religions, a non-physical body. It is also called *puryaṣṭaka* ('city of eight'). This latter term refers to a classification of the subtle body in accordance with the *tattvas, namely the five *tanmatras* or subtle elements (sound, touch, form, taste, and smell) and the *antah kāraṇa* or inner instrument (comprising *buddhi, *ahaṃkāra, and *manas). A Vedantic classification, however, says that the subtle body comprises seventeen parts, namely the five *prāṇas, ten organs of action and knowledge, manas, and buddhi.

The subtle body is the vehicle in which the soul (*jīva) transmigrates through *saṃsāra, and the repository of karmic seeds (*saṃskāras) which determine the physical body and individual destiny. Beyond the subtle body is the causal (*kāraṇa*) or highest (*parā*) body. The causal, subtle, and gross bodies correspond to the states (*avasthā) of deep sleep, dreaming, and waking.

The structure of the subtle body as elaborated in Tantrism comprises energy centres (*cakras) connected by channels or veins (*nāḍīs) through which life-energy (*prāṇa) flows, maintaining bodily functions.

Subud International Brotherhood. A *new religious movement started in Indonesia in 1933 by Muhammad Subuh Sumohadiwidjojo (1901–87), Pak Subuh, called Bapak ('father') by his followers. It claims to be a spiritual experience rather than a religion or belief system. The name Subud is an abbreviation of the Skt. terms *suśīla*, *buddhi*, and *dharma*, which are given the meanings: 'living according to the will of God', 'the force of the inner self within humanity', and 'surrender and submission to God', respectively. The whole (Subud) means 'right living, with all one's parts awakened'.

At the heart of the movement is *latihan* (or *latihan kejiwaan*), an Indonesian term meaning 'training' or 'exercise'. Latihan cannot be taught or acquired through imitation; it is said to arise spontaneously from within the individual after contact has been transmitted.

This movement, with members in some seventy countries, is responsible for many large enterprises, including banks and schools.

Suchness or **thusness** (*tathatā). Commonly used in Mahāyāna Buddhism to denote the essential nature of reality and the quiddity or true mode of being of phenomena. It is synonymous with 'emptiness' (*śūnyatā), but has more positive overtones.

Sudden enlightenment (belief that enlightenment does not need many years or lives of preparation): see HO-TSE; SOUTHERN AND NORTHERN SCHOOLS.

Śuddhādvaita (Skt., 'pure non-dualism'). The philosophical position of Vallabha (1473–1531 CE) and his successors. This school of *Vedānta accepts the *Vedas, the *Bhagavad-gītā*, the **Brahmasūtra*, and the **Bhāgavata Pur-*

āṇa as authoritative, and teaches that both the cause (*Brahman) and the effect (the phenomenal world) are 'pure' (i.e. real) and one. Śaṅkara's doctrine of *māyā is rejected, and Parabrahman (conceived of as *sat, cit, ānanda, and *rasa—being, consciousness, bliss, and 'sentiment' or love) is affirmed as both the material and efficient cause of the universe. The purpose of creation is described as 'divine play' (*līlā). This highest entity, Parabrahman, is personal, described as both 'perfect' (*purṇa*) and 'the best of beings' (*puruṣottama*) and having qualities such as knowledge (*jñāna) and activity (*kriyā*).

Śūdra. Fourth social, or occupational, division (*varna) in Hinduism. The origin of the word is uncertain. From *Ṛg Veda* 10. 90. 12, where the hierarchy is *rājanya* (rulers), *brāhmaṇas, *vaiśyas, and śūdras, it is assumed that they were already menials, though at least included in the Vedic community, even if, as not being 'twice-born', not wholly integrated. Their emergence in creation from under the feet of Puruṣa summarizes their position in society.

Suffering: see THEODICY.

Suffering servant. The figure in Deutro-*Isaiah who bears suffering in hope of redemption, perhaps an individual, but understood as Israel in *exile. It was applied to *Jesus.

Suffragan. A Christian *bishop, who gives his suffrage (help). It may be any bishop, subordinate to his *metropolitan or *archbishop. In the Church of England, it is a bishop appointed as an assistant to the bishop of a diocese.

Sufi Order in the West. Established in London in 1910 by Hazrat Inyat Khan (1882–1927), from Baroda, India. He was succeeded by Pir Vilayat Inayat Khan (b. 1916), eldest son of the founder. The stated aims of the Order are to provide a vehicle for the transmission of spiritual truth in a manner that is consistent with modern, Western culture, and generally to act as a bridge between East and West. This form of the *Sūfī way focuses on the evolution of consciousness by realizing the common ground on which all things rest. This is referred to as the state of 'the one', the reality of the absolute which people strive to attain and which is found in God, *Buddha, and *Christ.

Sūfīs (for suggested etymologies, see TAṢAWWUF). Muslims who seek close, direct, and personal experience of God, and who are often, therefore, described as mystics. Sufism is usually treated as a single phenomenon, although it is made up of different strands and styles. Sufism is a major part of Islam, and Sūfīs have been particularly important in the spread of Islam. By the 18th/19th cent. CE, at least a half (perhaps as many as three-quarters) of the male Muslim population was attached in some sense to a Sūfī *ṭarīqa (order). Thus although Sufism has often been contrasted with the forms of Islam concerned with *fiqh and *sharī'a (i.e. with the lawful ordering of Muslim life), and although there have historically been clashes between the two, there is no inherent or necessary conflict: Sūfīs in general have been insistent on the necessity for the proper observance of Islam (examples are *al-Muḥāsibī and his pupil *al-Junaid, who is known as 'the father of sober Sufism') and have themselves been critical of *antinomian tendencies or individuals in Sūfī movements—associated e.g. with Khurasān, or with the *Qalandars. The union between Sūfī devotion and sharī'a is associated particularly with *al-Ghaz(z)ālī and the great Indian teacher, Aḥmad Sirhindī (d. 1625 (AH 1034)): he was a Sūfī of the *Naqshbandī order who affirmed that while the experience of the unity of all being in God is real, it is neither the whole nor the end of religion: moral and virtuous life are as important—and to enforce this he wrote letters to his many followers throughout India. The Sūfī experience of absolute reality (*ḥaqīqa*) is not opposed to sharī'a but is its foundation.

The early history of Sufism is not yet clear. It seems to have emerged from a determination among some early Muslims not to be distracted by the rapid Muslim expansion over vast territories from the vision and practice of *Muḥammad in realizing the absolute sovereignty of God in life. Of this early attitude, al-*Ḥasan al-Baṣrī (Basra being an important centre of it) is a major example, and later Sūfī orders look back to him as a key link in the connection back to the Prophet. Also from Basra was the notable *Rabi'a al-'Adawiyya; but Sūfī devotion took root in many different places, often absorbing in each place something of its different atmosphere. Thus Khurasāni Sufism reflected its parched surroundings in an austere asceticism, producing such remembered figures as Fudayl ibn 'Iyad, Ḥātim al-Aṣamm (who left behind the four principles of Sūfī life, to remember that no one eats your daily bread for you, that no one performs your acts except yourself, that as death is hurrying toward you so address your life now to meet it, and that every moment of your life is under the eye and judgement of God), and Ibrāhīm ibn Adham. The latter was a prince who experienced a dramatic conversion when out hunting.

Or again Kashmiri Sufism, from the 14th cent. onward, drew on Hindu asceticism, even producing an order, the Rishis, whose name was derived from the word *ṛṣi (understood as 'a singer of sacred songs').

Since Sufism was a commitment to God in absolute trust and obedience, it (unsurprisingly) gave rise to intense experience of that relationship. Techniques were developed (e.g. *dhikr, *sama') which were capable of producing trance states of ecstasy. The realized condition of union with God produced such a sense of the absolute truth of God, and of the bliss of union with him, that poetry and teaching began to emerge in which the distinction between God and the self seemed to be blurred —or even obliterated: the disturbance this caused for those sensitive to the absolute transcendence of God can be seen in the fate of *al-Ḥallāj, although far more threatening in effect was the mystically monistic system of *ibn al-'Arabī. Any potential conflict between the *'ulamā and the Sufis was largely overcome by the work of al-Ghaz(z)ālī, who knew both positions at first hand, and demonstrated the part that both play in Islam.

From the experience of devotion to God, the Sūfī poets, especially in Persia, produced works of enduring beauty and power. Among the earliest was Pīr-i-Anṣār ('Abdullah al-Anṣārī, d. 1088 (AH 481)), of Herat in Khurasān.

Other memorable poets were Farīd al-Dīn *'Aṭṭār, ibn al-Fāriḍ, *Jāmī, and perhaps consummately *Jalāl al-Dīn Rūmī.

The wide extent and influence of Sufism led to attempts being made to give systematic order to its teachings and techniques—a notable example being Ali Hujwīrī (d. 1702). But even more important was the organization of Sūfī traditions into formal orders (*tarīqa, pl. turūq; *silsilah). For examples, see CHISHTI; MAWLAWIY(Y)A; NAQSHBANDIY(Y)A; QĀDIRIY(Y)A; SHĀDHILIY(Y)A; and Index, Sūfī orders. An adherent is known (in general terms, though these words also have a wider use) as *derwīsh, *faqīr, *marabout.

A leader is known as *shaykh.

Suhrawardī, Shihāb al-Dīn Yaḥyā, Shaykh al-Ishrāq (1154–91 (AH 549–87)). Muslim eclectic who established the *ishraqi* (Illuminationist) school of philosophy. He was born in Iran, and after years of wandering, settled in Aleppo. However, his unorthodox views led to his imprisonment and death, probably by execution—for which reason his followers called him al-Shaykh al-Maqtul (murdered) to distinguish him from two other famous *Sūfīs of the same family. He produced many works expounding the philosophy of Illumination, of which the best-known is *Kitab Hikmat al-Ishraq* (The Book of the Illuminationist Wisdom). In this he shows how humans can travel from darkness to light, not only metaphorically. He believed that the centre of light is in the point where the *Qur'ān was revealed, and that those living far away are in the position of those who are yearning to return. His influence continued particularly among *Shī'ites.

Suicide. The deliberate taking of one's own life is condemned in all religions, although exceptions on the margins (death accepted or embraced for religious reasons) are usually made. In Judaism, there is no explicit condemnation in the Bible, but it came to be prohibited, partly on the basis of the sixth commandment ('Thou shalt not kill'). However, suicide to avoid even greater offence (e.g. to avoid murder or idolatry) was regarded as praiseworthy: the reported suicides at Masada, to avoid falling into the hands of the Romans at the end of the Jewish revolt, 66–70, remained a model of martyrdom—see *kiddush ha-Shem. Among Christians, martyrdom is commended in the pattern of Christ who laid down his life for others, but the deliberate taking of one's own life is condemned on much the same grounds as those of the Jews, but with an added sense of the wrong done to family and society at large. Suicides could not, until recently, receive Christian burial. The sense of compassion and support needed for those tempted to commit suicide led to the founding of the Samaritans by Chad Varah in 1953. Islam shares the same kind of attitude: martyrs (*shahīd) are highly commended, but suicide (although barely mentioned in the *Qur'ān: see 4. 29) is strongly condemned in *ḥadīth.

In Eastern religions, the ambiguous border is not so much between martyrdom and suicide as between suicide and sacrifice. Among Jains, the religious relinquishing of the body is taken to a marked extreme in *sallekhanā. In Buddhism, the propriety of suicide to benefit another is recognized. But the consideration of *ahiṁsā (of doing no harm to a sentient being) makes suicide generally forbidden. Japanese *hara-kiri (*seppuku*) was originally a social rather than specifically religious act, but its endorsement by Zen Buddhism gave it a religious support.

Suiga Shintō or **Suika Shintō** (Jap., 'Shinto of grace and protection'). An eclectic school of *Shinto which was influenced by *neo-Confucianism. It was founded by Yamazaki Ansai (1619–82), a Buddhist priest turned Confucian scholar who attempted a grand synthesis of neo-Confucian metaphysical and ethical concepts with the traditions of the various Shinto schools of the early Tokugawa period.

Suigatsu (Jap., 'moon-reflected image'). A common summary in Japanese Buddhism of the transitory and non-substantial nature of all appearance.

Suijin matsuri (festivals of the water kami): see FESTIVALS AND FASTS.

Suika Shintō: see SUIGA SHINTŌ.

Sukh Asan (Pañjābī, 'sit at ease'). The Sikh ceremony during which the Gurū Granth Sāhib (*Ādi Granth) is formally closed for the night.

Sukhāvatī. The Western Paradise, ruled over by the Buddha Amitābha (*Amida). For *Pure Land Buddhism, it is the goal attainable by devotion to Amitābha, from which one cannot fall back into rebirth in other domains.

Sukhāvatīvyūha (Skt., *sukhāvatī*, 'place of happiness', + *vyūha*, 'description'). A Buddhist *Mahāyāna scripture. A *sūtra of the early *Ratnakūṭa collection, it is also known as *Amitābhavyūha*, *Amitābhaparivarta*, or *Aparimitāyur-Sūtra*, 'Sūtra of Unending Life'. The text includes a detailed description of Sukhāvatī and makes the point that whoever sincerely desires *enlightenment, with a mind fixed on Amitābha, will be reborn in that wonderful world. The *Sukhāvatīvyūha* is the textual base of the Japanese *Pure Land school of Buddhism, along with *Amityāyurdhyāna-Sūtra*. In Japanese, it is known as *Amida-Kyō*.

Sukhmanī (Pañjābī, 'hymn of peace'). Composition by Sikh Gurū *Arjan Dev. The Sukhmanī, *Ādi Granth pp. 262–96, is read daily in morning worship. It brings comfort, especially to the dying.

Sukkah, Sukkot (Heb., 'Booth', 'Festival of Booths'). The Jewish autumn festival, obedient to Leviticus 23. 42, 'You shall dwell in booths ...' The construction of the booth is discussed in the *Talmudic tractate *Sukkah*. The festival concludes with Shemini Atzeret and *Simḥat Torah. In biblical times, it was clearly connected with the agricultural year (Deuteronomy 16. 13–15), and, based on Leviticus 23. 40, the *four species are to be held during the worship services. In the days of the *Temple, a special ceremony of water libation was held, and the light of the candlesticks used to be reflected in the poured-out water.

Sūkṣma (Skt., 'subtle'). Usually in combination with *śarīra, the subtle body, especially in *Kuṇḍalinī and *Tantric yoga, the support of the *cakras.

Sulaimān (the Magnificent), al-Qānūnī ('the law-giver', 1494–1566 (AH 900–74)). *Ottoman caliph (*khalīfa) who led the empire to its highest points of achievement. Committed to good administration, he issued in 1530 (AH 937) the Kānūnnāmeh, a corpus of law to bring greater uniformity to the immense empire. He initiated public buildings and municipal works, encouraging the great architect Sīnān (1488–1587 (AH 895–996)), who built many of the best-known *mosques in Istanbul and Turkey, and rebuilt the Great Mosque in *Mecca.

Sulūk (Arab., 'journey'). Among the *Sūfīs, the mystic's progress on the way to God. It is a deliberate quest, beginning with one's initiation into a Sūfī order, followed, under the guidance of a *shaikh, by the methodical purification of the self through stages or stations (*maqāmat*). The Sūfī orders have their own individual programmes of stations for the sālik, the one who pursues this journey.

Sumbulon (Christian creed): see SYMBOLS.

Sumeru (sacred mountain in Indian religions): see MERU.

Summa. 'Total' or 'totality', used by medieval writers to denote a compendium of theology, philosophy, or canon law. They became handbooks for the *Scholastics, succeeding *Peter Lombard's *Sentences*, and consisted of 'questions' systematically arranged. The most famous are *Aquinas' *Summa Theologiae* and *Summa contra Gentiles*.

Sumohadiwidjojo, Muhammad Subuh (founder): see SUBUD.

Sundar Singh, Sadhu (1889–*c*.1929). Indian Christian teacher and mystic. Born of wealthy Sikh parents (though describing himself as a seeker, not a Sikh), he was converted to Christianity by a vision, and in 1905 was baptized into the Anglican Church. He wore the robe of a *sādhu to point to the possibility of Christianity in a Hindu context. His Eastern connections aroused great interest in Europe (shown in the writings of B. H. Streeter and N. *Söderblom among others), but in Germany also some accusations that he was a charlatan or a victim of his own fantasies. He was last heard of in Apr. 1929.

Sunday. As the Christian weekly day of worship it may perhaps be attested in the New Testament (Acts 20. 7; Revelations 1. 10: see LORD'S DAY), but emerges clearly in Rome in the 2nd cent. It was early understood as a weekly commemoration of Christ's resurrection on the first day of the week, but it may also owe something to the early Christians' desire to distance themselves from Jewish customs and worship on a day other than the *Sabbath.

Sundo (Chin., Shun-tao). The first Buddhist missionary to Koguryŏ, in Korea. Sundo travelled to Koguryŏ in 372, the second year of King Sosurim's reign (371–84), with an envoy dispatched by King Fu Chien (r. 357–85) of the Former Ch'in dynasty (351–94), presenting Buddhist images and scriptures to the Koguryŏ court. (Another tradition holds that Sundo came from the Eastern Ch'in (317–420) rather than the Former Ch'in.) In either case, this event is regarded as the first introduction of Buddhism to Korea.

Sunna (Arab., 'custom'). Customary practice which, in Islam, may refer to both bad and good examples in the past. But supremely the sunna refers to the way in which the Prophet *Muḥammad and his Companions (*Ṣahāba) lived, and to what they said and did (attending also to that concerning which they were silent). Thus Qur'ān is the fundamental authority, but the sunna forms the first living commentary on what Qur'ān means, and thus becomes equally the foundation for Muslim life: the *sunnat al-nabī*, the 'example of the prophet', controls Muslim life even in small details. Non-Shi'ite Muslims are therefore known as *Ahl al-Sunna wa'l-jamā'a*, the people of the sunna and of the gathered assembly, i.e. Sunnis. Shi'ites (*Shī'a) share most of the sunna with them, but place emphasis on the role of the Imām in guiding the community, and they also accuse Sunnis of suppressing *ḥadīth which support Shī'a beliefs and practices.

Suññattā: see ŚŪNYATĀ.

Suntarar (Tamil Śaivite): see NĀYAṆMĀR.

Sun Wu-k'ung. The monkey king, one of the Chinese *hsien (immortals).

Śūnyam. In Indian mathematics, the sign for 'nought' or zero. Its decimal potential, in combination with integers, enabled the Hindu imagination to create vast numbers—simply by adding to 1, 2, etc., an indefinite series of zeros. Equally, the emptiness of zero opened up the conceptualization of *Brahman without attributes (*nirguṇa), and pointed towards *śūnyatā in Buddhism. Among *Bāuls, the *guru is sometimes called śūnya.

Śūnyatā or **Suññattā** (Skt., Pāli, 'emptiness'; Chin., *k'ung*; Jap., *kū*; Korean, *kong*). In early Buddhism, the term suññatā is used primarily in connection with the 'no-self' (*anatman) doctrine to denote that the Five Aggregates (*skandhas) are 'empty' of the permanent self or soul which is erroneously imputed to them.

The doctrine of emptiness, however, received its fullest elaboration at the hands of *Nāgārjuna, who wielded it skilfully to destroy the substantialist conceptions of the *Abhidharma schools of the *Hīnayāna. Since there cannot be anything that is not the Buddha-nature (*buddhatā), all that appears is in truth devoid of characteristics. The doctrine of emptiness is the central tenet of the *Mādhyamaka school, and a statement of Nāgārjuna's views in support of it may be found in his **Mūla-Mādhyamaka-Nārikā*.

Emptiness thus becomes a fundamental characteristic of *Mahāyāna Buddhism. The teaching is subtle and its precise formulation a matter of sophisticated debate, since the slightest misunderstanding is said to obstruct progress towards final liberation. Emptiness is never a generalized vacuity, like an empty room, but always relates to a specific entity whose emptiness is being asserted. In this way up to twenty kinds of emptiness are recognized, including the emptiness of emptiness. The necessary indiscoverability of essences is the Mādhyamakan emptiness. It is important to distinguish this from *nihilism. In Yogācāra (*Vijñānavāda), emptiness is taught as the inability to think of an object apart from the consciousness which thinks of that object, i.e. the necessary indissolubility of subject and object in the process of knowing is the Yogācārin emptiness. It is important to distinguish this from idealism and solipsism.

Śūnyatāvādin (Skt., *śūnyatā*, 'emptiness', + *vādin*, 'teacher of'). Loosely used to denote a follower of the philosophy of *Nāgārjuna. The term first occurs in the *Vijñānakāya*, an *Abhidharma text of the *Sarvāstivādins where a śūnyatāvādin is described as someone who holds that the concept of person (*pudgala) is empty (*śūnya*). The term has been more generally applied to any adherent of his school, the *Mādhyamaka.

Supercommentaries. Jewish commentaries on the chief commentators on the *Pentateuch. Commentaries have been produced on the works of *Rashi, Abraham *ibn Ezra, and *Naḥmanides.

Supererogation, work of. A work which is not required as a matter of obligation in morality, but which is beneficial for the good of others or for the strengthening of spiritual or moral life. They include works done purely for the love of God.

The *counsels of perfection (poverty, chastity, obedience) are typically considered works of supererogation. For an example in Islam, see NĀFILA.

Supralapsarians (relation of election to fall): see PREDESTINATION.

Supremacy, Act of. An Act of 1559 declaring the Queen of England (Elizabeth I) to be 'the only supreme governor of this realm . . . as well in all spiritual or ecclesiastical things or causes as temporal'. The act was a revised form of Henry VIII's Act of 1534 repealed by Mary. It is intrinsic to the 'establishment' of the *Church of England.

Sura. Site of one of the Babylonian Jewish *academies. Sura was an important centre of *Torah study. It was established by *Rav in 219 CE. It was known as the 'yeshivah of the right', because its head sat on the right hand of the *exilarch at his induction ceremony. At the beginning of the 10th cent., the academy moved to Baghdād. *Sa'adiah Gaon became its head in 928. By the 12th cent. the town was in ruins.

Sura. One of a class of Hindu deities. They inhabit *Indra's heaven, but they have no strong role or identity—indeed, they may be derived from a mistaken view that the 'a' in *asuras is a negative, producing 'gods' (suras) and anti-gods (asuras).

Sūra. A division of the *Qur'ān (roughly equivalent to a 'chapter'). The term originally referred to a single portion of scripture, in this sense equivalent to *qur'ān*, a recitation. The word may come from the Syriac *ṣūrtā* (or *sūrthā*), a 'writing'. In the Qur'ān itself, it has the sense of a text of scripture. The Qur'ān is composed of 114 sūras in all, each one with a name, by which it is known to Muslims. Each sūra is classified as Meccan or Madinan according to whether it was first recited before or after the *Hijra, though it is accepted that some sūras contain verses from both periods. Each Sūra is composed of a number of *ayāt (singular, *āya*).

Sūrdās (15th/16th cent., b. *c.*1478). Hindu poet renowned for his devotion to *Kṛṣṇa as well as for his musical abilities. Little is known for certain of his life. He was blind (possibly, but not certainly, from birth). He met Vallabhacarya (see VAIṢṆAVA) and became a member of his movement. Of six works attributed to him, *Sūrsārāvalī* is based on the *avatāra of Kṛṣṇa, *Sāhityalaharī* deals with the *līlā of Kṛṣṇa. His most famous work is *Sūrsāgar*, based loosely on **Bhagavata Purāṇa*.

Suri (Jain teachers): see DĀDĀ GURŪS.

Surplice (Lat., *superpelliceum*, 'over-fur garment'). A Christian *vestment. It is a wide-sleeved loose linen garment reaching to the knees (or lower), worn over the cassock in the course of worship.

Sursum Corda (Lat.). The words 'Lift up your hearts' addressed to the congregation at the beginning of the *eucharistic prayer. The reply is 'We lift them up to the Lord'.

Sūrya, Savitar, or **Savitṛ** (nourisher). In Hinduism, the sun. As the source of heat and life, Sūrya is supreme among the *Ādityas, and one of the three chief gods of the *Vedas. As illumination, he resides within as the source of wisdom (*Maitri Upaniṣad* 6. 34). Later, he was superseded by *Viṣṇu. Sūryā is the daughter of Sūrya, who appears in *Ṛg Veda* 10. 6 ff. The Konārak, or 'Black Pagoda', was built at Orissa, in N. India, in the 13th cent. CE, as a temple to Sūrya. The surviving Great Hall is built as a replica of Sūrya's chariot.

Susanna and the Elders. Jewish *apocryphal work. It was added to the Roman Catholic canonical Book of Daniel as ch. 13 (following the *Septuagint), and was highly popular in the Middle Ages. In early Christian art, the story epitomized the salvation of souls.

Suso (German mystic): see HENRY SUSO.

Susoku-kan. Zen Buddhist practices of 'contemplation by counting the breath'. It is a group of practices in the early stages of *zazen, to help collectedness of mind and avoidance of distraction: (i) *shutsu-nyosoku-kan*, counting breaths in and out; (ii) *shussoku-kan*, counting out; (iii) *nissoku-kan*, counting in; (iv) *zuisoku-kan*, following the breath.

Sutra (Arab., 'to conceal, veil'). In Islam, an object (often a *rosary) which a worshipper places before him during *ṣalāt, in the direction of the *qibla, making a protected place, free from human (or demonic spiritual) interference (cf. *capella*—cloak pulled over one in prayer—chapel).

Sūtra (Skt., 'thread'). 1. In Hinduism, sūtras seem to have originated as manuals for those concerned with household and other rituals. Sūtra literature is written in a condensed prose. The *Kalpasūtras are concerned with ritual, and fall into three major categories: Śrautasūtras, Gṛhyasūtras, and *Dharmasūtras. As the names imply, the first deal with the performance of sacrifices (in complex detail), the second with home rituals including *saṃskāras, and the third with these and with other duties belonging to the *āśramas. They were extended in the verse-form *śastra literature. Sūtras are also sharp and elliptical works which are commented on in the *darśana (philosophical) works: e.g. *Jaimini, *Bādarāyaṇa, *Kaṇāda, *Patañjali.

2. In Buddhism, sūtras (Pāli, *sutta*) are the collections of the discourses or teachings of the *Buddha. In *Theravāda, they are gathered in the second part of the Pāli canon (*tripiṭaka), the Sūtra-(Sutta-) piṭaka. They are then divided

into five collections, *nikāyas (Skt., *āgama). In Mahāyāna, many additional sūtras have been preserved, some of which become foundational for particular schools of Buddhism (e.g. the **Lotus Sūtra*, **Śukhāvatīvyūha*, **Laṅkāvatāra-Sūtra*).

3. For Jain sūtras, see AṄGA.

Sūtrakṛta-aṅga (part of Jain scripture): see AṄGA.

Sūtra of the Garland of Buddhas (extensive and foundational Buddhist text): see AVATAMSAKA LITERATURE.

Sutta: see SŪTRA.

Sutta-nipāta (part of Buddhist Pāli canon): see KHUDDAKA-NIKĀYA.

Sutta-piṭaka (collection of suttas): see SŪTRA.

Suttavibhanga (division of Vinayapiṭaka): see TRIPIṬAKA.

Suttee (devotion through self-immolation of a widow): see SATĪ.

Su-yüeh (popular music): see MUSIC.

Suzuki, Daisetz Taitaro (1870–1966). Professor of Buddhist Philosophy at Ōtani University, Kyōto, from 1921, and an important scholar of *Mahāyāna Buddhism and *Japanese religion in general. Having started *Zen training under two separate masters at the age of 22, his academic work was always informed by a deep spiritual insight. He is chiefly known in the West for his popularization of Zen Buddhism.

Svabhāva. 'Self-nature' or 'Own-being': a property which, according to the *Mādhyamaka, is falsely ascribed to *dharmas, or the world of phenomenal reality. According to the *Abhidharma, however, it constituted the unique and inalienable 'mark' or characteristic by means of which phenomena could be differentiated and classified. Thus the schools of the *Hīnayāna, while denying a self of persons (*pudgala-nairātmya*), and explaining personal identity by recourse to the teaching of the Five Aggregates (*skandhas), nevertheless accepted the substantial reality of those elements (dharmas) which composed the aggregates and the world at large.

Svabhāvikakāya (the unity of the three manifestation forms of the Buddha): see TRIKĀYA.

Svadharma (Skt., *sva*, 'own', + *dharma*, 'duty, right'). In Hinduism, one's own right, duty, or nature; one's own role in the social and cosmic order. Svadharma is relative to one's *caste and stage of life (cf. *varṇāśramadharma), and to one's situation (cf. *āpaddharma). Svadharma or relative *dharma often conflicts with sādhāraṇa dharma, universal dharma, or *sanātana dharma, absolute or eternal dharma. For example, to kill is a violation of eternal dharma, yet a warrior's *svadharma (own duty, nature) is to kill.

Svāmi or **Swāmi** (Skt., 'owner', 'master'). Title of respect for a holy man or teacher.

Svaminarayan Movement. Founded by a high-caste *brahman, Sahajānanda Swami, known as Lord Svaminarayan, in Gujarat, India, in the early 19th cent. Since then there has been considerable segmentation. A follower of the *Vaiṣṇava teacher *Rāmānuja, Svaminarayan made qualified monism a fundamental precept and developed his movement in the *bhakti tradition of devotional worship. Svaminarayan is regarded as an *avatāra of *Viṣṇu who took on an earthly, human form in order to bring salvation to his followers. The movement spread from India to Britain in the 1950s, to become one of the largest Indian religions in that country. In 1995, it opened a large temple in Neasden (London), to be a centre for pilgrimage. Built at great expense, it revived skills of temple-carving and traditional decoration.

Svarga. In Hinduism, heaven, and especially the heaven of Indra, situated on one of the *Himālayas, usually Mt. *Meru. By proper performance of sacrifice, the good can hope to attain svarga, and in later texts (e.g. *Viṣṇu Purāṇa* 2. 2) may attain the form of *devas.

Svastika (Skt., *su*, 'well', + *asti*, 'is': i.e. 'all is well'). A cross with each extremity bent at right-angles to the right, an auspicious sign in Indian religions (found also in many other religions, e.g. as a sign of the infinite and of the sun among American Indians). For the svastika mountain, see KAILĀSA.

In Buddhism, the svastika is a symbol of the wheel of dharma (*dharma-cakra), or in Zen, the seal of the buddha-mind (*busshin-in*) transmitted from patriarch (*soshigata) to patriarch.

In the 20th cent., the svastika/swastika was adopted by the Nazis in Germany as the party emblem. It was mistakenly understood as an Aryan symbol, indicating racial purity and superiority.

Svatantrika-mādhyamaka (Buddhist philosophical School): see CANDRAKIRTI.

Svayambhū (Skt., 'unoriginated'). The capacity of objects to be self-existent, not dependent on the causal agency of another, and thus perhaps to sustain themselves from the idea concealed within them. It also represented an early attempt in Hinduism to recognize an unproduced Producer of all that is, an originator such as *Puruṣa, *Prajāpati or *Brahmā. In the *Purāṇas, it becomes the principle of indefinite cosmic elaboration, but in *Advaita and in the *Upaniṣads, it expresses the self-existent nature of *Brahman. *Vaiṣṇavites and *Śaivites apply it to *Viṣṇu and *Śiva respectively. In Buddhism, it is applied to the *Buddha as the one who is utterly independent of support in the apparent cosmos, and in Mahāyāna it is comparably applied to all buddhas, e.g. *Ādi Buddha.

Svedaja (Skt., 'born of sweat'). The fecundity in Hinduism of moist and humid conditions. It was linked to *tapas, so that the sweat of, e.g., a priest during rituals could be regarded as a sign of efficacious power.

Śvetāmbara ('white-clothed'). One of two major divisions among Jains, the other being *Digambara. For details of the issues between them, see DIGAMBARA. For their sacred texts, see AṄGA.

Śvetāśvatara Upaniṣad. One of the principal *Upaniṣads, belonging to the Black **Yajur Veda*, and one of the most profound and frequently referred to.

Swāmi: see SVĀMI.

Swaminarayan (manifestation of God and Hindu movement): see SVAMINARAYAN.

Sweat: see SVEDAJA.

Swedenborg, Emanuel (1688–1772). Speculative religious reformer and visionary. A severe religious crisis in 1743–5, accompanied by increasing dreams and visions, made him turn his attention to religious matters; and when a vision of *Jesus Christ resolved his crisis, he spent the rest of his life expounding his understanding of Christianity in *Neoplatonic terms. Among many works, the 8-vol. *Arcana Caelestia* (Heavenly Secrets) and *The True Christian Religion* (1771) give vivid descriptions of his spiritual experiences. His followers, after his death, organized, in 1787, the New (Jerusalem) Church, though this is meant to complement, not supplant, existing Churches.

Swiss Brethren (Protestant group): see ANABAPTISTS.

Sword of the Spirit. A *Roman Catholic lay organization founded in London in 1940 to defend and propagate Christian principles in national and international affairs. In 1965 its name was changed to the Catholic Institute for International Relations.

Syādvāda (Skt., *syāt*, 'perhaps'). Jain theory of knowledge which emphasizes the relativity and multifaceted nature of human judgement: it is therefore also known as *sapta-bhaṅgi-naya*, the 'dialectic of the seven steps'; and leads to *anekāntavāda. The Jains characteristically value the story of the blind men and the elephant, who feel only one part of the elephant and infer from that limited information what the elephant is like—a water pot (from the head), a winnowing basket (from the ears), a plough (from the tusks), a snake (from the trunk), a tree (from the legs), a rope (from the tail). The blind men then fall into furious argument, each one convinced that he alone possesses the whole truth. In contrast to the Western endorsement of the law of the excluded middle (either p or not-p), the Jains emphasize the provisionality of human judgements which allow several to coexist as contributions to truth, including some which appear to be mutually exclusive. See also NAYAVĀDA.

Syag (fence around Torah): see HOLINESS.

Śyāmā (Skt., 'black'). A form of the Hindu Goddess *Durgā/*Kālī.

Syllabus Errorum. A summary in eighty theses published in 1864 by *Pius IX of a number of papal pronouncements on a variety of issues, philosophical, theological, and political.

Symbolists: see SYMBOLS.

Symbols, symbolism (Gk., *sumbolon*, 'sign, token, pledge'; *sumballein*, 'cast together'). The representation in visible form of ideas, beliefs, actions, persons, events, etc., frequently (in the religious case) of transcendent realities, which bring the observer into connection and participation. So pervasive is the human use of symbols that E. Cassirer (*An Essay on Man*, 1944) called the human species *animal symbolicum*. Although it might seem obvious to define a symbol as that which stands for something which it represents (as a flag might be said to 'stand for' the country which it represents), in fact a symbol involves far more complex conditions of meaning—to be seen not least in the fact that symbols frequently stand for themselves, especially in the religious case (see R. Wagner, *Symbols that Stand for Themselves*, 1986): the symbolic actions of the Hebrew *prophets, for example, do not stand for (i.e. summarize in advance) a future event, but rather bring the reality of that event into being in the present. Beyond that, symbols may be non-referential and of effect in creating community and meaning (see A. P. Cohen, *The Symbolic Construction of Community*, 1985).

Since religions in that way are often evocative in their use of language, it is not surprising that the religious use of symbols can be paralleled in the turn to symbolism in arts and literature at the end of the 19th cent. The Symbolists were a loose association of artists and writers who turned strongly against the realist (and referential) ambitions of, for example, the Pre-Raphaelites or the neo-Impressionists, or of such writers as Flaubert and Zola. The importance of decoration in the symbolist sense is profoundly important in religious symbolism, though largely overlooked: there is an aesthetic satisfaction no matter what other purposes are being served. Most accounts of religious symbolism look at their function, especially as codes. An early meaning of *sumbolon* in Christianity is that of *creed, where the function of symbols in compressing (Gk., *sumballein*, 'to throw together') meaning and making it publicly available is emphasized. As C. S. Peirce realized, humans use different kinds of signs and symbols, each bearing some of the characteristics of the others. As a consequence of his work, the study of symbolism is firmly embedded in semiotics (Gk., *sēma*, 'a sign'). Peirce drew a distinction between three types of sign: icon, index, and symbol. An icon is a sign containing some of the qualities associated with the thing signified (e.g. maps and diagrams); an index is a sign which is in a dynamic relation with the thing signified and calls attention to what is signified (e.g. the column of mercury in a thermometer measuring temperature and indicating health or illness); a symbol is a conventional sign with an agreed connotation. Symbols are economies of statement and feeling which conserve successful accounts of context (success being measured crudely by persistence) and which evoke coherence by their power to unite immense diversities of human being and experience. But equally they set forward new opportunities of exegesis and action. For examples, see Index, Symbols. See also FEMININE SYMBOLS AND RELIGION; ICONOGRAPHY.

Symeon the New Theologian (949–1022). Byzantine mystic and spiritual writer. After entering the imperial service, he became a monk, first at Studios, then at St Mamas in Constantinople, where he became abbot. In 1005 he was forced to resign because of opposition to his teaching, and he was exiled. Though this was revoked, he remained in voluntary exile. Much influenced by the **Macarian Homilies*, he was a formative influence on *hesychasm. He is known as the 'new' or 'second' theologian, second only to *Gregory Nazianzen.

Symmachus ben Joseph (late 2nd cent. CE). Jewish *tanna. Symmachus was a disciple of Meir. He was the author of the principle, 'Money, the ownership of which cannot be decided, has to be equally divided' (*BBK* 46a), but is not to be identified with the Symmachus who translated the Bible into Greek (see also ONKELOS).

Synagogue (Heb., *bet *keneset*). Jewish meeting house and place of worship. The synagogue, in embryonic form, may perhaps date back to the period of the Babylonian *exile. By the 1st cent. CE, the synagogue emerges as a well-established institution. With the calamity of 70 CE, the synagogue became the main focus of Jewish religious life. Many of the rituals and customs of the Temple were adopted in the synagogue (e.g. the times of the Temple *sacrifices became the times of the synagogue prayers), and the synagogue also performed the function of a community centre. Different patterns of architecture have been followed in synagogue buildings. Many modern *Orthodox synagogues have a small synagogue nearby, known as a *bet ha-midrash, which is used for weekday services. In addition there are community halls and facilities for synagogue schools. The *Reform movement has built impressive synagogues (known as Temples in the USA); they have no special section for women; the bimah is generally placed in front of the Ark (so there is more room for seating) and there is often an organ and choir loft. Synagogues are grouped into organizations (e.g. The United Synagogue, The Federation of Synagogues, and the Union of Orthodox Hebrew Congregations (all British Orthodox organizations)) and rabbinic training is controlled by the organizations who sponsor the *rabbinical seminaries.

See Index, Synagogue.

Synagogue, The Great. Jewish institution mentioned in the *Mishnah. According to **Avot*, 'the men of the Great Synagogue' lived between the time of the *prophets and the time of the *rabbis. Most scholars date the period from the time of *Ezra, and the Great Synagogue was probably a representative body which met from time to time to pass resolutions.

Synanon Foundation. A *new religious movement. It was established in California in 1958 by Charles E. Dederich as a voluntary association of reforming alcoholics, soon developing into a therapeutic community for the treatment of narcotic addicts, and then into Social Movement and Alternative Society, a commune, with successful business operations and substantial real-estate holdings. In 1977 the Board of Directors proclaimed the Synanon Religion, with the so-called reconciliatory principle as its central tenet. Another important proposition is that individuals evolve by contributing to the community.

Synaxarion (Gk.). In E. Churches, a brief account of, or homily on, the life of a saint or the significance of a feast. The Greater Synaxarion is a liturgical book used in those churches, which contains short accounts of saints or feasts appointed to be read in the daily *office.

Synaxis (Gk., 'assembly'). In the early church, the service consisting of lessons, psalms, prayers, and sermon, probably derived from the worship of the *synagogue. It was later joined to the *eucharist.

Syncretism (Gk., explained by Plutarch with reference to the Cretans who, while habitually at odds with each other, closed ranks in the face of a common enemy). The amalgamation of religious beliefs and practices in such a way that the original features of the religions in question become obscured. The word has thus taken on a pejorative sense, derived from H. Usener who translated it (1898) as *religionsmischerei*, not so much a mixing as a confusing. The term is now usually used of those who are accused of abandoning a historic faith and practice in pursuit of some ecumenical religion which transcends the boundaries of existing religions. Despite this dismissive sense, all religions are syncretistic in the sense of absorbing and incorporating elements of other religions and cultures as they encounter them.

Synderesis (Gk., perhaps from *synteresis*, 'spark of conscience'). In Christianity, human knowledge (innate) of the first principles of moral behaviour. It is distinguished from conscience (although the two are sometimes used interchangeably) because the latter involves, not a basic intuition, but a judgement. In mystical theology, synderesis is the centre of the soul where mystical union occurs.

Synergistic controversy (on the relation between God's will and human freedom): see PREDESTINATION.

Synod (Gk.). A Christian church gathering for doctrinal and administrative purposes, constituted in many different ways in the different churches.

Synod of Dort (conference to prepare doctrine for Protestant Church): see DUTCH REFORMED CHURCH.

Synoptic Gospels. The three *gospels of Matthew, Mark, and Luke, so-called because their texts can be printed for comparison in a three-column 'synopsis'. The gospels share much of their subject-matter, and tell their stories in the same order and in many of the same words. The 'synoptic problem' is solved when these facts are accounted for. The most widely accepted solution (the 'two-document hypothesis') is that Mark is the earliest of the three and was used by both Matthew and Luke and that the additional matter common to Matthew and Luke was taken by them from a source *Q. Material peculiar to Matthew or to Luke is usually called 'M' and 'L' respectively.

Syrian churches. The churches whose traditional liturgical language is Syriac. The Syriac-speaking area in the ancient world included 'Syria', but its earliest and most important ecclesiastical centres were N. Mesopotamia (modern SE Turkey and N. Iraq) and Persia. Recently there has been a movement among these Syrian Christians to call themselves 'Assyrians' (but see ASSYRIAN CHURCH). All these churches share the heritage of Syriac literature before the 5th cent., e.g. the *Peshitta Bible and works of *Ephrem. After *Chalcedon their traditions gradually diverged.

The Syrian Orthodox Church descends from the *Monophysite movement in the patriarchate of *Antioch. The name *Jacobites is sometimes used in the West. The doctrinal position of the Syrian Orthodox is the same as that of the other *Oriental Orthodox churches.

The Syrian Catholic Church is the *Uniat body which came into existence from Roman Catholic conversions among the Syrian Orthodox. The hierarchy dates back to 1738. The present seat of the patriarch is Beirut. Their membership in the Middle East is *c*.80,000, with further churches in N. and S. America.

The *Maronite Church, a Catholic body, has had a separate existence from the Syrian Orthodox since the Middle Ages.

The Syro-Malankara Church is the product of a union with Rome among a group of Syrian Orthodox in India. They number *c*.200,000, with their own metropolitan of Trivandrum.

The *Church of the East is the descendant of the ancient Syriac-speaking church of Persia. It is more commonly known as the *Nestorian or *Assyrian Church; but none of these names is without its drawbacks. Total membership does not exceed *c*.50,000.

The Syro-Malabar Church is the largest body of *Malabar Christians. They have been Catholic since the time of Portuguese rule in India in the 16th cent. Relations with Rome were, however, often troubled until the church obtained its own hierarchy of native bishops in 1923. The liturgy is a slightly revised form of *Addai and Mari, now celebrated in the vernacular Malayalam.

The Chaldean Church is the Uniat body deriving from the Church of the East. Its numbers are also probably less than 50,000.

T

Taʿanit. Tractate of the Jewish *Mishnah and *Talmud. *Taʿanit* is concerned with the *halakhah related to fasts.

Tabarī: (Muslim scholar): see AL-TABARĪ.

Tabernacle (Heb., *mishkan*). The portable *sanctuary constructed by the Hebrew people in the wilderness. Exodus 25–31 and 35–40 describe the construction of the tabernacle, and Numbers 3. 25 ff. and 4. 4 ff. discuss its furnishings and the duties of the Levites (see LEVI).

In Christianity the word was originally applied to a variety of canopied structures in a church building, but most usually refers to an ornamental receptacle or cupboard for the *reserved sacrament.

Tabernacles, Feast of (Jewish festival): see SUKKAH.

Tablet in Heaven (source of the Qurʾān): see UMM AL-KITĀB.

Tablets of the Law/Covenant. The stones on which the Jewish decalogue (*ten commandments) were first inscribed. In the *aggadic tradition, the tablets of the law were created on the eve of the *Sabbath of the *Creation (*Avot* 5. 6) and they also contained the *oral law (*Ex.R.* 46. 1).

Tablīghī Jamāʿat (Urdu, 'Party which Propagates'). An Islamic movement which originated in India in 1923, and became a major international force for Islamic revival. It differs from other Muslim religious movements in that its founder, Mawlānā Ilyās (1885–1944), kept it free initially from political influences and zealously guarded it from being utilized for political purposes. He believed that spiritual regeneration of the individual should be the primary objective of any religious movement engaged in improving the condition of the Muslim community.

The movement has grown in popularity and strength, and has established many centres in African and Asian countries. In the 1960s Tablīghī Jamāʿat reached Japan, Britain, the USA, France, Belgium, Holland, and W. Germany, and won over numerous converts to Islam.

Taboo or **tabu** (Polynesian, *tapu*, 'marked off'). A power in relation to particular people, places, or objects which, if it is negative, marks them off as dangerous; it is thus related to *mana* (see MAGIC). More colloquially, the word has come to mean a prohibition against conduct which would invade the marked-off areas and thus disrupt the prevailing and desirable structures of life and society; hence the expression, 'taboos against . . .'.

Tabrīzī (Islamic Sūfī): see JALĀL AL-DĪN RŪMĪ.

Tabu: see TABOO.

Ta-ch'eng. Chin. for *Mahāyāna.

Tachikawa-ryū. A sect derived from *Shingon, accused by its opponents of *antinomian and immoral practices. It was founded (according to most accounts) by Ninkan in the 12th cent. While he was in exile during the civil wars of the Hōgen era, he both taught and studied with an adept (from Tachikawa) in the *Yin-yang school, and from this a kind of *Tantric system was developed, in which sexual union realized the unity of all appearance.

Ta-chu Hui-hai (8th cent. CE). Pupil of *Ma-tsu Tao-i, who cared for his teacher in his old age. While doing so, he produced the manuscript of a work on sudden enlightenment, which Ma-tsu read. He exclaimed, 'Here is a great pearl, the perfect and bright illumination which penetrates everywhere without impediment.' For that reason Hui-hai became known as Ta-chu, great pearl. His work was edited by Miao-hsieh and appeared as *Tun-wu ju-tao yao-men lun*, in which the southern school of Ch'an is integrated with the *Mahāyāna *sūtras.

Taesūng. Korean for *Mahāyāna.

Tafsīr (Arab.). Explanatory commentary on the *Qurʾān, generally a straightforward continuous comment on the text. At first, the term *taʾwīl was synonymous with tafsīr, but came later to designate more allegorical interpretation, while tafsīr was concerned more with philological explanation.

One who pursued the study of tafsīr was known as a *mufassir*: among the most famous are *al-Ṭabarī, the historian (d. 929/310); *al-Zama-khsharī (d. 1144/538); *al-Baiḍāwī (d. 1286/685); and in more modern times, the Egyptian scholar Muḥammad *ʿAbduh (1849–1905), whose commentary was edited by his follower *Rashīd Riḍāʾ as *Tafsīr al-Manār*.

See Index, Tafsir.

Tagore, Debendranath (1817–1905). Hindu reformer and leader of *Brahmo Samāj. He was primarily interested throughout his life in religion and education, especially in the role both can play in social reform and national development. He thus helped to lay the foundations of modern Indian society and political structure. From 1843, he successfully led the *Brahmo Samāj and founded *Tattvabodhini Patrika*, a journal of serious discussion, emphasizing the importance of maintaining the mother tongue, the need for the study of both science and religion, and the acceptance of both the best of Western culture and whatever was admirable in traditional Indian culture.

Tagore, Rabindranath (1861–1941). Probably the greatest modern Indian poet, and certainly the one most widely known internationally. He was the son of Debendranath *Tagore, and achieved recognition as a national poet when only in his twenties. The Eng. version of his lyrics, *Gitanjali*, won him the Nobel Prize for Literature in 1913. In addition to poetry, he excelled as a dramatist, essayist, and novelist. In 1912 he received an honorary doctorate from Calcutta University, and in 1913 a British knighthood; the latter he subsequently resigned in protest at the Jallianwala Bagh massacre. He was a close friend of Mohandas *Gāndhī, who, like so many others, honoured him with the title *Gurudeva*, and derived from him the inspiration to stand against the seemingly invincible strength of the British presence.

Ṭahāra (Arab., 'cleanliness'). Ritual purification in Islam. Purification is required before actions which are not lawful without ablutions—especially *ṣalāt, *circumambulation of the *Ka'ba, touching the *Qur'ān. Impurity is dealt with by wudu' and *ghusl: see ABLUTIONS (Islam).

Taḥrīf (Arab., 'corruption'). In Islam, an alteration of the written words, alteration when reading aloud, omission from or addition to the text, or wrong interpretation of an unaltered text. The charge, originally made against the Jews, was extended to the Christians also, of having somehow changed their scriptures (*Tawrāt and *Injīl respectively).

Ta Hsüeh (The Great Learning): see GREAT LEARNING.

Ta-hui Tsung-kao (Jap., Daie Soko, 1089–1163), Ch'an/Zen teacher in the *Rinzai school. He was the dharma-successor (*hassu) of Yüan-wu K'o-ch'in, and was a major advocate of training by use of *kōans. In this he opposed his friend, Hung-chih Cheng-chüeh, who accepted kōans, but put emphasis on quiet meditation, as in his brief text, *Mo-chao ming*, Jap., *Mokushomei* (The Seal of Silent Illumination). Ta-hui called this *jazen*, unwise Zen, dismissing those who practise it. Ta-hui gave to this position the name *mokushu zen*, i.e., 'silent-illumination zen'. Hung-chih called the way of Ta-hui *k'an-hua ch'an*, Japanese *kanna zen, 'Kōan-gazing zen', and these two names were adopted as the names of these two positions.

T'ai-chi (Chin., 'ridge-beam'). The supreme ultimate in Chinese philosophy and religion. It is the source of order and appearance in the **I-Ching*: 'In the changes, t'ai-chi produces the two energies [*yin-yang], which produce the four images [*ssu-hsiang*, the four possible combinations of Heaven and Earth, which give rise to the four seasons], from which arise the eight trigrams.' In *neo-Confucianism, t'ai-chi combines *li (structure) and *ch'i (primordial materiality), in an alternation of rest (yin) and activity (yang): from these arise the five elements (*wu-hsing) which constitute all existence.

T'ai-chi-ch'üan (Chin., 'power of the Great Ultimate'). An old form of physical and mental discipline in China. It consists of a sequence of stylized, graceful, slowly executed movements. In China it is commonly used as a daily exercise routine, but its roots lie in the great *martial arts tradition. It has sometimes been called 'shadow-boxing' in the West. See also GYMNASTICS, TAOIST.

T'ai-ch'ing (Taoist heaven of highest purity): see SAN-CH'ING.

T'ai-chi-t'u (Chin., 'diagram of the supreme ultimate'). The *yin-yang diagram, central to *Chou Tun-(y)i's explanation of how diversity arises from a single and unproduced source; hence *T'ai-chi Tu Shou*, the title of his work explaining the oscillation between activity and rest.

T'ai-hsi (embryo breathing): see CH'I.

T'ai-hsu (1889–1947). Chinese Buddhist monk, who did much to restore and revive Buddhism in China. He reorganized the *saṅgha, and founded the Buddhist Society of China (1929) and the Institute for Buddhist Studies. He argued that *Fa-hsiang is compatible with modern science, especially when combined eclectically with *Hua-yen and *T'ien-t'ai. His collected works were published in 64 vols.

T'ai-i (Chin., 'the supreme one'). The ultimate source of all appearance in *Taoism, which has received very different characterization in the many different forms of Taoism. In religious Taoism, he is personified as the supreme God; in philosophical Taoism, it is the unproduced source of all appearance; in interior Taoism, he is the controlling deity within the human system. T'ai-i is also equated, at times, with *t'ai-chi.

T'ai-I Chin-hua Tsung-chih (Teaching of the Golden Flower of the Supreme One). 17th-cent. Taoist text of the *ch'üan-chen tao (school of religious Taoism). It is a manual for circulating illumination through the body by breathing exercises, until the 'golden-flower' is formed. From this, the embryo of the immortal being can be produced.

T'ai-i Tao (Chin., 'way of the supreme one'). A school of religious Taoism (*tao-chiao), founded in 12th cent. CE, by Hsiao Pao-chen. From strict obedience to rules, the power to cure diseases, etc., is derived.

Tai-mitsu (Tendai esotericism): see ENNIN.

T'ai-p'ing Ching (Book of Supreme Peace). An early Taoist text, ascribed to *Yü Chi, which survives in differing forms, some only fragmentary. It was a basic text for *T'ai-ping tao.

Taiping Rebellion (1850–64). A major Chinese uprising which threatened to overthrow the Ch'ing dynasty. The Taiping's 'Heavenly Kingdom of Great Peace' (*T'ai-p'ing t'ien-kuo*) was a theocracy established and ruled by Hung Hsiu-ch'uan (1814–64). Influenced by Confucian utopianism and Protestant Christianity, Hung came to understand himself through dramatic visionary experiences to be the brother of *Christ Jesus and God's second holy son. The religio-political movement stressed the equality of the sexes, Christian education, and social welfare. As Hung Hsiu-ch'uan promised his followers reward in *heaven for *martyrdom on earth, zealous Taiping forces fought Ch'ing government troops with remarkable success. At the zenith of its wealth and power, however, the Taiping kingdom was shaken by internecine strife, and the religious community slowly began to disintegrate. Realizing the end was near, Hung Hsiu-ch'uan committed suicide in 1864. The Taiping Rebellion lasted for fourteen years and inspired many later anti-Ch'ing revolutionaries such as Sun Yat-sen and *Chiang Kai-shek.

The basic 'programme' of the rebellion is contained in *T'ien-t'iao shu* (Eng. tr., *North China Herald*, 14 May 1853), including a reapplied Ten Commandments.

T'ai-p'ing Tao (Chin., 'Way of Supreme Peace'). Early *Taoist school founded by *Chang Chüeh *c.*175 CE. It was a revolutionary, utopian movement, based on healing and confession of fault. For its alternative name, the Yellow Turbans, see CHANG CHÜEH.

Tairei (Mount Hiei): see MOUNT HIEI.

T'ai-shan. Sacred mountain in China. It is in Shantung province, and is therefore known as the 'sacred mountain of the east'. Its god, T'ai-yüeh ta-ti, is the ruler of the earth, and inferior only to the Jade Emperor (*Yü-huang). The mountain is ascended by about 7,000 steps, the Stairway to Heaven, lined by shrines and temples to other Taoist deities. It is one of the four sacred mountains (standing at the corners of China) which were visited by the emperors to mark out their territory.

T'ai-shang Kan-ying P'ien (Treatise on Action and Recompense). A text on Taoist morality. Life is lengthened or shortened according to one's conformity to the rules and advice offered.

T'ai-shang Tao-chün (Chin., 'supreme master of the Tao'). One of the highest deities of religious *Taoism. He is considered (as is *Lao-tzu) an incarnation of the *Tao, to make manifest the Tao in heaven, as Lao-tzu was to make it manifest on earth.

T'ai shih. 1. Taoist breathing exercises at a preliminary level, distributing saliva to other parts of the body.

2. The 'great beginning', the form of the world before it received form—i.e. formless, but with potential within it.

Taishō Issaikyō. Jap. edn. of the Chinese *tripiṭaka, ed. Takakusu in 100 vols. (1924–34).

Taittirīya Upaniṣad. *Upaniṣad belonging to the Black *Yajur Veda. It contains an ethical discourse, sometimes known as the 'Convocation Address', an exposition of the five sheaths of the Self, and the scale, or ladder, of perfections, leading up to the bliss of *Brahman.

T'ai-yüeh ta-ti (Chinese mountain God): see T'AI-SHAN.

Taizé Community. Christian Community, Roman Catholic in foundation, in the village of Taizé in France, engaged in reconciliation in the world and in the Church. It was founded by Brother Roger (Roger Schutz-Marsauche, b. 1915, known also as Roger Schutz) in 1940, but was closed down in 1942 by the Gestapo. In 1944 he returned with three brothers, and in 1949, seven brothers took monastic vows of celibacy, respect for authority, and common property. In 1982, the 'pilgrimage of trust' was inaugurated, to make apparent especially the yearnings and hopes of young people. Taizé has become a major place of pilgrimage and renewal. Pope *John XXIII spoke of the community as a sign of hope in the world—'Ah! That little spring time'.

Taizo-kai Mandara. Jap. for *garbha-dhātu maṇḍala*, the Womb Maṇḍala, one of two (with *vajra-dhātu maṇḍala*, the Diamond Maṇḍala) *maṇḍalas of central importance in esoteric (*mikkyō) Buddhism in Japan. The first has more than 200 deities contained within it, in thirteen divisions, the second has nearly 1,500 in nine. See also *SHINGON.

Taj Mahal. A monument and tomb, built at Agra in India by the Mughal emperor, Shah Jehān (1592–1666), for his favourite wife Mumtaz-i-Māhāl. Shah Jehān was also buried within it, their tombs being surrounded by a marble screen bearing the *ninety-nine beautiful names of Allāh. It was built between 1632 and 1647, and is now seriously threatened by air pollution.

Tajwīd (Arab.). *Qur'ān recitation. There are three major styles of tajwīd: (i) *tartīl*, slow and deliberate, in order to reflect on the meaning (73. 4); (ii) *ḥadr*, rapidly, in order to cover as much text as possible (e.g. in fulfilment of a vow, for merit, etc.); (iii) *tadwīr*, intermediate. The major treatise is Ibn al-Jazarī's *Al-Nashr fi'l-Qirā'āt al-'Ashr* (15th cent.; 2 vols., 1926).

Takbīr (Arab., the verbal noun from the reflexive verb *kabbara*, 'to magnify', 'to confess the greatness of'). A technical term, denoting the saying, by the Muslim, of *Allāhu akbar*, 'greater is God', in the prayer ritual, in the *ādhān, or call to prayer, and in personal devotion.

Takht (Pañjābī, 'throne'). 1. Five historical Sikh shrines where decisions taken by the *saṅgat are authoritative. The takhts are *Akāl Takht, *Amritsar; Harimandir *Sāhib, Paṭnā; Keśgaṛh Sāhib, *Anaṇḍpur; Hazūr Sāhib, *Nanderr; Damdama Sāhib, near Batinda in the Pañjab.

2. Wooden frame on which *Ādi Granth is installed in the *gurdwārā.

Takkanot (Heb., sing., *takkanah*). Directives enacted by Jewish scholars which have the force of law. The authority to enact takkanot is derived from Deuteronomy 17. 11. The difference between a takkanah and a *minhag is that a minhag is anonymous while a takkanah is deliberately made. The purpose of the takkanot is to deal with problems that emerged and which were not dealt with by the existing *halakhah. To be distinguished from the takkanot in general are the takkanot ha-kahal, which is Jewish legislation enacted not by halakhic authorities but by the communal leaders for members of their particular community.

Takuan Sōhō. Japanese Zen master of the *Rinzai school, Sōhō (1573–1645). He became a monk as a boy, and received the seal of recognition (*inka-shōmei) from Mindō Kokyō. He became abbot of Daitoku-ji in *Kyōto under orders in 1609, but retired after three days. Much later he was first abbot of Takai-ji in 1638. Famous for his skill in the ways of *calligraphy (*shōdō*) and tea ceremony (*chadō), he also, in *Fudochi Shimmyō-roku*, explored the relation between the way of the sword (*kendō) and the mental disposition of a Zen practitioner. He became known as 'the naked monk', since he had only one robe, and when he washed it, he remained in his room.

His writings were many, including poetry, but little has been translated. He explored in particular the meaning of Confucian thought in relation to Zen.

Takuhatsu (Jap.; Skt., *piṇḍapātika*). The practice of alms-begging, one of the disciplines undertaken by Buddhist monks.

Tala (Skt.). Darkness, either self-imposed by way of ignorance and evil behaviour; or as a group of seven 'places of darkness', i.e. hells.

Ṭalāq (Islamic divorce): see MARRIAGE AND DIVORCE.

Talbīyah (Arab.), ritual formula recited repeatedly by Muslims during *hajj (pilgrimage). They are the words attributed to Ibrahīm (*Abraham) when he summoned all people to the pilgrimage to *Mecca.

Tale of Genji (Japanese text): see MOTOORI NORINAGA.

Talfīq (eclecticism): see SCHOOLS OF LAW, MUSLIM.

Talion (i.e. *lex talionis*, 'law of retaliation'). A punishment which is equivalent to the offence. Most talions were abolished in *Talmudic times, and monetary payments were substituted (*BK* 8. 1).

Tallis, Thomas (*c*.1505–85). Church composer, often associated with *Byrd for their formative effect on composition. He was organist of Waltham Abbey until its dissolution in 1540. Subsequently he joined Byrd as organist at the Chapel Royal. His skill is shown at its height in a motet, *Spem in alium nunquam habui*.

Tallit, tallit katan. Jewish prayer shawl. On the four corners of the tallit, *zitzit (fringes) are attached. The tallit katan is a garment with fringes on the corners which is worn by strictly *Orthodox Jews all day under their clothes.

Talmid ḥakham (Heb., 'a disciple of the wise'). A Jewish rabbinical scholar. According to the *Talmud, a talmid ḥakham is the ideal type of *Jew, and even though a *mamzer, a talid ḥakham takes precedence 'over a *high priest who is an ignoramus' (*Hor*. 3. 8).

Talmud (from Heb., *lmd*, learn, study, teach). The body of teaching, commentary and discussion of the Jewish *amoraim on the *Mishnah.

There are two Talmuds: the Jerusalem (or Palestinian) Talmud which originated in *Erez Israel in *c*.500 CE, and the Babylonian Talmud which was completed in *c*.600 CE. Both works are commentaries on some or all of the Mishnaic orders of **Zera'im*, **Mo'ed*, **Nashim*, and **Nezikin*. The Babylonian Talmud also includes commentaries on *Kodashim* and *Tohorot*. The commentaries on the Mishnah are known as *gemāra. By the 11th cent. the supremacy of the Babylonian Talmud was finally established. The entire Talmud text contains *c*.2½ million words, one-third *halakhah and two-thirds *aggadah. Once it became an authoritative text, commentaries on it began to be produced, the most popular and influential being that of *Rashi which was completed in the 12th and 13th cents. by the *tosafists.

See Index, Talmud.

Talvaṇḍī Rāi Bhoi Dī. Birthplace of *Gurū *Nānak. It is situated in Shekhpurā tehsīl, about 65 km. west of Lahore. Now known as Nānkāṇā or Nānakiāṇā *Sāhib, this is the most important Sikh shrine in Pakistan. It is mentioned daily in the *Ardās.

Tam, Rabbenu (Jacob ben Meir, *c*.1100–71). French Jew and one of the leading *tosafists. His name *tam* ('perfect man') derived from Genesis 25. 27, 'Jacob was a *tam* dwelling in tents.' He headed the *yeshivah at Ramerupt, his birthplace, and became recognized as the greatest halakhic authority in his day. He issued many *responsa, generally taking a lenient line, and so far as possible he adhered to the text of *Talmud. His best-known work is *Sefer ha-Yashar* (Book of the Upright).

Tamas (Skt.). In *Sāṁkhya, one of the three strands (*guṇas) of material nature (*prakṛti).

In the external world, tamas is manifested as heaviness, darkness, and rigidity. In the individual it is reflected as fear, sloth, stupidity, indifference, etc., and is considered a negative force in humans.

Tambiah, Stanley Jeyaraja (b. 1929). Anthropologist of SE Asian Buddhist societies. Tambiah's *Buddhism and the Spirit Cults in North-east Thailand* (1970), based on fieldwork in a north-eastern Thai village, is still the most thorough and detailed of its kind. *World Conqueror and World Renouncer* (1976) is a more historically based account of Thai society as a whole, with particular reference to the institution of kingship.

Tambo, Oliver Reginald (1917–93). Christian leader, known as OR, who led the struggle for a free and democratic S. Africa. He was educated at mission schools in the Transkei, and was sponsored by the Anglican Province of S. Africa at St Peter's school, Rosettenville, and at the University of Fort Hare. He was dismissed from Fort Hare for 'subversive activities', and became a teacher. He retained the support of the Anglican Church as he translated his deep religious convictions into the political struggle for freedom. He was President of the ANC, 1967–90, and was accused by the S. African regime of being a communist and a terrorist.

Tamid (Heb., 'Continuous Offering'). A tractate of the order of *Kodashim* in the Jewish *Mishnah. *Tamid* describes the work of the *priests in the *Temple of Jerusalem.

Tamilnadu or **Tamil Nadu.** A state forming the southern area of India, at one time covering the areas where the Dravidian languages are prevalent (including Andhra Pradesh, Karnāṭaka, and Keralā). Its sense of separate identity is so strong that there have been movements for independence from the Indian republic. Although Aryan Hinduism from the north spread over Tamil areas, there has always been active interchange, with influence flowing in both directions. Thus although Tamilnadu is associated with devotional Hinduism (see ĀḶVĀRS) and especially devotion to *Śiva, in fact the name of Śiva occurs fairly late in Tamil texts, and is identified with the indigenous Mudalvan, with adaptation occurring in the transition. Again, Viṣṇu is known as Māl ('great one') and became associated with Tirumāl. One Tamil deity, Murukaṉ/Murugan, who is worshipped in a particularly frenzied sacred *dance, resisted assimilation altogether. This independence of Tamil religion is epitomized in *Tiruvaḷḷuvar's *Tirukkural*. Tamil religion is most usually associated with *bhakti poetry in which caste and ritual are reduced in importance, and the path to *mokṣa through devotion rather than knowledge (*jñāna) is prominent. See Index, Tamil religion.

Tammuz, fast of (17 Tammuz). A Jewish fast day (see FESTIVALS AND FASTS). The fast of Tammuz commemorates the breaching of the walls of *Jerusalem by the Babylonian Nebuchadnezzar in 586 BCE, and the Roman Titus in 70 CE.

Tammuz/Dumuzi (deities associated with death and the return of life): see DYING AND RISING GODS.

Tan. 1. Chin., 'cinnabar', the most important element in religious *Taoism, in the pursuit of immortality. In Outer *Alchemy, *wai-tan*, effort was devoted to purifying tan and converting it to gold, to prolong life. In Inner Alchemy, tan is understood to be the interactive energy of *yin-yang produced by appropriate breathing.

2. The slip of paper which designates the sitting-place of a Zen monk for *zazen.

3. Earth-bound component of the body in Zoroastrianism: see FRAVASI.

Tanabata (Jap. star festival): see FESTIVALS AND FASTS.

Tanach or **Tanakh.** Hebrew scriptures. Tanakh is an acronym for *Torah (*Pentateuch), Nevi'im (*Prophets), and Ketuvim (*Writings, Hagiographa).

Tanāsukh. Islamic word for rebirth of souls. Although it would apparently contradict the orthodox description of the *afterlife, it was nevertheless held to be true by some *Shī'a sects. Some *Ismā'īlīs believe in rebirth until the *Imām is recognized. More elaborately, the *Nuṣairīs have seven levels of rebirth: a sinner among them will be reborn as a Sunnī (or Jew or Christian), a *kāfir will be reborn as an animal. These beliefs can be reconciled (theoretically) with orthodox views, by pointing out that God bestows the soul (*nafs, *ruḥ*) to, and takes it away from, the body; in principle this could happen several or many times. But, in fact, it is rejected in mainstream Islam.

T'an-ching (Zen work): see LIU-TSU-TA-SHIH FA-PAO-T'AN-CHING.

Taṇḍava. In Hinduism, *Śiva's cosmic dance of creation and destruction. The name is said to come from the *ṛṣi Taṇḍi, who received *Śaivite teaching from the *Rudras. It is the turning of the wheel of life, through which Śiva goes out, through *līlā, to veil himself in the *māyā (appearance) of creation, and then withdraws, carrying with him his devotees into union with himself and escape from *saṃsāra (rebirth).

Tango no Sekku (Japanese boys' festival): see FESTIVALS AND FASTS.

Taṇhā (Pāli) or **tṛṣṇā** (Skt., 'thirst'). Thirsting or craving after the objects of the senses and the mind; according to the second Noble Truth (see FOUR NOBLE TRUTHS) in Buddhism, the root cause of all suffering. *Nirvāna is synonymous with the extinction of all thirsting.

Tan-hsia T'ien-jan (Jap., Tanka Tennen; 739–834). Chinese Ch'an/Zen master, dharma-successor (*has-su) of Shih-t'ou Hsi-chien. Nothing is known of his early life, beyond the fact that he studied *Confucianism and planned to be a state official, but on his way was diverted by a Ch'an monk who advised him that it would be wiser to seek to be a buddha, and sent him to *Ma-tsu. After his training with Shih-t'ou, he returned to Ma-tsu, and when asked what he had learnt, he sat on the shoulders of an image of *Mañjuśrī. The monks were outraged, but Ma-tsu said, 'My son, you are entirely natural'—hence his monastic name T'ien-jan, 'the natural'. He remained well-known for his unconventional behaviour.

Tan-huang. The oasis town in NW China, near which the caves of Mo-kao-k'u were found. These are the largest complex of Buddhist cultic caves, dating from about 5th cent. CE.

Tanḥuma. A group of Jewish *aggadic *midrashim containing many midrashim attributed to Rabbi Tanḥuma Bar Abba (late 4th cent. CE). *Tanḥuma* is based on the triennial cycle of *Torah reading observed in *Erez Israel.

Taniguchi Masaharu (founder): see SEICHŌ NO IE.

Tanjur (bstan.'gyur, 'translated doctrine'). The secondary part of the Tibetan Buddhist canon complementing the *Kanjur, and which comprises all treatises (Skt., *śāstra*) and commentaries on Buddhist doctrine available in Tibet prior to the 1959 Chinese invasion. The collection numbers many hundreds of volumes. See further TRIPIṬAKA.

Tanka Tennen (Jap. for Chinese Ch'an/Zen master): see TAN-HSIA T'IEN-JAN.

Taṅkhāh (Pañjābī, 'a fine'). Penalty imposed on lapsed Sikhs. The taṅkhāh imposed is normally *sevā (service) of the *saṅgat (congregation), e.g. minding shoes, sweeping the *gurdwārā, or else additional daily recitation of *nitnem (prayers from the *Ādi Granth).

T'an-luan (*c*.488–554). Chinese Buddhist monk generally considered to be the founder of the *Pure Land School in China. He was the author of the first known Chinese systematic work on Pure Land Buddhism, known as *Lun chu*, an abbreviation from *Wu-liang-shou ching yu-p'o-t'i-shê yüan sheng chi chu*. He taught the 'Easy Path' to enlightenment, by reliance on the power of Amitābha Buddha rather than the 'Difficult Path' or 'Holy Path' of the traditional practices.

Tanmātra (five elements): see AHAṂKĀRA.

Tanna. A Jewish *sage of the 1st and 2nd cents. CE. The tannaim (pl.) were teachers who handed down the *oral law and *midrashim and were distinguished in the *Talmud from the later scholars, the *amoraim.

Tan-t'ien (Chin., 'cinnabar fields'). In religious *Taoism, three regions of the body through which *ch'i flows and is to be directed: see TAN.

Tantra (beliefs, practices, etc.): see TANTRISM.

Tantra (Skt., 'extension', 'warp on a loom'). A text of *Tantrism. The word is also sometimes used as a synonym for *āgama and in a general sense for Tantric doctrine. Tantra denotes specifically *Śaiva and especially *Śākta texts, though a clear distinction is often difficult to make. Some *Vaiṣṇava texts are also called Tantras, such as the *Lakṣmi Tantra* of the *Pañcarātra. The teachings of the Tantras are esoteric, concerning macro-microcosmic correspondence, phonic evolution (see MANTRA), esoteric anatomy, and *Kuṇḍalinī *yoga. Central place is given to the transformation of desire (*kāma) to a spiritual end; the metaphor used is of removing a thorn by a thorn.

Tantras take the form of a dialogue between *Śiva and the Goddess (*Devī). Either the Goddess asks questions and Śiva replies (*āgama*), or vice versa (*nigama*). The distinction between *āgama* and *nigama* can also refer to that between Tantra and *Veda. The most important Śākta Tantras are the *Nityaṣodaśikārṇava*, the *Yoginīhṛdaya*, the *Tantrarāja*, the **Kulārṇava*, all written between 1000 and 1400 CE, and the 18th-cent. *Mahānirvāṇa Tantra*. See also TANTRIKA; TANTRISM.

Tantra-yoga (yoga associated with tantric analysis of the body): see KUṆḌALINĪ.

Tantrika (Skt., 'relating to Tantra'). A Hindu classification of ritual (*pūjā) in opposition to Vaidika (relating to *Veda). Tantric ritual follows the basic Vedic pattern of daily rites (*nitya), occasional rites (*naimittika*), and rites for the attainment of desires (*kāma), but differs in content. See also TANTRA; TANTRISM.

Tantrism (Skt., *tantra*, 'extension', 'warp on a loom'). A major current in Indian religious thought, in tension with the orthodox *Vedic tradition. It emphasizes the feminine aspect of a bipolar reality and advocates a practice (*sādhana) to unite these polarities and so attain freedom (*mokṣa).

The origins of Tantrism are obscure. Its roots may go back to autochthonous magic and fertility cults of pre- or non-*Aryan India, and certainly Tantrism arose on the edges of Aryan influence in N. India, Bengal, and Assam. In Hinduism, Tantra pervades the theistic traditions of *Śaivism, *Śaktism, and *Vaiṣṇavism. Tantrism also exerted considerable influence on Jainism. In a narrower sense Tantrism refers to doctrines and practices embodied in specific Śaiva and Śākta texts called Tantras.

Tantrism is multilevelled and Tantric texts range from crude magic to the sophisticated metaphysics of theologians such as *Abhinavagupta. Certain concepts, however, are common in Tantrism, for instance, the male–female polarity in which Śiva is passive and Śakti active. (Tantric Buddhism reverses this polarity with passive female *prajñā and active male *upaya*.) Tantrism maintains that the cosmos is hierarchical, created through a transformation of Śakti who manifests herself in the form of the *tattvas. From a state of union (*yāmala) with the Lord she evolves through various subtle levels to impure, gross creation. This cosmic hierarchy is recapitulated in the body which is regarded as a microcosm.

In Tantric sādhana the body is of central importance. *Maithuna is of central importance, especially in left-handed Tantra (see below), leading to the Indian definitions of Tantra: *mukti is *bhukti* ('enjoyment'), *yoga is *bhoga* ('sensual pleasure').

Tantric sādhana consists of *pūjā (worship) and yoga. In many ways Tantric pūjā follows Vedic pūjā and is of three kinds: *nitya*, to be performed daily; *naimittika*, to be performed on special occasions; and *kāma*, to affect a particular desire.

Tantrism has developed a sophisticated esoteric anatomy comprising of energy centres (*cakras) connected by channels (*nadis). This anatomy is visualized in Tantric yoga of which there are two important kinds, *mantra and *laya or *Kuṇḍalinī.

An important classification in Tantra is between the right-hand path (*daksinācāra) which interprets the five Ms (*pañca-mākāra) symbolically, and the left-hand path (*vāmācāra) which interprets them literally. Some left-hand sects such as the Śaiva Kāpālikas and the *Aghoris live in charnel grounds and are said to have consumed the flesh of corpses and scatological substances in order to achieve perfection and power (siddhi).

Though the development of Tantrism reached its peak about 1000 CE, it has never died out and has exerted considerable influence on modern religious movements such as the *Ananda Marga and Bhagavan Sri *Rajneesh movement.

For Buddhist tantrism, see also VAJRAYĀNA.

See Index, Tantrism.

Tanzīh (Arab., 'remove'). The insistence in Muslim theology on the way in which the attributes of God are not to be identified with the being of God. While it must be possible to have some idea of God (since otherwise he would be unknowable), the ideas and epithets are approximate and limited. Thus if he is called 'merciful', it is somewhat like what is recognized as merciful among human beings, but 'removed from' an exact and literal identification. Cf. ANALOGY; see also TASHBĪH; TA'WĪL; and see *bilā kaif* in *Allāh.

Tanzīl (sending down of revelation in Islam): see WAḤY; REVELATION.

Tao (Chin., 'way'). Central concept of *Taoism, supplying the name of this philosophical and religious system. In *Confucian usage, tao is (as the pictogram suggests) 'teaching', and 'the way humans should follow'. In *Lao-tzu (*Tao-te ching*), Tao becomes the source from which all appearance derives, the unproduced Producer of all that is, and the guarantor of its stability and regularity. In its manifestation, it appears as *Te, and human virtue is to live with discernment in accordance with Te expressing Tao, especially through *wu-wei.

Tao-an or **Shih Tao-an** (312–85). Chinese Buddhist monk, of key importance in the Chinese assimilation of Buddhism, and in the transition from *Theravāda to *Mahāyāna. Trained in both, he was also a pupil of Fo-t'u-teng, under whom he studied *Perfection of Wisdom texts and the *sūtras and practices of *dhyāna. He rejected syncretistic methods (*ko-i*) and insisted on disciplined life. This was balanced by devotion, especially to *Maitreya. In all these organized practices, the purpose was the penetration to the realization of the fundamental 'non-beingness' (*pen-wu*; Jap., *honmu*) as the absolute truth. In that way, he was pointing to the elaboration of *śūnyatā in Chinese terms. He wrote a commentary on *Sūtra on the Perfection of Wisdom*.

Tao-chia (philosophical Taoism, one of the two main streams of Taoism, along with tao-chiao): see TAOISM.

Tao-chiao (religious Taoism, one of the two main streams of Taoism, with tao-chia): see TAOISM.

Tao-ch'o (Buddhist patriarch): see MAPPŌ.

Tao-hsin (Jap., Dōshin; 580–651). Fourth patriarch in the Ch'an/Zen succession through *Bodhidharma: he was dharma-successor (*hassu) of *Seng-ts'an and master of Hung-jen. He instructed students in **Laṅkāvatāra Sūtra*, with emphasis on *zazen, and, settling on Mount Shuang-feng, gathered many students who formed a settled monastic community, a founding model for later Zen monasteries. His teaching includes the oldest text advocating *zazengi*, 'seated meditation'.

Tao-hsüan (596–667 CE). Chinese Buddhist who founded the Lü-tsung, School of Discipline. This was based on strict observance of Vinaya rules. It was transmitted to Japan in 754 by Chien-chen (*Ganjin) and became the foundation of the *Ritsu school. Tao-hsüan was also one of the earliest historian/biographers, producing the vast *Hsü kao-seng chuan* (Jap., *Zoku Kōsōden*), 30 vols. of biographies, including (book xvi) the first biography of *Bodhidharma.

T'ao Hung-ching (452–536). Taoist mediator of Mao Shan (see TAOISM), and follower of *Ko Hung who did much to consolidate Ko Hung's great achievements in systematizing Taoism and making it widely acceptable. His use of religious Taoist techniques to predict the future was sufficiently accurate for the emperor to invite him to live in the imperial court, but he refused to leave Mount Mao, where the emperor used to consult him—for which reason he became known as 'the prime minister of the mountains'. His major work was *Chen-kao* (Declarations of the Perfected), which gathered the Supreme Purity scriptures and gave an account of their revelation.

Tao-i (leader of Ch'an/Zen school of Hui-neng): see MA-TSU TAO-I.

Taoism or **Daoism.** Chinese religious and philosophical system, taking many different forms, and influencing other religions greatly, especially Buddhism. The two major forms of Taoism are philosophical, tao-chia (daojia), and religious, tao-chiao (daojiao); but both are intertwined (and not, as was once thought, incompatible alternatives).

Tao-chia goes back traditionally to *Lao-tzu and **Tao-te ching* (*Daode jing*). *Tao-te ching* proposes a transformation of character within, from which good society and behaviour will flow. Where a Confucian asks, 'What should I do?', a Taoist asks, 'What kind of person should I be?' This involves discerning the *Tao, the primordial source of order and the guarantor of the stability of all appearance. Tao is the unproduced Producer of all that is. Through the energetic initiative of creativity, i.e. through *Te, the inner and inexpressible nature of Tao nevertheless appears in manifest forms. To live in accord with Tao is to realize this order and nature and stability in one's own life and society. Te is then the virtue of the person who achieves that goal, especially through *wu-wei.

The political philosophy of Taoism requires the ruler to be equally 'invisible'. But since the ideal is never realized, the ruler has responsibility to enforce virtue; and this (especially *Tao-te ching* 6, 36, 65) has been criticized as encouraging despotism. This was reinforced indirectly by the second major figure/text of tao-chia, *Chuang-tzu, where the pursuit of absolute self-command and of the 'usefulness of the useless' is taken even further. In contrast, neo-Taoism, e.g. *Hsüan-hsüeh, rehabilitated Confucianism as an illustration of what wu-wei, properly understood, would mean in practice. By a different sort of contrast, the Seven Sages of the Bamboo Grove maintained that being in command of oneself and going with the grain of Tao allowed one to eat, drink, and be merry. The Seven Sages belonged to that part of the neo-Taoist revival known as *Ch'ing T'an, 'The School of Pure Conversations'.

Tao-chiao has had a far more diverse history, with many schools and teachings, and constant interaction with popular Chinese religion. The unifying thread is the search for the Way (Tao) of Great Equilibrium and the quest for immortality, though this may be understood literally, metaphorically, or as a temporary (quest for longevity) postponement of death. Because all nature is united in Tao, immortality cannot be achieved by emancipating some aspect of nature (e.g. a soul or spirit) in order to escape from nature; rather, it must be sought in the proper directing of the forces of nature within one's own body. The major areas of concern, emphasized in different ways in the different schools, are (i) inner hygiene, attention, especially through diet and gymnastic exercises, to the conditions of life; in the Inner Deity Hygiene School, the endeavour is to visualize and work with the deities who control the functions of the body, by making offerings to them of appropriate food and behaviour; (ii) breathing, attention to *ch'i (breath); (iii) circulation of the breath within the body, bringing its power deliberately to every part; (iv) sexuality, attention to the techniques leading to the retention of energy by retaining semen or controlling orgasm, and by sending this retained power through the body; (v) *alchemy, see especially KO HUNG; (vi) behaviour, attention to the kinds of moral behaviour which will be in harmony with the Tao; (vii) the search for the Isles of the Blessed where the immortals (*hsien) might be found who would reveal the secrets of their immortality.

While Tao-chiao rests on the same basic texts as Tao-chia, it rapidly produced many more (for the canon, see TAO-TSANG), and began to produce a proliferation of different schools. The first of these (in the sense that it produced deliberate organization and continuity) was *Wu-tou-mi tao, of *Chang Tao-ling and *Chang Lu. A different note was introduced by Wei Hua-ts'un (251–334): she had risen in the Celestial Master hierarchy, but then married and raised a family. After her family was grown up, she returned to her studies and received visions of the Immortals who entrusted to her the first sections of *Shang ch'ing*, writings which were to become the scripture of the new movement. From the connection with Mount Mao, the movement is known as Mao-shan. Religious Taoism is made up of many schools or sects: at least eighty-six major movements have been listed. Among these many schools, of early importance were *Ling-pao and T'ai-ping Tao (an early example of the revolutionary and somewhat *millennarian strand in religious Taoism, familiar in the *Boxer rebellion). Later schools of importance include *Cheng-i Tao and *Ch'üan-chen Tao.

Taoist canon (authoritative Taoist texts): see TAO-TSANG.

Tao-sheng or **Chu Tao-sheng** (355–434). Chinese Buddhist who founded the Nirvāna school (*nirvāna). Recognized early as a man of great insight, he went to Ch'ang-an in 405 and collaborated with *Kumārajīva. There he developed the arguments later accepted extensively, but at the time so revolutionary that he was expelled from the monastery—especially that all beings possess the buddha-nature (*buddhatā), and can realize this through sudden enlightenment. Nevertheless, it can and should be prepared for through meditation and study. Because even nirvāna is empty of self (*śūnyatā), he rejected *Pure Land tendencies to think of 'heavenly' rewards, but he insisted that the state of nirvāna has to be regarded as the highest, because undisturbed, bliss.

Tao-shih. The scholars and ritual functionaries of religious *Taoism (*tao-chiao*). In addition to local congregations, they came to take charge of organized communities, eventually developing monastic rules. See CHANG LU.

Tao-te Ching (The Book of the Way and its Power). A work attributed to *Lao-tzu (hence reference to it as *Lao-tzu*), foundation text of *Taoism. It is made up of 5,000 pictograms, hence the title, *Text of the Five Thousand Signs*. Trad. dated to 6th cent. BCE, it is more likely to come from 4th/3rd cent.; the oldest existing copy is *c.*200 BCE. The text expounds the *Tao as the unproduced and inexpressible source of all appearance, which nevertheless becomes manifest through *Te, through proper understanding of which the return to, and union with, Tao becomes possible.

Tao-te t'ien-tsun (ruler of Taoist heaven of highest purity): see SAN-CH'ING.

T'ao-t'ieh ('ogre masks'): see BRONZE VESSELS.

Tao-tsang. The *Taoist *'canon' of authoritative texts. After a list in Pan Ku's *Han Shu* (1st cent. CE), an early attempt to list such texts was made by *Ko Hung in *Pao Pu Tzu*. Lu Hsu Ching (5th cent.) was the first to divide Taoist writings into Three Caves (*tung/dung*); later Four Supplements were added. The first edition supported by the emperor appeared in the Tang dynasty, and contained anything (according to different accounts) between 3,000 and 8,000 rolls (texts), but it was lost or destroyed in the ensuing wars and rebellions. Further editions appeared until the Ming dynasty (1368–1644), when the Tao-tsang included nearly 8,000 rolls. There is no organizing principle, and many of the texts are concerned with immortality—with the foundations in Tao and *ch'i, with the cosmological support in *myths and *rituals, and with techniques for attaining immortality.

Tao-yin (Taoist exercise for guiding the breath to different parts of the body): see GYMNASTICS, TAOIST.

Tapa Gaccha (Jain sect): see GACCHA.

Tapas (Skt., 'heat'). *Asceticism conceived as a force of creative heat in Indian religions. This force is instrumental in the acquisition of spiritual power (*siddhi) and in gaining liberation (*mokṣa).

In the *Vedas, tapas has both a cosmic and a human aspect.

1. As a cosmic force it is the power underlying manifestation. For example, *Prajāpati creates the universe by heating himself (*Śatapatha Brāhmaṇa* 7. 1. 2, 13).

2. At a human level, tapas could be created in the fire sacrifice (*agnihotra) and in the sacrificial priest (*hotṛ) who manifested tapas by sweating.

With the *Upaniṣads and the development of *yoga, tapas becomes not a preparation for ritual but a means of realizing the self (*ātman) and gaining release (mokṣa). The practice of austerity produces inner heat; for example, in Buddhism the *Majjhima Nikāya* (1. 244) speaks of the heat obtained by holding the breath; and in Hinduism, the rise of *Kuṇḍalinī is associated with the arousal of heat.

Asceticism in some form is common to all yoga schools, though actual practices vary in intensity from mere celibacy to more extreme forms of asceticism such as never lying down, piercing the skin with a sharp instrument, bearing extremes of heat and cold, or, in Jainism, even slowly starving to death as a means of withdrawal from the world (*sallekhanā): see also ASCETICISM.

Taqīy(y)a (Arab., 'fear, guard against'). The dispensation for Muslims which allows them to conceal their faith when under persecution or threat or compulsion.

Among the *Shī'a, taqīya is equally, if not more, prominent, despite the redemptive beliefs focused on the death of *al-Ḥusain. One should not seek a martyrdom which serves no purpose: the prior obligation is to preserve oneself for the faith and for the community. In a situation of *jihād, taqīya no longer has the same priority.

Taqlīd (Arab., *qallada*, 'put a rope on the neck of an animal'). A word, in Islam, for authority in matters of religion, and particularly for the obligation to recognize established positions in *fiqh.

Tārā (Skt. 'Star', Tib. *sgrol.ma* or *drolma* 'She who saves'; possibly from Skt., *tārayati*, 'crossing, transcending'). Tibet's most important deity. She is a *bodhisattva who for many Tibetans has already become a *Buddha, having vowed—on being advised of the spiritual advantages of male rebirth—never to relinquish her female form. Tārā has the epithet 'mother of all the Buddhas', and is viewed with great affection by Tibetans. Originally she was a *Tantric deity, prominent in 7th-cent. *tantras. By the 8th cent. her cult was established at *Borobodur in Java, in itself showing the early extent of Tantric influence. Although her appearance in Tibet has been noted as 8th cent., it was not until the arrival of *Atiśa in 1042 that worship of Tārā became widespread.

Tibetan Buddhism recognizes twenty-one Tārās, according to the definitive text on her worship, *Homages to the Twenty One Tārās*, brought from India by Darmadra in the 11th cent. Each Tārā has a different function (averting disasters, wish-fulfilling, increasing wisdom, healing, etc.), each has a particular colour, *mudrā, and *mantra, and each emanates from Green Tārā as source. After the mantra of Chenrezi (**om maṇi padme hum*), the mantra of Tārā (*om tāre tuttāre ture svāhā*) is the most commonly heard on the lips of the Tibetan people.

Targum (Heb., 'translation'). A translation of the Hebrew scriptures into *Aramaic, conveying interpretation of the text. The best-known Targum is *Targum *Onkelos* which was regarded as authoritative. *Targum Jonathan* is the Targum to the *prophetic books, and *Targum Yerushalmi* is a largely *midrashic translation (or interpretation) of the *Hagiographa. *Targum Pseudo-Jonathan* is a late targum on the whole Pentateuch (Genesis 15. 14 mentions the wives of *Muḥammad as the wives of *Ishmael), but preserving the earlier interpretations. Several fragmentary targumim (pl.) have survived, together with an early form of the Palestinian targum tradition in Neofiti I. From all this it is clear that there was a relatively stable, though developing, targum tradition, which is unsurprising, given the connection between targumim and *synagogues.

Tariki (Jap., 'power of the other'). Liberation in Buddhism received through the help or power of another, especially *Amida/Amitābha. Liberation depending on one's own effort is *jiriki. The two are often called 'cat and monkey': a cat carries its kitten to safety, whereas a young monkey clings to its mother.

Ṭarīqa (Arab., 'path, way'; pl. *ṭuruq*). Originally (9th/10th cent. CE) a way of classifying the rules and methods by which a mystical approach to God might be sustained, it became a term for the different Sūfī systems themselves, along with their rules and rituals.

Tarka (Skt., 'reason', 'philosophy'). An activity of mind usually condemned by Buddhists. In the *Upaniṣads, tarka is held to be a preliminary, but inadequate, means for understanding the ultimate. The Buddhist canon generally speaks of tarka in the pejorative sense of vain speculation.

Tarn Tāran (Pañjābī, 'means of crossing ocean of life to salvation'). A Sikh shrine. Tarn Tāran lies 20 km. south of *Amritsar. Here Gurū *Arjan Dev constructed a *gurdwārā in honour of Gurū *Rām Dās and a pool whose water reputedly cures leprosy.

Tarpaṇa. Part of Hindu morning *ablutions. The morning cleansing with water is a basic obligation. Tarpaṇa is the point at which the worshipper makes a cup with his hands and pours the water back into the river while reciting *mantras. After sipping some water, he may then apply the distinguishing mark of his *saṃpradāya (tradition), e.g. three vertical lines (*tripuṇḍra*) for a Śaivite, three horizontal lines for a Vaiṣṇavite. It is followed by *saṁdhyā (morning prayer).

Taryag Mitzvot (the total of commands and prohibitions in Torah): see SIX HUNDRED AND THIRTEEN COMMANDMENTS.

Taṣawwuf (Arab., prob. form V *masdar* from √*ṣūf*, 'wool'). Muslim name for the commitment of those known as the *Sūfīs. If this etymology is correct, it may derive from the characteristic woollen garment worn by many early Sūfīs. Other etymologies have been proposed (e.g. *ahl al-ṣuffa*, those regularly sitting on 'the bench' of the *mosque in *Madīna; *ṣūfiyya*, those who have been purified; Banū Ṣūfa; Gk., *sophos*, 'wise', i.e. Sophists—although otherwise the Gk. letter sigma in transliteration becomes sīn not ṣād); but none seems convincing. By *abjad (numerical values to letters), taṣawwuf equals the Arabic for 'divine wisdom', but this is fanciful. For the nature of Sufism, see SŪFĪS.

Tashahhud (Muslim profession of faith): see SHAHĀDA; ṢALĀT.

Tashbīh (Arab., *shabaha*, 'liken, compare'). The issue raised in Islam by statements in the *Qur'ān which attribute to God human likenesses—e.g. a face, hands, and eyes—and which describe him talking and sitting. A fierce battleground in early Islam (see ALLĀH), it led to an avoidance of literal anthropomorphism by affirming *tanzīh (keeping God free from such reductions to human size), along with an agnostic acceptance of the language *bilā kaif* (see ALLĀH), without knowing how it is to be taken. The opposite view was to accept that nothing can be said of God beyond the extremely approximate and corrigible, and that God should be emptied of all attributes (*ta'ṭīl*): they cannot belong literally to his own nature or being, and simply reflect our perception of his dealings with us. An intermediate (but often suspect) position (*ta'wīl) took the statements of the Qur'ān to be allegorical. The issue has remained central to the major and continuing divisions of Islam. See also TANZĪH.

Tashlikh. Jewish *New Year ceremony. On the first day of *Rosh ha-Shanah (or on the second if the first day falls on the *Sabbath), the ceremony of symbolically casting sin into the sea is performed by running water. The tradition is not mentioned in the *Talmud and may have a pagan origin.

Tassels (on prayer shawl): see ZITZIT.

Tathāgata (Pāli, Skt.; Chin., *ju-lai*; Jap., *nyorai*; Korean, *yotae*: usually left untranslated; if translated then as 'Thus-Gone' or 'Truthfinder'). According to Buddhist tradition, the title chosen by the Buddha for himself. The title was intended to convey his identity as a perfect being, though the precise meaning of the word remains problematic. Etymologically it can be read as (i) 'thus-gone' (*tathā gata*) or 'thus-come' (*tathā āgata*), generally taken to mean 'one who has gone (or come)' i.e. attained emancipation; (ii) 'one come (*āgata*) to the truth (*tatha*)'. The etymology may itself be suspect, however, since it is not certain whether the word is Skt. or vernacular in origin.

Tathāgata-garbha. The 'Embryonic Tathāgata', a concept which emerges in *Mahāyāna Buddhism and in terms of which all living beings are regarded as potential *Buddhas by virtue of their participation in a universal 'buddha-nature'. In the course of time this embryonic seed or potency which exists in each creature will flower into full enlightenment, and since the potency is shared by all, the enlightenment will be a universal one. The sources which expound this teaching, such as the *Ratnagotravibhāga* and the *Tathāgatagarbhasūtra*, regard it as a third and final cycle in the development of Buddhist thought, being the culmination of both the Buddha's early teaching and its philosophical elaboration by the Mahāyāna. Its critics, on the other hand, saw it as dangerously close to the monistic doctrines of Hinduism as expounded by the *Advaita

Vedānta school of *Śaṅkara. See Index, Buddha-nature.

Tathatā (Skt., 'suchness'; Chin., *chen-ju*; Jap., **shinnyo*). Mahāyāna Buddhist attempt to express the absolute and true nature inherent in all appearance, and obviously contrasted with it *qua* appearance. It has no 'own nature' (*svabhāva), and is not other than the buddha-nature (*buddhatā, *bussho, *tathāgata-garbha), except of course that the 'two' cannot be compared or equated, because they have no characterized nature to be so compared. For that reason, the Buddha as *tathāgata is necessarily synonymous with tathatā (e.g. as argued in the **Diamond Sūtra*). See Index, Buddha-nature.

Tatian. Christian *apologist and ascetic. He was a pupil of *Justin Martyr in Rome between 150 and 165. His *Oratio ad Graecos* attacks Greek civilization as too evil to be reconciled with Christianity. In the Syriac Church he was venerated as the author of the **Diatessaron*, which remained in use until the 5th cent.

Ta'ṭīl (emptying God of attributes): see TASHBĪH.

Tattva (Skt., 'that-ness'). 1. In *Saṁkhya philosophy, in Hinduism, tattvas are the constituent subtle elements of *prakṛti; in Jainism, tattva is the categorical (i.e. true) constituent of appearance and release.

2. In Buddhism, tattva does not have the same technical philosophical sense. The proto-Mahāyānist *Prajñaptivādins defined tattva as the real phenomenon which underlies concept (*prajñapti*). In the *Vijñanāvāda (Yogācāra) this meaning is substantially retained, though now extended to take in the totality of entities. The *Ratnagotravibhāga* of *Asaṅga talks of reality (tattva) being devoid of the subject–object dichotomy, and other texts by the same author state that, since words and concepts do not partake of the nature of the things they denote, tattva is ultimately inexpressible.

Authors representing the Mādhyamaka tendency are careful not to use tattva in the Yogācārin sense in their effort to avoid all terms which may be taken as absolutes. *Nāgārjuna does, however, talk of the reality or truth (tattva) of the Buddha's teaching.

Tattvabodha (The Knowledge of the Truth). Short work of *Advaita Hinduism by *Śaṅkara, exploring the competence of *jīva—its relation to *Īśvara, its knowledge of its own relation to *ātman, hence to *Brahman.

Tattvabodhini Patrika (Indian journal): see TAGORE, D.

Tat-tvam-asi (Skt., 'That thou art'). One of the great sayings (*mahāvākya) which appears in **Chāndogya Upaniṣad* (6. 8. 7, 6. 9. 4, 6. 14. 3): the sage Uddālaka instructs his son Śvetaketu concerning Ultimate Reality (*Brahman) immanent as the Self (*ātman) in all beings: 'That which is the finest essence—this whole world has that as its self. That is Reality (satyam). That is the Self (ātman). That thou art, Śvetaketu.'

Tattvārtha Sūtra or ***Tattvārthadhigamasūtra.*** Jain text revered by both Śvetāmbaras and *Digambaras. It is attributed to *Umāsvāmi (also Umāsvāti, *c*.2nd cent. CE?), and consists of ten chs. of 357 sutras, expounding the seven *tattvas (principles). It is said that 'there is no Jaina doctrine or dogma which is not expressed or implied in these aphorisms' (K. B. Jindal), and it is recited daily in many temples.

Ta T'ung Shu (The Book of Great Unity/ Commonwealth). Major text written by *K'ang Yu-wei while in seclusion on Mount Hsi Chao Shan, 1884–5, though not published until 1901. It is an eclectic work, drawing on all resources which point to the abolition of social and labour divisions, so that (echoing Confucius), 'the world may become a common state'.

Tauler, Johann (*c*.1300–61). German Christian mystic. He became a *Dominican at Strasbourg in 1315 where he probably came under the influence of Meister *Eckhart and *Henry Suso. Famous as a preacher and director, especially of nuns, he became still more popular because of his devotion to the sick during the Black Death. His mystical doctrine, found mainly in his sermons, is firmly grounded in *Thomism, and concentrates on the practical consequences of God's indwelling, manifest particularly in humility and abandonment to the will of God.

Tāvatiṃsa Gods (33 Vedic gods): see COSMOLOGY (Buddhist).

Ṭawāf (Arab.). Ritual circuit of a sacred place or object, especially in Islam the *circumambulation of the *Ka'ba during the *ḥajj.

Tawbah (repentance): see SIN.

Tawḥīd (Arab., verb. noun of *waḥḥada*, 'make one'). Asserting the oneness of God, the supreme duty, and passion, of Islamic theology. His unity must be affirmed, in strenuous negation of all *dualism, idolatry, and superstition—i.e. of *shirk. Qur'ān 112, the Sūra of Unity, is the classic statement. In *Sūfī thought and poetry, tawḥīd means the unitive state in which the devotee transcends individuation in *fanā'.

Tawḥīd-i Ilāhī (Divine Faith of Akbar): see AKBAR.

Ta'wīl (Arab.). In Islam a term for commentary on the *Qur'ān. It was originally synonymous with *tafsīr, but it became associated later with commentary on the content of the Qur'ān, and eventually with allegorical interpretation, often in support of particular schools or parties of Islam. It was a method held in some suspicion because of the danger of 'explaining away' the uncongenial, and it came to be held that ta'wīl could never contradict the plain sense.

Tawrāt (Arab.; Heb., *Torah). The Quranic term for the scripture of the Jews, who thus qualify as *Ahl al-Kitāb, 'People of the Book' (scripture).

Taylor, Jeremy (1613–67). *Anglican *bishop and writer, 'the Shakespeare of the divines' (Emerson). He was chaplain to Charles I, and rector of Uppingham (1638–42). When the king's cause failed, he used his exile in Carmarthenshire to write his plea for toleration, *The Liberty of Prophesying* (1647), his influential devotional works, *The Life of Christ* (1649), *Holy Living* (1650), *Holy Dying* (1651), *Unum Necessarium* (1655), and various sermons. He was appointed bishop of Down and Connor in 1660. He regarded his *Ductor Dubitantium*, a comprehensive study of *moral theology, as his most important work.

Taz (Jewish halakhic authority): see DAVID BEN SAMUEL.

Ta'ziya (Arab.). An expression of condolence, but particularly the 'passion plays' of Shī'a Muslims. The plays focus on the death of *al-Ḥusain at *Karbalā', but they include figures from the earlier (biblical) history who bear witness that the sufferings of Ḥusain are greater than their own. The redemptive power of his martyrdom is effected through his intercession.

Te (Chin., 'power', 'virtue'). The means in Chinese thought, and especially in Taoism, through which the *Tao becomes manifest and actualized. The underlying character is made up of three elements, moving ahead, the eye, and 'heart-and-mind'. Philologically this suggests an underlying sense of a self-aware arising and disposition in a particular direction; but it may also include the sense of going in a straight direction. Te is thus the making particular of the potency of Tao, and is the inherent nature or quality which makes a thing what it is and what it ought to be. In Confucianism, Te is the quality possessed by wise and civilized people who are a model to their fellow-citizens.

Tea ceremony (Zen ceremony to overcome ordinary consciousness): see CHADŌ.

Teacher of Righteousness. The title given to the organizer of a Jewish sect in some of the documents of *Qumran. Attempts have been made to identify the Teacher, and possible candidates have included *Ezra, Onias III (the last Zadokite *high priest), Judah b. Jedidiah (a *sage martyred by Alexander Jannai), or Menaḥem b. Judah (killed by the captain of the *Temple in 66 CE).

Tebah (reading platform in Jewish synagogue): see ALMEMAR.

Te Deum. A Latin hymn to the Father and the Son, in rhythmical prose, beginning *Te Deum laudamus* ('We praise thee, O God'). According to tradition, it was a spontaneous composition of *Ambrose and *Augustine, who sang it antiphonally on the occasion of the baptism of Augustine by Ambrose. In fact, it is evidently a composition of at least three parts, only loosely connected.

Tefillah (Heb., prayer). The Jewish *Amidah prayer; also (for the *Sephardim), the *Prayer Book. Tefillah is also one of many terms (but the most common in the Bible) for prayer in general. The Hebrew root means 'to think, entreat, judge, intercede', and the reflexive means 'to judge oneself', and 'to pray'. With a strong emphasis on *blessings and *benedictions, Jewish prayer eventually (*c.*8th/9th cent. CE) led to the compilation of prayer books. If possible, Jews should pray facing in the direction of Jerusalem. Muḥammad initially followed this custom as well (see QIBLA).

Tefillat tal (Jewish prayer): see DEW, PRAYER FOR.

Tefillin. Jewish phylacteries. According to Exodus 13. 1–10, 11–16; Deuteronomy 6. 4–9 and 11. 13–21, a *Jew must bind 'these words for a sign upon your hand and a frontlet between your eyes'. This commandment is fulfilled by binding two small leather boxes containing these scriptural passages around the head and left arm by means of leather straps.

Teg(h) Bahādur, Gurū (1621–75 CE). Ninth Sikh *Gurū, poet and *martyr. Tyāg Mal, youngest son of Gurū *Hargobind and Nānakī, was born in *Amritsar and earned the name Tegh Bahādur, meaning 'hero of the sword'.

Since the dying Gurū *Har Krishan had indicated that his successor would be an older man from Bakālā, twenty-two local *Soḍhīs claimed the succession. According to tradition, Tegh Bahādur's gurūship was discovered and proclaimed by Makhaṇ Shāh Labāṇā, a merchant, who had vowed that if he escaped shipwreck, he would give 500 gold coins to the Gurū. On reaching Bakālā he gave a few coins to each claimant. When finally he met Tegh Bahādur and made a similar offering to him, the latter remonstrated, 'You promised 500 coins', so revealing his supernatural insight.

*Dhīr Mal, *Rām Rāi, and other Soḍhīs and their supporters harassed the Gurū, and the *masands refused him admission to the *Harimandir, Amritsar. Tegh Bahādur showed no resentment. In 1665 he founded *Anaṇḍpur, but, when harassment continued, he travelled eastward through Bengal to Āssām where he achieved a peaceful settlement between Auraṅgzeb's emissary and the rebel king of Kāmrūp.

The Gurū returned to Paṭnā, and then went to the *Pañjāb, which was troubled by Auraṅgzeb's persecution of non-Muslims. The Gurū journeyed slowly towards Delhi and was arrested in Āgrā. With five Sikhs he was escorted to Delhi, where he chose torture and death rather than Islam or the performance of miracles. He symbolically appointed the absent Gobind Rāi his successor.

On 11 Nov. 1675 he was beheaded on the site of the present *Sīs Gañj *gurdwārā.

Teheran (founding of as capital): see AL-MAJLISĪ.

Teilhard de Chardin, Pierre (1881–1955). French *Jesuit palaeontologist and theologian. He entered the Society of Jesus in 1899 and was ordained in 1911. His theories on the origin and development of humanity, first privately circulated among his fellow Jesuits, but later published, attracted a good deal of attention, especially *The Phenomenon of Man* and *Le Milieu divin*. He argued that the stuff of which the universe is formed increases in complexity as it evolves, and likewise increases in consciousness. Humanity is one peak in this process, which moves through ever more closely knit social relationships and integration of consciousness towards the Omega Point. This, theologically, he identified with *Christ. In 1962 the *Holy Office gave a warning that his works had to be read with caution; they were never formally condemned.

Teishin (Zen poet): see RYŌKAN DAIGU.

Teisho (Jap., 'presentation'). The presentation of Zen realization by a Zen master (*rōshi) during a period of *sesshin. The offering, usually based on a *kōan or *sūtra passage, is made to the *buddha. It is not an address to the assembled company, but a return of insight to its source.

Tejas (Skt.). Fire, energy, majesty, authority, in Hinduism. It may be of the gods, but can also be a visible aura surrounding a spiritual master, or one who is meditating.

Tekiden (Jap.). 'Authorized transmission' in Zen Buddhism of the *buddha-dharma from a master to his pupil (cf. HASSU), confirmed by the seal of recognition (*inka-shōmei).

Telakhon (Karen, 'fruit of wisdom'). A Buddhist-influenced *millennial movement among the Karen of Burma, founded in the mid-19th cent. by Con Yu. Their mythology speaks of a withdrawn high god, Ywa, whose offer of a Golden Book of knowledge and power was ignored by their ancestors; the millennium, with freedom from British and later Burmese oppression, would arrive when the Book was restored by the Karen's white younger brothers, and in preparation animal sacrifice was banned and a strict ethic adopted.

Teleological argument. A type of argument for God's existence starting from signs of order or purpose in the world; also known as the Argument from Design and the *Physico-Theological Argument. St Thomas *Aquinas' Fifth Way (*Summa Theologiae*, 1a, ii. 3) is an example of such an argument.

Templars or **Knights Templar.** The Poor Knights of Christ and of the Temple of Solomon. They were founded in 1118 by Hugh de Payens to protect pilgrims in the Holy Land. They resisted an attempt to merge them with the Hospitallers (known from 1530 as the Knights of Malta, founded to provide hospitality for pilgrims, but adding to this the care of the sick), but could not withstand an assault from the king of France (and the *Inquisition), and they were suppressed in 1312.

Temple

Judaism (also Temple Mount) The central place of Jewish worship in ancient times. The first Temple was built in *Jerusalem by King *Solomon. It was destroyed by King Nebuchadnezzar of Babylon in 586 BCE, and the fast of 9 *Av was instituted to commemorate the event. It was rebuilt after the return from *exile under the leadership of *Zerubbabel (Haggai 2) and was greatly enlarged and improved by King Herod the Great (1st cent. BCE). Within the walls lay the Temple Court open even to *gentiles; at the east end beyond the Gate Beautiful was the Court of Women which lay inside the consecrated area. Beyond this lay the Court of the Israelites, open to all male Jews, from which the sacrifices performed on the *altar in the Court of Priests could be viewed. Up further steps was the Temple proper, consisting of the porch, the *sanctuary which was furnished with the altar of incense, the table of *shewbread, and the golden *menorah, and finally the Holy of Holies. Temple ritual is described in the Mishnaic tractates, *Tamid*, *Middot*, and *Yoma*.

The building was destroyed by the Romans (again on 9 Av) in the siege of Jerusalem in 70 CE.

Hinduism See ART.

Jainism Although there has been occasional dissent among Jains (e.g. the Terapanth), the majority of Jains have regarded the building of temples and the revering of the fordmakers in them as meritorious; and they would describe themselves as *murtipujakas*, 'image-worshippers'. Jain temples reflect early descriptions of the first preaching hall of *Mahāvīra, and usually include a tower said to represent Jain *cosmography, but perhaps absorbed from Mount *Meru as the *axis mundi.

Japanese Religion (Jap., *tera, ji*) Centres for institutionalized Buddhist practice in Japan. Japanese Buddhist temples, both architecturally and religiously, were heavily influenced initially (6th–8th cents. CE) by the Chinese and Korean temple systems. Later, Japan adopted these systems to their own practices and developing sectarian movements.

Temples generally belong to one or another of the many sects of Japanese Buddhism, including some of the Buddhist '*new religions' of Japan. As such, they represent Japanese Buddhism in its sectarian and institutionalized form.

Temple, William (1881–1944). Christian *archbishop of Canterbury, prominent worker for social and ecumenical ends. He was ordained in 1910, retaining reflective doubts which he explored in subsequent works, *Mens Creatrix* (1917), *Christus Veritas* (1924), and *Nature, Man and God* (1934). His thought was imbued with the Oxford neo-Hegelianism of his youth, seeing the purposeful process of the universe leading to the central event of the *incarnation, where the highest possibility of the union of matter, life, mind, and spirit is displayed —and enacted.

Yet his academic reflection fell away in importance compared to his commitment to the application of his strongly incarnational belief. His progress in the Church (canon of Westminster, bishop of Manchester 1921, archbishop of York 1929, archbishop of Canterbury 1942) enabled him to set in motion or influence organizations in the direction of a gospel applied to society—e.g. COPEC (the Conference on Christian Politics, Economics and Citizenship), the Workers' Educational Association, Faith and Order. In an establishment style, he was one of the first of the *liberation theologians.

Temple of Heaven. The Hall of Annual Prayers in Bei-jing (Peking), where the 'Sons of Heaven', the Chinese emperors, received the Mandate of Heaven (*t'ien-ming) to rule. It goes back to the Ming dynasty (1368–1661), and is built in a spacious park outside the (former) Forbidden City. An annual sacrifice of burnt offerings was performed here by the emperor, at the time of the winter solstice.

Temple Scroll. Scroll of the Jewish *Qumran sect. The *Temple Scroll* was among those found in the *Dead Sea collection and dates from the end of the 2nd cent. BCE. It includes *halakhot on ritual *purity and impurity, rules for the celebration of the *festivals, the commandment to build the *Temple and statutes concerning the king's bodyguard.

Temptation of Christ. An episode in the gospels (Mark 1. 13; Matthew 4. 1–11; Luke 4. 1–13) in which Jesus after his *baptism is tempted by the *devil in the wilderness. The story is a usual subject of meditation in *Lent.

Tenchi kane no kami (parent Spirit of the Universe): see KONKŌ-KYŌ.

Ten Commandments. The Decalogue, the ten laws proclaimed by God to *Moses as the representative of the Jewish people. The Ten Commandments are recorded in Exodus 20. 2–14 and Deuteronomy 5. 6–18. Although they have been made a foundation for morality in general, they are in fact addressed only to adult Israelite males.

Tendai Shū (Chin., *t'ien-t'ai*). An academic school of Buddhism established in the 6th cent. CE, in China by *Chih-i on T'ian-t'ai Shan ('Heavenly Terrace Mountain'), and introduced to Japan in the 9th cent. by the Japanese monk *Saichō.

Sometimes called the Lotus school (i.e. Hokkeshū, from the Jap. for *Lotus Sūtra*, *Hokekyo*), Tendai evolved as a distinctively Chinese interpretation of the enormous variety of Indian Buddhist *sūtras available in Chinese translation by the 6th cent. Chih-i developed a comprehensive synthesis of this literature by arranging them chronologically into five periods of the *Buddha's career, four methods of teaching, and four types of doctrine.

In 788 a Japanese Buddhist monk named *Saichō (Dengyō Daishi, 766–822) established a small temple NW of *Kyōto on Mount Hiei. Saichō studied Tendai in China during the year 804, and after his return to Japan introduced it in his temple, Enryaku-ji, on Mount Hiei. With the emperor's approval he ordained 100 disciples in 807. The traditional Tendai synthesis of Buddhist teaching and practice was maintained by Saichō, but he also widened this tradition by introducing a number of doctrines and practices of the esoteric tradition of Buddhism, known in Japanese as *Shingon or 'True Word', which was being taught by his contemporary *Kūkai on Mount Kōya. Later, especially under his successor *Ennin, the esoteric tradition of Buddhism came to dominate Japanese Tendai even though Chinese T'ien-t'ai maintained its distance from it. A further synthesis of Japanese Tendai occurred when attempts were made to include Shinto beliefs and practices under the name *ichijitsu shintō* ('One-truth Shinto').

The Tendai school is also of major historical importance since it was, because of its synthesis of the major forms of Buddhist teaching and practice, the source of the four 12th-cent. 'Kamakura schools' of Japanese Buddhism. *Hōnen (1133–1212) the founder of Jōdo Shū (*Pure Land school), *Shinran (1173–1262) the founder of *Jōdo Shinshū (True Pure Land school), *Eisai (1141–1215) the founder of Japanese *Rinzai Zen, *Dōgen (1200–53) the founder of Japanese *Sōtō Zen, and *Nichiren (1222–82) the founder of the Nichiren school were all trained at Enryaku-ji. In the 10th cent., disputes between successors of Ennin and Enchin (814–91) led to two rival Tendai centres on Mount Hiei, with the Jimon-shū eventually setting up the Onjoji temple as its centre. A further schism in the 15th cent. was produced by Shinsei (1443–95), who introduced Pure Land elements and founded Tendai Shinsei-shū as a result. In recent years Tendai has looked for a revival through the *Ichigū o terasu undō* ('Brighten a corner') movement, which has sought to popularize Saichō's teaching, but Tendai remains small in comparison with other sects such as Nichiren or *Zen.

See Index, Tendai.

Ten Days of Penitence (period of repentance; Jewish Calendar): see PENITENCE.

Tenebrae. The special form of *mattins and *lauds for the last three days of *Holy Week. The name (Lat., 'darkness') comes from the practice of extinguishing fifteen candles, one at a time, during the service.

Tenjō tenge yuiga dokuson (Jap.). 'Above heaven, under heaven, I alone am worthy of honour', a statement which Zen Buddhists believe was made by the *Buddha Śākyamuni after his enlightenment. Far from being self-aggrandizing, it is a subtle statement of the realization that all appearances in the universe share the same buddha-nature (*busshō) and are equally empty of self (*śunyatā).

Teṉkaḷai and **Vaṭakaḷai.** The two rival religious movements within *Śrī-Vaiṣṇavism. In origin, this division goes back to different theological positions, taken by *Vedāntadeśika in relation to the teachings of Piḷḷai *Lokācārya, about the nature of *prapatti, *Lakṣmī, and divine grace. The former argued that the traditions inherited from the *Āḻvārs and *Rāmānuja had to be regarded together (as the *ubhaya-*Vedānta*, 'the twofold Vedic heritage') and as fulfilling orthodoxy, not as cancelling it. He implicitly objected to a one-sided emphasis on a locally restricted, vernacular tradition (namely, the *Āḻvārs, as interpreted by the Lokācārya). Grace had to be 'earned' through at least a minimum of human co-operation, which must include orthodox behaviour. His opponents viewed things differently. They regarded the Āḻvār heritage as supreme and produced a vast commentarial literature on the **Nālāyira-divya-prabandham* in Tamil. Not only did they read Rāmānuja's theology into the poems, but their exegesis derived from them also the blueprint of a totally novel form of religion. The novelty lay in the assumption of the unconditional availability of grace, with two important corollaries. First, no restrictions (as through *caste, etc.) must be imposed on it; and secondly, 'orthodox behaviour' was seen as creating the delusion of being able to merit divine grace. Through the teaching and organizing of Maṇavāḷa mā-muṉi (15th cent.) the obvious social, institutional, and cultural implications of all this were actualized and given a further economic and political dimension. Central in this was the question of control over temples (and their endowments).

The characteristic signs are a U containing a single vertical line for the Vaṭakaḷai (central line usually yellow) and the same supported on a stem for the Teṉkaḷai (central line red).

Ten lost tribes. The Jewish tribes who disappeared from history after the Assyrian conquest of 722 BCE. The *rabbis believed they were in *exile beyond the river *Sambatyon. Various identifications have been made. The *Falashas were said to be a lost tribe, as have been the British (i.e. the British Israelites), the Japanese, the Afghans, and certain Red Indian tribes.

Ten martyrs. Ten Jewish *sages martyred by the Romans. The first list of ten martyrs appears in the *midrash *Lamentations Rabbah*, and the legend was circulated particularly in mystical circles.

Ten Ox-Herding pictures (depiction of stages of Zen progress): see JŪGYŪ(-NO)-ZU.

Ten powers of a Buddha: see DAŚABALA.

Ten precepts (undertaken by Buddhist bhikṣus): see ŚĪLA.

Tenrikyo ('Religion of Heavenly Truth'). Japanese *new religious movement, eventually classified (1908) as a Shinto sect. It derives from the revelatory experiences of Nakayama Miki (1798–1887), especially in 1838. Adherents believe in Tenri-Ō-no-Mikoto, the creator of the universe. On one plot of land, man was created. The plot, *jiba*, is the centre of the main temple, with a pillar, the axis mundi, set up on it (*kanrodai*). Adherents live in the pattern of Nakayama's life and receive special help (*fushigi na tasuke*) as they do so.

Tenshō Kōtai Jingūkyō, Japanese *new religious movement, founded by Kitamura Sayo (1900–67). She received a revelation that the world was about to end, and in 1945 proclaimed herself universal saviour. Her followers believed her to be the successor of the *Buddha and *Jesus. The movement is known as 'the dancing faith', because of its use of dance to induce ecstatic and trance states.

Tenshō Kōtōroku (Zen text): see KŌAN.

Ten Wings (added commentary): see I CHING; SHIH-I.

Tenzin Gyatso (current Dalai Lama): see DALAI LAMA.

Tephillin (Jewish phylacteries): see TEFILLIN.

Tera or **O-tera** (Jap.). A temple or monastery. After a name, it appears as -dera, or -ji, the Sino-Japanese way of reading the character for tera —thus, *Sōji-ji.

Terapanth (Jain reforming sect): see BHIKṢU, ĀCĀRYA.

Teraphim. Household gods mentioned in the Hebrew scriptures. The teraphim appear in the story of *Jacob and Rachel (Genesis 31. 34) and of Michal and *David (1 Samuel 19. 13). They were condemned and removed by *Josiah in his reform of the cult (2 Kings 23. 24).

Terefah (unfit food): see FOOD.

Teresa, Mother (1910–97). Founder of the Missionaries of Charity, winner of the Templeton Prize and of the Nobel Peace Prize (1979). Born Agnes Gonxha Boyaxhiu she joined the Sisters of Loreto to work in India, where she went after a brief period in Ireland. Upon completing her noviceship in Darjeeling, she was sent to teach in Calcutta. In her spare time she worked among the very poor and the sick, and in 1948 she left the Sisters of Loreto, gained some medical knowledge, and returned to Calcutta to found her order. Her nuns, in their distinctive sari-like habit, are now to be found all over the world, working with the poorest in society. Mother Teresa became also a constant campaigner against both artificial birth control and abortion.

Teresa of Avila (1515–82). Spanish *Carmelite nun and mystic, canonized in 1622 and made a Doctor of the Church in 1970. She entered the Carmelite convent of the Incarnation at Avila in 1535. After years of a fairly lax discipline, she was drawn to a stricter life, encouraged by her extraordinary mystical experiences. In 1562 she founded the convent of St Joseph at Avila, the first of the houses of the Carmelite Reform (called 'discalced', i.e. without shoes). Her reform met with much opposition but she found support from, amongst others, St *John of the Cross. Alongside her reform, she wrote for her nuns several books on the spiritual life, especially her *Autobiography*, the *Way of Perfection*, and the *Interior Castle*.

Teresa of Lisieux (1873–97). *Carmelite nun. Born into a devout middle-class family she entered the Carmel at Lisieux when only 15. Within ten years she had died of tuberculosis. Under obedience she wrote her autobiography, and fame came to Teresa through the decision of the prioress (her sister) to publish an edited version of it. She was canonized in 1925. But Teresa's real importance lies less in the 'saint' propagated by her convent, than in the extraordinarily honest following of Christ in little things—the 'little way'—revealed more clearly in the original form of her writings published in recent times.

Terma (Tib., *gter.ma*, 'Treasure'). A class of texts in Tibetan Buddhism, of which the **Tibetan Book of the Dead* is an example, which were concealed rather than revealed upon their creation, thus requiring a discoverer (*terton* or *gter.ston*, 'treasure-finder') at a later date. The practice of burying texts was initiated during the first diffusion of Buddhism in Tibet by *Padmasambhava, who saw that the country was not then ready for his more advanced teachings. The first terma discoverer was the *Nyingma Sangye Lama (*c*.1000–80 CE), and although the practice has spread to other schools it has remained a predominantly *Nyingma activity.

Terracotta Warriors (Chinese tomb figures): see SIAN.

Tertiaries (lay Christians living under a rule associated with a religious order): see THIRD ORDERS.

Terton (discoverer of text): see TERMA.

Tertullian (*c*.160–*c*.225), Christian *father. He was born in Carthage and became a Christian before 197. He was the first important Christian writer in Latin, with a long and various list of works (the chronology of which is disputed). He eventually left the *Catholic Church in favour of *Montanism. His *Apology* (*c*.197) has the typical concerns of the *apologists of the time, resting on the view that there is a natural basis for the recognition of God's action in Christ—i.e. the argument that there is 'anima naturaliter Christiana', the soul naturally Christian'. In his *Apology* there already appears the rigorous commitment to the faith summarized as 'The blood of the martyrs is the seed of the Church'—though he wrote, 'We grow just as much as we are mown down by you, the seed is the blood of the Christians.' His moral and disciplinary works (e.g. *The Soldier's Crown*, *On Penitence*) are rigorous in their insistence on separation from pagan society. The corresponding rigour in his adherence to the faith is epitomized in his sentence, *Certum est quia impossibile est*, 'It is certain because it is impossible', (*De Carne Christi*). His theological works are mainly polemical. The most important are *De praescriptione haereticorum* (Against Heretics, following the model of *Irenaeus), *Against *Marcion*, and *Against Praxeas* (attacking *modalism and formulating a doctrine of the *Trinity).

Terumah or **terumot** (heave-offering): see TITHES.

Te-shan Hsüan-chien (Jap., Tokusan Senkan; 782–865). Ch'an/Zen master, dharma-successor (*hassu) of Lung-t'an Chung-hsin. Originally trained in the Northern school (see SOUTHERN AND NORTHERN SCHOOLS), and learned in the **Diamond Sūtra*, he was in some despair at its teaching that it may take thousands of *kalpas to attain buddhahood. Hearing of the Southern school, he set out to learn more of it, meeting an old woman on the way who sent him to Lung-t'an. Lung-t'an handed him a paper torch, and as he took it, Lung-t'an blew it out. He received immediate enlightenment. Next day, he took his commentaries on the *Diamond Sūtra* and set fire to them. After years of seclusion, he became abbot of Te-shan (hence his name), and taught many disciples in the style of *Ma-tsu, with much use of sticks (*shippei*, *kyosaku) and shouts (*katsu*: see HO).

Teshuva (Heb., 'repentance'). The renunciation of sin, appeal for forgiveness and return to righteous living in Judaism. Repentance is an important theme in the Hebrew scriptures and is the theme of the Ten Days of *Penitence. Forgiveness depends on true repentance, and, if another person is involved, restitution must be made.

Testaments of the Twelve Patriarchs. A *pseudepigraphical writing relating in twelve books the message that each of the twelve sons of *Jacob gave to his descendants on his deathbed.

Tetragrammaton (Gk., 'four lettered'). The four letters, YHWH/JHWH, of the Hebrew name for God. Traditionally the tetragrammaton is not pronounced, and in the biblical text, YHWH is read as *'Adonai' (my Lord) or 'Ha-*Shem' (the Name). The English 'Jehovah' is a vocalization of JHWH, inserting the vowels from Adonai.

Tetzel, John or **Johann** (1465–1519). *Dominican friar. Renowned as a preacher of *indulgences, he collected money for the building of St Peter's, Rome, and the purchase of Albert of Magdeburg's archbishopric. On 31 Oct. 1517, Luther published his famous ninety-five theses attacking the indulgence traffic. In 1519 the papal *nuncio von Miltitz endeavoured to restrain Tetzel in an attempt to reconcile those who were scandalized by his eloquent commercialism.

Tevah (raised platform for Torah reading): see BIMAH.

Ṭhag (Prakrit, *ṭhagga*; Sindhī, *ṭhagu*). The anglicized Thugs or Thugees. They were devotees of the Goddess *Kālī in the form of *Bhavānī, to whom they offered the victims of their attacks, plus a third of the proceeds. Known especially for strangling victims, any method was acceptable provided blood was not shed. The British largely eliminated the Thugs by 1861, but the cult, with its affinities with left-handed *Tantra, persists. There is still a temple devoted to Bhavānī at Mirzāpur, near Varāṇasī.

Thakur Siṅgh Sandwalia (president of Sikh movement): see SIṄGH SABHĀ.

Thanawīya (Arab., *thanā*, 'reiterate, double'). Dualism, suspect in Islam because of its necessary *shirk (association of anything as equal with God). Thanawīya was linked by Muslims with Mānī (Manichaeism), Mazdak (Zoroastrianism), and ibn Daiṣān. The threat arose with the conquest of Persia.

Thanksgiving Day. A national holiday in the USA on the fourth Thursday of Nov., to give thanks for the blessings of the past year. It is traditionally derived from the settlers in Plymouth, Mass. who observed a day of thanksgiving for their first harvest in the autumn of 1621.

Thanksgiving Psalms. Designation of one of the *Dead Sea Scrolls. It contains a number of poems, all of which begin, 'I thank thee, O Lord', or 'Blessed be thou, O Lord'.

Thaumaturgy (Gk., 'wonder-working'). The power to work miracles, hence 'thaumaturgical', religions endorsing the working of miracles, especially healing. The term 'thaumaturgus' is applied in Christianity to saints who have worked many miracles, e.g. St Gregory Thaumaturgus (213–68), who was made bishop of Neocaesarea and converted virtually the whole city—the first of many miracles.

Theatre and drama. Theatre, both East and West, has been, and often still is, closely connected to religious *ritual: the development of theatre and dramatic form is equally connected to liturgy. Conversely, liturgy and ritual share much in common with theatre and drama. In religious theatre, as in ritual and liturgy, meaning is expressed through the body, especially through the hands, often in coded and non-verbal languages, at least as much as it is through text—indeed, frequently there is no spoken text at all—hence the links with ballet: see DANCE. These connections remain particularly obvious in E. religions. In India, there is a continuing tradition of dance, which is not simply derived from ritual but is still an expression of it. The spread of Hinduism into SE Asia led to an integration with indigenous rituals, leading to many characteristic forms of ritual drama—e.g. in Bali and in Java in the 'shadow theatre' (a type of puppet theatre, *wayang kulit* or *wayang purwa*).

In Christianity, theatre remained closely connected to ritual through liturgical drama which issued eventually in the miracle plays (dramatizations setting forth the life, miracles, and/or martyrdom of a saint), the mysteries (cycles of plays in which the story of humanity was set forth from the fall of *Lucifer to the Last Judgement), and the moralities (dramatized allegories; early examples are *The Castle of Perseverance* and *The Summoning of Everyman*, more usually known simply as *Everyman*). In Spain, the *auto sacramental* was an even more direct development from the medieval morality plays, and led to the powerful transformations of the form effected by Calderón (1600–81). He wrote more than seventy *autos*, which expounded the meaning of faith, but which were devotional as well. In the 20th cent., there have been notable attempts in the theatre to explore Christian faith by dramatists who have strongly held Christian beliefs themselves, notably T. S. *Eliot and Charles Williams, and less successfully (because more obviously) Graham Greene.

See also RITUAL and DANCE; for Japan see NO DRAMA; for Shīʿa passion plays see TAʿZIYA.

The Family (new religious movement): see CHILDREN OF GOD.

Theism. The doctrine that there is one transcendent, personal God who freely created all that exists out of nothing, and who preserves and governs it. He is believed to be self-existent, present everywhere, all-powerful, all-knowing, and perfectly good, and therefore worthy of human worship. Theism is nowadays distinguished from *Deism: the latter denies God's personal governance of the world, usually by ruling out the possibility of providence, miracles, and revelation.

The Noise (cargo-cult): see PALIAU MALOAT.

Theodicy. The justification of God, in response to the charge that the evils of the world are incompatible with his omnipotence and perfect goodness. The word was coined by *Leibniz in his *Theodicy* (1710), in which he argued that this world is the best of all possible worlds. John Hick, in his *Evil and the God of Love* (1966) claimed to discern two traditions of Christian theodicy: the *Augustinian, which stresses the role of the *Fall, seeing evil as either sin or the result of sin; and the *Irenaean, which regards evil more as a feature of an evolving universe and the result of human immaturity: the world, with its tests, becomes 'a vale of soul-making'. Both positions (though without the specific appeal to the Fall) can be found in all theistic religions.

In Eastern religions, the issue of theodicy is not so acute, either because the understandings of cosmogony are diffused, or because there is no belief in a God who is responsible for creation (Jains and Buddhists). For Indian religions, the understanding of *karma in any case gives more direct answers to the questions of the occurrence and distribution of suffering. For Hindus, the sense of God participating in the conquest of evil is strong (e.g. *Kṛṣṇa in **Bhagavad-gītā*).

The term 'theodicy' received a different analysis in the work of *Weber, for whom theodicy is central in his understanding of religions. In his view, religions offer theodicies, not simply as abstract solutions to intellectual puzzles, but as programmes for action.

From the adopted theodicy of a particular religion flow social consequences which give to different societies their characteristic forms and actions (or lack of them). His extension of the concept of theodicy drew attention to the dynamic consequences of theodicy and the quest for salvation (or its equivalent) in the forming of religious societies. See also EVIL.

Theodore of Mopsuestia (*c*.350–428). Christian theologian and biblical commentator. He became bishop of Mopsuestia (in Cilicia, modern SE Turkey) in 392 and remained there the rest of his life. On account of his Christology, identified with *Nestorianism, he was condemned at the Council of *Constantinople in 553; as a consequence his works have mostly been lost in Greek. On the basis of Syriac versions, modern W. scholars have usually allowed that Theodore's thought is not unorthodox.

Theodore of Studios, St (759–826). Christian monastic reformer. In 799 the community of which he was abbot at Saccudium, moved to the monastery of Studios at Constantinople. This monastery, founded in 463, had followed the rule of the *Acoemetae, but had become almost extinct under the *Iconoclast emperor Constantine V. Under Theodore, however, it became the centre and model of E. monasticism. He was a man of personal sanctity and strong determination, and is widely venerated in the Orthodox Church. Feast day, 11 Nov.

Theodoret (*c*.393–*c*.466). Christian bishop of Cyrrhus near *Antioch, and theologian. He was a friend and admirer of *Nestorius and became a defender of the *Antiochene Christology against *Cyril of Alexandria. His writings against Cyril were later condemned at the second Council of *Constantinople (553). Theodoret's other works include erudite biblical commentaries, a *Religious History* giving an account of monks and *ascetics in Syria, a church history continuing that of *Eusebius to 428, an apology *The Cure of Pagan Maladies*, and an anti-*Monophysite work *The Beggar* (i.e. his opponent, who has 'begged' his various absurd doctrines).

Theogonies. Births of gods used to give an account of the origin of the cosmos—e.g. in Hesiod, or in the primordial sacrifice of *Puruṣa in *Ṛg Veda* 10. 90. Theogonies are thus a specialized form of cosmogony.

Theologia Germanica. Anonymous 14th cent. Christian treatise on mysticism. It greatly influenced *Luther, who edited it in 1518; though *Calvin rejected it (as 'a poison from the *devil'), and Pope Paul V placed it on the *Index. Of a tendency later known as *Quietism, the work advocates absolute acceptance of God's will, looking for union for its own sake.

Theology (Gk., *theos*, 'god', + *logos*, 'discourse'). Reflection on the nature and being of God. Initially, in Greek, the word was reserved for poets such as Hesiod and Homer who wrote about the gods. A distinction was then made between their *myth-based theology and the kind of philosophical enquiry undertaken by *Aristotle. The term is not natural to the Jewish understanding of God unfolded in scripture (though *Philo, with his Greek leanings, called *Moses *theologos*, the spokesman of God). The term was introduced by the Church fathers, but not yet as a separate discipline of human enquiry and reflection. *Theologia* means more naturally 'speaking of God', i.e. praise. The systematic organization of theology began especially with the *scholastics, as with the concern of *Aquinas to show that revealed truths were not believed unreasonably, and was taken in different (more Bible-controlled) directions by the *Protestant reformers. Theology, especially as a university discipline, and systematic theologies became increasingly valued, being, in time, broken up into different disciplines, e.g. dogmatic, doctrinal, systematic, pastoral, historical, biblical, etc. Theology thus developed as a highly coded and formal system, in which rules of appropriateness are generated within the system. Attempts to break out of the circularity (some have said sterility) of such a strongly coded system (e.g. in *liberation theology, or plural 'theologies of . . .') are unlikely to return theology to the human community of knowledge, since they themselves are evaluated from within the circle; but see *political theology.

The same is (so far) true of individual attempts to reconnect theology with life, e.g. of K. *Rahner, or of T. F. Torrance, who saw in modern science an exemplary way in which truth is achieved or attempted, not by detachment from reality, but by a relationship to reality which evokes new attempts; thus both theology and science begin with faith, understood as a rational, intuitive, but nevertheless cognitive apprehension of what is real. 'What is real' in the case of theology is God, who gave himself in an act of grace to be known in the Word made flesh. Theology develops the methods and constructs (e.g. *creeds) appropriate to its subject-matter, but it remains integrated to the whole endeavour of human enquiry and wisdom. Outside Christianity, 'theology' is not isolated from life in the same way, though *kalām in Islam came under suspicion of leading in that direction.

See Index, Theologians, philosophers; Theology.

Theophany (manifestation of divinity): see HIEROPHANY.

Theosophical Society. Organization founded in New York by Mrs H. P. Blavatsky and Colonel H. S. Olcott in 1875, to derive from ancient wisdom and from the insights of evolution a world ethical code. In 1882, it moved its headquarters to India, and became the Adyar Theosophical Society. Although intended to be eclectic, it drew increasingly on Hindu resources. An important advocate of the Society was Annie Besant.

Theotokos (Gk., 'God-bearer'). Title of the Virgin *Mary. It was used from *Origen onwards, and became both a term of devotion and a mark of accepting the divinity of Christ. The usual Latin equivalent is *Dei Genitrix*, 'Mother of

God', or less usually, *Deipara*, as in Bacon's *Confession of Faith*, 'The blessed Virgin may be truly and catholicly called *Deipara*' (*c*.1600).

Thera (Pāli, 'elders'). Senior monks (*bhikṣu) in Buddhism, determined either by age or accomplishment. Therī is the female equivalent, but here determination is more often by date of entry to the community.

Thera- and ***Therī-gāthā*** (part of Buddhist Pāli canon): see KHUDDAKA NIKĀYA.

Therapeutae (Gk., 'healers'). Jewish ascetic sect. The Therapeutae are described by *Philo in his *De Vita Contemplativa*. Many scholars believe that their way of life was copied by the early monks of the Christian Church.

Theravāda (Pāli, 'teaching of the elders (of the order)'; Chin., Shang-tso-pu; Jap., Jōzabu; Korean, Sangjwabu). An early school of Buddhism, derived from *Vibhajjavādins and associated with *Sthaviras. As the major survivor of this line, the term became synonymous with Buddhism derived from, and defensive of, the *Pāli canon—in contrast to *Mahāyāna. Theravāda is the form of Buddhism in Śri Lankā and SE Asia. Mahāyāna ('Large Vehicle') calls Theravāda '*Hīnayāna', 'Small Vehicle', and this term, despite its contemptuous associations, still persists. Theravāda, though strictly inaccurate, is preferable, even though Theravāda was simply one among many early Buddhist schools.

Thérèse of Lisieux (Carmelite nun): see TERESA OF LISIEUX.

Therī: see THERA.

Thessalonians, Letters to the. Two epistles of *Paul and books of the New Testament. They were probably written from Corinth *c*.51 and are thus the earliest of Paul's letters (possibly excepting *Galatians).

Theurgy (Gk., 'divine action'). The inducement of the direct action of God through a human agent. In contrast to black magic, which invokes power from forces opposed to God, theurgy utilizes help from angels or saints, as mediators of God's power.

Thich Quang Duc (Vietnamese Buddhist monk): see BUDDHISM IN SOUTH-EAST ASIA.

Third eye (divine-seeing eye in Hinduism): see DYOYA-DṚṢṬI.

Third Orders. Associations of (mainly) lay Christians, who are known as tertiaries, who live under an approved rule in association with a First (male) or Second (female) religious Order. They began to emerge in about the 12th cent., but the best-known was that of St *Francis, who wrote his own Rule for a Third Order (subsequently lost), which was approved in 1221.

Third Rome (Moscow): see SECOND ROME.

Thirteen principles of the faith. Principles of the Jewish faith drawn together by *Maimonides. They include the existence of God, the unity of God, the incorporality of God, the eternity of God, that God is the only hearer of prayer, that the *prophets were inspired by God, that *Moses is the supreme prophet, that the *Pentateuch was given in its entirety to Moses, that the *Torah is immutable, that God is omniscient, the reality of divine reward and punishment, that the *messiah will come and that the *dead will be raised (see RESURRECTION). These principles are printed in most editions of the Jewish *Prayer Book.

Thirty-Nine Articles. The articles of faith, designed in the 16th cent., to elucidate the particular tenets of the *Church of England, in contrast to the Catholic and reformed churches of the Continent. They were curtailed by Convocation in 1563 from the Forty-Two Articles of 1553, and were approved finally in 1571. They are commonly printed at the end of the *Book of Common Prayer*. The Articles are in no sense a creed, but only statements of the *Anglican position on dogmatic questions of the 16th cent.

Thirty-two marks (of a Buddha): see DVĀTRIṂŚADVARA-LAKṢANA.

Thomas, St. One of the twelve *apostles. According to John 20. 25–8 he doubted *Jesus' resurrection until Jesus appeared to him and invited him to touch his wounds. In later tradition, the *Acts of Thomas*, a 3rd-cent., ascetical, and probably *gnostic work, recounts Thomas's missionary work in India. The *Syrian 'Christians of St Thomas' in Kerala, S. India (along with some Western scholars) strongly defend this tradition as explaining the origin of their church. Feast day: 3 July in the Roman Catholic and Syrian Churches; 21 Dec. in the Church of England; 6 Oct. in the Greek Church.

The *Gospel of Thomas* is a Coptic document consisting of 114 secret sayings of Jesus to his disciples. This work is not to be confused with the *Infancy Gospel of Thomas*, a collection of miracle stories about the child Jesus.

Thomas à Kempis (*c*.1380–1471). Christian ascetical writer. His teaching, which was deeply influenced by the *devotio moderna* (see GROOTE, GEERT), stresses the importance of an inward devotion of love and obedience to Christ, which finds classic expression in the *Imitation of Christ*, of which he is probably the author.

Thomas Aquinas (Dominican philosopher and theologian): see AQUINAS.

Thomas Christians (Christians in India): see THOMAS, ST; UNIAT(E) CHURCHES.

Thomism. Christian philosophical theology based on the writings of St Thomas *Aquinas. Although some propositions of Aquinas were initially condemned, his system was established in the 16th cent. onwards (known as Second Thomism, but also, confusingly, as *Neo-Thomism/Neo-*Scholasticism) as the basis of Roman Catholic theology and education. This was powerfully reinforced by *Leo XIII in his *encyclical *Aeterni Patris* (1879) which gave rise to what is more properly known as Neo-Thomism. More recent writing on Aquinas has rejected the distorting lenses of the various Thomistic schools, and by returning to the text of Aquinas' works has emphasized the significant divergences between Aquinas and his commentators. (For transcendental Thomism, see RAHNER, K.)

Thread ceremony (Hindu ritual and one of the most important of the saṃskāras): see UPANAYANA.

Thread-cross (Tib., *mdos*). Implement used in the magical rites of *Tibetan religions, principally to deflect negative influences away from a person or community. The simplest form consists of two sticks bound together in the form of a cross with threads of five colours stretched over it to resemble a cobweb, but complex forms can be as much as eleven feet in height, resembling the *stūpa in shape and symbolism. The thread-cross can serve as a temporary residence for a deity in rites of 'creating good' (such as protection for travellers), but more commonly in rites of 'dispelling evil' (such as assisting a person bothered by demons). R. de Nebesky-Wojkowitz (*Oracles and Demons in Tibet*, 1956), has drawn attention to the finding of thread-crosses in S. Africa, S. America, Australia, and Scandinavia, as well as in several areas of India.

Three barriers kōan: see TOU-SHUAI TS'UNG-YUEH.

Three bodies (the ways in which the buddha-nature becomes apparant): see TRIKĀYA.

Three Children, Song of (apocryphal addition to Hebrew scriptures): see SONG OF THE THREE CHILDREN.

Three gems (three Vaiṣṇava texts): see PAÑCARĀTRA.

3HO (Sikh-derived movement): see HEALTHY, HAPPY, HOLY ORGANIZATION.

Three Hours' service. A Christian non-liturgical service held on *Good Friday from noon to 3 p.m., the time of Jesus' crucifixion.

Three Jewels (Skt., *triratna*; Pāli, *tiratana* Jap., *sanki*). In Buddhism, the three most precious things, *Buddha, *dharma, and *saṅgha. Taking refuge in them is the hallmark of all Buddhist practice. Since they are considered to be a unit, the translation 'Triple Jewel', though uncommon, is more appropriate.

In Taoism, see SAN-PAO. In Jainism, they are Right belief, Right knowledge, Right conduct, the path to liberation: see TATTVĀRTHA SŪTRA.

Three liberations (Skt., *vimokṣa*; Pāli, *vimokka*). A Buddhist meditation practice which concentrates on the realization that all appearances are empty of self (*śūnyatā), are without essential characteristics (*animitta*), and should be, in one's own case, detached from passion. To achieve this is to realize *nirvāna.

Three marks of existence (Pāli, *ti-lakkhaṇa*; Skt., *tri-lakṣaṇa*). In Buddhism the collective term for *anicca (impermanence), *dukkha (suffering), and *anattā (no-self). Although each comprises a topic of meditation in its own right conceptually they are interrelated. See also VIPASSĀNĀ.

Three Pillars of Zen. A term usually taken to refer to *dai-funshi, *dai-gidan*, and *dai-shinkon*. But it is also used more generally to refer to 'teaching, practice, and enlightenment', as in P. Kaplean's book, *The Three Pillars of Zen* (1980).

Three poisons (one of ten powers of a Buddha): see DAŚABALA.

Three refuges (basic Buddhist orientation of life): see TRIŚARAṆA.

Three-self policy (indigenizing commitment of Christian mission): see VENN, HENRY.

Three Stages School (School of Chinese Buddhism): see SAN-CHIEH-CHIAO.

Three steps (cosmic control of one of Viṣṇu's avataras): see VĀMANA.

Three vehicles (Mahāyāna account of the three stages of Buddhism): see TRIYĀNA.

Three ways. Three constitutive elements of spiritual and prayer life, associated especially with Christianity, but applied less systematically to other religions. The ways are *purgative, *illuminative, and *unitive.

Three weeks. Period between the Jewish fasts of 17 *Tammuz and 9 *Av (hence the Heb. name *ben ha-metsarim*, 'between the straits', from Lamentations 1. 3). The three weeks are a time of *mourning. Very pious Jews also abstain from meat and wine except on the *Sabbath.

Three Worlds (the constitutive levels of manifestation in the cosmos, in Indian religions): see LOKA.

Three worms (malevolent Japanese folk deities): see KŌSHIN.

Throne of God. Jewish vision of the transcendent power of God. God is described as sitting on a throne by the *prophets Micaiah (1 Kings 22. 19), *Isaiah (Isaiah 6), *Ezekiel (Ezekiel 1) and *Daniel (Daniel 7. 9). The imagery is also to be found in *Talmudic and *midrashic sources. Some mystical tracts speak of God's throne as his *'merkavah' (chariot). In the *Pentateuch, the *Ark of the Covenant is understood as the throne of God, (and in his *mercy seat). Many Jewish philosophers, such as *Sa'adiah Gaon and *Maimonides, interpreted all talk of God's throne as *allegory.

In Islam, the throne of God became a subject of controversy in the early years: how literally was it to be taken? The *Qur'ān speaks frequently of al-'Arsh (e.g. 7. 54, 9. 129) and of al-Kursi (the footstool, but often taken to be a synonym of al-'Arsh), notably in *āyat al-Kursi*, the verse of the Throne, 2. 256. Conflict arose because to take these verses literally would imply extreme anthropomorphism; to take them metaphorically might seem to impugn the direct meaning of the Qur'ān.

Thugs (devotees of the Goddess Kāli): see ṬHAG.

Thurible or **censer.** A metal vessel for the ceremonial burning of *incense, carried by a thurifer.

Ti (Chin.). Lord, God, especially in China as in *Shang-ti.

T'iao-ch'i (Chin., 'harmonizing the breaths'). A Taoist exercise in breathing. It is a preliminary to other exercises, e.g. *fu-ch'i, *hsing-ch'i*, *lien-ch'i, *t'ai-hsi*, *yen-ch'i. It consists in assuming the lotus position (*padmāsana), and breathing deeply, expelling contamination and calming the mind. See also CH'I.

Tibetan Book of the Dead. The name given by its first editor, W. Y. *Evans-Wentz, to the principal one of several Tibetan works referring to the afterdeath state, and which is properly called the *Bardo Todrol* (*bar.do'i.thos.grol*), Liberation by Hearing in the Intermediate State (*bardo). The *Bardo Todrol* is designed to be spoken to a person in the bardo as a guide towards enlightenment or, for one less able, as an aid to negotiating the experiences thrown up by mental construction in the journey towards rebirth. The text is an example of the *Nyingma *terma literature, supposedly written by *Padmasambhava in the 8th cent. CE, and concealed until its rediscovery by Karma Lingpa. Because Karma Lingpa had *Kagyü students, and because of ties between the Nyingma and *Sakya lineages, the *Bardo Todrol* has also passed into the Kagyü and Sakya traditions.

In the bardo, the disembodied consciousness looks back over his past life and assesses it, making resolutions for achievements in the next.

Tibetan religion. Covering $1\frac{1}{2}$ million square miles between Ladakh in the west, India, Nepal, Bhutan, and Burma in the south, Mongolia in the north and China in the east, Tibet forms the highest country in the world. It is necessary to distinguish between Tibet geographical (population six million) and Tibet political (in Chinese terms the Tibet Autonomous Region, population two million), since large parts of Amdo and Kham were assimilated into the provinces of Xinjiang, Qinghai, Gansu, Sichuan, and Yunnan following the 1950 annexation of Tibet by China. The number of Tibetan refugees in India and the West is around 150,000.

In its known history Tibet has been host to two principal religions: *Mahāyāna Buddhism (in its *Vajrayāna aspect), which is now represented by the four major schools of *Nyingma, *Sakya, *Kagyu, *Geluk, and the indigenous *Bön religion, also now divided into different schools, which has come to resemble Tibetan Buddhism in most respects.

The first Tibetan king truly to adopt Buddhism was Trisong Detsen (*c.*741–97), the 'Tibetan *Aśoka'. He built the first Tibetan monastery at *Samyé, invited the Indian missionaries *Śāntarakṣita, *Kamalaśīla, and *Padmasambhava, and ensured Tibetan Buddhism would develop along Indian rather than Chinese lines. Perhaps in response to this as much as in defence of the native Bön, King Langdarma (*c.*803–42) seized power from King Ralpacan (*c.*805–36), and began a programme of persecution of Buddhism so ruthless that historians now isolate 'first and second diffusions' of Buddhism in Tibet. Langdarma was himself assassinated by a Buddhist monk, propelling the country into two centuries of anarchy.

The 'second diffusion' began in the 11th cent. In 1012 the heirs of those monks who had escaped to the east moved into central Tibet and founded the Gyal Lukle monastery. Simultaneously, sympathetic descendants of the broken royal line which had escaped to the west encouraged translators such as Rinchen Zangpo (c.958–1055) to study with Indian teachers and bring back *sūtras and *tantras. The influence of *Atisa, who arrived in 1042, has endured to the present. For the next nine centuries Tibetan Buddhism developed its own character. It may have assimilated something of the native Bön tradition, but it owes far more to Indian Vajrayāna.

As can be seen from the biographies of the *Dalai and *Panchen Lamas, Tibet has paid for its own pre-Buddhist imperialism by relentless cycles of Mongolian and Chinese invasion. It had survived with its independence and religion unscathed until the 1950 annexation by China and the driving into exile of the present Dalai Lama. After that, the systematic dismantling of Tibetan religion and culture began. The accusation of genocide against China by the International Commission of Jurists in 1960 had no effect in obstructing the policy, and by the time Mao died in 1976, 1.2 million Tibetans are estimated to have died as a result of the occupation.

Today, religious activity (banned completely 1966–79 along with the use of Tibetan clothing and even food bowls) remains subject to strict controls. A few monasteries (on tourist routes) have been renovated, and a limited number of monks (who must be vetted by the Communist Party committees governing each monastery) are now permitted. Though monastic education is reappearing, the use of *tantric imagery remains subject to stringent restrictions (this has been likened to a ban on representing Mary in Catholicism), and it is outside Tibet that Tibetan religions currently flourish, with a particular growing appeal for Tibetan Buddhism in the West.

See Index, Tibetan religion.

Tibetan Wheel of Life (*Srid.pa'i.'khor.lo*). Pictorial representation of the cycle of *saṃsāra and the single most common example of Tibetan art, valued for its clear embodiment of much Buddhist teaching. The wheel itself is held by Shinje (Skt., *Yāma), Lord of Death, to whom all life is subject, and is made to turn by the *three poisons at the centre—ignorance, desire, and hatred in the form of a pig, cockerel, and snake, usually shown chasing each other's tails. Clockwise on the outer rim are symbolized the twelve causes of existence of the *patīcca-samuppāda, and between the centre and the outer rim is the main body of the picture—the six realms of existence depicting all possibilities of birth: gods (*lha*), semi-gods (*lha.ma.yin*), animals (*byal.sang*), hell (*dmyal.ba*), hungry ghosts (*yi.dvags*), and humans (*mi*). These are to be understood as psychological as much as physical states. For the additional representations in Buddhism, see BHAVACAKRA.

T'ien. Chinese supreme source of power and order, usually translated as Heaven. Initially associated with *Shang-ti (see HEAVEN AND EARTH, SACRIFICES TO), T'ien achieved independent importance during the Chou *dynasty. T'ien was early associated with a moral life. To live according to the way of Heaven (and for an emperor according to *T'ien-ming, the Mandate of Heaven) becomes a summary of the goal of the appropriate life, however defined. The arrival of Buddhism led to T'ien being divided into different realms (along Buddhist lines), and led also to T'ien becoming the impersonal power of nature which brings things into appearance. This was congenial to Taoists, who could relate T'ien to *Tao. It follows that T'ien bears many different meanings: it is a place where gods, spirits, and immortal beings live; it is a supreme order, or a personal Lord, governing the cosmos in all its manifestations; or it is the unity of that cosmos as a single system.

T'ien-chih (will of heaven): see T'UNG CHUNG-SHU.

T'ien Fang (Chin., 'cube of heaven'). Chinese Muslim name for the *kaʿba.

T'ien-ku (Chin., 'heaven's drum'). *Taoist exercise to drive off harmful influences/spirits before breathing exercises. The drumming noise is produced by finger motions on the back of the head.

T'ien-ming (Chin.). The Heavenly Mandate, a concept developed in Chou philosophy (c. 8th cent. BCE) to define legitimate rulers. The concept is attributed to *Mencius. It holds that an emperor lacking in virtue has forfeited the right to rule. This right is then granted from *T'ien to the conqueror who establishes the next dynasty. T'ien-ming was developed further during the Han dynasty, and thereafter it was received by emperors in the *Temple of Heaven. It could be recalled by heavenly disapproval (expressed through portents and signs), and rulers would then have to amend their rule.

T'ien-shang Sheng-mu ('Holy Mother in Heaven'). A Chinese Goddess of seas, protector of seafarers, and patron saint of fishermen and boat-people. She is one of the most popular divinities on the SE coast of China and its adjacent islands. The common people call her affectionately Ma-tsu (Lord Mother).

T'ien-shih (Chin., 'celestial master'). Title of Taoist masters, descendants of *Chang Tao-ling, of the *wu-tou-mi tao, and of its successor, *cheng-i tao. A t'ien-shih has little actual authority, though he may formally recognize the head of Taoist congregations or communities. The Western equation of t'ien-shih with 'the pope' of Taoism is wide of the mark.

T'ien-t'ai, Tiantai, or **Fa-hua-tsung** (Chin., 'School of the Celestial Platform'). School of Chinese Buddhism derived from *Chih-i (538–97), who lived on Mount T'ien-t'ai. Because of its veneration of the **Lotus Sūtra* it is also known as the Lotus school. T'ien-t'ai looked back on previous Buddhist history and sought a way of giving status to its diverse teachings, classifying the Buddha's teaching into *'five periods and eight schools', and allowing that his teaching was adapted, in successive periods of his life, to different levels of attainment (*upāya-kauśalya). The *Lotus Sūtra* contains the consummation and highest level of teaching. T'ien-t'ai approximates to the teaching of *Nāgārjuna, whom it sees as its patriarch. T'ien-t'ai was taken to Japan by *Saichō, where it is known as *Tendai. See Index, Tendai.

T'ien-t'iao shu (T'ai-p'ing text): see BOOK OF HEAVENLY COMMANDMENTS.

T'ien wang (four world protectors in Buddhism): see CELESTIAL KINGS.

Tijāniy(y)a. Muslim *Sūfī order (*ṭarīqa) founded by Abu'l-'Abbās *Aḥmad al-Tijānī (1737–1815 (AH 1150–1230)). He was admitted to the *Qādiriy(y)a (and other orders) before founding his own order, based on Fez, having received a direct commission from a vision of the Prophet *Muḥammad in the desert. Members of the order are called *aḥbāb* ('friends'), and are forbidden to join any other *ṭarīqa (order), because their line of descent is directly from Muḥammad, and not via other teachers/guides. They adjusted to W. rule, especially to the French, and are therefore strong in parts of Africa which were formerly French colonies.

Tikhon of Zadonsk, St (1724–83). Russian *bishop and writer on religious and spiritual matters. Born of poor parents, he studied at the seminary in Novgorod, where he later became professor, taking monastic vows in 1758. In 1761 he was consecrated bishop and in 1763 became bishop of Voronezh. He resigned in 1767 and retired to the monastery of Zadonsk from 1769. Both as bishop and recluse he displayed deep pastoral concern and devoted himself to those in need. He is unusual in *Orthodox spirituality in his experience and understanding of the *dark night of the soul, though otherwise he is deeply rooted in the ascetic and mystical traditions of *Russian Orthodoxy. He is believed to be the model for Zosima in Dostoevsky's *The Brothers Karamazov*.

Tikkun. Jewish *kabbalistic term for cosmic repair. Tikkun is particularly associated with the thought of Isaac *Luria.

Tikkun Ḥatsot. Jewish ceremony, mainly among *kabbalists, held at midnight in order to make repair and restitution by means of penitence (see TESHUVAH) in response to the exile (*galut) of God's presence following the destruction of the *Temple.

Tikkun Soferim (Heb., 'repair of the *Scribes'). Changes in the text of the Heb. *Bible. The *rabbis attribute eighteen tikkunim (pl.) to the men of the Great *Synagogue, who changed the text because it showed lack of respect to God.

Tikkun tal: see DEW, PRAYER FOR.

Tilak, Bāl Gangādhar (1856–1920). Indian politician and patriot, who perceived the importance of religion in political matters, especially in relation to self-government. For his forthright articles in 1908, he was deported to Mandalay for six years. In prison in Mandalay he wrote his famous book *Srimad *Bhagavad Gītā Rahasya* (The True Import of the Gītā), which saw 'the religion of the Gītā, combining spiritual knowledge, devotion and action' as the foundation of India's revival. Tilak died on 1 Aug. 1920, and because the people came in such large numbers to pay their last respects to the national hero, the cremation took place at Chowpati Beach, Bombay.

Tilaka or **puṇḍra.** Marks in Hinduism, made on the body, usually the forehead, to indicate caste or sect membership. The single spot of red, white, or yellow in the middle of the forehead is the sign of marriage. Lines of *ash (puṇḍra) are worn by male ascetics, three vertical lines in V formation for devotees of *Viṣṇu, three horizontal lines for those of *Śiva, twelve to different parts of the body for those of Śrī-*Kṛṣṇa.

Tillich, Paul Johannes Oskar (1886–1965). Christian Protestant theologian. He was born in Prussia, and after education at Berlin and Tübingen, and ordination in 1912, he served as a chaplain in the First World War, receiving the Iron Cross. He became professor at Union Theological Seminary until he retired in 1955. He then became professor, first at Harvard, then at Chicago. He was a major and innovative theologian, taking his point of departure from Schelling: symbols, as human creations of meaning (participating in the reality to which they point) mediate between bare objects and conventional signs. But humans are always involved existentially in questions (arising from limitation and above all from awareness of the personal ending which is to come) and predicaments (situations which seem to lead to self-defeat). These questions and predicaments have no solution (and are thus empty symbols in quest of meaning) until they are brought into relation with religious symbols which offer the meaning sought. This is the basis for the principle of correlation which led him to explore the theology of culture. In so far as forms of cultural expression set forth something of unconditional importance, they are expressing that which is religious. Unconditional meaning (*Gehalt*) breaks into the form of a cultural work in such a way that the content of the work can be seen to be a matter of indifference in relation to it. Tillich was later to call the unconditional meaning 'ultimate concern'. Religion then becomes the state of being unconditionally concerned about that which concerns one unconditionally. Thus 'God' is in no way a synonym for 'ultimate concern'. Indeed, that which is truly God, the God above God, cannot be spoken of except as being-itself: 'God does not exist. He is being itself beyond essence and existence. Therefore to argue that God exists is to deny him.' But 'God' enters our vocabulary because the ground of being enters our lives as the answer to the question implied by human finitude. Time is thereby not simply transition but *kairos*, opportunity.

Not surprisingly, Tillich's ideas are communicated, not simply in technical works (e.g. *Systematic Theology*, 3 vols., 1953–63), but also in sermons (e.g. *The Shaking of the Foundations*, 1948; *The Eternal Now*, 1963) and lectures (e.g. *The Courage to Be*, 1952).

Ti-lo-pa (989–1069). One of the eighty-four *mahāsiddhas of Indian Tantric Buddhism, and the first human teacher in the *mahāmudrā tradition. He passed on his powers and teachings to Nā-ro-pa, through whom they were transmitted into the *Kagyü school in Tibet.

Time. Religious understandings of time rest on human awareness of transition in daily activities, in the movement from birth to death, and in the unfailing periodicity of the sun, moon, stars, and seasons. Much of the religious understanding of time seeks to find connections between these, and to interpret their significance. Therefore, a primary source for a religion's perception of time is to be found in its *cosmology, which is generally replete with time-related characteristics. The cosmology of the natural world is often endowed with a *soteriological meaning by using it as a metaphorical milieu for the spiritual path through time, leading to an eternal goal of enlightenment or salvation.

Based on common features found in many (but not all) ancient religions throughout the world, a pattern of cyclical religious behaviour has been observed among these traditions in which there is a regularly recurring need to return to some mythical beginning.

M. *Eliade associated what is termed 'sacred' time with such cyclically governed religious times and 'profane' time with ordinary daily temporal existence. Sacred time was experienced in a ritualistic yearly repetition of some mythical creation act, often involving an hero-god who brought about creation and order by fighting and overcoming the forces of darkness, evil, and chaos.

This primitive cyclical experience can be compared with that of the early Israelites, suggesting that they began to deal with this terror from a considerably different spiritual viewpoint, namely that of faith. It was this faith that was the undercurrent nourishing the seeds for the gradual growth over many centuries of a sense of time as progressive and non-cyclical, i.e. with events related significantly to each other. The organization of this into the *Deuteronomic history was an important step in distinguishing 'times' as revealing the purposes of God.

This biblical view of time, or 'times', was later expressed primarily in terms of two Gk. words, *kairos* and *chronos*, endowing time roughly with quality and extensiveness, respectively. *Kairos* had the general purport of 'decisive moment', or 'opportunity'. On the other hand, chronos could mean time in general, duration, lifetime, or age.

The early Christians quite naturally continued the Israelite tradition of 'event-oriented' time. With the Christians, in addition to the biblical events, there were further decisive sacred events, compressed, of course, into a much shorter period of time. By far the most crucial of these were the crucifixion and resurrection of *Jesus, but continuing with 'the *acts of the *apostles'. Although it was not viewed so in biblical times, for Christians in later centuries and today Jesus as *Christ stands at the centre of history, BC (before Christ) and AD (*anno Domini*, in the year of the Lord) years being numbered from this time. In general, therefore, in the biblical period, time seems to have been experienced and viewed on three different levels. The first is that of human subjectivity, time as realized in the worldly and religious life of persons and communities. The second is the cosmic level based on the understanding of the order of the natural world, which exhibits a manifold diversity of temporal aspects. The third level is that realized by the divine encounter with God; it is God's eternal time.

It is the interplay of these last two levels that provides the fabric of the Judaeo-Christian, as well as the Islamic, cosmologies. They are 'one-time' cosmologies characterized by one unrepeatable beginning and evolving redemptively to a specified end, involving an *eschatology of final salvation and judgement.

In contrast to the Western religious view of sequential and progressive time, set in a cosmology with an unrepeatable beginning and ending, the Eastern view of time exhibits a cohesive interrelation of both cyclical and non-cyclical characteristics. The cyclical is evident in Hinduism in the earliest times when the *Vedic altar was considered to be time itself, with 360 bricks for the days and 360 stones for the nights. However, the usual diversity of thought in Indian religion is already apparent in the *Sūtras and the religious philosophy of the six major schools (*darśana) of Hindu thought, with major differences in the understanding of time. However, all six schools do adhere to some common time-related views, perhaps because the problem of time was a central concern in the historical development of these positions. Thus the concept of repeated creation and dissolution of the universe is accepted by all schools, except the *Pūrva-Mīmāṁsā; and all, with the Upaniṣads, maintain that being cannot arise from nothing; it is uncaused, indestructible, beginningless, and endless.

The awesome periodicity of the Indian cosmology is often cited by Western writers as the basis for a general claim that a strictly cyclical view of time characterizes this tradition. This claim has only very limited validity. First, the yugas are not equal in duration, nor in moral content, and even if they were, it is the karmic growth and progression of the soul through this periodicity that is the essential soteriological feature. Secondly, there is a voluminous scriptural literature in the tradition that meticulously expounds an incredibly broad spectrum of time concepts, most of which are not cyclical.

Nevertheless, the concept of rhythmic repetition, but in altered form, also found its way into the cosmologies of most Buddhist schools. Again the cosmologies provide a milieu for the path to salvation. In this case it means transcending the samsaric cycle of births, deaths, and all attendant suffering, and escaping time with achievement of *nirvāna. However, the concept of time differs fundamentally in Buddhism from Brahmanism. For the Buddhist, flux and change (*anicca) characterize the world, so that change is the ultimate reality; nothing is exempt from change. The position on this doctrine is so fundamental that the world is seen not as matter undergoing change, but as change bringing about 'matter'. Inseparable from this doctrine is the equally fundamental conviction concerning the reality of the moment. All being is essentially instantaneous. Each moment is a creation entirely new, never seen in the same way before: 'The moment is change manifested' (L. Kawamura). Consistent with this is the understanding of *anātman (no-self).

However, no one theory of cosmic time or the duration of its divisions is accepted by all schools of Buddhism, and speculation on such matters was discouraged by the Buddha as not directly relevant to the quest for liberation. Such speculation as did occur was based upon Hindu notions of endlessly recurring continuities of time, and it is from this procession of saṃsāra that the Buddhist seeks release. Thus time in itself has no eschatological significance and there is no doctrine of an apocalypse.

Among the Jains, time is understood as an ongoing series of ṛevolutions of a wheel, rising up from the lowest point, and turning over the top into descent. The downward half is known as *avasarpini*, starting from the apex of a golden age, and descending through six spokes or ages to the *kaliyuga (*duhsama*) in which Jain teaching and practice disappears. The uprising is known as *utsarpini*. The cycle is driven by itself, not by the intervention of any god or other agent. During each cycle of the wheel, the *tīrthaṅkaras appear in order.

In this survey of the time-related views of major world religions there are two general features that are common: (i) the value placed on the living moment; (ii) the attempt to relate and reconcile lived time with some form of divine eternity, whether it is endless time, the totality of all time, or absolute timelessness. The general scientific or philosophic view of time as a chain of mathematical instants, an unrepeatable succession of experienced moments, or an irreversible continuous flow, is enriched by the religions which bestow a sacredness to each living moment; thus it is value-endowed time. Furthermore it is a goal-directed time that is set in a context of divine eternity or against a timeless transcendent background of reality with which the believer strives to find unity.

Time of ignorance (period in Arabian society prior to Islam): see JĀHILĪYYA.

Timothy, St. Companion of *Paul. According to *Acts he was circumcised by Paul and accompanied him on his second missionary journey. His name is joined to Paul's at the head of seven of his letters. By tradition he was the first bishop of Ephesus and was martyred there on 22 Jan. 97.

The two Letters to Timothy are two of the *Pastoral Epistles in the New Testament, professedly by Paul to his deputy Timothy in Ephesus.

Tinkling cymbal (allusion in Christian scripture): see CHARITY.

Tipiṭaka (Pāli, 'Triple Basket'): see BUDDHIST SCRIPTURES; TRIPIṬAKA.

Tiracchāna-kathā (Pāli, 'animal talk'). Worldly chatter or gossip, regarded by Buddhists as unseemly, especially for *bhikṣus (monks).

Tīrath (Hindī, Pañjābī), 'Pilgrims' bathing place'. Gurū *Nānak rejected the Hindu practice of ritual bathing at tīraths (see TĪRTHA) as irrelevant to salvation. He used the imagery of tīrath to describe the nature of true, interior religion. This message is clearly expressed in his verses, e.g. Ādi Granth 687 and 789, 'The true tīrath is the divine *Nām.'

Tirmidhī (Muslim collector of Ḥadīth): see AL-TIRMIDHĪ.

Tīrtha (Skt., 'ford', 'crossing place'). In Indian religions, a recurrent metaphor for a sacred place where one can cross over easily and safely to the far shore of liberation (*mokṣa): a *limen* or threshold. Tīrthas are the focus of devotion and *pilgrimage (tīrthayātrā) throughout India and can be found at actual fords across rivers and by tanks, lakes, and the seashore, as well as up mountains, in forests, and in cities. These thresholds between heaven and earth are charged with a power and purity which afford a spiritual crossing and are often associated with great events relating to the heroes of myth and legend or the appearances of the gods. Tīrtha can also refer to a holy person or path which affords access to the sacred. Hence the twenty-four great Jain teachers are referred to as *tīrthaṅkaras, 'builders of the ford'; see also TĪRATH.

Tīrthaṅkara (Skt., 'builders of the ford'). In Jainism, the title given to the twenty-four omniscient spiritual teachers who have displayed the way of salvation across the ocean of suffering and existence, thus a synonym for *jina. With the exception of *Ṛṣabha (first), *Pārśva (twenty-third), and *Mahāvīra (twenty-fourth), the Jain canon gives a highly stereotyped description of their lives. Jain temples today house identical images of all twenty-four tīrthaṅkaras, which are distinctively identifiable only from the totem which is commonly associated with each: (1) Ṛṣabha (bull), (2) Ajita (elephant), (3) Sambhava (horse), (4) Abhinandana (ape), (5) Sumati (heron), (6) Padmaprabha, (7) Supārśva, (8) Candraprabha, (9) Suvidhi (crocodile), (10) Śītala (wishing tree), (11) Śreyamsa (rhinoceros), (12) Vasupujya (male buffalo), (13) Vimala (boar), (14) Ananta (hawk/bear), (15) Dharma (thunderbolt), (16) Śānti (deer), (17) Kunthu (goat), (18) Ara (diagram), (19) Malli (water jar), (20) Manisuvrata (tortoise), (21) Nami (blue lotus), (22) Nemi (conch shell), (23) Pārśva (snake), (24) Mahāvīra (lion). See Index, Tirthankaras.

Tirukkuṛaḷ: see TIRUVAḶḶUVAR.

Tirumaṅkai-Āḻvār (Hindu poet): see ĀḺVĀRS.

Tirumuṟai ('canon' of Tamil Śaivism): see MAṆIK(K)AVACAKAR.

Tiruvaḷḷuvar (*c*.5th cent. CE). Author of a major work in Tamil, *Kuraḷ* or *Tirukkuṛaḷ*. The work reviews three of the four ends of human life (*puruṣhartha): *aram* (*dharma), *porul* (*artha), and *inpam* (*kāma), but not the final end of *mokṣa. It is uncertain to which religion the author actually belonged: he has been claimed by Jains and Christians as well as Hindus. Its ethical stress and openness of manner have led to its being translated many times. It is regarded by Hindus in S. India as a sacred text, and for that reason is often called Tamilveda.

Tisarana (the three fundamental Buddhist commitments): see TRIŚARAṆA; THREE JEWELS.

Tishah be-Ab(v) (day of mourning in Jewish calendar): see AV, NINTH OF.

Tithes

Judaism (Heb., *ma'aser*). Money or goods levied for the maintaining of sacral institutions. Several types of tithe are mentioned in the Hebrew scriptures. According to Numbers 18. 24, the 'first tithe' was given to the *Levites after the 'heave-offering' (*terumah*) had been separated from it for the *priest. The 'second tithe' (Leviticus 27. 30–1; Deuteronomy 14. 22–6) was a tenth part of the 'first tithe'. The laws of tithes are compiled in the tractate *Ma'aserot* in the *Mishnah.

Christianity In Europe a system of tithes came into legal force in the early Middle Ages (e.g. in England in 900), as a tax for the support of the Church and relief of the poor. The levy consisted of a tenth part, originally of the produce of lands ('praedial' tithes) and later of the profits of labour also ('personal' tithes). The system did not survive the secularization of continental European states after the *Reformation.

For regulated giving in other religions, see ZAKĀT; DASWANDH.

Ti-ts'ang. Chin. for *Kṣitigarbha, a *bodhisattva who helps children and has power over the six realms of rebirth.

Titus, Letter to. One of the *Pastoral Epistles of the New Testament, professedly by Paul to his assistant Titus in Crete.

TM: see TRANSCENDENTAL MEDITATION.

Tobacco. Prohibited for Sikhs. The use of tobacco is specifically prohibited in the *khaṇḍe-dī-pāhul (initiation) ceremony of *khālsā Sikhs, and is avoided by Sikhs, both *sahajdhārī and *keśadhārī.

For its possible prohibition for Muslims, see KHAMR.

Tobit, Book of. Book of the Jewish *apocrypha. Tobit contains the story of the righteous Tobit whose sight was restored after his son Tobias had been guided by an *angel. It became a favourite subject in Christian art, often with Tobit's dog (5. 16), the only one mentioned favourably in the Bible.

Todai-ji (temple-complex): see NARA BUDDHISM; BODHISENA.

Toda Jōsei (co-founder): see SŌKA GAKKAI.

Tōgaku (China-derived music): see MUSIC.

Tohorah (Heb., 'purification'). The Jewish ceremony of washing the dead before burial. The justification for tohorah is the Ecclesiastes verse, 'As he came, so shall he go' (5. 15). *Progressive Jews have abandoned the practice. See also PURITY.

Tōji. A temple in *Kyōto, built in 796 by the emperor Kanmu when the capital was relocated there. In *c*.830, it was given to *Kūkai to serve as the centre of *Shingon, after which it was called Konkōmyō-shitennō-kyōō-gokokuji, or Kyōō-gokokuji for short. The beautiful five-storey *pagoda was reconstructed in the 17th cent.

Tokudo (Jap., 'attainment of going beyond'). The ceremony in Zen Buddhism through which a layperson is initiated into Buddhism, or a monk is ordained.

Tokugawa period. The period in Japan between 1600 and 1868 when power was held by the Tokugawa clan. Because of a strong emphasis on the worth of the traditions and past glories of Japan, it led to a revived interest in *Shinto, and laid the foundations for *Kokugaku (the School of National Learning).

Tokumitsukyō (Zen Buddhist movement): see MIKI TOKUHARU.

Tokusan Senkan (Ch'an/Zen master): see TE-SHAN HSUAN-CHIEN.

Toledot Yeshu (Heb., 'The Life of Jesus'). A Jewish life of Jesus. *Toledot Yeshu* was compiled, from more ancient sources, in the 10th cent. It claims that Jesus' mother was raped. Jesus himself had supernatural powers, but his magic was exorcised by the *sages. Some of his *miracles, such as the resurrection, are given a natural explanation. Several versions of the work have been preserved.

Tolstoy, Leo (1828–1910). Russian novelist and advocate of reform. He spent a period in the army and a further period travelling in Europe, studying educational and social reform. On his return in 1862 he married and wrote his greatest novels, *War and Peace* and *Anna Karenina*. The rest of his vast literary output was on moral and religious subjects, directly through essays, and indirectly through short stories and his novel, *Resurrection*. He became increasingly critical of the formalism of the *Orthodox Church. He was eventually excommunicated.' He made huge demands of God in pursuit of an anguished humility, which made Gorky observe that the relationship of Tolstoy with God reminded him of 'two bears in one den'. He preached a gospel of love and moral goodness, and dispensed with dogma and ritual, though occasionally (e.g. in *The Death of Ivan Ilych*) he suggests that humans discern truth in an act of absolute renunciation, even of their achievement through good works.

Tomitsu. (esoteric Buddhism): see ENNIN.

Tomurai. Japanese funeral rites. At the approach of death, people plead with the soul not to depart, but when it is clear that it has nevertheless gone, a bowl of rice is placed by the head of the deceased for sustenance in the spirit world, with a sword or sharp knife on the other side for protection against evil spirits. The body is washed and dressed in white before being placed in the coffin. Words of comfort may be spoken (e.g. by Buddhist functionaries), and the body is then buried or cremated. A week later, on *shonanuka* ('seventh day'), a posthumous name is bestowed. Mourning continues for seven weeks. Commemorations are made, especially at Bon (see ULLAMBANA; FESTIVALS AND FASTS). When these are complete, the last being called exactly that, *tomurai age*, 'completion of the rites', the spirit has become one with the ancestral *kami.

Tonghak (Eastern learning): see KOREAN RELIGION.

Tongyō (Jap., 'sudden enlightenment'). The attainment of sudden or immediate enlightenment in Zen Buddhism, in contrast with the gradual progress (*zengyō) through long training, meditation practice, etc. Tongyō-tonshu is 'sudden enlightenment and sudden practice' (i.e. all meritorious acts are performed in a short time), tongyō-zenshu is 'sudden enlightenment and long practice'.

Tonsei or **tonzei** (Jap.). Retreating from the world, the Buddhist practice of world-renunciation; tonsei-sha is one who has renounced. After the Kamakura period, tonsei became a more formal group of those who simply wished to live in seclusion.

Tonsure (shaving of the top of the head): see HAIR.

Tooth Relic Temple. More accurately known as Dalada Maligawa, the shrine in Śri Lankā in which the relic of the Buddha's tooth is kept. It is now in Kandy, but there were several earlier shrines after the tooth was brought to Śri Lankā in the 4th cent. CE. It is an object of constantly maintained devotion, and it is brought out in procession once each year.

Torah (Heb., 'teaching'). The teachings of the Jewish religion. In the *Pentateuch, the term 'Torah' can mean all the laws on a particular subject (e.g. Leviticus 7. 2) or the summation of all laws (e.g. Deuteronomy 4. 44). It is also used to refer to the Pentateuch in contrast to the *Prophets and *Hagiography (as in *Tanach), and later a distinction was made between the *written and the *oral law. The purpose of Torah is to make *Israel 'a kingdom of *priests, a holy nation' (Deuteronomy 33. 4). In a famous exchange *Hillel summarized Torah in the maxim, 'What is hateful to you, do not to your fellow' (*B.Shab.* 31a), and Akiva maintained that its overriding principle was 'Love your neighbour as yourself' (Leviticus 19. 18). *Maimonides laid down in his *thirteen principles of the Jewish faith that Torah is immutable and that it was given in its entirety to Moses. The belief in the divine origin of both the written and oral Torah remains the touchstone of *Orthodox Judaism. The *Karaites accepted the written, but not the oral law, while the *Progressive movements tend to distinguish between the moral and ritual law. See Index, Torah.

Torah, reading of. The practice of reading the Jewish *Torah publicly. The Babylonian *Talmud refers to a fixed cycle of readings (*B.Meg.* 29a), with the entire *Pentateuch being read over the course of three years. By the 12th cent., it became the universal practice to read it over an annual cycle. Before and after the reading the Torah *scroll is carried in procession around the synagogue. The readers recite particular *benedictions before and after their reading which is normally chanted (see CANTILLATION).

Torah ornaments. The coverings of the Jewish *Torah *Scrolls. The scrolls are rolled on two staves known as *azei ḥayyim* ('trees of life'). On the top of the staves are two finials, the *rimmonim*, and these are covered with an open crown (*keter*). The *Sephardim encase the scrolls in a double-hinged wooden box decorated with leather or metal. The *Ashkenazim cover their scrolls with a decorative mantle, often richly embroidered, on which a breastplate is suspended. The breastplate is reminiscent of the costume of the *high priest. In order to avoid touching the parchment of the scroll, a pointer, the *yad* ('hand'), is used.

Torah she-be'al peh (Torah transmitted by mouth): see HALAKHAH.

Torah she-bi-khetav (Torah which is written): see HALAKHAH.

Torii. The gateway into *Shinto temples, standing also before sacred rocks, bridges, etc. They are made generally of two posts supporting two horizontal lintels. Worshippers bow to the gods as they pass through them. Their shapes and design vary greatly.

Torma (*gtor.ma*, 'scattered (oblation)'; Skt., *bali*, 'offering'). Sacrificial cake-offering in Tibetan Buddhism, made of barley flour, brightly decorated with coloured butter and shaped according to ritual requirements. It is so called because almost invariably it is scattered for eating by birds and animals after the ceremony, though occasionally it may be consumed during the ritual. Tormas may be offered to *bodhisattvas, *ḍākinīs, local spirits, even as bribes to satisfy demons. Tormas often play a part in empowerment (Skt., *abhiṣekha; Tib., *dbang.bskur*) rituals, where the empowerment to perform the practice of a particular deity is given by the lama first projecting the deity into the torma, and then anointing the disciple with it.

Toronto Blessing. The term was first coined by British churches for the claimed experience of a new wave of the Holy Spirit beginning in 1994. At the end of Jan. 1994 a small *charismatic church in Toronto, of the Vineyard denomination (the 'Airport Vineyard') experienced what they believed to be a new and concentrated outpouring of the Spirit night after night. The Airport Vineyard church has since been recognized as 'a worldwide renewal centre'. Various manifestations deemed to be evidence of the presence of the Spirit have become synonymous with 'Toronto': they include falling or resting in the Spirit, laughter, shaking, and crying. In Dec. 1995, the founder and overseer of the Vineyard churches, John Wimber, released the Airport Vineyard from the Vineyard denomination for reasons of growing unhappiness with the emphasis on the extraordinary manifestations of the Spirit, and because he no longer felt able to exercise oversight over the Church and its activities. After Jan. 1996, the church continued to exist as an independent church. Despite the controversy, testimony continued strongly of those claiming to have been greatly blessed by God.

Torquemada, Tomas de (1420–98). Grand Inquisitor in Spain. A *Dominican, he joined the *Inquisition in 1482, and was responsible for about 2,000 executions and for the expulsion of those Jews from Spain (in 1492) who refused *baptism. His methods were summarized in the handbook, *Instrucciones de la santa Inquisición* (1484).

Torrance, T. F. (Christian theologian): see THEOLOGY.

Tortoise oracle. Ancient Chinese method of divination, similar in antiquity and use to the *oracle bones. Unlike the latter, however, the tortoise oracle was not forgotten to later Chinese history and in fact enjoyed considerable fame in art, literature, and philosophy. The cosmic tortoise is known from ancient myths as the foundation of the world, but it is from traditions which coalesced around the **I Ching* (Book of Changes) that the sacred and mysterious significance of the tortoise is largely derived. The legend that the earth is supported by a tortoise is apparently attributable to the **Lieh-Tzu*; other legends explain the symbolism of the tortoise as more fully cosmic, since the round and vaulted shell represents the heavens, the flat underside the square earth with the four legs denoting the four quarters of earth.

Tortosa, Disputation of. A Jewish–Christian disputation held in Tortosa in 1413–14. The disputation was the longest of the medieval disputations. It was presided over by the *pope and was predominantly a missionary exercise on the part of the Christians. The Christian side was led by the *apostate, Geronimo de Santa Fé, who was always allowed to conclude the discussion. Jewish participants included Zerahiah ha-Levi, Astruc ha-Levi, Joseph *Albo, and Mattathias ha-Yizhari. Many Jews were baptized as a consequence.

Tosafot (Heb., 'additions'). Collections of comments on the Jewish *Talmud. The tosafot grew out of the French and German schools which aimed to develop and enlarge the Talmudic commentaries of *Rashi. The tosafot are records of discussions between teachers and pupils in the *yeshivot. The tosafot literature is vast: it extended to commentary on *Pentateuch commentary and even on the *halakhot of *Alfasi. It is normally included in editions of the Talmud so 'a page of *gemāra' means the text, Rashi's commentary (known as *perush*), and tosafot (collectively described by the acronym GaPaT).

Tosefta. A collection of works by the Jewish *tannaim. The Tosefta parallels and supplements the *Mishnah. It dates from *c.*2nd cent. CE, and has the same six orders as the Mishnah.

Tōshōdai-Ji (temple-complex): see NARA BUDDHISM.

Totemism. The practices and beliefs relating to the identification of a totem object. The word totem is taken from the Ojibwa of Canada, the word *dotem/oteman* signifying, 'he is a relative of mine'. Ojibwa clans are named after animal species, so that the totem idea expresses membership of the same exogamic group. However, the word 'totem' was applied, far more loosely, to animals, plants, or other objects associated with a social or kinship group, often regarded by the group as sacred. Totemism thus became the cornerstone of far-reaching theories of religion, e.g., *Durkheim and *Freud. However, totemism is neither an institution nor a religion, but is rather a classificatory device which mediates between conceptions of the natural world and social categories and relations. It is a mode of thought in which relations are established through totemic emblems of such a kind that a single, unified cosmos is envisaged and established.

Totum simul (Lat., 'everything' + 'at the same time'), a synonym for *eternity, derived from *Boethius.

Tour of Victory (journeys of pre-eminent Indian philosopher): see ŚAṄKARA.

Tou-shuai Ts'ung-yueh (1044–92). Ch'an/Zen master of the Ōryō lineage of *Rinzai, and dharma-successor (*hassu) of Pao-feng K'o-wen. He is remembered for the 'three barriers' *kōan (*Mumonkan* 47).

Tower of Silence (place where Zoroastrians and Parsis dispose of dead bodies): see DAXMA.

Toyouke Okami (Ise shrine deity): see ISE.

Tōzan Ryōkai (co-founder of school of Buddhism): see TUNG-SHAN LIANG-CHIEH.

Tractarians. The early leaders of the *Oxford Movement, so-named from the series of *Tracts for the Times* (1833–41) in which their ideals were expounded. The name is therefore also used for those of a *high church tendency.

Tradition. The formal transmission of information (both verbal and non-verbal) in religions. In non-text religions, the process of tradition is all the more vital since there is no independent repository of information in written form, whether designated as *scripture or not—hence the foundational importance of *myth and *ritual in all religions. In Judaism, tradition became the authoritative interpretation and application of *Torah, handed down, initially in oral form, from teacher (*rabbi) to pupil. This tradition became of such importance that it was designated 'second Torah', *Torah she be'al peh* ('Torah transmitted by word of mouth'; see HALAKHAH). More widely, tradition in Judaism is referred to as *masoret*, which in the *Talmud includes custom, law, history, and folklore. Tradition (see ḤADĪTH) is equally formal in Islam, since *Muḥammad and his companions were the first living commentators on *Qur'ān. In Christianity, the status of tradition is more complex (and controversial), since one part of the Church (the *Roman Catholic) has given to tradition (as the unfolding of scripture) a defining role in some matters of salvation: that which is at best dimly alluded to in scripture, or only to be inferred (e.g. *purgatory, the *Assumption of the Blessed Virgin Mary) can be defined by the pope *ex cathedra: such definitions are *infallible and irreformable—i.e. tradition has become equivalent to scripture. The formality of transmission in other religions can be seen in the importance of the *saṃpradāyas among Hindus (see also VEDA), and the succession lists and transmission procedures and rituals among some Buddhists.

Traducianism (the generation of souls): see CREATIONISM (2).

Traherne, Thomas (*c.*1636–74). *Anglican clergyman, and *Metaphysical poet. His main work remained unpublished until the beginning of the 20th cent., when his *Poems* and *Centuries of Meditation* appeared. Trusting the divine intuitions of childhood, he expresses a strong sense of the mystical embrace.

Trailokya (regions of the cosmos in Buddhism): see LOKA (BUDDHISM).

Transcendental anthropology: see RAHNER, KARL.

Transcendentalists, New England: see EMERSON, R. W.

Transcendental meditation. Taught by *Maharishi Mahesh Yogi and comprising 'a specific and systematic mental technique which can be easily learnt and enjoyed by anyone, whatever his opinions or beliefs'. The Indian-based philosophy holds that this (*mantra) technique leads practitioners to 'the field of pure consciousness'. This alone 'is the self-sufficient reality of life'. Transcendental meditation is widely used, especially in America where it enters into the worlds of education, business, and welfare. This is in accord with Maharishi's aim of transforming society, especially through the World Government of the Age of Enlightenment.

Transcendental Thomism see RAHNER, KARL; NEO-THOMISM.

Transfiguration of Christ. The story recorded in the first three gospels (Mark 9. 2–13, etc.) according to which Jesus took on a glorious appearance alongside Moses and Elijah. The Feast of the Transfiguration on 6 Aug. has been observed in the East since before 1000 CE, and in the West since 1456.

Transmigration: see REBIRTH.

Transmission outside the scriptures (transmission of teaching and truth directly from teacher to pupil): see FUKASETSU.

Transubstantiation. In Catholic theology of the *eucharist, the change of the substance (underlying reality) of the bread and wine into the substance of the body and blood of Christ, leaving the 'accidents' (i.e. the appearances of the bread and wine) intact, so that the faithful do not literally touch Christ's body. The term was recognized at the Lateran Council of 1215, and was formally defined at *Trent in 1551. The E. Church entertains an essentially identical doctrine to transubstantiation, but many modern Orthodox theologians avoid the term because of its associations with Latin *scholasticism.

Trapeza (Greek altar): see ALTAR.

Trappists. Popular name (from La Trappe) for *Cistercians derived from the reform instituted by the abbot Armand de Rancé in 1664. Its rule is particularly severe (hence they are known as Cistercians of the more strict observance).

Trent, Council of (1545–63). A council of *Roman Catholic *bishops and superiors of *religious orders, reckoned by that church to be the 19th *ecumenical *council. It was convoked only after pressure from the Emperor Charles V, who hoped for reconciliation between Catholics and *Protestants in his German dominions. It met in three sessions at

Triento in N. Italy, 1545–9, 1551–2, and 1562–3. Protestant representatives attended only the second of these sessions, with no lasting effect. The fathers of the council rejected Protestant sacramental theory and *Luther's doctrine of *consubstantiation, in the latter case endorsing the theory of *transubstantiation. Among the ecclesiastical reforms there was an attempt to abolish pluralism, an insistence that bishops must reside in their sees, a provision of better education for, and closer control over, the clergy, and a reform of the Roman *curia. It also reasserted the traditional teaching on a number of issues such as *indulgences, the existence of *purgatory, and the veneration of *saints. It was, perhaps, the single most significant element in the *Counter-Reformation.

Tretā-yuga. The second of the four *yugas, or divisions of *time, in Hinduism. It lasts 1,296,000 years: sacrifice begins, but righteousness declines; it is the yuga during which *Rāma appears as *avatāra (incarnation).

Triads (secret societies): see SECRET SOCIETIES.

Tribes, the twelve. The traditional composition and division of the Jewish people. The twelve tribes were supposedly descended from the sons and grandsons of the patriarch *Jacob. They include Reuben, Simeon (Levi), Judah, Issachar, Zebulun, Benjamin, Dan, Naphtali, Gad, Asher, Ephraim, and Manasseh.

Tricivara (wearing a robe made of three pieces, in Buddhism): see DHŪTANGA.

Trickster (term introduced by D. G. Brinton, *Myths of the New World*, 1868). A hero, and also anti-hero, in many religions and cultures. Although the Trickster was identified particularly in the stories of N. American Indians, the recognition of similar characteristics in a wide range of stories has led to the emergence of a kind of composite figure, of one who subverts and satirizes the norms of society, and yet who emerges as hero: Brer Rabbit is a familiar example.

Tridharma (Skt., 'three teachings'). An Indonesian group which bases its beliefs on a combination of those of *Buddha, *Confucius, and *Lao-Tzu. It was founded in Jakarta in 1938 by Kwee Tekhoay, a Chinese writer.

Trika(śāsana). *Kashmir *Śaiva system which postulates three fundamental sources of all appearance: *Śiva, who creates from his imagination the world as though independent of himself, whereas it is always an expression of his will; *Śakti as the energy through which this is achieved; and Aṇu as the individualized *ātman who takes local initiatives. The system was elaborated by Vasugupta (770–830), whose main works are *Śiva-Sūtra* and *Spanda-Kārikā*.

Trikāya (Skt., 'three bodies'; Chin., *san-shen*; Jap., *sanshin*; Korean, *samsin*). A doctrine which came to prominence in *Mahāyāna Buddhism according to which the *Buddha manifests himself in three bodies (trikāya), modes, or dimensions.

Several centuries after his death, these three facets of the Buddha's nature were articulated in the form of a doctrine developed initially by the *Sarvāstivāda school, but quickly taken up and elaborated by the Mahāyāna. According to this development, the Buddha, and all Buddhas were, in their essential nature, identical with the ultimate truth or absolute reality. This is their first 'body'. At the same time, Buddhas have the power to manifest themselves in a sublime celestial form in splendid paradises where they teach the doctrine surrounded by hosts of *bodhisattvas and supernatural beings. This is their second body. Furthermore, motivated by boundless compassion, they project themselves into the world of suffering beings (e.g. the human world) disguised in an appropriate manner through the use of skilful means (*upāya-kauśalya) so as not to frighten and alarm, but instead to provide that which is most necessary and useful. This is their third body.

A Buddha in human form is called a Nirmāṇakāya (Skt., 'transformation body') and one in celestial form is called a *Saṃbhogakāya (Skt., 'enjoyment body'); the identification of these two bodies with particular figures varies with the lineage (see BUDDHIST SCHOOLS). The unmanifest form is the Dharmakāya (Skt., 'dharma body') which is synonymous with *Tathatā (Skt., 'Thus-ness') and *Tathāgatagarbha (Skt., 'womb *or* embryo of the Buddhas'). In the Tantric tradition, the Dharmakāya is said to be manifest as an *Ādi-Buddha (Skt., 'Original Buddha')—identified in different lineages as *Vajradhara, *Vairocana, *Samantabhadra, etc. —who is non-dual with his unmanifest ultimate nature. The unity of the Trikāya is sometimes taught as a fourth aspect, *Svabhāvikakāya* (Skt., 'essential body').

Trikona yantra (Skt., 'triangle'). Hindu diagram of two intersecting triangles. The downward-pointing triangle represents masculinity and God, the upward femininity and *śakti.

Trilocana (Skt., 'three-eyed'). Epithet of *Śiva in Hinduism. According to *Mahābhārata*, *Pārvatī, his consort, covered his eyes in play, and a burning third eye burst forth in his forehead. Śiva is often portrayed with a third eye, surmounted by a crescent moon, and he uses it destructively—e.g. of *Kāma, for evoking amorous thoughts in Pārvatī. The 'third eye' is also claimed by adepts, especially in Tibet, to give spiritual vision: see ŪRṆĀ.

Triloka (three constituent domains in the cosmos): see LOKA.

Trimārga (Skt., 'three ways'). The three major ways through which Hindus can approach *mokṣa (release). They are *karma-mārga (the way of action, especially of sacrificial ritual), *jñāna-mārga (the way of knowledge, especially associated with *Upaniṣads and *Vedānta), and bhakti-mārga (the way of devotion to God).

Trimūrti (Skt., 'of three forms'). The Hindu recognition of threefold interaction being necessary for creation and dissolution, hence especially the three interrelated manifestations of the divine: *Brahmā, *Viṣṇu, and *Śiva. As Brahmā diminished in importance, the 'social' necessity of being (cf. TRINITY) led to Viṣṇu or especially Śiva being represented in threefold activity.

Trinity, The. A predominantly Christian understanding of the inner nature of the Godhead. Trinitarian understandings of God may arise primarily from revelation, as Christians affirm, but they are more widely embedded in a belief that there is an analogical relationship between God and the created or manifest world (see ANALOGY): since in this world it is only possible to be a self in a field of selves, the inference is drawn that the interior nature of God must be relational, and not monistically abstract. Among Hindus, the relational character of God may be dipolar, with opposites united in a single character and action, but equally, as in the *Trimūrti emphasis, it may be of far greater complexity. None of this contradicts the insistence in Islam (though many Muslims suppose that it does) on *tawḥīd, the absolute unity of God, since whatever God may turn out to be, it can only be God that God turns out to be—though it so happens that that nature is relational: see also SAN-I in Taoism; TRIKĀYA in Buddhism.

It is, however, in Christianity that the Trinitarian nature of God has been most complexly explored, affirming that there is the one God, who exists in three persons: Father, Son, and *Holy Spirit. The basis for this doctrine in the Bible consists of threefold formulae like Matthew 28. 19; 1 Peter 1. 2, and Isaiah 6. 3. These passages in no way predicate a God who is eternally three in one, but they set the terms for later thinking toward that end. In the 3rd and early 4th cents., against *Sabellianism and *Arianism, the Son and Father were defined as distinct yet coequal and coeternal. In the late 4th cent. the *Cappadocian Fathers took the final step by understanding the Holy Spirit as of the same status. God was then to be spoken of as one *ousia* (being) in three *hypostases (persons), and this has remained the orthodox formulation.

Many modern scholars have said that, given the essential mystery of the doctrine, the two kinds of conceptions need not be considered incompatible: the doctrine of the Trinity is a necessary consequence of *Christology, and takes seriously the necessity for interrelation in the formation of all appearance or reality. The *patristic concept of *circumincessio* (Gk., *(em)perichoresis*), the inner involvement of the Three Persons, anticipates the current social model of the Trinity, of three distinct realities, inseparably requiring each other to be the sort of reality they are, and therefore also only one reality.

Trinity Sunday. In W. Christian churches, the first Sunday after *Pentecost. Its observance was made binding on the Church by Pope John XXII in 1334.

In the **Book of Common Prayer* the Sundays until Advent are numbered 'after Trinity'.

Tripiṭaka (Skt., 'Triple Basket'; Chin., *San-ts'ang*; Jap., *Sanzō*; Korean, *Samjang*). The threefold collection of authoritative texts in Buddhism. It is used more loosely in *Mahāyāna Buddhism to mean the entire body of the Buddhist scriptures, corresponding to the Pāli Tripiṭaka in its general meaning, although the content and arrangement of the Mahāyāna canons, of which the chief are the Chinese Tripiṭaka and the Tibetan canon, are significantly different.

The Pali Tripiṭaka is the most fundamental collection extant, though it is believed that each of the original eighteen schools of Buddhism had tripiṭakas of their own. It is divided into three parts, *Sutra/Sutta Pitaka (discourses), *Vināya (rules for the *saṅgha) and *Abhidharma/*Abhidhamma (philosophical and psychological analysis). During the *Mahāyāna period, new texts were added to the canon, both Mahāyāna sūtras and *śāstra material, written by influential thinkers such as *Nāgārjuna. At a later date still, *Tantric material was introduced. This explains why the old threefold division is obscured in the Chinese and Tibetan tripiṭakas (the Tib. tripiṭaka is divided between *bka-'gyur*, containing works attributed to the Buddha himself, amounting to more than 100 vols., and *bstan-'gyur*, 220 vols. of mainly commentaries). See also KOREAN TRIPIṬAKA.

*Buddhaghosa records the early fivefold division of the Sutta piṭaka into *Dīgha Nikāya,

*Majjhima Nikāya, *Saṃyutta Nikāya, *Aṅguttara Nikāya, and *Khuddaka Nikāya (not all of which is recognized as canonical by all schools). In the Indian (Skt.) canon (little of which has survived outside translation), the corresponding divisions of the Sūtra piṭaka are Dīrghāgama, Madyamāgama, Saṃyuktāgama, Ekottarāgama, and Kṣudrakāgama: more is included in the āgamas than in the nikāyas, the arrangement is often different, and the texts also may be different in details of expression; the differences do not affect the overall content of teaching.

The *Vinaya piṭaka is divided into three parts: Suttavibhaṅga, containing the Pātimokkha casuistic rules; the Khandhaka, containing complementary rules which address communal life and ceremonies, and seek to avert schism; and the Parivāra, ancillary works which amount to an appendix making the earlier parts more manageable.

The Abhidhamma piṭaka is made up of logical and philosophical analysis gathered under headings (*mātikā*) which give brief notes on the doctrine in question. In the *Theravāda tradition, there are seven books; other schools have different collections, but all undertaken in the same style.

The development of the sūtra tradition led to four major collections: Prajñāpāramitā (*Perfection of Wisdom), (Mahā)ratnakūṭa (found mainly in 5th-cent. Chinese translations, sūtras which seem to be a compendium of Mahāyāna teaching), Buddhāvataṃsaka (see AVATAṂSAKA for an example), and Mahāsaṃnipāta (a diverse collection showing an interest in *magic).

The addition of Tantric texts represents the last stage of the Buddhist canon. They are now divided into four groups: (i) Kriyātantra, describing relatively obvious and accessible rituals; (ii) Caryātantra, more advanced 'outer ritual' and the beginnings of 'inner yoga'; (iii) Yogatantra, the workings of 'inner yoga' in meditation and trance; (iv) Anuttarayogatantra, esoteric rituals, often concerned with the workings of sexual symbolism, accessible only to the initiated.

Triple Body (of the Buddha): see TRIKĀYA.

Tripuṇḍra (three marks indicating allegiance): see TARPAṆA.

Tripuṭi (Skt., 'threefold sheath'). The Hindu analysis of appearance in terms of a metaphysic of relationships. If there is one field of reality, nevertheless it exists or appears in the relationship of subject, object, and the relation between the two—as lover, beloved, and love created between them. In Hinduism, such a metaphysic of perception contributes to illusion and has to be transcended.

Triratna (three fundamental commitments of a Buddhist): see THREE JEWELS.

Trisagion or **Trisyatoe.** Christian *hymn beginning 'Agios O Theos' ('holy God'), of great antiquity, and now embedded in the *liturgy. It is reputed to be the hymn of praise sung by the *angels in heaven.

Triśalā. Mother of Vardhamāna *Mahāvīrā. Śvetāmbara sources recount how Triśalā experienced fourteen dreams (the *Digambaras claim sixteen) before Mahāvīrā's birth, which were portents of the birth of a great teacher. These dreams are recalled today by Jains when they celebrate the five auspicious moments (*kalyāṇakas*) in Mahāvīrā's life, of which the first is conception.

Triśaraṇa (Skt.; Pāli, *tisaraṇa*, 'threefold refuge'). Basic Buddhist orientation of life, taking refuge in the *Three Jewels (*triratna*): the *Buddha, the *dharma, and the *saṅgha.

Triśula (Skt., 'trident'). *Śiva's emblem in Hinduism, denoting his threefold role (*trimūrti) in creating, sustaining, and destroying; or his use of the three *guṇas. Śaivites frequently set up a triśula before worship (*pūjā).

Trisvabhāva (three aspects, central teaching of Vijñānavāda): see VIJÑĀNAVĀDA.

'Trito-Isaiah' (chapters in biblical book): see ISAIAH.

Trivikrama (cosmic version of Hindu god): see VĀMANA.

Triyāna (Skt., 'three vehicles'). The *Mahāyāna Buddhist analysis of the three vehicles that bring one toward *nirvāna: (i) *śravaka-yāna = *Hīnayāna; (ii) *pratyeka-yāna; (iii) *bodhisattva-yāna = Mahāyāna.

Troeltsch, Ernst (1865–1923). Christian historian of culture and religion. He became professor of systematic theology at Heidelberg in 1894, and professor of 'religious, social and historical philosophy and the history of the Christian religion' at Berlin in 1915. The latter title points effectively to Troeltsch's general position. Historical relativism (or 'historicism') suggests that cultural values are embedded in history and change over time. No religions (including Christianity) express absolute values which are exempt from this process; and the recognition that this is so is the consequence of the modern historical consciousness—and that is why Troeltsch maintained that the modern age began with the Enlightenment, not with the Reformation, which he regarded as a medieval phenomenon. But in that case, is there anything about religion which persists and endures through the vicissitudes of time? Here, Troeltsch, like R. *Otto, took a *Kantian line, and argued that there is an *a priori* religious mode of consciousness, which brings religions, in all their variety and relativity, into being. In *Die Absolutheit des Christentums* ... (1902; The Absoluteness of Christianity ...) he claimed that Christianity is 'relatively absolute' (*relativer absolutismus*) as a religion because it, more than any other religion, affirms the value of personal and ethical beings, locating this character in God and exhibiting it in Christ. His development of the *Church–Sect (and mysticism) typology has remained influential. In his major work, *Die Soziallehren der christlichen Kirchen und Gruppen* (1912; The Social Teaching of the Christian Churches), he argued that underprivileged and less educated populations are the driving force in religious creativity, since they feel more and ask less.

Tṛṣṇa (Skt., 'thirst'). 1. In Hinduism, tṛṣṇa is the longing for life which keeps one bound to *saṃsāra (continuing rebirth); it must be contested by deliberate exercise (*sādhana).

2. In Buddhism, it is more closely analysed. See under its Pāli form, *taṇhā.

Trungpa, Rinpoche Vidyadhara Chögyam (1939–87). Tibetan Buddhist of Kagyü and Nyingma schools. He was recognized as the eleventh Trungpa Tulku when 1 year old and began training, including *Vajrayāna. He escaped to India when the Chinese invaded Tibet, and in 1963 received a Spalding award to study at Oxford. In 1967, he co-founded Samyé-Ling Tibetan Centre in Scotland, and married. Conflict in Scotland meant that in 1970 he left for N. America, where he founded several centres. He also established the Vajradhātu Association of Buddhist Churches. His autobiography (co-authored) is *Born in Tibet* (1977), and he wrote many other works mediating Tibetan Buddhism to the West.

Tsaddik (Ḥasidic leader): see ZADDIK.

Ts'ai-shen. *Taoist god of prosperity, one of the most important gods of religious Taoism (*tao-chiao*), and of folk religion. He is usually portrayed with a dark face and heavy moustache.

Ts'ao Kuo-chiu (one of eight immortals): see PA-HSIEN.

Ts'ao-shan Pen-chi (Jap., Sōzan Honjaku; 840–901). Co-founder, with his teacher (of whom he was dharma-successor, *hassu) *Tung-shan Liang-chieh, of *Ts'ao-tung. He stayed with him only three years or so, but perfectly understood what Tung-shan was attempting to say, eventually expressed in the Five Ranks (see also GO-I). The histories list nineteen disciples, but within four generations his line ended. His true succession lies in *Sōtō.

Ts'ao-tung (Jap., Sōtō). Ch'an/Zen school of Buddhism, the name being derived from the graphs of the two founders, *Tung-shan Liang-chieh and Ts'ao-shan Pen-chi, who in turn received their names from the mountains of their monasteries. In its Chinese form, it is also known as 'The Five Ranks', from its fivefold approach to recognizing the identity of the absolute and the relative, the one and the many. The stanzas of the Five Ranks are now regarded as the consummation of the *kōan process. See further GO-I. Ts'ao-tung is one of the Five Houses of Ch'an Buddhism in the period of the Five Dynasties; but its future lay in Japan as *Sōtō.

Tseng-tzu (supposed author of **Hsiao Ching*): see HSIAO.

Tshar (sect of Sakya): see SAKYA.

Tsha-tshas. Small clay or dough images of holy persons, *chörtens, symbols etc., in Tibetan Buddhism, which may be made with herbs, ground relics, or the ashes of a dead *lama mixed in. They are used as amulets.

Tsimtsum (contraction in Godhead): see LURIA, ISAAC BEN SOLOMON.

Tsitsit (fringes on a prayer shawl): see ZITZIT.

Tso-ch'an. Chinese for *zazen.

Tsong Khapa (Lobsang Drakpa, *blo.bzang.-sgrags. pa*; 1357–1419). Eminent Tibetan scholar and founder of the *Geluk school of Tibetan Buddhism.

At the age of 40, and as probably the most learned man of his era, Tsong Khapa joined the *Kadam monastery of Radreng (*rva.sgreng*). Here, in 1402, Tsong Khapa completed his *magnum opus*, *The Great Graduated Path* (*lam.rim. chen.mo*), which was principally based on *Atiśa's *Bodhipathapradīpa*, and has become the root text of the Geluk school. As elsewhere in his voluminous writings, Tsong Khapa emphasizes *Prāsaṅgīka-madhyāmaka as the highest form of reasoning and stresses the correct understanding of relative reality as that which, while not possessing even a conventional own-being, can nevertheless be demonstrated by reasoning to be not non-existent. At the heart of *The Great Graduated Path* is the thesis that, while tantra may be necessary in order to become a fully enlightened Buddha, a prior study of sūtra is absolutely necessary for a preliminary development of wisdom and compassion. In another important work, *The Great Graduated Path of Mantra* (*sngags.rim.chen.mo*), which discusses the four classes of tantra, Tsong Khapa defines the relationship of tantra to sūtra as that between method and wisdom.

In 1408, Tsong Khapa established the Great Prayer (*smon.lam.chen.mo*), a New Year festival held in the *Jokhang, which won him much devotional support. In 1409, Tsong Khapa had enough followers to found his own monastery of Riwo Ganden ('Joyous Mountain'), and although initially calling his order the 'New Kadam', they soon became known as the Geluk. Tsong Khapa's views were similar to those of Atiśa, and it is unclear whether Tsong Khapa had reformed a Kadam tradition which had become lax, or whether the Geluk simply grew out of the Kadam under the impetus of his own personal renown. The founding of Drepung (*'bras.sprungs*) followed in 1416, and of Sera in 1419, the year of Tsong Khapa's death when his body was embalmed and placed inside a *chörten at Ganden.

Tsou Yen (4th/3rd cent. BCE). One of the earliest Chinese philosophers to systematize a naturalism based on *yin-yang—hence the Yin-yang school (or more fully Yin-yang Wu-hsing-chia, Yin-yang Five Phases School). Through the interaction of male–female, light–dark, heavy–light, heaven–earth, and other opposites, the *T'ai-chi, the primordial foundation, works its way into manifestation by use of the five elements (*wu-hsing).

Tso-wang (Chin., 'sitting forgetting'). *Taoist technique of meditation in which the mind floats completely free from content and association and is at one with Tao. Its attainment is described in *Chuang-tzu* 6. 7.

Tsukimi (moon festival): see FESTIVALS AND FASTS.

Tsung (ancestral): see CHINESE RELIGION.

Tsung-chiao (religion): see CHINESE RELIGION.

Ts'ung-jung Lu (collection of kōans): see KŌAN.

Tsung-mi (5th patriarch): see FIVE WAYS OF CH'AN/ZEN; HUA-YEN.

Ts'un-ssu (Chin., 'sustaining the thought'). *Taoist method of meditation, concentrating on a particular object. This may be literal or conceptual (e.g. the three treasures, *san-pao), or it may be the visualization of the inner deities.

Tsuya (Jap., 'all night'). The Japanese practice of keeping vigil over the dead; the relatives, friends, and acquaintances of the dead keep a watch over his or her soul all night before the day of the funeral ceremony.

Tübingen School. A group of scholars of early Christianity who were influential in the mid-19th cent. They were led by F. C. *Baur and included E. Zeller, A. Hilgenfeld, A. Schwegler, and (for a time) A. Ritschl. In their view, influenced by *Hegel's conception of history, the early church was divided into a Jewish party led by Peter and a gentile party led by Paul. The opposition of the two parties was resolved only in the *'catholic' synthesis of the 2nd cent., at which time the bulk of the New Testament was written. Baur's influence declined after the 1840s, and the work of A. *Harnack and J. B. Lightfoot is usually said to have led to the abandonment of its positions.

Tu bi-Shevat. Jewish *festival of *New Year for trees. This festival is celebrated on 15 Shevat. In Israel, the festival has become one of thanksgiving for the revival of the land, accompanied, often, by ceremonial tree-plantings by children.

Tucci, G. (1894–1984). Italian explorer and orientalist, the most influential scholar of Indian and Tibetan *Mahāyāna Buddhism of recent times. He organized a total of eight expeditions to Tibet, and in 1948 he stayed in Lhasa as a personal guest of the fourteenth Dalai Lama and was the only W. Buddhist scholar to spend time at the monastic citadel of *bSam-yas*. Among his more important publications are *Tibetan Painted Scrolls* (1949), *The Religions of Tibet* (1980), *The Theory and Practice of the Mandala* (1949), and *Storia della filosofia indiana* (1957).

Tukārām (*c.*1607–1649). Hindu poet, who, after an unhappy second marriage, turned to religion, starting with the worship of Viṭhobā at Paṇḍherpur. He studied the **Bhāgavata* of *Eknāth, and after a period of study and meditation, began composing verses in Abhaṇga metre. His Abhaṇgas number 6,000–8,000 and are devotional in character, with practical advice for the ordinary man and woman.

'Tukutendereza' (revivialist chorus: 'We praise thee, Jesus'): see EAST AFRICAN REVIVAL.

Tulasīdās: see TULSĪDĀS.

Tulku (Tib., *sprul.sku.*, 'Transformation Body'). A title applied in Tibetan Buddhism to a reincarnate *lama, i.e. to one who is understood to have already attained lamahood in a previous life. Thus the present fourteenth *Dalai Lama, for example, is considered to be the same 'person' as the first Dalai Lama, successively reincarnating within the same office.

Tulsi (leader of Jain sect, the Terapanth): see BHIKṢU, ĀCĀRYA.

Tulsīdās or **Tulasīdās** (1532–1623). Indian poet and devotee of *Rāma. He retold the

*Rāmāyaṇa in Hindi. His *Ramcaritamānasa* (The Holy Lake of the Deeds of Rāma) is far from being a translation, and remains a profoundly influential spiritual encouragement (sometimes called 'the Bible of North India'). Later, he wrote *Kavitāvali* poems (of that metre) to Rāma, and *Vinaya-patrikā*, the petition to Rāma, and at least seven other works.

Tummo (one of the Six Doctrines of Naropa): see NĀRO CHOS DRUG.

T'ung Chung-shu (*c*.180–*c*.105 BCE). Confucian philosopher who effected the connection between the assumptions underlying the Yin-yang school (*Tsou Yen) and the state, thus opening the way for *Confucianism to become the state religion. His major work is *Ch'un-ch'iu fan-lu* (Profound Meaning of the Spring and Autumn Annals). T'ien has a will and creates all things for a purpose: for humans, that purpose is to sustain order. For this reason, *t'ien-ming (Mandate of Heaven) is conferred on the emperor who must respond to this trust with moral excellence. In this way, *t'ien-chih* (the will of heaven) is expressed in the world. It is manifest especially in the Three Bonds of yang and yin which hold society together: ruler (yang) and subject (yin), father and son, husband and wife.

Tung-shan Liang-chieh (Jap., Tōzan Ryōkai; 807–69). Co-founder, with his pupil *Ts'ao-shan, of *Tsao-tung. He began his temple education when young, and was soon recognized as exceptional, and was sent, eventually, to Yün-yen T'an-sheng, through whom he acquired power to 'understand the sermons of inanimate things', i.e. to hear them silently eloquent of their undifferentiated nature. He became dharma-successor (*hassu) of *Yün-yen.

Tun-huang (Dunhuang). Town in NW of Kansu province in China, a major staging post on the Silk Road trading route. Because it was the point of access to China for Buddhist *missionaries travelling on the overland route from India, it became an important Buddhist centre. The major remains of this presence are in the Mo-kao (Mogao) Caves, also known as the Caves of a Thousand Buddhas, the oldest Buddhist shrines in China.

Tun-wu ju-tao yao-men lun (Zen text on enlightenment): see TA-CHU HUI-HAI.

Turban (Pañjābī, 'pagg', 'pagṛī'). Headdress of male *keśadhārī Sikhs from boyhood. Although not one of the *Five Ks, the turban distinguishes male *khālsā Sikhs as the *keś* (uncut hair) must be covered in this way.

Turbulent priest: see BECKET, THOMAS À.

Turin Shroud (Christian relic): see SHROUD OF TURIN.

Turīya (Skt., 'the fourth'). The accomplished state of absolute consciousness in Hinduism, beyond waking, dreaming, and deep sleep. It is the realization of the *ātman as *Brahman. The four states are described and analysed in **Māṇḍūkya Upaniṣad* 12.

Turner, Victor (1920–83). British social and cultural anthropologist latterly working in the USA, best known for his investigations of the meaning, nature, grounds, and functions of Ndembu (Zambia) rituals and symbols. His interest in Ndembu *rites of passage, where liminal periods are important, encouraged Turner to advance the theory of communitas: as well as structured interaction, all societies require contexts of anti-structure; contexts in which bare, and so equal, individuals can recognize their 'humankindness'. At the end of his life, he came to realize that the emphasis in his work (and his teaching of other anthropologists) had been wrong, and that he should have recognized that *biogenetic structuralism was correct in returning a genetic contribution to human (and thus religious) behaviours: see his 'Body, Brain and Culture', *Zygon* (1983), 221 ff.

Tu-shun or **Fa-shun** (557–640). First patriarch of the Chinese Buddhist *Hua-yen school. Beginning life in the army, he became a monk at 18 and originated the theory of the 'ten gates', which were reworked by *Fa-tsang, the founder of the school.

Tuṣita (Skt., 'contented ones'). Buddhist heaven inhabited by the 'contented gods' (*deva). It is the domain of all *buddhas who need to reappear only once more on earth to work out the last remnants of *karma. It is the domain also of *Maitreya.

T'u-t'an chai (Tao ritual): see CHAI.

T'u-ti. A Chinese deity, the 'earth god', an ubiquitous deity worshipped in almost every village or district of China. His dwelling is the sacred space of the community, whether it is a simple mark or a modest roadside shrine.

Hou-t'u is an earlier name for Earth God. 'Hou' denotes fertility or the generative force in Chou times. 'Hou-t'u' therefore denotes the generative force of the earth.

Fu-teh Chen-shen (God of Prosperity and Virtue) is a later name for Earth God. It was given by religious *Taoism in the Sung dynasty (960–1279). 'Chen-shen' is a Taoist designation for divinity, connoting immortality. As Fu-teh Chen-shen, Earth God has become a member of the Taoist pantheon.

Tutu, Desmond Mpilo (b. 1931). Archbishop of Cape Town, and determined opponent of apartheid (see DUTCH REFORMED CHURCH). He was ordained Anglican priest in 1961. He became bishop of Johannesburg (1985–6) and archbishop in 1986. His opposition to apartheid, conducted with dignity and non-violence, earned him the Nobel Peace Prize in 1984. He is the author of *Crying in the Wilderness* (1982) and *Hope and Suffering* (1984).

Tvaṣṭṛ. The craftsman of the gods in Hinduism. The ability to create new forms from formless stone, wood, etc., is a manifestation of divine power embodied in Tvaṣṭṛ (*Atharva Veda* 12. 3. 33), and only animals with testicles (i.e. begetters) can be offered to him in sacrifice. He is one of the *Ādityas.

Twelfth Night. A Christian observance, the evening preceding *Epiphany (twelve days after *Christmas). It commemorated the different epiphanies of *Christ, e.g. to the shepherds, to the *magi, to the world when he changed water to wine. When the feast was adopted in the West, it became an occasion for festivity and games.

Twelvers, The (Shi'a movement): see ITHNĀ 'ASHARĪYA.

Twelve Tribes (division of the Jewish people): see TRIBES, TWELVE.

Twice-born. An epithet of the first three *varnas, *brahmans, *kṣatriyas, and *vaiśyas, since the males of these three groups are seen as achieving a second, spiritual, birth (*dvija, 'twice-born') at the investiture of the sacred thread (*upanayana).

'Twice-born' is also used of those who have undergone a 'born-again' experience in religion. Although it is usually used of Christians who have undergone a reconversion experience, William *James recognized it as a category in all religions.

Tyāgarāja (1767–1847). Born Tyāgabrahmam, the *primus inter pares* of three S. Indian composers, the others being Muttusvami Dīkṣitar (1777–1835) and Śyāmā Śāstri (1762–1821). Tyāgarāja was a devotee of *Rāma, who resisted invitations to become a court musician—many of his compositions were spontaneous reactions to places of pilgrimage. He believed profoundly that music rested in the primordial creativity of sound (see MANTRA), and that music combined with *bhakti would lead more directly to *mokṣa (release) than any other route, including *yoga.

Tylor, Sir Edward Burnett (1832–1917). The 'father' of cultural anthropology, whose most influential work was *Primitive Culture* (2 vols., 1871). In his view (first expressed in 1866), animism is the earliest form of religion, to be studied through 'survivals'.

Tyndale, William, or **Huchens** (*c.*1494–1536). Biblical translator and religious reformer. He was born in Gloucestershire, and worked for his BA and MA at Magdalen Hall, Oxford, 1506–15. From Oxford, he may have gone to Cambridge before becoming tutor to the children of Sir John Walsh in Gloucestershire (important for *Lollardy) in 1522. After failing to gain patronage in London, Tyndale went probably to Wittenberg, but then to Cologne and to Worms (all connected with the Protestant *Reformation). His translation of the New Testament was published in Worms in 1526 and was smuggled to England. The Pentateuch came next (Antwerp, 1530), the first translation ever made of Hebrew into English; *Joshua* and *II Chronicles* followed. His New Testament was ceremoniously burnt in London in 1526, and his own life was in danger from English spies and Henry VIII's allies. In 1535 he was imprisoned in the castle of Volvorde, and after trial for heresy he was strangled and burnt at the stake, 6 Oct. 1536, praying that God would 'open the King of England's eyes'. His translations were not immediately used in England (when the Great Bible, see COVERDALE, was finally printed), but they underlie some 80 per cent of the *Authorized Bible (1611).

Typology (Gk., *typos*, 'example, figure'). A method of exegesis which takes a text as having a symbolic or anticipatory reference in addition to its apparent historical sense. It is characteristic of traditional Christian readings of the Old Testament.

Tyrrell, George (1861–1909). *Modernist theologian. An Irish *Protestant by birth, he became a *Roman Catholic and joined the *Jesuits in England. He became increasingly dissatisfied with *scholasticism, and stressed the experiential aspects of religion and the relativity of theology and doctrinal formulations (e.g. in *Through Scylla and Charybdis*, 1907, and more radically in *Christianity at the Crossroads*, 1909). Expelled from the Jesuits in 1906, he suffered minor excommunication in 1907, and was refused Roman Catholic burial.

Tzitzit (fringes on a prayer shawl): see ZITZIT.

Tzu (Chin., 'ancestor'). Respect for, and sustenance of, ancestors is as central in Chinese religion as in any other. They are commemorated on plaques, before which food and offerings are left, and with which conversations are held, so that ancestors remain a part of the family.

For the importance of sustaining ancestors in appropriate ways, see HUN; KUEI.

Tzu Ssu (author of Confucian text): see CHUNG YUNG.

U

U (Jap., 'being'). Existent appearance, in Japanese Buddhism, in contrast to *mu. It is therefore the constituent cause of appearance, as well as the state produced by the working out of *karma.

UAHC: see UNION OF AMERICAN HEBREW CONGREGATIONS.

Ubiquity (Lat., *ubique*, 'everywhere'). The claim, in general, that God is present to all events and circumstances, i.e. is omnipresent. In *Luther, ubiquity is the presence of Christ to each enactment of the *Lord's Supper.

Ucceda-diṭṭhi (nihilism): see UCCHEDAVĀDA; NIHILISM.

Ucchedavāda (Pāli, Skt., 'the doctrine of the cutting-off (of the soul and the body)'). Annihilationism (*nihilism), the doctrine of no afterlife in any form whatsoever, the belief that personal identity perishes with the body at death. It and its antithesis, *eternalism, occur in the Buddhist *Nikāyas as the two most common forms of misrepresenting reality.

Ucchiṣṭa (Skt., 'left over'). The remnants/remainders of a sacrifice in Hinduism. The continuing power within them helps to sustain the world (*Atharva Veda* 11. 7).

Uchimura Kanzō (1861–1930). Pioneer Japanese *Protestant leader and founder of the Non-Church (Mukyōkai) movement.

Uchimura spent four years studying in the USA at Amherst College and Hartford Seminary, returning in 1888. Two years later, he became a teacher in the new government academy to prepare students for the Imperial University. On 9 Jan. 1891, the teachers were compelled to participate in a ceremony that became standard procedure for all schools in the Japanese empire until the end of the Second World War. This was to make a low bow of obeisance before a personally signed copy of the Imperial Rescript on Education, which had been promulgated the previous autumn. Some Christian teachers absented themselves from school to avoid the issue of possible idolatry. Uchimura refused to do this, and in the presence of sixty professors and over 1,000 students he went forward but did not bow.

Uchimura was assured by Christian friends that bowing in this case was not an act of worship, and after reflection he decided to conform. The incident, however, became a *cause célèbre*, and Uchimura was forced to resign his post. He continued to support himself by teaching, but from 1892 he turned seriously to writing.

Uchimura was primarily concerned for Christian freedom, and in the context of his own time and place this meant the spiritual independence of Japanese Christians *vis-à-vis* the almost overwhelming cultural influence of W. forms of Christianity. For this reason Uchimura was able to speak with telling power to members of Japanese churches as well as to those of Mukyōkai, to non-Christians as to Christians. He affirmed *both* Japan *and* Jesus, and was often attacked from each side.

Uchiwamaki (fan festival): see NARA BUDDHISM.

Udāna. 1. In Hinduism, 'breathing upwards', the *prāṇa which unites the physical and metaphysical aspects of human form.

2. In Buddhism (solemn utterances): see KHUDDAKA NIKĀYA.

Udāsī (Pañjābī, 'withdrawn, dejected', from Skt., *udas*, 'grief'). 1. Ascetic Sikh order. The Udāsīs revere Gurū *Nānak and the *Ādi Granth, claiming as their founder Srī Chand, Gurū Nānak's unmarried elder son. They emphasize celibacy (*brahmacarya) in contrast to the mainstream Sikh ideal of *grahastī, and so perpetuate *Nāth principles within Sikhism.

2. Gurū Nānak described the true udāsī or renunciant in *Vār Rāmkalī, Ādi Granth, p. 952.

3. In the *janam-sākhīs, udāsī refers to the travels of Gurū Nānak, perhaps because during these he assumed the appearance of travelling mendicants.

Udayana (1025–1100 CE). A Hindu theologian of the *Nyāya-Vaiśeṣika tradition who established arguments for the existence of God (*Īśvara) by means of the Indian syllogism. The main argument in his 'Handful of the Flowers of Logic' (*Nyāyakusumāñjali*) is a form of the *cosmological argument that the universe must have a maker as its cause because it has the nature of an effect.

Uddālaka Āruni (character in the Chandogya Upaniṣad): see CHANDOGYA UPANIṢAD.

Udgātṛ or **Udgātar.** One of four chief priests in a Hindu *sacrificial ritual. He chants the hymns of the **Sāma Veda*, the chant being called udgītha.

Uemura Masahisa (1858–1925). Pioneer Japanese *Protestant Christian leader. Uemura was a member of the original Yokohama Band. A characteristic of early Japanese Protestantism was the formation of 'bands' of young Christians, the best-known other bands being the Sapporo Band, from which came *Uchimura Kanzō, and the Kumamoto Band, from which came Niijima Jō. Enduring great privation in order to continue his education under American missionaries, Uemura never graduated formally from any school but read widely.

In 1890 he began publication of the bimonthly magazine *Nihon Hyōron*. His first important theological work, *Shinri Ippan* (Universal Truth), was published in 1884. He participated as a leader of growing importance in the organizational development of the *Nihon Kirisuto Kyōkai* (The United Church of Christ in Japan).

Uemura showed his independence of spirit when he published a statement in support of *Uchimura Kanzō, after the famous disloyalty incident in 1891. Uemura was the first to propose the ordination of women as elders in the *Nihon Kirisuto Kyōkai* and in spite of opposition was able to secure the adoption of this policy, perhaps the first instance of the ordination of women as elders in the history of the Presbyterian-Reformed tradition anywhere in the world.

Ugarit (*Ras Shamra). Ancient city of the Middle East. Archaeological excavations, especially of the Ugaritic texts, at Ugarit have had an important effect on biblical studies: the city is not mentioned in the Bible, but its social structure in the Late Bronze Age casts light on *Canaanite culture and religion.

Ŭich'ŏn (1055–1101). Korean Buddhist monk. Ŭich'ŏn founded the Ch'ŏnt'ae (*T'ien-t'ai) sect in Korea in the year 1097 and, in addition, laboured to bring about a reconciliation between the 'doctrinal school' (*kyojong*) and the 'meditational school' (*sŏnjong*). He compiled a catalogue of scriptural commentaries and treatises, altogether 1,010 titles in 4,740 fascicles, and, on the basis of this work, endeavoured to publish supplements to the Korean Buddhist canon existing at that time.

Ŭisang or **Master Taesŏng Wŏn'gyo** (625–702). Korean Buddhist monk, who studied *Hua-yen Buddhism under Chih-yen (602–68). The second patriarch of the Hwaŏm (Chinese Hua-yen) sect, he founded the Pusŏk subsect of Hwaŏm in Korea, and established Hwaŏm as the ideological foundation of the Silla dynasty (668–935). His *Diagram of the Hwaŏm One-Vehicle World*, a *mandalic, meditational device of 210 Chinese characters, has been highly acclaimed by E. Asian Buddhists as a superb compendium of Hua-yen thought. He had ten Hwaŏm monasteries built, convertible to forts in the event of foreign invasion.

Uji (equivalence of being and time): see DOGEN.

Ujigami. Japanese *kami of the kinship group, eventually personified as the ancestor god. An ujiko is a child of the Ujigami, so the word is also used of Shinto worshippers.

Ujiko: see UJIGAMI.

Ujjayini (Ujjain, originally Avanti). One of the four sacred Hindu cities where a *kuṃbhamela is held once every twelve years.

'Ulamā (Arab., pl. of *'alīm*, one who possesses *'*ilm*, 'knowledge'). The learned and qualified in Islam, in matters of law, constitution, and theology. Through them the *ijma' (consensus) of the community is expressed, and they are the guardians of tradition, both in a general and technical (*ḥadīth) sense. In Shī'a Islam, the nearest equivalent in practice is the *mujtāhid*, though the term 'ulamā is applied.

Ullambana (from Skt., *avalambana*, 'hanging down'). Rituals performed to save deceased people from torments after death—such as being suspended upside down. In China, Ullambana is held on the fifteenth day of the seventh month to help hungry ghosts (*preta): offerings of food and wealth (often in paper or representational form) are made to succour them. In Japan, Urabon (or more simply Bon) is held on 15 July or 15 Aug.

Ultimate concern: see TILLICH, PAUL.

Ultimate salvation (in contrast to proximate): see GREAT TRADITION, LITTLE TRADITION.

Ultramontanism (Lat., *ultra montes*, 'beyond the mountains', i.e. the Alps). A movement emphasizing the pre-eminence of *Roman authority in the Church. It was opposed from the 17th cent. onwards to *Gallicanism in France, Josephinism in Austria, and similar attempts elsewhere to promote the development of national churches independent of Roman, but under state, control. In the 19th cent., ultramontanism was closely associated with support for the *papacy's temporal power, and for the doctrine of papal *infallibility.

Umā. Non-Vedic Hindu goddess, first mentioned in *Kena Upaniṣad*, where she mediates between Brahmā and other gods.

'Umar al-Khayyām (Muslim mathematician and poet): see OMAR KHAYYAM.

'Umar ibn al-Khattāb (d. 644 (AH 23)). Second caliph (*khalīfa) and main architect of the Arab Islamic empire. Originally he was an enemy of Islam, but had a sudden conversion four years before the *hijra. In *Madīna, 'Umar's energy of will, piety, wisdom, and organizing ability made him second to the Prophet *Muḥammad in authority and prestige. The Prophet nicknamed him *faruq*, 'distinguisher' (between truth and falsehood). As second caliph (*khalīfa) he organized the Islamic conquests and the administration of the empire. Traditions reveal, however, that he was feared rather than loved, and at the height of his power he was assassinated at Madīna.

It was during 'Umar's caliphate that Muslim religious and political institutions arose which were to be the model for future generations. Among these were: the *dīwān* ('stipend register'), a form of welfare state by which annual stipends were paid to all Muslims from the public treasury; regulations for non-Muslim subjects (*dhimmi); military garrisons which later became the great cities of Islam, e.g. Kūfā and Fustat; the office of *qāḍi (judge); religious ordinances such as obligatory nightly prayers in the month of *Ramaḍān; civil and penal codes; the hijra *calendar; and the standardization of the text of the *Qur'ān.

Orthodox *Sunni sources praise 'Umar for piety, justice, and make him a model for all the virtues of Islam. In contrast, *Shī'a sources retain an animus against the man who blocked the claims of *'Alī.

Umāsvāmi or **Umāsvāti** (*c.*2nd cent. CE). Jain disciple of the revered *Kundakunda. To him is attributed the **Tattvārtha Sūtra*. He and his *Sūtra* are claimed by both of the two major divisions among the Jains, *Digambara and Śvetāmbara, the former calling him Umāsvāmi, the latter Umāsvāti.

Umayyads (Arab., *al-dawlah al-Umawiyyah*). The first hereditary dynasty of caliphs (*khalīfa) in Sunni Islam. The founder of the dynasty was *Mu'āwiyya, the son of *Abu Sufyān, of the Umayyah (hence the name) clan of the *Quraysh of *Mecca. Under the Umayyads, the Muslim Empire increased at a rapid rate, stretching by 732 from the Atlantic and the borders between Spain and France in the West, to the borders of China and India in the East—in that year Charles Martel halted the Arab advance at Poitiers and Tours. In Spain, the foundations were laid for a great flourishing of trade, crafts, architecture, and learning—the final expulsion of the Muslims did not take place until the 17th cent. But elsewhere the Umayyads ruled more severely and autocratically. The last Umayyad caliph, Marwan II, 'the wild ass of Mesopotamia', was beheaded in Egypt in 750 (AH 132). The 'Abbāsids succeeded, although an Umayyad dynasty continued in Spain, known as the Western Caliphate.

Umbanda. A Brazilian cult which, because of its syncretizing tendencies, has also become a general term for all forms of a new eclectic and *syncretist religious complex in urban Brazil. The spiritual world is composed of many spirit powers drawn from sources such as the following: (i) *caboclos*, spirits of great Amerindian leaders or of spiritualized natural forces; (ii) *pretos velhos*, spirits of the old or wise among Negro slaves, (iii) *crianças*, spirits of children who died young; (iv) *orixas*, spirits of African ancestors or deities, especially Yoruba; (v) spirits of *Jesus, the Virgin *Mary, or the saints of Portuguese folk Catholicism, often equated with the previous group; and (vi) other spirits and occult powers as understood in the sophisticated French spiritualism articulated by Alan Kardec (1804–69), which attracts the higher social classes.

'Umma (Arab., pl. *umam*). People, community, a powerful and sometimes visionary concept in Islam. The word has various uses in the *Qur'ān, but it is used especially in contrast to the social divisions of humanity. While the Qur'ān required Muḥammad to establish an Arab 'umma out of the disunited tribes, it also envisaged the creation of a single 'umma transcending the continuing divisions in the world. The first implementation of this in practice can be seen in the Constitution of *Madīna.

'Umm al-Kitāb (Arab., 'Mother of the Book'). The 'heavenly pattern' of the *Qur'ān itself. This original is thought of as pre-existent 'in a tablet preserved' in heaven (85. 21). From it, the revelations of the Qur'ān were sent down gradually to the Prophet *Muḥammad. The term 'Umm al-Kitāb is also used for the *Fātiḥa, which is said to contain the essentials of the whole Qur'ān. The tablet is known as al-Lawḥ.

Ummī (Arab.). A term used in Qur'ān 7. 157 and 158, *al-rasūl al-nabī al-ummī* ('the prophet, messenger, the unlettered one'), denoting Muḥammad. It is traditionally (and generally by Muslims) understood as meaning that Muḥammad was totally unable to read or write, so emphasizing the miracle (*i'jāz) of the *Qur'ān, with its surpassing eloquence coming into being via a complete illiterate. If, however, ummī is read as expressing a distinction from the Jews (who were 'people with a book'), then it must mean 'scriptureless', i.e. 'illiterate' in being, as yet, without an Arabic scripture.

Ummon School. One of the *'five houses' (*goke-shichi-shu*) of Ch'an Buddhism, founded by *Yun-men Wen-yen (Jap., Ummon Bun'en), hence known as Yun-men-tsung (Ummon-shu).

The best-known representative of the school in China is *Hsüeh-tou Ch'ung-hsien; eventually the school was absorbed into *Rinzai.

'Umra. Muslim *pilgrimage, specifically the 'lesser pilgrimage' within the boundaries of the *Masjid al-Ḥarām in *Mecca. The rites of 'Umra consist of: *ṭawāf ('circumambulation' of the *Ka'ba); kissing the *Black Stone; *sa'y (running) between the two elevations of al-Ṣafā' and al-Marwa. 'Umra, along with the ḥajj itself, has origins in the pagan period, but the rites were given an Islamic character by the *Qur'ān and by Muslim practice.

Unam Sanctum (bull): see EXTRA ECCLESIAM ...

Unction. The religious use of oil for *anointing; and in Christian use specifically the rite of anointing of the sick. The practice has its authority in the New Testament (Mark 6. 13, James 5. 14 f.), and in the Middle Ages came to be numbered among the seven *sacraments. In the early cents., it was connected with recovery from illness, but thereafter the rite became so closely connected with repentance and the whole *penitential system that it was commonly postponed until death was approaching. Thus the name 'extreme unction' by which the rite was long known probably derives from its reception *in extremis*.

Underhill, Evelyn (1875–1941). Christian spiritual writer. Born into an unreligious upper middle-class family, she quickly showed an interest in the religious capacities of the human soul, culminating in her great work, *Mysticism* (1911). As an Anglican, she exercised an enormous influence through her books (among them, *Worship*, 1936) and spiritual direction, both with individuals and in the giving of retreats.

Underworld. Domain in which the dead are (or were) believed to have continued existence —'life' would be too strong a word (see SHEOL). Whereas it was once thought that all the dead ended up in the same place somewhere beneath the earth, it was later believed that the evil were separated from the good, and that only the evil were in the underworld, which then became a place of punishment. In this way *hell developed from the underworld.

U-Netanneh Tokef (Heb., 'let us declare the importance'). Jewish *piyyut recited on *Rosh ha-Shanah and Yom Kippur (*Day of Atonement). It was written *c.*8th cent. CE, and announces that God is full of forgiveness

Ungan Donjō (Ch'an/Zen master): see YUN-YEN T'AN-SHENG.

Uniat(e) Churches. More properly Eastern Catholic or Eastern-rite Catholic Churches. Churches in union with *Rome, but retaining their own language, customs, and *canon law—e.g. allowing marriage of the clergy and communion in both kinds. The name 'Uniates' is a disparaging term used by the *Orthodox Church with unhappy memories of what this form of association with Rome has implied. Apart from the several different rites (Antiochene, Alexandrian, Chaldean, Armenian, *Melkite) which entered into union mainly because of the assistance the connection might bring, the *Maronite Church has a history distinct from Orthodoxy. In India, the attempt of the Portuguese to impose W. discipline on the St Thomas Christians created various divisions. Two groups entered into union with Rome, the *Malabar Christians and the Malankara Church. In fact, far from reinforcing local tradition, all of these unions led to a process of Latinization, which demonstrated to Orthodoxy at large that this was a process of proselytization, not of seeking a union of equals. The Eastern Catholic Churches rapidly became an obstacle to union, rather than a step towards it.

Unification Church: see MOON, SUN MYUNG.

Uniformity, Acts of. Four acts of Parliament (1549, 1552, 1559, 1662) which regulated the worship of the Church of England and the use of the **Book of Common Prayer*. The 1662 Act, part of the Restoration settlement, contained as an annex the *BCP* still in use, and required all ministers to assent to it. This Act remains on the statute-book, but has been radically amended by 1974 legislation allowing *alternative services.

Union of American Hebrew Congregations (UAHC). Association of *Reform Jewish congregations in the USA and Canada. The organization, founded in 1873, was responsible for the foundation of the *Hebrew Union College.

Union of Orthodox Jewish Congregations of America (UOJCA). Association of *Orthodox Jewish congregations in the USA. The organization was founded in 1898.

Unitarianism. A religious movement connected with Christianity. Unitarians are those who reject the Trinitarian understanding of God. Although there are many antecedents, the specific point of origin for the movement is usually taken to be the work of *Servetus, and of the Sozzinis (i.e. *Socinianism). The first Unitarian congregation in England was formed in 1774, and in the USA in 1782, but the movement did not become fully organized until the Baltimore sermon of W. E. Channing in 1819, on 'Unitarian Christianity'. The American Unitarian Association was founded in 1825. In 1961, the Unitarians merged with the *Universalists, the joint movement becoming known as the Unitarian Universalist Association. It is characterized by an emphasis on members seeking truth out of human experience, not out of allegiance to creeds or doctrines. There is no hierarchical control, each congregation being self-governing. There are more than a thousand congregations, mainly in the USA and Canada.

Unitarians. Arab. *al-Muwaḥḥidūn* can be translated as 'the Unitarians', and it occurs particularly, in Islam, in *Ismā'īlī and *Sūfī movements, where the unity of Being is stressed, with human (or sometimes all) appearances being manifestations of that one Being. See also Almohads in *Ibn Tumart; Druzes.

Unitas Fratrum: see MORAVIAN BRETHREN.

United Church of Christ. The body formed in the USA by the union of the Congregational Christian churches with the Evangelical and Reformed in 1961.

United Reformed Church. The body formed by the union of the *Congregational Church of England with the *Presbyterian Church of England, which came into being in Oct. 1972. Negotiations with the *Churches of Christ resulted in the majority of its churches joining the URC in 1981.

United Synagogue. Association of *Ashkenazi Jewish congregations in Great Britain. The organization was established by Act of Parliament in 1870. It supports the British *Chief Rabbinate, the London *Bet Din, and all the *synagogues which accept the authority of the Chief Rabbi.

United Synagogue of America. Association of *Conservative Jewish *synagogues in the USA and Canada. The organization was founded by Solomon *Schechter in 1913.

Unitive Way. Third and last of the *Three Ways in prayer. In this, after experiencing the *purgative and *illuminative ways, the soul is united with God by love: hence the imagery of spiritual betrothal and marriage, which itself suggests the indefectible state of cleaving to God characteristic of this way.

Universal Church of the Kingdom of God. An evangelistic church founded in Brazil in 1977 by Edir Macedo, called *bishop. The church emphasizes faith healing, and evokes generous giving on the part of the faithful (estimated in 1995 at about $15 million a week). The church became publicly controversial in 1995 when, after a television attack was made on the Virgin *Mary, the attorney-general in Brazil ordered an investigation of the church for alleged tax fraud and for alleged links with drug cartels.

Universal House of Justice (*Baytu'l-adl-i a'ẓam*). The Supreme ruling body of the *Bahā'ī Faith. Formulated in the writings of *Bahā'u'l-lāh and his successors, the House of Justice was first elected in 1963 by ballot vote by the members of all national Bahā'ī Assemblies. At present, the House of Justice is re-elected every five years and comprises nine members. Bahā'īs regard its judgements as divinely guided and authoritative.

Universalism

Judaism The claim, in contrast to particularism, that a religion is true for all humanity. Judaism is universalistic in that it recognizes the absolute sovereignty of God and that *messianic redemption is for all humankind. It is particularist in that it perpetuates the survival of the Jewish people as a separate entity.

Christianity The doctrine that all beings will in the end be saved. It starts from the conviction that a loving God cannot impose eternal punishment (in *hell), and that eternal bliss cannot be complete while any are excluded. A separate movement/denomination had begun in the 18th cent. (especially in N. America), receiving impetus from Hosea Ballou, *Treatise of the Atonement* (1805). It merged in 1961 with the *Unitarians, to become the Unitarian Universalist Association.

Universal love (*chien ai*, of Mo Tzu): see JEN.

Unknowability of God: see APOPHATIC THEOLOGY.

Unknown Christ of Hinduism: see PANNIKAR, RAIMUNDO.

Unleavened bread: see MAZZAH.

Unnō (Jap., 'cloud robe'). A Zen term, comparable to *unsui, for the cloudlike detachment of the Zen life.

Unsui (Jap., *un*, 'cloud', + *sui*, 'water'). *Zen monks who exemplify the homeless life, drifting like clouds and forever moving like water.

Untouchables. The fifth, and lowest, category (*pañchama*) of Hindu society. To it belonged the offspring of mixed-caste unions, tribals, and foreigners, and those with defiling occupations, such as the *Chāmar (leather-workers) and Dom (scavengers and funerary specialists).

Some castes were so polluting they were not only untouchable but unseeable, such as the Vannān of S. India whose job was to wash the clothes of other untouchables, and who might leave their homes only during darkness since even the sight of one of them was enough to pollute a higher caste person.

Untouchables lived outside village boundaries, and were not allowed to draw water from wells used by higher castes. Education was prohibited; they were not allowed to read the sacred texts, and only by patiently accepting their humble lot was salvation possible for them.

The Constitution of modern independent India has abolished untouchability in theory, but in practice, especially in rural areas, the concept still survives. Reform movements, or individuals (see e.g. AMBEDKAR, B. R.), have tried to eradicate it, so far without success. *Gāndhī attempted to improve the image of untouchables by giving them the name 'Harijans' (Children of God); officially they are termed 'Scheduled Castes', but terminological change does not necessarily effect status change.

UOJCA: see UNION OF ORTHODOX JEWISH CONGREGATIONS OF AMERICA.

Upādāna (Pāli, Skt.; lit., 'that which fuels a process' or 'keeps it going'). Grasping, clinging, attachment; according to Buddhism the mark of human behaviour generally. There are four types: grasping after sense objects, speculative philosophies (*diṭṭhi-vāda), rules and rituals (see SĪLABBATA-PARĀMĀSA), and theories of a soul (*atta-vāda*).

Upadhye (ritual officiant in Jain worship): see PŪJĀ.

Upāgama A supplementary text to an *Āgama: see also Śaiva-Āgama.

Upanayana. Sometimes called 'the thread ceremony', or 'sacred thread' ceremony, this is one of the most important rites of passage in Hinduism. It is a ceremony that marks a boy's transition from childhood to his student life, when traditionally he would come under the authority of his guru, or teacher, and be instructed in sacred lore and Skt. He becomes *dvija ('twice-born') and assumes the duties and responsibilities of his caste. He eats for the last time with his mother; he will now join the men of the family, eat with them, and be served by the womenfolk. Brahman boys receive the thread, which is usually of cotton, though it may vary from caste to caste, at the age of 8, *Kṣatriyas at 11, and Vaiśyas at 14. *Śūdras do not go through the ceremony.

Nowadays the receiving of the thread (*yajñopavītā*) is the most important part of this ceremony; its connection with the commencement of religious education is usually forgotten. The thread runs over the left shoulder and under the right arm, except during funerary rites, when it is reversed. It is renewed annually, and the old thread is burnt on the sacred fire.

Upāṅga (auxiliary aids): see VEDĀṄGA.

Upaniṣad (Skt.). In Hinduism, the genre of texts which end or complete the Vedic corpus. For this reason they are also called *Vedānta, 'the end of the Veda'. The word 'upaniṣad' itself is usually understood to mean 'esoteric teaching', the preferred etymology (*upa* + *ni* + *śad*, 'to sit close by') referring to the proximity necessary for the transmission of such teachings. The Upaniṣads, as texts, developed out of the earlier speculations on the Vedic ritual contained in the *Brāhmaṇas and *Āraṇyakas. In number they are counted by some as being over 200; traditionally, there are 108, listed at the beginning of *Muktika Upaniṣad*. Nine show a clear relationship to preceding brāhmaṇas or āraṇyakas. Six more are commented on or mentioned by Śaṅkara. *Radhakrishnan, in his work *The Principal Upaniṣads* (1953), included eighteen. The central teaching of these early upaniṣads is that the Self (*ātman) is identical to the ultimate ground of reality (*Brahman). He who realizes this finds liberation (*mokṣa) from the cycle of suffering (*saṃsāra) embodied in birth, death and rebirth. This speculative perspective, extolling the way of knowledge (*jñānamārga), became a point of departure for much of Indian philosophy, particularly the various schools of Vedānta. The later Upaniṣads, composed under Purāṇic, *Tantric, or devotional influences, are less philosophical and more sectarian. Their importance is not so much for the history of philosophy in India as for an understanding of its popular religion.

The major Upaniṣads are **Aitareya*, **Bṛhadāraṇyaka*, **Chandogya*, *Īśa*, **Kaṭha*, **Kauṣītaki*, **Kena*, **Mahānārāyaṇīya* **Maitri*, **Māṇḍūkya*, **Muṇḍaka*, **Praśna*, **Śvetāśvatara*, **Taittirīya*. See Index, Upaniṣad.

Upapātaka (minor sin): see MAHĀPĀTAKA.

Uparama (one of six great Hindu virtues): see ṢATKASAṂPATTI.

Upāsaka (fem., *upāsikā*; Pāli, 'one who sits close by'). Buddhist layperson, who has taken refuge in the *Three Jewels (*triratna*) and undertaken the five precepts (*śīla).

Upāsakādhyana-aṅga (Jain text): see AṄGA.

Upāsana (Skt., 'act of sitting'). A word of varied though related meanings in Indian religious thought. It can mean ritual worship, devotional worship, and meditation. In his commentary on the **Vedānta Sūtra*, *Rāmānuja equates upāsana with devotional meditation and knowledge of *Brahman (5. 1. 1). This is a higher kind of knowledge which has the character of devotion (*bhakti) and consists in direct intuition of Brahman.

Upa Veda. Secondary *Veda in Hinduism, attached to, but having no other connection with, revealed Veda. They are (i) *Āyur Veda*, on medicine; (ii) *Ghāndharva Veda*, on music and dance; (iii) *Dhanur Veda*, on archery and military skills; (iv) *Sthāpatya Veda*, on architecture (sometimes referred to as *Śilpa Śastra*).

Upāya-kauśalya ('skill in means'). Adaptation of teaching in Buddhism to the level of the audience's existing attainment. The concept of 'skilful means' is of considerable importance in *Mahāyāna Buddhism and is expounded at an early date in texts such as the **Lotus Sūtra* and the teachings of **Vimalakīrti Sūtra*. At the root of the idea is the notion that the *Buddha's teaching is essentially a provisional means to bring beings to *enlightenment, and that the teachings which he gives may therefore vary: what may be appropriate at one time may not be so at another. The concept is used by the Mahāyāna to justify what appear to be its innovations in doctrine, and to portray the Buddha's early teachings as limited and restricted in accordance with the spiritual potential of his early followers. In the Mahāyāna, skilful means comes to be a legitimate method to be employed by buddhas and *bodhisattvas whenever the benefit of beings would seem to warrant it. Although this involves a certain degree of duplicity, such as telling lies, the Buddha is exonerated from all blame, since his only motivation is compassionate concern for all beings.

Upekkha (Pāli, 'equanimity'). Fundamental Buddhist state of equilibrium in the mind. It is one of the seven constituents of enlightenment, and one of the four cardinal virtues (with *metta, *karuṇā, *muditā), which controls the other three.

Uposatha (Pāli, 'fasting'; Skt., *upavasatha*; Jap., *fusatsu*). Buddhist observance on the days of (initially) new and full moon, now of the quarter moons. For laypeople (*upāsaka) it involves a day of more careful observance, sometimes by undertaking an additional three rules (*śīla), and by assembling at the local monastery, for worship, instruction, and renewal of vows to keep the precepts (śīla). Monks are under obligation to attend a ceremony in which (or before which) acknowledgement of fault against the *pratimokṣa is made. The pratimokṣa is recited at this ceremony.

Uppalavaṇṇā or **Utpalavarṇā** (5th cent. BCE). One of the best-known (with *Khemā) women *arhats who attained enlightenment through the teaching of the Buddha. She was named by the Buddha, with Khemā, as the ideal model of bhikkhunī.

Ur. Ancient city of the Middle East. The city of Ur is referred to in the Hebrew scriptures as the place of origin of the *patriarchs (Genesis 11. 28, 31), although originally it was not realized that Ur was a place. Since the letters form the Hebrew word for 'fire', it was believed that Abram/*Abraham came from the fire of the Chaldaeans. This was taken to be the fire of persecution, hence the elaboration of many stories concerning Abram's refusal of idolatry. Although resting on a mistake, these stories persist into Islam.

Urabe family (Shinto family of diviners): see YOSHIDA SHINTŌ.

Urabe Shintō (Shinto school): see YOSHIDA SHINTŌ.

Urabon (rituals for the dead): see ULLAMBANA.

Urbi et Orbi (Lat., 'to the city and to the world'). The blessing given by the *pope on solemn occasions, initially from any one of the basilicas in Rome, but now from St Peter's. The custom was revived in 1922 after an interval of fifty years, becoming increasingly an occasion of adulation of the pope.

Uriel. An *angel mentioned in the Jewish book of *1 *Enoch*. Uriel is one of the four angels placed around God's throne (*Num.R.* 2. 10).

Urim and Thummim. A priestly device for telling oracles in the ancient Israelite religion. The *high priest wore the Urim and Thummim on his breastplate. It was used for questioning God on behalf of the ruler (Numbers 27. 21) and it seems to have given a 'yes-or-no' answer (1 Samuel 23. 10–12). The underlying meaning of the two words is not known.

Ūrṇā (Skt., 'wool'). A circle of hair between the eyebrows. In both Hindu and Jain understanding, this is, or conceals, the jewel or ornament of the 'third eye', which is derived from *Śiva's production of his third, burning, eye: see TRILOCANA.

'Urs (Arab.). Bride and bridegroom, hence marriage. From this, it is also the collective name for ceremonies observed at the anniversary of the death of a *Sūfī saint or *murshid*. The death of a saint is regarded as a time of reunion with his Lord and therefore considered a happy occasion. Each Sūfī order celebrates its particular annual 'urs programme.

Urvan (soul): see FRAVASI.

Uṣas (Skt., 'dawn'). Hindu goddess of the dawn, restorer of life and bounty.

Use. A local modification of the prevailing Christian *rite (especially the Roman rite). These uses, which differed from the parent rite only in details, came to be standardized and employed over wide areas.

Usha, synod of. 2nd-cent. CE convention of Jewish *sages. After the persecutions at the close of the *Bar Kokhba revolt, a synod met at Usha to reactivate the *Sanhedrin.

'Ushr (Arab., 'tenth part'). The tithe on property owned by Muslims, often levied for public assistance, in distinction from *kharāj*, which was levied on property owned by non-Muslims.

USPG (United Society for the Propagation of the Gospel). Christian missionary society formed in 1965 by the amalgamation of the SPG and the Universities' Mission to Central Africa.

Ussher, James (1581–1656). Anglican *archbishop of Armagh, Ireland. A scholar of vast learning, he was an authority on such diverse subjects as the letters of *Ignatius (of which he distinguished the seven genuine ones) and the early history of Ireland. He is probably best remembered today in connection with his scheme based on the genealogies, according to which, e.g. the world was created in 4004 BCE.

Uṣūl (Arab. pl. of *aṣl*). Root or principle. In Islam, the word is used for a branch of learning, especially uṣūl al-*hadīth, uṣūl al-*fiqh, and uṣūl al-*kalām (earlier uṣūl al-dīn); and also for the sources of those disciplines, *Qur'ān, ḥadīth (together, *sunna), *ijma', and *qiyās at least: claims to further sources would be disputed. Uṣūliy(y)a is used for what in English might be called *fundamentalism.

Uṣūlī (school of Shi'ite law): see BIHBAHĀNĪ.

Usury. The lending of money at interest. The exacting of interest on loans to a fellow-Jew is forbidden in the Hebrew scriptures (Exodus 22. 24), including loans to a resident alien (Leviticus 25. 35–7) but it is permitted on loans to a 'foreigner' (Deuteronomy 23. 20 f.). In the Middle Ages, Jews were excluded from trade and craft guilds, and money-lending became a common Jewish activity. The Christian Church forbade usury to Christians in 1179, but the canon law did not apply to Jews. The stereotype of the Jew in the late Middle Ages was thus of an avaricious usurer (e.g. Shakespeare's Shylock, Marlowe's Barabbas).

For usury in Islam, see RIBĀ.

'Uthmān b. Affān (d. 655 (AH 35)). Third caliph (*khalīfa), who was an early convert to Islam. He married the Prophet *Muḥammad's daughters, Rukaiya and (after her death) Umm Kulthum. Upon election as caliph he promised to follow and develop *'Umar's policies of uniformity in religion and government. It was during his time that Islamic conquests reached their peak, bringing with them novel problems of the relation between the original community and the newly acquired territories. 'Uthmān, already old, was unequal to these difficulties. He began to rely on his 'Umayyah family, and was consequently accused of nepotism and corruption. Opposition to 'Uthmān came to be represented in the figures of *'Ā'isha (Prophet Muḥammad's favourite wife) and *'Alī, with the introduction of a religious accusation that 'Uthmān was not following the precepts of the Qur'ān and the Prophet. 'Uthmān's circulation of the official edition of the Qur'ān, to preserve uniformity in religion, precipitated a chain of events that led to his assassination: the *Qurra* ('Qur'ān-reciters') had been the expositors of the sacred text and had exercised great influence over the new converts, which gave them religious prestige and authority in the provinces. 'Uthmān's official Qur'ān deprived these monopolists of control over divine revelation. The religious grievance over the Qur'ān now became allied to social, economic, and political discontent; anti-'Uthmān feeling spilled over into open rebellion. Rebel forces from Egypt, Kūfā, and Basra advanced on Madīna, declared 'Uthmān unfit to rule, and murdered him. The bloody end to 'Uthmān's rule marks a turning point in Islamic history: political and religious unity was at an end and the period of schisms and civil wars had begun. The murder of 'Uthmān raised the complex issue of just murder and unjust killing, and this too created further division amongst the Muslim community: had 'Uthmān acted in ways that contravened Islam, and, if so, had he so ceased to be a Muslim that he could be treated accordingly and be legitimately killed? For the main parties to this dispute, see ĪMĀN.

Utpalavarṇā (woman arhat): see UPPALAVAṆṆĀ.

Uttara-Mīmāṃsā (Skt., 'latter discussion/revered thought'). One of the six philosophical systems (*darśana) of early Hinduism. Generally related to *Vedānta, it is linked to *Bādarāyaṇa and the *Vedānta-* or *Brahma-Sūtra*. Where *Jaimini's *Pūrva-Mīmāṁsā deals with karma-kāṇḍa, or the duties required by the *Veda, Uttara-Mīmāṁsā explores the religious and philosophical speculations of the Upaniṣads. The *Vedānta Sūtra* then becomes the major text on which subsequent commentaries are made.

V

Vāc (Skt., from *vac*, 'speech'). The Hindu goddess of speech, the manifestation of sound. From early Vedic times, reliance on the sacred oral teachings 'heard' by the *ṛṣis, properly intoned and accented, thrust the folk-divinity Vāc into prominence. In the *Tantric tradition she is also celebrated as Para-vāc, Transcendental Speech, the mother of all sacred *mantras.

Vacanam (form of religious verse): see BASAVA.

Vāhana (Skt., 'vehicle'). The bird or animal on which a Hindu, Jain, or Buddhist deity is conveyed. In post-Vedic Hinduism, the vehicles are associated iconographically with the deities in question and are linked to their attributes, e.g. *Agni, a ram; *Bhairava, a dog; *Brahmā, a swan (*haṃsa); *Durgā, a tiger (or lion); *Gaṇeśa, a rat; *Garuḍa, a bird; *Indra, an elephant; *Kāma, a parrot; *Śiva, a bull; *Varuna, a fish; *Yama, a buffalo.

Vāhigurū or **Wāhegurū** (Pañjābī, 'praise to the Gurū'). Used by Sikhs as name for God. Vāhigurū is frequently heard in the proclamation *Srī Vāhigurūjī kā *khālsā: Srī Vāhigurūjī kī *fateh* (The khālsā is God's: God's is the victory). In the early *janam-sākhīs, however, Vāhigurū was not a name for God but an ascription of praise either to God or to the Gurū (i.e. *Nānak). From its repetition in meditation (see NĀM SIMARAN) Vāhigurū naturally came to be regarded as God's name.

Vaibhāṣika. An influential Buddhist school of the Hīnayāna, closely related to the *Sarvāstivāda, which flourished in NW India principally in Gandhāra and Kashmir. Their name derives from a great treatise known as the *Vibhāṣā*, compiled in the early centuries of the Christian era as a commentary on a fundamental work of the *Abhidharma tradition, the *Jñānaprasthāna* (Basis of Knowledge) of Katyāyanaputra, a Sarvāstivādin philosopher. The commentary is an encyclopaedia of Vaibhāṣika philosophy.

Vaikuṇṭha. *Viṣṇu's paradise (and thus also an epithet/name), variously located, e.g. on Mount *Meru, or in the depths of the ocean. As Baikunth, 'heaven' enters into the teaching of Gurū *Nānak, but only in a demythologized form: Baikunth is the bliss of union with God.

Vailala Madness. The best-known of the early *cargo movements, in the Gulf division of Papua. In 1919, an old man, Evara, had trance experiences and prophesied that a steamer would come with the spirits of their ancestors and a cargo of European goods; others had similar visions depicting a coming *millennium and sometimes featuring God or *Christ. Traditional rituals and objects were attacked, gardens and trade were abandoned, and a new *ascetic ethic enjoined *Sunday observance, cleanliness, and rejection of personal adornment. It spread rapidly and did not die out till about 1931, but is still remembered as an idealized time of wonders. It was much more than mere anti-white hysteria, for it arose from resentment at the inadequacy of the old ways in comparison with those of the whites.

Vairāgya (Skt., 'absence of passion'). An attitude of genuine dispassion and freedom from worldly desires. It is considered a primary requisite for aspirants in most systems of Indian spiritual discipline.

Vairocana (Skt., 'the illuminator', 'he who is like the sun'). 1. In Hinduism (as Virocana), an *asura who attempted, with Indra, to find the self (*ātman): see *Chandogya Upaniṣad* 8. 7.

2. In Buddhism, one of the five transcendent Buddhas, associated with the *bodhisattva *Samantabhadra and the earthly buddha Krakuccanda. He is often depicted making the hand-clasped sign (*mudra) of supreme wisdom. Vairocana became identified with the Ādi-buddha as the personification of *dharma-kāya. Vairocana is no longer an epitome of the absolute and undifferentiated nature of all appearance, to be approached only through aeons of insight-meditation, but becomes Mahāvairocana, accessible through cult and ritual. In Japan, Birushana is central in *Shingon.

Vaiśākhi (Indian spring festival): see BAISĀKHĪ.

Vaiśālī (Skt.; Pāli, Vesālī). City north of the *Gaṅgā (Ganges), location of the Second Buddhist *Council.

Vaiśaradya (Skt.), four certainties, the mark of a *Buddha. He is certain that: (i) his enlightenment is irreversible; (ii) all defilements (*āsava) are exhausted; (iii) all obstacles are overcome; (iv) the way of overcoming reappearance (*saṃsāra) has been proclaimed.

Vaiśeṣika (Skt., 'referring to the distinctions', *viśeṣa*). The oldest of the six early Hindu philosophical systems (*darśana) related to *Nyāya.

Founded by Kaṇāda, to whom *Vaiśeṣika Sūtra* is attributed, it begins with *dharma and the authority of the *Veda. But it then proceeds to the analysis of the six categories or objects of experience (*padārthas*) and makes no mention of God or gods. Later Vaiśeṣika could not regard all appearance as coming together from nowhere, and therefore postulated an unproduced Producer of all that is, i.e. God. Vaiśeṣika led on to the multiple systems of Nyāya, often known as Nyāya-Vaiśeṣika.

Vaiṣṇava. An adherent of Vaiṣṇavism, one of three major forms of Hindu devotion (*bhakti), along with *Śaivas and *Śaktas. Vaiṣṇavism is the cult of *Viṣṇu, initially connected with Viṣṇu as the sun, pervading all things with light and spiritual enlightenment (*Ṛg Veda* 3. 62. 10). He was assimilated with *Nārāyana, cosmic energy, and was later associated with *Kṛṣṇa-Vāsudeva, until the relation between all three became one of dynamic manifestation. Viṣṇu came to be regarded as *Īśvara, Supreme Being, and also as *Brahman theistically conceived. He becomes manifest in incarnate forms (for the list of these see AVATĀRA), especially in times of crisis or need, and it is mainly in these forms that he is worshipped. Vaiṣṇavism has divided into many schools and sects. Of enduring importance have been *Caitanya and his contemporary Vallabha (*c*.1479–1531). Vallabha's *Śuddhādvaita Vedānta (pure non-duality vedānta) mediates between *Śaṅkara and *Rāmānuja, by maintaining the goodness and purity of both world and self as parts of what truly is, namely Kṛṣṇa, so that while appearances are an expression of *māyā, the bliss-relation of the parts to the whole, and thus of *ātman to *Brahman, is not: thus bhakti (devotion) is the realization of this, and is the true path to *mokṣa (release). For face markings, see TILAKA. See also NIMBĀRKA; RĀMĀNANDA; ŚRĪ-VAIṢṆAVISM.

Vaiśvadeva. A Hindu household ritual, offering homage to the gods, especially *Agni who bears offerings to the heavens. Fire is fed with consecrated fuel, and offerings are thrown into it, accompanied by *mantras.

Vaiśvānara (Skt., 'relating to all people'). An epithet of *Agni (fire). Agni Vaiśvānara is regarded as the author of *Ṛg Veda* 10. 79 and 80. He represents the fire of digestion.

The term is then applied in *Vedānta to the waking state of human beings, one of the four states, the others being deep sleep, dreaming, and sublimity (*turīya).

Vaiśya. The third of the four Hindu social categories, or *varna. Traditionally the Vaiśyas were traders and businessmen, or peasant farmers. Vaiśyas are often vegetarian, and zealous in religious observance; they have a particular devotion to *Lakṣmī, goddess of wealth.

Vajra (Skt.; Tib., *rdo.rje*, 'diamond', 'thunderbolt'). 1. In Hinduism, the weapon of *Indra. Although often described as his 'thunderbolt', the adamantine ('diamond') connections of vajra mean that it is equally described as hard and sharp—the splitter. The association may simply be in the connection between lightning and thunder.

2. Double-headed ritual implement in *Tibetan Buddhism, used in conjunction with a bell (Skt., *ghaṇṭā*; Tib., *dril.bu*). The bell is always held in the left hand where it represents wisdom, emptiness (*śūnyatā) *nirvāna, and the feminine principle; the vajra is always held in the right hand where it represents skilful means (*upāya-kauśalya), compassion, *saṃsāra, and the masculine principle.

Vajracchedika-[Prajñapāramitā-] Sūtra: See DIAMOND SŪTRA.

Vajradhara. In Tantric Buddhism, the source of the Five Jīnas or *Dhyāni-Buddhas. He is identified with the Absolute or primordial reality which is the source of all enlightenment.

Vajrayāna (Skt., 'thunderbolt-' or 'diamond-vehicle'). The *Tantric aspect of *Mahāyāna Buddhism, which sees itself as a succession built upon the preliminary stages of Hīnayāna and of Sūtrayāna (the *sūtra aspect of Mahāyāna Buddhism). Followers of Vajrayāna see the Sūtrayāna as a long path, developing only compassion and wisdom; the Vajrayāna, however, is seen as a swift path (Tib., *myur.lam*) offering enlightenment in the present lifetime by the development of method. The term Vajrayāna is often (mistakenly) used synonymously with Tibetan Buddhism; in fact, Tibetan Buddhism teaches all three vehicles according to personal advancement, and stresses that while Sūtrayāna may be taught separately from Vajrayāna, Vajrayāna may not be taught separately from Sūtrayāna, but rather as an extension of it.

Vajrayoginī (a Tantric form of Durgā): See CHINNAMASTA.

Vajroli mudra (Skt.). A Tantric practice of reabsorbing, into the penis, semen discharged during intercourse. Semen (*bindu), breath (*prāṇa), and thought (*citta) correspond in *Tantrism, and through reabsorbing the semen, the Tantric adept seeks to arrest breath and thought.

Vāk (goddess of speech/sound): see VĀC.

Vakh (verse sayings): see LALLĀ.

Vāk laina. The way in which Sikhs get advice from the Gurū Granth Sāhib (*Ādi Granth), by prayer, followed by opening the book 'at random'. The book is held between the hands, the hands are moved slowly outward, and the reading begins at the first line of the first complete hymn on the left-hand page. A vāk commences the installation of the Gurū Granth Sāhib each day.

Valabhī, Assembly of. A Jain Assembly at which an attempt was made to formalize something approaching a canon of sacred texts. It was held in 453 CE (though by some reckonings in 466). Since there is no record of the unclad (i.e. *Digambaras) attending, it seems to have been a Śvetāmbara endeavour. The main works accepted are described under *aṅga.

Valentine, St. Roman Christian martyr of the 3rd cent. The association of St Valentine's Day (14 Feb.) with lovers and choosing of a 'Valentine' has nothing to do with the martyr, but probably derives from customs of the Roman festival of Lupercalia in honour of the goddess Februata Juno, when boys drew by lot the names of unmarried girls (mid-February). The suggestion of Francis *de Sales that the names of saints to be emulated should be drawn as Valentines has not caught on.

Valentinus (2nd cent. CE). *Gnostic theologian. According to his orthodox opponents (*Irenaeus, *Tertullian, *et al.*) he lived at Rome, *c.*136–*c.*165, and only left the Catholic Church after failing to be elected bishop. His sect, the Valentinians, was the largest of the gnostic bodies. He produced a variety of writings, including the earliest commentary on the gospel of *John and perhaps the **Gospel of Truth*.

Vallabhā (exponent of Vaiṣṇava): see VAIṢṆAVA.

Vālmīki. Legendary author of the epic **Rāmāyaṇa*, which he claimed to have visualized in the *Vedas; in fact, *Rāmāyaṇa* bears signs of different layers of composition, but Vālmīki may have been a *kuśīlava* ('bard') who introduced the *śloka*, the epic metre of two lines, each of two parts with eight syllables in each, which was used also for much of **Mahābhārata*. To him is attributed another epic work, **Yoga-Vaisiṣtha*, but there is no real historical evidence for him. For the community revering Vālmīki, see BĀLMĪKĪ.

Vāmācāra (Skt., 'left-handed conduct'). A spiritual path, especially in *Tantrism, which is counter to established social ways. Since the present age (*Kali-yuga) is the most decadent, ascetic spiritual practices are no longer effective. In this age a Tantric must 'rise with the aid of those things which make most men fall'. For many this includes deriving power from meat, liquor, sex, and other normally restricted things.

An underlying tenet of the left-handed path is that the world is itself a manifestation of Śiva-Śakti. The process of creation is an act of enjoyment, not suffering; hence to fully realize this ultimate reality, the yogin must not only attain transcendent realization of Śiva-Śakti (*mokṣa), but must also participate in creation, enjoying it with the full realization, 'I am Śiva.'

Vāmana (Skt., 'dwarf'). In Hindu mythology, the form (the fifth) *avatāra which *Viṣṇu adopted in order to trick the demon king *Bali into restoring the world to the gods. When Bali agreed to give him three paces of land, the dwarf grew to an enormous size so that his first two steps covered earth and heaven, and Bali had to offer his own head for the third step. (This cosmic version of Vāmana is known as *Trivikrama*, Skt., 'three steps'.) Vāmana is the fifth *avatāra in the standard list, and his is the only avatāra story which has a clear connection with the Viṣṇu of the **Ṛg Veda*.

Vānaprastha. The third of the four *āśramas, or stages of life, of the Hindu. The term meant literally 'forest departure', a time of retirement when a householder, having raised his children and made them independent, devoted himself, with or without his wife's company, to preparing for death and the next stage of his existence.

van der Leeuw, G.: see PHENOMENOLOGY.

Vanity of vanities: see ECCLESIASTES.

Va Postori (followers): see AFRICAN APOSTLES.

Vār (Pañjābī, 'ballad'). Any of a set of twenty-two hymns of praise in the *Ādi Granth.

Varāha (Skt., 'boar'). In Hindu mythology, the form which *Viṣṇu assumed in order to raise the earth from the cosmic ocean. In its earliest forms this story is a creation myth, and the boar is identified with the creator god *Prajāpati. Later it is identified with *Brahmā and then with Viṣṇu, eventually being regarded as the third *avatāra of the standard list.

Vārāṇasī (Indian sacred city): see KĀŚĪ.

Vardapets (unmarried clergy): see ARMENIAN CHURCH.

Varna (Skt., perhaps from *vṛ*, 'veil', hence 'colour'). 1. The four social orders, or categories, of Hindu society, *Brahmans, *Kṣatriyas, *Vaiśyas, and *Śūdras. These divisions date from the time of the early *Aryan settlement in N. India, and, according to the **Ṛg Veda*, were created by the gods from the body of *Puruṣa, the first man. Into these four major divisions the castes (*jāti) later fitted. Some maintain there is a fifth category, the Harijans, or *untouchables, while others place them within the Śudra division, dividing this into two segments, 'clean' and 'unclean'. The three upper varṇa are termed *'twice-born', since the male family members go through a thread ceremony (*upanayana) which implies a spiritual rebirth, marking the transition into adulthood, and the student stage (*āśrama) of life. Reading, writing, and the pursuit of knowledge were regarded as irrelevant for the Śūdra way of life, so that varna was excluded from the thread ceremonies.

The word varna means 'colour', hence the hypothesis that the system reflects an observed difference in appearance between the fair-skinned Aryan ('noble') invaders from the north and the darker skinned indigenous inhabitants (*dāsas*, 'slaves').

2. See BINDU.

Varṇāśramadharma. The code of conduct by which a Hindu should live, according to his ascribed status by birth (*varna), his stage of life (*āśrama), and the *dharma, or appropriate duty laid down for each of these. Interpretation of the four aims of life—dharma (moral righteousness), *artha (prosperity), *kama (pleasure), and *mokṣa (release from the cycle of existence)—will be influenced by varna and āśrama. Conformity to varṇāśramadharma provides the ideal Hindu social order.

The most authoritative formulation is in the **Manusmṛti*. It remains the orthodox Hindu ideal, although it is seldom if ever followed exactly according to *Manusmṛti*.

Varuṇa. Early Hindu god, prominent in the Vedic period. Possibly connected with *vṛ* ('veil'), he was associated with the all-covering sky, but in the *Vedas his activities resemble those of *Indra and *Agni. He was connected with oceans and rivers, though in later mythology Indra has taken precedence over him, and he has been reduced to the god of death.

Vāsanās (Skt., 'underlying desire'). 1. In Hinduism, the underlying desires, memories, ambitions, etc., which form character, and which can surface at any moment. They are thus close to (sometimes synonymous with) *saṃskāras(z).

2. In Buddhism, they contribute to the storehouse consciousness, *ālaya-vijñāna.

Vaṣaṭ or **Vauṣat.** Ritual exclamation in Hinduism uttered by the hotṛ (see ṚTVIJ) priest at the end of the sacrificial offering verse. Once it is uttered, the oblation is cast in the fire. Vaṣaṭ summons the gods and unifies the cosmos in the offering.

Vasiṣtha. Prominent *ṛṣi of the Vedic Hindu period. To him is attributed *Ṛg Veda* 7. 18; and to him also the victory of the *Brahmanas over the *Kṣatriyas is ascribed.

Vassa. Three-month rain period (sometimes referred to as a 'Buddhist *Lent') when Buddhist *bhikkhus remain in their monasteries for more intense meditation, and when laymen may join the community for a brief period. Vassa begins with the *festival of Poson.

Vasu (sphere of existence): see ĀDITYAS.

Vasubandhu (4th/5th cent. CE). Buddhist philosopher, said to be a younger brother of *Asaṅga. According to tradition, Vasubandhu was originally a follower of *Sarvastivāda (in *Hīnayāna). When the teachings of the Mahāyāna were revealed to him, Vasubandhu quickly came to see its superiority and embraced the *Vijñānavāda school which his brother had established. Vasubandhu's major works include the *Abhidharmakośa*, a scholastic compendium, and the extensive *Vijñapti-mātratā-siddhi*, a work on idealism. Shorter works are the *Triṃśikā* and the *Viṃśatikā*, which summarize the essence of the Vijñānavāda system.

Vasudeva. In Hindu mythology, a prince of the Vṛṣṇi clan, son of Śura, and father of *Kṛṣṇa and *Balarāma.

Vāsudeva. Manifestation of *Viṣṇu in power, worshipped as such by *Vaiṣṇavas. It is often regarded, both within the Vaiṣṇava tradition and by W. scholars, as a patronymic from Vasudeva, and thus another name for *Kṛṣṇa, but this derivation is by no means certain. In Purāṇic texts, the word vāsudeva is often said to mean 'dwelling in all things', and as such may have been the name of a tribal god who became identified with Kṛṣṇa and with the all-pervading *Viṣṇu.

Vasumitra. Teacher of the *Sarvāstivāda school of Buddhism who put forward a thesis to defend the school's basic tenet that entities (*dharma) exist in the past and future as well as in the present. According to Vasumitra, dharmas exist in a noumenal or latent condition in the future until they attain their moment of causal efficacy (*karitra*) in the present. This marks their entry into a functional relationship with other phenomena. When this moment is past they once again enter into a noumenal mode which is now described as 'past'.

Vaṭakaḷai (religious movement within Śrī-Vaiṣṇavism): see TEṈKAḶAI.

Vatican. A city-state of some 109 acres, occupying the Vatican hill on the west bank of the Tiber in *Rome. Created by the Lateran Treaty of 1929 between the kingdom of Italy and the *Holy See, it now provides a base for the *pope and the *curia. 'The Vatican' may also refer to the central, hierarchical organization of *Roman Catholicism, hence Vatican Catholicism.

Vatican Council, First, or **Vatican I** (1869–70). A *Roman Catholic *council. Called by *Pope *Pius IX. This council adopted only two constitutions, despite the advance preparation of fifty-one *schemata*. The constitution on *faith, *Dei Filius*, dealt with God as creator, *revelation, faith, and faith's relationship to reason, adopting positions similar to those of St Thomas *Aquinas. The *schema* on the *Church was not voted on; instead, the question of the *papacy was brought forward, although many (e.g. J. H. *Newman) regarded this as inopportune. The constitution *Pastor Aeternus* defined the primacy of the pope and also his *infallibility when he speaks **ex cathedra*, i.e. when as chief pastor of the Church he defines a doctrine on faith or morals to be held by the whole Church.

After Italian troops occupied Rome, the Council was suspended in Oct. 1870. It never reconvened, and the incompleteness of its work led to a serious imbalance in RC Church teaching.

Vatican Council, Second, or **Vatican II** (1962–5). A *Roman Catholic *council. In calling for an *ecumenical council, *Pope *John XXIII spoke of his desire for *aggiornamento in the RC Church, for 'a new *Pentecost'. He lived to see only the first session: the Council's work was concluded under his successor, *Paul VI (pope 1963–78). The debates showed deep disagreements on many issues, sometimes leading to the rejection of draft *schemata* prepared before the Council. Sixteen documents were eventually produced, five of which are particularly important. The Constitution on the Church (*Lumen Gentium*) gave a deep theological analysis of the nature of the Church, and defined the authority of *bishops and the position of the laity. The Constitution on Revelation (*Dei Verbum*) outlined the nature of *revelation, *scripture, and *tradition; it laid down canons for biblical interpretation and encouraged greater use of the Bible in *theology, *liturgy, and private devotion. The Pastoral Constitution on the Church in the Modern World (*Gaudium et Spes*) dealt with the Church's attitude to human life and culture, and to marriage, economic development, war, and other contemporary issues. The Constitution on the Liturgy set out a theology of the liturgy and principles for reform (e.g. through wider use of the vernacular; see LITURGICAL MOVEMENT). The Decree on Ecumenism explained the RC Church's attitude to other Christians, and outlined a programme for reunion.

Despite the ensuing period of great turbulence, the Council succeeded in producing the greatest changes in the RC Church since the Council of *Trent in the 16th cent.

Vātsīputrīya (Skt., followers of Vātsīputra). A school of early Buddhism. According to tradition Vātsīputra was a *Mahāsaṅghika who claimed to have supernaturally received an *Abhidharmic text in nine sections from *Śāriputra and *Rāhula. This is known as the *Śāriputra-Abhidharma*. Vātsīputra probably lived in the early 3rd cent. BCE in Kośala (E. India) and it seems that the Vātsīputrīyas flourished in that region until the 11th cent. CE.

Their texts, which do not survive, were written in Apabhraṃśa and treat positively the notion of personal identity (*pudgala*). The Vātsīputrīyas were therefore *Pudgalavādins.

Vaudois (adherents of Christian reform movement): see WALDENSES.

Vaughan, Henry (1622–95). Welsh doctor and *Metaphysical poet, known as the Silurist. His main work, *Silex Scintillans* (The Flashing Flint) was influenced by G. *Herbert. Aware of the restlessness of human nature and of the experience of the absence of God, he is especially remembered for vivid images of mystical vision.

Vāyu (Skt., *va*, 'blow'). Indian god of wind and warfare. He was born from the breath of *Puruṣa and was the first to drink *soma. He is the subtle pervader of all space and one of the guardians (see LOKAPĀLA) of the quarters. He came to be seen as the vital guarantor of *prāṇa.

Veda (Skt., 'knowledge'). The body of sacred knowledge held to be the basis of true belief and practice among Hindus. Through it the knower contacts the divinities, or discovers the universal foundation of things, thereby attaining to his desires and overcoming all that is undesirable. The Veda is *śruti, and is thus authoritative, in that it is held to be eternal (*sanātana) and of non-human origin (*apauruṣeya*). In ancient times, it is held, the Veda was 'heard' (śruti) or 'seen' by priestly seers (*ṛṣis), and it is the families descended from these seers who have preserved it through oral transmission. Originally the Veda consisted of two parts: *mantras (verses of invocation and praise) and *Brāhmaṇas (discussions of the proper use of mantras in ritual settings, and explanation of the mythic background of the verses). Later the Veda was extended to include two further groups: *Āraṇyakas and *Upaniṣads. The mantra portions were organized into collections (*samhitās) associated with particular aspects of the *Vedic *sacrifice and with particular priests. Of these, three were at first recognized as Veda: the **Ṛg Veda*, **Sāma Veda*, and **Yajur Veda*. Later a fourth was included, the **Atharva Veda*. To each of these four collections Brāhmaṇas, Āraṇyakas, and Upaniṣads were appended. In addition to these strictly Vedic compositions a number of other texts became associated with the Veda, including the *Vedāṅga, the Upavedas, and the ritual sūtras. Finally the sanctity of the Veda was extended by some to include the *Itihāsa and the *Purāṇas as the 'fifth veda'.

Vedanā (sensing): see SKANDHA.

Vedāṅga (Skt., 'the limbs of the *Veda'). The group of auxiliary texts in Hinduism developed over many centuries to preserve and explicate the Veda, especially in relation to ritual. They are sometimes considered part of the Veda, but strictly lie outside and are reckoned as *smṛti, not *śruti. The Vedāṅga are written mostly in *sūtra style and are traditionally six in number: *śikṣa* (phonetics); *chandas* (metre); *vyākaraṇa* (grammar); *nirukta* (etymology); *jyotiṣa* (astronomy and calendar); *kalpa* (ceremonial). The additional 'limbs' are the Upāṅgas, four in number: *purāṇa, *nyāya, *mīmāṃsā, and *dharmaśāstra.

Vedānta (Skt., 'Veda' + 'end'). The end, i.e. culmination, of the *Vedas, especially as contained in the last section of the *Veda, the *Upaniṣads. However, Vedānta understood as the culmination of the Vedas in ordered reflection (i.e. as a philosophical and religious tradition) rests also on the **Bhagavad-gītā* and on the **Brahma Sūtra* of *Bādarāyaṇa (also known as *Vedānta Sūtra*) which attempted to bring order and harmony to the scattered reflections in the Upaniṣads on the nature of *Brahman and the relation of Brahman to the created order, in particular the continuing presence of Brahman within it as *ātman. These three works became the basis of the philosophy of Vedānta, and became the subject of commentaries leading to the diverse interpretations of Vedānta, of e.g. *Śaṅkara, *Rāmānuja, and *Madhva. Cf. also *Uttara-mīmāṃsā See Index, Vedanta.

Vedāntadeśika (Skt., 'teacher of the *Vedānta'). One of the most outstanding figures in post-*Rāmānuja *Śrīvaiṣṇavism. His real name was Veṅkaṭeśa or Veṅkaṭanātha, and he died *c.*1370 CE, aged nearly 100. He became regarded as the figure-head of the Vaṭakaḷai (see TEṆKAḶAI). More than a hundred works in Tamil and Skt., on every aspect of Śrīvaiṣṇava thought and practice, were written by him. These include not only theological treatises like the *Rahasyatrayasāram* or *Tattvaṭīkā* (a commentary on the *Śrī-Bhāṣya*) or philosophical works like the *Nyāyasiddhāñjana* and *Nyāyapariśuddhi*, but also poetic works (including a drama, two *mahakāvyas*, and thirty devotional poems in *kāvya*-style).

Vedanta Society. A Hindu movement formed in New York in 1896 by Swami Vivekananda, a disciple of Sri *Ramakrishna. It is the W. branch of the Ramakrishna Math (monastery), based at Belur near Calcutta, and was established for the purpose of acquainting the West with the spiritual heritage of India in return for the scientific, educational, and other material benefits of the West.

Vedānta Sūtra (Hindu text): see BRAHMASŪTRA.

Vedas (more comprehensively, *Veda). The four collections which lie at the foundation of Hindu scripture, **Ṛg Veda*, **Sāma Veda*, **Yajur Veda*, **Atharva Veda*. They constitute the foundation of revealed (*śruti) scripture.

Vedi (Hindu altar): see ALTAR.

Vedic. Adjective applied to the language, literature, religion, mythology and ritual pertaining to the *Veda. Generally it indicates the archaic period in Indian culture preceding the classical. Vedic language encompasses the Skt. composed prior to its codification in *Pāṇini's Grammar which set the rules for classical Skt. For Vedic literature, see VEDA. Vedic religion (sometimes called *Brahmanism) can be distinguished from the religion which grew out of it, now usually referred to as Hinduism. Some of the more notable differences between the two religions are seen in their mythology and ritual. Vedic mythology presents a pantheon of deities many of which are solar or meteorological in some of their aspects. These deities are summoned to the human plane in the Vedic rituals (*yajñas*, see *sacrifice). Of the many deities of the Vedic pantheon, few survive into Hinduism and those that do are transformed in character. Similarly, the Vedic ritual, though preserved among some *Brahmans to this day, gives way to a ritual centred not in yajña but in *pūjā.

Vegetarianism. The conscious avoidance of eating animal flesh, frequently extended to fish, and sometimes to animal products. In the East, it is most closely associated with Hindu, Jain, and Buddhist traditions: see FOOD.

Veil (in Islam): see ḤIJĀB.

Veneration of the Cross. A ceremony of the Latin *rite for *Good Friday, in which clergy and people solemnly kiss the foot of a crucifix at the entrance to the sanctuary. In the Middle Ages it was called 'creeping to the cross'. A comparable ceremony in the Orthodox Church takes place on the feast of the *Exaltation of the Cross.

Venial sin. In Christian *moral theology, a sin which is less grave or deliberate than *mortal sin and so does not deprive the soul of sanctifying *grace. On the basis of John 5. 16 the *fathers posited two classes of sins, but the modern distinction goes back to the *scholastics, especially Thomas *Aquinas. According to the theology of *penance, there is no obligation to confess venial sins. For the Hindu distinction between major and minor offences, see MAHĀPĀTAKA.

Venite. Psalm 95, so-called from its first words in Lat.: *Venite exultemus* ('O come, Let us worship').

Venn, Henry (1796–1873). Christian organizer of missionary work, and one of the founders of the *CMS (Church Missionary Society). On the basis of Matthew 28. 19, he envisaged the emergence of national churches with their own indigenous characteristics. This vision is summarized in the 'three-self' policy—though that concept and phrase may have originated from Rufus Anderson: the churches should be self-governing, self-supporting, self-propagating.

Veronica, St. A woman of Jerusalem who, according to legend, offered her head-cloth to Jesus to wipe his face on the way to his crucifixion. When he gave it back, his features were impressed on it. A 'veil of Veronica' seems to have been at Rome since the 8th cent. The legend was probably written in its present form in the 14th cent. to explain the relic. The incident is now devotionally important as the sixth of the *stations of the cross. Feast day, 12 July.

Versicle. In Christian worship, a short sentence, often taken from the Psalms, which is said or sung and answered by a 'response', e.g. between priest and congregation. Versicle and response are often denoted by the symbols ℣ and ℟.

Verstehen (understanding): see HERMENEUTICS.

Vesak or **Vesākha Pūjā** (Skt., Vaiśākha). Major *Theravādin Buddhist *festival, celebrated at full moon in May. It commemorates the birth, enlightenment, and parinibbāna (*nirupadhiśeṣa-nirvāṇa) of the *Buddha.

Vespers. The evening *office of the W. Church.

Vestments. The liturgical dress of the Christian clergy. It derives not, as formerly believed, from the vestments of the ancient Jewish priesthood, but mainly from the secular dress of Roman antiquity retained inside the Church.

See also LITURGICAL COLOURS.

In the Orthodox E., the vestments evolved in a parallel way, and correspond mostly to those of the W. The vestments of the priest are the *sticharion, epitrachelion, girdle, epimanikia, and phainolion. Bishops wear the sakkos, omophorion, and epigonation. There are no special liturgical colours.

VHP (Indian political party): see BHARATYA JANATA PARTY.

Via Dolorosa. The route in Jerusalem which Jesus is supposed to have followed from the judgement-hall of *Pilate to his crucifixion on Mount *Calvary. It is marked by fourteen *stations of the cross.

Via eminentiae (Lat., 'the way of eminence'). The way in which one may arrive positively at the discernment that God is, and to some extent what God is; contrast *via negativa.

Via media (Lat., 'the middle way'). The *Anglican Church in so far as it holds within itself both Catholic and Reformed beliefs and practices (and people), and in so far as it mediates between the two extremes of Christendom. Via media is then used of other central (and often reconciling) positions, e.g. Buddhism as a *middle way.

Via negativa or **Via negationis** (Lat., 'way of negation'). Realization that since God is not a universe or an object in a universe, 'he' is not open to observation or description. It follows that God can only be spoken of *analogically or poetically; and that it is easier to say 'what God is not' rather than what God is. This awareness occurs, in different forms, in all theistic religions, e.g. in *ein-sof, *bila kaifa, *neti neti, *nirguṇa-brahman. This is *apophatic, as opposed to kataphatic theology.

Vianney, Jean-Baptiste Marie, St (1786–1859). French priest, better known as the Curé d'Ars, because of his pastoral ministry in that village. He was born near Lyons and received little formal education. He was dismissed from two seminaries in his attempt to become a priest, but was eventually ordained at Grenoble in 1815. In 1818 he began his ministry in Ars-en-Dombes, a village of about 230 of those whom he regarded as souls, not people.

The life of the village was transformed, and soon penitents came to him in vast numbers: during his last years, he spent up to eighteen hours a day in the confessional. He was made patron of parish priests in 1929.

Viaticum (Lat., 'provision for a journey'). Holy *communion given to those close to death, to give them strength and grace for the next stage of their history.

Vibhajjavādin (Pāli, 'Distinctionist'). A school of early Buddhism belonging to the Elder (*Sthavira) tradition which at the Buddhist Council of Pāṭaliputra in 250 BCE was adjudged to embody the orthodox teachings of the *Buddha. The appellation thus seems to be an alternative designation for the *Theravāda school, and may be derived from the Buddha's basic methodological practice of making a 'distinction' between extreme views of all kinds in his teachings.

Vibhaṅga (Skt., 'distribution', 'division', 'classification'). A Buddhist commentarial work. In the Pāli *Tripiṭaka, a vibhaṅga consists of a detailed exposition of any short section of scripture (*uddesa*). In this sense many discourses of the Sutta Piṭaka may be considered to be vibhaṅgas in their own right. The second book of the Abhidhamma Piṭaka has the straightforward title Vibhaṅga, since it comprises a classification and definition of the various elements of existence. The Vibhaṅga may represent part of the most original Abhidharmic system common to all schools.

Vibhāṣā (Vaibhāṣika text): see VAIBHĀṢIKA.

Vibhūti. 1. In Hinduism, superhuman powers, especially associated with *Śiva, but also listed by *Patañjali in *Yoga Sūtra* 3. 16–55. Since they include knowledge of past and future, previous births, hour of death, etc., they are virtually identical with siddhis/*iddhis. More generally, they are the inspirations of musicians, artists, etc.

2. The ashes with which *Śiva smeared his body (as do his devotees), having the power to restore the dead to life.

Vicar (Lat., *vicarius*, 'substitute'). Title of certain Christian priests. In the Church of England a vicar is the priest of a parish whose *tithes were the property of a monastery in medieval times and thereafter of a 'lay rector'. Since the time of Pope Innocent III (1198–1216) the title 'Vicar of Christ' based on John 21. 15 ff., has been a title reserved to the pope.

Vicar-General. In the Roman Catholic Church a priest appointed by a *bishop to assist in administering his diocese.

Victory, Tour of (period in life of Indian philosopher Śaṅkara): see ŚAṄKARA.

Videhamukti (Skt., 'bodiless' + 'liberation'). *Mokṣa through knowledge that one is not one's body but rather *ātman. One becomes in consequence disembodied or discarnate.

Vidyā (Skt.) or **vijja** (Pāli). 'Knowledge', the total and integral knowledge which precedes and comes after the incomplete non-knowledge (*avidyā) or ignorance which binds people to the wheel of transmigration (*saṃsāra). Vidyā penetrates *māyā and thus enables us to apprehend all things (however apparently different) as they really are. In Hinduism, it is of two types: (i) apara-vidyā, lower knowledge, acquired through intellect; (ii) para-vidyā, higher, spiritual knowledge, leading to enlightenment and liberation (*mokṣa).

Vidyā is defined more precisely than *jñāna, which also means knowledge. There were originally four branches of vidyā: trayī-vidyā, knowledge of the triple *Veda; *ānvīkṣikī*, metaphysics and logic; *daṇḍa-nīti*, the art of government; and *vārttā*, or agriculture, trade, and medicine. A fifth, ātma-vidyā, the knowledge of the *ātman, was added later.

Vidyāraṇya or **Madhavācarya** (14th cent. CE). Hindu philosopher who expounded the *Advaita Vedānta of *Śaṅkara. His *Pañcadaśi* became a basic work of this school.

Vigil. A night service before a Christian festival.

Vigraha (Skt., 'form'). The divine represented in Hinduism through a manifest form. An image is consecrated by *mantras and other rituals, but does not 'become' God: it becomes the mediating vehicle through which the divine becomes real to the worshipper.

Vihāra (Skt., 'dwelling'). Originally a Buddhist monastic retreat during the rainy season, later becoming a permanent monastic establishment. The rock-carved vihāras of the Western Ghats, usually associated with a *caitya hall, are among the earliest surviving examples of Buddhist architecture, though Jain vihāras (1st and 2nd cents. BCE) are found in Orissa. Of the rock-carved variety, Bhājā, dating from the early Śunga period (2nd cent. BCE) is a good example, consisting of a central rectangular chamber surrounded by individual cells. Later vihāras are simply an elaboration on this basic theme, in which a central courtyard (very often enclosing a railed *Bo Tree, shrine room, and ambulatory) is encompassed by monks' cells, sometimes reaching several storeys with veranda attached.

The vihāra is a fundamental feature of all Buddhist cultures. The Indian state of Bihar is so called because of the large number of vihāras which at one time covered the landscape.

Vijñāna (Skt., 'knowing'). 1. In Hinduism, knowledge which penetrates ritual and sacrifice, and understands its meaning. It is therefore the highest state of consciousness in which the meditator sees *Brahman, not just in the condition of *samādhi, but in the whole of everything. In *Vedānta, this is 'seeing Brahman with open eyes'.

2. In Buddhism (Pāli, *viññāna*), the fifth of the five *skandhas. As 'perception', it is contrasted with *jñāna ('understanding'). Its importance was enhanced in *Vijñanavāda (Yogācāra), because it is the basis of the 'storehouse consciousness' (*ālaya-vijñāna), which contains the seeds of all *dharmas (constituents of manifestation).

Vijñānavāda. Buddhist school of idealism, also known as Yogācāra ('yoga-practice') or the doctrine of 'Mind-Only' (*citta-mātra*). The school developed in the 4th cent. CE, and its leading exponents were Maitreyanātha, *Asaṅga, and his brother *Vasubandhu. Its literature is extensive and includes the **Laṅkāvatāra Sūtra*, **Samdhinirmocana Sūtra*, and the **Avataṃsaka Sūtra*, as well as many treatises composed by its followers.

The basic postulate of the school is that consciousness itself is the fundamental and only reality, and that the apparent diversity of the empirical world is the product of instability and obscuration in the individual field of consciousness. The standard form of the doctrine distinguishes eight functions or aspects of consciousness, the most fundamental being the *ālaya-vijñāna ('Receptacle Consciousness', or storehouse consciousness) which is the foundation of personal identity. Due to the effect of previous actions (*karma) the ālaya becomes tainted and unstable, and proceeds to manifest itself in a dualistic form whereby the notions of 'self' and 'other' arise. This is the second aspect, the 'defiled consciousness' (*kliṣṭa-mano-vijñāna*). The division of consciousness is carried further through its operation in the six sense-modalities (touch, taste, smell, hearing, sight, and thought) which completes the list of eight functions. An image commonly used to describe this scheme is that of the ocean: its depths are like the ālaya, and the operation of the six senses are compared to the waves which disturb its surface stirred by the wind of *karma. For the Vijñānavāda enlightenment is achieved through the recognition of the ālaya as the only reality and the consequent cessation of dualistic imaginings.

The Vijñānavada introduced a doctrine of 'three aspects' (*trisvabhava*) to describe the ways in which the ālaya manifests itself.

The doctrine of 'Mind-Only' had a profound influence in all *Mahāyāna Buddhist countries and became especially popular in the Far East.

Vijñapti-mātra. The doctrine of 'mere imagining' or 'thought only' associated with the *Vijñānavāda school of Buddhist idealism. According to this teaching the empirical world of objects is regarded as the product of pure ideation, with no reality beyond the consciousness of the perceiving subject. In terms of the doctrine of Vijñapti-mātra, enlightenment is the realization of the imaginary status of phenomena and the non-substantiality of the self and external objects.

Vikalpa (Skt., *vi* + *klṛp*, 'variation', 'diversity'). In Buddhist philosophy, the imaginative tendency of unenlightened minds. The Pāli term *vikappa* is not used in a technical sense in the *Tripiṭaka of the *Sthaviravādins, but it is common in *Mahāyāna philosophical works, particularly of the Yogācāra (*Vijñānavāda) variety. The *Abhisamayālaṅkāra* considers both 'subjectivity' (*grāhaka*) and 'objectivity' (*grāhya*) to be the result of imagining (vikalpa). Vikalpa is said to come to an end in the enlightened state, when one comes to understand reality freed from all thought-construction. A common synonym for this state is 'gnosis devoid of imagining' (*nirvikalpajñāna*).

Vikāra (Skt., 'transformation'). The means, in Hinduism, especially in *Sāṁkhya, whereby one substance is changed into another, as cream into butter, etc. Thus *prakṛti is able to manifest all forms of appearance.

Village Awakening Councils (Buddhist self-development organizations): see SARVODAYA.

Vilna Gaon (Jewish spiritual leader): see ELIJAH BEN SOLOMON ZALMAN; MITNAGGEDIM.

Vimalakirti (bodhisattva): see BODHISATTVA.

Vimalakīrti Sūtra or ***Vimalakirti-nirdeśa-sūtra*** (Teachings of the *Bodhisattva Unstained-Glory). Major *Mahāyāna text. A measure of its popularity is the number of translations: into Chinese (eight times), Tibetan (three times), Sogdian, and Khotanese. The Skt. original has not survived.

The Sūtra, which was composed not later than 2nd cent. CE, has been especially popular with the laity, since the protagonist is himself a lay householder. Thus the world-renouncing monastic ethos of the Hīnayāna is rejected, and the status of the laity legitimized as part of the broad re-evaluation of religious ideals undertaken by the Mahāyāna.

Vimānavatthu (part of Buddhist Pāli canon): see KHUDDAKA NIKĀYA.

Vimokkha (Pāli), **vimokṣa** (Skt., 'liberation', 'deliverance'). A term occurring in early Buddhism in connection with two classificatory lists. First: the Eight Liberations or Stages of Liberation. These form a slight variant on the eight *jhānas as a system of classifying stages of attainment in developing concentration meditation (*samādhi).

Second: the Three Doors to Deliverance (vimokkha-mukha). When a person resolves to attain *nirvāna, he cannot make nirvāna itself a subject of meditation, for it is 'inconceivable', not an object of thought. He therefore makes his way towards nirvāna by making impermanence (*anicca), suffering (*dukkha), and no-self (*anatman), respectively, his subjects of meditation.

Vimokṣa: see VIMOKKHA.

Vimutti (Pāli, 'freedom', 'release', 'deliverance'). Freedom from suffering (*dukkha), the goal of the Buddhist path. Canonical Buddhism distinguishes two kinds: freedom through understanding (pañña-vimutti) and freedom of mind (ceto-vimutti). The former means final release from suffering, the ending of rebirth, *nirvāna, and is so named because it is brought about by understanding (*prajña) which develops out of the practice of insight meditation (*vipassanā). The latter represents the qualified freedom from suffering which arises out of the practice of concentration meditation (*samādhi), Ceto-vimutti can only become permanent and unshakeable (*akuppa*), synonymous with final release, if it is combined with paññā-vimutti, that is, if the meditator cultivates insight as well as concentration.

Vinaya ('that which separates'). The rules which govern the *saṅgha, and thus lives of Buddhist *bhikkhus and bhikkunīs. It is one of the three parts ('baskets') of the *Tripiṭaka. It is divided into three parts: *Sutta Vibhaṅga* (*Sūtravibhaṅga*, also known as *Vinayavibhaṅga*), which has incorporated an earlier disciplinary text, *Pratimokṣa Sūtra*: it thus becomes a statement and explication of the *pratimokṣa rules. The second part is *Skandhaka* (*Khandhaka*, 'Chapters', also called *Vinayavastu*), of more diverse materials, and itself divided into *Mahāvagga* ('Greater Section') and *Cūlavagga* ('Smaller Section'): in addition to rules governing rituals and communal occasions, e.g. *uposatha, *vassa, admission to the order, *schism, it contains a partial biography of the *Buddha and an account of the first two *Councils; it also establishes the importance of *sīmā*, 'boundary', which establishes much more than territory: it designates a sacred space in which all new members of the community are ordained, thus securing the continuity of the community. The third part is *Parivāra*, a kind of appendix which organizes the material of the other parts in ways which make it easier to learn. See also TAO-HSÜAN; RITSU.

Vincent de Paul (founder): see VINCENTIANS.

Vincentian Canon. A threefold (but never realized) criterion of *Catholic doctrine: *quod ubique, quod semper, quod ab omnibus creditum est* ('what has been believed everywhere, always, and by all'). It was formulated by St Vincent of Lérins (d. before 450) in his *Commonitorium*, a guide to *heresy and to determining the true faith.

Vincentians. The most usual name for the Congregation of the Mission (CM), a Roman Catholic religious order founded by St Vincent de Paul in 1625. He had been moved by the plight of a poor woman in 1617, and established Les Dames de Charité, an early expression of organized charity. From this developed Les Filles de la Charité, who, in addition to collecting money, committed themselves to service. As dispensers of charity and as missionaries, they are also known as Lazarists, from the priory of St. Lazare, Vincent's headquarters in Paris.

Vinculum (bond in marriage): see MARRIAGE (Christianity).

Vindhyācalavāsini. 'Dweller on the Vindhya', perhaps originally a tribal goddess of the Vindhya hills, but later a form of *Kālī, worshipped by the *Ṭhags.

Vindhyavāsinī (Skt., 'she who lives on the Vindhya mountains'). Name of a goddess in a well-known Hindu temple. The shrine stands near Mirzapur, E. Uttar Pradesh, and has been famous since at least the 7th cent. CE, even with N. Indian court poets.

Viññāna (consciousness): see VIJÑĀNA (2).

Vinobā Bhāve, Ācārya (1895–1982). Hindu reformer who succeeded, and developed the ideas of, *Gāndhī. Drawn to an ascetic life, he burnt his school certificates and eventually joined Gandhi's *āśrama at Sabarmati. In 1921, Gandhi sent him to start a new āśrama at Wardha, and in 1941 he was the first *satyāgrahi to be arrested in the civil disobedience movement. In 1951, the idea came to him of a middle way between Communist insurrection and landholding aggrandizement by asking large landholders to donate surplus land to the landless. The principle of *sarvodaya, 'welfare for all', was not in fact far from Communism.

Violence. An aspect of human behaviour often bound up with emotions (especially anger), which religions cannot ignore—and often express. Opinion is divided as to where violence should be located along the nature–nurture spectrum. Those favouring natural processes or *psychodynamic theory hold that religious activities reduce violence if they function cathartically, but increase violence if they result in frustration. An additional consideration is that religions often put 'violence'—if that is what it is—to religious ends, examples here being *sacrifice, head-hunting, many male rites of *initiation, and the justification of war (*just war) on religious grounds.

Vipāka (Pāli, Skt., 'ripen'). The coming to fruition, in Buddhism, of an act—the consequence of the law of *karma.

Vipāka-sūtra-aṅga (Jain text): see AṄGA.

Vipassanā (Pāli), **vipaśyanā** (Skt., 'see clearly', 'penetrate an object thoroughly'). Insight into the truths of impermanence (*anicca), suffering (*dukkha), and no-self (*anātman); the form of *meditation which has the personal apprehension of these specific truths of Buddhism as its object. Together with tranquillity (*samatha) it represents the twofold dimension to Buddhist meditational practice. But it is superior to the latter because it is concerned with that aspect of meditation which is distinctively Buddhist, and because it alone produces the form of understanding, prajña, through which liberation takes place. It is the central focus of meditational training in *Theravāda Buddhist centres.

Vipaśyanā: see VIPASSANĀ.

Virabhadra. A fearsome manifestation of *Śiva, created to threaten Dakṣa and wreck his great sacrifice when he forgot to invite Śiva to it.

Viraśaivas ('heroic Śaivas'): see LIṄGĀYAT.

Virgin Birth of Christ. The Christian doctrine that *Jesus was conceived by the Virgin *Mary by the operation of the *Holy Spirit and without sexual relations with a man (one should strictly speak of 'virginal *conception*'; that Mary remained a virgin even in giving birth is a later idea).

Among modern Christians belief in the virgin birth is often taken as a touchstone of orthodoxy, both by *Catholics, for whom it is involved with *mariology, and *Protestants. Some liberal theologians have criticized the doctrine as setting Christ's humanity apart from ours. They have also drawn attention to the widespread claim of virgin births in many religions (e.g. Mahāmāyā and the *Buddha, *Kuntī/Pṛtha and Karna, *Zoroaster and the saviour, Saoshyant), and have suggested that this is a reverential theme introduced for apologetic reasons. Even stronger criticisms have been made by feminist writers and theologians, who point out that Mary is not even accorded the participation of parthenogenesis if perpetual virginity (see above) is affirmed.

Vīr Siṅgh (Sikh writer): see SIṄGH SABHĀ.

Virūpa (Tibetan siddha): see SIDDHA TRADITION.

Virya (Skt.; Pāli, *viriya*). Effort and exertion of will in Buddhism; it appears in the eightfold path (*aṣṭangika-marga), as one of the four perfect exertions, of the five powers (*bala), and of the seven factors of enlightenment.

Vishishtadvaita (qualified non-duality): see VIŚIṢṬĀDVAITA-VEDĀNTA.

Vishnu (Hindu god): see VIṢṆU.

Viśiṣṭādvaita-vedānta. The teaching and school, in Hinduism, of qualified non-duality, in contrast to *Advaita. The name is derived from *viśiṣṭa* ('distinct', 'particular to') and *advaita* ('not-dual'). Although introduced by the *Vaiṣṇava writer, Yamunācārya, the school is usually associated with *Rāmānuja. The world, selves, and God are all real, but the world and self depend on God, since God creates the cosmos out of his *subtle body by transforming it into a gross one—though he does not prevent faults or blemishes occurring. Selves depend in such a way that they are sustained in continuing, independent existence, even after liberation (*mokṣa). But they remain part of the whole body of *Brahman as attributes, Brahman being 'all that is'. Since the highest mode of being is personal (i.e. higher than inanimate, or non-relational being), Brahman is personal, i.e. containing the relational within his being 'all that is'.

Visitandines (Christian Order): see DE SALES.

Visiting the sick (Heb., *bikkur holim*). A major commandment in Judaism. The way in which this should be done is carefully described, including the wise advice never to sit on the bed. From this general requirement (at least as old as Ecclesiasticus 7. 35) it passed into the fundamental teaching associated with *Jesus in the parable of the separation between the sheep and the goats (Matthew 25).

Viṣṇu. The 'pervader', or perhaps, the 'one taking different forms', a Hindu god of little importance in the *Vedas, but subsequently a major deity, and a member of the Hindu 'trinity' (*trimūrti). He is the preserver of the universe and embodiment of goodness and mercy. For *Vaiṣṇavites, he is the supreme deity, *Īśvara, from whom all created things emanate. As Īśvara, he becomes incarnate (*avatāra) at moments of great crisis (for list, see AVATĀRA). Īśvara is the material cause of the universe, omnipresent to it, and sustaining it in life. Through his presence, he is the refuge of all who need his help. Īśvara exists in five forms, *para, vyūha, vibhava, antaryāmin*, and *ārcāvatāra*. In his transcendent being, he is called *para, as in Parabrahman, Paravāsudeva. He manifests his power through four *vyūhas*—*Vāsudeva, Saṁkarṣana, Pradyumna, and Aniruddha—thereby being able to create and being available for worship. Viṣṇu is usually depicted standing, holding weapons, or reclining on *Śeṣa, the serpent. Because of his pervasive presence, images of Viṣṇu are extremely important, whether in the home or in temples—some of which have consequently evoked magnificent architecture. See Index, Viṣṇu.

Viṣṇu Purāṇa. In Hinduism one of the eighteen *Mahāpurāṇas. It may have been compiled towards the end of the 3rd cent. CE, or near the beginning of the 4th. Unlike most *purāṇas, it is a unified and clearly structured composition, with a consistent theological viewpoint discernible throughout. *Viṣṇu is identified with *Brahman, and his omnipresence and omnipotence are constantly emphasized.

Viṣṇuśaram (compiler of *Pañcatantra*, collection of legends): see PAÑCATANTRA.

Viṣṇuyaśas. A prominent Hindu *brahman. One of his descendants will be born at the end of the *Kali-yuga, as *Kalki(n), the *avatāra, of the future, of *Viṣṇu. His coming will restore peace and innocence to the earth (*Viṣṇu Purāṇa* 4. 24).

Visualization (*dmigs.pa*). An essential component of *meditation in Tibetan Buddhism. Though it has been linked with *Theravādin *nimitta practice, visualization does characterize *Vajrayāna as a step away from *Hīnayāna and other forms of *Mahāyāna meditation which rely to a great extent on awareness (*samatha) and insight (*vipassanā). Principal subjects for visualization are *maṇḍalas and deities, and to be able to visualize them well means to be able to see their every detail as indistinguishable from common reality—a feat said to require at least one lifetime of total devotion to the skill. Visualization has four stages: projection, which is the creation of the appearance; pride, which is the identification of the self with that which is visualized; recollection of purity, which is the contemplation of the meaning of the practice and the nature of the deity; absorption, which is the reintegration of the deity into the *yogin.

Visuddhimagga ('Path of Purification'): see BUDDHAGHOSA.

Viśva-devās (Skt., 'all gods'). In the *Ṛg Veda*, all the gods together. But the concept is more subtle than that of a collective polytheism: it expresses the way in which one god can incorporate the powers and characters of all others.

Viśva Hindu Paraśad (Indian political group): see BHARATYA JANATA PARTY.

Viśvakarman (Skt., 'all-creating'). The Hindu *Vedic creative power, the personified divine architect of the universe.

Viśvāmitra. Famous Hindu *ṛṣi, said to be composer of the third maṇḍala of the *Ṛg Veda* which contains the most sacred *mantra, *Gāyatrī (3. 62. 10).

Viśvanātha (Skt., 'lord of the universe'). In Hinduism:

1. Manifestation of *Śiva at Kāśī, where a temple bears his name.
2. Author of *Rāghava-Vilāsa*, a life of *Rāma, and *Sāhita-darpana*, a treatise on poetry.

Viśvarūpa-darśana. The vision in Hinduism of the universal divine form, celebrated especially in *Bhagavad-gītā* 11, when it is manifested to *Arjuna.

Vitakka or **vitarka** (Pāli, Skt., 'thought-conception'). In Buddhist psychology the initial application of the mind to its object. It is defined as laying hold of the object of thought and directing attention towards it.

Vital, Ḥayyim ben Joseph (1542–1620). Jewish *kabbalist. Vital was the principal student of Isaac *Luria in Safed and arranged and elaborated on his teachings. *Ez ha-Ḥayyim* (Tree of life) is a record of these teachings, and this was re-edited by his son and circulated under the title *Shemonah She'arim* (Eight Gates). Vital also produced an autobiography (*Sefer ha-Hezyonot*, Book of Visions), commentaries on the *Talmud, volumes of sermons, a commentary on the **Zohar*, and various *halakhic *responsa. As the chief formulator of the Lurianic kabbalah, he was an important influence on the development of later Jewish *mysticism.

Vitarka: see VITAKKA.

Viṭhobā (Mahārāṣtra deity): see NĀMDEV.

Viṭṭhala (Mahārāṣtra deity): see NĀMDEV.

Vivāha (Hindu marriage): see MARRIAGE.

Vivasvat (social law): see ĀDITYAS.

Viveka (Skt., 'discrimination'). In *Sāṁkhya philosophy, the direct intuitive discrimination between *puruṣa (pure consciousness) and *prakṛti (materiality), and the goal of the Sāṁkhya system. In *Advaita Vedānta viveka is considered one of the four requisites of a seeker after knowledge of Brahman and is defined by *Śaṅkara as: 'an (intellectual) discrimination between what is eternal and what is non-eternal' (*Brahmasūtrabhāṣya* 1. 1).

Viveka-cūḍāmaṇi (The Crest Jewel of Discrimination). A work on the distinction between reality and appearance by *Śaṅkara.

Vivekānanda (1863–1902). A devout follower of *Ramakrishna, and founder of the Ramakrishna Mission which now has more than a hundred centres throughout the world. After a meeting with Keshab Chandra *Sen, he joined the *Brahmo Samāj. All his life he acted on the principle that all people hold within themselves the means to achieve their full potential.

It was after becoming a disciple of Ramakrishna that Vivekānanda received his new name, and the honourable title of 'swāmi'. After six years of contemplation in the Himālayan region he carried out, with missionary zeal, tours of S. and W. India, becoming the most noteworthy teacher of modern *Vedānta. In 1893 a *World's Parliament of Religions was held in Chicago. Swami Vivekānanda represented Hinduism with outstanding success, and, through the power of his oratory and his impressive appearance, became known worldwide.

Vizier (Muslim government minister): see WAZĪR.

Vladimir, St (d. 1015). Prince of Kiev and 'apostle of Russia'. Brought up a pagan, he invited Greek missionaries to his realm and became a Christian in 988. His motives cannot have been unconnected with the desire for an alliance with Byzantium, and he married Anne, sister of the emperor Basil II, shortly after. Vladimir set about the conversion of his people by enforcing *baptism by law. He is remembered as pious and even scrupulous, wondering whether the death penalty could be used by a Christian prince. Feast day, 15 July.

Vodou, vodum, vodun, voodoo, or **voudou** (Fon, in Benin, *vodu*, 'deity' or 'spirit'). The name given to the folk religion of Haiti, developing since the 18th cent. among the rural and urban poor, but despised by the other classes until intellectuals began to defend it in the 1930s as the Haitian national religion. French *Roman Catholic elements are synthesized with African religious and magical elements derived from slaves of Dahomean origin. In 1996, the African origins of Vodou were reaffirmed when the ban on Vodou was lifted in Benin, and its validity as an indigenous religion was recognized. The effective divinities are the capricious *loa*, representing ancestors, African deities, or Catholic *saints. They communicate through dreams or descend during the cult ritual and 'ride' their devotees while in a trance state; to encourage this, the *loa's* own symbolic patterns (*veves*) are laid out in flour on the ground. For the first half of this century the RC Church launched ineffective anti-vodou campaigns, aided in 1941 by the government forces destroying vodou temples. After 1957, the ruling Duvalier family courted vodou for political reasons

Vohu Manah (the Good Mind): see AMESA SPENTAS.

Void (in Buddhism): see ŚŪNYATĀ.

Von Hügel, F.: see HÜGEL, F. VON.

Voodoo: see VODOU.

Vorgriff (pre-hension): see RAHNER, KARL.

Voudou: see VODOU.

Vows. Promises or commitments to undertake, or abstain from, particular actions, lifestyles, etc. All religions offer the opportunity to formalize one's intentions in this way, to such an extent that there can be uncertainty about whether a vow once made can be revoked. Thus in Judaism vows are not required of Jews in the Bible, but once made they have to be carried out with precision (Deuteronomy 23. 22–4). Vows are thus inviolable (1 Samuel 14. 24 ff.; Judges 11. 30 ff.), but the *rabbis evolved an elaborate system for the annulment of vows in the tractate *Nedarim*. Jewish law uses three terms for vows, *neder* (general), *nedavah* (freewill offering), and *shebu'ah* (to pursue or not to pursue a course of action).

Some early Christians followed the practice of taking vows (Paul, e.g., taking the temporary vow of a Nazirite, Acts 21. 22–6), although *Jesus had warned against letting a dedication of something to God through *qorban* take precedence over more fundamental obligations (Mark 7. 11). Vows came to be understood as a social act through which a person donates himself or herself to another (marriage vows), or to God in a religious community.

For examples of vows in other religions, see BODHISATTVA VOW; FIVE GREAT VOWS (among

Jains); SHIGUSEIGAN (the four great vows in Zen); VRATA; see also Index, Vows.

Vrata (Skt., 'will'). The Indian religious commitment of the will to some religious end—e.g. pilgrimage, chastity, devotion. Vows are fundamental to Jains, in the sense that they constitute the Jain commitment: see FIVE GREAT VOWS. For vrata in the sense of celebration, see FESTIVALS AND FASTS.

Vratya. One bound by a vow. Vratyas appeared as groups of people (bound perhaps by common vows) in NE India, perhaps the first of the *Aryan invaders. They had their own distinct beliefs and customs which they took with them as they migrated east to Magadha. Their religion was assimilated into the **Atharva Veda*. They persisted as groups of religious functionaries.

Vṛndāvana (Skt., 'grove of a multitude'). A sacred forest in India by the river Yamunā, near Mathurā, the birthplace of *Kṛṣṇa. It is a place particularly sacred to *Vaiṣṇavas. The modern town is also known as Brindavan.

Vṛtra (Skt., 'storm-cloud'). In Hinduism, the dark cloud of ignorance and sloth, personified as a demon-serpent, vanquished by *Indra.

Vṛtti (Skt., 'wave'). In Hinduism, the thoughts of the waking and dream states which wash over consciousness like waves, and prevent the seeing of truth.

Vulgate (Lat., *versio vulgata*, 'popular version'). The Lat. version of the Christian *Bible of widest circulation where Latin continued to be used. Mainly the work of *Jerome, it was intended to end the confusion of varying readings in the existing 'Old Latin' MSS of the Bible. The Council of *Trent (1546) pronounced the Vulgate the only authentic Lat. text of the scriptures. A full critical edition by the *Benedictines was begun at the direction of Pope Pius X in 1907.

Vulture Peak (mythical mountain): see NICHIREN.

Vyāhṛti. The Hindu utterance of sacred sounds, *mantras, etc., especially the sacrificial utterances of *Prajāpati, *bhūr, bhuvar, svar*, 'the three clear ones'. *Manusmṛti* 2. 76 calls them 'the great vyāhṛtis', and they are recited by *brahmans after *Oṃ at the beginning of each day's prayer.

Vyākhyā-prajñapti-aṅga (Jain text): see AṄGA.

Vyāsa (Skt., 'collector'). Collectors and compilers of Hindu works, especially Veda-vyāsa, the compiler of the *Vedas. Traditionally, this is said to be Śaṣvata, though clearly many were involved.

Vyūha (manifest power of Viṣṇu): see VIṢṆU.

W

Waco, Texas: see BRANCH DAVIDIANS.

Wager, Pascal's: see PASCAL.

Waḥdat al-shuhūd; Waḥdat al-wujūd (unity of consciousness, unity of being): see AḤMAD SIR-HINDĪ.

Wahhābīya. An ultra-conservative, puritanical Muslim movement adhering to the *Ḥanbalite law, although it regards itself as *ghair muqallidīn*, non-adherent to parties, but defending truth. It arose in Najd in the Arabian peninsula during the 18th cent. Its founder, Muḥammad ibn 'Abd al-Wahhāb (1703–87 (AH 1115–1201)) found a champion in the tribal leader Muḥammad ibn Sa'ūd of the Dar'iya region, and from then on the Saudis became the main supporters of the movement. They believe that the Muslims have abandoned their faith in One God (*tawhid) and have distorted Islam through innovations (*bid'a) which run counter to pure Islam. The Wahhābīs accept only the *Qur'ān and the authentic *Sunna, and all Muslims who do not accept their creed are regarded as heretics, especially the *Shī'a, who are considered as archenemies of Islam.

During the 19th cent., the Wahhābīs in alliance with the Sa'ūd family began to expand territorially. Within the new kingdom of Saudi Arabia, the Wahhābīs became dominant in conservative control, introducing *mutawwi'ūn*, 'enforcers of obedience', a kind of private religious police, monitoring not only public but also private conformity to Islam (since before Allāh there is no distinction between private and public).

Wāhigurū (Sikh acclamative name of God): see VĀHIGURŪ.

Waḥy (Arab., 'to suggest, put something in someone's mind'). The idea of 'revelation' in Islam. The term waḥy is used especially for the giving of the *Qur'ān, itself described as a 'revelation revealed' (*waḥy yūḥā*, 53. 4). Waḥy refers also to revelation given to former prophets, as to *Moses (20. 13), and is indirect, for humans cannot see Allāh (42. 50). The *ḥadīth give details as to the manner of revelation, and the way in which Muḥammad himself was affected physically by the force of the message he received.

The more common term for the giving of the Qur'ān is 'sending down', from the verbal root *n-z-l*, hence *nazzala anzala*, 'cause to descend'.

Wahyguru (Sikh acclamation): see VAHIGURU.

Wai-ch'i (breathing in Chinese religion and medicine): see CH'I.

Wailing Wall (*ha-Kotel ha-Ma'aravi*). Western Wall of the Jewish *Temple in *Jerusalem. The Wailing Wall was all that remained of the Temple after its destruction by the Romans in 70 CE. It is a place of *pilgrimage and the most holy place in the Jewish world. Since 1967, when it came into *Israeli hands, the area in front of the wall has been cleared and converted into a large paved area where Jews can gather and pray.

Wai-tan (external alchemy): see ALCHEMY.

Wajd (Arab., *wajada*, 'find, know by experience'). Ecstasy or rapture, a *Sūfī term for a state of mental and physical excitement that manifests itself when the heart of the devotee is undergoing divine illumination.

Wājib (duty in Islam): see FARḌ.

Waka (Japanese verse form): see HAIKU.

Waldenses/Waldensians or **Vaudois.** Adherents of a reforming movement which began in the 12th cent., in the *Roman Catholic Church and became a *Protestant Church. It originated with a Frenchman, Pierre Valdès (Peter Waldo), when he obeyed the command of Christ to sell all that he had and give it to the poor (Matthew 19. 21), and set out (much as, in different ways, did *Francis and *Dominic) to recover the Church as Christ intended. When the small group who gathered around him ('the poor men of Lyons') were banned by Pope Lucius III (at the Council of Verona) from unauthorized preaching in 1184, they organized an alternative Church. They continued to be victims of persecution (including the massacre in 1655 which evoked Milton's Sonnet, 'On the Late Massacre in Piedmont'), but survived long enough to be granted religious freedom in 1848. They number now about 20,000.

Waldo, Peter (founder of Waldenses): see WALDENSES.

Walī (Arab., *waliya*, 'protect'). A benefactor or protector in Islam. In the *Qur'ān it is used especially of God ('God is the walī of those who believe', 2. 257), and it is a title of *Muḥammad. Conversely, a walī is a friend of God, and is the title of one particularly devoted to God.

The veneration of walīs became a highly popular part of Islam, particularly focused on their tombs. Thus Baghdād has been called 'the city of the walīs', because so many are venerated there—e.g. *al-Junaid, Sīdī *'Abd al-Qādir al-Jili, Shihāb al-Dīn al-Suhrawardī. Among the *Sūfīs, elaborate hierarchies of awliyā' (pl.) were produced, along with levels or stages, in the progress towards wilayat, becoming a walī.

Wali Allah or **Waliullah** (Indian Islamic reformer): see SHAH WALIULLAH.

Walking object indices (apparent people providing cross-reference to the world): see PHENOMENOLOGY.

WALUBI. Acronym for Per-*WAL*-ian *U*mat *B*uddha *I*ndonesia, or All-Indonesia Federation of Buddhist Organizations. It was founded in Jogyakarta in 1978 to promote union among Indonesia's 3 million Buddhists. The Federation includes both *Theravāda and *Mahāyāna Buddhist groups (the former having strong links with Dhammayutika temples in Thailand via the Phra Dhamma-Dūta missionary programme) and Buddhayana, a syncretistic combination of both these branches of Buddhism plus Kasogatan, a local type of Javanese Buddhism. Monks and lay Buddhists are strongly represented in most branches of WALUBI. See also TRIDHARMA.

Wandering Jew. Figure in a Christian legend of a Jew who, as a consequence of rejecting *Jesus, is condemned never to die, but to wander homeless through the world until the Second Coming (*Parousia) of Christ, or until his last descendant shall have died. When the last descendant dies, the Wandering Jew 'attains the happiness of eternal sleep'.

Wang An-shih (reformer): see CH'ENG HAO.

Wang-pi (important figure in neo-Taoism): see HSÜAN-HSÜEH.

Wang Yang-ming (Jap., Ō Yōmei; 1472–1529). Chinese philosopher, soldier, and statesman, of the Ming dynasty. He was a follower of the Confucian school who incorporated into his own teachings Buddhist and Taoist insights. His principal tenets include the unity of knowledge and action and the paradoxical identity between mind and heart (*hsin*) and *li ('principle', referring to being, and to virtue). The Yang-ming school became very popular in late Ming China (16th cent.), and spread as well to Japan, as Yōmei-gaku, where it gained adherents among the lower *samurais, many of whom worked actively for the success of the Meiji restoration in the 19th cent.

Wanshi Shōgaku (Chinese Ch'an/Zen master): see HUNG-CHIH CHENG-CHUEH.

Waqf (pl., *awqāf*). Legal term in Islam, to prevent something (by dedication) falling into the possession of another, hence especially the dedication of land, buildings, etc., to religious purposes, or for family endowments. The alienation of waqf land in Israel/Palestine has been a particular source of grievance to Palestinian Muslims.

War: see JUST WAR.

Ward, Mary (founder): see INSTITUTE OF THE BLESSED VIRGIN MARY.

Warrior-monks (Japanese): see AKUSŌ.

Warsaw Ghetto: see GHETTO.

War Scroll. One of the *Dead Sea scrolls found near *Qumran. The *War Scroll* is an *apocalyptic work describing the conflict at the end of time between the Sons of Light and the Sons of Darkness.

Wasan (Jap., 'song of praise'). In Buddhism, a song/hymn celebrating a *buddha, *bodhisattva, *soshigata, etc., or some Buddhist theme. Especially famous is *Hakuin's *Zazen wasan*.

Wāṣil B. 'Aṭā', Abū Hudhaifa (699–748 (AH 80–131)). Leading *Mu'tazilite theologian in Islam. He belonged to the associates of *Ḥasan al-Baṣrī, though he separated from his views enough to start the school of the Mu'tazilites (a separation once thought to be the origin of the name). He held four distinctive views: (i) the qualities/attributes of *Allāh are not eternal; (ii) humans possess free will (cf. *Qadarites); (iii) a Muslim who sins is in an intermediate state between that of a Muslim and that of a *kāfir; (iv) it is possible to judge that one of the parties in the murder of *'Uthmān, and in the battles of the Camel and Siffīn (see 'ALĪ) was wrong.

Watarai Nobuyoshi (1615–90). A Shinto scholar and religious leader of the early Tokugawa period in Japan. As a descendant of the famous Watarai line of priests, who were the hereditary officiants at the outer shrine of *Ise, Nobuyoshi reversed the flagging fortunes of his school of Shinto. Since the 13th cent., Watarai Shinto had developed a complex syncretic system synthesizing *Confucian and Buddhist ideas within a Shinto framework. His major work, the *Yōfukuji*, is the most important source of his own religious ruminations, which largely follow the traditional doctrines originally set forth in the Five Books of Shinto (*Shintō gobusho*).

Watarai Shinto: see ISE; WATARAI NOBUYOSHI.

Watcher. A heavenly being in the biblical book of *Daniel. The *Septuagint translates the term as *angel. Watchers also appear in *pseudepigraphic and later *mystical books.

Watchman Nee (Ni To Shang/Duo Sheng, 1903–72). Founder of the Christian-based Little Flock Movement in China. He was converted while a student at Trinity College, Foochow (Fuzhou), and having been baptized, he began preaching. His *fundamentalist approach insisted on the necessity for the human spirit to be broken in order to be released into union with the Spirit of God, so that soul and body can be kept in subjection and obedience. He established Assemblies, which by 1949 had reached *c.*500 in number. He was arrested in 1952 and remained in captivity for the rest of his life. The Little Flock Movement now numbers nearly a million.

Watch-night. A dedication service held on New Year's Eve. Derived from early Christian *vigils, it came, by way of *Moravianism, into 18th-cent. *Methodism.

Watchtower, The (magazine of Jehovah's Witnesses): see JEHOVAH'S WITNESSES.

Wato (Jap., 'word-head'). The key point, line, or word in a *kōan.

Watts, Alan (1915–73). Comparative religionist, theologian, philosopher, and student of mysticism. This Californian *'guru' greatly influenced the counter-culture of the 1960s. Writing with particular public success in *The Way of Zen* (1957) and *Psychotherapy East and West* (1961), he argued that people in the West are in a state of confusion, seeking solace in satisfying their egos. The solution is to change consciousness, to realize that everything is interrelated as necessary components of one process.

Watts, Isaac (1674–1748). English hymnwriter. He was for a time pastor of a prestigious *Independent congregation in London, but was forced into a long retirement by ill health. Watts's *hymns include many still in common use.

Wayang kulit/purwa (Javanese theatre): see THEATRE AND DRAMA.

Way of Supreme Peace (early Taoist school): see T'AI-PING TAO.

Wazīr (Arab., *wazara*, 'he carried a burden'). Minister in Muslim governments, anglicized as vizier. Under the Caliphs (*khalīfa), wazīrs were advisers who on occasion ran the entire government—e.g. the Barmecides, until they were eradicated by Harūn al-Rashīd; or Niẓam al-Mulk under the Saljuqs.

Weber, Max (1864–1920). Major scholar and sociologist, who is regarded, alongside E. *Durkheim, as a founder of the *sociology of religion.

Weber's essay *The Protestant Ethic and the Spirit of Capitalism* (1904–5) encapsulates the central tenets of Weber's sociological approach to religion. Popular accounts notwithstanding, Weber did not claim that *Protestantism caused capitalism. Rather, by postulating an 'elective affinity' between the ethic of Protestantism and the spirit of modern rational capitalism he articulated one specific link in a complex causal chain of socio-cultural elements. Rejecting the determinism of both *Hegelian idealism and Marxian materialism, Weber saw religion as a potential independent variable in a multivariate formula: a proactive as well as a reactive element in social life.

For Weber, the study of religion is not an end in itself but simply an indispensable means of understanding human society. From this perspective, religion represents humanity's continuous effort to impose intellectual and moral order on the chaos of existence and, in the process, to discover the ultimate meaning of the cosmos for both individuals and collectivities. Contributing their own distinctive solutions to the problem of meaning (for example, in *theodicies which explain the existence of suffering and evil), the great world religions provide the main focus of Weber's vast comparative-historical analysis of civilizations and constitute the essential background to his penetrating account of the emergence of the modern world.

The transformation of a collective desire for salvation from a diffuse sentiment to a new religious dispensation is, according to Weber, the achievement of the *prophet. By claiming a special gift of divine grace (*charisma), this type of religious leader (whether in exemplary or ethical guise) challenges the legitimacy of the established religious and social order and attempts a breakthrough into a realm of new values. In decisively breaking with tradition, the prophet initiates a more systematized cultural order and is thus a prime mover in the process of rationalization which dominates Weber's broad vision of social dynamics and underlies his dark ruminations on the fate of the world.

(See further IDEAL TYPE).

Wee Frees (Scottish Free Church): see FREE CHURCHES.

Weeks, Feast of (Jewish festival): see SHAVU'OT.

Weeping Sūfīs. *Sūfīs who seek to stay close to God by constant weeping, or who do not resist weeping when they hear of the mercy of God.

Wei (learning and effort): see HSÜN TZU.

Wei Cheng (guardian of the emperor, and of temples): see DOOR GODS.

Wei Hua-tsun (founder of Tao-chiao movement): see TAOISM.

Weil, Simone (1909–43). Religious philosopher of intense personal commitment. Born into a non-practising Jewish family, she taught in various French schools between 1931 and 1937, while at the same time being politically active on behalf of the humiliated—all whom she identified as exploited, such as factory-workers, peasants, and the colonized, or, historically, the Provençal *Cathars. In 1934–5 she worked in a factory, and in 1936 worked in the front line in the Spanish Civil War as a cook. Out of these experiences came her early appeals, not simply for greater justice in the distribution of power in relation to work, but for the transformation of the process of work in the direction of its humanization. In 1942, she left France to join the Free French in England. Here she became deeply and dialectically involved in Catholic Christianity. She was never baptized (for that reason she has been called 'a Saint outside the Church') and remained fiercely critical of the hierarchical organization of Christianity.

In all religions (and outside them) the awareness of God is possible and has left its mark. The mark of truth is goodness.

Wei P'o-yang or **Pai-yang** (2nd cent. CE). Foundation figure in religious *Taoism (*tao-chiao*), who attempted to unify the practices of *alchemy with Taoist philosophy and **I Ching*. His major work, *Chou-i ts'an-t'ung-ch'i* (very roughly, the unifying and harmonizing of the three ways, Lao-Tzu, and *I Ching*) aims to show how life can be prolonged and the cosmic forces brought into harmony and balance.

Wei-t'o. Chinese general, regarded by Buddhists as the guardian of the South. He wears a helmet and holds a *vajra, with which he destroys opponents of the *Buddha's teaching.

Wellhausen, Julius (1844–1918). German *biblical critic. Wellhausen put forward the theory in his *Die Composition des Hexateuchs* (1887) that the *Pentateuch was compiled from four separate sources. Although his views were to a great extent accepted by most modern biblical scholars, they remained anathema to *Orthodox Jews and to those Christians who maintain the Mosaic authorship of the Pentateuch.

Wenceslas, St (*c*.907–29). Bohemian prince and *martyr. The son of Duke Wratislaw and Drahomira, he was brought up a Christian by his grandmother, St Ludmilla. After his father's death, he took over the government from his mother in *c*.922. In pursuit of the religious and cultural improvement of his people he formed friendly links with Germany. This, and pagan opposition to him, led to his murder by his brother Boleslav. He was soon venerated as a martyr, and by the end of the century had come to be regarded as the patron *saint of Bohemia. The connection with the carol is one of imagination, not fact.

Wen-ch'ang. Taoist god of writing and literature. He is invoked by those taking exams. Chinese aspiring to education put up a plaque representing him with the wish-fulfilling sceptre (*ju-i*).

Wen-shu-shih-li. Chin. for Mañjuśrī, bodhisattva associated with wisdom and the conquest of ignorance.

Wesley, Charles (1707–88). Brother of John *Wesley and hymn-writer. In 1738 he experienced a conversion like that of his brother, and became an itinerant preacher until 1756, settling finally in London in 1771. Charles Wesley is generally considered the most gifted of Anglican writers of hymns. He is recognized in the Church of England Lesser Festivals, 24 May.

Wesley, John (1703–91). Founder of *Methodism. After ordination in 1725 and a brief curacy, Wesley became fellow of Lincoln College, Oxford (1726), where he was a member of a small religious society nicknamed the 'Holy Club' and also dubbed 'Methodists' because of their emphasis on discipline and self-examination. In 1735 he undertook missionary work in Georgia, but, burdened by disappointment and a sense of personal need, he returned home in 1738. Influenced by *Moravians, he experienced conversion at a meeting in Aldersgate St, London ('I felt my heart strangely warmed'), and thereafter became a passionate evangelist, constantly preaching in the open air throughout England, Scotland, and Ireland, as well as sending preachers to N. America. Travelling on horseback approximately 8,000 miles a year, he recorded his experiences and frequently hostile receptions in his *Journal*. He had no wish to secede from the *Church of England; but opposition, and the necessities of the mission field in America (which caused him to ordain Thomas Coke as Superintendent or *bishop) led to increasing separation. He and Charles *Wesley are recognized in the Lesser Festivals of the Church of England, 24 May.

Westcott, Brooke Foss (1825–1901). Anglican scholar and bishop. He became Regius Professor of Divinity at Cambridge in 1870, and with F. J. A. Hort prepared their widely-used edition of the Gk. New Testament (published 1881). As bishop of Durham from 1890 he somewhat surprisingly made social problems his special concern, and was long remembered (cf. *Manning) for his mediation in the coal strike of 1892.

Western Buddhist Order or **Friends of the Western Buddhist Order.** An eclectic movement established in London, England, in 1967 by Venerable Sangharakshita, an Englishman who had studied extensively in India, writing prolifically (e.g. *A Survey of Buddhism*, 1957).

There is no exclusively monastic membership of this Order, which attempts to make known the Buddhist path by using a language appropriate to the contemporary Western world. All who participate are known as 'friends', and *saṅgha refers to the whole community, but those who advance with commitment can be ordained as mitras, and then as Order Members. There is some argument among Buddhists whether this eclecticism represents the true Westernization of Buddhism (cf. the diffusions into Tibet), or whether it is an erosion of tradition.

Western Paradise (ruled over by the Buddha Amitābha): see SUKHĀVATĪ.

Western schism: see ANTIPOPE.

Western Wall: see WAILING WALL.

Westminster Confession. A credal statement of *Calvinistic Christianity, drawn up for Presbyterian Churches, 1643–6. In the end its compromise was overtaken by events, with the restoration of Charles II in 1660, and the re-establishment of the Anglican Church. But it remained a credal foundation for the Presbyterian Church in Scotland.

Wheel of Life (symbol of the cycle of rebirth): see TIBETAN WHEEL OF LIFE.

Whichcote, B. (philosopher): see CAMBRIDGE PLATONISTS.

Whirling dervishes (ecstatic Muslims): see DERWĪSH.

White Eagle Lodge. Spiritualist movement whose teachings are based on communications from White Eagle, a Native American, who spoke through Grace Cooke. The movement teaches that God the eternal spirit is both Father and Mother, and that the divine Son, or Cosmic Christ, dwells in every living thing, giving unity and harmony to the Cosmos.

Whitefield, George (1714–70). *Calvinistic preacher and leader in the *Evangelical Revival. Born in Gloucester, Whitefield was educated at Oxford, where he associated with the *Wesley brothers. His skill as a communicator was at its best in his outdoor evangelistic preaching to vast crowds. His ardent Calvinism brought him into conflict with J. Wesley, but the two men retained their friendship, Wesley preaching the sermon at Whitefield's funeral. He visited America for extended preaching tours on seven different occasions, eventually dying there.

Whitehead, A. N. (philosopher): see PROCESS THEOLOGY.

White Horse Monastery/Temple (Buddhist monastery in China): see PAI-MA-SSU.

White Lake of the Ascetics: see PILGRIMAGE (Jain).

White Lotus School (school of Buddhism): see PAI-LIEN-TSUNG; T'IEN-T'AI.

White Lotus Society. Chinese folk movement, with strong millenarian beliefs. It consisted of a number of organizations, developing from (11th cent.) a relatively simple devotion to *Amida under lay leadership into the practice of magic, healing, and exorcism. In the 14th cent., its eclectic tendency absorbed Taoist elements and expectation of the imminent advent of *Maitreya. The preparatory conflict with the evil rulers of their day (e.g. among *Red Turbans) led to their prohibition and persecution. The White Lotus Rebellion of 1796–1805 and the *Boxer Rebellion illustrate the continuing power of the movement.

White shamanism: see SHAMANS.

Wicca (witchcraft): see WITCHCRAFT.

Wiesel, E. (Jewish writer): see HOLOCAUST.

Wig, wearing of: see HEAD, COVERING OF.

Wilberforce, William (1759–1833). *Evangelical *Anglican and reformer. Born in Hull, he became MP for the city in 1780. He later took the county seat for Yorkshire and worked tirelessly in Parliament for the abolition of the slave-trade. His *Practical View of the Prevailing Religious System of Professed Christians* (1797) exposed the nominal Christianity of many in 'the Higher and Middle Classes' and became a religious best-seller for forty years. He is recognized in the Lesser Festivals of the Church of England, 29 July.

Wild ass of Mesopotamia (name for last Umayyad caliph): see UMAYYADS.

Wilfrid, St (634–709). English *bishop. As abbot of Ripon, he introduced the *Benedictine rule, and at the Synod of Whitby (664) he helped to secure the Roman (against the *Celtic) dating of *Easter (see also HILDA). He is remembered as a cosmopolitan churchman and proponent of closer relations between the English Church and Rome. Feast day, 12 Oct.

William of Ockham or **Occam** (14th cent.). Christian philosopher. He studied at Oxford but, since he did not complete his master's degree, he remained an inceptor, hence his nickname, Inceptor Venerabilis. He began to write logic and commentaries, especially on Aristotle's *Physics*. Here he argued against prevalent views which allowed the intellect to constitute individuals as universals, never perceiving them directly as such, but knowing them to be so by reflection. To Ockham, individuals alone are real, as they are and as they can be observed; and what can be known is the individual, not some unperceivable universal. In this insistence on observation, he has been regarded as the forerunner of Bacon, Newton, and *Descartes. His name has been given to the principle of ontological economy (popularly known as 'Occam's razor'), *entia non sunt multiplicanda praeter necessitatem* ('entities ought not to be multiplied beyond necessity'), i.e. that in accounting for phenomena, one should not posit more (especially by way of cause or reality) than is necessary to give a satisfactory or true explanation; and as such it might seem to call in question the propriety of invoking God to account for anything. The principle is derived from Aristotle, and is referred to by Grosseteste as *lex parsimoniae*, but the words do not occur in the surviving works of Ockham.

William of St-Thierry (*c*.1085–1148). Christian theologian and mystical writer. Born at Liège and probably educated at Laon, he became a *Benedictine and *c*.1120 was appointed Abbot of St-Thierry, near Reims. He had long been a friend of St *Bernard of Clairvaux, whose life he wrote, but did not join the *Cistercians until 1135, owing to Bernard's resistance. In his writings he shows wide reading of the Fathers, Greek as well as Latin, and (especially in his *Golden Letter*) develops an understanding of the soul's knowledge of God through love which lays bare and fosters a kind of kinship with God.

Williams, Roger (*c*.1604–83). Advocate of religious toleration, and an American colonist. After ordination (probably in 1629) he became chaplain to Sir William Masham, but separatist views compelled him to seek religious freedom in N. America (1630). He established a settlement which he named 'Providence' (1636), and founded Rhode Island where he formed the first *Baptist church in the colonies.

Wine: see ALCOHOL; KHAMR.

Wine Ode, The: see OMAR KHAYYAM.

Wird (Arab.). A time of private prayer (cf. *du'ā') in Islam (in addition to *ṣalāt), and also the formula of prayers recited on these occasions (also known as *ḥizb*). Awrād (pl.) are usually made up of passages from the *Qur'ān, and among Sūfīs are recited at least seventy times morning and evening.

Wisdom (Heb., *ḥokhmah*, *binah*, 'discrimination'). An ethical and religious quality of life as advocated by the Hebrew scriptures. Wisdom is sometimes used in the sense of 'intelligence' (e.g. Ecclesiastes 2. 3), but it came to symbolize a particular cultural tradition within Judaism. The wisdom books of the *Bible are *Proverbs, *Job, and *Ecclesiastes. The *Apocrypha includes *Ecclesiasticus* (**Ben Sira*) and the **Wisdom of Solomon*.

Wisdom (in Mahāyāna Buddhism): see PERFECTION OF WISDOM LITERATURE; PARĀMITĀ.

Wisdom of Solomon. One of the books of the *Apocrypha. The author's familiarity with Gk. philosophy places him as a Jew of Alexandria in the period 2nd cent. BCE–1st cent. CE. The terms used of Wisdom in ch. 7 passed into Christian theology as applied to Christ.

Wise, Isaac Meyer (1819–1900). Pioneer of *Reform Judaism. He was born in Bohemia and emigrated to the USA in 1846. From 1854, he was *rabbi of the Cincinnati congregation of B'nai Jeshuran. He founded the periodical, *The Israelite*, in 1854, organized the 1855 *Rabbinical Conference in Cleveland, and was a key figure in the founding of the *Hebrew Union College in 1875. He agreed that *Torah was the source of authority, but only the Decalogue (see TEN COMMANDMENTS) was absolutely obligatory —all else was open to interpretation.

Witchcraft (from *wicca*). The belief that human affairs and features of the environment can be ordered, controlled, and changed by skilled practitioners whose powers are usually believed to be innate. Witchcraft is closely associated with *magic, but its techniques are derived from within or given by a supernatural agent, rather than (as often with magic) learnt. The belief that the agent was the *devil led to ferocious persecution of witches in medieval Christian Europe. Although witchcraft thus has had, in the past, a strongly negative connotation, it has been reassessed more recently in increasingly positive terms, in two main ways. First, anthropologists have described its positive role in small-scale societies, in healing, reducing hostilities and social tensions, reinforcing social order, supplying plausible meanings to inexplicable events, providing surrogate action in crises (e.g. the *evil eye). Second, the increasing emancipation of women from the control of men in religions has led to a re-evaluation of the role of women as witches (since women have always far outnumbered men as witches), and to the postulation that 'witchcraft' represents an unbroken religious tradition which men opposed because it empowered women. This tradition is often known as Wicca (or Wicce, from the Old English, the root of which means 'to bend' or 'shape'), but it is embedded in a wider neo-Paganism. According to Starhawk, a leader of the recovery of Wicca, 'Followers of Wicca seek their inspiration in pre-Christian sources, European folklore, and mythology. They consider themselves priests and priestesses of an ancient European *shamanistic nature religion that worships a goddess who is related to the ancient Mother Goddess in her three aspects of Maiden, Mother and Crone.'

Wittgenstein, Ludwig (1889–1951). Austrian philosopher. He studied mathematical logic with Bertrand Russell in Cambridge in 1912–13, fought in the Austrian army in the First World War, and wrote his *Tractatus Logico-Philosophicus* (1921; tr. 1922) whilst a prisoner of war in Italy. He gave up philosophy for several years, but resumed work in it in the late 1920s. He returned to Cambridge, and became Professor of Philosophy there in 1939. Apart from a single article, he published nothing further in his own lifetime: his later works were all published posthumously, starting with the *Philosophical Investigations* (1953).

Wittgenstein's later philosophy took a different direction from that of the *Tractatus*, and was critical of it in many respects. But in both cases he was concerned with the relation between language and the world. The *Tractatus* sees meaningful language as ultimately analysable into basic propositions, which picture the world. Since *ethics, aesthetics, and religious language do not picture anything, they are relegated to the realm of the mystical and inexpressible. In his later work, however, Wittgenstein disclaimed any attempt to give a unitary account of the nature of language. Instead, he saw language as composed of many different 'language-games', a term used to indicate that uses of language are rule-governed and go with activities and practices; he also compared language to a set of tools, each having its own use.

Wittgenstein wrote little about religion as such, though interesting observations about it are scattered throughout his works. In 1938 he gave some lectures on religious belief, in which he presented the distinctiveness of such beliefs as lying in the ways in which they express certain reactions and regulate our lives.

It is Wittgenstein's later philosophy in general, however, that has had more influence on the philosophy of religion and theology than his few writings on religion as such. Whereas the Logical Positivists (who were much influenced by the *Tractatus*, though it can be argued that they misunderstood it) dismissed religious language as meaningless because unverifiable in empirical terms, Wittgenstein's later philosophy seemed to offer a more tolerant approach which would permit the inclusion of religious language amongst meaningful uses of language. For religious language-games are just as much parts of human life as other uses of language, and indeed Wittgenstein includes 'praying' in his list of common language-games, in *Philosophical Investigations* § 23; and there is no superior vantage point from which this, or any, language can be assessed.

If this account is correct, the philosophy of religion and much theology should be concerned more with coming to understand the distinctive nature of religious beliefs and practices, through a perspicuous description and analysis of them, than with shoring them up with intellectual defences. We are, however, left with the questions of what kind of truth religion and theology might have, and how it is discerned.

Woking Mosque: see AḤMADĪYYA.

Wolff, Joseph (1795–1862). Christian missionary to the Jews (and others) of the orient. Although the son of a *rabbi, Wolff converted to Christianity and devoted the latter part of his life to bringing the Christian message to the Jews of Palestine, Mesopotamia, Turkey, Persia, Kurdistan, Khurasan, Bukhara, India, and the Yemen. He wrote several accounts of his travels which provide lively and interesting details about the eastern communities.

Womb Maṇḍala (maṇḍala in exoteric Buddhism): see TAIZO-KAI MANDARA; SHINGON.

Women. The status of women in religions has, in the past, been tied closely to the reproductive cycle, both that of humans, and that of crops and herds. The controls of evolution and of natural selection (of course not known or understood) established boundaries within which, either the replication of genes and the nurture of children succeeded, or the family/group/community/village went to extinction. Religions, as the earliest cultural systems of which we know, have created strong protections for replication and nurture, often by way of controls over behaviour—hence the preoccupation of religions with sexual behaviours and food. Characteristically, societies developed a necessary division of labour, based on biology but extended symbolically, with women responsible for the upbringing of the family and for related activities in preparation of food (both in cooking and in the fields), and with men relating to a wider environment, e.g. in hunting, warfare, political relations. The feminine is thus often celebrated in religions as the source of life and gift of fertility. There is some (disputed) evidence that the feminine, as Mother Goddess, was the primordial focus of worship: at a time when the male contribution to reproduction was not realized, this is unsurprising. Equally unsurprising (from a genetic point of view) is the way in which men consequently took control of the reproductive cycle. That control is mirrored in the increasing dominance of patriarchal religion. Even in India, where the feminine has remained central in worship, and where the Goddess may still be the single focus of devotion for many Hindus, the Goddess on her own is usually destructive and fierce, and only fruitful in relation to a consort, such as *Śiva. The subordination of women to men became widespread in all religions: exceptions are very much exceptions to the rule. Combined with profound fears about the dangers surrounding sexuality (elaborated in complex ritual customs to deal with 'purity and danger', the title of a relevant study by Mary Douglas), this led to literal separations of women from men, especially in worship (for example, in *synagogue or *mosque or in the *Roman Catholic refusal of the *ordination of women, or, until 1992, of girl servers near the altar).

While it is true that the increasing emancipation of women in many parts of the world has led to major adjustments in the place accorded to women in most religions, the phrase 'place accorded to' reveals the continuing truth: men remain predominantly in control and allow some women some greater access to authority and decision-making. A classic example was the 'Letter to All Women' issued by Pope John Paul II in 1995. While it was remarkable in apologizing for the oppressive record of the Church in relation to women, the document as a whole adopted the usual male strategy of congratulating women on the gifts of their characteristic natures, while at the same time making it clear that those natures prohibited women from undertaking certain roles reserved for men.

Judaism The Hebrew scriptures teach that woman was created as a 'helper' to men (Genesis 2. 23–4). Her chief duty was to be childbearing (Genesis 3. 16), and a good wife and mother was cause for praise (Proverbs 31. 28). The *rabbis exempted women from all time-bound positive commandments (see SIX HUNDRED AND THIRTEEN COMMANDMENTS) (*Kid*. 1. 7), and female education was not encouraged. In 1994, a Commission, convened by the Chief Rabbi of the UK, issued a far-ranging report on the status of women in Orthodox Judaism, recommending that the exclusion of women from *kaddish, the separation of women from men in synagogue by *mechitzah* ('partition') should be ended or modified, and that a pre-nuptial covenant, guaranteeing the supply of the *get* (bill of divorce: see MARRIAGE AND DIVORCE, JUDAISM) in the case of divorce, should be supplied. *Progressive Jews stress the absolute equality of men and women and have female as well as male rabbis, *cantors, and *synagogue leaders. See also NIDDAH.

Christianity Early Christianity was an egalitarian movement in which women played a prominent part. Not only did *Jesus give and receive much in ministry to and from women (with an openness which went against the norms of his day), but women clearly played an important part in the life and running of the early Church. The early churches reaffirmed traditional and cultural attitudes, leading to the continuing subordination of women to the authority of their husbands, and to men in the Church (e.g. 1 Corinthians 14. 34; Ephesians 5. 22 f.; Colossians 3. 18; 1 Timothy 2. 11 f.; Titus 2. 4 f.). The Church subsequently has endeavoured (generally speaking) to confirm that subordinate status of women. The Church has thus, historically, admired women from a distance, insisting on their special and higher vocations, while at the same time regarding them as inherently the source of sin, because of their descent from *Eve, and certainly not to be admitted to the male preserves of decision-making and priesthood. The Virgin *Mary became the role model, calling sexuality into question and exhibiting the way to salvation through perfect obedience. Yet clearly there are many RC and Orthodox Christians who are, despite discouragement, committed to the realization within time of that final vision, in which the Christian attitude to all oppressed groups is summarized, when there shall be 'neither Jew nor Greek, slave nor free, male and female' (Galatians 3. 28).

Islam In Islam, it is believed that women and men are different but equal. The advent of Islam brought great advantages to the status and protection of women, and women, especially *'Āisha, played an important part in the early years of Islam, as they have continued to do. Women are not the source of sin (Eve,

Ḥawwā, is not named in the *Qur'ān, which makes it clear that both Adam and Eve were equally at fault: see e.g. 2. 36 f.), though they may be the source of particular impurity after childbirth and menstruation. Women, and mothers in particular, are deeply honoured. Women have access to education and retain control of their own property. At the same time, certain inequalities between women and men, together with the fact that some customs have become virtual obligations in some parts of the Muslim world, have raised questions about the implementation of Qur'ān and *ḥadīth in this area. Thus the veil (*ḥijāb), or more total covering of *chaddor*, is not required by Qur'ān, which only commands modesty in dress (24. 31); the widespread practice of female circumcision is not required at all; polygamy is envisaged in the Qur'ān, but not polyandry; men may marry women of the *ahl al-Kitāb, but women may not marry such men. In any case, the authority of men over women remains, derived from two verses in particular: having affirmed mutual rights for women, 2. 228 states, 'But men have *darajah* over women.' *Darajah* means 'rank' or 'degree' or 'precedence', and may simply be restricted to the different ways in which men and women can initiate divorce, but it is often taken in a more general sense. In another verse (4. 34/8), it is said that men are *qawwumūn* over women (because they have to support them) and that women suspected of ill-conduct must be admonished, banished to their beds, and beaten. *Qawwamūn* is usually taken to mean 'standing over', i.e. having authority; but the meanings of the Qur'ān are not fixed, and the word may legitimately mean 'standing in attendance'; and in any case, the beating cannot be painful and is largely symbolic. Even so, for many Muslim women these particular aspects of the assymetry between men and women raise searching questions about the (theoretically possible) rethinking of the meaning of *sharī'a in the spirit of Muḥammad's own support for the worth and dignity of women. As matters stand, the experience of many Muslim women, as they report it, is one of which Muḥammad could scarcely have approved, and which the Qur'ān did not intend.

Hinduism The status and role of women in Hinduism are complex. At the level of home and society, they are revered, yet at the same time they are dependent on men and are to be guarded by them. In the *Dharmaśāstras, they are ritually impure and a source of impurity (and therefore, e.g., not to study or recite *mantras): their husbands are their *gurus, and their domestic duties are their rituals. Their devotion to their husbands is their highest good (especially if consummated in *satī), and yet, according to **Manusmṛti* 2. 213 f., they are incapable of achieving absolute devotion. Nevertheless, at the same time, feminine images of the divine are more obvious in Hinduism than in other religions (with the possible, but limited, exception of devotion to *Mary in Christianity, where she is only associated with the divine). Even then, goddesses usually appear as consorts with male gods, and are beneficial in co-operation with them, otherwise being, in general, destructive. Women are prominent in myths, and in life they have been even more prominent in *bhakti (devotion to God). Women are recognized by Hindus as a source of immense power, but they remain, nevertheless, firmly under patriarchal control.

Buddhism The *Buddha's attitude towards women was not radically different from that of his contemporaries: for those pursuing the religious life, women are a temptation and a snare; but in the context of lay society, the role of women as wives and mothers was crucial to the stability of the social order. The Buddha frequently cautioned monks to be on their guard when dealing with women lest they be overcome by lust and craving.

However, from the outset women were allowed to become nuns, although with more severe rules imposed on them. Regarding the role of women in lay life the Buddha upheld the traditional values of his time.

Jainism The status of women in relation to enlightenment is a specific issue between *Digambaras and Śvetāmbaras, with the latter regarding gender as usually irrelevant: see DIGAMBARA.

Sikhism The recurring image in the *Ādi Granth of the soul offering itself to God as a chaste woman surrenders to her husband reveals the traditional relationship. In accordance with the ideal of *grahastī, Sikhs are expected to marry, and motherhood is an honoured role. Sikh teaching condemned the once-prevalent practices of female infanticide and *satī. Women participate in *gurdwārā *worship and are prominent in preparing *Gurū-ka-laṅgar. They may read the scriptures publicly or sing, and serve as management committee members.

Won Buddhism (Korean, *won*, 'circular'). Korean Buddhist movement, founded by Soe-tae San (1891–1943). He spent his early years in ascetic practice until achieving enlightenment in 1915. In 1924, he founded the Association for the Study of Buddha-Dharma, though under the Japanese occupation, it was relatively unknown. After 1946, the school gained many adherents. Its teaching combines the goal of seeing the *Buddha in all things (and living consistently with this perception), with 'timeless and placeless' Zen, i.e. Zen meditation does not depend on allocated places and times.

Wŏnhyo (618–86). Korean Buddhist scholar-monk. Wŏnhyo founded the Punhwang (or Haedong) subsect of the Hwaŏm (*Hua-yen) sect, integrated various Buddhist thoughts through his notion of the 'harmony of disputes' (*hwajaeng*), and popularized Buddhism through dance and song. A prolific writer, his works include *Kisillonso* ('Commentary on *Awakening Mahāyāna* Faith') which had a profound influence on Buddhists in E. Asian countries.

Woolman, John (Quaker committed to abolition of slavery): see FRIENDS, THE SOCIETY OF.

World-affirming, World-denying (categorization of sects): see SECTS.

World Alliance of Reformed Churches: see PRESBYTERIANISM.

World Buddhist Sangha Council: see SAṄGHA.

World Council of Churches: see ECUMENISM.

World Fellowship of Buddhists. Founded in 1950 by a Sinhalese Buddhist, Malalasekera. Its objective is to spread understanding of Buddhism and to reconcile the divergent styles and teachings of Buddhism.

World protectors (in Buddhism): see CELESTIAL KINGS.

Worlds, The four. Jewish *kabbalistic doctrine. The kabbalists identified four stages in the creation process which correspond to the four letters of the *tetragrammaton: the world of Azilut (the source of all being), Beriah (creation), Yezirah (formation), and Asiyyah (angelic world).

World's Parliament of Religions. A meeting of representatives of the major world religions at Chicago in 1893. The meeting was sponsored by the League of Liberal Clergymen, who saw the encounter of religions as an opportunity of extending religious vision and morality by co-operation rather than by proselytizing conflict. A further World Parliament of Religions was held in 1993, to mark the centenary of the first, also in Chicago. Attempts to establish a World Council of Religions were coolly received. Instead, the possibility of Centres for Interfaith Study were envisaged, which might then form networks of consultation. A Global Ethic was proposed, drawing together the common elements in the *ethics of different religions.

Worldwide Church of God: see ARMSTRONG, H. W.

Worms, Concordat of: see CONCORDAT.

Worms, Diet of. The imperial diet of 1521 at which M. *Luther defended his teaching before the emperor Charles V. He refused to recant. According to an early tradition he concluded his answer with the famous words 'Here I stand. I can do no other. God help me. Amen.' A few weeks later he was declared an 'outlaw' by the papacy and his teachings were formally condemned.

Worship. The offering of devotion, praise, and adoration to that which is deemed worthy of such offering, usually God. Worship of that which is less than God as though it is equivalent to God, especially if it is addressed to particular images, is *idolatry. In non-theistic religious, worship is more usually expressed as gratitude to the enlightened guide or guides, as with Buddhists and Jains.

More often, however, worship is associated with the adoration of the supreme Being, the unproduced Producer of all that is, from whom all things and all events ultimately come, and to whom all things return. This sense of the transcendence of God necessarily evokes worship. From this sense of the absolute majesty, holiness, and supremacy of God derives Israel's life of worship, of the constant recognition of God in *Temple, *sacrifice, *Psalms, *pilgrimage, and eventually *synagogue, *liturgy, and *Prayer Book—epitomized in *kiddush ha-Shem. By wearing the *tefillin, an observant Jew bears on his body a constant worship of God.

Christians inherited this sense of God's independence from, and yet concern for, the universe which he has created—and in particular they inherited the Psalms, which from the start informed their religious intelligence and became the backbone of prayer and devotion. But Christianity recognizes in *Jesus the *incarnate presence of God, through whom praise and worship is offered to the Father—in other (less contingent) words, transcendence and immanence are held together in the reality of Jesus' own prayer.

Islam shares the Jewish sense of the absolute uniqueness and oneness (*tawhīd) of God. Since this and its consequences (not least in belief and behaviour) are made known in the *Qur'ān, the very chanting of the Qur'ān (even without a knowledge of what it means) becomes an act of worship. But the acknowledgement of God is so fundamental that it becomes a daily obligation in *ṣalāt, and an annual obligation in *ṣawm, the month-long fast in *Ramaḍān—both of these being among the *Five Pillars of Islam. But Muslim devotion goes far beyond obligation, spectacularly so in the case of the *Sūfīs.

An attitude of worship and devotion is equally characteristic of Hindus and it defies brief description. Worship (*pūjā) is held and sustained in the home (where there is likely to be a small shrine devoted to a particular deity), but it readily flows out into temples and shrines, and into many practices of particular devotion. Since Hindus in general believe that *Brahman becomes manifest in many different ways, there are many different forms of the deity. More formal communal worship may be expressed through *dance and drama, or through the singing in groups of *kīrtana and *bhajana* ('songs of praise'). These are usually associated with *bhakti, a particularly powerful tradition of devotion and praise. But for the Hindu, the human relation to the divine is possible at all times: every circumstance can be an occasion of the divine. It is this which underlies the importance in worship of *mantra, *maṇḍala, and *yantra. For the Hindu, worship is as natural as birth and death: it is the bridge which connects the one to the other.

See also YASNA; Index, Worship.

Wrathful deities. Deities who, in Buddhist *tantra, convey the transcendence of *dosa (hate), itself one of the three major impediments to the attainment of enlightenment. Wrath is thus the purified form of hate, turned against the self in its emotional indulgence. Wrathful deities are depicted in fierce and fearsome guises, but this is intended to represent the attitude necessary to transform hate into wrath against itself (and the other 'poisons' of the mind).

In W. religions, the wrath of God is the righteous anger of God against wrong-doing, which in the Bible often carries with it punishment of wrong-doers, combined (in Christianity and Islam) with the threat of eternal punishment. The wrath of God thus becomes an invitation to moral seriousness.

Wrekin Trust. A *New Age movement established in Britain by Sir George Trevelyan (1906–96), who became an advocate of 'alternative spirituality' after hearing a lecture on Rudolph Steiner's anthroposophy in 1942. The Trust was established to encourage the exploration of the spiritual nature of humans and of their universe through residential courses, conferences at New Age centres and elsewhere, and through publications.

Writings or **Hagiographa.** The third section of the Hebrew scriptures (see TANAKH). The Writings contain: *Psalms, *Proverbs, *Job, the *Song of Songs, *Ruth, *Lamentations, *Ecclesiastes, *Esther, *Daniel, *Ezra, *Nehemiah, and 1 and 2 *Chronicles.

Wu (Chin., 'not/non-being'). Key concept in *Taoism, denoting the absence of qualities perceivable by the senses, but not 'non-existent'. It is the basic characteristic of *Tao, whose emptiness of attributes does not deprive it of character and effect. To understand the emptiness of character in the Tao which nevertheless is its truth is to be drawn into becoming an expression of the same in one's own life, through active inactivity (*wu-wei). Thus wu may also be the word through which the state of that realization is expressed.

Wu-ch'ang (Chin., 'five constants'). The five cardinal virtues in *Confucianism: (i) *jen, empathy; (ii) *i, propriety; (iii) *li, rights and customs observed; (iv) *chih*, insight, wisdom; (v) *hsin*, mutual trust. They have their corresponding types of relationship (*wu-lun*), which form the basis of society: (i) parent and child; (ii) ruler and subject; (iii) husband and wife; (iv) older and younger children; (v) friend and friend.

Wu-chen Pien (Treatise on Awakening to Truth). Work of Cheng Po-tuan of the inner elixir school (see NEI-TAN). He rejected the outer elixir (*wai-tan*) quest for external means to immortality, contending that all humans contain what is necessary within.

Wu-chi (Chin., 'summit of nothingness'). According to Taoists, the primordial, unconfined, limitless source to which all manifestation returns; cf. FU.

Wu-ch'in-hsi (Chin., 'movement of the five animals'). *Taoist exercises, developed by Hua T'o (2nd/3rd cent. CE), to resist ageing, by adapting the different means through which animals distribute *ch'i within the body. The five are bear, bird, monkey, stag, tiger.

Wu-chi-t'u (diagram of emptiness): see CH'EN T'UAN.

Wuḍū' (minor ablution in Islam): see ABLUTIONS.

Wu-hsing, also known as **wu-te** (Chin., 'five movers'). Five virtues, the five elements which work as agents, fundamental in Chinese and Taoist understanding of the cosmos and history. The five are not physical substances, but the metaphysical forces associated with the nature of the substances. The five are wood, fire, earth, metal, water. The basic identifications are obvious, connected with the seasons and the cycle of life: spring, summer–autumn, winter. Earth mediates between the four, sustaining and being sustained by them.

Wu-lun: see WU-CH'ANG.

Wu-men Hui-k'ai (1183–1260). Chinese Buddhist. Successor of Wu-tsu Fa-yen in the Yang-ch'i line of *Rinzai, although in an offshoot represented in the teacher Yüeh-an Shan-kuo, whose dharma-successor (*hassu) he became. He was also taught by Yueh-lin, who set him the *mu* *kōan; after six years he had not progressed through it, and he resolved not to sleep until he did so. In a desperate state, he heard the midday drum, and reached enlightenment.

Wu-men-kuan (collection of Zen kōans): see KŌAN.

Wu-shan (federation of Ch'an/Zen monasteries): see GOSAN.

Wu-shih Ch'i-hou (Chin., 'five periods, seven stages'). *Taoist analysis of progress to the goal. First: (i) the mind is always on the move; (ii) the mind calms down; (iii) calm and movement are in balance; (iv) calm predominates by concentration on an object of meditation; (v) the mind rests and is not 'kept going' by external inputs. Next: (i) anxiety then subsides; (ii) the appearance reverts to that of a child at rest, but supernatural powers develop; (iii) the condition of immortal (*hsien) is attained; (iv) *ch'i is perfected, and the perfect being (*chen-jen) emerges; (v) *shen-jen is attained; (vi) harmony with all forms is attained; (vii) perfect harmony with *Tao is realized in the practice of life.

Wūtai (mountain): see PILGRIMAGE.

Wu-t'ai-shan ('Five Terrace Mountain'). Place of pilgrimage for Chinese Buddhists who venerate *Mañjuśri (Chin., Wen-shu). It is in Shansi province. Nearly sixty of the monasteries survive from the more than 200 of its heyday (6th cent. CE).

Wu-te (five virtues): see WU-HSING.

Wu-tou-mi Tao ('five pecks of rice Taoism'). School of religious *Taoism (**tao-chiao*), founded by *Chang Tao-ling (2nd cent. CE) and his grandson, *Chang Lu. Those wishing to join paid five pecks of rice to the functionaries (*tao-shih), hence the name. The leaders were called *tien-shih, celestial masters, and this is another name for the school, the Celestial Master, or Heavenly Master, School. It has continued to the present day, more respectfully known as *cheng-yi*, 'the Orthodox way'.

Wu-tsu Fa-yen (exponent of kōans): see KŌAN.

Wu-tsung (814–46). Chinese emperor (841–6) of the T'ang dynasty, who espoused the claims of religious *Taoism (*tao-chiao*) for the attainment of immortality. The Taoist hierarchy (*tao-shih) urged the suppression of their rivals, the Buddhists, and edicts were issued which led to the virtual destruction of institutional Buddhism.

The principle from this was established that a religion in China will only be allowed if the state permits it; and that 'foreign' religions are suspect. This principle (and often specific appeal to Wu-tsung) remains to the present day.

Wu-wei (Chin., 'not/non-doing'). The mode of being and action in *Taoism which 'goes with the grain' of the way of Tao in bringing manifest forms into appearance. It is not total lack of activity, but, rather, active inactivity which allows the way of Tao to be expressed.

Wyclif(fe), John (*c*.1329–84). English philosopher, theologian, and proponent of reform. He was resident in Oxford for most of his life. His views were not wholly original, and were somewhat protected by the fact that they were normally expressed within the university. However, he engendered controversy by stressing the importance of civil powers within the Church, which scandalized the *pope and leading clergy. He is chiefly remembered for his opposition to *transubstantiation and his support for vernacular scripture. Some of his ideas were preserved in Wycliffe's *Wicket*, but his major achievements were to provide a translation of the Bible in English, and to put forward views on the Church which were later promoted by the *Lollards. He is recognized in the Church of England Lesser Festivals, 6 Oct.

X

Xavier, Francis (Jesuit priest and missionary): see FRANCIS XAVIER.

Xenoglossolalia (speaking in a language unknown to the speaker but known to the hearer): see GLOSSOLALIA.

Xerophagia (Gk., dry nourishment). An intensification, in E. Churches, of the *Lenten fast during the beginning (Monday to Thursday) of *Holy Week. Water is allowed, but otherwise only bread, onions, and salt, with herbs and garlic.

Xi'an: see SIAN.

Xizang Autonomous Region. Chinese name for Tibet (see TIBETAN RELIGION; DALAI LAMA).

Y

Yab-Yum (Father-Mother). The iconographical representation of two deities in ritualized intercourse (Skt., *maithuna) in Tibetan Buddhism. Although such Tantric representations have a long Indian history, the Yab-Yum, with an active female astride and facing a passive male, is a peculiarly Tibetan style. While the function of the Yab-Yum is primarily as an instructive *symbolism that may also serve as a basis for *visualization, its actual enactment through the taking of Tantric consorts is not unknown.

Yad (pointer): see TORAH ORNAMENTS.

Yad Fāṭima (symbol/charm of power): see HAND OF FĀṬIMA.

Yad Vashem (memorial to victims of the *Holocaust): see ḤASIDEI UMMOT HA-ʿOLAM.

Yahad (Heb., 'Unity'). A term used in the *Dead Sea Scrolls to express the unifying spirit of the sect. The members of the group are described as 'men of the yahad'.

Yahrzeit (lit., 'year's time'). The anniversary of a death in Judaism. *Kaddish is recited, and a twenty-four hour memorial candle is lit.

Yahweh. The God of Judaism as the *tetragrammaton, YHWH, *may* have been pronounced. By Orthodox and many other Jews, God's name is never articulated, least of all in the Jewish liturgy.

Yahwist. The supposed editor of one of the hypothetical sources of the Jewish *Pentateuch. According to *Wellhausen, the Pentateuch was compiled from four separate sources. The oldest source, known as J because it uses the *tetragrammaton to refer to God, was composed by the Yahwist, and is thought to date from the 9th cent. BCE. However, in recent years the documentary hypothesis has come under question once more.

Yahya. Islamic form of *John the Baptist.

Yajamāna (instigator of sacrifice): see SACRIFICE (HINDU).

Yajña (Hindu sacrifice): see SACRIFICE (HINDU).

Yajñavalkya. Hindu sage at the court of King *Janaka, to whom *Vājasaneyi-saṁhitā*, known also as *White *Yajur Veda*, is attributed. The adherents of the school which he founded were then called Vājasaneyins. Other works attributed to him include **Śatapatha Brāhmaṇa*, to which *Bṛhadāranyaka Upaniṣad* is attached.

Yajñopavītā (receiving of the thread in Hindu 'sacred thread' ceremony): see UPANAYANA.

Yajur Veda (Skt.). The *Vedic collection of sacrificial prayers (*yajus*) used by the Adhvaryu priest. Of the four *Vedas, it most reflects the Vedic sacrifice in its ritual character and full scope. The *Yajur Veda* has two major divisions: the *Black Yajur Veda* existing in four versions and the *White Yajur Veda* existing in two versions. The titles appear to have arisen as polemical terms used by the followers of the White school to characterize the purity of their tradition. Keith estimated the recension of the *Black Yajur Veda* at not later than 600 BCE.

Yakkha (Pāli; Skt., *Yakṣa). 1. In Buddhism, historical and legendary communities. References to Yakkhas belong to three main types or classes: (i) the records of Buddhist contact with individual Yakkhas or communities of Yakkhas; (ii) the records showing the actual process of amalgamation of the Yakkha tribes with the 'cultured peoples'; (iii) the records which preserve the myths and legends of the Yakkhas as they persisted in society long after the Yakkhas lost their tribal identities.

2. Supernatural beings in Buddhism (cf. Hindu *yakṣa) who may be neutral in their relations to humans, but who more often are malevolent.

Yakṣa. Collective name for supernatural beings in Hinduism, who inhabit the countryside and forests, but became especially associated with the sacred trees in villages. They can assume any form, and often appear as the servants of *Kubera, the god of wealth. They can be beneficent or malevolent, but are usually known as *punyajana*, 'good beings', to propitiate them in advance.

In Jainism, they are attendants on each of the twenty-four *tīrthaṅkaras.

Yakushi. Jap. for *Bhaisajya-guru Buddha.

Yakushi-ji (temple-complex): see NARA BUDDHISM.

Yā Latīf (Islamic prayer): see PRAYER.

Yali Movement. A *cargo cult on the Rai coast of New Guinea, especially among the Tangu people. Yali Singina. After his death in 1975 the movement was reorganized as the Lo-

Bos ('law-boss') movement based on the town of Madang, with weekly meetings for confessions of law-breaking, moral and social discipline, and messages from Yali or the spirits.

Yalkut (Heb., 'compilation'). Title of several Jewish *midrashic anthologies. The best-known Yalkut are the *Yalkut Shimoni* (13th cent.) which covers the whole Bible, the *Yalkut ha-Makhiri* (14th cent.), and the *Yalkut Reuveni* (17th cent.) which has been arranged to correspond to the weekly readings of the *Torah *Scroll.

Yama (Skt., 'restraint'). 1. The god of death in Hinduism and Buddhism, also called *Dharma Rāja, possibly connected with the Iranian *Yima. In the **Ṛg Veda* he appears in books 1 and 10 presiding over the ancestors or 'fathers' (*pitṛ) in the third (highest) heaven of the sky (*svarga) realm (above atmosphere, *bhuvah*, and earth, *bhūr*). In the **Kaṭha *Upaniṣad*, Yama bestows highest knowledge. Post-Vedic mythology in contrast portrays Yama as a judge and punisher of the dead in a lower world where the soul (ātman, *jīva, *puruṣa) goes after death and receives its sentence. The *Mahābhārata* depicts Yama as clothed in red with glaring eyes, holding a noose with which to bind the souls of the dead. This image is embellished in later mythology where he is a terrible deity inflicting torture upon souls. Yama is associated with the south, the realm of the dead.

In Buddhism, Yama is the Lord of the Underworld. In some respects, he is replaced by *Māra. The canonical account of Yama is contained mainly in the two almost identical *Devadūta Suttas* in **Majjhima Nikāya* 3. 179 ff., and **Anguttara Nikāya* 1. 138 ff.

In the post-canonical Buddhist literature, Yama is depicted as the overlord of the purgatory system who assigns to beings the punishments they must undergo in expiation of their karmic misdeeds. In *Tantric Buddhism, Yama is a fierce deity. Tibetan iconography and the **Tibetan Book of the Dead* (*Bardo Thodol*) portray Yama, who appears at death, as standing in a halo of flames, adorned with human skulls and heads, holding in his left hand the mirror of karma (which reflects the good and bad deeds of the deceased) and in his right hand the sword of wisdom (*prajña).

2. The first limb of eight-limbed (*aṣṭaṅga*) or *rāja *yoga comprising five ethical rules: (i) non-injury (*ahiṁsā), (ii) truthfulness (*satya), (iii) non-stealing (*asteya*), (iv) celibacy (*brahmacarya), and (v) greedlessness (*aparigraha*). Commitment to these is the Great Vow (Mahāvrata).

Yamabushi (mountain ascetics): see FUJISAN; SHUGENDŌ.

Yāmala (Skt., 'pair'). 1. The goal of the *sādhaka's spiritual practice (*sādhana) conceived as the union of *Śiva and *Śakti.

2. An old group of texts in *Tantrism such as the *Brahma-yāmala*, *Rudra-yāmala*, and *Jayadratha-yāmala*. These are Śaiva texts with *Bhairava as the central deity but with strong Śākta tendencies. Dating from the 6th to the 9th cents. CE, they are a source of Śaiva and *Kaula developments in Kashmir (see KASHMIR ŚAIVISM).

Yamamoto Gempō (1866–1961). Prominent Zen Buddhist of his time, sometimes called 'the 20th-cent. *Hakuin'. A foundling, with poor eyesight, he was virtually illiterate. He abandoned his wife and home to seek Zen training, receiving the seal of recognition (*inka-shōmei) from Sōhan. He specialized in the way of writing (*shōdō*: see ART (CH'AN/ZEN)), and the Zen of indifference—remaining fond of wine and women.

Yama no Kami (mountain deities): see FESTIVALS AND FASTS (JAPANESE).

Yamaoka Tesshu (1836–88). Zen layman who became the major exponent of the way of the sword (*kendō). He was also an outstanding calligrapher and painter.

Yamazaki Ansai (1618–82). A leading Japanese advocate of *Shushigaku during the Tokugawa (1600–1868) period. His school stressed *Chu Hsi's moral and ethical teachings, with an emphasis on memorization and moral rigour. Eager to reconcile *neo-Confucian metaphysics with *Shinto theology, Yamazaki Ansai also formulated his own school of Shinto called Suika Shintō; in the end, Shinto is in control.

Yamoussoukro (site of basilica in the Ivory Coast): see BASILICA OF NOTRE DAME DE PAIX.

Yāmuna (known in Tamil as Āḷavandār; 10th/11th cent.). One of the early leaders of the *Śrīvaiṣṇava movement in S. India. Six works are attributed to him in which the foundations of the Śrīvaiṣṇavite devotion and of *Viśiṣṭādvaita can be found.

Yamunā or **Jumna.** One of the seven Hindu *sacred rivers.

Yāna ('path, course', 'journey', 'vehicle, carriage'). A 'way' of progress, especially in Buddhism. The term is best known in *Mahāyāna Buddhism, but it occurs in early Buddhism as well. Texts in the *Pāli canon refer to the eightfold path as yāna (*Therīgāthā* 389). The *locus classicus* for the later use of the term is ch. 3 of the **Lotus Sūtra* (*Saddharmapuṇḍarīka Sūtra*), which relates the parable of the burning house. In order to entice his sons (all beings) out of an old and decaying house (*saṃsāra) that is engulfed by fire (suffering), the father (the Buddha) offers three kinds of cart (*ratha*) pulled by goats, deer, and bullocks. Wishing to have these toys, the children rush out of the house. But the father gives them all the third and best kind of cart, the one drawn by great (mahā) white bullocks. This cart is the great vehicle (mahā-yāna). (The other two are vehicles suited to people of lesser spiritual aspirations.) It is explicitly stated in this chapter that the Buddha's action is skill-in-means (*upāya-kauśalya). He offers three kinds of yāna but only actually gives one—the mahā-yāna or buddha-yāna or eka-yāna ('single vehicle')—which leads all beings to become Buddhas (*Lotus Sūtra* 3. 89–91).

This running together of the terms *upāya and yāna is crucial to understanding the meaning of yāna in Mahāyāna texts, and it has a number of far-reaching consequences that totally transform its usage (compared with early Buddhism). First, yāna refers to the various means (upāya) that are used by the Buddha to bring beings to enlightenment.

Secondly, because these devices are really only modifications of the one truth, yāna also means that one truth or liberation itself.

Thirdly, because this eka-yāna is the same as the Buddha, it can never be limited or defined or even pointed to. Here we enter the paradoxes of Mahāyāna metaphysics. One cannot get at the beginning, middle, or end of this one great vehicle (*Aṣṭasāhasrikā-Prajñāpāramitā Sūtra* 23); hence in the last analysis, there is no yāna and no one who rides it (*Laṅka* 135). It is just like space, which contains all forms but itself has no form and can never be got hold of. In typical Mahāyāna style, therefore, we are offered everything and nothing at the same time.

Yang (constituent energy in the universe): see YIN-YANG.

Yang-ch'i Fang-hui (school of Ch'an/Zen Buddhism): see YŌGI SCHOOL.

Yang-ch'i-tsung (the Chinese name): see YŌGI SCHOOL.

Yang Chu (fl. *c.*450 BCE). Early Chinese philosopher. He seems to have taught a doctrine of self-preservation in opposition to hedonism. No complete work of his survives, but he is often referred to in later works such as *Lü-shih ch'un ch'iu* (Mr Lü's Springs and Autumns), which may preserve authentic fragments from his writings or sayings.

Yang-hsing (Chin., 'nourishing the life principle'). Collective term for Taoist exercises to prolong life and attain immortality, whether addressed to body (*yang-sheng) or mind (*yang-shen).

Yang-shan Hui-chi (Jap., Kyōzan Ejaku; *c.*810–*c.*887). Ch'an/Zen master, dharma-successor (*hassu) of Kuei-shan Ling-yu (see KUEI-YANG TSUNG), and so renowned that he became known as 'the little Śākyamuni'. His parents opposed his early inclination to become a monk until he presented them with two of his chopped-off fingers as a mark of his determination. He visited many masters, including *Ma-tsu and *Pai-chang, but found perfect connection with Kuei-shan. The two are regarded as co-founders of the Igyo school, with its emphasis on the ninety-seven circles of contemplation.

Yang-shen (Chin., 'nourishing the mind'). Taoist practice, especially of the inner deity hygiene school (see TAOISM), to prevent the inner deities from leaving the body.

Yang-sheng (Chin., 'nourishing the body'). Taoist practices, especially through breathing and directing the breath (*ch'i) to prolong life and attain immortality.

Yannai (3rd cent. CE). Jewish *amora. Yannai was of *priestly descent and a pupil of R. Ḥiyya. Yannai established an academy, and his rulings are frequently quoted in the *Talmud.

Yantra (Skt., 'instrument for supporting'). A geometrical design representing the cosmos used in Hindu liturgy (*pūjā) and meditation (*dhyāna), especially in *Tantrism. Though akin to *maṇḍala, yantra differs in that it can be a three-dimensional object of worship made of stone or metal plates. Like maṇḍala, the yantra is a symbol of cosmogonic development from the absolute in the centre to the material world at the outer edges, and like maṇḍala is the visual equivalent of *mantra. Yantras often have a seed (*bīja) mantra inscribed upon them. In Tantric pūjā, the yantra, if made of stone or metal, is invested with power and meditated upon as the deity. The most famous yantra is the *Śrīyantra.

Ya'qūb. Islamic form of *Jacob.

Yaqui Church. A body in N. Mexico and Arizona. It derives from *Jesuit missions among the Yaqui people in Mexico from 1617 until the Jesuits were suppressed in 1767. Left on their own, with Yaqui religion now defunct, they integrated the new *Roman Catholic form with community life, and resisted Mexican government efforts to assimilate them. Many Yaqui migrated to Arizona in the late 19th cent. and now there are community villages centred upon the church at Guadalupe, Old Pascua, New Pascua, and Barrio Libre, with a total of some 5,500 members, and up to 3,000 scattered elsewhere. The great cycle of open-air ritual dramas features the biblical events in *Holy Week.

Yarmulke (Yid., etym. uncertain; the tradition that it is a corruption of the Heb. for 'in fear of God' is unlikely). Skull cap worn by *Orthodox Jewish men. The yarmulke is worn by the observant at all times as a sign of humility before God. The less orthodox only cover their heads for prayer. The *custom is of relatively recent origin (*c.*17th cent.) and its religious basis lies in the proscription of *gentile practices (i.e. of uncovering the head as a sign of respect). See also HEAD, COVERING OF; HAIR.

Yasna (from *yaz*, 'sacrifice, worship'). Worship among Zoroastrians (the word is akin to *yajña). Yasna is an obligation in general, originally undertaken in close proximity to the creations of *Ahura Mazda, in conditions of great purity, and only later in temples. Yasna is also the daily ritual of Zoroastrians, with offerings to fire and water (*zaothra*). The offering is made by a *zaotar/zot*, and is not congregational. The offering to fire, which initially involved blood sacrifice, creates a sense of bonding between animals and humans, in which the souls of humans, and of domestic and wild animals, are equally reverenced. Yasna is also the name of the liturgical text recited during the ritual, the central section of which, Staota yesna, is believed to be the most powerful *manthra* (cf. Skt., *mantra). Of central importance are the *Gāthās.

Yaśovijaya (1624–88). Jain logician who set himself the task of reconciling conflicting sects. He studied at *Kāśi (Benares), concentrating especially on logic. He endeavoured to show the interior correspondences and meanings of external religious acts, e.g. in *Jñānasāra*. His attempt to heal divisions among the Jains had as much success as such endeavours generally have, i.e. very little.

Yasukuni shrine (Shinto shrine in Tokyo): see KAMIKAZE.

Yathrib. Original name of al-*Madīna

Yati (Skt.). One who practises a discipline in Indian religions, an *ascetic.

Yaum al-Dīn. The Day of Judgement in Islam, succeeding immediately the day of resurrection (*yaum al-Qiyāma), so that the two can be regarded as parts of the same event, and are often virtually synonymous. It is the day when each person's deeds will be weighed on an exact balance (Qur'ān 7. 8 f.; 21. 47; 23. 103 f.; 101. 6–9)

Yaum al-Qiyāma. The day of resurrection in Islam. Referred to frequently in the *Qur'ān as a matter of certainty (against the scepticism of *Muḥammad's opponents), it is likened to the power of God to bring new life from the dead earth. The descriptions of what it will be like are frequent and detailed.

Yavez (pen-name): see EMDEN, JACOB.

Yavneh (centre of early rabbinic Judaism): see JABNEH; ACADEMIES.

Ya-yüeh (elegant music): see MUSIC.

Yazatas (worshipful beings): see AHURA MAZDA.

Yazīdīs (religious movement): see YEZĪDĪS.

Yazrain ('two inclinations'): see INCLINATION, GOOD AND EVIL.

Year (religious): see CALENDAR.

Yehuda (common Jewish name derived from the son of the Jewish patriarch, Jacob): see JUDAH.

Yehudai ben Naḥman or **Yehudai Gaon** (8th cent.). Head of the Jewish *academy of *Sura. He was the first *gaon to write a book, the *Halakhot Pesukot*, and the first to compile *responsa. He rested his decisions entirely on the Babylonian *Talmud, and through his influence the Babylonian rather than the Palestinian Talmud became the basis of halakhic decisions.

Yelammedenu (Aram., 'let him pronounce'). The opening word of each sermon in the 4th-cent. **Tanḥuma*. It thus has become an alternative title for *Tanḥuma*.

Yellammā (Ellammaṉ, Eḷammā, Yēlū, and many further forms). A goddess of folk Hinduism, venerated particularly in Mahārāṣṭra, Karṇāṭaka, and further south, by the lower *castes. The most likely etymology of her name is from a Dravidian *ēḻ*, 'seven', and *ammaṉ*, 'mother, goddess', and thus alludes to a belief, found all over W. India, in the 'seven sisters' or 'seven mothers'. The main ritual centres of her worship are the temples of Mahūr (E. Mahārāṣṭra) and Saundattī (Karṇāṭaka), but in simpler form her worship is performed all over the area in the villages.

Yellow Hats. In early Western writers on Tibetan Buddhism, the *Geluk school, who distinguish themselves from other schools by their wearing of yellow hats. See also RED HATS.

Yellow Turban rebellion (Taoist rebellion): see CHANG CHÜEH.

Yen-ch'i (Chin., 'swallowing breath'). A Taoist exercise in embryonic breathing (*tai-hsi*), which controls the level from which breath is exhaled. It is usually linked to *lien-ch'i.

Yen-t'ou Ch'uan-huo (Jap., Gantō Zenkatsu; 828–87). Ch'an/Zen master, dharma-successor (*hassu) of Te-shan Hsuan-chien. His death, murdered by robbers, caused the problem of 'Yen-tou's cry': far from accepting death with equanimity, he uttered a cry heard for miles around. *Hakuin solved the problem when he attained enlightenment and said, 'Indeed, Gantō is alive, strong, and well'.

Yeshivah (pl. yeshivot). Institute of Jewish *Talmudic learning. The term 'yeshiva' is applied to the *academies of Jewish learning in Babylonia and *Erez Israel in which the *amoraim studied the *Mishnah (see TALMUD), to the academies of *Sura and *Pumbedita in the *geonic period, and to later local Talmudic institutions. By the mid-16th cent., many yeshivot were supported and governed by local community councils. The curriculum centred on the Talmud and its commentaries, although *minhagim, *posekim, and *responsa were also studied.

Yeshivah of the right (academy for Torah study): see SURA (1).

Yeshiva University. Jewish *Orthodox institution of higher education. Yeshiva University was founded in 1897 in New York as the Rabbi Isaac Elhanan Theological Seminary for advanced *Talmudic study.

Yeẓer ha-ra'/ha-tov (evil/good inclination in Judaism): see INCLINATION, GOOD AND EVIL.

Yezīdīs, also **Yazīdī.** A religious community found among the Kurds of Iraq, Turkey, Syria, Germany, Armenia, and Georgia. Its nucleus was a Muslim *Sūfī brotherhood founded in Iraq by the Arab sheikh Adi b. Musafir (*c*.1075–1162 CE), a descendant of the *Umayyad caliphs (*khalīfa). In the 14th–15th cents., a distinct religion emerged and was adopted by a number of the semi-independent Kurdish tribes. Expansion of the Ottoman Empire and subsequent persecutions caused massive defections to Islam. But the religion survived in the Sheikhan district N. of Mosul (Iraq), and in the Jebel Sinjar mountains to the West. Yezidis are also found in SE Turkey (many of them now in Germany), the Jebel Siman mountains west of Aleppo (Syria), and in Armenia and Georgia. The total number of Yezīdīs is around 200,000, of whom half live in Iraq.

The distinctive feature of the religion—a monotheistic faith incorporating many Jewish, Christian, and Muslim traditions—is the belief that the fallen angel *Lucifer has been pardoned by God for his disobedience and that those who venerate him are the elect of humankind.

Yezīdīs are forbidden to use the term *Satan, whom they call Melek Taus ('Peacock Angel'). A large bronze image of a peacock is paraded at important festivals and for many years replicas were carried by alms-gatherers among Yezīdī villages. The Yezīdīs are not, however, devil-worshippers, as they have sometimes been called.

The tomb of Sheikh Adi at Lalish (a mountain valley north of Mosul, often itself called 'Sheikh Adi') is the principal shrine of the Yezīdī religion. A five-day festival there in mid-Oct., attended by many pilgrims, includes ritual dancing, singing, and feasting, as well as secret ceremonies associated with the great peacock and with a spring of water called Zemzem that gushes out of the rock beneath Sheikh Adi's tomb. The secular arm of the community is represented by the Mir of Sheikhan, who lives at Baadri, immediately south of Lalish. The Chol dynasty was established in the 17th cent., and was accorded semi-divine status. But the Mir's civil authority was curtailed by the extension of Ottoman bureaucracy in the 19th cent., followed by the British occupation of Iraq (1918–32, 1941–5).

Yezirah, Sefer (Heb., 'Book of Creation'). An early Jewish mystical work. There is no scholarly consensus as to the date or place of origin of *Sefer Yezirah*. It was certainly in existence by the 10th cent. *Sefer Yezirah* was an immensely influential text in the development of *kabbalistic thought and early Jewish philosophy.

YHWH. Name of the Jewish God: see TETRAGRAMMATON.

Yibbum (Jewish obligation to ensure male descent): see LEVIRATE MARRIAGE.

Yidam (Tib., *yi.dam.*, 'bound in thought'). A class of tutelary deities in Tibetan Buddhism corresponding to the Indian *Iṣṭadevatā. It also parallels the Western concept of the *guardian angel, in that the yidam inspires, guides, and protects, although restricted in role to the context of *Tantric practice. The yidam selected by the *yogin may be that of his school or monastery, but often the choice is determined by personal feeling. Yidams are classified in appearance as *wrathful, semi-wrathful, and peaceful, and are often considered as 'aspects' of well-known *bodhisattvas.

Yiddish (contracted from *Yidish-daytsh*, i.e. Jewish-German). Language used by *Ashkenazi Jews. Yiddish is related to German, but has many Slavic, Hebrew, and *Aramaic words, and it is written in the Hebrew script.

Yigdal (Heb., 'May he be magnified'). Jewish *liturgical hymn. The hymn is based on *Maimonides' *Thirteen Principles of the Jewish faith. A Christian version (made by T. Olivers, 18th cent.) is sung as 'The God of Abraham praise . . .'.

Yi Li. *Ceremonials and Rituals*, one of the collections of ritual texts included in the *Confucian Classics. While undated, they are probably from late Chou times (roughly 5th–3rd cents. BCE), although they may contain much earlier material.

Yima. Iranian mythological king, who presided over a perfect place (known as *var*) where neither death nor winter were able to enter until someone sinned. When a *taboo was broken, Yima saved his people by taking death upon himself, and thus became the first mortal.

Ying-chou (island of the immortals, China): see FANG-SHIH.

Yin-Hsiang. Chin. for *mudra.

Yin-yang. The two opposite energies in Chinese thought, from whose interaction and fluctuation the universe and its diverse forms emerge. They are the polar extremes of the unbounded *Tao of the supreme and ultimate source (*t'ai-chi), and from their intermingling arise the five elements (*wu-hsing), which give rise to the myriads of forms, and to history and time. The yin-yang symbol expresses this interaction, with the two spots (white in the dark, dark in the white) indicating that each of the two contains the seed of the other and is about to produce the replication of its opposite in interaction. All oppositions can be mapped onto yin and yang, yin representing e.g. the feminine, yielding, receptive, moon, water, clouds, even numbers, and the yang the masculine, hard, active, red, the sun, and odd numbers. Combined with wu-hsing (five phases), these represent the organizing categories of the Chinese world-view.

Yin-yüan (introduced Ōbaku-shū to China in 17th cent.): see ŌBAKU-SHŪ.

Yishtabbaḥ (Heb., 'praised shall be [your name]'). A Jewish *benediction. The Yishtabbaḥ concludes one section of the *Shaḥarit service. It contains thirteen individual praises which, according to the *Zohar*, activate the thirteen attributes of God. It is recited standing.

Yizkor (Heb., 'he shall remember'). Jewish memorial *prayer. The Yizkor is said for close relatives on the last day of *Passover, on the second day of *Shavu'ot, on Shemini Atzeret (see SUKKOT), and on the *Day of Atonement.

Yoga (Skt., 'yoking', 'joining'). The means or techniques for transforming consciousness and attaining liberation (*mokṣa) from *karma and rebirth (*saṃsāra) in Indian religions. The mind (*manas, *citta) is thought to be constantly fluctuating, but through yoga it can be focused, one-pointedness (*ekāgrata) developed, and higher states of consciousness (*samādhi) experienced. Such control of consciousness, which is taught by a *guru, also results in the attainment of paranormal powers (*siddhi).

Techniques of meditative absorption (*dhyāna, samādhi) were developed in the *Śramana tradition which constrained Jainism and Buddhism, emphasizing control of consciousness as the means of liberation. Although the early *Upaniṣads speak of the interiorization of the sacrifice, the actual term 'yoga' and technical terms such as āsana do not appear until the late Upaniṣads (500 BCE onwards).

Classical yoga is referred to as one of the six systems of Indian philosophy (*darśana). Expressed in *Patañjali's *Yoga Sūtra* (2nd–3rd cents. CE) it represents a refinement of ideas and practices found in the Upaniṣads. Patañjali states the goal of yoga to be quite simply the 'cessation of mental fluctuation' (*cittavṛtti *nirodha) which results in higher levels of consciousness or absorptions (samādhi) and the purification of the self (*ātman). The *Yoga Sūtra* advocates *rāja or eightfold (aṣṭaṅga) yoga.

The *Bhagavad-gītā* addresses yoga specifically, in that here *Kṛṣṇa is the object of the yogin's meditation. The *Gītā* advocates three kinds of yoga, *karma yoga, the performance of action without attachment to its result, *jñāna yoga, knowledge of God, and *bhakti yoga, devotion to God (which the *Gītā* evidently regards as the highest).

Yoga became associated with the theistic traditions of *Vaiṣṇavism, *Śaivism, and *Śaktism, the object of meditation becoming the deities of those traditions. During this period (900–1600 CE) various yoga techniques were developed along with ideas about the physiology of the subtle body (*liṅga/*sūkṣma śarīra)—for example in the Yoga Upaniṣads. The *Nath tradition developed *Haṭha yoga, though the latter is not confined to this one tradition. The yoga of *Tantrism places particular emphasis on practices involving sound and vision, that is the *visualization of *maṇḍalas, *yantras, and deities (*devatā), *mantra, and kuṇḍalinī yoga. Tantrism also uses sexual intercourse (*maithuna) as a form of yoga.

Today yoga is an integral part of Hinduism. Important modern Hindus have advocated various kinds of yoga. For example, *Aurobindo advocated a form of Tantric yoga, calling it

Integral Yoga, *Rāmakrishna practised bhakti yoga, and *Ramana Maharṣhi the yoga of knowing the identity of the self and God. Many of the new religions encourage the practice of some kind of yoga. For example, the *Vedānta Society practises jñāna yoga, ISCKON/Hare Krishna (*International Society . . .), bhakti yoga, and the 3HO (*Healthy, Happy, Holy Organization) a form of Tantric yoga. Haṭha yoga has become very popular in the West, though more as an aid to health than as a soteriology.

See Index, Yoga.

Yogācāra (Buddhist school of idealism): see VIJÑĀ-NAVĀDA.

Yogānanda, Paramahamsa (1893–1952). Founder of the Hindu Self-Realization Fellowship. Taking Yukteśvar as his *guru, he went to lecture in the USA in 1920 and stayed there, founding a Yoga Institute in Los Angeles in 1925. He travelled extensively, extending the Fellowship, and advocating Kriyā-yoga, *yoga based on practical efforts. His own account is in *Autobiography of a Yogi* (1946).

Yoga Sūtra. The text of classical *yoga attributed to *Patañjali and composed during the 2nd or 3rd cents. CE. The text comprises 195 aphorisms (*sūtras) and is divided into four sections (*pada*) on (i) *samādhi or concentration, (ii) *sādhana or practice, (iii) *vibhūti or magical powers, and (iv) *kaivalya, the condition of isolation or freedom. The *Sūtra* is a systematic exposition of the theory and practice of eight-limbed (*aṣṭāṅga) or *rāja yoga.

Yogatantra (division of Tantric texts): see TRIPIṬAKA.

Yogi (Skt., 'one who is joined'). A participant in one of the schools of *Yoga. More casually, the word is used of Hindu *ascetics in general.

Yoginī. An initiated female partner in Hindu *Tantric *maithuna; female deities in the service of *Durgā; adepts possessed of *magic powers.

Yōgi school (Chin., Yang-ch'i-tsung/p'ai; Jap., Yōgi-shu). School of Ch'an/Zen Buddhism, originating with Yang-ch'i Fang-hui. In the phrase 'five houses and seven schools' (*goke-shichishu), the latter indicates a twofold derivation from *Lin-chi, Yōgi and Ōryū, the two lines of *Rinzai. Its best-known representative was *Wu-men Hui-k'ai.

Yohanan (form of Jewish name): see JOHANAN.

Yōka-genkaku (Ch'an/Zen master): see YUNG-CHIA HSÜAN-CHÜEH.

Yŏlban. Korean for *nirvāna.

Yoma (Heb., 'the day'). Fifth tractate of the order *Mo'ed* in the Jewish *Mishnah (and *Talmuds). *The* day is the *Day of Atonement, with which the tractate deals.

Yōmei-gaku. Jap. term for the heterodox *neo-Confucian teachings of *Wang Yang-ming (Jap., Ō Yōmei, 1472–1529), also known as the School of Mind or Intuition. Nakae Tōju (1608–48) is considered the school's founder in Japan, which also included the *samurai reformer Kumazawa Banzan (1619–91). The school's politically activist teachings attracted numerous followers during the Tokugawa (1600– 1868) period's final decades, including figures like Ōshio Chūsai (Heihachirō), Sakuma Shōzan, and Yoshida Shōin, whose students became leaders of the Meiji Restoration of 1868.

Yom Haatzma'ut (Independence Day). The anniversary of the State of *Israel's Declaration of Independence. It is observed as an annual public holiday on 5 Iyyar.

Yomi (death): see IZANAGI AND IZANAMI.

Yom Kippur (Jewish festival): see DAY OF ATONEMENT.

Yom Kippur war. So-called because on this day in 1973 (6 Oct.) Egypt and Syria attacked Israeli positions in the Sinai peninsula and on the Golan heights.

Yom tov (Heb., 'a good day'). General term for a Jewish *festival.

Yom tov sheni galuyyot (second days of festivals): see SECOND DAYS.

Yoni (Skt., 'source'). In Hinduism, the female origin of all appearance. In particular, it is the female sexual organ, symbolized as a triangle. By *śaktas, it is venerated, either on its own, or in conjunction with the *liṅga.

Yon mchod (patron and priest, pattern of relationship between China and Tibet): see 'PHAGS-PA BLO-GROS-RGYAL-MTSHAN.

Yōsai (Tendai monk): see EISAI.

Yose b. Yose (early composer of piyyutim): see PIYYUT.

Yoshida family (Jap.). In *Shinto, a family of diviners serving in the emperor's court in ancient times, later serving as hereditary priests in the Yoshida Shrine and Hirano Shrine of *Kyōto. Before 1387, they were known as the Urabe family. The members of this family were recognized as scholars of classical and Shinto studies. Urabe Kanekata was a 13th-cent. scholar who compiled *Shaku nihongi*, an important commentary on the **Nihon-shoki*; and his son Kanefumi wrote the earliest extant commentary on the *Kojiki. The famous writer Yoshida Kenkō (c.1283–c.1352), author of the *Tsurezuregusa* (Essays in Idleness), was also of this family. Their greatest Shinto scholar was Yoshida Kanetomo (1435–1511), who organized and systematized the Yoshida traditions and founded the school known as *Yoshida Shintō, through which the Yoshida family played a prominent role within Shinto up until the Meiji Restoration in 1868.

Yoshida Shintō (Jap.). A school of *Shinto which draws on Confucianism, Taoism, and *Shingon Buddhism, but considers Shinto as the central root or foundation. The Shinto learning passed on in the *Yoshida priestly family since the Heian period was summarized and systematized by Yoshida Kanetomo (1435–1511), restoring the ideological independence of Shinto. This school of Shinto called itself 'Shinto of the Original Source' (*Gempon Sōgen Shintō*) because of its belief in a supreme primordial *kami, Daigen Sonshin (Venerable Kami of the Great Origin), who preceded heaven and earth and was the source of the myriad kami. Yoshida Shintō was widely spread in Japan from the later medieval period until the Meiji Restoration and was influential in appointments to the priesthood, decisions about religious ceremonies, and the like. It was also called Yui-itsu Shinto ('unique Shinto') and Urabe Shinto.

Yotae. Korean for *tathāgata.

Yotzer (Heb., 'He creates'). The Jewish *benedictions which frame the *Shema'. In the plural (Yotzerot) it stands for all the liturgical hymns (*piyyutim) chanted during the morning service.

Young, Brigham (Mormon leader in 19th cent.): see MORMONS.

Yüan-ch'i (Chin., 'primordial breath'). The fundamental energy in which *yin and yang are still closely interactive in producing the universe. The yüan-chi is now dispersed, but can be summoned together again in the *Taoist breathing exercises which distribute it to the whole body.

Yuan-chueh-ching (Skt., *Purṇa-buddha Sūtra*; Jap., *Engaku-kyo*). 'The Sūtra of Perfect Enlightenment', a Ch'an/Zen sūtra supposedly translated into Chinese by Buddhatrāta in 693 (but it is not certain that there was a Skt. original). The *Sūtra* tells how twelve *bodhisattvas (including *Mañjuśri and *Samantabhadra) are instructed on the nature of perfect enlightenment.

Yüan-shih t'ien-tsun (Taoist deity): see SAN-CH'ING.

Yüan-wu K'o-ch'in (Jap., Engo Kokugon; 1063–1135). Master of the *Yōgi lineage of *Rinzai, dharma-successor of Wu-tsu Fa-yen, and major figure in the development of *kōan-based Zen. He was head of different monasteries, and was favoured by the northern emperor, Hui-tsung, who called him Fo-kuo Ch'an-shih, 'Zen master of the buddha fruit'. His major work was the joint-compilation of *Hekiganroku*, the *Blue Cliff Record*—see KŌAN.

Yü Chi or **Kan Chi** (d. 197 CE). *Taoist scholar and practitioner of the skills of religious Taoism in effecting cures, etc. He wrote *T'ai-p'ing ching-ling shu* (The Book of Supreme Peace and Purity), which became foundational for *T'ai-p'ing Tao—though according to tradition, he received the book miraculously, rather than writing it.

Yuga (Skt.). An 'age' in Hinduism, one of the four periods into which a world cycle is divided: (i) kṛta (or satya)-yuga, the golden age when there is unity (one god, one *veda, one ritual), in which the *varnas perform their roles without oppression or envy; (ii) *tretā-yuga when righteousness begins to decline by a quarter and sacrifice begins; (iii) dvāpara-yuga, when righteousness again declines by a quarter, the Vedas split into four, and few study them; (iv) *kali-yuga, further decline by a quarter, when disease, despair, and conflict dominate. At present, we are in (iv), which began 3102 BCE, so that one should not be optimistic about the general prospect for the world.

Yugyō-ha (school of wanderers): see JISHŪ.

Yü-huang (Chin., 'Jade Emperor'). Deity of wide importance in Chinese folk religion and religious *Taoism (*tao-chiao*). He is one of the three Pure Ones (*san-ch'ing), who determines all that happens in heaven and on earth. His earthly deputies are T'ai-yüeh ta-ti (mountain deity who rules the earth and all people, deciding the moments of birth and death), Cheng-huang (guardians of cities who guide the souls of the dead), Tsao-chün (the lord of the hearth, who observes all that happens in the home), and T'u-ti (guardians of particular parts of cities or towns). He is portrayed usually on a throne in a robe decorated with *dragons, holding a string of thirteen pearls and a ceremonial plaque. His feast day is the ninth day of the first lunar month.

Yuige (Jap., 'poem left behind'). A verse left by a Zen teacher for his pupils, when he knows that death is near. In it, he expresses his quintessential understanding of Zen, gathered in a lifetime. For examples, see YÜAN-WU K'O-CH'IN; WU-MEN HUI-K'AI.

Yui-itsu Shinto (school of Shinto): see HONJI SUIJAKU; YOSHIDA SHINTŌ.

Yukta (Skt.). In Hinduism, one who has attained realization of, and union with, *Brahman permeating all appearance, and lives in that condition of freedom from all appearance.

Yün-chi Ch'i-ch'ien (11th cent. CE). Taoist encyclopaedia, containing, in many vols., a survey of all the works and practices addressed to the prolonging of life and attaining of immortality up to that time. It contains much early Taoist work that no longer survives in any other form.

Yung-chia Hsüan-chüeh (Jap., Yōka Genkaku; 665–713). Last of the great masters of the school of *Hui-neng. He combined the philosophy of *T'ien-t'ai with Ch'an practice, and related both to *Mādhyamaka. These views are reflected in a poem attributed to him, *Shōdōka*, 'Hymn on the Experience of *Tao/truth'.

Yun-kang/Yungang (Chin., 'Cloud Hill'). Complex of caves 16 km. west of the N. China town of Ta-t'ung (Datong), with cave temples containing among the greatest expressions of Chinese Buddhist art.

Yün-men Wen-yen (Jap., Ummon Bun'en; 864–949). Founder of the Ch'an/Zen *Ummon school. He was dharma-successor (*hassu) of *Hsueh-feng I-ts'un. A ruler from the Liu family built a monastery for him on Mount Yün-men (hence his name), where many disciples gathered. Yün-men used the stick-and-shout method (*katsu* see HO, *kyosaku), but is better known for his careful use of word structures in dialogue, leading into *kōans—e.g. he would offer different answers, or answer for the student, or make the answer a question. He is particularly renowned for introducing 'one-word barriers', single-word, challenging answers (though in fact they may be of more than one character), thus: 'What are the words of the revered Buddhas and great patriarchs?' 'Dumplings'; 'What is Zen?' 'It'; 'What is the eye of the true *Dharma?' 'Everywhere'.

Yunus. *Jonah in the *Qur'ān.

Yun-yen T'an-sheng (Jap., Ungan Donjō; *c.*780–841). Ch'an/Zen master, dharma-successor (*hassu) of Yueh-shan Wei-yen, and master of *Tung-shan Liang-chieh, co-founder of *Ts'ao-tung. Several formative exchanges (*mondō) between the two have been recorded —for an example see TUNG-SHAN.

Yūpa (Skt., 'post'). Stake to which, in Hinduism, a sacrificial victim is tied. It is regarded as the tree of life, uniting earth and heaven (cf. SKAṀBHA), and was clearly associated with *liṅga power. It is often eight-sided, and when anointed, it was addressed as 'the tree of divine sweetness'.

Yūsuf. Islamic form of *Joseph.

Z

Zabuton (Jap., 'sitting mat'). The mat on which *zazen is practised; cf. ZAFU.

Zacuto, Moses ben Mordecai (1620–97), Jewish *kabbalist. For much of his life Zacuto lived in Italy and was a member of the Venetian *yeshivah. Although initially drawn to the *Shabbatean movement, he rejected it after the *apostasy of *Shabbetai Zevi. He edited the kabbalistic *Zohar Ḥadash* (1658) and annotated the work of *Luria and *Vital under the acronym of ReMeZ (Rabbi Moses Zacuto). His poems have been collected in various anthologies, and his great dramatic poem, *Tofteh Arukh* (1715), attained great popularity.

Zaddik (Heb., 'righteous man'). A model of Jewish behaviour who is much praised in biblical literature. The zaddik (*tsaddik*) is the name given to the *ḥasidic leader whose charismatic personality is devoutly admired among his followers. He is believed to have attained mystical union with God, and employs his powers for the benefit of his community. He keeps court to which the individual Ḥasid makes *pilgrimage, and he is perceived as the ladder between Heaven and earth.

Zaddik, Joseph ben Jacob Ibn (d. 1149). Spanish poet and philosopher. Zaddik was the author of *Sefer ha-'Olam ha-Katan* (ed. 1854), which was praised by *Maimonides. It explores what constitutes 'everlasting good' and comes to the conclusion that 'knowing God and doing his will' leads to the greatest happiness.

Zadok (11th cent. BCE). Israelite *priest. Zadok was a descendant of *Aaron and together with Abiathar was King *David's chief priest. At David's behest, he anointed *Solomon the next king of Israel, and Solomon appointed Zadok's son as the *high priest of the *Temple. From then on, the high priesthood remained in the Zadokite family until the *Maccabean era.

Zadokites (Heb., 'Benei Zadok', 'Sons of Zadok'). Members of the ascetic community at *Qumran. According to the *Dead Sea Scrolls, 'the sons of Zadok are the elect of *Israel, called by name, who arise in the latter days'.

Zaehner, Robert Charles (1913–74). Spalding Professor of Eastern Religions and Ethics at Oxford from 1953. Although a specialist in Persian, from 1953 he became absorbed in the textual traditions of India. He expounded and criticized the Hindu classics 'from inside' and correlated them with the Catholicism to which he had been converted in 1936. His major works are *Mysticism, Sacred and Profane* (1957), *At Sundry Times* (1958), *Hindu and Muslim Mysticism* (1960), *Dawn and Twilight of Zoroastrianism* (1961), *Hinduism* (1962), *The Bhagavad-Gītā* (1969), *Concordant Discord* (1970). Towards the end of his life, he became increasingly preoccupied with the problems of rationality and unreason, good and evil, the latter given full rein in his last book *Our Savage God* (1974).

Zafarnāmā (Pers., 'epistle of victory'). Guru *Gobind Siṅgh's reply to *Auraṅgzeb *c.*1705, included in the *Dasam Granth. Gobind Singh wrote the Zafarnāmā in Dīnā, S. Pañjāb, after leaving *Anaṇḍpur and suffering defeat.

Zafu (Jap., 'sitting cushion'). Round, black cushion, on which *zazen is practised: cf. ZABUTON.

Zagu (death on the mat in Zen): see DAISHI.

Ẓāhiriy(y)a, al. Those who derive law governing Muslim life from the direct text (ẓāhir) of the *Qur'ān and *Sunna. Their view rejected *hermeneutical methods of relating Qur'ān and Sunna to life—not only *ray'y, istiṣḥāb*, *istiḥsān, but also *qiyās; and *ijma' could only be accepted as the consensus of the *Companions.

Zaidīy(y)a, al-, Zaidis, or **Zaydis** (sometimes called 'Fivers' because they seceded over the fifth *Imām), a sect of *Shī'a Muslims, in contrast to the *Ithna 'Asharīy(y)a (Twelvers) and the *Seveners (see also ISMĀ'ĪLIY(Y)A). When the fourth Shi'ite Imām, 'Ali Zayn al-'Ābidīn, died in 713 (AH 95), the Zaidis followed Zaid rather than his brother, Muḥammad al-Baqīr, as Imām. Zaid al-Shahīd rebelled against the *Umayyad caliph in 737 (AH 121), but was killed in battle. Strict in their observance, they reject *mut'a and *Sūfī claims. The Imām is not a matter of succession (hence there can be periods without an Imām) but of recognition.

Zakāt. The third *Pillar of Islam, the official alms tax levied on certain types of property and payable by every adult Muslim of sufficient means. The word is borrowed from the Heb. *zakūt*, and the Arab. root *zakā* is itself connected with the meaning of purity. This is elaborated by some commentators: the believer gives a portion of his wealth to Allāh, and so can 'purify' the rest and use it with a good conscience. In the *Qur'ān, almsgiving is often cited along with prayer as a duty of the Muslim:

'Perform the prayer, and give the alms' (2. 43, 110, 277).

The percentage to be paid on property varies for different classes of goods, and interpretations differ between the schools of law.

Zakkai, Johanan ben (leading Jewish sage): see JOHANAN BEN ZAKKAI.

Zalman, Schneur (founder of movement in Judaism): see SHNE'UR ZALMAN OF LYADY.

Zamakhsharī (Muslim grammarian): see AL-ZAMAKHSHARĪ.

Zammai, also **Sanmai.** Japanese pronunciation of *samādhi. Sanmai-do is a meditation hall; in particular, it is a shrine built near a graveyard for the performance of hokke-zanmai rituals for the benefit of ancestors, and thus also any hokke-zanmai-in temple of *Tendai.

Zamzam. The sacred well of *Mecca, also called the well of *Ismāʿīl, because, according to tradition, Jibrīl (*Gabriel) opened it to save Hagar and her son in the desert. Important in the *ḥajj, pilgrims hope to dip in, or touch with, its waters the clothes in which they will be buried.

Zanāna (often transliterated as 'Zenāna', as in the Zenana Missionary Society). The women's quarters in Muslim homes in India.

Zaotar (officiating priest): see MAGI; YASNA.

Zaothra (offerings): see YASNA.

Zaqen mamre (contumacious and obstinate teacher): see REBELLIOUS ELDER.

Zarathustra (founding prophet): see ZOROASTER.

Zasu (Jap., 'master of the seat'). The ruling functionary in a Buddhist institution (school, temple, etc.). As a title, it is especially associated with Enryaku-ji on Mount Hiei.

Zat Sikh form of *jāti, *caste.

Zawj or **al-zawaj** (marriage): see MARRIAGE (ISLAM).

Zaydiy(y)a (sect of Shīʿa Muslims): see ZAIDĪY(Y)A.

Zazen (Jap., 'sitting' + 'absorption'; Chin., *tso-ch'an*). Basic meditation practice in Ch'an/Zen, the gateway to enlightenment. Associated above all with *Dōgen (his way of Zen is sometimes called *shikan taza*, 'zazen alone'), it is described in his classic work *Fukanzazengi*:

If you wish to attain enlightenment, begin at once to practise zazen. For this meditation you need a quiet room; food and drink should be taken in moderation. Free yourself from all attachments and bring to rest the ten thousand things. Think not of good or evil; judge not on right or wrong; maintain the flow of mind, will, and consciousness; bring to an end all desire, all concepts and judgments!

To sit properly, first lay down a thick pillow and on top of this a second (round) one. One may sit either in the full or half cross-legged position. In the full position one places the right foot on the left thigh and the left foot on the right thigh. In the half position, only the left foot is placed upon the right thigh. Robe and belt should be worn loosely, but in order. The right hand rests on the left foot, while the back of the left hand rests on the palm of the right. The two thumbs are placed in juxtaposition. Let the body be kept upright, leaning neither to the left nor to the right, neither forward nor backward. Ears and shoulders, nose and navel must be aligned to one another. The tongue is to be kept against the palate, lips and teeth firmly closed, while the eyes should always be left open.

Now that the bodily position is in order, regulate your breathing. If a wish arises, take note of it and then dismiss it! If you practise in this way for a long time, you will forget all attachments and concentration will come naturally. That is the art of zazen. Zazen is the Dharma gate of great rest and joy. (Tr. Dumoulin.)

Zazengi (seated meditation): see TAO-HSIN.

Zeal (Gk., *zelos*, 'be hot, boil'). Enthusiasm which may become intemperate, and thus an ambiguous religious emotion. The *Septuagint used *zelos* to translate Heb., *qana*, 'to be dyed red', which expresses the visible change of appearance of those under strong emotion. In Jewish scripture, the zeal of God expresses his involvement in his chosen people, and this zeal may be expressed as anger or mercy. Conversely, people are full of zeal for God, (Psalm 69. 5), but *zealots are not unambiguously good people. In the New Testament, the same ambiguity continues: Paul regarded himself as a zealot for the *traditions of Judaism when he tried to destroy the new movement which became Christianity (Galatians 1. 14), and *zelos* (or *zeloi* in the plural) are included in his list of vices in Galatians 5. 20 and 2 Corinthians 12. 21. Yet equally, he praises the Christians at Corinth for their zeal for the good of others.

Zealots. Jewish resistance fighters in the Jewish–Roman War, 66–73 CE. The movement stemmed from the activities of Judah the Galilean who 'incited his countrymen to revolt'. In the War against the Romans, one of the sons of Judah seized the fortress of Masada and took command of the Jewish forces in Jerusalem until his murder in 68. The majority of the Zealots died in the siege of Jerusalem; Masada fell in 73, and those who fled to Egypt were rounded up, tortured, and executed.

Zeami Motokiyo (Japanese playwright and actor): see NŌ DRAMA.

Zechariah. Eleventh of the *Minor Prophets in the Hebrew scriptures and Christian Old Testament. The book is attributed to Zechariah, son of Berechiah, and three of the prophecies are dated between the second and fourth year of the reign of King Darius (520–518 BCE).

Zekut(h) Abot(h) (merit of the fathers): see MERITS OF THE FATHERS.

Zelanti (Lat., *zelantes*, 'those who are eager'). Franciscans in the Franciscan Controversy of the 13th cent., who opposed any modification of the Rule as established by St *Francis in 1221 and revised by him in 1223. The Relaxati supported modification of the Rule. The term is also used of other strongly committed, and usually conservative, groups.

Zemban (Jap., 'Zen board'). Board used in long sessions of *zazen to prop up the chin in order not to fall forward if drowsiness sets in.

Zemirot (Heb., 'songs'). According to the *Sephardim, the verses and *psalms recited before the main part of the Jewish morning service. According to the *Ashkenazim, they are the hymns sung during and after the *Sabbath meals. Twenty-five of the better known ones are printed in many editions of the *Prayer Book.

Zenana (Missionary Society): see ZANĀNA.

Zen arts: see ART.

Zen Buddhism (Jap., *zenna* or *zenno*, from reading Chin., *ch'an-na* or *ch'an*, a Chin. version of *dhyāna). A coalition of related ways for attaining realization, even beyond enlightenment, of the true nature underlying all appearance including one's own—and above all, that there is no duality within appearances, but only the one buddha-nature (*buddhatā, *bussho).

Ch'an emerged as part of the *Mahāyāna development, though naturally it traces its lineage back to the *Buddha Śākyamuni. Bodhidharma is recognized as the key figure in the transition to China. Conflict set in over the sixth patriarch, leading to the division into *Southern and Northern schools, with the difference of emphasis summarized in the saying, 'Suddenness of South, gradualness of North'. The Southern school developed into many independent schools, often in relation to other forms of Chinese Buddhism. Tsung-mi lists seven schools (though he includes the Northern school as one), but of these, only two developed important and continuing lines, those established by *Ma-tsu Tao-i and by Shih-tou Hsi-ch'ien, in the third generation after *Hui-neng. Ma-tsu was dynamic and *kōan-based); Shih-tou was quieter and more reflective. From these two derive the 'Five Houses and Seven Schools' (*goke-shichishū), replicating these differences of emphasis: from Shih-tou, *Tsao-tung (Jap., *Sōtō), *Yün-men (*Ummon) and *Fa-yen (*Hogen); and from Ma-tsu, *Kuei-yang (Igyo) and *Lin-chi (*Rinzai); Lin-chi produced two further divisions (hence the 'seven schools'), Yang-chi (*Yōgī) and *Hüang-lung (Ōryu).

As Ch'an faded in China, the different schools and emphases flowed into Korea and into Japan, as indicated in the equivalent names above, but the two which have been of the greatest importance are *Rinzai and *Sōtō. Foundation figures for Rinzai were *Eisai and Enni *Ben'en; the dominant figure is that of *Hakuin who led the revival of the 18th cent. Sōtō adherents regard *Dōgen as the key figure. The general truth to be realized is that there is only the buddha-nature underlying all appearance; when one realizes that this also is what one is, all differentiation ceases and one rests in that nature. To know this intellectually is very different from realizing it as experienced truth; and Zen developed many ways of seeking and seeing that unity—hence the immense cultural consequences of Zen. See also ZAZEN; ART; and Index, Zen practice.

Zendō. Zen hall (also dōjō, 'way hall'). Large hall in Zen monasteries, in which *zazen is practised.

Zengyō (Jap.). 'Gradual enlightenment', the step-by-step approach to enlightenment associated with the northern school of Ch'an Buddhism (see SOUTHERN AND NORTHERN SCHOOLS) —as opposed to sudden enlightenment (*tongyō).

Zenjō. Jap. for *dhyāna; hence zenjō-bikuni, a nun; zenjo-mon, a monk.

Zenrin-Kushu (Collection of Sayings from the Zen Forest). An anthology of Chinese wisdom, from Ch'an, Confucian, and Taoist sources, compiled by Ijūshi, 1688.

Zephaniah. *Prophet of the 7th cent. BCE. The Book of Zephaniah is the ninth of the *Minor Prophets, and the author is probably reacting to the abuses current in the days of King Manasseh (687–642 BCE).

Zera'im (Heb., 'Seeds'). One of the six orders of the *Mishnah. Apart from the first tractate, it deals with the agricultural laws pertaining to *Erez Israel.

Zerubbabel (6th/5th cent. BCE). Post-exilic Jewish leader. Zerubbabel worked with Joshua the *high priest as leader of the returned exiles from Babylon and as builder of the *Temple in *Jerusalem. Zerubbabel's activities are described in the books of *Ezra, *Nehemiah, *Haggai, and *Zechariah.

Zhen dong (*gzhan.stong*, 'Emptiness of Other'). At one time a heretical theory in Tibetan Buddhism that contributed to the downfall of the *Jonang school, but which was later resurrected to underpin the great eclectic *Rimé movement of the Tibetan Renaissance. The theory asserts that the two levels of truth—ultimate truth (*paramārtha satya*) and conventional truth (*saṃvṛti satya*)—are two distinct 'entities', in other words that ultimate truths (i.e. emptinesses) are empty of being the objects that are the basis of their imputation, and that objects (e.g. tables) are empty of being the emptiness that may be imputed on them. This involves the belief that a conventional truth (tables are just tables) is true from a conventional point of view, and that an ultimate truth (emptiness is empty of any phenomenal basis of imputation) is only true from a standpoint of meditative insight at which point all phenomena apparently cease. The *Geluk, who adopt the *rang dong theory and who condemned the Jonang for heresy, point out several errors, notably that the separation and independence of the two levels of truth amounts to substantialism by reifying the 'absolute'; that their understanding of an ultimate truth contradicts the Prajñāpāramitā (*Perfection of Wisdom) by separating emptiness from form; and that the absence of emptiness can never be true at any level.

Zikhronot (Heb., 'remembrances'). A *benediction in the *Musaf prayer of *Rosh ha-Shanah.

Zikr (remembrance of God): see DHIKR.

Zimra (Jewish halakhist): see DAVID BEN SOLOMON.

Zimzum, also **tsimtsum** (Heb., 'contraction'). Jewish *kabbalistic doctrine. The kabbalists taught that, in order that *creation could take place, God had in some sense to make a space for it. See further, LURIA, ISAAC BEN SOLOMON.

Zinā' (Arab.). Sexual intercourse outside the permitted relationships (which, in Islam, include concubines as well as marriage). Zinā' is dealt with particularly in *Qur'ān, sūra 4. The punishment by *rajm appears in *ḥadīth, not in Qur'an. See also ḤADD.

Zindiq (Pers., *zand*, 'free thinking'). A heretic, in Islamic law, whose teaching endangers the community. The penalty for public expression may be in this life death, and certainly in the next, damnation. Initially it appears to have referred to *dualists, e.g. the *Manichaeans.

Zinzendorf, Count (supporter of Moravians): see MORAVIAN BRETHREN.

Zion. A hill in the city of *Jerusalem. The term Zion can refer to the city of Jerusalem, to the whole of Judea or just to the *Temple mount. By the 1st cent. CE, Mount Zion included the Upper City which was surrounded by a wall.

Zion Christian Church. The largest independent church in S. Africa. It was founded by Enginasi Lekganyane (d. *c*.1948), a Pedi who had been influenced by a mission from J. A. Dowie's Christian Catholic Apostolic Church in Zion in Illinois; he separated from Eduard of Basutoland's Zion Apostolic Faith Mission in 1925 to form his own church in the Transvaal. Enginasi was succeeded briefly by one son and at his death by another, Eduard (1922–67), a progressive leader who in the 1960s attended the Dutch Reformed Church seminary at Turfloop near Zion City; his son, aged 13, became head in 1967, under a council.

Zionism. International, political, and ideological movement dedicated to restoring *Erez Israel to the Jewish people. The desire to return to the land of *Israel has been preserved in the *liturgy and folk consciousness of the Jews of the *diaspora since the time of the destruction of the Temple in *Jerusalem in 70 CE. Modern political Zionism was first conceived by Theodor *Herzl, and the movement was launched at the First Zionist Congress of 1897. Its stated aim was 'to establish a home for the Jewish people in Palestine secured under public law'. Early Zionism was not supported wholeheartedly by the Jewish community. Many of the *Orthodox believed that the return to Zion would only be effected by divine intervention, and that it was wrong for human beings to anticipate divine providence. At the other extreme, members of the *Progressive movements were anxious to play down the ethnic and nationalistic aspirations of Judaism and were convinced of their successful future in the countries of the *diaspora. Today, Zionist activities are organized under the auspices of the World Zionist Organization which embraces all the various unions, federations, and associations. See Index, Zionism.

Zionist Churches. A general term loosely used for the less orthodox, more *Pentecostal and more African *new religious movements in southern Africa, embracing several million Bantu and distinguished from the *Ethiopian churches. Both the size of membership and the degree of Christian content vary considerably, but the more Christian movements resemble the *Aladura in W. Africa.

Zitzit (Heb., 'fringes'). Tassels attached by Jews to garments worn to fulfil the commandments of Numbers 15. 37–41 and Deuteronomy 22. 12. As a positive time-bound commandment, *women do not have a duty to wear zitzit.

Ziyāra. Visit to a Muslim holy place or tomb, especially to *Muḥammad's tomb in *Madīna.

Zōbō (period in pure Land Buddhism): see SHŌZŌMATSU.

Zohar, Sefer ha- (Heb., 'Book of Splendour'). The central literary work of the *kabbalah. The *Zohar* is a collection of several books, many of which are supposedly the work of *Simeon b. Yoḥai (2nd cent. CE). It is a mystical commentary on the *Pentateuch and parts of the Hagiographia, and much of it is arranged according to the weekly portions of the *Torah. It first appeared in Spain and is thought to have been composed by *Moses b. Shem Tov de Leon who lived in the late 13th cent. The *Zohar* has been crucially important in the development of the kabbalah, and many commentaries have been written on it, the best known being *Ketem Paz* (1570) by Simeon Labi of Tripoli, *Or ha-Hammah* (publ. 1896) by Abraham b. Mordecai Azulai, the 18th-cent. *Mikdash Melekh* of Shalom Buzaglo, and *Elijah ben Solomon's *Yahel Or*.

Zoku Kōsōden (Buddhist biographies): see TAO-HSÜAN.

Zōmatsu (age of spurious dharma): see SAICHŌ.

Zoroaster. The name by which the ancient Iranian prophet Zarathustra has been known in the West. *Parsis often date him around 6,000 BCE, following Greek texts which misinterpret ancient Iranian sources. The significance for them is that he is the first of the world's religious prophets. There has been much W. scholarly debate over the dating. Until the 1980s the date most commonly given was the 6th cent. BCE (Gershevitch and *Zaehner), but more recently much earlier dates around 1200 BCE have been generally accepted (Boyce, Gnoli).

His teaching has been preserved in seventeen hymns, the *Gāthās, **Yasna* (hereafter *Ys.*) 28–34 and 43–53. Zoroaster was a practising priest (the only one of the great religious prophets known to have been such), and these hymns were meditations on the liturgy (*Yasna) cast into rather esoteric mantic poetry. They are, therefore, extremely difficult to translate and interpret, so that accounts of them differ considerably. Fundamental is the prophet's conviction that he had seen God, the Wise Lord, *Ahura Mazda, in a vision. He believed that he personally had been set apart for his mission from the beginning, a conviction which resulted in a stress on personal responsibility in religion. There are, he taught, two opposing forces, the Bounteous Spirit of Mazda and the destructive power of *Angra Mainyu who created respectively life and non-life. Each person's eternal fate would be determined by the choice (s)he made between them (*Ys.* 30. 3). Zoroaster called upon his followers to worship the good Mazda, who he declared, in a series of rhetorical questions, is the creator of all things.

Central to Zoroaster's belief in Ahura Mazda are the *Amesha Spentas, a system of seven spirits which in later tradition at least were opposed to seven evil spirits. He therefore saw a cosmic divide between the forces of good and evil. He used the term which later referred to the expected saviour, Sōšyant, at least partly to refer to the work of himself and his followers, but also probably with a future sense as in the developed eschatology.

Zoroaster says that he was cast out by kinsfolk, rejected by many of his contemporaries, and refused hospitality when travelling. Clearly his teaching provoked opposition from the priests of his day. According to tradition, he was slain (at the age of 77) by invaders while sacrificing at the altar. Among Orthodox Parsis, he is often seen as a manifestation of the divine, almost as an *avatāra. He is the great role model for all Zoroastrians.

Zoroastrianism. The religion of the followers of the prophet known in the West as *Zoroaster (Zarathustra to his followers). However, by the 7th cent. BCE, his teaching had spread across the Iran plateau, and when Cyrus the Great established the Persian Empire in the 6th cent., Zoroastrianism became the official state religion and so held sway from N. India to Greece and Egypt.

In the 3rd cent. there was a revolt when the Sasanians from the SW of the country, Persia proper, overthrew the Parthian northerners. They legitimated their rebellion by presenting their rule as a reassertion of Zoroastrian power, publicity which has affected generations of W. scholars (e.g. R. C. *Zaehner's *Dawn and Twilight of Zoroastrianism*, 1961). The Sasanian era was perhaps the time of the greatest courtly splendour in Iran. The monarchs threw their considerable power behind the official priesthood (magi), so Church and State were spoken of as 'brothers, born of one womb and never to be divided'. Once the authority of the chief priests had been declared, deviance from their teaching became not only *heresy, but treason. Whether that teaching was what historians consider 'orthodox' Zoroastrianism may be doubted. It seems rather to have been the 'heresy' of Zurvanism (*Zurvan), which not only contravened traditional Zoroastrian teaching on free will, but also questioned the essential goodness of the material world. The Sasanian period is the only era in Zoroastrian history where there is clear evidence of the oppression of other religions. Whether this was royal fervour or Zurvanite teaching is not known, but there were attempts to convert or suppress Jews and Christians (*Naujote).

The 1,200 years of Zoroastrian imperial history came to an end in the 7th cent. CE with the rise of Islam. The last Zoroastrian king, Yazdegird III, fled and was killed by one of his own people in 652. After the initial conquest, the imposition of Muslim rule on the lives of the people was a gradual affair. There was some ambivalence over the position of Zoroastrianism as a religion of the book (*ahl al-kitāb), though in Islamic times the *Avesta had emerged as the holy text of the religion. Ever-increasing Muslim oppression forced the diminishing number of Zoroastrians to retreat from the big cities near trade routes to the desert cities of Yazd and Kerman and their neighbouring villages. In the 10th cent., a band of Zoroastrians left the homeland to seek a new land of religious freedom, and settled in India where they are known as the *Parsis, or the people from Pars (Persia).

In 20th cent. Iran, the Zoroastrians experienced a revival of their fortunes. Due largely to the efforts of a Parsi, Manekji Limji Hataria, the *jizya had been removed in 1882, and grinding poverty was eased. He and others laboured hard to make educational and medical provisions for the oppressed Zoroastrians, so that, at the start of the 20th cent., they had improved in learning, health, and wealth as a number of merchants began to flourish. In 1906, a parliament, the Majles, was established and a Zoroastrian was elected. In 1909, all minorities were given one representative, including the Zoroastrian representative, Kay Khosrow Shahrokh. When the Majles deposed the last Qajar monarch and enthroned the prime minister as Reza Shah Pahlavi, the physical circumstances of Zoroastrians improved considerably. They were generally seen as the true, the ancient, Iranians, and were recognized as reliable, industrious, and able.

When the Islamic Republic under Ayatollah *Khumayni assumed power in 1979, many Zoroastrians feared for their future. Those who remained in the homeland have not suffered the persecution they feared, but their rights in law are not equal to those of Muslims; their opportunities in education and the professions are restricted. Always there is the fear of an outbreak of fanaticism. The future of the world's oldest prophetic religion in its homeland seems delicately poised as the third millennium begins.

Zucuto, Abraham ben Samuel (1452–1515). Historian and astronomer. Zucuto was the author of the astronomical work, *Ha-Hibbur ha-Gadol*, under the patronage of the bishop of Salamanca. After the expulsion of the Jews from Spain in 1492, he settled first in Portugal (where he advised Vasco da Gama) and then N. Africa. He also wrote *Sefer ha-Yuhasin*, a history of the *oral law based largely on original research, on which Moses b. Israel *Isserles subsequently wrote notes (publ. 1580).

Zugot (Heb., 'pairs'). The pairs of Jewish *sages who maintained the chain of *oral law. The zugot are seen as the link between the *prophets and the *tannaim (*Pe'ah* 2. 6).

Zuhd (Arab., *zahada*, 'abstain'). Abstinence in Muslim life, at first from sin and from all that separates from God; then (for those pursuing a *Sūfī path) from all that is created in order to cling only to the Creator.

Zunz, Leopold (Yom Tov Lippmann; 1794–1886). Jewish historian. Zunz was among the founders of the 'Science of Judaism'. Zunz became editor of *Zeitschrift für die Wissenschaft des Judentums* in 1823, the purpose of which was to redefine Judaism in accordance with the spirit of the times. He hoped that Jewish Studies would be recognized as an academic subject taught in secular universities. Although this aim was not realized in his lifetime, his work was continued after his death by the specially created Zunz Foundation (Zunzstiftung).

Zurvan. 'Time' in *Zoroastrianism, speculation on which subject appears to have given rise to a 'heresy' so powerful that it was dominant in Sasanian if not Achaemenid times. Essentially it appears to have been an intellectual interpretation of the doctrine rather than a formal cult, since there is no evidence of a separate priesthood or temples. Probably under Greek philosophical influence, Time was seen as the source and controller of all things, as the unity behind the polarity of the twin spirits of good and evil, *Ahura Mazda and *Angra Mainyu. If the idea of twins requires a father, then Zurvan was that father. But Time as the controller of all things led to a doctrine of predestination, fundamentally at variance with 'orthodox' teachings on free will (*Fravasi).

Zushi (Jap.). A small shrine or sanctuary dedicated to the *Buddha or to a transmitter of *dharma.

Zutra, Mar. Three Jewish *exilarchs of the 5th and 6th cents. CE. Mar Zutra I (d. *c.*414), known as 'the pious', was famous for his compassion and exemplary character. Mar Zutra II (d. 520) defeated the Persians and set up an independent Jewish state, 513–20. His son, Mar Zutra III, was traditionally born on the day his father was executed. He left Babylon and eventually settled in *Erez Israel.

Zwingli, Ulrich (1484–1531). Swiss *Reformer. After *ordination in 1526, he became pastor at Glaurus, where he devoted himself to the study of *Erasmus, biblical languages, *patristic theology, and the memorization of the *Pauline epistles. In 1516 he became chaplain of the Cloister at Einsiedeln where blatant abuses strengthened his desire for reform. He was appointed *priest at the Zurich 'Great Church' in 1518, gradually using his expositions to encourage reform. Zwingli defended his views in sixty-seven theses, on which he wrote *Auslegung und Gründe der Schlussreden*, i.e. his own commentary, and obtained the active support of the Zurich City Council, but a second disputation in 1523 led to a breach with two of his more radical colleagues, Conrad Grebel and Felix Manz, with Zwingli fearing that their 'Free Church' convictions would alienate the magistracy. Zwingli opposed their views about believers' *baptism, insisting on the baptism of all infants. At the same time, he encountered further theological difficulty over relationships with the *Lutherans, with the 1529 Colloquy of *Marburg failing to reconcile the *eucharistic views of German and Swiss Protestants. The Swiss Cantons fought over their divergent ecclesiastical loyalties, and the intensely patriotic Zwingli was killed at the battle of Cappel in 1531.

Zwingli placed great emphasis on the work of the *Holy Spirit. Thus although (as with *Luther) scripture has supreme authority, only the Spirit enables perception of its truth: prayer precedes perusal. Baptism he related to *covenant theology, and the *Last Supper he understood, not as initiating a sacrificial *mass, but as mediating the opportunity for faith to perceive the presence of Christ and to receive the benefits thereof.

TOPIC INDEX

Note In this Index of general topics, the entries are to headwords of articles in the main text of the book. An entry followed by → means that the entry will be found in the main text under the headword given—e.g., JPIC appears in the index under Acronyms and Abbreviations; the reader is then directed to the article, Cosmology, in the main text where it is discussed.

Where topics in the Index can provide further information to each other, cross-references are denoted by see/see also followed by small capitals—e.g. Mysticism see also SUFI BELIEFS.

In each topic, general entries, or those dealing with several religions, come first, followed (where applicable) by those related to particular religions.

The Index does not include accents, breathings, or italics.

Mahasiddha; Mani; Mrtyunjaya-siddhi; Nada; Nadi; Nyasa; Pingala; Pranayama; Rsi; Sai Baba; Sakti; Soma; Svedaja; Vibhuti; Visnu; Vyuha; Yantra **Jain**: Gandharas **Japanese**: Dosojin; Himorogi; Musobi; O-mamori **Muslim**: Baraka **Taoist**: Ch'i; Chiao; Ching; Huang-ching; Te **Tibetan**: Abhiseka; Kadam; Padnasambhava; Six Doctrines of Naropa; Thread-cross; Yab-yum **Zoroastrian**: Magi; Yasna

Practice Abstinence; Alchemy; Almsgiving; Anti-Semitism; Asceticism; Celibacy; Charms; Circumcision; Hair; Pilgrimage; Praxis; Purity; Zeal **Buddhist**: Abhibhavayatana; Adibrahmacariyaka-sila; Astangika-marga; Bhumi; Bodhi; Bodhisattva; Bodhisattva vow; Dhuta; Gotra; Kung-fu; Kusala; Mudita; Nien-fo; Sravaka; Takuhatsu; Three Jewels; Triyana; Upasaka; Uposatha; Vijnapti-matra; Virya; Yab-yum **Chinese**: Fang-shih; Feng-shui; T'ai chi ch'uan **Christian**: Agape; Ascetical theology; Imitation of Christ; Intention; Judaizers; Martha; Pietism; Sacramentals **Hindu**: Adityavarna; Apaddharma; Artha; Asrama; Bali; Bhakti; Brahmacarya; Grhastha; Kamasastra; Karma-kanda; Karma-yoga; Nyasa; Sadhaka; Sadhana; Trimarga; Vairagya; Vajroli mudra; Varnasramadharma **Jain**: Prabhavana **Japanese**: Bushido; Do; Hara-kiri; Martial arts; Samurai **Jewish**: 'Aliyah; Hasidim; Head covering; Hekdesh; Hevra kaddisha; Imitation of God; Mezuzah; **Muslim**: 'Abduh, Muhammad; al-Halal wa'l-Haram; 'Itikaf; Nafila; Niyya; Qibla; Sadaqa; Sawm; Wali; Zakat **Sikh**: Grahast(h)i; Gurmukh; Seva **Taoist**: Ch'i; Ching; Fang-chu shu; Fu-lu; Gymnastics; Nei-kuan; Nei-tan; Pa-tuan-chin; Pi-ku; Shou; T'ien-ku; Wu-ch'in-hsi; Wu-wei; Yang-hsing; Yang-shen **Tibetan**: Kyabdro **Zen**: Banka; Dai-funshi; Kendo; Kissako; Kyudo; Samu; Sesshin; Takuan Soho; Unsui

Prayer Affective prayer; Aridity; Illuminative way; Intercession; Midnight vigil; Prayer; Retreat; Rosary; Three ways; Unitive Way **Buddhist**: Kaji **Christian**: Abba; Accidie; Anamnesis; Andrewes, L.; Angelus; Baker, A.; Benedict; Bernard of Clairvaux; Book of Common Prayer; Breviary; Caussade, J. P. de; Collect; Contemplation; de Sales, Francis; Epiclesis; Evening prayer/evensong; Fenelon, F.; Gerson, J.; Groote, G.; Hesychasm; Horologion; Hugel, F.; Ignatius Loyola; Jesus Prayer; John Climacus; John of the Cross; Kyrie; Law, W.; Litany; Lord's Prayer; Luis of Granada; Merton, T.; Novena; Office; Opus Dei; Ordinal; Pater noster; Quietism; Recollection; Rogation days; Teresa of Avila; Thomas a Kempis **Hindu**: Yajurveda **Jewish**: 'Al het; Aleinu le-Shabbeah; Aleinu le-shabbeah; 'Amidah; Ashamnu; Avelei ha-Rahamim; Avinu Malkenu; Davven; Dew; El male rahamim; Ge'ul(l)ah; Hashkivenu; Kavvanah; Kiddush; Kol nidrei; Ma'aravot; Ma'ariv; Mahzor; Malkhuyyot; Mizrah; Moon, Blessing; Perek Shirah; Selihot; Sheli'ah; Tallit; Tefillah; Wailing Wall **Muslim**: Adhan; Du'a; Fatiha; Istikhara; Jum'a; Laylat al-Qadr; Nafila; Qibla; Rak'a; Sajjada; Salat; Shafa'a; Wird **Shinto**: Norito **Sikh**: Ardas; Gukta; Gurbani; Gurdwara; Nitnem; Rahiras; Sohila **Tibetan**: Prayer wheel **Zoroastrian**: Khorda Avesta; Naujote; Prayer and worship (Zoroastrian)

Preaching Buddhist: Dhamma Cakkappavattana Sutta; First sermon **Christian**: Andrewes, L.; Bunyan, J.; Calvinistic Methodists; Chrysostom; Cuthbert; Dominic; Eckhart; Henry Suso; Kerygma; Moody, D. L.; Niemoller, M.; Savonarola; Simeon, C.; Spurgeon, C. H.; Tetzel, J.; Wesley, C.; Wesley, J.; Whitefield, G. **Jewish**: Aggadah; Dov Baer; Kranz, J.; Maggid; Yelammedenu **Muslim**: Khutba **Zen**: Teisho

Priest Anointing; Mahant **Chinese**: Chang Lu **Christian**: Absolution; Archpriest; ARCIC; Armenian Church; Bishop; Canons Regular; Cardinal; Chantry; Clergy; Confession; Herbert; Ignatius; Oratory; Orders; Ordinal; Presbyter; Rector; Secular clergy; Staretz; Vicar **Hindu**: Agni; Atharva Veda; Atharvan; Brahman; Drona; Ksatra; Ordination; Priest; Rtvil; Sacrifice; Sama Veda; Udgatr; Yajur Veda **Japanese**: Guji; Norito; Shinto **Jewish**: Aaron; Aaronides; Breastplate; Ephod; Ezekiel; Hallah; Hasmoneans; High priest; Holiness Code; Levi; Leviticus; Maamad; Melchizedek; Sadducees; Urim and Thummim; Zadok **Zoroastrian**: Atas

Progressive Judaism Baeck, Leo; Haskalah; Montefiore, C.; Progressive Judaism

Prophets Prophet **Christian**: Monatanus **Jewish**: Abraham; Amos; Elisha; Ezekiel; Habakkuk; Haggai; Hosea; Isaiah; Jeremiah; Joel; Jonah; Micah; Nahum; Nathan; Obadiah; Samuel; Zechariah; Zephaniah **Muslim**: Abraham; Adam; David; Dhu 'l-Nun; Harun; Hud; Isaac; Jesus; John the Baptist; Muhammad; Nabi; Nubuwah; Rasul; Salih; Seal of the Prophets **Zoroastrian**: Avesta; Zoroaster

Psychology see ANTHROPOLOGY

Pure Land Amida; Amitabha; Genshin; Gose; Hokyo-darani; Honen; Honganji; Hui-yuan; Ichinen; Ippen; Isshin; Jakuhitsu Genko; Jiriki; Jishu; Jodo; Jodo Shinshu; Kannen;

Karuna; Kuya; Mappo; Myokonin; Nembutsu; Nien-fo; Ojo; Pai-lien-tsung; Pure Land; Raigo; Shinran; Shojo Daibutsu; Sraddha; Sukhavati; Sukhavativyuha; T'an-luan; Tariki

Puritans Baxter, R.; Bunyan, J.; Calvinism; Covenant services; Hooker, R.; Puritans; Sabbath; Wahabiya

Qur'an al-Ash'ari; Aya; Bada'; Eve; Fatiha; Furqan; I'jaz; Ijma'a; Ijtihad; Qur'an; Satanic verses; Sura; Tafsir; Tajwid; Tashbih; Ta'wil; Umm al-Kitab; Ummi; 'Uthman; Zahiriy(y)a

Qur'anic figures Abraham; Adam; David; Dhul-Nun; Harun; Ishaq; Ishmael; Jesus; Job; Mary (Islam); Messiah (Islam); Nasara; Yahya

Rabbinics Academies; Aggadah; Aharonim; Amoraim; Avot; Bet din; Chief rabbi; Codifications of law; Exempla; Hakham; Halak(h)ah; Haskamah; Hermeneutics (rabbinic); Kelal; Midrash; Mishpat Ivri; Mitzvah; Oral law; Prosbul; Rabbi; Rabbinical conferences; Rabbinical seminaries; Semikah; Synagogue; Takkanot; Talmid hakham; Talmud; Tikkun soferim; Women; Yeshivah

Rabbis, teachers, etc. Aaron ben Jacob; Aaron of Baghdad; Abba; Abba bar Kahana; Abba Saul; Abbahu; Abbaye; Aboab; Abrabanel, Isaac; Abraham ben David; Abulafia, Me'ir; Adret, Solomon; Ahad-ha-Am; Akiva; alFasi; Amoraim; Asher b. Jehiel; Ashkenazi, Z. H.; Bacharach, Jair; Baeck, Leo; Benamozegh, Elijah; Capsali, M.; Caro, Joseph; David ben Samuel; David ben Solomon; Duran, S.; Edels, S.; Eger, Akiba; Einhorn; Eisendrath; Eleazar; Eliezer ben Hyrcanus; Elijah ben Solomon; Eybeschuetz, J.; Falk, J.; Feinstein, M.; Finkelstein, L.; Four Captives; Frankel, Z.; Gamaliel; Geiger; Hafets Hayyim; Hai ben Sherira; Herzog, I. H.; Hillel; Hirsch, S. R.; Holdheim; Horowitz, I.; Ishmael ben Elisha; Johanan ben Zakkai; Judah ben Samuel; Judah ha-Nasi; Judah Loew; Kaplan, M.; Karelitz, A. Y.; Kohler, K.; Kook, A. I.; Landau, E.; Levinsohn; Lubavi(t)ch; Luria, Solomon; Manasseh ben Israel; Mannheimer; Meir; Meir ben Baruch; Nahman; Nahmanides; Rabbah bar Nahmani; Rabbi; Rashi; Rav; Rava; Rishonim; Sa'adiah Ga'on; Sages; Samuel ben Hophni; Samuel ha-Naggid; Savoraim; Schechter; Shammai; Sherira; Simeon bar Yohai; Simeon ben Gamaliel; Sofer, Moses; Soloveichik; Spektor, I. E.; Symmachus; Talmid hakham; Tam; Tanna; Wise, I. M.; Yannai; Yehudai ben Nahman; Zugot

Rama Adam's Bridge; Adhyatma Ramayana; Agastya; Ahalya; Avatara; Ayodhya; Dasahra; Hanuman; Hiranyakasipu; Kubera; Laksmana; Rama; Ramanada; Ramlila; Ravana; Sankaradeva; Sita; Treta-yuga; Tulsidas; Tyajagaraja; Vaisnava

Reading **Buddhist**: Banka; Honen; Hongan; Ichinen **Christian**: Diptychs; Lectio divina; Lectionary; Office of readings; Pericope **Hindu**: Pandita **Japanese**: Butsumyo-e **Jewish**: Bar mitzvah; Bible; Bimah; Birkat ha-Torah; Bridegroom of the Law; Cantillation; Daf Yomi; Haftarah; Hakhel; Masorah; Petihah; Scroll of the Law; Sedarot; Simhat Torah; Torah reading **Muslim**: 'Itikaf; Tajwid **Sikh**: Bhog; Hukam; Path; Rumala; Sukh asan; Vak laina **Zen**: Choka

Rebirth Anagamin; Apaya; Bhava; Bhavacakra; Divyavadana; Dukkha; Eko; Gaki; Gandharva; Gati; Gilgul; Goindval; Kaivalya; Merit; Metempsychosis; Moksa; Nirvana; Nusairi; Ojo; Origen; Punamrtyu; Punarajati; Punya; Pure Land; Rebirth; Ruten; Sagga; Sakadagamin; Samcita-karma; Samsara; Samskara (2); Shoji; Srotapanna; Subtle body; Tanasukh; Trsna; Tulku

Reform Judaism Assimilation; Bat Mitzvah; Conservative Judaism; Einhorn, D.; Eisendrath, M. N.; Friedlander, D.; Geiger, A.; Halakhah; Haskalah; Hebrew Union College; Holdheim, S.; Jacobson, I.; Jew; Kohler, K.; Mannheimer, I. N.; Mendelssohn; Montefiore, C.; Rabbinical conferences; Reform Judaism; Synagogue; Union of American Hebrew Congregations; Wise, I. M.

Reformation Adiaphorism; Anabaptists; Anticlericalism; Augsburg Confession; Beza, T.; Bucer, M.; Bullinger, H.; Calvin; Carlstadt; Catechism; Church; Confession; Covenanters; Coverdale, M.; Cranmer; Huguenots; Hus; Knox, J.; Latimer, H.; Lollards; Luther, M.; Marburg, Colloquy of; Melanchthon; Melville, A.; Mennonites; Millenarianism; Munzer, T.; Non-Conformists; Predestination; Presbyterian; Protestantism; Radical Reformation; Reformation; Ridley, N.; Tyndale, W.; Waldenses; Zwingli, U.

Relics Relics **Buddhist**: Bo Tree; Buddha's tooth; Dagbara; Pagoda; Sanchi; Sarira; Stupa; Tan-hsia T'ien-jan; Tooth Relic Temple **Christian**: Invention of the Cross; Shroud of Turin; Veronica **Tibetan**: Chorten

Religion, study of see STUDY OF RELIGION

Religions African Religion; African-American religion; Ainu; Aladura; Babis; Baha'i faith; Bon; Brahmanism; Buddha-sasana; Buddhism; Bungan; Bwiti; Cao Dai; Chinese religion; Christianity; Confucianism; Daikyo; Druzes; Falashas; Folk religion; Gnosticism; Hinduism; Islam; Jainism;

Tibetan: Torma **Zoroastrian**: Yasna
Saints Abercius; Advocatus diaboli; Agnes; Aidan; Alban; Albertus Magnus; Ambrose; Andrew; Anne; Anselm; Antony; Antony of Padua; Aquinas; Athanasius; Augustine; Augustine (of Canterbury); Barlaam and Joasaph; Barnabas; Bartholomew; Basil; Beatification; Becket; Becket, T.; Bede; Bellarmine, R.; Benedict; Bernadette; Bernard of Clairvaux; Bollandists; Bonaventura; Boniface; Bridget of Sweden; Brigid; Cabrini, F.-X.; Campion, E.; Canisius; Canonization; Catherine; Catherine of Alexandria; Catherine of Siena; Cavasilas; Cecilia; Chrysostom; Clement of Alexandria; Clement of Rome; Columba; Communion of saints; Cuthbert; Cyprian; Cyril; de Sales, Francis; Dominic; Elmo; Ephrem; Fisher, J.; Francis; Francis Xavier; George; Gregory I; Gregory Palamas; Gregory VII; Hagiography; Hilda; Hippolytus; Hugh; Ignatius; Irenaeus; Isidore; Jerome; John of Damascus; John of God; Joseph; Joseph of Arimathea; Justin; Luke; Macarius; Mark; Martha; Matthew; Matthias; Maximus; Melito; Mesrob; Monica; More, T.; Nimbus; Patrick; Patron saint; Paul; Peter; Peter Damian; Polycarp; Possessors; Purusottama; Saint; Sebastian; Seraphim of Sarov; Sergius; Simeon the Stylite; Simon; Stanislaw; Stephen; Teresa of Avila; Teresa of Lisieux; Theodore of Studios; Thomas; Timothy; Vladimir; Valentine; Veronica; Vianney, J.B. M.; Vincentians; Wenceslas; Wilfrid
Saivite see SIVA
Sakti Agama; Annapurna; Bhairavi; Bhutasiddhi; Bindu; Cakra puja; Camunda; Candi; Devi; Duti puja; Feminine symbols; Gitagovinda; Kala; Kali; Kapalika; Kashmir Shaivism; Kaula; Kumari Puja; Kundalini; Laksmi; Mahavidyas; Mahesevari; Mandala; Nyasa; Prakrti; Sahasrara; Saivism; Sakti; Saktism; Sri Yantra; Tantra; Tantrism; Trikona; Vamacana; Yamala; Yoni
Scripture reading see READING
Scripture see CANONICAL COLLECTIONS
Secret societies Boxer rebellion; Ch'eng-i Tao; Eight Trigram Societies; I-kuan Tao; Nusairi; Pai-pien-tsung; Secret societies; Societies, Chinese; White Lotus Society
Sects, movements, etc. Abrahamites; African Independent Churches; Afro-Brazilian cults; Agnihotri; Aghori; Ahmadiy(y)a; Amaravikkhepikas; Anagarika; Annatitthiya Paribbajakas; Anthroposophical Society; ARE; Armstrong, H. W.; Atlanteans; Azali Babis; Baul; Bayudaya; Black Jews; Branch Davidians; Cargo Cults; Cults of affliction; Deima; Druzes; Eckankar; Emin Foundation; est; Ethiopianism; Exegesis; Fellowship of Isis; Godianism; Grail Foundation; Gymnosophists; Hahalis Welfare Society; Hallelujah; Indian Ecumenical Conference; Indian Shaker Church; Israelite Mission; Jon Frum; Jordanites; Kitawala; Kuga Sorta; Macumba; Manseren, Koreri; Maria Lionza; Metaphysical movements; Moon, S. M.; Mormons; Nazarite Church; Neo-Paganism; New Age; New religious movements; New Thought; Pagan Pathfinders; Paliau Maloat; Peoples' Temple; Pocomania; Pormalim; Providence Industrial Mission; Radhasoami Satsang; Rastafarians; Reformed Ogboni Fraternity; Rizalistas; Santeria; Scientology; Sects; Self-Realization Fellowship; Servants of the Light; Shango; Silva Mind Control; Sociology of religion; Subud; Synanon Foundation; Telakhon; Theosophical Society; Transcendental Meditation; Tridharma; Umbanda; Unitarianism; Universal World Harmony; Vailala Madness; Valentinians; White Eagle Lodge; Yali Movement
Buddhist: Bharatiya Buddha Mahasabha; Buddhist schools; Chenzei; Dainichi Nonin; Eighteen Schools of early Buddhism; Fa-hsiang; Five Houses; Five periods, eight schools; Fujifuse; Goke-shichishu; Hoa Hao; Hua-yen; Jishu; Jodo Shinshu; Kegon; Kuya; Mahasamghikas; Mahayana; Mula-sarvastivada; Nara Buddhism; Nichiren Shoshu; Nichiren Shu; Obaku-shu; Prajnaptivada; Pramana; Prasanghika; Pudgalavadins; Pure Land; Ritsu; San-chien-chiao; San-lun; Sanron-shu; Sarvastivada; Sautrantikas; School of the Three Stages; Shingon; Shugendo; Southern and Northern Schools; Sthaviravada; Tendai; Theravada; T'ien-t'ai; Ts'ao-tung; Ummon; Vaibhasika; Vatsiputriya; Vibhajjavadin; Vijnanavada; Walubi; Western Buddhist Order; Won Buddhism **Chinese**: I-kuan Tao; White Lotus Society
Christian: Adventists; African Apostles; African Greek Orthodox Church; African Israel Church Nineveh; African Methodist Episcopal Church; Aiyetoro; Aladura; Alumbrados; Amish; Anabaptists; Assemblies of God; Bedwardites; Bogomils; Braid(e) Movement; Calvinistic Methodists; Campbellites; Catholic Apostolic Church; Children of God; Christadelphians; Christian Fellowship Church; Christian Science; Church Army; Churches of Christ; Doukobhors; East African revival; Evangelical Alliance; Evangelicals; Feden Church; Fifth Monarchy; Friends;

perennis; Philosophy of religion; Psychodynamic theory; Psychology of religion; Religionsgeschichtliche Schule; Renan, E.; Retrogressive rituals; Reuchlin, J.; Rhys Davids; Rites of passage; Sacred and profane; Schopenhauer, A.; Sects; Secularization; Shahrastani; Sociology of religion; Stcherbatsky, T.; Suzuki, D. T.; Symbols; Syncretism; Tabu; Tambiah, S. J.; Theodicy; Totemism; Tradition; Trickster; Troeltsch, E.; Tubingen School; Tucci, G.; Turner, V.; Tylor, E. B.; Violence; Weber, Max; Wellhausen, J.; Zaehner, R. C.

Stupas Amaravati; Anuradhapura; Bharut; Borobudur; Caitya; Chorten; Dagaba; Gilgit; Gorinsotoba; Kusinagara; Nalanda; Nipponzan Myohoji; Pagoda; Relics; Sanchi; Sarnath; Shwedagon; Sian; Sotoba; Stupa; Thread-cross; Toji

Sufi beliefs 'Abd al-Karim al-Jili; Abdal; al-Insan al-Kamil; al-Niffari; Baraka; Barzakh; Bast; Dhikr; Dhu 'l-Nun; Fana'; Faqir; Ghaiba; Hadd; Hal; Kashf; Khidr; Qabd; Qutb; Sama'; Shath; Sufis; Suluk; Tawhid; 'Urs; Wajd; Wali; Waqfa; Wird; Zuhd

Sufi orders Beshara; Derwish; Hamallism; Hasan al-Banna; Mawlawiy(y)a; Naqshbandiy(y)a; Ni'mat Allah Wali; Nurbakhshiy(y)a; Qadiriy(y)a; Safavids; Shadhiliy(y)a; Silsilah; Sufis; Tariqa; Tijaniy(y)a; Yezidis

Sufis 'Abd al-Karım al-Jili; 'Abd al-Qadir al-Jilani/Jili; Abu Madyan; Ahl al-Suffa; Ahmad al-Badawi; Ahmad al-Tijani; Ahmad Sirhindi; al-Bistami; al-Busiri; al-Ghaz(z)ali; al-Hallaj; 'Ali Hujwiri; al-Junaid; al-Muhasibi; al-Niffari; al-Sanusi; al-Shadhili; al-Shibli; 'Attar; Chishti; Dhu 'l-Nun; Hasan al-Basri; Ibn (al-)'Arabi; Ibrahim b. Adham; Iqbal, M.; Jalal al-Din; Jami; Khirqa; Ma'ruf al-Kharki; Ni'mat Allah Wali; Rabi'a; Salman al-Far(i)si; Shah Waliullah; Sufis; Tassawuf; Weeping Sufis

Sutra reading see READING

Symbols A; Adi; Agni; Allegory; Amitayus; Amoghasiddhi; Amulets; Anointing; Art; Astamangala; Bija; Blood; Chaur(i); Civil religion; Diksa; Durkheim; Eliade; Evans-Pritchard; Feminine symbols; Festivals; Food; Geertz; God; Goddess; Habit; Hair; Halo; Iconography; Initiation; Jung; Kingdom of God; Lotus; Magic; Mandala; Mudra; Myth; Ophites; Psychology of religion; Pundarika; Ritual; Sacrament; Sunyam; Svastika; Symbols; Taboo; Tantra; Tillich; Time; Turner; Typology; Vajrayana; Vodou; Yantra **Buddhist**: Aksobhya; Astamangala; Avalokitesvara; Bodhicitta; Body, speech, and mind; Bo-tree; Chorten; Cintamani (2); Dainichi; Dhamma-cakka; Dhyani-buddhas; Gandhara; Hotei; Laughing Buddha; Mandala of the Five Jinas; Manjushri; Pagoda; Raga; Stupa; Trikaya; Vairocana; Vajradhara **Chinese**: Beijing; Bronze vessels; Chiang Kai-shek; Dragons, Chinese; I Ching; Lung; T'ai-i Chin-hua Tsung-chih; Tortoise Oracle; Wu-hsing; Yin-yang **Christian**: Alb; Antidoron; Burning bush; Candlemas; Candles; Chi-Rho; Cross; Crucifix; Dove; Elevation; Evangelists; Halo; Ichthus; Icon; IHS; Labarum; Lamb; Ordination; Ostrich eggs; Pallium; Pelican; Phoenix; Sacred Heart; Saints **Hindu**: Agastya; Anata; Ardhanari; Asvamedha; Bindu; Danda; Danielou; Devi; Dhruva; Durga; Duti puja; Garuda; Go; Gopi; Hamsa; Hanuman; Jnana-mudra; Kulamava Tantra; Kumbha; Linga(m); Maithuna; Makara; Mala; Mandira; Narmada; Nath; Nyasa; Purusa; Rsabha; Sahasrara; Sri yantra; Trikona; Trisula; Upanayana; Vamacara; Varaha; Yantra; Yoni **Jain**: Parsva **Japanese**: Dosojin; Fumie; Ninigi; Ryobu Shinto; Shintai **Jewish**: Abraham; Adam Kadmon; Auschwitz; Bahir; Candles; Catacombs; David; Eruv; Eternal light; Falasha; Four species; Gartel; Hanukkah; Haroset; Hosea; Jacob; Kabbalah; Kittel; Magen David; Menorah; Moon; Philo; Prophets; Shiddukhin; Tashlikh **Muslim**: Adhan; al-Farabi; Crescent moon; Hajj; Hand of Fatima; Jami; Khirqa; Miraj; Omar Khayyam **Sikh**: Five Ks; Gurdwara; Hargobind; Ik Onkar; Karah prasad; Khanda; Langar; Nihang; Nisan Sahib; Panj kakke; Turban **Taoist**: Ch'ang; Ch'ang-sheng pu-ssu; Ho; Lung; Pa-hsien **Tibetan**: Bhavacakra; Dorje; Kadam; Lama dancing; Mahamudra; Om mani padme hum; Thread-cross; Tibetan Wheel; Tsha-tsha; Yab-yum **Zen**: Denne; Enso; Han-shan; Hassu; Ho; Hosso; Kuei-yang-tsung **Zoroastrian**: Atas; Naujote; see also ICONOGRAPHY

Synagogue Aliyah; Almemar; Ark; Art (Judaism); Bar mitzvah; Bat mitzvah; Bet (ha-) Midrash; Bimah; Bittul ha-Tamid; Cairo Genizah; Candles; Cantor; Day of Atonement; Eternal light; Ezrat nashim; Finkelstein, L.; Genizah; Haftarah; Hagbaha, Gelilah; Hakkafot; Hallel; Hekdesh; Hummah; Kaddish; Keter; Kiddush; Kristallnacht; Maaravot; Mehizah; Minhah; Minyan; Mizrah; Musaf; Music; Ner tamid; Parochet; Pentateuch; Petihah; Sabbath; Scroll of the law; Sedarot; Shammash; Shtetl; Shtibl; Shul; Sukkot; Synagogue; Women (Judaism)

Tafsir see HERMENEUTICS (MUSLIM)

Talmud Aramaic; Avodah Zarah; Avot; Baraita; Berakhot; Bertinoro, Obadiah;

Israel; Aliyah; Ark; Art (Jewish); Avot; Bible; Bimah; Birkat-ha-Torah; Breast-plate; Bridegroom; Caro; Chosen people; Codifications of law; Da'at Torah; Din Torah; Elijah ben Solomon; Enoch; Ethics (Jewish); Golden Rule; Hagbaha, Gelilah; Hagbahah, gelilah; Hakhel; Halakah; Judaism; Kallah; Karaites; Kelal; Ket(h)er Torah; Maimonides; Mitzvah; Oral law; Pentateuch; Petihah; Pilgrimage (Judaism); Rebellious elder; Revelation; Scroll of the Law; Simhat Torah; Sinai; Six hundred and thirteen commandments; Sura; Synagogue; Tawrat; Torah; Torah ornaments

Torah reading see READING

Tradition see CUSTOMS

Translation Abraham bar Hiyya; al-Biruni; Amoghvajra; An Shih-kao; Aquila; Arabic; Aramaic; Aristeas, Letter of; Authorized Version; Bible; Boethius; Buddhabhadra; Bu-ston; Coverdale; Eknath; Fa-hsien; Fa-tsang; Hermeneutics; Hsuan-tsang; Hui-yuan; Ibn Hasdai; I-Ching; Jerome; Kagyu; Ke-yi; Kumarajiva; Marpa; Melanchthon; Nyantiloka; Onkelos; Padmasambhava; Pure Land; Quran; Rhys Davids; Sakya; Septuagint; Tao-te Ching; Targum; Tyndale

Upanisads Aitareya; Brahmasutra; Brhadaranyaka; Chandogya; Isa; Katha; Kausitaki; Kena; Mahanarayaniya; Mahavakya; Maitri; Mandukya; Mundaka; Prasna; Svetasvatara; Taittiriya; Upanisad

Vaisnava see VISNU

Vedanta Anubhava; Badarayana; Bhagavad-gita; Brahman; Brahma-sutra; Cit; Darsana; Drg-drsya-viveka; Karma; Mahasunya; Mithya; Nididhyasana; Nimbarka; Nirguna-Brahman; Prakrti; Ramanuja; Saccidananda; Sankara; Satkasampatti; Sri Harsa; Sri-Vaisnavism; Suddhadvaita; Upanisad; Uttara-mimamsa; Vaisnava; Vallabha; Vedanta; Vivekananda

Virtues Buddhist: Abhabba-tthana; Alobha; Anagamin **Christian**: Seven virtues **Hindu**: Abhaya-mudra; Abhaya-vacana; Ananda; Aparigraha; Asparsa

Visnu Abhaya-mudra; Acarya; Alvars; Ananta; Angkor; Avatara; Bhagavad-gita; Bhagavan; Bhagavata-purana; Brahma; Brahman; Buddha; Daityas; Dattatreya; Dhruva; Ganga; Garuda; Gaya; Govinda; Hara; Hari-hara; Hayagriva; Hiranyakasipu; Hiranyaksa; Jagannatha; Janardana; Kalki; Krsna; Kurma; Laksmi; Madhu; Mahendra; Matsya; Mayon; Mohini; Nara; Narasimha; Narayana; Nath; Padma-purana; Pancaratra; Parasurama; Prapatti; Rama; Ramanuja; Samkarsana; Sankaradeva; Sesa; Tamilnadu; Trimurti; Vaikuntha; Vaisnava; Vamana; Varaha; Vasudeva; Vasudeva (2); Visnu

Vows Abhiseka; Aparigraha; Hair; Oaths; Vows; Vrata **Buddhist**: Amida; Bhaisajyaguru; Bodhisattva vow; Homon; Hongan; Hui-yuan; Jikkai; Jujukai; Sila **Christian**: Baptism; Confirmation; Crusade; Francis Xavier; Habit (Christian); Jesuits; Nun; Opus Dei **Hindu**: Kapalika; Vratya; Yama (2) **Jain**: Ahimsa; Anuvrata; Brahmacarya; Diksa (Jain); Five great vows; Gunasthana; Jainism; Prayascitta; Sallekhana **Jewish**: Kol nidrei; Korban; Leviticus; Nazirite; Oaths **Muslim**: 'Itikaf; Itiqaf; Waqf **Pure Land**: Hongan **Taoist**: Chai **Zen**: Homon; Shiguseigan

Women 'A'isha; Ambapali; Anandamayi Ma; Anne; Bernadette; Beruryah; Bhago, Mata; Bhatra; Brahma Kumari; Bridget of Sweden; Brigid; Butler, J. E.; Cabrini, F.-X.; Catherine; Cecilia; Day, D.; Deaconess; Deborah; Deva-dasi; Devi; Digambara; Draupadi; Duti puja; Eshet hayil; Eve; Ezrat nashim; Fatima; Feminine symbols; Feminist theology; Friends; Gopi; Gujari; Hadassah; Hadewijch; Hafsa; Hagar; Hijab; Hilda; Hildegard; Julian of Norwich; Khadija; Khema; Lingayats; Ma.gcig Lab.sgron; Mahaprajapati; Martha; Mary; Mary Magdalene; Mehizah; Menstruation; Miko; Mikveh; Mirabai; Monica; Mubusha, Alice M.; Nashim; Niddah; Nivedita; Nun; Purdah; Rabi'a; Rachel; Rebecca; Ruether, R. R.; Ruth; Salafiy(y)a; Salat; Sati; Savitri; Sita; Starhawk; Teresa of Avila; Teresa of Lisieux; Trisala; Uppalavanna; Veronica; Weil, S.; Witchcraft; Women; Zanana

Worship Altar; High place; Idolatry; Incense; Joss; Worship **Buddhist**: Caitya; Daimoku; Puja; Sampai **Chinese**: Altar of Earth **Christian**: Benediction; Choir; Forty Hours Devotion; Monstrance; Name of Jesus; Precious Blood; Sacred Heart **Hindu**: Acara; Aradhana; Arati; Arti; Bahya-puja; Bhakti; Bhutasiddhi; Darsana; Deva-dasi; Duti puja; Go; Istadevata; Mandir(a); Murti; Panj Pir; Pranapratistha; Prayopavesana; Puja; Ramaprasad; Sadhana; Tantrika; Tantrism; Upasana; Vigraha **Jain**: Puja **Japanese**: Ema; Fushimi Inari; Iwasaka **Jewish**: Avodah Zarah; Corban; Keter Malekuth; Levi; Moloch worship; Omer **Muslim**: Adhan; 'Ibadat; 'Itikaf; Sajjada; Salat; Takbir **Shinto**: Fushimi Inari; Ise; Shinsen; Shintai **Sikh**: Ardas; Bairagi; Divan; Japji; Mattha tekna; Sadh sanghat **Tantric**: Cakra puja; Kumari puja **Tibetan**: Torma **Zoroastrian**: Atas; Prayer and worship

INDEX OF CHINESE HEADWORDS

WADE–GILES → PINYIN CONVERSION TABLE

Wade–Giles	Pinyin
A-lo-pen	A-luo-ben
An Shih-kao	An Shigao
Ch'an	Chan
Ch'ang	Chang
Ch'ang-an	Chang'an
Chang Chüeh	Zhang Jue
Chang Hsien	Zhang Xian
Chang Hsiu	Zhang Xiu
Chang Kuo-lao	Zhang Guolao
Chang Ling	Zhang Ling
Chang Lu	Zhang Lu
Chang Po-tuan	Zhang Boduan
Chang san-feng	Zhangsanfeng
Ch'ang-sha Ching-ts'en	Changsha Jingcen
Ch'ang-sheng Pu-ssu	Changsheng Busi
Chang Tao-ling	Zhang Daoling
Chang T'ien Shih	Zhang Tianshi
Ch'an-na	Channa
Ch'an-tsung	Chanzong
Chao-chou Ts'ung-shen	Zhaozhou Congshen
Ch'eng	Cheng
Ch'eng-chu	Chenzhu
Ch'eng Hao	Cheng Hao
Ch'eng-huang	Chenghuang
Ch'eng I	Cheng Yi
Cheng-i tao	Zhengyidao
Cheng-kuan	Zhengguan
Ch'eng-shih	Chengshi
Cheng-yi	Zhengyi
Ch'eng Yi	Cheng Yi
Chen jen	Zhenren
Ch'en T'uan	Chen Tuan
Chen-yen	Zhenyan
Ch'i	Qi
Chiang-I	Jiang Yi
Chiao	Jiao
Ch'ieh-lan	Qielan
Ch'ien ai	Qian ai
Chien-chen	Jianzhen
Ch'ien tzu wen	*Qian zi wen*
Chih	Zhi
Ch'i-hai	Qihai
Chih-che	Zhizhe
Chih-i	Zhiyi
Chih-kuan	Zhiguan
Ch'i-kung	Qigong
Chih Tao-lin	Zhi Daolin
Chih-tun	Zhidun
Ch'in	Qin
Ching	Jing
Ch'ing-ming	Qingming
Ch'ing-t'an	Qingtan
Ching-te Ch'üan-teng-lu	*Jingde Quangdenglu*
Ching-t'un	Jingtun
Chinju	Jingru
Chin-lien	Jinlian
Chin-tan	Jindan
Chou	Zhou
Chou Lien-ch'i	Zhou Lianqi
Chou Tun-(y)i	Zhou Dunyi
Chu	Zhu
Ch'üan-chen tao	Quanzhendao
Chuang chou	Zhuangzhou
Chuang-tzu	Zhuangzi
Chu Hsi	Zhu Xi
Chu-hung	Zhuhong
Ch'un Ch'iu	*Chun Qiu*
Chung-Kuo-Shih	Zhongguoshi
Chung-li Chuan	Zhonglizhuan
Chung-yang	Zhongyang
Chung Yüan	Zhong Yuan
Chung Yung	*Zhong Yong*
Chün tzu	Junzi
Fa	Fa
Fa-chia	Fajia
Fa-hsiang	Faxiang
Fa-hsien	Faxian
Fa-ju	Fazhu
Fa-jung	Farong
Fa-lang	Falang
Fang-chang	Fangzhang
Fang-chung shu	Fangzhongshu
Fang-shih	Fangshi
Fang Yen-kou	Fang Yangou
Fa-shun	Fashun
Fa-tsang	Fazang
Fa-yen Wen-i	Fayan Wenyi
Fei-sheng	Feisheng
Feng-kan	Fenggan
Feng-shui	Fengshui
Fen-yang Shan-chao	Fenyang Shanzhao
Fu-ch'i	Fuqi
Fu-lu (pai)	Fulu (bai)
Han Hsiang-tzu	Han Xiangzi
Han-shan	Hanshan
Han Shu	*Hanshu*
Han Yü	Han Yu

PINYIN→ WADE–GILES CONVERSION TABLE

A-luo-ben	A-lo-pen
An Shigao	An Shih-kao
Baduanjin	Pa-tuan-chin
Bagua	Pa-kua
Bailianzong	Pai-lien-tsung
Baimasi	Pai-ma-ssu
Baiyunguan	Pai-yün Kuan
Baizhang Huaihai	Pai-chang Huai-hai
Baizhangqinggui	*Pai-Chang-Ch'ing-Kuei*
Bajiao Huiqing	Pa-chiao Hui-ch'ing
Baxian	Pa-hsien
Bigu	Pi-ku
Biqiu	Pi-ch'iu
Biyanlu	*Pi-yen-lu*
Bukong Jingang	Pu-k'ung Chin-kang
Caishen	Ts'ai-shen
Caodong	Ts'ao-tung
Cao Guojiu	Ts'ao Kuo-chiu
Caoshan Benji	Ts'ao-shan Pen-chi
Chan	Ch'an
Chang	Ch'ang
Chang'an	Ch'ang-an
Changsha Jingcen	Ch'ang-sha Ching-ts'en
Changsheng Busi	Ch'ang-sheng Pu-ssu
Channa	Ch'an-na
Chanzong	Ch'an-tsung
Cheng	Ch'eng
Cheng Hao	Ch'eng Hao
Chenghuang	Ch'eng-huang
Chengshi	Ch'eng-shih
Cheng Yi	Ch'eng I
Cheng Yi	Ch'eng Yi
Chen Tuan	Ch'en T'uan
Chenzhu	Ch'eng-chu
Chun Qiu	*Ch'un Ch'iu*
Cunsi	Ts'un-ssu
Dacheng	Ta-ch'eng
Dachu Huihai	Ta-chu Hui-hai
Dahui Zonggao	Ta-hui Tsung-kao
Danxia Tianran	Tan-hsia T'ien-jan
Dao	Tao
Daoan	Tao-an
Daochuo	Tao-ch'o
Daodejing	*Tao-te Ching*
Daodetianzun	Tao-te t'ien-tsun
Dao Hongjing	T'ao Hung-ching
Daojia	Tao-chia
Daojiao	Tao-chiao
Daosheng	Tao-sheng
Daoshi	Tao-shih
Daoyi	Tao-i
Daoyin	Tao-yin
Daozang	Tao-tsang
Datongshu	*Ta T'ung Shu*
Daxue	*Ta Hsüeh*
Deshan Xuanjian	Te-shan Hsüan-chien
Di	Ti
Dicang	Ti-ts'ang
Dongshan Liangjie	Tung-shan Liang-chieh
Doushuai Congyue	Tou-shuai Ts'ung-yueh
Dunhuang	Tun-huang
Dunwu rudao yaomen-lun	*Tun-wu ju-tao yao-men lun*
Dushan	Tu-shun
Emei, Mount	O-mei, Mount
Emito, Mount	O-mi-t'o
Fa	Fa
Fajia	Fa-chia
Falang	Fa-lang
Fangshi	Fang-shih
Fang Yangou	Fang Yen-kou
Fangzhang	Fang-chang
Fangzhongshu	Fang-chung shu
Farong	Fa-jung
Fashun	Fa-shun
Faxian	Fa-hsien
Faxiang	Fa-hsiang
Fayan Wenyi	Fa-yen Wen-i
Fazang	Fa-tsang
Fazhu	Fa-ju
Feisheng	Fei-sheng
Fenggan	Feng-kan
Fengshui	Feng-shui
Fenyang Shanzhao	Fen-yang Shan-chao
Fulu (bai)	Fu-lu (pai)
Fuqi	Fu-ch'i
Ge Hong	Ko Hung
Geyi	Ko-yi
Gong'an	Kung-an
Gu, Ku	Ku, K'u
Gui	Kuei
Guifeng Zongmi	Kuei-feng Tsung-mi
Guishan Lingyu	Kuei-shan Ling-yu
Guiyangzong	Kuei-yang-tsung
Hanshan	Han-shan
Hanshu	*Han Shu*
Han Xiangzi	Han Hsiang-tzu
Han Yu	Han Yü
Heqi	Ho-ch'i
Heshang	Ho shang
Heshanggong	Ho-shang kung
He Xiangu	Ho Hsien-ku
Hongren	Hung-jen
Hong Xiuchuan	Hung Hsiu-ch'uan
Hongzhi Zhengque	Hung-chih Cheng-ch'üeh
Huahu Jing	*Hua-Hu Ching*

Xiao	Hsiao
Xiao Jing	*Hsiao Ching*
Xin	Hsin
Xing	Hsing
Xingqi	Hsing-ch'i
Xinxing	Hsin-hsing
Xinxinming	*Hsin-hsin-ming*
Xi Wang Mu	Hsi Wang Mu
Xiyun	Hsi-yün
Xuansha Shibei	Hsüan-sha Shih-pei
Xuantian Shangdi	Hsüan-t'ien Shang-ti
Xuanxue	Hsüan-Hsüeh
Xuanzang	Hsüan-tsang
Xuedou Chongxian	Hsüeh-tou Ch'ung-hsien
Xuefeng Yicun	Hsüeh-feng I-ts'un
Xu Gaoseng zhuan	*Hsü Kao-seng chuan*
Xun Qing	Hsün Ch'ing
Xunzi	*Hsün Tzu*
Xutang zhiyu	Hsü-t'ang Chih-yü
Yang	Yang
Yangqi Fanghui	Yang-ch'i Fang-hui
Yangqizong	Yang-ch'i-tsung
Yangshan Huiji	Yang-shan Hui-chi
Yangshen	Yang-shen
Yangsheng	Yang-sheng
Yangxing	Yang-hsing
Yangzhu	Yang Chu
Yanqi	Yen-ch'i
Yanton Chuanhuo	Yen-t'ou Ch'uan-huo
Yayue	Ya-yüeh
Yichuan	I-ch'uan
Yiguandao	I-kuan Tao
Yijing	*I-Ching, Yi Ching*
Yijing	I-Ching
Yikong	I-k'ung
Yingzhou	Ying-chou
Yinxiang	Yin-Hsiang
Yinyang	Yin-yang
Yinyuan	Yin-yüan
Yixuan	I-Hsuan
Yongjia Xuanchue	Yung-chia Hsüan-chüeh
Yuanqi	Yüan-ch'i
Yuanshi tianzun	Yüan-shih t'ien-tsun
Yuanwu Keqin	Yüan-wu K'o-ch'in
Yuanzhuejing	*Yuan-chueh-ching*
Yuhuang	Yü-huang
Yu Ji	Yü Chi
Yungang	Yün-kang
Yungan Tansheng	Yün-yen T'an-sheng
Yunji Qiqian	*Yün-chi Ch'i-ch'ien*
Yunmen Wenyang	Yün-men Wen-yen
Zengzi	Tseng-tzu
Zhang Boduan	Chang Po-tuan
Zhang Daoling	Chang Tao-ling
Zhang Guolao	Chang Kuo-lao
Zhang Jue	Chang Chüeh
Zhang Ling	Chang Ling
Zhang Lu	Chang Lu
Zhangsanfeng	Chang san-feng
Zhang Tianshi	Chang T'ien Shih
Zhang Xian	Chang Hsien
Zhang Xiu	Chang Hsiu
Zhaozhou Congshen	Chao-chou Ts'ung-shen
Zhengguan	Cheng-kuan
Zhengyi	Cheng-i
Zhengyidao	Cheng-i tao
Zhenren	Chen jen
Zhenyan	Chen-yen
Zhi	Chih
Zhidun	Chih-tun
Zhi Daolin	Chih Tao-lin
Zhiguan	Chih-kuan
Zhiyi	Chih-i
Zhizhe	Chih-che
Zhongguoshi	Chung-Kuo-Shih
Zhongjiao	Tsung-chiao
Zhonglizhuan	Chung-li Chuan
Zhongyang	Chung-yang
Zhong Yong	*Chung Yung*
Zhong Yuan	Chung Yüan
Zhou	Chou
Zhou Dunyi	Chou Tun-(y)i
Zhou Lianqi	Chou Lien-ch'i
Zhu	Chu
Zhuangzhou	Chuang chou
Zhuangzi	Chuang-tzu
Zhuhong	Chu-hung
Zhu Xi	Chu Hsi
Zi	Tzu
Zi Si	Tzu Ssu
Zong	Tsung
Zongmi	Tsung-mi
Zongronglu	*Ts'ung-Jung Lu*
Zou Yan	Tsou Yen
Zuochan	Tso-ch'an
Zuowang	Tso-wang

Oxford Paperback Reference

The Concise Oxford Dictionary of Quotations
Edited by Elizabeth Knowles

Based on the highly acclaimed *Oxford Dictionary of Quotations*, this paperback edition maintains its extensive coverage of literary and historical quotations, and contains completely up-to-date material. A fascinating read and an essential reference tool.

The Oxford Dictionary of Humorous Quotations
Edited by Ned Sherrin

From the sharply witty to the downright hilarious, this sparkling collection will appeal to all senses of humour.

Quotations by Subject
Edited by Susan Ratcliffe

A collection of over 7,000 quotations, arranged thematically for easy look-up. Covers an enormous range of nearly 600 themes from 'The Internet' to 'Parliament'.

The Concise Oxford Dictionary of Phrase and Fable
Edited by Elizabeth Knowles

Provides a wealth of fascinating and informative detail for over 10,000 phrases and allusions used in English today. Find out about anything from the 'Trojan house' to 'ground zero'.